GARRY FILAFILO
765-0485

MW00748984

PUBLISHER'S NOTICE
Pages 679 to 682 are out
of order. We apologize
for this inconvenience.

Management Concepts and Canadian Practice

SECOND CANADIAN EDITION

This book is dedicated to Aurelia Starke
and to our sons, Eric and Grant

Preface

This book is written for students who want management theory to be clearly linked with management practice. It is balanced throughout, with emphasis on both practical problems and current theory. The objective is to convey to students the importance, and the excitement, of a career in management.

The text is organized into 6 major sections as follows:

Section I: Introduction   This section discusses the basic concept of management and introduces the major management functions. It also describes the external environment of the firm and how this environment creates both problems and opportunities for managers.

Section II: Planning and Decision Making   This section focuses on the first major function of management. The basic planning process that is relevant at all organizational levels is presented, as is the strategic planning process. This section contains an in-depth discussion of management by objectives at a major Canadian company.

Section III: Organizing   The key elements involved in the organizing function are the focus of this section. Both the formal and informal structures of organizations are analyzed.

Section IV: Influencing This section stresses the "people" aspect of the manager's job. Included in this section are chapters on motivation, leadership, communication, conflict, change, stress, corporate culture, and organization development.

Section V: Controlling The importance of ensuring that plans become reality is the focus of this section. The basic controlling process is discussed, and several important controlling techniques are described.

Section VI: Situational Applications The concluding section of the text deals with situations that require particular management skills. Included in this section are chapters on small business, international business, and the social responsibility of business.

Changes in the Second Edition

Every chapter in the second edition has been revised and updated. The following comments on selected chapters indicate the kinds of improvements that have been made in the second edition:

Chapter 2: The External Environment Much new data on the Canadian managerial environment has been added. This includes trends in male and female participation in the labor force, Canadian productivity in relation to that of other industrialized countries, the size of the Canadian work force, unemployment rates, employment in various sectors of the economy, and union membership trends. This type of information conveys to students the dynamic nature of the environment that Canadian managers must cope with.

Chapter 3: The Planning Process Additional information on organizational objectives has been added to this chapter. As well, the material on management by objectives which was formerly in Chapter 4 has been moved into this chapter.

Chapter 4: Strategic Planning This is an entirely new chapter. It focuses on long-range planning, particularly from the top-management perspective. The strategic planning process, strategic planning techniques, and dominant corporate strategies are treated here.

Chapter 5: Decision Making New material on the decision-making process and decision-making techniques has been added. Examples illustrate how the decision-making process and techniques are used by managers.

Chapter 9: Power and Politics This is a new chapter dealing with some of the subtle, but important, aspects of management. Power is contrasted with authority, and the concept of organizational politics is discussed in depth. Included in this discussion is an assessment of the importance of organizational politics in decision making, and an analysis of the arguments for and against politics.

Chapter 11: Motivation   New material has been added on intrinsic/extrinsic motivation, flextime, and on the relationship between motivation, ability, and performance.

Chapter 12: Leadership   The distinction between leaders and managers is developed in more depth, and new material on transactional and transformational leaders has been added. New material on charismatic leadership is also included in this chapter.

Chapter 14: Organizational Conflict, Change, and Stress   This is a new chapter, made up of material from several chapters in the first edition, as well as new material written for this edition.

Chapter 15: Corporate Culture and Organization Development   This is also a new chapter, made up of some material from the first edition, and some new material. The important topic of corporate culture is presented here, including material on how to identify corporate culture, and the impact of corporate culture on organizational performance.

Chapter 17: Control Techniques   New material on control techniques such as net present value and just-in-time inventory systems has been added to this chapter.

Chapter 19: Managing Multinationals   New information on Canadian multinationals and the issue of foreign ownership has been added to this chapter.

Chapter 20: Social Responsibility and Business Ethics   More material on business ethics and on the responsibility of Canadian business to society has been added to this chapter.

Features of the Revised Edition

Each chapter in this revised edition contains a variety of features designed to stimulate student interest and understanding of the field of management. Each chapter includes the following features:

Key Terms   At the beginning of each chapter a list of key terms appears. These alert the student to items of particular importance that will appear in the chapter. Mastery of these terms is important for a full understanding of the field of management. Within the chapter, each key term is highlighted in color in the margin for easy location. All key terms are also listed and defined in the glossary at the end of the text.

Learning Objectives Each chapter outlines a set of objectives to help students anticipate the important points that will be made in the chapter. Once students have finished reading the chapter, they can return to the objectives to determine how well they have mastered the material.

Opening Incident Each chapter begins with an incident which is based on an actual occurrence in a management setting. The incident deals with a specific problem that is relevant to the subject matter of the chapter. Students are encouraged to think about the problem before they begin reading the chapter.

Opening Incident Revisited At the end of each chapter, the opening incident is reviewed and analyzed using material that was presented in the chapter. Students can compare the solution they developed before reading the chapter, and can note how the chapter material was helpful in developing a workable solution to the problem.

Talking to Managers Almost every chapter contains an interview with a practicing manager. These managers, ranging from company presidents to first-line supervisors, are asked specific questions about how they carry out the functions of management. A significant part of each interview focuses on material that is presented in the chapter. The responses of these practicing managers to a variety of questions helps students see how management theory is carried out in practical situations. There are seven new interviews in this edition of the text.

Management in Practice Inserts Each chapter contains several inserts describing how actual Canadian companies are using various tools of management in their day-to-day operations. These inserts give students valuable insights into the practice of management in Canada. There are over 100 of these inserts in the text, approximately 70 percent of which are new with this edition.

Summary The material in each chapter is concisely summarized. The summary is not a substitute for reading the chapter, but it does help students to see the main points in the chapter and the logic of their presentation.

Review Questions A substantial number of review questions are included at the end of each chapter. These questions relate directly to the factual material that is presented in the chapter. The questions determine how well students can recall specific important facts that they should know. Essay and integrative questions are contained in the Instructor's Manual.

Exercises Two or three exercises are presented at the end of each chapter. To do these exercises, students usually interview a practicing manager on a particular topic, or survey a number of managers to get their views on an issue. The exercises relate directly to material that is presented in the chapter.

Case Studies Each chapter contains two or more short case studies. These describe situations and problems that can be analyzed using the material presented in the chapter. At the end of each case, several questions guide students in their analysis. All cases are based on actual situations. There are 47 short cases in the text, approximately half of which are new with this edition.

Comprehensive Case Studies Fourteen comprehensive case studies are included at the end of the text. Six of these cases are new in the second edition. These cases are considerably longer and more detailed than those that appear at the end of each chapter. The comprehensive cases generally raise several issues that are important in the practice of management. These cases further build student analytical skills and convey to the student the complicated nature of management. All cases are based on actual situations; company names are often disguised.

References A list of books and articles that are relevant to the chapter material is presented at the end of each chapter. Students who wish to read further on certain topics will find this list useful. Students wishing to do group or individual projects as required by the professor will also find the list of references helpful in getting started.

All of the features described above are designed to enhance student interest while conveying the key elements in the practice of Canadian management. Our sincere desire is that the text will encourage the reader to consider one of the most challenging and rewarding careers possible — management.

Acknowledgements

I owe special thanks to the acquisitions editor, Yolanda de Rooy, to the project editor, David Jolliffe, and to the editor, Chelsea Donaldson, for their dedicated efforts toward helping me complete this text. Special thanks go to Diana Sokolowski for her help in the preparation of the manuscript.

The following people helped by reviewing the text material. Their comments were gratefully received, carefully read, and implemented wherever possible.

Robert A. Boudreau, University of Lethbridge
Olga L. Crocker, University of Windsor
Lorne A. Fingarson, British Columbia Institute of Technology
Brian Harrocks, Algonquin College
Jim Mason, University of Regina
John Redston, Red River Community College
Elizabeth Reid, consultant
William J. Riddell, Seneca College
Garry E. Veak, Southern Alberta Institute of Technology
William C. Wedley, Simon Fraser University

Contents in Brief

PART ONE   INTRODUCTION   1

Chapter   1   Management   2
Chapter   2   The External Environment   56

PART TWO   PLANNING AND DECISION MAKING   93

Chapter   3   The Planning Process   94
Chapter   4   Strategic Planning   141
Chapter   5   Managerial Decision Making   178

PART THREE   ORGANIZING   225

Chapter   6   The Organizing Process   226
Chapter   7   Authority, Responsibility, and Organizational Structure   253
Chapter   8   Group Behavior and the Informal Organization   292
Chapter   9   Power and Politics   321
Chapter 10   Staffing the Organization   347

PART FOUR   INFLUENCING   385

Chapter 11   Motivation   386
Chapter 12   Leadership   434
Chapter 13   Communication   474
Chapter 14   Organizational Conflict, Change, and Stress   510
Chapter 15   Corporate Culture and Organization Development   542

PART FIVE   CONTROLLING   567

Chapter 16   The Controlling Process   568
Chapter 17   Control Techniques   598

PART SIX   SITUATIONAL APPLICATIONS   643

Chapter 18   Managing Small Businesses   644
Chapter 19   Managing Multinationals   681
Chapter 20   Social Responsibility and Business Ethics   716

COMPREHENSIVE MANAGEMENT CASE STUDIES   752

CONTENTS

PART I   INTRODUCTION   1

CHAPTER 1   MANAGEMENT

Key Terms   2
Learning Objectives   3
Opening Incident   3
Management in Various Settings   4
The Profit-Oriented Business Firm   5
  Forms of Business Ownership   7
Not-for-Profit-Organizations   11
Manufacturing versus Service Organizations   12
What is Management?   13
Who are Managers and What Do Managers Do?   13
The Management Functions   15
Planning   15
Talking to Managers — David Leighton   16
Organizing   18
Influencing   18
Controlling   19
Coordination   19
Management Functions at Various Managerial Levels   21

Managerial Roles 22
Managerial Skills 23
Conceptual Skills 24
Technical Skills 24
Human Skills 25
The Relationship Between Skills and Functions 26
Basic Schools of Management Thought 26
The Classical School of Management 27
   Scientific Management 27
   General Management Theory 30
The Behavioral School of Management 30
   Human Relations 30
   Modern Behavioral Science 31
Other Schools of Management Thought 32
Opening Incident Revisited 34
Summary 35
Review Questions 36
Exercises 37
Case Studies
   From Engineering to Management 37
   From Assistant Foreman to President 38
   A Business Opportunity 39
Endnotes 40
References 41

APPENDIX TO CHAPTER 1   CAREERS IN MANAGEMENT

Gaining Insight into Yourself 43
Talk to Professionals 44
The Testing Center 45
   Interest Tests 45
   Aptitude Tests 45
   Personality Tests 45
   Intelligence Tests 46
Career Objectives 46
Entry-Level Positions in Management 47
The Risk Factor 47
Entry-Level Management 48
Management Training Programs 48
From Professional to Management 49
From Sales to Management 50
The Search for the Right Industry 50
The Search for the Right Company 51
The Résumé 51

Matching Yourself with the Right Company   52
Initial Problems on the Job   53
The Young Brat Syndrome   54
Making Changes   54
Politics   54
The Free Spirit   54
The Boss   55

CHAPTER 2   THE EXTERNAL ENVIRONMENT   56

Key Terms   56
Learning Objectives   56
Opening Incident   57
The External Environment   58
Government   60
Competitors   64
The Work Force   67
Unions   71
Shareholders   73
Suppliers   74
Customers   74
The General Public   74
The Systems Approach: The Business System   75
Resources/Inputs   76
Processing Resources/Inputs   76
Outputs   77
Management and Standards   77
Dynamics of a Business System   77
The Situational Approach   79
Talking to Managers — Dr. John Evans   80
External Environment   82
Objectives of the Organization   82
Technology   82
Structure   83
Personnel   83
Managerial Styles   84
Balancing the Situational Factors   84
Opening Incident Revisited   85
Summary   86
Review Questions   87
Exercises   88
Case Studies
The Toy Environment   88
Northern Forest Products Company   89
Endnotes   90
References   91

PART II THE PLANNING PROCESS 93

CHAPTER 3 PLANNING AND DECISION MAKING 94

Key Terms 94
Learning Objectives 94
Opening Incident 95
The Planning Process: An Overview 96
Mission 96
Organization Objectives 98
Characteristics of Good Objectives 99
Types of Objectives 99
  Economic Objectives 99
  Service Objectives 100
  Personal Objectives 100
Establishing Objectives 101
Problems Encountered in Establishing Objectives 102
  Real versus Stated Objectives 102
  Multiple Objectives 103
  Goal Distortion 103
Standards 104
Performance Results Standards 105
Process Standards 106
Plans 106
Policies 108
Procedures and Rules 109
Procedures 109
Rules 109
Contingency Planning 111
Unintended Side Effects of Plans 112
Planning Through Management by Objectives 113
Background of MBO 114
The MBO Process 115
Top Management's Philosophy, Support, and Commitment 115
Establish Long-Range Goals and Strategies 115
Establish Specific Shorter-Term Organization Objectives 117
Establish Individual Performance Objectives 117
Appraise Results 118
Take Corrective Action 118
Setting Objectives 118
Who Should Set Objectives? 118
Objectives for Individuals 119
Group Objectives 120
Benefits of MBO Programs 124
Summary Evaluation of MBO 127

Potential Problems with MBO   128
MBO: Assessing its Overall Effectiveness   129
Opening Incident Revisited   129
Summary   130
Review Questions   131
Exercises   131
Case Studies
  The Apple Farmer   132
  MBO At York Investments Ltd.   133
  Objectives and Plans at West-Can   134
  Undue Influence?   136
Endnotes   136
References   137

CHAPTER 4   STRATEGIC PLANNING   141

Key Terms   141
Learning Objectives   142
Opening Incident   142
The Strategic Planning Process   145
Formulating Strategy   145
Determining the Mission   145
Assessing the Internal Environment   147
Assessing the External Environment   148
  Forecasting   150
Selecting a Strategy   151
Implementing Strategy   152
Setting Objectives   152
Establishing Functional Strategies   153
Monitoring Strategy   153
Talking to Managers — Robert Black   154
The Levels of Strategic Planning   156
Corporate-Level Strategic Planning   156
SBU-Level Strategic Planning   156
Functional-Level Strategic Planning   158
Strategic Management Techniques   158
The BCG Matrix   158
  Placing SBU's on the BCG Matrix   159
  Stars, Questions Marks, Cash Cows, and Dogs   160
  Implications of BCG Analysis   161
General Electric's Nine-Cell Planning Grid   161
The Product Life Cycle   162
The McKinsey Seven S Framework   163
Grand Strategies   164
Concentration   165

Market Development   165
Product Development   165
Integration   165
Diversification   166
Joint Ventures   168
Retrenchment   168
Opening Incident Revisited   170
Summary   171
Review Questions   172
Exercises   172
Case Studies
  Layton Hardware   173
  A Strategic Management Consultant   174
Endnotes   174
References   175

CHAPTER 5   MANAGERIAL DECISION MAKING   178

Key Terms   178
Learning Objectives   178
Opening Incident   179
Making Decisions   180
Making Personal versus Professional Decisions   181
  Personal Decisions   181
  Professional Decisions   181
Making Routine versus Nonroutine Decisions   182
  Routine Decisions   182
  Nonroutine Decisions   182
Requirements for Decision Making   183
The Presence of a Decision Maker   184
Problem Content   184
Courses of Action   184
Payoff Relationships   184
State of Nature   184
Basic Approaches to Decision Making   185
The Intuitive Approach   185
The Systematic Approach   186
  Observation of Events   186
  Hypothesis Formulation   186
  Experimentation   187
  Verification   187
Which Approach is Better?   187
The Decision Making Process   187
The Problem Analysis Phase   189
  Develop Standards   190

Observe Deviations From the Standard   190
Describe the Deviation Specifically   191
Determine the Cause of the Deviation   191
The Decision Making Phase   191
State Objectives of the Decision   191
Develop Alternative Solutions   192
Evaluate Alternative Solutions   192
Choose the Best Alternative   193
The Implementation Phase   193
Action Planning   193
Implement the Solution   194
Follow Up   194
Factors Affecting the Decision-Making Process   195
Risk   195
Time   195
Talking to Managers — Dr. Heleen McLeod   196
Degree of Acceptance and Support by Equals and Superiors   198
The Manager's Ability as a Decision Maker   198
Organization Politics   199
Decision-Making Techniques   199
The Decision Matrix   199
Decision Trees   202
Brainstorming   202
Nominal Grouping   204
Delphi Technique   205
Individual versus Group Decision Making   205
Advantages of Group Decision Making   206
Disadvantages of Group Decision Making   207
Management Information Systems   208
A Definition of an MIS   208
The Need for an MIS   209
Information Needs at Different Levels of Management   209
Developing an MIS   210
Implementing an MIS   211
Computers and MIS   215
Choosing a Computer for the MIS   215
Microcomputers   215
Minicomputers   216
Mainframe Computers   216
The Impact of the Computer on Management   217
Opening Incident Revisited   217
Summary   218
Review Questions   219
Exercises   220
Case Studies
Maintenance Expenses   220
A Request for Special Favors   221

Northlands Hospital   221
Endnotes   222
References   223

PART III   ORGANIZING   225

CHAPTER 6   THE ORGANIZING PROCESS   226

Key Terms   226
Learning Objectives   226
Opening Incident   227
Objectives   229
Environmental Factors   230
  The External Environment   230
  The Internal Environment   230
Functions   231
Specialization of Labor   232
  Advantages of Specialization   233
  Disadvantages of Specialization   234
Departmentation   235
Grouping Similar Functions   235
  Sufficient Volume of Work   235
  Tradition, Preferences, and Work Rules   236
  Functions Similar to Others in the Organization   236
  Separation of Functions to Prevent Conflicts of Interest   236
  Combining Dissimilar Functions to Allow Coordination   236
Bases of Departmentation   237
  Departmentation by Function   237
  Departmentation by Product   237
  Departmentation by Customer   238
  Departmentation by Geographic Territory   238
  Departmentation by Project   239
Departmentation: A Combination Approach   240
Differentiation   240
Organizing at the Supervisory Level   243
Opening Incident Revisited   245
Summary   245
Talking to Managers — Victor Rice   246
Review Questions   248
Exercises   249
Case Studies
  The Organization of Quality Control   249
  Materials Organization at Newco   250
Endnotes   251
References   251

CHAPTER 7   AUTHORITY, RESPONSIBILITY, AND
ORGANIZATIONAL STRUCTURE   253

Key Terms   253
Learning Objectives   254
Opening Incident   254
Delegation   256
Responsibility   257
Authority   258
Division of Authority   258
Amount of Authority: Centralization versus Decentralization   259
  Size and Complexity of the Organization   261
  Geographic Dispersion of the Organization   261
  Competence of Personnel Available   261
  Adequacy of Communications System   262
  Uniformity of Policy Desired   262
  Cost of Decisions   262
  History of the Organization   262
Accountability   263
Organizing Principles   264
Unity of Command   264
Equal Authority and Responsibility   265
The Scalar Principle and the Chain of Command   265
Span of Management   265
  Factors Affecting the Span of Management   267
Organizational Structures   268
The Functional Structure   269
  Advantages of the Functional Structure   271
  Disadvantages of the Functional Structure   271
The Divisional Structure   272
  Advantages of the Divisional Structure   272
  Disadvantages of the Divisional Structure   273
The Line Organization   273
The Line and Staff Organization   275
  Functional Authority   279
Project and Matrix Organizations   280
Talking to Managers — Tom Ward   284
Opening Incident Revisited   286
Summary   286
Review Questions   287
Exercises   288
Case Studies
  Misco Paper Converters   288
  Managing Growth at Sharp's   289
Endnotes   290
References   291

CHAPTER 8   GROUP BEHAVIOR AND THE INFORMAL
ORGANIZATION   292

Key Terms   292
Learning Objectives   292
Opening Incident   293
Group Behavior   295
Comparing Formal and Informal Organizations   296
Norms   298
Roles   298
Leadership   299
Structure   299
Cohesiveness   302
Size   302
Synergism   303
Benefits and Costs of the Informal Organization   303
Benefits of the Informal Organization   303
  Assists in Accomplishing Work   303
  Helps to Counter Weaknesses in the Formal Structure   304
  Broadens the Effective Span of Management   305
  Compensates for Violations of Formal Principles   305
  Provides an Additional Channel of Communication   305
  Provides Emotional and Social Support for Employees   305
  Encourages Better Management   306
Costs of the Informal Organization   306
  May Work Against the Formal Organization   306
  Reduces Degree of Managerial Control   307
  Reduces the Number of Practical Alternatives   307
  Increases the Time Required to Complete Activities   307
Talking to Managers — Charles McDougall   308
Status   310
Status Sources   310
Status Symbols   312
Status Functions   314
Opening Incident Revisited   315
Summary   315
Review Questions   316
Exercises   316
Case Studies
  The Young Accountant   317
  A View of the River   318
Endnotes   318
References   319

CHAPTER 9   POWER AND POLITICS   321

Key Terms   321
Learning Objectives   321
Opening Incident   322
Power   323
Types of Power   323
Power versus Formal Authority   325
The Significance of Power to the Manager   326
Organization Politics   327
The Universality of Political Behavior   329
Talking to Managers — Jerry Gray   330
The Dynamics of Political Behavior   332
How Managers View Political Behavior   334
Is Political Behavior Positive or Negative?   336
Opening Incident Revisited   341
Summary   341
Review Questions   342
Exercises   342
Case Studies
   Power Play   343
   The Return of Thomas Palatuk   344
Endnotes   345
References   345

CHAPTER 10   STAFFING THE ORGANIZATION   347

Key Terms   347
Learning Objectives   348
Opening Incident   348
Management of Human Resources   349
Staffing   350
Training and Development   350
Compensation   350
Health and Safety   352
Employee and Labor Relations   352
Personnel Research   352
Legal Aspects of Staffing   352
Antidiscrimination Laws   353
Health and Safety Laws   355
Labor Relations Laws   355
Compensation Laws   356
The Staffing Process   357

Human Resource Planning   359
  Job Analysis   359
  Job Description   359
  Job Specifications   360
  Work Load Analysis   360
  Work Force Analysis   361
Recruitment   362
The Selection Process   364
  Preliminary Interview   364
  Evaluation of Application Form   364
  Testing   364
  Interviewing   365
  Talking to Managers — Brian Peto   368
  Background and References Checks   371
  Management Approval   372
  Physical Exams   372
Placement on the Job: Orientation   372
Special Considerations in Selecting Managerial Personnel   373
Determining Executive Needs   374
Techniques For Identifying Managerial Talent   375
  Personal Characteristics   375
  The Assessment Center   375
Opening Incident Revisited   377
Summary   378
Review Questions   379
Exercises   379
Case Studies
  The Harried Department Head   380
  Expansion Plans At Eagle Aircraft   381
Endnotes   381
References   382

PART IV   INFLUENCING   385

CHAPTER 11   MOTIVATION   386

Key Terms   386
Learning Objectives   386
Opening Incident   387
The Process of Motivation   389
Talking to Managers — Peter Thomas   390
Intrinsic and Extrinsic Motivation   392
Motivation, Ability, and Performance   394
Philosophies of Human Nature   395
McGregor's Theory X and Theory Y   396

Argyris' Maturity Theory   397
Motivation: The Self-Fulfilling Prophecy   398
Motivation Theories   399
Maslow's Hierarchy of Needs   400
Alderfer's E-R-G Theory   402
Herzberg' Motivation-Hygiene Theory   402
McClelland's Needs Theory   406
   Need for Achievement   406
   Need for Power   406
   Need for Affiliation   407
Expectancy Theory   408
Reinforcement Theory   409
Equity Theory   412
The Role of Money in Motivation   412
Job Design and Motivation   415
Job Rotation   416
Job Enlargement   416
Job Enrichment   417
Quality Circles   418
Flextime   421
Motivation Lessons From the Japanese   422
Motivation: Implications for Management Practice   423
Opening Incident Revisited   424
Summary   425
Review Questions   427
Exercises   427
Case Studies
   The Problem Chemist   428
   A Birthday Present for Kathy   429
Endnotes   430
References   431

CHAPTER 12   LEADERSHIP   434

Key Terms   434
Learning Objectives   435
Opening Incident   435
Leadership Defined   436
Leaders versus Managers   436
Leadership, Management, and Performance   438
Transactional versus Transformational Management   439
Basic Leadership Styles   440
One-Best-Way (Universalist) Leadership Theories   440
The Trait Approach to Leadership   441
Likert's Systems of Management   442

System II — Benevolent Autocratic 443
System III — Consultative 443
System IV — Participative Team 443
Talking to Managers — Edwin Mirvish 444
Blake and Mouton's Managerial Grid 447
Situational Theories of Leadership 449
The Ohio State Leadership Studies 449
The Ohio State Leadership Studies 449
The Path-Goal Theory of Leadership 451
The Leadership Continuum 452
Fiedler's Contingency Leadership Model 453
Hersey and Blanchard's Situational Leadership Theory 454
Vroom and Yetton's Leadership Decision-Making Model 458
General Factors Affecting Choice of Leadership Style 460
Factors Related to the Manager 461
Factors Related to the Workers 462
Factors Related to the Situation 462
Opening Incident Revisited 464
Summary 465
Review Questions 466
Exercises 467
Case Studies
  A Natural Born Leader 468
  The Unhappy Salesman 468
Endnotes 470
References 471

CHAPTER 13   COMMUNICATION   474

Key Terms 474
Learning Objectives 474
Opening Incident 475
The Communication Process 477
What Should Be Communicated? 479
Organizational Channels of Communication 480
Formal Downward Channels 481
Formal Upward Channels 481
Informal Communication Channels 481
Barriers to Communication 486
Technical Barriers 486
  Timing 487
  Communication Overload 487
  Cultural Differences 487
Language Barriers 488
  Vocabulary 488
  Semantics 489

Psychological Barriers 491
  Knowledge of What you Want to Say 491
  Filtering 492
  Lack of Trust and Openness 492
  Jealousy 493
  Perception Set Differences 493
Facilitating Communication 494
Empathy 494
Listening 495
Improved Reading Skills 496
Observation 496
Word Choice 496
Body Language 496
Actions 497
Transactional Analysis 498
  Parent 498
  Child 498
  Adult 498
Effects of new Technologies 499
Talking to Managers — Michael Cowpland 500
Opening Incident Revisited 503
Summary 503
Review Questions 504
Exercises 504
Case Studies
  A Failure to Communicate 505
  The Management Trainee 505
  Assuming the Worse 506
Endnotes 507
References 508

CHAPTER 14   ORGANIZATIONAL CONFLICT, CHANGE, AND STRESS 510

Key Terms 510
Learning Objectives 510
Opening Incident 511
Organizational Conflict 512
Two Views of Conflict 512
  The Traditional View 512
  The Current View 514
Sources of Conflict 515
Interpersonal Conflict Management 517
  Force 517
  Withdrawal 517

Smoothing 517
Compromise 517
Mediation and Arbitration 517
Superordinate Goals 518
Problem Solving 518
Structural Conflict Management 518
Procedural Changes 518
Organizational Changes 519
Physical Layout Changes 519
Expand Resources 520
Organizational Change 520
The Change Sequence 521
Recognition of the Need for Change 521
Identifying the Change Method 524
Unfreezing the Status Quo 524
Moving to a New Condition 524
Refreezing to Create a New Status Quo 525
Sources of Resistance to Change 525
Insecurity 525
Possible Social Loss 526
Economic Losses 526
Inconvenience 526
Resentment of Control 527
Unanticipated Repercussions 527
Union Opposition 527
Reducing Resistance to Change 527
Make Only Necessary Changes 528
Attempt to Maintain Useful Informal Relationships 529
Build Trust 529
Provide Information in Advance 529
Encourage Participation 529
Guarantee Against Loss 530
Provide Counseling 530
Stress Management 530
Talking to Managers — Joanne Klassen 532
Executive Burnout 534
Opening Incident Revisited 535
Summary 535
Review Questions 536
Exercises 537
Case Studies
Rumors of a Change at Duncan Electric 537
A Line-Staff Conflict 538
Endnotes 538
References 539

CHAPTER 15   CORPORATE CULTURE AND ORGANIZATION
             DEVELOPMENT   542

   Key Terms   542
   Learning Objectives   542
   Opening Incident   543
   Corporate Culture   544
   Identifying A Corporation's Culture   545
   Corporate Culture and Organizational Performance   546
   Factors that Determine Corporate Culture   546
   The Participative Culture   550
      Values of Participation   550
      Limits of Participation   550
   Talking to Managers — Judith Jossa   552
   Organization Development   554
   Organization Development Techniques   554
      The Survey Feedback Method   554
      Team Building   556
      Process Consultation   557
      Sensitivity Training   558
      Management by Objectives   559
      Job Enrichment   559
      The Managerial Grid   559
   Management Development   559
   Opening Incident Revisited   561
   Summary   561
   Review Questions   562
   Exercises   562
   Case Studies
      A Change of Culture   562
      Creighton Ltd.   563
   Endnotes   564
   References   565

PART V   CONTROLLING   567

CHAPTER 16   THE CONTROLLING PROCESS   568

   Key Terms   568
   Learning Objectives   568
   Opening Incident   569
   The Controlling Process   570
   Establishing Standards   570
   Observing or Measuring   573
   Comparing Performance with Standards   574

Correcting Deviations if Necessary   574
The Dynamics of Corrective Action   575
Talking to Managers — Sharon Matthias   576
Discipline Principles   578
Controlling and the Business System   579
Controlling Inputs   580
Materials Controls   580
Personnel Selection Controls   580
Capital Controls   580
Controlling the Process   581
Controlling Output   581
Evaluation of Employee Performance   582
Quality and Quantity Controls   582
Controls Through Financial Analysis   583
Establishing Strategic Control Points   583
Control and Levels of Management   587
Reasons for Negative Reactions to Controls   589
Inappropriate Controls   589
Unattainable Standards   590
Unpredictable Standards   590
No Control of the Situation   590
Contradictory Standards   590
Overcoming Negative Reactions to Controls   591
Justify Controls   591
Make Controls Understandable   591
Establish a Realistic System   591
Give Timely Feedback   591
Give Accurate Feedback   592
Opening Incident Revisited   592
Summary   593
Review Questions   594
Exercises   594
Case Studies
A Question of Standards   594
Flextime   595
Endnotes   596
References   596

CHAPTER 17   CONTROL TECHNIQUES   598

Key Terms   598
Learning Objectives   599
Opening Incident   599
Non-Financial Control Techniques   600
Rewards and Punishments   600
Selection Procedures   601
Socialization and Training   601

Talking to Managers — Stephen Butler   602
The Management Hierarchy   604
The Management Audit   604
Management by Exception   605
Quality Control   606
  Acceptance Sampling   608
  Control Charts   608
Inventory Control   609
  Economic Order Quantity   611
  The ABC Inventory Method   612
  The Just-In-Time Inventory System   613
Network Models   615
  PERT   616
  The Critical Path Method   621
Financial Control Techniques   621
Budgets   622
  Types of Budgets   622
  An Illustration of Budgetary Control   623
  Benefits of the Budgeting Process   624
  Limitations of the Budgeting Process   625
  PPBS and ZBB   625
Break-even Analysis   626
Net Present Value   628
Profit Centers   628
Ratio Analysis   629
Auditing   633
The Use of Control Techniques by Managers   633
Opening Incident Revisited   635
Summary   636
Review Questions   638
Exercises   639
Case Studies
  Pooling Our Knowledge   639
  A New Product Decision   640
  Ratio Analysis at Norcan Ltd.   640
Endnotes   641
References   641

PART VI   SITUATIONAL APPLICATIONS   643

CHAPTER 18   MANAGING SMALL BUSINESSES   644

Key Terms   644
Learning Objectives   644
Opening Incident   645

Small Business in Canada 646
What is a Small Business? 649
The Role of the Entrepreneur 649
Becoming a Small Business Owner 651
Talking to Managers — Dick Smeelen 652
Why Some People Want Their Own Business 654
Franchising and Small Business 654
Factors Affecting the Management of Small Businesses 656
Economic Factors 656
Political/Legal Factors 657
Social Factors 658
Objectives 659
Technology 660
Organizational Structure 661
Personnel 662
Pitfalls in Starting a Small Business 663
Lack of Experience in the Business 664
Lack of Capital 664
Poor Location 664
Inadequate Inventory Management 665
Excessive Investment in Fixed Assets 665
Poor Credit Policies 665
Taking Too Much Cash Out of the Business 666
Unplanned Expansions 666
Having the Wrong Attitude 667
Government and Small Business 667
Government Assistance to Small Business 667
Government Regulation of Small Business 669
Checklist for Going into Business 670
Opening Incident Revisited 673
Summary 674
Review Questions 674
Exercises 675
Case Studies
  The New Business 675
  The Lethbridge Inn 676
  The Photography Studio 677
Endnotes 679
References 679

CHAPTER 19 MANAGING MULTINATIONALS 681

Key Terms 681
Learning Objectives 681
Opening Incident 682
What is a Multinational Company? 683

The Development of Multinationals 687
Factors Affecting the Management of Multinationals 688
Economic Factors 688
Political/Legal Factors 690
Social Factors 692
Objectives of the Multinational 693
Technology and Multinationals 697
Talking to Managers — Bernard Lamarre 698
Multinational Organizational Structures 700
Personnel Management in Multinationals 703
  Types of MNC Employees 704
  Personnel Problems in MNCs 705
A Final Word on Multinationals 707
Opening Incident Revisited 708
Summary 708
Review Questions 709
Exercises 710
Case Studies
  The Overseas Transfer 710
  International Expansion 711
Endnotes 712
References 713

CHAPTER 20   SOCIAL RESPONSIBILITY AND BUSINESS
ETHICS 716

Key Terms 716
Learning Objectives 716
Opening Incident 717
The Social Contract 718
Obligations to Individuals 719
Obligations to Other Organizations 720
Obligations to Government 720
Obligations to Society in General 720
The Changing Role of Business in Society 721
Corporate Social Responsibility 723
A Definition of Social Responsibility 723
Factors Affecting Corporate Social Responsibility 726
The Social Audit 729
The Debate About Social Responsibility 730
Arguments Favoring Social Responsibility 731
Arguments Against Social Responsibility 731
Talking to Managers — Dorothy Dobbie 732
An Evaluation of the Debate 735
Ethics 736
A Model of Ethics 736

Business Ethics 737
Ethical Dilemmas Facing Managers 738
Illegal versus Unethical Behavior 739
Factors Affecting Managerial Ethics 740
  Government Regulation 740
  Codes of Ethical Behavior 740
  Social Pressures 742
  Individual Ethics versus Corporate Demands 742
A Managerial Code of Ethics 743
Opening Incident Revisited 744
Summary 745
Review Questions 746
Exercises 747
Case Studies
  Dilemma at Can-Roc Ltd. 747
  The Hiring of a Friend's Daughter 748
Endnotes 748
References 749

COMPREHENSIVE MANAGEMENT CASE STUDIES 752

WESTCORP 754
MAIDS, MAIDS, MAIDS, INC. 759
CITY OF FASOFURN, ONTARIO 764
ELECTRONICS UNLIMITED 770
ATLANTIC STORE FURNITURE 774
SCOTT TRUCKS 778
EASTERN TEL 783
KRYZOWSKI AND SONS LTD. 788
CENTRAL DECAL LTD. 792
NORTH HILL REGIONAL CENTRE 796
DUKE AND NOBLE 799
SLOW WHEELING 804
AGGRAVATION AT ANC 807
GOOD SAMARITAN SERVICES 813

GLOSSARY 818
INDEX 832

I

Introduction

1

Management

KEY TERMS

business firm
profit
sole proprietorship
partnership
corporation
shareholders
common stock
preferred stock
board of directors
corporation bylaws
not-for-profit
  organizations
management
effectiveness
efficiency

lower-level
  managers
middle managers
top management
planning
organizing
influencing
motivation
leadership
communication
controlling
coordination
decision making
interpersonal role
informational role

decisional role
conceptual skill
technical skill
human skill
classical school of
  management
scientific
  management
behavioral school of
  management
human relations
  movement
Hawthorne effect
behavioral science

LEARNING OBJECTIVES

After completing this chapter, you should be able to
1. Define and describe management and explain the work of managers.
2. Relate the importance of service industries in the economy.
3. Identify the different forms of business ownership.
4. Identify and describe the management functions of planning, organizing, influencing, and controlling.
5. Explain the managerial roles — interpersonal, informational, and decisional — and the important managerial skills — technical, human and conceptual.
6. Describe the classical and behavioral schools of management.
7. Identify and describe the various schools or approaches to the study of management.

OPENING INCIDENT

Lawton Manufacturing Ltd.

Marshall Cizek graduated from high school 10 years ago and immediately went to work as a maintenance mechanic for Lawton Manufacturing Ltd. The maintenance department, comprised of eight people, was responsible for routine maintenance and repairing factory machinery. Cizek liked his job, got along with his colleagues, and considered himself happy. In the past year, however, he had begun to think about a promotion. Graham Tonks, the plant superintendent, often praised Cizek's work and his cooperative attitudes. This spring, when the head of the maintenance department left Lawton for another position, Tonks appointed Cizek to replace him.

Cizek energetically threw himself into his new job. He wanted to make his department the most efficient in the entire plant. He came to work early, stayed late, and became a dominating presence in the maintenance area. He continued his technical interests in the machinery, often doing repairs himself. He disliked paperwork, so he spent most of his time in the plant, dealing with what he called "problems on the firing line."

After several months as head of mainte-nance, Cizek was called into the plant superintendent's office for a talk. Tonks began by asking Cizek why his reports were always late and often incomplete. Tonks went on to state that he was concerned about growing inefficiency in the maintenance area. In Tonks's opinion, Cizek was not giving proper leadership to either maintenance and repair or the people in his department. Tonks noted that several maintenance workers had complained about Cizek meddling in the technical details of their work. The superintendent was sympathetic, saying that he had high regard for Cizek's technical skills; but Tonks reminded Cizek that he was now a manager and, unless Cizek could begin to manage the maintenance department more productively, he would have to be replaced.

Cizek left work that day feeling dispirited. That evening he played softball with some friends; after the game, he talked over his problem with Jim, one of his close friends. After listening to Cizek for about half an hour, Jim said: "You know, Marshall, a baseball player can't play every position on the team."

Did you know that almost half of all new Canadian businesses fail in the first six years of operation?[1] In over 75 percent of these cases, managerial incompetence and inexperience are the causes of the failure. The costs of poor management to individuals and to Canada's economic stability are great. Not only are financial and physical resources wasted when businesses fail, but individuals may suffer psychological damage. Clearly, business failure can often be avoided through good management practices: a reason why management is a subject of increasing importance.

The Canadian economy comprises both large and small organizations. In these organizations, people work together to accomplish goals that are too complex or large in number to be achieved by a single individual. Throughout life, Canadians have contact with a variety of organizations, such as hospitals, schools, churches, businesses, colleges, universities, and government agencies. The most significant factor in determining the quality of performance and success of such organizations — and the quality of life in Canada — is the quality of its management.

Why are some managers successful, while others are not? This question requires a complicated answer. In this book we examine a variety of factors that influence managerial success. For now, we will simply say that successful managers are those who are able to carry out effectively the basic functions of management — planning, organizing, influencing, and controlling. We should also note that successful managers foster the cooperation and goodwill of others inside and outside the organization. Managers must work through others to achieve success.

In this book, we provide you with knowledge about the fundamental concepts and techniques used by effective managers in all types of organizations. The material is presented from the standpoint that there is no one best way to manage. In order to illustrate the concepts, examples of how management is actually practiced are presented. While our primary focus is on the management of profit-oriented business firms, most concepts and principles will also apply to not-for-profit organizations such as schools, churches, government, and charitable organizations.

MANAGEMENT IN VARIOUS SETTINGS

In Canada, there are many different kinds of organizations. Consider this list:

Falconbridge Nickel	Eldorado Nuclear	Winnipeg Blue
Ron's Hairstyling	Ltd.	Bombers
Shop	Algonquin College	Scott Mission

Canadian National Railways	Canadian Wildlife Federation	Shoppers Drug Mart Perth's
Eaton's	Canada Post	Women's College Hospital
Revenue Canada	The YMCA / YWCA	
Shopsy's	Canadian Kidney Foundation	Air Canada
Imperial Oil		Jim's Taxi
The Canadian Mint	Creditel	Loto Canada
Canadian Broadcasting Corporation	Canadian Imperial Bank of Commerce	Underground Gourmet
	Inuit Tapirisat	Safeway
Mienke and Mienke Meat Market	Atomic Energy of Canada	The United Way Cashway Lumber

Some of these organizations operate in the private sector and pursue a profit (for example, Falconbridge Nickel, Shoppers Drug Mart, Jim's Taxi, Perth's, and Cashway Lumber). Some of these private sector firms produce a physical product (for example, Imperial Oil), some produce intangible services (for example, Winnipeg Blue Bombers), and others produce both physical goods and intangible services (for example, Underground Gourmet).

Some of these organizations operate in the public sector and do not pursue a profit (for example, The YMCA/YWCA, The United Way, the Canadian Broadcasting Corporation, and the Canadian Kidney Foundation). Some of these public-sector firms produce a physical product (for example, Eldorado Nuclear Ltd.), some produce intangible services (for example, Canada Post), and others produce both physical goods and intangible services (for example, the Canadian Mint).

All of the privately owned firms are profit-oriented; some of the government-owned organizations are also profit-oriented (for example, Air Canada), but many others are not (for example, The Canadian Mint, Canada Post, Atomic Energy of Canada).

All organizations — whether they are profit-oriented or not-for-profit, whether they produce a physical product or an intangible service, whether they are private sector or public sector — need managers in order to function effectively. The general work that managers do (making decisions and allocating resources) is similar in all organizations. However, the specific jobs that need to be done vary depending on whether the organization is profit-oriented or not-for-profit. We will now consider the differences between profit and not-for-profit organizations, and between manufacturing and service organizations, in more detail so that the role of managers is clearer.

The Profit-Oriented Business Firm

business firm

Business firms play an integral role in the Canadian economic system. A **business firm** is an entity that seeks to make a profit by gathering and allocating productive resources to satisfy demand. This demand may be for either goods or services.

Although some people think that business firms are found only in the private sector, a government organization which pursues a profit is also a business firm. Like any private-sector firm, it tries to gather and allocate resources in such a way that a profit is made.

The business firm is the basic building block for the making of economic decisions in Canada. Through business firms, resources are organized for production, and land, labor, and capital are first asembled, then converted into products and services that can be sold. This activity is directed and guided by managers. (See Figure 1-1.)

Business activity, regardless of whether the firm conducting it is publicly or privately owned, requires decision making to produce and sell goods and services at a profit. It requires buying as well as selling. Thus, the market plays a role. How resources are used depends mainly on choices made by firms and consumers. Both are primarily guided by market prices. The firm is the key to the market's operations because it guides the flow of resources through the marketplace. The firm is an input-output system. The inputs are productive resources the firm buys in the market. The outputs are the goods it makes and sells in the market. Both input and output depend on market prices, although in some instances decisions will be guided by social and political considerations in addition to economic ones.

Resources and the goods made from them are both scarce. Therefore, they command prices. The firm's costs of doing business (converting resources from one form to another) must be less than its revenues if it is to earn a profit. To determine how profitable it is, a firm must keep records of its costs and sales. Accounting traces the effects of resource flows on profits. **Profit** is the difference between the cost of inputs and the revenue from outputs. People form business firms to produce and sell consumer-demanded goods and services so that they can make a profit. However, profit does not appear until it is earned, and there is no guarantee that a firm will succeed.

profit

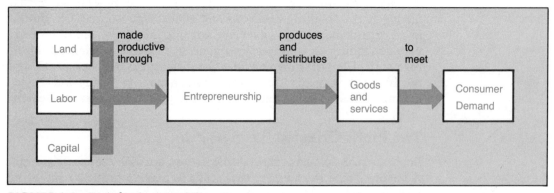

FIGURE 1-1   Basic business activity

If revenues are greater than costs, a profit is earned. Profit may be increased by raising prices, lowering costs, or selling more units. But most firms cannot raise prices much without reducing sales. Most of them try to increase profit by cutting costs and/or increasing the number of units sold. If a firm's revenues and costs are equal, it earns no profit. It only breaks even. Few people, however, go into business to break even. This is especially true if there is no "owner's salary" included in the firm's list of expenses. Firms that just break even give their owners no economic return from being in business.

Any after-tax profit earned by a firm is reinvested in the firm and/or is distributed to its owners. For many firms, reinvested profit is the major source of funds to finance their growth. The owners, in effect, are willing to reinvest their profit in the firm rather than taking it out and spending it themselves.

While it is an accepted fact in capitalist economies that all types and sizes of business firms seek profit, there is some argument whether profit should be their only objective. Governments have profitability in mind when they form business firms, but they also take into account other social and political factors. Later, we discuss the social responsibility of business. At any rate, it's one thing to seek profit and another to make it.

Forms of Business Ownership

Business firms vary in size from single-owner firms to giant corporations owned by thousands of people. A business firm may be a sole proprietorship, a partnership, or a corporation.

sole proprietorship

The sole proprietorship is the oldest and still the most common form of legal ownership in Canada. A **sole proprietorship is a business** owned and managed by one person. That person, however, may have help from others in running the business. The sole proprietor is the classic case of the entrepreneur. Only a sole proprietor can say: "I am the company" or "This is my business." Ron's Hairstyling Shop and Jim's Taxi are sole proprietorships.

partnership

A second form of business firm, a **partnership**, comes into being when two or more individuals agree to combine their financial, managerial, and technical abilities for the purpose of operating a company for profit. Mienke and Mienke Meat Market is a partnership. Many law firms and accounting firms are run as partnerships.

corporation

The third form of business ownership, the **corporation**, can be defined as "an artificial being, invisible, intangible, and existing only in contemplation of law." Unlike a sole proprietorship or partnership, the corporation has legal existence apart from its owners. It can buy, hold, and sell property in its own name, and it can sue and be sued. Originally, the corporate form of ownership was used most frequently for charitable, educational, or public purposes. In order to incorporate, a charter was required from the federal government. That is why the corporation is legally separate from its owners. It is a creation of government authority. Eaton's, Imperial Oil, Shopsy's, Safeway, Falconbridge Nickel, Creditel, and Shoppers Drug Mart are corporations.

shareholders

Shareholders are persons who own the common and preferred shares of a corporation. The number of votes a shareholder has depends on the number of shares he or she owns. It is not a case of "one person, one vote," and this explains why many small shareholders do not vote their shares in large corporations. For example, a person who owns 10 shares of INCO may choose not to vote. Control of such a corporation can be effective if a group of shareholders pools its votes to get a voting majority. In some cases, a person with 10 percent or even less of a corporation's stock can exercise much control over its affairs. Most corporations have thousands of shares and hundreds of shareholders. Some, however, remain quite small in terms of number of owners and the number and market value of shares outstanding.

A shareholder need not, and generally does not, participate in managing the corporation. Ownership and management are separate. Most of the shareholders in Canada do not participate in managing the corporations of which they are part owners. The shareholders come from many backgrounds — for example, schoolteachers, plumbers, or salaried executives.

Shareholders are the direct owners of a corporation. There are, however, millions of other people who have an indirect ownership in many corporations. For example, the members of many labor unions make payments to their union pension funds. Some of this money is used to buy shares in corporations. Thus, the union members are indirect owners of stock.

A shareholder owns a partial interest in the whole corporation. Suppose you own one share of stock in Norcen Energy Resources. You are not entitled to walk into the corporation's headquarters and demand to see the "property" you own. The property is owned by the corporation. What you own is a small part of the entire corporation. The value of that part varies with changes in the value of the shares of stock which you own. This is determined by the supply of, and demand for, the shares on the market.

common stock

The two basic types of stock are common stock and preferred stock. **Common stock** shows ownership in a corporation. It is voting stock and all common shareholders enjoy the same rights. Common shareholders have a right to earnings that remain (residual earnings) after the corporation has met the prior claims of bondholders and preferred shareholders. The actual payment of a common stock dividend from these residual earnings does not occur until the board of directors declares a common stock dividend. If the corporation goes bankrupt, the common shareholders are the last to receive any proceeds from the sale of the corporation's property. Creditors, bondholders, and preferred shareholders are all paid before the common shareholders. Thus, common shareholders are the residual owners of a corporation.

preferred stock

Preferred stock also shows ownership in a corporation. Preferred shareholders usually cannot vote their shares, but they do enjoy certain preferences with respect to dividends and assets. As we have seen, they have a right to receive the dividend indicated on their share certificates before common shareholders receive any dividends. This dividend also is not owed until declared by the corporation's board of directors. If the corporation goes out of business and pays off its debts, preferred shareholders have the right to receive their share of any remaining assets before the common shareholders receive anything.

The number of votes a shareholder has in elections of board members and other business voted on at shareholders meetings depends on the number of shares he or she owns. Each share of common stock carries one vote; thus, a person with 20 shares has 20 votes.

board of directors

A corporation's board of directors is elected by its shareholders. (See Figure 1-2.) The **board of directors** is a group of people who are

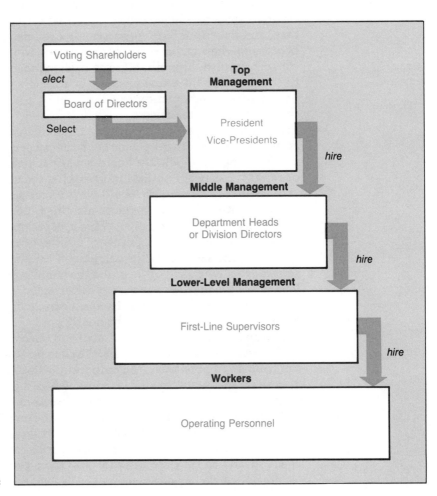

FIGURE 1-2
Corporate structure

Board of Directors

given the power to govern the corporation's affairs and to make general policy. This power comes from the corporate charter and the corporation's shareholders. In small corporations the major shareholders often manage the business. But in larger corporations, with thousands of shareholders, the board of directors is accountable for guiding the affairs of the business. It's easy for a board to keep itself in power as long as it does a good job in the opinion of voting shareholders. Unseating a board member can be tough. The board of directors elects its own officers. These board officers usually include a chairperson of the board, a vice-chairperson, and a secretary. The board holds periodic meetings.

corporation
bylaws

Although the shareholders have the authority to draw up the corporation's bylaws, they usually leave it up to the board. **Corporation bylaws** are the rules by which the corporation will operate. They include: place and time of meetings, procedure for calling meetings, directors' pay, duties of corporate officers, regulations for new stock issues, and procedures for changing the bylaws.

Another task of the board is selecting the corporation's officers, or its top managers, who include the president, vice-president(s), secretary, and treasurer. The corporation's officers are employees of the board and they are also the corporation's top management. These officers, in turn, hire other, lower-level managers to help in running the corporation. In actual practice, boards sometimes select only the president, or chief executive officer (CEO), and he or she then selects the other corporate officers.

The board is accountable to the shareholders for the actions of the corporate officers. In other words, the board performs the function of a "watchdog." As such, the board usually has the authority to accept or reject the officers' actions in managing the corporation.

In some corporations the board plays a very active role in managing the corporation. It holds frequent meetings and has a lot of say in the firm's day-to-day management. This is especially likely to be the case in small, closely held corporations. On the other hand, some boards are content to select only the company president. The president then selects other corporate officers and the board merely acts as a "review board" for the president and the other officers' decisions. In this case, the president pretty well runs the entire corporation, subject to "rubber stamp" approval by the board.

The distinctions between the board and the corporate officers often are blurred. In some corporations the chairperson of the board is also the company's president. The corporation's other top managers may also be on the board. In such a case, the board members who are not corporate officers are called "outside directors."

Board members have certain legal obligations. They must act in the best interest of the shareholders and be reasonable and prudent in doing their jobs. They must be as careful in managing the corporation's affairs as they are in managing their personal affairs. In the

MANAGEMENT IN PRACTICE

Things Have Changed in the Boardroom

Recruiting members for a company's board of directors is becoming an increasingly difficult job. There are two reasons for this. First, as Patrick O'Callaghan, a partner with Caldwell Partners International, notes, directors' responsibilities and workload are much more significant now than previously. The days are gone when a person could sit on the boards of eight or ten major companies and attend a couple of meetings a year. Now, most directors sit on only two or three boards because each one requires considerable work.

The second reason has to do with increased expectations about directors' liability for their decisions. Federal and provincial regulations have made directors substantially more responsible to shareholders, employees, and customers. Shareholders have grown more sophis-

ticated and are now more likely to sue board members for bad decisions. Directors are also being held personally liable if an ex-employee wins a suit for wrongful dismissal. Liability insurance is also a problem. Premiums have increased substantially, dollar coverage has decreased, deductibles are higher, and insurers are excluding more types of claims.

A survey done in 1985 by the Conference Board of Canada revealed that 16 percent of the companies surveyed had experienced at least one legal action against their directors, and some had had as many as 15 legal actions. More than 70 percent of Canadian companies pay for liability insurance for their directors.

SOURCE Adapted from Patricia Lush, "Being a Director Means Being a Worker," *The Globe and Mail* (March 16, 1987): B1, B8.

---

past, board members have been held liable only for illegal acts and fraud. More recently, however, some courts have even held directors liable for using poor judgment.

Not-for-Profit Organizations

Many organizations in Canada do not have profit as their objective; in fact, business firms are the only profit-oriented organizations in Canadian society. Examples of not-for-profit organizations include the Scott Mission, The United Way, the Canadian Wildlife Federation, the Canadian Red Cross, The YMCA/YWCA, the Canadian Kidney Foundation, and Inuit Tapirisat — to name just a few.

not-for-profit
organizations
 Not-for-profit organizations usually stress service objectives instead of profit. The Canadian Union of Public Employees, for example, provides expert service for its members regarding grievance and wage negotiations. The Fort Richmond Community Club provides services for people in its local area. The YMCA/YWCA provides a variety of social services.

In spite of the differences between profit-oriented and not-for-profit organizations, two crucial similarities make management im-

NB

1) All organizations have objectives to remain in existence

2) People must be directed and motivated towards organizations goals

portant to both of them. First, all organizations have objectives that must be reached if the organization is to remain in existence. Second, in both types of organizations, people must be directed and motivated toward the organization's goals. Since managers direct the efforts of other people in accomplishing organization goals, it is clear that both kinds of organizations need managers.

The importance of these similarities can be shown by analyzing the activities of two organizations that appear very different — the Canadian Wildlife Federation and Imperial Oil. Although it is a not-for-profit organization, the CWF needs managers to ensure that it reaches its objectives of protecting and managing wildlife in Canada. To reach these objectives, individuals in the CWF must be motivated to make the public aware of its goals and to act in ways consistent with preserving wildlife. Imperial Oil also needs managers to reach its goals of providing oil products to Canadian consumers so that it can make a profit. Managers at Imperial Oil must also motivate their employees so that these goals can be reached. Thus, even though these two organizations have markedly different goals, they both need managers to help them reach their goals.

Manufacturing versus Service Organizations

In the past, when business management was discussed, most people thought of the operation of buildings with smokestacks, assembly lines, and workers with lunch pails. While the factory system is still inportant to Canada's economic system, working conditions have changed drastically in the past few decades.

Most business organizations in Canada are involved in providing services rather than physical products. Service organizations do not produce tangible products; rather, they create intangible services. Banks, insurance companies, schools, government, and businesses with involvements as diverse as transportation, real estate, and personal grooming are all service organizations that do seek to make a profit. Service organizations employ about two of every three Canadians. Service industries also account for a substantial part of the expenditures of Canadian households.

A complicating factor in dealing with the manufacturing versus service issue is the fact that many organizations are involved in both. IBM, for example, manufacturers computers, but its after-sales service and its advice to customers on how best to use the computer are clearly service activities. IBM is not an isolated example; many large manufacturing firms are both service and manufacturing organizations.

Regardless of whether a firm is involved in service or manufacturing, or both, management is important. Resources must be properly allocated so that organization goals can be reached. This is the job of managers.

WHAT IS MANAGEMENT?

Most likely, you will be employed by some type of organization and, as a result, be working with managers. Understanding what is involved in managing is important even though you probably will not start out as a manager. Knowledge of basic management concepts will be beneficial to you either as a worker or as a manager. If you have plans for a management career, you should gain a full understanding of what managers do and what management is all about.

management

There are almost as many definitions of management as there are books on the subject. Most definitions of management do share a common idea — **management** is the process of accomplishing organization objectives through the efforts of other people. Objectives, or goals, are the final results expected. For example, your immediate objective may be to pass this course, while your long-term goals may be to complete your schooling and obtain a good job. The objective of business firms is to make a profit by providing goods and/or services to customers. In order for a business firm to achieve this goal, the managers in the firm must perform four main functions:

- Determine what is to be achieved (planning).
- Allocate resources and establish the means to accomplish the plans (organizing).
- Motivate and lead personnel (influencing or directing).
- Compare achieved results to planned goals (controlling).

Thus, management is the process of planning, organizing, influencing, and controlling to accomplish organization objectives through the coordinated use of human and material resources.

effectiveness

efficiency

Managers must be both effective and efficient as they carry out the management process. **Effectiveness** means achieving the goals that have been set. **Efficiency** means achieving the greatest output possible with a given amount of inputs. Stated another way, effectiveness means doing the right things, while efficiency means doing things right.

Note that one of the functions of management is directing (leadership). Some people feel that leaders are concerned mainly with effectiveness, while managers are concerned mainly with efficiency. (This issue of leaders vs. managers is examined in more detail in Chapter 12.)

WHO ARE MANAGERS AND WHAT DO MANAGERS DO?

In a sense, everyone is a manager. People manage their lives by planning, organizing, directing, and controlling their skills, talents, time, and activities. Parents manage their jobs, households, and children; children manage their allowances; and students manage their time if they expect to succeed in various subjects in school.

Take the example of Laurie Steen, an accounting major at a university. Her objective is to pursue a career as a chartered accountant. In order to accomplish her goal, she must first complete her B.Comm. degree. Next, she must find a job articling in one of the CA firms. While she is working in the profession, she will be taking further specialized accounting courses toward the Uniform Final Examination, which must be passed by all people who wish to become a CA. In order to accomplish her goal, Laurie must be a good manager of her time. She must plan her schedule, organize her time and financial resources, and evaluate or control her own performance to maintain her grades. Laurie uses management concepts to achieve her objectives.

Managers in business and in not-for-profit organizations also pursue objectives, but those of the organization, not their own. Pursuit of a common goal can lead to the grouping of managers. For instance, the term "management" is sometimes used to refer collectively to all the managers in a firm. This usage is most often heard in connection with negotiations between workers or unions and their supervisors. The uppermost managers in an organization — usually called executives — may also be referred to collectively as management.

Because management so frequently refers to a firm's top executives, people sometimes forget that managers occupy other positions within large organizations. Actually managers operate at most levels within every type of organization — large or small, private sector or public sector, business or not-for-profit. As shown earlier in Figure 1-2, there are three basic levels of managers.

3 levels of managers

lower-level managers

Lower-level managers, often referred to as supervisors or first-line supervisors, are responsible for managing employees in daily operations. In a manufacturing firm, a factory supervisor is responsible for ensuring that the assembly line runs properly and that the right type of product is produced. In a government office, the supervisor of clerical staff ensures that paperwork is processed correctly and on time.

middle managers

Middle managers, such as department heads, are concerned primarily with the coordination of programs and activities that are necessary to achieve the overall organization goals, as identified by top management. In a manufacturing company, sales managers and production superintendents are middle managers. In government organizations, department heads are middle managers.

top management

Top management includes the chief executive officer, the chairperson of the board, the president, as well as vice-president(s). In not-for-profit organizations, the top manager is sometimes called the executive director. These individuals are responsible for providing the overall direction of the organization.

In the final analysis, a manager is anyone, at any level of the organization, who directs the efforts of other people in accomplishing organization goals. Wherever a group of people work together to achieve results, a manager is present.

School principals, meat market supervisors, service station operators, and factory supervisors are managers, just as the presidents of Air Canada, London Life Insurance, Imperial Bank of Commerce, and Falconbridge Nickel are managers. The prime minister is a manager, too, as are government agency heads, university deans, church pastors, and military commanders.

Managers are responsible for making decisions concerning the use of a firm's resources to achieve results. Managers are the catalysts who establish goals; plan operations; organize various resources — personnel, materials, equipment, capital; lead and motivate people to perform; evaluate actual results against the goals; and develop people for the organization.

The success of a particular business manager cannot be judged exclusively on short-run output. In other words, a manager may be said to be effective if his or her unit is earning a profit, or reducing costs, or increasing the market share for the company's products, or other such measurable results. Naturally, these accomplishments are important to any organization. However, a major challenge and, indeed, obligation of any manager is the development of people under his or her direction; in so doing, long-term goals may be achieved more effectively. Developing competent and well-trained people who can be promoted to more responsible positions is a significant part of a manager's job. This is an excellent long-run measure of the effectiveness of a manager and contributes to the growth and success of the firm whether it is a manufacturing or service organization.

THE MANAGEMENT FUNCTIONS

In every organization, the work done by managers concerns the functions of planning, organizing, influencing, and controlling to achieve the organization objectives. A separate section of this text is devoted to each of these four management functions, which are introduced here.

Planning

planning

Planning is the process of determining in advance what should be accomplished and how to do it. Ideally, plans should be stated in

Photo by Ellen Tofflemire

**David Leighton
Nabisco Brands Ltd.**

Academics, as we all know, are a funny breed. Great for discussing the price elasticity of Oreo cookies but lousy at making the brand profitable — right? Wrong, says David Leighton, vice-chairperson of Nabisco Brands Ltd., the $938.5 million (annual sales, 1984) maker of Oreos, among about 500 other brand products, including Planters peanuts, Ritz crackers, Dr. Ballard's pet foods and Oh Henry! candy bars. As someone who has straddled both the

academic and business communities for much of his long career, Leighton is quite convinced that the intellectual rigor of the academic can be harnessed to the bottom line.

Leighton has taught business at such universities as Harvard and Western. As well, he ran the Banff Centre for Continuing Education for 12 years, until 1982. In 1983, he was made chairperson of Nabisco.

Q: The stereotype of the executive and the entrepreneur is anti-intellectual. You were an academic, yet you are in a top executive position in a large company — heavily involved in marketing, no less. How are you received and perceived?

Leighton: I was sitting next to Jim Gillies (a professor of business at York University) at a board meeting yesterday. I commented that we were in "academic row." He replied that he had the same problem — all his academic friends think he's a businessman, and all his business friends think he's an academic.

The transition from academic to executive was relatively easy for me. I was on the Nabisco board for years, so I became a familiar figure to the key executives here. But there are some obstacles. I don't think anybody really believes that an academic could run something profitably. You tend to get slotted into a staff role or to become a resident philosopher or guru.

I point out periodically that while in Banff, I ran a business with 350 employees, and had to negotiate labor contracts, look at the computer-based information systems and decide on capital investments. The Banff Centre just happened to be an academic institution.

Q: How much real intellect is involved in managing a corporation these days?

Leighton: Much more than what used to be the case. First of all, the job is more demanding. You can't be a chief executive officer of a company this size today, having come up through the ranks and being solely concerned with the production and sale of your product.

Today you're dealing with government at every level all the time. You're also dealing with international situations and worrying about the dollar and investment strategy. All of these things call for a broader-range senior manager. The business schools have been catalysts in the process. The people running the divisions of this company are all MBAs. Twenty or 30 years ago none of them would have been. I'm not saying the MBA is the be-all and end-all, but the degree indicates a breadth of intellectual experience that is broader than the previous system of coming up through the ranks.

Q: Twenty years ago Canadians were considered weak marketers. Is that still so?
Leighton: Not in the food business or packaged goods. The sophistication in marketing here is as good as it is in New York. What's made us improve? Partly the high degree of competition, which is more intense now than 20 years ago. Our business schools have helped a great deal. Multinational corporations have also provided a tremendous stream of know-how back and forth.
We can't operate a company in Canada at a significantly lower level of expertise than the American company. A high proportion of the key jobs in our company in the US are filled by Canadians. I'm almost arguing that it is more sophisticated here, that you can get general management experience earlier and faster in Canada that in the US because it's not quite so far to the top.

Q: All your products are in mature industries so there's nowhere much to go. Over the last two years, hasn't all your growth come from acquisitions?
Leighton: A significant amount has also come out of R & D. In this battle, we're convinced the prize is going to the company that has the best research. Our parent has just invested $60 million in an R & D center. We get a lot out of that. A good example is the work they did developing the "Crisp and Chewy" cookies

that have been a major part of the cookie war with Procter & Gamble Inc. That may seem like a trivial kind of product innovation but there was a lot of very imaginative R & D and technical work involved.

Q: Nine out of 10 new products fail. Can you improve on those odds?
Leighton: We'd better, or we won't last very long. That number has been kicked around for a long time and I've never been very sure about what counted as new products. The well-managed companies, such as Procter & Gamble, have a much higher success ratio. Ours is better too — that's one of the jobs of management. The trick is to understand the market and have a very clear strategy; and also to be tough on incrementalism — those modest little changes in the package, or those features which may boost your market share a point or two and make a product manager look like a hero.

Q: Where does the multinational fit into economic strategy?
Leighton: I'm an internationalist. One of the potentially saving graces of the modern economy is the development of multinationals. They've been unjustly pilloried for political reasons by people who didn't understand what they were doing. It was like trying to hold back the tide. In this corporation and others, there are enormous benefits to the economy and to this country in terms of employing and using its brainpower. The attitude we've taken toward international investment and multinationals is crazy.
And in the Third World, there's a certain onus on the country involved to look after its own affairs and to channel the investment and knowhow of those multinationals. The response varies from country to country. Most multinationals are responsible, thinking, long-term investors prepared to deal on a straightforward basis. Quite often, they literally don't know what is best for the local economy and rely on the pressure of the local groups to push them in a given direction.

specific terms so that they provide clear guidance for managers and workers. For example, when Coca-Cola decides to gain market share by developing new products, management has to make specific decisions about how this is to be achieved. It is not enough to say that the overall objective of a company is to "make a profit" or "be the leader in the industry." Its plans must be specific and must indicate how the overall goal is going to be achieved. Molson's might want to achieve a 30 percent share of the Canadian beer market and a 15 percent return on investment. In order to accomplish these goals, the company must develop step-by-step plans for producing and marketing its products. The overall organization objective is translated by managers into goals for each part of the firm; this is the planning process. The planning function — including decision making — is discussed in detail in Chapters 3 to 5.

Organizing

organizing

Organizing is the process of prescribing formal relationships among people and resources to accomplish goals. The organizing function is concerned with developing a framework that relates all personnel, work assignments, and physical resources to one another. This framework is usually termed the "organizational structure" and is designed to facilitate the accomplishment of the organization's objectives.

Since firms' goals and resources differ, the organization structure in each firm is unique. Firms within one industry may have similar organization structures (for example, Steel Company of Canada and Algoma Steel), but no two structures are exactly the same. Firms that provide different products or services may have very diverse organization structures (for example, Imperial Oil and Algonquin College).

Chapters 6 and 7 discuss organizing as a formal process. Of course, the formal organization must take into account the informal relationships and group behavior patterns that exist among organization members. These are the subject of Chapters 8 and 9. An important aspect of organizing is ensuring that the right people with the right qualifications are available at the right places and times to accomplish the purposes of the organization. This is called "staffing" and is the subject of Chapter 10.

Influencing

influencing

motivation

Influencing is the process of determining or affecting the behavior of others. This involves motivation, leadership, and communication. It also involves managing organizational conflict and change, and developing employees capabilities. **Motivation** is the willingness to put forth effort in the pursuit of goals. Motivating workers often means simply creating an environment that makes them want to work. Part of this environment is the direction provided by the manager. Each worker may require a different means of motivation. A manager cannot motivate a worker to produce unless the worker chooses to respond. But managers can often create a situation where workers will want to work harder. We discuss motivation in greater detail in Chapter 11.

leadership

Leadership is getting others to do what the leader wants them to do. A good leader is one who motivates others to put forth their best efforts. As will be seen in Chapter 12, leaders may depend in part on charisma or other outstanding personal characteristics. Good leadership more often results from learning what motivates individual workers and using this knowledge to direct their activities. The leadership style that works best will vary depending on the characteristics of the leader, his or her employees, and the situation.

communication

Communication is the transfer of information, ideas, understanding, or feelings between people. Much of a manager's day is spent communicating. Supervisors, for example, tell workers what needs to be done. They also report to upper-level management, summarizing their unit's activities, seeking support and guidance, and representing subordinates. Communication will be discussed further in Chapter 13.

The way in which managers motivate and lead workers and communicate with superiors and subordinates affects and is affected by corporate culture. The culture can be one of openness and support, or one of autocracy and fear.

Controlling

controlling

Controlling is the process of comparing actual performance with standards and taking any necessary corrective action. The purpose of establishing controls is to ensure proper performance in accordance with plans. In the event of unsatisfactory performance, corrective action can be taken. For instance, if a company's costs for producing a product are higher than planned, management must have some means of recognizing the problem and taking the appropriate action to correct the situation. Controls can also work on the positive side. If sales exceed expectations, work shifts can be added at existing plants or new capacity can be purchased or leased.

An aspect of the controlling function that relates uniquely to the human resource is disciplinary action. This is action taken to correct undesired behavior and ranges from a verbal warning to outright dismissal. The control function is discussed in Chapters 16 and 17.

Coordination

coordination

Some management writers consider coordination as a separate function of management. However, in our view **coordination** involves the integration of the functions of planning, organizing, influencing, and controlling. Being a manager should not be viewed as performing separate and distinct functions. For instance, the planning function is usually thought of as preceding controlling, but results of the controlling process may cause future plans to be altered. Coordination is necessary throughout the management process and in this text will not be considered as a separate and distinct function of management.

Managers must coordinate the functions, physical resources, and personnel of their firm so that the organization goals can be achieved efficiently and effectively. As such, coordination represents an overall concern of all managers and is achieved when people, resources, and functions blend together harmoniously to achieve quality results.

MANAGEMENT IN PRACTICE

Management Functions and Polar Exploration

The management functions of planning, organizing, staffing, directing, and controlling are obviously important in business organizations. But these functions are also important in many other kinds of organizations. Consider the race between the British and Norwegians in 1911-1912 to see who would be the first to reach the South Pole. To get there, it was necessary to set up a base camp on the Antarctic Ocean, then walk or ski approximately 1200 kilometres to the Pole and return. All of this took place in the most hostile environment on earth. Temperatures ranged from 0^0 C to -45^0 C and much travelling at altitudes up to 3500 metres (10 000 feet) was required.

The Norwegians, led by Roald Amundsen, won the race primarily because they were better managed. Their expedition was planned several years in advance and strict attention to detail was evident. For example, the organization of supplies and the laying out of supply depots on the way to the South Pole was a triumph of organization that ensured the Norwegians enough food to make it safely back to their base camp after they reached the Pole. Amundsen carefully selected the five men to make the run for the Pole, and he demonstrated insightful leadership in motivating these men in the context of a small group. The group had confidence in their leader, and Amundsen allowed his men to participate in many of the important decisions that had to be made during the expedition.

By contrast, the British expedition, led by Robert Scott, was poorly managed. The planning of the important details of the expedition was left to the last minute, and the organization and laying out of the crucial supply depots left much to be desired. Scott's leadership ability was limited, and there was dissension in the ranks because Scott was not sensitive to the dynamics of the small group. Scott did not inspire confidence in his men and he did not allow participation in important decisions. Although Scott also reached the South Pole (one month after Amundsen), his group of five paid dearly for his lack of management competence — they died of starvation and exposure while attempting to get back to their base camp.

SOURCE Adapted from Roland Huntford, *The Last Place on Earth* (New York: Atheneum, 1985).

decision making

A task that managers perform in carrying out each of the management functions is decision making. **Decision making** is the process of generating and evaluating alternatives and making choices among them. Perhaps no other attribute so frequently distinguishes the excellent manager from mediocre ones as does decision-making skills.

Management Functions at Various Managerial Levels

As illustrated in Figure 1-3, the basic functions of planning, organizing, influencing, and controlling are performed by managers at every level within an organization. The amount of time and effort devoted to each function, however, will likely depend on the level of a manager. As shown in the diagram, the amount of time that lower-level managers spend on planning is much less than that spent by top management. The lower-level manager must devote considerable time and effort in influencing and controlling the work of others — accomplishing routine tasks and putting out daily fires. As managers move to higher levels in the organization, a greater percentage of their time is devoted to planning and less to influencing (although

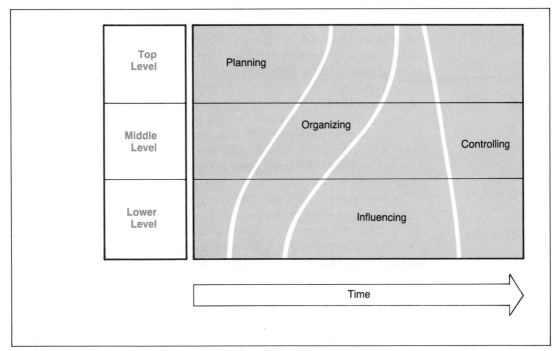

FIGURE 1-3 Management functions at various managerial levels

they may spend increased time influencing external groups like government, unions, or consumers). The amount of time spent on the controlling function is fairly consistent at all levels of management except for the uppermost level, such as for the president or chief executive officer. At this high level, the chief executive is concerned with overall control of resources essential to the survival of the firm. Finally, the amount of time devoted to the organizing function is fairly consistent at all levels.

MANAGERIAL ROLES

Management writers have long recognized that, when the complexities of managerial work are reduced to the four functions of planning, organizing, influencing, and controlling, much of the dynamics of what a manager does on a day-to-day basis is lost. In an attempt to overcome this problem, Henry Mintzberg of McGill University has developed a view of managerial work that captures some of the uncertainty, complexity, frustration, and excitement of the typical management job.[2]

Mintzberg did a detailed analysis of the work behavior of five chief executive officers. Overall, he found that managers worked long hours, were involved in intense activity, and often were interrupted before they could finish the task they were working on. Because of these factors, a manager's job can be frustrating and tiring, but also very rewarding.

More specifically, Mintzberg notes that managers are given formal organizational authority to run their own units, and they derive status from this authority. This status, in turn, causes them to get involved personally with subordinates, peers, and superiors. Each of these groups provide managers with the information they need to make decisions.

The formal authority and status aspects of management jobs result in managers playing three major roles as they carry out their work duties. The **interpersonal role** requires the manager to interact with other significant people both inside and outside the organization. When playing this role, a manager may be a figurehead (for example, performing ceremonial duties like breaking ground for a new building) a leader (for example, motivating subordinates), or a liaison (for example, dealing with people outside the firm).

The second major managerial role is the **informational role**. This role requires the manager to both gather and disseminate information. The manager may be a monitor (for example, analyzing travel

interpersonal role

informational role

costs of salespeople), a disseminator (for example, giving subordinates information they can use to perform their jobs better), or a spokesperson (for example, forwarding desired information to individuals outside the manager's unit or outside the organization).

decisional role

The third major managerial role is the **decisional role.** This role requires the manager to use the information available to make decisions to help the manager's unit function effectively. When carrying out this role, the manager may be an entrepreneur (for example, identifying a new product opportunity), a disturbance handler (for example, settling conflicts among subordinates), a resource allocator (for example, deciding how resources should be distributed within the manager's department), or an negotiator (for example, resolving a potential grievance with the union steward).

Mintzberg's "roles" approach to management gives considerable additional insight into what is required in the demanding job of managing. As you think about these roles, you'll have no difficulty concluding that the day-to-day work of a manager can be busy and challenging.

MANAGERIAL SKILLS

To be effective, a manager must possess and continually develop several essential skills. Figure 1-4 illustrates three categories of skills important to a manager's overall effectiveness. The relative signifi-

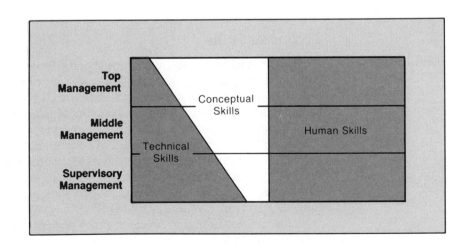

FIGURE 1-4
Skills at various
levels of
management

cance of each skill varies according to level of management, but the best managers recognize that they must develop and practice all three to be effective in accomplishing organizational and personal goals. They dare not concentrate their efforts on only one of these areas, even though it may be the most important one at their level in the organization. It is the combination of skills that is vital to managerial success. With this clearly in mind, let us now consider the three categories separately.

Conceptual Skills

conceptual skill

The ability to comprehend abstract or general ideas and apply them to specific situations is **conceptual skill.** It is through the exercise of conceptual skills that the manager understands the complexities of the overall organization, including how each subunit contributes to the accomplishment of the firm's purposes. These skills are crucial to the success of top-level executives, who must be concerned with the big picture—assessing opportunities and deciding how to take advantage of them. For instance, the "Great Burger War" might be equated to a chess game, in which Wendy's must not only plan its own action but anticipate the initiatives of McDonald's and Burger King. A mistake here can mean disaster.

The further down in the organization one looks, the less vital conceptual skills are. Middle managers need moderate conceptual skills but not as much as top managers. Supervisors typically have the least need for conceptual skills because they usually are given fairly specific guidelines. Supervisors are primarily concerned with their department and other closely related departments, and these relationships are more clearly defined. A Wendy's restaurant manager, for example, does not have to consider the restaurant design. That complex matter has been decided at higher levels.

Technical Skills

technical skill

Technical skill is the ability to use specific knowledge, methods, or techniques in performing work. This category of skills is very important to job success for supervisors. They need technical skills partly because they must train new workers, but also because knowing how the job should be performed helps the supervisor monitor daily work activities. If corrections are needed, the technically skilled supervisor is much better qualified to make them. Managers at every level in the Wendy's organization are concerned with how to make the perfect hamburger, but it is the store manager who must answer the customer's question, "Where's the beef?"

As one moves to higher levels of management within the organization, the importance of technical skills usually diminishes because managers at those levels have less direct contact with day-to-day problems and activities. Top management has perhaps the least need for technical skills. Many upper-level managers have technical backgrounds, but, unlike supervisors, they seldom use their technical skills on a day-to-day basis. For instance, the president of an engineering firm, although trained as an engineer, is not likely to design a new machine personally. However, we do not wish to overstate the case. Some chief executives are highly respected by subordinates for their technical expertise. Undoubtedly this makes them better managers.

Human Skills

human skill

The ability to understand, motivate, and get along with other people is **human skill**. Human skills are about equally important at all levels of management. Activities requiring human skills include communicating, leading, and motivating. For example, a Wendy's store manager must interact with workers, customers, and suppliers. Wendy's president must communicate with and influence other executives and directors in the company and persons outside the organization, such as investment bankers.

MANAGEMENT IN PRACTICE

Can a Non-Lawyer Manage a Law Firm?

The Toronto law firm of Borden & Elliot has hired John Herrick as its chief operating officer. Herrick spent over 30 years producing and marketing products such as Cheerios; he admits that he has no experience in the legal business. He was hired because the law firm wanted someone who had a lot of experience in managing people. Borden & Elliot is believed to be the first law firm in Canada to have hired a non-lawyer for such a crucial position. This idea has already been implemented in several US law firms.

The idea in hiring Herrick is that the lawyers will practice law and Herrick will manage the business. Borden & Elliot is really saying that they are a business firm and need to be managed like one. One of Herrick's first jobs will be to draw up a strategic plan for the firm. He will therefore be helping the partners decide on the growth rate of the firm, and the specific areas the firm should get involved in.

Milton Zwicker, a specialist in law office management, thinks it is inevitable that other law firms will follow Borden & Elliot's lead. He predicts that eventually the chief operating officer in law firms will be given authority to decide on professional policy matters like the hiring of lawyers (Herrick does not have this authority).

Some lawyers at other Bay Street firms have doubts about Borden & Elliot's decision to hire a business manager. They are not sure what his role is going to be. Other lawyers worry about losing power to a chief operating officer. Lawyers have always had a great deal to say about what goes on in the firm, but if Zwicker's predictions come true, that will change.

SOURCE   Adapted from Marina Strauss, "Veteran Businessman Gets Chance To Make A Legal Firm Businesslike," *The Globe and Mail* (January 22, 1987): B6.

MANAGEMENT IN PRACTICE

Managers of the Future

The turbulent eighties have brought the demand for managers with a unique set of skills. Perhaps the most important of these is an ability to articulate the corporation's purpose and set of values. A company's survival in the marketplace will be dependent on the manager's adeptness in communication. Tom Watson of IBM and Robert Noyce of Intel Corporation achieved this, and the potency of their messages gave their companies market dominance. Unfortunately, others, such as Ford and Xerox, were not as quick to see the importance of communication and their market shares declined.

Managers will have to become as nimble as entrepreneurs because changes are occurring at a rapid pace. Research and development in technology and new markets should be the focus of a manager's decisions, not short-term productivity.

According to Franz Tyaack (chief executive officer) of Westinghouse Canada, Inc., today's management system is outdated and worn out. It is a system perfected around 1900 which works on the premise that the blue-collar workforce is composed largely of poorly educated, recently arrived immigrants. This militaristic model is prevalent in both public and private North American enterprises. Under this system, human resources are wasted and there is much job dissatisfaction. The task for tomorrow's manager is to understand his or her business well, know when changes are necessary, and communicate effectively with employees.

SOURCE Adapted from M. A. Wente, "Remaking the Management Mind," *Canadian Business* (January 1983): 23, 24, 82, 83.

The Relationship between Skills and Functions

The difference between management skills and management functions can be confusing. However, the relationship is really quite straightforward — management skills are necessary to perform management functions. For example, communication and people skills are necessary to perform the influencing function; technical skills are necessary to perform the controlling function; and analytical and conceptual skills are needed to perform the planning function. Since managers perform the functions of planning, organizing, influencing, and controlling, they ought to have some competence in each of the managerial skills. The emphasis on the various skills changes as a manager moves from the supervisory level to top management.

BASIC SCHOOLS OF MANAGEMENT THOUGHT

The emphasis in this book is on the current state of management thinking. But just as political science students must consider the history of government, management students must have at least a passing familiarity with what has gone before in the field of management. The history of management obviously extends several thousand years into the past. Moses, for example, is credited with having employed the first management consultant (his father-in-law) to help design the organization through which Moses governed the Hebrews. But it was not until the late nineteenth century that management began to be considered a formal discipline. To place the recent history of management thought in some perspective, although at the risk of oversimplification, we will discuss two schools of management thought in terms of the historical development of the field. Then we will show how one expert has categorized the modern theories of management without regard to their connection to history.

The Classical School of Management

classical school of
management

The oldest and perhaps most widely accepted school among practitioners has been called the **classical school of management** thought. This is the approach to management thought that arose mainly from efforts between 1900 and 1940 to provide a rational and scientific basis for the management of organizations. This is sometimes referred to as the traditional school of management.

As a result of the Industrial Revolution, people were brought together to work in factories. This system stood in marked contrast to the handicraft system whereby people worked separately in small shops or in their own homes. Thus, industrialization created a need for the effective management of people and other resources in the emerging organizations. In other words, there was a need for efficient planning, organizing, influencing, and controlling of work activities.

In response to the growth of large organizations in the late nineteenth century and during the early twentieth century, there was an intensified interest in management as a process and as a science. It was apparent to many that management could be made more effective and efficient. The primary contributions of the classical school of management include the following:

- The application of science to the practice of management.
- The development of the basic management functions: planning, organizing, influencing, and controlling.
- The articulation and application of specific principles of management.

Classical management concepts have significantly improved the practice of management, leading to substantial improvements in performance within organizations.

Scientific Management

Frederick Taylor, who made major contributions to management thinking around the turn of this century, is often called the Father of Scientific Management. Taylor was supported in his efforts by Henry

scientific
management

Gantt, Frank and Lillian Gilbreth, and Harrington Emerson. All of these Taylor disciples became famous in their own rights. Together with Taylor they revolutionized management thinking. **Scientific management** is the name given to the principles and practices that grew out of the work of Frederick Taylor and his followers and that are characterized by concern for efficiency and systematization in management. Taylor was convinced that the scientific method should apply to the management process. The scientific method provides a logical framework for the analysis of problems. It basically consists of defining the problem, gathering data, analyzing the data, developing alternatives, and selecting the best alternative. Taylor believed that following the scientific method would help to determine the most efficient way to perform work. Instead of abdicating responsibility for establishing standards, for example, management would scientifically study all facets of an operation and carefully set a logical and rational standard. Instead of guessing or relying solely on trial and error, management would go through the time-consuming process of logical study and scientific research and develop answers to business problems. Taylor's philosophy can be summarized in the following four principles:

- Developing and using the scientific method in the practice of management (finding the "one best way" to perform work)
- Using scientific approaches to select employees who are best suited to perform a given job
- Providing employees with scientific education, training, and development
- Encouraging friendly interaction and cooperation between management and employees but with a separation of duties between managers and workers.

Taylor stated many times that scientific management would require a revolution in thinking by both the manager and the subordinate. His purpose was not solely to advance the interests of the manager and the enterprise. He believed sincerely that scientific management practices would benefit both the employee and the employer through the creation of a larger surplus. The organization would achieve higher output, and the worker would receive more income.

The greater part of Taylor's work was oriented toward improving management of production operations. The classic case of the pig iron experiment at the Bethlehem Steel Company illustrates his approach.[3] The task he studied at Bethlehem was so simple, most managers would tend to ignore it. Laborers would pick up 92-pound pigs (chunks of iron) from a storage yard, walk up a plank onto a railroad car, and place the pigs in the car. In a group of 75 laborers, the average output was about 12.5 tons per man per day. In applying the scientific method of study to this problem of getting work done through others, Taylor developed (1) an improved method of work, (2) a prescribed amount of rest on the job, (3) a specific standard of

MANAGEMENT IN PRACTICE

Scientific Management in Troubled Times

Until very recently, the scientific management ideas of Frederick Taylor were widely accepted. During the period 1920-1970, managers seemed to have the view that managing was like following a recipe. If the right ingredients were put into the business, an acceptable level of profit would automatically result.

Recently, the environment of business has become complex, and management writers are now saying that high performing companies are those that stress corporate culture rather than management techniques. Corporate excellence is more likely to result from motivated people than from the application of scientific management techniques. Viewing the manager as a tradesman is therefore "out"; viewing the manager as an entrepreneur is "in."

It is understandable that a techniques-oriented system developed under the influence of scientific management. Managers at all levels in organizations were rewarded for short-term performance, even if this performance was gained at the expense of the long-run viability of the company. The new view, strongly influenced by the Japanese system of management, is that managers must concern themselves with the long-run health and survival of the firm. If they don't, they will discover that they are unable to compete as the environment of business changes.

SOURCE   Adapted from Maurice Hecht, "Real Managers Don't Need Theories Anymore," *Executive* (January 1984): 32-35.

output, and (4) payment by the unit of output. Using this approach, the average output per worker rose from 12.5 tons to 48 tons. Under the incentive system, the daily pay rose from $1.15 to $1.85, an amount substantially higher than the going rate.

Taylor's dedication to systematic planning and study of all kinds of processes pervaded his entire life. With a specially designed tennis racket, he became part of the National Doubles Tennis Championship team. When he played golf, he used uniquely designed clubs for any predictable type of lie. When he used a particular putter, his friends refused to play because of its accuracy. A famed novelist reported that Taylor died of pneumonia in a hospital, probably with his stopwatch in his hand.

Frank and Lillian Gilbreth concentrated on motion study to develop more efficient ways to pour concrete, lay bricks, and perform many other repetitive tasks. After Franks' death, Lillian became a professor of management at Purdue University. Until her death in 1972, she was considered the First Lady of Management. H. L. Gantt developed a control chart that is used to this day in production operations. The Gantt chart is considered by many to have been the forerunner of modern PERT (program evaluation and review technique) analysis (discussed in detail in Chapter 17). Harrington Emerson set forth "twelve principles of efficiency" in a 1913 book of that title. Certain of Emerson's principles state that a manager should carefully define objectives, use the scientific method of analysis, develop and use standardized procedures, and reward employees for good work. His book remains a recognized management classic.

General Management Theory

In contrast to Taylor, Emerson, Gantt, and the Gilbreths, Henri Fayol and C. I. Barnard attempted to develop a broader theory concerned with general management. (Although Frederick Taylor and Henri Fayol were contemporaries, the two apparently never knew of one another's work. Fayol's major contribution to management literature, *Industrial and General Management*, was not translated into English until long after Taylor died and, in fact, after Fayol himself had died.) Fayol's thesis was that the fundamental functions of any manager consist of planning, organizing, commanding, coordinating, and controlling. He attempted to develop a number of general principles designed to improve the practice of general management.

Chester Barnard's ideas, expressed in his classic book, *The Functions of the Executive*, have significantly influenced the theory and practice of management for nearly half a century.[4] For years, Barnard was president of New Jersey Bell Telephone and also held a number of important public service posts. Barnard believed that the most important function of a manager is to promote cooperative effort toward the goals of the organization. He believed that cooperation depends on effective communications and a balance between rewards to, and contributions by, each employee.

The Behavioral School of Management

In the 1920s and 1930s, some observers of organizations became convinced that scientific management was shortsighted and incomplete. In particular, Elton Mayo and F. J. Roethlisberger began to point out that the approaches advanced by scientific management were not necessarily the most efficient, nor did they always work as intended.[5] These researchers believed the human aspects of business organizations had been largely ignored. The **behavioral school of management** is the approach to management thought that is primarily concerned with human psychology, motivation, and leadership as distinct from simple mechanical efficiency. The behavioral school of management thought includes what has come to be called the human relations movement, as well as modern behaviorism.

behavioral school
of management

Human Relations

The field of human relations emerged from the work of Elton Mayo. The **human relations movement** is the name given the trend that began in the 1920s and that reached its high point in the 1940s and 1950s toward treating satisfaction of psychological needs as the

human relations
movement

primary management concern. The project that had the most to do with the beginning of the concern for human relations in business was the Hawthorne experiments, conducted in the Chicago Western Electric Company plant (the Hawthorne works) between 1927 and 1932. In these experiments, researchers attempted to prove the validity of certain accepted management ideas. Several of the experiments attempted to determine the relationship between working conditions and productivity.

In one study, the researchers set up *test groups*, for which changes were made in lighting, frequency of rest periods, and working hours, and *control groups*, for which no changes were made. When rest periods and other improvements in working conditions were introduced, productivity of the test groups increased, as expected; however, the researchers were surprised when output increased again when the various improvements in working conditions, such as rest periods, were removed.

Mayo and the other researchers concluded that their own presence had influenced the behavior of the workers being studied. The influence of behavioral researchers on the people they study has come

Hawthorne effect

to be called the **Hawthorne effect**. A management corollary is that when employees are given special attention, output is likely to increase regardless of the actual changes in the working conditions. Mayo and Roethlisberger followed up the early experiments at the Hawthorne plant with an investigation of cliques, work groups, and other informal relationships in organizations, and an intensive interviewing program. The basic conclusions reached as a result of the interviewing program were that the psychological needs of individuals have a significant impact on group performance and that employees often misstate their concerns.

Much behavioral research supports the thesis that reasonable satisfaction of the needs and desires of employees will lead to greater output. This suggests that any management approach that ignores or de-emphasizes the human element may result in only partly accomplished objectives.

Modern Behavioral Science

Since the early experiments at the Hawthorne plant, the human relations approach has evolved into modern behavioral science. The

behavioral science

term **behavioral science** refers to the current stage of evolution of the behavioral school of management, which gives primacy to psychological considerations but treats fulfillment of emotional needs mainly as a means of achieving other, primarily economic, goals.

In recent years, there has been renewed interest in developing techniques to utilize people more effectively in organizations. The contributions of such well-known behavioral scientists as Abraham Maslow, Douglas McGregor, Chris Argyris, Frederick Herzberg, and

Rensis Likert have provided considerable insight into ways of achieving managerial effectiveness. We will discuss the contributions of each of these behavioral scientists in considerable detail in Chapters 10 and 11. At this point, brief mention of the basic precepts of modern behaviorism will suffice.

Behavioral scientists have often criticized classical management theory and scientific management for not being responsive enough to human needs. The behaviorists' specific criticisms include the following:

- Jobs have been overly specialized.
- People are underutilized.
- Managers have exercised too much control and have prevented employees from making decisions they are competent to make.
- Managers have shown too little concern about subordinates' needs for recognition and self-fulfillment.

Behavioral scientists argue that the design of work has not changed to keep pace with changes in the needs of today's employees. In today's complex, affluent, and rapidly changing society, they say, employees cannot be treated like interchangeable parts. Today's worker has a higher level of education and tends to have higher expectations of the work environment than did workers of the past. Modern behaviorists say employees of the 1980s desire diverse and challenging work. This desire has placed increased pressure on management to be responsive to change and to provide an environment designed to meet human needs.

Other Schools of Management Thought

While our discussion has so far focused on the classical and behavioral schools of management, it should not be concluded that these two schools represent the only possible theoretical approaches to management. Harold Koontz, in attempting to clarify what he has described as a "management theory jungle," has identified 11 approaches to the study of management.[6] Each of the schools in Koontz's classification is identified and briefly described in Table 1-1.

One of the most important recent schools of management thought to emerge is the contingency, or situational, school. Gordon Allan, president of Gordon Allan Consultants of Toronto, noted as far back as 1971 that managers must be flexible and adapt to the characteristics of specific situations if they hope to be effective.[7] They must be able to change their managerial style to fit the demands of the situation. Failure to do so will result in inappropriate management behavior, in less satisfied employees, in lowered organization productivity, and in an overall reduction in organization effectiveness.

TABLE 1-1 Koontz's Classification of the Theories of Management

Empirical or Case Approach	In this school, management is studied through case examples of the successes and failures of practicing managers. This approach can assist managers in developing basic generalizations to support theories or principles of management. However, this method of learning about management may create illusions for current managers because the future is quite likely to be considerably different from the past. An analysis of past experiences of managers may not prove to be very helpful in solving current managerial problems.
Interpersonal Behavior Approach	According to this school of thought, management is concerned with accomplishing results through others. Therefore, the study of management should concentrate on interpersonal behavior and the study of psychology. This school focuses on the study of motivation and leadership. While the study of human behavior in organizations is important, a manager's knowledge of management is incomplete if that is all he or she understands.
Group Behavior Approach	Using research findings in sociology, anthropology, and social psychology, this approach explains management in terms of group behavior. According to this view, effective management requires a thorough understanding of behavioral patterns of group members within the organization. However, rigid adherence to the group behavior approach may cause managers to place too much emphasis on organization behavior and not enough on other equally fundamental concepts of management.
Cooperative Social Systems Approach	An outgrowth of the interpersonal and group behavior approaches, the cooperative social systems school of management has also been referred to as the "organization theory" approach. While all managers do perform in a cooperative social system, this approach does not explain many of the complexities of modern management. Social systems is a broader concept than management, and it overlooks a number of principles, techniques, and factors that are important to effective management.
Sociotechnical Systems Approach	The sociotechnical systems approach is based on work done at the Tavistock Institute in England. It was discovered that the technical system — the machines and methods used — has a strong influence on the social system within the working environment. Personal attitudes of group members were strongly influenced by the technical system of the workplace. A major task of management is to make sure that the social and technical systems are harmonious. While closely related to industrial engineering, the approach has made a significant contribution to the practice of management. It does not, however, provide an overall theory of management.
Decision Theory Approach	The major responsibility of managers is to make decisions, according to the decision theory approach to management. While many who study and/or practice management agree that decision making is an essential skill, this approach overlooks other skills and requirements of management. In some cases, the actual making of the decision may be relatively straightforward.
Systems Approach	The systems approach to management concentrates on the effective and efficient use of resources to produce desirable products and/or services. The systems approach requires that the physical, human, and capital resources be interrelated and coordinated within the external and internal environment of an organization.
Mathematical or Management Science Approach	This school or approach to management uses mathematical models, concepts, and symbols in solving managerial problems, particularly those requiring decisions. Advocates of the school argue that management can be made more scientific through the use of mathematical and simulation models. Many advocates argue that the mathematical or management science approach offers a complete school of management. Other theorists and practitioners believe that mathematical models are tools of analysis, not a separate school of thought.
Contingency or Situational Management	Contingency or situational management refers to managers' abilities to adapt to meet particular circumstances and restraints a firm may encounter. In other words, managerial action depends upon circumstances within the situation. That is, "no one best approach" will work in all situations. Applying a situational approach requires that managers

diagnose a given situation and adapt to meet the conditions present. The difficulty with this approach is that few management writers have prescribed precisely what a manager should do in a given situation.

Managerial Roles Approach

Henry Mintzberg observed and studied what managers actually do in managing and identified the primary roles of managers. He concluded that executives do not always perform the traditional managerial functions of planning, organizing, directing and controlling, but instead perform a variety of other activities. According to Mintzberg, managers have three dominant roles: interpersonal, informational, and decision making. In the interpersonal role, a manager acts as a figurehead, leader, and liaison person. In the informational role, a manager serves as a monitor, disseminator, and spokesperson. In the decision-making role, a manager acts as entrepreneur, disturbance handler, resource allocator, and negotiator. A difficulty that arises is that the roles Mintzberg identifies inadequately describe managerial activities and functions. Such important roles as those of goal setting, strategy identification and implementation, developing the organization, and selecting and developing managers are not included.

Operational Approach

The operational approach to management indicates that the foundations for management science and theory are drawn from a number of other schools and approaches. The operational approach recognizes that there are significant concepts, principles, theories, and techniques that comprise the effective practice of management. This approach draws on pertinent knowledge from other fields of study including political science, sociology, social psychology, psychology, mathematics, economics, decision theory, general systems theory, and industrial engineering. We believe that the operational approach provides a logical framework for the study of management theory and practice.

SOURCE Harold Koontz, "The Management Theory Jungle Revisited," *Academy of Management Review* 5, no. 2 (April 1980). Reprinted with permission of the author and *Academy of Management Review*.

Henry Mintzberg, "The Manager's Job: Folklore and Fact," *Harvard Business Review* 53, no. 4 (1975): 49-61.

OPENING INCIDENT REVISITED

Lawton Manufacturing Ltd.

Marshall Cizek had a rather unpleasant introduction to the practice of management — perhaps because he did not understand what management is all about. In this chapter, we defined management as the accomplishment of organizational objectives through the efforts of other people. Cizek's experience suggests that he was ignoring this fundamental aspect of management. He was trying to do most of the work himself; he was acting as if he was still a maintenance mechanic whose job was to repair machinery. This situation had changed, but Cizek didn't seem to realize it.

In order to become effective managers, individuals must understand what the functions of management are. Planning, organizing, influencing, and controlling are introduced in Chapter 1 and are discussed in detail in the remaining chapters of this text.

In his new position, Cizek became a lower-level manager. As such, he should have been making certain decisions about how to spend his time. Figure 1-4 indicates that managers at the lower levels in an organization must allocate varying amounts of time to all the basic functions of management, but most should be spent on influencing others. Cizek allocated very little time to any of the functions and was particularly remiss with respect to influencing. As a result, he had little real influence with his subordinates. In fact, they had gone to the plant superintendent about his "meddling" in their work, rather than talk to him.

Overall, Cizek did not seem to understand the difference between managing the work of others and actually doing the work himself. Until he understands this distinction, he will have serious troubles in any management position.

SUMMARY

Effective management is essential to the success of every organization: whether the organization is a profit-oriented firm or a not-for-profit organization; whether it operates in the public or private sector; whether it produces a physical product or an intangible service; or whether it is a sole proprietorship, partnership, or a corporation. Management influences the lives of all members of an organized society. All individuals can gain from a better understanding of and appreciation for management as a means of functioning more effectively in an organization. The study of management provides:

- A knowledge of and insight into the responsibilities of managing people and other resources
- An understanding of the problems of operating a business firm
- An opportunity to learn the skills essential to making effective managerial decisions
- An understanding of basic principles of management
- The ability to identify and cope with internal and external environmental forces that affect performance
- The skills and attitudes required to continue your professional development.

Canadian society is dominated by large organizations in which people must work together effectively to accomplish goals. The degree of success of any organization — business or nonbusiness — is determined to a great extent by the quality and overall effectiveness of management. What is management? Who is a manager? What do managers do? What roles do managers play in work performance? What skills are needed for good management? In answering these questions, it is important to realize that there is no one best approach to management that is effective in every situation.

Management is the process of planning, organizing, influencing, and controlling to accomplish organization goals through the coordinated use of human and material resources. A manager is anyone, regardless of level within a firm, who directs the efforts of other people in accomplishing goals. A manager is the catalyst who makes things happen by *planning* what is to be achieved, *organizing* personnel and other resources to achieve the plan, *influencing* or *directing* people, and comparing results achieved to the planned performance (*controlling*). In order to be effective, managers need to possess and develop technical, human, and conceptual skills. These skills must all be employed in the proper proportion, based on the particular level occupied by the manager.

While we can agree that every organization requires good management, there is considerable disagreement as to the most effective way to manage. Historically, two different approaches to management have developed. The classical school, including the work of Frederick

Taylor, Henri Fayol, and C. I. Barnard, attempted to provide a rational and scientific basis for management. Major contributions of scientific management include the application of the scientific method to management and the classification of the basic management functions.

The behavioral school of management is concerned with the human element in the organization. The early human relations era, which resulted primarily from the Hawthorne experiments in the late 1920s and early 1930s, evolved into behavioral management science. Behavioral scientists have criticized classical management theory as being unresponsive to the needs of employees, overspecializing jobs, underemploying and overmanaging people, and showing too little concern about a person's need for recognition and self-fulfillment. In today's world, management has little choice but to be more responsive to the needs of employees if improved performance is desired. Harold Koontz identified 11 schools of management. One of the eleven — the operational approach — indicates that the foundations of management science and theory are drawn from approaches found in other disciplines. Another of these schools — Allan's contingency approach — stresses the flexibility required when the basic functions of management are performed.

REVIEW QUESTIONS

1. Define management. Who is a manager and what does a manager do?
2. List some factors that may account for the success and effectiveness of a manager.
3. Why is the study of management important?
4. List and briefly describe three managerial roles and three managerial skills important to effectiveness. How are the skills relevant to managers operating at different levels in the organization?
5. What is the classical school of management? Identify the basic contributions of this school of management.
6. Frederick Taylor is known as the Father of Scientific Management. Why? What is scientific management and Taylor's philosophy?
7. Identify briefly the contributions to management theory of:
   a. Henri Fayol
   b. C. I. Barnard
   c. H. L. Gantt
   d. Harington Emerson.

8. Discuss the behavioral school of management. How and why did the movement originate?

9. What specific criticisms did behavioral scientists have of traditional or classical management theory?

10. Harold Koontz coined the phrase "the management theory jungle" to describe the various approaches to the study of management. What do you believe he meant, and what were the various schools of management he identified?

EXERCISES

1. Interview three managers from different types of organizations (for example, talk to the manager in a bank, a retail store, a manufacturer, or a college/university). Have a list of prepared questions including, but not limited to, the following:
   a. How did you become a manager?
   b. What does your job as a manager entail? Describe your major functions.
   c. Why are you a manager?
   d. What skills are necessary for success as a manager?
   e. What advice would you give a person interested in a career in management?
   f. Is management a profession?
   g. Can a person learn to be a better manager? if so, how?

2. Review the employment classified ads in the *Globe and Mail* or a Saturday edition of a large city newspaper. Make a list of the types of managerial jobs available, the companies offering employment, and the qualifications needed to obtain the positions. What is your basic conclusion after this review, regarding the availability of managerial positions and the qualifications necessary to obtain such a position?

CASE STUDY

From Engineering to Management

Jack Esselmont had recently received a promotion to the position of manager of engineering at Keystone Home Products Ltd., a medium-sized firm producing a diverse line of consumer household products. Esselmont had an electrical engineering degree and had been with the company for nine years since graduating from Queen's University.

Esselmont's record as a design engineer was excellent. He had developed three new products, one of which was now marketed in the United States and England. The department Esselmont worked in was widely respected as an industry leader in innovative product design and in research and development.

Not only was Esselmont a good engineer, he

was also popular with almost everyone in the company. Throughout his nine years with Keystone, Esselmont had kept up to date in his field by reading engineering journals, and by attending meetings of electrical engineers where new technical developments were discussed. Because of his technical and engineering experience with the company and his ability to get along with people, top management felt confident in promoting Jack Esselmont to the position of manager of engineering.

For the first few months, Esselmont's department ran fairly smoothly. He continued to be heavily involved in actual research and new product design, but his subordinates didn't seem to mind too much — at least, they didn't say anything. As time went on, however, Esselmont began to feel frustrated because managing the department was starting to interfere with his ability to do the research and design work that he liked so well. He tried to compensate by working longer hours, but Esselmont found he didn't have the "creative spark" he used to.

The situation continued to deteriorate, as Esselmont found himself becoming less interested in both the management and the research functions in his department. He felt "burned out," lacking the motivation to do his job. To make matters worse, some of his engineers began to express the views that Esselmont was too heavily involved in research and design work, that he should concentrate on managing, so the engineers could do what they were paid for.

At about this time, Esselmont heard rumors that top management was having serious doubts about his ability to manage the engineering department. These rumors concerned him deeply, so he decided to make an appointment with his boss to see if he could straighten out the mess he had got into.

QUESTIONS

1. What is the basic problem confronting Jack Esselmont as a manager? What are the causes?
2. How does being a manager differ from being an engineer? Be specific.
3. Did top management make a mistake in promoting Esselmont to the position of engineering manager?
4. What skills are important for Esselmont as a manager? Why?
5. Does being a good engineer guarantee success as a manager? Why or why not?

CASE STUDY

From Assistant Foreman to President

Today, Phillip Garrick becomes president of Canadian Controls Ltd., a producer of high-quality control mechanisms. When the previous president announced his retirement, Garrick had been identified as the likeliest choice to assume the post. He was respected for his competence in the field and for his ability to work with employees at all levels of operations. Garrick is early this morning, not so much to work, as to think. Sitting in his new office, his thoughts go back to his earlier days with the company.

Twenty years ago, Garrick had graduated from a community college. With a diploma in industrial management and no business experience, he had been hired as assistant foreman on the production line. "Those were the days," thinks Garrick. "Seemed as though there was a problem to solve every minute. Thank goodness for the standard procedures manual and a foreman who was patient enough to answer all my questions. Didn't have to make too many critical decisions back then."

Garrick's thoughts pass next to the time when he was taken off the production line and promoted to middle management. "Noticed a few changes," he remembers. As foreman, he had been primarily concerned with meeting daily production requirements; as production manager, he had had to plan weeks, often months, in advance. Just as at the lower level of management, the people and communication problems remained; Garrick seemed to think the reports he then had to write were much longer. Still, the major change was that he had had to do more creative thinking. Chuckling, he recalls the time he'd gone to the files for a standard procedure to respond to an unusual problem confronting him and found there wasn't one; he'd felt momentarily frustrated that he had to handle the problem without assistance. However, as his analytical, decision-making, and conceptual abilities increased, he found himself using his technical skills less.

Phillip Garrick's promotion five years ago to vice-president of planning was a major accomplishment in his career, as he had been in a tight competition with three well-qualified managers. He'd heard through the grapevine that he had been promoted over the others mostly because he was able to think for himself. But even his past training had not fully prepared Garrick for the demands of this job; he had had to learn much of it on his own. Rather than think weeks or months into the future, as vice-president of planning, Garrick had to envision years ahead.

Garrick recalls that at first he had not realized how many people outside of production he had to coordinate. Marketing and finance had to be tied into production; although the process of planning for all three departments had been a difficult one, Garrick realized that his conceptual and decision-making skills had increased significantly through it. He had long left behind the "good old standard procedures manual."

Today, as Garrick looks at the gold plate bearing his current title as "President," he wonders what changes are in store for him at this top level of management. What new requirements will be placed on him? A twinge of excitement and challenge tells him he knows he can face and cope with them. What skills must he develop to continue to be successful?

QUESTIONS

1. As the president of Canadian Controls, what specific skills will Garrick need to be effective? Reference to Figure 1-4 provides insight into this question.
2. How do the demands of different levels of responsibility change as a manager progresses up the hierarchy of an organization?
3. What general recommendations would you offer Garrick?

CASE STUDY

A Business Opportunity

While working on their seminar case, which was due in three days, Fred Dillinger, an accounting major, and Katherine Mandu, a marketing major, discussed what they were going to do when they graduated from Southern Alberta Institute of Technology (SAIT) in a few weeks. During their discussion they were joined by Rocky Allen, an administration major, who had a similar concern. As it turned out, Rocky had just received a $100 000 bequest from the estate of his uncle Woody and was thinking of starting a business. Fred indicated that he had just received a scholarship of $50 000 for maintaining a 3.75 grade point average in accounting over his six quarters at SAIT, and he was also considering starting his own business. Katherine revealed that she had just been awarded $75 000 from Economics instructor Keynes for being the only student to earn an A in Economics 201 in his fifty years at SAIT. She went on to tell them that not only was she interested in being in business but she had a great idea about which one to try.

Katherine had done a marketing survey of the students at SAIT and had found that they would welcome an establishment that would provide such activities as pool, bowling, and mini golf, while supplying beer, as long as it was not too far from SAIT. Through her research she discovered a company that would supply a prepackaged pool hall, bowling alley, games arcade, miniature golf, and pizza center for $200 000 delivered. They also guarantee that their package would pass the Alberta Liquor Control Board requirements for the serving of beer.

Rocky and Fred became quite excited by Katherine's idea; the three decided to approach it the way they had learned to do case studies. They gathered the following facts:

- The package would cost $50 000 to erect.
- The business would require a C-1 lot of at least 30 m × 45 m.
- Equipment would cost $2500 per month to lease.
- Preopening costs (advertising, promotions) would run about $10 000.
- Two locations are available:
  - The former "Filler's Station" directly across from SAIT, for $200 000.
  - A former Imperial service station and restaurant, "EAT HERE AND GET GAS," about 4 km away for $150 000.
- The first location can be purchased with a downpayment of $60 000 and monthly payments of $1654.26 (15 years at 12 percent). Monthly utilities are $525. Monthly taxes are $500.
- The Imperial station can be purchased with a downpayment of $45 000 and monthly payments of $1240.70 (15 years at 12 percent). Monthly utilities are $525. Monthly taxes are $414.
- The package can be purchased with a downpayment of $20 000 and monthly payments of $2321.68 (15 years at 13.75 percent).
- Wages and salaries would be $3 000 per month.

- Rocky, Fred, and Katherine can only borrow an extra $5000 each.
- Currently, a "safe" investment would generate a 10 percent return.
- Rocky, Fred, and Katherine can each find a job with an annual income of about $24 000 if they choose not to go into this business.
- A gross profit of $19 500 per month could be produced by this business at the location of the former "Filler's Station."
- A gross profit of $15 000 per month could be produced by this business at the location of the former Imperial station.

SOURCE Adapted from a case by Garry E. Veak, Southern Alberta Institute of Technology. Reprinted by permission.

QUESTIONS

1. Advise Katherine, Fred, and Rocky about what form of business — sole proprietorship, partnership, or corporation — makes the most sense for their proposal. (None of them wants to be a minority owner.) Why is your choice more suitable than the other two? (*Hint:* Consult an introduction to business text's section on forms of business ownership.)
2. Indicate what will be involved in each of the basic management functions for this type of organization.
3. Suppose these SAIT graduates make their proposal a reality. Should they hire managers, or manage the business themselves?

ENDNOTES

[1] *The Canadian Business Failure Record* (Dun and Bradstreet Canada Ltd., 1985): 4.

[2] Henry Mintzberg, "The Manager's Job: Folklore and Fact," *Harvard Business Review* 53, no. 4 (1975): 49–61.

[3] Frederick W. Taylor, *The Principles of Scientific Management* (New York: Harper, 1911): 41–47.

[4] Chester I. Barnard, *The Functions of the Executive* (Cambridge, Mass.: Harvard University Press, 1938).

[5] F. Roethlisberger and W. J. Dickson, *Management and the Worker* (Cambridge, Mass.: Harvard University Press, 1935).

[6]Harold Koontz, "The Management Theory Jungle Revisited," *Academy of Management Review* 5, no. 2 (April 1980).

[7]Gordon Allan, "Management Flexibility," *The Canadian Personnel and Industrial Relations Journal* 18 (May 1971): 13–21.

REFERENCES

Ackoff, Russell. *Management in Small Doses*. New York: Wiley and Sons, 1986.

Boone, Louis E., and Johnson, James C. "Profiles of the 801 Men and 1 Woman at the Top." *Business Horizons* 23, no. 1 (February 1980): 47–53.

Carroll, Stephen, and Gillen, Dennis. "Are Classical Management Functions Useful in Describing Managerial Work?" *Academy of Management Review* 12, (January 1987): 38–51.

Cook, Curtis W. "Guidelines for Managing Motivation." *Business Horizons* 23, no. 2 (April 1980): 61–70.

Cornelius, Edwin, and Lane, Frank. "The Peer Motive and Managerial Success in a Professionally Oriented Service Organization." *Journal of Applied Psychology* 69, (February 1984): 32–39.

Cummings, L. L. "The Logics of Management." *Academy of Management Review* 8, no. 4 (October 1983): 532–538.

Drucker, Peter F. *Management: Tasks, Responsibilities and Practices*. New York: Harper, 1974.

_____. "Management: The Problems of Success." *Academy of Management Executive*, (February 1987): 13–20.

Fayol, Henri. *General and Industrial Management*. New York: Pitman, 1949.

George, Claude, Jr. *The History of Management Thought*. Englewood Cliffs, N.J.: Prentice-Hall, 1972.

Hay, Christine D. "Women in Management: The Obstacles and Opportunities They Face," *Personnel Administrator* 25, no. 4 (April 1980): 25–31.

Hecht, Maurice. "Real Managers Don't Need Theories Anymore." *Executive* 26, no. 1 (January 1984): 32–35.

Huntford, Roland. *The Last Place on Earth*. New York: Atheneum, 1985.

Kantrow, Alan M. "Why Read Peter Drucker?" *Harvard Business Review* 58, no. 1 (January-February 1980): 74–83.

Koontz, Harold. "The Management Theory Jungle Revisited." *Academy of Management Review* 5, no. 2 (April 1980): 175–189.

McFarland, Dalton. *The Managerial Imperative: The Age of Macromanagement*. Cambridge, Mass.: Ballinger Publishing Co., 1986.

McGregor, Douglas. *The Professional Manager.* New York: McGraw-Hill, 1967.

Mintzberg, Henry. "The Manager's Job: Folklore and Fact." *Harvard Business Review* (July-August 1975): 49–61.

_____. *The Nature of Managerial Work.* New York: Harper, 1973.

Newman, William H., ed. *Managers for the Year 2000.* Englewood Cliffs, N.J.: Prentice-Hall, 1978.

Olivia, Terence A., and Capdevielle, Christel M. "Can Systems Really Be Taught? (A Socratic Dialogue)." *Academy of Management Review* 5, no. 2 (April 1980): 277–281.

Pfeffer, Jeffrey. "The Theory-Practice Gap: Myth or Reality?" *Academy of Management Executive,* (February 1987): 31–32.

Ralston, David; Anthony, William; and Gustafson, David. "Employees May Love Flextime, But What Does It Do To Organizational Productivity?" *Journal of Applied Psychology* 70, (May 1985): 272–279.

Roethlisberger, F. J., and Dickson, W. J. *Management and the Worker: An Account of a Research Program Conducted by the Western Electric Company Hawthorne Works, Chicago.* Cambridge: Harvard University Press, 1939.

Scott, W. E. and Podsakoff, P.M. *Behavioral Principles in the Practice of Management.* New York: Wiley and Sons, 1985.

Stewart, Rosemary. *Choices for the Manager.* Englewood Cliffs, N.J.: Prentice-Hall, 1982.

Strauss, Marina. "Veteran Businessman Gets Chance to Make a Legal Firm Businesslike." *The Globe and Mail* (January 22, 1987): B6.

Sullivan, Jeremiah. "Human Nature, Organizations, and Management Theory." *Academy of Management Review* 11, (July 1986): 534–549.

Walker, Dean. "The Brains Behind Nabisco." *Executive* (July 1985): 48–51.

Wells, Jennifer, ed. "Remaking the Management Mind: How Companies and Business Schools are Trying — Painfully — To Change Their Ways." *Canadian Business* 56, no. 10 (October 1983): 36.

Wente, M.A. "Remaking the Management Mind." *Canadian Business* 56, no. 1 (January 1983): 23.

Whitely, William. Managerial Work Behavior: An Integration of Results From Two Major Approaches." *Academy of Management Journal* 28, (June 1985): 344–362.

APPENDIX

Careers in Management

To be successful in a job search, you need to know much more than that you desire a career in management. The number and types of managerial positions are many. If you are to be happy in a chosen career, the best position that meets your specific needs must be obtained. This is precisely what this appendix is about — finding the right job that will lead to a career in management.

Your job search should progress through a series of important steps. This appendix begins by showing how to gain valuable insight into what you desire from a career. It is followed by a discussion of how to identify career objectives. Next, the types of careers available in management are presented, after which the actual sequence for searching for the right job is discussed. Finally, we present some job realisms. The overall purpose of this appendix is to identify what entry level management positions are available and how you can obtain the best match with a firm.

GAINING INSIGHT INTO YOURSELF

Successful managers come from a wide variety of experiences. Some know immediately that they want to be managers. Others believe that they want to be in management and learn later on that management is not their cup of tea. There are individuals who may be extremely successful as a manager in one situation and a dismal failure in another environment.

The number of students who graduate from a college or university without a clear understanding of their career goals is astounding. It is difficult to achieve a goal if you do not know what you want to accomplish. Statements such as "I want to be a manager," or "I want to be in a job where I can work with people," are not sufficient. You must be willing to go into much greater depth to gain a realistic appreciation of what you desire to accomplish in a career.

First, you must develop a realistic understanding of who you are and what you desire out of life. Once this has been accomplished, you will be in a much better position to identify what career you desire. The following discussion is directed primarily toward students who have little or no business experience and are unsure of their career goals.

Just as no two personalities are exactly alike, so each of us has different strengths and weaknesses. People who are serious about an attempt to gain better insight into their career objectives will need to know their strengths and weaknesses. It is through the recognition of your strengths that you are encouraged toward a particular career. A knowledge of your weaknesses will show you what skills or attributes need to be developed further, and what sorts of difficulties you may have in accomplishing certain goals.

Talk to Professionals

People who are successful in their jobs are a valuable resource from which to uncover career information. It is likely that you, your parents, or close friends know individuals who would be willing to share career information with you. Most likely these people would be willing to talk to you about the demands of a particular job. Prior to setting up an interview with such a person, it would be wise to identify some questions you would like answered. To get your mind working, some potential questions are provided below:

- What type of entry-level position would be available to a person with my education and experience?
- If I didn't start off in a managerial position, how long would it typically take to progress to a first-level managerial position?
- What type of training does your firm regularly provide for management personnel?
- What is the typical salary range for a person like myself starting with your firm?
- What would be the typical duties a new employee would be expected to perform?
- How supportive is your firm when an employee makes a mistake?
- Whom should I contact if I am interested in a position similar to yours?
- What's your firm's policy regarding promotion from within?
- What type of preparation or qualifications does a person need for a career with your firm?

The list could go on and on. The point to be stressed is that you should ask the questions that concern you the most. The benefits are numerous. You are now in a position to discover if a particular job might be interesting. The professional is not under the pressure of conducting an interview and will answer questions candidly. Also, if this type of job proves interesting, you have gained valuable information that can be used in future job interviews. Confidence is built up because you can now talk intelligently about the position you are applying for. You are also able to learn the typical salary range for a specific position. This information is important because a recent college graduate can be realistic about salary expectations by not asking for too much or too little.

The Testing Center

A resource that often goes unused by students is their school's testing center. You might say, "Why should I use the testing service? There is nothing wrong with me." Perhaps this myth has been built up because it has been assumed that only people who are really "messed up" ought to be tested. Nothing could be further from the truth. The unique feature of the testing center is that you can discover many things about yourself prior to going for an interview. You can be absolutely honest because only you and your counselor will see the results. Since many companies give similar tests to their job applicants, it is likely you will feel much more relaxed when these tests are administered. If you wait until after graduation to utilize a similar service, it may be quite expensive. Fees of over $5 000 are sometimes charged for these services.

The purpose of using the testing services is to gain an insight into yourself that may prove beneficial when seeking a job. Some of the topics you may desire to explore in greater detail relate to interests, aptitude, personality, and intelligence. Each will be briefly discussed from the standpoint of how the tests can be beneficial in selecting the best job.

Interest Tests

You might be surprised at the number of students who do not know what they want to do once they graduate. One of the authors of this book changed majors five times! In the "old days," he did not have the opportunity to use a modern testing service. Interest tests are designed to help a person identify career fields. If the test interpretation supports your belief in what is desired in a career, there is a good chance that the situation has been properly assessed. You are reinforced in the belief that the proper decision has been made. On the other hand, you may discover that there are other areas that you did not initially recognize. Knowledge of these additional interests can provide you with the stimulus to evaluate other alternatives.

Aptitude Tests

At times, our abilities and our interests do not match up. A person may have an interest in being a brain surgeon but not the aptitude for the career. Aptitude tests assist individuals in determining if they have the natural inclination or talent needed for a particular job. These tests are valuable in determining a person's probability for success in a selected job.

Personality Tests

There are jobs for which certain personalities have proved to be more useful than others. Personality tests assist a person in determining if he or she possesses the proper personality for a particular job. Although it is difficult to generalize about which qualities may be beneficial on a particular job, you should benefit from the interpretation of the test results. Corporations, like individuals, have distinctive personalities. People tend to be attracted to organizations that provide the means for meeting their goals and aspirations. A person may be quite successful in one firm and a failure in another merely because of personality differences.

Intelligence Tests

If a career field requires a certain level of intelligence, it is best to find out if you meet the minimum levels before pursuing this career. Through hard work a person may meet the entry requirements, but what will the results be in the long run? Instead, a more realistic job, with just as much challenge, may need to be considered. We cannot all be Albert Einsteins! Intelligence tests assist in this endeavour.

The testing service should not be expected to provide all the answers. Test results should be reviewed only as indicators and should never be thought of as providing the final decision concerning your entry into a profession. However, if the results of the tests suggest an alternative career path would be warranted, it may be beneficial to reevaluate personal goals. A conference with a respected instructor may provide some assistance. You will do well to remember that we are often pushed into careers not of our choosing because of well-intentioned, but perhaps misinformed, friends.

CAREER OBJECTIVES

Once you have a thorough understanding of your abilities, likes and dislikes, you are in a much better position to develop realistic career objectives. It is at this juncture that you can either enhance or diminish your chances of obtaining a position that will lead to the career of your choice. Take for instance these two career objectives, which were found on résumés of recent graduates:

I. *Career Objective:* To obtain a position where I can work with people, perhaps in management.
II. *Career Objective:* To obtain an entry-level position in personnel management that provides the opportunities for ultimately progressing into a middle-management position.

The personnel director who showed these career objectives to one of the authors was amazed at how many graduating students are not capable of identifying what they desire in their first job. Always remember these two general guidelines:

• Be as specific as possible in identifying the type of job you would like. This point becomes quite obvious when comparing career objective I and career objective II. The company needs to know the type of job you are interested in if it is to be capable of evaluating your credentials. The personnel director is also in a position to see whether a person has given serious consideration to the type of job he or she prefers.

- In the objective statement, provide an indication of your goals over the next five years. Most personnel directors recognize that a person does not want to stay forever in an entry-level position. But they also want to know if prospective employees are realistic in their expectations.

Once you have clearly thought out your career objectives, you are, for the first time, in a position to evaluate the firms that have the potential for satisfying these goals. It is not a task that is accomplished overnight. Often this is the most agonizing part of the job search, but it is likely one of the most important.

ENTRY-LEVEL POSITIONS IN MANAGEMENT

Having decided that you ultimately want to be a manager, the decision must be made as to what avenues are available to lead you to this goal. But now a problem arises. What types of managerial positions are available? Few first-level managerial positions are open to recent graduates with minimal work experience. The discussion of possible entry-level positions in management will begin by examining the risk factor, and its importance in determining whether you are given an opportunity to secure a particular job. Next, four of the many possible avenues for obtaining entry-level management positions will be discussed. As each type of entry-level position is presented, you should consider the significance of the risk factor.

The Risk Factor

A major factor in determining the type of managerial positions that may be available to recent graduates relates heavily to the risk factor that a company assigns a particular position. Risk is the probability of a particular decision(s) having an adverse effect on the company. A low-risk managerial job is one in which if a mistake is made, there is a minimal potential loss for the firm. A high-risk managerial job is one in which a mistake by the manager may have a major impact on the organization. The types of managerial positions that are available may be viewed on a continuum that goes from low risk to high risk.

Typically, the lower the risk, the greater the opportunities available for a recent graduate with minimal work experience. A person who desires to enter management after graduation must usually search for these low-risk positions. It will do little good to set your sights on a job that is associated with high risk; these positions are likely reserved for individuals who have already proved themselves in lower-risk jobs.

The risk continuum is like a thermometer: the better the impression a person makes on the individual(s) doing the hiring in a firm, the higher the temperature rises. For many management positions you may want, however, there will be no movement on the thermometer. This means that there is no chance for that particular job. But if you have done your homework, it is likely that the temperature will rise at least enough to permit you to get an entry-level position. It may not mean that you will go immediately into management.

The concept of risk as it applies to different firms is often not consistent. There are organizations that rapidly place inexperienced new employees in positions of responsibility. One manufacturing firm may hire recent industrial management graduates and place them immediately into first-level supervisory positions. Another firm that manufactures a similar product may have a policy of placing only experienced individuals into first-line managerial positions. It is necessary for you to study the risk factor as it applies to specific firms.

Risk should also be considered from the standpoint of how much security a person desires from his or her job. There is a common myth currently circulating among some students that their risk of failure will be less in a major corporation as opposed to a smaller one. They reason that a large firm will take the time to train a person on a job prior to placing the employee in a position of responsibility; job security is therefore enhanced. This myth should be dispelled. A firm, no matter what size, is in business to make money. If economic conditions do not warrant keeping an employee, the large firms as well as the small ones reduce the number of employees.

Entry-Level Management

As we discussed above, there are instances where a person with limited work experience can progress immediately into management. The risk factor will have to be low, but there are entry-level management positions. Many of these positions carry the title of assistant manager. Decisions typically are made under the supervision of a manager with experience. These jobs offer young graduates the opportunity to get their feet wet without fear of making that one wrong decision that could be detrimental to a career. Many of these positions are in retail management with titles such as assistant manager of a department or grocery store.

Management Training Programs

A smaller number of the entry-level management positions involve a formal management training program (MTP). In an MTP, you are given formal training, for a period ranging from three months to two years, in the job that you ultimately will be filling. You are often exposed to both classroom and experiential training so as to get the overall "big picture" of operations within the firm. Along with the formal classroom training, you may work in production one month, marketing the next, and accounting the following month. Once the training program is completed, you will be placed in a managerial position.

A point that should be remembered is that formal management training programs are often quite expensive for a firm. The firm does not receive benefits from the employee until the training is complete. Thus, it is likely that a highly competitive screening process will be used. The company must feel that the individual will become a productive long-term employee before the employee is permitted to enter the training program. If an MTP is desired, young graduates must thoroughly convince the company representatives of their potential and that the risk factor in hiring them is not excessive.

From Professional to Management

Many people graduate in a technical field such as accounting, computer science, or engineering. Perhaps management was not their initial goal, but they may later see their future in management. It is likely that a person must first prove ability in the technical aspect of the job before being considered for a managerial position.

There are times when this path to a managerial position can be a delicate transition. A person who has always been associated with the technical aspect of a job may have difficulty in moving into a managerial position. A good engineer or accountant will not always become an effective manager. But since many firms believe that their first-level supervisors must have technical ability, managers often come from the ranks of technical and professional staff members.

One individual progressed from a technical job to a managerial position in the following way: On receiving his M.S. in geology, he went to work for Columbia Exploration Ltd. After being with the firm four years, he was identified as a high potential individual, meaning that he had impressed his supervisors as possessing certain managerial qualities. In preparation for moving him into management, he was placed in assignments outside the geology department and moved to other locations in the firm for training. He worked for several months in the human resources department, supervising a task force of three people in developing a management by objectives program. He was then moved to the systems development department where he again directed a task force in reorganizing a geology department. Finally, after approximately eighteeen months, he was transferred back into geology as a manager. The company viewed the additional corporate exposure as vital in the career progression of this manager.

From Sales to Management

An option that is being used increasingly by graduates is to progress to a management position through an entry-level sales job. A person who is in sales is in a position to learn the operations of the entire company. Thus, many graduates have found that the quickest path to a managerial position is through sales. It is likely this situation has occurred because approximately 50 percent of all entry-level positions open to graduates are in sales.

Some firms make it mandatory to progress through sales before any of their employees can enter management. For instance, one large insurance company has initiated a program to attract bright graduates into their management ranks. In this program, new employees spend three months at the home office working in various departments and another three months observing in the field. They are then required to produce as a salesperson for one year. At this point, they have the option of going into management or remaining in sales.

The point that should be clearly understood is that a sales position can lead to managerial positions in areas other than sales. Many people have been able to go from sales to other departments, such as production. Because salespeople have been dealing with the customer, who purchases the product, it is reasoned that they provide valuable input if placed in the production area of the business.

THE SEARCH FOR THE RIGHT INDUSTRY

A good starting point in a job search is to identify the growth industries. Industries that are projected to grow rapidly in the future would be the target for your analysis, to identify several of the best companies operating within the industry.

Examples of *fast-growth* industries include: computer products, health-care products and services, electronics, energy-related, banking and financial services, various leisure-time industries, and various types of service industries. *Slow-growth* industries include education, transportation (particularly railroads), and steel.

Thus, you should follow this procedure:

- Identify growth industries.
- Pinpoint or select for further study and analysis the industries that would seem to fit your goals, needs, or interests.
- Determine the three or four "leading" firms in the industry. These firms may not be the largest, but they may be growing or predicted to grow at a rapid rate over the next several years.
- Seek interviews with the companies you select from your analysis as described above. The procedure to be followed will be discussed in the following section, "The Search for the Right Company."

- Finally, be concerned about the specific entry-level position, fully recognizing that if you perform well, you won't be in this position long — probably not more than one or two years.

Naturally, there are excellent opportunities available in some industries that are identified as slow growth. This discussion should not be taken to mean that a person should not apply to firms in the slow-growth industries. The authors merely suggest that considerable thought should be given to the selection of which industry should be pursued.

THE SEARCH FOR THE RIGHT COMPANY

You have now accomplished a thorough self-assessment, developed an appreciation of your career goals, determined companies in growth industries, and obtained an overview of the types of jobs that are available to begin a career in management. But you cannot start your career until a job offer is obtained. This section will concentrate on the remaining steps you need to take in order to obtain the management position of your choice.

The Résumé

In many instances, the first contact that a prospective employee has with the person in charge of hiring is through a résumé. As such, the résumé becomes an extension of your personality. The résumé sells in your absence. It should be designed to present you in the best possible perspective. Any deficiencies can be explained during the interview, but it is difficult to accomplish this task if the opportunity to participate in the interview is not available.

Through experience and through contacts with numerous personnel directors, some guidelines have been developed that may prove to be beneficial in the preparation of a résumé. They are:

- Present your most significant accomplishments and attributes. If it is the truth, it is not bragging.
- The order of the presentation of items on a résumé is dictated by your strengths. If you have high grades, stress your grades; if you have a significant amount of work experience, this item should receive top priority.
- Companies are placing additional emphasis on activities outside the classroom such as membership and offices held in social and business organizations. If you have been particularly active in various campus organizations, highlight these endeavors.
- The amount of school expenses that you personally paid is also receiving additional attention. A statement such as "paid 50 percent of college expenses" is often quite helpful.

- If you are willing to be mobile, this should be stressed. For a company that has offices throughout Canada, a geographical preference of "None" would likely receive more attention than one that said "Toronto." Naturally, if geographical preference is truly a restriction, it should be stated as such.
- If you have work experience, you should stress this fact. A firm recognizes that individuals who are working to finance their way through school will not likely have fancy titles. They are interested in determining how you performed while employed. It is satisfying for a recruiter to call one of your past employers and receive statements such as "He is a hard worker" or "She did not constantly watch the clock."
- If you have work experience you should describe the functions that were performed while working. Merely listing the position titles does not give the recruiter significant insight into what type of work you actually performed. Action phrases such as "was responsible for," "coordinated the activities of," and "in charge of" are much more descriptive.
- If references are to be placed on a résumé, permission should be requested, even if the reference is a good friend. References can assist you by tailoring their comments to meet the requirements of the job that you are seeking.

Matching Yourself with the Right Company

The next step in searching for the right company is to identify the firms that can afford you the greatest opportunity to achieve career objectives. Identification of these firms is a task that often proves quite difficult for students seeking their first job, but it is one that must be done. Here you will be attempting to identify firms that meet your specific needs.

There are numerous sources from which to obtain the names of suitable firms. A great deal of information can be found in *trade journals* that apply to the particular firm in which you are interested. Also, a large amount of useful data may be found in publications such as *The Financial Post* and *The Globe and Mail*. You should select only the firms that have the potential for fulfilling your own specific needs.

Once a list of prospective companies has been developed, you still are not in a position to send out a résumé. A certain amount of research remains. Data concerning each company should be obtained so you can send a personal cover letter to each firm. This also includes obtaining the name of the person to whom the letter must be addressed. In the cover letter, state your reason for wanting a job with this company. Remember that the *only* reason a firm will consider a person for employment is that they expect the services rendered will make money for the company.

The job search does not stop here. The waiting process now begins. This stage is also quite difficult. But because you have done your homework, we will now assume that you have an invitation to visit a company. Before leaving on a trip, additional research, or at least a review of your previous research, may be necessary. Much more information than last year's sales is necessary. In addition, it may be wise to develop a list of questions that you as a prospective employee would like to ask about the company. The interview is a two-way street; the interviewee is attempting to determine if this particular company is a good place to work, and the firm is evaluating the individual for his or her potential to fit into the organization.

If the interview goes well and you believe that the company has the potential to satisfy your career objectives, it is customary to write a letter expressing your sincere interest. In this letter you should also tell precisely why you feel qualified to take a position with the company — perhaps a comment such as, "the work that a quality control inspector with your firm performs appears extremely interesting and challenging. I am confident that I possess the type of personality to be capable of working with the people on the line, my supervisor, and top management." On the other hand, if you discover after your visit that the position is not what you expected, a courteous letter should be written thanking them for their interest but telling the company representative that you do not believe a proper match exists.

Approximately one day after the follow-up letter has been received by the company, place a phone call to the person who interviewed you. During this call, you should ask intelligent, searching questions, as well as again expressing interest in the firm. Once the call has been completed, you have had the opportunity to visit with the company representatives four times: by resume, in person, by letter, and by phone.

Once an offer has been tendered, you must decide whether it should be accepted or rejected. This usually poses no problem, unless several offers are received. In deciding between two or more offers, the job with the greatest long-run potential should be selected. Try to pick a company you can be comfortable with, including its head office location. This job is not necessarily the one with the highest starting salary. It is often tempting to take the highest salary offer without considering all other factors. But success on the first job after graduation can have a tremendous impact on your entire career. It should be chosen with care.

INITIAL PROBLEMS ON THE JOB

Recent graduates have conquered a major hurdle in their lives. They may feel that the world's problems are now going to be solved. But from a realistic viewpoint, certain cautions should be observed. This section is not intended to frighten or disillusion you, but to give you a realistic appreciation of the work environment. Although a job has been secured, there are numerous initial job threats that you should be aware of.

The Young Brat Syndrome

Not all employees of a firm will welcome a new graduate with open arms. Although top management may realize that it is important to bring bright, young, college-educated people into the firm, this enthusiasm may not be shared by all. Graduates may find themselves working either with or for people without a degree. The starting salary of graduates may be more than that of employees who have been with the firm for a long time. Some may even perceive a new graduate as a threat. Graduates have found that out of necessity their degree may need to be played down. In time people will discover that you have your degree and will likely respect you more for not bringing it to their attention.

Making Changes

After graduation, your mind is filled with new ideas or approaches that have been learned in the classroom. But the company may have been successfully accomplishing a task in a certain manner for many years. To you, it may be obvious that changes need to be made, and it may come as quite a shock when your ideas are not immediately accepted. Although your first inclination may be to start making changes, it may be best to first establish a good working relationship with members of the department and gradually bring forth new ideas.

Politics

The hardest lesson a young person must learn is that hard work and long hours do not guarantee advancement. In reality, obtaining a promotion or raise may depend on who one knows and with whom one plays golf or tennis. You must be alert to the different power groups at work within the organization.

The Free Spirit

Just as each of us has a different personality, companies are also different in their attitudes toward standards of appearance. If a graduate goes to work for a firm in which all of the company's managerial personnel wear suits, conformity will likely be the order of the day. Resistance to this image can only result in difficulties. If a person wants to be less conventional, there are firms that are more likely to accept this attitude.

The Boss

New graduates often feel that their superior is not as intellectually enlightened or supportive as they believe a person in that position should be. Assuming that you desire to maintain that position (a reasonable alternative might be to quit or request a transfer), you must accept that the supervisor is still the boss. If you desire to progress in that firm, an overt effort must be made to support the activities of the department. Expressing doubt concerning the superior's abilities to other employees can only hurt your chances for advancement. If you wish to make changes, they must be accomplished within the system.

2

The External Environment

KEY TERMS

unions	system	technology
shareholders	system approach	structure
social responsibility	open system	centralized
ethics	situational approach	decentralized
	objective	

LEARNING OBJECTIVES

After completing this chapter you should be able to
1. Describe the major external environment factors that can affect a firm.
2. Describe the major changes that have occurred in the external environment during the twentieth century.
3. Explain the systems approach to management and describe the basic components of a business system.

4. Describe the situational approach to management and identify the major situational factors successful managers must balance.

OPENING INCIDENT

Farlane Mining and Smelting Ltd.

James Farlane is the president of Farlane Mining and Smelting Ltd., which has operations at eight locations in Ontario and Quebec. As Farlane arrived at his office one day, several problems that had been building for weeks came to a head. The most pressing problem concerned the latest union contract. Negotiations were not progressing well and the union was threatening to go on strike at midnight the next day. The main point of disagreement was a wage increase for union members that the company thought it could not afford.

Over the past two years, the company had been directed to meet federal pollution regulations with its smelter. In the last three months, some emission-control devices had been installed; an inspector was due that day. Farlane knew that, for the smelter to meet the legal requirements, the company would need substantially more equipment than had already been bought. In Farlane's assessment, the company simply could not afford to spend more on pollution-control equipment because the increase in the company's cost structure would make it uncompetitive. Farlane was sensitive, however, to the adverse reactions of townspeople who lived near the smelter; he'd read articles in the local papers expressing increasing dissatisfaction with the company for polluting the air and water. The debates over acid rain had produced additional negative publicity for Farlane's company. Farlane feared the federal inspector would not be sympathetic to the pollution-control efforts made so far.

Farlane thought ahead to the company's upcoming annual meeting. He knew the company's shareholders would not be happy when he reported a 13 percent decline in earnings per share. The reasons for this decline were clear — wage increases granted to employees, expenditures for pollution-control equipment and generally depressed prices in the industry — but Farlane knew that the shareholders wanted earnings per share to grow, not decline.

Farlane had also noticed a recent trend among the company's customers; they were pressuring the company to lower prices on several products. Farlane had requested marketing reports to track the pricing of the company's competitors, fearing his customers might switch. Farlane was troubled about this problem because a drop in sales would make all the other problems facing him that much more difficult to resolve.

In Chapter 1, we introduced the concept of management; we also talked about what managers do in business and nonbusiness organizations. That discussion was directed largely toward the specific activity of managers *within* an organization. James Farlane's experience indicates that managers must also be concerned about activities *outside* the firm they work for. Changes in the environment external to an organization can have a major impact on it.

In this chapter we describe the eight major external environment factors that managers must deal with if they are to be successful. We then discuss two complementary problem-solving ideas — the systems approach and the situational approach — that help managers to cope effectively with the external environment. The systems approach views the business organization as part of a larger system of interrelated parts. This approach assumes that changes in the external environment also affect the internal workings of the firm. The situational approach builds on the systems approach and helps the manager to realize that different external situations require different managerial styles.

THE EXTERNAL ENVIRONMENT

Managing an organization is not done in a vacuum. Many interacting external factors can affect the performance of managers and the firms they work for. Figure 2-1 shows the major external environment factors that can affect firms in Canada: (1) government, (2) competitors, (3) the work force, (4) unions, (5) shareholders, (6) suppliers, (7) customers, and (8) the general public. Each of these can constrain the behavior of a firm's managers. These external factors can work singly or in combination, and their impact may be difficult to predict.

As shown in Figure 2-1, these eight external environmental factors can be placed in one of two basic categories. The general environment is composed of those factors which have an overall influence on the organization, but the firm can do little to change this environment. For example, a business firm can do little to change the size of the work force or to change the attitudes of the general public. The general environment is very similar for all firms.

The direct action environment is composed of those factors which have a specific impact on the business. The firm *can* influence the factors in the direct action environment. For example, a business firm can develop a new product to deal with competition, or it can lobby government to change a law that is hurting the firm, or it can bargain with a union about work rules, and so on. The firm may or may not be successful in this activity. The direct action environment is unique for each organization.

Several general observations about all eight factors can be made. First, managers at different levels in the management hierarchy have differing degrees of involvement with the external environment of the firm. Generally speaking, the closer to the top of the firm's hierarchy managers are, the more their work will be affected by the external environment. First-line supervisors have relatively little

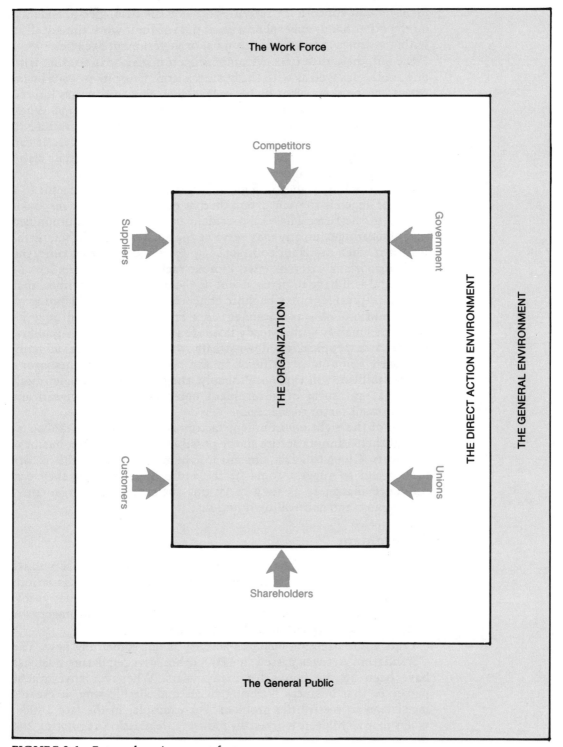

FIGURE 2-1   External environment factors

management concern for activities outside the firm; vice-presidents, on the other hand, may spend a great deal of their work time dealing with consumer groups, labor unions, or government agencies.

Second, these external environment factors may be in conflict with one another as well as with the business firm. Customers want lower prices and workers want higher wages; but, since a firm has limited resources, it cannot satisfy fully the demands of both groups. When faced with conflicts like this, managers often try to compromise to satisfy some of the demands of each group. However, this tactic can be frustrating since each group may be persuasively vocal in its claim that all its needs should be met.

Third, the importance of a given external environment factor to a manager depends to some extent on that manager's specific responsibilities in the firm. The vice-president of personnel in a unionized manufacturing company may serve as the head of the firm's bargaining team when the labor contract is up for review. At that time, the most important external environment factor the vice-president of personnel will have to manage will be the union; at other times, that same vice-president may be more concerned with general labor market conditions. A superintendent in a pulp and paper mill may be concerned mainly with a steady flow of raw materials from suppliers. But, if townspeople living downstream from the mill report suddenly increased amounts of effluent in the river, that same manager's responsibilities will expand. Probably, the plant superintendent will find that an aspect of government becomes the most significant environment factor to manage.

Each of the eight environment factors is complex. A brief discussion of them cannot capture all the possible ways they affect business managers. Given this fact, our purpose here is to describe the factors briefly and to suggest some of the more obvious ways they can influence managers as they carry out their planning, organizing, influencing, and controlling functions.

Government

One of the most obvious external factors Canadian managers must deal with is the law — federal, provincial, and municipal legislation. Government legislation covers a wide range of business activities, having a direct impact on the organization and its managers. A sample of such legislation is shown in Table 2-1.

Legislation affecting business activity is not something new. The Conciliation Act was passed in 1900; other laws regulating business have been on the books for many years. Whenever government perceives that business is acting in an undesirable way, it creates legislation to rectify the problem. For example, in the late 1800s, when many children worked in industry, legislation regulating the

TABLE 2-1   Canadian Legislation Affecting Business Activity

Federal Law	Major Provisions
Conciliation Act	Assists in the settlement of labor disputes through voluntary conciliation.
Industrial Disputes Investigation Act	Provides for compulsory arbitration of labor disputes by a government-appointed board.
Privy Council Order 1003	Recognizes the right of organized labor to bargain collectively with management.
Canada Labour Code	Deals with the personnel practices of firms, with provisions on fair employment practices, standard hours of work, employee health and safety, and discrimination in employment practices.
Canadian Human Rights Act	Ensures that any individual who wishes to obtain a job has an equal opportunity to compete for it, by prohibiting discrimination (on the bases of age, race, sex, religion, marital status, and ethnic origin) in the recruitment, selection, promotion, and dismissal of personnel.
Food and Drug Act	Prohibits the sale of food that contains any harmful substance; also prohibits misleading food advertising.
Textile Labelling Act	Regulates the labelling, importation, and sale of consumer textile articles.
Canada Water Act	Controls water quality in fresh and marine waters.
Environmental Contaminants Act	Establishes limits on the amount of airborne substances that may be discharged into the atmosphere.
Combines Investigation Act	Prohibits a wide variety of business practices which lessen competition and/or harm the consumer. Includes prohibitions on (1) mergers and monopolies which lessen competition, (2) misleading advertising, (3) illegal trade practices — for example, setting abnormally low prices in an attempt to bankrupt competitors, (4) bait and switch selling — baiting a consumer with an advertised low price and then switching the consumer to a higher-priced item, (5) resale price maintenance — manufacturer's attempts to force retailers to sell above a minimum price, and (6) promotional allowances — given to some buyers but denied to others.
Weights and Measures Act	Regulates weighing and measuring devices; also concerned with the implementation of the metric system in Canada.
Hazardous Products Act	Regulates the labelling, advertising, and sale of potentially dangerous products.
Consumer Packaging and Labelling Act	Ensures adherence to packaging and labelling guidelines. All prepackaged goods must, for example, state the quantity in English and French in metric units.

MANAGEMENT IN PRACTICE

Pollution and Profitability

The new pollution legislation in Ontario is having a major impact on a pulp and paper mill at Terrace Bay. The Municipal-Industrial Strategy for Abatement (MISA) is an ambitious pollution reduction program that contains more rigorous pollution control standards than previous legislation.

The mill at Terrace Bay is owned by Kimberly-Clark of Canada Ltd. The company has already spent $30 million on pollution control in the last five years, but MISA will require it to spend about $26 million more. The company claims it cannot afford to install additional pollution control equipment. The mill has lost $86 million in the past eight years, and local management has been ordered to turn the mill around or it will be closed. Significant layoffs have already occurred.

The company was recently granted an extension (until 1990) to meet effluent requirements. There were immediate protests that the government wasn't serious about its new law. Faced with this pressure, Environment Minister James Bradley reduced the extension to one year. Upon hearing this, the company threatened to close the mill and lay off 1200 workers. Premier David Peterson then stepped in and tried to negotiate a compromise. The province may decide to help the company clean up the pollution in an attempt to save the jobs at the mill.

SOURCE Adapted from Kimberley Noble, "Pulp Mill Test of New Pollution Policy," *The Globe and Mail* (January 26, 1987): B1-B2.

employment of children was passed. This legislation directly affected business firms by prohibiting children below a certain age from working.

The federal laws described in the table show also that all areas of the firm are affected by government activity. Personnel managers, for example, must be up to date on legislation regarding discrimination in employment practices. Production managers must be aware of pollution laws. Marketing managers must abide by advertising and pricing regulations. Government legislation, therefore, has a profound impact on all areas of the typical business firm.

On certain occasions, government legislation can be controversial. Foreign ownership and investment in Canada is one controversial area. In an attempt to reduce the perceived negative impact of foreign ownership on Canadian business, the former Liberal government established the Foreign Investment Review Agency (FIRA) to screen new foreign investment in Canada. Its purpose was to ensure that significant benefits from foreign investment accrued to Canada. This federal legislation had a major impact on companies that wanted to be bought by foreign firms because they could be prevented from doing so by FIRA. Many complaints were levelled at FIRA during the 1970s and early 1980s; the argument was made by business managers that the agency had made Canada an unattractive place for foreigners to invest. When the Progressive Conservative government was elected in 1984, it quickly changed the name of the agency to Investment Canada and embarked on a strategy of encouraging "appropriate" foreign investment.

Controversy can also erupt between business and government at the provincial level. Consider Quebec's language law (Bill 101). This legislation, designed to protect and promote the French language, contained provisions prohibiting certain business practices conducted in English. All signs, menus, and employment advertisements, for instance, had to be printed in French only. Many business firms complained about the costs incurred to alter their firms to French only. They pointed out that much of their commerce was with businesses elsewhere, where the language of business is English. The language law and other legislation of the Quebec provincial government have caused many business firms in the 1980s to move out of the province. The long-run effect of this legislation on business activity in Quebec is not yet clear.

A further complication developed in 1986, when the Supreme Court of Canada ruled that Bill 101 violated the Charter of Rights. Because the legislation was enforced for a period of time and then declared unconstitutional, uncertainty has been created about what a business firm can and cannot do. This uncertainty is not conducive to business activity.

As a third example of controversial legislation, consider the dispute about metric conversion in Canada. Many Canadian consumers were opposed to converting to metric because it would require them to learn a new system of measurement. Many business firms, however, wanted to convert to metric because it is more straightforward than the imperial system and because it would make trade with European countries easier. The federal Liberal government announced its commitment to metric conversion in 1972, and changes began to be noticeable by the late 1970s. Various pockets of resistance were evident — for example, in Ontario, some gasoline dealers and small grocery stores continued pricing by imperial measures — but the shift was clearly happening. As much of the general public — the voters — still expresses resistance to metric use, legislators are still under some pressure to delay metric conversion. They point to the United States, where conversion is voluntary and very slow. However, many Canadian business firms have expressed opposition to any change of policy because they have already spent a great deal of money on metric conversion. In addition, the education system has converted wholly to metric measures. Likely, most businesses with direct contact with the general public will continue to use both systems simultaneously; that way, they meet the requirements of both external environment factors.

Competitors

Unless an organization is in the unusual position of having a monopoly in the market it serves, it will have to cope with competitive goods and services. A decision made by one firm may have a substantial impact on other firms in the market. Gasoline prices provide a common example. In recent years, service stations have watched their competitors very closely; in some cities prices vary little, within a tenth of a cent per litre. Weekend "gas wars" have erupted — to the delight of consumers — with service stations near one another lowering their prices several times a day in response to competitors' reductions.

Business firms operating in Canada must cope not only with domestic competition, but also with competition from firms headquartered outside Canada. International competition may not always be quite as obvious as domestic competition, but its overall effect can be profound.

One way to assess Canada's international competitiveness is to examine our record of imports and exports. As shown in Figure 2-2,

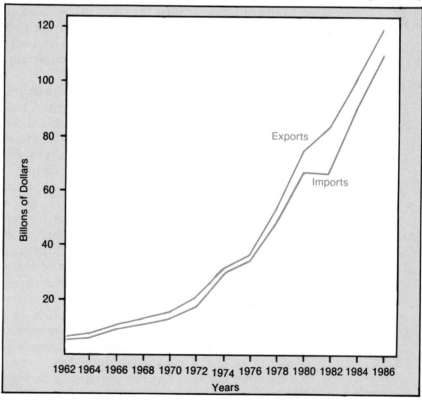

FIGURE 2-2   Canadian imports and exports of merchandise, 1962–1986, selected years

SOURCE   *Bank of Canada Review* (May 1987): S136.

Canada's exports have consistently exceeded imports during the last decade. However, these figures are heavily influenced by our favorable balance of trade with the US. It is evident from the table that Canada imports more from many of its other major trading partners than it exports to them (see Table 2-2). China and Russia are important exceptions.

Another competitive aspect of international trade is the rate of productivity growth among various countries. The growth rate has varied widely over time and across countries. During the period 1973-1983, Canada's growth rate was lower than that of all the major western European countries, Japan, and the US (Japan's was by far the highest). More recently, Canada's record has been somewhat better, but our low productivity growth rate is an area of concern.

Another way to look at this issue is to examine Canada's manufacturing productivity record. As shown in Figure 2-3, Canada at one

TABLE 2-2   Major Trading Partners of Canada for 1986

Merchandise Exports to Major Countries	(millions)	Merchandise Imports from Major Countries	(millions)
USA	$93 170	USA	$77 667
Other Asian nations	10 259	Other Asian nations	13 854
Japan	5 932	Japan	7 625
UK	2 713	UK	3 724
Central America and Antilles	1 553	West Germany	3 452
West Germany	1 310	Central America and Antilles	2 085
USSR	1 219	South Korea	1 749
China	1 105	Taiwan	1 743
Middle East	1 104	Italy	1 670
France	1 006	France	1 584
Netherlands	998	Mexico	1 179
South Korea	965	Hong Kong	1 041
Belgium and Luxembourg	834	Brazil	820
Oceania	831	Netherlands	694
Brazil	786	Oceania	686
Italy	701	Belgium and Luxembourg	620
Australia	650	China	566
Taiwan	601	Venezuela	516
Venezuela	415	Australia	504
Mexico	403	Algeria	322
Hong Kong	327	USSR	25
Algeria	190		

SOURCE   Statistics Canada, *Canadian Statistical Review*, cat. no. 11-003E, February 1987, p. 120. Used by permission of the Minister of Supply and Services Canada.

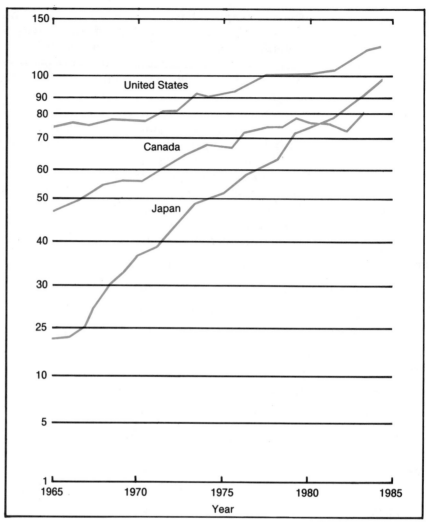

FIGURE 2-3   Output per hour in total manufacturing: US, Canada, and
Japan

SOURCE   Donald J. Daly, "Canadian Manufacturing and International Competition,"
(November 21, 1985).

time had a considerable lead over Japan in output per hour in total
manufacturing, but Japan surpassed Canada in 1980, and continues
to widen its lead.

Both domestic and foreign competition are of major concern to
business firms. In Canada, consumers are free to purchase the items
that they prefer, regardless of whether the goods are produced domes-
tically or in a foreign country. Given this fact, business firms must
compete with both domestic and foreign companies if they are to
remain viable.

The Work Force

The number and characteristics of individuals in the work force form a major external factor that business firms must take into account. In 1983, the Canadian work force was comprised of approximately 12 million people, nearly double the figure for 1961.[1] (See Figure 2-4.) Throughout the 1980s, the work force will continue to increase in size but at a much lower rate than that experienced over the last 20 years. It is also likely that the high national unemployment levels evident in the early 1980s will continue throughout the decade. (See Figure 2-5.)

The industries that will absorb these additional workers will likely be different from those that dominate current employment in

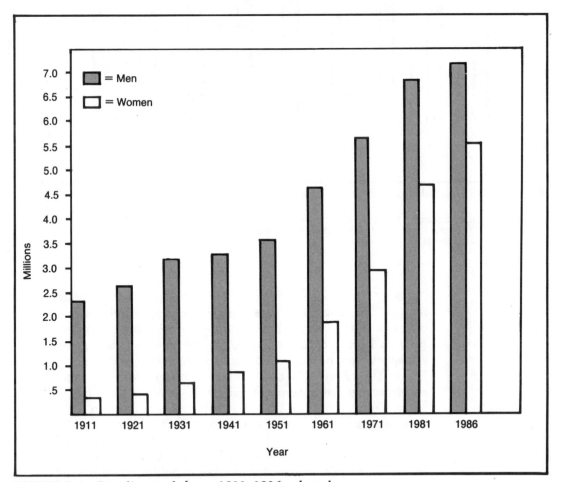

FIGURE 2-4   Canadian work force, 1911–1986, selected years

SOURCES   *Historical Statistics of Canada*, F. H. Leacy (ed.), Series D8–55 (1911–1971); also, *The Labour Force*, 71–001 (1981 and 1986). Used with permission of the Minister of Supply and Services Canada.

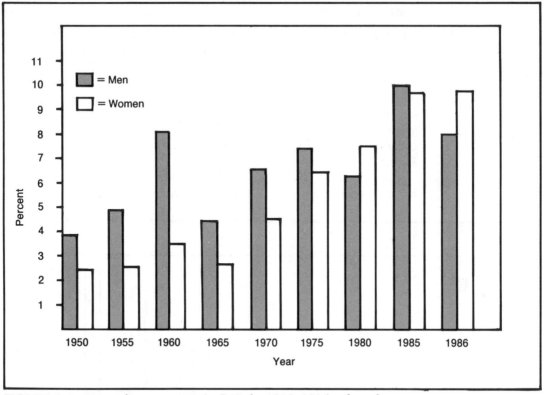

FIGURE 2-5   Unemployment rates in Canada, 1950–1986, selected years

SOURCES   *Historical Statistics of Canada*, F. H. Leacy (ed.), Series D 223–247 (1950–1975);
also, *The Labour Force*, 71–001 (1980, 1985, and 1986). Used by permission of the
Minister of Supply and Services Canada.

Canada. The goods-producing industries, such as construction, mining, and manufacturing, are expected to remain relatively stable in terms of employment. But job opportunities in service industries, such as health care, trade, repair and maintenance, government, transportation, banking, and insurance are expected to increase.[2] (See Figure 2-6.) Employment in service industries will likely constitute an increasing proportion of total employment in Canada.

The composition of the labor force is also changing. While the participation rate for men continues to decline, it is rising sharply for women.[3] (See Figure 2-7.) Women currently have improved opportunities to move into occupations that traditionally have been closed to them; for example, computer sales, public accounting, and top management. This trend is expected to continue.

The number of "service" workers is also expected to increase more rapidly than the number of "product" workers through 1990. The increased use of computers and the shift from goods-producing to service-producing firms are largely responsible for this pattern. The

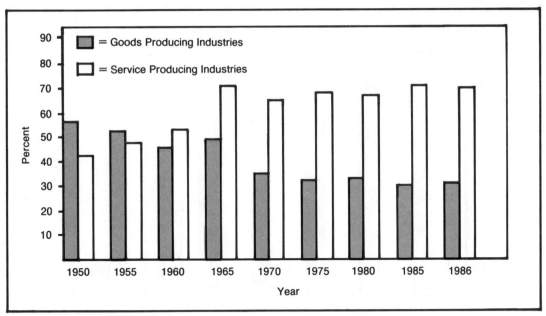

FIGURE 2-6   The proportion of total Canadian employment in goods-
producing and service-producing industries, 1950–1986,
selected years

SOURCES   *Historical Statistics of Canada*, F. H. Leacy (ed.), Series D266-317 (1950–1975);
also, *The Labour Force*, 71-001, (1980, 1985, and 1986). Used by permission of the
Minister of Supply and Services, Canada.

MANAGEMENT IN PRACTICE

Career Versus Nursery

A growing number of Canadian women are jumping off the management ladder to bring up a baby. This movement is interesting, given the fact that it was not until recently that women began occupying important management positions in companies. The challenge for firms is whether they are willing to make short-term concessions to women in management during their childbearing years. These concessions include part-time work, extended maternity leave, and assigning work that can be done at home. As more and more young women enter the management ranks, these creative alternatives to the normal nine-to-five routine will become more important.

One recent study done at the University of Michigan found a reversal of the trend of previous years of rising participation of women in the executive ranks. Childbearing may be a factor here. Researchers also noted a decline in the percentage of women vice-presidents in relation to the number of women promoted to other management jobs.

Dorothy Mikalachki, a researcher at the University of Western Ontario, argues that business firms should view a woman's contribution to the firm from a longer term perspective than they currently do. Companies spend a lot of money training women, and this longer term perspective would allow both parties to benefit. London Life, for example, provides eighteen weeks maternity leave and, for women earning over $25 000, makes up some of the difference between unemployment insurance payments and the woman's salary.

SOURCE   Adapted from Dorothy Lipovenko, "Moms Choosing Nursery Over Career," *The Globe and Mail* (February 26, 1987): B1, B2.

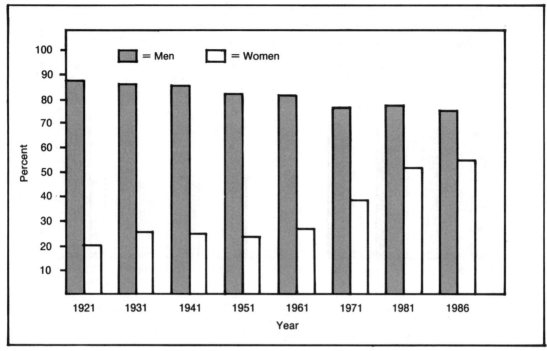

FIGURE 2-7   Employment participation for men and women, 1921–1976, selected years

SOURCES   *Historical Statistics of Canada*, F. H. Leacy (ed.), Series C-85-97 (1921–1971); also, *The Labour Force*, 71-001 (1981 and 1986). Used by permission of the Minister of Supply and Services, Canada.

MANAGEMENT IN PRACTICE

Day Care Centers

There is a growing involvement by Canadian companies in the child care needs of their employees. High quality day care at an affordable price enables both parents to work and reduces the stress caused by worry over their child's welfare.

Magna International Inc. of Markham, Ontario operates the Rolls Royce of child care centers in Canada. It recently opened a $1 million facility that looks more like a country club than a day care center. The center takes care of 56 children of company employees; the children range in age from six weeks to five years. Employees of Magna can drop their children off just minutes before starting work at the company. The fee is $50 per week — less than half the actual cost of the child's care.

One of the pioneers of employer-financed day care centers is Lavalin Inc. of Montreal which has operated a high quality center since 1981. Lavalin's center cares for 80 children and rivals the center at Magna. More recently, Global Communication and two other companies have joined in a cooperative venture to take care of the children of all three companies' employees.

SOURCE   Adapted from Wilfred List, "Country Clubs For Kids Open Eyes To Daycare Costs," *The Globe and Mail* (December 29, 1986): B8.

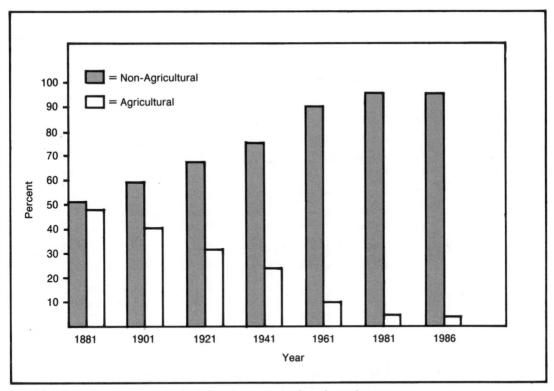

FIGURE 2-8   Canadian agricultural and non-agricultural employment,
1881–1986, selected years

SOURCES   *Historical Statistics of Canada*, F. H. Leacy (ed.), Series D1-7 (1881–1961); also, *The Labour Force*, 71-001 (1981 and 1986). Used by permission of the Minister of Supply and Services Canada.

trend started many years ago and is evidence that our economy has reached a high level of industrial maturity. This can also be seen in the steadily declining employment in agriculture. (See Figure 2-8.)

Unions

unions

Unions are groups of employees who have joined together for the purpose of presenting a united front in dealing with management. Unions are an external environment factor because they are third parties dealing with company management. The union, rather than the individual employee, negotiates an agreement with the firm; so, while individual employees are part of the internal environment of the firm, their union is a part of the external environment. There are many large unions in the Canadian business environment (see Table 2-3).

TABLE 2-3   The Ten Largest Unions in Canada (1985)

	Number of Members
1. Canadian Union of Public Employees (CLC)	296 000
2. Nat. Union of Prov. Gov't. Employees (CLC)	245 000
3. Public Service Alliance of Canada (CLC)	181 500
4. United Steelworkers of America (AFL/CIO/CLC)	148 000
5. United Food and Commercial Workers (ALF/CIO/CLC)	146 000
6. United Automobile, Aerospace and Agricultural Implement Workers of America (CLC)	135 800
7. Social Affairs Federation (CNTU)	93 000
8. International Brotherhood of Teamsters, Chauffeurs, Warehousemen and Helpers of America (Independent)	91 500
9. Quebec Teaching Congress (Independent)	90 000
10. United Brotherhood of Carpenters and Joiners of America (AFL/CIO)	73 000

SOURCE *Labour Organizations in Canada*, 1985, p. xxii. Reproduced by permission of the Minister of Supply and Services Canada.

Through collective bargaining, organized labor has influenced the pattern of employee-management relations in business firms. In Canada, approximately 30 percent of the total labor force is unionized.[4] (See Figure 2-9.) Even among nonunion firms that try to

MANAGEMENT IN PRACTICE

Unionization at Eaton's

For many years, Eaton's employees have been nonunion. However, in 1984, the Retail, Wholesale, and Department Store Employees Union was certified as the bargaining agent for employees at two Eaton's stores. A retail analyst from a Montreal brokerage firm had predicted a union drive because department stores had frozen wages and reduced staff levels dramatically during 1980-1982. A research and education director for the Ontario Retail Council believes there were also other contributing factors. Part-time jobs used to be taken by people who were between jobs, but that era has passed. People have begun relying on these jobs, and the lower wages associated with them have become unacceptable.

To discourage further inroads by labor unions, retail outlets will need to improve working conditions and employee wages and benefits. However, this may reduce profits and put downward pressure on share prices.

SOURCE   Adapted from Frances Phillips, "Union Claims Second Eaton's Store," *The Financial Post* (April 21, 1984): 4.

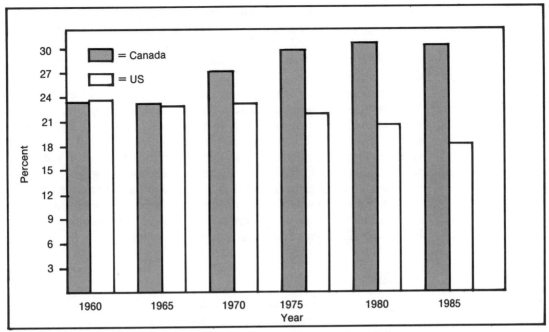

FIGURE 2-9   Union membership as a proportion of the total work force,
US and Canada, 1960–1985, selected years

SOURCES   *Labour Organizations in Canada* (1985): xxv; also *Statistical Abstract of the United States* (1984): 439; also Reinecke and Schoell, *Introduction to Business* (Allyn and Bacon, 1986): 244.

maintain their nonunion status, unions have an impact. Current wage levels, fringe benefits, and working conditions for millions of employees reflect decisions made by unions and management through collective bargaining.

Shareholders

shareholders

People who are owners and who share in a corporation's profit (or loss) are referred to as **shareholders**. They are vitally interested in the firm's operating effectiveness. The price of the shares and the dividends paid are also of major concern to shareholders. Managers actually operate the firm but, since the shareholders own the company, managers must be sensitive to the needs of shareholders as an external environment factor.

Because shareholders have a monetary investment in the firm, they may at times challenge programs considered by management to be beneficial to the organization. Managers may be forced to justify the merits of a particular program in terms of how it will affect future profits. For instance, if managers recommend that equipment be bought that will lower pollutants, they will likely have to justify the purchase to shareholders with regard to how it affects the long-term profitability of the firm. Shareholders are concerned with how expenditure decisions relate to increasing revenues or decreasing costs.

Another means by which some shareholders have influenced some firms is through shareholder activism. A small group of shareholders may try to force a corporation to take a certain action in order to avoid negative public relations. For example, during the 1960s, a group of Dow Chemical shareholders asked the firm to stop manufacturing items used in the war in Vietnam. The last thing most corporations want is criticism of the firm in the headlines of major newspapers.[5] Such action was virtually unheard of before 1960 and, although shareholder activism's goals are rarely fulfilled, it usually succeeds in increasing the firm's sensitivity to its public image.

Suppliers

A manufacturing firm cannot operate effectively unless it is continuously supplied with needed raw materials. Lack of adequate supplies can cause the manufacturing process to be inefficient or to cease altogether — even if the firm has sufficient capital and employees. Managers must try to minimize the negative impact of supplier failure. For instance, a steel strike can affect a manufacturing firm's ability to produce its regular product. Similarly, a computer company which produces data-processing services would likely have to delay its operations if it was unable to secure the needed forms to process the customer's output. Suppliers of both service and goods-producing industries can be a crucial external factor. When supplies fail, managers should have contingency plans ready.

Customers

The people who actually use a firm's products and services also must be considered part of the external environment. Because sales are critical to a firm's survival, managers have the task of ensuring that its business practices do not antagonize the members of the market it serves. If customers or consumers think a firm's employment, pricing, or pollution policies are unreasonable, for instance, they may refuse to buy the firm's products or services.

The General Public

Canadian society as a whole also exerts considerable pressure on managers. The general public is not always willing to accept the actions of business without question. Pressure has been brought to bear on business with respect to such issues as product safety, minority and women's rights, and advertising.

As an external environment factor, the general public can affect managers through government. Public pressure can be effective if a sufficiently large segment of society elects representatives who will support legislation to control the business activities at issue. In the 1970s and 1980s, for example, public concerns about pollutants have been expressed so widely that business firms are now much more conscious of how their activities will affect air and water quality. The general public can also act directly to affect an organization; consider the impact "right-to-life" advocates have as members of hospital boards.

social
responsibility

ethics

Two concepts — corporate social responsibility and business ethics — must be considered when discussing the public as part of the external environment. **Social responsibility** is the implied, enforced, or felt obligation of managers, acting in their official capacities, to serve and protect the interests of groups other than themselves. **Ethics** are contemporary standards or principles of conduct that govern the actions and behavior of individuals within the organization. Both these issues are discussed in detail in Chapter 20.

If a firm is to remain acceptable to the general public, its managers must be able to explain its purpose satisfactorily. This can be a most difficult challenge. Recent surveys have indicated that the general public does not have a favorable perception of business; as many as 50 percent of those surveyed have expressed displeasure with the actions of business. The public also has an exaggerated view of overall business profitability. When asked what a typcial business firm earns on each dollar of sales, many people think profits are almost thirty cents (30 percent) per dollar of sales when in reality profits are usually about five cents (5 percent) on each sales dollar.

Managers must remember that the employees of the firm are also members of the general public, and each will have an influence over a large number of people who are not directly connected with the firm — their families, friends, and neighbors. If employees are kept informed of management's perspective on issues, they can do much to help communicate this information to the general public.

THE SYSTEMS APPROACH: THE BUSINESS SYSTEM

In order to be successful, managers must understand and be capable of coping with the many environment factors that confront them each day. Managers must also be able to see how the functions of planning, organizing, influencing, and controlling interrelate. A concept that helps managers to perform the management functions and to respond effectively to environment factors is the systems approach. A **system** is an arrangement of interrelated parts designed to achieve objectives. The **systems approach** is a way of viewing the firm in terms of the interrelationships of its internal components with each other and with the external environment. Through the systems approach, managers are better able to understand and work with the various units within the organization to coordinate the accomplishment of the goals of the firm.

Successful managers have found that the systems approach aids significantly in managing organizations. In any organization, management's job is to use resources (inputs) in an efficient manner to produce or achieve desirable products and/or services (outputs). Although the systems approach is useful in managing any type of organization, our illustration of its usage is applied specifically to a business firm. (See Figure 2-10.)

Resources/Inputs

A business enterprise uses certain inputs that are processed into outputs (products and/or services). This interaction with the external environment suggests that organizations are operating in an **open system**; that is, the organization depends on other systems for its inputs. Just as people cannot live long without food and water, a dynamic business system cannot survive without resources that keep it alive. These resources or inputs may be human (employees to run the plant) or nonhuman (fuel for the factory, supplies or information). The resources needed by the system vary according to the objectives or goals of the firm. If, for example, a watch manufacturer has the objective of making high-quality watches, the inputs needed are likely to be highly trained craftspeople and quality equipment and materials. A manufacturer of lower-quality watches may need different inputs, such as mass-production equipment and less-skilled employees.

Processing Resources/Inputs

Resources or inputs are processed within the organization to create desired outputs in the form of products or services. This processing involves every aspect of the firm except managerial talent. It includes the necessary equipment, employees, and structure needed to convert resources into outputs. The processor for a university would be the faculty, the nonmanagerial staff, and the buildings required to maintain the university. The president, vice-presidents, deans, department heads, and other managerial personnel are not considered part of the processor; they oversee its operation. The desired outputs of the processor vary with the objectives of the firm. The Ford Motor Company takes steel, aluminum, and glass and converts them into automobiles and trucks. A hospital changes patients into healthy people; a school changes uninformed students into knowledgeable ones; and a retail store changes products on the shelves into desired consumer goods.

Outputs

The products and services of a firm are the outputs of the conversion process. Once inputs (physical, human, capital) are converted to outputs, they return to the external environment. These outputs should conform to the objectives and goals of the firm (discussed in greater detail in Chapter 3). The output of IBM is largely information-processing machinery, while the output of Ontario Hydro is energy. A different system may be required for each firm, to reflect its goals and the output required.

Management and Standards

Analyzing the business system still further, note the information feedback to management (the arrow in Figure 2-10 from outputs to management). Managers use this information to ensure that outputs are being produced according to standard. Standards provide management with basic guidelines for desired performance. If standards are not being achieved, management must make changes to correct any deviations; these may be a result of incorrect inputs, such as defective parts or unqualified employees. As inputs are processed and transformed into outputs, a problem could result because of low morale among employees. Whatever the cause, management's task is to identify any deviations and make corrections in line with company objectives.

Dynamics of a Business System

All of the components of any firm — resources, processor, output, management, and standards — operate as a system. But it cannot be a closed system that fails to take into consideration the external environment. The external environment affects how the business system operates. For instance, the union may decide to strike, and thereby shut down the processor. Suppliers may not be able to provide the material necessary to keep the processor going. Government legislation may be passed that places certain restrictions on the firm. Competitors may develop an innovative product that makes the firm's current products obsolete.

The business system is dynamic, constantly changing. The systems approach provides managers with a means of viewing the interrelationships of internal and external factors. Many factors must be considered if the goals of the organization are to be achieved.

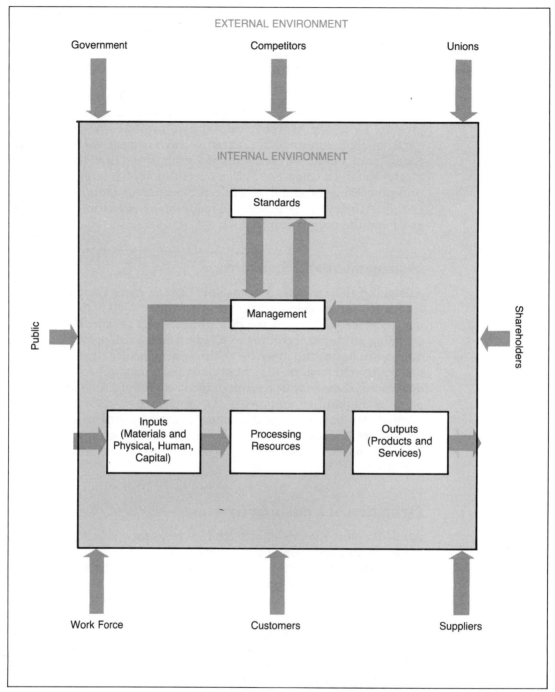

FIGURE 2-10   The business system

THE SITUATIONAL APPROACH

situational
approach

Managers use the systems approach to management to analyze inter-relationships that exist within all organizations. Another concept — the situational approach — builds upon the systems approach and provides managers with a broader appreciation of the management process. The **situational approach** stresses management flexibility in adapting to the particular circumstances and constraints that a firm may encounter. It is not a new concept; in *The Prince* [1512], Nicoló Machiavelli wrote:

> Therefore, you ought to know that there are two ways to fight: by using laws, and by using force. The former is characteristic of man; the latter, of animals. ... Therefore, since a prince must perfect his knowledge of how to use animal attributes, those he must select are the fox and the lion. Since the lion is powerless against snares and the fox is powerless against wolves, one must be a fox to recognize snares and a lion to frighten away wolves.

Machiavelli was telling his prince that he must be capable of making decisions based on the demands of a particular situation; nothing is consistently either yes or no. In using this approach, managers recognize that many different types of situations can exist and they should use a variety of strategies to respond to them. (The situational approach to management in general should not be confused with situational theories of leadership, which are discussed in Chapter 12. The former is a philosophy of management, while the latter are specific to one function of management.)

The need for a situational approach to management can be demonstrated by contrasting different types of organizations. It would be inappropriate to try to manage a college or university in the same way as a large manufacturing corporation. Though the management functions are the same in all types of organizations, their performance depends on the situation. Both the systems and situational approaches are important to managers in the performance of their jobs.

Although there is an unlimited number of specific circumstances or constraints managers may encounter, they may be classified in six major categories:

- External environment
- Objectives
- Technology
- Structure
- Personnel
- Managerial style

Not only must managers recognize that these factors exist, they must be capable of aligning or synchronizing them through the help of the systems approach to achieve the best results. Situationally oriented

Dr. John R. Evans
Allelix Inc.

Looking for ways to take part in what's expected to be a $100 billion, worldwide market arising from the application of biological processes and mechanisms to industrial and commercial uses? Consider a visit to Allelix Inc.'s brand new $20-million biotechnology center in the city of Mississauga, adjacent to Toronto.

Allelix is probably Canada's major entry in the race to endow organisms with abilities that will create products in fields as diverse as forestry, medicine, and food. Basically, Allelix's work force of 90 scientists (a research scientist in biotechnology can expect to make up to $60 000 a year, five years after his or her Ph.D.) is trying to gain genetic control of certain enzymes that can produce desirable products. Running an operation dedicated to the industrialization of this microscopic world calls for a special blend of intellectual, entrepreneurial, and administrative skills. It took

more than a year to find and attract the men who filled the jobs, in June 1982, of president, scientific director, and commercial director. In February 1983, Allelix rounded out top management by appointing 54-year-old John Evans as chairman and chief executive officer.

Q: We laymen are mildly terrified of work being done in biotechnology. Are we justified in our fears?

Evans: Those involved in this field face major ethical considerations. No one can rule out that some variant in a process might be harmful. But, consider these two important aspects. First, experience suggests that mutants — the ones we change in these organisms — tend not to survive very well. We have to nourish them and support them, and sometimes they die out when we try to scale up. This lack of the adaptive processes that characterize natural organisms is a protection.

Second, wherever one is producing new organisms, one must impose control systems. In a facility like ours, even though we don't believe there is a danger and even when we're using standard organisms that already exist, we use careful control systems so that they are separately vented and looked after. If we came up with an organism that seemed to have toxic effects, we should have to be extraordinarily careful with it. Most of the organisms we deal with are already present in nature, and all we're doing is changing one characteristic. It's pretty hard to imagine that's going to be a threat to society down the road.

Q: It's been more than 30 years since the proposal for the structure of DNA. Where are we now in terms of developing commercially useful products using biotechnology?

Evans: First-generation biotechnology firms dealt primarily with products for humans: insulin, growth hormones, interferons, blood products. That began in the early 1970s and those companies are just now bringing to market a few of the products that are a little simpler in their characteristics. In the next five years, we'll see quite a lot of such products.

Q: Your challenge must be in selecting areas of research.

Evans: That's the greatest dilemma because we don't have an established marketing system to send back directing signals about which niche to cultivate. You see some general market opportunities which you can assess but you don't know whether the science will be far enough advanced to take you to those.

A company such as ours at this stage has a heavy orientation to "science-push" rather than "market-pull" in determining its activities. We have very few marketing people on staff and we have a great diversity of product possibilities. We supplement our own market analysis by working with people who are major commercial actors in different fields.

I expect that there will be three different approaches to commercialization. Where we have a major flow of product possibilities and where the market is not already dominated by difficult-to-budge entities, we will develop products at Allelix itself or spin off Allelix subsidiaries to handle the production side and, maybe, even the marketing aspect up to distributor level. The second option is for us to licence out the products to a group that already has a position in the market. Some of our earliest products may go in that direction because we don't want to develop the necessary management until we know more about where our best lines are likely to emerge. A third possibility is joint ventures, in which we join with somebody who can bring something to the table in a commercial position, both in terms of market analysis and in marketing and distribution skills.

Q: So research and development is the main thrust?
Evans: I would hate to see that disappear from Allelix. The aim is certainly not to run a little research and then market. I hope that at the end of a decade Allelix will be a very strong research and development enterprise with a knowledgeable group that attracts others to work with it in scientific areas. I hope it would also have proven most effective in identifying commercial niches.

Q: Your scientists are coming together here for the first time. How does the lack of shared previous experience affect Allelix?
Evans: In any organization, there's a tendency to seek a compartmental comfort. We hope that won't happen because interactions among scientists in major areas of scientific activity

are of great importance. The key breakthroughs will come in the overlapping areas of scientific development. A management challenge is to create an atmosphere that encourages crossing the classical scientific disciplinary boundaries to allow linkage of the intelligence that exists in different areas. If people are rewarded for moving their own projects forward exclusively, they're going to be reluctant to give their time to helping others move their projects forward. We have to give value to the support an individual gives to a project outside his or her area.

Q: You offered scientific staff equity in Allelix. Is this a strong motivator?
Evans: I thought it would be. But so far, it is not. The critical issue is whether this is going to be a reasonably stable enterprise or a fly-by-night. Some biotechnology groups have depended on hype to float an equity issue. A great strength of Allelix is that its shareholders have made a commitment which will sustain the core scientific staff for eight to ten years. That means a chance to get some worthwhile intermediate and long-term product development under way. In other companies, there's a tendency to press on short-term issues that could go to market quickly; these aren't as rewarding financially or scientifically to the individuals concerned.

Q: Where does Canada stand against other countries in this technology?
Evans: The overwhelming leader is the United States. Over the last 20 years, Americans have made major investments in the basic biological sciences and in molecular biology, stimulated by cancer research programs. The amount of private-sector investment through the large chemical, pharmaceutical, and agribusiness companies is enormous. It's primarily a private-sector and university development there. If you think of the United States in the first rank, and Japan and Europe in the second rank, then Canada is in the third. Whether we can move up into the second rank depends on whether we can bring some kind of coordinated approach to industry, universities, and government laboratories.

SOURCE Adapted from Dean Walker, "Allelix Offers a New Hybrid That Could Take Root," *Executive* (April 1984): 52-57. Reprinted by permission.

managers must be constantly aware of these factors and the manner in which they interact. Managers should recognize that no one best approach to management meets the needs of all organizations.

External Environment

Earlier in this chapter, we discussed the main factors that comprise the external environment. These factors constantly affect the way managers perform their assigned tasks. The situational approach counsels managers to be aware of possible pressures or changes in the external environment and to solve problems with the objectives of the organization in mind.

Objectives of the Organization

objective

An **objective** describes the result a firm wants to accomplish. For example, a beverage company may want to achieve a 20 percent market share for a new soft drink. Or, a nightclub might want to reduce employee turnover to five percent during its next fiscal year.

Objectives are influenced by the external environment of the firm. If environment changes are dramatic enough, objectives may have to be completely abandoned. For example, when saccharine was banned by legislation in 1977, companies making products using saccharine had to remove them from grocers' shelves. Knowing the government was preparing this legislation, the saccharine producers had to re-think their product strategies. This, in turn, forced them to set different profit objectives with products that did not contain saccharine.

In highly uncertain environments, such as ones for professional sports teams, objectives may be subject to rapid change. In more stable and predictable environments, such as those for Bell Canada or B.C. Hydro, managers are able to establish more specific and steady objectives. As external environment requirements change, the objectives of a firm that desires to survive and prosper must also change.

Technology

technology

Knowledge about how to use skills, methods, and equipment to convert resources into desired products and/or services is called **technology**. In the situational approach to management, technology can be characterized on the basis of how well it is understood. If the technology is well understood and a firm knows exactly what it is doing, a routine can be developed and applied uniformly. If the technology is complex and rather uncertain, the organization is more dependent on people for effective operation. The technology for manufacturing hand calculators is more straightforward than that for teaching students. In turn, the technology for teaching students is better developed than the technology for curing mental illness.

MANAGEMENT IN PRACTICE

Managing Milk Production with Robots

The use of robots to milk cows is closer to becoming a reality. Researchers have found that cows like to be milked, and that they will return to a milking station up to five times in one day if they can be milked on demand. The more they are milked, the more milk they produce, so attempts are being made to allow milking on demand. One study in Holland showed that milk output increased 30 percent if a cow was milked three times a day instead of two.

This is where the milking robot comes in. A robot milking machine could be placed in the corner of a field and a cow could go to the machine whenever it felt like being milked. The machine would recognize the cow from an electric radio necklace around the animal's neck. The milking machine would be attached to the udders by a vacuum, and would automatically release when the milk supply began to dry up. These robot milkers could be installed on the backs of trucks, and at the end of the day could simply be driven to an unloading site.

Such machines are now being developed, and field trials may take place as early as 1990. The effect on the dairy business would be to increase productivity and reduce labor costs.

SOURCE   Adapted from "The Land Of Milk and Robots," *The Winnipeg Free Press* (November 15, 1986): 51.

Structure

structure

As used here, **structure** means the manner in which the internal environment of the firm is organized or arranged. If most major decisions are made primarily by top-level executives, the organization is **centralized**. If lower-level supervisors and managers are permitted to make significant decisions, the structure is more **decentralized**. Organization structures are discussed in Chapter 7.

centralized

decentralized

Personnel

"Hire good people and let them use their strengths" is the general philosophy toward personnel held by many effective managers. But because each employee differs in terms of goals, aspirations, background, experiences, and personality, some employees are a better match with one organization than another. It has been found that employees tend to move toward the firm that possesses an environment most compatible with their goals and needs. If a firm has a need for individuals with skills that are different from those currently available in the organization, changes may have to be made. This is a predicament facing Canadian workers of the future. Technological changes will affect thousands of jobs over the next 20 years. For instance, robots are taking the place of some automobile assembly-line workers, and other applications are sure to follow. Managers need a work force that can keep pace with the technological advances of the firm, either through retraining or hiring personnel with different skills.

Managerial Styles

There are many managerial styles. One popular way of categorizing leadership styles is to assess the amount of authority a manager delegates to subordinates. This creates a continuum of managerial styles, with the extremes being "autocratic" and "democratic." With the autocratic style a manager's attitude is, "I will make all the decisions." With the participative style a manager encourages worker involvement in decision making. The situational approach says that different styles are workable under different conditions. This important issue is examined in more depth in Chapter 12.

Balancing the Situational Factors

Thus far we have discussed the systems and situational approaches as if they were separate and distinct. This is not really the case, since the systems approach provides a manager with the ability to balance the situational factors. It is how these factors interact, rather than any one factor taken separately, that is significant.

Both the systems and situational approaches must be interrelated if a manager is to be effective; the organizational system must take into consideration the situational factors. (See Figure 2-11.) These factors must be balanced if good results are to be achieved. As the situational factors change, the system may need to be modified. For

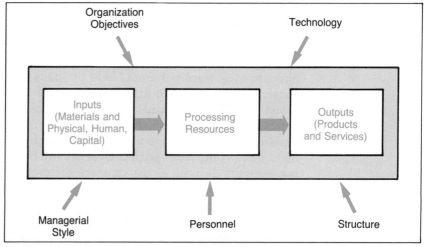

FIGURE 2-11   Management from a systems and situational viewpoint

instance, if the objectives of the firm alter (e.g., the firm switches to diversification as opposed to concentration on only one product), the situational factors will likely be out of balance. New technologies may be required in order to achieve the new objectives. New workers will likely be needed; if the structure is not one that can accommodate these new employees or if the firm finds that it is having difficulty recruiting the type of people necessary to bring about these changes, the situational factors will need further realignment. As the situation is altered, the system must change to adapt.

A manager must be capable of recognizing when situational factors are unbalanced, and of bringing them back into line by changes to the system. Maintaining proper alignment of the situational factors ensures that the firm is operating at all times with the best system to meet the objectives of the organization. Underwood, the leading producer of typewriters many years ago, failed to recognize the growing trend toward office mechanization. This trend was the impetus for the development and sale of electric typewriters, which later became standard equipment in virtually every office. Underwood, however, continued to produce manual typewriters. A competitor, IBM, recognized the trend and brought its system into alignment with the environment. IBM adapted its organization objectives, technology, structure, personnel, and management approach to meet the needs of a changing environment. IBM has since become the leading manufacturer of electric typewriters and many other electronic office products. Underwood (which merged with Olivetti in 1966 to become Underwood-Olivetti) belatedly noted the changing market conditions and entered the electric typewriter business, but it has been unable to reestablish its former dominant position in the typewriter industry.

OPENING INCIDENT REVISITED

Farlane Mining and Smelting Ltd.

Manager James Farlane was experiencing pressure from a variety of factors in the environment external to his company, and he was wondering if he could satisfy all of them. The material in this chapter indicates that eight significant environment factors can affect any business firm. For Farlane Mining and Smelting, at this particular time, four have assumed prominence: (1) the union, (2) government, (3) shareholders, and (4) customers. Each of these groups is asking for something that will cost the company money. Since monetary resources are limited, Farlane cannot agree to exactly what each group wants. Rather, he will have to compromise — try to give each group enough of what it wants and still keep the firm in business.

Farlane must contend with the further complication that one group or environment factor may be in conflict with another as well as with the company. For example, the union wants higher wages, but shareholders want higher earnings per share. The goals of these two groups are in conflict since money is limited.

As another example, the federal government requires the company to install more pollution-control equipment, which will cost money; at the same time, some customers want lower prices. Decreasing prices would reduce both profits and the company's ability to buy more pollution-control equipment. It will also reduce their ability to pay higher wages.

There are no easy solutions to the problems facing Farlane Mining and Smelting. But, since firms that cannot satisfy the demands of important external environment groups run the risk of being forced out of business, Farlane must do something. He might present the company's financial problems to the union and see if it will consider wage concessions in return for job security. A number of companies across Canada in the last several years have used this strategy successfully. He might also try to get an extension on complying with federal pollution regulations, giving the company time to sort out some of its other problems and generate the capital necessary to purchase the additional pollution-control equipment. The government is likely to be reasonable about such an extension; after all, it does not want to bankrupt the firm.

Farlane's presentation to the shareholders at the annual meeting must point out these conflicting pressures and must demonstrate the need for shareholder patience. The crises will pass. If the proper actions are taken, earnings per share should increase and shareholders will benefit in the future. Farlane may not be able to do much about the customers. In a free economy, customers can purchase wherever they are getting the best deal. Farlane Mining and Smelting must remain competitive if it is to stay in business. The requested marketing survey will indicate which competitors are likely to pose the major threat; Farlane may try an advertising campaign stressing product quality as a counter strategy, rather than lowering the prices.

This series of crises demonstrates the complex interaction of the various external environment factors facing business managers. To be successful, managers must be able to cope with considerable uncertainty and anxiety. They must also be able to find creative ways to satisfy the conflicting demands of groups in the firm's external environment.

SUMMARY

The job of managing is not accomplished in a vacuum. Many interacting external factors can affect a manager's performance. Major external environment factors include: government, competitors, the work force, unions, shareholders, suppliers, customers, and the general public.

One of the most important external factors managers must cope with is the law, the maze of regulations from federal, provincial, and municipal governments. Such regulations range from protection of the air, water, and land to prohibition of discrimination in hiring based on age, race, color, sex, religion, or national origin. Regarding competition, managers must remember that a decision made by another firm may affect their own company. The nature of the Canadian labor force as a whole will be quite different as more women and white-collar workers enter the work force; increased use of technology will also bring changes to employment practices. Unions, too, must be considered an external environment factor because they become essentially third parties when dealing with the firms in which unionized employees work. Shareholders are vitally interested in the firm's operation and, since they own the company, their needs must be considered by managers. Managers must be aware of suppliers in the external environment, because lack of supplies could cause the manufacturing process to be reduced or to stop, even though the firm has sufficient capital and employees. The customers — the people who buy and use a firm's products or services — are a crucial factor in the firm's external environment. Finally, the general public can affect managerial decisions, usually working through its elected representatives to legislate changes to business practices.

The systems approach is a concept that helps managers to perform the management functions and to respond to external environment considerations effectively. A system is an arrangement of interrelated parts designed to achieve objectives. Successful managers have found that the systems approach is a significant aid because it leads them to consider the factors inside and outside the firm that have an impact on one another and on the firm itself. In any organization, managers use resources (inputs) in an efficient way to produce or achieve desirable products and/or services (output). Standards provide managers with basic guidelines for desired performance. All the components of any firm — input, processor, management, and standards — operate as a system.

The situational approach to managing builds on the systems approach, giving managers a greater appreciation of the management process. The situational approach requires that managers adapt to meet particular circumstances and constraints that a firm may encounter. Although the number of such circumstances and constraints is unlimited, they can be classified into six major categories: the external environment, objectives, technology, structure, personnel, and managerial styles. Not only must managers realize that these factors exist, they must be capable of aligning or synchronizing them through the situational and systems approaches to achieve the best results.

REVIEW QUESTIONS

1. Identify and describe the eight environmental factors that can affect a manager.
2. What is the difference between the general environment and the direct action environment?
3. How has the Canadian work force changed during the twentieth century?
4. How have unemployment rates for men and women varied since World War II?
5. What trends have been evident in the goods-producing and service-producing industries since 1950?

6. How do trends in union membership in Canada and the US compare?
7. Define a system. Why does a manager need to understand the systems approach?
8. What are the components of a business system? How do they interrelate?
9. Define the situational approach to management. Identify and define the six categories of situational factors that a manager must align in order to achieve the best results.

EXERCISES

1. Consider the following objectives from two different firms:
   Firm A: Our goal is to be an innovator in the creation of new products and services.
   Firm B: Our goal is to mass produce products that have a proven record of success.
   Given these different objectives, how might the situational factors of technology, structure, personnel, and managerial style be different? Are there factors from the external environment that would be different for each firm?
2. Listed below are three different managerial positions. Describe and discuss the major environment factors that would likely affect these positions.
   a. President of Falconbridge Nickel Ltd.
   b. President of a community college or a university.
   c. Owner and operator of a 7-11 convenience store in a major Canadian city.
   d. Manager of a nuclear power station.

CASE STUDY

The Toy Environment

Carson Toys Ltd. produced a line of children's toys. The company had always been successful, but recent reports showed that sales of two of Carson's most successful nonseasonal toys were down substantially. If allowed to continue, this would have a negative effect on profits, so Jonathan Carson, president of Carson Toys, called in Martha Bucyk, the vice-president of marketing, for an explanation. She gave several possible reasons for the decline.

First, Bucyk said that she had been told by several Carson salespersons that some customers were placing trial orders with a toy manufacturer in Taiwan. This manufacturer produced two high-quality toys which were very similar to two of Carson's toys. The major difference was the price. In Canada the imported toys sold at retail for 75 percent of the retail price of Carson's two toys. Bucyk suggested that retail toy buyers were growing more price conscious, because the uncertain economy in Canada was causing customers to demand more for their money.

Bucyk also suggested that the recent increase in the cost of plastic had led to a reduction in the thickness of the plastic used to make several Carson products, including the two problem products. She thought that this had hurt the company's reputation for making quality toys. In fact, Carson had received 150 letters from retail customers complaining about "shoddy" toys, and three customers said they were reporting the problem to Consumer and Corporate Affairs Canada. They claimed that their children had received cuts on their hands from jagged pieces of plastic, which became exposed when the toys broke during normal play. Bucyk and Carson worried about this. They knew that three competitors had removed several unsafe toys from the market. Bucyk suggested, however, that this was a production problem and not directly her concern.

Bucyk's third suggestion for decreased sales was the declining birth rate in Canada. The two problem toys appeal to children between the ages of two and four, she pointed out, and so, with the number of potential users declining, Carson Toys cannot be surprised if sales also decline.

She suggested, too, that many parents were complaining about the tremendous volume of advertising aimed at children and that the constant bombardment of television commercials was "bad" for them. Carson had concentrated its advertising on Saturday-morning children's television shows and several parents had written to Carson and accused the company of "taking advantage" of children. Bucyk also knew that the government was investigating these complaints from parents and that restrictive legislation was possible. As a result, the company had decided several months ago to reduce its advertising. However, they may have been too late and these complaints may have caused the decline in sales.

Finally, Martha Bucyk reminded Carson that more and more toys were now being sold through "price-cutting" discount stores. Carson had always refused to sell through discount stores because many toy store owners said they would stop buying their products if they did. The discount stores had become a major problem, Bucyk noted, and something had to be done in order for Carson to remain competitive in non-discount stores.

QUESTIONS

1. List and describe briefly the external environment factors affecting Carson Toys Ltd.
2. How are these environment factors causing problems for Carson Toys Ltd.?
3. Develop a plan of action for dealing with each one of these environment factors.

CASE STUDY

Northern Forest Products Company

As the largest employer in a remote Ontario community, Northern Forest Products (NFP) is an important part of the local economy. NFP employs about 30 percent of the local work force, and there are few alternative job opportunities available.

William Jamieson, the personnel director for NFP, recently had to make a difficult decision. With the soft demand and excess capacity in the pulpwood industry, he knew that sooner or later the word would come down from above that operations needed to be streamlined and operating costs reduced.

Jamieson received the news at a private meeting with the president. He was told that NFP would have to cut employment by 20 percent within the next six months. Jamieson was asked by the president to develop a plan to achieve the necessary cuts. He knew that the president would probably not adopt his plan without revisions, but he also knew that the president was expecting him to come up with a workable first effort.

As Jamieson began developing his plan, he thought first about how the union would react. The laid-off workers would have to be let go in order of seniority, according to the union contract. But the union would try to protect as many jobs as possible. Jamieson knew that all management's actions during this period would be intensely scrutinized by the provincial government to ensure that no regulations regarding extended layoffs were being violated. He had to make sure that the company had its act together so that it didn't get any negative publicity. He remembered reading about a government minister's negative remarks about Inco when it had planned to lay off some workers because of low prices for nickel on world markets. He certainly didn't want that kind of publicity for NFP.

Then there was the matter of the impact on the surrounding community. Jamieson knew that the economy in many northern communities in Canada was shaky, and the community in which NFP operated was no exception. He knew that cutbacks would reduce worker income and that this, in turn, would negatively affect many of the small businesses in town. He remembered the concerns that were evident in Lynn Lake, Manitoba when there was talk of shutting down the gold mine there. He knew that cutbacks at NFP would create the same kinds of concerns. He also knew that government officials would want to know what the company was doing to minimize the impact of the layoffs.

Jamieson believed that, from an economic perspective, the company really had no choice but to make the cuts. He also felt under pressure from the president, and since the president was his boss, he really felt he had no alternative but to develop a plan for implementing the cuts. He was well aware that several competitors of NFP had recently laid off substantial numbers of workers. To keep sales from being further depressed, he had to ensure that NFP was competitive. A cost advantage of even two or three percent would allow competitors to take away many of NFP's customers.

A major reason for the cutbacks was to protect the interests of the shareholders and to maintain the financial viability of the company. In general, the company's shareholders seemed to be far more concerned with their return on investment than they were with the firm spending a lot of time worrying about employment levels.

At his meeting with the president, Jamieson had been reminded that, just like every other manager in the company, his first responsibility was to increase the wealth of the shareholders, because they were the ones who had taken the financial risks by investing their money in the company.

Jamieson tried to keep all these things in mind as he began writing his report to the president.

QUESTIONS

1. List the elements in the company's environment that will affect Jamieson's suggested plan. To what extent are these environmental factors contradictory?
2. Is Jamieson's idea that shareholders' interests should come first justified? Discuss.

ENDNOTES

[1]F. H. Leacy (ed.), *Historical Statistics of Canada.* Series D8–55; also *The Labour Force*, 71–001.

[2]F. H. Leacy (ed.), *Historical Statistics of Canada.* Series D266–317; also *The Labour Force*, 71–001.

[3]F. H. Leacy (ed.), *Historical Statistics of Canada.* Series C85–97; also *The Labour Force*, 71–001.

[4]*Labour Organizations in Canada*, 1985: xxv.

[5]David Vogel, "Ralph Nader's All Over the Place: Citizens versus the Corporation," *Across The Board* 1 (April 1979): 26–31.

REFERENCES

Allen, Robert E., and Keaveny, Timothy J. "Does the Work Status of Married Women Affect Their Attitudes Toward Family Life?" *Personnel Administrator* 26 (June 1979): 63–66.

Appley, Lawrence A. "New Directions for Management." *Supervisory Management* 26 (February 1981): 9–12.

Bruce, Harry. "Perfectly Unclear." *Canadian Business* 60 (March 1987): 84–85, 114.

Chisholm, Derek. "Bailing Out Insolvent Banks." *Canadian Business Review* 12 (Winter 1985): 19–21.

Dam, André van. "The Future of Management." *Management World* (January 1978): 3–6.

Davis, Tim R. V. "The Influence of the Physical Environment in Offices." *Academy of Management Review* 9, no. 2 (April 1984): 271–283.

Fram, Eugene H., and Deubrin, Andrew. "Time Span Orientation: A Key Factor of Contingency Management." *Personnel Journal* 60 (January 1981): 46–48.

Gooding, Wayne. "High-tech Adjustment Can Be Tough." *Financial Post* (January 14, 1984): S3.

Graeff, Claude L. "The Situational Theory: A Critical View." *Academy of Management Review* 8, no. 2 (April 1983): 285–291.

Grayson, C. Jackson. "Productivity's Impact on Our Economic Future." *Personnel Administrator* 24 (December 1979): 21, 23.

Jacobs, Bruce. "Keeping Fast-Track Managers on the Rise." *Industry Week* (November 10, 1980): 34.

Lees, David. "Besieging the Banks." *Canadian Business* 59 (September 1986): 76–80, 109–115.

Leslie, C. E. "Critical Issues Confronting Managers in the '80s." *Training and Development Journal* 34 (January 1980): 14–17.

Lipovenko, Dorothy. "Moms Choosing Nursery over Career." *The Globe and Mail* (February 26, 1987): B1–B2.

List, Wilfred. "Country Clubs for Kids Open Eyes to Daycare Costs." *The Globe and Mail* (December 29, 1986): B8.

Luthans, Fred, and Stewart, Todd I. "A General Contingency Theory of Management." *Academy of Management Review* 2 (April 1977): 181–195.

Marsh, Robert M., and Minnari, Hiroshi. "Technology and Size as Determinants of Organizational Structure of Japanese Factories." *Administrative Science Quarterly* 26 (March 1981): 33–57.

Mintzberg, Henry. "The Manager's Job: Folklore and Fact." *Harvard Business Review* (July-August 1975): 49–51.

Nicholson, Joan; Cooper, Toby; Peterson, Russell; Henderson, Hazel; and Densen, James. "How Business Treats Its Environment." *Business and Society Review* 33 (Spring 1980): 56–65.

Noble, Kimberly. "Pulp Mill Test of New Pollution Policy." *The Globe and Mail* (January 26, 1987): B1–B2.

Rieder, George A. "The Role of Tomorrow's Manager." *Personnel Administrator* 24 (December 1979): 27–31.

Rosen, Gerald R. "Can the Corporation Survive?" *Dun's Review* 114 (August 1979): 40–42.

Schwartz, Gail G., and Niekirk, William. "New Shakedowns in the Workplace." *Canadian Business* 57 no. 5 (May 1984): 85.

Stout, Russell. "Formal Theory and the Flexible Organization." *Advance Management* 446 (Winter 1981): 44–52.

"The Land of Milk and Robots." *The Winnipeg Free Press* (November 15, 1986): 51.

Wooton, Leland M. "The Mixed Blessings of Contingency Management." *Academy of Management Review* (July 1977): 431–441.

II

The Planning Process

Planning and Decision Making

KEY TERMS

mission
objectives
standard
performance
  results
  standards
process
  standards

plans
standing plans
policy
procedure
standard operating
  procedures
rule

contingency
  planning
management by
  objectives
activity trap
action plans

LEARNING OBJECTIVES

After completing this chapter you should be able to
1. Describe the planning process.
2. Explain what the term "mission" means.
3. Explain the types of organization objectives a firm must consider.
4. Define standards and recognize the various types of standards that may be established.

5. Distinguish among a policy, a procedure, and a rule.
6. Describe the concept of contingency planning and its importance to managers.
7. Explain what management by objectives is, and identify the essential elements in the MBO process.
8. Describe the benefits and potential problems of MBO.

OPENING INCIDENT

Algonquin Food Products Ltd.

William Klassen, marketing department manager at Algonquin Food Products Ltd. was reviewing a memo from the president. Marie Beliveau, the accounting department head, stopped by his office and asked him if he wanted to go for coffee.

"Yes, I need a break from this goals memo from the president," replied Klassen. "You know, I'll never understand him or this so-called participation planning system. Here's another memo that dictates the latest objectives my department is supposed to achieve. No one in my department had a chance to discuss these objectives. Most of them are unrealistic and many are unattainable."

"Frustrating, isn't it?" agreed Beliveau. "My department couldn't meet the last set of objec-tives, and nothing I say seems to make a difference."

"Why doesn't the president ask us about the goals before he decides to impose them?" Klassen continued. "Isn't that how our Management-by-Objectives system is supposed to operate? And another complaint I have is about all these forms we have to fill out! I'm not sure the president even reads them. But, if he does, he'll probably use them against me this time next year. I really can't see how any of this is going to increase the performance in marketing."

Beliveau chuckled, "Come on, Bill; give up on trying to change the president for now. Let's get a cup of coffee and talk about more pleasant things."

All managers need to be effective planners. Whether the organization they work for sells products or services, operates in the private or public sector, or is a profit-oriented or not-for-profit organization is immaterial. Each of these types of organization needs planning. Managers are responsible for planning — it is one of the four basic management functions.

In Chapter 2, we noted that organizations face uncertainty in their external environment. Some people might argue that such uncertainty makes planning fruitless. However, a systematic consideration of the constraints and opportunities in the external environment may lead to strategies that allow an organization to cope more effectively. Managers who undertake such studies understand the value of planning. Without it, the organization is simply hoping that things will work out all right.

Some managers do not like to spend time planning. They prefer to be active, energetic individuals, accustomed to making rapid decisions and achieving goals daily. Because much of their work has this day-to-day perspective, they have difficulty thinking about the future. But, in order to continue meeting realistic daily goals, managers must be prepared for the future.

Planning is important at all levels of management, although its focus differs from the bottom of the firm to the top. There are four major differences. First, lower-level managers must develop plans that will fit the overall objectives established by top management. Second, the amount of time spent on planning by lower-level managers is not as great as by top management. Third, the timeframe for planning is shorter for lower-level managers. Finally, lower-level managers focus more on internal factors, while top management deals with both internal and external factors.

This chapter is organized around a model of the planning process. The concept of an organizational mission is discussed first. We then discuss organization objectives. We note several different types of objectives and discuss the benefits of and problems with setting objectives. The differences among plans, policies, and procedures in the planning process is also noted. The chapter concludes with an in-depth discussion of management by objectives (MBO).

THE PLANNING PROCESS: AN OVERVIEW

As we saw in Chapter 1, planning is the process of determining in advance what should be accomplished and how it should be done. The planning process is shown in Figure 3-1. This process is appropriate whether planning is done by top, middle, or lower-level managers. The planning process is dynamic and should be constantly evaluated and modified to conform to current and anticipated situations.

MISSION

mission

The process begins with the development of a mission statement. The **mission** is the organization's continuing purpose or reason for being. The expressed mission statement of Holiday Inns, for example, is "Making people feel welcome — all over the world." Holiday Corporation considers itself the world's largest hospitality company and not just a motel chain. Holiday Corporation's managers know that, "and to make a profit doing this" is an implied continuation of the mission statement. Obviously, the company must make a profit

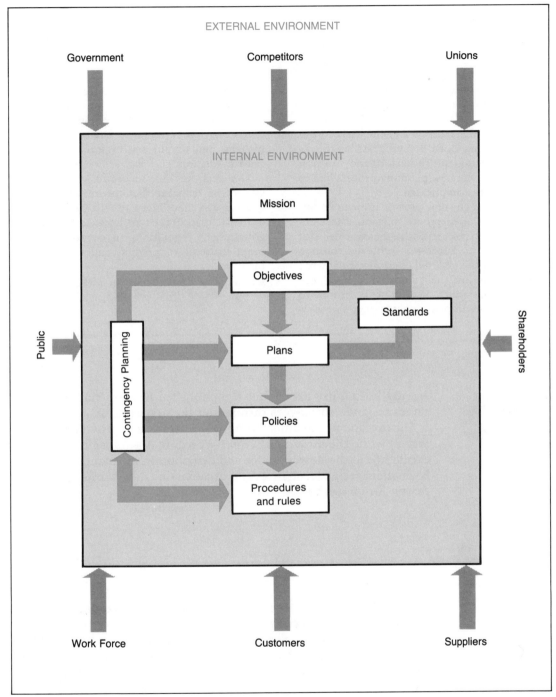

FIGURE 3-1   The planning process

MANAGEMENT IN PRACTICE

Planning at CWNG

Until a few years ago, Canada Western Natural Gas (CWNG) was able to develop business plans for up to five years in advance. The onslaught of the recession in the early 1980s changed all that. Once, planning had been just a matter of basing future performance on past performance; the new planning process had to be much more complicated.

The focus of the new process is on an understanding of the corporate mission, the company's objectives, and the basic rules for achieving them. Success is achieved through awareness of the external environment and the impact it has on the company. CWNG has created a planning and control group to support the main planning group at the com-

pany. Strengths and weaknesses in the planning system are constantly being evaluated. An assessment of management's responsibility to customers, governments, shareholders, employees, and suppliers is important for a successful business.

The real key to successful planning for CWNG is realizing that future prospects for growth and development will be much less dramatic than in the past because of increased government regulation, an economy that is more difficult to predict, and several other factors.

SOURCE Adapted from "Forecasting and Planning," *Oilweek* (January 30, 1984): 14, 15, 17.

---

serving hospitality needs, but the published mission statement still serves to guide employees throughout the organization.

The mission of Canadian National Railways is to provide transportation, while the mission of Great West Life Assurance is to achieve excellence in the development and distribution of financial services. Each managerial level in every organization has a mission — its reason for existence.

ORGANIZATION OBJECTIVES

objectives

Specific objectives, or goals, can be established once the mission is understood. **Objectives** are the desired end results of any activity. Objectives should be set at each managerial level in the organization; however, lower-level objectives must be consistent with objectives of top management. For example, a top management objective for General Motors of Canada might be to "provide automobiles that satisfy consumer desires for safety, comfort and style"; a lower-level objective in the same company might be to "produce 42 Chevettes each hour at the Brantford plant."

Characteristics of Good Objectives

Well thought-out objectives should have four basic features: (1) they should be expressed in writing; (2) they should be measurable; (3) they should be specific as to time; and (4) they should be challenging but attainable.

Placing the goals in written form increases understanding and commitment. Confusion as to what the goals actually are is less likely to occur when they are written.

Measurability suggests that the goals should be quantified whenever possible. It would be much better to set a goal of increasing profits by 10 percent during a certain period than just to say, "We want to increase profits." A one percent increase would meet the latter goal.

Objectives should be specific as to time. Individuals need and want to know when an objective should be accomplished. Also, a goal that is set without a time limit cannot be challenging. In the above example, are the profits to be increased by 10 percent this year or this century?

Finally, an objective that is too easily accomplished provides little satisfaction when completed. On the other hand, an unattainable goal is more likely to frustrate workers than to encourage them.

Types of Objectives

The creation of specific organization objectives is no simple task. As we discussed in Chapter 2, numerous external factors exert their influence on a firm. These external environment factors are competition, shareholders, customers, unions, suppliers, the labor force, the general public, and government. Because of these external factors, an organization usually has more than one objective, and the emphasis may change depending on the impact of a particular environment factor or group of factors. At least three main types of objectives can be identified for Canadian business firms.

- *Economic objectives* — survival, profit, and growth
- *Service objectives* — creation of economic value for society
- *Personal objectives* — goals of individuals and groups within the organization.

Economic Objectives

Survival is a basic objective of all organizations: the one goal common to all. Whether an organization is producing products or services that are useful takes second place to the concern of just staying in business. A firm cannot easily account to higher societal objectives when it does not know whether it can meet the next payroll. An anonymous fellow once noted: "It's difficult to remember that your initial objective was to drain the swamp when you're up to your neck in alligators."

In order to survive, a business firm must at least break even — that is, it must generate enough revenues to cover costs. But business firms want more than mere survival — they are in business to make a profit. Profit provides a vital incentive for continued, successful operation.

Not-for-profit organizations obviously do not pursue profit, but they do have economic objectives that focus on the organization's survival. Their goal is to continue to provide their services to those who need them. The United Way, for example, sets an objective each year specifying the amount of money it needs to carry out its programs.

Growth may be a major objective of both profit and not-for-profit organizations. In an effort to avoid failure, an organization may seek unrestricted growth. Sometimes this growth can become an end in itself, blinding the organization to economic objectives. There are, of course, certain advantages that come with expansion. In profit-oriented companies, growth may help them to compete more effectively in the marketplace. In not-for-profit organizations, growth may help them to generate revenues more effectively and to have more impact on society.

Service Objectives

Profit alone is often viewed as the primary motive for being in business. While it is true a business firm cannot survive for long without making a profit, the old question, "Which comes first, the chicken or the egg?" may have meaning when discussing the profit versus the service objective. If a firm cannot consistently create a product or service that consumers want or can use, it will not stay in business long enough to make a profit. To accomplish the economic objective, a firm must produce goods consumers want. The creation of economic value constitutes the major goal of business organizations within Canada's economic system.

Service objectives are often even more important in not-for-profit organizations. In fact, they may be the major reason the organization exists. For example, agencies running provincial drug- and alcohol-abuse programs do not provide a profit to the government, but their service is beneficial to society in general.

Personal Objectives

Organizations are made up of people who have different personalities, backgrounds, experiences, and goals. Most likely, their personal goals are not identical to the objectives of the organization. If the difference between an individual's goals and those of the company is significant, that employee may choose to withdraw from the firm.

However, "withdrawal" does not necessarily mean departure from the organization. For instance, an employee may not feel that he or she can afford to quit. Major differences between the employee's goals and the organization's goals can result in withdrawal through minimum work effort, absenteeism, and even sabotage. Employees are not the only ones whose goals, when they differ from those of the organization, can affect that organization. For instance, a shareholder can cease to provide support for the organization by selling his or her shares.

If the organization is to survive, grow, and earn a profit, it must attempt to provide a match between its goals and the goals of groups who have contact with the firm. Some possible goal differences between the organization and these various groups may be seen in Table 3-1. It is not unusual for particular groups or members to feel their personal goals are in conflict with the goals of other individuals related to the organization. For instance, some customers may believe that higher wages will make the prices of products higher, while the union may believe that shareholder dividends are too high. Managers have the difficult task of reconciling these conflicts.

Establishing Objectives

Objectives are established by an organization's managers. When these objectives are developed, the mission of the firm and the desires of the shareholders must be considered. Because diversity of personality, background, experience, and personal goals exists among individuals, the objectives of two firms may differ, even though they both produce similar products.

TABLE 3-1   Possible Goal Differences between the Organization and Groups who Have Contact with the Firm

Group	Possible Goal
Organization	Maximize profits
Management	Earn promotions, higher salaries, or bonuses
Employees	Increase wages and bonuses
Government	Obtain adherence to all government legislation, laws, and regulations
Competition	Attain a greater share of the market
Customers	Buy quality product at lowest price
Shareholders / owners	Increase dividends
Public	Protect the ecological environment
Unions	Gain greater influence for union members

The person or persons charged with the responsibility of establishing overall corporate objectives vary from business to business. At times, the president or chairperson of the board provides the major thrust in goal creation. At other times, a group of top-level executives develops corporate goals. Whatever the source, these objectives provide the course toward which future energies of the firm will be directed.

Objectives should be well thought out and concisely stated. They should not constrain lower management to the degree that no further decision making is possible. An objective permits the greatest possible freedom for lower-level management while still providing direction to achieve a specific result.

Overall organization objectives should be accompanied by priorities that should not be altered too frequently. Obviously, major decisions have far-reaching and drastic effects on areas such as personnel requirements, managerial styles, and organizational structure. For instance, a firm dedicated to maintaining a high-quality product will have as a priority the recruitment of well-trained or experienced employees. And a more participative structure may be required to attract and keep skilled employees. Thus, once a particular corporate objective has been stated, the effects of the decision will be felt throughout the organization for a long time.

Problems Encountered in Establishing Objectives

Numerous difficulties can arise when creating objectives. Here are three types of problems that may be encountered.

Real versus Stated Objectives

The real goals of any organization may be at odds with its stated goals. Objectives are often the result of power plays and pressures that come from circumstances in the marketplace or from internal tensions. The personal goals of the board of directors, outside creditors, lower-level managers, employees, shareholders, and labor unions are bound to be different. Because of these differences, the stated goals are at times different from the real goals of the organization. Goals are often significantly altered by individuals and groups who seek to adapt the organization to their narrower purposes. For example, a manager may claim that his objective is to make decisions that will benefit the company, but he actually makes decisions only after considering how his own career will be affected.

To determine the real goals of an organization, one must look at the decisions and actions that occur from day to day. Managers' actions speak louder than words. What functions or groups actually receive the major share of the resources? What type of behavior is accorded the greatest rewards by managers? A prison may specify its major objective as rehabilitation of prisoners; but, if it has only two counselors on its payroll, while it employs 500 guards, the facts tell against the stated goal. A manufacturing firm may say its chief objective is to produce high-quality products; but, if it employs only a few quality-control inspectors and does not stress the importance of quality to its workers, the firm's real objective is inconsistent with its stated objective.

Multiple Objectives

At times, an organization may have multiple and sometimes conflicting goals that must be recognized by management. For instance, what is the major service goal of a university? Is the primary objective of the university to provide education for students, or to conduct research to advance the state of knowledge, or to provide community service? In some universities, research is given the first priority in money, personnel, and privilege. In others, the teaching goal is dominant. In still others, an attempt is made to be all things to all people. However, given limited funds, priorities must be established in most cases. One can debate the priority of goals for such institutions as a mental hospital (therapy? or confinement?), a prison (rehabilitation? or confinement?), a vocational high school (skill development? general education? or keeping young people off the streets?), a medical school (training students for medical practice? or for basic research?), or an aerospace firm (research information? or usable hardware?). At some point, choices and priorities must be made.

Goal Distortion

Once overall objectives and a pattern of priorities are established for an organization, managers must set and pursue goals that conform to them. Unfortunately, managers occasionally get sidetracked and emphasize the achievement of goals that are not significant to the overall organization. This problem can arise when an unimportant goal is easy to quantify, while an important goal is difficult to quantify. For example, in universities, the primary goal of excellence in education is difficult to quantify. Administrators may, therefore, be tempted to overstress what can be quantified — for instance, the number of books and articles published by faculty members. Books or articles may indeed contribute to excellence in education, but the contribution is difficult to measure, while the books and articles themselves are easily quantified.

As another example, a government agency may measure how many dollars it distributes to its constituency because this is easy to monitor. It may then argue that it is effective because it has distributed increasingly large amounts of money over time. It may not be obvious whether the agency is really achieving its goals by spending more money.

Goal distortion also occurs when one department in an organization overemphasizes its particular functions and loses sight of the overall objectives of the organization. In a business firm, for example, marketing managers may pursue sales with great vigor. This is not surprising, since that is marketing's function. However, if they pursue sales to the exclusion of other important organization objectives (for example, researching new areas of their marketplace), the total organization may suffer. If the organization permits its aggressive marketing department to be more important than its after-sales service department, then this imbalance also creates goal distortion. Organizations that stress departmentalized activities always risk goal distortion because personnel and managers in each functional area may become so involved in that specific area that they lose sight of the organization's overall objectives.

STANDARDS

Managers need to express objectives and plans to employees and they need ways to find out if objectives are being met. Both these needs are met by standards, policies, procedures and rules.

standard

A norm, or criterion, to which something can be compared is referred to as a **standard**. Standards specify what constitutes proper behavior or conditions; they help determine whether objectives in the form of plans have been achieved. As such, they provide the link between planning and controlling. Referring once again to Figure 3-1, we can see that standards provide a way of determining if a plan is being properly implemented. It would be foolish to establish objectives and not be able to determine if they have been achieved. But, as is described in Chapter 16, standards provide the starting point for the controlling process.

performance
results standards

process standards

In business, standards can be created to cover nearly every aspect of a situation. Standards can be divided into two main categories. **Performance results standards** deal with the end result of work, while **process standards** deal with work as it is being done. Examples of both types of standard are seen in Table 3-2.

TABLE 3-2   Examples of Standards

Type of Standard	Example
Performance Results	
Quantity	Forty units should be produced each day.
Quality	Each part should have a mass of 1.5 kg $\mp$ 0.01 kg.
Time	Project is scheduled for completion by January 1.
Cost	Labor costs should not exceed $2 per unit.
Process	
Function	The procedure in handbook A-1 should be followed when writing up a sales order.
Personnel	The probationary period for new employees is three months.
Physical factors	Only two workers at a time are permitted in the security area.

Performance Results Standards

The major areas to be evaluated with performance results standards relate to:

- The quality of work
- The quantity of work
- The time needed to complete work
- The cost of work

Quality standards are usually derived from the design of the firm's products or services. For a physical product, standards would exist for consistent quality of form, dimensions, strength, color, and durability. Often quality-control inspectors collect information from production and compare it with established requirements. For a service, quality standards would exist for consistent, fair treatment of all customers.

Quantity standards relate to the number of items produced during a specific time period. For instance, a factory time study may result in a requirement that 50 units per hour be produced by a certain machine operator. An employment interviewer for a personnel agency may be required to place a minimum of 15 applicants a week. In an automobile assembly plant, the standard might be 60 vehicles produced each hour on the assembly line.

Standards governing time are often related to the quantity standards as shown in those examples. The most common example of a time standard relates to completion of a report on a particular date. Most firms' annual reports must be completed in time for presentation at the annual meeting of their shareholders.

Cost standards are established to ensure that a project is completed within set cost limits. These standards are extremely important, for it is embarrassing and financially unwise to complete a project on time only to find that the costs are significantly higher than expected and they wipe out whatever profits might have been realized. Annual and monthly budgets constitute a well-known example of cost standards. Standard cost systems are also designed to enable managers to make more effective decisions governing ongoing action.

Process Standards

Managers attempt to specify and control performance through process standards. For example, a hotel may hire a highly qualified chef for its finest restaurant; this would be a standard of personnel. Or the hotel may develop standards for the best service through job descriptions and standard operating procedures for all hotel staff. These are standards of function. Finally, standards that attempt to provide superior physical factors in terms of equipment, furnishings, lighting, ventilation, or privacy may be drawn up. These are physical factors standards. The operating assumption here is that the best people, using the latest in methodology and equipment, might reach maximum efficiency without having to establish specific standards of quality, quantity, time, and cost. Process standards can be applied for manufacturing firms, but are often crucial to service organizations.

PLANS

plans

Objectives are concerned with the end results desired. **Plans** are statements of how objectives are to be accomplished. Planning is a task that every manager, whether a top-level executive or a first-line supervisor, must perform. Stating an objective does not guarantee its accomplishment. A plan must be developed to tell people what to do in order to fulfill the goal. There are usually more ways than one to accomplish a goal. The plan states which approach is to be taken. Specifically, planning should answer the following questions:

- What activities are required to accomplish the objectives?
- When should these activities be carried out?
- Who is responsible for doing what?
- Where should the activities be carried out?
- When should the action be completed?

MANAGEMENT IN PRACTICE

Planning in the Real Estate Development Industry

Canadian real estate developers had tremendous success during the 1960s and 1970s in developing both commercial and residential real estate. The downtown areas of many Canadian cities attest to that. However, the recession of 1981-1983 caused these developers to revamp their planning processes (which had been fairly rudimentary) to cope with the changed economic environment.

A study of six major Canadian real estate developers by Peter Barnard Associates of Toronto revealed similar planning processes across the six companies. Most plan five years in advance and rely heavily on information from the sales staff in the field. The information filters up to the chief financial officer who puts a business plan together and ensures that it is consistent with overall corporate objectives.

Executives in this industry are enthusiastic about the benefits of planning. In spite of the fact that the real estate development industry must respond quickly to opportunity, systematic planning is not seen as something that "gets in the way of quick action." Rather, it gives management a framework in which to decide on the investment opportunities that best suit the company. In the companies surveyed, planning also encouraged dialogue between corporate planners and divisional managers, something that is often missing in large organizations.

SOURCE   Adapted from Rod Lawrence, "Developers Adjust to Change," *Executive* (February/March 1983): 51–53.

MANAGEMENT IN PRACTICE

Planning in High-Tech Industries

Denzil Doyle opened Digital Equipment of Canada Ltd.'s first sales office in the 1960s. When he resigned as president of Digital in the early 1980s, the company was selling $250 million worth of computers each year and employed over 1700 people. At present, he is the head of Doyle-tech Corporation, a Kanata, Ontario company that helps high-tech companies get organized and running.

Doyle stresses the critical importance of a business plan. In his view, nothing significant happens to a high-tech idea until people with the idea develop a business plan and then give that plan to venture capitalists for considera-

tion. Doyle says that the business plan for a high-tech venture should include a clear statement of why investors should put their money into the venture. The product should also be described and its benefits stated. Market share objectives, channels of distribution, costs of marketing, pricing, and product strategies should also be included. Detailed revenue projections using different assumptions (for example, optimistic and pessimistic) should also be presented.

SOURCE   Adapted from Alan Morantz, "Denzil Doyle: A Man for the High-Tech Season," *Executive* (August 1983): 22-24.

standing plans

Plans that remain roughly the same for long periods of time are referred to as **standing plans**. The most common kinds of standing plans are policies, procedures, and rules.

POLICIES

policy

A **policy** is a predetermined, general course or guide established to provide direction in making decisions. As such, policies should be based on a thorough analysis of organization objectives. Policies cover the important areas of a firm such as personnel, marketing, research and development, production, and finance. A company that collects debts may have a policy that says: "No collection agent shall accept from any client or debtor gifts that are substantial enough to cause undue influence on the decision-making behavior of the collection agent." This policy does not tell the agents exactly what gifts they can accept, but it does state that the agents must not let these gifts interfere with their collection responsibilities.

To formulate policies, managers must have knowledge of, and skill in, the area for which the policy is being created. However, there are certain generalizations that apply to the establishment of policies. The most important has already been stated: policies must be based on a thorough analysis of organization objectives. There are several other general principles that can help managers create appropriate policies.

- *Policies should be based on known principles and, as much as possible, on facts and truth.* It is a fact that each province has passed legislation for safety in the work place. It is not a fact that a satisfied employee is automatically a productive employee.
- *Subordinate policies should be supplementary, not contradictory, to superior policies.* A policy for a company division should not conflict with an overall corporate policy.
- *Policies of different divisions or departments should be coordinated.* They should be directed toward the entire organization rather than favoring a particular department, such as sales, engineering, purchasing, or production, to the detriment of the whole.
- *Policies should be definite, understandable, and in writing.* If a policy is to guide actions, persons concerned must be aware of its existence; this requires the creation of understandable directives in a definitive written form. These sets of guides record the memory of the organization, which it uses to help cope with future events.
- *Policies should be flexible and stable.* The requirements of policy stability and flexibility are not contradictory; one is a prerequisite to the other. Stable policy alters only in response to fundamental and basic changes in conditions. New government regulation can represent such a basic change in conditions that it can have a major impact on a firm's employment policies. The higher the organizational level, the more stable the policy must be. Changing the direction of the enterprise is a much more complex

and time-consuming task than changing the direction of a department or section. The higher the organizational level, the more policy resembles principle; conversely, the lower the level, the more it resembles a rule.

- *Policies should be reasonably comprehensive in scope.* Policies conserve an executive's time by making available a previously determined decision. Managers should organize their work in such a way that subordinate personnel can handle the routine and predictable work, while they devote time to the exceptional events and problems. If the body of policies is reasonably comprehensive, the cases that arise that are not covered by policy constitute exceptions.

PROCEDURES AND RULES

When a firm's broad policies have been established, more specific plans may need to be created to ensure compliance with them. Procedures and rules might be thought of as restrictions on the actions of lower-level personnel. They are usually established to ensure adherence to a particular policy. Although the terms *procedure* and *rule* are similar, they refer to discrete ideas.

Procedures

procedure

A **procedure** is a series of steps established for the accomplishment of some specific project or endeavor. Many organizations have extensive procedures manuals and instructions designed to provide guidelines for managers and workers lower in the organization. The stable body of policies and procedures, written and unwritten, that governs an organization is called **standard operating procedures (SOP)**. For most policies, there are accompanying procedures to indicate how that policy should be carried out.

standard operating procedures (SOP)

Procedures are developed to assist in the implementation of plans or to indicate steps to be taken for repeated activities. For example, most companies have a clear procedure for reimbursing salespeople for their monthly travelling expenses. Salespeople fill out a form indicating where they travelled during the last month; they also attach any appropriate receipts. If they do not follow this procedure, their travel expense cheque may be held up or not approved.

Rules

rule

A **rule** is a specific and detailed guide to action, set up to direct or restrict action in a fairly narrow manner. For example, a company with a printing shop may have a "no smoking" rule there because many flammable chemicals are used in printing.

Examples of policies, procedures, and rules are given in Table 3-3. While policies are easy to discern, it is clear from the examples that procedures and rules may overlap. In fact, taken out of a sequence of steps, a procedure may actually become a rule.

Policies, procedures, and rules are designed to direct action toward the accomplishment of objectives. If managers could be assured that all persons doing work were thoroughly in agreement with and completely understood basic objectives, then policies, procedures, and rules would not be needed. Apparently, objectives at times are unclear and even controversial. Thus, all organizations have a need for policies, procedures, and rules that are more definitive and understandable than the overall objectives on which they are based.

TABLE 3-3 | Examples of Policies, Procedures, and Rules

Policy:	It is the policy of the company that every employee is entitled to a safe and healthful place in which to work, and to prevent accidents from occurring in any phase of its operation. Toward this end the full cooperation of all employees will be required.
	Management will view neglect of safety policy or program as just cause for disciplinary action.
Procedure:	The purpose of this procedure is to prevent injury to personnel or damage to equipment by inadvertent starting, energizing, or pressurizing equipment that has been shut down for maintenance, overhaul, lubrication, or setup.
	1. Maintenance persons assigned to work on a job will lock out the machine at the proper disconnect with their own safety lock and keep the key in their possession.
	2. If the job is not finished before shift change, the maintenance person will remove the lock and put a seal on the disconnect. A danger tag will be hung on the control station stating why the equipment is shut down.
	3. The maintenance person who will be coming on the following shift will place his or her lock on the disconnect along with seal.
	4. Upon completion of the repairs, the area supervisor will be notified by maintenance that work is completed.
	5. The supervisor and the maintenance person will check the equipment to see that all guards and safety devices are securely in place and operable. Then the supervisor will break the seal and remove the danger tag from the machine.
Rules:	The following rules are intended to promote employee safety.
	1. The company and each employee are required to comply with provisions of the provincial health and safety regulations. You will be informed by your supervisor on specific OSHA rules not covered here that apply to your job or area.
	2. Report all accidents promptly that occur on the job or on company premises — this should be done whether or not any injury or damage resulted from the incident.
	3. Horseplay, practical jokes, wrestling, throwing things, running in the plant, and similar actions will not be tolerated as they can cause serious accidents.
	4. Observe all warning signs, such as "No Smoking," "Stop," etc. They are there for your protection.
	5. Keep your mind on the work being performed.

6. Familiarize yourself with the specific safety rules and precautions that relate to your work area.

7. Approved eye protection must be worn in all factory and research lab areas during scheduled working hours or at any other time work is being performed.

8. Hearing protection is required when the noise level in an area reaches limits established by provincial legislation.

9. Adequate hand protection should be worn while working with solvents or other materials that might be harmful to hands.

10. Wearing rings or other jewelry that could cause injury is not allowed for persons performing work in the factory area.

11. Good housekeeping is important to accident prevention. Keep your immediate work area, machinery, and equipment clean. Keep tools and materials neatly and securely stored so that they will not cause injury to you or others.

12. Aisles, fire equipment access, and other designated "clear" areas must not be blocked.

13. Learn the correct way to lift. Get help if the material to be lifted is too heavy to be lifted alone. Avoid an effort that is likely to injure you.

14. Only authorized employees are allowed to operate forklifts and company vehicles. Passengers are not allowed on lift equipment or other material-handling equipment except as required in the performance of a job.

15. Learn the right way to do your job. If you are not sure you thoroughly understand a job, ask for assistance. This will often contribute to your job performance as well as your job safety.

16. Observe safe and courteous driving habits in the parking lot.

CONTINGENCY PLANNING

contingency
planning

Robert Burns wrote: "The best laid schemes of mice and men / Go oft awry" — a sentiment still applicable in today's business world. Events can occur so rapidly that plans may be useless before they can be fully implemented. Even if a plan is properly developed, external and internal disturbances often occur that result in its modification or even elimination. Prudent managers recognize that unforeseen events can happen and that they must anticipate such disruptions and deal effectively with the new conditions. **Contingency planning** is the development of alternative plans to be placed in effect if certain unexpected events occur.

Referring again to Figure 3-1, note that contingency planning encompasses all phases of the planning process. Suppose, for instance, that a paint firm's competition alters its product in a way that affects the product plans of the firm. A contingency plan must have already been decided upon, or the firm could lose business. Changes in the firm's plans could affect not only long-range planning but also policies, procedures, rules, and even standards. Examples that reinforce the need for contingency planning are numerous. For instance, a new government policy may have a drastic effect on a long-range business plan; it can even change organization objectives. A new regulation calling for the total removal of lead from paint would affect the plans of both firms in the earlier example. Also, an unanticipated stoppage in the supply of a raw material, as with the oil embargoes of the 1970s and 1980s, makes contingency planning necessary.

Contingency planning does not mean that a firm has to wait for an unanticipated situation to occur before it responds. Management should attempt to anticipate these contingencies as far as possible. Naturally, not all situations can be anticipated, but managers who try to anticipate possible deviations stand a much better chance of coping with new situations.

A disaster recovery plan for a computer installation is a common example of a contingency plan. Organizations that use computers become very dependent on them. This is true for practically every modern company. But what happens when the system fails? Sabotage and vandalism are human-made disasters to which computer systems may be vulnerable. Fires, floods, rainstorms, tornadoes, and hurricanes are natural threats that often disable computer systems.

The plan for recovery typically involves provisions for backups (not only for the information contained in the computer but also for the functions the computer performs). Think what the cost might have been if G. D. Searle had lost the data from the years of testing NutraSweet. The data processing personnel for a large firm may make daily or weekly copies of master files and place them in a secure location. Contingency plans are made to obtain these files if and when they are needed. Some other aspects of a data processing contingency plan might be damage assessment, emergency processing, and methods to keep system users informed about restoration efforts. Reciprocal emergency processing agreements and mutual aid pacts between firms are often used in contingency plans. Contingency planning is increasingly important in the field of data processing, but it applies to most other aspects of the organization as well.

UNINTENDED SIDE EFFECTS OF PLANS

Every plan is likely to have certain undesired effects, and managers must anticipate the negative as well as the positive results. In many instances, a possible counterproductive effect of a plan can be headed off by appropriate action. For example, if a top manager suddenly asks for weekly output figures in kilograms, he or she may cause frantic juggling of orders to ensure high kilogram runs by week's end. This misguided objective, in turn, is likely to lead to missing some delivery promises for smaller orders. Rather than abolish the new output reports, thereby harming the control function, the top manager can ask for such reports on a semimonthly basis. The additional time should provide the flexibility for lower managers to meet both delivery dates and kilogram output standards. Looking at an important index too frequently can produce some undesirable side effects.

One unintended side effect of planning is that the individuals who have to carry out the plan may resist it. This opposition is particularly likely if employees feel that the plan has negative implications for their long-term employment prospects, or if the plan upsets normal working patterns. For example, if management develops a plan for installing a new computer complex, employees may resist it for fear of losing their job to the computer. Or, employees may resist attempts by management to change the objectives that the organization is pursuing. People who have worked in an organization for a long time become comfortable with the objectives they are used to pursuing, and any significant change in these can cause serious employee opposition. In situations where executives want to institute plans that are a major departure from past practice, it is important that they get as many employees as possible committed to the change. The issue of implementing change in an organization is discussed in detail in Chapter 14.

PLANNING THROUGH MANAGEMENT BY OBJECTIVES

management by objectives (MBO)

If we accept that planning is a major function of management, we must be concerned with how it can best be accomplished. Although each firm's requirements are unique, and each firm approaches planning somewhat differently, focusing on the objectives of the organization is a logical starting point. During the past two decades, few other developments in the theory and practice of management have received as much attention and application as MBO. **Management by objectives (MBO)** is a philosophy of management that emphasizes the setting of agreed-on objectives by superior and subordinate managers and the use of these objectives as the primary basis of motivation, evaluation, and control efforts. Above all else, MBO represents a way of thinking that concentrates on achieving results. It forces management to plan explicitly as opposed to simply responding or reacting on the basis of guesses or hunches. It provides a more systematic and rational approach to management and helps prevent "management by crisis," "firefighting," or "seat-of-the-pants" methods. MBO emphasizes measurable achievements and results and may lead to improvements in both organizational and individual effectiveness.[1] The approach depends heavily on active participation in objective setting at all levels of management.

Background of MBO

Peter Drucker first described management by objectives in 1954 in *The Practice of Management*.[2] According to Drucker, management's primary responsibility is to balance conflicting demands in all areas where performance and results directly affect the survival, profits, and growth of the business. Drucker stated that specific objectives should be established in the following areas:

- Market standing
- Innovation
- Productivity
- Worker performance and attitude
- Physical and financial resources
- Profitability
- Managerial performance and development
- Public responsibility.

Drucker argued that the first requirement of managing any enterprise is "management by objectives and self-control." As originally described, an MBO system was designed to satisfy three managerial needs.

First, *MBO should provide a basis for more effective planning.* Drucker had in mind what might be called the systems approach to planning — that of integrating objectives and plans for every level within the organization. The basic concept of planning should consist of *making it happen* as opposed to *just letting things happen.* According to Drucker, MBO is a planning system requiring each manager to be involved in the total planning process by participating in establishing the objectives for his or her own department and for higher levels in the organization.

Second, *MBO improves communications within the firm by requiring that managers and employees discuss and reach agreement on performance objectives.* In the process, there is frequent review and discussion of the goals and plans of action at all levels within the firm.

Finally, *Drucker thought that the implementation of an MBO system would encourage the acceptance of a behavioral or more participative approach to management.* By participating in the process of setting objectives, managers and employees develop a better understanding of the broader objectives of the organization and how their goals relate to those of the total organization.[3]

activity trap   One of the foremost advocates of MBO contends that special efforts must be undertaken to avoid the **activity trap**.[4] *This is the tendency described by George Odiorne, for some managers and employees to become so enmeshed in carrying out activities that they lose sight of the reasons for what they are doing.* As a result, such persons often justify their existence by the energy and sweat expended and avoid questioning whether they have accomplished any result necessary to organizational effectiveness.

THE MBO PROCESS

The MBO process is illustrated in Figure 3–2. Notice that MBO requires top management support and commitment and involves five steps. These aspects of MBO are discussed below.

Top Management's Philosophy, Support, and Commitment

Any MBO program is doomed from the start without the absolute and enthusiastic support of top management. It is because of the lack of top-level commitment that so many MBO programs fail. To be effective, MBO must be consistent with the philosophy of top management. Implementing an effective MBO program is difficult if the chief executive lacks trust in the subordinates or is not personally committed to a participative style of management. A chief executive cannot introduce MBO by simply giving an order or a directive. Lower-level managers must be convinced of the merits of the system and meaningful participation in the process. MBO relies on the participative approach to management; this requires the active involvement of managers at all levels in the organization.

Establish Long-Range Goals and Strategies

Every successful MBO program must have long-range goals and the strategies to accomplish these goals. Long-term plans are developed by thoughtful determination of the basic purpose or mission of the organization. We noted earlier that to develop long-range goals, the top management of a firm must answer such questions as these:

- What is the basic purpose of the organization?
- What business are we in and why?
- What business should we be in?

Long-range planning is essential if top management is to identify areas needing improvement.

Long-term goals and strategic planning can be illustrated by considering a company whose mission is to produce and market agricultural implements. Several long-term goals and strategies consistent with this mission may be developed. The company may have as a goal both to increase its rate of return on shareholder investment to 15 percent after taxes and to achieve a share of 25 percent of the total Canadian market for agricultural implements within seven years. This is a long-range goal because it extends beyond one year. The firm's strategic plan — the means to attain the stated goal — might include substantial quality improvements in the agricultural implements they pro-

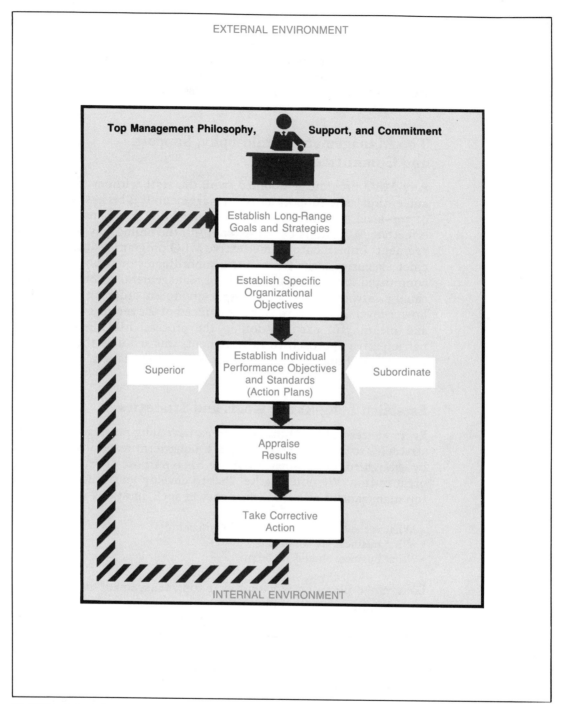

FIGURE 3-2   The MBO process

MANAGEMENT IN PRACTICE

Management by Objectives at Counsel Corporation

Counsel Corp. is a fast-growing financial management firm. It has three main lines of business — financial services, real estate, and health care. The company was founded in 1979, but already has $1.1 billion of assets under its administation.

The top managers give much of the credit for their success to management by objectives. All employees are required to take courses on how to set objectives, and managers take courses on

performance appraisal. By February of each year, each employee has signed an agreement detailing how much he or she will be paid and what bonuses they will receive if they meet their objectives. The overall goals for the company are published in the annual report.

SOURCE Adapted from Virginia Galt, "Counsel Corp. Finds Niche In Yuppie, Old-Age Market," *The Globe and Mail*, (January 9, 1987): B1-B2.

duce. These changes might create a greater demand for the firm's products. If the firm is able to control costs and generate greater sales volume, its long-term goals should be attained.

Establish Specific Shorter-Term Organization Objectives

After long-range goals and plans are established, top management must set specific short-term objectives to be attained within a given time period. These objectives must support the overall purpose and key result areas. Usually they are expressed as precise and quantifiable targets covering such areas as productivity, market, and profitability. Returning to the agricultural implements manufacturer, specific organization objectives might be:

- Increase sales of self-propelled combines to 8000 units — an increase of 10 percent over last year.
- Reduce production costs per combine produced by five percent over last year.
- Increase investment in new product design by 10 percent over last year.
- Increase profits by 10 percent over last year.

Each of these would be further subdivided into department objectives consistent with attaining these organization goals.

Establish Individual Performance Objectives

Establishing performance objectives and standards for individuals is known as action planning. The crucial phase of the MBO process requires that challenging but attainable objectives and standards be established through an interaction with superiors and subordinates.

action plans **Action plans** require clear delineation of what specifically is to be accomplished and when it is to be completed. For example, a salesperson and his sales manager might have agreed on the following standards for the salesperson's own performance: (1) increase sales of combines in the north Saskatchewan region by 10 percent by June 30, and (2) reduce travel expenses by five percent by June 30.

Appraise Results

The next step in the MBO process is to measure and evaluate actual performance as compared to the goals and standards established. Having specific standards of performance provides managers with a basis for such a comparison. When goals are specifically stated and agreed on by both the manager and the subordinate, self-evaluation and control become possible. We discuss performance appraisal in detail in a later chapter.

Take Corrective Action

Although an MBO system provides the framework for goal setting, managers in the organization must take action to correct areas where results are not being accomplished according to the plans. Such action may take the form of changes in personnel, structure, or even the goals themselves. Other forms of corrective action may include providing additional training and development of individual managers or employees to enable them to achieve the desired results. Corrective action should not automatically have negative connotations. Original objectives can be renegotiated without any penalty or fear of dismissal.

SETTING OBJECTIVES

The actual setting of objectives is the heart of the MBO approach (refer to Figure 3-2) and is one of the most difficult steps in the process. Managers must decide how much involvement subordinates should have in setting objectives, and whether objectives should be targeted for individuals or for groups.

Who Should Set Objectives?

MBO objectives may be set (1) by the superior, (2) by the subordinate, (3) jointly, or (4) jointly with the aid of a staff specialist. (See Chapter 7 for a discussion of the staff specialist concept.) When superiors are completely in charge of goal setting, problems often occur. Rather than involving subordinates in the process, they impose a specific, quantitative, and time-bounded goal on employees. This is not MBO. It should probably be referred to as RBO (rule by objectives). The following conversation between the president of a holding company and the president of one of its subsidiaries illustrates RBO. The subsidiary president had expressed doubt as to whether he could meet the budget goal. The holding company president's reply was: "Do I pay you a lot of money? Do I argue with you over what you want to spend? Do I bother you? Then don't tell me what the goals should be. . . . My board and my shareholders want me to make my numbers. The way I make my numbers is for you guys to make your numbers. So, make your numbers!"[5]

Most MBO programs require some type of joint determination of objectives between superiors and subordinates. The advantage of having an MBO specialist is that he or she assures that meetings will actually take place and that help and advice will be available. The joint process can comprise any number of variations. The closest to RBO would be an initial determination of goals by the superior; these would be given to the subordinate, whose reaction would be requested. At the other extreme, the subordinate could set his or her goals and give them to the superior for a reaction. A middle ground is to have both superior and subordinate come to the meeting with a set of tentative objectives; final objectives will be agreed on after some negotiation.

Objectives for Individuals

In order for MBO to achieve maximum results, objectives for each individual should be carefully developed. They should be limited in number, highly specific, challenging, and attainable. The number of objectives for each individual should range from four to eight. Having more than eight may lead the employee to spread himself or herself too thinly, thereby diminishing overall effectiveness. Each objective should be assigned a priority, perhaps ranging from one to three. In this way, should time and resources prove to be more limited than anticipated, the individual has a basis for deciding which objective to pursue.

Perhaps the most important characteristic of good objectives is that they should be stated in specific terms. In most instances, this means quantification and measurability. For example, goals have far less impact when stated in such terms as "improve the effectiveness of the unit," "keep costs to a minimum," or "be alert to market changes." At the performance review, the employee should be able to look back and definitely answer the question, "Did I do it or not?" For instance, a goal stating that production will be increased by 1000 units is much clearer than one that merely encourages increased production. Therefore, in writing objectives, a special attempt should be made to phrase them in terms of volume, costs, frequency, ratios, percentages, indexes, degrees, or phases. It is particularly important to place time limits on each objective. In 10 of 11 studies that examined the impact of such specific goals on performance, evidence was found supporting the contention that specifically stated goals increased the level of accomplishment.[6]

Developing challenging and attainable objectives requires a delicate balance of opposing forces. Yet both are essential in motivating the subordinate. Obviously, managers desire that objectives be set at such a level that employees must make special efforts. However, some researchers have pointed out that, if promotion and salary are related to success in attaining objectives, as they should be, the participatory approach may well be asking the subordinate to construct a "do-it-yourself hangman's kit."[7] Jean Bishop, a hospital supply sales representative, might indicate to her sales manager that she plans to sell $200 000 in surgical instruments and supplies during the next three months. Since no one in the company has ever accomplished this level of sales in a three-month period and since Jean sold only $200 000 during the entire last year, it is highly unlikely that she will attain her goal. Jean has just hung herself because her goal is unrealistic and unattainable.

In the initial phases of new MBO programs, one of the more common errors is the establishment of objectives that are unattainable. This is particularly the case if the time period for review is 6 to 12 months. Anything seems possible with that much time. The superior must not allow excessively high goals to be set because this may cause a decline in the future expectations and performance of the individual. Attention must be given to obstacles that affect accomplishment, for example the availability of resources necessary for performance. The impact of other personnel on the subordinate's performance must be recognized and discussed.

Research indicates that challenging objectives lead to greater accomplishment only if the subordinate truly accepts the goal as reasonable and only if goal accomplishment actually leads to organization rewards. Challenging goals with a history of past success will lead to continued success. A series of failures creates a mental set that makes attainment increasingly more difficult. Subordinates with self-assurance do well in relation to challenging goals. The subordinates' assessment of the probability of success should be that they have at least a 50-50 chance of achieving the objectives.

Group Objectives

The accomplishment of goals often requires that individuals cooperate as a team. There are many factors that can affect the attainment of group or team objectives. For instance, a sales manager may set a specific objective of selling 50 000 units by March 1, but it cannot be done if production does not manufacture that number of units. One highly recommended approach to overall goal setting involves team meetings to establish group goals. Team goal setting requires an open and supportive corporate culture. In general, MBO is more effective and achieves more positive results when applied in an organization with an open and supportive culture. Consider this instance: "a medium-size service company experimented with the team approach and decided to ignore individual objectives altogether, reasoning that too much interlinking support and cooperation are required to blame or reward any individual for the production of any single end result."[8]

If team goal-setting sessions are to be used as a prelude to the more typical individually oriented meeting, some training in group processes will most likely be necessary. It is difficult enough for a manager to establish an open and participatory climate with an employee. It is far more complex and challenging to try to do so in a group. Training programs directed toward this end go under the title of organizational development, a subject discussed in Chapter 15. The following is a suggested sequence in an MBO team approach: (1) team meetings of top executives to set overall organizational objectives; (2) team meetings at unit level; (3) individual person-to-person goal-setting sessions; (4) individual reviews of accomplishments; (5) team meetings at unit level to review progress and accomplishment; and (6) review at the top level to determine the degree of overall organization success.[9] The team goal-setting process improves the chances of success of the MBO program because it improves coordination and communication within the organization.

MANAGEMENT IN PRACTICE

Application of MBO at Investments Syndicate Limited

Investors Syndicate has used MBO since 1974 to motivate its sales force in selling a wide range of financial services. Investors is a private corporation and a wholly owned subsidiary of Power Corporation. It has over 1000 salespeople across Canada, making it the largest direct sales force of any company in the financial sector. Investors also owns Great West Life Assurance Company and Montreal Trust. Its major competitors are banks, trust companies, and insurance companies. Investors Syndicate has offices in every major metropolitan area of Canada. It also has offices in

smaller cities such as Kelowna, British Columbia; Red Deer, Alberta; Dauphin, Manitoba; St. Catharines, Ontario; and Ste-Hyacinthe, Quebec. Its salespeople are paid on a straight commission basis.

During the early 1970s, top management of Investors observed that MBO was a useful management technique being used by a variety of business organizations. Representatives from Investors attended MBO seminars; they reported that the concept might be successful for Investors in the sales function. (A partial organization chart of the sales function at Investors is shown in Figure 3-3.) After reading a great deal of literature on the subject of MBO, top management concluded that, if MBO were to succeed, five key concepts would have to be stressed:

Concept 1: *Company purpose* The basic reason the company is in existence (its mission) must be understood by all employees. The mission of Investors is to satisfy clients in need of general and comprehensive financial planning. Through product development and an efficient sales distribution system, Investors assists in implementing financial plans and providing effective on-going service.

Concept 2: *Activities* The tasks that employees must perform so that the company can fulfill its mission must be clearly stated. In the sales area, this means calling on commercial and household clients and informing them of the wide range of financial services that are available from Investors. It also includes salespeople studying to improve their product knowledge, communication skills, prospecting abilities, and administration of their franchise.

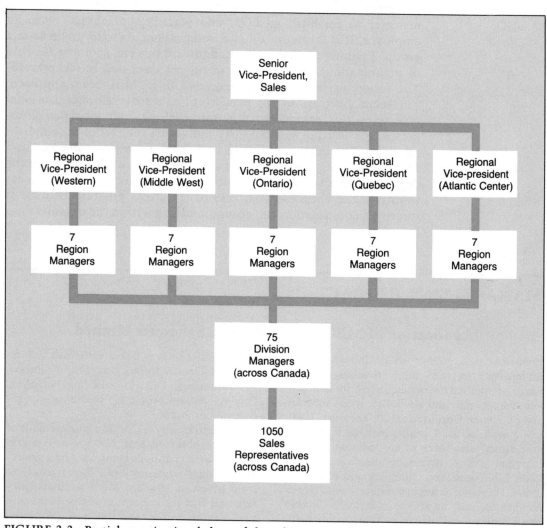

FIGURE 3-3 Partial organizational chart of the sales area at Investors

Concept 3: *Responsibilities* The "key result areas" in which each employee must perform well need to be outlined. The Concept 3 activities are grouped into related areas, usually of four to five key responsibilities.

Concept 4: *Measurement* Effectiveness standards and performance indicators must be developed.

Concept 5: *Objectives* The specific results (objectives) that each salesperson will attempt to achieve must be stated.

These five concepts are constantly referred to at Investors. When the vice-president of sales asks for a "Concept 5", the staff know what it is and the criteria that are valid for it.

Concepts 3, 4, and 5 are used to set objectives and to plan the activity the salesperson will engage in to achieve these goals. These three concepts form the basis for the "Objective Record Sheet." (An example is shown in Figure 3-4.) Concepts 3 to 5 form the action part of the MBO program. When a salesperson has set an objective (for example, two sales calls per

	OBJECTIVE RECORD SHEET/ RELEVE D'OBJECTIFS
Time-frame	*REGION-DIVISION*
FULL YEAR	CONCEPT 3. (Major Responsibilities/Responsibilités Majeurs) PERSONNEL (REGION MANAGER)
	CONCEPT 4. (Measurements/Mesures) PER DIVISION: No. of Interviews; No. of Tests; No. of Terminations; Net Increase; No. sent to Career Development Seminars; $ spent on personnel prospecting

		Priority/ Priorité
		1

CONCEPT 5. (Objectives/Objectifs)
To hire 24 reps — approximately 12 for each division — 8 of these hirings to be experienced — female market to be explored.

Dates	**PROGRAM OF ACTIVITIES/ PROGRAMME D'ACTIVITÉS**	**Objectives Objectifs**	**Results Resultats**
Jan. & Sept.	1) Hold Management meeting to set up Co-op Personnel recruiting budget.	2	2
Jan., Mar., Apr., Jun., Oct. & Dec.	2) Hold Career Information nights in conjunction with Division Managers.	6	5
	3) Handle all screening personally up to the In-Depth Interview.	—	—
	4) Make 6 contacts personally each month.	6	6
Jan., Apr., Jul., Oct.	5) Ask all representatives for names of possible recruits at least quarterly.	4 ea.	
	M Dionne _____ MANAGER/DIRECTEUR		
ACTUAL PERFORMANCE/RESULTATS OBTENUS:			

FIGURE 3-4
Objective
record sheet

day), that same person must establish an activity plan to achieve the objective. The lower half of the Objective Record Sheet requires the salesperson to indicate the activity plan in detail.

The MBO Process

The MBO process begins when the vice-president of sales develops general goals for the entire sales force. These general goals may be based on, for instance, last year's performance or on desired growth over last year's performance. This sets the stage for Planning Week which is held annually in 35 regional centers across Canada during the first week of December. The purpose of Planning Week is to give salespeople the opportunity to: (1) review their personal, career, and financial accomplishments of the past year, (2) relate individual results to the goals, objectives, and plans of the total company, and (3) think through and restate their personal, career, and financial goals for the coming year. During Planning Week, sales representatives meet with their division managers and set specific sales objectives for the next year.

The setting of objectives involves working through five distinct steps:

Step 1: *Determining Franchise Operating Costs* Since each sales representative in essence owns a franchise, the first step is to determine the costs of operating each franchise. Once expenses are projected, the salesperson can compute the level of income required to make the franchise profitable.

Step 2: *Determining Personal Requirements* Each salesperson then decides on personal financial needs; for instance, each asks: "How much money do I need to live on for the next year?"

Step 3: *Determining Total Financial Requirements* Steps 1 and 2 are combined to establish the salesperson's total financial requirement for the upcoming year. Thus, the franchise operating costs (Step 1), personal requirements (Step 2), and the profit requirements (Step 3) determine the salesperson's total financial requirement for the year.

Step 4: *Activity Plan* This requires the preparation of a plan of action to achieve the goals developed in Steps 1, 2, and 3. Detailed guidance is provided here, so that the salesperson can set realistic objectives. The activity plan tells the salesperson in very specific terms how many sales calls he or she must make in order to reach the sales objective. An example is shown in Figure 3-5. The example is a realistic one taken from actual company records. It says that, if the salesperson wants to make $30 000 per year, he or she will have to make 46 approaches per week (an approach is an attempt to contact a possible client).

Step 5: *Productivity* The final step involves the completion of the "Sales Information System — MBO Summary Sheet." (See Figure 3-6.) Detailed instructions for completing this important document are also given to salespeople. The information it contains becomes the basic data for planning throughout the company.

Financial Requirements	$	30,000	**Approaches Objective**		2,025
divided by: income per sale ratio ÷		200	divided by: number of weeks to be worked in the coming year ÷		44
Sales Objective		150	**Weekly Approaches Objective**		46
multiplied by: presentations per sale	×	3	Convert sales objective to a production objective:		
Presentations Objective		450			
multiplied by: contacts per presentation	×	3	Average production per sale		15,000
Contacts Objective		1,350			
multiplied by: approaches per contact	×	1.5	multiplied by: sales objective	×	150
			Production Objective		$2,250,000

FIGURE 3-5 Activity plan

SALES INFORMATION SYSTEM — MBO Summary Sheet
PLANNING WEEK MBO SUMMARY SHEETS

REPRESENTATIVE NAME	REP. NO.	REGION OFFICE	R.O. NO.	DIVISION OFFICE	DIV. NO.

ACTIVITY MONTHLY

MONTHLY	ACTUAL 1983 PRODUCTION 1983	APPS	PLANS	MBO 1984 PRODUCTION 1984	% INC. (Dec.)	APPS	PLANS
January							
February							
March							
April							
May							
June							
July							
August							
September							
October							
November							
December							
TOTAL							

PRODUCTION INCREASE _____ % Rep. _____
Div. _____

ACTIVITY BY PRODUCT

PRODUCT	ACTUAL 1983 YTD S.I.S.	EST. DEC.	TOTAL 1983	MBO 1984	DIFF. 83-84	% INC. (Dec.)
Income Deferral Certificates						
MAP — Guaranteed						
Equity Funds						
Debt Funds						
RRSP — GIC						
MAP — Equity						
Annuities						
Group Products						
GIC — Montreal Trust						
Insurance						
Dollar Averaging						
Money Builder						
RHOSP						
GIC — Investors						
Installment GIC						
Term Certain Annuity						
Investors Real Property Fund						
Canamerica Money Fund						
TOTAL						

Reg. Mgr. _____
R.V.P. _____

FIGURE 3-6 Sales information system — MBO summary sheet

PRODUCTION QUALIFICATIONS AND BENEFITS			
$15,000 per week average	Qualifies a new representative to attend the Career Development Center — Initial Seminar — to be presented with Qualified Financial Planner Certificate.	$1,000,000	Qualifies you for overwriting on all personal production.
		$1,500,000	Qualifies you for the No Limit Performance Bonus.
$20,000 per week average	Qualifies a new representative to attend the Career Development Center — Advanced Seminar — to be presented with Advanced Financial Planner Certificate.	$2,000,000	Qualifies for you the Millionaire plaque, for free personalized Millionaire stationery and calling cards plus an announcement in your local newspaper.
$500,000	Qualifies you for free personalized letterhead.	$8,000,000	Qualifies you to receive Investors' beautifully designed diamond ring in recognition of an outstanding sales achievement.

FIGURE 3-7   Production qualifications and benefits

division managers. They discuss the objectives with each of their salespeople and come to a consensus on what individual sales goals will be. Each division manager then forwards the proposed objectives for his or her division to the appropriate regional manager. This process continues all the way up to the vice-president of sales (refer to Figure 3-3) who gives final approval to the total company sales objectives for the coming year.

Negotiation is an important element of the MBO process at Investors. On occasion, a salesperson will set a goal that the manager considers to be either too low or too high. When this occurs, negotiation between the salesperson and the manager is needed until a goal is developed that is satisfactory to both. Investors has found that resolving problems through negotiation early in the planning process helps prevent major disagreements later.

Recognition is also an important part of the MBO system at Investors. Various awards are given for different levels of sales performance, and these awards are publicized. (See Figure 3-7.) Each salesperson works at his or her own level of ability; most salespeople earn awards and are recognized for their achievements. Each salesperson therefore feels that he or she is making a positive contribution to the company, as well as to his or her career.

Summary of MBO at Investors

Investors has found that the MBO system is well suited to its sales function. The goals of salespeople can be stated in quantitative terms and the salesperson can tell clearly whether or not he or she has achieved the goals originally established. Senior Vice-President of Sales, Sterling McLeod believes that the MBO system is valuable; he notes that Investors' salespeople often set much more challenging goals for themselves because of this system. The company has reached or exceeded its objectives each year since the MBO system was introduced. Between 1980 and 1983, Investors' sales nearly doubled, despite the fact that the Canadian economy was in a recession.

McLeod notes that about 75 percent of Investors' salespeople conscientiously fill out the MBO forms, and that MBO has made a noticeable difference in their sales performance. A few salespeople, however, view MBO as something of a game of paper shuffling and, for them, MBO may not be so helpful. In such cases, McLeod says, Investors' managers must sell MBO to the staff instead of trying to enforce it. In McLeod's view, many companies that have tried to enforce MBO discovered that their employees resisted the system instead of enthusiastically using it to improve their own financial well being.

McLeod also points out that by itself MBO would not have had such a dramatic impact; Investors simultaneously emphasized career planning using MBO. Together, the two uses of the planning system have had very positive effects.

Overall, MBO appears to have boosted the performance of salespeople at Investors Syndicate. Once the salespeople have set specific goals, they are motivated to perform the activities necessary to achieve them. The return they get, in terms of personal satisfaction and recognition by the company, completes this process.

SUMMARY EVALUATION OF MBO

Benefits of MBO Programs

Proponents of MBO have claimed the following benefits:

1. *Results in better overall management and the achievement of higher performance levels.* MBO systems encourage a results-oriented philosophy of management that requires managers to do specific planning, develop action plans and consider the resources needed.
2. *Provides an effective overall planning system.* MBO helps the manager avoid management by crisis and firefighting.
3. *Forces managers to establish priorities and measurable targets or standards of performance.* MBO programs sharpen the planning process. Rather than just saying "do your best" or "give it your best shot," specific goals tend to force specific planning. Such planning is typically quite realistic because the progam calls for a scheduled review at a designated future date. Subordinates make sure that they can obtain the resources necessary for goal accomplishment and that obstacles to performance are discussed and removed. MBO forces planning a logical sequence of activities before action begins.
4. *Clarifies the specific role, responsibilities, and authority of individuals.* Objectives must be set in key areas, and individuals responsible must be given adequate authority to accomplish them. A production plant superintendent who has a goal of producing 10 000 units a day must be given the authority to organize and direct resources to achieve the desired level of production.
5. *Encourages the participation of individual employees and managers in establishing objectives.* If the process of MBO has been undertaken on a joint and participatory basis, the chances are that commitment to company objectives will be increased.
6. *Facilitates the process of control.* Periodic reviews of performance results are scheduled, and information collected is classified by specific objectives. Subordinates report what was accomplished rather than concentrating on descriptions of what they did or how hard they worked. MBO also stimulates improvement in the performance of superiors, who are forced to clarify their own thinking and to communicate this to subordinates.
7. *Provides an opportunity for career development for managers and employees.* Personal development goals are often part of the set of objectives developed in joint sessions. MBO results identify the areas where employ-

ees need additional training. Establishment of priorities provides realistic guides for effort, as well as enabling the concrete demonstration of goal accomplishment. This, in turn, makes possible a more realistic and specific annual performance review, which is crucial in deciding on promotions, pay increases, and other organizational rewards.

8. *Other specific strengths of an MBO system might include:*
   a. Lets individuals know what is expected of them.
   b. Provides a more objective and tangible basis for performance appraisal and salary decisions.
   c. Improves communications within the organization.
   d. Helps identify promotable managers and employees.
   e. Facilitates the enterprise's ability to change.
   f. Increases motivation and commitment to employees.[10]

Potential Problems with MBO

Although there are numerous benefits attributed to MBO, certain problems may be encountered, such as the following:

- MBO programs often lack the support and commitment of top management.
- Goals are often difficult to establish.
- The implementation of an MBO system can create excessive paperwork if it is not closely monitored.
- There is a tendency to concentrate too much on the short run at the expense of long-range planning.
- Some managers believe that MBO programs may be excessively time-consuming.

In fact, there is strong evidence that MBO has not generally worked out well as a complete system. Toronto management consultant Gordon Allan has pointed out that management by objectives may cause rigidity in the organization if objectives are simply developed by top management and imposed on lower-level managers.[11] In order for an organization to cope with rapid change, develop new products or services, and keep in tune with its external environment, it must develop objectives that take into account the skills, needs, abilities, and aspirations of the people who must achieve them.

In spite of its flaws, MBO still provides a good model for planning. The central principles of MBO have been incorporated into all kinds of organizations and continue to have a major impact. These principles include specific, verifiable objectives; evaluation of performance on the basis of goal accomplishment; and integration of individual objectives with organizational objectives. When these concepts are established as part of a rigid MBO structure, they have not tended to work out too successfully, but individually, they are sound concepts.

TABLE 3-4   MBO Effectiveness as Applied in 185 Organizations

Research Approach	Positive	Mixed	Not Positive	Ratio Positive: Not Positive
Case Studies	123	8	10	12:1
Surveys	9	2	1	9:1
Quasi-experiments	20	3	4	5:1
True experiments	1	2	2	1:2
Totals/average	153	15	17	9:1

SOURCE   From Jack N. Kondrasuk, "Studies in MBO Effectiveness," *Academy of Management Review* 6, no. 3 (1981): 425. Used with permission.

MBO: Assessing its Overall Effectiveness

In a review of 185 studies, Jack N. Kondrasuk found that there are numerous arguments, pro and con, regarding the effectiveness of MBO.[12] Many organizations have adopted MBO on faith, often as a result of questionable case studies or unsubstantiated testimonies. One researcher concluded, "There is relatively little empirical evidence to demonstrate the impact of MBO on any aspect of organizational or individual behavior, including job performance."[13]

As illustrated in Table 3-4, MBO did achieve positive results in 153 out of 185 organizations — a ratio of 9 to 1, positive to not positive. Case studies and surveys show a much higher level of effectiveness for MBO than do experiments. "Positive results" do not necessarily mean that respondents thought MBO to be worth the effort. According to the researcher, "There are tendencies for MBO to be more effective in the short term [less than two years], in the private sector, and in organizations removed from direct contact with the customer. We may conclude that MBO can be effective, but questions remain about the circumstances under which it is effective."

OPENING INCIDENT REVISITED

Algonquin Food Products Ltd.

The way MBO has been implemented at Algonquin Food Products certainly leaves something to be desired, at least according to William Klassen. Several of the potential problems mentioned in this chapter have become problems at Algonquin. Klassen is particularly upset that he is never consulted about what goals are realistic and attainable for his department. As noted in the chapter, when unrealistic goals are imposed by a supervisor, subordinates are generally not enthusiastic about pursuing them.

Klassen is also concerned that the MBO system is merely a "paper mill." If employees feel that MBO only means filling out forms each year, they aren't likely to think it can be useful; in such a company, it probably won't be. Klassen also believes that no one will look at his results. This implies that top management is not genuinely committed to the MBO process at Algonquin. Klassen fears that, even if top management does look at his performance goals, the MBO system will be used against him rather than to help his department perform better in the future.

In general, Algonquin has violated most of the basic rules about MBO. Therefore, the system will likely not be beneficial to the firm. A close reading of this chapter should help you think of ways top management at Algonquin could have avoided the situation that has developed. The material on the MBO process is particularly important; an understanding of what MBO is supposed to do reduces the chance of faulty implementation.

SUMMARY

Effective planning can have a major impact on the productivity of managers at all levels in an organization. Planning is determining in advance what should be accomplished and how to do it.

The planning process begins with a mission statement. The mission is the organization's continuing purpose or reason for being. Specific objectives, or goals, can be established once the mission is understood. Objectives are the end results desired. Objectives should have four basic characteristics: (1) they should be expressed in writing, (2) they should be measurable, (3) they should be specific as to time, and (4) they should be challenging but attainable. At least three main types of objectives can be identified: economic, service, and personal. Some problems encountered in establishing objectives include: real versus stated objectives, multiple objectives, and quantitative versus nonquantitative objectives.

Objectives are concerned with the end results desired. Plans are statements of how objectives are to be accomplished. Standards specify what constitutes proper behavior. Performance results standards deal with the end result of work, while process standards deal with work as it is being done.

Plans that remain roughly the same for long periods of time are referred to as standing plans. The most common kinds of standing plans are policies, procedures, and rules. A policy is a predetermined general course or guide established to provide direction in decision making. A procedure is a series of steps established for the accomplishment of some specific project or endeavor. A rule is a very specific and detailed guide to action, which is set up to direct or restrict action in a fairly narrow manner.

Events can occur so rapidly that plans may be useless before they can be fully implemented. Contingency planning is developing different plans to be used if certain hindrances occur. Contingency planning makes it unnecessary for a firm to wait for a problem to occur before it prepares to respond.

Management by objectives (MBO) is a systematic approach to planning that focuses on achieving goals. The steps in the MBO process are: (1) gain management's support and commitment, (2) establish long-range goals and strategies, (3) establish specific organizational objectives, (4) establish individual performance objectives and standards (action plans), (5) appraise results, and (6) take corrective action.

In order for MBO to achieve maximum results, objectives for each individual should be carefully developed. They should be limited in number, highly specific, challenging, and attainable. The accomplishment of most goals requires that individuals cooperate as a team.

REVIEW QUESTIONS

1. What are the steps involved in the planning process?
2. What is the purpose of a mission statement?
3. Describe the characteristics of good objectives. What are the three main types of objectives?
4. Describe the two major types of standards. Give examples of each type.
5. What are the specific questions that planning should answer?
6. Distinguish, by definition and example, among policies, procedures, and rules.
7. What is meant by the term "contingency planning?"
8. What are some possible unintended side effects of plans?
9. What is management by objectives (MBO)? Describe the basic steps in the MBO process.
10. Briefly discuss the benefits and problems with MBO.

EXERCISES

1. What do you believe would be the missions of the following firms?
   a. Ford Motor Company
   b. Air Canada
   c. Peat, Marwick, Mitchell & Co.
   d. Toronto Blue Jays
   e. The Girl Guides
   f. Revenue Canada

2. Assume that your objective is to obtain a 4.0 grade point average next term. Develop a plan stating policies, procedures, and rules that could help you achieve this goal.

3. Apply the management by objectives concepts discussed in this chapter to the development of clear-cut personal goals for yourself for next year. Be sure to include specific action plans to ensure goal accomplishment.

4. Visit a firm in your area that uses MBO and ask several managers within the company about their reaction to the program. This is an excellent class project that could be part of a tour of a local business.

CASE STUDY

The Apple Farmer

Bill Lester was up early. When the sun began to peek over the horizon, he was already at his orchard thinking about how to accomplish the day's work. Within an hour, he would have 30 workers in the field picking his bumper crop of apples. Bill needed to be there early to think about how the pickers were to be kept supplied with baskets and the trucks efficiently scheduled to deliver the apples to the broker's warehouse with a minimum of handling.

There were many other matters to attend to. The pickers were paid according to the amount they picked, so careful records had to be kept. The apples had to be picked at just the right ripeness or Bill would be docked a certain percentage when they were inspected at the warehouse. Even simple details like not having drinking water available for the pickers could significantly slow down the harvest.

Bill thought about how complicated apple farming was. He and his father had planted the trees 12 years earlier. They had spent what then seemed to be a lot of extra money to get the finest strain of hybrid trees that were available. These trees produced 50 percent more than ordinary trees and had a longer bearing life. It was necessary to prune and spray the trees every year, to irrigate them during dry periods, and to cultivate and fertilize the area covered by the roots. It was also useful to treat the ground to eliminate bore worms and to supply "blossom fast" liquid to the trees to decrease the likelihood that they would shed their blooms before the fruit buds were properly formed.

Bill was the third generation of Lesters to run the business, and this orchard was the best ever. It would not be the best for long though. The previous fall he had planted 300 acres with a new type of tree that was expected to do even better. Bill had become moderately wealthy growing apples, but he knew his success had not happened by accident. He hoped to pass on to his son, then aged 12, not only the finest orchard in the Okanagan, but also a legacy of scientific farming and disciplined hard work.

Even as the first pickers were arriving that morning, Bill was looking forward to the fall. He thought of how he would prune and trim his trees so that they could withstand a cold winter, in case one occurred, and produce an even larger crop the following year.

QUESTIONS

1. How is the planning process Bill should follow similar to that followed by a manager of a modern office or factory?

2. What kinds of contingency plans would you recommend that Bill make? Why?

3. In what areas of Bill's agribusiness should plans be made, and over what time frames should those plans extend?

CASE STUDY

MBO at York Investments Ltd.

York Investments Ltd. provides a wide range of financial services to consumers and business firms. The company introduced a management by objectives (MBO) program two years ago. Top management of the firm was convinced that MBO would significantly improve the company's overall effectiveness in planning and would provide a system for more accurate evaluation of personnel. Prior to the implementation of MBO, the company had no formal planning system and had used a performance appraisal system that primarily evaluated such factors as quantity of work, quality of work, judgment, and adaptability. The performance factors were rated from 1 (very poor, unacceptable performance) to 5 (exceptional performance). All personnel including managerial employees were evaluated using this system. The considerable dissatisfaction with this rating system was the primary reason why York Investments decided to implement MBO. At the beginning of each year, overall company objectives as well as department goals are formulated and communicated to managers throughout the firm. The following is a description of the company's MBO program as it is applied in the Accounting Services Department.

Jean Stelmach, the accounting services manager, has four supervisors reporting to her. These supervisors are responsible for accounts payable, accounts receivable, payroll, and customer services. At the beginning of each year, Stelmach discusses the company and department objectives with each of her four supervisors.

The payroll supervisor is George Patrick, a CMA who has been with York for 9 months. He had four years of experience in payroll operations at another company. He is considered to be a competent supervisor, with eight clerks reporting to him. The department processes the payroll for almost 1000 employees. Patrick and Stelmach had agreed on the following goals for the payroll department during Patrick's first year as supervisor:

1. Establishment of a consistent account reconciliation program for the 160 payroll-related accounts in the general ledger by June 1.
2. Establishment of a cross-training program for the payroll clerks by June 1.
3. Creation of written documentation for all payroll department procedures by September 1 (in accordance with the company's broader statements on policy and procedure).
4. Reduction of employee turnover to 15 percent during the year.

During the year, the company experienced rapid growth, adding an average of 10 employees per month. Turnover of clerical personnel in the payroll department began in February. Within the first four months, payroll lost three experienced employees. These personnel changes required considerable on-the-job training of new employees. Near the end of the year, Stelmach reviewed the progress of the payroll section with Patrick. The results were as follows:

Objective 1 Not accomplished. A consistent reconciliation program has not been implemented.

Objective 2 Not accomplished. A cross-training program has not been devised. Several duties have been reassigned as new employees were hired, and some jobs have been slightly redesigned.

Objective 3 Not accomplished. Written documentation has increased, but no substantial progress was made during the year toward developing an overall detailed payroll procedures manual.

Objective 4 Not accomplished.

Stelmach expressed disappointment with the overall performance of payroll. She asked Patrick why payroll had experienced these problems. Patrick agreed the results were not attained as planned but believes employee turnover greatly affected payroll. "Of the three people I hired," he said, "only one was as effective as those who quit."

QUESTIONS

1. If you were Jean Stelmach, how would you rate the performance of George Patrick, the payroll supervisor?
2. Evaluate the MBO program as it is used by the company. Does it meet the criteria for a successful program as discussed in the chapter?
3. Should Patrick be retained? Why or why not?

CASE STUDY

Objectives and Plans at West-Can

West-Can Stores Ltd. operates a chain of convenience stores in western Canada. (See Figure 3-8 for a partial organizational chart of the company.) Duties for store managers are specific; top management of the company believes that profitability is possible only if a tight rein is kept on operations at the retail level.

Top management strives for uniformity of operation in all areas, including ordering, stocking, customer check-out procedures, and managers' attitudes. Because of the routine nature of work and because of a concerted effort by top management to foster conformity in store managers' duties, there tends to be little discretion on the part of managers regarding day-to-day store operations.

This general lack of freedom to make decisions extends to the supervisory level. Virtually all supervisors are promoted from the ranks of "successful managers" within West-Can. As a result, those individuals who conform best to the established orientation are promoted. Typically, a supervisor is responsible for three to five stores. Normal duties include picking up the previous day's receipts, verifying daily accounting records, monitoring the physical condition of the stores, and making employment recommendations. Most matters not recognized as standard operating procedures are resolved at a higher managerial level.

The authority of district managers is also limited, though to a lesser extent than that of supervisors. Typically, district managers are responsible for approximately 15 stores, with three supervisors reporting directly to them. Although their district is considered a profit center, their ability to control profits is restricted to routine matters. From a practical standpoint, the success or failure of a district manager depends on the degree of conformity he or she is able to obtain from managers within his or her area of responsibility.

Any decisions that are not covered by standard operating procedures must be made by the division manager. The division manager is also responsible for establishing objectives and formulating plans. All division managers are promoted from the ranks after successfully accomplishing the duties of a store manager, supervisor, and district manager.

Bob Harrison was recently promoted to division manager, moving up through West-Can's ranks in only 10 years. The area manager called Harrison in last Wednesday and questioned him about his objectives and plans for the coming year. When Harrison said he did not have them and was not really sure what was expected, the area manager became rather puzzled.

"Bob," the area manager said, "you are expected to do much more creative thinking now than in the past. You can let your subordinates take care of daily routines. Your job is much more encompassing. The very survival of West-Can depends on how well your objectives and plans are formulated."

Harrison returned to his office in a state of controlled panic. He really had no idea how to go about setting objectives because higher managers had always told him clearly what to do. He thought back to his positions as store manager, supervisor, and district manager. In each of those jobs he had felt quite secure because operating procedures had been spelled out for him. Now he felt as if his area manager had set him adrift with no guidelines. What was he going to do?

QUESTIONS

1. Why does the area manager believe the "very survival" of West-Can depends on how well district managers' objectives and plans are formulated?

2. Harrison's situation is not uncommon. How could a firm ensure that people such as Bob are equipped to handle the planning function?

3. Assess the managerial style at West-Can.

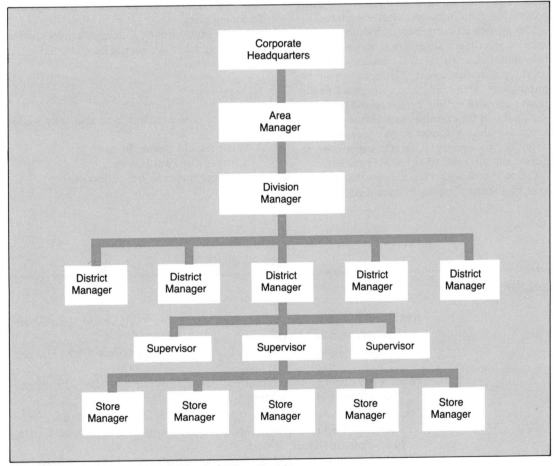

FIGURE 3-8   Organizational chart of West-Can Stores

CASE STUDY

Undue Influence?

Heather Odom is the head of the purchasing department of a large federal government agency. Her department is responsible for purchasing items ranging from paper clips to computer software; annual purchases of the department exceed $10 million. Odom has two people reporting to her who contact and buy from visiting salespeople. One Monday morning, Odom is called into her boss's office. Her supervisor informs her that Paul Hayles, one of Odom's purchasing agents, has been accepting substantial gifts from potential suppliers.

The agency has a policy forbidding acceptance of gifts from suppliers if these gifts are substantial enough to cause undue influence on the purchasing agent. The agency believes purchasing agents might be influenced to buy from suppliers willing to sweeten a deal with such gifts. In the extreme, such influence could cause purchasing agents to buy inferior products for the agency. Odom's supervisor requests a quick resolution to this problem.

Odom meets with Hayles later that day and asks him about the gifts. Hayles readily admits he accepted gifts from three different suppliers and that he purchased some items from them. However, Hayles denies that he had purchased the items because he had been given a gift by the salesperson. Odom reminds Hayles of the agency's policy forbidding acceptance of suppliers' gifts which might influence purchasing behavior. Hayles says he is aware of the policy and reassures Odom that his purchasing decisions are not influenced by the gifts. Odom is under the impression that Hayles will continue to accept gifts.

After Hayles leaves, Odom sits in her office wondering what she should do and what she'll tell her supervisor.

QUESTIONS

1. What is the problem here and why has it arisen?
2. What should Odom do now:
    a. regarding Paul Hayles?
    b. in her report to her supervisor?

ENDNOTES

[1] Anthony P. Raia, *Managing by Objectives* (Glenview, Ill.: Scott, Foresman, 1974): 10–12.

[2] Peter F. Drucker, *The Practice of Management* (New York: Harper, 1954).

[3] Peter F. Drucker, *Management Tasks, Responsibilities, Practices* (New York: Harper, 1974).

[4] See George S. Odiorne, *Management by Objectives* (Belmont, Cal.: Pitman, 1965), and *Management Decisions* (Englewood Cliffs, N.J.: Prentice-Hall, 1969).

[5] Wendell L. French and Robert W. Hollman, "Management by Objectives: The Team Approach," *California Management Review* 17, no. 3 (Spring 1975): 19.

[6] Raia, 14–18.

[7]Gary P. Latham and Gary A. Yukl, "A Review of Research on the Application of Goal Setting in Organizations," *Academy of Management Journal* 18, no. 4 (December 1975): 829.

[8]W. J. Reddin, *Effective Management by Objectives* (New York: McGraw-Hill, 1971): 16.

[9]Richard E. Byrd and John Gowan, "MBO: A Behavioral Science Approach," *Personnel* 51, no. 2 (March-April 1974): 48.

[10]Harold Koontz, "Making MBO Effective," *California Management Review* 20 (Fall 1977): 5.

[11]Gordon G. Allan, "Management Flexibility," *The Canadian Personnel and Industrial Relations Journal* 18 (May 1971): 13–21.

[12]Jack N. Kondrasuk, "Studies in MBO Effectiveness," *Academy of Management Review* 6, no. 3 (1981): 419–430.

[13]Kondrasuk, 419–430.

REFERENCES

Allen, David. "Establishing a Financial Objective — A Practical Approach." *Long Range Planning* 12 (December 1979): 11–16.

Allen, L. A. "Managerial Planning: Back to the Basics." *Management Review* 70 (April 1981): 15–20.

Anderson, Carl R., and Paine, Frank T. "Managerial Perceptions and Strategic Behavior." *Academy of Management Journal* 18 (December 1975): 811–823.

Babock, R., and Sorensen, P. F. Jr. "MBO Checklist: Are Conditions Right for Implementation?" *Management Review* 68 (June 1979): 59–62.

Bologna, J. "Why MBO Programs Don't Meet Their Goals." *Management Review* 69 (December 1980): 32.

Bowman, Edward H. "Risk/Return Paradox for Strategic Management." *Sloan Management Review* 21 (Spring 1980): 17–31.

Camillus, John C., and Grant, John H. "Operational Planning: The Integration of Programming and Budgeting." *Academy of Management Review* 5 (July 1980): 369–379.

Denny, W. A. "Ten Rules for Managing by Objectives." *Business Horizons* 22 (October 1979): 66–68.

Dowst, S. "Classify Your Objectives." *Purchasing* (April 25, 1979): 38.

Ford, C. H. "MBO: An Idea Whose Time Has Gone?" *Business Horizons* 22 (December 1979): 48–55.

Ford R. C. "MBO: Seven Strategies for Success." *SAM Advanced Management Journal* 42 (Winter 1977): 4–13.

Ford, R. C., et al. "Ten Questions about MBO." *California Management Review* 23 (Winter 1980): 48–55.

"Forecasting and Planning." *Oilweek* (January 30, 1984): 14.

Fox, H. W. "Frontiers of Strategic Planning: Intuition or Formal Models." *Management Review* 70 (April 1981): 44–50.

Galt, Virginia. "Counsel Corp. Finds Niche in Yuppie, Old Age Market." *The Globe and Mail* (January 9, 1987): B1–B2.

Goldstein, S. G. Mike. "Involving Managers in System-Improvement Planning." *Long Range Planning* 14 (February 1981): 93–99.

Gup, Benton E. "Begin Strategic Planning by Asking Three Questions." *Managerial Planning* 28 (November 1979): 28–31.

Hailden, B. T. "Date and Effective Corporate Planning." *Long Range Planning* 13 (October 1980): 106–111.

Haines, W. R. "Corporate Planning and Management by Objectives." *Long Range Planning* 10 (August 1977): 13–20.

Herbert, Theodore T. "Strategy and Multinational Organization Structure: An Interorganizational Relationships Perspective." *Academy of Management Review* 9, no. 2 (April 1984): 259–270.

Jackson, J. H. "Using Management by Objectives: Case Studies of Four Attempts." *Personnel Administrator* 26 (February 1981): 78–81.

Kahalas, Harvey. "Planning Types and Approaches: A Necessary Function." *Managerial Planning* 28 (May-June 1980): 22–27.

Koontz, H. "Making MBO Effective." *California Management Review* 20 (Fall 1977): 13–15.

Kudla, R. J. "Elements of Effective Corporate Planning." *Long Range Planning* 9 (August 1976): 82–93.

Lebell, D., and Krasner, O. J. "Selecting Environmental Forecasting Techniques from Business Planning Requirements." *Academy of Management Journal* 20 (July 1977): 373–383.

Levinson, Harry. *Ready, Aim, Fire: Avoiding Management by Impulse.* Cambridge, Mass.: The Levinson Institute, 1986.

Lindsay, W. M., and Rue, L. W. "Impact of the Organization Environment on the Long Range Planning Process: A Contingency View." *Academy of Management Journal* 23 (September 1980): 385–404.

Lopata, R. "Key Indicators: Simpler Way to Manage." *Iron Age* (January 26, 1981): 41–44.

Lorange, Peter. *Implementation of Strategic Planning.* Englewood Cliffs, N.J.: Prentice-Hall, 1982.

McCaskey, Michael B. "A Contingency Approach to Planning: Planning with Goals and Planning without Goals." *Academy of Management Journal* 17 (June 1974): 281–291.

Martin, John. "Business Planning: The Gap between Theory and Practice." *Long Range Planning* 12 (December 1979): 2–10.

Michael, Steven R. "Feedforward versus Feedback Controls in Planning." *Managerial Planning* 29 (November-December 1980): 34–38.

————. "Tailor Made Planning: Making Planning Fit the Firm." *Long Range Planning* 13 (December 1980): 74–79.

Migliore, R. Henry. *MBO: Blue Collar to Top Executive*. Washington, D.C.: Bureau of National Affairs, 1977.

Muczyk, J. P. "Dynamics and Hazards of MBO Application." *Personnel Administrator* 24 (May 1979): 51–61.

Naylon, T. H. "Organizing for Strategic Planning." *Managerial Planning* 28 (July 1979): 3–9.

Pack, R. J., and Vicars, W. M. "MBO — Today and Tomorrow." *Personnel* 56 (May 1979): 68–77.

Pearson, G. J. "Setting Corporate Objectives as a Basis for Action." *Long Range Planning* 12 (August 1979): 13–19.

Pekar, Peter P. "Planning: A Guide to Implementation." *Managerial Planning* 29 (July-August 1980): 3–6.

Ratcliffe, Thomas A., and Logsdon, D. J. "Business Planning Process — A Behavioral Perspective." *Managerial Planning* 28 (March 1980): 32–38.

Robinson, Richard B. Jr., and Pearce, John A. II. "Research Thrusts in Small Firm Strategic Planning." *Academy of Management Review* 9, no. 1 (January 1984): 128–137.

Schneier, C. E., and Beatty, R. W. "Combining BARS and MBO: Using an Appraisal System to Diagnose Performance Problems." *Personnel Administrator* 24 (September 1979): 51–60.

Simmons, William W. "Future of Planning." *Managerial Planning* 29 (January-February 1981): 2–3.

Snyder, N., and Glueck, W. F. "How Managers Plan the Analysis of Manager's Activities." *Long Range Planning* 18 (February 1980): 70–76.

Stephenson, E. "Assessing Operational Policies." *Omega* 6 (1976): 437–446.

Stoffman, David. "Waking Up To Great Meetings." *Canadian Business* 59 (November 1986): 75–79.

Taylor, Bernard. "Strategies for Planning." *Long Range Planning* (August 1975): 437–446.

Thomapoulis, Nick T. *Applied Forecasting Methods*. Englewood Cliffs, N.J.: Prentice-Hall, 1980.

Thune, Stanley S., and House, Robert J. "Where Long-Range Planning Pays Off." *Business Horizons* 13 (August 1970): 81–87.

Tosi, H., et al. "How Real Are Changes Induced by Management by Objectives?" *Administrative Science Quarterly* (June 1976): 276–306.

Townsend, Robert. *Up the Organization*. Greenwich, Conn.: Fawcett, 1971.

Vancil, Richard F., and Lorange, Peter. "Strategic Planning in Diversified Companies." *Harvard Business Review* 53 (January-February 1975): 81-90.

Vesper, Volker D. "Strategic Mapping — A Tool for Corporate Planners." *Long Range Planning* 12 (December 1979): 75–92.

Weitzul, J. B. "Pros and Cons of an MBO Program." *Best's Review* 81 (January 1981): 72–73.

Wente, M. A. "Remaking the Management Mind." *Canadian Business* 56 no. 1 (January 1983): 23.

Wiehrich, H. "TAMBOL Team Approach to MBO." *University of Michigan Business Review* 31 (May 1979): 12–17.

Word, E. Peter. "Focussing Innovative Effort through a Convergent Dialogue." *Long Range Planning* 13 (December 1980): 32–41.

4

Strategic Planning

KEY TERMS

strategic planning
forecasting
demand forecasting
trend line
cyclical variation
seasonal demand
random demand
moving average
exponential
    smoothing
regression analysis
time series analysis
corporate-level
    strategic planning

strategic business
    unit
SBU-level strategic
    planning
functional-level
    strategic planning
stars
cash cows
question marks
dogs
product life cycle
grand strategy
concentration
market development

product
    development
integration
forward integration
backward
    integration
horizontal
    integration
diversification
conglomerate
    diversification
concentric
    diversification
retrenchment

LEARNING OBJECTIVES

After completing this chapter you should be able to
1. Distinguish between strategy formulation and strategy implementation.
2. Describe the strategic planning process.
3. Explain the impact of the environment on strategic planning.
4. Describe the various levels of strategic planning.
5. Describe the techniques used in strategic management.
6. Identify several grand strategies that emerge from the strategic planning process.

OPENING INCIDENT

Allyn and Bacon, Publishers

Allyn and Bacon is a publisher of educational textbooks. In 1983, they decided to expand their Canadian publishing activities. Until that time, the Canadian books that Allyn and Bacon had published were the result of almost random opportunities identified by sales representatives in their discussions with university professors and community college teachers. The company's efforts to find new projects increased with its decision to expand its Canadian publishing. A new editor, Dennis Bockus, was hired from a rival company; he along with the salespeople, uncovered publishing possibilities in business, chemistry, education, engineering, English, environmental studies, French, history, political science, psychology, social work, and sociology. Clearly, there were more opportunities than could be evaluated in a year. A strategy was needed to determine which projects would get top priority.

In order to develop this strategy, a two-day meeting was arranged at a rural inn with Bockus, Gerry FitzGerald (the general manager), and Jerry Smith (the marketing manager) in attendance. At this isolated place, the managers were free from the normal interruptions that would occur at their regular office. Their goal for the two-day meeting was to determine what objectives they should set for the company's publishing program during the next two to three years. FitzGerald was left to decide how a strategy could be developed that would satisfy the needs of the three managers and win their support.

In Chapter 3, we discussed the planning process. That process remains essentially the same at each level in the organization. In addition to the regular planning process that goes on at all levels of organizations, managers must give some thought to where the organization as a whole is going. **Strategic planning** is the determination of overall organizational purposes and objectives and of how they are to be achieved.

strategic
planning

Strategic planning usually covers a time frame extending five years or more into the future. Of course, this time frame can vary depending on the purpose of the organization and its technology. For example, it may be unrealistic for the Toronto Argonauts to plan 10 years into the future, because too many factors can change — a star player may retire early due to an injury, or a rookie may develop much faster than expected. A strategic plan for two or three years would be more realistic. On the other hand, strategic planning for Canadian General Electric may cover more than 10 years, and for B.C. Forest Products plans may be set for the next 30 years or more.

The strategic planning period depends to a large extent on how far the organization can look into the future with a reasonable expectation of being accurate. What should be the strategic plan of Pepsi-Cola Canada Ltd., if it aims to be number one in the soft drink industry? Should the company diversify by developing other soft drinks, add new product lines other than soft drinks, open new production plants, and/or expand into other markets? How long should such changes take to be implemented?

Logically, firms that establish an overall strategic plan ought to be more effective than those that do not develop such a plan. In recent years, strategic planning has received increased emphasis in Canadian business firms. Firms that recruit executives for other companies report that increasingly, their clients want managers with some background in strategic planning and forecasting. As further evidence of the importance of strategic planning, consider the fact that many companies have established planning departments responsible for developing three-, five-, and ten-year plans for their organizations. Most of the top Canadian firms have a position called "vice-president of planning" or some variation on that title. Even firms that do not have a vice-presidential planning position usually have permanent committees that are actively involved in strategic planning.

The specific tasks to be accomplished in strategic planning are determined by corporate objectives and the types of business in which the firm is engaged. Table 4-1 gives some examples of types of businesses which would benefit from strategic planning.

There are some major differences in the way organizations do strategic planning. Generally speaking, the larger the organization, the more formalized and visible the strategic planning process is. In smaller organizations, it is done informally, or perhaps not at all. Strategic planning may be done by an individual (usually the chief executive officer) or by a strategic planning group. Many companies use in-house strategic staff specialists who assist and advise managers in strategic planning. Others retain consultants to assist in designing and implementing strategy. Consultants are particularly useful for providing marketing and other research, which can be used as an informational base for strategy decisions. Since many firms cannot afford full-time strategic staff specialists, consultants are a useful way to get the data needed to make strategic decisions.[1]

Although many organizations have strategic specialists, every manager should think in strategic terms, because every manager is responsible for achieving corporate objectives. However, since many managers have a specific interest (e.g., finance, production, marketing,

TABLE 4-1   Long-Range Planning Projects

Primary Product / Service of Firm	Type of Planning Projects
Automotive tires	Assets effects of energy crisis New product diversification Help ailing product lines
Computers	Research new business markets Acquisitions Venture analysis
Aircraft	New product development
Natural gas	Acquisitions Raw materials supply research Diversification
Catalog order and retail department store	Expansion of facility Corporate financing Marketing directions
Railway transportation	Major construction projects Capital expenditure Market growth
Steel	Overall industry or business capital Spending policies and trends Timing of major investments
Pharmaceuticals	Plant location planning New product development Overall business strategy
Cosmetics and toiletries	Expansion New business Resource allocation
Petroleum	Finding new energy sources New / expanded petrochemical plants Technology and personnel needs

personnel, etc.) they tend to think mainly in terms of that area. Organizational strategists are needed so that the overall focus of the organization is given some attention. Organizational strategists are those persons who spend a large portion of their time on matters of vital significance to the organization as a whole. In general, organizational strategists are found at the top two levels of management. In-house staff specialist groups and some consultants are also organizational strategists.

In this chapter, discussion of the important issue of strategic planning is organized as follows: First, a model of the strategic planning process is presented and discussed. Second, we describe strategic planning at different levels in the organization, and third, some techniques that facilitate strategic planning are presented. These techniques help managers decide what the organization should be doing and what it should not be doing. The chapter concludes with a discussion of several overall corporate strategies that grow out of the process of strategic planning.

THE STRATEGIC PLANNING PROCESS

As shown in Figure 4-1, the strategic planning process is made up of two basic activities — strategy formulation and strategy implementation. Strategy formulation requires managers to make a decision about which basic strategy the organization will pursue. Strategy implementation involves actually putting the strategy into practice, i.e., executing the strategic plan. The elements involved in both strategy formulation and strategy implementation are described in subsequent sections. However, the emphasis will be on strategy formulation, since the strategic planning process is similar to the basic planning process discussed in Chapter 3. (In strategic planning, more emphasis is given to the mission of the organization as a whole, and to the external environment in which organizational activity takes place.)

Figure 4-1 portrays strategic planning as a sequential process. However, no diagram can capture all of the real-world complexities involved in strategic planning.[2] In many organizations, the steps may not occur in the sequence shown. In others, certain steps may be repeated several times. In still others, personal preferences may override systematic analysis when strategic decisions are made. Since all organizations are made up of people, and since people are not completely rational, the strategic planning process will always involve subjective perceptions, biases, and judgments. Keep these things in mind as the strategic planning process is analyzed.

FORMULATING STRATEGY

Determining the Mission

The first step in the strategic planning process is the determination of the organization's mission. As noted in Chapter 3, the mission is the organization's continuing purpose, or its reason for being. A mission

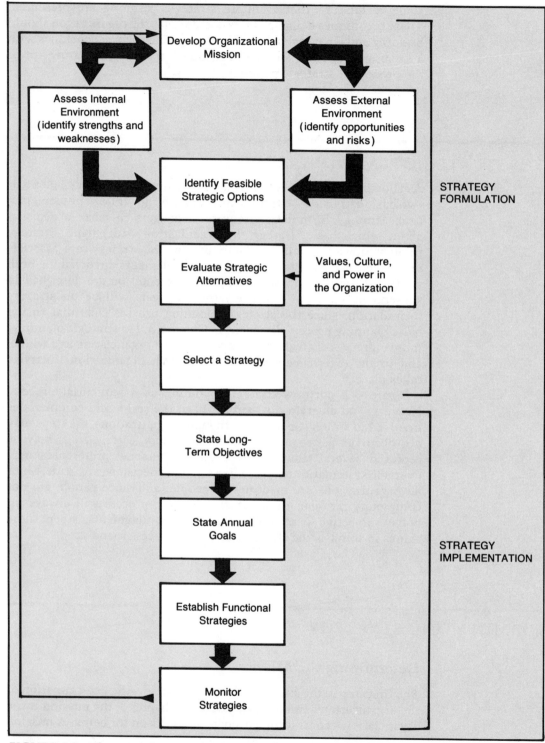

FIGURE 4-1   The strategic management process

statement answers the question, "What are we attempting to do, and for whom?" A good mission statement specifies the products or services that will be provided, the primary market that will be served, and the technology that will be used to produce and deliver goods and services.[3]

The mission statement can be very long or very short. A high-fashion dress shop might state as its mission "We will serve the fashion-conscious woman by selling high-quality dresses and stressing personal attention to the customer." This mission statement identifies the product that is being sold (high-fashion dresses), the primary market (women with substantial disposable income), and the technology to be used (personal attention to customers through salespeople, rather than mass checkout counters).

Sears Canada Inc. is "committed to satisfying customers by providing products and services of superior value through both personal shopping and catalogue ordering from coast to coast."[4] This mission statement identifies the product that is being sold (products and services of superior value), the primary market (all Canadians), and the technology (once again, retailing, but with an emphasis on both personal attention and catalogue sales).

The mission of Canadian General Electric is the manufacture, sale, and service of high-technology systems and equipment for industrial and commercial customers around the world.[5] The market (international), products (high-technology systems), and technology (manufacturing, sales, and service) are indicated in their statement of mission.

It may take managers considerable time to develop a good mission statement, and there may be disagreements among managers about what the organization's mission should be. Nevertheless, the top managers in an organization should spend time developing the firm's mission statement, because that statement motivates organizational members to achieve goals, acts as a criterion for allocating scarce resources, establishes a distinctive corporate culture, and ensures that the work of organizational members will be consistent.

Many organizations include their views on related issues in their mission statement. Statements about the importance of the free enterprise system, corporate profitability, growth, survival, public image, social responsibility, and corporate philosophy all complement the basic mission statement and convey to both the workers and the public what the organization thinks is important.

Assessing the Internal Environment

Once the mission has been determined, the organization must be assessed to determine its strengths and weaknesses. The outcome of this process is the identification of the corporation's distinctive competence — the area where it is particularly strong.[6] For example, one firm might have a highly efficient mass production system, while another might be unusually competent in custom production. Still another might not have any competence in the actual production of goods, but may be expert at providing intangible services that complement the physical product.

The identification of strengths immediately implies the existence of weaknesses. If a firm is primarily involved in manufacturing certain products and only marginally involved in engineering them, it would not be well advised to get involved with products that require considerable engineering expertise. As a practical matter, a firm may be reluctant to state its weaknesses, so particular attention must be paid to ensuring a realistic assessment of them.

Assessing the External Environment

In earlier chapters, it was noted that the organization's external environment consisted of various groups — customers, suppliers, unions, government, etc., that affect the organization from without. These same environmental groups can also bring social, political, technological and economic forces to bear on the strategic planning process.

The social environment of planning involves ethical and moral considerations and the responsibilities strategic managers have to people because of their humanity, rather than because of any legal, economic, or political forces that may exist. Some people argue that strategic planners should be completely rational. However, every manager experiences the emotions of friendship, love, pity, admira-

MANAGEMENT IN PRACTICE

Strategy in the Far North

Iqualit (formerly called Frobisher Bay) is the administrative center for the eastern half of the Northwest Territories. Until 1986, Nordair offered the only jet service between Baffin Island and southern Canada. But then a company called First Air started turboprop service on that run and undercut Nordair's fare. Now First Air uses a jet on the route.

First Air has traffic rights between Montreal and Iqualit, Ottawa and Toronto, and Montreal and Ottawa, but it doesn't plan to use the latter two because of the heavy competition on those runs. Its strategy is to emphasize the less

heavily travelled routes where competition is not so keen. At present, First Air is a major cargo carrier in the Arctic. Most of its work comes from mining companies or from the federal government.

One problem for the airline is that of finding and keeping Inuit staff. First Air tries to have at least one Inuktituk speaker on each flight to or from the North.

SOURCE Adapted from Matthew Fisher, "It Isn't The Sun Run, But It's A Living," *The Globe and Mail* (January 7, 1987): B1-B2.

tion, and so forth. These emotions influence the behavior of organizational strategists, and therefore of organizations.

The political facet of the environment is made up of laws and regulations, as well as of courts and governmental officials who interpret and enforce the laws. It also involves other groups and institutions in society that wield power. The increasing burden of laws and regulations is of concern to every manager. Many government agencies, some with overlapping areas of responsibility, restrict organizational activity; if laws are inconsistently applied, they create uncertainty for strategists. In addition to government, many other groups and institutions in society hold power: consumer advocacy groups, environmental groups, religious organizations and minority rights groups, to name a few. Organizational strategists both influence and are influenced by these groups.

The technological environment is the sum total of machines, materials, and knowledge that go into the production of goods and services. Technological innovations account for many of the success stories in business and are a significant concern for corporate strategists. Henry Ford built a great company on the assembly line method of manufacturing, while Jobs and Wozniak used microchip technology to create the Apple Computer.

Economic forces are considered by many to be the most important aspect of the organization's external environment. When Nobel Laureate Milton Friedman said "The only social responsibility of business is to earn a profit within the rules of the game," he was stressing

---

MANAGEMENT IN PRACTICE

Corporate Strategy at the Bank of Montreal

The Bank of Montreal is in the midst of deciding whether to "make or buy" the structures which it will need to help it get into new areas of financial services. Chairperson William Mulholland notes that although the bank has not decided on specific methods of expansion at this point in time, it is committed to the general principle of broadening the range of financial services offered to consumers. This will probably involve expansion into areas that have so far been restricted to investment dealers and insurance and trust companies.

Mr. Mulholland noted that changes in banking regulations will allow the bank to get into the provision of non-traditional financial services, but that simple access to new markets does not guarantee success. As well, he said the Bank of Montreal will not rush into new areas on a broad scale. Grant Reuber, president of the Bank of Montreal, said the bank is sharpening its focus and establishing its priorities before it makes major moves. He noted that the bank at present is not intending to buy a securities business.

SOURCE Adapted from Virginia Galt, "Bank of Montreal To Decide How to Add Services," *The Globe and Mail* (January 20, 1987): B1-B2.

the economic importance of business firms.[7] In *The Wealth of Nations*, Adam Smith suggested that if entrepreneurs pursued their own economic interests, society would benefit.[8] Whether or not a person agrees with these observations, it is clear that the economic environment has a major impact on the strategic planning process.

The level of economic activity facilitates or inhibits the performance of a particular company. When times are good, all kinds of businesses prosper, but many firms go out of business at the first sign of economic downturn. Since strategic planning concerns the long run, forecasting the state of the economy is a major consideration for planners.

Forecasting

forecasting

Attempting to predict what will occur in a firm's future is called **forecasting**. It involves identifying opportunities and threats in the firm's external environment. A firm will be more successful if its strengths match those conditions that are being forecast in its external environment.

demand
forecasting

trend line

Several terms commonly used in forecasting are illustrated in Figure 4-2. An attempt to estimate the demand for a firm's product is called **demand forecasting**. The four basic components in demand forecasting are long-term trend (the trend line), cyclical variation, seasonal demand, and random demand. The **trend line** estimates the

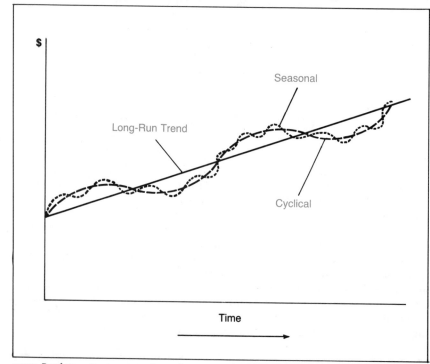

FIGURE 4-2
Forecasting

NOTE: Random patterns are not shown because we do not know when they will occur.

cyclical variation

seasonal demand

random demand

moving averages

exponential
smoothing

regression analysis

time series analysis

long-run demand (5 years or more) for the product. **Cyclical variation** (periods of 1 to 3 years) occurs around the trend line. A business recession may cause sales to be unusually depressed, while a recovery period may cause sales to be unusually buoyant. **Seasonal demand** (periods of less than one year) causes the demand for some products to fluctuate dramatically. The demand for electric razors, for example, is heavily concentrated in the holiday seasons. **Random demand**, by definition, follows no pattern; it therefore cannot be predicted.

Many forecasting techniques are available to business planners. **Moving averages** are used to smooth out the effects of random demand on a company's product. **Exponential smoothing** is used to predict the demand for different products with different growth rates. **Regression analysis** is used to predict sales of one item — the dependent variable — based on knowledge of one or more other items — the independent variable(s). **Time series analysis** is a variation of regression analysis; it is an analysis of past demand or sales to find a trend over time.[9]

MANAGEMENT IN PRACTICE

Corporate Strategy in the Christmas Tree Business

Keith Horton is a professional forester who operates Horton's Magic Hill Tree Farm. The farm sells about 10 000 Christmas trees each year at a retail price of about $18 each. Although the actual sale of trees is obviously concentrated in the month of December, much long-range planning and management activity are necessary on a year-round basis.

Horton says that there is a seven-year period from planting to harvest. Genetic research and pruning also take time, and pesticides and herbicides must be applied regularly to protect the crop.

The Christmas tree industry is a cyclical one and forecasting can be difficult. The kind of tree consumers prefer can change over time. For instance, in the late 1950s too many Scotch

pines were planted and this led to excess supply; by the late 1960s, many tree farmers were forced out of business because they couldn't get the prices they needed. That created a shortage of trees during the 1970s, but by the mid-1980s, three times as many trees were being planted as were harvested.

Although the Christmas tree business is flourishing, some companies are diversifying into related products like garlands and Christmas wreaths where growth potential promises to be even greater. Most of these products are exported to the northeastern United States.

SOURCE Adapted from Kimberley Noble, "How A Seasonal Trade Branches Out," *The Globe and Mail* (December 24, 1986): B1, B2.

Selecting a Strategy

After the organization's managers have developed a mission statement and have assessed both the internal and external environments, they must make a decision about which specific strategy to adopt for the organization. This requires a systematic decision process (see

MANAGEMENT IN PRACTICE

A Change in Strategy at Canadian National

Ronald Lawless is the new chief executive officer at Canadian National Railways. In his view, CN is one of the least forward-looking companies in the industry, has too heavy a debt burden, and too many employees for the output that is produced. He also sees threats to the company from "leaner" competitors. He says that CN must be prepared to offer lower rates and better service than its competitors or risk losing business.

CN plans to keep its rail division, which generates 85 percent of the corporation's revenues. Other divisions will be sold off. The corporation's chain of hotels, for example, may be bought by Canadian Pacific. Other divisions are being examined to see if they fit into CN's long-term corporate strategy. CN is currently the least productive railway in North America; it also has the oldest locomotive fleet. Lawless wants CN to become the lowest-cost transportation system in Canada. To do this may mean getting rid of almost all of the other activities CN is now engaged in. This includes hotels, exploration, real estate, and communications. Profit will be the key criterion in deciding which activities to keep and which ones to get rid of.

SOURCE Adapted from Cecil Foster, "CN Gets Set For New Competitive Challenge," *The Globe and Mail* (May 4, 1987): B1, B5.

Chapter 5) which involves (1) identifying feasible strategic options, (2) evaluating the options that are identified, and (3) picking the option which promises the most benefit for the organization. During this process, the values held by various individuals in the organization can have a substantial influence on the outcome. So also can the culture of the organization (see Chapter 15) and the power of the various managers making strategic decisions (see Chapter 9).

The strategy that is eventually selected must be consistent with the organization's overall mission, its strengths, and the external environment. Once again, keep in mind that strategy selection is not simply a matter of rational choice. Emotional considerations play a big role in some organizations. If a powerful top executive wants the company to get involved in manufacturing and selling a certain product, the company will probably do so, even if a strictly rational analysis shows that the firm should not do so.

IMPLEMENTING STRATEGY

Setting Objectives

Once a basic strategy has been agreed upon, the organization must implement the strategy it has selected. The first part of implementation involves setting objectives for both the long- and short-run. In the area of long-run objectives, an organization may set an objective of a 10 percent return on investment. Long-run or strategic objectives should possess all the characteristics of objectives that were noted in Chapter 3: They should be time-framed, measurable, specific, and challenging. However, they will deal with broader issues that are of concern to the organization as a whole.

Often, managers do not attempt to maximize overall corporate results. Rather, they "satisfice." This means that they accept the first satisfactory outcome they discover.[10] If top management of a company believes that 10 percent is a reasonable return on invested funds, it may approve any objective that exceeds that amount.

Corporate strategists are often more concerned with setting general directions than with setting specific objectives. As long as sales and profits show an upward trend (adjusted for inflation), top management may be happy. Many organizations do not have specific objectives, yet they continue to survive. However, these organizations could almost certainly improve their performance by setting challenging, specific, time-framed objectives.

In addition to long-run objectives, managers must be concerned with setting year-to-year goals. These goals will still deal with overall organizational issues, but will focus organizational activity over a one-year time span.

Establishing Functional Strategies

Once short- and long-term goals have been set for the organization as a whole, each part of the organization must develop its own detailed strategy. For example, if the basic strategy that has been selected involves development of a new line of products, each of the functional areas in the firm (marketing, production, and finance) must do certain things to ensure the success of the strategy. Marketing, for example, must do market research, sales forecasting, and sales training. Production will probably have to purchase new equipment and train personnel to make the new products. The finance department must determine sources of funds that are available to finance the new products. Getting these diverse areas to work together can be very difficult.

Monitoring Strategy

Once a strategy is implemented, it must be monitored to determine if it is having the desired effect. In some cases, it is obvious whether the strategy is a success or failure, but in most cases results will not be so clear cut. For example, if profits from a new product are not as high as expected, company management will be faced with a tough choice: whether to continue putting resources into that product or to pull out and minimize possible losses. To make the monitoring stage more

TALKING TO MANAGERS

Robert F. Black
Eddie Black's Limited

His great-grandfather made and sold boots in Beaverton, Ontario. His grandfather owned a store at Spadina and Lonsdale in the old village of Forest Hill, when those streets weren't much more than wagon trails. His father started Eddie Black's radio and appliance store in 1930. "We are," acknowledges Robert F. Black, president of Eddie Black's Limited, the Ontario chain of specialty photography stores, "a merchant family."

The descendants of these storekeepers now have 100 crisply designed outlets in Ontario and a space-age photofinishing laboratory in a $5-million headquarters on the outskirts of Toronto. Careful market analysis and astute investment have kept up a pace of growth that did not pause for the recent recession. Sales grew to almost $59 million last year from $28.4 million in 1978. Profits have almost kept pace too — earnings last year were about $5.6 million, up from just under $2 million in 1978.

Bob Black's been a part of the company since working during the Christmas school break in 1945 at his father's store. He just never went back to school. This put an end to his plans to become a veterinarian, but gave him his first spin as an entrepreneur.

Q: You are adding about a dozen stores a year. Why are they all in Ontario?
Black: Look at the marketplace. Outside of Ontario, going east, we'd have to go to Montreal. We weren't anxious to go into the Quebec environment of the last few years. Going west, the marketplace is Winnipeg, which is not as big as North York [a part of metropolitan Toronto], and then Calgary and Edmonton. It's not too enticing to go 1500 km to find 500 000 people.

Q: Yet, you must be close to saturation in Ontario.
Black: That's becoming true. Ontario growth is not as buoyant as it was five years ago. Every community now has a shopping center and we're in most of them.

Q: What's the strategy? go to the United States?
Black: It's a possibility. We could locate an office 500 km south of Toronto and pick up 20 million people in a 250 km radius.

Q: Who is your main competition?
Black: The department stores are fairly strong competitors in cameras and allied products. The specialty stores compete more for the carriage trade with sophisticated products for the serious amateur or some professionals. We don't chase that business. We gave up the semiprofessional business years ago because we felt that the well-informed customer would not be particularly loyal. We thought it might be more sensible to go to where the people are and offer convenient facilities for the middle-of-the-road picture taker who likes good quality but is not deeply involved. That's why we wanted to try shopping centers in the 1950s when they were new.

Q: How do you win out in competition in that middle area?
Black: We try to be innovative. When the photography business began to grow after

World War II, most of the people in it were either studio operators or people who liked taking pictures. There weren't many people in the business with merchandising know-how. On the other hand, we were raised in merchandising by a high-profile entrepreneur. My father was not a good executive in managing finances, inventory and warehousing, but he was a great entrepreneur. We saw the weakness of running a company without proper systems. When we finally took over, we had to dismiss a lot of my father's employees because the systems had been poor and the temptations too great.

Q: What gives you an edge?
Black: Our mix of merchandise and how we blend the finishing work and equipment sales.

Q: Is the money in selling film and processing rather than cameras?
Black: It is and it isn't. Certainly, the margin in popular cameras, from 5 percent to 30 percent, would make a shoe merchant sick. But the equipment is not only technical, it is also fashionable. So we're vulnerable there. When we have a 5 percent markup and an item stops selling, it's difficult to clear out. We have to stay on top of everything with sophisticated inventory control. From the perspective of margins, cameras provide our lowest profits. The average person shoots about 6 or 7 rolls of film a year. At $10 a roll, that's $60 to $70 a year spent by the average camera user who will have spent anything from $15 to $500 for the camera.

Q: The technology has changed and middle-priced cameras can be quite sophisticated. What has that meant to the average shooter?
Black: We were lucky when we decided to go out into the shopping centers. Then, cameras had become much simpler, and more people could take more pictures more easily.

Q: For a while there was a surge in popularity of instant photography. Did that scare you?
Black: It did. At Christmas 1976, 40 percent of all cameras sold processed the film in the camera. That rattled us because there is virtually no profit in selling instant cameras or instant film. Shortly after Christmas we had a session to decide what to do. We'd already

started offering a larger print for Kodak's Instamatic Camera. To make us noticeable against instant pictures, we decided to print 4" × 6" (10 cm × 15 cm) pictures on all film sizes. That wasn't exactly new; other finishers had offered it as an option. However, we sold nothing but those prints. We spent $500 000 to convert equipment and had to train staff. In the spring of 1977, we produced the larger prints across the board. To convey bigness, we created our elephant symbol and had a commercial made right in a shopping center with an elephant delivering a roll of film to our counter. We had albums created to fit the pictures. We promoted it very strongly. It was highly successful. That was a gamble that really paid off. Instant pictures never did come back to the acceptance of 1976. They eventually settled into a niche as a party novelty, a fun thing.

Q: Is there a new threat now from electronic photography?
Black: It's coming. It's been set back for a while by innovations in film. Electronic photography isn't just over the horizon; it's down the road somewhere.

Q: What are you doing about the exploding market for videotape records?
Black: We're not in the VTR business yet. But we want that business when it comes. When a VTR becomes one-piece and truly portable, we'll be in there.

Q: How do you personally exercise control over what's going on?
Black: We have a concept of central distribution. Everything funnels out from one central source: finishing supplies, toilet paper, paper clips, whatever. Things work better when managers can walk around and be part of everything. I can walk into the lab or a store and, from 35 years' experience, know from what's happening whether it's right or wrong. We also look at the computer printouts, read reports, check inventory — do all that. But managers still need that personal contact to know that they're satisfied with what's happening.

SOURCE Adapted from Dean Walker, "Black's *Is* Photography: And Don't They Know it," *Executive* (January 1984): 36-39. Reprinted by permission.

effective, it is imperative that management set clear objectives during the strategy implementation phase. If the strategy is not yielding the results that were planned for, alterations can then be made.

THE LEVELS OF STRATEGIC PLANNING

Many different kinds of organizations use strategic planning. If an organization is very large, strategic planning is not limited to the very top level of management. Rather, it is carried out at several different levels within the organization. Figure 4-3 illustrates how the three strategic planning levels correspond to organizational levels in a typical large company.

Corporate-Level Strategic Planning

corporate level strategic planning

Corporate-level strategic planning is the process of defining the overall character and purpose of the organization, the businesses it will enter or leave, and how resources will be distributed among those businesses. Corporate-level planners seek to answer such questions as:

- What are the purposes of the organization?
- What image should the organization project?
- What are the ideals and philosophies the organization desires its members to subscribe to?
- What is the organization's business or businesses?
- How can the organization's resources best be used to fulfill corporate objectives?

Corporate-level strategic planning is primarily the responsibility of the organization's top executives. The major focus here is on formulating strategies to accomplish the organization's mission.

SBU-Level Strategic Planning

strategic business unit

Large organizations are usually divided into strategic business units (SBU's). **A strategic business unit** is any part of a business organization that is treated separately for strategic planning purposes. In general, an SBU engages in a limited number of businesses. For example, at Bristol Aerospace activities are grouped into three SBU's: (1) aircraft maintenance, (2) manufacturing of engine components, and (3) manufacturing of rockets and accessories.

Many companies set up SBU's as separate profit centers, sometimes giving them a great deal of autonomy. Other companies maintain tight control over their SBU's, and enforce corporate policies and standards on all levels in the organization.

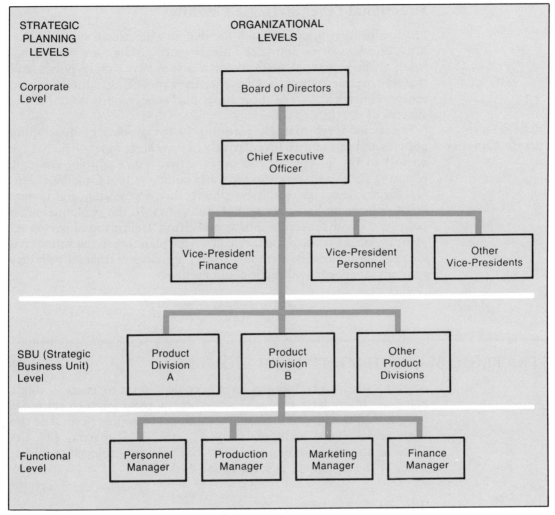

FIGURE 4-3   The levels of strategic planning

SBU-level strate-
gic planning

SBU-level strategic planning is the process of determining how an SBU will compete in a particular line of business. At the SBU level, strategic questions include the following:

- What specific products or services does the SBU produce?
- Who are the SBU's customers?
- How can the SBU best compete in its particular product or service market?
- How can the SBU best conform to the total organization's ideas and philosophies and support organizational purposes?

Generally speaking, SBU-level strategic planning is the responsibility of vice-presidents or division heads. In single SBU organizations, senior executives have both corporate-level and SBU-level strategic planning responsibilities.

Functional-Level Strategic Planning

Practically every organization is divided into functional subdivisions. Most business firms define the functions of production, marketing, finance, and personnel. Military installations have supply, police, and maintenance departments. Churches have preaching, education, and music ministries. Each of these functional subdivisions is vital to the success of the organization.

functional level
strategic planning

Functional-level strategic planning is the process of developing policies and procedures for relatively narrow areas of activity that are critical to the success of the organization. For example, strategic planning for the finance function at a company like Canadian General Electric involves establishing budgeting, accounting, and investment policies and allocating SBU cash flows. In the personnel area, policies for compensation, hiring and firing, training, and personnel planning are of strategic concern. Strategic planning in the functional areas is not concerned with day-to-day activities; rather, it provides general, longer-range direction and guidance.

STRATEGIC MANAGEMENT TECHNIQUES

A wide variety of techniques have been developed to assist strategic planners. Many large companies use several techniques to get more insight into the important issue of strategic planning. Several of the most widely used techniques are (1) the BCG matrix, (2) the General Electric planning grid, (3) the product life cycle concept, and (4) the McKinsey Seven S framework.

The BCG Matrix

Large organizations are typically involved in producing many diverse products. For strategic planning to be done properly, there must be some systematic way of making decisions about the array of products that the firm is selling. Many large firms use a two-dimensional diagram to concisely display various attributes of their businesses (SBU's). One of the best-known ways of doing this was developed by the Boston Consulting Group (BCG).

The BCG matrix is illustrated in Figure 4-4. Each SBU can be assessed in terms of its market share and the growth rate of the market it is involved in. Each circle on the BCG matrix represents a different SBU. The BCG matrix greatly simplifies the strategic planning process, and gives a strong visual impression of the company's mix of businesses.

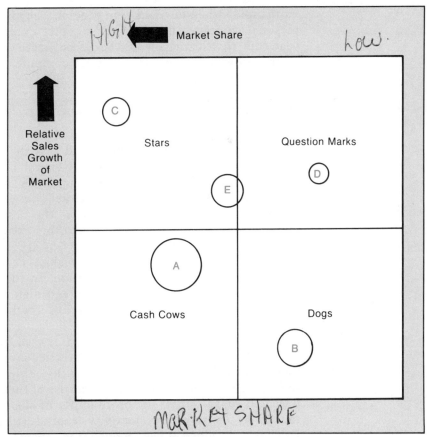

FIGURE 4-4   The BCG Matrix

Placing SBU's on the BCG Matrix

The matrix shows three things about each SBU. First, the area of each circle is proportional to the sales revenue of the respective business. SBU-A is the largest contributor to the firm's total sales, while SBU-E is the smallest. The others are intermediate.

Second, the relative position of a circle along the horizontal axis is determined by the SBU's market share as compared with that of its largest competitor. For example, in the personal computer business, Apple is very large, having sold over 500 000 units. However, IBM sells more than twice as many PC's as Apple. So if IBM was developing this kind of chart, it would place its personal computer business at the extreme left of the BCG matrix, while Apple would place its business further to the right.

Third, the vertical axis of the BCG matrix measures the overall market growth rate, not the growth rate in sales of the individual business. A business that is gaining market share will be growing more rapidly than the market in general. The rate of growth of IBM's personal computer business has recently exceeded 30 percent per year. Still, this business would be placed on the vertical axis according to the growth rate of the personal computer business in general (about 20 percent a year).

Stars, Question Marks, Cash Cows, and Dogs

An implicit assumption of the BCG analysis is that market share in a given business signifies strength, and that the market growth rate signifies opportunity. This is why General Electric, for example, demands that each division of the company be, or become, dominant in its field. Businesses with high market shares in high growth-rate industries are called **stars.** They offer the best profit and growth opportunities for the company. At the other extreme, SBU's with low market shares in low-growth industries are called "dogs." Their market shares suggest competitive weakness and the slow industry growth-rate suggests market saturation. In the middle ground are SBU's with either a low growth-rate and high market share ("cash cows") or a high growth-rate and low market share ("question marks").

The major focus of the BCG analysis is cash flow. SBU's that hold high market shares in low-growth industries should not be expanding their investment because other, better investments are available. But these SBU's typically earn profits because of their high market share. Research suggests that the profitability of such companies depends mostly on employee productivity, capital utilization, and pricing policies, not added investment.[11] Since there is no need for added investment in the business, the profits can be used to finance the corporation's other businesses (particularly stars). This is why businesses with a high market share in a slow growth market are called **cash cows.**

Usually, when a company enters a new business it starts with a low market share. Because the market is new (even if it is growing rapidly), any new entry faces an uncertain future. So low market-share businesses in high growth industries are called **question marks** on the BCG matrix. They typically require large amounts of cash to develop into stars. Sometimes, however, a question mark business grows so rapidly and becomes so profitable that it can generate the cash flows required for its own growth.

Businesses in low growth, low market-share situations are called **dogs** because they usually do not contribute to the business. The low growth in the industry, coupled with low market share, means that opportunities for cash flows are very limited. Dogs which are well managed by strategies such as vigorous cost control may make a reasonable contribution to the overall firm, but poorly managed dogs should be candidates for divestiture.

stars

cash cows

question marks

dogs

Implications of BCG Analysis

The corporate-level strategist who uses the BCG approach must ask, "What are the strategic implications for the corporation as a whole?" and "What does BCG analysis say about resource allocation and about the disposition of the various SBU's? BCG proponents argue that the corporation's overall cash-flow must be balanced. There should be enough cash cows in the business portfolio to fund the cash needs of the stars and question marks. Positions on the matrix imply certain strategies. Sales or liquidation is recommended for dogs and perhaps weak cash cows. Growth is the right path for question marks and stars. Efforts should be made to get back the investment from cash cows.

Resource allocation is an important but often overlooked used of the BCG matrix.[12] BCG analysis should not be limited to buy-sell decisions; it can also be used to distribute resources within the corporation.

The BCG matrix has some limitations. Fundamentally, strategic analysis requires a company to examine more than just market share and growth rates. Other factors, such as the company's distinctive competence and executive preferences, cannot be ignored. It may also be difficult to exactly define a market and its growth rate. As well, the BCG matrix deals with either high or low growth-rates and market shares, and does not stress the average case.

General Electric's Nine-Cell Planning Grid

An approach that is similar to the BCG matrix was developed at General Electric. Their grid (see Figure 4-5) is based on two variables: (1) industry attractiveness (made up of factors like market growth-rate, competition, seasonality, cyclical qualities, and so forth), and (2) business strength (made up of factors like relative market share, profit margins, knowledge of customers, management capability, and so forth). Each of these factors is weighted and scored and this allows a quantitative (but subjective) assessment to be made for each factor. The two variables are each broken down into three levels, so a nine-cell grid results.

Three overall strategies are suggested, based on the position of the SBU on the grid. The first is to invest in a product to generate growth. This is equivalent to the stars category in the BCG matrix, and would apply when business strength and market attractiveness were both high. The second strategy involves divestiture. This is equivalent to the dog category in the BCG matrix, and is recommended in cases where business strength and market attractiveness are both low. The third strategy is to manage the equivalent of cash cows and question marks. This approach is appropriate when business strength is average and market attractiveness is medium.

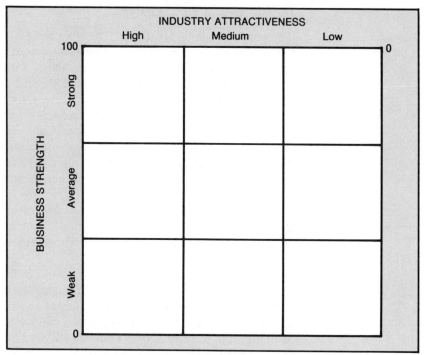

FIGURE 4-5   General Electric's planning grid

The General Electric grid's main advantage over the BCG matrix is its refinement into three categories instead of only two. In addition, the grid requires a systematic assessment of the multiple components that make up the variables of business strength and market attractiveness.

The Product Life Cycle

product life cycle

All products follow a general pattern that includes the stages of introduction, growth, maturity, and decline. This is referred to as the **product life cycle**. Corporate strategists who value stability in sales and earnings will tend to develop a diverse group of products. But to gain maximum benefit from their product line, they will also tend to promote a balance of products and services across product life cycle stages.

Figure 4-6 illustrates the product life-cycle curve. Although every product goes through the life-cycle stages, some products may regain popularity through the conscious efforts of strategists. For example, Arm and Hammer baking soda was well into the decline phase of the cycle when renewed growth was generated through the company's successful national advertising campaign, which touted new uses for baking soda.

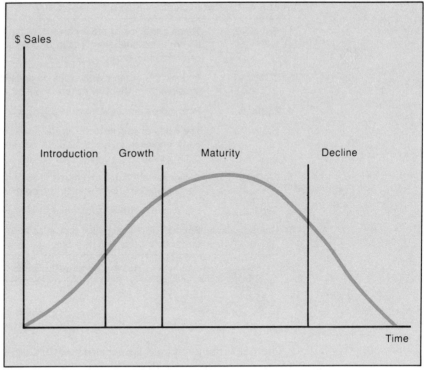

FIGURE 4-6   The product life-cycle

For most products, the life cycle is quite consistent, with variations only in the length of the stages and the amount of sales and profits earned at each stage. So, many companies try to have a certain number of products or services in each stage of the product life cycle at all times. As one product goes into the decline stage, another will be experiencing sales growth, and the company will have a stable source of profits from those products in the maturity stage.

The McKinsey Seven S Framework

The Seven S framework is illustrated in Table 4-2. In their best-selling book *In Search of Excellence*, Peters and Waterman say that corporate strategists have tended to rely on the "hardware" of organizations — structure, strategy, and systems — and have ignored the "softer" elements.[13] Two other authors, Athos and Pascale, also argue that the four soft elements can no longer be regarded as frosting on the corporate cake.[14] They are indispensable parts of any corporate commitment to long-term success. Proponents of the Seven S framework believe a balanced emphasis on all seven s's is required for corporate success.

TABLE 4-2   The McKinsey Seven S Framework

1. Structure:	Those attributes of the organization that can be expressed through an organizational chart (span of control, centralization versus decentralization, etc.).
2. Strategy:	Actions the organization plans or undertakes in response to or in anticipation of the external environment.
3. Systems:	Procedures and processes regularly followed by an organization.
4. Staff:	The kinds of specialties or professions represented in an organization)"engineering types," "used car salesmen," "MBAs," "computer jocks").
5. Skills:	Distinctive attributes and capabilities of the organization and its key people in comparison with its competition.
6. Style:	Patterns of behavior and managerial style of senior managers.
7. Shared values:	Spiritual or philosophical principles and concepts that an organization is able to instill in its members.

SOURCE   Adapted from Anthony G. Athos and Richard T. Pascale, *The Art of Japanese Management: Applications for American Executives* (New York: Simon & Schuster, 1981).

The McKinsey Seven S framework offers a concise way of viewing corporate culture, the shared values, beliefs, and habits of an organization. (Corporate culture will be discussed further in Chapter 15.) The Seven S model is useful for three purposes:

- It helps managers and analysts understand the corporate culture in their organization.
- It helps strategists compare their organizations with others along each of the seven dimensions, thereby identifying organizational strengths and weaknesses.
- As a tool of strategy implementation, the Seven S model can help managers to systematically make changes to the corporate culture which they consider vital to success.

GRAND STRATEGIES

grand strategy

To this point, we have described the strategic planning process and some specific techniques for helping managers do strategic planning. The outcome of strategic planning is the selection of a grand strategy. A **grand strategy** is the overall plan of major actions the firm has decided upon as a means of reaching its long-term objectives. While each firm's grand strategy is really unique, since it is made up of so many specific details, several basic grand strategies that are often practiced by business firms have been identified. These include

(1) concentration, (2) market development, (3) product development, (4) integration, (5) diversification, (6) joint ventures, and (7) retrenchment.

Concentration

concentration

When a company grows by producing and selling more of what it already produces, it is using a strategy of **concentration**. In the extreme, this means that company resources are concentrated on a single product in a single market. In times of economic downturn, a company using this strategy can experience severe difficulties. However, the detailed knowledge about marketing and producing the product which management possesses can make the firm a strong competitor, and many small companies and some larger ones have successfully used this strategy.

Market Development

market development

If a firm is concerned about the risks of overspecialization that are evident in the concentration strategy, it might try market development. **Market development** means marketing the firm's existing products (with minor changes) to customers similar to the firm's current customers. To achieve this, the firm makes minor changes in its products so they will appeal to a broader market segment. The firm might also decide to expand geographically to reach consumers in other markets. Like concentration, this strategy is quite conservative and does not require company management to become knowledgeable about new products or markets.

Product Development

product development

A somewhat more risky strategy is **product development**, which involves introducing changes in the company's current products or creating entirely new products. The idea is to sell these additional products to existing customers with whom the company has a good reputation. Annual changes in automobile styles and the development of new automobile brands are examples of the product development strategy.

Integration

integration

A commonly used term among organizational strategists is **integration**, meaning the unified control of a number of successive or similar operations. When companies combine, this is integration. Integration also includes taking over a portion of an industrial or commercial process that previously was done by other firms. Integration need not involve ownership, only control. Thus, supply and marketing

forward
integration

backward
integration

horizontal
integration

contracts are forms of integration. Integration toward the final users of a company's product or service (for example, when Tandy Corporation opened its Radio Shack stores) is **forward integration**. When a company takes control of any of the sources of its inputs, including raw materials and labor, this is called **backward integration**. Southland Corporation's purchase of the petroleum refinery that supplies gasoline to the company's Seven-Eleven stores is an example of backward integration. Buying or taking control of competitors at the same level in the production and marketing process is called **horizontal integration**. When Prentice-Hall Inc., a publishing company, took over Allyn and Bacon Inc., another publishing company, that was horizontal integration.

There are several advantages to integration:[15]

- improved marketing and technological intelligence
- superior control of the firm's economic environment
- product differentiation advantages.

Each type of integration can accomplish different objectives. For example, if the objective is to decrease the cost of inputs, one way to do this would be to buy out suppliers that earn profits producing the inputs (backward integration). If the strategic objective is to obtain additional market share, horizontal integration might be tried. A single company can be involved in all three types of integration.

Backward and forward integration are usually designed to capture additional profits or obtain better control. Backward integration does this for the supply channels. Forward integration does this for distribution channels. Obviously, if a supplier or an intermediate customer is thought to be making exorbitant profits, vertical integration may be tempting. Vertical integration may also be justified when a company can efficiently perform the functions of suppliers or intermediate customers. However, if better control of supply or distribution channels is the only objective, it may be better not to buy the business. There may be better ways to ensure control, such as making franchise agreements with intermediate customers and long-term supply agreements with suppliers. Besides, taking over customers or suppliers is costly and often involves a company in an unfamiliar business.

Diversification

diversification

Diversification involves increasing the variety of products or services made or sold. This is usually done in an attempt to smooth out the fluctuations that the firm experiences in the demand for its products or services.

conglomerate
diversification

Diversification may be conglomerate or concentric. **Conglomerate diversification** means developing businesses that are not related to

concentric
diversification

the firm's current business. **Concentric diversification** means developing businesses that are related to the firm's current businesses.[16] Reduction of risk is usually the goal of diversification. A company that is involved in a number of different businesses avoids having all its eggs in one basket. Ideally, when some of a conglomerate firm's businesses decline, others will be on the increase.

Countercyclical firms are those that experience increasing sales even though the economy in general is declining. Such businesses are unusual. The do-it-yourself hand tool market is one of those exceptions. When times are tough, people tend to repair their own automobiles, and need tools to do so.

Using diversification as a strategy, a company can develop a group of SBU's whose valleys and peaks occur at different times in the business cycle. Concentric diversification may not appear to serve the risk reduction objective as well as conglomerate diversification. However, concentric diversification tends to be more successful in improving profitability, probably because the managers of the concentrically diversifying firm know something about the business they are buying and are therefore more effective at running it.[17]

MANAGEMENT IN PRACTICE

Corporate Strategy at Vulcan

Vulcan Packaging Inc. of Toronto is the company that developed Explosafe — an aluminum alloy mesh designed to prevent containers of flammable liquids, chemicals, and gases from exploding. However, the company has never been able to sell any significant amounts of the product, nor has it made any profit on it. It does make money from manufacturing steel drums, tin cans, and plastic pails — in fact, it is the largest manufacturer of metal and plastic industrial containers in Canada. At its 1986 annual meeting, it was announced that the company was giving up on Explosafe.

Since 1973, the company has spent $10 million trying to market the product. On many occasions, it seemed that big profits were just around the corner, but somehow the orders never materialized. Shareholders were initially patient, but by the late 1970s, they were asking pointed questions about the viability of the product. Eventually, the company decided to downplay the importance of Explosafe in its corporate strategy. Vulcan has now decided to emphasize a new line of products in the consumer packaging area, particularly in plastics. But some industry analysts fear that the company is in danger of once again spreading itself too thinly in areas that it doesn't know very much about.

The company's president says that the recession of 1981-82 convinced him that (1) Vulcan had to broaden its product base so that it wouldn't be vulnerable to economic swings, and (2) that the company had to develop a much more realistic view of the place of Explosafe in the company's long-term strategy.

SOURCE   Adapted from Kimberley Noble, "Vulcan Does Its Best Packaging in Projecting Company Image," *The Globe and Mail* (December 15, 1986): B1, B5.

MANAGEMENT IN PRACTICE

A New Strategy for Alcan

Alcan Aluminum is the world's largest producer of aluminum, and much of its output is made in Quebec, where hydroelectric stations provide cheap power. But Alcan has recently run into problems, and its future is uncertain. Demand for aluminum is not increasing, and the company posted a $185 million loss in 1985.

In the summer of 1986, 70 senior managers met for a week at an isolated resort to develop a new strategy for Alcan. Alcan has given up its strategy of trying to encourage the wider use of aluminum. Instead, it will be more selective about the markets for its products and will diversify into more promising lines of business. Through new subsidiaries, Alcan has become involved in areas like aerospace, ceramics, and computer wafers. By the 1990s, Alcan wants 25 percent of its sales to come from products that it doesn't even make currently. It also wants to increase return on investment from 9 to 14 percent.

Industry analysts have expressed some concern that, because Alcan's management has experience only in aluminum, diversifying into new product lines may cause the company serious difficulties.

SOURCE Adapted from "Alcan Charts New Course But Outlook Is Cloudy," *The Winnipeg Free Press* (November 19, 1986): 47.

Diversification often occurs as a by-product of bargain hunting by corporate strategists. Even if their preference is for a related merger candidate, corporate-level strategists often acquire an SBU in an entirely different business because it seems to be greatly underpriced. Diversification can also be the product of a simple desire for growth. During the 1970s, many companies acquired businesses that were unrelated to their existing strengths.

Joint Ventures

Sometimes, a single firm does not have the resources or expertise to develop a product or service. It may then join together with one or more other firms on a particular project. For example, a number of insurance companies may get together to write insurance for a client because none of them individually could afford to pay off if a claim was made. Or, a group of banks might get together and loan a business (or a foreign government) money. Some firms are reluctant to use this strategy, because it reduces their flexibility by requiring them to consult with other companies before they take action.

Retrenchment

retrenchment

Retrenchment means the reduction of the size or scope of a firm's activities. This strategy is normally applied only when a major crisis

MANAGEMENT IN PRACTICE

Hostile Takeovers: Canada vs the United States

During the last few years, many so-called "hostile takeovers" have occurred in the US. This happens when a corporate "raider" sets out to gain voting control of a company against the wishes of the management of the company. The raider tries to achieve this control by offering significantly more than the current market price of the stock in order to induce shareholders to sell their shares. Most hostile takeovers have occurred in the United States, not in Canada. Why is this so?

There are several reasons why hostile takeovers are less common in Canada. First, many Canadian business managers think that the practice of management is more "gentlemanly" in Canada than in the US. Jack Fraser, president of Federal Industries Ltd. (which has been involved in numerous friendly takeovers), says that Canadian managers are less adversarial than their American counterparts.

Second, under Ontario's security law, takeover artists who offer to pay 15 percent or more above the market price for stock during a takeover attempt must make the same offer to all shareholders, not just a selected group, as they can in the US. The cost of acquiring so many shares is a powerful deterrent against corporate raiders.

Finally, almost all the large Canadian companies that raiders might be interested in are "closely held," that is, one shareholder or a small group of shareholders owns a large proportion of the company's common stock. Thus, a raider would find it impossible to buy controlling interest if this small group of people refused to sell their shares.

SOURCE   Adapted from John Partridge, "Takeover," *The Globe and Mail* (January 3, 1987): D1, D7.

MANAGEMENT IN PRACTICE

Retrenchment at AMCA International

In April 1986, William Holland took over as chief executive at AMCA International (formerly Dominion Bridge). He immediately set out to reduce the size of the company in an attempt to return it to profitability. His aim was to cut 40 percent from the company's revenue base, and even more from its massive debt, which currently stands at about $570 million (US).

Mr. Holland's predecessor, Kenneth Barclay, had attempted to transform the old Dominion Bridge by using a grand strategy of acquisitions. However, an article in *Forbes* magazine characterized the strategy as a random expansion that resulted in disaster. Holland disagrees with that assessment, but does say the company overleveraged its balance sheet and that the problem must be rectified.

The retrenchment includes reductions in staff and head-office expenses. Holland feels that corporate overhead must be cut by about 50 percent (to one percent of revenue). Corporate staff have also been reduced from 225 to 75.

SOURCE   Adapted from John Partridge, "AMCA's Return To Health, Image Rests on Lean Plan," *The Globe and Mail* (January 21, 1987): B1-B2.

(usually financial) is facing the firm. Most corporate strategists resist this strategy, and will seriously consider it only if the survival of the firm is at stake.

There are two major ways that retrenchment is usually done: cost reduction or asset reduction. Costs can be reduced by laying off workers, cutting down on advertising and employee training, leasing instead of buying, and so forth. Asset reduction is accomplished by selling land the company is not using, selling corporate aircraft and automobiles, getting out of certain lines of business and selling the freed-up assets, and so forth.

If these actions are not sufficient, the company may have to retrench further. If retrenchment still fails, the top management of the firm may have no alternative but to sell the business.

OPENING INCIDENT REVISITED

Allyn and Bacon, Publishers

In the opening incident, FitzGerald, Bockus, and Smith were trying to set objectives for Allyn and Bacon's publishing program for the next two to three years. How did they do it?

First, the three managers tried to define the corporation's identity: why does Allyn and Bacon exist, and what does the Canadian company hope to accomplish? The mission statement that they finally created defined their concern with producing educational materials — rather than just books — for Canadian post-secondary use (not just subjects that had specific Canadian content).

The second step in the managers' planning process was to analyze the external environment facing them. They examined the patterns of enrollments in various subject areas and agreed that they would not publish in areas of small or declining enrollments. They also evaluated the textbooks available from Allyn and Bacon's competition; the managers found that, in some high enrollment areas, so many good textbooks had already been published that it did not make sense to publish more.

The third step was for the three managers to identify honestly the strengths and weaknesses of their company and to capitalize on its strengths. They decided that, in the short-run, the company would take on a limited number of projects so that the marketing department could put full emphasis on each project.

The three managers now had the basis for a corporate strategy. The company would not pursue certain subject areas because the market was too small or because the competition was too well entrenched. The subject areas not excluded for these reasons would form the basis for Allyn and Bacon's Canadian publishing strategy. Bockus could now request specific market research from Smith's personnel. Further, Bockus could establish information networks in these subject areas and ignore the others. This strategy would make him far more efficient in his work.

One interesting development that was difficult for FitzGerald and Bockus to anticipate was the takeover of Allyn and Bacon by Prentice-Hall, a competitor in the educational publishing business. The takeover occurred near the end of 1986. A number of the individuals who formerly worked for Allyn and Bacon now work for Prentice-Hall, but Bockus and Fitz-Gerald decided to pursue other interests they had. One of the outcomes of the merger is that Prentice-Hall sales representatives now find they are selling books they used to compete with. The business world is ever-changing!

SUMMARY

Strategic planning is the determination of overall organizational purposes and the means of achieving those purposes. The strategic planning process involves both strategy formulation (deciding what to do) and strategy implementation (doing it).

Before a strategy can be selected, the organization's managers must decide what the organization's mission is. They must then assess the firm's strengths and weaknesses and the risks and opportunities that are evident in the external environment. An important part of this environmental assessment is forecasting. Various strategic options must be identified and evaluated before a specific organizational strategy is chosen.

After a strategy is selected, it must be implemented. This requires the setting of both long- and short-term objectives. Each of the functional areas of the organization must establish strategies that are consistent with the organization's overall strategy. Whatever strategy is implemented must be monitored to see if it is having the desired effect.

There are three levels of strategic planning in organizations: corporate level (defining the overall character and purpose of the organization); SBU-level (determining how a particular strategic business unit will compete in a particular line of business); and functional level (developing policies and procedures for functional areas of activity like finance, marketing, and production).

There are many techniques designed to help managers in the strategic planning process. The Boston Consulting Group has developed a system for making strategic product decisions based on market share and growth rate. General Electric's planning grid is a system for making strategic product decisions based on industry attractiveness and the business strengths of the company. The product life cycle shows sales and profits of the typical product during the phases of introduction, growth, maturity, and decline. It allows strategic decisions to be made at various points in the life cycle of the product. The McKinsey Seven S framework identifies seven elements that are important for strategic success — structure, strategy, systems, staff, skills, style, and shared values.

There are several grand strategies that grow out of the strategic planning process. A grand strategy is the overall plan of major actions the firm has decided upon as a way to reach its long-term objectives. Grand strategies include: (1) concentration (producing and selling more of what a company already produces); (2) market development (selling the firm's existing products, with minor changes, to new customers who are similar to the firm's current customers); (3) product development (developing new products to sell to the firm's existing customers); (4) integration (unifying control of a number of successive operations); (5) diversification (increasing the variety of products or services sold); (6) joint ventures (joining with other firms to provide a product or service); (7) retrenchment (reducing the size or scope of a firm's operations).

REVIEW QUESTIONS

1. Define strategic planning. What is the difference between strategy formulation and strategy implementation?
2. What is a strategic business unit (SBU)?
3. Who are the organizational strategists?
4. List and briefly describe each step in the strategic planning process.
5. What are the major environmental elements that affect the strategic planning process?
6. Identify the major elements of the following strategic management techniques:
   a. Boston Consulting Group Matrix
   b. General Electric Planning Grid
   c. Product Life Cycle
   d. McKinsey Seven S Framework
7. What are the three levels of strategic planning found in organizations?
8. Describe the grand strategies that grow out of the strategic planning process.
9. What is the difference between concentric and conglomerate diversification? Between horizontal and vertical integration? Between market and product development?

EXERCISES

1. Write an appropriate mission statement for each of the following:
   a. Chrysler Canada
   b. Procter and Gamble
   c. The Toronto Argonauts
   d. The University of British Columbia
   e. The United Way
   f. The Canadian Armed Forces
2. Place the following businesses on the BCG matrix, based on your knowledge and reasonable assumptions about them:
   a. General Motors' automobile business
   b. Tandy Corporation's Radio Shack computer business
   c. Canadian General Electric's small-appliance division
   d. Sharp's electronic calculator division

3. Interview a top executive from a manufacturing firm to determine what the firm's mission is. Try to find out if the company has a well-defined process for selecting a corporate strategy.

CASE STUDY

Layton Hardware

Layton Hardware Stores is a chain of twelve retail outlets located in small towns in Ontario. The parent corporation, Layton Merchandisers, Inc., is owned by the Layton family of Toronto. The company has steadfastly refused to vary from the plan that has worked since the first Layton Hardware stores were opened during the 1940s. The plan is simple: only one store is opened in each town, and the towns must be between 8000 and 15000 population at the time. Inventories are tightly controlled, and no item is stocked unless it turns at least four times a year. Each store is managed by a carefully selected local citizen who is paid 50 percent of the profits the store generates. All purchasing is done by the central office in Toronto, although most items are shipped directly from hardware wholesalers and manufacturers to the individual stores. The store buildings are rented. After an initial infusion of capital, each store is required to pay its own way. If it does not, it is closed.

Layton Merchandisers had opened no new stores for several years, although the existing stores were quite profitable. The company had never done much borrowing, so the high profits resulted in increasing cash balances, even after paying family members director's fees, salaries, and so forth.

Until 1984, the excess funds were invested in guaranteed investment certificates. That year, the board of directors — made up of the founder's two sons, a nephew, and a niece — decided that the company should go into the restaurant business. The board decided that Layton Merchandisers would invest $3 million and build five new seafood restaurants. They would feature pond-raised rainbow trout and would be located in towns similar to those where the Layton Hardware stores were.

The restaurant business was separately incorporated as Rainbow Restaurants, Inc. By mid-1987 three restaurants were opened. The system was patterned as much as possible after the Layton Hardware chain. Restaurant managers were paid on a percentage of the profit basis. Purchasing was done centrally, and each restaurant was required to support itself after the initial investment. It became clear within a year, however, that the first two restaurants would have to be closed unless additional funds were provided.

QUESTIONS

1. As clearly as you can, state what you believe to be the corporate mission of Layton Merchandisers, Inc.
2. List the strategies discussed in the case that you would consider SBU-level strategies and the ones that are corporate-level strategies. Explain your answer.
3. What kind of integration occurred when Layton Merchandisers went into the restaurant business? Discuss.
4. Do you believe that the company is likely to be successful in the restaurant business? Why or why not?

CASE STUDY

A Strategic Management Consultant

Martin Sloan is a management consultant who helps companies develop strategies for overcoming personnel problems. He is a member of a three-person firm, headquartered in Toronto, that advertises nationally in publications such as *The Globe and Mail*. His clients include banks, manufacturing firms, hospitals, contractors, and computer firms.

In one recent situation, Martin worked with a large manufacturing firm. Before talking to anyone other than the chief executive, Martin asked that a memorandum be prepared saying that he had been retained to help the company seek ways to improve its internal operations. Then, he conducted a series of interviews with the company's 37 managers, starting with the chief executive and working on down. Each manager was asked to identify any problems or opportunities that existed within the firm and to suggest how the company might go about addressing them.

After this initial series of interviews, each taking about an hour, Martin prepared an interim report. With the president's permission, he met with the managers as a group and discussed the conflicts and frustrations that had been mentioned — without revealing who had mentioned them. He also discussed the opportunities that had been stated by at least two of the managers.

The major problem which came up time and time again was that the chief executive was too involved in the details of the operation and didn't give his subordinates as much discretion as their abilities justified. There was no consensus about the opportunities.

After the initial series of interviews and the interim report, Martin again visited with several of the managers whom he considered to be especially well informed. They went over the problems and opportunities that had received some agreement. Then, Martin went back to Toronto to prepare his final report. His intention was to clear the report with the chief executive and then ask for another meeting of all the managers, preferably to be held in the evening, over a meal. He expected the meeting to last for several hours.

QUESTIONS

1. Explain why a business firm with 37 managers might hire a management consultant.
2. What is likely to happen when the chief executive receives the final report highlighting his own tendency to get too involved in the details of the operation?
3. What additional work needs to be done to produce a complete strategic planning process? What problems might arise during the process?

ENDNOTES

[1] Richard B. Robinson Jr., "The Importance of Outsiders in Small Firm Strategic Planning," *Academy of Management Journal* 25 (March 1982): 80–93.

[2] Frederick Gluck, Stephen Kaufman, and A. Steven Walleck, "The Four Phases of Strategic Management," *Journal of Business Strategy* 2 (Winter 1982): 11–12.

[3] John A. Pearce and Richard B. Robinson, *Strategic Management* (Homewood, Ill.: Richard D. Irwin, 1985): 80.

[4]Sears Canada Inc. Corporate Profile, *Annual Report*, 1985.

[5]Canadian General Electric Corporate Profile, *Annual Report*, 1985.

[6]Charles C. Snow and Lawrence G. Hrebiniak, "Strategy, Distinctive Competence, and Organizational Performance," *Administrative Science Quarterly* 25 (1980): 317–335.

[7]Milton Friedman, *Capitalism and Freedom* (Chicago: University of Chicago Press, 1962).

[8]Adam Smith, *The Wealth of Nations* (New York: Modern Library, 1937).

[9]For an indepth analysis of forecasting techniques, see S. Makridakis, S. C. Wheelwright, and V. E. McGee, *Forecasting: Methods and Applications*, second edition, New York: Wiley, 1983.

[10]Herbert A. Simon, *The New Science of Management Decision* (New York: Harper & Row, 1960).

[11]Ian C. MacMillan, Donald C. Hambrick, and Diana L. Day, "The Product Portfolio and Profitability," *Academy of Management Journal* 25 (December 1982): 733–755.

[12]Frederick Gluck, "The Dilemmas of Resource Allocation," *Journal of Business Strategy*, (Fall 1981): 67–71; also Philippe Haspeslagh, "Portfolio Planning: Uses and Limits," *Harvard Business Review* 60 (January-February 1982): 58–73.

[13]Thomas J. Peters and Robert H. Waterman Jr., *In Search of Excellence* (New York: Harper & Row, 1982).

[14]Anthony G. Athos and Richard T. Pascale, *The Art of Japanese Management* (New York: Simon & Schuster, 1981): 83–84.

[15]Kathryn Rudie Harrigan, "A Framework for Looking at Vertical Integration," *Journal of Business Strategy* 3 (Winter 1983): 30–37.

[16]In a technical sense, the term *related diversification* is better than *concentric diversification*, but the latter term has gained more widespread use.

[17]Richard A. Bettis, "Performance Differences in Related and Unrelated Diversified Firms," *Strategic Management Journal* 2 (October-December 1981): 379–393.

REFERENCES

"Alcan Charts New Course But Outlook Is Cloudy." *The Winnipeg Free Press* (November 19, 1986): 47.

Anderson, Carl R., and Paine, Frank T. "Managerial Perceptions and Strategic Behavior." *Academy of Management Journal* 18 (December 1975): 811–823.

Arnold, William, and Brown, John. "Tracking Strategy in the Airlines: PWA 1945-1984." *Canadian Journal of Administrative Sciences* 3 (December 1986): 171–203.

Athos, Anthony G., and Pascale, Richard T. *The Art of Japanese Management: Applications for American Executives.* New York: Simon & Schuster, 1981.

Bettis, Richard A. "Performance Differences in Related and Unrelated Diversified Firms." *Strategic Management Journal* 2 (October-December 1981): 379–393.

Bowman, Edward H. "Risk/Return Paradox for Strategic Management," *Sloan Management Review* 21 (Spring 1980); 17–31.

Fisher, Matthew. "It Isn't The Sun Run, But It's A Living." *The Globe and Mail* (January 7, 1987): B1–B2.

Fox, H. W. "Frontiers of Strategic Planning: Intuition or Formal Models." *Management Review* 70 (April 1981): 44–50.

Friedman, Milton, *Capitalism and Freedom.* Chicago: University of Chicago Press, 1962.

Galt, Virginia. "Bank of Montreal To Decide How to Add Services." *The Globe and Mail* (January 20, 1987): B1–B2.

Gluck, Frederick. "The Dilemmas of Resource Allocation." *Journal of Business Strategy* (Fall 1981): 67–71.

Gluck, Frederick, Stephen Kaufman, and A. Steven Walleck. "The Four Phases of Strategic Management." *Journal of Business Strategy* 2 (Winter 1982): 11–12.

Gup, Benton E. "Begin Strategic Planning by Asking Three Questions" *Managerial Planning* 28 (November 1979): 28–31.

Gupta, Anil and Govindarajan, Vijay. "Resource Sharing Among SBU's: Strategic Antecedents and Administrative Implications." *Academy of Management Journal* 29, (December 1986): 695–714.

Hardy, Cynthia. "Strategies for Retrenchment: Reconciling Individual And Organizational Needs." *Canadian Journal of Administrative Sciences* 3, (December 1986): 275–289.

Harrigan, Kathryn. "Vertical Integration and Corporate Strategy." *Academy of Management Journal* 28, (June 1985): 397–425.

_____. *Strategic Flexibility: A Management Guide for Changing Times.* Lexington, Mass.: D. C. Heath and Company, 1985.

_____. "A Framework for Looking at Vertical Integration." *Journal of Business Strategy* 3 (Winter 1983): 30–37.

Haspeslagh, Philippe. "Portfolio Planning: Uses and Limits." *Harvard Business Review* 60 (January-February 1982): 58–73.

Judla, R. J. "Elements of Effective Corporate Planning." *Long Range Planning* 9 (August 1976): 82–93.

MacMillan, Ian C.; Hambrick, Donald C. and Day, Diana L. "The Product Portfolio and Profitability: A PIMS-based Analysis of Industrial-Product Businesses." *Academy of Management Journal* 25 (December 1982): 733–755.

Martin, John. "Business Planning: The Gap between Theory and Practice." *Long Range Planning* 12 (December 1979): 2–10.

Naylon, T. H. "Organizing for Strategic Planning." *Managerial Planning* 28 (July 1979): 3–9.

Noble, Kimberley. "Vulcan Does Its Best Packaging In Projecting Company Image." *The Globe and Mail* (December 15, 1986): B1, B5.

_____. "How A Seasonal Trade Branches Out." *The Globe and Mail* (December 24, 1986): B1–B2.

Odiorne, George. *Strategic Management of Human Resources.* San Francisco: Jossey-Bass, 1984.

Partridge, John. "Takeover." *The Globe and Mail* (January 3, 1987): D1, D7.

_____. "AMCA's Return To Health, Image Rests on Lean Plan." *The Globe and Mail* (January 21, 1987): B1–B2.

Pearson, G. J. "Setting Corporate Objectives as a Basis for Action." *Long Range Planning* 12 (August 1979): 13–19.

Peters, Thomas J. and Waterman, Robert H. Jr. *In Search of Excellence.* New York: Harper & Row, 1982.

Polyczynski, James J., and Leniski, Jason. "Inviting Front-Line Managers into the Strategic Planning and Decision Making Process." *Appalachian Business Review* 9 (1982): 2–5.

Robinson, Richard B., Jr. "The Importance of 'Outsiders' in Small Firm Strategic Planning," *Academy of Management Journal* 25 (March 1982): 80–93.

Schoeffler, S., Buzzell R. D. and Haney, D. F. "Impact of Strategic Planning on Profit Performance." *Harvard Business Review* (March 1974): 137–145.

Simon, Herbert A. *The New Science of Management Decision.* New York: Harper & Row, 1960.

Smith, Adam. *The Wealth of Nations.* 1776; New York: Modern Library, 1937.

Taylor, Bernard. "Strategies for Planning." *Long Range Planning* (August 1975): 437–446.

Thune, Stanley S., and House, Robert J. "Where Long-Range Planning Pays Off." *Business Horizons* 13 (August 1970): 81–87.

Uttal, Bro. "The Corporate Culture Vultures." *Fortune,* (October 17, 1983): 66–72.

Vancil, Richard F., and Lorange, Peter. "Strategic Planning in Diversified Companies." *Harvard Business Review* 53 (January-February 1975): 81–90.

Vesper, Volker D. "Strategic Mapping — A Tool for Corporate Planners." *Long-Range Planning* 12 (December 1979): 75–92.

Wren, Daniel A. *The Evolution of Management Thought.* 2nd ed. New York: Wiley and Sons, 1979.

5

Managerial Decision Making

KEY TERMS

decision making
personal decisions
professional
  decisions
routine decisions
non routine
  decisions
decision maker
problem content
payoff relationships

state of nature
intuition
scientific method
hypothesis
risk
decision matrix
brainstorming
nominal grouping
Delphi technique

management
  information
  system
data
  information
microcomputer
minicomputer
mainframe
  computer
telecommuting

LEARNING OBJECTIVES

After completing this chapter you should be able to
1. Define decision making.
2. Distinguish between personal and professional decisions.

3. Distinguish between routine and nonroutine decisions.
4. Distinguish between intuitive and systematic approaches to decision making.
5. Explain the rational decision-making process and indicate the kinds of things that can go wrong when managers make decisions.
6. Identify the factors affecting the decision-making process.
7. Describe five techniques for helping managers make decisions.
8. Describe the role of management information systems in managerial decision making.
9. Understand the impact of computers on management.

OPENING INCIDENT

Mackie Real Estate

Mackie Real Estate is a small but rapidly growing firm in a western Canadian city. The company's two main activities are traditional residential real estate sales and speculative buying and selling of commercial property. For the latter activity, the four managers of the firm meet once a month to determine if any good opportunities exist.

At the last meeting a dispute arose over the speculative purchases. One manager had heard that the provincial government was likely to purchase one of three blocks of land in the next six months in order to build a power plant. If the company could buy the land first and then sell it to the government, Mackie could realize a tidy profit. The managers' dispute centered on which of the three available blocks of land the company should buy.

Block 1 costs $40 000. The managers estimate that there is a 0.2 probability that the government will purchase Block 1 for its power plant. If it does, the company could make a $40 000 profit; if the government doesn't buy it, Mackie will still make a $5000 profit because the land is inflating in value.

Block 2 costs $60 000, and the managers estimate that there is a 0.5 probability that the government will build the power plant on it. If it does, the company will make a $50 000 profit; if it doesn't, Mackie will lose $25 000 because the land will decline in value.

Block 3 costs $100 000 and the probability of the government buying it is 0.3. If it does, the company could make $110 000; if it doesn't, Mackie will lose $35 000.

Which purchase should Mackie's managers make?

Managers make decisions. The manner in which they resolve organization problems determines their success as managers. In fact, decision making can be viewed as virtually synonymous with managing, since it accounts for a large portion of managers' jobs. Merely because individuals have managerial titles does not mean that they can manage. Many individuals with elaborate titles are not managers because they are not decision makers. The key to whether a person should be classified as a manager is whether he or she has the authority to choose from among alternatives, to make the needed decision, and to implement it.

Managers who have the authority but refuse to make decisions are not carrying out their jobs. One of the most important qualities for success as a manager is not to procrastinate in making decisions, hoping problems will go away if ignored. True, a decision to do nothing may, in its broadest sense, imply that a choice has been made. However, a pattern of failure-to-decide does not give a person the right to be called a manager.

Increasingly, managers are being measured by the results of their decisions. Companies do not want dynamic failures; they want individuals who are properly equipped to make correct decisions. This does not mean that managers must be right 100 percent of the time; no one is perfect. But, successful managers have a higher ratio of success to failure than less successful managers.

In this chapter, we define, and identify the requirements for, decision making. We then examine two basic approaches to decision making as well as the key steps in making a decision. We also describe several factors that affect the decision making process and several techniques which help managers make decisions. Since a crucial element in decision making is the information available to managers, we end the chapter with a discussion of management information systems and the role of computers in decision making.

MAKING DECISIONS

decision making

Decision making is the process of evaluating alternatives and making a choice among them. We call it a process because the work of analysis leading up to any decision is of the utmost importance; indeed, it is the essence of management.

Everyone makes decisions every day. However, before anyone even thinks about actually making a decision, he or she either is confronted with a problem or sees an opportunity. Thus, people make problem decisions or opportunity decisions. Once an individual identifies the choice as a problem or an opportunity, he or she must identify and analyze the alternatives that are available. The alternative that promises to resolve the problem most effectively, or takes best advantage of the opportunity, is chosen after careful analysis. The choosing of this alternative is defined as the decision point.

To place decision making in perspective, we need to distinguish between personal and professional decisions and between routine and nonroutine decisions.

Making Personal versus Professional Decisions

Although a similar thought process exists in making either personal or professional decisions, managers should be aware of the differences between the two. Here is a brief overview of personal and professional decision making.

Personal Decisions

personal decisions

A wide variety of decisions are considered personal. Decisions to study, to go on a date, to watch television, or to go to bed early are examples of **personal decisions** made routinely by university and college students. Personal decisions can, of course, affect business firms. If you purchase a Ford instead of a Chevrolet, you will have a positive effect on the Ford Motor Company and a negative effect on General Motors.

A portion of any manager's time is spent discussing employees' personal problems and what can be done about them. Managers should recognize that employees experiencing difficulties in their personal lives may bring these problems to the job. Thus, a manager may be involved to some degree in the personal decisions of employees, whether the manager wants to be or not.

Professional Decisions

professional decisions

Virtually every gainfully employed person is required to make **professional decisions** — decisions that are part of the work he or she performs. Professors make decisions concerning the nature of the information they present to their students. Physicians diagnose problems and prescribe treatments. Scientists formulate hypotheses and design experiments for testing them. Managers of baseball teams, football coaches, politicians, plumbers, and clergy — in fact, most employed people — are required to make decisions as part of their professional lives. Yet the administrator in a business organization is labelled a manager, whereas many of the other decision makers are not. Managers are expected to be professional decision makers; their reason for being a manager is to make decisions.

Why are organization managers labelled professional decision makers whereas people in many other occupations are not? The answer is visibility. The manager of an organization operates in an open environment. A managerial decision affects many people (customers, shareholders, employees, the general public). The business manager sees the results of decisions reflected in the firm's earnings report, the welfare of employees, and the economic health of the community and the country. Decisions made by business managers may be no more crucial that those made by physicians or scientists, but their decisions affect a greater number of people. Managers' careers cannot be made by only one good decision. Their careers must be marked by a series of decisions that are acceptable. Hence, Levitt contends, unlike the lawyer, scientist, or physician: "The manager is judged not for what he knows about the work that is done in his field, but by how well he actually does the work."[1] To survive, the manager must be able to make professional decisions.

Making Routine versus Nonroutine Decisions

Managers are continually confronted with the need to make a variety of decisions. Professional decisions may range from major issues, such as whether to build a new plant or enter a new business, to rather routine decisions, such as deciding from which supplier to purchase the washroom paper towels. The two basic categories of professional decision making are routine and nonroutine.

Routine Decisions

routine decisions

Most managers make numerous routine decisions daily in the performance of their jobs. **Routine decisions** made by managers are governed by the policies, procedures, and rules of the organization, as well as by the personal habits of the managers. Decisions related to appropriate disciplinary action if an employee has violated company safety rules, or to settling disputes among employees over vacations, may be governed by company policies, procedures, and rules. Deciding when to go to lunch or how to organize daily activities are examples of routine personal decisions that may be determined largely by habit.

Since routine decisions are relatively straightforward, they free managers for more challenging and difficult problem solving. Many organizations set policies, procedures, and rules that provide a framework for decision making. Some firms have routine decisions made by a computer system; these are often called programmed decisions. However, managers are little more than robots if they simply adhere to the rule book and do not exercise personal judgment.

Nonroutine Decisions

nonroutine decisions

While routine decisions may take up a considerable portion of a manager's time, individuals make or break it as managers on the basis of the success of their nonroutine decision-making ability. **Nonroutine decisions** are those made when managers deal with unusual problems or situations. Decisions to expand to foreign markets, build a new production plant, or buy a more advanced computer system are examples of nonroutine or out of the ordinary situations. While these are examples of nonroutine decisions made by top management,

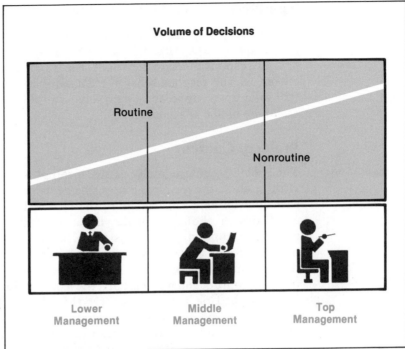

FIGURE 5-1
Managerial levels and
the amount of
routine versus
nonroutine decisions

managers at all levels in the organization make nonroutine decisions. For instance, nonroutine decisions made by a lower-level manager might include firing an employee or changing the layout or work flow procedures in his or her department.

Figure 5-1 illustrates the relationship between the level of management and the proportion of routine and nonroutine decisions made at each level. As managers progress to higher levels, their proportion of nonroutine decisions increases. Nonroutine decisions require managers to exercise creativity, intuition, and good judgment in solving nonroutine problems. (Recall also that in Chapter 1 we noted that the level of management also influences the relative importance of management skills and functions.)

REQUIREMENTS FOR DECISION MAKING

As previously stated, the most important quality that a business manager needs is the ability to make correct decisions. This one quality often separates the successful from the less successful managers. Certain factors that must be present before a decision can be made are: a decision maker, a problem, various alternatives, payoffs, and states of nature.

The Presence of a Decision Maker

decision maker

While Harry Truman was president of the United States, he kept a plaque on his desk that stated: "The buck stops here." He was the person responsible and he made the final decision. The **decision maker** has the responsibility for choosing the course of action that will take up an opportunity or solve a problem within the area for which he or she is accountable.

Problem Content

problem content

The **problem content** includes the internal or external environment within which the problem exists, the decision maker's knowledge of that environment's factors, and the changed environment that will exist after a choice is made. Because of the significance of the particular context of a decision, what may be optimum in one organization may result in complete failure in another. For instance, if a nonunion firm decided that, because of reduced sales, 10 percent of its work force must be laid off, the least productive workers would likely be the first to be laid off. On the other hand, a unionized firm facing the same circumstances would have to adhere to the labor-management agreement; it would likely lay off employees with the least seniority, even if these workers were highly productive.

Courses of Action

When facing a problematic decision, a manager should develop more than one alternative from which to choose. Alternatives may be many or few in number. They may merely represent the option of doing something or doing nothing. A good decision maker, however, attempts to identify and analyze as many alternatives as possible within given time and resource restrictions.

Payoff Relationships

payoff relationships

The various courses of action must be analyzed with the decision's objective in view. **Payoff relationships** are established to measure the costs or profits of alternative courses of action. When the profits and costs associated with a particular alternative cannot be expressed mathematically, managers may have difficulty making the decision. For example, decision making is easier if a manager can state that a particular decision will save $50 000, instead of just expressing an opinion that costs will be lowered.

State of Nature

state of nature

The **state of nature** refers to the probability that various situations could occur for a course of action. For example, when a weather reporter says: "There's a 20 percent chance of rain," rain would be one possible state of nature and no rain would be another. If the state of nature never varied, decisions would be much easier to make. Choice is required when the precise relationships among alternatives are known and the problem is to identify the probability of success or failure in terms of the decision's objective. Or, choice may be required when precise relationships among alternatives are *not* known, and the future environment is uncertain. Anyone who has played five card draw poker understands uncertainty about the future and the imprecise relationships that can exist. The good decision maker, like a good poker player, studies the situation thoroughly in the hope that his or her decisions will be correct more often than not. Because of the unpredictability of states of nature, most decision makers will never be 100 percent correct.

BASIC APPROACHES TO DECISION MAKING

Two basic approaches to decision making are the intuitive approach and the systematic approach. Each is briefly discussed below.

The Intuitive Approach

intuition

Individuals who rely on intuition make their decisions based on accumulated experience. **Intuition** is insight acquired through experience and accomplishments rather than through a formal reasoning process. Experience has a reputation for being a good teacher. You will discover that many business recruiters place major emphasis on the business experience students have gained while in university or college and on extracurricular activities they have participated in. The recruiters believe the learning process for a particular job may be shortened if a student has been active in other endeavors while in school. But business managers who make decisions relying only on intuition base judgment on their "feel" for the situation. Alternatives are chosen on the basis of a hunch, and solutions are judged on the basis of whether or not they work. If such decision makers confront situations to which they have not been exposed previously, wrong decisions may result. The intuitive approach to decision making has several obvious shortcomings:

- Learning from experience is usually random.
- Although experience is valuable, no one can assess its value. No one can guarantee that experience equals learning.
- What is learned through experience is necessarily limited by any individual's experiences.

MANAGEMENT IN PRACTICE

Intelligence and Decision Making

Intelligence, as measured by IQ tests, seems to be related to a person's success in school, but it apparently doesn't have much to do with how successful a person is in his or her business career. Successful executives generally score fairly well on IQ tests, but that is not what distinguishes them from unsuccessful executives. Accordingly, psychologists are increasingly searching for something called "practical intelligence."

This involves discovering the mental processes that are critical in work situations. Recent research suggests that the most successful executives are those who are cognitively complex; they have the ability to plan strategically without being locked in to one course of events and they have the capacity to acquire

much information on which to base decisions, but they are not overwhelmed by that information. They are also able to grasp relationships among rapidly changing events.

Professor Siegfried Streufert assessed managerial thinking styles in a simulation in which executives spent several hours making decisions based on data such as investments abroad, raw materials, and the stability of foreign governments. He found that executives who displayed greater cognitive complexity did a better job of making decisions which took into account the complicated relationships among these factors.

SOURCE   Adapted from Daniel Goleman, "Super IQ Not the Key to the Executive Suite," *Globe and Mail* (August 21, 1984): L9.

- Conditions change and experiences of the past may not be good indicators of current or future conditions.[2]
- The question may be asked, "Do you have 20 years of experience or do you have one year of experience 20 times?"

The Systematic Approach

scientific method

The systematic approach to decision making emphasizes the use of the scientific method in problem solving. The **scientific method** can be divided into four distinct but interrelated phases: observation of events, formulation of hypotheses, experimentation, and verification.

Observation of Events

The first step in the scientific method requires a full exploration of the relationships among the elements of a system and of how and why they produce a particular outcome. The process begins by observing an occurrence and then asking why it happened.

Hypothesis Formulation

hypothesis

The second step in the scientific method involves formulating an explanation of the hows and whys of the observed event. A **hypothesis** is a tentative statement of the nature of relationships that exist in a particular system. A hypothesis provides a possible explanation of the cause that brought about the observed effect. For instance, you might formulate the hypothesis that a relationship exists between turnover and job satisfaction.

Experimentation

The third step in the scientific approach to decision making is experimentation. A manager subjects the hypothesis to one or a series of tests to determine whether the tentatively stated relationship does in fact exist. Tests either support the hypothesis or prove it to be unsound.

Verification

The final step in the scientific method is verification of the findings obtained from the experiment. Sometimes this may take the form of another experiment or a series of experiments. Such is the case when a marketing researcher finds that a sample market is highly receptive to a new product and then verifies these results in additional test cities when the product is actually sold to consumers.

Which Approach Is Better?

The professional decision maker must adopt an approach that uses the best features of both the intuitive and the systematic approaches. All information that managers are able to obtain should be used to assist in making decisions. Intuition is an essential part of decision making because experience can provide valuable insight into what may occur if a certain decision is made. The systematic approach, on the other hand, forces the decision maker to evaluate critically what is known and to recognize what is unknown before jumping to a decision based solely on a hunch. Professor Ralph C. Davis's classic statement summarizes the need for a bond between these two approaches in this discussion of the professionally trained exscutive:

- A man who has nothing but background is a theorist. A man who has nothing but practical experience is a business mechanic. A professionally trained executive is one in whom there is an effective integration of these two general types of experiences, combined with adequate intelligence regarding the types of problems with which he must deal.[3]

THE DECISION-MAKING PROCESS

Managers make decisions by choosing among various courses of action. The issue may be as simple as deciding whether or not to work overtime or as complicated as deciding on the overall strategy of the firm. If an organization is to be successful, it must have managers

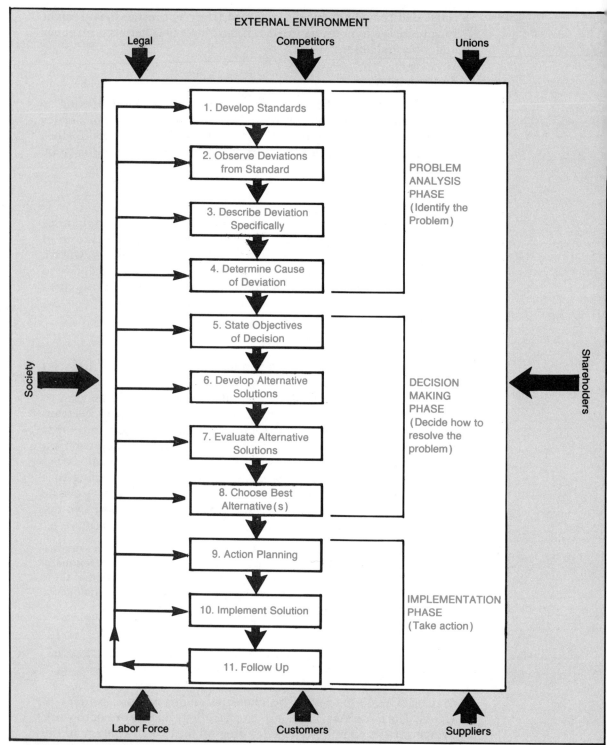

FIGURE 5-2   The decision-making process

who are willing and able to make decisions in the best interest of the firm. As such, decision makers are the architects of organizations. They have the ability to develop solutions to problems that occur in their areas of responsibility.

The process that should ideally be followed when making decisions is illustrated in Figure 5-2. Decision making does not take place within a vacuum; all decisions must be made within the constraints of the organization's internal and external environment.

The elements in the external environment remain the same as those identified in Chapter 2. Variations in any of these factors can have a big impact on decision making. For example, intense competition in a certain market may lead to a management decision to withdraw from that market. Or, shareholder pressure to make certain products or conduct business in certain countries can influence management decisions.

In a similar manner, the internal environment facing managers influences the decisions those managers make. For example, if a manager wants to pursue a certain course of action but his or her boss strongly opposes it, the manager will probably decide not to do it, even though it may be a rational action to take.

The relative influence of the internal and external factors may change, based on whether the decision is made by top, middle, or lower-level managers, but the basic process does not. For example, a company president will have to give serious consideration to share-holder views when making a decision about whether to merge with another firm. A production supervisor, on the other hand, will be more influenced by internal company policy when thinking about terminating an employee.

There are three major phases in the decision-making process: (1) problem analysis — identifying the problem; (2) decision making — deciding how to resolve the problem; and (3) implementation — putting the decision into practice. These three phases are elaborated in the following sections. In discussing each of these phases, the ideal situation is described; however, since the ideal is rarely achieved, the discussion also notes the kinds of things that can go wrong in each phase.

The Problem-Analysis Phase

In this stage, the decision maker's only goal is to come to a clear understanding of what the problem is. The importance and difficulty of doing so should not be underestimated. Countless examples exist of organizations or individuals who wasted time and money pursuing inappropriate solutions based on faulty problem analysis. To avoid this type of mistake, decision makers should proceed through the following steps.

Develop Standards

Before a manager can assess whether or not a problem exists, a standard must be in place. Standards are relevant for all kinds of organizations — public or private, profit-pursuing or not-for-profit, manufacturing or service. The standards may be stated qualitatively or quantitatively (preferably the latter), and individuals in the organization must have a clear idea of what the standards are. So, for example, a manufacturing firm may set a standard by stipulating the units per hour that are to be produced of a certain product; a hospital may set a standard for occupancy rates; an airline will probably have a standard percentage of seats that must be filled; a government agency may have a standard governing the number of clients that should be served in a particular time period. Overall, the standard indicates to members of the organization what their required performance is.

Unfortunately the development of standards can be a highly controversial and conflict-filled activity. Why are conflicts over standards so common? First, the individuals affected (either workers or management) may fear that they will be allowed no input into setting the standards. They may therefore fear being confronted with an unreasonable task. Second, even if they are involved in setting the standard, they may feel that the way in which the standard is measured is inappropriate and will make their performance seem inadequate. Third, they may feel that measurement occurs at an inappropriate time. For example, if performance is measured on a day when many regular workers are off sick, it may appear that productivity in a particular department is not up to par. Fourth, workers may object to specific standards because they feel that management will use performance statistics against them. Whatever the reason, the setting of standards is a very difficult activity in many organizations; it should not be approached as a simple job that must be done quickly in order to "get on with more important things." If the standards are not realistic and/or have no support, any kind of productivity measurements will be met with great resistance.

Observe Deviations from the Standard

The next logical step in the problem-analysis phase is to observe performance (either machine or human) and determine whether there is any deviation from standard. The deviation may, of course, be on the high side or on the low side; the idea is to determine whether organizational performance is close to what was predicted when standards were originally set. Several questions must be answered in this phase:

- Is there agreement among managers and employees that a deviation exists?
- How bad is the deviation, i.e., is it significant enough to cause a major disruption in progress toward the goal originally set?
- Is there a trend in the deviation, i.e., is it a random thing or is there a pattern?

Describe the Deviation Specifically[4]

The old saying, "a problem that is well-defined is a problem that is already half-solved" is an oversimplification, but its point is well taken: we cannot proceed to a solution until it is clear what the problem is. This step requires that the observed deviation be described in detail, which involves stipulating the location, magnitude, and timing of the deviation. Any additional information that gives the decision maker a better understanding of the deviation should also be gathered at this point.

The major practical problem with this step is that people avoid it altogether. Typically, what happens is this: an individual makes a cursory observation of a situation, observes a deviation from standard, and then immediately leaps to a conclusion about what caused the deviation. This very fundamental error is the major pitfall that must be avoided in the problem-analysis phase. In our society, where decisive action is admired, it is not surprising that individuals try to determine immediately the cause of a deviation rather than first carefully describe the deviation. Failure to describe the deviation accurately, however, often results in failure to find the cause of the problem.

Determine the Cause of the Deviation

If Steps 1, 2, and 3 have been handled properly, a successful conclusion to the problem-analysis phase is very likely. If clear standards are set, if the deviation from standard is observed, and if this deviation is well understood, the cause can be much more easily determined. Step 4, therefore, requires the use of the information that has been gathered in the previous three steps.

The Decision-Making Phase

Once the cause of the problem is known, the decision maker must decide how to resolve it. Deciding upon the specific solution to the problem is the goal of this phase. To do this, several steps are required.

State Objectives of the Decision

For problem decisions, the objective is to solve the problem that has just been defined in Step 4. For opportunity decisions, the objectives must first be stated. These objectives deal with issues such as maximizing profit, maximizing productivity, reducing rejects, improving customer service, etc.

Once again, human idiosyncracies can cause serious problems in stating objectives. To start with, there may be little agreement on the objectives that the organization should pursue. A manufacturing firm may wish to do some state-of-the-art manufacturing, but the finance people in the firm may feel that this is inadvisable and that production should continue to work in areas that it is familiar with. This will no doubt cause a disagreement and no objectives can be set until the disagreement is resolved. Even with specific issues resolved, the general objectives of one segment of the firm may be in disagreement with the objectives of the other segments. The classic example of this is the dispute that routinely occurs between production and marketing people, with the former wanting long production runs and standardized products and the latter wanting speedy delivery and a wide variety of products. Each of these areas has a perfectly legitimate goal, yet conflicts of this nature mean that objective setting is difficult. Organizational politics also play a role in the setting of objectives. If the corporation president wants to pursue a certain goal it may be difficult for organizational members to object successfully. Stated more generally, any powerful individual in an organization may be able to stipulate objectives that push the organization in a certain direction.

Develop Alternative Solutions

At this step, the decision maker develops as many possible solutions to the problem as can be generated. The greater the length and diversity of the list of alternatives, the greater the likelihood that a workable solution will be found. Creativity is important in this step, since innovative solutions often resolve problems when traditional solutions will not.

The practical problems to be anticipated here are two-fold; First, when individuals attempt to develop alternative solutions, they typically suggest those that have worked for similar problems they have encountered in the past. While these suggestions can be useful, they often lead to the implementation of solutions that really do not confront the problem at hand. The major reason this happens is that individuals do not expend the effort needed to develop a long list of alternative solutions. Rather, they develop a couple of alternatives that look feasible and then spend considerable time arguing about the relative merits of those solutions. Second, the conservative nature of most decision makers means that innovative alternatives are dismissed because "we've never done it that way." Thus, people are either unwilling or unable to seriously consider innovative alternatives.

Evaluate Alternative Solutions

Once the list of potential alternatives has been developed, they must be analyzed systematically to determine which one is best. To do this, some sort of criterion must be developed so that the alternatives can be compared with each other. Some of the techniques for accomplishing this are discussed later in this chapter.

The major problem with this step is that (like Step 3 in the problem-analysis phase) individuals often avoid it altogether. Although it appears strange that such a crucial step would be avoided, this is precisely what occurs. Why is this so? First, people are often not motivated to take the time, or expend the effort, to make a decision properly. Second, the decision maker may feel that the analysis required is beyond his or her capability. So, a shallow analysis is done and a decision is made on that basis. Third, there may be disagreements among individuals working on a problem about the proper method to use to evaluate the alternatives. These difficulties constitute a formidable list and it is not surprising that Step 7 is so often avoided by decision makers. Once again, it cannot be overemphasized that the consequences of failing to do this step properly are significant. Individuals who avoid the evaluation of alternatives will often find that the alternatives they pick will have many unexpected negative features. Proper evaluation increases the likelihood that the negative features will be recognized before the decision is made.

Choose the Best Alternative

Once Steps 1-7 (for problem decisions) or Steps 5-7 (for opportunity decisions) have been completed, the decision maker can choose the best alternative. The alternative that is best will, of course, depend on the criterion that the decision maker has chosen. Once a particular alternative has been chosen, the decision-making phase has been completed.

The problems that are encountered in Step 8 are largely the result of failure to adequately conduct Steps 1-7. For example, if objectives have not been stated clearly in Step 5, the decision maker will be unable to tell whether the alternative chosen is the best one. Likewise, if a proper analysis has not been done in Step 7, there will probably be numerous disputes about what the best alternative is. Or, if the deviation from standard has not been described adequately, the decision maker cannot be sure that the solution chosen is solving the actual problem.

The Implementation Phase

In this phase, the decision maker must convert thoughts into action. This really requires the decision maker to consider the most effective way to introduce change (this topic is discussed in detail in Chapter 14). Three steps are required.

Action Planning

Once the problem has been defined and a solution has been developed to resolve it (the "problem analysis" and "decision-making" phases, respectively) a specific plan of action must be developed. This requires the decision maker to think about such questions as: (1)

should employees participate in the implementation plan or should they simply be required to implement the decision? (2) what kind of coordination is required between the decision maker and those who will implement the decision? (3) who will monitor the implementation to see if it is working properly? and (4) what criteria will be used to determine if the proposed solution really solves the problem?

Implement the Solution

Two key concepts must be kept in mind in this phase: the quality of the decision and the acceptance of the decision. A high-quality decision that is not accepted by those who must live with it is useless. Suppose a manager decides that resolution of a certain problem requires the implementation of a new requisition system. No matter how quality-oriented this system is, if subordinates will not accept it, it will not succeed. Likewise, if a solution is implemented strictly because the employees will accept it, and the decision itself is of low quality, it is unlikely that it will resolve the problem. These quality and acceptance aspects appear to be multiplicatively related — a low score on either of the variables results in a fairly low overall effectiveness score.[5]

The practical problems with Step 10 can be a nightmare of frustration for the decision maker. The literature of organizational behavior is full of examples of attempts by managers to implement changes, only to find that those affected have vigorous objections. Problems like this can be avoided by allowing those who will be affected by the change to participate in the actual decision-making phase, but this process can take considerable time and money.

Follow Up

Once the proposed solution has been implemented, management must monitor the extent to which that solution really resolves the problem. Often a solution that appears perfect runs into considerable technical or human difficulties once it is implemented. A control system must therefore be in place to detect whether or not the solution really has resolved the problem.

The greatest practical difficulty with Steps 9-11 is bridging the gap between thinking and action. Steps 1-8 are largely mental while Steps 9-11 require both mental and physical action. While many individuals are very strong at Steps 1-8, they may not have the interest, inclination, or ability to make the leap from thinking to action. In addition, the particular manner in which the solution is implemented and followed up is critical.

As the above discussion shows, the decision-making process is long and complicated, and many things can (and do!) go wrong at each step of the way. Knowledge of both the technical and human elements in the organization is important if the decision maker is to make and implement decisions successfully.

FACTORS AFFECTING THE DECISION-MAKING PROCESS

There are numerous factors which affect the decision making process in organizations. Five factors which are particularly important are discussed below. They are (1) the level of risk, (2) the time available to make the decision, (3) the degree to which the decision maker is accepted by others, (4) the decision maker's ability, and (5) organization politics.

Risk

risk

Risk is a probability that an incorrect decision may have an adverse effect on an organization. Risk is a factor that all managers consider, consciously or unconsciously, when making decisions. The president of a small book publishing firm, for example, is thinking of paying a $50 000 advance to a well-known author to write a book. If the book sells well, the firm could make $250 000; if it doesn't sell well, the publisher will lose the $50 000 advance, plus about $30 000 in developmental and promotional costs. The president decides that the risk of losing $80 000 could put the company out of business. The $50 000 advance is too high a risk; if the author will not accept less, the publisher must try another alternative.

The purchasing manager at General Motors frequently signs contracts for automobile parts that exceed $1 million. The risk involved in each decision to sign, however, is typically low. The parts will be used and, as part of vehicles, will be sold. But, even the loss of $1 million would not have as disastrous an effect on General Motors as the loss of $80 000 would to the publisher. The relative risk must be weighed in each decision. Generally, as risk related to a decision increases, more time and effort will be devoted to the process of making that decision.

Time

The amount of time a manager can devote to making a decision is often critical. A manager would prefer to have sufficient time to develop and analyze thoroughly all alternatives prior to making a decision. Most business people are not afforded this luxury; they must make decisions under pressure, when they often do not have sufficient time to analyze all alternatives. Suppose, for instance, that a customer of yours offers to purchase your product in bulk, but at a slight discount. Although the firm will make a profit on this order, the profit is not as large as normally obtained. Today you have no other orders to choose from; tomorrow you may have. However, the decision must be made today or your buyer will go to another manufacturer. You are truly under time pressure. It is much easier to make decisions when you have enough time to analyze all the alternatives; managers often do not have the extra time to decide.

TALKING TO MANAGERS

Dr. Heleen McLeod
Alberta Education

Heleen McLeod is the Director of Special Educational Services for Alberta Education. The mandate of this branch is to develop policies which will result in the initiation, maintenance, and improvement of educational programs to meet the special educational needs of gifted, talented, or disabled students in all Alberta schools. McLeod studied at the University of Alberta, receiving a Ph.D. in Counselling Psychology and an M.Ed. in Educational Psychology. She was Assistant Superintendent with the Edmonton Public School Board and held positions of Supervisor Teacher Staffing, Director of Counselling Services, Teacher, and Counsellor with that board. In addition, McLeod has been employed as a consulting psychologist to the Edmonton General Hospital and to the Westfield Diagnostic and Treatment Centre and has operated a private psychology practice.

Q: Is there some particular aspect of your job that requires unusually careful attention during decision making?

McLeod: Yes — determining how money to be spent on special educational needs for students will be allocated to, and spent in, the various school jurisdictions in the province. As one might expect, this can be a very emotional issue, so Special Educational Services has had to take great care when making allocation decisions.

Q: Could you briefly indicate how you make these allocation decisions?

McLeod: We are in the midst of changing the system. Previously, each school system applied for money to provide programs for special-needs students (those with mental or learning disabilities, physical or multiple disabilities, and deaf or blind children). Our branch then reviewed the applications and decided on the basis of established criteria how much money each school jurisdiction would receive. School jurisdictions that knew how to play the application game and had good programs already in place got a larger proportion of the funds, while jurisdictions that weren't as adept at the application process or hadn't developed programs received less.

About a year ago, Alberta Education decided to change this procedure. We changed some of the criteria for allocating funds. For example, we used to require that a given school have three to five special students within a certain category before we would allocate funds to set up a special class. Now we allocate money on the basis of a commitment to provide services to students with special educational needs. To demonstrate such commitment, we require that the school board have policies relating to serving those special educational needs. So, our emphasis has gone from being funding-based to being policy-based. Now, we provide a block rate of $135 per resident student to each school jurisdiction, to be spent on such special programs and services. We have decentralized decision making, since the school jurisdiction is expected to use block funding in the most appropriate way. An obvious result of this system is that school jurisdictions have increased responsibility to provide good services with the money they are allocated. With increased discretion on how to spend the money, they can be more responsive to local needs and conditions and can no longer simply blame "the government" if things don't go well.

Q: How did you decide on this new system for allocating funds?

McLeod: This is only part of a new management and finance plan, which is a current thrust of Alberta Education. This plan is meant to provide — within policy directions established by the province — increased local responsibility, flexibility, and discretion to school jurisdictions regarding the use of provincial funds. Initially, committees were set up to develop the new system and to prepare people for the change. Interestingly, some departmental staff thought that school jurisdictions wouldn't use wisely the money they were given. But we finally agreed that we had to decentralize decision making in order to get better decisions. Decision making regarding the use of special educational funds now rests with the local school jurisdictions instead of the province, with Alberta Education regional offices monitoring the use of funds. Our committees also identified some potential snags in the new system. For example, if a very small school division were to have an unusually large number of disabled students, the $135 per student might be insufficient. We therefore decided to set up a contingency fund for such situations.

Q: What is your philosophy of decision making in the day-to-day aspects of management?

McLeod: Well, as a general statement, I try to push decision-making as far down the hierarchy as possible. I feel that the people who work for me will be more motivated to do their jobs well if they have the right to make many of the decisions that affect them.

Q: Can you give a specific example?

McLeod: We are in the process of developing a manual that will explain all the details and implications of the management and finance plan. I met with my staff and discussed what the objectives of the manual were, but indicated that they would decide what should actually go into the manual. This is a major job, and they will have to make many decisions before it is eventually completed. Once it is completed, I hope they will feel a sense of ownership for it. Likely, they would not feel that way if all details of the finished manual were simply imposed on them from above. Expecting them to make many of the decisions about what to include will also increase their understanding of the new system.

Q: What do you do if a subordinate suggests something that you don't agree with?

McLeod: I try to think objectively about it and try to ensure that I don't disagree simply because I didn't think of it first. Even if I don't agree with the idea, I may allow the subordinate to proceed on the project because, after all, that person has worked more closely on it than I have and may have more insights about the problem. I have very competent staff members and they understand the organization in which we work. However, if I can't agree with a project or the way it is being done, the project may need to be adjusted or discontinued. I don't think we've ever come to the point of not going ahead with a project, since generally we can work differences through by discussing them and coming to an understanding of each other's point of view. On occasion, I will discuss issues with my supervisor or directors of other branches to get a fresh point of view on the matter.

My supervisor takes the same approach with me on many occasions. I send status reports on various projects to him and make suggestions for how I think things should be done. He retains the right to reject my suggestions, but he doesn't generally exercise that right. That motivates me to work harder on a given project.

One of the things I have to do is make sure that suggestions my subordinates make are politically acceptable. People lower in the hierarchy may not be aware of the agendas of certain people further up the line. So, I try not to reject new ideas, but they must be presented in a way that is acceptable.

Q: What do you feel is necessary for good management decision making?

McLeod: Three things. First, you must have good information on which to base your decision. While you can get overwhelmed by data if you're not careful, you need sound and sufficient information to make good decisions. Second, you need to involve people in the decision-making process. If you simply try to impose a decision on them, they will usually resist it. Third, you must recognize that the rational decision may not be the one that will be implemented. Emotional considerations play a big role in many decisions.

Degree of Acceptance and Support by Equals and Superiors

New managers are not immediately accepted. Perhaps the manager is in a division where most of the other managers are much older; perhaps the manager is the only high-ranking female in an old-fashioned organization. If the acceptance and support by other managers is lacking, it is up to the individual to overcome the problem. Vanessa Ward, a supervisor of computer programmers for a major store operation, got support for her decisions by using the following tactics:

When I took the job, I really didn't realize what I was getting into. But I soon learned that no one liked the programming department. The previous chief programmer had just rammed things down the throats of other managers. Top management was committed to putting everything on the computer, so the chief programmer was given free rein. I knew that I couldn't conduct myself that way. Unlike the previous supervisor, I was younger than most of the managers that I had to work with. They thought that I was a "whiz kid." I tried to dispel that impression by seeking their advice before I made changes that affected their departments. I became a politician. Although I was overwhelmed by the workload, I made it a point to have coffee or visit with at least one other manager every day. It took a while, but now I believe we have an excellent working relationship with everyone, from accounting to purchasing.

Vanessa was able to overcome her problem by establishing a good working relationship with other managers. She realized that gaining the acceptance of other managers was an important aspect of getting the job done.

A lack of acceptance on the part of subordinates can also limit a manager's ability to make decisions and get them implemented. Solutions requiring close cooperation may not even be feasible if subordinate acceptance is lacking. Perhaps the best way for a manager to gain acceptance is to earn subordinates' respect. Making an effort to improve communication and involve workers in the decision-making process helps develop a feeling of mutual respect. When Lee Iacocca came to Chrysler, he kept his reputation for working harder than anyone else, coming to work early and staying late. It was also clear that he knew his job and was willing to put out extra effort to get the job done. Any manager who wishes to gain subordinate acceptance may have to work hard to get it.

The Manager's Ability as a Decision Maker

Perhaps the most important factor affecting decision making is a manager's ability. No matter how willing managers are to make decisions and be responsible for them, they need to have the *ability* to make good decisions. To a considerable degree, good decisions are dependent on systematic use of the decision-making process illustrated in Figure 5-2.

Organization Politics

Successful managers in all kinds of orgainizations know that rational factors are not the only ones to consider when making decisions. As we saw in the discussion of Figure 5-2, the politics of an organization can influence managerial decision making. Status, power, prestige, convenience, and ease of implementation can all influence decision makers. This means that managers may debate at length which alternative is the politically correct one. For example, if a company is trying to decide whether to break into a new market, some people in the organization may favor it and some may oppose it. Each side will try to influence the other by bringing to bear both rational and political arguments. The final decision may be based partly on rational grounds — the company thinks it will make more money — and partly on political grounds — the president wants to do it. The issue of organization politics is discussed in detail in Chapter 9.

DECISION-MAKING TECHNIQUES

In this section, we will discuss five of the most popular and/or heavily researched decision-making techniques: (1) the decision matrix, (2) decision trees, (3) brainstorming, (4) the nominal-grouping technique, and (5) the Delphi technique. The first two can be used in either a group or individual setting, while the last three require a group setting.

The Decision Matrix

decision matrix

Managers are often faced with problems in which the alternatives are known but the criteria for making the decision are numerous and the weights for these criteria are disputed. In these situations, a **decision matrix** is very useful. Consider the following problem:

A company is considering the purchase of a new computer system. After preliminary analysis, they have decided that they will buy either computer system A or computer system B. System A is very user-friendly, is fairly high priced, and is not particularly flexible. System B is moderately user-friendly, is very flexible, and is moderately priced. The managers agree that user-friendliness is about equal in importance to cost, and that flexibility is only half as important as the first two criteria. Which system should the company buy?

Figure 5-3 indicates how the decision matrix could be used to make a decision in this situation. The following steps are necessary:

WEIGHTS	.4	.4	.2	
CRITERIA ALTERNATIVES	Cost	User-Friendliness	Flexibility	TOTAL
System A	4	10	3	6.2
System B	7	5	10	6.8

FIGURE 5-3   The decision matrix for the manager's problem

MANAGEMENT IN PRACTICE

Using the Decision Matrix at SAIT

Some time ago, the Southern Alberta Institute of Technology (SAIT) wished to choose a supplier for petroleum products. There were three companies willing to handle such a contract. The SAIT purchasing department decided to use a decision matrix to determine the successful supplier. The following steps were necessary:

1. *Listing the alternatives.* These form the rows of the matrix. In this case there were three alternatives (companies A, B, and C).
2. *Choosing the necessary criteria.* These formed the columns of the matrix. In this case, the criteria were discounts, assurance of supply, credit terms, and equipment loans.
3. *Weighting the criteria.* The important thing to keep in mind is the relationship between the weightings. In this case, the purchasing department decided that assurance of supply was the most important criterion, and it was given a weight of 150. Discount was second at 120, equipment loan was third at

75, and credit terms were least important and were given a weight of 20.
4. *Rating the criteria.* This is done by starting with the first criterion and rating each alternative on that criterion. In this case, the ratings were done as follows: Assurance of supply was judged on the basis of a firm's reputation, location, management, and financial condition. Firm A received eight points, B received ten, and C received nine. Discount was decided on by using ratios. Firm A received 10 points because its discount was best, at 20 percent; B's discount was 18 percent so it received $18/20 \times 10 = 9$ points; C's discount was 12 percent, so it received $12/20 \times 10 = 6$ points. Equipment loan was related to the value of the equipment offered by each company. Firm C offered $21 000 worth of equipment and was given 10 points. A offered $7000 worth of equipment and received $7/21 \times 10 = 3.33$ points. B offered no equipment and received 0 points. For credit terms, Firm C offered 30 days and received 10 points. A and B both

offered 10-day credit terms and received $10/30 \times 10 = 3.33$ points.

5. *Calculating the final scores.* For each alternative, multiply the weight for each criterion times the value for each criterion, and add up the weighted ratings for each alternative. Based on the above information, the scores for the three companies are as follows:

Company A — $8(150) + 10(120) + 3.3(75) + 3.3(20) = 2713.5$
Company B — $10(150) + 9(120) + 0(75) + 3.3(20) = 2646.0$
Company C — $9(150) + 6(120) + 10(75) + 10(20) = 3020.0$

Company C was chosen because it had the highest score. See the decision matrix below for a summary of this problem.

ALTERNATIVES	WEIGHTS	120	150	20	75	
	CRITERIA	Discount	Assurance of Supply	Credit Terms	Equipment Loans	TOTAL
Company A		10	8	3.33	3.33	2716.35
Company B		9	10	3.33	0	2646.60
Company C		6	9	10	10	3020.0

FIGURE 5-4   The decision matrix for SAIT

1. List the alternatives that are to be analyzed. These form the rows of the matrix. In this case there are only two alternatives.
2. Develop the criteria that are to be used to make the decision. These form the columns of the matrix. In this case, there are three criteria — flexibility, user-friendliness, and cost.
3. Weight the criteria. The problem is most easily dealt with if the total of the weights equals 1 or 10 or some other convenient number, but any weighting system could be used. Note the weight for each criterion above the criterion. In this case, the criteria have been weighted based on the managers' preferences stated in the problem.
4. Start with the first criterion and assess each alternative on that criterion. In this case, the first criterion is cost, so each computer system should be assessed on that basis. (The higher the cost, the lower the score the system would receive.) Go to the second criterion and assess each alternative on that criterion. In this case, the managers have used a scale of one to ten for each criterion. Assess other criteria in the same fashion.

5. For each alternative, multiply the weight for each criterion times the value for each criterion to get a total score for each alternative. Computer system A's total score is 6.2, which is determined by multiplying $.4(4) + .4(10) + .2(3)$. Computer system B's total score is 6.8, which is determined by multiplying $.4(7) + .4(5) + .2(10)$.

6. Choose the alternative with the highest score. In this case, computer system B would be chosen, because its score is about 10 percent higher than system A's score. If the scores of the alternatives are very close, managers can refine the analysis further by considering additional criteria.

The decision matrix may be used in either an individual or a group setting. In the former, the manager simply decides on the criteria that will be used to assess the problem, and the weights that should be given to each criterion. In a group setting, there may be major disagreements about the criteria that should be used and/or the weights that should be attached. Considerable group discussion may therefore be necessary to determine what the criteria and the weights should be. This is an excellent way of getting people to think about the problem and this activity increases the likelihood that a better decision will be made.

Decision Trees

Decision matrices are useful for making decisions when the important aspects of a problem (e.g., payoffs) are not easily stated in dollar terms. In situations where a manager is able to quantify payoffs, and reasonably estimate the likelihood of certain future events occurring, decision trees can be very helpful. To demonstrate how decision tree analysis works, see the Management in Practice insert entitled "A Decision Making Problem."

Brainstorming

brainstorming

Brainstorming is an idea-generating technique wherein a number of persons present alternatives without regard to questions of feasibility or practicality. Through brainstorming, individuals are encouraged to identify a wide range of ideas. Usually one individual is assigned to record the ideas on a chalkboard or writing pad. Brainstorming may be used at any stage of the decision-making process but is most useful as a means of generating alternatives once a problem has been stated.

Brainstorming is fairly widely used in some companies and is generally thought to be quite effective. However, several research studies have shown that people working individually generate more creative solutions than do brainstorming groups. Apparently, the group suppresses people's willingness to suggest alternatives that they fear will be judged as unacceptable.

MANAGEMENT IN PRACTICE

A Decision-Making Problem

Suppose you are considering two possible part-time positions at a pizza restaurant that has recently opened. One of the positions is for an assistant manager and the salary is based on commission. The alternative is as a pizza cook for which you will be paid $6.00 an hour.

Because the pizza house is relatively new, the sales potential of the business has not been established. However, based on experience within the community, you estimate that there is a 20 percent chance of high sales, a 50 percent chance of average sales, and a 30 percent probability of low sales. You recognize that these states of nature will have an impact on the amount of money you could receive from the assistant manager's position. As an assistant manager, you estimate the payoff for high sales will be $10.00 an hour, for average sales it will be $7.00 an hour, and for low sales it will be $2.00 an hour. However, you will receive $6.00 an hour no matter what the sales are if you choose the job as a pizza cook. The payoff relationship between each alternative and the states of nature is provided in Figure 5-5. You are now in a position to analyze the two alternatives.

Which job should you take? One way to make the choice is to compute the expected value of each job. The expected value is computed by multiplying the probability of each state of nature by the payoff associated with each and adding the results. For this problem, you will have two expected values because you have two job alternatives. They are as follows:

$$\text{pizza cook} =$$
$$0.2(6.00) + 0.5(6.00) + 0.3(6.00) = \$6.00$$

$$\text{manager} =$$
$$0.2(10.00) + 0.5(7.00) + 0.3(2.00) = \$6.10$$

For the expected earnings for the pizza cook position, multiply the probability of the high sales state of nature (0.2) by the payoff associated with high sales ($6.00). Add to that total

the sum of the probability of the average sales state of nature (0.5) times its payoff ($6.00) plus the probability of the low sales state of nature (0.3) times its payoff ($6.00). The job value of the pizza cook position is $6.00. Do the same analysis for the assistant manager job; the expected value for it is $6.10. If you want the job that has the highest expected value, you will take the assistant manager position.

However, you should consider other facts before you make the decision. Your financial situation may prevent you from accepting the risk of receiving only $2.00 an hour if sales are poor. You may have other jobs available to consider. You may think the experience gained from the assistant manager job outweighs any money you might earn. Full evaluation of the solution, of course, cannot be done until the job is actually taken.

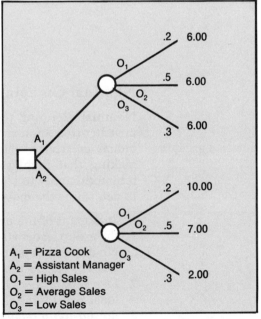

FIGURE 5-5   Decision tree for the job-choice problem

MANAGEMENT IN PRACTICE

But You Can't Quantify That!

Quantifying significant variables when making decisions is useful because many decision-making techniques require numerical values. However, difficulties arise when decision makers attempt to quantify, for instance, the value of a park to community residents, the value of preserving a vanishing species of animal, or the value of a human life. Can such variables be quantified? Why quantify them?

Suppose an automobile manufacturer is alerted to a design flaw in a current model that may be dangerous to human life. Should the manufacturer correct the flaw? Suppose that, after doing some research, the company concludes that: (1) the flaw will cost $20 million to fix, (2) 23 people will die if it is not fixed, and (3) class-action suits against the company by relatives of those killed will amount to $10 million.

In purely quantitative terms, the company should not fix the flaw because at most it will cost them $10 million and 23 deaths. However, this alternative implies that the manufacturer has a quantitative value for a human life: $434 782 ($10 million ÷ 23 people). This sounds very mercenary; if the manufacturer did not fix the flaw, it would likely not be willing to admit that it made the decision on this basis.

However, the fact remains that the value of a human life can be quantified in a given situation — but the decision maker would have to be unusually heartless. Most people prefer to talk in generalities about issues like this and managers prefer to say: "You can't quantify that!"

Nominal Grouping

Nominal grouping represents an attempt to move away from the unstructured approach of brainstorming and yet to encourage individual creativity.[6] **Nominal grouping** is an approach to decision making that involves idea generation by group members, group interaction only to clarify the ideas, and ranking the ideas presented to determine the most appropriate solution. The steps are as follows:

1. *Statement of the problem:* After the nominal group is assembled, the group leader states the decision problem clearly but succinctly. No discussion is allowed, although group members may ask questions to clarify the problem.
2. *Idea generation:* Group members silently record and number their ideas for solving the problem.
3. *Round-robin recording:* The group members alternatively present their ideas while the group leader lists them on a flip chart or chalkboard. The process continues without discussion until all of the ideas have been recorded.

4. *Clarification of ideas:* Under the leader's guidance, group members question one another to clear up any confusion about what each idea means. No evaluation is allowed yet.
5. *Preliminary voting:* Each group member independently ranks the best of the decisions presented. The ideas that receive the lowest average ranks are eliminated from further consideration.
6. *Discussion of revised list:* Individual group members question one another to clarify the ideas that remain. The purpose is not to persuade but to understand.
7. *Final ranking:* Group members rank all of the ideas. The one with the highest total ranking is adopted.

This technique is called *nominal grouping* because members act independently. Thus, they form a group in name only, or nominally. An important feature of this technique is that it allows the members to meet face to face but does not restrict individual creativity as traditional group discussions often do.

Delphi Technique

Delphi technique   The **Delphi technique** is a formal procedure for obtaining consensus among a number of experts through the use of a series of questionnaires. The procedure is similar to nominal grouping but participants do not meet. In fact, ideally the experts do not know who else is involved. The steps in the Delphi technique are as follows:

1. The problem is presented to group members in a questionnaire that asks them to provide potential solutions.
2. Each expert completes and returns the questionnaire.
3. Results are compiled and provided to the experts, along with a revised and more specific questionnaire.
4. The experts complete the second questionnaire. The process continues until a consensus emerges.

The Delphi technique avoids allowing the respondents to be influenced by the personalities of the other participants, but does make provision for the sharing of ideas. Unlike nominal grouping, the end result is a consensus decision. This method was conceived by the Rand Corporation to forecast how seriously a nuclear attack would affect the United States. It is expensive and time consuming and generally has been limited to important and futuristic ideas.

INDIVIDUAL VERSUS GROUP DECISION MAKING

In the previous section, we noted that certain systematic decision-making techniques can be used on either an individual or group basis, while others are designed specifically to be used in groups. The question is, do groups or individuals make better decisions? It is important to answer this question since there are so many work groups and committees in decision-making roles in organizations.

Before addressing the question, however, we must define what "better" means. The criteria normally used to define a better decision are (1) quality of the decision, (2) individual satisfaction with and acceptance of the decision, and (3) the time required to make the decision. The research findings on these criteria are quite clear: (1) the quality of group decisions is higher than the quality of the average individual decision, but lower than the best individual decisions, (2) individual satisfaction and acceptance is enhanced when decision-making authority is delegated to groups, and (3) groups require more time to reach a decision than do individuals.[7]

Advantages of Group Decision Making

There are several advantages inherent in group decision making. First, groups usually have a greater knowledge base that can be brought to bear on the problem. This is an almost automatic outcome, since more than one person is involved.

Second, the number of approaches to resolving the problem is usually greater in groups because each group member thinks along somewhat different lines. Individuals can get into ruts thinking about a problem in isolation, but approaches that group members perceive as unfruitful will be challenged.

Third, the group format allows increased participation by a variety of individuals. Although participation per se does not guarantee a high-quality decision, it does increase member satisfaction. If we accept the idea noted earlier that the effectiveness of a decision is a function of both quality and acceptance, member satisfaction is an important goal to pursue. Consider the following equation:[8]

$$ED = Q \times A$$
$$\text{where } ED = \text{effectiveness of the decision}$$
$$Q = \text{quality of the decision}$$
$$A = \text{acceptance of the decision}$$

The practical implications of this simplified equation are straightforward: if either decision quality or acceptance is low, decision effectiveness drops sharply. Thus, concern must be shown for both quality and acceptance. Participation clearly deals with the acceptance issue; if individuals have participated in making a decision, they are more likely to support its implementation than if the decision has simply been imposed on them. On an organizational level, individuals who represent various areas of the organization can be appointed to decision-making groups, and this can enhance the implementation of changes that affect more than one area. The recent trend toward appointing employees to Boards of Directors is an example of this idea.

MANAGEMENT IN PRACTICE

Japanese Decision Styles

Although it is unusual, there are some North Americans working for major Japanese companies, and they have some interesting observations about Japanese decision-making styles. Thomas Cappiello, a public relations manager for the trading company Nissho Iwai, notes that a good leader in Japan is not one who makes decisions, but rather one who finds out what the decision is. In a similar vein, Geoffrey Tudor of Japan Airlines points out that, if Japanese managers try to make an important decision unilaterally, they are removed from their jobs — in a face-saving way. John Macklin, an executive for Fujitsu, observes that, if a company president wants a certain decision

made, he or she may first plant the idea with a few subordinates; then let them do the analysis on the problem and make the decision. The president will then compliment them on a good idea and decision.

Apparently these practices are widespread. In terms of individual participation in decisions, this type of environment can be very motivating. Ronald McFarland, a supervisor at Isuzu Motors, says that one satisfying aspect of Japanese companies is that even the ideas of new employees are listened to.

SOURCE Adapted from "Outsiders in Japanese Companies," *Fortune* (July 12, 1982): 114-128.

Disadvantages of Group Decision Making

The most practical disadvantage of group decision making is the time required to make decisions. In one sense, this may not be a disadvantage because the extra time that is taken usually results in a better decision. However, in most organizations there is a sense of urgency about decisions, and groups or committees have a reputation for being slow. Thus, decisive individuals can experience frustration as they await the decision of a group, or participate in the group process. The old saying, "If you don't want any action taken on an important issue, give it to a committee" represents the frustration many managers have experienced with committees.

A second problem with group decision making is that certain individuals invariably dominate the discussion; as a result, the dominant individuals' preferences may be accepted and other (perhaps better) ideas will never be discussed.[9] This is one of the most significant problems in group decision making. As one writer has noted:

... groups fail to reach their full potential because of problems associated with the interaction process ... groups perform at a level generally better than the competence of their average member, but rarely as well as their most proficient member.[10]

The Delphi technique, nominal gouping, and social-judgment analysis are all techniques that have been developed to overcome these problems with interactions among people in groups.

A third problem with groups is the potential for "groupthink," the tendency for group members to suppress critical comments in the interest of maintaining group solidarity and a feeling of togetherness.[11] Because individuals fear being labeled as uncooperative by other group members, they do not voice concerns about the direction the group is taking, even if there are logical grounds for being concerned.

Finally, groups may make decisions that are simply a compromise between the various views held by individual members. This is particularly likely when a group must make a decision on a controversial issue. By definition, controversial issues will elicit opposing views. After a brief discussion, the group may conclude that a decision favoring either side is unacceptable, so a compromise solution is chosen. Unfortunately, this kind of decision has several shortcomings: First, it may please no one. In a compromise no one gets exactly what they want, so everyone in the group may be unhappy. Second, a compromise simply avoids the issue that was causing the controversy. Good decisions are not made when important issues are ignored. Third, a compromise may result in a low-quality decision. If people cannot agree on something and a compromise is quickly accepted to get the problem solved, other possible solutions to the problem may not even be analyzed to see if they are superior.

MANAGEMENT INFORMATION SYSTEMS

In this chapter, we focus on managerial decision making. In several places, we stress the importance of managers having good information on which to base decisions. Management information systems (MIS) help managers perform the basic functions of management.

A Definition of an MIS

management
information
system

All organizations have some sort of system — either simple or sophisticated — for getting the information they need to make decisions. A **management information system** (MIS) can collect, analyze, organize, and disseminate information from both internal and external sources so that managers can use it to make decisions beneficial to the organization. A good MIS gives managers information on past and present organization activities and makes some projections about future activities. An effective MIS provides managers with information that is timely, accurate, and useful. In short, the MIS helps managers perform the four basic functions of management — planning, organizing, influencing, and controlling.

Because computers have had such an impact on information, many people assume that a computer must be a part of any business MIS. A computer is not an automatic element of an MIS, although increasing numbers of organizations are using computers in their MIS because they can analyze large amounts of data quickly. We discuss the role of computers in MIS later; for now, keep in mind that: (1) a computer need not be used in an MIS and (2) even when one is used, a computer is only one part of the total MIS.

A crucial distinction in discussions of MIS is the difference between data and information. **Data** are unanalyzed facts about an organization's operations. Data become information only when used for some sort of analysis. **Information** is anything relevant and useful to practicing managers, including analyzed data. A good MIS takes data and converts them to information managers can use to help make decisions.

data

information

The Need for an MIS

Managers in all organizations rely on information to make decisions. For instance:

- Production managers need information on plant capacity utilization in order to determine whether plant expansion will be necessary if demand increases. They also need regular information on such items as production costs, labor costs, order backlogs, and machine breakdowns.
- Marketing managers need information on sales trends so that they can coordinate their activities with those of the production people. They also need information on new product development, new product sales trends, selling costs, marketing research, and sales territories.
- Personnel managers need information on workforce turnover and absenteeism, employee skill levels, labor markets, and wage levels in order to decide how to mobilize the firm's human resources in the most effective way. Managers in each functional area constantly need information in order to make good decisions. This information can be supplied by the MIS.

Information Needs at Different Levels of Management

Managers at different levels in the organization (top, middle, and lower) need different kinds of information, and they usually need it at different time intervals.

Top management uses the MIS to set overall corporate policies and strategy to ensure the organization's growth and survival. Because these kinds of decisions have a long-term impact, this information is generally needed at most quarterly, and perhaps only yearly. The most useful information for top management deals with whether the general direction of the organization is profitable and whether changes would increase the chance that goals will be reached.

TABLE 5-1   Information Requirement by Division Category

Characteristics of Information	Management Level	
	Operational	Strategic
Source	Largely internal	External
Scope	Well defined, narrow	Very wide
Level of aggregation	Detailed	Aggregate
Time horizon	Historical	Future
Currency	Highly current	Quite old
Required accuracy	High	Low
Frequency of use	Very frequent	Infrequent

SOURCE   G. Anthony Gorry and Michael Scott Morton, "A Framework for Management Information Systems," *Sloan Management Review* (Fall 1971): 59. Reprinted by permission.

Middle managers put into operation the overall plans and strategies that top management has developed. They use the MIS to set up control procedures and to allocate resources. Because this information is more specific, middle managers need information on a weekly or monthly basis. The information most useful to middle managers indicates whether the operational systems put into place can reach top management's overall objectives.

Lower-level managers ensure that the goods or services offered by the organization are actually produced. They use the MIS to determine what raw materials they need, to develop work schedules, and to make sure that materials and people are in the right place at the right time so that production activities are not held up. Because these activities are very detailed, lower-level managers need information on an hourly or daily basis. The information most useful at this level centers on whether goods and services have been produced on schedule and whether customers are getting the products they want when they want them.

Table 5-1 summarizes these and other ideas regarding the different information needs at different management levels.

Developing an MIS

An MIS may be developed for a particular department in an organization, or one may be developed for the total organization. When an organization decides to develop a company-wide MIS, it must realize that it will probably take many months before the new system is fully operational. Determining the information needs of an organization is not a simple matter, so considerable time must be allocated to the process. As well, top management must give its wholehearted support to the development process; without it, the MIS will probably not generate the information that the organization really needs, nor will it be used by those who are supposed to benefit from it.

Robert G. Murdick has proposed that the development of an organization-wide MIS proceeds essentially through four stages.[12] In the first stage, an MIS task force is selected to determine the information needs of the company. This study includes the internal and external environment of the firm and the influence these areas have on the information that is needed. The information needs of all the major areas of the firm are identified, and any possible constraints on the development of the system are noted.

In the second stage, the task force proposes various MIS designs that might be used. The performance requirements the organization will need of its MIS are identified. Managers and workers in the organization are asked for their input into the system.

In the third stage, the proposed MIS design is tested to see whether it will generate the information that is needed. Based on feedback from managers in the firm, necessary revisions to the system are made..

In the final stage, many specific operational activities are performed. For example, forms for data collection are designed, training programs are written, computer software is developed (if a computer is part of the system), and files are developed. This stage concludes with a final test of the new system. The same four stages are used for a department-wide MIS.

Implementing an MIS

The implementation of an MIS constitutes a major change in an organization. Great care must be taken to ensure that the change will be accepted by the people who must work with the new system. Whenever an organization decides to install an MIS, it runs the risk of making all sorts of mistakes. We next look at some mistaken assumptions often made during the implementation process and then present some suggestions for avoiding such problems.

Russell Ackhoff has described the five most common misapprehensions people have about an MIS.[13]

- More information is better. Often, an MIS is introduced on the assumption that managers suffer from a shortage of relevant information. While managers may lack some of the information they should have, it is more likely that they have an overabundance of irrelevant information. They may therefore be spending excessive amounts of time analyzing information that is not very helpful to them. If an MIS simply generates additional irrelevant information, the MIS is not serving its purpose.
- Managers actually need all the information they request. Managers often ask for a great deal of information, particularly on issues about which they

may not know very much. They do this because they think that more information may help them break through to a solution. If the designer of the MIS gives managers all the information they request, this MIS may simply worsen the information overload referred to in the first point.

- If managers are given all the information they need, they will make better decisions. Just having information on which to base a decision does not guarantee managers will make a good decision. If managers cannot use information effectively, those managers will not make good decisions no matter how much information is provided.
- More information communication means better performance. In most cases, an MIS can provide more current information about what the various parts of a firm are doing. Some people assume that this alone will allow managers in all parts of the firm to coordinate their activities and that this coordination will increase the performance of the total organization. These results are certainly possible, but information dissemination alone does not constitute either communication or coordination.
- Managers do not have to understand how the MIS works in order to use it. MIS designers try to make the system as easy as possible to use, but usually do not stress that managers understand it. As a result, managers may be unable to evaluate the system properly and may end up being controlled by the MIS instead of the other way around.

Any one of these misconceptions can reduce the effectiveness of the MIS. Fortunately, many lessons have been learned during the last 20 years about MIS. An MIS can be implemented effectively with the following general guidelines in mind.

Perhaps the most fundamental lesson that has been learned is that the manager/user must be involved in the MIS development process. Management information systems are normally developed by systems analysts who have technical expertise but, possibly, little knowledge of the manager's job. Therefore, they must get input from the managers who are actually going to use the system. Managers who are consulted by systems analysts in the design and implementation of the MIS are more likely to accept and use the system and are more able to revise the system as the needs of management change. If the manager/user is bypassed initially, he or she may never accept or use the system.

Time and cost factors associated with the system must be accurately assessed. During the early stages of MIS design, all concerned parties must have a reasonable estimate of what the MIS will cost and when it will be operational. It is frustrating for users to be told repeatedly that the system "isn't quite ready yet." Top management become displeased when their new system is not only behind schedule, but also costlier than originally planned.

"Human problems" need attention. The introduction of an MIS can lead to significant changes in the way people relate to one another and to the amount of information they have about each other. In both these cases, people may become unhappy. Suppose a company institutes a computerized MIS and finds that its most effective approach is to combine the purchasing and inventory functions. The people in these two areas my be unhappy that the distinctive nature of their work has disappeared. They may also be required to work with new people. These kinds of problems should not be underestimated; productivity may be affected negatively as people try to retaliate against the system that imposed an uncomfortable working environment on them. An MIS that is technically sound but is opposed by the firm's employees likely will not work as well as an MIS that has some technical flaws but is enthusiastically supported by workers and managers.

The MIS performance goals must be stated at the outset. Both designers and users must understand just exactly what the MIS is supposed to achieve once it is operational. In many instances, managers are surprised to learn that the MIS will not do something they assumed it would do. Careful specification of just what management can expect from the system before it is implemented is important in avoiding problems further down the line.

Understandable training and directions for users must be provided, especially when a computer is part of the MIS. Many managers are fearful of computers, so systems analysts must provide easy-to-understand directions and training manuals. If not, the chances are that system use will decline. Training and documentation must be geared to managers, not computer experts.

MANAGEMENT IN PRACTICE

An Example of an MIS

Now that we have described the basic idea of MIS, we present a brief example of how it works in practice. We consider an MIS at work in the personnel area of an organization.

The goal of the personnel function is to ensure that appropriate human resources are available when the organization needs them. (The personnel function is described in detail in Chapter 10.) In order to do a good job, personnel managers need information about several aspects of human resource management. (See Figure 5-6.) They need (1) information about potential employees and their characteristics, (2) financial data about payroll and budgets, and (3) job data regarding the number and types of jobs that need to be filled. These three factors constitute the inputs to the MIS. The information developed through these three input areas is combined into data bases. These data bases can be manipulated to provide outputs, such as wage and salary programs, promotion plans, and fringe benefit reports. The entire system of inputs, transformation, and output makes up the MIS. It allows personnel managers to make sound decisions regarding the use of the firm's human resources.

An MIS can be developed for any area of the firm — production, marketing, or engineering — or for the entire firm.

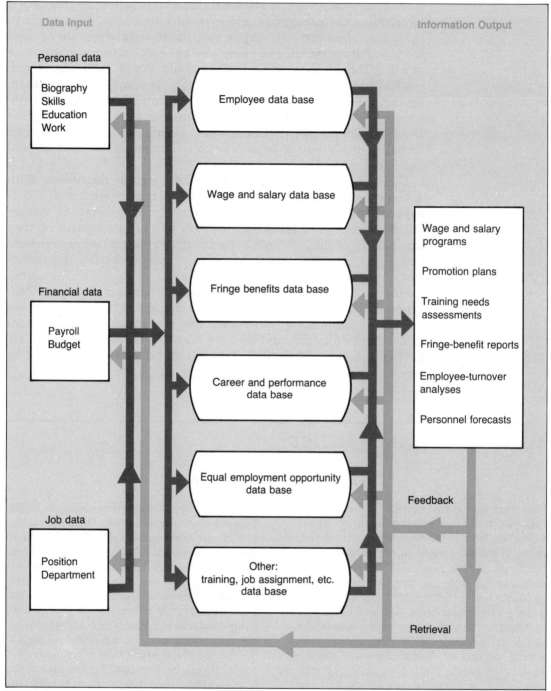

FIGURE 5-6   An example of an MIS

SOURCE   Lawrence J. Gitman and Carl McDaniel Jr., *Business World* (New York: Wiley, 1983): 182. Reprinted by permission.

COMPUTERS AND MIS

Because an MIS is likely to include a computer, its manager/users need to be somewhat computer literate. This does not mean that managers must become data-processing experts any more than it means that they must become professional accountants. But, just as managers need some accounting knowledge to understand and interpret financial reports, so they also need to know something about what computers can and cannot do. At the minimum, managers need to know enough about computers to make good decisions regarding their use.

Computers were first used in business firms in the early 1950s, shortly after they were developed. Early use was restricted to extremely mechanical, high-volume work like processing employee paycheques and keeping track of inventory. As computer technology improved, computer usage expanded in business. During the 1960s and 1970s, computer programs were developed to deal with frequently recurring routine decisions. We referred to these as programmed decisions earlier. Computers make fine tools for an MIS. Further changes in computer technology now occur with such tremendous speed that we cannot forsee uses that may eventually develop. Managers must be aware of such innovations and how they can benefit their organization in order to remain competitive.

Choosing a Computer for the MIS

Too many firms purchase or lease a computer and then attempt to design their MIS around the computer. If a computer is needed to provide accurate, timely, and useful information, the computer should be chosen on the basis of how well it converts raw data into useful information. Choosing a computer may not be an easy task, since a wide variety of computers is available. The selection should be made with the firm's specific needs in mind, to fit the design of its MIS.

There are three generally accepted categories of computer: microcomputers, minicomputers, and mainframe computers.

Microcomputers

microcomputer

The smallest version is the **microcomputer**. The availability of microcomputers has permitted many smaller firms to buy their own computer system. But microcomputers are not just for small businesses. Large corporations use thousands of them. Because of their flexibility, micros make the job of management much simpler. The microcomputer can be an invaluable tool for the busy executive; it can show financial trends, answer "what if" questions, and even keep the executive's calendar. Some managers who previously wrote memoranda in longhand now zip them out on the keyboard. Micros can give executives access to corporate data bases or sophisticated programs when they are hooked up to a mainframe system. They are used in research and development laboratories, on shop floors, and in hospitals. Microcomputers acquire data, take measurements, and control all kinds of processes in ways that greatly simplify manufacturing and production. They can be used in remote locations such as offshore oil well platforms. They also work well in adverse environments, such as on ships and airplanes. Micros can automatically change the settings of valves and other control devices in response to changes in physical conditions, such as pressure and temperature. Industrial robots often depend on microcomputers to help them do factory assembly operations formerly too complex for mechanization.

In every kind of organization and at every level, microcomputers simplify the job of administration. Traditional office paperwork is created and processed using computers. Because microcomputers can communicate with one another, many written reports and other documentation have actually been eliminated. Word processing software is available to assist in entering, arranging, correcting, retrieving, and printing all types of business information and correspondence.

Minicomputers

minicomputer

Between the mainframe computer and the microcomputer is the **minicomputer**. A mini may look much like a micro. Minis have faster internal processing speeds and larger memories. They are also likely to have a larger number of terminals and other peripheral devices. Minis were developed because they could meet particular needs at signficantly lower costs than could large computer systems. They are also much easier to install and have fewer environmental restrictions.

Mainframe Computers

mainframe
computers

At the upper end of the spectrum are **mainframe computers**, costing millions of dollars and capable of handling vast amounts of data. Included in this category are the IBM Model 158 and 168 and the Burroughs B7800 and B7900. Amdahl Corporation, Cray Research, and Control Data Corporation have developed huge "supercomputers" to meet the information-processing needs of such types of organizations as national laboratories, university research centers, financial service companies, and service bureaus. Many of these systems can do millions of computations per second. Simulation, design and engineering work, as well as applications requiring large data bases, can be handled effectively when large-computer capabilities are available.

The Impact of the Computer on Management

telecommuting

The rapid developments in computer technology are having an enormous impact on managerial decision making. Some computer equipment can be carried in a briefcase, permitting a manager to work almost anywhere. Computer hookups from office to home have added a new dimension to the work-at-home routine, called **telecommuting**. Moving the computer terminal into the home has permitted businesses to reach labor markets that might not otherwise be reached. However, managers must be trained to cope with this new working relationship. Some managers find it quite difficult to supervise workers they do not see regularly. Also, some workers find working at home an isolating experience because they are left out of office politics, gossip, and coffee breaks with friends.[14]

The office of the future is expected to change dramatically because of the computer. Specialized work stations are being created for professionals and managers.[15] These work stations should provide executives with access to information by the touch of a button.

In spite of the positive aspects of information synthesis offered by a computer, some middle and lower-level managers are worried. While it is true that they will be able to monitor their subordinates more effectively, they know that they in turn will be monitored more closely by their superiors. This monitoring could create anxiety and unhappiness, especially for managers who may be insecure about their positions. Some managers may dislike the fact they they must supply information to the MIS specialists rather than directly to their superiors. Such managers may feel a loss of control. Another potential problem for middle and lower-level managers is that the MIS allows top management to centralize decision making; some middle and lower-level managers may consider they have lost some discretion. It is also feared that a computerized MIS will actually do away with some managerial positions.

Top management does not share these concerns because generally it is benefiting from the MIS. The managers at the top of the firm with an effective MIS will be getting timely, accurate information about what is going on throughout the organization; they feel in control. As a result, they are usually favorably impressed by an MIS. However, top management should be aware of other managers' concerns and try to allay them.

OPENING INCIDENT REVISITED

Mackie Real Estate

The managers at Mackie Real Estate can use mathematical analysis to help decide which speculative investment to make. Since they are able to attach numbers to the important variables in the problem, they can use the kind of analysis that was used in the part-time job problem in this chapter.

The expected value of each of the three alternatives must be computed. For each alternative there is a chance of gaining — if the government later buys the block of land the company buys now — and a chance of losing — if the government does not choose the block of land the company buys. The general formula for expected value is: the probability of gaining multiplied by the amount won plus the probability of losing multiplied by the amount lost. The expected values for the three alternatives are:

Block 1 = 0.2(40) + 0.8 (5) = 12.0
Block 2 = 0.5(50) + 0.5(—25) = 12.5
Block 3 = 0.3(110) + 0.7(—35) = 11.5

Based on this simple analysis, Mackie should buy Block 2 because its expected value is the highest. However, other important factors must be taken into account. How much money does the company have to use for speculation?

In this case they have $100 000; so, they could buy both blocks 1 and 2 and have more of a chance than by buying only one block. Another factor concerns the relative risk preferences of the managers. Are they risk-takers or risk-averse? If they are risk-averse, they will buy Block 1, because they can't lose any money on it no matter what happens. If the Mackie managers are risk-takers, they will want to buy Block 3 because they can make the most money if the government chooses it. Another factor is lost investment opportunities elsewhere. Can this company invest its money and do even better elsewhere than it can with any of these three alternatives?

This brief analysis shows that even when the facts to make a decision are quantified, considerable uncertainty may still exist about what the best course of action is. Each decision will be affected by many variables and, likely, no two individuals would develop and analyze them in precisely the same way.

SUMMARY

Decision making is the process of evaluating alternatives and making a choice among them. One of the most important managerial jobs is making good decisions. Routine decisions are those that recur frequently. Nonroutine decisions are those made when managers deal with non-recurring, unusual situations.

Before a decision can be made, certain basic requirements must be satisfied. A decision must be made by a manager with the authority to implement it. Problem content, courses of action, and payoff relationships must be identified. A major consideration is identifying the probabilities in the state of nature for a particular decision.

There are two basic approaches to making decisions. The intuitive approach relies on experience rather than a formal reasoning process. Alternatives are judged on the basis of whether or not they will work. Intuition has several shortcomings, the major one being that a person may not learn from experience. The other approach is a systematic one using the scientific method. This involves observing events, formulating hypotheses, and testing those hypotheses. Professional decision makers use the best features of both of these approaches.

The rational decision-making process is made up of three major phases: (1) the problem analysis phase — determining exactly what the problem is; (2) the decision making phase — deciding how to resolve the problem; and (3) the implementation phase — putting the solution into effect. Factors which influence the decision making process include the time available to make the decision, the level of risk inherent in the decision, the degree to which the decision maker is accepted by others, the decision maker's ability, and organizational politics.

There are many decision-making techniques which are available to help managers make decisions. Decision matrices are useful whenever a choice is to be made between alternatives with multiple characteristics. Decision trees can be used when payoffs are quantified and probabilities can be stated with some confidence. Brainstorming is an idea-generating technique whereby a number of persons present alternatives without regard to their feasibility or practicality. Nominal grouping involves unrestrained idea generation by individual group members followed by presentation of those ideas without discussion. This is followed by group discussion to clarify and evaluate the ideas, and the final decision is made on the basis of individual ranking of each alternative. The Delphi technique is a formal procedure for obtaining consensus among a number of experts through the use of a series of questionnaires.

A management information system (MIS) is an organized way of obtaining information on which to base management decisions. The MIS should be designed to provide information with the following characteristics: timely, accurate, available, concise, relevant, and complete. The general steps that should facilitate the development of a useful MIS include: (1) study the present system, (2) develop a priority of information, (3) develop the information system, and (4) choose a computer.

REVIEW QUESTIONS

1. Define and discuss the process of making decisions. How important is it to a manager?
2. Distinguish between personal decisions and professional decisions. Why are managers expected to be professional decision makers?
3. What five factors must be present before a decision can be made?
4. What is the difference between the intuitive approach and the systematic approach to decision making? Which approach is better?
5. What are the three major phases in the decision-making process? What does each one involve?
6. What is the main advantage in using systematic decision-making methods such as the weights and criteria method and decision trees? What is the main disadvantage?

7. What effect do risk, time, and organization politics have on managers when making decisions?
8. What is an MIS? Discuss some benefits and some potential disadvantages of using a computer in an MIS.
9. What is telecommuting? How might it affect organizations if its use increases?

EXERCISES

1. List five decisions that you made today. Did you use a systematic approach, or did you rely on intuition? Why did you use the approach you used?
2. Develop a decision-making problem in which there are three courses of action and two states of nature. (Remember that the probabilities must total 1.0.) Solve the problem using a decision tree. Would you have made the same decision using intuition?
3. Interview a manager who has recently made an important decision. Ask the manager to describe each step that was used in the process. Is the process the manager used consistent with the decision-making process illustrated in Figure 5-2? If not, why not?

CASE STUDY

Maintenance Expenses

"You've got a problem and I want you to make a decision about it," said George LeBeau, manager of distribution for *The Daily Herald*. The remark was directed at Tom Sifton, supervisor of the truck drivers who deliver the newspapers to the surrounding towns and local drop-off stations. There are 30 drivers who drive the delivery trucks, sometimes hundreds of miles in one day.

LeBeau continued, "I've been watching the maintenance costs on the trucks and right now our costs are up 20 percent over last year. I've already talked with the maintenance foreman and he assures me that the same maintenance programs are being followed this year as last. That means your drivers are responsible for the increased costs. What do you propose to do about it?"

"I'm not sure," replied Sifton.

"What do you mean you're not sure?" said LeBeau. "The facts speak for themselves. You

certainly can't argue with the facts now, can you?"

"Well, I still have some checking to do before I can decide," said Sifton.

"I can't see what checking there is to do. You've got to come to a decision quickly before the V.P. has us both in on the carpet. I just know in my bones he's seen the same figures," said LeBeau. "He will want to know what we're doing about the increased costs, so you give me a decision by this time tomorrow."

"I'll do my best," replied Sifton, as he walked out of LeBeau's office.

QUESTIONS

1. Comment on LeBeau's handling of this situation. What about Sifton's?
2. Use the decision-making process in Figure 5-2 to analyze this situation. Make suggestions about what LeBeau and Sifton should do.

CASE STUDY

A Request for Special Favors

Bill Paquette is the manager of the payroll department at Plains Insurance Company. Bill reports to the company comptroller. A major function of the department is processing the biweekly payroll for the more than 1000 employees of the company. The work load in payroll is oriented toward tasks and deadlines. The work load is even more demanding during holiday periods, such as Thanksgiving, Christmas, and New Year's.

At the beginning of December, Betty Friesen, a 20-year-old clerk, informs Paquette that she needs to take a week of vacation between Christmas and New Year's in order to "visit her family during the holidays." Since the payroll is processed every other week, it has been customary for the payroll department manager and clerical personnel to schedule vacations during the weeks that the payroll is not processed. Betty, an efficient worker, has been employed since March and became eligible for one week of vacation in October. (An employee is eligible for one week of vacation after 6 months, or for two weeks on the completion of one year.) At the time Friesen was hired, specific vacation arrangements were not discussed, only the minimum time for eligibility.

Friesen's request for a one-week vacation during the holiday period will make it difficult for the payroll department to meet its deadlines. The department will lose two days during the period because Christmas Eve and Christmas Day are holidays. Paquette is concerned about getting the payroll processed that week; with Friesen away, the deadlines will be more difficult to meet.

Paquette and Friesen discussed work load requirements during the week in question. He told her the department needs her effort that week, particularly since it is a short week. Friesen responded by saying: "My husband has made plans for us to go and he says we're going." Paquette considers Friesen a satisfactory worker, but wonders about her commitment to the job and company. He is also concerned about the effect on other members of the department if he approves Friesen's vacation request.

QUESTIONS

1. What decision should Bill Paquette make regarding Betty Friesen's request for vacation? Demonstrate how Paquette could make the decision using the decision-making process developed in this chapter.
2. In making the decision, what additional situational factors should be considered, other than the fact that Friesen intends to take the time off against the wishes of her supervisor?

CASE STUDY

Northlands Hospital

You are a director at Northlands General Hospital, which currently employs 450 nurses. One of the problems you are facing is that you do not have enough nursing coordinators to adequately supervise the clinical staff in your area. You have therefore decided to hire another nursing coordinator. Staff procedures at Northlands require that the job be posted and that résumés be collected and analyzed before a person is chosen for the job. Both internal and external candidates may be considered. The process is now at the stage where you must analyze the three resumes you have received.

You could promote Jenny Barnes (B.N.). She

is 41, married, with one child. She has worked in your area for 11 years. Jenny is familiar with all the nursing staff in your unit, and she has a good working knowledge of the clinical area. She is well liked by everyone and is available to start immediately. She has no supervisory experience per se, but she is sincere, reliable, and would certainly like to get the $2000 raise that goes with the job (she currrently earns $29 000 per year). Your evaluation of Jenny after interviewing her was summarized as follows: "Jenny seems very friendly and cooperative and quite happy with her job. She feels that her greatest strengths are her knowledge of the clinical area and her ability to get along with people.

A second candidate, George Heddon (R.N., B.N.), has been identified by your personnel department. George is 55, single, and is currently a nursing coordinator at a hospital in Vancouver. He has over 20 years experience and comes well recommended. You met him a few weeks ago at a conference in Calgary and were impressed by his credentials, personality, and ambition. If you opt for George as your nursing coordinator, you'll have to wait thirty days since he'll need that much time to wrap up his current job and his personal affairs. You'll have to assume half of his $2000 relocation expense. Since he's already at a supervisory level, he'll require a raise from $30 000 to $34 000.

The third candidate is Marlene Rempel (R.N.). She is 32 and is divorced. She is currently working at another hospital in the city, and has been in that position for four years. She has some supervisory duties in her present job. In checking into her references, you have found that she is considered to be the most capable nurse in the hospital where she works. She is highly qualified from a technical perspective, and she has a reputation for being very up-to-date on new developments in patient care. She is outgoing, cheerful, and very confident. She has strong views on the critical role of nurses in proper patient care, and she can be somewhat argumentative with doctors regarding some aspects of patient care. Marlene is available in 60 days, and she will have to be paid $27 000.

QUESTIONS

1. Which person should be chosen for the job? What technique is most appropriate for making this decision? Why?
2. What other information might you want to have before making this decision?

ENDNOTES

[1]Theodore Levitt, "The Managerial Merry-Go-Round," *Harvard Business Review* 52 (July-August 1974): 120.

[2]First four items adapted from Alvar O. Elbing, *Behavioral Decision in Organizations* (Glenview, Ill.: Scott, Foresman, 1970): 14.

[3]Ralph C. Davis, *The Fundamentals of Top Management* (New York: Harper, 1951): 55.

[4]The most impressive analysis of this phase of the process appears in C. Kepner and B. Tregoe, *The Rational Manager: A Systematic Approach to Problem Solving and Decision Making* (Princeton: Kepner-Tregoe, Inc., 1976).

[5]See the discussion of individual and group decision making later in this chapter for a formal statement of this idea.

[6]A. L. Delbecq and A. H. Van de Ven, "Group Process Model for Problem Identification and Program Planning," *Journal of Applied Behavioral Science* 7 (1971): 466–492.

[7]C. R. Holloman and H. W. Hendrick, "Adequacy of Group Decisions As a Function of the Decision Making Process," *Academy of Management Journal* 15 (1972): 175–184.

[8]Norman R. F. Maier, "Assets and Liabilities in Group Problem Solving: The Need for an Integrative Function," *Psychological Review* 74 (1967): 239–249.

[9]For a review of this problem, see J. D. Steiner, *Group Process and Productivity* (New York: Academic Press, 1971); also J. Rohrbaugh, "Improving the Quality of Group Judgment, Social Judgment Analysis, and the Delphi Technique," *Organizational Behavior and Human Performance* 24 (1979): 73–92.

[10]J. Rohrbaugh, "Improving the Quality of Group Judgments."

[11]Irving Janis, *Victims of Groupthink* (Boston: Houghton Mifflin, 1972).

[12]Robert G. Murdick, "MIS Development Procedures," *Journal of Systems Management* 21, no. 12 (December 1970): 22–26.

[13]Russell L. Ackhoff, "Management Misinformation Systems," *Management Science* (December 1967): 147–156.

[14]"The Potential For Telecommuting," *Business Week* (January 26, 1981): 94.

[15]"Will The Boss Go Electronics, Too?" *Business Week* (May 11, 1981): 106.

REFERENCES

Archer, Earnest R. "How to Make a Business Decision: An Analysis of Theory and Practice". *Management Review* 69 (February 1980): 54–61.

Bass, Bernard M. *Organizational Decision Making.* Homewood Ill.: Richard D. Irwin, 1983.

Brown, Rex V. "Do Managers Find Decision Theory Useful?" *Harvard Business Review* 51 (May-June 1970): 78–89.

Daniel, D. W. "What Influences a Decision? Some Results from a Highly Controlled Defense Game." *Omega* 8 (November 1980): 409–419.

Donaldson, Gordon. *Decision Making At The Top.* New York: Basic Books 1983.

Fischoff, Baruch, and Goitein, Bernard. "The Informal Use of Formal Models." *Academy of Management Review* 9, no. 3 (July 1984): 505–512.

Grayson, C. Jackson, Jr. "Management Science and Business Practice." *Harvard Business Review* 51 (July-August 1973): 41–48.

Grindlay, Andrew, "MIS Organization: Perhaps It's Time to Change." *Business Quarterly* 48, no. 4 (Winter 1983): 9–17.

Grove, Andrew, S. "Decisions, Decisions." *Canadian Business* 57, no. 2 (February 1984): 62.

Harrision, J. Richard, and March, James G. "Decision Making and Post-decision Surprises." *Administrative Science Quarterly* 29, no. 1 (March 1984): 26–41.

Henderson, John C. "Influence of Decision Style on Decision Making Behaviour." *Management Science* 26 (April 1980): 371–386.

Hogarth, Robin M., and Mankridakis, Spyors. "Value of Decision Making in a Complex Environment — An Experimental Approach." *Management Science* 27 (January 1981): 93–107.

Hughes, Robard Y. "A Realistic Look at Decision Making." *Supervisory Management* 25, no. 1 (January 1980): 2–8.

Kirby, Peter G. "Quality Decisions Start with Good Questions." *Supervisory Management* 25, no. 8 (August 1980): 2–7.

Magrum, Claude T. "Determining the Right Regimen of Managerial Exercises." *Supervisory Management* 26, no. 2 (February 1981): 26–30.

McCall, Morgan, and Kaplan, Robert. *Whatever It Takes: Decision Makers at Work.* Englewood Cliffs, N.J.: Prentice-Hall, 1985.

McKenny, J. L. and Keen, P.G.W. "How Managers' Minds Work." *Harvard Business Review* 52, no. 3 (May-June 1974): 79–90.

Mayer, Alan D. "Mingling Decision Making Metaphors." *Academy of Management Review* 9, no. 1 (January 1984): 6–17.

Motherwell, Catheryn, "No Office Grind, No Office Laughs." *The Globe and Mail* (April 27, 1987): B1, B11.

Munro, Malcolm, and Wand, Yair. "On Empirical MIS Research: The Case of Information Requirements Analysis." *Canadian Journal of Administrative Sciences* 3, (December 1986): 359–375.

Pitz, Gordon F. Sachs, Natalie J.; and Heerboth, Joel. "Procedures for Eliciting Choices in the Analysis of Individual Decisions." *Organizational Behaviour and Human Performance* 26, no. 3 (December 1980): 396–408.

Roy, Delwin A., and Simpson, Claude A. "Export Attitudes of Business Executives in a Smaller Manufacturing Firm." *Journal of Small Business Management* 19 (April 1981): 16–22.

Simon, Herbert A. *The New Science of Management Decision.* rev. ed. Englewood Cliffs, N. J.: Prentice-Hall, 1977.

_____. "Rational Decision Making in Business Organization." *American Economic Review* 69, no. 4 (September 1979): 493–513.

_____. "Making Management Decisions." *Academy of Management Executive,* (February 1987): 57–64.

Tjosvald, Dean. "Effects of Crisis Orientation on Manager's Approach to Controversy in Decision Making." *Academy of Management Journal* 27, no. 1 (March 1984): 130–138.

Trevino, Linda. "Ethical Decision Making in Organizations: a Person-Situation Interactionist Model." *Academy of Management Review* 11, (July 1986): 601–617.

Vroom, Victor H. "A New Look at Managerial Decision Making." *Organizational Dynamics* 1, no. 4 (Spring 1973): 66–80.

Wanous, John, and Youtz, Margaret. "Solution Diversity and the Quality of Group Decisions." *Academy of Management Journal* 29, (March 1986): 149–158.

Wright, Peter. "The Harrassed Decision Maker: Time Pressures, Distractions, and the Use of Evidence." *Journal of Applied Psychology* 59, no. 5 (October 1974): 555–561.

III

Organizing

6

The Organizing Process

LEARNING OBJECTIVES

After completing this chapter you should be able to
1. Define and describe the organizing process.
2. Describe a function and specialization in terms of organizational structure, and identify the benefits and limitations of specialization.
3. Describe and give examples of the process of vertical and horizontal differentiation.
4. Describe functional similarity and identify the factors that determine the extent to which it can be applied.
5. Identify and describe the primary means of departmentation.

OPENING INCIDENT

Richter's Hardware Stores

Karl Richter grew up in Winnipeg's North End. He exhibited an entrepreneurial attitude early in life and, by the time he graduated from university with a degree in marketing, he had already been involved in several small-scale operations. He returned home after graduation in 1964 to take over his father's hardware store and to refine his entrepreneurial skills. He thought this would give him an opportunity to put into practice some ideas he had learned at university.

Richter threw himself into work with great vigor. After carefully analyzing the Winnipeg market, he added some completely new product lines, expanded others, and discontinued some altogether. He streamlined record-keeping by instituting a mechanized data processing system. Within three years, profits and sales had increased dramatically. Encouraged by this success, Richter opened two new stores in Winnipeg in 1967. These were also successful and, by 1970, the company employed 51 people. (See Figure 6-1.)

Richter decided to expand farther west in the next few years, since the Winnipeg market was getting saturated. He branched out regionally to include such cities as Brandon, Portage La Prairie, Dauphin, and Regina. By 1980, the company employed 103 people at 16 different locations. Richter observed that these regionally dispersed stores were reasonably successful, but not as profitable as the new Winnipeg Stores.

Over the next several years the company expanded to include Saskatoon, Calgary, and Edmonton. By 1984, the company had 29 stores and 203 employees. At this point, difficulties began to crop up. The financial statements for 1984 showed that the company overall was still making a profit, but far below expectations. Richter therefore called a meeting of the three vice-presidents to get their views on what was wrong.

The meeting was not pleasant. All three complained that in the last several years their jobs had become almost impossible. The marketing

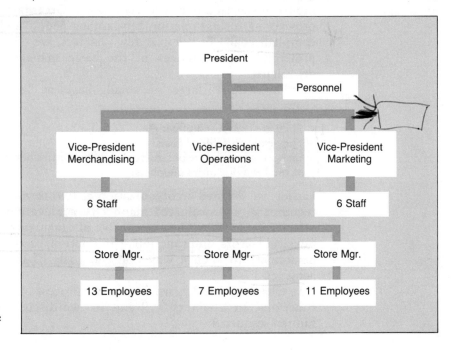

FIGURE 6-1
Richter's hardware
stores

vice-president complained that she was forced to spend promotion money in new markets that she really didn't know much about. She noted that her travel expenses were up considerably. The merchandising vice-president complained that he was unsure about what product lines to carry in the different regions. He implied that the marketing vice-president didn't seem interested in cooperating with merchandising. He noted several sales ads that had recently appeared in local papers for products the company didn't even have in stock. The marketing vice-president retorted that it wasn't her job to coordinate the two functions.

The operations vice-president wasn't happy either. He claimed that regional store managers paid little attention to his suggestions for store operations. The regional store managers pointed out that the operations vice-president didn't have any knowledge about their local markets and that he shouldn't try to impose unreasonable ideas on them from the head office.

Richter listened to these and other complaints for three hours. He heard of discord among members of the top management team and apathy among employees at the retail outlet. Head office employees in the marketing, operations, and merchandising functions seemed reasonably content, but some couldn't see how their particular job fit into the total scheme.

Richter knew the company could not survive financially if it had another couple of years like the last one. After the meeting with his vice-presidents, he was concerned about the satisfaction and motivation levels of his employees.

The managerial function of organizing is important for all types of organizations — universities, military units, churches, hospitals, government agencies, or manufacturers. Once the objectives and plans have been developed and stated, managers must organize; they must design a structure that will bring together human resources and inputs to function in an orderly manner. **Organizing** is the process of prescribing formal relationships among people and resources to accomplish goals. In the next few chapters, we discuss the concepts, principles, and practices of the basic management function of organizing.

organizing

Organizations, large or small, have at least three common characteristics:

1. • They are composed of people.
2. • They exist to achieve goals.
3. • Each has some degree of structure that results in a definition and limitation of the behavior of its members.

Earlier, we defined an organization as two or more people working together in a coordinated manner to achieve certain goals. To be effective, managers must be capable of organizing human resources, physical factors, and functions (production, marketing, finance, and personnel) in such a way that the goals of the organization are achieved.

In Chapters 6 and 7, we discuss the process of organizing through functions. In Chapters 8, 9 and 10, we discuss the organizing of human resources.

OBJECTIVES

As Figure 6-2 illustrates, organizing is a three-step process. It begins, just as planning does, with a consideration of the overall objectives of the organization. On the basis of these objectives, managers must

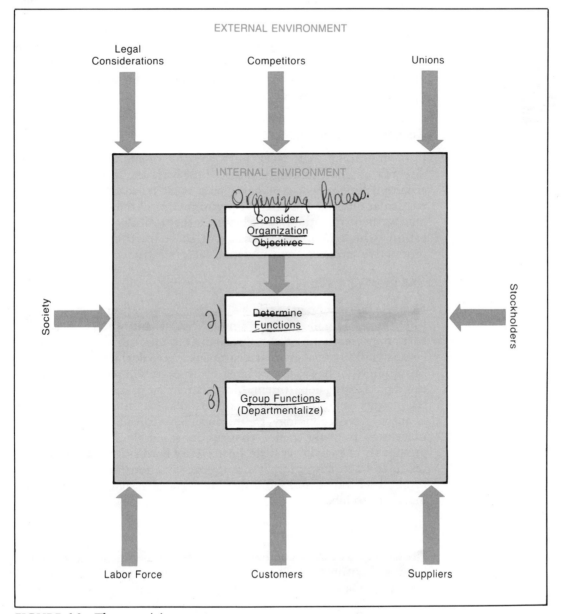

FIGURE 6-2   The organizing process

2 determine the functions or activities necessary to the organization. 3 Finally, the appropriate departments must be set up to execute the required tasks.

Everything the manager does should be directed toward goal accomplishment. Organizing is no exception. It should have as its purpose arranging people and resources in the best way possible to support the organization's objectives. Consider a drug store chain whose major purpose is to earn high profits through discount merchandising. This purpose dictates that the organization be able to respond quickly to competitors while keeping internal costs at a minimum. There is no room, for example, for four or five levels of highly paid managers. A typical store manager might direct a number of moderately paid department supervisors who not only manage groups of workers but do work themselves.

Environmental Factors

It is important that every phase of the organizing sequence be directed at goal accomplishment; however, the approach to goal accomplishment that a manager uses must be compatible with the particular internal and external environments of the firm. Otherwise, management runs the risk of having a theoretically effective organization, which in practice turns out to be inefficient or counterproductive, because environmental factors intrude.

The External Environment

External environmental effects on the organization include things like laws and public concern about clean air and water. These pressures may create the need for personnel to monitor any substances a company discharges. Also, if a company has to deal with a wide range of suppliers, or has to buy in large volumes, it will require a sophisticated purchasing department. More than in the past, rapidly changing technology can influence an organization's structure. Recent changes in automotive technology, for instance, have forced automobile manufacturers to make major changes in assembly lines, which had previously changed very little since Henry Ford's time. As changes in the manufacturing process occur, organizations must be able to respond with new and more flexible ways of assigning persons and machines to jobs.

The Internal Environment

Organizing to attain company objectives is also influenced by the internal environment. The boss's view of the company's strategic and operating plans will often limit the way a manager can organize resources to carry out those plans. Such personal preferences on the part of upper management may not actually be stated in the official mission statement, but anyone working within an organization must be aware of these factors. It is well known at Chrysler Corporation that Lee Iacocca places emphasis on product quality as well as on low cost. Therefore, managers at Chrysler must create organizational units that tightly control quality *and* contain no "extra fat", in the form of additional management levels or positions.

The more management takes external and internal environmental factors into consideration, the less likely these factors are to intrude. Foresight at this stage of the organizing process can help to avoid more serious problems in setting functions and departmentalizing, the two subsequent stages in the process.

FUNCTIONS

function

Once objectives have been established, the organizing process begins. Managers determine the types of functions or work that must be performed within the organization. A **function** is a type of work activity that can be identified and distinguished from other work activities. On a hockey team, several distinct functions must be performed effectively if the team is to win games. Players perform the functions of checking, shooting, penalty-killing, defending, and goal-keeping. A good team has specialists for each of these activities. A baseball team needs a pitching staff consisting of starters, short-relievers, long-relievers, and a stopper. Infielders and outfielders specialize in defense at a particular position, like first base or short-stop, but must also perform well offensively. Most teams also hire specialists for both batting and running bases.

Basic work functions can be defined in any organization. The major functions of a manufacturer are production, marketing, and finance. For a retailing company, the basic functions are buying and selling of merchandise and extending credit. The major functions in a bank include depositing or receiving customers' money and making loans to borrowers. At a university or college, teaching, research, and service are the primary functions that must be performed.

However, saying that the primary functions at a retail store are buying and selling does not provide an adequate basis for organizing a store. Selling sporting goods is certainly different from selling lingerie. It is appropriate to consider these as two separate functions. There are also a number of supporting functions that require special

MANAGEMENT IN PRACTICE

The Organizing Process at CSL

Bruce Lougheed was a systems engineering manager for 10 years with a major computer company; recently, he resigned his position to form a computer services company, which he has named Computer Systems, Limited (CSL). Lougheed and two partners, Gerry Zakus and Marion Spence, are making plans to develop a computer services firm specializing in the development, installation, and maintenance of computer software systems for life insurance companies.

The goal for CSL is to provide high-quality, specialized computer services to life insurance companies at a profit. After establishing the objectives for the new company, the three partners determine that the functions CSL must accomplish include: systems engineering and design, programming development, and the installation and maintenance of computer systems. Based on these functions, the human resources required for CSL are: highly trained systems analysts, computer programmers, and marketing personnel, as well as a clerical support staff. In addition to the personnel required, physical resources such as capital, computer equipment, office space, and office furnishings are essential. The partners must determine not only the type of personnel needed but also the number of specialists

needed for each major function. Recruiting will be Zakus's major task. In addition, the company must secure sufficient capital, from banks, shareholders or other sources, to begin and continue operations. Spence will be responsible for finding the funds to lease office space, purchase or lease equipment, employ and compensate personnel, and pay for supplies.

Lougheed realizes that he must coordinate the functions and the physical and human resources into a workable, organizational structure. He decides that three departments are needed: (1) systems design and programming, (2) installation and maintenance, and (3) marketing. In this newly formed company, personnel will perform a wide variety of tasks; but, as CSL grows, they will perform more limited, specialized functions. Once the functions have been grouped into a coordinated organizational structure, Lougheed will assign appropriate levels of responsibility, authority, and accountability to all employees. The final phase of the organizing function is the assignment of specific work activities. For instance, the marketing manager must call on potential customers, design promotion and advertising, and recruit and train sales personnel.

---

skills. For example, store buildings must be maintained, shelves must be stocked, money must be collected from the cash registers, and someone must approve checks. In other words, functions must be described in great detail. Generalities will not suffice.

Specialization of Labor

In his 1776 book, *The Wealth of Nations*, Adam Smith explained how he was able to increase the productivity of a group of pin makers more than a thousand-fold through specialization (division) of labor. **Specialization of labor** means the division of a complex job into simpler tasks so that one person or group may carry out only identical

specialization
of labor

or related activities. A purpose of organizing, like everything else the manager does, is to improve productivity, and specialization of labor is one way of achieving this. Specialization is particularly efficient in mass-production industries. In fact, though, most work activities performed in most organizations are of a specialized nature. A stocker in a Safeway store, for example, normally would not be expected to operate a cash register.

Organizations have endless options as to the degree of specialization associated with each job. For instance, if a company produces small transistor radios, several different approaches might be available:

- Each employee may assemble the entire radio (low specialization).
- Each employee may assemble one component of the radio (moderate specialization).
- Each employee may perform a few routine operations such as putting the knobs on for tuner and volume control (high specialization).

Advantages of Specialization

Specialization, or work simplification, offers the following advantages:

- Allows workers to concentrate skills on a narrow range of work, thus increasing work output.
- Permits managers to supervise a large number of employees.
- Facilitates the selection and training of workers to perform identical activities, so that jobs can be learned in less time.
- Leads to more efficient utilization of workers because they can develop and practice specialized skills.
- Contributes to consistently better quality in products or services.
- Facilitates the achievement of complex goals.

A worker who is able to concentrate skill and effort on a small number of tasks can usually achieve a higher level of output than a worker who must perform a large number of tasks. In manufacturing electronic components, output per worker tends to be much higher when employees perform highly specialized work activities. Similarly, high performance results are apparent in many fast-food restaurants where employees perform specialized functions, such as cooking hamburgers or french fries, in contrast to more traditional restaurants where employees perform a wide variety of jobs.[1]

In addition to higher output, specialization may permit a manager to supervise a larger number of employees. A manager may be able to supervise 30 to 50 workers who perform the same specialized tasks. If workers perform diverse tasks, the number of employees a manager can supervise effectively is fewer.

Generally, a more specialized job can be learned more quickly than a job involving numerous work activities. When training time is reduced, workers become productive at a faster rate. For instance, the time required to train a worker to cook french fries or prepare milkshakes is minimal compared to the time required to learn all the jobs performed in a fast-food restaurant.

Work simplification leads to a more efficient utilization of employees because they can develop and practice their specialized skills. A worker can be more efficient and produce more by concentrating on one or a few activities. A professional football player is usually a highly trained specialist; rarely does one player perform more than a few specialized activities. Most place kickers in professional football specialize only in kicking extra points and field goals. Quarterbacks, linemen, and running backs all specialize in what they do best. By specializing, the players continually refine and improve their individual skills.

Specialization contributes to consistently higher-quality products and services. In an age of specialization, most people are employed as specialists. Many students who choose to pursue a degree or diploma in business administration specialize in accounting, computer science, finance, management, or marketing.

Finally, specialization facilitates the achievement of complex goals. The successful completion of any complex project usually requires many different specialists. For example, the development of Canada's oil resources in the oceans or the prairie tar sands would not be possible without the work of thousands of specialists. A large amount of knowledge about ecology, climate, production processes, and extraction techniques is critical to the success of Canada's energy plans.

Disadvantages of Specialization

Despite the advantages of the specialization of labor, its application may not always be desirable. In fact certain jobs have become oversimplified. Too much specialization in the design of jobs may create boredom and fatigue among employees; for example, most people would find it difficult to work on an assembly line tightening bolts 1000 times a day. Typically, the highest degree of specialization is found in assembly line work, which sometimes results in high employee turnover, absenteeism, and a deteriorating quality of output. These negative consequences of specialization may cause an increase in operational costs.

Another disadvantage of specialization is that it can cause employees and managers to become too involved in their own area of specialization. When people in organizations work at highly specialized jobs, they may fail to see the overall objectives of the organization. Specialization can also lead people to think that their specific function is the most important, when, in fact, all the different functions must be integrated and coordinated to be effective.

Specialization has been well-entrenched in Canada for many years because Frederick Taylor's scientific management ideas have had a major impact on managers. Some companies, however, are finding that specialization doesn't always lead to higher productivity. Many of them are begining to experiment with alternative ways to achieve high productivity. Currently, the most popular approach is *job enrichment*, in which jobs are designed so that workers do a larger, not a smaller, part of a function. We discuss job enrichment further in Chapter 11.

DEPARTMENTATION

departmentation

The process of grouping related functions or major work activities into manageable units is known as **departmentation**. The purpose of departmentation is to contribute to the more effective and efficient use of resources. In this section, we will first discuss how functions should be grouped in an organization. Then, common types of departments will be described.

Grouping Similar Functions

Ideally, each department or division in the organization should be made up of people performing similar tasks. This is the concept of functional similarity, which guides us in the creation of sections, departments, and divisions. Jobs with similar objectives and requirements are grouped to form a section. A person with the background necessary to supervise these functions effectively should be assigned as the manager. For example, a construction company might employ a plumbing crew, an electrical crew, and so forth. Each different crew performs a group of related functions. At a restaurant chain, the data processing section performs only tasks involving computers and does not become involved in other functions, like managing the restaurants.

As important as functional similarity is, there are a number of factors that affect our ability to achieve it throughout the organization. Several of these are discussed below.

Sufficient Volume of Work

Sometimes the volume of work is inadequate to allow specialization. In small firms, personnel have to cope with a wide assortment of jobs. But with increases in volume, the concept of functional similarity can be applied more rigorously. For example, let us compare the operations of a small grocery store with those of a large supermarket. In the small store, one person might perform such functions as stocking shelves, working in the produce section, checking, and bagging groceries. In the large supermarket, personnel will tend to specialize in one or only a few of the basic functions. It is common to have individual managers of the produce section and of the stocking, checking, and bagging functions.

Tradition, Preferences, and Work Rules

Although two tasks may be similar, traditions, work rules, and personal preferences may prevent their assignment to the same individual. For example, installing electrical conduit (the steel pipe that protects electrical wire) is quite similar to running water piping; however, few plumbers would be willing to run conduit, and electricians would usually object to installing water pipes. This is because of the set of behavioral expectations, duties, and responsibilities that individuals associate with a given position.[2] In unionized organizations, formal work rules often prohibit the assignment of plumbers to electrical work or electricians to plumbing and other such violations of tradition.

Functions Similar to Others in the Organization

A third complicating factor is that a particular function is often similar to several other functions. For example, inventory control would appear to fit logically with the purchasing function. The purchasing department buys the material and thus has need for records of inventory levels; however, production uses these materials and in scheduling, must work with these same inventory records. Inventory control could be placed in either section.

Separation of Functions to Prevent Conflicts of Interest

Sometimes similar functions are not combined because doing so might create conflicts of interest. Quality control is intimately involved in production; inspectors frequently work side by side with production employees. The inspector, however, should not be unduly influenced by the production manager's interest in quantity and costs. Thus, inspection, although similar to production, should be separate from production to protect its independence.

Combining Dissimilar Functions to Allow Coordination

Finally, there are occasions when two dissimilar functions must be combined for purposes of effective action and control. Although purchasing is clearly different from selling in a factory organization, buying and selling are so interdependent in department stores that one person is often made responsible for both. The theory is that a well-bought dress or hat is half-sold.

Bases of Departmentation

There is no standard way to divide an organization into departments. Even companies in the same industry often have vastly different kinds of departments; however, it is possible to identify five bases on which departmentation normally occurs. The resulting kinds of departments are: (1) functional, (2) product, (3) customer, (4) geographic territory, and (5) project.

Departmentation by Function

Departmentation by function is perhaps the most common means of grouping related functions. (See Figure 6-3.) Departments are formed on the basis of specialized functions, such as production, marketing, engineering, finance, or personnel. Departmentation by function helps managers to use efficiently the resources of the organization. However, it can also create problems for managers, in the sense that employees may become more concerned with their own department than with the overall company. Departmentation by function is especially useful for firms whose external environment is stable and where technical efficiency and quality are important.[3]

Departmentation by Product

The product basis of departmentation is used when top management wants to emphasize product lines. This type of departmentation enhances the use of specialized knowledge of particular products or services and is often used by large companies that have diverse products. For example, a large electronics firm might be organized into three product divisions, as shown in Figure 6-4.

Firms manufacturing and selling technologically complex products are often structured this way.[4] Since 1916, General Motors has been divided into five product divisions: Chevrolet, Pontiac, Oldsmobile, Buick, and Cadillac. Because of what GM executives call "creeping complexity," the company recently reorganized into only two divisions — one comprised of Chevrolet, Pontiac, and GM Canada and a

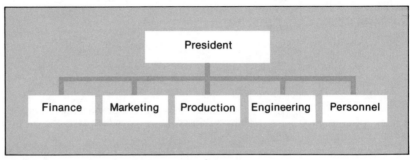

FIGURE 6-3   Departmentation by function

FIGURE 6-4
Departmentation
by product

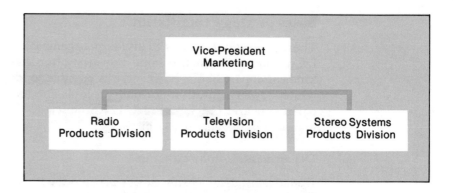

second comprised of Buick, Cadillac, and Oldsmobile. Small cars will be designed and manufactured by the first division and intermediate and large cars by the second division.[5]

Departmentation by Customer

Departmentation by customer is used by organizations that have a special need to provide high quality service to different kinds of customers. As illustrated in Figure 6-5, a manufacturing company might have industrial, government, and consumer products divisions. Large retailers and banks use customer departmentation, because businesses and members of the general public require different services from such organizations.

Departmentation by Geographic Territory

Departmentation according to geographic territory is used by organizations that have physically dispersed and/or independent operations or markets to serve. The marketing function of the company shown in Figure 6-6 is organized into the Western, Central, and Atlantic regional divisions. Geographic departmentation offers the advantages of better service from local or regional personnel, often at less cost.

FIGURE 6-5
Departmentation
by customer

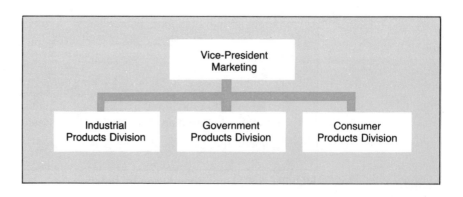

FIGURE 6-6
Departmentation by
geographic territory

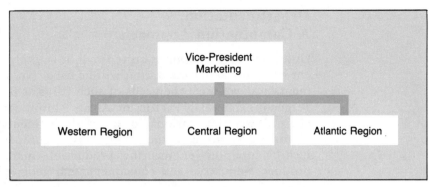

Departmentation by Project

When the work of an organization consists of a continuing series of major projects, departmentation by project is normally used. This is especially common in the construction and aerospace industries. Figure 6-7 shows how a typical construction operation might be departmentalized. In this example, each project superintendent is responsible for a separate contract under the direction of the general superintendent. Such an organization changes frequently as projects are completed and new ones started. The superintendent who is now in charge of Project A may transfer to a new project or back to headquarters or be laid off when Project A is finished. In addition, the plumbing supervisor currently working on Project A may move to Project C when the plumbing on Project A is complete. We discuss project departmentation in more detail in Chapter 7.

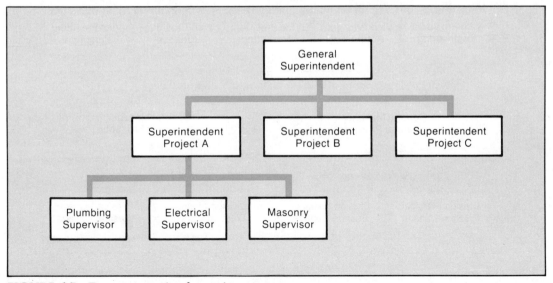

FIGURE 6-7   Departmentation by project

Departmentation:
A Combination Approach

Unless the organization is quite small, it is likely that several different bases for departmentation will be used. No one form of departmentation can meet the needs of such firms as Bell Canada, Massey Ferguson, Canadian Pacific, or Alcan Aluminum. An organization chart illustrating various forms of departmentation is shown in Figure 6-8. In this case, the manufacturing company is departmentalized by function (engineering, production, marketing, and so on), product (industrial and consumer), and geographic territory. The precise form of departmentation a firm chooses must be based on its particular needs.

DIFFERENTIATION

In a newly formed small organization, an owner/manager usually performs all the major functions of the business, such as providing the necessary financing, procuring materials, designing the product, and making and selling the product. As the volume of business grows,

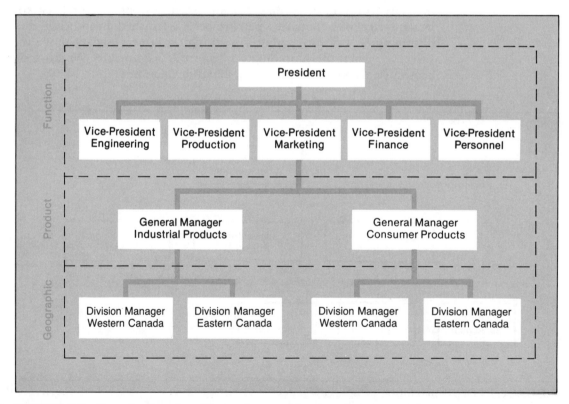

FIGURE 6-8   Organization chart illustrating combination departmentation

MANAGEMENT IN PRACTICE

Departmentation in Practice

In practice, it may or may not be easy to decide what basis of departmentation a company is using. Consumers Distributing, for example, is organized at the top level as shown in Figure 6-9. This firm is clearly organized using departmentation by function; the key functions that the company must perform (store operations, finance, or development) are the basis for the various departments.

The basis for departmentation is not as clear at Continental Group of Canada Ltd. There are elements of both functional departmentation (finance, operations) and product departmentation (metal products and automotive). (See Figure 6-10.) This combination of departments is more common in Canadian firms than any one of the types of departmentation used alone.

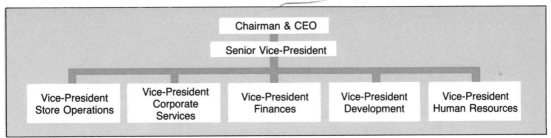

FIGURE 6-9 Departmentation by function at Consumers Distributing
SOURCE *Annual Report*, Consumers Distributing (1980).

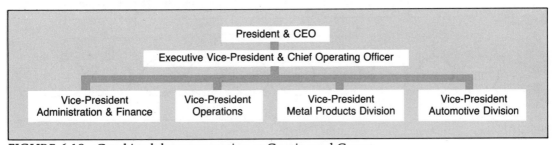

FIGURE 6-10 Combined departmentation at Continental Group
SOURCE *Annual Report*, Continental Group of Canada.

the work required will increase beyond the capacities of one person. At this point, additional personnel are employed.

vertical
differentiation

The process of creating additional levels in the organization is defined as **vertical differentiation**. Initially, there are just two levels, managerial and operative (see section A in Figure 6-11); functions that require special expertise and which are considered vital, like sales and finance, often continue to be done by the manager.

As the volume of business continues to grow, additional personnel will be added and more operative functions differentiated and allocated. The process of forming additional units at the same level in the organization is called **horizontal differentiation**. The result is shown in section B of Figure 6-11.

horizontal
differentiation

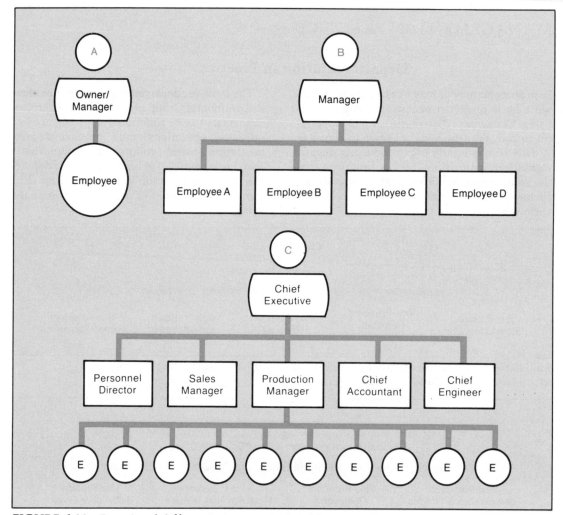

FIGURE 6-11   Functional differentiation: vertical and horizontal

Ordinarily, horizontal differentiation occurs because the original manager finds that certain functions can be more effectively and economically performed by a specialist. For example, a manager may find sales a weak area because of ineffective or inadequate training programs. Therefore, a sales trainer would be employed to take over that phase of the business, so the manager can devote more time to other areas. Horizontal growth usually occurs at the supervisory levels first, and at lower levels later, as additional workers are required. As the organization grows, horizontal differentiation usually results in those functions that are the most complex and are least similar to any other functions in the firm being split off.

As shown in section C of Figure 6-11, horizontal differentiation usually results in several functional departments being created. If the organization continues to grow, further vertical and horizontal differentiation will be needed. Figure 6-12, on page 244, shows how manufacturing might be further subdivided, resulting in an additional level of managers. When differentiation occurs, coordination is required. **Coordination** is the process of ensuring that persons who perform interdependent activities work together in a way that contributes to overall goal attainment. Coordination assumes greater importance as the organization becomes more complex.

coordination

The ideal result of the process of differentiation is to facilitate the accomplishment of the organization's goals through the use of specialists. The benefits of creating additional specialists in any organization — profit or non-profit — must exceed their costs. If a firm has doubled the size of its sales force without splitting the training function off from the work of the sales manager, then the organizational benefits and the increased efficiency of employing a sales training specialist may be greater than the cost to the company.

ORGANIZING AT THE SUPERVISORY LEVEL

Thus far we have viewed organizing as if it were strictly the province of top-level management. Organizing is important for any manager, even first-line supervisors. Organizing decisions at this level might include determining who will work on a particular project this week, how the workplace will be arranged, and the like.

Numerous factors can have a major influence on the supervisor's ability to organize. First, supervisors may find it difficult to reassign workers if there is a union. In some nonunion firms, people can be readily moved to respond to the needs of the situation. Delta Airlines attributes much of its success to workers' willingness to perform a multitude of tasks; for example, a Delta ticket agent may sometimes load baggage.

Second, in some firms, virtually every aspect of the supervisor's job is controlled by standard operating procedures. The supervisor may have little discretion in rearranging people or tasks except as prescribed by the procedure manual.

Third, some bosses are willing to give supervisors considerable flexibility. Others tell the supervisors exactly what to do. If the boss is inflexible, it may be a waste of time for the supervisor to try to reorganize.

Fourth, if workers are qualified in a variety of tasks, organizing flexibility is increased. For instance, a punch press operator may also be qualified on a drill press. This worker can be assigned to either job.

Finally, supervisors who have considerable influence within the organization are usually in a much better position to make changes. These supervisors can also arrange human and physical resources with little interference.

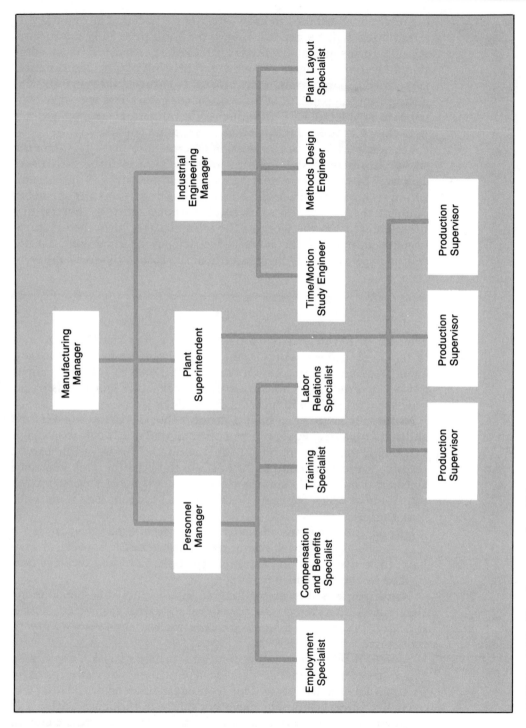

FIGURE 6-12 Development of staff departments

OPENING INCIDENT REVISITED

Richter's Hardware Stores

Karl Richter had made numerous improvements to his hardware chain, but their success has been limited. The basic problem here is that Richter has concentrated on expansion without giving much thought to the structural implications of doing so. Richter has added product lines and expanded regionally without adequately preparing existing managers and without altering his head office's perspective of the organization.

Some of the specific manifestations of this problem came out in the dispute between the marketing and merchandise vice-presidents. The lack of coordination between them is probably caused by the company's unstructured growth. This problem would not have arisen back in the days of the smaller company because these two managers would have been operating in only the Winnipeg market; coordinating their product lines and inventory would have been easier. The expanded structure has contributed to the lack of coordination by forcing managers into specialized jobs without allowing them to see the organization-wide perspective; they have difficulty making suggestions about how to head off these problems.

An additional problem is that Richter has added new outlets at various locations and is running into the problem of distance from his head office. The vice-president of marketing in Winnipeg really didn't know about some of these distant markets, yet her job was to advertise in them. This kind of problem could be resolved by changing the structure to set up a regional office in certain areas instead of doing everything from head office.

The structure of the company is based on function. During expansion, this basis contributes to the company's problems because the top management is having increasing difficulty coordinating the diverse regions where Richter has stores. One obvious alternative is to use another basis of departmentation. Perhaps the most reasonable is departmentation by geographic territory. Richter might appoint two vice-presidents, one for the Winnipeg area, and one for the outlying region. Each of these vice-presidents would be in charge of marketing, merchandising, and operations managers. If growth continues, a third vice-president could be added, dividing the outlying region.

SUMMARY

An organization is defined as two or more people working together in a coordinated manner to achieve group results. Organizing is prescribing formal relationships among people and resources to accomplish goals. In organizing, it is first necessary to consider organizational objectives before attempting to determine the kind of organization needed to accomplish those objectives. Next, management must determine the functions, or activities, that will be required. Finally, a number of departments, or separate organizational units, are set up, each designed to carry out a separate function or group of functions.

Specialization of labor means breaking a complex job down into simple tasks so that one person or group may carry out only identical or related activities, resulting in increased output. Specialization is especially essential for the achievement of efficiency in mass-production industries.

**Victor Rice
Massey-Ferguson**

Few envied Victor Rice in 1980 when he took over the chief executive's slot at farm-machinery giant Massey-Ferguson Ltd. Rice, then 39, was faced not only with the job of convincing a diverse and far-flung group of nervous creditors that Massey was worth more alive than dead, but also with the task of completely restructuring the core businesses and reorganizing the company into profit-oriented divisions.

The financial restructuring was perhaps the most pressing problem. A severe loss, equal to 30 percent of its net worth, crippled Massey in 1978, just as its consolidated debt climbed to US $2.5 billion. Rice had to perform like a virtuoso in 1981 and 1983 to convince 150 creditors in different jurisdictions to postpone debt repayment and convert debt and interest owed into equity.

Meanwhile, a worldwide slump in farm-machinery sales saw Massey's business shrivel like so many acres of parched corn in a Depression drought. Sales shrank on average more than 16 percent annually from 1978 to 1983.

Throughout all of this, Rice has managed to rewrite Massey's corporate job description, transforming the company into a number of individual profit-oriented divisions and establishing strict rules for expected returns on assets employed in each (about double the prevailing interest rate).

Q: You once said that Massey-Ferguson got into its mess because of "terrible management." What mistakes are you avoiding that your predecessors made?
Rice: I'm probably making as many mistakes — I just hope they're not as catastrophic!

This job can be depressing sometimes. When I took over, we had 68 000 people; today it's about 20 000. You can either accuse me of "massacring families" or you can say I've managed to keep 20 000 people employed.

Everybody talks about Chrysler and its mammoth recovery. They certainly did a lot of very good things. But I would argue that we've done precisely the same things. The one significant difference is that the car market went up and our market has continued to go down. What we've got now is a very small corporate headquarters that spends its time doing three things: legal and accounting services; monitoring divisional performance, in terms of return on assets employed; and setting corporate strategy.

The success of the strategic direction I set for the company probably will not be known until after I've retired. Of course I'm making mistakes. The question is whether, with the development of hindsight, they prove to be major or minor ones.

Q: You believe the market for agricultural equipment will stay depressed, whereas competitor John Deere believes it will bounce back. Here we have two huge companies making long-term strategic decisions based on entirely different viewpoints. Does the fate of one of these companies depend on which of you is right and which is wrong?

Rice: In the long run, yes. John Deere is a well-run, highly successful company, but with something like 70 percent of its business in North America. It's financially strong, but if its long-term view of the North American market is wrong, then its strategic direction will come back to haunt it.

We are clearly going down a different path. I took over as president at the end of 1978, and in 1979 this company launched its first-ever detailed strategic plan. It took us over a year to put it together. We did get one thing wrong. We knew the farm-machinery market was going to go down. We did not know it was going to keep going down, and down, and down.

We have a long-term corporate thrust: when we've finally got the company stabilized, we will start growing other businesses. The first small step in that path was the Rolls Royce engine acquisition last year, and we have other twinkles in our eye. It was amusing — back at the beginning of 1980 — we were looking at a 15-20 year horizon, when I wasn't even sure we were going to survive until lunchtime!

Q: During the crisis, you were able to hang on to a number of your best people. How did you manage?

Rice: The average age of the top 100 executives is late 30s or early 40s. There are a lot of people who have been given an awfully big responsibility at a young age. Another thing. We never — not for one second in the whole process — lost our faith that we could do it.

Q: It can't have been that simple. Surely you must have awakened in the night wondering how you'd survive.

Rice: Oh, I did. Frequently. I can remember thinking, as I drove into the office in the dim, dark days, that I had no idea how to solve this problem. But then there'd be a combination of people brainstorming, coming up with crazy ideas. There was tremendous excitement. That excitement remains today. This is a company that's gone through the worst possible times and survived.

Q: As comptroller in the mid-1970s, you saw the crisis coming and tried to draw attention to it, but you didn't have much success in getting the directors to take it seriously. Could some steps have been taken then that might have averted the crisis, or were the directors, many of whom were of an older generation, too keen on protecting their entrenched interests?

Rice: With hindsight, the answer is yes: earlier retrenchment — facing up to reality — would certainly have helped. The particular management group you mention had already been through a period when the company had problems, and it had returned Massey to stability. In the early 1970s came the greatest period of growth in the farm-machinery industry. Every year, demand rose, and Massey was more profitable than ever. It's difficult to look back on that environment and say that many people were doing the wrong thing. The fundamental reason that caused this company's problems is that it dramatically overexpanded, using debt when it should have raised equity.

Q: So you're really saying that Massey made the same basic error that everybody was making then?

Rice: It was worse in Massey's case because of injudicious investments. For example, it got into the construction-equipment business, which cost us US $450 million.

I'm not a person who goes to seminars often but I admire Peter Drucker. Six years ago I joined a small group of about 60 people — chairmen and chief executives of all sorts of companies — for a session with Drucker. He said, "I look around this room and see people in their 30s to late 50s and you're all successful, all running companies. Yet none of you has any experience! All of your business experience has been in the post-war era, and the post-war era has been steadily booming. The last couple of years, with the oil shock and volatile rates and increasing inflation, are very uncomfortable, and all of you are grappling to get control of it until things return to normal. Well, the abnormal period was the post-war era. What you are wrestling with now, what you think is abnormal, is normality."

The process of grouping related functions or major work activities into manageable units is known as departmentation. Functions should be grouped according to the following guidelines: (1) similar functions; (2) sufficient volume of work; (3) tradition, preferences, and work rules; (4) functions similar to others in the organization; (5) separation of functions to prevent conflicts of interest, and (6) combining dissimilar functions to allow coordination.

It is possible to identify five bases on which departmentation normally occurs. Departmentation by function is formed on the basis of specialized functions, such as production, marketing, engineering, finance, and personnel.

Departmentation by product is concerned with organizing according to the type of product being produced and/or sold by the firm. Departmentation by customers is used by organizations that have a special need to provide better service to different types of customers. Departmentation by geographic territory is used by organizations that have physically dispersed and/or independent operations or markets to serve. When the work of an organization consists of a continuing series of major projects, departmentation by project normally occurs. Unless the organization is quite small, however, it is likely that several different bases for departmentation will be used.

The process of creating additional levels in the organization is defined as vertical differentiation. Initially there are just two levels, managerial and operative. As the volume of business continues to grow, additional personnel will be added and more operative functions differentiated and allocated. The process of forming additional units at the same level in the organization is called horizontal differentiation. When differentiation occurs, coordination is required. Coordination is ensuring that persons who perform interdependent activities work together in a way that contributes to overall goal attainment.

Numerous factors have a major influence on the supervisor's ability to organize. First, supervisors may find it difficult to reassign workers if there is a union. Second, in some firms, virtually every aspect of the supervisor's job is controlled by standard operating procedures. Third, some bosses are willing to give supervisors considerable flexibility, while others are not. Fourth, if workers are qualified in a variety of tasks, organizing flexibility is increased. Finally, supervisors who have considerable influence within the organization usually are in a much better position to make changes.

REVIEW QUESTIONS

1. Define organization. What are the three common characteristics of an organization?

2. Describe the process of organizing. What tasks must managers perform in the organizing process?
3. In terms of the organizing process, define a function. What types of functions are needed for a community drama group? a football team? a fast food restaurant? a small-appliance assembly plant?
4. Define specialization of labor. What are the advantages and disadvantages?
5. What guidelines should be used in grouping functions?
6. Define *departmentation*. What are the primary bases of departmentation?
7. Distinguish by example and definition between horizontal and vertical differentiation.
8. What are the factors that can have a major influence on the supervisor's ability to organize?

EXERCISES

1. Specialization has both advantages and disadvantages. List the specialized education and training required for the following professions. Which profession(s) is(are) possible with your present level of education and training? Which could you achieve?
   a. Electrical draftsman
   b. Neurosurgeon
   c. Machine operator
   d. College president
   e. Personnel manager
2. Assume that you are production manager for a small firm. The firm currently is experiencing much growth and success with its product line, and sales have tripled in the past year. As a result, you have hired forty new employees over the last six months to keep up with production demands. Describe the horizontal and vertical differentiation that you would implement in the company for maximum efficiency as the organization continues to grow.

CASE STUDY

The Organization of Quality Control

Richard Boas is production manager for Memorand Ltd., a small component parts manufacturer in the Maritimes. He has been with the firm for 15 years and has progressed from foreman to his current position. Boas is completely dedicated to the company and its future. He has passed up numerous opportunities for higher paying more prestigious positions with competing firms because he likes his job and the employees.

Kathy Wells is currently in charge of the quality control section with Memorand and reports directly to Boas. She has been with the company for 10 years, having started as department secretary to Boas. He has supported Wells getting a degree and has allowed her to take time off to attend classes at the local university. After several years of attending courses, she recently obtained a degree in operations management with a specialty in quality control. Because of the patience and support Boas gave her, Wells has a strong loyalty to Boas and to Memorand.

Memorand has been awarded a very lucrative contract by CBU Ltd., with the provision that Memorand produce the parts within three weeks. If Memorand completes the order on time, it may obtain additional contracts from CBU that would increase overall company sales by at least 10 percent a year. The order comes at a time when business has been relatively bad for Memorand — the firm has been considering a reduction of its work force.

On the second day of production, Wells discovered a problem and requested a meeting with Boas. This conversation took place:

Wells: Dick, the quality of the parts we're making for CBU is not as good as those we normally make. I believe we should slow down and inspect all the parts to ensure that we don't send out an inferior product.

Boas: Are the parts below standard?

Wells: No, but about 45 percent of the parts are marginal. I believe that, if we want to improve our chances of obtaining additional orders, we must slow down the production line.

Boas: If we slow down the production line, Kathy, we won't make the deadline we promised CBU. If we don't make the deadline, most likely Memorand will not even have a chance to receive follow-up contracts. I expect you to meet the production schedule like everyone else.

After receiving such a firm demand, Wells left the office. She thought her position was right but didn't know what more to do.

QUESTIONS

1. Would you reorganize the reporting relationships of the production department and the quality control section to ensure that the conflict experienced by Wells and Boas would not occur in the future? Why or why not? If you would reorganize, how?
2. If you agree with Wells, what do you think she should do? Discuss.
3. Do you believe Boas was correct in his assessment of the situation? Discuss.

CASE STUDY

Materials Organization at Newco

Newco Manufacturing Company, based in Hamilton, Ontario, employed 210 workers in the production and assembly of small electrical motors. Tom Baryluk, the new materials manager, knew one of his first tasks was to improve the organization in his department. Baryluk reported to the vice-president of manufacturing, Charles McDowell. Baryluk had 12 people in his department; they performed functions like stocking, receiving, inventory control, purchasing, and outside sales.

Because the workflow was not easily predictable, the previous materials manager told the department's personnel to do whatever they thought necessary. Jobs included working the parts issue windows while mechanics were ordering parts, stocking the parts bins when time permitted, receiving parts when deliveries were made, and shipping orders to customers. These same employees answered the phone and handled outside sales as required. Frequent employee complaints had been made about inadequate pay, unclear work assignments, and lack of competent leadership.

Baryluk had received a rather detailed account about the materials operations from McDowell. McDowell described the materials department as performing poorly, because of a lack of overall direction, ineffective organization, and incompetent personnel. McDowell described several of the department's personnel as "dope heads" or "long hairs" who did as little work as possible. The turnover rate had been over 200 percent per year for the past three years. McDowell suggested that Baryluk "clean house" by firing most of the employees in the department and start with a fresh crew.

Baryluk was surprised by McDowell's comments and concerned about the complaints of the personnel in the department. He considered finding a new position, but chose not to leave the company until he had given the assignment his best efforts for at least a few months.

QUESTIONS

1. Using concepts and principles discussed in this chapter, what actions would you recommend Baryluk take to improve the materials department?
2. What type of organization chart would you recommend Baryluk develop?
3. Should Baryluk "clean house" as suggested by McDowell? Why or why not?

ENDNOTES

[1]"The Fast-Food War: Big Mac Under Attack," *Business Week* (January 30, 1984): 45.

[2]W. G. Astley and A. H. Van de Ven, "Central Perspectives and Debates in Organization Theory," *Administrative Science Quarterly* (June 1983): 248.

[3]R. L. Daft, *Organization Theory and Design* (St. Paul, Minnesota: West Publishing, 1983): 227.

[4]T. T. Herbert, "Strategy and Multinational Organization Structure: An International Relationships Perspective," *Academy of Management Review* (April 1984): 263.

[5]"Can GM Solve Its Identity Crisis?" *Business Week* (January 23, 1984): 32-33.

REFERENCES

Alexander, E. R. "Design of Alternatives in Organizational Contexts: A Pilot Study." *Administrative Science Quarterly* 24 (September 1979): 382–404.

Bobbitt, H. R. Jr., and Ford, J. D. "Decision-Maker Choice as a Determinant of Organizational Structure." *Academy of Management Review* 5 (January 1980): 13–23.

Cherman, C. "Organizing for Strength." *Personnel Journal* 58 (July 1979): 437–438.

Dalton, D. R.; Todor, W. D.; Spendelini, J.; Fielding, J.; and Porter, L. W. "Organization Structure and Performance: A Critical Review." *Academy of Management Review* 5 (January 1980): 61–64.

Gerwin, D. "Relationships between Structure and Technology at the Organizational and Job Levels." *Journal of Management Studies* 16 (February 1979): 70–79.

Handy, C. "Shape of Organizations to Come." *Personnel Management* 11 (June 1979): 24–27.

_____. "Through the Organizational Looking Glass." *Harvard Business Review* 58 no. 1 (January-February 1980): 24–27.

Herbert, Theodore T. "Strategy and Multinational Organization Structure: An Interorganizational Relationships Perspective." *Academy of Management Review* 9, no. 2 (April 1984): 259–270.

Huber, G. P., et al. "Optimum Organization Design: An Analytic Adoptive Approach." *Academy of Management Review* 4 (October 1979): 567–578.

Naylor, T. H. "Organizing for Strategic Planning." *Managerial Planning* 28 (July 1979): 3–9

Pavett, Cynthia M., and Lau, Alan W. "Managerial Work: The Influence of Hierarchical Level and Functional Specialty." *Academy of Management Journal* 26, no. 1 (March 1983): 170–177.

Scanlon, K. "Maintaining Organizational Effectiveness — A Prescription for Good Health." *Personnel Journal* 58, no. 5 (May 1980): 381–386.

Slocum, J. W. Jr., and Hellriegel, D. "Using Organizational Designs to Cope with Change." *Business Horizons* 22 (December 1979): 65-76.

Walker, Dean. "Massey: Act III." *Executive* (May 1985): 46–50.

7

Authority, Responsibility, and Organizational Structure

KEY TERMS

delegation	chain of command	line and staff
responsibility	span of management	organization
authority	organizational	staff departments
centralization	structure	personal staff
decentralization	organizational chart	advisory staff
accountability	functional structure	service staff
unity of command	divisional structure	control staff
principle	line organization	functional authority
scalar principle	line departments	project organization
		matrix organization

LEARNING OBJECTIVES

After completing this chapter you should be able to
1. Distinguish between authority, responsibility, and accountability.
2. Identify the advantages and disadvantages of centralization and decentralization.
3. Define delegation and describe the reasons for delegation.
4. Explain the basic principles related to authority, responsibility, and accountability.
5. Define span of management and identify the factors affecting it.
6. Identify the basic types of organizational structures and the advantages and disadvantages of each.

OPENING INCIDENT

The Faculty of Administration

Frank Singh was the head of the management department in the Faculty of Administration at a large university. John Gebhart was an Associate Dean in the same Faculty. Singh and Gebhart had attended college together and both had come to the university about 15 years ago. They remained good friends, often lunching together and talking over Faculty business. Two years ago Gebhart had given up the position of head of the management department to become the Associate Dean for Graduate Studies and Research. Singh had been chosen as Gebhart's replacement. (See Figure 7-1 for the current organizational structure of the Faculty of Administration.)

One function Singh performed as department head was assigning classes to the members of his department. Recently he completed this activity and sent each member in his department his or her schedule for next year, including Gebhart's classes. Soon after the schedules were distributed through the faculty mailboxes, Gebhart approached Singh about his schedule, noting that he had been assigned two sections of the Organizational Behavior course in the MBA program. Gebhart asked Singh if the two sections could be combined so that both full- and part-time students could be handled in one class. Singh said that he was reluctant to do so. He had heard various faculty members complaining that administrators (as-

sociate deans and department heads) only taught two classes per year, while regular faculty members were required to teach five classes. He was afraid that, if he let Gebhart teach only one class, the criticism would be even greater and he would be accused of "playing favorites." (It was well-known that Singh and Gebhart were friends.)

When Singh expressed this concern tactfully, Gebhart said that he wasn't interested in faculty members' views about the teaching loads of administrators. Gebhart said that he was working hard at his job and that members of Singh's department shouldn't question how many classes administrators teach. Singh raised his own concern that members of his department might accuse him of favoritism if he assigned only one course to Gebhart. Singh said he would like to leave Gebhart's schedule as it was, with Gebhart teaching two sections of the Organizational Behavior course.

At this point, the two were interrupted in their discussion and the matter was left unresolved. Since it was Friday afternoon, Singh had the weekend to mull over his problem. He didn't want this incident to affect his friendship with Gebhart, but he also didn't want to be accused of favoritism by members of his department. Either result might reduce his ability to lead the management department effectively.

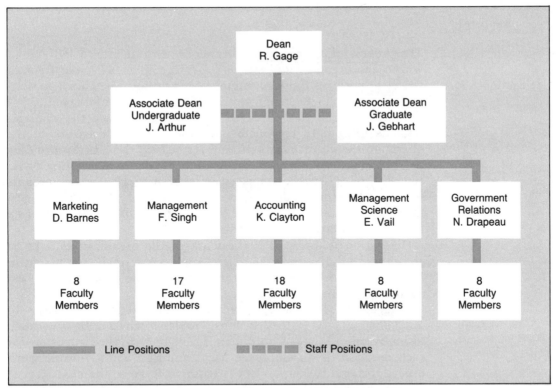

FIGURE 7-1   Organizational structure of the Faculty of Administration

The incident with Singh and Gebhart illustrates just how frustrating it can be when functional relationships are unclear and/or when expectations are ambiguous. In order to perform effectively in any organization, managers must have a clear understanding of what's expected of them and what levels of responsibility and authority they possess. The primary purpose of an organizational structure is to clarify and communicate roles of managers and other personnel within the firm. As described in Chapter 6, organizing is the process of bringing together functions, human resources, and inputs for the purpose of achieving the objectives of the firm. We have already discussed the various functions that must be performed and how these functions might be grouped for optimal productivity. In this chapter, we will discuss patterns for organizing functions that take into account the people and the formal relationships that exist in organizations.

What concepts and principles should managers understand and apply in performing the organizing function? We first discuss the ideas of delegation of responsiblity, authority, and accountability. Next, we present several guidelines that can be used by managers to determine how well they are performing the organizing function. In the final section of the chapter, we discuss the concept of organizational design and the main types of organizational structures.

DELEGATION

delegation

The process of assigning specific work assignments to individuals within the organization and of providing them with the right or power to perform those functions is **delegation**. The ability to delegate is one of the most significant skills a manager can have.

There is some risk involved in delegation, since the manager remains ultimately responsible for the success or failure of the operation. Some managers attempt to reduce the risk by avoiding delegation and doing tasks themselves. However, delegation of responsibility and authority is essential if managers are to provide opportunities for the development of their staff. One of the biggest mistakes a manager can make is to be unwilling or unable to delegate some responsibility and authority.

Delegation is essential if the work of the organization is to be accomplished effectively and efficiently. Some of the more significant reasons why delegation is important to the organizing process are illustrated in Figure 7-2.

Delegation of responsibility and authority generally leads to quicker action and faster decisions. Problems can be dealt with much faster by subordinates if they do not have to go to their superiors for each decision. If an employee has a question about routine work procedures and the supervisor is required to go to the next level of management for a decision, the action is delayed and both employee and supervisor may become frustrated waiting for a decision. In

FIGURE 7-2
Reasons for
delegation

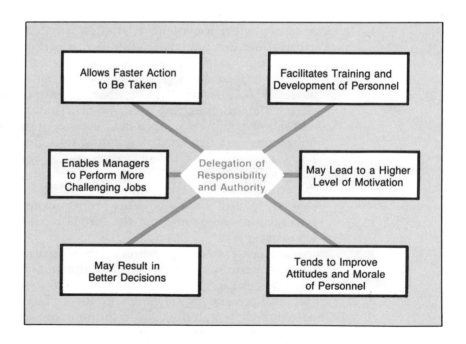

general, when routine matters are handled at a higher level than necessary, time is wasted and work output is reduced.

Delegation is an important facet of training and developing personnel in the organization. Employees or managers cannot learn to perform certain functions or make decisions unless they are given the opportunity. Delegation of responsibility and authority is essential if the firm wants to develop its personnel to assume more challenging and demanding jobs in the future. In addition, delegation may lead to higher levels of motivation among personnel since they believe they are being trusted and their managers have confidence in their abilities. Delegation not only builds the confidence of personnel but also improves attitudes and morale generally.

Through delegation of routine matters, managers are freed to perform especially challenging jobs. Delegation is a way of extending managers' capabilities; evidence suggests that managers recognize this. A recent study of graduating MBA's and practicing managers revealed that the more varied the tasks a manager is assigned, the more delegation is necessary.[1]

Despite these reasons for delegating responsibility and authority, certain potential problems should be considered:

- If employees do not tell their managers what they are doing, the managers may lose control and may not have time to correct any problems that occur.
- Delegation can fail if the degree of responsibility and authority is not clearly defined and understood.
- If an employee given responsibility or authority does not possess the ability, skills, and/or experience to accomplish the jobs or make decisions, delegation can prove disastrous.
- Problems can result if an employee is given responsibility for a job but is not given sufficient authority to perform the task.

RESPONSIBILITY

responsibility

Responsibility is an obligation to perform certain work activities. For example, if James Lewis, a manager, is responsible for the data processing center he has an obligation to plan, organize, influence, control, and coordinate the work of computer operators and analysts. That's not all. He also has the obligation for the maintenance of the computer equipment and programs, plus numerous other activities that are essential to the success of the data processing department.

Responsibilities or obligations to perform certain functions must be clearly defined. Nothing is more frustrating to managers or workers than being unclear about the nature, scope, and details of their specific job responsibilities. For instance, consider the following conversation between Suzanne Belle, a lower-level manager for a large insurance company, and her superior, Phil Reeve:

Belle: Is my unit responsible for processing the new commercial fire insurance policies or should Joe Davis's unit handle them?

Reeve: I don't think it really matters too much which unit handles these new policies as long as it's done correctly and thoroughly.

Belle: But what am I expected to do?

Reeve: I'll get back to you later on this — I'm busy at the moment.

Obviously, Reeve's responses create ambiguity for Belle. She doesn't know what her specific responsibilities are with regard to the new commercial fire insurance policies and gets no clarification from Reeve. Accomplishing the objective of processing the policies may be quite difficult. In order to perform any job adequately, an individual must understand the objectives, functions, and specific responsibilities it entails. As was illustrated in Figure 6-2, objectives, functions, responsibilities, and authority must be closely integrated for the most effective organization.

Personnel in the organization are delegated responsibilities or work assignments by their superiors. When a manager delegates a responsibility to a subordinate, a relationship based on an obligation exists between the two. However, managers should remember an important point: they cannot relieve themselves of any portion of the original responsibility; delegation allows only for someone else to do the work. Responsibility is a series of obligations established between two management levels in an organization.

AUTHORITY

authority

Once managers have assigned responsibilities, they must delegate the authority necessary to accomplish the job. Viewed in terms of management, **authority** is the right to decide, to direct others to take action, or to perform certain duties in achieving organization goals. The concept of authority comprises at least three key characteristics:

- Authority is a right.
- Exercising authority involves making decisions, taking action or performing duties.
- Authority is used to achieve the organization's goals.

Division of Authority

Delegation of authority and delegation of responsibility cannot and should not be separated. In fact, a widely accepted basic principle of management states that authority should *equal* responsibility. In other words, a manager who is given a job to do (responsibility) should have adequate authority (or rights) to get the job done.

The concept sounds good in theory. Yet one of the most common complaints of lower-level managers is that they have more responsibility than authority. Authority deals with rights; these rights must relate directly to the responsibility delegated. For example, if a supervisor is made responsible for staffing a department, he or she can be delegated any one of these degrees of authority:

- Rights to recruit, screen, and hire all personnel
- Rights to recruit, screen, and hire, subject to prior approval from a higher-level manager
- No rights to recruit and screen (This function has been delegated to the personnel department, but the supervisor can accept or reject candidates.)
- No rights to hire. (The supervisor must take whomever the personnel department sends.)

In the last instance, the supervisor is responsible for getting a job done but lacks the authority to perform the job adequately by hiring personnel he or she considers best qualified.

Amount of Authority:
Centralization versus Decentralization

Management must determine the appropriate degrees of responsibility and authority to be delegated. If, generally, a limited amount of authority is delegated, the organization is usually characterized as centralized. If, generally, a significant amount of authority is delegated to lower levels, the organization is described as decentralized.

Centralization and decentralization are theoretical extremes, with many gradations between. The real issue is not *whether* a company should decentralize but rather how much. In determining how decentralized an organization is, the nature and location of decision making must be assessed. In a structure using **centralization**, individual managers and workers at lower levels in the organization have the right to initiate only a rather narrow range of decisions or actions. By contrast, in a decentralized organization, the scope of authority to make decisions and take action is rather broad for lower-level managers and workers. For example, in a highly centralized organizational structure, top management makes all decisions regarding the hiring or firing of personnel, or the approval of purchasing of equipment and supplies. In a decentralized structure, lower-level managers may make these decisions.

Although recent trends in Canadian businesses seem to favor decentralization, a decentralized organization cannot be assumed to be better or more effective than a centralized organization. **Decentralization** is advocated by those who believe that lower-level managers should be given responsibility to make decisions. Such advocates believe that, when all decisions and orders come from one central source, organization members tend to act like robots — unthinking

centralization

decentralization

MANAGEMENT IN PRACTICE

Decentralization: A Key to Good Decisions

A rigid hierarchy in an organization may be the cause of poor decisions by top management and poor implementation by workers. The larger the hierarchy, the more information is filtered on its way up and down. Stephen Ferris, a management consultant for Berkley Developmental Resources, Inc. in Toronto, says that many top executives are isolated from the realities of the world around them because they have surrounded themselves with yes-men who screen out bad news and allow only good news to pass through. Too often a manager is so far removed from the lower levels in the organization that he or she has never even been into the factory or met a customer.

The remedy for this kind of problem is a more decentralized structure that stresses smaller work units, multidirectional communication (lateral, diagonal, and vertical), and shared decision making. Gordon Fehr, CEO of Pfizer Canada, Inc. of Montreal, says that his firm tries to have its decisions made as far down the hierarchy as possible. The best decisions are made by the people who know the work and the consequences of different actions. He thinks that decentralized decision making improves the effectiveness of decisions and the productivity and commitment of employees.

SOURCE Adapted from M. A. Wente, "Remaking the Management Mind," *Canadian Business* (January 1983): 24.

---

executors of someone else's commands. Decentralization usually creates a climate for more rapid growth and development of personnel, a primary responsibility of managers.

In addition to the different impacts on human behavior evident between decentralization and centralization, other factors can affect managers' decisions. Centralization generally:

- Produces uniformity of policy and action
- Results in less risk of errors by subordinates who lack either information or skill
- Utilizes the skills of central and specialized experts
- Enables closer control of operations.

Decentralization generally:

- Produces speedier decision making by reducing consultation
- Results in decisions that are more likely to be adapted to local conditions
- Results in greater interest and enthusiasm on the part of subordinates to whom authority has been entrusted (These expanded jobs provide excellent training experiences for possible promotion to higher levels).
- Allows top management to use its time for more study and consideration of the basic goals, plans, and policies of the organization.

To what extent should authority be decentralized? Top management of an organization, in making this decision, must consider the organization's size and complexity, its geographic dispersion, the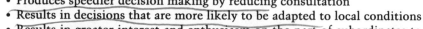

Degree of decentralization determined by [handwritten margin note]

competence of its personnel, the adequacy of its communications system, the degree of organizational uniformity, the risk of costly poor decisions, and the history of the organization.

Size and Complexity of the Organization

The larger the organization, the more authority managers are forced to delegate. If the firm is engaged in many separate businesses, the limitations of expertise will usually lead to decentralization of authority to the heads of these units. Each major product group is likely to have different production problems, varying kinds of customers, and varied marketing channels. If speed and adaptability to changing conditions are necessary for success, decentralization is a must.

Geographic Dispersion of the Organization

When the difficulties of size are compounded by geographic dispersion, the organization has a greater need for decentralization. General Motors is a prime example of decentralization because of size and geographic dispersion. However, not every decision or every function should be decentralized. Control of operations may have to be pushed down to lower levels in the organization, while control of financing may remain centralized. Because of the increasing complexity of government legislation affecting employment practices, centralization of labor relations is often established for purposes of uniformity throughout the company.

Competence of Personnel Available

A major limiting factor in many organizations is the adequacy or inadequacy of its personnel. If the organization has grown under centralized decision making and control, subordinates may be ill-equipped to start making major decisions. They were hired and trained to be followers, not leaders or decision makers. In some convenience store chains this deficiency has developed into a major problem. Store managers are promoted to supervisors because they are able to perform basic store functions, not because they make sound decisions. Supervisors are promoted to general managers not because they have made good decisions, but because they can ensure that lower managers follow standard operating procedures. A person who eventually makes it to the top is not equipped to cope with making decisions that are not based on established practices and procedures.

The chain will have few managers who are proven capable of independent thought and action; many may already have left the centralized firm.

Adequacy of Communications System

Size, complexity, and geographic dispersion lead to the delegation of larger amounts of authority to lower levels in the organization. Managers can seek to avoid decentralization through the development of a communication system that provides for speed, accuracy, and for the availability of the great amounts of information needed for top management to exercise centralized control. In effect, although size and geography may preclude being on the spot, a firm can try to control subordinates by detailing standards of performance and process and by ensuring that information flows quickly and accurately to the central authoritative position.

Uniformity of Policy Desired

If top management wants all its employees to behave consistently with respect to certain policies, the organization will be highly centralized. For example, if top management wants all customers to pay the same price for a certain product, it will not give its salespeople the authority to set or change prices. If, however, top management wants to "charge what the traffic will bear," it might allow salespeople to charge different prices to different customers. Top management must realize that, in a decentralized organization, not all lower-level managers will make the same decision when confronted with a certain problem. Therefore, it is important that all employees follow a uniform policy — for example, obeying antitrust laws — then the organization will have to be centralized. If uniformity of policy is not critical, the organization may be increasingly decentralized.

Cost of Decisions

If the cost to an organization of a bad decision is going to be high, the right to make that decision will likely be centralized. The right to make decisions with low monetary risk may be given to lower-level managers. For example, a foreman would probably be allowed to spend a small amount of money on machine maintenance, but that same foreman would not have the authority to buy new machinery.

History of the Organization

The way in which the organization has grown over the years also influences the amount of decentralization. If the organization has grown by acquiring other organizations, it will tend to be more decentralized. This is because the addition of new products or services may involve top management in areas where it has no particular expertise. The managers of the acquired companies will likely have considerable freedom in running them.

If a company grows simply by selling more of what it is already involved in, it may remain fairly centralized. This is because top management of the company knows a great deal about its products and services and hence is able, if it wishes, to centralize decision-making authority at the top of the organization.

ACCOUNTABILITY

accountability

No organization can function effectively without a system of accountability. **Accountability** is any means of ensuring that the person who is supposed to do a task actually performs it and does so correctly. Situations can rapidly get out of control when people are not held accountable.

Before a manager can be held accountable for results, certain conditions should be present. First, responsibilities must be thoroughly and clearly understood. An individual who is unaware of what is expected cannot be properly held accountable. Second, the person must be qualified and capable of fulfilling the obligation. It would be inconceivable to assign the responsibility and authority for performing engineering or accounting functions to individuals having no previous educational background and/or experience in these areas. Finally, sufficient authority to accomplish the task must be delegated. Assigning a manager the total profit responsibility for a department but no authority to hire or fire employees might mean that insufficient authority has been delegated. This manager would probably object to being held accountable for results.

Since it is so closely related to responsibility, a manager's accountability cannot be delegated to someone else. Managers are usually accountable not only for their own actions and decisions but also for the actions of their subordinates. An extreme case of this is the naval tradition that the captain must go down with the ship.

Accountability can be established in several ways. The first method is through personal inspection by the manager. After assigning a person to do the task, the manager observes to see that it is done properly. The second method is to have the subordinate complete reports and give them to the manager. However, because it is human nature to want to be seen in the best possible light, such reports might be biased in favor of the subordinate. A third method is through reporting done by others. A quality control inspector might report the number of defective units for each worker to the manager. Customers may report poor service or faulty products. This method of accountability is not in the hands of the person held accountable and is therefore reasonably free of bias.

ORGANIZING PRINCIPLES

During the twentieth century a large number of organizing principles have been developed by research scholars and practicing managers. These principles are generally helpful for managers who would like some guidelines on how to be effective in their work. However, there are exceptions to these principles, so they must be applied in a flexible way. The main organizing principles are summarized in Table 7-1. We will discuss each point briefly.

Unity of Command

unity of command
principle

The **unity of command principle** is the belief that each person should answer to only one immediate superior; each employee has only one boss. Unity of command enables better coordination, more complete understanding of what is required and tighter discipline. An employee with two or more bosses can receive contradictory orders.

Although unity of command is a sound concept, it does have certain limitations. In large organizations especially, a person may

TABLE 7-1   Organizing Principles

Principle	Definition of	Rationale	Possible Causes of Violation	Possible Results of Violation
Unity of command	A person should report to only *one* boss	Clarity and understanding, to ensure unity of effort and direction, and to avoid conflicts	Unclear definition of authority	Dissatisfaction or frustration of employees and perhaps lower efficiency
Equal authority and responsibility	The amount of authority and responsibility should be equal	Allows work to be accomplished more efficiently, develops people's skills, and reduces frustration	Fear on the part of some managers that subordinates might "take over"	Waste of energies and dissatisfaction of employees, thereby reducing effectiveness
Scalar Principle	There should be a clear definition of authority in the organization	Clarity of relationship avoids confusion and improves decision making and performance	Uncertainty on the part of the employee or a direct effort by the employee to avoid chain of command	Poor performance, confusion, and/or dissatisfaction
Limited span of management	There is a limit to the number of employees a manager can effectively supervise	Increased effectiveness in direction and control of a manager	Overloading a manager due to growth in number of personnel	Lack of efficiency and control, resulting in poor performance

need to be accountable to more than one boss. At Sears, for example, store managers are expected to follow the directives from the central personnel office as well as from their direct superiors.

Equal Authority and Responsibility

We have already noted that authority should equal responsibility. When this happens, the likelihood is much higher that work will be performed more efficiently and with a minimum amount of frustration on the part of personnel. By not delegating an adequate amount of authority along with responsibility, managers are wasting employee energy and resources; dissatisfaction often results.

Suppose, for example, that a sales manager is given the responsibility for achieving certain sales goals, but is not given the authority to discipline or reward salespeople. This situation is undesirable because the sales manager cannot do what is necessary to motivate the salespeople to achieve the organization's sales goals. Nor is this an extreme case; many organizations inadvertently create situations where authority and responsibility are not equal. In universities, for example, department heads may face this problem. They are often given the responsibility for developing high performance in teaching and research among faculty members, without the authority necessary to attain it.

The Scalar Principle and the Chain of Command

scalar principle

chain of
command

The **scalar principle** is the philosophy that authority and responsibility should flow from top management downward in a clear, unbroken line. If the scalar principle is followed, there is a clear chain of command for every person in the organization. The **chain of command** is the line along which authority flows from the top of the organization to any individual. A clear chain of command clarifies relationships, avoids confusion, and tends to improve decision making, thus often leading to more effective performance. When the scalar principle is followed, superiors and subordinates communicate by going through channels.

Span of Management

span of
management

The number of employees a manager can effectively supervise is referred to as the **span of management**. The span of management, or span of control as it is sometimes called, is a fundamental principle related to the organizing function. Limiting it enables the manager to achieve maximum effectiveness in organizing, motivating, and controlling personnel. According to the span of management principle, the number of employees a manager can effectively supervise or control is limited. The precise number or "span" varies according to the situation.

Determining the number of potential relationships a manager might have to deal with given a certain number of subordinates was the subject of research by A. V. Graicunas, a management consultant during the 1930s. Graicunas derived a formula to determine the potential interactions or relationships that were possible when a manager had a given number of employees.[2] Graicunas's formula is:

$$R = n + n(n - 1) + n(2^{n-1} - 1)$$

where R represents the number of relationships or interactions and n is the number of subordinates reporting to the manager.

According to Graicunas's formula, a manager with two employees would have six potential relationships to monitor. For example, if Ed has two subordinates, Joan and Sasha, the following interactions are possible.

Number of Relationships

2	Ed may meet and talk with Joan *or* Ed may meet and talk with Sasha	= *direct relationships*
2	Ed may meet and talk with Joan, with Sasha present *or* vice versa	= *group relationships*
2	Joan may interact with Sasha without Ed *or* Sasha may meet with Joan without Ed	= *cross-relationships*
6		

As Table 7-2 shows, each additional employee a manager supervises creates a substantial number of additional relationships.

TABLE 7-2 Possible Relationships with Different Number of Employees

Number of Employees	Potential Number of Relationships
1	1
2	6
3	18
4	44
5	100
6	222

Factors Affecting the Span of Management

In most private and public-sector organizations, spans of management have historically been relatively narrow, usually ranging from 6 to 15 employees per manager. More restricted spans of management permit closer supervision of personnel but tend to create tall organizational structures with a large number of levels; this may cause communication difficulties. Larger or wider spans result in relatively fewer levels, or "flat" organizations, and greater freedom for the individual employee. (See Figure 7-3, in which both organizations have a total of 29 employees.) While managers agree that the span of management is a fundamentally valid concept, the exact number of subordinates that one manager can effectively supervise cannot be determined precisely. However, a number of factors affect the span of management:

FActors

- Complexity of the work
- Degree of similarity to other work
- Degree of interdependence with other work
- Stability of the organization and situation

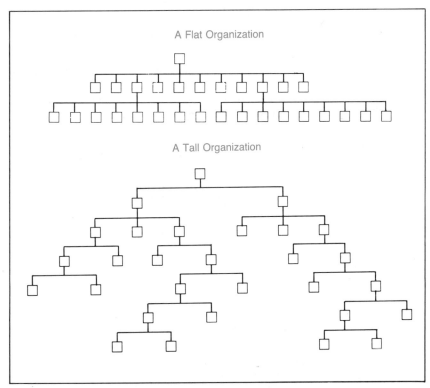

FIGURE 7-3   Flat and tall organizational structures

Factors

- Degree of standardization of the work
- Qualifications, skills, expertise, and experience of the manager
- Qualifications, skills, experience, and motivation of the employees
- Type of technology.

In general, the more complex the work, the narrower the span of management. The span can be wider if a manager is supervising employees performing similar jobs. If jobs are closely interlocked and interdependent, a manager may have greater problems with coordination, creating the need for a rather limited span of management. Similarly, if the organization is operating in a rapidly changing environment, a narrow span may prove to be more effective. On the other hand, the establishment of numerous standards increases predictability and provides the basis for effective control.

Another key factor affecting the span of management is the qualifications of managers and nonmanagerial personnel. Managers and employees who are highly skilled, experienced, and motivated generally can operate with wider spans of management and with less supervision. But narrow spans may result in a higher commitment to the organization.[3]

Finally, technology can have a significant impact on the span of management. Joan Woodward, a British researcher who conducted studies in 100 English manufacturing firms, discovered that the type of technology had a significant impact on the spans of management actually used in businesses. Woodward classified production technology into three groups:

- Unit or small-batch processing (made-to-order goods such as custom-tailored clothing)
- Mass production (assembly-line operations)
- Process production with continuous long runs of a standardized product (such as oil, chemicals, or pharmaceuticals).

She discovered that spans of management were widest in those firms using mass production technology. The jobs in mass production tend to be more routine and similar, thereby leading to wider effective spans of management.[4] Unit and process production had narrower spans.

ORGANIZATIONAL STRUCTURES

organizational structure

The formal relationships among groups and individuals in the organization are called **organizational structure**. The organizational structure provides guidelines essential for effective employee performance and overall organizational success. The structure clarifies and communicates the lines of responsibility and authority within the firm and assists management in coordinating the overall operation.

Although we usually think of large companies when we discuss organizational structures, every firm, large or small, has a structure. It may or may not have an organizational chart. Small businesses may have simple structures that are easily understood; in fact, the organizational structure may be informal and highly changeable in a small, uncomplicated business. By contrast, large, diverse, and complex organizations usually have a highly formalized structure, but that does not mean the structure is so rigid that it cannot change, perhaps even frequently.

Determining the most appropriate organizational structure is not a simple matter. Considerable experimentation and analysis is necessary before a firm is in a position to adopt a suitable structure for its particular kind of work. Even so, changes in the firm's external environment or in its overall objectives may necessitate further structural experimentation or analysis. The frequency with which some companies reorganize is an indication of how actively they are searching for the most workable structure. Newly formed high-technology companies are likely to reorganize frequently; but, as noted earlier, some long-established Canadian industrial firms may also introduce structural changes to improve their effectiveness.

organizational
chart

The structure of an organization is shown in its **organizational chart**, which depicts diagrammatically a firm's formal structure at a point in time. An organizational chart does not indicate the extent to which authority is delegated, what the organization's objectives are, the comparative importance of the various jobs in the organization, or the informal relationships that spontaneously arise in the organization over time. (The informal organization is discussed in Chapter 8.)

A cursory glance at the organizational charts of several different organizations reveals what appears to be an almost infinite variety of structures. However, a close examination of these structures shows that most of them fit into one of two basic categories: functional or divisional.

The Functional Structure

functional
structure

The oldest and most commonly used structure is the **functional structure**, similar in concept to departmentation by function. Both are established on the basis of the key functions the organization must perform in order to reach its objectives. In Chapter 6, we showed how departmentation by function would look in a traditional manufacturing firm. (Refer to Figure 6-3.) Examples of how a functional structure looks in various other organizations are shown in Figure 7-4.

An analysis of these examples clearly shows that the work of the various functional areas must be coordinated by some higher authority. In the manufacturing firm in Figure 6-3, the functions of person-

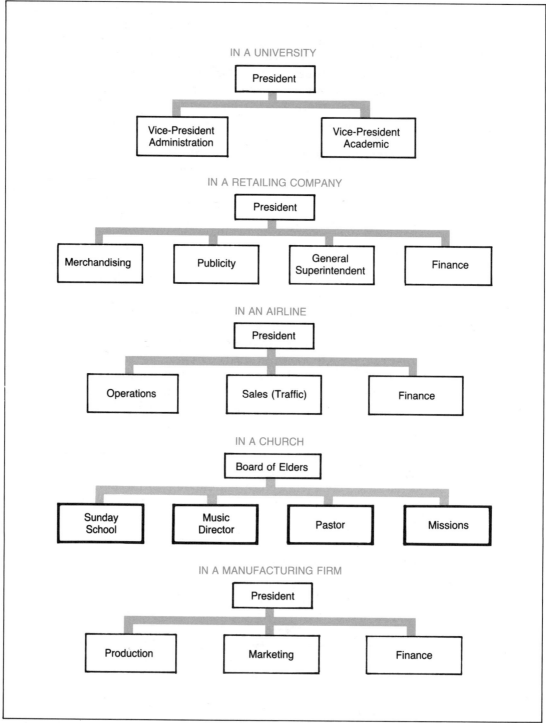

FIGURE 7-4 Functional structures in various kinds of organizations

nel, engineering, production, marketing, and finance are coordinated by the president because not one of these functional areas can by itself achieve organization goals.

Advantages of the Functional Structure

Functional structure is common because it has several advantages. First, it encourages specialization of labor. Specialization normally leads to efficiency in the performance of tasks. A person who is a specialist in marketing, for example, will likely do a better marketing job than a person who must know a little about marketing in addition to other jobs. The functional structure therefore promotes a career path for people with specialized skills. Second, employees understand the structure. It is easy for employees to understand that specialized functional areas exist in the firm and that these specialized areas must work together. As well, employees in each of the areas work with people who have training similar to theirs; task accomplishment is enhanced because these employees see that they have something in common with their coworkers. Finally, functional structure eliminates duplication. In the functional structure, there is only one marketing department, or one production department. With only one department for each of the key functions, little duplication of activities occurs. It is very unlikely that two departments would each be working on, say, the effects of advertising on sales without being aware that another group was working on the same question. Rather, all work is centrally coordinated; duplication is minimal.

Disadvantages of the Functional Structure

The functional structure can have some disadvantages. Employees do not have a systems perspective. Perhaps the major failing of the functional structure is that employees become overly concerned with activities in their own specialized area and are not concerned enough about coordinating their work with other areas of specialization. A classic example of this problem is the conflict that arises between marketing and production in many firms. Marketing wants a diverse product line and short delivery times in order to maximize sales; production wants a limited product line and long production runs in order to minimize costs. Another potential problem with functional structure is that no one function is accountable for results. Since no single function can achieve organization goals by itself, each one can argue that it is blameless if the organization as a whole doesn't perform well. If a company suffers a financial loss, who is to blame? marketing? production? personnel? finance? The answer is usually not clear.

A serious disadvantage of a functional structure is the lack of training for top management. Since each manager in a functional structure works in a specialized area, he or she may not be getting good training for truly top management positions. The top person in an organization must be able to see how all parts of the organization work together, but a person who has come up through the ranks in a specialized area may have difficulty seeing the significance of functional areas outside his or her own specialization. As a result, certain functions (those of the person's previous experience) may get preferred treatment, and the total organization suffers.

The Divisional Structure

divisional
structure

The functional structure's disadvantages can make it inappropriate for some companies. In fact, many companies have adopted instead the **divisional structure:** the organization is broken down into divisions; each division operates as a semiautonomous unit and as a profit center. The divisions may be formed on the same basis as departmentation by product, customer, or geography. (Refer back to Figures 6-4, 6-5, and 6-6). Whatever basis is used, each division operates almost as a separate business. Divisional performance can be assessed each year by the parent company because each division behaves as a separate company. Firms with this structure are often called conglomerates.

Advantages of the Divisional Structure

The divisional structure is suitable for some companies because it facilitates expansion. If the parent company wishes to expand into additional lines of work, it can simply add another division to focus on this new line of work. Since many companies are very interested in growth, this advantage is important.

Accountability is also increased. Each of the divisions is responsible for reaching its own profit targets; thus, there is much more discipline than in the functional structure. Managers within each division must think constantly in terms of actions that will generate profits for the division.

A further advantage of the divisional structure is that expertise is built within each division. If a division is organized around products, the managers within that division will have detailed knowledge about those products. If a division is organized around geography, managers in that division will have detailed knowledge about local markets. Knowledge of this type benefits the division and increases the chance of good performance. Finally, divisional structure allows for training for top management. Since the head of a division is really acting in the role of a chief executive overseeing all functional areas, the divisional structure is a good training ground for top managers. A person who successfully headed a division could likely take over an independent company because of his or her previous experience as a top manager.

Also, since one firm will have several divisions — each with its own top management — it will have a pool of experienced managers as candidates for promotion.

Disadvantages of the Divisional Structure

In spite of these substantial advantages, the divisional structure has some potential problems. Certain activities, for example, may be duplicated. It is quite likely that two (or more) divisions in a conglomerate could be working on the same problem. If these different divisions do not communicate with each other about what they are doing (and often they do not), costly duplication can result. If two divisions are working on a new rust-inhibiting paint but are unaware of each other's work, much less may be accomplished and higher costs incurred than if their work were coordinated. This duplication of effort is probably the greatest disadvantage of the divisional structure. A further disadvantage may be that specialists' communication is limited. Each division in a conglomerate will have specialists (chemists, engineers, or geologists) with skills that are relevant for that division. The communication between, say, engineers working in different divisions may be infrequent. Various studies have shown that ideas often emerge when specialists have in-person discussions about problems they are working on.

Another serious disadvantage is that the conglomerate may have no strategy for adding divisions. One of the criticisms of the divisional structure is that the parent company can become involved in such a diverse set of activities that no one has an overview of the entire organization. In the 1970s, for example, many conglomerates were forced to get rid of certain divisions because they were performing poorly, but no one in the parent company knew enough about the divisions' activities to take appropriate remedial action.

Whether an organization uses a functional or divisional structure, it must make a decision about whether or not to use staff experts. If it decides not to use them, the firm maintains a simple line organization; if it does use them, the firm has a line and staff organizational structure. The distinction between these two organizational structures is discussed below.

The Line Organization

line organizations

line departments

Line organizations are those that have only direct, vertical relationships between different levels within the firm. They include only line departments. **Line departments** are those departments directly involved in accomplishing the primary purpose of the organization. In a typical manufacturing firm line departments include production, finance, and marketing. In a line organization, authority follows the chain of command. Figure 7-5 is an illustration of a simple line organizational structure.

Several advantages are associated with the pure line organization structure.

ADV

- A line structure can simplify and clarify responsibility, authority, and accountability relationships within the organization. The levels of responsibility and authority of personnel operating within a line organization are precise and understandable.
- A line structure promotes fast decision making and allows the organization to change directions more rapidly, since few people must be consulted when problems arise.
- When pure line organizations are small, close communication between management and employees is easily promoted and all personnel usually have an opportunity to know what's going on within the firm.

DISADV 1)

Despite these advantages, line organization also has certain disadvantages. The major disadvantage is its increasing lack of effectiveness as the firm grows larger. At some point, speed and flexibility do not offset the lack of specialized knowledge and skills. In other words, a line structure may force individual managers to wear too many hats,

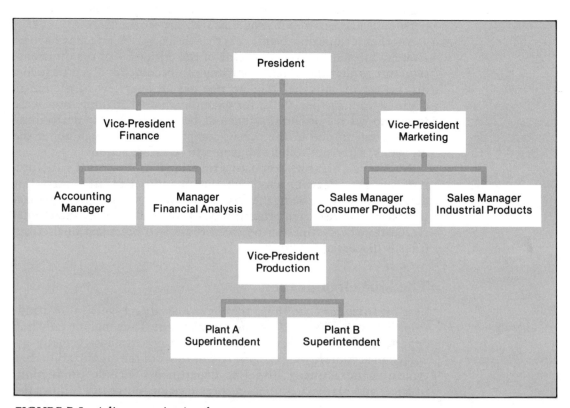

FIGURE 7-5   A line organizational structure

thereby reducing their effectiveness. In a line organizational structure, the firm may become overly dependent on one person or a few key people who can perform numerous jobs. If the organization is to remain purely line, one solution is for management to seek help by creating additional levels of organization to share the managerial load. This, however, will result in a lengthening of the chain of command and a consequent loss of some of the values of speed, flexibility, and central control.

The Line and Staff Organization

Suppose Bill Smith starts a company and over a period of several years the firm grows and becomes quite successful. Smith (now president) heads an organization that looks like the one shown in Figure 7-6. This is a line organization: all the positions in the organization are in the direct line of authority from the top of the firm down to the bottom. Each level in the organization is subordinate to the ones above it, and there are no advisory specialists. This structure might work very well as long as the company does not get too large. However, with increased growth the need for specialized experts almost surely will emerge. If these experts are added to the organization, the structure is called a line and staff organization.

line and staff
organizations

Line and staff organizations are those organizations that have direct, vertical relationships between different levels as well as specialists responsible for advising and assisting other managers. Such organizations have both line and staff departments. **Staff departments**

staff
departments

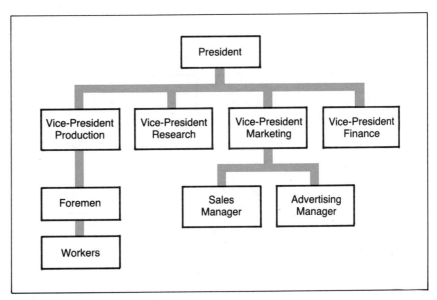

FIGURE 7-6   A line organization in a production-oriented organization

are departments that provide line people with advice and assistance in specialized areas. Depending on the organization, these experts might be personnel experts, legal advisors, market researchers, accountants, industrial engineers, or computer programmers. Bill Smith's company might now look like the one shown in Figure 7-7.

The line and staff structure preserves the authority relationships in organizations in the face of primary and secondary goals. In the line and staff organization, certain functions are considered central to goal attainment (line functions), and others are considered secondary (staff functions). The principle of line and staff relationships states that line personnel have command authority in their functional areas; staff personnel, on the other hand, have the right to provide advice to line personnel in their (staff) field of expertise. Keep in mind that staff personnel (for example, the director of marketing research in Figure 7-7) have line authority over the people in their own department.

Strictly speaking, it is incorrect to say that line functions are more important and staff functions are less important, since in some

SEE HANDOUT ✳ ✳

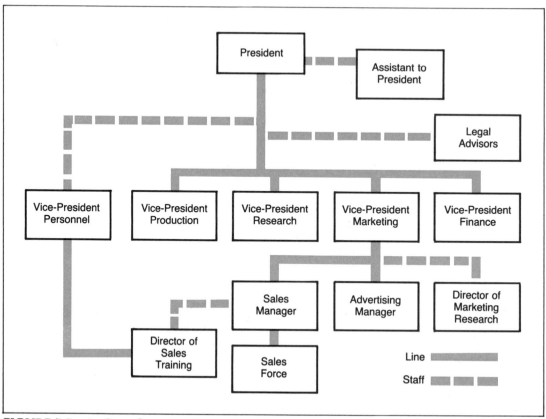

FIGURE 7-7   Outline of a typical line and staff structure in a production- oriented organization

instances staff functions, while secondary in relation to goals, are nevertheless very significant. In these situations, staff people usually possess functional authority, which can make them equivalent to the line, although such situations are generally temporary.

An example of the prominence of a staff expert in a coal mine operation would be a safety engineer. While safety is not a primary function of the organization — it is not the organization's main objective to produce safe mines — safety is nevertheless so crucial to productivity that the safety engineer is given the equivalent of line authority. This permits the production manager of the mine to retain full (line) authority and accountability over the complete operation of the mine but, should the situation require, allows the safety engineer to exert influence in matters of mine safety. In this instance, the production manager would likely have a general safety orientation and training, whereas the safety engineer would be highly specialized in the field of safety engineering.

personal staff

advisory staff

service staff

control staff

Four separate types of specialized staff units can be identified: (1) personal, (2) advisory, (3) service, and (4) control. **Personal staff** (for example, the executive assistant to the president) assist specific line managers but generally do not act for them in their absence. **Advisory staff** (for example, personnel, marketing research) advise line managers in areas where the staff has particular expertise. **Service staff** provide a specific service to line managers (for example, testing and interviewing of prospective applicants by the personnel department). **Control staff** (for example, accounting, quality control) are those with the responsibility for controlling some aspect of organizational performance, although theoretically they still only provide advice.

It is possible for one unit to perform more than one of these functions. For example, the personnel department may *advise* line managers on the appropriateness of recognizing a particular labor union, provide a *service* by procuring and training needed personnel, and exercise *control* by auditing salaries to ensure conformity to line-approved pay ranges.

Some staff units, by contrast, may perform only one of the four functions. For example, a staff economist may *advise* the establishment of long-range plans, a maintenance staff unit *repairs* plant equipment, and a quality control staff *enforces* authorized product standards. The potential for conflicts in coordination between line and staff tends to be greatest in a control relationship, and least in an advice relationship. Advice can be ignored, but service is needed, and control is often unavoidable.

There are both advantages and disadvantages to a line and staff organizational structure. The primary advantage is that it uses the expertise of specialists. The actions of a manager can be made more systematic by concentrated and skillful analysis of business problems. In addition, the manager's effective span of management

MANAGEMENT IN PRACTICE

The Executive Assistant

The executive assistant position exists in many organizations. People who are executive assistants are usually one of three types. First, they can be staff people brought up from the ranks. For example, Lyn Johnson is the executive assistant to the president of Shell Oil. In her position she organizes most of the president's official encounters with people outside Shell Oil. This involves assisting the president in choosing speaking engagements, helping with speech writing, and keeping him up to date on a variety of issues.

Another kind of executive asistant is the one with a few years of line experience, who is a "comer" in the company but needs some high-level experience. Ben Heineman of Northwest Industries takes bright young executives, makes them his special assistant for a couple of years, and then puts them into top line positions. One former assistant, for example, became president of one of Northwest's chemical subsidiaries and then moved up to vice-president of Northwest.

The third type of executive assistant is one who may be as old or older than the boss. This may be a person who realizes that he or she won't make it to a top line position, but who likes having the power that goes along with reporting to a top executive.

Other people in the organization are often suspicious of executive assistants because they don't know how much power the assistant has or how favorably the boss views the assistant. Another potential problem is that the executive assistant can lose his or her own identity in the shadow of the boss. One executive assistant quit soon after his boss did because he found he had no reputation or identity as an executive in his own right.

SOURCE   Adapted from Walter Kiechel, "The Executive Assistant," *Fortune* (November 15, 1982): 177 – 180.

---

can be widened — he or she can supervise more people. Some staff personnel may operate as an extension of a manager to assist in coordination and control.

Despite the fact that a line and staff structure allows for increased flexibility and specialization, it may create conflicts. When a firm introduces various specialists into its organization, its line managers may believe they have lost authority over certain specialized functions. These managers do not want staff specialists telling them what to do or how to do it, even though they recognize the specialists' knowledge and expertise. To maintain good working relations, a firm should introduce staff personnel without destroying unity of command. The right of the line manager still remains, although the ability to exercise this right may have been considerably weakened. The problem is not so much the type of structure as the individual personnel within it. Some staff personnel have difficulty adjusting to the role of adviser, especially if line managers are reluctant to accept their advice. Staff personnel may resent not having authority, causing further conflict.

Functional Authority

functional
authority

A pure line structure makes limited use of specialists. The line and staff organizational structure frequently uses specialists. If a staff specialist is given authority over a line manager with regard to the staff person's specialty, a **functional authority** relationship has been created. Functional authority is typically limited to the areas in which the staff person is an expert. The chain of command of line authority and the notion of single accountability is broken, creating multiple accountability.

Although few firms are established completely on a functional authority basis, increasing numbers of companies have some staff specialists who have functional authority over some line executives. If a firm considers a function to be crucial, it may need the specialist to exercise direct, rather than advisory, authority. The violation of single accountability is undertaken deliberately. The possible losses resulting from confusion or from conflicting orders from multiple sources may be more than offset by increased effectiveness in the performance of the specialty.

Good examples of specialties that have been given functional authority in many organizations include quality control, safety, and labor relations. (See Figure 7-8.) Quality control is a prominent

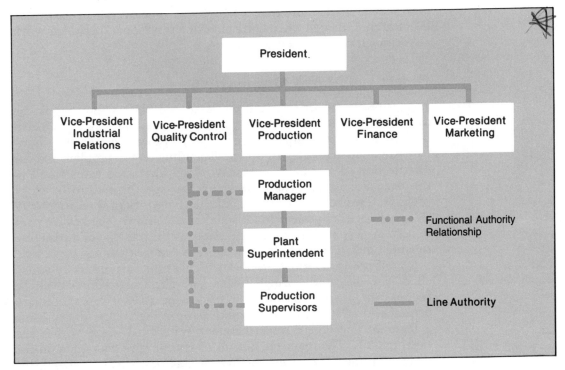

FIGURE 7-8   Functional authority

function in most manufacturing organizations, and its level of authority and stature within organizations has increased over the years. A staff quality control department would merely advise; if, however, that unit is given the authority, or right, to issue orders (for example, to correct defects) in its own name, it has functional authority.

Likewise, safety and labor relations specialists may exercise functional authority over personnel in other areas of the organization, but only in relation to their specialties. A safety manager may issue compliance guidelines and give direct interpretations of provincial health and safety regulations; a labor relations specialist often will have complete authority in contract negotiations with the union. In each of these examples, the traditional chain of command has been split. As long as this splitting process is restricted, coordination and unity of action are not in real danger. Many organizations that use functional authority attempt to confine its impact to managerial rather than operative levels. Thus, a department supervisor may have to account to more than one superior, but the employees are protected from this possible confusion.

Despite the advantages of functional authority, two potential problems can result: (1) the conflicts from the violation of the principle of single accountability, and (2) the tendency to keep authority centralized at higher levels in the organization. If functional authority is used extensively, the line department supervisor may become little more than a figurehead. The overall structure can become complicated when corresponding functional specialists work at various levels in one organization.

Project and Matrix Organizations

The primary concern of line and line and staff structures is the distribution of authority through emphasis on vertical, rather than horizontal, relationships. However, work processes may flow horizontally, diagonally, up, or down, depending on the problem and the distribution of available talents. Work requirements often result in the need for organization based on the specific nature of work projects. Two forms of organizing that have emerged to cope with this challenge are project and matrix organizations. The key element in both project and matrix organizations is the creation of a structure in which managers and professionals have more than one superior.

project organization

A **project organization** provides a highly effective means by which all of the necessary human talent and physical resources can be focused for a time on a specific project or goal. It is a temporary organizational structure designed to achieve specific results by using a team of specialists from different functional areas within the organization. The team focuses all of its energies and skills on the assigned project. Once the specific project has been completed, the project team is broken up and personnel are reassigned to their

MANAGEMENT IN PRACTICE

How to Use a Task Force

A task force is a group of people brought together for a specified period of time to work on solving a specific problem facing an organization. The task force's mandate can range from searching for a new president, to deciding which computer system to buy. Ideally, a task force should address matters that relate to the future, not try to solve problems from the past. The task force should come up with concrete recommendations that management can act on.

Task forces are often not used properly. To increase the chance that they will be effective, the following guidelines are suggested:

1. Membership should be representative of those who have insights into the issue being examined.

2. The size of the task force should be limited to six to eight people.
3. The mandate of the task force must be clear to the members.
4. The role of the chair is crucial. An outside facilitator may be needed to ensure proper discussion of sensitive issues.
5. Deadlines must be strictly enforced. The manager who sets up a task force must set realistic deadlines and then let the task force do its work without interference.

SOURCE Adapted from Andrew Campbell, "Task Force Offers Great Potential, But Strong Discipline Is Required," *The Globe and Mail* (April 27, 1987): B7.

regular positions in the organization. Many business firms and government agencies make use of project teams or task forces to concentrate their efforts on a specific project assignment, such as the development of a new product or new technology or the construction of a new plant.

The project organization is used extensively by Canadian firms. The construction of hydroelectric generating stations is a case in point. These large-scale projects are headed by a project manager who oversees all aspects of the construction. When the station is completed, it is turned over to the operating people and then becomes part of the traditional structure of the provincial hydroelectric utility. Project organization is also used in the technological development in the prairie tar sands. The extraction of energy resources from this area is a unique and complex activity; project organization has proven useful for coordinating the many elements needed to extract oil from the tar sands.

Project organization is most appropriate when work is:

- Definable, in terms of both a specific goal and target date for completion
- Unique and unfamiliar to the existing structure
- Complex, with respect to interdependence of activities and specialized skills
- Critical, in terms of possible gain or loss
- Temporary, with respect to duration of need.

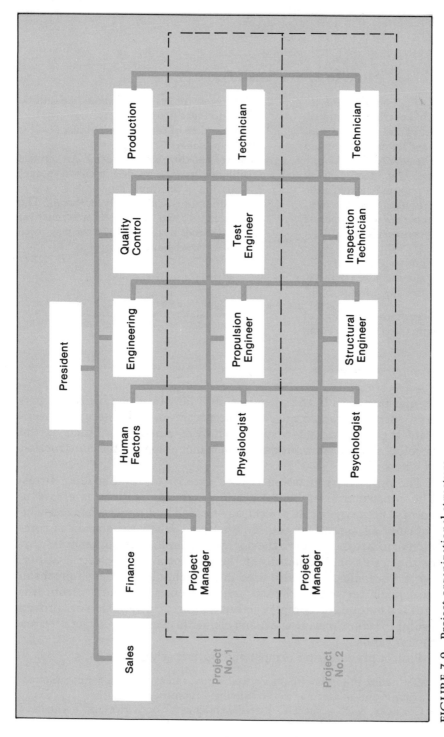

FIGURE 7-9   Project organizational structure

Figure 7-9 illustrates a simplified project organization within an existing structure. Personnel are assigned to the project from the existing structure and work under the direction and control of the project manager. The project manager specifies what effort is needed and when work will be performed, while the individual department managers may decide who in their unit is to do the work and how it is to be accomplished. Home base for most personnel is the existing department — engineering, production, purchasing, personnel, or research and development.

The authority over the four project members is shared by both the project manager and the functional managers in the existing structure. The specialists are temporarily on loan to spend a portion of their time on the project assignment. Since a deliberate conflict has been established between the project manager and managers within the existing structure, personnel authority will obviously be a crucial issue. The authority relationships are overlapping, presumably in the interest of ensuring that all problems will be covered.

Project managers and department heads are often forced into using means other than formal authority to accomplish results. Informal relationships become more important than formal prescriptions of authority. In the event of conflict and dispute, discussion and consensus are required rather than forceful compliance by threat or punishment. Full and free communication, regardless of formal rank, is required among those working on the project. More attention is allocated to roles and competence in relation to the project than to formal levels of authority.

matrix
organization

Project organizations are temporary attachments to existing structures. When this concept is introduced as a more permanent structure, it is usually referred to as a **matrix organization**; this format is often used when the firm must be highly responsive to a rapidly changing external environment. For example, an electronics firm operating in a highly competitive market with rapidly changing technology might find that the matrix organization facilitates quick response to this environment. The matrix organization, however, requires the use of an effective coordinating mechanism to offset the negative effects of dual authority.[5] Matrix organizational structures have been used successfully in such industries as banking, chemicals, computers, and electronics.

Matrix organizations have functional managers and product managers. Functional managers are in charge of such specialized resources as production, quality control, inventories, scheduling, and selling. Product managers are in charge of one or more products; they are authorized to prepare product strategies and call on the various functional managers for the necessary resources. When a firm moves to a matrix organizational structure, its functional managers must realize that they will lose some of their authority and will have to take some direction from the product managers, who have budgets to purchase internal resources.

Tom Ward
Genstar Shipyards Ltd.

Tom Ward is Operations Manager for Genstar Shipyards Ltd., a Vancouver firm that specializes in the custom building and repair of icebreakers, research vessels, ferries, tugs, and barges. The company has sales in excess of $30 million and employs 200 to 400 workers. It is the second largest shipyard on Canada's west coast; in peak periods, it has delivered a new ship every two months. Ward is responsible for the overall operations of the shipyard. His duties include: (1) reviewing and approving project cost estimates that have been developed by the shipyard's estimators and engineers, (2) writing proposals for custom-built vessels, and (3) setting work schedules once a shipbuilding contract has been awarded to the company. He is a member of the management committee and reports to the president.

Ward works closely with two full-time new construction project managers (PMs), who have degrees in marine engineering in addition to considerable shop floor experience. Each ship the company builds is treated as a project, and the PMs have the responsibility of seeing that each project is finished on schedule, to specification, and within budget. Some projects employ up to 400 people, making the PM's job a major administrative function. Each PM has a small clerical staff to assist in this work.

Q: What is the dollar value of a typical project, and how long does it take to complete?

Ward: The value of each project varies widely and can range from a low of about $2 million for a small tugboat, to a high of nearly $60 million for a state-of-the-art icebreaker. Projects run from a minimum of four months to a maximum of two years.

Q: What does a PMs job involve?

Ward: The project manager is responsible for the initial development of a master schedule for the vessel's design and construction. In conjunction with the estimating, technical, and purchasing departments, he identifies items of machinery and outfit which are critical to this schedule; if necessary, he will negotiate with the ship owners and designers to modify the specifications to allow equipment to be used whose availability and quality satisfies both the shipyard's schedule and cost budgets and the owners' performance requirements. During this period, the PM interacts with all departments having input into both the technical and the commercial aspects of the construction contract; he also familiarizes himself with the overall intent, requirements, preferences, and priorities of the customer. Once there is an agreement that the master schedule satisfies both the ship owners' and builders' requirements, the PM is responsible for seeing that the schedule and budget are adhered to. After launching and completion of outfitting, the PM oversees the trials of the ship and her delivery to the owner. He will then act as the main contact between the shipyard and owners during the guarantee period — usually one year after delivery.

Q: What kind of authority does a PM have?

Ward: The PM derives most of his authority from reporting to the same level that the shipyard superintendents report to. He has specific authority to decide the construction sequence and how many workers will be assigned to each phase of the project. He makes these decisions after consulting the project plans and the time-frame in which the project must be completed. He does not have authority to hire, lay off, or fire workers employed on the project — this remains with the worker's functional supervisor, the department foreman; but the PM works with all the foremen to determine when the work force should be increased or decreased. Shipyards employ many different trade skills — steelworkers, welders, carpenters, painters, pipefitters, electricians, and machinists — and the PM must be knowledgeable about the collective agreement the company has with various trade unions.

The PM also approves purchase orders being placed with outside suppliers and subcontractors. Throughout the project, he is required to keep a close eye on costs committed to purchase orders, and he has to work closely with the accounting department in approving accounts payable. In the event of any dispute arising with these outside sources, the PM's approval is required for payment of their invoices. In many companies, the PM does not have this type of authority, but we have found that it is beneficial.

Q: Do the workers on a project report to the PM or the foreman?

Ward: The workers report to the foreman, and the foreman takes direction from the PM. The PM can often decide which worker he wants assigned to a project. If the PM and the foreman disagree about which particular tradesmen or how many of them in a specific trade will be on which project, the PM can appeal to the foreman's superintendent. He usually gets his way on staffing issues, because those levels on our projects are so important and both understaffing or overstaffing can have a serious effect on the project schedule and cost.

Q: Are there other disagreements that arise between a PM and the foremen?

Ward: Yes. For example, a foreman might think work on some aspect to the ship's construction ought to be done in a particular way, and the PM might think it should be done in some other way. If the disagreement is a question of sequencing the work, the PM will usually prevail; but, if the disagreement is about specific trade practices, the foreman will generally get his way. As another example, a foreman may try to assign more tradesmen to a project than the PM thinks necessary. The foreman may do this to give himself a cushion in meeting his schedule. In these cases, the PM usually wins out because he has the total project schedule and budget in mind, whereas the foreman may be thinking only of the work that his particular crew is doing.

Q: Do the two PMs ever have disagreements with each other?

Ward: Sometimes. However, it is important that a high level of communication and trust exist between the two PMs because they must think about how all the shipyard's contracts can be most effectively dealt with. Each PM is drawing from the same common pool of tradesmen and helpers, so they must be flexible in their demands and keep the good of the total company in mind when making their respective staffing decisions. The better the quality of each worker loading schedule developed from the master construction schedule, the less will be the potential for conflict in this area.

Q: What kind of skills does a PM have to possess to be effective?

Ward: Three basic skills, really. First, the PM must be very strong in his interpersonal skills. He has to be able to instill enthusiasm and push the project forward at as fast a pace as possible. However, should a disagreement arise between a PM and a foreman, the PM must be sensitive enough to know when to push hard for his point of view and when to ease off. Second, the PM must have good administrative skills so that he can keep track of the total project, its physical progress, and the extent of committed costs at all times. Finally, he must possess good technical skills so that he can communicate effectively with the technical people on the project. This allows the PM to assess accurately how well the work is progressing and to deal with any technical problems that might arise.

Q: On balance, how has the project management structure worked for Genstar Shipyards?

Ward: It is really the only structure that makes sense for us. Since time is of the essence in every construction contract we enter into and costs have to be closely monitored, the project structure is necessary. It focuses our efforts on the activities that are needed to get the job done, and that helps us meet our time deadlines. It is very gratifying to see a finished ship leaving.

Despite limitations, the effectiveness of the project and matrix structures demonstrates that people can work for two or more managers and that managers can effectively influence those over whom they have no clear authority. The possibility of conflict and frustration is a risk, but the opportunity for prompt, efficient goal accomplishment is great.

OPENING INCIDENT REVISITED

The Faculty of Administration

Frank Singh, head of the department of management, was wondering how to resolve the scheduling problem that had arisen between himself and John Gebhart, the associate dean of the faculty. Singh was concerned that he would get complaints no matter what decision he made. If he agreed with Gebhart, he would be accused of favoritism; if he agreed with members of his department, Gebhart would be dissatisfied.

This incident demonstrates how problems can arise in organizations when authority and responsibility are not equal and when job responsibilities are not clearly stated. Singh believes he has the responsibility to assign Gebhart's class load, but doesn't feel he has the authority to do so. The inequality of authority and responsibility is causing Singh some difficulty, but the solution to his problem is quite straightforward. Singh shouldn't be deciding how many classes Gebhart should teach because Gebhart doesn't report to Singh. Figure 7-1 clearly shows that Gebhart reports to the dean, not to Singh. Therefore, the only person who has the authority to determine Gebhart's teaching load is the dean. The dean should decide what proportion of Gebhart's time should be spent teaching and what proportion should be spent on administrative work; once this information is conveyed to Singh, he can assign the number of classes that the dean thinks is appropriate. Singh should not get caught up in trying to make a decision he has no authority to make.

Situations like this can and do arise frequently in organizations. Why? Perhaps people get so involved in trying to get their work done that they forget to analyze fundamental issues, such as equating authority and responsibility.

SUMMARY

Determining the appropriate levels of responsibility and authority is essential to sound organizing. Derived from functions, responsibility is an obligation to perform certain work activities. It is crucial to the success of a firm that responsibilities be clearly defined. Once responsibilities have been assigned to personnel, superiors must then delegate enough authority to get the job done. Authority is the right to decide, to direct others to take action, or to perform certain duties in achieving an organization's goals. A basic principle of management is that authority should equal responsibility. The process of making specific work assignments to individuals within the organization and giving them the authority to perform these functions is known as delegation. Delegation is an important concept if work is to be accomplished and people in the organization are to develop expertise. Once authority has been delegated, an individual can then be held accountable for results. Accountability is the final responsibility for results that a manager cannot delegate to someone else.

Depending on the extent of the delegation of authority, an organization is said to be either centralized or decentralized. In a centralized organization, decisions are made primarily by top management, whereas in a decentralized structure, lower-level managers in the organization play a more active role in making decisions. The four important principles of authority, responsibility, and accountability that must be considered in the delegation process are:

- Single accountability: A person should have only one superior
- Authority should equal responsibility
- A chain of command: Clear definition of authority (through channels)
- Span of management: A limit to the number of people a manager can supervise effectively.

The means for organizing the functions, resources, and the formal relationships is the organizational structure, of which there are two basic types: functional and divisional. Within both these general categories we can find three other structural variations: line, line and staff, and project or matrix. A line structure is the simplest and most basic. The line and staff structure allows for increased flexibility and specialization with the introduction of staff specialists who serve as advisers. However, it creates conflict over authority. In the line and staff structure, staff specialists are given authority to issue orders in designated areas of work. Finally, project and matrix organizational structures provide a means by which all of the necessary human talent and physical resources are allocated for a time to a specific project.

REVIEW QUESTIONS

1. Define and illustrate the following:
   a. responsibility
   b. authority
   c. accountability.
2. What is meant by centralization and decentralization?
3. What are the advantages and disadvantages of centralization and decentralization?
4. Briefly describe the primary factors to be considered in determining the degree of centralization that is appropriate for an organization.
5. What is meant by delegation? Identify four reasons for delegating and four limitations of delegation that managers should consider.

6. Identify and briefly define four significant principles of management governing authority, responsibility, and accountability relationships. What are some possible causes for and results of the violation of these principles?
7. What are the advantages and disadvantages of wide and narrow spans of management? What factors affect the span of management?
8. Identify the two basic types of organizational structures. Draw a chart to illustrate each.
9. Briefly discuss the strengths and weaknesses of each type of organizational structure identified in question eight.
10. What is the difference between a "line" and a "line and staff" organizational structure?
11. What is functional authority? Why is it used?
12. Under what circumstances are project and matrix organizational structures most appropriate?

EXERCISES

1. Analyze the organizational charts of a local retail store, a bank, a manufacturing company, and your college or university. How is each organized and what are the bases of departmentation used? What changes, if any, would you suggest in the structure of these organizations? Draw new charts if necessary.
2. Go to the library and review two current journal articles describing corporate reorganizations. At the next class meeting report to the class one example of a company that has been reorganized. In your three-minute presentation briefly describe the company as well as the reasons for and the advantages of the reorganization.

CASE STUDY

Misco Paper Converters

When Dick Valladao and George Smeltzer, owners of Misco Paper Converters, began their business, it was only a part-time operation. The operation involved buying rolls of brown kraft paper, such as that used for grocery bags, cutting it into various shapes and sizes, bundling the sheets together, and shipping the bundles to industrial customers. The pieces of paper were used for various purposes: as vapor barriers in electronic equipment, to place between glass or china plates and bowls prior to shipping, and as a protective wrapping for many small manufactured items.

As the business grew and became more profitable, Dick and George decided to leave their jobs and work at Misco full time. They had been doing the work in a small metal building behind George's house, but when they went into the business full time they rented a 2000-square-meter warehouse. They also purchased a shear press and a stripper in addition to the press and stripper they already owned, as well as a truck to pick up the raw paper at the paper mill and to make some deliveries. Usually the bundles of paper were shipped by common carrier to customers, some of which were as much as 600 miles distant.

Dick and George found it necessary to hire six operators. The operation was simple. The paper was fed off the large rolls through a stripper, which cut it to the appropriate widths. The stripping machine was set to clip the paper off every fifty feet or so. Then the strips were stacked on top of one another on a set of rollers that allowed the paper to be fed back into one of the shear presses. When a stack of strips was fifty layers thick, it was fed into the shear press, which clipped it to the appropriate length. The resulting rectangular stacks of brown paper were tied with twine and stacked onto shipping pallets. When a pallet was full, it was set aside to wait for shipment.

At first, George and Dick worked with the operators as a team, with each worker doing whatever needed to be done. Each person soon learned to operate the forklift, the strippers, and the shear presses and tie bundles as well. Dick and George felt themselves to be relative equals, so neither attempted to exercise authority over the other. As time went on, however, Dick began to think that the whole operation could be accomplished more efficiently if some kind of structure were imposed.

QUESTIONS

1. Do you believe that anything is to be gained at Misco by establishing an organizational structure, including specialization and lines of authority and responsibility? Explain your answer.
2. Assuming that George and Dick decided to set up a typical kind of organization, how should they decide who is to be chief executive? Should they have to decide that at all? Explain.

CASE STUDY

Managing Growth at Sharp's

At 07:00, O.C. Sharp unlocks his office door. He has been arriving at this same office at this precise hour, six days a week for the past 19 years; that was when he took over as president of Sharp's Department Stores from his father, who had turned a family-operated dry goods business into a three-store firm. Under O. C. Sharp, the business has grown to a 16-store firm in 10 Ontario cities. O. C. Sharp is considered by business colleagues to be a shrewd businessman and a far-sighted planner, even though some question his paternalistic attitudes toward his employees.

During his 19 years as chief executive at Sharp's, Sharp pioneered the development and implementation of modern management systems, including MBO, as well as extensive planning, policy, and procedure systems. The organization and its president have a reputa-

tion as an effective and efficient machine. (Figure 7-10 shows the current organizational chart at Sharp's.).

Sharp obviously knows how to operate a department store successfully; few others have the success he enjoys in this highly competitive field. Each store in the firm handles operations in the same way because Sharp has constantly overseen the writing and revision of "operating procedures." These "OPs", as Sharp calls them, give step-by-step methods for all phases of operation; they are discussed and updated at monthly managers meetings. Sharp, the four vice-presidents, and all store managers attend these meetings. A typical meeting would involve four to five hours reviewing, discussing, and updating the OPs and the remaining time on discussions of merchandise, buying, scheduling of company-wide sales, store expansion

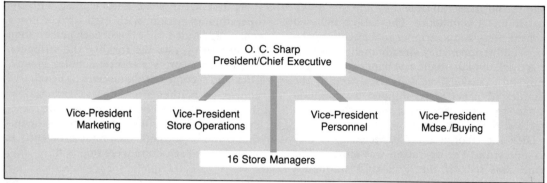

FIGURE 7-10 Organizational structure of Sharp's

plans, and selection and training of personnel.

On this particular morning, though, Sharp's mind keeps turning over a conversation he'd had the day before with one of the vice-presidents. They had both been expressing disappointment over recent stunted sales volume and the slow-down in the growth rate of the business. Sharp recognized some time before that he had been finding it increasingly difficult to add new stores. He'd always believed he could manage a chain of 25 or 30 stores with equal success using his OP system. What's troubling him this morning is the realization that he can't seem to stay on top of all activities in the 16 stores he has now. He wonders if he needs to change some facet of the business, or if he's just getting too old to manage as president.

QUESTIONS

1. What do you think is the source of Sharp's Department Stores' recent slump? If O. C. Sharp consulted you, what advice would you give him?
2. Refer to Figure 7-10. Evaluate the strengths and weaknesses in the current organizational structure of Sharp's Department Store chain.
3. What changes to the organizational structure or the reporting relationships would you suggest, in order to respond to any weaknesses you've found?

ENDNOTES

[1] J. D. Ford and W. H. Hegarty, "Decision Makers' Beliefs About the Causes and Effects of Structure: An Exploratory Study," *Academy of Management Journal* (June 1984): 281.

[2] A. V. Graicunas, "Relationships of Organizations," *Papers on the Science of Administration*, eds. L. Gulick and L. Urwick (New York: Columbia University Press, 1947).

[3] L. W. Fry and J. W. Slocum, Jr., "Technology, Structure, and Workgroup Effectiveness: A Test of a Contingency Model," *Academy of Management Journal* (June 1984): 236.

[4] Joan Woodward, *Industrial Organization: Theory and Practice* (London: Oxford University Press, 1965); 52–62.

[5] J. L. C. Cheng, "Interdependence and Coordination in Organizations: A Role-Systems Analysis," *Academy of Management Journal* (March 1983): 160–161.

REFERENCES

Arnold, John D. "The Why, When, and How of Changing Organizational Structures." *Management Review* (March 1981): 17–20.

Benson, Robert. "Delegation: A Tough Skill to Learn but Worth the Cost." *Canadian Business* (December 1982): 138.

Campbell, Andrew. "Task Force Offers Great Potential, But Strong Discipline is Required." *The Globe and Mail* (April 27, 1987): B7.

Gibson, James L.; Ivancevich; John M.; and Donnelley, James H. Jr., *Organizations: Behavior Structure and Processes.* Dallas: Business Publications, 1981.

Graeff, Claude L. "The Situational Theory: A Critical View." *Academy of Management Review* 8, no. 2 (April 1983): 285–291.

Haynes, M. E. "Delegation: There's More to It Than Letting Someone Else Do It." *Supervisory Management* 25 (January 1980): 9–15.

Herbert, Theodore T. "Strategy and Multinational Organizational Relationships Perspective." *Academy of Management Review* 9, no. 2 (April 1984): 259–270.

Joyce, William. "Matrix Organization: A Social Experiment." *Academy of Management Journal* 29, (September 1986): 536–561.

Karasek, R. A. Jr. "Job Demands, Job Decision Latitude for Job Redesign." *Administrative Science Quarterly* 24 (June 1979): 285–308.

Logges, J. G. "Role of Delegation in Improving Productivity." *Personnel Journal* 58 (November 1979): 776–779.

Ouchi, W. G. "Relationship between Organizational Structure and Organizational Control." *Administrative Science Quarterly* 22 (March 1977): 206–216.

Peters, T. J. "Beyond the Matrix Organization." *Business Horizons* 22 (October 1979): 15–27.

Potter, B. A. "Speaking with Authority: How to Give Directions." *Supervisory Management* 25 (March 1980): 2–11.

Rousseau, D. M. "Assessment of Technology in Organizations: Closed versus Open Systems Approaches." *Academy of Management Review* 4 (October 1979): 531–542.

Waterman, H. Jr.; Peters, J.; and Phillips, R. "Structure Is Not Organization." *Business Horizons* 23, no. 2 (June 1980): 14–26.

Wente, M. A. "Remaking the Management Mind." *Canadian Business* (January 1983): 24.

Group Behavior and the Informal Organization

KEY TERMS

group	role	synergism
informal group	contact chart	grapevine
informal organization	sociogram	status
norms	cohesiveness	status symbol

LEARNING OBJECTIVES

After completing this chapter you should be able to

1. Explain what the informal organization is and why it exists within every formal structure.
2. Explain how group goals, norms, roles, leadership, and structure differ in both the formal and informal organizations.

3. Describe the importance of cohesiveness, size, and synergism in the informal organization.
4. Identify the benefits and costs of the informal organization.
5. Explain the concept of status, status sources, and status symbols.

OPENING INCIDENT

Mary Soo's Lesson

Mary Soo was excited to have her new job at Jay-Mar Garments. She had been looking for a job for nearly six months. During the interview, Mary had been told that she would be paid on a piece-rate basis (a certain amount of money for each garment she produced). She was looking forward to this system because she was a fast worker. At other jobs she had held, she was paid on an hourly basis, and even though she produced more than the other workers, she received the same amount of money. Mary viewed the new job as an opportunity to show her skills.

Mary was friendly and had no trouble fitting in to the work group, at least at first. In short order, she was exceeding the production quota for her job. After receiving one particularly good paycheque (with a $50 bonus for extra production), she ran into one of her coworkers, Pat Allman. After telling Pat about her bonus, Mary was surprised when Pat replied, "You shouldn't produce so much. Management will simply reduce the piece rate and then we'll all be paid less for doing the same amount of work."

Despite Pat's disapproval, Mary continued to work hard and earn big bonuses. Before long she noticed that many of her coworkers were going out of their way to avoid her. Several of them finally spoke to her privately and told her in strong terms that she had better reduce her output. Faced with this pressure, Mary let her production drop back to normal. Gradually, her coworkers began to be friendly again.

To this point, we have talked about managers occupying positions in the formal structure of organizations without much reference to them as people. Chapters 6 and 7 outlined the types of formal structures and functions managers must consider when organizing. Chapters 8, 9, and 10 consider how the human element affects and is affected by the organizational structure.

In a general sense, inserting the human element into an organization blunts the clear, logically designed official structure that so appeals to some managers. These managers are proud of the formal structure they have created, precisely because it is logical and orderly. (See Figure 8-1.) Everyone knows exactly who he or she reports to and the task each is expected to do. Some managers believe their organizing function is fulfilled, and that their work will run itself, once they have developed orderly formal structures.

This is a false hope. When the orderly structure designed by managers is peopled, it is often drastically altered to conform to people's wants and needs. The way a company is formally organized

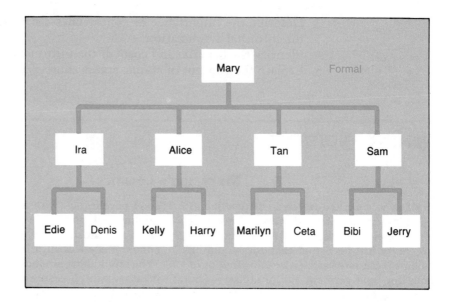

FIGURE 8-1
The formal
organization

and the ways employees actually interact may be enormously different. An illustration of the way the informal group operates within the formal organization is shown in Figure 8-2. Mary, the president by title, actually has little influence; Alice is recognized as the most influential decision maker (even by Mary herself). Ira, Tan, and Sam defer to and confer with Alice rather than Mary; all three compete with one another for Alice's attention, hoping for promotion if Mary steps aside. Alice is so busy she hasn't noticed that Kelly and Harry, who report to her, dislike each other and try constantly to undermine one another's efforts. Denis, taking advantage of the hostility between Kelly and Harry, deals more often with Alice than with his own supervisor, Ira. Edie, who also reports to Ira, wonders who's really in control and who should be doing Denis's neglected work. Marilyn and Ceta, although they report to Tan as his employees, are both more interested in him as a member of the opposite sex. Bibi, Ceta's friend, is more interested in the romance in the adjacent area than in working for her supervisor, Sam. Jerry, who also reports to Sam, spends much of his time trying to influence Mary because he is sure she will one day take back her rightful authority.

Overall, Figure 8-2 makes one key point: employees often do not conform to the formal structure that has been prescribed. Rather, they develop spontaneous friendships and relationships based on criteria that are not derived from the formal structure. They sometimes choose their own informal leaders and allegiances; these leaders may or may not be those selected by the formal organization. Managers must be aware of the informal organization if they want their formal structures to work toward effective organizing.

In this chapter, we examine the nature of the informal organization

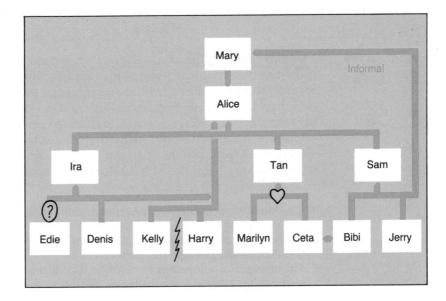

FIGURE 8-2
The informal
organization

and show how it can have both a positive and negative influence on the formal organization. We begin by briefly noting the importance of groups in organizations and how they are an integral part of the informal organization. Next, we systematically compare the key features of formal and informal organizations. The benefits and the costs of the informal organization are examined, and we conclude with a discussion of the important role of status in organizations. The objective of this chapter is to give you an appreciation of the factors a manager must consider when dealing with the informal organization. Failure to deal with such issues effectively will almost certainly guarantee managerial failure.

GROUP BEHAVIOR

group

informal group

A **group** is two or more people joined together to accomplish a desired goal. Within a company, many different groups exist. Our concern here, though, is primarily informal groups. An **informal group** is defined as two or more persons associated with one another in ways not prescribed by the formal organization. The informal group includes workers who are especially close friends and have their own cliques. Two or three people might belong to the same church or baseball team, or they might go fishing or have parties together. There are job-related groups, too, within work groups. If you work close to a person who does similar work, you will probably communicate with that person much more than with others. Managers need to understand all of these kinds of groups if they are to accomplish their jobs effectively.

COMPARING FORMAL AND INFORMAL ORGANIZATIONS

informal organi-
zation

The **informal organization** refers to the patterns of behavior and influence that arise out of the human interaction occurring within the formal structure. While formal and informal organizations are similar, they have some important differences. Because the informal organization can exert a strong influence on employee behavior, managers must understand its nature, how it works, in what ways it affects behavior, and how it can be used in the management of organizations. Examples of behavior in the informal organization are many and varied. Here are a few:

- A production worker restricts output to conform to the norm of the rest of the work group.
- Management plans a major announcement for employees but the message is leaked earlier through the grapevine.
- The manager of a department may find that during the baseball season the leader of the company baseball team appears to exert more influence than the line managers.
- A potentially conflict-laden meeting proceeds rationally — most of the disagreements on issues were worked out the night before over a few drinks.

In general, the informal organization emerges because the formal structure does not satisfy all employee and organization needs. The exact form the informal organization will take depends on the specific deficiencies in the formal structure and on the particular needs of employees. Managers do not have a choice as to whether or not the informal organization will develop; informal relationships *will* be formed within any formal structure. Managers should try to understand, rather than to suppress, the informal organization and to channel its energies toward organization goals.

Another reason for the existence of the informal organization is the human need for predictability and stability in interpersonal relationships and social processes. The formal organization is unable to provide them, since formal structures are generally designed from a mechanical, rational perspective, not a behavioral one. The personal relationships that develop from on-the-job interaction provide the necessary security and predictability that individuals need, resulting in the informal structure parallel to the formal one.

The formal and informal organizations have common attributes, but the manifestations of these attributes differ significantly. Informal organizations represent the human side of organizations, and are dependent on the nature of individuals in the organization; formal organizations, since they are not spontaneous, are usually highly structured and give less emphasis to human considerations. In one sense, the formal organization is "how it should be" and the informal organization is "how it actually is." Table 8-1 summarizes many of

TABLE 8-1 A Comparison of Formal and Informal Organization
Characteristics

Characteristic	Informal Organization	Formal Organization
Structure		
Origin	Spontaneous	Planned
Rationale	Emotional	Rational
Characteristics	Dynamic	Stable
Representation	Contact Chart	Organization Chart
Position terminology	Role	Job
Goals	Member satisfaction	Profitability or service to society
Influence		
Base	Personality	Position
Type	Power	Authority
Flow	Bottom up	Top down
Control mechanisms	Norms	Threat of discipline, firing, demotion
Communication		
Channels	Grapevine	Formal channels
Networks	Poorly defined, cut across regular channels	Well defined, follow formal lines
Speed	Fast	Slow
Accuracy	Moderate	High
Membership		
Individuals included	Only those "acceptable"	All individuals in work group
Interpersonal relations	Arise spontaneously	Prescribed by job description
Leadership role	Result of membership agreement	Assigned by organization
Basis for interaction	Personal characteristics, ethnic background, status	Functional duties or position
Basis for attachment	Cohesiveness	Loyalty

the differences between formal and informal structures. In the discussion that follows, several key differences between formal and informal organizations, noted in the table, are analyzed in more detail.

Norms

norms

The formal organization has its performance standards, and the informal organization has its **norms,** or standards of behavior expected from group members. Those who violate group norms are pressured to conform. This informal pressure is often more powerful than official sanctions used by managers to enforce conformity to organization standards. A worker who is a good producer — highly acceptable to the formal organization — may be ostracized by the informal organization until his or her production falls back in line with the informal group's norms. Group norms are unwritten rules that new members, if they are to remain members, gradually learn. Norms that are frequently understood include: how hard one should work, whether one should be friendly, the degree to which one should cooperate with managers, and whether one should be innovative.

Roles

role

The concept of role is broader than that of its counterpart in the formal organization — the job. A **role** consists of the total pattern of behavior expected of a person. In the formal organization it includes, but goes beyond, the official content of the job description. If a person is officially designated a supervisor, pressure may be exerted to dress, talk, and act like other supervisors in the organization. If managers in a firm dress formally, the manager who fails to wear the proper "uniform" is not fulfilling the expected role.

Individuals in an informal group also are expected to act out a role. The amount of support an informal group of employees gives its managers has a major impact on the roles of the group members. If the group decides it should not support a decision made by top management, the pattern of its behavior (role) may reflect indifference or slowing down on the job. Failure to conform to the expected role may result in a member's psychological ejection from the informal group.

A person may have many roles that he or she must play. For instance, when working toward his doctorate, one of the authors was a student, a teacher, a consultant, and a military officer. For each of these activities, the author needed a different role; failure to change roles immediately at the proper time often resulted in difficulties. Being a military officer on the weekend with considerable authority, followed on Monday morning by the learning role of a doctoral student was sometimes not easy. Supervisors working in firms who return to school part-time often encounter similar difficulties.

Leadership

In the formal organization, managers are placed in their position of authority by top management. By assuming a particular managerial position, an individual is formally designated as leader of the group. However, this formally designated person may not be the most influential person in the group. Some other person, known as the informal leader, may fill that role. The informal leader is not chosen in the same way as the formal leader; rather, he or she emerges gradually. No formal election is held; yet other employees usually have little difficulty identifying the informal leader of their group or section.

The informal group leader is usually the individual who best satisfies the needs of the group. For example, if a major need of the group is security, the individual who can best reach this goal for the group will be the informal leader. If technical expertise is important, then a highly skilled technician may emerge as the informal leader. The important point here is that the informal leader may well be someone whom management does not formally recognize as having any authority. Yet if the informal group puts great weight on that person's views, management cannot ignore that fact in its decision making.

Structure

Although it is sometimes difficult to chart, the informal organization has its own structure. As with the formal structure, informal groups may also have different levels in a chain of command. Sometimes managers may chart the informal organizational structure, but the members themselves rarely diagram their structure. Successful executives know that an organizational chart cannot capture who has the real influence and authority in an informal organization.

The informal structure constantly changes as different members enter into and exit from the group. The structure is heavily based on the communication patterns that develop among group members. If many people attempt to get advice from one individual, this individual is often the informal leader and the structure develops around this person. Just as formal organizations have vice-presidents, the informal group may have a second-in-command. The informal structure evolves and changes, rather than being formally laid out, but it is often more effective than the structure of the formal organization.

contact chart

One means by which the structure of an informal organization may be studied is through the use of a **contact chart**. This chart identifies the connection that an individual has with other members of the organization. Many contacts do not follow the formal organization chart. (See Figure 8-3.) In various instances, certain levels of management are bypassed; others show cross-contact from one chain of command to another. Based on the number of workers contacting individual 19, he or she appears to be very popular and is likely an informal leader.

One difficulty with a contact chart is that it does not show the reasons for relationships that develop. Also, these contacts could work either for or against the organization. Individual 19 in Figure 8-3 could be assisting other employees in doing their work or could be stirring up trouble for the organization and promoting disharmony among company employees. Once managers have identified the ma-

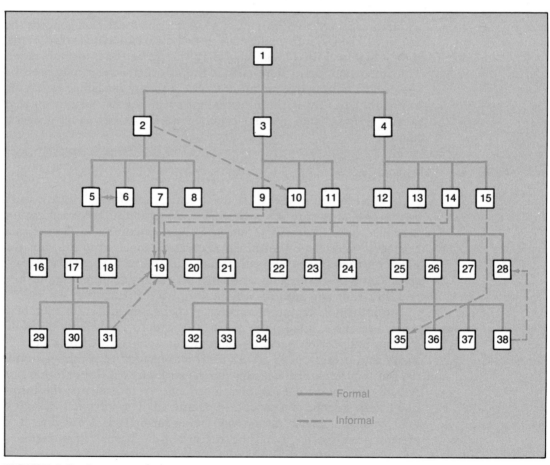

FIGURE 8-3   A contact chart

jor contact points, they are in a position either to encourage or discourage the individual leader within the work group.

A contact chart is used to chart informal relationships throughout the organization. A technique which can be used to chart informal relationships within a particular group is sociometric analysis. The outcome of this type of analysis is a sociogram, an example of which is shown in Figure 8-4. The **sociogram** illustrates how the members of a group interact with each other; it is developed by observing the actual behavior of group members. Through such observation it is possible to answer important questions, such as which group member has the most influence, which group members do not adhere to group norms, which individuals are excluded from the group, and which person is the informal group leader.

sociogram

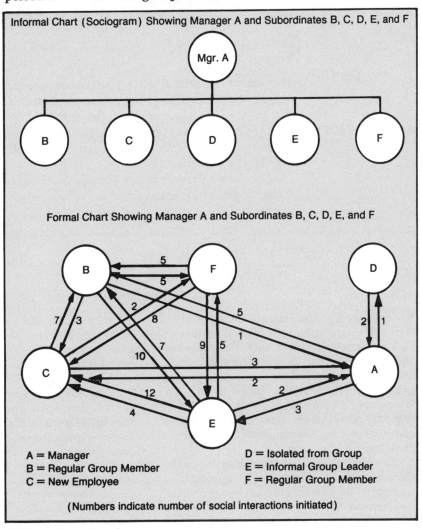

FIGURE 8-4   A sociogram

Cohesiveness

cohesiveness

The degree of attraction that the group has for each of its members is referred to as **cohesiveness**. It has importance for both the formal and informal organizations. It is identified by such attitudes as loyalty to the group, a feeling of responsibility for group effort, defending against outside attack, friendliness, and congeniality. Cohesive informal work groups are powerful instruments. For instance, a highly cohesive group whose goals are in agreement with organization objectives can use this strength to assist the firm in increasing productivity. On the other hand, a highly cohesive group that is not in agreement with organization objectives can have an extremely negative effect on the accomplishment of the firm's goals. Because of this potential power, some managers attempt to reduce group cohesion in order to maintain control.

Size

The size of the formal work group is determined by the needs of the organization; the size of the informal organization is determined by the kind of satisfaction that the informal group members want. Because interpersonal relationships are the essence of informal organizations, the informal group tends to be small, so that its members may interact frequently.

Since many organizations consist of thousands of members, the initial approach to managerial organizing must be formal in nature:

MANAGEMENT IN PRACTICE

Executive Bonding

A number of Canadian companies are sending their executives on non-traditional outings as part of their experience with the company. Sheraton Corp., for example, regularly sends its executives to Collingwood, Ontario for swimming, skiing, and sleigh rides. Kai Habranson, vice-president of Sheraton, feels that the environment there lessens tensions and opens up communication between managers.

One program involves "roughing it" in the Canadian bush. David Clark, president of Campbell Soup of Toronto, along with six of his vice-presidents, went on an Outward Bound program near Lake Superior in September 1986. The trip included paddling on the lake for four days, being alone in the wilderness for one day, and scaling a sheer granite cliff. Clark says the experience resulted in "team bonding." After the seven men returned, they spent time discussing how what they had learned on the trip could be applied to business management. The trip cost the company $9000 plus air fare, but Clark feels it was well worth it.

SOURCE   Adapted from Dorothy Lipovenko, "One Way To Cut Management Flab," *The Globe and Mail* (January 1, 1987): B1-B2.

the design of official units, definition of jobs, and establishment of relationships for authority, responsibility, and accountability. Within this formal organization, many small, informal work groups will be spontaneously established and — so managers hope — will be aligned with overall organization objectives.

Synergism

synergism

Synergism means the whole is greater than the sum of its parts. In the context of an organization, synergism can mean that, when two or more people work together, they can do more in total than would have been possible by each person working separately. Synergism also comprises the possibility of accomplishing tasks that could not have been done at all by two people working alone.[1] The concept of synergism has implications for both the formal and informal organizations. Managers need to recognize that greater effort may be achieved when two workers cooperate. However, through the synergistic effect, the informal organization achieves more power because people in groups have much more influence than each individual has alone.

BENEFITS AND COSTS OF THE INFORMAL ORGANIZATION

Managers often have mixed emotions about informal work groups. On the one hand, the work group is capable of contributing to greater organizational effectiveness. On the other, the informal organization *can* work against the best interests of the organization. If managers are properly trained to understand and work with informal groups, the benefits should exceed the costs. (See Figure 8-5.) Without proper attention, however, the scale may tip the other way.

Benefits of the Informal Organization

Managers cannot destroy the informal organization — fortunately, because it is capable of providing significant benefits to an organization. These potential values are discussed below.

Assists in Accomplishing Work

For a manager to be effective, his or her subordinates must be permitted a certain degree of flexibility in performing their assigned tasks. Requiring advance approval of every move is detrimental to productivity. If people in a business acted only when they were told

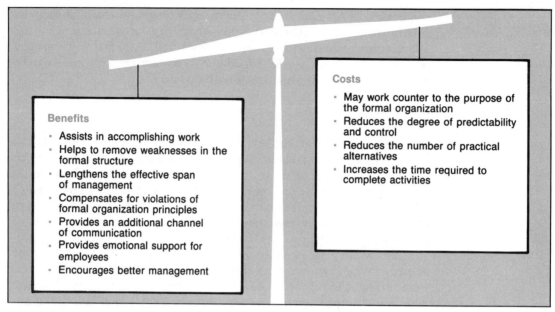

Benefits

- Assists in accomplishing work
- Helps to remove weaknesses in the formal structure
- Lengthens the effective span of management
- Compensates for violations of formal organization principles
- Provides an additional channel of communication
- Provides emotional support for employees
- Encourages better management

Costs

- May work counter to the purpose of the formal organization
- Reduces the degree of predictability and control
- Reduces the number of practical alternatives
- Increases the time required to complete activities

FIGURE 8-5   Benefits and costs of the informal work group

to act, followed standard instructions to the letter at all times, and contacted others only when duly authorized, the business would have to cease operations.

Occasionally, a formal command will be unsuitable or inadequate for the situation. If the atmosphere in an organization is prominently traditional, subordinates may exhibit "malicious obedience" by executing a command faithfully, despite personal knowledge that their action will ultimately result in failure. Unions working to rule provide an example of this tactic. Many managers have discovered that subordinates can follow every directive to the letter and yet fail miserably. If more faith is placed in informal relationships, subordinates may voluntarily adapt the formal order to the requirements of the actual situation. When a work group is loosely structured, it is often able to achieve objectives more effectively.

Helps To Counter Weaknesses in the Formal Structure

The formal organization often has a number of gaps that the informal group can fill. Consider a person who is promoted to a position that exceeds his or her capabilities. This condition is not unusual for a newly promoted manager. He or she must be given time to get used to the position and, possibly, to make some mistakes because of inexperience. While the new manager is learning how to do the job properly, the informal organization can fill in the gaps in his or her knowledge and experience. For example, experienced employees can show the new manager how certain tasks are done and why they are done that way. The formal organizational chart says the new manager is the boss but, by informally acknowledging temporary weaknesses caused by inexperience, help may be obtained from subordinates. As the new manager gains more experience, this kind of reliance on the informal organization will decline.

Broadens the Effective Span of Management

As we indicated in Chapter 7, the number of people a manager can supervise effectively is limited. If individuals and small groups are permitted to interact more cohesively, their manager need not devote as much time to each individual worker. This informal cooperation could contribute to a broadening of a manager's formal span of management.

Compensates for Violations of Formal Principles

The development of informal relationships can compensate for the violation of certain traditional principles of formal organizations, such as the idea that authority should equal responsibility. As a result, employees try to develop informal contacts with personnel over whom they have no formal authority. Favors are traded and friendships form. Employees quickly learn that the formal prescription of authority is often not a sufficient base for operation. This informal compensation still does not negate the desirability of having responsibility equal authority, however.

Provides an Additional Channel of Communication

grapevine

The informal means by which information is transmitted in an organization is called the **grapevine**. To some traditional managers, the grapevine constitutes an obstacle, to be destroyed. They seek to channel and control most, if not all, communications through the official chain of command. However, the grapevine can add to organizational effectiveness if managers use it for their own purposes. Clues to the changing informal structure can be gained through the grapevine; managers can even circulate unofficial information through the grapevine.

Use of the grapevine does not decrease the importance of the official channels of communication and command. Although the grapevine can spread much information in a short time, it cannot provide the authority necessary for much of the action that will take place.

Provides Emotional and Social Support for Employees

Many managers find out the hard way that employees need emotional support while they are working. Over half of all voluntary resignations in Canadian businesses are estimated to occur within the first six months of a person's employment. These are often a result of poor hiring and orientation procedures, where the new employee is given little help in joining and being accepted within work groups. Friendships, or at least speaking acquaintances, are essential to a satisfactory working environment for most people. In one hospital, the termination rate among janitorial personnel was high; research disclosed that the janitorial staff felt isolated and uncomfortable when working alone among physicians, nurses, and patients. Hospital management formed cleanup teams of janitors; the new work teams reduced the negative feelings, and the turnover rate declined considerably.

Encourages Better Management

Awareness of the nature and impact of the informal organization often leads to better management decisions. A manager who enjoys good informal relations with coworkers, and who is sensitive to the nature and effects of relations among his or her subordinates, will be much more effective in motivating employees. Organizational performance can be greatly affected by the workers who grant or withhold cooperation and enthusiasm. Means other than formal authority must be sought to develop attitudes that support effective performance.

Costs of the Informal Organization

If a manager is hostile toward informal work groups or tries to suppress their activities, the drawbacks of the informal organization are more likely to emerge. We discuss some of the possible costs below.

May Work against the Formal Organization

Most managers realize that individuals and groups can and sometimes do work in opposition to the formal goals of an enterprise. If the goals of the informal group were always the same as those of the formal organization, few managers would oppose its existence. However, on occasion, informal organizations engage in tactics like work restriction, pressuring workers into disregarding company requirements, disloyalty, insubordination, and unauthorized actions that hurt the company. When these tactics are used, they usually frustrate and anger managers, who then try to suppress the informal organization. Unfortunately, attempts at suppression will take time and will probably make the informal organization dig in its heels even more.

Reduces Degree of Managerial Control

Some managers feel uncomfortable with the informal organization because they believe it reduces their control over subordinates' work performance. Some subordinates may have much more informal influence than their position on the formal organizational chart suggests. A basic purpose of structure is to ensure predictability and control of individual behavior, so that individuals will work effectively toward organization goals. Accomplishing this purpose depends, however, on people interpreting and executing formal guidelines. Managers must recognize and accept the positive effects of more flexible management, but they also must accept the risks that accompany this lower degree of control. The informal element can and does add much to an organization's effectiveness; it also can and does add more uncertainty.

Reduces the Number of Practical Alternatives

A study of military combat units during World War II concluded that the natural unit of personal commitment was the informal group, not the total formal organization.[2] The soldiers reported that one of their major reasons for moving forward in combat was to avoid letting the other fellow down. The solidarity developed in the informal group greatly strengthened the motivation of individual members.

The significance of this finding creates problems in businesses when it is necessary to transfer personnel. If natural groups are broken up by moving individual members in and out of them, a degree of motivation and cooperation is reduced. This potential loss may mean that managers should think in terms of moving groups around, rather than individuals. If managers wish to capitalize on the considerable values issuing from the development of primary work groups, they must lose some flexibility in the making of decisions.

Increases the Time Required To Complete Activities

If the cooperative efforts of the informal work groups can be aligned with the objectives of the firm, managers have the best of both worlds. The collective power generated can be quite phenomenal. Managers will find, however, that informal work group activities, such as gossiping, betting pools, long coffee breaks, and general horseplay, are time consuming, and may be detrimental to efficient operations. These acts will tax the patience of managers who have specific goals to reach within strict deadlines. Yet, if an effective work group is to be established, some of these activities will have to be permitted — and some even encouraged. Managers must realize that, despite concern for goal accomplishment, they must allow the group time and opportunity to maintain itself in good working order. People can usually sustain action for a longer period of time under an informal atmosphere than they can when in a rigid, controlled, and formal situation.

Charles W. McDougall
Royal Victoria Hospital

Charles W. McDougall is an administrator at the Royal Victoria Hospital in Montreal. The 863-bed hospital is associated with McGill University and provides major research and teaching components, along with patient care. McDougall reports to the vice-president of corporate affairs, who reports to the president. About 60 percent of his time is devoted to project administration, including the planning of new building and renovation being undertaken by the hospital. The remainder of his time is spent managing such line functions as maintenance of buildings, care of equipment, and security. In total, he is responsible for coordinating the efforts of about 75 people, most of whom are consultants, and administering a budget of about $16 million per year.

Q: What are the main formal groups that must interact within the hospital?

McDougall: We have over 200 physicians located full-time in the hospital. There are senior administrators, finance people, nurses, hospital service workers, laboratory workers, professional service workers, and members of the auxilliary services. Many of the groups are represented within their professions or by unions, of which we have 17 locals.

Q: How are the interests and concerns of all these various groups represented and served in the operation of the hospital?

McDougall: A lot of the actual policy of the hospital is determined by committees. About a third of my time is related to committee activities. I serve on seven major committees, including the Property Committee, the Management Advisory Committee, the Management Information Systems Master Group, the Equipment Committee, the Space Committee, the Building Coordinating Committee, the Interdepartment Coordinating Committee, and about eight planning task forces. A basic function of the committees is to rationalize the competition for limited resources.

Q: Is there a lot of competition among members of the committees? One would expect the politics to become intense in the effort to sway a committee to one or another point of view.

McDougall: First of all, let me explain that the committees do not vote; they work by consensus, although the chairperson may exert considerable influence to establish a consensus in some situations. Members do tend to argue from the background base that they represent and to favor the needs of their own constituents, but no one wants to close the door completely on anyone. After all, they all need to work together in the future. Resources do tend to be spread around. Of course, the way that happens may sometimes be an extension of self-interest. Security has a very low profile and low priority in the allocation of resources for equipment, but, if a few microcomputers have been stolen from various departments and offices, funds for security cameras to watch the unguarded exits may be approved hastily. Without that kind of incident, the security director lacks the power base to have his requests supported.

The workings of most of the committees are quite smooth, but in the Space Committee, groups get very territorial. Department directors "own" space within the hospital. When they need additional space for some reason, they can usually only get it by expropriating space from someone else. Committee work becomes more difficult on such occasions.

Q: Are there situations in which the existence of informal relationships or groups undercuts or, perhaps, enhances the accomplishment of management policy?

McDougall: The situation at the Royal Victoria Hospital seems to work against the formation of informal groups. Perhaps there are so many formal structures created by the departments and the interdepartmental committees that most possible informal groups have been made formal.

Informal relationships still exert considerable influence, of course. There was a situation a while ago when the president authorized the creation of some new office space for one department. This was a small department, and the new space would represent a significant increase in its size. The decision was made without the approval of the Space Committee. In my mind, the decision occurred primarily due to the informal relationships that exist around the president. The chief of that particular unit is a physician with an international reputation. Keeping key people from becoming world travellers is a legitimate concern, but now I have the problem of where to place the dominoes. So far I have managed to relocate the occupants of three offices that adjoin the department. Finding the additional required space is proving more difficult.

Unlike other places I have worked I have little social interaction here outside the formal structures. There is almost an ethic among managers that discourages social intercourse.

In some ways this situation makes a manager's work more difficult. Socialization produces some commonality of goals. I once worked for a hospital where several managers met every two weeks to play penny-ante poker. Many of the hospital's problems were sorted out at those games. Here I don't have access to such chances to talk things over in a relaxed social setting. This situation here may result in more rational decision-making processes, but it is certainly more demanding. I feel that I am more effective as a manager when I can work through informal channels as well as formal ones.

STATUS

Thus far we have noted that the formal organization attempts to organize jobs rationally so that organizational goals will be achieved. We also noted that the informal organization may facilitate or inhibit the achievement of organizational goals. Consider the following example of the interaction between the formal and informal organizations. A manufacturing firm has three vice-presidents: finance, marketing, and production. From a strictly structural perspective, each of these vice-presidents is equal to the others. But everyone in the organization knows that one of the vice-presidents really has much more influence than the other two. Situations like this are common in organizations because of status differences between individuals in a given group.

status

A person's rank or position in a group is called **status**. The concept of status has considerable effect on the morale and productivity within an organization. Status is a component of human relationships in all aspects of life, as well as in business. In this section, we examine the sources of status in business organizations, the symbols that denote status levels, and the functions of a status system.

Status Sources

The sources of status, or social rank, can be of both an informal and a formal nature. Examples of these sources are:

Formal	Personal
Occupation or job	Education
Organizational level	Age
Job title	Seniority
Salary	Ethnic origin
Authority	Religion
	Parentage
	Gender
	Competence
	Associates

Certain jobs are accorded more prestige than others. In the most general sense, white-collar jobs have higher status than blue-collar jobs. But within this broad classification additional distinctions are made. For example, electricians have more status than cleaners, even though both are blue-collar jobs. Computer programmers have more status than office clerks, even though both are white-collar jobs. Even finer distinctions can be made. Long-distance telephone operators have more status than local operators; cafeteria personnel who serve beef have higher status than those who serve fish; and graduate students have higher status than undergraduates.

The status of an occupation depends on: (1) the rank accorded the occupation by one's peers or by society, and (2) the job's level within the enterprise structure. The former is defined by the informal organization, while the latter is indicated by the formal organization. The status given a job by the informal organization may or may not be consistent with the status given to it by the formal organization. For example, a maintenance crew may occupy a relatively low position on the formal organization chart, but, because they do critical repair work that keeps the entire factory running, they may have very high status. Their status may also be high because they can move around the factory, whereas other workers must stay at one machine.

MANAGEMENT IN PRACTICE

No Place for Big Egos at Deacon Morgan

Campbell Deacon is chairman of Deacon Morgan McEwen Easson Ltd. Neither Deacon nor his vice-president, Anthony Edwards, have an office. And they say they never will because all the action at their company is in the large open space where brokers, traders, and finance people do their work. The work atmosphere is very casual — people wear shirtsleeves and address each other by their first names.

The firm has grown rapidly since its beginning in 1986. Integrating new people into the firm has been an important activity and it has gone very smoothly, because the team concept has been stressed. One strategy has been to hold Friday afternoon parties with all the staff, so people can catch up on what has happened during the week.

Mr. Deacon says that big egos are not in fashion in the company. He says the company is just one of the "little guys" having fun, and is not trying to take over the world.

SOURCE Adapted from Patricia Lush, "Big Egos Out Of Place At Deacon," *The Globe and Mail* (March 31, 1987): B1-B2.

MANAGEMENT IN PRACTICE

Status Symbols at Ontario Hydro

Most large companies spell out status symbols quite clearly, and Ontario Hydro is no exception. It has very detailed specifications regulating office size and furnishings for its managers. For example, the office sizes are as follows:

Chairman	56 m^2
Executive Vice-President	46 m^2
Vice-President	37 m^2
Directors	32 m^2

Office furnishings are also specified in detail. For example, directors get no extras except two plants and a couch; vice-presidents are allowed three plants and several pieces of furniture; the executive vice-president gets even more plants and furniture; and the chairman gets two glass walls, a television and videotape machine, even more furniture, and custom white carpet.

SOURCE Adapted from Jerry Amernic, "The Perks of Power," *The Financial Post Magazine* (November 1, 1982): 78.

TABLE 8-2   Status Symbols

Visible Appurtenances	Top Dogs	V.I.P.'s	Brass
Brief cases	None — they ask the questions	Use backs of envelopes	Someone goes along to carry theirs
Desks, office	Custom made (to order)	Executive style (to order)	Type A, "Director"
Tables, office	Coffee tables	End tables or decorative wall tables	Matching tables, type A
Carpeting	Nylon — 1-inch pile	Nylon — 1-inch pile	Wool-twist (with pad)
Plant stands	Several — kept filled with strange exotic plants		Two — repotted whenever they take a trip
Vacuum water bottles	Silver	Silver	Chromium
Library	Private collection	Autographed or complimentary books and reports	Selected references
Shoe shine service	Every morning at 10:00	Every morning at 10:15	Every day at 9:00 or 11:00
Parking space	Private — in front of office	In plant garage	In company garage — if enough seniority

Status Symbols

status symbol

A visible, external sign of one's social position is known as a **status symbol**. A stranger can enter an office and, if aware of status hierarchies, be able to recognize who has status quickly by reading the various symbols. Status symbols do vary from firm to firm; most firms provide managers in the higher-status positions with increasingly elaborate office furnishings. In one organization, however, the high-status positions are given antique roll-top desks, whereas lower jobs come equipped with new, shiny, modern furniture. Symbols sometimes change with the times. Some typical items that can be status symbols (or perquisites) in business are:

- Job titles
- Pay
- Bonus or stock plans
- Size and location of desk or office
- Location of parking space or reserved parking
- Type of company car assigned
- Secretaries or researchers
- Privacy
- Use of executive clubs or sports facilities
- Cocktail party invitations

TABLE 8-2 continued

No. 2s	Eager Beavers	Hoi Polloi
Carry their own — empty	Daily — carry their own — filled with work	Too poor to own one
Type B, "Manager"	Castoffs from No. 2s	Yellow Oak — or castoff from Eager Beavers
Matching tables, type B	Plain work table	None — lucky to have own desk
Wool-twist (without pad)	Used wool pieces — sewed	Asphalt tile
One medium-sized — repotted annually during vacation	Small — repotted when plant dies	May have one in the department or bring their own from home
Plain painted	Coke machine	Water fountains
Impressive titles on covers	Books everywhere	Dictionary
Every other day	Once a week	Shine their own
In company properties — somewhere	On the parking lot	Anywhere they can find a space — if they can afford a car

- Office furnishings, including rugs, pictures, tables, and bookcases
- Privileges, including freedom to move about, not punching a time clock, and freedom to set working hours and to regulate coffee breaks
- Ceremonies of induction
- Number of windows in office.

Many status symbols are within the control of managers and constitute the basis for conflicts. Executives have been caught down on their hands and knees, measuring to compare the sizes of offices. Windows are counted, steps from the president's office are paced off, secretaries who can take fast dictation are sought (even though the supervisor may never give dictation), parking space is fought for, and company cars are wangled. A humorous illustration of the importance of status is shown in Table 8-2.

Some companies have tried to abolish all status symbols by equalizing privileges, offices, and furnishings. Other companies have eliminated executive dining rooms; some use open-landscaped offices. In most universities, the position of department head is rotated among department members, thereby reducing the status attached to the position. In some businesses, windowless buildings have been constructed, office sizes are standardized, and only one type of company car is available.

MANAGEMENT IN PRACTICE

Status Symbols at Crows Nest Resources

Large companies are not alone in specifying status symbols. Even small firms seem concerned about spelling out what managers at various levels are allowed to possess in the way of status symbols. Crows Nest Resources is a Calgary-based coal mining company with only 600 employees. Its office area specifications are as follows:

President	30 m²
Vice-Presidents	28 m²
Managers	21 m²
Others	14 m²

As far as furnishings are concerned, the president gets two plants and expensive Chippendale furniture; the vice-presidents get one plant and walnut furniture; managers get no plants and even cheaper furniture; and others get nothing beyond a desk.

SOURCE Adapted from Jerry Amernic, "The Perks of Power," *The Financial Post Magazine* (November 1, 1982): 78.

Generally speaking, these official attempts to do away with status symbols fail. People want to distinguish their position in the company from the position occupied by other people, and status symbols fulfill this desire. If certain status symbols are not formally allowed, others will emerge. If no one's office has a window, some other criterion (desk size, thickness of carpet, size of plants) will be used to rank people. An individual wants other people to know where he or she stands in the status hierarchy, and status symbols indicate that position with more impact than a job title alone.

Status Functions

Status produces certain positive conditions within the organization. First, status assists in meeting people's social needs. Most employees want the respect of others. Recognition of their abilities and accomplishments becomes tangible through status symbols. Also, status facilitates informal channels of communication in the organization. Even a person's job title conveys subtle messages that help other people process information; an opinion about a computer coming from an electronics expert with programming experience (whose job title states these credentials) is likely to be more valuable than the opinion of a computer salesperson — even if the information is identical. Status can carry influence that helps people weigh alternatives. Clearly, status can act as motivation for managers or for employees who wish to become managers. The perquisites and influence of status provide incentive for managers to perform well and be considered promotable. Nonfinancial incentives can be as satisfying as additional money; if many managers are paid the same salary, the managers may feel motivated to compete for the nonfinancial status symbols. Higher-level managers can develop more comprehensive and coordinated incentives to provide further motivation and, by their awarding of status symbols, indicate approval or disapproval toward managers.

OPENING INCIDENT REVISITED

Mary Soo's Lesson

Mary's problems at Jay-Mar Garments were caused primarily by her lack of insight into the informal organization and the importance her coworkers placed on it. Many workers enter a new job with the desire to produce a lot and thereby improve their financial well-being. They may also receive considerable satisfaction from doing the job well. But the world of work is not simply a matter of pursuing one's own goals. In Mary's case, she has entered a situation where people who are experienced with the piece-rate payment system are suspi-cious of management. Apparently, some events occurred in the past at this company that convinced the workers that producing more would not be to their benefit.

Mary has two basic alternatives. She can decide to produce at a high level and try to cope with the cold shoulder from her coworkers. Or, she can produce at a level that is "acceptable" to the group and be welcomed as a member in good standing. The former alternative is much more difficult to handle than the latter.

SUMMARY

The formal organization establishes what employees should do through organizational charts and job descriptions. However, the formal structure is only one element of organizations. Another struc-ture — the informal organization — invariably emerges as a result of the spontaneous interaction of people at work. The informal organi-zation exists within all formal organizations. It cannot be suppressed or done away with.

A group exists when two or more people join together to accom-plish a goal. Both the formal and informal organizations have goals, but managers often do not want to recognize the existence and goals of the informal organization. The structure of the informal organiza-tion is spontaneous and dynamic while the structure of the formal organization is planned and stable. Influence in the informal organi-zation is based upon an individual's personality and power, while influence in the formal organization is based upon formal position in the hierarchy. Information flows rapidly through the informal organization's "grapevine," but may flow very slowly through the formal organization's communication channels. The informal organization exists to satify its members needs, while the formal organization exists to achieve organizational goals.

There are both positive and negative aspects associated with the informal organization. On the positive side, the informal organization assists in accomplishing work, helps to remove weaknesses in the formal structure, broadens the effective span of management, compensates for violations of formal organizational principles, provides an additional channel of communication, provides emotional and social support for employees, and encourages better management. On the negative side, the informal organization may work against the purposes of the formal organization, reduce the degree of predictability and control in the organization, reduce management flexibility, or increase the time required to complete activities.

A person's rank or position in a group is referred to as status. Status symbols are the visible signs of a person's social position. Status assists in meeting the needs of individuals, aids in the communication process, and serves as a motivational tool for management.

REVIEW QUESTIONS

1. What is the informal organization? Describe how it differs from the formal organization in terms of goals, norms, leadership, communication, and structure.
2. Why does an informal organization emerge within every formal structure?
3. What is group cohesiveness? Is it good or bad for the formal organization?
4. What are the costs and benefits of the informal organization?
5. What is the most effective way for managers to deal with the informal organization?
6. What is the purpose of a contact chart?
7. What is status? What are the three functions of status?

EXERCISES

1. Develop a contact chart for an organization of which you are a member. Interpret the results.
2. Think of three groups that you currently belong to. What are the status symbols in each of the groups? How do the symbols differ? Why do they differ?

3. Interview an acquaintance who has been in the work force for more than five years. Ask the person to tell you about how the informal organization operates in his or her firm. How consistent is the person's description with that given in the chapter?

CASE STUDY

The Young Accountant

Dave Maddala was recruited to work as an accountant for Bradford Ltd., a manufacturer specializing in producing oil-field parts. Dave brought with him an impressive record from his university years; he had been both an excellent student and highly involved in all forms of campus activities. Also, Dave worked intensely for the chartered accountancy firm that employed him while he studied for his CA exams. Generally, people felt comfortable around Dave, and his opinions were well respected by students, faculty, and fellow workers.

Donald Dean, the department head, took great pride in having hired Maddala once he was fully qualified. Dean bragged to his superiors about how he had been able to attract Maddala to Bradford Ltd. As expected, when Maddala began with Bradford, he started with the same intensity that had earned him such respect previously. Maddala learned the job quickly and within a short time was identifying and initiating changes that could improve operations. He followed the chain of command and cleared each modification with Dean. This pleased Dean, for he was able to take credit for the changes with his superiors.

In the department, 10 other accountants reported to Dean. They soon came to recognize Maddala's expertise; they began to go to him with their particular problems, since Maddala's easy-going personality made it easy for others to talk to him. Even though Maddala was junior in age, he was regarded as a true professional. As time went on, employees would even go to him with their personal problems.

A strange situation ultimately developed. If an employee had a problem, he or she would first go to Maddala. If he could not solve it, he would go to Dean. Upward communication was going entirely through Maddala.

Although Dean did not have a reputation for political sensitivity, he recognized what had evolved. Although the department had gained in efficiency since Maddala had joined the firm, Dean did not like his loss of power. He even felt that his career was in jeopardy. Dean reasoned that the only way to eliminate this threat was to ensure that Dave was either transferred or pressured to resign.

Dean immediately began a harassment campaign. He reprimanded Maddala in front of his peers. Anything Maddala recommended, Dean immediately disapproved. It did not take long for the other employees to recognize that, if they associated with Maddala, they were in trouble. Various forms of subtle discipline were in store for those who even spoke to Maddala. Ultimately, Dean's strategy worked; Maddala quit. But, six of Dean's best accountants also resigned and his department was thrown into complete confusion.

QUESTIONS

1. Why did Dave Maddala become an informal leader?
2. To what extent was Maddala a threat to his supervisor, Donald Dean? How noticeable and influential are status, power, and politics in this situation? Discuss.
3. How can a strong informal group affect the operations of a department such as accounting?
4. Evaluate Dean's position at Bradford Ltd. once Maddala resigned.

CASE STUDY

A View of the River

The professors of the Faculty of Administration at a major Canadian university were scheduled to move into a new building in May, 1987. One of the items on the agenda of the October, 1986 monthly meeting was a report by the Building Committee regarding security in the new building. The new building was the culmination of much hard work by the Faculty's dean, the student body, and the business community.

The building was extremely attractive and all faculty members were looking forward to occupying their new offices. All offices in the new building were larger (and much nicer) than the current offices that faculty members occupied. As well, all Faculty offices in the new building had a window (this was not true in their present quarters). Some offices overlooked the river that flowed by the campus and others overlooked the parking lot. The offices overlooking the river were considered to be the most desirable and had been picked first when faculty members were given the opportunity to choose their new office.

During the discussion of the security issue, one professor raised the question of what procedures had been used to allow faculty members to pick their new office. The response was that a special committee had been set up to determine criteria for the assignment of offices in the new building. That committee had reported at a previous faculty meeting, and had proposed that the criteria be rank and seniority (in that order). Thus, full professors would get

to pick before associate professors, and associate professors would get to choose before assistant professors. The proposal also meant that a full professor who had been with the Faculty for, say, two years would get to pick before an associate professor who had been with the Faculty for 20 years. This proposal had been approved. The administrative assistant for the Faculty had then implemented the system, and all professors picked from the offices that were still available when their position on the priority list was reached.

As this issue was reviewed, several people expressed dissatisfaction with the criteria that had been used to establish the priority list (most of those who complained were professors who had been forced to pick offices overlooking the parking lot because all the offices overlooking the river had already been taken). A major discussion then occurred about whether the process should be done over again, this time using different criteria. At the end of the discussion it was agreed that the process would not be repeated, but for any new office allocations it might be reconsidered.

QUESTIONS

1. Why were certain professors unhappy with their new offices, even though they were much improved over their present quarters?
2. Can you develop a procedure for making this allocation that will make everyone happy?

ENDNOTES

[1] Arthur D. Sharplin, Northeast Louisiana University, unpublished working paper (December 1981).
[2] Samuel A. Stouffer, et al., *The American Soldier* (Princeton: Princeton University Press, 1949): vol. 2, 1974.

REFERENCES

Allen, R. W., et al. "Organizational Politics: Tactics and Characteristics of Its Actors." *California Management Review* 22 (Fall 1979): 77–83.

Amernic, Jerry, "The Perks of Power." *The Financial Post Magazine* (November 1, 1982): 76.

Astley, W. Graham, and Sachdewa, Paramjit S. "Structural Sources of Intraorganizational Power: A Theoretical Synthesis." *Academy of Management Review* 9, no. 1 (January 1984): 104–113.

Briscoe, Dennis R. "Organizational Design: Dealing with the Human Constraint." *California Management Review* 23 (Fall 1980): 71–80.

Cobb, Anthony T. "An Episodic Model of Power: Toward an Integration of Theory and Research." *Academy of Management Review* 9, no. 3 (July 1984): 482–493.

Franklin, J. E. "Down the Organization: Influence Processes across Levels of Hierarchy." *Administrative Science Quarterly* 20 (June 1975): 153–164.

Hall, R. H., et al. "Patterns of Interorganizational Relationships." *Administrative Science Quarterly* 22 (September 1977): 457–474.

Harragan, Betty Lehan. *Games Mother Never Taught You.* New York: Warner Books, 1977.

Herker, C., and Aldrich, H. "Boundary Spanning Roles and Organization Structure," *Academy of Management Review* 2 (April 1977): 217–230.

Hodge, John. "Getting Along with the Informal Leader." *Supervisory Management* 25 (October 1980): 41–43.

Lincoln, J. R., and Miller, J. "Work and Friendship Ties in Organizations: A Comparative Analysis of Relational Networks." *Administrative Science Quarterly* 24 (June 1979): 181–199.

Lipovenko, Dorothy. "One Way To Cut Management Fat." *The Globe and Mail* (January 1, 1987): B1–B2.

Lucas, H. C. Jr. "MIS Affects Balance of Power." *Management Accounting* 61 (October 1979): 61–68.

Lush, Patricia. "Big Egos Out of Place at Deacon." *The Globe and Mail* (March 31, 1987): B1–B2.

March, James G., and Feldman, Martha S. "Information in Organizations as Signal and Symbol." *Administrative Science Quarterly* 26 (June 1981): 171–186.

Mayes, B. T., and Allen, R. W. "Toward a Definition of Organizational Politics." *Academy of Management Review* 2 (October 1977): 672–678.

McKenna, R. F. "Blending the Formal with the Informal System." *Journal of Systems Management* 26 (June 1975): 38–41.

McQueen, Rod. "Brawl in the Family." *Canadian Business* (March 1984): 62.

Miles, R. H., and Perreault, W. D. Jr. "Organizational Role Conflict: Its Antecedents and Consequences." *Organizational Behavior and Human Performance* 17 (October 1976): 19–44.

Miller, J. "Isolation in Organizations: Alienation from Authority, Control, and Expressive Relations." *Administrative Science Quarterly* 20 (June 1975): 260–271.

Mintzberg, Henry. "Power and Organization Life Cycles." *Academy of Management Review* 9, no. 2 (April 1984): 207–224.

Moschis, G. P. "Social Comparison and Informal Group Influence." *Journal of Marketing Research* 13 (August 1976): 237–244.

Pfeffer, Jeffrey. *Power in Organizations.* Marshfield Ma.: Pitman, 1982.

Quick, J. C. "Dyadic Goal Setting and Role Stress: A Field Study." *Academy of Management Journal* 22 (June 1979): 241–252.

Quinn, R. E. "Coping with Cupid: The Formation, Impact, and Management of Romantic Relationships in Organizations." *Administrative Science Quarterly* 22 (March 1980): 57–71.

Roos, L. L. Jr., and Hall, R. I. "Influence Diagrams and Organizational Power." *Administrative Science Quarterly* 25 (March 1980): 57–71.

Schmidt, S. M., and Kochan, T. A. "Interorganizational Relationships: Patterns and Motivations." *Administrative Science Quarterly* 22 (June 1977): 230–234.

Schriesheim, C. A. "Similarity of Individually Directed and Group Directed Leader Behavior Description." *Academy of Management Journal* 22 (June 1979): 345–355.

Power and Politics

KEY TERMS

power   coercive power   expert power
legitimate power   referent power   organization politics
reward power

LEARNING OBJECTIVES

After completing this chapter you should be able to
1. Explain what power is and how it is different from authority.
2. Describe five types of power.
3. Define the term organizational politics and explain why it is found in every organization.
4. Understand the arguments for and against organizational politics.

OPENING INCIDENT

The Publishing Department

Ginny DeVor is one of 46 employees in the publishing department of a large government agency. She has been on the job for three years. While having coffee with several colleagues one afternoon, she learns that the head of her department is being promoted to a new job in another agency. Not surprisingly, there is much discussion and rumor about who the new head will be.

The department is presently composed of two distinct groups of people — the younger climbers and the older, more established workers. There is animosity between the two groups on several issues, including the criteria for promotion. The young workers feel that performance should be the criterion, while the older workers argue that seniority should be used. DeVor is a member of the younger group and would like to become the new head. She also knows that Carl Ryan, the informal leader of the older group, assumes he will get the job because he has been in the department for 11 years.

Several years ago, the department adopted the practice of using a four-person selection committee to recommend to the agency director who the new department head should be. Members are elected to the selection committee at a meeting of the entire department. The director is not required to accept the committee's choice, but he is reluctant to ignore it because he really believes in participative management.

In the month before the election of the selection committee members, DeVor makes a point of cultivating friendships. In one-on-one meetings with various members of the department, she determines their likes, dislikes, fears, and hopes. She makes a point of going to lunch with various groups in the department and participates discreetly in ongoing discussions about the qualities the new head should possess. Before long, she finds that all the members in the young group — and even some of the older workers — are quietly urging her to apply for the head's job.

Given this support, DeVor becomes more open in her strategy. In the week before the meeting when the selection committee will be elected, she consults many members of the younger group; they agree to nominate four members from their group and then concentrate all their votes on those four candidates. They also agree to nominate seven or eight members from the older group in order to split that group's votes over a larger number of nominees.

At the meeting, four candidates favorable to DeVor are elected. Various supporters come by her office after the meeting to congratulate her and to say the important activity in choosing a new head has already been done. All that remains is the formality of the selection committee going through the motions of selecting the new head.

One month later, it is announced that Ginny DeVor is the new department head.

In the last chapter we introduced the idea of the informal organization and indicated its main features. The basic point in that discussion was that management cannot formally structure everything that goes on in the organization. In this chapter, we continue with this theme.

We begin by discussing the important concept of power. The difference between power and authority is noted, and the various kinds of power are described. We then introduce the concept of organization politics and describe some tactics of political behavior. The chapter concludes with an analysis of the positive and negative aspects of organizational politics.

POWER

power

We noted in Chapter 7 that authority is the right to command others. **Power** is the ability to influence the behavior of another person. Managers in organizations have little trouble understanding the role and importance of power. In one study, each of 10 department managers was asked to rank himself or herself, along with 20 other department managers, based on how much influence each had.[1] Only one manager asked what was meant by "influence." The overall results showed that there were virtually no disagreements in the ranking of the top five and bottom five managers on the list, even though ranking 21 people is not an easy task.

Power is an emotionally laden term, particularly in cultures that emphasize individuality and equality. To label a manager pejoratively as a power seeker is to cast doubt on that manager's motives and actions. Some of these negative views are the result of earlier writings which suggested that power is evil, that it corrupts people, that it is largely comprised of brute force, and that the amount of power is in limited supply.

Not a great deal of systematic analysis of power in organizations has been conducted. This research may have been neglected because most people — including students, managers, and the general public — *want* to believe that all behavior in organizations is rational.[2] Management students would rather believe that they are entering a career in which they rationally allocate resources for the good of society than that they will be involved in power struggles with other people. Practicing managers may want to believe that their careers are based on rational considerations of merit, not on power. Similarly, the general public takes comfort in the belief that businesses allocate the resources of society in an efficient and rational way.

Types of Power

There are many kinds of power, and not all are under the control of management. A popular listing of five main types of power is presented below.[3]

legitimate power

Legitimate power results from a person being placed in a formal position of authority. It results from a person occupying a certain position in the organizational structure and being granted formal authority. For example, individuals feel obligated to do what their manager says. Legitimate power is synonymous with authority.

reward power

Reward power is derived from a person's ability to reward another individual. Reward power may be formal or informal. Formal reward power might depend on the manager's ability to obtain a promotion or a pay raise for a worker. The informal group might reward a person through acceptance by coworkers. In the story at the beginning of the previous chapter, Mary Soo was rewarded by the informal group for decreasing her output.

coercive power

Coercive power is derived from the ability to punish or to recommend punishment. From a formal standpoint, the manager might fire a worker; the informal group might punish an individual by imposing the silent treatment, as happened to Mary Soo when she started doing too much work. Both are examples of coercive power.

referent power

Referent power is based on a liking for or a desire to be like the power holder. The particular personality and characteristics of an individual will affect the degree to which other persons wish to identify and be associated with that person. US President John F. Kennedy is known to have possessed this form of power to a remarkable degree. His admonition, "Ask not what your country can do for you but what you can do for your country," resulted in thousands of volunteers for the Peace Corps.

Charisma refers to personal qualities that allow an individual to influence others. This concept is closely related to the concept of referent power. Individuals with charisma possess referent power because their followers believe that the individual's goals are good, or right, or desirable. (The concept of charismatic leadership is discussed more fully in Chapter 12.)

expert power

Expert power comes from the possession of special knowledge or skills. Even if an individual has limited formal authority, expertise in a particular area will give him or her considerable influence. Famed oil-well firefighting expert "Red" Adair is well known by roughnecks (oil-field workers) the world over for his knowledge of how to put out oil-well fires. This expertise gives him the ability to go aboard an oil drilling platform anywhere in the world and immediately start to issue orders that will be obeyed without question.

Expert power possessed by subordinates is often difficult for management to accept. For example, if a computer programmer becomes so knowledgeable and competent as to be considered indispensable to the organization, problems can result. The supervisor may feel unable to even reprimand the programmer for fear that person will quit or sabotage the supervisor.

This illustrates a potential problem with line and staff organizations: the line has the legitimate power, whereas the staff depends on expert power. The formal right to manage a firm remains with line managers, but the capacity to manage it has been diluted and spread among a number of experts.

MANAGEMENT IN PRACTICE

A Power Struggle at Birks

Henry Birks & Sons Ltd. is the largest jewelry chain in Canada (1983 sales were $265 million). The firm has 4000 employees and 111 stores across Canada; it also has 68 stores in the United States. The firm was started in 1879 in Montreal by Henry Birks. Down through the years, succession had passed from eldest son to eldest son without any hint of disagreement. At least that was true until 1976 when a family member was fired and an internal power struggle began.

The fired family member, Robbie Birks, sued for $3 million for wrongful dismissal. In addition, his father Victor, vice-chairman of Birks, was fired with three days' notice after 53 years of service. He also sued the company, claiming that a voting trust agreement he had signed in

1968 should be annulled because he did not understand the impact it would have on his control of the company. Victor Birks won his suit in a court decision handed down in 1980, but that decision was overturned in 1983; the opposition (headed by Drummond Birks) essentially gained complete control of the company.

Industry observers predict that Drummond Birks will continue to head the company for many years and, when he retires, one of his three sons will take over the business. Whether there will be further disagreements at that time remains to be seen.

SOURCE Adapted from Rod McQueen, "Brawl in the Family", *Canadian Business* (March 1984): 62–68.

Power versus Formal Authority

The concept of power extends far beyond that of formal authority. A person's total power can be represented by the following formula:

$$\frac{\text{Total}}{\text{Power}} = \frac{\text{Legitimate}}{\text{Power}} \pm \frac{\text{Reward}}{\text{Power}} \pm \frac{\text{Coercive}}{\text{Power}} \pm \frac{\text{Referent}}{\text{Power}} \pm \frac{\text{Expert}}{\text{Power}}$$

A person's total power is the total of all these forms of power. The only power given by the manager's position in the organization is legitimate power, but the formula shows that total power can be strengthened or weakened by reward, coercive, referent, and expert power. For instance, a supervisor with little legitimate power might still be quite powerful because he or she is an expert in the field. On the other hand, a manager with considerable legitimate power might be virtually powerless because of a lack of job knowledge.

When an experienced manager with a good reputation is promoted to a new position, that manager probably already has great referent and expert power. As time passes, this will be supplemented by legitimate power, based on the respect people have for the manager's position; and by reward and coercive power, resulting from the manager's ability to reward and punish.

MANAGEMENT IN PRACTICE

A Power Struggle at Kruger Inc.

Bernard and Gene Kruger are the patriarchs of Kruger Inc., an international paper and packaging firm based in Montreal. The company's assets are valued at more than $750 million. Although Gene, the older brother, tended to dominate Bernard, the two managed to get along quite well for many years. But when Gene's son joined the company and started following in his father's footsteps, the family began to fall apart.

In 1927, when the boys' father died, Gene took over operation of the company at age 25. Bernard joined the firm in 1928 at the age of 16. Over the next several decades they worked together harmoniously, although Gene's insistence on controlling sometimes caused some tension between them.

Both men had sons, who were appointed to the Board of Directors in the 1960s. At this point, the real troubles began. Joseph (Gene's son) took an active role in the company, and by the late 1970s was making many major decisions. Bernard discovered that his position was being eroded by his nephew. Joseph was acting more and more like his father; he even began to

overrule decisions made by Bernard. Bernard was willing to tolerate this kind of behavior from his brother, but not from his brother's son. In 1979, Bernard retired to reduce the friction that had developed.

After his retirement, Bernard realized that he was in an awkward position, because his brother and nephew controlled his sources of income. So he began asking about finances. However, he was unable to find out from Gene and Joseph how much he was owed. In a face-to-face meeting with his brother, he was told to get a lawyer if he didn't like the way things were being handled.

In 1982, Bernard sued his brother, alleging that Kruger Inc. had cut off his $40 000 annual pension, fired his secretary, canceled his company credit cards, and stopped his dividend payments (which were Bernard's major source of income) even though the company had net earnings of over $12 million. What was once a close family relationship had been destroyed.

SOURCE   Adapted from Anne Beirne, "Kruger vs Kruger," *Canadian Business* (January, 1986): 61– 66.

The Significance of Power to the Manager

Research has shown that a good manager must have a concern for acquiring and using power. In a number of studies, it was found that over 70 percent of managers have a higher need for power than does the general population.[4] And the better managers have a stronger need for power than a need to be liked by others. This need for power is not a desire to be dictatorial, nor is it necessarily a drive for personal enhancement. Rather, it is a concern for influencing others on behalf of the organization. It is a need for socialized power rather than for personal power. When managers feel a greater need to be liked than to influence others, they tend to be less effective.

The control of situational factors, both in and out of the organization, is of significant concern to modern managers. It has been noted that when organizations grow so large and complex that no one individual has the capacity to manage all of the interdependencies, a dominant managing group will develop. This coalition is sometimes formalized into a presidential or executive office. It will exist, however, whether or not it is actually recorded on a chart. If the president of the firm heavily depends on the vice-president of finance to develop the crucial programs, that vice-president is likely to be a member of the dominant coalition and have actual power in excess of that suggested by the official chart.

ORGANIZATION POLITICS

Organization politics is one of the most pervasive yet elusive concepts in organizations. An understanding of this subject is crucial for anyone with serious career aspirations toward top management. In today's complex organizations, individuals do not move rapidly up the hierarchy unless they have a good grasp of the political aspects of their work environment.

Consider the results of a study which analyzed 149 managers in a manufacturing firm over a five-year interval.[5] During the period, 47 percent were promoted, 14 percent were given a lateral transfer, 22 percent stayed in their jobs, and 17 percent were demoted. The individuals who were promoted exhibited the following characteristics: (1) they understood the complex nature of the organization and the overlapping responsibility that resulted; (2) they recognized that it was more important to get along with their peers than with their subordinates, if they wanted to get ahead in the company; (3) they felt they had great freedom on the job; (4) they recognized that good performance was not automatically rewarded; and (5) they recognized that it was more important to seize the opportunity to become known than simply to do a good job and hope for the best.

These comments by successful practicing managers are probably not unusual. To demonstrate the diversity of situations in which political activity is important, consider the following examples from actual organizations:

- Bill reports to the vice-president of marketing for a provincial utility. He is aggressive and considers himself top-management material. By ingratiating himself with the vice-president's secretary, Bill is able to gather considerable evidence that the vice-president is frequently out of the office on nonbusiness activities. Bill informally presents this evidence to certain key members of the board of directors who belong to the same country club that Bill's father does. Two months later the vice-president is fired and Bill is chosen as his replacement.
- Joanna and Kirk are management trainees for a major food marketing company. They do not particularly like each other. Both are in line for a promotion and both are members of the new-product committee. At a meeting of the committee, Kirk makes what appears to be an impressive

presentation. However, Joanna observes aloud that his argument contains a major logical flaw. Although no decision is made at that time, Joanna notices that Kirk's proposal is quietly dropped from the agenda for the committee's next meeting. When the next promotion is announced, Joanna gets it.

- Marsha is a sales representative with a major computer manufacturer. One Thursday afternoon her boss informs her that an important customer is arriving at the airport and that she is to pick him up. Marsha feels complimented that her boss has chosen her for the job. Moments later, however, Marsha's boss says: "By the way, don't take your car. It isn't good enough for the customer. I think it's time you bought a new one." Marsha feels threatened by this comment, since she can't afford a new car.

- Louis is a finance professor in a large business school in central Canada. He has very strong views about nearly everything and he expresses them vigorously at faculty meetings. When Louis first came to the university, his comments had some impact, but as time passed people paid less and less attention to him. A recent faculty meeting was typical. The Strategic Planning Committee chairman presented a report proposing a new administrative position for the faculty. With the best of intentions, Louis asked what experience other universities had had with this type of position. Several committee members gave vague responses, and it was clear that the Strategic Planning Committee had not analyzed the issue in much depth. Louis therefore suggested that this analysis be done before a person was hired for the proposed position. He was amazed and infuriated when his suggestion was rejected and the committee's recommendation was approved instead.

- Ron is the top regional sales manager of a major food products company. He is also an excellent golfer. Last week he was asked to join a foursome composed of his boss (the national sales manager), the vice-president of marketing (his boss's boss), and the president of the firm. Ron knew that these people were critical to his career, and he wanted to make a good impression. So he played his best and shot a 71, the lowest score by far in the group. He left the golf course in great spirits. When Ron entered his boss's office the next morning he was greeted by: "Ron, what in the world were you trying to prove yesterday? *Nobody* beats the president at golf!" His boss then curtly dismissed him. Ron felt depressed about the incident for several days.

Incidents like these happen every day in organizations. They demonstrate that some individuals (Bill and Joanna) are able to assess the realities of organization life and then act in a way that is beneficial to their careers. Other individuals (Marsha, Kirk, Louis, and Ron) seem to have difficulty doing so.

organization politics

Organization politics refers to the activities of individuals within organizations as they try to develop and use power to achieve their own desired outcomes.

The individuals participating actively in organization politics are working with and through many people. As such, politics transcend the traditional structural boundaries. In the process of these interactions, the medium of exchange is power. The shrewd office politician acquires power and transfers it to another person when it can purchase something of value. Organization politicians use this medium of exchange to exert pressure on others in the network in order to gain their desired result. Just like the accountant, the office politician has a balance sheet. When power is transferred, something is received in return. To the politician, a favor given now is power to be extracted in the future. Thus, everyone is a politician to a certain extent; some are better at it than others.

Perhaps the most important issue that arises in dealing with organization politics has to do with where one draws the line between reasonable and unreasonable political behavior. Consider the brief list of examples presented earlier. Is it acceptable to let the president win at golf? Is it acceptable to use the vice-president's secretary to gather negative information about the vice-president? These are difficult questions, and you should keep these issues in mind as you consider the issue of organization politics in the remainder of the chapter. Remember: in your career you will almost certainly be faced with decisions such as these, and you will have to make a choice based on your individual background, training, and knowledge.

The Universality of Political Behavior

Political behavior in organizations is both universal and inevitable. It can be observed in all kinds of organizations — manufacturing firms, government agencies, service organizations, churches, the military, or universities. In this sense, political behavior is like the informal organization; any attempt to suppress it is certain to fail because the forces that encourage it are so potent.

What are these forces? Perhaps the most fundamental is self-interest — what people do to improve their own financial situation, status, or ego. While most people understand such behavior, they also recognize that, since organizations are made up of many different people, their self-interests are likely to clash. When people observe that what they are pursuing may be thwarted by someone else — as happens frequently — political behaviors are likely to be used.

Another reason political behavior is so widespread is that an organization has limited resources. An organization must therefore decide which of many possible goals it will pursue. Various groups or individuals in the organization will normally be in conflict with one another over which goals are going to be pursued and, in the process of trying to win, these groups are likely to indulge in political behavior. Such tactics are particularly likely if little objective evidence exists about the goals the organization should pursue.

Self-interest and limited resources guarantee that political behavior will be evident in all organizations. Some individuals believe that, in certain kinds of organizations, political behavior doesn't exist. For

Jerry Gray
University of Manitoba

Jerry Gray is Professor of Management and Associate Dean of the Faculty of Management at the University of Manitoba. He received his Bachelor's degree in business administration from the University of Evansville, his Master's degree in management at Southern Illinois University, and his Ph.D. in business administration from the University of South Carolina. He has taught management and organizational behavior at the University of Manitoba since 1970.

Dr. Gray has conducted executive development seminars for many different public and private sector organizations. He is a popular speaker at conferences, and a recognized authority on leadership training, motivation theory, organization design, and supervision. He is noted for his ability to translate complex theories of human behavior into practical terms for managers. Dr. Gray has written books and articles in the area of organizational behavior, and he is president of J. L. Gray & Associates, a consulting firm specializing in human resource development. He was formerly the head of the Department of Business Administration at the University of Manitoba.

Q: How would you define the term "organization politics?"

Gray: I think of politics as the informal part of organizational behavior that is designed to protect the specific interests of individuals and groups. I say it is "informal" because you will never see political behavior described in a company policy manual, and much of our management theory excludes it.

Q: You have extensive experience in both management and management consulting. Can you relate an incident of political behavior that you have encountered?

Gray: One typical example I encountered occurred in a large Crown corporation. The director of training was openly opposed to a particular training program that was being pushed by his manager. The director did not want the program because it didn't fit into his own plan for training programs in the corporation. At the outset, he grudgingly followed his manager's orders and conducted the training program. As time went on, however, he became more vocal in his opposition, even to the point of attempting to sabotage the program. After a year of putting up with this, his boss transferred him to a remote outpost where he no longer had a voice in training programs. As is typical in corporate politics, the manager concluded the transfer with a testimonial speech, in which he praised the director's "dedication and hard work in the area of training." To the outsider, the transfer appeared to be a promotion. But everyone inside knew the real reason for the transfer, and another lesson in corporate politics was learned.

Q: How widespread is political behavior in organizations?

Gray: I believe that corporate politics is the most predominant form of behavior in organizations. It's literally everywhere and knows no level. Vice-presidents engage in as much (if not more) political behavior as clerical employees. The only difference between people is the tactics and strategies they use.

Q: Why is politics so widespread?

Gray: I think the main reason is that people learn that they can get things done more effectively and efficiently by working with people they know. Once these interpersonal relationships are formed, many of the formal barriers come down. Since organizations must decide how to allocate scarce resources, individuals learn that their own self-interest is served if they can establish groups or coalitions that see the world the way they do. Therefore, all organizations consist of these coalitions that are working in ways the formal system does not sanction. For example, if an employee needs a new chair, the chances of getting the chair are much greater if the employee knows someone in the purchasing department.

Q: Can students be effectively taught about organization politics or is it something that a person has to experience to understand?

Gray: I think students can be taught the details of political behavior, but I don't think we can (or should) teach people to behave in a political way. I have had occasion to point out to individuals some aspects of their behavior that are not politically wise, but in the final analysis it is their decision whether they want to "play the political game" or not. In some cases, they decide they do not want to play and then they suffer the consequences. I also believe that a certain proportion of political behavior is determined by an individual's personality, and no amount of teaching will overcome that aspect. There are some people who are simply better at political behavior than others. Experience in organizations will help students appreciate corporate politics more, since some of them refuse to believe that such behavior exists until they see it.

Q: Should students know about organization politics before they begin their careers?

Gray: Most definitely. But knowing about it does not guarantee that one can play the game well. I'm always amazed at the people in organizations who seem completely oblivious to the political behavior around them. I give my students a simple formula: learn the corporate political game and then decide whether you're going to play it.

Q: People who don't like political behavior in organizations sometimes propose that organizations be made more rational and "fair." Is that possible?

Gray: The definition of "fair" is open to debate. Each individual will have a different definition of what is fair. There are some who maintain that political behavior is the fairest way of allocating resources, since decisions are based upon more complete information than would otherwise be the case. Also, it is impossible to legislate fairness. Those organizations that have tried have found the outcome to be less satisfactory than they had hoped. In one case with which I'm familiar, an organization reduced its employee selection process to an ineffective bureaucratic nightmare by trying to legislate fairness. The situation began when an unsuccessful applicant filed a grievance on a selection board interview on the grounds that the successful applicant was asked questions that he had not been asked, and that made the other applicant look good. A new policy was then developed that required all applicants to be asked the same questions. But then another grievance was filed on the grounds that later interviewees learned of the questions by talking to earlier interviewees and thus had more time to come up with good answers to the questions. The organization then developed another policy requiring that all applicants must receive the questions a week in advance. The end result was that the usefulness of the selection board was substantially reduced, and the organization found it difficult to find people willing to serve on it.

I think it is possible for political behavior to become a problem in organizations if it is too prevalent. But to attempt to eliminate it is foolish and shows a very shallow understanding of human behavior in organizations.

instance, might not charitable organizations pursuing goals that society values have no political behavior because employees use their energies to pursue those goals? Unfortunately, this view ignores the two realities we've noted: individuals pursue their own self-interests, and the resources of organizations are limited. Individuals who ignore these realities may be surprised, shocked, and dismayed at the behavior of others. Conversely, those who take these realities into account will find that they are better prepared for life in the workplace.

The Dynamics of Political Behavior

If all actions could be foreseen, perhaps organization members would have little need to behave politically, since all conflicts could be resolved in some rational manner acceptable to everyone. However, inasmuch as such circumstances are unlikely to arise, individual members must be prepared to adjust to varying conditions and pressures. Though going exclusively by the official rules could, under certain circumstances, be construed as one form of political behavior, adjustment or accommodation usually involves a bending of the rules, an exchange of favors, or offers of a reward for cooperation. Some management students are shocked to discover that merely doing their job will not earn them the rewards they might expect.

To make the implications of politics clearer, consider this situation. An engineer heading up an industrial engineering department has developed a new procedure for processing work in the production department. According to the formal rules she would elect to follow the first suggestion listed below. The others listed are *not* formally required and can be construed as various forms of adjustment and accommodation.

- The engineer submits the recommendation for approval to the line executive. She provides supporting data and presents persuasive arguments. This failing, the engineer appeals to a common line superior who will decide the case and issue an order accordingly.
- The engineer attempts to get to know the line executive on a personal basis through casual conversation, enquiries about respective backgrounds, and the like.
- The engineer attempts to simulate a friendship that is not genuine.
- The engineer arranges to go to lunch with the line executive in the company dining room to promote her views on a casual basis.
- The engineer invites the line executive to lunch, at her own expense.
- The engineer offers to exchange favors that are possible within the regular operating rules and policies; for example, she agrees to do an immediate restudy of a particular job rate that has caused serious difficulties between the line executive and the union.

MANAGEMENT IN PRACTICE

Competing for the Top Spot at W.R. Grace

Peter Grace has been the chief executive at W.R. Grace since 1945. Recently he decided to let three individuals compete to determine who would take over his job when he retires. The competitors — J.P. Bolduc, Terrence Daniels, and Paul Paganucci — were all promoted to the position of vice-chairperson in November of 1986; at the same time, it was announced that one of them would be chosen to succeed Mr. Grace. Two senior executives in their early 60s, who would normally have been in line for the job, were passed over completely.

The announcement comes amid some difficult times for the company. In 1985, a German corporation owning 26 percent of the company's shares decided to sell out. Since Grace was worried about a hostile takeover, it had to find the money to buy the shares. In addition,

the performance of several of Grace's business lines had not been good. To cope with these and other problems, corporate staff has been reduced by almost one third. The change in the executive pecking order simply added to the mood of uncertainty at the company.

Analysts are not quite ready to believe that any of the three candidates will ever replace Grace. They point out that he has already outlasted one generation of candidates by "moving back the finish line," i.e., putting off his retirement. Although Mr. Grace is 73, he says he works as hard as anybody at the company. Even Mr. Grace concedes that things could change and that there is no guarantee that any one of the three will take over his job.

SOURCE   Adapted from Daniel F. Cuff, "Three Executives Jockeying For Top Post At W.R. Grace," *The Globe and Mail* (March 20, 1987): B2.

- The engineer agrees to a favor involving a slight bending of procedures and policies; for example, she agrees to delay introduction of a new method and rate, even though fully developed and ready to go, at the request of the line executive.
- The engineer agrees to a favor involving a more serious bending of the procedures and policies; for example, she "discovers" that the particular job rate noted above is too tight, when it is not, and loosens it up for the benefit of the line executive.
- The engineer agrees to cover for the line executive if, for example, the line executive wishes to use the industrial engineering department as an excuse for failing to meet schedules because of presumed work interferences.
- The engineer, with the assistance of understanding accountants, agrees to a transfer of industrial engineering budget funds to the line executive's department.

Many other possible actions could be tried to persuade the line executive to cooperate. The available alternatives depend on the extent of power possessed by the two parties. In instances where one individual has control over items or services that can be adapted to personal as well as organizational use, the power is even greater. Cases are on record in which personal furniture has been constructed on company time with company materials, or personal cars have been repaired in company motor pools. (See Table 9-1 for a list of political tactics that are frequently observed in organizations.)

TABLE 9-1 Commonly Used Political Tactics

Image building Engaging in activities designed to create and maintain a good image. Includes dressing appropriately, drawing attention to one's successes, being enthusiastic about the organization, adhering to group norms, and having an air of confidence about work activities.

Selective use of information Using information selectively to further one's career. Includes withholding unfavorable information from superiors, keeping useful information from competitors, interpreting information in a way that is favorable to oneself, and overwhelming people with technical information they don't understand.

Scapegoating Insuring that someone else is blamed for a failure. Individuals who are skillful organizational politicians make sure that they will not be blamed when something goes wrong and that they will get credit when something goes right.

Forming alliances Agreeing with several key people that a certain course of action will be taken. If a conflict develops, the people in the coalition will get their way because they are strong enough as a group to impose their will on others.

Networking Insuring that one has many friends in positions of influence.

Compromise Giving in on an unimportant issue in order to gain an ally who will be on your side when an issue of importance to you arises at a later date.

Rule manipulation Refusing an opponent's request on the grounds that it is against company policy, but granting an identical request from an ally on the grounds that it is a "special circumstance."

The degree of political behavior is limited not only by formal organization restrictions but also by personal codes of ethics and conscience. The fact that at times office politics may be unethical should not preclude a discussion of the subject. That such actions as those listed in the example just given do exist in various business firms is undeniable. Few businesses are run completely and rigidly by the book, and political behavior cannot be condemned outright. Some accommodations are constructive, whereas others may be destructive of both organized activity and individual morals.

How Managers View Political Behavior

How do practicing managers view the issue of politics within organizations? In one study, 428 Canadian managers in public-and private-sector organizations were given a series of statements and asked to agree or disagree with them.[6] There were several interesting findings. First, 60 percent of the repondents felt that most casual talk at work was political in nature, and 70 percent agreed that politics was common in their organizations.

Second, a majority of the respondents agreed that political behavior is self-serving and detrimental to the organization in which it occurs. Overall, political behavior was viewed as bad, unfair, unnecessary and conflict-oriented. When respondents were asked to write a brief story demonstrating political behavior in action, 84 percent of the stories portrayed it as being nonrational.

Third, people at lower levels in organizations perceived more politics than people at higher levels. People at lower levels apparently saw themselves as "victims" of political behavior. We can speculate that people at upper levels saw less politics because they felt that they achieved their position not through political behavior, but through meritorious service.

Fourth, there was no difference in the perceived level of political behavior in public- and private-sector organizations. If we recall our earlier notion that individuals pursue their own self-interests regardless of the setting, this finding is not surprising.

Fifth, over 70 percent of the respondents agreed that successful and powerful executives act in a political fashion. They also felt that a person must be a good politician to get ahead in organizations.

Finally, political behavior was most frequently perceived in areas where there were no explicit policies or procedures to guide people.

MANAGEMENT IN PRACTICE

Politics at Manitoba Hydro

Manitoba Hydro is a provincially owned and operated utility whose mandate is to promote efficiency and economy in the supply and use of electric power. In 1979, the Tritschler Commission conducted hearings about alleged mismanagement in the organization. Among other conclusions, the commission reported that Manitoba Hydro had predicted power shortages that never materialized, had underestimated construction costs of new generating plants, and had expanded when its financial position was weak.

Several political principles and how they operated at Manitoba Hydro are noted below:

Principle 1. Groups within organizations vie with one another for status and power. In a province where 90 percent of the electricity is generated by water, it is not surprising that hydraulic construction engineers were a powerful group.

Principle 2. Changes in the external environment of the organization will favor one group over another. The rapid growth in demand for

electricity in the 1960s increased the power of the hydraulic engineers within the organization.

Principle 3. Organizational power considerations are as important, if not more so, than economic or rational considerations in making organizational decisions. At Manitoba Hydro, hydraulic engineers produced the demand forecasts and did the planning for future generating stations. Impartial decisions were therefore not likely to be made.

Principle 4. Powerful groups will use political means to stay in power. When the predicted demand for electricity did not materialize, the engineers attempted to manipulate the environment to increase demand. For example, rates were kept artificially low and deals were made to sell power to the United States.

SOURCE Adapted from Roger Hall, "Some Emerging Principles of the Politics of Organizational Decisions" (Paper presented at the Administrative Sciences Association of Canada Conference, 1980).

Political behavior was easy to observe in the areas of promotions and transfers, delegation of authority, and interdepartmental coordination. Although it may appear that objective criteria exist for issues such as promotion, most of the incidents written by the respondents mentioned that people got promoted because of "pull' rather than because they met the objective criteria for promotion.

This study indicates once again the universality of political behavior in organizations and the fact that most people have reservations about it. It suggests that individual managers face a real dilemma: they must either "join the parade" and behave in a political fashion in order to further their career, or decide to opt out of such behavior, realizing that in so doing they may be seriously reducing their chances of getting ahead. This is, of course, a decision that each individual must make, given his or her personal value system and beliefs about what is right.

Is Political Behavior Positive or Negative?

Until recently, the majority of people who analyzed organizations or worked in them assumed that political behavior was negative. However, many researchers and managers are now accepting the idea that political behavior has positive aspects. At least political behavior is now accepted as a fact of organization life; an improved understanding of it can lead to better results for both organizations and individuals. However, many people still see it as undesirable, so the debate about organizational politics is still very lively. Table 9-2 summarizes the arguments for and against politics. These arguments are analyzed in the paragraphs that follow.

TABLE 9-2   Arguments For And Against Political Behavior

Arguments Against	Arguments in favor
1. People are treated unfairly when political decisions are made.	1. Determining what is "fair" is a subjective process and is a vague argument.
2. Political behavior distorts the decision-making process in organizations and results in decisions that are bad for the organization.	2. In a free society people must be allowed to pursue their own interests, as long as their behavior is not illegal.
3. The use of power allows an organization to ignore internal and external groups that may be unhappy with the organization.	3. Political behavior forces an organization to behave in a way that is consistent with important internal and external groups.
4. Politics is time consuming and inefficient.	4. Political processes are very fast because decision makers can get the "real story" on an issue through their own personal network of contacts.
5. Political processes give certain people too much power.	5. Those who get power are those who have demonstrated an ability to solve the organization's key problems.

Argument 1: People are sometimes treated unfairly when political decisions are made. Ethnic minority groups argue, for example, that employment decisions are made not on the basis of competence, but on the basis of ethnic origin. (This practice is, of course, illegal, but that doesn't stop it from happening.) Opponents of political behavior also argue that it causes decisions to be made on mysterious criteria by an "in group" that does not really have to answer to anyone. The existence of this in group (frequently called the "old-boy network") is often considered unreasonable in a democratic society. The implication of the argument is that the old-boy network will make decisions based on something other than rational grounds and that competent people may not be given a chance to show their merit; thus, overall organization performance will suffer.

Counterargument: Some people argue that the old-boy network benefits organizations because it is efficient: (1) decisions can be made quickly and accurately on the basis of personal contacts, and (2) the organization benefits because the decision maker feels confident about the results. Information is crucial in making good decisions, and supporters argue that political decision-making gives better results than decision making on a traditional basis.

Argument 2: Political behavior can distort the decision-making process so that decisions made may be bad for the organization or for society as a whole. Opponents of political behavior feel that the political maneuvering that goes on in organizations is caused by individuals' desires to improve their career prospects. While this motivation is not negative by itself, it is often carried to extremes. The motivation of self-interest is strong in most people, often strong enough to induce them to further their own careers without regard to the harm they may cause to individuals, the organization, or society as a whole. An example is the executive who is brought in to shape up a weak division. Typically, some drastic actions are taken in the short run, and performance often does improve noticeably. After a couple of years, the executive may be promoted to another position on the basis of his or her successful past performance. But what happens after the executive leaves the division? Sometimes productivity declines and it appears that the executive is really missed. However, performance might have declined anyway, if, for example, he or she generated increased profits only at the expense of reduced training, maintenance, or other such expenditures. Thus, the executive's pursuit of personal goals (promotion) induced him or her to make decisions that were bad for the organization.

Counterargument: Even supporters of political behavior agree that some executives behave this way; they respond by pointing out that, in a free society, individuals should be allowed to pursue their self-interest as long as they are not breaking the law. Advocates of political behavior also point out that individuals will always debate about what goals an organization should pursue and the behavior that is acceptable in the pursuit of these goals. When disagreements arise,

MANAGEMENT IN PRACTICE

Whistleblowers

Stephen Hayes (not his real name) is a structural engineer who designed a tunnel for an amusement park. It was to be supported by reinforced concrete, but the amusement park's owner had substituted a light-gauge metal because it was cheaper and quicker to set up. Hayes was concerned that the tunnel might collapse and kill or injure people, so he inspected it daily. When he found a crack in it, he exercised his authority as a structural engineer and closed the ride. The park's owner was infuriated that his ride was closed for an entire day during the peak season.

Hayes is an example of a whistleblower — a person who speaks out about things they believe are illegal or unethical. Not surprisingly, there is much concern that these people will lose their jobs because of their whistleblowing. Many engineers at a seminar in Toronto in 1985 reported that they were pressured to overlook safety violations; many of them did not report the violations because they felt they would have lost their job had they done so.

Ad Varma is a Canada Post clerk who, in 1984, made allegations of waste and mismanagement to his superiors. Fellow workers tried to convince him not to, but he went ahead anyway. He was fired, but was later reinstated after his case became public. Most whistleblowers learn that, at the minimum,

going public scuttles their chance of promotion.

Some companies try to create a legitimate forum for employee complaints. At IBM Canada, for example, a program called "Speak Up" has been introduced. Employees note their complaint or concern on a form and give the form to a coordinator. The questioner's name is removed and locked in a safe. The rest of the form is directed to the appropriate manager and a written response is returned to the employee within 10 days. If still unsatisfied, the employee can request an anonymous telephone conversation with the manager in question. In 1984, 350 employees spoke up.

Overall, however, many people are skeptical of business' ability and motivation to police itself. Some people have suggested legislation to protect individuals who want to speak out (and some states in the US already have such legislation), but others argue that legislation will be largely ineffective in this area. Company loyalty is a big issue with managers, and those who speak out against the company are demonstrating a lack of dedication in many managers' minds.

SOURCE Adapted from Lawrence Archer, "The Moral Minority," *Canadian Business*, (January, 1986): 56–59.

they must be resolved in some way. Supporters of political behavior argue that the most effective and efficient mechanism for resolving these conflicts is the use of power. Hence, political behavior is functional for individuals and organizations because it provides a mechanism for resolving conflicts that might otherwise be unresolvable.

Argument 3: The use of political manipulation and the use of power allow an organization to ignore internal and external groups that may be unhappy with what the organization is doing. The essence of the criticism is that certain individuals and groups inside and outside organizations are prevented from being heard because the people in power ignore them. What's worse, the people in power stay there by using all sorts of unfair tactics. The most obvious example is the refusal of corporations to do voluntarily what consumer groups believe they should do, such as controlling pollution or not publishing pornography. Consumer advocates respond by attempting to get laws passed requiring that these actions be taken by corporations.

Counterargument: It can also be argued, however, that political behavior forces an organization to behave realistically, both internally and in its relations with its external environment. While it is true that in every organization people at the top try to retain their positions, many pressures for change are also at work, both internally and externally. If the organization does not deal with these changes, it will find itself in deep trouble. For example, many of the traditional manufacturing industries in Canada find themselves unable to compete with foreign firms because they are unwilling or unable to adapt to fundamental changes in their industry. Often, political behavior on the part of certain managers in the firm is the only way to move the organization in a direction that will ensure survival.

Argument 4: Organization politics is inefficient and time-consuming because the negotiation, bargaining, conflict, and strategy development that is so evident in political behavior takes up people's time unduly. Some people express concern that people in organizations will expend so much effort on political behavior that they will have little time or energy left for pursuing organization goals. As a result, overall performance will suffer.

Counterargument: Others argue that political decisions are made as quickly as rational decisions. Rational processes take a great deal of time, too, because information must be formally gathered and analyzed, and its meaning debated by many people; political processes are more informal and tend toward private rather than public discussions of various issues. Therefore, political decisions may be made more quickly than those made on a rational basis.

Argument 5: Perhaps the most fundamental criticism of political behavior is that political processes allow certain individuals to have too much power while other individuals have too little. Central to this criticism is the argument that power corrupts people and that power differences between people should therefore be minimized. The best way to do this is to eliminate political behavior.

Counterargument: In response to this criticism, we may consider three points. First, it is not possible to minimize power differences between people because of the pyramidal structure of organizations, and because people differ in their ability and inclination to behave politically. Second, the most powerful individuals and departments in organizations are usually those who cope with important uncertainties the organization is facing. Power is therefore a way of inducing people to act (for example, to cope with uncertainty) in ways that increase organizational effectiveness. Third, individuals

MANAGEMENT IN PRACTICE

Organization Politics and Your Career

During your formal studies, you will take many different courses that are designed to give you a better understanding of complex organizations. Courses in quantitative methods, principles of marketing, accounting, capital budgeting, production, etc., all emphasize systematic and rational approaches to organizational decision making. Many students never question the accuracy or utility of this view of organizational life.

Now that you have been exposed to another point of view — the political one — you have several questions to answer:

1. Do you think that the political view of organizations is a realistic one?
2. Are you disappointed that organizations are not places where strictly rational criteria are always used to make decisions?
3. What does this imply about the rational and systematic management techniques you will learn during your school years?
4. Will what you learn in school be helpful in furthering your career in the organization where you work?
5. How do you feel about engaging in some of the political tactics mentioned in this chapter?

These are interesting and difficult questions, but you will benefit by asking them now, and then carefully considering how and why you answered the way you did.

---

who are able to solve key problems rise to positions of power, further increasing organizational effectiveness. At a society-wide level, an interesting trend is evident regarding the kinds of individuals who become chief executives. In the early twentieth century, the major problem facing organizations was how to satisfy rapidly increasing demand. In this environment, production-oriented people often became presidents of corporations. By the 1930s and 1940s, production problems had been largely resolved and the main problem was how to sell what was being produced. Then, sales-oriented people rose to positions of power. More recently, the unsettled financial environment has given finance- and accounting-oriented people more power to attain positions as chief executives.

We believe that, managed properly, political behavior and the use of power can be helpful to an organization. Unfortunately, the current understanding of organization politics does not allow us to state simple rules for effectively managing politics and the use of power. Keep in mind that any attempt to regulate political behavior closely may be doomed to failure. Somehow, people always find ways to get around the rules that other people make. Perhaps the following quote helps to compromise all the conflicting perspectives:

> Power — because of the way it develops and the way it is used — will always result in the organization suboptimizing its performance. However, to this grim absolute, we add a comforting

caveat: If any criteria other than power were the basis for determining an organization's decisions, the result would be even worse.[7]

OPENING INCIDENT REVISITED

The Publishing Department

Ginny DeVor in the publishing department wanted to be promoted ahead of an older, more experienced person who was an informal leader of an important group. DeVor's success was, in part, a result of her sensitivity to organization politics.

DeVor's tactics consisted of cultivating friendships before the time when these friendships could be used to secure votes. In order to get the job, DeVor knew that the selection committee's decision must favor her; the most direct approach was to influence the nomination and election of committee members. With four sympathetic members on the selection committee, DeVor realized the committee likely would choose her as the new department head.

DeVor's behavior in the opening incident is quite consistent with the definition of politics presented in this chapter. Carl Ryan was probably unhappy with the outcome because he wanted the job. If Ryan was insensitive to or aloof from office politics, he may have disapproved of the tactics used by DeVor's supporters; he would probably say they were unfair.

Whether the political activities behind DeVor's appointment as department head are in themselves positive or negative is difficult to say. At the individual level, some people are hurt and some people are helped by political behavior. At the organizational level, if political behavior results in a more capable individual being promoted, the organization benefits and the net effect is positive. Of course, the definition of "capable" is crucial. In this case, some would argue that DeVor was more capable than Ryan because she saw what was necessary to get the job. Individuals who aspire to positions of authority must be sensitive to influential organization characteristics, and DeVor certainly was sensitive. On the negative side, this perspective of "capable" might allow DeVor to rationalize doing whatever is necessary to get her preferred decisions in her daily job performance, which could be undesirable to the publishing department or the agency itself.

All individuals must make their own decisions about how involved they will get in organization politics. Clearly, all sorts of people are prepared to become heavily involved in an attempt to further their careers. Their activities will have an impact on other members of the organization as well as on people in the society at large.

SUMMARY

Power is the ability to influence the behavior of another person. The concept of power is important since managers cannot accomplish all their work simply by relying on their formal authority. There are several types of power. These include legitimate power (resulting from a person's place in the formal hierarchy), reward power (derived from a person's ability to reward others), coercive power (derived from a person's ability to punish others), referent power (based on a liking for a person or a desire to be like that person), and expert power (resulting from the possession of special knowledge about a particular area).

Organization politics is the behavior that individuals engage in as they try to develop and use power to achieve their own personal goals. Political behavior is found in all types of organizations because resources are scarce and because each person is interested in improving their own situation. Some tactics that are used when people behave politically are image building (trying to create a good image for oneself), selective use of information, scapegoating (blaming someone else when something goes wrong), forming alliances, networking, compromise, and rule manipulation (selectively applying rules to gain advantages over others).

One study of Canadian managers found that they viewed political behavior negatively, but that it was widespread in organizations. Lower level participants perceived more political behavior than upper level managers, but there was no difference in the amount of politics in public- and private-sector firms. Managers felt that political behavior was necessary if a person wanted to get ahead in the organization.

There are five major arguments against the use of political behavior: (1) people are treated unfairly, (2) politics distorts the decision-making process, (3) the wishes of internal and external groups are ignored by those in power, (4) politics is inefficient and time consuming, and (5) politics gives certain people too much power. However, it can also be argued that political behavior is good for organizations; that political decision-making is effective and recognizes the various contributions that different individuals and groups make to the organization; and that organization politics makes an organization very sensitive to its internal and external environment.

REVIEW QUESTIONS

1. Define the term "power." Discuss the five types of power.
2. Define the term "organizational politics."
3. Why is political behavior found in all kinds of organizations?
4. Describe several political tactics that are commonly used.
5. How do practicing managers view political behavior?
6. Summarize the major arguments against political behavior as well as the major arguments in favor of it.

EXERCISES

1. Using the formula for total power presented in this chapter, state the kinds of power, and how much total power, each of the following individuals might possess:

    a. Guard in a maximum security prison

    b. President of Air Canada

    c. A community college student

    d. A pastor of a church

    e. A computer repair technician

2. Ask a manager that you are acquainted with to describe an example of political behavior in his or her organization. Were there positive and negative outcomes from the political incident? Is the manager reluctant to talk about political behavior?

3. Consider an organization that you are a part of. What kinds of political behavior are evident in the organization?

4. Collect three articles from your local newspaper that relate to the use of power. Describe how power was used to obtain results or why it failed to achieve results.

CASE STUDY

Power Play

Robert Henri grew up on a farm near Bedford, Québec. His parents were disciplinarians, conservative in their views, and over the years helped him to develop a strong sense of right and wrong. He had been happy through childhood because his parents stressed the value of hard work and harmony in the family.

After Henri graduated with an engineering degree from Laval University, he went to work for Latimer Hydraulics, a firm which specialized in the custom manufacture of liquid pumping systems for agriculture and industry. Customers approached the company with a specific problem and its hydraulic engineers would design a system to meet the customer's need. Since the systems were custom-made, testing them was an important function.

Henri was a first-rate engineer, and his boss, Charles Toland, soon recognized Henri as a valuable addition to the company. Henri was given increased responsibility in a variety of areas and he always performed well. Four years after Henri joined the firm, a major contract was landed by Latimer Hydraulics. The contract involved building a state-of-the-art system for Creighton Manufacturing, and Henri was named chief engineer on the project. In that role he had the responsibility of overseeing all aspects of the contract, including final testing of the system.

Design and production went well for the first four months. The work was proceeding on time, and preliminary test results were positive. However, three weeks before the new system was due, Henri received the results of a test on a major component of the system, indicating that it did not work. The tests were repeated, but the results were the same. Henri therefore began to redesign in order to remedy the defect. He also informed Toland that additional time would be needed to complete the project. At that point the following conversation took place:

Toland: I'm sorry, but I can't give you any additional time to complete the project. The customer needs it in three weeks. Just sign the test report saying that the system works and we'll get it working later. We've done that before when we had problems.

Henri: I can't do that. The system doesn't work! It wouldn't be right.

Toland: As the chief engineer, you've got to sign the test report.

Henri: I won't sign it until the system is working.

Toland: Now, Robert, listen to reason. This contract is going to put Latimer on the map! You want to be part of that, don't you? Now sign the report.

Henri: You can sign it if you want. I won't be part of a deception like that. It's unethical.

Toland: Well, I'm going to have to sign it. I'm sorry to say this, but I'm going to remove you as chief engineer, effective immediately.

Disappointed and somewhat shocked, Henri continued to argue his point. Toland seemed unable to understand. The next day, Henri resigned.

Several months later, Henri read in the paper of a problem that had developed between Latimer Hydraulics and Creighton Manufacturing involving a pumping system that didn't work. The paper noted that, after some negotiations between Latimer and Creighton, a satisfactory arrangement had been worked out. It also noted that Charles Toland had been promoted to executive vice-president of Latimer Hydraulics.

QUESTIONS

1. What factors contributed to Robert Henri's resignation? What could he have done to avoid the situation that led up to it?
2. Evaluate Toland's decision as a manager.
3. What would you have done in this situation?

CASE STUDY

The Return of Thomas Palatuk

In 1982, Thomas Palatuk entered the University of Toronto and began working toward his B.Comm. degree. In the summer of 1985, he got a temporary job in the Systems and Procedures department at Burrows Ltd., a firm that manufactured and sold a variety of industrial products.

One of the responsibilities of the Systems and Procedures department was to monitor the budgeting process at Burrows to ensure that expenditures were orderly and that budgets were not exceeded. Palatuk found that he was required to follow rigid work procedures, but he didn't mind too much since he was just learning the job and the procedures gave him clear guidance about what to do. In his job, his main emphasis was checking computer printouts containing budget data for various departments. If a deviation was found, he informed his supervisor, Neil Mitchell, and Mitchell followed up on it with the head of the department in question.

At the end of the summer, Mitchell called Palatuk in and complimented him on the work he had done. Mitchell indicated that Palatuk should apply at Burrows for a career position when he graduated the next spring. Palatuk thanked Mitchell and said he would certainly consider it.

After interviewing several companies during his fourth year, Palatuk decided to go to work full time for Burrows. Palatuk reasoned that he knew something about the company, and had worked well there on a temporary basis, so he felt good about his choice. He was told that he would again be working for Mitchell, but this time in a position of considerably increased authority and discretion. On his first day with the company, he was greeted enthusiastically by Mitchell, and the following conversation took place:

Mitchell: I'm glad you chose to go with us full-time. I have just the job for you.

Palatuk: What have you got in mind?

Mitchell: Well, last summer you worked in an area that really didn't let you exercise all your skills. You were limited to checking computer printouts for budget deviations.

Palatuk: Oh, I didn't mind too much. You've got to start somewhere.

Mitchell: Well, that's true, but I've got a much more important project for you to work on. Top management has decided to implement a management audit that will complement our financial auditing system. The purpose of the management audit is to assess the quality of our management team.

Palatuk: That is an important area in any company. In one of my personnel courses, we did a major term-project on the issue of management audits. I think that should be helpful.

Mitchell: That's great! I wasn't aware that you already had some relevant experience in this area. I'm putting you in charge of a three-person task force. You will have the authority to gather data on each of the company's managers and to write a report to top management indicating the current expertise Burrows possesses in its management ranks.

Palatuk: What kind of authority do I have to gather information?

Mitchell: You have the full authority of the Systems and Procedures department behind you. As well, each of the managers knows that the top management group in the company supports this management audit.

Palatuk: What kinds of data am I supposed to gather?

Mitchell: We've already got a questionnaire worked out. You and your team simply administer it and analyze the data that the managers provide. If you wish, you can develop additional questions to ask the managers and include those as well.

Palatuk: When do I start?

Mitchell: Right away. I'll show you your office and introduce you to the other members of the audit team. Let's go.

QUESTIONS

1. What problems might Palatuk encounter as he conducts the management audit? For each potential problem you identify, explain why it might develop.

2. What can Palatuk do to reduce the chance that problems will develop during the audit procedure?

ENDNOTES

[1] G. R. Salancik and J. Pfeffer, "Who Gets Power — And How They Hold On To It: A Strategic Contingency Model of Power," *Organizational Dynamics* 5 (1977): 3.

[2] J. Pfeffer, *Power in Organizations* (Boston: Pitman, 1980): 7.

[3] J. P. French and B. Raven, "The Bases of Social Power," in *Studies in Social Power*, ed D. Cartwright (Ann Arbor: University of Michigan Institute for Social Research, 1959): 150–167.

[4] David C. McClelland and David H. Burnham, "Power is the Great Motivator," *Harvard Business Review* 54 (March-April 1976): 102.

[5] F. H. Goldner, "Success vs Failure: Prior Managerial Perspective," *Industrial Relations* (October 1970): 457–474.

[6] J. V. Gandz and V. V. Murray, "The Experience of Workplace Politics," *Academy of Management Journal* 23 (1980): 237–251.

[7] Salancik and Pfeffer, 20.

REFERENCES

Archer, Lawrence, "The Moral Minority." *Canadian Business* (January 1986): 56–59.

Beirne, Anne. "Kruger vs Kruger." *Canadian Business* 59 (January 1986): 61–66.

Brass, David. "Men's and Women's Networks: A Study of Interaction Patterns and Influence in Organizations." *Academy of Management Journal* 28 (June 1985): 327–343.

Christy, Jim. *The Price of Power: A Biography of Charles Eugene Bedaux.* New York: Doubleday, 1984.

Goh, Swee. "Uncertainty, Power, and Organizational Decision Making: A Constructive Replication and Some Extensions." *Canadian Journal of Administrative Sciences* 2 (June 1985): 177–191.

Gray, Barbara, and Ariss, Sonny. "Politics and Strategies Change Across Organizational Life Cycles." *Academy of Management Review* 10 (October 1985): 707–723.

Guff, Daniel. "Three Executives Jockeying for Top Post at W. R. Grace." *The Globe and Mail* (March 20, 1987): B2.

Kakabadse, Andrew, and Parker, Christopher, (eds). *Power, Politics, and Organizations.* New York: Wiley, 1984.

Kram, Kathy, and Isabella, Lynn. "Alternatives to Mentoring: The Role of Peer Relationships in Career Development." *Academy of Management Journal* 28 (March 1985): 110–132.

Medcof, John. "The Power Motive and Organizational Structure: A Micro-Macro Connection." *Canadian Journal of Administrative Sciences* 2 (June 1985): 95–113.

Mulder, Mauk; deJong, Rendel; Kippelaer, Leendert; and Verhage, Jaap. "Power, Situation, and Leaders' Effectiveness." *Journal of Applied Psychology* 71 (November 1986): 566–570.

Remick, Helen (ed). *Comparable Worth and Wage Discrimination: Technical Possibilities and Political Realities.* Philadelphia: Temple University Press, 1984.

Schick, Allen; Birch, Jeffrey; and Tripp, Robert. "Authority and Power in Organizational Decision Making: The Case of a University Personnel Budget." *Canadian Journal of Administrative Sciences* 3 (June 1986): 41–64.

Zey, Michael. *The Mentor Connection.* Homewood, Ill.: Dow Jones Irwin, 1984.

10

Staffing the Organization

KEY TERMS

staffing
human resource
  planning
recruitment
selection
training and
  development
organizational
  development
performance
  appraisal
compensation

health
safety
staffing process
job analysis
job description
job specification
work load analysis
work force analysis
recruitment
employment
  requisition
screening interviews

employment
  application
validity
reliability
interview
patterned
  interview
unstructured
  interview
stress interview
orientation
assessment center

LEARNING OBJECTIVES

After completing this chapter you should be able to
1. Identify and briefly describe the basic functions related to human resources that must be accomplished if the firm's employment needs are to be met.
2. State the predominant laws that affect the staffing process.
3. Describe what is involved in human resources planning and recruitment.
4. Explain each phase of the selection process.
5. State some special considerations involved in selecting managerial personnel and identify some techniques for identifying managerial talent.

OPENING INCIDENT

Condor Steel

Douglas Gardner is the plant superintendent of Condor Steel's rolling mill in Hamilton. He has been with the company for 27 years, is highly regarded, and runs the mill with a very firm hand. His mill has the highest efficiency rating of the eight mills operated by Condor.

As is typical of large Canadian manufacturers, the personnel department at Condor plays a substantial role in recruiting both office and factory workers. It cannot, however, dictate to line management who they should hire. Recently, Karen Mercato, the personnel administrator, developed a list of candidates for a newly established quality control managerial position in the plant. When Mercato and Gardner met to discuss the candidates, the following exchange took place:

Gardner: I've looked over these candidates and, in my mind, the only person who could handle the job is Bill Prosser. He's been in the plant for seven years and has some on-the-job training that will be valuable. I've talked to him on several occasions and I know I could work well with him because we see eye-to-eye on production.

Mercato: Of course, you have the final say on hirings, but I think I should warn you that

you'll have problems if you choose Prosser. I know Monica Stewart really wants that job and she has been here longer than Prosser. Remember that she has some formal academic training in quality control. Gilles Ferrier is also a strong candidate — he held a quality control position at Inland Steel before he came to work for Condor. Do you think you should ignore these two candidates?

Gardner: Stewart and Ferrier may look good on paper, but they just won't work out. I have a sixth sense about people on the job. Besides, neither of them are compatible with what I want to do. Take Stewart, for example. She won't be able to cope with all the hassling she'll get from the guys in the plant. Ferrier is tough, but he hasn't earned respect out there because he hasn't worked in the plant long enough. The person who takes this job will have to work under pressure, and will have to be strong to take the deadline demands. Prosser is the only one who will fit in, so I'm going to choose him.

Mercato: Doug, you can't refuse a job to candidates on the grounds that they won't fit in or because they're the wrong sex. You'll have to form some more valid reasons for not considering them. Either Ferrier or Stewart may file a complaint with the human rights commission saying they weren't fairly considered for the job.

Gardner: That's ridiculous! I've considered them fairly and I've concluded that they won't be able to handle the job. You know, Karen, I'm getting sick and tired of government rules about who we can hire, promote, and fire. In our business, we've got to make hard, quick decisions so that the mill works at peak efficiency. The company's got to remain competitive so that we can beat out foreign competition. Why don't you let me run this mill the way I see fit? So far I've done that very well without advice from outsiders and I'm going to continue my way until somebody forces me to do otherwise.

Mercato: Well, Doug, I hope we don't have any legal hassles over this. A commission enquiry could cost Condor a lot of money and goodwill.

Gardner: Don't worry about it. I'll handle it.

The success of a firm depends to a great extent on its effectiveness in selecting quality personnel. A firm will not profit if it has high market potential for a product or service but no capable personnel to direct its effort to achieve the market potential. The need for sound selection and development practices is crucial for all types of organizations — banks, retail stores, manufacturing plants, hospitals, schools, and professional sports teams.

In this chapter we examine human resource management. We first describe the basic human resource management activities to be performed if an organization is to make effective use of its personnel. Second, we note the legal framework within which an organization's human resource management operates. Government regulation has become increasingly important in recent years and will have a substantial future impact on the personnel function. Third, we describe in detail the key elements in the staffing process. Finally, we discuss the special problems that are encountered in executive recruitment.

MANAGEMENT OF HUMAN RESOURCES

Managers must work with the firm's human resources if organization goals are to be achieved. The firm must attract, select, train, motivate, develop, and retain qualified people. Employees must also be permitted to satisfy at least some of their own personal needs. Six basic activities are necessary if a firm is to utilize its human resources effectively: (1) staffing, (2) training and development, (3) compensation, (4) health and safety, (5) employee and labor relations, and (6) personnel research.[1]

Staffing

staffing

Staffing is the process of ensuring that the organization has qualified workers available at all levels in order to achieve company objectives. The staffing process primarily involves planning, recruitment — and selection, the focus of this chapter.

human resource planning

recruitment

selection

An organization should determine in advance how many workers and what kinds of skills are needed to accomplish the firm's objectives. This analysis of future personnel requirements is **human resource planning. Recruitment** involves encouraging individuals with the needed skills to make application for employment with the firm. **Selection** is the process of identifying those individuals who will best be able to assist the firm in achieving its goals. These three tasks must be carefully coordinated if the firm is to manage its human resources to its best advantage.

Training and Development

training and development

Training and development (T&D) programs help individuals, groups, and the entire organization to become more effective. Training is needed because people, jobs, and organizations are always changing. T&D should begin at the time individuals join the firm and continue throughout their careers. Large-scale T&D programs are called **organizational development** (OD). The purpose of OD is to alter the firm's internal environment so that employees can become more productive.[2]

organizational development

performance appraisal

A management technique that is closely associated with T&D is performance appraisal. Through **performance appraisal**, employees are evaluated to determine how well they perform their assigned tasks. Managers identify both strong points and areas for improvement; any obvious deficiencies can often be amended through T&D programs.

Compensation

The issue of what constitutes a fair day's pay has been a major concern of managers for decades. Employees must be provided with adequate and equitable rewards for their contributions to the organization's goals. **Compensation** includes all rewards individuals receive as a result of their employment. As such, it includes more than monetary income. The reward may be one or a combination of:

compensation

- Pay: The money that a person receives for performing jobs.
- Benefits: Additional financial rewards other than base pay, such as paid holidays, medical insurance, and retirement programs.

- Nonfinancial rewards: Nonmonetary rewards that an employee may receive, such as enjoyment derived from the work performed or from a pleasant working atmosphere.

MANAGEMENT IN PRACTICE

How Much are Managers Worth?

Many top executives in Canada earn over $500 000 per year. Some earn over $1 million and a few over $2 million. Many chief executives refuse to discuss the issue of executive compensation, or get upset when they are asked what they do to deserve such high salaries. Others are willing to offer opinions. Charles Bronfman, Seagram Distillers' deputy chairman, earned $944 520 in cash and bonuses in 1986. He says he feels adequately paid and has actually asked for lower compensation. On the other hand, he notes that the 20 percent ownership in Du Pont that Seagram bought in 1981 for $53 per share is now worth $110, so that might suggest that executives at Seagram should be paid much more money than they are getting.

Besides the question of absolute salaries paid to top executives, there is the issue of whether their salaries should move up and down in relation to their company's performance. Does this happen? Sometimes, but it is not hard to find cases where executive salaries go up while company profit goes down. At Imperial Oil Ltd., for example, profit fell 37 percent from 1985 to 1986, yet Chairman Arden Haynes' total compensation package went up 12 percent (to $660 000). Similar situations were evident in many other companies, including Bell Canada Enterprises, Canadian Occidental Petroleum, Canadian Pacific, and Westcoast Transmission Co. Ltd.

SOURCE   Adapted from John Partridge, "How Top Pay Matches Performance," *The Globe and Mail* (May 12, 1987): B1 – B2.

MANAGEMENT IN PRACTICE

What's Happening to the Year End Bonus?

More and more Canadian companies are foregoing that long-standing tradition, the Christmas bonus. At Inco, for example, a company spokesperson noted that the firm has lost nearly $1 billion during the last three years and simply cannot afford to pay bonuses. Other firms have abandoned the bonus in favor of a tougher management strategy — paying for performance.

In the past, Christmas bonuses were given on the assumption that workers were nice people and they deserved something extra at the end of the year. In recent years, however, the feeling has emerged that bonuses should be tied to actual employee performance. Herb Brown, president of the Profit-Sharing Council of Ca-nada, argues that the traditional Christmas bonus was taken for granted, but performance-related bonuses improve employee satisfaction and let them see how their work affects the bottom line.

Some companies are staying with the Christmas bonus idea because they feel that the bonus improves employee morale. Some large firms like Dofasco and Molson have such a large revenue base that cutting the Christmas bonus will not significantly affect their balance sheets. Maintaining the bonus, however, may prevent a loss of goodwill among employees.

SOURCE   Adapted from Barbara Aarsteinsen, "Turkey! Bonus? Ho! Ho!," *The Globe and Mail* (November 29, 1986): B1, B4.

Health and Safety

health

safety

Health refers to the employees' physical and mental well-being. **Safety** involves the protection of employees from injuries caused by work-related accidents. These topics are important to managers because employees who enjoy good health and work in a safe place are more likely to be productive; forward-thinking managers support safety and health programs. In fact, organizations today *have* to concern themselves with their employees' safety and health, because of the extent of government legislation in this area.

Employee and Labor Relations

As we noted in Chapter 2, millions of Canadian workers belong to labor unions. Business firms are required by law to recognize unions and bargain with them in good faith; this relationship has become an accepted way of life for many employers. However, the majority of workers in Canada (68 percent) still do not belong to unions. Nevertheless, people in nonunion organizations are often knowledgeable about union goals and activities. Often, nonunion firms try to satisfy the needs of their employees in order to persuade them that a union is not necessary for individuals to achieve their personal goals. Thus, unions influence even organizations that are not unionized.

Personnel Research

The personnel manager's research laboratory is the work atmosphere. Research needs permeate all human resource management. For instance, research may be conducted to determine the type of workers who will be most helpful to the firm. Or, it may be directed toward determining the causes of certain work-related accidents. Or, it may involve study and analysis of compensation packages that might increase worker motivation or satisfaction. Personnel research will be increasingly important to all kinds of organizations in the future.

LEGAL ASPECTS OF STAFFING

The main external environment factor that affects managers involved in the staffing function is legislation concerning human resource management. When managing human resources, managers must deal with four basic categories of laws: (1) antidiscrimination laws, (2) health and safety laws, (3) labor relations laws, and (4) compensation laws.

MANAGEMENT IN PRACTICE

The Impact of Human Rights Legislation

Years ago, a company could hire anyone it liked. Times have changed. With the advent of the Canadian Human Rights Act and its provincial counterparts, management has found that it must be careful not to violate anyone's human rights.

Take the case of the man who applied for a job as a coach cleaner for Canadian National Railways. The company originally refused to hire him because he had curvature of the spine. But three medical specialists testified at a Canadian Human Rights Commission hearing that the man's condition would not affect his ability to do the job. The man was awarded $15 400 in lost wages and was promised that he would be given the next coach cleaner position that came open.

While awards like this are the exception rather than the rule, the case demonstrates the kinds of issues that are now being scrutinized in Canada. In 1982, the Canadian Human Rights Commission handled 444 complaints. Almost half of these were dismissed; 96 others were settled by conciliation, and 61 were either withdrawn or settled during the investigation. Regardless of the outcome of the case, companies have found that dealing with alleged human rights violations is time-consuming and frustrating. Recruitment practices must therefore be closely monitored to ensure that human rights violations do not occur.

SOURCE Adapted from Keith McLean, "Legal Liability: Why Your Hiring Practices May Be Discriminatory," *Canadian Business* (February 1984): 114–115.

Antidiscrimination Laws

The key federal antidiscrimination legislation is the Canadian Human Rights Act of 1977. The goal of this Act is to ensure that any individual who wishes to obtain a job has an equal opportunity to compete for it. The Act applies to all federal agencies, Crown corporations, and business firms that do business interprovincially. Thus, it applies to firms such as the Bank of Montreal, Air Canada, Telecom Canada, Canadian National Railways, and many other public and private sector organizations that operate across Canada. However, even with such wide application, the Act affects only about 10 percent of Canadian workers; the rest are covered under provincial human rights acts.

The Canadian Human Rights Act prohibits a wide variety of practices in the recruitment, selection, promotion, and dismissal of personnel. The Act specifically prohibits discrimination on the basis of age, race and color, national and ethnic origin, physical handicap, religion, gender, marital status, or prison record (if pardoned). Some exceptions are permitted with respect to these blanket prohibitions. Discrimination could not be charged in the case of a blind person who was refused a position as a train engineer, bus driver, or crane operator. Likewise, a firm could not be charged for discrimination if it did not hire a hearing-impaired person as a telephone operator or as an audio engineer.

These situations are fairly clear-cut, but many others are not. For example, is it discriminatory to deny women employment in a job which requires routine carrying of objects with a mass of more than 50 kg? Ambiguities in determining whether discrimination has occurred are sometimes circumvented by referring to the concept of "bona fide occupational requirement." This concept means that an employer may choose one person over another based on overriding characteristics of the job in question. If a fitness center wanted to hire only women to supervise its women's locker room and sauna, it could do so without being discriminatory because it established a bona fide occupational requirement.

Even with reference to the bona fide occupational requirement concept, uncertainties remain. Consider three cases: Would an advertising agency be discriminating if it advertised for a male model of about 60 years of age for an ad that is to appeal to older men? Would a business firm be discriminating if it refused to hire a person as a receptionist because the applicant was overweight? Would a bank be discriminating because it refused to hire an applicant whom the personnel manager felt wouldn't fit in because of his appearance?

We might speculate that the advertising agency is not discriminating, the business firm might or might not be discriminating, and the bank would probably be accused of discrimination, but we can't be sure. The human rights legislation cannot specify all possible situations; so, many uncertainties remain regarding what the law considers to be discriminatory and what it considers to be acceptable. Nevertheless, the spirit of the legislation is clear, and managers must try to abide by it.

Enforcement of the federal Act is carried out by the Canadian Human Rights Commission. The commission can either respond to complaints from individuals who believe they have been discriminated against, or launch an investigation on its own, if it has reason to believe that discrimination has occurred. During an investigation, data are gathered about the alleged discriminatory behavior and, if the claim of discrimination is substantiated, the offending organization or individual may be ordered to compensate the victim.

Each province has also enacted human rights legislation to regulate organizations operating in that one province. These provincial regulations are similar in spirit to the federal legislation, with many minor variations from province to province. All provinces prohibit discrimination on the basis of race, national or ethnic origin, color, religion, sex, and marital status, but some do not address issues like physical handicaps, criminal record, or age. Enforcement of provincial legislation is handled by provincial human rights commissions.

Health and Safety Laws

The purpose of health and safety laws is to ensure that employees do not have to work in situations that are dangerous to their physical or mental well-being. These laws are an outgrowth of the undesirable conditions that existed in many Canadian firms at the close of the nineteenth century and the beginning of the twentieth century. While much improvement is evident, Canada still has some problems in the area of workplace health and safety. In one study of six western industrialized nations, Canada had the worst safety record in mining and construction, and was next to worst in manufacturing and railways.

In Canada, each province has developed its own workplace health and safety regulations. Provincial health and safety laws are very similar from province to province. The Ontario Occupational Health and Safety Act of 1978 is illustrative; parts of it are described briefly below.

The Ontario Act requires that all employers make sure that equipment and safety devices are used properly. Employers must also indicate to workers the proper way to operate machinery. At the job site, supervisors are charged with the responsibility of seeing that workers use equipment properly. Workers are also required by the Act to behave appropriately on the job. Employees also have the right to refuse to work on a job if they believe it is unsafe; a legal procedure exists for resolving the dispute.

Provincial health and safety regulations provide for the establishment of joint health and safety committees. These committees must be composed of people from both managerial and worker levels. Their purpose is to identify possible hazards in the work place and to make suggestions as to how these hazards can be reduced. The Ministry of Labor in each province also appoints inspectors to enforce health and safety regulations. If the inspector finds a sufficient hazard, he or she has the authority to clear the work place. In most provinces, inspectors can come to a firm unannounced to conduct an inspection.

Labor Relations Laws

One of the crucial areas many Canadian managers must handle is labor relations laws. These laws affect both union and nonunion firms, although union firms will have more daily experience with them. During the past 80 years, several major pieces of federal legislation have been passed dealing with labor relations. The key acts are noted in Table 10-1.

In addition to the various federal acts, each province has enacted a

TABLE 10-1   Four Federal Labor Relations Acts

Industrial Disputes Investigation Act	The first major legislation dealing with labor-management relations, it prohibited work stoppages while a 3-person board (one person each from labor and management, and a neutral chairperson) investigated the dispute.
Privy Council Order 1003	This order guaranteed labor's right to organize and bargain collectively with management
Industrial Relations and Disputes Investigation Act	Similar to PCO 1003, but applied only to employees of the federal government.
Public Service Staff Relations Act	Gave government workers the right to strike or to have compulsory arbitration.

labor relations act. Each is similar to the federal Act in its provisions, but each contains many minor variations. The provincial acts prohibit a wide variety of practices by both labor and management. For example, a manager cannot interfere with the formation of a union, nor can a manager discriminate against a person who is involved in the formation of a union. A union cannot ask management to dismiss an employee simply because the employee has been expelled from the union, nor can the union interfere with the formation of an employers' association.

Compensation Laws

The federal and provincial governments have all enacted legislation regarding compensation for employment. These laws stipulate such matters as minimum wages, hours of work per day or week before

---

MANAGEMENT IN PRACTICE

Equal Pay for Equal Work Adjustments

The Canadian Human Rights Commission has approved a settlement that will affect the pay of about 140 former and current female government employees. These employees will get adjustments averaging nearly $4000 per year for six years (for home economists) and over $4600 for six years (for physical therapists).

The Professional Institute of the Public Service of Canada, which negotiated the settlement, said it agreed that the two female-dominated groups should receive salaries equal to those paid to a male-dominated group of agriculture and forestry workers. The Institute used a nine-point job rating plan which compared jobs on factors such as education, experience, responsibilities, skills, etc. Salaries for the home economists and physical therapists had been about $11 000 per year lower than those of the agriculture and forestry workers.

SOURCE   Adapted from "Equal-Pay Adjustments Slated," *Winnipeg Free Press* (September 19, 1985): 19.

overtime must be paid, statutory holidays, overtime rates, maternity leave, and termination of employment. As with other human resource legislation, compensation laws differ slightly in each jurisdiction. Managers must be aware of the federal laws and the provincial or territorial laws where their organization operates.

One important aspect of compensation laws concerns the question of pay equity for women. Recent statistics show that, on average, women earn about 64 percent of what men earn. The conclusion that there is discrimination against women seems fairly widely accepted, but remedies to resolve this problem are controversial. Several provinces are currently considering legislation which will require employers to pay men and women equal salaries if they are doing work of equal value.

MANAGEMENT IN PRACTICE

Equal Pay for Work of Equal Value

Many managers in private sector firms strongly oppose the concept of equal pay for work of equal value. They agree that pay inequities exist, but they say that it will cost business firms too much money to resolve the inequities. One study prepared for the Ontario Labor Ministry estimated that it would cost approximately $10 billion for the public and private sectors in Ontario to establish equitable payment for jobs of equal value. Yet the cost cannot be used as an easy defense: In one case, the Québec Human Rights Commission ruled that 24 female office employees of the Québec North Shore Paper Co. were performing work of equal value to that done by male production workers. The company was required to increase the secretaries' salaries by $701 and give them over $1000 in back pay.

Companies that already use good job evaluation systems may not have excessive difficulty coping with the concept of equal pay for work of equal value. For example, Nova Corp. of Calgary estimates that it will cost less than one-half of one percent of its revenues to comply with the principle of equal pay for work of equal value. Other companies argue, however, that implementing the concept will reduce their competitiveness at precisely the time when Canadian industry must become more competitive if they are to survive in world markets.

SOURCE   Adapted from Gordon Pitts, "Equal-Pay Issue: Business Uneasy," *The Financial Post* (August 31, 1985): 1 – 2.

THE STAFFING PROCESS

staffing process

The **staffing process** involves planning for future personnel requirements, recruiting individuals, and selecting those recruits who are most likely to fulfill the needs of the firm. Figure 10-1 illustrates the basic steps in the staffing process. In the sections that follow, we discuss each of these steps.

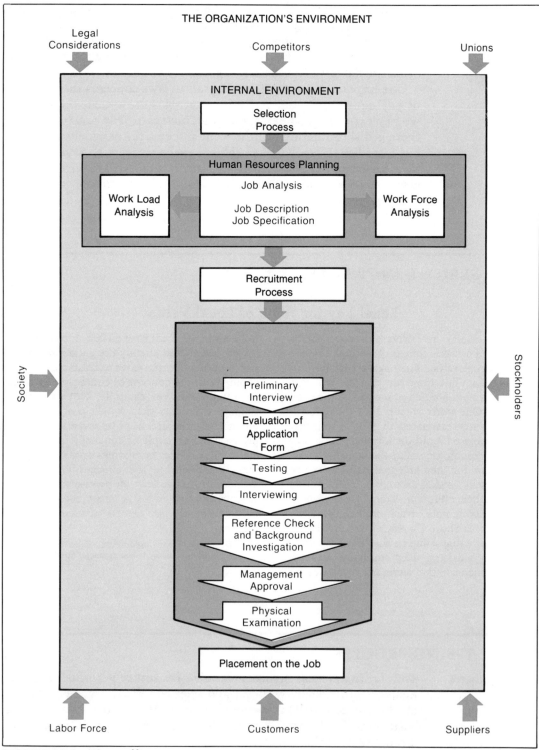

FIGURE 10-1 The staffing process

Human Resource Planning

Planning is necessary to assure that the organization will have the right number and kinds of people available to work when and where they are needed. Human resource planning, when performed properly, can:

- Enable managers to anticipate shortages and surpluses of labor, and to develop plans for avoiding or correcting problems before they become serious
- Permit forecasts of recruitment needs for both numbers and types of skills sought
- Help analyze sources of labor in order to focus recruitment efforts on the most likely sources
- Identify replacements or backup for present key managers from either inside or outside the organization
- Integrate personnel plans with financial plans and forecasts.[3]

Job Analysis

job analysis

The process of determining the human qualifications required to perform each job is a **job analysis.** It requires identifying the responsibilities and operations of a job, leading to the development of a job description and job specification. Several methods may be used in conducting job analyses including:

- Observations of and interviews with present employees performing the jobs
- Questionnaires completed by present employees or supervisors of the work
- Analysis by experts
- A diary of activities performed by present employees.

Job Description

job description

The job description is a product of job analysis. As shown in Figure 10-2, a **job description** summarizes the purpose, principal duties, and responsibilities of a job. A job description includes statements on:

- Duties to be performed
- Supervision given and received
- Relationships with other jobs
- Equipment and materials needed
- Physical working conditions.

Job descriptions facilitate the recruitment process by clarifying the specific nature, objectives, and responsibilities of a particular position. They are also a helpful tool in the orientation and training of new employees. While job descriptions exist in many large firms, managers sometimes do not understand or use them properly. For instance, some managers believe that having job descriptions restricts flexibility and creativity in staffing the organization. However, to be useful to managers, job descriptions must be translated into a statement of human requirements.

Job Description
Great West Life Assurance Company

JOB TITLE Senior Benefits Clerk	CLASSIFICATION	C5
DEPARTMENT Personnel Benefits	DEPT. 158 *WA 85·04·23*	
DIVISION Corporate Resources	COMMITTEE SECRETARY	

General Purpose

To assist in the initial set up and maintenance of benefit records (manual and computer) for the on-going administration of all Company Benefit Programs for Staff and Agents. To provide Staff and Agents with up-to-date information regarding their benefits, ensuring that this information is correct and promptly received.

Duties

1. Maintains computer and manual records of benefit programs for Staff and Agents.
2. Checks the calculation and coding of benefits for new staff and agents, terminations, and changes.
3. Processes and approves staff and agents changes to benefits, for instance, group life, AD&D, Dependent Life, Health and Dental (excluding Evidence of Insurability Forms).
4. Assists in year-end procedures and preparation of benefit summaries.

5. Provides assistance and advice and answers questions on all Benefit Plans (for example, questions on health and dental claims) for Staff and Agents on a daily basis, both by phone and in written form.
6. Prepares pension quotations for checking by the Personnel Benefits Administrator.
7. Checks the calculation of pension refunds.
8. Is responsible for calculation of deferred annuities and issuing certificates.
9. Assists in annual indexing of pension and disability pensions.
10. Is responsible for conversions of life, health, and disability conversions and health extensions.
11. Assists in preparation of monthly premium statements.
12. Is responsible for ensuring long-term disability payments and benefit deductions are handled accurately.

FIGURE 10-2   A job description

Job Specifications

job specification

The statement of the minimum acceptable human qualities necessary to perform the job is the **job specification**. The job specification pinpoints such characteristics required for the job as: education, experience, personality, and physical abilities. Because of antidiscrimination legislation, organizations need to be able to show that other characteristics are job related. The job specification is the standard to which the applicant is compared in each step of recruitment.

Work Load Analysis

Not only must we know the type of person required for a job but also the number of people necessary to meet organization needs. Determining the number of personnel needed by an organization requires a prediction of future work loads.

13. Is responsible for the administration of all applications, changes, and balancing of the Individual Retirement Annuity Plan.
14. Assists in the administration of the Profit-Sharing/Savings Plan in respect of the annual enrollment, terminations, re-entries, and withdrawals.
15. Is responsible for annual enrollment and processing of applications for Accidental Death and Dismemberment Insurance.
16. Handles special projects: for instance, ad hoc increases, statistical studies, and benefit surveys.

Job Specifications

I. Education and Experience High school education with an aptitude for analytical and mathematical work. Some Company experience in an area using mathematical skills and well-developed communication skills: 2–3 years' experience preferred.

II. Responsibility Level Works with confidential information (salaries, increases, personal family information).
Reports to Personnel Benefits Administrator under general supervision.

III. Contacts Extensive phone and written contact with Staff and Agents (at all levels) regarding their benefits.
Extensive phone and written contact with other departments, Commission Administration, Payroll, Staff and Agents Claims, Marketing Actuarial Programming, and Group Pensions.
Some outside Company contacts — Trustees of Profit-Sharing/Savings Plan, other insurance and trust companies.

IV. Job Knowledge Detailed knowledge about all the Company Benefit Plans and how to calculate benefits under these plans.
Detailed knowledge of coding procedures and how to read computer output to ensure that there are no errors.
Good knowledge of department routines and procedures, especially those occurring at year-end.

V. Supervisory Responsibility Nil.

JOB ANALYST *WA* CHECKED BY *KH* APPROVED BY *EH* DATE ___85.04.23___

---

work load analysis

Work load analysis involves estimating future types and volume of work to be performed. It requires that forecasts of work volume be prepared. These forecasts are then translated into person-hour requirements. Work programs are often stated in terms of units produced, products assembled, boxes packed, customers called, or vouchers processed. These are then converted into the number of person-hours by a time study of the units or by averaging past work experience. For example, to produce a specified number of products will require 1000 person-hours of work during a 40-hour work week. By dividing 1000 person-hours by 40 hours, the personnel needed is calculated as 25 workers.

Work Force Analysis

work force analysis

After determining the number of workers required, personnel research needs a work force analysis. A **work force analysis** consists of identifying the skills of current personnel to determine if work loads can be handled by these employees. If the work cannot be performed by the present work force, individuals will have to be recruited from outside the firm. In some organizations a computerized personnel data bank (human resource information system) assists in providing this information. The following is typical of the information included:

- Personal history: age, sex, marital status, and similar data
- Skills: education, job experience, and training
- Special qualifications: membership in professional organizations and special achievements
- Salary and job history: present salary, past salary, dates of raises, and various positions held
- Company data: benefit plan, retirement information, and seniority
- Capacity of individual: test scores and health records
- Special preferences of the individual: geographic location and work assignments

Recruitment

recruitment

employment requisition

Recruitment involves encouraging individuals with the needed skills to make application for employment with the firm. In most large organizations, this begins with an employment requisition. An **employment requisition** is a form issued to activate the recruitment process; it typically includes such information as the job title, starting date, pay scale, and a brief summary of principal duties. Personnel recruitment can range from locating qualified individuals within the firm, to a sophisticated and extensive search for a new president.

Personnel can be recruited using internal and/or external sources of qualified applicants. There are advantages and disadvantages of both internal and external sources of applicants. Internal recruitment, or promotion from within, is an important source of personnel for positions above the entry level. Promotion from within has several advantages; it

- Increases morale of employees
- Improves the quality of selection since an organization usually has a more complete evaluation of the strengths and weaknesses of internal applicants than of those from outside the firm
- Motivates present employees to prepare for more responsible positions
- Attracts a better quality of external applicants for entry-level jobs if chances for promotion from within are good
- Assists the organization to use personnel more fully.

Despite the advantages of internal recruiting, several disadvantages should be considered; two of these are: (1) the supply of qualified applicants may be inadequate; and (2) internal sources may lead to inbreeding of ideas — current employees may lack new ideas on how to do a job more effectively.

External sources of applicants permit an organization to overcome the disadvantages of recruiting internally. The major advantage of external recruitment is the new ideas that come into the firm with new people. If a firm promotes strictly from within, its personnel may develop a narrow view of the business and may fail to adopt innovative or creative ideas that will help the firm prosper. External recruitment is also needed to maintain a constant labor force since workers do retire, leave the firm, or die.

Keep in mind the distinction between sources and methods of recruitment. Sources of recruitment refers to the location of potential employees. Possible sources of recruitment include high schools and vocational schools, technical schools, community colleges, universities, competitors, and unsolicited applicants. Methods of recruitment are the means by which job applicants may be encouraged to seek employment with the firm. Some methods are advertising, employment agencies, recruiters, and employee referrals. Essentially, the firm must first determine where potential employees may be found

MANAGEMENT IN PRACTICE

Executive Recruiting

Jo Ann Compton is an executive search consultant — often called a "headhunter" — who works for the Coopers & Lybrand Consulting Group. Her job is to find top executives for other companies. As an example of her work, consider the following: A manufacturing company was looking for a vice-president of human resources. They hired Compton to help pick the right person for the job. To begin with, she talked to 89 people; of those, the 35 most promising were interviewed. After reflecting on the interviews, Compton narrowed the field to nine candidates, whom she interviewed a second time. Finally, she presented a "short list" of four candidates to top management of the company. Several weeks later, the company picked one of the four candidates, a person with an M.B.A. and experience in the oil and gas industry.

Requests for hiring services come from all sorts of companies, but Compton notes that most companies are very cautious about who they pick. They are very conscious of the bottom line as a result of the recession in the early 1980s, and most executive searches cost between $15 000 and $35 000. This may seem high, but Compton estimates that the cost of an error in choosing a person for a top job can be as much as $100 000. One other interesting statistic: the people most frequently chosen for high paying positions are those who are not even looking to change jobs. The next most frequently chosen are those who are dissatisfied in their current job and have quietly passed the word that they are looking for a change. The least successful candidates are those that are actively looking for a job.

SOURCE   Adapted from "Average Executive Search Fee $15 000 to $35 000," *The Globe and Mail* (March 23, 1987): B17.

and then use the appropriate methods to encourage them to apply. Only when a firm has applicants for a job can the selection process begin.

The Selection Process

The ultimate objective of recruitment is to select individuals who meet the requirements of the job. This is primarily a matter of comparing applicants' skills, knowledge, and education to the requirements of the job description/job specification. The steps in the selection process are shown in Figure 10-1.

Preliminary Interview

screening interviews

Screening interviews are typically used to eliminate the obviously unqualified applicants for such reasons as excessive salary requirements, inadequate education, inability to speak coherently, or lack of job-related experience. An applicant who appears to qualify for a position is asked to complete an employment application.

Evaluation of Application Form

employment application

Almost all organizations use a form for employment application in selecting new employees. The **employment application** collects objective biographical information about an applicant, such as education, work experience, special skills, general background, and references. (See Figure 10-3, on pages 366-367, for an example of an employment application.) Information obtained from the employment application significantly assists managers in selecting quality personnel. Some organizations design and use a weighted application form by determining relationships between biographical facts and job success. For example, one bank discovered that newly hired secretaries are least likely to quit the job if they are over 35 years of age, married, not college graduates, and have more than three years experience.[4] Biographical analyses can also be used to predict the quality of job performance. However, in the rapidly changing environment of the last few years, much new legislation has come into existence limiting the kinds of data that can be gathered about prospective employees. Managers must, therefore, be careful to stay within provincial and federal guidelines when developing and using application forms. Remember that information requested on an employment application should not lead to discrimination against applicants. Questions referring to an applicant's age, sex, race, religion, national origin, or family status may violate government regulations.

Testing

Traditionally, testing has been an integral component in the selection process. Tests have been used to screen applicants in terms of skills, abilities, aptitudes, interests, personality, and attitudes that cannot be objectively judged in other ways. Tests to determine specific skills such as typing or shorthand are in wide use. However, in recent years many organizations have reduced or eliminated their psychological and intelligence pre-employment testing programs because some tests have been found to be instruments of discrimination.

validity

In order to meet legal requirements, tests must possess both validity and reliability. **Validity** of tests is concerned with the relationship between the score on the test and actual job performance. A test is valid if the score on the test can predict job success. Validity is highly specific in nature. A test may be valid for one objective and invalid for another. For instance, an IQ test may be valid for measuring abstract intelligence, but it will probably be far less valid in predicting the on-the-job success of a supervisor.

reliability

Reliability is concerned with the degree of consistency of test results. If a test possesses high reliability, a person tested a second or third time with the same test, under the same conditions, will obtain close to the first score.

An organization choosing to use testing in the employment process should be careful to avoid potential discriminatory aspects of tests and use tests only as an aid in the process, not as the determining factor.

Interviewing

interview

The **interview** is the most widely used and probably the most important method of assessing the qualifications of job applicants. In general there are several objectives in interviewing job applicants:

- Assessing potential for advancement
- Determining the ability to get along with others
- Assessing personality
- Determining if the person will fit into the organization.

patterned interview

The selection process can choose between two basic types of interviews: direct (patterned) and nondirect (unstructured). In recent years, increased interest has been shown in the use of a directed or patterned interview. In **patterned interviews**, the interviewer follows a predetermined series of questions in interviewing applicants. The interviewer asks questions and records the applicant's responses. The patterned interview usually yields complete, consistent, and reliable information about an applicant. Also, its use permits easy comparison of several applicants and minimizes interviewer bias and prejudices.

unstructured interview

Unstructured interviews have no predetermined interviewing strategy or list of questions. Broad, open-ended approaches, such as "Tell me about yourself," are part of the unstructured interview. The

THE **Great-West Life** ASSURANCE COMPANY • HEAD OFFICE - WINNIPEG, CANADA

APPLICATION FOR EMPLOYMENT CAN.

SURNAME	GIVEN NAMES (CIRCLE NAME USED)		
PRESENT ADDRESS		POSTAL CODE	HOW LONG?
TELEPHONE	ALTERNATE TELEPHONE	SOCIAL INSURANCE NUMBER	
HAVE YOU EVER APPLIED FOR EMPLOYMENT WITH THIS COMPANY? NO ☐ YES ☐ WHEN?	HAVE YOU EVER BEEN EMPLOYED BY THIS COMPANY? NO ☐ YES ☐ WHEN?		
DATE AVAILABLE TO COMMENCE EMPLOYMENT	TYPE OF WORK FOR WHICH YOU ARE NOW APPLYING	PERMANENT ☐ TEMPORARY ☐	SUMMER ☐ PART-TIME ☐
ARE YOU LEGALLY ENTITLED TO WORK IN CANADA? ☐ YES ☐ NO		SALARY EXPECTED	
LANGUAGES: ENGLISH - ☐ WRITTEN ☐ SPOKEN	FRENCH - ☐ WRITTEN ☐ SPOKEN	OTHER - ☐ WRITTEN ☐ SPOKEN	

EDUCATION	NAME OF SCHOOL	ENTERED MONTH YEAR	LEFT MONTH YEAR	GRADE/LEVEL COMPLETED	DEGREE/DIPL. OR CERT. OBTAINED	OVERALL AVERAGE	COURSE TAKEN AND/OR MAJOR SUBJECT
HIGH SCHOOL		NOT REQUIRED	NOT REQUIRED				
UNIVERSITY OR							
COMMUNITY COLLEGE							
OTHER							

IF COMPLETED HIGH SCHOOL WITHIN LAST 2 YRS. LIST COURSES, THEIR NUMBERS AND MARKS FOR FINAL YEAR. UNDERLINE SUBJECT LIKED MOST, CIRCLE SUBJECT LIKED LEAST.

HAVE KNOWLEDGE OF TYPING ☐ (WORDS PER MIN. DICTAPHONE ☐ CALCULATORS ☐	COMPUTER LANGUAGES ☐ WORD PROCESSING ☐ KEY PUNCH ☐	SPECIFY ____ TYPE OF EQUIP. ____ TYPE OF EQUIP. ____	OTHER SKILLS
PLANS FOR FUTURE EDUCATION			

LIST PREVIOUS EMPLOYMENT IN ORDER BEGINNING WITH THE PRESENT OR LAST EMPLOYER

COMPANY		POSITION	DATE STARTED	REASON FOR LEAVING
ADDRESS	TELEPHONE NO.	SUPERVISOR OR MANAGER	MONTH YEAR DATE LEFT	
DEPARTMENT		SALARY START $ FINISH $ PER ____	MONTH YEAR	
BRIEFLY OUTLINE DUTIES PERFORMED				
COMPANY		POSITION	DATE STARTED	REASON FOR LEAVING
ADDRESS	TELEPHONE NO.	SUPERVISOR OR MANAGER	MONTH YEAR DATE LEFT	
DEPARTMENT		SALARY START $ FINISH $ PER ____	MONTH YEAR	
BRIEFLY OUTLINE DUTIES PERFORMED				

FOR COMPANY USE (EMPLOYMENT HISTORY CONTINUED ON REVERSE)

DEPARTMENT NUMBER	TYPING W.P.M.	SOURCE	TEST SCORE	START DATE	SALARY	PREV. EXPER. GWL ☐ YRS.___	TRAINING UNIV. ☐
DIVISION NUMBER	DATE TESTED			REPLACING		OTHER ☐	BC ☐ HS ☐
JOB NAME		CLASS					
REPORTING TO LOCAL	PROB. ☐ REGULAR ☐			INTERVIEWER(S)		YRS.___	OTHER

E15CAN-7-82M

FIGURE 10-3 An employment application form

EMPLOYMENT HISTORY CONTINUED

COMPANY	POSITION	DATE STARTED	REASON FOR LEAVING
ADDRESS TELEPHONE NO.	SUPERVISOR OR MANAGER	MONTH YEAR / DATE LEFT	
DEPARTMENT	SALARY / START / FINISH / $ / $ PER _____	MONTH YEAR	
BRIEFLY OUTLINE DUTIES PERFORMED			

COMPANY	POSITION	DATE STARTED	REASON FOR LEAVING
ADDRESS TELEPHONE NO.	SUPERVISOR OR MANAGER	MONTH YEAR / DATE LEFT	
DEPARTMENT	SALARY / START / FINISH / $ / $ PER _____	MONTH YEAR	
BRIEFLY OUTLINE DUTIES PERFORMED			

REFERRED FOR EMPLOYMENT BY	NAMES OF ACQUAINTANCES EMPLOYED BY THIS COMPANY

LIST HOBBIES, CLUBS TO WHICH YOU BELONG OR HAVE BELONGED*, SPORTS, POSITIONS OF LEADERSHIP HELD, AND OTHER SPARE-TIME ACTIVITES

*NOT REQUIRED TO LIST THOSE WHICH WOULD DISCLOSE RACE, RELIGION, COLOUR, SEX, AGE, MARITAL STATUS, POLITICAL BELIEF, NATIONALITY, PHYSICAL OR MENTAL HANDICAP, ETHNIC OR NATIONAL ORIGIN OR FAMILY STATUS.

GIVE BELOW TWO REFERENCES WHO ARE NEITHER RELATIVES NOR FORMER EMPLOYERS

NAME	ADDRESS	TELEPHONE NO.	OCCUPATION
NAME	ADDRESS	TELEPHONE NO.	OCCUPATION

Are you aware of any current health condition or disability that could affect performance on the job and/or attendance record?
☐ No ☐ Yes   If Yes, please elaborate.

_____

_____

_____

Do you require reasonable accommodation or special work conditions to perform the type of work for which you are applying? ☐ No ☐ Yes
If Yes, please elaborate.

_____

_____

_____

In connection with my application for employment I hereby consent that The Great-West Life Assurance Company conduct and/or cause to be conducted a personal investigation. I understand that any misleading or incorrect statements render this application void, and, if employed, may be cause for my termination.

_____   _____   _____
         DATE   CITY   SIGNATURE

Brian Peto
Credit Union Central

Brian Peto is the Personnel Supervisor at Credit Union Central, an organization which is a co-operative financial intermediary within the province of Manitoba. Credit Union Central provides financial opportunities, services, representation, and leadership for member organizations, the majority of which are credit unions. Credit Union Central is often called "the credit unions' credit union." While it does perform some of the traditional functions of a credit union (for example, making loans), its major focus is on the provision of services to other credit unions on a basis similar to that of a trade association.

Past President of the Human Resource Management Association of Manitoba, Peto received his diploma in Business Administration from Red River Community College in 1975; he is currently working on a B.A. in administrative studies. He started his career working full-time for Eaton's as a Personnel Representative. He joined Macleod's in 1977 and helped develop its personnel support function. From 1980 to 1984, Peto was the personnel manager at Burroughs Canada, a major computer manufacturer. In 1984, he joined Credit Union Central of Manitoba. As personnel supervisor, Peto is responsible for developing and administering many of the personnel services that are sold to Manitoba credit unions, such as analyzing compensation packages, recruiting individuals for managerial positions, and evaluating organizational effectiveness.

Q: How is the personnel services activity at Credit Union Central different from that in most personnel departments?
Peto: The difference is that we provide personnel services to independent credit unions around the province of Manitoba. Each credit union is completely autonomous and doesn't have to use our services if it doesn't want to. This contrasts with the situation normally found in companies that have their own personnel departments; staff feel duty-bound to use them whether they do good work or not. For example, if a manager in a credit union doesn't like the quality of service we're providing, he or she can go to some other organization and contract with it to do the work. Or, if a credit union is trying to recruit a general manager, it could use a management consulting firm to find one. This doesn't often happen, however, because we have a proven track record in providing good personnel services. The important point is that we don't have any authority over the line managers in the credit unions.

Q: Do the various credit unions in Manitoba have their own personnel departments?
Peto: Some credit unions are large enough to have full-time personnel staff, but even then they rely on Central's human resource department for support. The majority of credit unions do not have their own departments and therefore rely on the "trade association" principle in using our resources.

Q: What specific kinds of services does your department provide to the credit unions in Manitoba?
Peto: Basically, our service can be divided

into the two main areas of personnel services and training. Personnel services include recruitment, personnel policy development, employee benefits, compensation, relocation, and counseling. As far as training goes, we concentrate on the training of management and staff of credit unions, as well as the training of volunteers who serve on the boards of the credit unions.

Q: Can you give us a couple of specific examples?

Peto: Well, suppose the board of directors of a credit union wanted to hire a general manager. Normally the directors would come to us and indicate what kind of a person they are looking for; that's often somewhat dependent on the size of the credit union — they range in size from two employees to over 100. Based on the directors' preferences, we then draw up a job specification and begin advertising the opening for potential candidates. For some of these jobs, we get many applicants, so we may have to do considerable screening. After the screening, and in conjunction with the board directors, we develop a short list of candidates that they will want to interview. We are normally asked to attend these interviews in order to answer candidates' technical questions about working conditions, conditions of employment, or moving policies, and to help the board with the interview process. The board directors then make the final decision about who will get the job.

As another example, we provide training for tellers at credit unions in two main areas: how to sell services that credit unions offer, and how to do the technical work required in a teller's job. Our department sets up this training and designs it with the credit unions in mind. I would like to point out again that, if a credit union doesn't like what we're doing, it can stop using our training services. So we've got to be responsive to their needs.

Q: In your experience, what role does the personnel department play in most organizations?

Peto: In all four of the companies I've worked for, the personnel function has definitely been a staff function. I have always been in the role of consultant to line managers and have rarely had any authority over their activities. So, I

have had to prove that the work of the personnel department is valuable to them. I think I have been able to do that successfully, and I've noticed that, once line managers accept that the personnel department is doing a good job, they come to rely on it for a wide range of services. In order to get to the point where personnel is seen as a desirable service, people who work in it must be able to empathize with line managers and see the organization from their perspective.

Q: How do you ensure that work gets done in the proper way and at the right time?

Peto: I think it is important to make sure people understand exactly what they are supposed to do. It is not enough to give brief directions and then assume that workers are clear on what is to happen. Taking a little more time on the front end to ensure that the worker knows exactly what to do is an important part of the controlling function of a manager's job. It is also important for a manager to check work in progress and to give workers enough authority to do the work properly. For example, if I ask one of my employees to develop data on salary ranges for the credit union system, they must have the authority to gather these data. Of course, they also have to exercise discretion when factoring in market peculiarities and other variables that might distort the data. Once they have salary ranges for one class of jobs — for example, tellers — I usually have them check with me on what they have done so far. If the research looks good, they can then proceed to the next phase, which might be salary ranges for branch managers or secretaries.

Q: How much discretion can you give workers and still carry out your control responsibilities?

Peto: Quite a bit. I've found that, if you make it clear that you expect people to make their own decisions and not come running to the boss all the time, that they will usually exercise good judgment. If you have high expectations, you'll get high performance from people. Feedback is also very important in the control process. You've got to let people know how they're doing, whether it's good or bad. It's easier to give people good news than bad news, but feedback in both areas is necessary.

unstructured interview may be useful in assessing such characteristics of an individual as ability to communicate, personal values and personality.

Other types of interviewing techniques have also been used for special purposes. One of these techniques, the group interview, has been frequently used in the selection of managerial trainees. Group interviews are used where a small group of five or six applicants is observed and evaluated in discussions by two or more company managers or interviewers. Another technique, the panel interview, is a situation in which an applicant is interviewed by several people at the same time.

stress interview

The stress interview is another approach that is sometimes used in the selection of managers and potential managers. The **stress interview** deliberately puts the applicant on the defensive — perhaps by having the interviewer say something like "I don't think you're qualified for this job" — and then observes how the applicant reacts. The logic here is that managerial jobs contain much stress and, if an applicant can handle stress during an interview, he or she may make a good manager.

Regardless of the type of method used, the interview is the most important element in the selection of new personnel. Since most managers must rely on interviewing when selecting new employees or evaluating candidates for promotion, following sound practices is essential. The following guidelines are helpful in conducting effective interviews:

- Plan for the interview: review job specification and description as well as the applications of candidates.
- Create a good climate for the interview: try to establish a friendly, open rapport with the applicant.
- Allow sufficient time for an uninterrupted interview.
- Conduct a goal-oriented interview: seek the information needed to assist in the employment decision.
- Avoid certain types of questions: try not to ask leading questions or questions that may imply discrimination.
- Seek answers to all questions and check for inconsistencies.
- Record the results of the interview immediately on completion.[5]

Over the years, the interview, much like testing, has received considerable criticism concerning its ability to predict success on the job. In interviewing an applicant for employment, many factors influence the decision of the interviewer. For example, the interviewer may allow a first impression of an applicant to influence unduly the outcome of the interview. The personnel manager may be a great believer in the importance of initial impressions in evaluating applicants for jobs. He or she may place considerable emphasis on an applicant's handshake, speed of walking, and eye contact. If the applicant has a firm handshake, maintains good eye contact when meeting others, and keeps up with the personnel manager's fast walking pace, the applicant may be considered both confident and aggressive. Many managers rely on similar but sometimes questionable practices in selecting personnel.

Interviews can be instruments of discrimination and, for this reason, they have received close scrutiny in recent years. Charges of possible discrimination have led to an increase in the use of the patterned interview, since it has significantly higher reliability and validity than other methods of interviewing.

An effective means of assessing the success of an organization's interviewing process is to compare performance of employees with the evaluation of these same employees when they were first interviewed for the job. This objective evidence is an indication of the effectiveness or validity of the interview in predicting job success for that organization.

Background and Reference Checks

Once an applicant successfully clears the interviewing hurdle, the practice of many organizations is to conduct background and reference checks. The purpose of checking a person's background and references is to verify the information provided by the applicant in the interview and on the employment application.

Reference checks may or may not yield useful information. Suppose an employee left a previous job because he was not performing up to par. Would a reference check detect this? If the applicant's former manager didn't want to hurt the person's chances of getting another job, or was relieved to get rid of a problem employee, she might not indicate that the employee was a problem. In this case, the person doing the reference check would not really find out anything useful. Another problem with reference checks is the increasing concern about employee privacy. Possibly, as privacy laws become more refined, employers will be reluctant to say much about former employees for fear of being prosecuted for releasing confidential information. Some organizations now have official policies that bar managers from disclosing any information about former employees beyond the years worked and the positions held. Even recommendations are not permitted.

Although a reference check often provides enough information to verify information on the application, there are times when it does not. Often it is necessary to perform a background investigation into the applicant's past employment history. The background investigation may be helpful in determining if past work experience is related to the qualifications needed for the new position. Another reason for background investigations is that credential fraud has increased in recent years.[6] It has been found that between 7 and 10 percent of job applicants are not what they present themselves to be.[7] A frequently used but perhaps questionable way of verifying background information is the polygraph, or lie detector.

Management Approval

In most large organizations, many of the selection steps are performed by a personnel department. However, the personnel department does not usually make the final decision as to who is selected for a particular position. Under most circumstances, the manager or supervisor who will be the immediate superior of the new employee will make the final hiring decision. The selection decision is usually made after interviewing all the applicants and reviewing the recommendations of the personnel department. The immediate supervisor knows the needs of his or her department and is in the best position to evaluate the qualifications and characteristics of prospective employees. The supervisor or manager should be able to identify factors in the applicant's background or work experience that would help the new employee fit into the department.

Physical Exams

After a prospective employee has successfully completed the other phases in the selection process, he or she must usually pass a physical exam. The physical exam has at least three basic goals:

- To determine if the applicant can meet the physical demands of the job
- To provide a record to protect the organization against claims for previously incurred injuries
- To prevent communicable diseases from entering the firm.

Placement on the Job: Orientation

orientation

Orientation is a formal and informal process whereby new employees are introduced to their company, jobs, and members of the work group. Once applicants have been selected and have joined the firm, several days may be spent in orientation. The purposes of orientation are the following:

- To create a favorable impression on the new employee of the organization and its work
- To help ease the new employee's adjustment to the organization
- To provide specific information concerning the task and performance expectations of the job.[8]

Every new employee goes through an orientation period regardless of whether the firm has a formal orientation program. New recruits must learn the ropes if they are to succeed. Much new-employee orientation takes place on an informal basis — during coffee breaks, at lunch, or during work — through interaction with longer-term employees. However, most organizations have formal orientation programs designed to acquaint new personnel with the formal items they should know. Table 10-2 lists these important items.

TABLE 10-2   Orientation Outline

1. History and nature of the business

2. Goals of the company

3. Basic products/services provided by the firm

4. Organizational structure

5. Policies, procedures, and rules covering such areas as:
   a. Work schedules
   b. Salaries and payment periods
   c. Physical facilities
   d. Attendance and absenteeism
   e. Working conditions and safety standards
   f. Lunch and coffee breaks
   g. Discipline and grievance
   h. Parking

6. Company benefits
   a. Insurance programs
   b. Pension and/or profit sharing plans
   c. Recreational programs — bowling, tennis, golf, etc.
   d. Vacations and holidays

7. Opportunities
   a. Advancement, promotion
   b. Suggestion systems

8. Specific departmental responsibilities
   a. Department functions
   b. Job duties/responsibilities/authority
   c. Introduction to other employees in work group

SPECIAL CONSIDERATIONS IN SELECTING MANAGERIAL PERSONNEL

In recruiting and selecting nonmanagerial personnel, it is usually possible to use more objective factors in identifying potentially successful employees. However, subjective judgment is often particularly important in selecting managerial personnel. In selecting managers, many intangible factors — such as people skills, leadership ability, planning and decision-making skills, attitudes, and personal characteristics — are the focus of evaluation. These intangibles may be much more difficult to assess than such factors as typing ability, filing ability, and manual dexterity, which are measures for lower-level workers.

The recruitment and development of quality managerial personnel is essential to the continuing success of every organization. Because of this need, organizations must be concerned with identifying persons with managerial potential.

MANAGEMENT IN PRACTICE

Promotions in the Banking Industry

Canada's five major banks rank in size among the top 100 banks in the world. Thus, the position of chairperson and CEO carries a lot of power: power to squeeze a developing country, to veto major corporate loans, and even to dictate how a business in trouble should operate.

There used to be a standard way of becoming a bank chairperson and CEO in Canada. The age-old rags-to-riches notion was very true: start working at a bank at age 16 and gradually work up to a top management position.

The Bank of Montreal was the first bank to bring in outsiders rather than promoting someone from within the bank itself. These outsiders gave the bank a fresh outlook and an open mind on modernization.

Merely promoting from outside is not a guarantee of long-term success, however. William Mulholland was brought into the Bank of Montreal in the mid-1970s to "shake up the organization." Profits went up sharply after his arrival and, by 1981, earnings per share were $6.16. Recently, earnings per share have slid to $3.87; critics say that Mulholland's style was right for turning the bank around, but not right for running it on a long-term basis.

SOURCES Adapted from Roderick McQueen, "Heirs Apparent," *Canadian Business* (February 1983): 26, 28 and "Bank of Montreal Loses Ground to Rivals," the *Globe and Mail* (November 24, 1984): B1.

Determining Executive Needs

Decisions concerning the number of executives required by an organization involve a comparison of: (1) predicted future needs, and (2) present inventory of talent. Determining needs for managerial personnel requires an inventory of personnel currently available within the organization. The inventory is not simply a counting of heads; it includes a catalog of present and potential abilities and attitudes. It is an assessment not only of skills, experience, and abilities but also of personal motivation. Sometimes, a person who appears to be properly prepared for a promotion indicates a desire to transfer, to change occupational area, or to remain on the present job.

In making up the inventory, a decision must be made about which personnel to include. Certainly, present lower- and middle-managers will be included. In some companies all salaried personnel compensated on a monthly or semimonthly basis are included. Each lower-level manager may be asked to submit recommendations of employees with the potential for advancement. For each individual included, detailed information must be gathered to supplement and update existing data, such as education, experience, performance ratings, health, psychological test results, recreational interests, hobbies, and civic involvement. Such data can be computerized in order that: (1) assessment as to current adequacy of talent reservoirs can be made, and (2) searches can be made to fill particular vacancies arising.

Many companies maintain backup organizational charts to show listings of available talent for each key managerial position in the organization. These charts usually include the names of at least two individuals as replacements for each key position. They also include an assessment of eligibility for promotion for each of the key positions.

Techniques for Identifying Managerial Talent

Identifying individuals with potential executive talent has become an increasingly significant activity in large organizations. In general, the activity has taken two directions: (1) determining the material personal characteristics or behaviors that seem to predict managerial success, and (2) establishing managerial talent assessment centers.

Personal Characteristics

Over the years, considerable interest has been shown in determining the personal characteristics related to managerial success. Major companies, such as AT&T, Sears, General Electric, and Standard Oil, have engaged in research within their firms to identify a series of traits or characteristics necessary for success. The studies related such measures of job performance as the productivity, salary level, and quality of work of successful managers with the personal characteristics and attitudes of these managers. Some of the characteristics of managers included in these studies were grades in college, level of self-confidence, organized and orderly thought, personal values of a practical and economic nature, intelligence, nonverbal reasoning, and general attitudes.

While a few studies did show a relationship between these kinds of factors and managerial success, for the most part, studies of personal characteristics of managers have not yielded very accurate predictions.

The Assessment Center

assessment center

In an effort to improve managerial selection, researchers have recently developed a second technique for identifying talent. This approach involves using an **assessment center**, designed to provide the systematic evaluation of the potential of individuals for future management positions. The basic assessment center idea was developed in the 1950s by AT&T and has grown in popularity in both Canada and the United States. In the typical assessment center, a series of activities is developed to test the potential manager's skills, abilities, attitudes, and judgment. Table 10-3 illustrates a three-day assessment center schedule, which evaluates executive candidates on a number of different bases.

In determining the predictive accuracy of assessment centers, the initial study at AT&T was most impressive. Assessor ratings were not communicated to company management for a period of eight years in order to avoid contaminating the results. In a sample of 55 candidates who achieved middle-management ranks during that period, the center correctly predicted 78 percent of them.[9] Of 73 persons who did not progress beyond the first level of management, 95 percent were correctly predicted by the assessment staff. As a result, this company has maintained its centers, processing an average of 10 000 candidates a year. Reviewing ratings and actual progress of 5943 personnel over a ten-year period demonstrated a high validity of assessment center predictions.[10]

The assessment center procedure usually has five steps. The first step involves participants in several activities, designed to test the effectiveness of their behavior in simulated but realistic management

TABLE 10-3   A Typical Schedule for an Assessment Center

Day 1	Orientation of dozen candidates
	Break-up into groups of four to play a management game (observe and assess organizing ability, financial acumen, quickness and efficiency of thinking under stress, adaptability, leadership)
	Psychological testing (measure and assess verbal and numerical abilities, reasoning, interests, and attitudes) and/or depth interviews (assess motivation)
	Leaderless group discussion (observe and assess aggressiveness, persuasiveness, expository skill, energy, flexibility, self-confidence)
Day 2	In-Basket exercise (observe and assess decision making under stress, organizing ability, memory and ability to interrelate events, preparation for decision making, ability to delegate, concern for others)
	Role-playing of employment or performance appraisal interview (observe and assess sensitivity to others, ability to probe for information, insight, empathy)
	Group roles in preparation of a budget (observe and assess collaboration abilities, financial knowledge, expository skill, leadership, drive)
Day 3	Individual case analyses (observe expository skill, awareness of problems, background information possessed for problems, typically involving marketing, personnel, accounting, operations, and financial elements
	Obtainment of peer ratings from all candidates.
	Staff assessors meet to discuss and rate all candidates
Weeks later	Manager with assessor experience meets with each candidate to discuss assessment, with counseling concerning career guides and areas to develop

situations. For example, a participant might be asked to chair a committee meeting or do a performance appraisal. While the participant is going through these exercises, several assessors observe.

The second step requires individual assessors to draw some conclusions about the participant's planning ability, leadership skills, and communication skills.

In the third step, the assessors pool their individual evaluations and develop a group consensus about how well each of the participants performed during the simulations.

Step four is the preparation of the assessment center report. This report summarizes the participant's behavior during the simulations and notes the participant's strong and weak points.

The final step involves giving the assessment center report to the participants and having one-on-one discussions with them about its contents. The report can also be given to the personnel department staff to help them decide what additional training and development individuals might need or want.

OPENING INCIDENT REVISITED

Condor Steel

The material in this chapter is relevant to the hiring situation apparent at the Condor Steel Mill run by Doug Gardner. The legal aspects of recruiting, hiring, and promoting people have changed substantially in the past 20 years, and managers must consider them. Formerly, managers had considerable discretion in these areas, but many laws now exist that prohibit activities which used to be widely accepted.

Two problem areas are raised in the Condor incident. The first is the issue of overt discrimination against women in promotions. Gardner is convinced that Stewart cannot handle the quality control job because she couldn't cope with the "hassling she'll get from the guys in the plant." Mercato and Gardner do not mention any bona fide occupational qualification for the job in question; Gardner may put Condor into difficulty if Stewart goes to the Human Rights Commission.

Second, Gardner is ignoring Ferrier, another qualified individual who also has a good claim on the job, because his experience is from another firm. Gardner has apparently decided that Prosser is the man who can best handle the

job, but how he came to this conclusion is not clear. Gardner obviously likes Prosser — and may feel he can control him — but beyond that he provides very little evidence that Prosser is better suited for the job than the other two candidates.

Gardner says he has a "sixth sense about people on the job," but this evidence will not be acceptable if one of the candidates goes to the Human Rights Commission. Gardner is apparently relying on subjective factors in this decision, which may cause him legal problems.

From Gardner's point of view, he is being unduly dictated to by government and his decision making is being interfered with by Mercato. Gardner looks back on his successful career and wonders why he has to defend his choice to a personnel officer who isn't even a line executive. This incident shows the kind of conflict that can arise between line managers and staff specialists. Each party is competent in his or her area and, when faced with a person who disagrees, each may defend his or her position vigorously.

SUMMARY

People are the most important asset of any organization. Most firms today realize that acquiring and developing quality human resources is essential if the organization is to survive and grow. In most large firms, a human resource or personnel department is responsible for administering the organization's staffing function. However, every manager, regardless of function, must understand and participate in the staffing process.

The six basic functions related to human resources are staffing, training and development, compensation, health and safety, employee and labor relations, and personnel research. Staffing primarily involves personnel planning, recruitment, and selection. Training and development programs are designed to assist individuals, groups, and the entire organization in becoming more effective. Compensation includes all rewards individuals receive as a result of their employment. Health and safety programs are designed to enable workers to have a safe and healthy work place. Employee and labor relations involve dealing with a union or developing an atmosphere where employees believe a union is unnecessary. Personnel research is directed toward gaining a better understanding of human relations problems.

Every manager involved with human resource management is affected by government legislation. Both the federal and provincial levels of government in Canada have passed laws that affect the way managers deal with the recruitment, hiring, promotion, and dismissal of employees. The key federal legislation is the Canada Human Rights Act, which prohibits discrimination on the basis of race and color, national origin and culture, gender, physical handicap, marital status, age, religious beliefs, and pardoned prison record.

The staffing process involves planning for future personnel requirements, recruiting individuals, and selecting from those recruits employees who fulfill the needs of the firm. The process of determining the human qualifications required to perform the job is called job analysis. A job description summarizes the purpose, principal duties, and responsibilities of the job. The statement of the minimum acceptable human qualities necessary to perform the job is the job specification. Workload analysis involves estimating the types and volume of work that needs to be performed if the organization is to achieve its objectives. Work force analysis consists of identifying the skills of current personnel to determine if workloads can be handled by these employees.

In most large organizations, an employee requisition is issued whenever a job becomes available. Recruitment may then begin. The ultimate objective of recruitment is to select individuals who are most capable of meeting the requirements of the job. Selection from among those recruited applicants is the next step. The steps in the selection process are: (1) screening interview, (2) completion of application, (3) testing, (4) interviews, (5) reference checks, (6) management approval, (7) physical exam. Once individuals have been selected, they need an orientation to the organization.

REVIEW QUESTIONS

1. Describe and discuss the different phases in the staffing process.
2. Distinguish between job description and job specification.
3. What are the major federal and provincial laws that affect the staffing process?
4. Describe the advantages and disadvantages of promotion from within.
5. What are the general objectives that need to be achieved in interviewing job applicants?
6. What steps are involved in the personnel selection process?
7. What is the purpose of an assessment center? Discuss.

EXERCISES

1. Assume you are a personnel director hired by firms of various types to help fill their job vacancies. What phase(s) of the personnel selection process do you believe would require special attention in selecting candidates for each of the following positions?
   a. Faculty member for a major university that stresses research
   b. A general laborer for a construction firm
   c. A skilled welder for work on an assembly line
   d. A senior secretary who is required to take dictation and type 70 words per minute
   e. A first-level production supervisor.
2. Consult the personnel wanted section of a major weekend newspaper. Evaluate the positions that are available for the following career fields. Can you detect a general pattern of job requirements that are needed for an applicant?
   a. Personnel manager
   b. Computer specialist
   c. Car salesperson
   d. Production supervisor

CASE STUDY

The Harried Department Head

Ron Colindale was the head of the department of management at a large university. Total university enrollment for the past year had been approximately 20 000 and was increasing slowly each year, despite earlier predictions that it would decline in the 1980s. Demand for spaces in the business school was even higher than that for the university as a whole. For example, the previous year 1345 students applied for admission to the business school; only 485 were admitted because of limited teaching staff.

Unlike many other faculties on campus, the business school was actively recruiting teachers in an attempt to satisfy the demand for management education. As a department head, Colindale was responsible for recruiting, but he was rapidly becoming frustrated by the rigid rules and regulations he had to follow. Two factors were at the root of his frustration: (1) very few people who had a PhD in business could be attracted to teaching, and (2) recruiting rules were very strict. Colindale had discovered, for example, that, if he wanted to hire an American, he had to prove that no equally qualified Canadian applicants were available. Colindale didn't have any particular preference for American faculty but, since many more candidates with PhDs were produced in the United States than in Canada, he would have more candidates to choose from.

Explicit directions had been provided for the wording and publication timing of advertisements Colindale wanted to place in various university journals. The wording directions concerned both the Canadian-American issue and the gender bias issue. Although no laws demanded that a certain number of women be hired, the university required that equal opportunity be heavily emphasized in the ads. Colindale considered himself personally supportive of equal opportunity, but he found himself starting to worry about satisfying the restrictions confronting him. For the timing deadlines, Colindale's ad had to appear in at least two consecutive issues, at least 60 days before the closing date for applications.

The rules and regulations did not stop there. Once Colindale had received curriculum vitae from various candidates, he had to meet with a committee of faculty members from his department. This committee — one member of which had to be a woman — would choose the three most promising applicants and invite them for an interview. Several lengthy meetings occurred, during which Colindale and one committee member disagreed persistently about the qualifications of several applicants.

Collindale finally had the following discussion with the Dean of the Faculty of Business, Gene Moeller:

Colindale: You know, Gene, this recruiting is starting to get me down.
Moeller: What's the problem?
Colindale: Well, all these rules and regulations make it difficult to do an efficient job of staffing my department. Every time I turn around there's another restriction. Making sure I'm adhering to all these rules sure takes a lot of time.
Moeller: But these rules are designed to ensure equal treatment for all applicants.
Colindale: I know, but I have to get special permission to make decisions that managers in other organizations could do in the normal course of their work.
Moeller: Like what?
Colindale: Well, take the initial screening of applicants: surely I should be able to do that on my own? I could then present my short list of candidates to the recruiting committee and we could decide which candidates to have in for an interview. I have spent hours involved in detailed discussions of every applicant with all the committee members. I don't have the time to do that and keep up my teaching, administrative work, and research.

Moeller: I'd like to help, but I'm afraid you don't have any alternative in this area. The recruiting rules are quite specific. But you've done a good job so far; keep up the good work and don't let it get you down. Well, it's time for the dean's council meeting, Ron. Nice talking to you.

QUESTIONS

1. What circumstances have motivated the university to state recruiting regulations so specifically?
2. What federal laws are relevant for this case?
3. What should Ron Colindale do? Why?

CASE STUDY

Expansion Plans at Eagle Aircraft

David Johnson, personnel manager for Eagle Aircraft, was a little anxious as he checked through his in-basket that morning. He had just returned from a week in Mexico. His friend Carl Edwards, vice-president of marketing, had called the night before to tell him about a meeting of the company's executive council. "It was a great meeting," Edwards had said. "I don't think the future has ever looked brighter for Eagle."

Edwards had gone on to tell Johnson about the president's decision to expand operations. He continued, "Everyone at the meeting seemed to be completely behind the president. Joe Davis, the controller, stressed our independent financial position; the production manager had done a complete work-up on the equipment we are going to need, including availability and cost information. And I have been pushing for this expansion for some time, so I was ready. I think it will be good for you too, David. The president said he expects employment to double in the next year."

Johnson found nothing in his mail about the meeting. He decided not to worry about it. "I suppose they'll let me know when they need my help," he thought.

Just then he looked up to see Rex Scherer, a production supervisor, standing in the doorway. "David," said Scherer, "the production manager jumped me Friday because maintenance doesn't have anybody qualified to work on the new digital lathe they are installing." "He's right," Johnson replied, "we'd better get hot and see if we can find someone." It was going to be another busy Monday.

QUESTIONS

1. What deficiencies do you see in planning at Eagle Aircraft?
2. How might the planning situation at Eagle Aircraft be improved?
3. When should Johnson start to work on finding the maintenance person for the digital lathe? Why?

ENDNOTES

[1] This section is based on the discussion in R. Wayne Mondy and Robert M. Noe III, *Personnel: The Management of Human Resources* (Boston: Allyn and Bacon, 1981): 8–11.

[2] Lester A. Digman, "Let's Keep the OD People Honest," *Personnel* 56 (January-February 1979): 23.

[3] Lewis E. Albright, "Staffing Policies and Strategies," *ASPA Hand-*

book of *Personnel and Industrial Relations,* edd. Dale Yoder and Herbert Heneman (Washington, D.C.: Bureau of National Affairs, 1974): vol. 1, 4–21.

[4]Stanley R. Jovack, "Developing an Effective Application Blank," *Personnel Journal* 49 (May 1970): 421.

[5]C. Harold Stone and Floyd L. Ruch, "Selection, Interviewing, and Testing," in *ASPA Handbook of Personnel and Industrial Relations,* edd. Dale Yoder and Herbert G. Heneman (Washington, D.C.: Bureau of National Affairs, 1979): 152–154.

[6]Kenneth Cooper, "Those 'Qualified' Applicants and Their Phony Credentials," *Administrative Management* 38 (August 1977): 44.

[7]Scott T. Rickard, "Effective Staff Selection," *Personnel Journal* (June 1981): 477.

[8]Diana Reed-Mendenhall and C. W. Millard, "Orientation: A Training And Development Tool," *Personnel Administrator* 25 (August 1980): 40.

[9]Douglas W. Bray and Donald L. Grant, "The Assessment Center in the Measurement of Potential for Business Management," *Psychological Monographs* 80 (1966): 24.

[10]James R. Huck, "Assessment Centers: A Review of the External and Internal Validities," *Personnel Psychology* 26 (Summer 1973): 198.

REFERENCES

Aarensteinsen, Barbara. "Turkey? Bonus? Ho! Ho!," *The Globe and Mail,* (November 29, 1986): B1, B4.

Breaugh, J. A. "Relationship between Recruiting Sources and Employee Performance, Absenteeism, and Work Attitudes." *Academy of Management Journal* 24 (March 1981): 142–147.

Bucalo, J. "Personnel Directors: What You Should Know Before Recommending MBO." *Personnel Journal* 56 (April 1977): 176–178.

Byham, William C. "Assessment Centers for Spotting Future Managers." *Harvard Business Review* 40 (July-August 1970): 158.

Campbell, Andrew. "Hiring for Results — Interviews that Select Winners." *Business Quarterly* 48, no. 4 (Winter 1983): 57–61.

Collins, E. G. C., and Blodgett, F. B. "Sexual Harassment: Some See It — Some Won't." *Harvard Business Review* 59 (March-April 1980): 77–94.

Cronshaw, Steven. "The Utility of Employment Testing for Clerical/Administrative Trades in the Canadian Military." *Canadian Journal of Administrative Sciences* 3, (December 1986): 376–385.

Davies, G. S. "Consistent Recruitment in a Graded Manpower System." *Management Science* 22 (July 1976): 1215–1220.

Dhanens, T. P. "Implications of the New EEOC Guidelines." *Personnel* 56 (September 1979): 32–39.

"Equal Pay Adjustments Slated," *Winnipeg Free Press,* (Sept. 19, 1985): 19.

Forsythe, Sandra; Drake, Mary; and Cox, Charles. "Influence of Applicant's Dress on Interviewer's Selection Decisions." *Journal of Applied Psychology* 70, (May 1985): 374–378.

Gandz, Jeffrey, and Rush, James C. "Human Rights and the Right Way to Hire." *Business Quarterly* 48, no. 1 (Spring 1983): 70–77.

Greer, Charles R. "Countercyclical Hiring as a Staffing Strategy for Managerial and Professional Personnel: Some Considerations and Issues." *Academy of Management Review* 9, no. 2 (April 1984): 324–330.

Heflich, D. L. "Matching People and Jobs: Value Systems and Employee Selection." *Personnel Administration* 26 (January 1981): 77–85.

Henderson, J.A. "What the Chief Executive Expects of the Personnel Function." *Personnel Administration* 22 (May 1977): 40–45.

Higgins, James M. "A Manager's Guide to the Equal Employment Opportunity Laws." *Personnel Journal* 55 (August 1976): 406–412.

Hoffman, W. H., and Wyatt, L. L. "Human Resources Planning." *Personnel Administration* 22 (January 1977): 19–23.

Hollingsworth, A. T., and Preston, P. "Corporate Planning: A Challenge for Personnel Executives." *Personnel Journal* 55 (August 1976): 386–389.

Lawshe, C. H. "Inferences from Personnel Tests and Their Validity." *Journal of Applied Psychology* 70, (February 1985): 237–238.

Malinowski, F. A. "Job Selection Using Task Analysis." *Personnel Journal* 60 (April 1981): 288–291.

Marr, R., and Schneider, J. "Self-Assessment Test for the 1978 Uniform Guidelines on Employee Selection Procedures." *Personnel Administration* 26 (May 1981): 103–108.

McLean, Keith, "Legal Liability — Why Your Hiring Practises may be Discriminatory." *Canadian Business* 57, no. 2 (February 1984): 114–115.

McQueen, Roderick. "Heirs Apparent." *Canadian Business* 56, no. 2 (February 1983): 26.

Partridge, John. "How Top Pay Matches Performance," *The Globe and Mail* (May 12, 1987): B1–B2.

Pitts, Gordon. "Equal Pay Issue: Business Uneasy." *The Globe and Mail* (August 31, 1985): 1–2.

"Probing Before Hiring Can Ease Personnel Grief." *Executive* 26, no. 2 (February 1983): 40–45.

Ritts, Morton. "Career Coaching." *Canadian Business* 59 (September 1986): 62–66.

Salter, Michael. "Helping Employees with Personal Problems Pays Off." *Financial Post* (February 11, 1984): 18.

Strauss, Marina. "Average Executive Search Fee $15 000 to $35 000." *The Globe and Mail* (March 23, 1987): B17.

"Training: A Good Way to Spot Future Executives." *The Financial Post* (May 5, 1984): 24.

Walker, Dean. "Peter Thomas: The Selling of a Salesman." *Executive* (February 1985): 34–37.

IV

Influencing

Motivation

KEY TERMS

motivation
extrinsic motivation
intrinsic motivation
Theory X
Theory Y
self-fulfilling
  prophecy
hierarchy of needs
E-R-G theory
hygiene factors
motivators

need for
  achievement
need for power
need for affiliation
expectancy theory
expectancy
valence
reinforcement
  theory
organizational
  behavior
  modification
  (OBM)

equity theory
job design
job rotation
job enlargement
job enrichment
quality circles
flextime
Theory Z
Seven S model

LEARNING OBJECTIVES

After completing this chapter you should be able to
1. Define motivation and explain some basic philosophies of human
   nature.

2. Distinguish between the motivation theories of Abraham Maslow and Clayton Alderfer.
3. Explain the motivation theory of Frederick Herzberg.
4. Describe the work of David McClelland as it relates to motivation.
5. Explain how expectancy theory, organizational behavior modification, and the self-fulfilling prophecy might be applied in business.
6. Explain job design and its relationship to job enrichment and job enlargement.

OPENING INCIDENT

Baylor's Department Store

George Homenchuk was the vice-president of operations for Baylor's Department Store in Edmonton. For the past 20 years the store had surveyed its customers annually about their feelings toward the store. The last three surveys had shown a disturbing trend — customers felt that the salesclerks in the store where unfriendly and not very helpful. These feelings had been reflected in sales; the data Homenchuk had before him revealed that both absolute sales volume and profit margins had declined for the last three years.

Homenchuk believed the problem was very serious, so he called a meeting of Baylor's executive committee to deal with it. In attendance were the vice-presidents of marketing, finance, personnel, and merchandising. After a lengthy meeting, with considerable input from the personnel vice-president, the executive committee decided that the real problem was low motivation levels among salesclerks. These low motivation levels apparently had resulted in indifferent attitudes toward customers. Several executives at the meeting commented that rumors had filtered up to them that clerks on the floor were not happy because they felt they were being ignored by management.

The vice-president of personnel, Lise Daniels, pointed out that Baylor's conducted attitude surveys of employees from time to time, and these revealed: (1) salesclerks did not find their jobs interesting; (2) they received little feedback on how well they were doing; and (3) they felt that there were inequities across departments in terms of workload. A discussion then ensued about how these attitudes could be improved. Daniels pointed out that, since the salesclerks were on straight salary, they were all paid the same amount of money regardless of their sales. She suggested that the clerks be put on commission; if so, Daniels argued, salesclerks would show much more interest in customers and therefore would sell more. She cited evidence from a number of organizations showing that the introduction of an incentive system had resulted in increased output by employees and increased profit for the organization.

Some of the members of the executive committee thought that this step was rather drastic and that employee turnover would surely increase if the system were implemented. They cited evidence from companies where this had happened. Other members thought that an incentive scheme really wouldn't solve the problem of poorly motivated employees because money wasn't a good motivator of people. In view of these disagreements, Homenchuk scheduled a second executive committee meeting for one week later, to allow the members time to mull over the problem and come up with a workable solution.

The problem facing Baylor's Department Store is, unfortunately, a common one in all kinds of organizations. Increasingly, researchers and employers report that today's employees do not respond to managers in the more compliant way their earlier counterparts did. Apparently the prosperity of the post-war era has caused fundamental changes in the way workers view their jobs — although recessions can cause reversals of this trend. Managers cannot ignore employees' views of their jobs without ignoring the basic management function of influencing.

Influencing is the management function of directing or stimulating the members of an organization to follow its plans and objectives, to work efficiently, and to help the firm to prosper. Managers can influence employees — as well as other managers — through motivation, through their leadership, through effective communication and handling of conflict, and through the development of the organization's culture. Chapters 11 to 15 deal with each of these topics. This chapter discusses motivation.

Throughout history, managers in diverse kinds of organizations have made a variety of assumptions about what motivates workers. Threats and abuse were common in slave labor organizations; even paid workers were thought to work only out of economic necessity. In the 1930s and 1940s the view that money was the only effective motivator was widespread. In the 1970s and 1980s, however, workers have increasingly been saying that they want something more from their jobs. They talk of wanting to be "fulfilled" by their job and by doing work that has "meaning." Comments like these imply that money by itself is not sufficient to motivate workers. Unfortunately, they don't suggest any specific motivators that managers can use to influence workers to produce enthusiastically.

Managers need to keep informed about worker needs, attitudes, and desires. Many workers appear to be generally suspicious of management, unimpressed by money, and unconcerned about productivity. Motivating workers with these views presents a genuine challenge to managers in the 1980s. This challenge exists when managing either service or production workers. Until recently, more attention was directed at production workers; now, office workers are also becoming more difficult to motivate. Some are refusing transfers and promotions in the interest of pursuing leisure-time or family-oriented activities. Absenteeism is becoming common and a general apathy seems to pervade the office ranks in some firms.

In view of these developments, a manager must ask: "How can I create a climate that will motivate my employees to perform most effectively and efficiently?" To answer this crucial question, we analyze what is known about human motivation and how these findings can be applied in the work place. We begin by defining the term "motivation" and by noting the two basic types of motivation. We then describe several philosophies of human nature and show

how these philosophies influence managerial behavior and subordinate motivation in the work place. In the third section of the chapter, we present the most popular motivation theories. They provide considerable insight into human behavior and are useful for improving our understanding of what motivates various employees. The fourth section is a discussion of the role of money as an employee motivator. The fifth section analyzes the important issue of job design and how it influences employee motivation. The chapter concludes with a discussion of what are usually called "Japanese management techniques" and indicates how these techniques can have a positive impact on employee motivation.

THE PROCESS OF MOTIVATION

motivation

Motivating the modern Canadian worker is considerably more complex than the simple application of the carrot-and-stick approach used by many managers in the past. **Motivation** is the perseverance and enthusiasm employees exhibit as they work toward organizational goals. In an organization, personnel are motivated if they perform their jobs efficiently, effectively, and eagerly.

Everyone has certain needs. A person cannot be motivated until a need is activated; this need activation is referred to as a motive. Motives explain why people engage in certain behavior; they are the drives or impulses within an individual. In Figure 11-1, one model of motivation is illustrated.

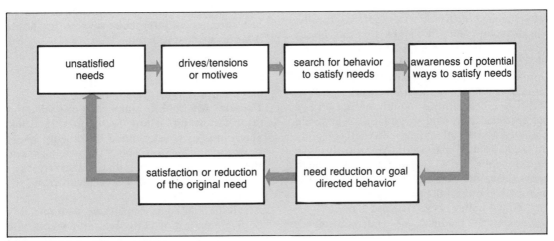

FIGURE 11-1   The motivation process

**Peter Thomas
Century 21**

When it comes right down to it, selling may be what made North America great. Certainly, salesmanship sets the style for the North American dream. Perhaps that is why Peter H. Thomas, a grade 12 graduate who has made himself a millionaire many times over by launching and operating several successful enterprises, likes to think and talk of himself as a salesperson. The ever-optimistic 46-year-old has even written a 160-page book (his second) on the subject. *Windows of Opportunity* (Key Porter Books, 1984) is jammed with enough enthusiasm and 10-second wisdom to get any salesperson out on the road again in the morning, armed with a shoeshine and a smile.

Thomas, a graduate of Dale Carnegie's course in winning friends and influencing peo-

ple, got his sales start in the mid-1960's. He was selling mutual funds in Edmonton just when the concept of "people's capitalism" was booming and Bernie Cornfeld and his Investors Overseas Services were about to show how far and fast a fellow could rise — and fall — when the idea was hot and the sales pitch just right. Thomas started buying and selling real estate shortly after that. In 1974 he obtained the master franchise for Canada for Century 21. Today he owns 74 percent of Century 21 Real Estate Canada Ltd., and acts as its president and chairperson.

Thomas has gone on to establish other franchises with the same fervor he put into Century 21. Triexcellence of Canada Inc., an idea hatched by the Century 21 people in (where else?) California, is aiming to do for used-car dealers what Century 21 did for real-estate independents — establish credibility for system members by promoting a higher degree of professionalism. Ditto for Mr. Build, another California creation, launched in Canada last summer as a franchise system for home maintenance contractors.

Q: Books are a lot of work and don't make much money. Why did you bother?
Thomas: My book is a new way of packaging information on selling techniques. I think about my own sales force getting up every morning and hearing about the economy and the strikes. Mix that in with the distractions of family life, and it all takes away from the simplicity of the job.
A salesperson's job is really very simple. My book breaks it down into five components: you prospect, you set the stage, you present, you

close, you follow up. Although it looks like I won't make money on it, one of my motivations in writing it was to produce a manual for my own sales force.

Q: Did you also think writing a book would help you gain a higher profile?
Thomas: Well, yes. I might be the chairperson of the board of Century 21, but the bottom line is that I'm a sales manager and I make my living attracting, motivating and recruiting salespeople. The reason I didn't publish the book myself was to establish its authenticity.

I read that sort of stuff all the time to remind me how I make my living. I used to sell products. Now I sell my ideas. I sold the idea of Century 21 to Canada to the extent that it handled $3 billion worth of real estate last year. Triex consists of selling car dealers on the idea of putting their salespeople in green jackets and doing a few things I ask them to do. I'm selling. That means, just as I say in the book, that I have to find a prospect; I have to set the stage so we can relate to each other; I have to give my presentation; I have to close; and then I have to handle service after the sale. Whether you're selling vacuum cleaners or a deal to the most sophisticated chairman of the board, the rules are the same.

Q: Does the pleasure in selling come from a sense of power?
Thomas: I don't feel any sense of power. I feel a sense of accomplishment. I don't want to feel powerful; I've never felt that way. I take an individual car salesperson or real-estate salesperson and tell them our program is for them because it will be good for them. They come with 1000 reasons why they won't join, and I

come up with 1000 reasons why they should. It's an interplay, a two-hour dialogue. When I leave there with a cheque and a customer, I feel good.

Q: You belong to the National Speakers' Association. What do you get out of that?
Thomas: The secret of my success is my ability to attract people who are better than me — fantastic top-notch professional people, in all areas. One of the ways you meet such people is to be kind of fantastic yourself. Be a properly dressed, hard-working, loyal, trustworthy individual with integrity. Get those kinds of people around you. One of the ways I find them is through the National Speakers' Association. It's exposure. Exposure lets me meet the winners face to face out there — we find each other.

I've just encouraged the number one salesperson in the real-estate business in the US to join us. She's going to be selling Mr. Build franchises on the West Coast. That one person will do more than 15 lightweights. Look at my fellow in Toronto who sells Triex franchises. A good marketing person might sell two Triex franchises in one month; last month, this one guy sold 10.

Q: You say you enjoy getting up and at it every morning. Where does all that steam come from?
Thomas: I have a psychologist friend in Vancouver and we talk. What makes Sammy run?. First of all, Sammy doesn't drink. Sammy is a marathon runner. Sammy has been married for 23 years to the same woman; Sammy's not running around looking for all that. He's a very satisfied guy.

An aroused need (motive) will cause a person to search for a way to satisfy the need. Once a way is found, it will be followed with some type of behavior directed toward a particular goal that the person has learned will satisfy the need. For example, a person may feel a need to associate with other people. He or she will search out other individuals and associate and interact with them in the hope of obtaining the goal of friendship.

This simple explanation of motivation does not represent the complexity of the process. Any single act by a particular person may be reflecting a number of different needs. Striving for a promotion may be caused by a need for material possessions or by a need for recognition. The same act by another person may be caused by a different set of needs. One person may seek friendships to satisfy his or her need for association with other people, whereas another individual may wish to use friendships for advancing a career. For yet another, it may be a combination of both these reasons. Furthermore, the same need can be expressed in different ways. One person seeks recognition through hard work; another seeks it by being the office clown or practical joker.

To motivate employees to perform well, managers have traditionally relied on the use of rewards (increased pay, job security, good working conditions) or punishments (dismissal, demotions, reprimands). However, current managers cannot rely on the manipulation of pay, benefits, or working conditions to motivate workers to perform effectively. Rather, managers must create a work atmosphere that will bring out the potential within every person. Specifically, managers should create a work atmosphere in which employees will want to be productive, contributing members of the organization.

To achieve this goal, managers must be aware of basic human needs and how these needs influence work behavior. Managers cannot assume that all people are alike, but they can assume that there is a reason for each subordinate's behavior. Managers should not condemn any act as stupid or senseless because, in the eyes of the person who committed it, the behavior makes sense. Instead, managers should try to understand why the behavior occurred. Stated more formally, managers must understand the forces that instigate behavior.

Intrinsic and Extrinsic Motivation

People work for many different reasons. When they work, they receive rewards of two basic types. Extrinsic rewards (for example, pay, promotions, compliments) are independent of the task the person performs and are administered by other people. Intrinsic rewards (such as a feeling of accomplishment for doing a task well) are an integral part of the task and are administered by the person

extrinsic
motivation✗

intrinsic
motivation✓

doing the task. **Extrinsic motivation** exists when a person works hard at a task because of the promise that some obvious reward will be forthcoming if a good job is done. **Intrinsic motivation**, on the other hand, exists if the person enthusiastically performs a task in the absence of any obvious external reward for doing so.

Consider two examples. Suppose that you feel that the work of the United Way is very important, and you volunteer to work on their annual fund-drive team. You work very hard doing your part. If the fund drive reaches its goal, you will probably feel a great sense of satisfaction for having done something that you feel is socially useful. You did not expend all that energy because someone promised you a reward, but rather because you felt the work of the United Way was important. When the job was completed, you rewarded yourself for doing well and were not dependent on someone else to give you rewards.

As another example, suppose you are a salesperson working on commission. You know that if you close a big sale, there will be a bonus in it for you. So you work very hard and make the sale. In this case, you have been extrinsically motivated by the promise of a reward for making a sale. There might also be an element of intrinsic motivation here if you get some pleasure out of doing a good job, but other people will usually assume that you are working for the money.

Both intrinsic and extrinsic rewards can motivate people. Intrinsic rewards can be particularly powerful because they involve people's normative beliefs about what is right or wrong. If an organization is full of people who honestly feel that the company is selling a very useful product or service, or that the company is an unusually good corporate citizen, the firm will benefit from the enthusiasm that these people feel. To maximize employee performance, a manager should determine the need structure of each individual and then allow them to work in such a way that intrinsic motivation is maximized. For a variety of reasons this is usually not possible, so most organizations rely on extrinsic motivators (primarily money) to motivate workers.

Both intrinsic and extrinsic motivation are usually present in the work place. Although it might seem that this should give managers twice as many opportunities to motivate workers, problems may arise when there is interaction between intrinsic and extrinsic motivation. In one experiment, students worked on several interesting puzzles. One half of the subjects were paid for working on the puzzles and the other half were not. Subjects were given free time during the experiment when they could do whatever they wished. The activity they engaged in during their free time was taken as an indication of their intrinsic motivation. Students who were not paid for working on the puzzles spent significantly more free time working on the puzzles than did subjects who were paid.

The possibility that intrinsic motivation is reduced when extrinsic rewards are given has interesting practical implications. In the extreme it suggests that if the pay of workers is tied completely to performance, only extrinsic motivation will be evident and none of the benefits of intrinsic motivation will remain. More realistically, it is probably the case that several other factors also influence the relationship between extrinsic and intrinsic motivation. For example, the nature of the task may be an important intervening variable. If the reward the employee receives is an integral part of the task (for instance in commission selling), giving extrinsic rewards may not reduce intrinsic motivation. When the reward is not an integral part of the task, extrinsic rewards may reduce intrinsic motivation.

Motivation, Ability, and Performance

Researchers and practicing managers generally accept the idea that employee performance is the result of many factors, some of which are not known to the manager, and some of which may not even be consciously understood by the worker. They also agree that the two most important variables in explaining employee performance are employee motivation and employee ability. These variables appear to be related as follows:

$$\text{performance} = \text{motivation} \times \text{ability}.$$

As we have noted, motivation is evident if employees eagerly and enthusiastically perform a task. Ability refers to a person's task competence. The distinction between ability and motivation is relevant for many situations. For example, if two offensive linesmen are vying for a starting position, they may do so with equal enthusiasm. However, if one of them weighs 80 kg and the other weighs 115 kg, the coach will likely pick the heavier player. In a business situation, two salespeople may pursue customers with equal vigor, but if one sells much more than the other, the sales manager would have to conclude that one has more ability at sales.

Admittedly, these two examples are somewhat extreme. Most managers face situations where the difference between ability and motivation is not quite so clear, and where performance may not be very clearly defined. Nevertheless, an understanding of the formula noted above gives considerable insight into an important part of a manager's job: getting employees to perform at a satisfactory level. The formula allows managers to assess various situations much more effectively because they can emphasize the variable that seems to be causing unsatisfactory performance. In some situations employee motivation levels are the problem, but in others ability is the issue. The solutions to the problems of lack of ability and lack of motivation are quite different; managers will obviously be more effective if they define the problem correctly.

MANAGEMENT IN PRACTICE

Productivity Improvement at Cardinal

Cardinal Meat Specialists of Mississauga, Ontario sells meat to retail outlets such as The Keg and Swiss Chalet restaurants. In 1982, it introduced a productivity gain-sharing program in an attempt to increase employee productivity. The program measures productivity gains on a division basis (not an individual one) and the value of all productivity gains is evenly split between management and workers. For example, a 30 percent gain produces a 15 percent bonus to each worker's paycheque.

The program has worked very well at Cardinal. Productivity increased 17 percent within 10 weeks of the program's introduction. It continued to increase, and in 1983 productivity was 34 percent higher than before the program was introduced. As well, absenteeism and turnover have declined to nearly zero, according to Jack Boulet, the controller at Cardinal.

SOURCE   Adapted from Sandra Bernstein, "Morale Booster: Productivity Gain Sharing Helps You Get More From Your Workers," *Canadian Business* (April 1984): 122.

In the formula provided here, a very low score on either motivation or ability will result in low performance overall. For example, people who are extremely nervous about speaking in front of a large audience (low ability) will not perform well at this task, no matter how motivated they are. The formula also implies that a high score on one variable can overcome a moderate score on the other variable. Thus, a person with relatively low ability but high motivation might outperform another person with high ability but low motivation. This situation occurs frequently in professional sports, when a supposedly superior team gets beaten by a team with less talented players.

PHILOSOPHIES OF HUMAN NATURE

In order to create an atmosphere conducive to a high level of employee motivation, managers must gain some understanding of basic philosophies of human nature. The assumptions that managers make regarding other people's behavior are a major factor in determining the climate for motivation. Some supervisors, for instance, still believe that employees are basically uninterested in what the organization is doing and are there simply because of economic necessity. These supervisors reason that such employees certainly won't have much of value to say about how to improve the organization's performance. Other supervisors might assume just the opposite. Managers' positive or negative views of human nature have a major impact on the motivational levels of the people working for them.

McGregor's Theory X and Theory Y

Douglas McGregor stressed the importance of understanding the relationship between motivation and philosophies of human nature.[1] In observing the practices and approaches of traditional managers, McGregor concluded that managers usually attempt to motivate employees by one of two basic approaches. He referred to these approaches as Theory X and Theory Y. **Theory X**, or the traditional view of management, suggests that managers must coerce, control, or threaten employees in order to motivate them. In contrast, McGregor proposed an alternative philosophy of human nature; **Theory Y** suggests that managers basically believe people are capable of being responsible and mature. Thus, employees do not require coercion or excessive control by the manager in order to perform effectively. McGregor's basic belief was that Theory Y is a more realistic assessment of people.

Theory X

Theory Y

Table 11-1 illustrates the different assumptions of these two philosophies of human nature. The Theory Y assumptions represent a high degree of faith in the capacity and potential of people. If managers accept the Theory Y philosophy of human nature, they will seriously consider managerial practices such as: (1) abandonment of time clocks, (2) flexible working hours on an individual basis, (3) job enrichment, (4) management by objectives, and (5) participative decision making. All these practices are based on the belief that abilities are widespread in the population and each person can be trusted to behave in a responsible manner. Thus, management would create an atmosphere that would permit workers to realize their potential. McGregor did not advocate Theory Y as the panacea for all

TABLE 11-1　A Comparison of McGregor's Theory X and Theory Y Assumptions about Human Nature

Theory X	Theory Y
The average person inherently dislikes work and will avoid it if possible.	The expenditure of physical and mental effort in work is as natural as play or rest.
Because of the dislike of work, most people must be coerced, controlled, directed, and threatened with punishment to get them to perform effectively.	People will exercise self-direction and self-control in the service of objectives to which they are committed.
The average person lacks ambition, avoids responsibility, and seeks security and economic rewards above all else.	Commitment to objectives is a function of the rewards associated with achievement.
Most people lack creative ability and are resistant to change.	The average person learns, under proper conditions, not only to accept but to seek responsibility.
Since most people are self-centered, they are not concerned with the goals of the organization.	The capacity to exercise a relatively high degree of imagination, ingenuity, and creativity in the solution of organizational problems is widely, not narrowly, distributed in the population.

SOURCE　Based on Douglas McGregor, *The Human Side of Enterprise* (New York: McGraw-Hill, 1960).

managerial problems. The Theory Y philosophy is not utopian, but McGregor argued that it does provide a basis for improved management and performance.

Argyris's Maturity Theory

The research of Chris Argyris has also aided managers in developing a more complete understanding of human behavior. Argyris emphasized the importance of the process of maturity. He suggested that there is a basic difference between the demands of the mature personality and the demands of the typical organization. Argyris concluded that, if plans, policies, methods and procedures are prescribed in detail, an employee will need to be submissive and passive, which suggests a Theory X type of organization. In this type of organization, subordinates are expected to concentrate on the orders as given and not question or attempt to understand these orders in a broader perspective. In brief, such a detailed prescription may ask individuals to work in an atmosphere where: *Theory X - immature treatment*

- They are provided minimal control over their workaday world.
- They are expected to be passive, dependent, and subordinate.
- They are expected to have a short time-perspective.
- They are induced to perfect and value the frequent use of a few shallow abilities.
- They are expected to produce under conditions leading to psychological failure.[2]

When the mature employee encounters these conditions, three reactions are possible:

- An employee may escape by quitting the job, being absent from work, or attempting to climb to higher levels in the firm where the structure is less rigid.
- A person can fight the system, exerting pressure on the organization by means of informal groups or through formally organized labor unions or ombudsmen.
- The most typical reaction by employees is to adapt by developing an attitude of apathy or indifference. The employee plays the game, and pay becomes the compensation for the penalty of working.

According to Argyris, adaptation is the least representative of good mental health.

Managers cannot assume that all employees are mature, as defined by Argyris, or that they are Theory Y types, as defined by McGregor. These assumptions may be valid when managers are dealing with highly educated professional, technical, and managerial employees, but security may mean more to the industrial worker than to the highly educated professional. The industrial worker may value the freedom of private thought permitted by the highly structured and repetitive tasks that others may find boring.

It could be argued that a highly structured atmosphere *requires* employees to act in an immature manner. In fact, managers have conditioned employees to prefer that type of behavior. Many people can and have adjusted to the kinds of tightly regimented work situations that Argyris contended demand immature behavior. One need only observe workers on an assembly line to recognize the truth of this interpretation. The resulting atmosphere is one of indifference and apathy, which may be a successful, acceptable adaptation. However, only a fraction of the jobs in Canadian business are of the highly structured, totally controlled type. To the degree that an open job market operates effectively, some matching of varying human needs and organization demands will be possible.

The philosophies of human nature discussed here provide the basis for a manager's approach to motivation and leadership. As such, the theories of both McGregor and Argyris should be kept in mind as we discuss human motivation in this chapter and leadership in Chapter 12.

Motivation: The Self-Fulfilling Prophecy

self-fulfilling
prophecy

One major problem that managers can counter with their influence is the **self-fulfilling prophecy**: the observable tendency for subordinates to give the manager what the manager expects from the subordinate. J. Sterling Livingston argues that:

- A manager's expectations of employees and the way he or she treats them largely determine their performance and career progress.
- A unique characteristic of superior managers is their ability to create high performance expectations that subordinates fulfill.
- Less effective managers fail to develop similar expectations and, as a consequence, the productivity of their subordinates suffers.
- Subordinates, more often than not, appear to do what they believe they are expected to do.[3]

The work of McGregor and Argyris suggests a solution to the problem of the self-fulfilling prophecy: a manager should develop high expectations of subordinates rather than low expectations, since both tend to be self-fulfilling prophecies. A manager communicates expectations both verbally and nonverbally. The manager's facial expressions, eye contact, body posture, or tone of voice can indicate approval and high expectations — or just the reverse.

Numerous studies support the notion of the self-fulfilling prophecy. In one such study, 18 elementary school teachers were informed that about 20 percent of their students were intellectual "bloomers." The teachers were told that these youngsters would achieve remarkable progress during the school year. In actuality, the 20 percent sample of students was chosen at random and did not differ in intelligence or abilities from the remainder of the students in the classes. The only variable was the teacher's expectations of the group.

The students actually did achieve significantly greater progress during the school year. Thus, the teachers' expectations of the students became a self-fulfilling prophecy.

Similar results have been achieved by managers. More often than not, if managers have high expectations of their employees, the employees' performance will meet those expectations. For example, the high expectations of the manager of a large computer center at a major university substantially changed the life and work of a janitor. The manager believed that the janitor, with limited formal education, had the potential to become a computer operator. The computer center manager had high expectations and believed that the cleaner could learn the new job. After several months of training, the former janitor did become a successful computer operator, and eventually even trained others. This example illustrates how the high expectations of one person can have a significant positive impact on the actions of another.

Many businesses have not developed effective managers rapidly enough to meet the needs of their organization. As a consequence, organizations are not developing their most valuable resource — talented young men and women. In fact, the self-fulfilling prophecy seems to have the greatest potential impact on younger employees and managers. By failing to create high expectations or provide training and development for their personnel, firms are experiencing high costs from excessive employee turnover. Also, managers who fail to communicate high expectations may significantly damage the attitudes and career aspirations of younger personnel.

Managers who are interested in high productivity must treat their employees in ways that contribute to high performance, career development, and personal satisfaction. Effective managers who have high expectations of subordinates tend to build the employees' self-confidence and develop their performance capabilities. By contrast, ineffective managers tend to create a negative climate and to have low expectations of subordinates. As a result, the employees' level of motivation and performance is lower, and their self-esteem and careers may be damaged.[4]

MOTIVATION THEORIES

There are nearly as many theories of motivation as there are psychologists who develop them. None of the theories provides a universally accepted approach that explains all human behavior. However, a basic understanding of these theories is useful to managers as they attempt to motivate people in their organizations. Our purpose in presenting different theories of human motivation is not to identify one as superior. Rather, it is to develop a thought process that will ultimately lead managers to understand human motivation and how it affects their specific work situation.

Maslow's Hierarchy of Needs

Many psychologists believe that there are certain prevalent patterns or configurations of human needs, in spite of obvious individual differences. A common approach to establishing this need pattern is to develop a universal need hierarchy. Abraham Maslow has proposed one widely accepted pattern, which is illustrated in Figure 11-2. Examples of how an organization might help satisfy these basic needs are also presented. Maslow states that individuals are motivated to satisfy certain unsatisfied needs. His theory of human motivation is based on the following assumptions:

- Needs that are not satisfied motivate or influence behavior. Satisfied needs do not motivate behavior.
- Needs are arranged according to a hierarchy of importance.
- An individual's needs at any level on the hierarchy emerge only when the lower-level needs are reasonably well satisfied.[5]

hierarchy of needs

According to Maslow's **hierarchy of needs** theory, an individual's needs are arranged in a hierarchy from the lower-level physiological needs to the higher-level need for self-actualization. The physiological needs are the highest priority because, until they are reasonably satisfied, the higher-level needs will not emerge to motivate behavior.

A person is never completely satisfied on any need level but, if a sufficient amount of gratification of lower-priority needs exists, he or she then seeks to satisfy upper-level needs. Maslow suggested that a typical person might be 85 percent satisfied in physiological needs, 70 percent in safety needs, 50 percent in love needs, 40 percent in self-esteem needs, and 10 percent in self-actualization needs.

The use of the universal needs hierarchy by a manager in motivating employees is based on the idea that reasonably well-satisfied needs do not motivate. Therefore, if an individual's lower-level needs are fairly well satisfied, managers cannot use these needs to motivate behavior. Thus, pay might not be a motivator for people whose physiological and safety needs are well satisfied.

While Maslow's theory of human needs is widely known and accepted by many practicing managers, several research studies have contradicted it. These studies suggest that only two or three distinct categories of needs exist, not the five Maslow proposed. In addition, some critics question the order of the hierarchy of needs. While considerable importance is placed on physiological needs if they have not been satisfied, a person might not move up the hierarchy in an orderly or predictable manner once the physiological needs are satisfied. A clear-cut pattern of the progression of needs that require satisfaction has not emerged. According to Maslow, a need that has been relatively well satisfied ceases to motivate. This may be the case

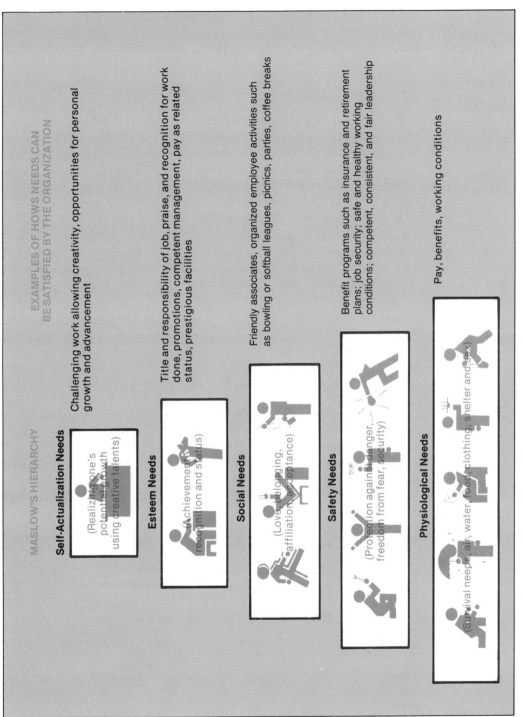

FIGURE 11-2 Maslow's need hierarchy and how needs are satisfied by the organization

SOURCE Abraham H. Maslow, "A Theory of Human Motivation," Motivation and Personality, 2d ed. (New York: Harper and Row, 1970). Reprinted by permission of author and publisher.

for the physiological, security, and social needs. But such a conclusion may not be warranted regarding the upper-level needs of esteem and self-actualization, achievement, recognition, or acceptance of responsibility.

Alderfer's E-R-G Theory

Clayton Alderfer has developed a more modern version of Maslow's needs hierarchy, which he referred to as the existence-relatedness-growth, or E-R-G theory.[6] Alderfer's theory is an attempt to make Maslow's theory more consistent with knowledge of human needs. Table 11-2 illustrates the relationship between Alderfer's and Maslow's theories of human needs. Alderfer's classification condenses Maslow's ideas into three categories of needs.

- Existence Needs (types of physical or material needs)
- Relatedness Needs (relationships with other people)
- Growth Needs (all forms of creative efforts to achieve or gain recognition to satisfy needs for esteem and attain a high degree of personal fulfillment).

E-R-G theory

Existence and relatedness needs, once satisfied, may fail to motivate; however, the importance of growth needs to the individual may increase as they are satisfied. According to the **E-R-G theory,** each level becomes increasingly abstract and more difficult to satisfy. While some individuals follow a logical progression in satisfying needs from levels one through three, some people experience frustration. A person who is unable to satisfy growth needs reverts back one level and concentrates on the more concrete relatedness or existence needs. For example, an assembly-line worker who has a job that fails to satisfy his or her need for recognition or personal satisfaction might concentrate on improving his or her personal relationships and friendships with other employees and on gaining additional pay and job security.

Herzberg's Motivation-Hygiene Theory

One of the most widely known and controversial theories of motivation is the motivation-hygiene theory of Frederick Herzberg.[7] His

TABLE 11-2. Alderfer's and Maslow's Theories: A Comparison

Needs theories	Level 1	Level 2	Level 3
Maslow's hierarchy of needs theory	Physiological needs	Social needs, security needs	Self-fulfillment needs, esteem needs
Alderfer's E-R-G theory	Existence needs	Relatedness needs	Growth needs

theory grew out of research on factors that led to job satisfaction. Herzberg proposes that job satisfaction and job dissatisfaction are not opposite ends of the same continuum. Instead, there exist two significantly different classes of job factors, one of which influences job satisfaction, and the other job dissatisfaction. In other words, there are two different continuums.

One class, referred to as hygiene factors, makes up a continuum ranging from "dissatisfaction" to "no dissatisfaction." As illustrated in Figure 11-3, hygiene factors relate to the environment and are external to the job. Herzberg indicates that these factors do not cause job satisfaction; rather, their absence causes dissatisfaction. Hygiene factors "maintain" an employee; they do not make a person healthy but rather prevent unhealthiness. An organization that meets the hygiene needs of its employees will eliminate dissatisfaction but will not motivate employees to work harder.

The second class of factors, referred to as motivators, makes up a continuum leading from "not satisfied" to "highly satisfied." As illustrated in Figure 11-3, the work itself, recognition, achievement, possibility of growth, and advancement are all **motivators**. These are concerned with the work itself rather than its physical, administrative, or social atmosphere. If the worker is to be truly motivated, the job must contain motivators.

Herzberg's theory suggests that a clear delineation exists between motivators and hygienes. Pay, for example, is categorized as a hygiene factor for each individual, but pay may be a dissatisfier to some individuals and a satisfier to others. Thus, it can be argued that hygiene and motivation factors should not be considered as absolute categories.

Specific criticisms of Herzberg's theory include:

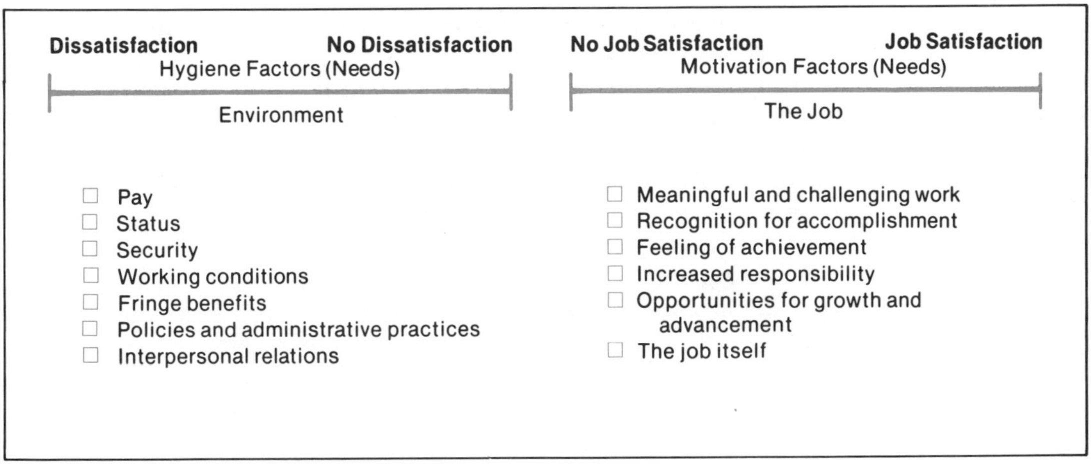

(margin labels: hygiene factors; motivators)

Dissatisfaction	No Dissatisfaction	No Job Satisfaction	Job Satisfaction
Hygiene Factors (Needs)		Motivation Factors (Needs)	
Environment		The Job	

Hygiene Factors (Environment):
- ☐ Pay
- ☐ Status
- ☐ Security
- ☐ Working conditions
- ☐ Fringe benefits
- ☐ Policies and administrative practices
- ☐ Interpersonal relations

Motivation Factors (The Job):
- ☐ Meaningful and challenging work
- ☐ Recognition for accomplishment
- ☐ Feeling of achievement
- ☐ Increased responsibility
- ☐ Opportunities for growth and advancement
- ☐ The job itself

FIGURE 11-3 Motivation and hygiene factors

- The research methodology used by Herzberg is the "critical-incident" technique, which involves asking people to reflect on past experiences. Some critics claim this technique causes people to recall only their most recent experiences. Also, analysis of the responses derived from this approach is highly subjective.
- The theory is most applicable to knowledge workers — managers, engineers, accountants, and other professional-level personnel. It is not possible to say that the findings apply equally to other occupational groups. Most studies have shown that, when the employees are professional- or managerial-level employees, the theory is applicable. However, studies of lower-level or manual workers are less supportive of the theory.
- The theory focuses too much attention on "satisfaction" or "dissatisfaction" and not enough on the performance level of the individual. Satisfaction may or may not be directly related to job performance.

Despite these criticisms, Herzberg's two-factor theory has made a significant contribution toward improving managers' basic understanding of motivation. Managers should be aware of the potentially successful application of the theory, especially as the work force becomes increasingly better educated and develops higher expectations of management.

There is a fairly close relationship between Maslow's hierarchy of needs theory and Herzberg's motivation-hygiene theory. (See Figure 11-4.) Herzberg's "motivators" are similar to the esteem and self-actualization needs in Maslow's hierarchy. The hygiene factors closely correspond to the physiological, safety, and social needs. Herzberg's basic contention is that most organizations give inadequate attention to the motivation factors in the work place. Most of the efforts of managers are concentrated on meeting the low-level needs, which are satisfied by the hygiene factors. But, just because the hygiene or maintenance needs are satisfied — by good pay, benefits, or working conditions — does not mean that the individual's performance will be positively influenced. To achieve effectiveness, the organization must satisfy both the hygiene and the motivation needs of its employees. Most organizations have given considerable attention to the hygiene needs but inadequate attention to the motivation needs of their personnel. This imbalance is understandable. since hygiene needs can be met in a more tangible or specific manner than can the motivational needs. It may be easier to provide employees with improved pay, fringe benefits, or working conditions than with a job that is more responsible or challenging.

Advocates of Herzberg's two-factor theory of motivation suggest that managers can assist employees in meeting their motivational needs by providing employees with more challenging and responsible jobs. According to Herzberg, increasing the level of autonomy, skill variety, task significance, and feedback will lead to better job performance and more satisfied employees. (This is known as job enrichment, and will be discussed later in this chapter.)

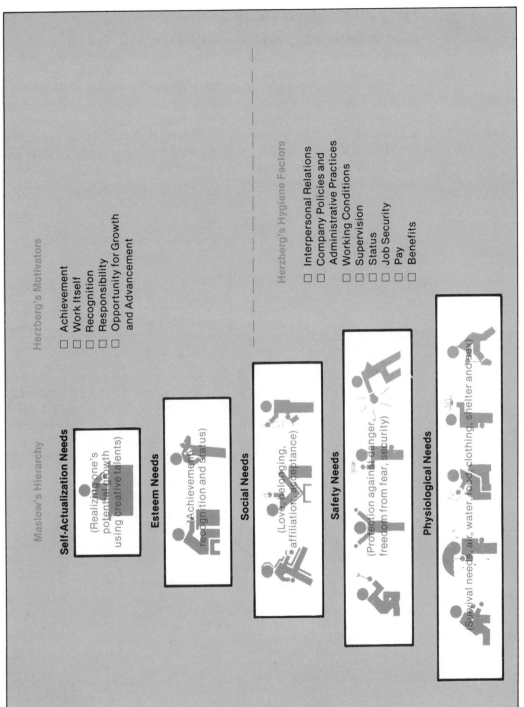

FIGURE 11-4 Maslow and Herzberg related

McClelland's Needs Theory

Whereas Maslow's theory stresses a universal hierarchy of naturally existing needs, the research of David McClelland emphasizes that certain needs are learned and socially acquired as the individual interacts with the environment. McClelland's "manifest needs theory" is concerned with how individual needs and environmental factors combine to form three basic human motives: the need for achievement (*n Ach*), the need for power (*n Pow*), and the need for affiliation (*n Aff*). As previously noted, motives explain behavior. McClelland conducted numerous studies in an attempt to define and measure basic human motives.

Need for Achievement

need for achievement

Tues Feb 27 ✗

moderate risk taker.

IE GAMBLER is NOT N/ACH

A person with a high **need for achievement** (*n Ach*) is an individual who:

- Wants to take personal responsibility for finding solutions to problems
- Is goal oriented
- Seeks a challenge — and establishes moderate, realistic, and attainable goals that involve risk but are not impossible to attain
- Desires concrete feedback on performance
- Has a high level of energy and is willing to work hard.

People exhibiting a high *n Ach* have found the above pattern of behavior personally rewarding. McClelland's research has shown that a high *n Ach* is probably a strong or dominant need in only a small proportion of the population. Persons high in the need for achievement gravitate toward entrepreneurial and sales positions. In these occupations, individuals are better able to manage themselves and satisfy the basic drive for achievement.

Need for Power

need for power

A high **need for power** means that an individual seeks to influence or control others. Such an individual tends to be characterized by the following types of behavior:

- Is concerned with acquiring, exercising, or retaining power or influence over others
- Likes to compete with others in situations that allow him or her to be dominant
- Enjoys confrontations with others.

McClelland suggests that two basic aspects of power exist: positive and negative. Positive power is essential if a manager is to accomplish results through the efforts of others. Negative power is evident when an individual seeks power for his or her own personal benefit; negative power may be detrimental to the organization.[8]

Need for Affiliation

need for
affiliation

The **need for affiliation** is related to the desire for affection and establishing friendly relationships. A person with a high need for affiliation is an individual who:

- Seeks to establish and maintain friendships and close emotional relationships with others
- Wants to be liked by others
- Enjoys parties, social activities, and bull sessions
- Seeks a sense of belonging by joining groups or organizations.

To varying degrees, everyone possesses these three motives. However, one of the needs will tend to be more characteristic of an individual than the other two.[9] People in a given culture may have the same needs, but the relative strength of those needs differs. Each of the three motives evokes a different type of satisfaction. For example, the achievement motive tends to evoke in managers a sense of accomplishment, whereas a manager may have a feeling of being in control or influencing others when the power motive is prevalent. According to this theory, the probability that an individual will perform a job effectively and efficiently depends on a combination of:

- The strength of the motive or need relative to other needs
- The possibility of success in performing the task
- The strength value of the incentive or reward for performance.

The most effective mixture of these three motives depends on the situation. In studies of over 500 managers, it was concluded that the most effective managers have a high need for power, a moderate need for achievement, and a low need for affiliation. These managers tended to use their power in a participative manner for the good of the organization. Managers had a moderate need for achievement, but it was not strong enough to interfere with the management process. Persons with high needs for both power and achievement have high managerial motivation, but they may not make the best managers.[10] After all, management is the achievement of goals through the efforts of others, not shoving others aside to do the work alone.

Outstanding sales personnel tend to be high in the need for achievement and moderately high in the need for power. Entrepreneurs who develop ideas and promote specific enterprises tend to be high in achievement motivation. They delight in solving problems personally and in getting immediate feedback on the degree of success. Entrepreneurs sometimes are unable to make the transition to top management positions. Their need for personal achievement gets in the way of the requirements for effectively influencing the organization's employees.

Expectancy Theory

Managers must develop an understanding of human needs and the variety of organizational means available to satisfy the needs of employees. However, the needs approach to motivation as developed by Maslow, Alderfer, and Herzberg does not adequately account for differences in individual employees or explain why people behave in certain ways. Victor Vroom developed an approach to motivation known as expectancy theory that attempts to explain behavior in terms of an individual's goals, choices, and expectations of achieving these goals.[11] **Expectancy theory** assumes that people can determine which outcomes they prefer and make realistic estimates of the chances of obtaining them. The key concept of expectancy theory is that motivation depends on: (1) an individual's **expectancy** (his or her perception of the probability) that a particular outcome will occur as a result of certain behavior, and (2) the value (**valence**) an individual places on a specific outcome.

expectancy theory

expectancy

valence

Expectancy theory can be stated mathematically as follows:

$$\text{Motivation} = \text{Expectancy} \times \text{Valence}.$$

These factors — expectancy and value — determine motivation. Both must be present before a high level of motivation can occur — a high expectancy or a high value alone will not ensure motivation. For example, if an employee had a low expectancy (perceived little chance) of receiving a pay increase but placed a high value on money, the employee would not be highly motivated to work hard to obtain the increase.

All employees in an organization do not share the same goals or values regarding pay, job security, promotions, benefits, or working conditions. For example, a supervisor in the systems and programming division places a high value on receiving a promotion to a more challenging and responsible position. She perceives that excellent performance in her current supervisory position is essential to achieving her desired promotion. Her manager recognizes the value that she places on a promotion, and lets her know that there is a high probability she can be promoted if she performs effectively in her current position. Thus, she will seek to perform well in order to achieve the promotion. Another employee, an office supervisor, values stability and job security and is not interested in a promotion because he does not want more responsibility. Thus, he will not be motivated by an opportunity for a promotion.

A key factor in the expectancy model is what the employee perceives as desirable, not what the manager believes the employee should consider to be desirable. A manager's ability to motivate employees therefore depends on a thorough knowledge of each individual employee's background, goals, or experiences. The manager needs to identify what sparks motivation in each employee.[12]

A major contribution of expectancy theory is that it explains how the goals of employees influence their behavior on the job. The employees' behavior depends on their assessment of the probability that the behavior will actually lead to the attainment of the goal.

A manager who wishes to use the expectancy model of motivation should:

- Ensure that employees have sufficient training to do the task assigned
- Remove organizational obstacles to good performance
- Instill in employees the confidence to perform well
- Select organization rewards that will meet specific employee needs
- Communicate clearly the relationship between rewards and performance
- Administer the reward system consistently and equitably so that employees will perceive a relationship between performance and the rewards they receive.

Reinforcement Theory

reinforcement
theory

Reinforcement theory is based primarily on the research of B. F. Skinner and has been increasingly applied in business situations. **Reinforcement theory** is the idea that human behavior can be explained in terms of the previous positive or negative outcomes of that behavior. People tend to repeat behaviors that they have learned will produce pleasant outcomes. Behavior that is reinforced will be repeated; behavior that is not reinforced will not be repeated.

Skinner contends that people's behavior can be controlled and shaped by rewarding (reinforcing) desired behavior while ignoring undesirable actions. Over time, the reinforced behavior will tend to be repeated, whereas the unrewarded behavior will tend to be extinguished and will disappear. Punishment of undesired behavior is to be avoided since it may contribute to feelings of restraint and acts of rebellion. Thus, over a period of years, the conditioner can control human behavior without the person becoming aware of being controlled. In his book, *Beyond Freedom and Dignity*, Skinner says that people can be controlled and shaped while at the same time feeling free.[13]

Skinner's theory of shaping behavior is useful to managers, but one should not assume that human behavior is simple to understand and/or modify. Obtaining immediate feedback is a form of instant reward related to behavior on the job. The primary technique suggested by Skinner is organizational behavior modification.

organizational
behavior modification (OBM)

Organizational behavior modification (OBM) is the application of Skinner's reinforcement theory to organizational change efforts. OBM rests on two fundamental concepts: (1) people act in ways they find personally rewarding, and (2) behavior can be shaped and determined by controlling the rewards. In OBM, rewards are termed "reinforcers" because the goal is to encourage the rewarded behavior. Which reinforcers actually work in motivating people is determined by trial and error, and by experience. What is succesful with one

MANAGEMENT IN PRACTICE

Behavior Modification at Burroughs Memorex

Burroughs Memorex is one of Canada's major producers of computer products. In the early 1980s, its Winnipeg plant was experiencing several problems, including poor quality, failure to meet schedules, high scrap costs, and less-than-ideal labor relations. In an attempt to resolve these problems, the company introduced a behavior modification program called Performance Management.

The first step was to train 75 managers and supervisors how to use behavior modification properly. Once the training had been completed, supervisors identified their "key result areas." They then began applying behavior modification principles in order to improve performance in these key result areas. Both verbal and written positive reinforcement were given to employees who had achieved the standards which had been set. Output graphs were also posted in the factory so that all workers could see the extent to which they were achieving quality and output goals. An incentive system for rewarding good suggestions was also implemented.

The behavior modification program has had dramatic effects. Consider the following: In 1981, the "arrival quality" of the plant's shipments was only 59 percent — only 59 per cent of the customers were happy with the product and how it worked when it arrived at their plant. The workers set a goal of 80 percent arrival quality in 1982; they actually achieved 83 percent. They then set a goal of 90 percent for 1983 and achieved 91 percent. Arrival quality during 1984 was 93 percent.

Another example: Scrap costs on a certain part in 1981 were running at $6500 per week. One employee discovered that these costs were incurred by improper handling of the product; he therefore wrote up a 20-minute training program that indicated the proper way to handle the part. His program is now used to train all people who handle the part in question. After being made aware of the cause of the problem, the employees set a goal to reduce scrap costs to $2500 per week. Feedback graphs were also posted in all departments who handled the part and appropriate reinforcement applied for improved performance. Scrap costs are now down to $400 per week.

SOURCE Interview with Carole Postnieks, Manager of Training and Development, Burroughs Memorex, Inc.

---

employee may not work with another because needs and wants differ. Praise is used most frequently because it is most readily available. It becomes less effective whenever it becomes predictable or is continuously applied. Money is also used, as are public or private letters of commendation, time off, and increased status.

In OBM, punishment is rejected as a reinforcer because it suppresses the undesired behavior while at the same time stimulating anger, hostility, aggression, and rebellion. And at times, it is difficult to identify the punishment. In one prison, placing prisoners in solitary confinement on bread and water turned out to be a status symbol and led to repetition of offenses. When the bread and water was changed to baby food, the status symbol disappeared, leading to a significant reduction in the number of undesirable acts. When undesired behavior is not rewarded, it tends to disappear over time.

In reinforcing desired behavior in a positive fashion, managers must allocate the rewards soon after the behavior occurs so that the person perceives a clear and immediate link. Fast and accurate feedback of information to the performer in itself constitutes a reinforcer.

Organizational behavior modification has been used successfully in a number of organizations to improve performance. In one firm, positive reinforcement was used to reduce absenteeism.[14] Each day an employee came to work on time, he or she received a playing card. At the end of the week, the highest poker hand received $20. Over a three-month period, the absenteeism rate of the experimental group decreased 18 percent, whereas that of a control group actually increased. One telephone company identified these desirable behaviors among its operators: (1) service promptness in answering calls, (2) shortness of time taken to give information, (3) use of proper references in handling the call, and (4) attendance.[15] Praise and recognition were adopted as the dominant reinforcers. The results were a 50-percent improvement in attendance and above standard productivity and efficiency levels.

The Emery Air Freight OBM program was a major success story.[16] It used the simple reinforcers of information feedback and praise to condition employee behavior. In responding to customer questions about service and schedules within a standard 90-minute period, performance moved from 30 percent of the standard to 90 percent within a few days. Employees were provided with feedback charts through which they could monitor their own performance. Employees who did not achieve the desired results were reminded of the goal, then praised for their honesty. This 90 percent achievement remained stable for over three years. As a result of the application of OBM, estimated savings to Emery Air Freight were placed at $650 000 per year.

If a manager wants to use OBM, the following actions are necessary:

- Identify the desired performance in specific terms; for example, improving attendance rates or answering a certain number of questions in a certain period of time.
- Identify the rewards that will reinforce the desired behavior; for example, praise, money, time off.
- Make the reward a direct consequence of the behavior.
- Select the optimum reinforcement schedule.

Despite the successes achieved by behavior modification, it has been criticized as being a manipulative and autocratic approach to management because employees are conditioned to change their behavior in the direction required by management and the organization. Some critics argue that OBM is not consistent with the theories of such behavioral scientists as Maslow, Argyris, or McGregor. The assumption underlying their theories is that people are motivated by their own internal needs and are capable of a degree of self-control; OBM assumes that the causes of human behavior are in the environment and therefore external to the individual.

Equity Theory

equity theory

Equity theory assumes that individuals consider the ratio of their inputs on the job to the outcomes they receive and then compare this ratio with the input/outcome ratio of others doing similar work.[17] If the worker perceives an inequity, he or she will be motivated to resolve the inequity. Managers must deal with employees who continually compare the pay and rewards they are receiving with the rewards other employees receive. The degree of perceived equity is important to each employee. When an employee receives compensation from the organization, his or her perceptions of equity are affected by: (1) comparison of the compensation received to such factors as input of effort, education, or training, and (2) comparison of the perceived equity of pay and rewards received to that of other people. For example, even though an employee values money and expects that it will be paid if he or she performs, comparisons will be made to the rewards received by others. Thus, if the employee likes money and believes that an $800 raise will be forthcoming if he or she performs well, motivational force will decrease if he or she perceives that other employees are receiving $1000 for the same performance level.

THE ROLE OF MONEY IN MOTIVATION

The role of money in motivation has been debated vigorously for many years. In the early part of the twentieth century, Frederick Taylor's views about money were widely accepted. (See Chapter 1.) In Taylor's view, workers would do a job in a certain way only if they were given the monetary incentive to do so. By the 1930s, this "economic man" view of workers was challenged by research like the Hawthorne studies which suggested that workers were also motivated by intangible factors such as friendship, respect, and a sense of belonging.

The function of pay in our society today is quite complex. Each of the motivation theories discussed makes some direct or indirect statement about the role of money in motivation; in the following paragraphs, we present some summary comments about the role of money in motivation by referring to these motivation theories.

One of the difficult aspects of compensation is that financial rewards have multiple meanings. In addition to being the obvious means by which workers can satisfy basic needs, pay can be an indication of social status, social value, and competence. Therefore, workers can also satisfy higher-order needs with their paycheques. To complicate the situation even more, their perceptions of the degree to which their lower-order needs are satisfied may change as their income rises; so while workers may have their basic needs relatively satisfied, a pay increase may serve only to increase their level of expectations regarding the lower-order needs. For example, if eating hamburgers four times a week satisfies people's need for food, increasing their wages may simply cause them to change their eating habits from hamburger to steak as a result of higher expectations of satisfaction. Possibly, eating steak may also satisfy other needs, like status.

Perceptions of need satisfaction are determined by expectations, which are in turn determined by comparisons with what other individuals are receiving relative to the responsibility of their jobs. Individuals generally feel an inequity if comparisons show that they are receiving less than others with similar inputs. Equity theory is very useful here, since it states that the relative levels of perceived pay are as important as absolute levels of actual pay.

Consider the concept of piece-rate or commission-payment (incentive) systems and their potential impact on motivation. Perhaps a useful way to determine their impact is to examine the assumptions that underlie the incentive system concept:

- Employees desire to make more money and will change their behavior to meet this objective (Taylor's "economic man" assumption).
- Employees can see a relation between their efforts and the rewards they receive (expectancy theory).

MANAGEMENT IN PRACTICE

Increasing Motivation through Profit Sharing

Palliser Furniture of Winnipeg instituted a profit-sharing plan in 1978. Of the firm's 800 employees, all 600 who are eligible belong to the plan. David DeFehr, head of management information systems at Palliser, says the plan works as follows: 20 percent of the company's profits go into a pool; payout from the pool has ranged from 0 percent to 17 percent of an individual worker's salary, depending on the year's profits. The employee can take the cash, or put it into a deferred profit sharing plan which works like an RRSP.

The plan has resulted in better employee morale and significant productivity gains for the company. Employees also are more interested in their work, produce higher quality output, and maintain equipment better than they did before the system was implemented.

SOURCE   Adapted from Jack Francis, "Profit Sharing Gaining Ground," *Winnipeg Free Press* (June 8, 1984).

- Employees attach a net positive value to increasing their efforts to produce more (expectancy theory).
- Earning extra money will allow employees either to increase their perception of needs satisfaction or to satisfy needs not currently satisfied (Maslow).
- Employees have the ability to increase output (physiological assumption).
- Other conditions in the work atmosphere do not override the desire to increase output for financial rewards (Herzberg, expectancy theory).
- The worker perceives that other individuals in his or her comparison group receive similar rewards for similar efforts (equity theory).

Not surprisingly, many piece-rate and commission payment systems are less than successful in view of all the criteria they must meet.

Gellerman has noted that, in order for money to motivate, pay increases must be extremely large to create the feeling of "wealth."[18] If a worker sees that increased effort will lead to a significant change in his or her standard of living, then pay can be considered a motivator. For this reason, incentive systems at higher echelons of organizations tend to meet with more success than do those on production-line systems. If top executives improve their performance, they stand to gain considerably from their efforts, since some company bonus systems increase executive pay by as much as 50 percent. Production workers, on the other hand, are limited to much smaller absolute increases.

Herzberg maintains that pay is not a motivator but a hygiene: if it is satisfactory, workers will not be dissatisfied. If pay meets their expectations, they will do nothing differently because of it. Only when pay does not meet expectations do employees change their behavior. Consistent with both equity theory and Gellerman's position, payment above expectations will probably change behavior as the individual attempts to reduce the dissonance associated with the increased pay. Payment below expectations causes dissatisfaction and prevents a positive work climate from being established. The key point in this philosophy is that providing workers with what they expect will have no appreciable effect on their behavior.

The varied role that pay can assume is further demonstrated through McClelland's *n Ach* theory. In the most literal sense, the high achiever is not motivated by pay. However, in actual job situations, it is easy to see how a supervisor can misinterpret the individual's motives and assume that the need for money — instead of the need for achievement — is operating.

In summary, if money is to motivate behavior, employees must both desire it and believe that it will be forthcoming if they behave in the manner prescribed. Determining the importance of money to employees requires knowledge of each individual's current need level. If employees have a need for higher pay and expect to receive it if they perform more effectively, then pay can motivate performance.

JOB DESIGN AND MOTIVATION

Can managers enhance employee motivation, improve job satisfaction, and maximize production all at the same time? J. Richard Hackman and Greg R. Oldham contend that it is possible to improve the quality of work life while increasing worker productivity.[19]They challenge several traditional assumptions, including the following:

- The basic nature of work is fixed and cannot be changed.
- Technology and work processes determine job design.
- All management can do is properly select and train personnel.

job design

Work or job design has been identified as an approach that can assist in increasing productivity. **Job design** is the process of altering the nature and structure of jobs for the purpose of increasing productivity. Job design is concerned with the specific tasks to be performed, the methods used in performing them and how the job relates to other work in the organization. In their book, *Work Redesign*, Hackman and Oldham assert that, if managers wish to create a climate for a high level of motivation, reliable feedback on performance must be provided; there must be a sense that the worker is accountable for specific results and a feeling that the job has meaning beyond pay.[20] Workers get more satisfaction from completing a "whole and identifiable piece of work" than from producing indistinguishable pieces. Because of this, job design becomes an important concept in creating a motivational climate for today's work force.

Technological constraints on job design include the type of equipment and tools needed as well as the particular work layout and methods used in producing the product or service. Technology may make job redesign difficult, and perhaps expensive. For example, adapting or redesigning an assembly line may not be technically or economically feasible.[21]

Economic factors affect job design as well. Top management must decide if sufficient resources are available to the organization should it wish to redesign some or all of its jobs. Suggestions to redesign jobs may improve output and the level of worker satisfaction, but the cost may be prohibitive. Managers must continually balance the benefits of job design with the costs.

Job design is also affected by government requirements or regulations. Management may wish to design a job in a way that might increase worker performance but would violate labor laws or environmental or safety standards. Some proponents of work redesign have even urged the federal government to legislate guidelines for changes in work design.

If a company has a union, job design can be affected by the philosophy, policies, and strategies of the union. Typically, the contract between the company and the union specifies and defines the types of jobs, duties and responsibilities of workers. Unions have traditionally opposed many work redesign experiments. They have perceived them as attempts by management to squeeze more work out of the worker without any increase in wages. In order to maintain harmony and work efficiency, managers must foster cooperation with the union over job redesign.

Important considerations in job design are the abilities, attitudes, and motivation of personnel within the organization. Obviously, the design of particular jobs depends on the ability or training of present or potential employees. It would be ridiculous to design a job to make it considerably more complex than the ability level of employees available for the position. The ability and willingness of employees to be trained can limit job redesign.

Finally, management philosophy, objectives, and strategies may determine the feasibility of job redesign. Top management must be committed to the concept. Job redesign may grant employees greater authority in determining how their jobs are performed and how they are managed. Thus, managers who identify with McGregor's Theory X assumptions would likely have difficulty with job redesign because it might give workers more discretion than the manager thinks is desirable.

Some approaches to job redesign require only minor changes in attitudes and behavior (for both managers and workers), while others require substantial change. Several approaches are discussed below.

Job Rotation

job rotation

The simplest approach to job redesign is **job rotation**, whereby employees are rotated through several very similar jobs. For example, a production-line worker might be rotated every two weeks through several assembling jobs that require about the same level of skill. While job rotation does increase the variety in a worker's job, its impact on efficiency or productivity is doubtful. As a result, job rotation probably does not have a significant positive effect on employee motivation.

Job Enlargement

job enlargement

Job enlargement involves a horizontal expansion of worker duties, so that the worker learns several different jobs involving somewhat different skill levels. For example, a production-line worker may work at several different jobs during the course of a day. These jobs would require the worker to use various skills. Compared to job rotation, job enlargement is more likely to increase worker motivation, but it also falls short of truly changing the worker's view of work. As a result, job enlargement is not likely to cause a substantial increase in worker motivation.

Job Enrichment

job enrichment

The most dramatic type of job redesign is called job enrichment. Strongly advocated by Frederick Herzberg, **job enrichment** refers to basic changes in the content and level of responsibility of a job so as to provide for the satisfaction of the motivation needs of personnel.[22] The individual is provided with an opportunity to derive a feeling of greater achievement, recognition, responsibility, and personal growth in performing the job. Although job enrichment programs have not always achieved positive results, such programs have demonstrated improvements in job performance and in the level of satisfaction of personnel in many organizations.

According to Herzberg, a number of principles are applicable in implementing job enrichment:

- Increasing job demands: changing the job in order to increase the level of difficulty and responsibility of the job.
- Increasing a worker's accountability: allowing more individual control and authority over the work, while retaining accountability of the manager.
- Providing work scheduling freedom: within limits, allowing individual workers to schedule their own work.
- Providing feedback: making timely periodic reports on performance to employees — directly to the worker rather than to the supervisor.
- Providing new learning experiences: work situations should encourage opportunities for new experiences and for the personal growth of the individual.

If these five principles are adhered to, the result will be a substantially redesigned job for many workers, particularly those in mass production industries and in firms with repetitive clerical operations.

Consider the changes in job design that occurred in one company that manufactured pumps for washing machines. Prior to the implementation of job enrichment, the work was done in the traditional assembly-line fashion, with the pump (containing 27 parts) assembled by six workers, each assembling a small part of the pump. Each pump required approximately 1.75 minutes to complete. In a two-step process, the job was enriched so that eventually one worker assembled the entire pump, inspected it, and placed his or her identifying mark on it. After the change, the company reported that: (1) assembly time had dropped to 1.5 minutes per pump, (2) product quality increased, and (3) cost savings were evident.[23]

This example demonstrates several of the principles of an enriched job noted above. First, by assembling the entire pump, the worker experienced increased job demands. Second, because the inspection function remained with the worker, the worker received feedback on how well the job had been performed. Third, the worker was allowed to determine individual work pace and procedures for completing the job, thereby increasing job freedom.

Quality Circles

quality circles

Another technique that has been shown to be effective in enhancing motivation and achieving improved quality and productivity in several hundred American and Canadian companies is a concept known as quality circles.[24] In most firms, **quality circles** (QCs) consist of periodic meetings of small groups of employees who brainstorm ways to improve the quality and quantity of work.[25]

Consider how quality circles operate at Great-West Life Assurance Company, a large insurance company with a Canadian head office in Winnipeg. The company has an active productivity improvement program, which is based on the idea of employee participation in decision making and the use of quality circles. At present, 10 to 15 percent of Great-West's staff are members of quality circles; the goal is to increase eventually to 30 percent participation. Most of the quality circles operate in Winnipeg, but recently they have also been set up in Toronto and Vancouver, and in Denver, its American head office.

MANAGEMENT IN PRACTICE

Quality Circles at TRW

The Thompson Products Division of TRW in St. Catharines, Ontario implemented quality circles because it felt they would allow workers more involvement in their work and would promote improvements in cost reductions, product quality, productivity, and manager/worker teamwork.

To implement the concept, a steering committee made up of a cross section of workers and managers was formed. Each quality circle is made up of volunteers; maximum group size is 15 members. The groups meet once a week for one hour prior to the end of their shifts. A quality circle facilitator has been appointed from company staff to train quality circle group leaders.

The first quality circle was started in the die build area, which is concerned with the die sinking operation for dies used in the forge shop. After some initial experimentation with team size, a quality circle composed of 10 people was formed. After only two months, the circle members made a presentation to management indicating how they wished to solve several important problems. Management was impressed with the quality of both the presentation and the recommended solutions.

The benefit derived from use of quality circles goes beyond the specific problems that are solved. It also has allowed the firm to implement the behavioral theories of Maslow, Herzberg, McGregor and others. Using these motivation theories on the job also allows employees to satisfy more of their own personal needs.

SOURCE Adapted from L. J. Knight, "Quality Circles in Action: A Canadian Experience," *CTM: The Human Element* (February 1983): 20–21.

MANAGEMENT IN PRACTICE

Quality Teams at
Burroughs Memorex's Winnipeg Plant

As part of a program to improve product quality and plant operations, Burroughs Memorex, Inc. implemented quality teams at its Winnipeg plant in 1981. Each quality team is made up of 8 to 10 people who meet once a week for one hour to brainstorm ways to improve operations. Problems may be raised by team members, or management may request that the team consider how to solve a particular problem. Although team membership is voluntary, 90 percent of eligible employees are participating. Quality team meetings take place on company time, but several teams have worked on projects on their own time.

Burroughs's use of the team concept differs from that of other companies in several significant ways. First, managers are involved on quality teams; in fact, they were the first to be trained. In many other companies, quality circles are composed solely of workers.

Second, all quality team members receive formal training in quality control and behavior modification — 32 hours in total. This training gives them valuable insights into what quality teams are supposed to accomplish and how they work.

Third, each team identifies levels for the ideas it comes up with. Level 1 solutions can be implemented without managerial approval; level 2 solutions must be submitted for managerial consideration because they affect other departments; level 3 solutions are taken to managers at the idea stage so that more information can be gathered regarding their feasibility.

Fourth, the formal presentations the quality teams make to higher levels of management are not so much designed to get approval, as they are to gain positive reinforcement for the people on the quality team.

Finally, because quality teams were implemented after a successful behavior modification program had been started, a high level of trust had developed between workers and management. This earlier program made the quality team concept easier to implement and it was received with enthusiasm.

SOURCE Interview with Carole Postnieks, Manager of Training and Development, Burroughs Memorex, Inc.

Quality circles at Great-West Life are called "Innovative Change Teams" (ICTs). The objectives of the ICTs are to:

- Build an attitude of continuous improvement and problem prevention through creative thinking, open communications, and teamwork.
- Provide all employees with the opportunity to contribute ideas for change and to participate in decisions affecting their work.
- Achieve an enhanced quality of working life for employees, a higher level of productivity, and a superior quality of service to customers.

Each ICT is made up of volunteer members who meet once a week on company time to consider ways to do higher quality, more effective work. There are no monetary rewards for participation in an ICT. Each group has a leader who has received formal training in leading an

ICT. The leader of a newly formed ICT is usually the group's supervisor, but the leader position often rotates after the group has been meeting for a while. Group leaders also train their group members. An agenda is prepared for each meeting; it may include discussion of several minor items, or the entire meeting may be devoted to a major issue. When a group has completed a given project — large projects may take six months or more — a presentation is made to management. All team members are encouraged to take part in these presentations.

ICTs at Great-West Life have become involved in both quality- and productivity-improvement projects. Projects have been completed in four general areas: (1) procedures/processes, (2) communications, (3) education and training, and (4) internal environment. A sample of the kinds of projects that have been completed in each of these areas is shown in Table 11-3.

At Great-West Life, ICTs have been set up to improve productivity and quality over the long run. As a result, the company has not yet begun to stress quantitative measurement of their impact. This will be possible once the idea of quality circles is firmly entrenched and employees feel comfortable with it. At present, the program looks promising; both employees and managers feel that quality circles have resulted in a higher quality of service, improved productivity, and improved employee satisfaction.

TABLE 11-3   Sample of Quality Circle Projects at Great-West Life

Procedures/Processes
Improved system for receiving information from policyholders
Improvements to central file systems in several departments
Improved productivity in the Group Insurance Renewal Calculation
Improved use of central photocopy service to reduce cost and improve staff productivity

Communication
Developed newsletter to communicate information on new procedures, projects, and people
Improvements to circulation file system
Identified opportunities for improving productivity in the underwriting departments

Education and Training
Preparation of manual which provides medical and occupation information in uncomplicated language
Development of orientation program for new staff in Real Estate Accounting Department
Development of a "Helpful Hints Guide" to improve the use of computer terminals in the Actuarial Systems Department

Internal Environment
Recommendations on upgrading typewriter equipment to improve productivity
Redesigned office layout to improve efficiency
Improved telephone system

MANAGEMENT IN PRACTICE

Quality Circles at the Jim Pattison Group

Jim Pattison is one of Canada's best known entrepreneurs. In the late 1970s, he visited Japan and became interested in quality circles. Quality circles at his company involve regular meetings and workshops among nonmanagerial personnel. These sessions are designed to improve communications among workers, which in turn should improve worker efficiency and product quality.

There are now more than 100 quality circles in the Pattison Group, and they are starting to show results. One company in the group, EDP, specializes in financial packages for business.

A quality circle was introduced there in 1980 and, as a result, the number of jobs having to be redone has dropped from 15 percent to less than three percent.

The Pattison Group can quote many examples of how quality circles have improved company operations. One circle discovered that a better type of paint existed for a certain job; they also discovered that the company already had some of that paint in its storeroom.

SOURCE Adapted from *Executive* (April 1984): 30.

Flextime

flextime

During the past two decades, organizations have started to allow more flexibility in the working pattern of their employees. They have done this in the hope that giving employees some freedom in their working hours will increase their job satisfaction and productivity. First introduced in Germany in the 1960s, **flextime** is a system which requires all workers to be at the workplace at certain core hours during the day, but allows workers flexibility in choosing when they will work the remaining hours in each day. Technically speaking, flextime does not involve job redesign, but since it does involve a change in the way employees see their job, we have included it here.

The details of flextime generally work as follows. Management decides which hours of the day are "core hours." These are the hours when it is absolutely essential that all workers be at their jobs. In many firms, the core hours are 10 a.m. to 2 p.m. A person who likes to arise early might start work at 7 a.m. and finish at 3 p.m., while a person who likes to sleep late might not come in until 10 a.m. and then stay until 6 p.m.

A large number of studies have been conducted to determine the impact of flextime on employee morale, turnover, and productivity. Generally speaking, the introduction of flextime is associated with an increase in morale, a decline in employee absences and turnover, and an increase in productivity.[26] In one well-controlled study, flextime led to a significant reduction in employee absences and a small increase in productivity.[27]

Like almost any technique, flextime does have some potential drawbacks. Perhaps the key problem is the perception by some first-line supervisors that they lose some control over subordinates when flextime is implemented. Two obvious concerns are (1) communicating with, and (2) coordinating the work of subordinates with staggered hours. Overall, however, flextime appears to be a system which can be implemented with little cost and which generally yields benefits in employee satisfaction and productivity.

MOTIVATION LESSONS FROM THE JAPANESE

William Ouchi's book *Theory Z* and Richard Pascale and Anthony Athos's *The Art of Japanese Management* describe management practices in a number of progressive North American companies that are similar to those successful Japanese firms have been using for years.[28] Ouchi identified Hewlett-Packard, IBM, Procter and Gamble, and Eastman Kodak as Theory Z organizations. **Theory Z** refers to an organization that shows a strong relationship between the company and its employees and demonstrates unusual responsibility toward its employees; the employees in turn show great loyalty toward the company. Theory Z companies tend to keep employees for their entire working life and avoid layoffs. The companies usually enjoy low employee turnover, low absenteeism, and high employee morale. The workers are more involved in their jobs with the company, a factor that leads to increased productivity and performance. Theory Z companies often develop their own traditions, ideals, and culture that fosters a 'family' atmosphere. This atmosphere within the organization tends to bond its members — employees and managers — thereby facilitating decision making and communications within the company. All these practices have much in common with Japanese patterns and practices. Companies in North America have not necessarily imitated Japanese practices but have developed their own management style through the recognition of the types of employees who make up today's work force.

Theory Z

Pascale and Athos identify many of the same companies mentioned in the Ouchi study — Eastman Kodak, IBM, and Hewlett-Packard — as practitioners of the Theory Z style of management. However, they also include: Delta Airlines, Boeing, and 3M as companies with management styles similar to Japanese firms. Pascale and Athos present what they refer to as a **Seven S model**. This model attempts to identify what makes enterprises succeed or fail. The seven S's are:

Seven S model

Strategy	Plan or course of action leading to the use of resources to achieve goals
Structure	Manner in which the firm is organized — type of departmentation, and responsibility and authority of managers

Systems	Policies, procedures, and methods that managers use in making decisions, implementing change, or communicating with others in the organization
Staff	"Demographic" characteristics of personnel within the firm
Skills	Distinctive capabilities of key personnel
Style	Patterns of behavior of key managers in achieving the organization's goals; cultural style of the organization
Superordinate goals	The overall purpose of the organization — guiding values and principles that integrate individual and organizational purposes.[29]

The first three elements, strategy, structure, and systems, are known as the "hard S's." They are the more traditional elements that a company relies on for effective management. The other four factors, or "soft S's," are often not adequately addressed by firms. Pascale and Athos argue that the more successful and progressive companies address all seven S's and give particular attention to the four soft S's. They place significant emphasis on what they refer to as "superordinate goals" — the glue that holds the other six S's together.

Well-managed companies such as those described in Ouchi's *Theory Z* and Pascale and Athos's *The Art of Japanese Management* usually have superordinate goals expressed in terms of the firm's responsibility to its employees, to its customers, and to the surrounding community. Thus, superordinate goals assist the firm in becoming more internally unified and self-sustaining over a period of time. For instance, at IBM, the goal of never sacrificing customer service is an example of a superordinate goal. Outstanding companies are usually quite advanced in their grasp of strategy, structure, and systems, but, unlike less successful firms, which rely primarily on these three S's, the best managed companies usually show great sophistication in the four soft S's as well. The most effective firms link their purposes and methods to human values as well as to economic measures such as profit and efficiency.[30]

MOTIVATION: IMPLICATIONS FOR MANAGEMENT PRACTICE

From our discussion of the theories of motivation, several implications for managers can be derived. Management should recognize that many factors affect job performance, including: (1) skills and abilities of personnel, (2) levels of education and training of employees, (3) existing technology, and (4) equipment and tools available to perform the job. A manager may not be able to motivate an employee to better job performance if the employee does not possess the education, skills, training, and equipment to perform the job effectively. If any of these factors is inadequate, performance may be adversely affected. Employees may possess the necessary skills and be highly motivated to perform a certain job effectively, but their overall performance level may be quite low because they do not know how to do the job. This problem is sometimes overlooked by managers, who believe that an employee is simply not motivated when in fact the employee does not understand what he or she is required to do, or lacks the proper training or equipment to perform efficiently and effectively. It does little good, and may cause considerable harm, if managers persist in driving employees in an effort to motivate them, when motivation is not the problem.

The following summary observations about motivation are useful:

- Managers must keep in mind that effective motivation is not so much something that a manager "does" to an employee as it is the creation of the climate where personnel will want to be productive and creative in their work.
- Managers must try to develop a better understanding of human behavior if they hope to create a climate that encourages greater employee performance and satisfaction.
- Human needs that are reasonably well satisfied do not motivate behavior. The lower-level needs on Maslow's hierarchy (physiological, safety, and social) are fairly well satisfied for most employees and therefore have little significant influence in motivating behavior. Thus, management should devote more of its attention toward providing a climate for the satisfaction of upper-level needs, such as esteem and self-actualization.
- Personnel have generally been underutilized and overmanaged. Organizations should try to provide more responsible and challenging jobs that allow a greater degree of individual self-control.
- Many managers hold Theory X assumptions regarding the behavior of their subordinates. These managers have created a climate of distrust and one that encourages immature actions on the part of employees. These conditions do not lead to more effective performance or a higher level of employee satisfaction.

OPENING INCIDENT REVISITED

Baylor's Department Store

If you were a member of the executive committee and attended the second meeting called by the vice-president of operations, what useful comments could you make about the role of money in motivation after reading this chapter? If you accept Herzberg's view of motivation, you would probably disagree with Lise Daniel's incentive scheme as a solution to the motivation problem, Herzberg does not see money as a motivator. He would instead propose a restructuring of the job so that it would be psychologically rewarding to employees and would motivate them to sell enthusiastically.

If you accept Maslow's arguments, the role of money as a motivator is less clear. Money could be a motivator for any need, but is particularly important for physiological and safety needs. For some needs, however, money is only one of the ways to achieve satisfaction. The need for status, for example, may be satisfied by having a certain job title even though the job does not pay very well. Thus, the role of money in motivation, according to Maslow's theory, is dependent on the level of the hierarchy at which the individuals find themselves, as well as on the general view of money the individuals have.

Equity theory says that money may be a motivator if people are underpaid or overpaid. If the person perceives an inequity involving pay, he or she will be motivated to resolve it.

This motivation may, of course, be positive or negative, as the person may produce more or less. Baylor's, in this case, would have to determine if salary schedules for salesclerks are perceived to be equitable before implementing the incentive scheme.

Expectancy theory argues that money is a motivator if it is positively valent and no organization factors inhibit task performance. In the case of Baylor's, management would have to ensure that these two criteria are satisfied before an incentive scheme could be successfully implemented.

SUMMARY

Motivation is one of the most important and frequently discussed subjects in management. Today's employees are better educated, more highly skilled, and often do not respond to the traditional values that motivated employees 20 or 30 years ago. Motivation is the process of influencing or stimulating a person to take action by creating a work atmosphere in which the goals of the organization and the needs of the people are satisfied. In an organization, personnel are said to be motivated if they perform their jobs effectively and efficiently, and are enthusiastic while doing so. Management has traditionally relied on the use of rewards, such as increased pay, job security, good working conditions; or punishment, such as dismissal, demotions, or withholding rewards, to motivate employees. But today, management cannot rely on the manipulation of pay, benefits, or working conditions to motivate personnel. Motivation is a much more complicated process.

Managers must attempt to understand human nature and employees' basic needs if they are to create a climate for motivation. McGregor's Theory X and Theory Y and Argyris's maturity theory can help managers to develop a better understanding of human behavior. The theories of Maslow, Herzberg, McClelland, Vroom, Skinner, and Alderfer are also helpful to managers as they attempt to gain a more complete appreciation of basic employee needs and the reasons for their behavior.

Maslow's hierarchy of needs is a widely accepted theory, which suggests that people are motivated by unsatisfied needs. According to Maslow, a person's needs are arranged in priority from the basic physiological to the more complex self-actualization needs. The important point for managers is that needs that are fairly well satisfied do not motivate behavior. Alderfer's E-R-G theory classifies needs into three levels in order of progression — existence, relatedness, and growth. Each level of need becomes increasingly difficult to satisfy. Herzberg's motivation-hygiene theory classifies human needs into two categories — hygiene factors and motivators. The hygiene factors correspond to the lower-level needs on Maslow's hierarchy, while the motivators represent upper-level needs. Herzberg contends that, despite the fact that most managers and organizations concentrate on satisfying the hygiene needs, this action does not motivate employees. He believes firms should direct more attention to the motivators and to enriched jobs; but, at the same time, firms should not forget to be concerned about the hygiene needs. McClelland's theory stresses that certain needs are learned. He argues that each person's need for achievement, power, and affiliation affects his or her behavior in the work place.

The needs approach to motivation as developed by Maslow, Alderfer, and Herzberg does not adequately explain individual behavior differences in accomplishing goals. Vroom's expectancy theory of motivation attempts to explain behavior in terms of an individual's goals, choices, and his or her expectations of achieving those goals. Employees are motivated by what they expect as a reward for their behavior. Skinner contends that behavior can be controlled and shaped by reinforcing desired behavior. The primary approach suggested by Skinner is organizational behavior modification (OBM), which has been successfully applied in a number of organizations. Under this approach, people act in the way they find most rewarding and, by controlling rewards, management can direct or modify employee behavior.

In addition to the major theories of motivation, managers should also develop an understanding of the role of money as a motivator. There is no simple relationship between pay and employee motivation, but an assessment of the popular motivation theories gives some insight as to whether money is likely to be a motivator in a particular situation. If money is desired by an employee and the employee can see a clear connection between effort expenditure and money, it will likely be a motivator of behavior for that person.

Job design is the process of altering the nature and structure of jobs for the purpose of increasing productivity. Job design is concerned with the specific tasks to be performed, the methods used in performing the tasks, and how the job relates to the others in the organization. Some of the factors affecting work design include: technology, economy, government, unions, and management philosophy. Job rotation and job enlargement involve a horizontal expansion of duties, but add no responsibilities to the job. Job enrichment, on the other hand, creates basic changes in the content and level of responsibility of a job in an attempt to provide for the satisfaction of the needs of personnel.

Another technique that has been shown to be effective in enhancing motivation and achieving improved quality and productivity in several hundred North American companies is a concept known as quality circles. In most firms, quality circles consist of periodic meetings of small groups who get together to brainstorm ways to improve the quality and quantity of work.

North American firms are becoming increasingly interested in the motivation practices of Japanese companies, since Japanese workers are strongly committed to the firms they work for and are, as a result, extremely productive. Some policies of Japanese firms include lifetime employment, a high degree of responsibility toward employees, and an avoidance of employee layoffs.

REVIEW QUESTIONS

1. How would you define motivation?
2. Compare and contrast McGregor's Theory X and Theory Y. What are some examples of managerial practices that are consistent with a Theory Y philosophy of human nature?
3. What is Argyris's maturation theory? How does it apply to motivation?
4. What is the notion of the "self-fulfilling prophecy?" How is it related to management and motivation?
5. Relate Herzberg's theory of motivation to the theories developed by Maslow and Alderfer.
6. Describe McClelland's theory of human motives. How does it relate to motivation, and what are the basic characteristics of individuals described by the theory?
7. What is expectancy theory, and how can managers use it in the motivation process? Provide examples.
8. Briefly describe organizational behavior modification. How can it be used in motivating people? Give illustrations.
9. What is the role of money as a motivator? How important is the issue of equity of pay in terms of motivation? Discuss.
10. What is meant by job enrichment, and how does it differ from job enlargement? How would you apply job enrichment? Give an example.
11. What are quality circles and how successful have they been in improving the quality and quantity of work?
12. What characterizes "Theory Z" type companies? How do the seven S's relate to motivation in organizations?

EXERCISES

1. Interview three managers — for example, a bank president, a college dean, and a local retailer. Ask these managers to describe their approach to motivating personnel within their organization. Compare their comments with the concepts of motivation presented in this chapter.

2. Using Maslow's hierarchy of needs as a guide, describe how your various needs have been satisfied on any job(s) you have held. Were any of your needs not met? Why or why not? How could they have been satisfied?

CASE STUDY

The Problem Chemist

Martin Stahl was the head of the research and development lab of Beltronics Ltd., a large manufacturing firm involved in the manufacture of plastic products for both consumer and industrial markets. In his role as laboratory head, Stahl supervised 11 chemists, all of whom had PhDs in chemistry. The R & D laboratory had a dual responsibility: (1) to do pure research on various chemical compounds and how they behaved, and (2) to take any promising results from the pure research output and see how they could be applied in the manufacture of plastic products.

The R & D lab had an excellent reputation inside and outside the company. A steady stream of new ideas and compounds had emerged from the lab over the last 10 years, and several major patents had been obtained during that period. Most of the members of Stahl's department had also published articles about their work in chemical trade journals. Stahl encouraged this because it gave the company a good reputation and it provided feedback and status to the chemists.

Stahl was on good terms with all but one of the staff chemists. Gary Blaski had been hired seven years ago to give some additional expertise in the pure research area. Blaski had gone to school with one of Stahl's group and, on that person's recommendation, Stahl had hired Blaski. However, within about one year of Blaski's hiring, Stahl began to have problems with him. In Stahl's view, although Blaski was a fine chemist, he didn't seem to be motivated to do the kind of work the R & D lab was doing. Blaski showed little enthusiasm for the job, was often absent, and had a very low productivity level as measured by new patents granted, trade journal publications, and research projects completed.

Stahl had several discussions with Blaski about his performance, but Blaski rejected Stahl's position and argued that research can't be rushed. These discussions were often frustrating for Stahl, but he had gradually learned some things about Blaski. For example, he realized that Blaski craved recognition of any sort, no matter how insignificant. Stahl had attempted to use this knowledge to motivate Blaski by suggesting that Blaski get some of his work patented; this would mean considerable recognition. Blaski seemed interested in the idea, but somehow nothing ever came of it.

As time went on, Stahl became more and more unhappy with Blaski's nonchalant attitude and his subpar performance. He began increasing pressure on Blaski to improve his performance, but the interpersonal relations between the two worsened. Stahl noticed that Blaski seemed to be more and more unhappy; on one occasion Blaski offered the opinion that the other chemists didn't seem to like him. He even commented that his former school buddy seemed to be avoiding him. When asked why, Blaski said he didn't know, but that it was unfair that his peers didn't recognize his abilities.

One afternoon Blaski came to Stahl's office and requested permission to take time off from work (with pay) to attend a meeting of industrial chemists being held in another city. The following conversation took place:

Blaski: I'd like to go to the Industrial Chemists Association meetings. I think it's appropriate that the company pay for my travel and accommodations since I will be improving my work-related expertise by attending this meeting. I know you have reimbursed other people in the lab, and I think I should be treated the same way.

Stahl: I'm sorry, but I can't grant the request. Before laying out money for things like this, I need to see a considerable improvement in your work here.

Blaski: What do you mean?

Stahl: You know exactly what I mean. Your nonchalant attitude has got to change and your productivity must improve.

Blaski: I've told you this before, but you just don't listen. You can't rush research.

Stahl: The other chemists don't seem to be having any trouble meeting my productivity standards. I must not be "rushing" them. Why are you the only person who can't seem to do the job?

Blaski: You just don't realize that each person is unique. You're trying to make me fit into a certain mold and that's been weighing on my mind and reducing my productivity. If I were given more freedom to do my own thing, I would be more productive.

Stahl: When you demonstrate some productivity you'll get some freedom!

After Blaski left, Stahl wondered if he had been too harsh with him. However, he was at the end of his rope and had exhausted all the avenues he knew of to motivate Blaski.

QUESTIONS

1. Use each of the motivation theories in this chapter to analyze this problem. What solutions would each theory suggest?
2. Comment on Blaski's performance problems using the formula
   $$performance = ability \times motivation.$$
3. What should Stahl do to motivate Blaski?

CASE STUDY

A Birthday Present for Kathy

Bob Rosen could hardly wait to get back to work Monday morning. He was excited about his chance of getting a large bonus. Bob is a machine operator with Ram Manufacturing Company which makes electric motors. He operates an armature winding machine. The machine winds copper wire onto metal cores to make the rotating elements for electric motors.

Ram pays machine operators on a graduated piece-rate basis. Operators are paid a certain amount for each part made, plus a bonus. A worker who produces 10 percent above standard for a certain month receives a 10 percent additional bonus. For 20 percent above standard, the bonus is 20 percent. Bob realized that he had a good chance of earning a 20 percent bonus that month. That would be $287.

Bob had a special use for the extra money. His wife's birthday was just three weeks away. He was hoping to get her a new Chevrolet Citation. He had already saved $450, but the down payment on the Citation was $700. The bonus would enable him to buy the car.

Bob arrived at work at seven o'clock that morning, although his shift did not begin until eight. He went to his work station and checked the supply of blank cores and copper wire. Finding that only one spool of wire was on hand, he asked the fork truck driver to bring another. Then he asked the operator who was working the graveyard shift, "Sam, do you mind if I grease the machine while you work?"

"No," Sam said, "that won't bother me a bit."

After greasing the machine, Bob stood and watched Sam work. He thought of ways to simplify the motions involved in loading, winding, and unloading the armatures. As Bob took over the machine after the eight o'clock whistle, he thought, "I hope I can pull this off. I know Kathy will be happy not to be grounded while I'm at work."

QUESTIONS

1. Explain the advantages and disadvantages of a graduated piece-rate pay system such as that at Ram.
2. Explain Bob's high level of motivation in terms of needs theory, reinforcement theory, and expectancy theory.

ENDNOTES

[1] Douglas McGregor, *The Human Side of Enterprise* (New York: McGraw-Hill, 1960).

[2] Chris Argyris, *Personality and Organization* (New York: Harper, 1957).

[3] J. Sterling Livingston, "Pygmalion in Management," *Harvard Business Review* (July-August 1969).

[4] John L. Single, "The Power of Expectations: Productivity and the Self-Fulfilling Prophecy," *Management World* (November 1980): 19, 37-38.

[5] Abraham Maslow, *Motivation and Personality* (New York: Harper, 1954).

[6] Clayton P. Alderfer, "A Critique of Salancik and Pfeffer's Examination of Need Satisfaction Theories," *Administrative Science Quarterly* 22 (December 1977): 658-672.

[7] Frederick Herzberg, *Work and the Nature of Man* (Cleveland: World, 1966).

[8] David C. McClelland and David H. Burnham, "Power is the Great Motivator," *Harvard Business Review* 54 (March-April 1976): 103.

[9] David R. Hampton, Charles E. Summer, and Ross A. Webber, *Organizational Behavior and the Practice of Management* (Glenview, Ill: Scott, Foresman, 1978): 11-15.

[10] M. J. Stahl, "Achievement Power and Managerial Motivation: Selecting Managerial Talent with the Job Choice Exercise," *Personnel Psychology* (Winter 1983): 786.

[11] Victor Vroom, *Work and Motivation* (New York: Wiley, 1964).

[12] C. W. Kennedy, J. A. Fossum and B. J. White, "An Empirical Comparison of Within-Subjects and Between-Subjects Expectancy Theory Models," *Organizational Behavior and Human Performance* (August 1983): 124.

[13] B. F. Skinner, *Beyond Freedom and Dignity* (New York: Knopf, 1971).

[14] Ed Pedalino and Victor U. Gamboa, "Behavior Modification and Absenteeism," *Journal of Applied Psychology* 59 (December 1974): 694-698.

[15] W. Clay Hamner and Ellen P. Hamner, "Behavior Modification and the Bottom Line," *Organizational Dynamics* 4 (Spring 1976): 12.

[16] "At Emery Air Freight: Positive Reinforcement Boosts Performance," *Organizational Dynamics* 1 (Autumn 1973): 41-50.

[17] J. S. Adams, "Toward An Understanding of Inequity," *Journal of Abnormal and Social Psychology* 67 (1963): 425.

[18] S. W. Gellerman, *Management by Motivation* (New York: American Management Association, 1968).

[19]J. Richard Hackman and Greg R. Oldham, *Work Redesign* (Reading, Mass: Addison-Wesley, 1980).

[20]Hackman and Oldham.

[21]John F. Runcie, " 'By Days I Make the Cars,' " *Harvard Business Review* (May-June 1980): 106–115.

[22]Frederick Herzberg, "One More Time: How Do You Motivate Employees?" *Harvard Business Review* 46 (January-February 1968): 53–62. See also Frederick Herzberg, "Motivation and Innovation: Who are Workers Serving?" *California Management Review* 22, no. 2 (Winter 1979).

[23]M. D. Kilbridge, "Reduced Costs Through Job Enlargement: A Case," *Journal of Business* 33 (1960): 74–80.

[24]"Will the Slide Kill Quality Circles?" *Business Week* (January 11, 1982): 108–109.

[25]"The New Industrial Revolution," *Business Week* (May 11, 1981): 85–98.

[26]R. T. Golembiewski and C. W. Proehl, "A Survey of the Empirical Literature on Flexible Workhours: Character and Consequences of a Major Innovation," *Academy of Management Review* (October, 1978): 837–853; also S. D. Nollen, "Does Flextime Improve Productivity?" *Harvard Business Review* (September-October, 1979): 12, 16–18, 22.

[27]J. S. Kim and A. F. Campagna, "Effects of Flextime on Employee Attendance and Performance: A Field Experiment," *Academy of Management Journal* (December, 1981): 729–741.

[28]William Ouchi, *Theory Z: How American Business Can Meet the Japanese Challenge* (Reading, Mass: Addison-Wesley, 1981); Richard Pascale and Anthony Athos, *The Art of Japanese Management: Applications for American Executives* (New York: Simon and Schuster, 1981).

[29]Pascale and Athos, 81.

[30]Pascale and Athos, 178.

REFERENCES

Armstrong, J. "How to Motivate." *Management Today* 12 (February 1977): 60–63.

Berry, L. E. "Motivation Management." *Journal of Systems Management* 30 (April 1979): 30–32.

Brockner, Joel, and Hess, Ted. "Self-Esteem and Task Performance in Quality Circles." *Academy of Management Journal* 29 (September 1986): 617–622.

Collison, Robert. "The Japanese Fix." *Canadian Business* (November 1981): 37.

Cook, C. W. "Guidelines for Managing Motivation." *Business Horizons* 23 (April 1980): 61–69.

Davis, Tim R. V. "The Influence of the Physical Environment in Offices." *Academy of Management Review* 9, no. 2 (April 1984): 271–283.

Eastmond, Archie, "Motivation in the Broker's Office." *Canadian Insurance* (September 1982): 14.

Erez, Miriam, and Arad, Revital. "Participative Goal Setting: Social, Motivational, and Cognitive Factors." *Journal of Applied Psychology* 71 (November 1986): 591–597.

Francis, Jack. "Profit Sharing Gaining Ground." *Winnipeg Free Press* (June 8, 1984): 46.

Gallagher, W. E. Jr., and Einhorn, H. J. "Motivation Theory and Job Design." *Journal of Business* 49 (July 1976): 358–373.

Gayle, J. B., and Searle, F. R. "Maslow, Motivation, and the Manager." *Management World* 9 (September 1980): 18–20.

Giblin, E. J. "Motivating Employees: A Closer Look." *Personnel Journal* 55 (April 1976): 68–71.

Hackman, J. R. "Is Job Enrichment Just a Fad?" *Harvard Business Review* 53 (September 1975): 129–138.

Hatuany, N., and Puick, V. "Japanese Management Practices and Productivity." *Organizational Dynamics* 9 (Spring 1981): 4–21.

Keys, J. Bernard, and Miller, Thomas R. "The Japanese Management Theory Jungle." *Academy of Management Review* 9, no. 2 (April 1984): 342–353.

Kim, Jay S. "Effect of Behavior Plus Outcome Goal Setting on Feedback Satisfaction and Performance." *Academy of Management Journal* 27, no. 1 (March 1984): 139–149.

Klimoski, R. J., and Hayes, N. J. "Leader Behavior and Subordinate Motivation." *Personnel Psychology* 33 (Autumn 1980): 543–555.

Knight, Lou. "Quality Circles in Action: A Canadian Experience." *CTM: The Human Element* (February 1983): 20.

Latham, Gary P., and Steel, Timothy P. "The Motivational Effects of Participation versus Goal Setting on Performance." *Academy of Management Journal* 26, no. 3 (September 1983): 406–417.

Marks, Mitchell; Mirvis, Phillip; Hackett, Edward; and Grady, James. "Employee Participation in a Quality Circle Program." *Journal of Applied Psychology* 71 (February 1986): 61–69.

McClelland, D. C., and Burnham, D. H. "Power Is the Great Motivator." *Harvard Business Review* 54 (March 1976): 100–110.

Miller, William B. "Motivation Techniques: Does One Work Best?" *Management Review* (February 1981): 47–52.

Neider, L. L. "Experimental Field Investigation Utilizing an Expectancy Theory View of Participation." *Organizational Behavior and Human Performance* 26 (December 1980): 425–442.

Nonaka, Ikujiro and Johanssen, Johnny. "Japanese Management: What About the 'Hard' Skills?" *Academy of Management Review* 10 (April 1985): 181–191.

Norris, Dwight R., and Beibuhr, Robert E. "Attributional Influences on the Job Performance — Job Satisfaction Relationships." *Academy of Management Journal* 27, no. 2 (June 1983): 424–430.

Odiorne, G. S. "Uneasy Look at Motivation Theory." *Training and Development Journal* 34 (June 1980): 106–112.

Ouchi, William G. "Organizational Paragrams: A Commentary on Japanese Management and Theory Z Organizations." *Organizational Dynamics* 9 (Spring 1981): 36–42.

_____. "Theory Z Corporations." *Industry Week* (May 4, 1981): 49–51.

Parson, Mary. "The Play's the Thing." *Canadian Business* 59 (May 1986): 68–72.

Peters, Thomas J. "Putting Excellence into Management." *Business Week* (July 21, 1980): 196–205.

Pinder, C. C. "Concerning the Application of Human Motivation Theories in Organizational Settings." *Academy of Management Review* 2 (July 1977): 384–397.

Quick, J. C. "Dyadic Goal Setting within Organizations: Rolemaking and Motivational Considerations." *Academy of Management Review* 4 (July 1979): 377–380.

Rosenthal, Robert. "The Pygmalion Effect Lives." *Psychology Today* (September 1973): 56–60.

Runcie, John F. " 'By Days I Make the Cars.' " *Harvard Business Review* (May-June 1980): 106–115.

Schmitt, N., and Son, L. "Evaluation of Valence Models of Motivation to Pursue Various Post High School Alternatives." *Organizational Behavior and Human Performance* 27 (February 1981): 135–150.

Silburt, David. "Secrets of the Super Sellers." *Canadian Business* 60 (January 1987): 54–59.

Speigel, D. "How Not to Motivate." *Supervisory Management* 22 (November 1977): 41–45.

Trautman, L. J., et al. "Managing People: Choosing the Right Motivator." *Mortgage Banker* 40 (August 1980): 34–37.

Ungson, Gerardo Rivera, and Steers, Richard M. "Motivation and Politics in Executive Compensation." *Academy of Management Review* 9, no. 2 (April 1984): 313–323.

Leadership

KEY TERMS

leadership
manager
leader
transactional
 managers
transformational
 managers
autocratic leader
participative leader
democratic leader
laissez faire leader
trait approach
Likert's systems of
 management

leadership
 continuum
managerial grid
Ohio State
 leadership studies
initiating structure
consideration
path-goal theory
Fiedler's
 contingency
 leadership model
leader-member
 relations

task structure
leader position
 power
situational
 leadership theory
task behavior
relationship
 behavior
task-relevant
 maturity
leadership decision-
 making model

LEARNING OBJECTIVES

After completing this chapter you should be able to
1. Describe leadership and define the types of power a leader may possess.
2. Identify and describe the major leadership theories which advocate a universal leadership style.
3. Identify and explain the major situational leadership theories.
4. Describe the integrated approach to leadership.

OPENING INCIDENT

Mission Chapel

The Mission Chapel is a nondenominational church located in the downtown section of a large Canadian city. The chapel's choir has 45 volunteers and performs each Sunday from September through June.

There are two distinct types of people in the choir. Ten people are experienced singers, with many years of formal music and voice training. The remaining 35 people have little or no musical training but are in the choir because they like to sing. The experienced singers are expected to help the inexperienced ones; in addition, the experienced singers do solo performances on a regular basis.

The choir director, Carolyn Barnes, is known throughout the city as an excellent musician. In addition to directing the chapel choir, she judges various musical competitions held throughout the year and is the producer of a popular local music show on television. Barnes is paid a token salary of $5000 per year for conducting the chapel choir. Practice is held for two hours on Wednesday evenings, at which time the choir works toward the goal of a good performance at the regular church service.

Barnes runs the choir with a firm hand. She decides which music is to be performed, the date on which it will be performed, who the soloists will be, the nature and timing of special concerts, and the structure of the Wednesday night practices.

In her opinion, she is very effective, since the current choir has placed first in all three competitions it has entered in the past 18 months. Morale of the choir seems very high and turnover is fairly low (10 percent).

In spite of this success, Barnes has noticed two things that disturb her. First, absenteeism is running at 20 percent at both the practice sessions and the regular Sunday services. She has tried to solve this problem by pointing out to choir members the importance of regular attendance, but this lecture has been ineffective. Second, certain of the choir members continually talk and laugh during the practice sessions. This joking is annoying to Barnes and on several occasions she has made it clear that she will not tolerate it. These comments have not had any effect and the problems have continued. Barnes wonders if her leadership style is appropriate for the situation and if she should change it in an attempt to solve these two problems.

Influencing through motivation can be most effective when a manager shows clearly that he or she is a leader. What does it take to be an effective manager? What is the most effective leadership style?

These questions have perplexed and challenged managers for generations. Literally thousands of research studies have been conducted to try to answer them. However, such studies of leaders and the leadership process have not yielded any set of traits or behaviors that are consistently related to effective leadership. The basic conclusion that can be drawn from these studies is that there is no one most effective leadership style. What we do know is that effective leadership is absolutely essential to the survival and overall growth of every organization.

Despite high salaries and excellent opportunities in large corporations, there continues to be a shortage of competent leaders. The lack of capable leadership is not just confined to business organizations but has also been felt in government, churches, education, and all other types of organizations. The problem is not a lack of people who *want* to be leaders or managers, but rather a scarcity of skilled people who are *capable* of performing effectively in leadership positions. The primary challenge of leadership is to guide an organization toward the accomplishment of its objectives. The leader achieves this by directing and encouraging employees of the organization to attain the highest level of performance possible within the limitation of available resources, skills, and technology.

This chapter will begin by defining leadership and comparing it to management. A distinction will also be drawn between transformational management and transactional management. Next, we examine three universalist leadership theories. These theories assume that there is one best way to lead followers, regardless of the situation. By way of contrast, the next section examines several contingency leadership theories, which are based on the idea that the most effective leadership style depends on a variety of situational factors. The chapter concludes with a discussion of the general factors which influence managers' styles of leadership.

LEADERSHIP DEFINED

leadership

Leadership is the ability to motivate followers to pursue the goals the leader wishes to achieve. What the leader wants may or may not be consistent with the goals of the organization the leader belongs to. So, a leader may or may not have a positive effect on the achievement of an organization's goals. In this chapter, we are primarily concerned with managers as leaders.

Leaders versus Managers

manager

We need to make a distinction between the terms "leader" and "manager." A **manager** is one who performs the functions of planning, organizing, influencing, and controlling and who occupies a

leader

formal position in an organization. For example, the sales manager is the individual who manages the sales staff of the company. A **leader** is anyone who is able to influence others to pursue certain goals. Is this sales manager both a manager and a leader? Not necessarily. The sales manager is certainly a manager because of the formal position he or she occupies. Whether the sales manager is also a leader depends on his or her ability to influence the sales staff to pursue certain goals.

Zaleznik argues that leaders can be distinguished from managers by virtue of their (1) orientation toward goals, (2) view of their work, (3) attitude toward human relations, and (4) view of themselves.[1] In his view, managers reactively adopt impersonal goals which arise out of the necessities of organizational life, while leaders are more active and shape ideas instead of simply responding to them. Managers view their work as that of facilitating the combination of people and ideas, while leaders view their work as finding new ways of resolving long-standing problems. Managers relate to people on the basis of their role in the decision-making process, while leaders relate to people in more intuitive and empathetic ways. Finally, managers see themselves as an integral part of the system they work in, while leaders see themselves as quite separate from the system.

The difference between leaders and managers can be clearly seen when we consider the concept of charismatic leadership. People with charisma have personal abilities and characteristics that allow them to have an unusually strong influence on the behavior and attitudes of others. While some managers seem to have charisma (for example, Lee Iacocca of Chrysler), we normally think of managers as individuals who systematically plan, organize, and control subordinates.

In the political and religious realm, however, charismatic leadership is much more visible. Various political and religious leaders — for example, Churchill, Hitler, Gandhi, Jesus Christ — demonstrated a high degree of charisma. The followers of charismatic leaders have high motivation because they believe the leader is extraordinarily gifted. The followers are also devoted, loyal, give unquestioned obedience to the leader's commands, and trust the leader. Because of all these factors, the leader is able to bring about dramatic change through the followers.

Charismatic leaders possess three key characteristics: (1) self-confidence, (2) dominance, and (3) a strong conviction about the rightness of their beliefs.[2] The charismatic leader models a value system for followers and is able to convey a transcendental goal. Martin Luther King, for example, was able to convey to followers his conception of what life could be like for blacks in his famous "I have a dream" speech in the 1960s. The charismatic leader also expects high performance from followers. For example, Churchill's speech about "England's finest hour" during World War II was based on his expectation that the Nazi's could be defeated — even though the situation looked hopeless at the time.

Leadership, Management, and Performance

Generally speaking, a good manager is a good leader, but a good leader may not be a good manager. If we accept the idea that one of the functions of management is to direct, then a good manager should be a good leader. But the converse may not be true, because the leader may be directing followers toward a goal that is not functional for the organization. Consider the following actual situation.

A team of consultants had prepared a feasibility study for the president of a newly formed mobile home manufacturer. The study recommended that the new plant produce a relatively low-priced mobile home because the firm was in a low-income geographic area. However, the company hired a production manager with an excellent reputation who had several years of experience with a manufacturer of higher-priced, higher-quality mobile homes. Against the advice of the consultants and without the knowledge of the board of directors, the production manager decided to direct his production supervisors and workers to produce a higher-priced mobile home. The results proved to be disastrous for the newly established company. The sales staff was not able to sell these high-priced units; the firm had invested over $350 000 of its working capital in an inventory of mobile homes that it could not sell. This was a major factor contributing to the firm's bankruptcy within nine months of its start-up. In this illustra-

MANAGEMENT IN PRACTICE

Leadership at Gray Coach

William Verrier became president and chief executive officer of Gray Coach Lines Ltd. of Toronto during 1986. Prior to his arrival, the company was considered a laggard in an industry that has been experiencing many problems. Now, profits at Gray Coach are at record levels, worker morale is high, and the company is setting operational standards for the industry.

Before coming to Gray Coach, Mr. Verrier was executive vice-president and chief operating officer of Eastern Provincial Airways. He has many ideas he wants to try out in the bus industry, some of which involve making bus transportation more like plane transportation. For example, he is considering the idea of plush double-decker buses, equipped with comforta-ble chairs, bar-grills, and hostesses. He also wants to introduce credit cards, and a comprehensive reservation system to reduce congestion at terminals.

Mr. Verrier notes that applying these new ideas will require that the bus industry be dragged out of the dark ages. There is much resistance to the adoption of his new ideas, but he intends to pursue them vigorously. Some critics are withholding judgment on the success of Mr. Verrier's plans. They point out that so far he has increased profits not by increasing ridership, but by cutting costs.

SOURCE Adapted from Cecil Foster, "An Iconoclastic Boss Is Turnaround Artist For Gray Coach," *The Globe and Mail* (March 2, 1987): B6.

tion, the production manager exercised effective leadership because he significantly influenced the behavior of his workers. However, he was an ineffective manager because he had the employees pursuing goals that were not in the best interest of the company.

Thus a company can fail even though it has leaders who have been effectively influencing the behavior of others to accomplish goals, if these goals are inappropriate for the company. Also, it should be noted that a person can have the title of manager but have very little influence over the behavior and actions of others. Or, an individual might not carry the title of manager but be an important informal leader exercising considerable influence over the behavior of others in the work group.

Transactional versus Transformational Management

transactional managers

transformational managers

In the past few years, management writers have made a distinction between transactional and transformational management. **Transactional managers** have a traditional view of management functions. They stress planning for the future, setting up a structure to achieve the plans, and controlling the system so that it performs well. **Transformational managers** stress additional activities such as revitalizing the organization, communicating the organization's vision and culture to employees, molding employees into effective performers, and getting employee commitment to the organization's goals.

Three specific activities are involved in transformational management: (1) creation of a vision (the leader provides the organization with a vision of a desired future state); (2) mobilization of commitment (the critical mass in the organization accepts the leader's vision); and (3) institutionalization of change (new patterns of behavior are adopted which are consistent with the new vision).[3] The transformational leader must recognize that people will have mixed emotions about major changes, and must help them to move from their initial negative reaction to such changes to more positive ones. Transformational leaders can ease the transition by replacing the organization's past glories with a strong vision of future opportunities.

In a very general sense, major changes are sweeping through North American society, and traditional managers will *have* to develop transformational skills in order to survive. They will need a longer-term perspective on problems facing our society, and will increasingly be called upon to make decisions that will benefit not only the business firm, but also society at large. Transformational management involves getting organizations and the people in them, to take on new challenges. Transformational management is based on the idea that leadership makes a difference in the way business copes with change.[4]

BASIC LEADERSHIP STYLES

autocratic leader

participative leader

democratic leader

laissez faire leader

Four basic leadership styles have been identified: autocratic, participative, democratic, and laissez-faire. An **autocratic leader** is a person who tells subordinates what to do and expects to be obeyed without question. This style is typical of a person who accepts McGregor's Theory X assumptions, described in Chapter 10. A **participative leader** is a person who involves subordinates in decision making but may retain the final authority. A **democratic leader** is a person who tries to do what the majority of subordinates desire. Participative and democratic leaders tend to make Theory Y assumptions. The **laissez-faire leader** is uninvolved in the work of the unit. It is difficult to defend this leadership style unless the leader is supervising expert and well-motivated specialists, such as scientists. In fact, practically every leader who has attained recognition for effectiveness — from Winston Churchill to Billy Graham to Lee Iacocca — has done so by being deeply involved and active in pursuing a certain goal.

MANAGEMENT IN PRACTICE

Participative Management at Algoma Steel

Since the mid-1970s, Algoma Steel has increasingly used participative management to make decisions in several important areas of the company's operations. For example, the company was dissatisfied with its safety record, so it instituted joint safety committees. Both union and management people sit on these committees, whose primary goal is to make the work place healthier and safer to work in.

Another area of participation concerns compensation plans. The company formerly had many different plans; this meant that workers in one department might earn a higher bonus than workers in another department. These inequities across departments made workers unhappy. Now, one incentive plan has been cooperatively developed for the entire plant, and all workers in the plant are paid a bonus based on the tonnage shipped from the plant.

Attitude surveys taken by the company suggest that there is a definite improvement in the workers' perceptions of the company, and a better cooperative spirit between workers and management.

SOURCE Adapted from Dean Walker, "Flexibility Means Profitability," *Executive* (February 1982): 61–62.

ONE-BEST-WAY (UNIVERSALIST) LEADERSHIP THEORIES

Leadership research began in earnest in the early twentieth century and has been steadily increasing in volume. Leadership theories which were developed before 1970 often had a universalist flavor: they assumed that there was one best way to lead subordinates regardless of the situation the leader found himself or herself in.

Three of the most popular universalist leadership theories are: (1) the trait approach, (2) Likert's System IV Management, and (3) Blake and Mouton's Managerial Grid.

The Trait Approach to Leadership

The leader has always occupied a strong and central role in traditional management theory. Most of the early research on leadership attempted to (1) compare the traits of people who become leaders with those who remain as followers and (2) identify characteristics and traits possessed by effective leaders. The **trait approach** to leadership is the evaluation and selection of leaders based on their physical, mental, and psychological characteristics. Research studies comparing the traits of leaders and nonleaders have found that leaders tend to be somewhat taller, more outgoing, more self-confident, and more intelligent than nonleaders. But a specific combination of traits has not been found that can differentiate leaders or potential leaders from followers. Clearly it is difficult to identify a leader from an initial impression.

Considerable research has been conducted to compare the traits of effective and ineffective leaders. Traits such as aggressiveness, ambition, decisiveness, dominance, initiative, intelligence, physical characteristics (looks, height, and weight), self-assurance, and other factors were studied to determine if they were related to effective leadership. The underlying assumption of much trait research has been that leaders are born, not made. Although it has been demonstrated that this is not the case, some people still believe there are certain inborn or acquired traits that make a person a good leader. No studies have conclusively shown that physical traits can distinguish effective from ineffective leaders.

The trait approach to the study of leadership is not dead, however. Edwin Ghiselli has continued to conduct research in an effort to identify personality and motivational traits related to effective leadership.[5] Ghiselli identified thirteen trait factors. Subsequent research studies of these trait factors have ranked them in order of significance, as illustrated in Table 12-1. The six most significant traits are defined as follows:

- *Supervisory ability:* The performance of the basic functions of management, including planning, organizing, influencing, and controlling the work of others.
- *Need for occupational achievement:* The seeking of responsibility and the desire for success.
- *Intelligence:* Creative and verbal ability, including judgment, reasoning, and thinking capacity.
- *Decisiveness:* Ability to make decisions and solve problems capably and competently.
- *Self-assurance:* Extent to which the individual views himself or herself as capable of coping with problems.

trait approach

TABLE 12-1   Ghiselli's Managerial Traits

Traits	Importance Value*
Supervisory ability (A)	100
Occupational achievement (M)	76
Intelligence (A)	64
Self-actualization (M)	63
Self-assurance (P)	62
Decisiveness (P)	61
Lack of need for security (M)	54
Working-class affinity (P)	47
Initiative (A)	34
Lack of need for high financial reward (M)	20
Need for power (M)	10
Maturity (P)	5
Masculinity-femininity (P)	0

SOURCE: James F. Gavin, "A Test of Ghiselli's Theory of Managerial Traits," *Journal of Business Research* (February 1976): 46. Reprinted by permission.
Note: A = ability trait; P = personality trait; M = motivational trait.
*100 = very important; 0 = plays no part in managerial talent.

- *Initiative:* Ability to act independently and develop courses of action not readily apparent to other people. Self-starter — able to find new or innovative ways of doing things.

Notably absent from the list of significant traits is gender. Although the majority of managers are males, most research has concluded that this may be because of sex role stereotyping. In fact, some researchers believe that there are no significant differences at all in leadership behavior between the sexes.[6]

In spite of the contributions of Ghiselli, the trait approach to the study of leadership has left many unanswered questions concerning what is required for effective leadership. Perhaps one of the major problems with the trait approach is defining who is effective. Does the mere fact that a person has a powerful position make that individual a leader?

Likert's Systems of Management

Likert's systems of management

Rensis Likert, former director of the Institute for Social Research at the University of Michigan, developed a universal theory of leadership. Likert's theory consists of a continuum of styles ranging from autocratic to participative. **Likert's four systems of management** are:

System I, Exploitative Autocratic; System II, Benevolent Autocratic; System III, Consultative; and System IV, Participative Team. Only the last style — System IV — was in the long run deemed best for all situations.[7]

System I — Exploitative Autocratic

In this kind of organization, managers make all the decisions. They decide what is to be done, who will do it, and how and when it is to be accomplished. Failure to complete work as assigned results in threats or punishment. Under this system, management exhibits little confidence or trust in employees. A typical managerial reponse under this system is: "You do it my way or you're fired." In System I, a low level of trust and confidence exists between management and employees.

System II — Benevolent Autocratic

In System II organizations, managers still make the decisions, but employees have some degree of freedom and flexibility in performing their jobs so long as they conform to specific procedures. Under this system, managers take a very paternalistic attitude: "I'll take care of you if you perform well." With System II, a fairly low level of trust is present between management and the employees; employees use caution when dealing with management.

System III — Consultative

In System III organizations, managers consult with employees prior to establishing goals and making decisions about work. Employees have a considerable degree of freedom in deciding how to accomplish their work. A manager using System III might say to an employee: "I'd like your opinion on this before I make the decision." Management tends to rely on rewards, as opposed to punishments, to motivate employees. Also, the level of trust between the employees and management is fairly high. This system creates a climate in which employees feel relatively free to discuss work-related matters openly with management.

System IV — Participative Team

System IV is Likert's recommended system or style of management. The emphasis in a System IV organization is on a group participative role with full involvement of the employees in the process of establishing goals and making job-related decisions. Employees feel free to discuss matters with their managers, who display supportive rather than condescending or threatening behavior. Likert argues that the entire organization should be designed along System IV lines, with work being performed by a series of overlapping groups. The leader provides a link between the group and other units at higher levels in

Edwin Mirvish

Edwin ("Honest Ed") Mirvish may be the last of an unusual brand of entrepreneurs. He owns and runs an apparently eclectic clutch of Toronto retail and real estate operations, restaurants, and theatres which employs 1000. Yet, at age 69, as always, he's directly and personally involved in almost everything. It's management by personality. Mirvish himself is the glue which binds together the businesses. As a manager, Mirvish has a thing or two to teach the whiz kids from our business schools. He has no secretary. He doesn't need one to devise his systems for him. He's figured out his own and they work: keep in touch by talking to the right people and reading the right reports; make decisions today; trust the people you hire and encourage them to carry out their ideas (he once told an employee that it was all right to make mistakes — at least they told him she was working); gamble only when you can afford to lose.

As an entrepreneur, though, Mirvish is a classic. He started with nothing but a formula for retailing that worked (sell for cash, buy for credit) that led him to create what's said to be North America's first discount stores in 1948. He knows his customers — whether they're the patrons of his classy theatre, the Royal Alexandra Theatre, or customers in Honest Ed's, which does about $50 million in sales a year. Devotees of Honest Ed's can pick up such bargains as toothpaste for $0.99 or a set of glass utility tables for $4.99. Decisions are made by "feel." There are no long-term plans, no decision trees. Perhaps there will be a meeting or two within the small group which helps Mirvish run the empire, where ideas will be shouted across the table. Definitely, no management consultants. Mirvish has no partners — that would mean explaining his decisions. It would also mean sharing financial details — something Mirvish, like many, is loath to discuss.

Q. Honest Ed's sales volume is about $50 million a year. How does that compare with conventional department stores?

Mirvish: I'm not sure how it compares now; but for many years we were doing more dollars per square metre than most retail businesses. One reason is we've never branched out; we have just one location. And we do not have stock problems. Stock comes in every day and is held beneath or above the counter. We don't have stockrooms because I've always had the fear we'll forget what's sitting out there.

Each of our 14 buyers manages his own department. So it's all very tight and our gross per square metre and our turnover are both very high. The whole store turns over 24 times a year. That may not be unusual in drugs or groceries but, in our case, it also includes shoes and clothing and furniture.

Q. There have been a lot of changes in the world in the 35 years Honest Ed's has been in business. How has your approach changed to keep abreast?

Mirvish: I try to keep in touch with what's happening. I'm at the store every day from eight until noon. And those 14 buyers must keep in touch too. I don't like them sitting in their offices too much. I want my buyers out on the floor so that, when we have a hundred-degree day, they will send the truck down and pick up a few hundred electric fans and sell them that day. We were the last to go into computer cash registers because, by the time a computer tape is fed into an office and the office digests it, it may be snowing outside. Our whole business is based on simplicity. Perhaps that's because I had little formal education.

Q. How do you stay in touch with the tastes and needs of your customers out there?

Mirvish: Every Tuesday and Friday we have a meeting with the 14 buyers. We go over everything, thrash it out, and resolve what's to be done. I don't feel that much out of touch. I feel the same as I ever did because I still walk in that door, I see and talk to the customers. It's up to my buyers to be up to the minute. They have to know this changing world's markets. They have a lot of freedom and unlimited money, but once every 4 weeks they have to answer for their turnover.

Q. Retailers tend to have high staff turnovers, yet you keep your people for years. Do you pay better than most stores?

Mirvish: Keeping help has to do with more things than pay. Because we have only one location, and I am involved, I get to know our people. We try to be interested in them as people. That has a lot to do with it. We used to have a retirement plan so that people would retire at 65. When I got to be 64, I changed the plan because I didn't want to be out of work. So now we have people here who are 75 and they still do a good day's work. The main thing is to find the time to be involved. There are people here who started when I only had 3 or 4 employees. Now the store must have nearly 400. Many of them grew and developed with me. Because we didn't go according to the book but by trial and error, they understand my way of thinking and I understand them.

Q. What do you look for when you hire?

Mirvish: We never hire at the top. Anyone who works for us starts as a young person. We look for stability. If someone has been out of school 3 years and has had 10 jobs, we don't take another look at that application.

Q. Have you a long-term plan?

Mirvish: No. Everything I've done has really been a development, an evolvement. The important thing always is to fulfill the needs that are there today. It's too hard to know what they'll be 5, 10 years down the road.

Q. Although you've had no long-term plans, there are things that you deliberately did not do. You could have taken Honest Ed's national, for example.

Mirvish: I never did that because I'd find it boring. It's not something I want to be involved in. Once you are making a living, you're making a living. I don't want to sit and look at a bunch of charts. I want to be out where the action is. If your goal is just to make money, you're going in a different direction. My goal is for the work I'm doing to be enjoyable and rewarding.

Q. How do you keep all these things going and continue to put your personal stamp on everything?

Mirvish: I've never had a secretary. I'm in the store every morning from eight to noon. I get a report on the day-before's business. It tells how many customers went through the store, how much each department did. If there's a trend, I can catch it. I'm in direct touch with each of the 14 department buyers. At noon I'm at the restaurant. From two-thirty to six, I'm at the theatre. Then I go home. I don't work evenings.

I have good managers. My people look after the housekeeping. One of the most important things in any business is the housekeeping. You won't have good turnover if your housekeeping isn't good. There are people responsible for the housekeeping at Honest Ed's, and the housekeeping in Mirvish Village, in the theatre and the restaurants.

If they change a menu they discuss it with me; but our menus are not big, they're simple. We take counts of everything. If something's not popular, it's out. It is not really that complicated. We have a thousand employees in Toronto but, over the years, I've surrounded myself with people who feel comfortable with me and I feel comfortable with them.

SOURCE   Excerpted from Dean Walker, "From Discounts to Show Biz, Ed Mirvish Does It His Way", *Executive* (November 1983): 34–38. Reprinted by permission.

the organization. This concept is often referred to as the linking-pin theory. Decision making is widespread throughout the enterprise, with the power of knowledge usually taking precedence over the power of authority.

Measurement of the type of style in the Likert framework is usually accomplished by having the employees assess the organization culture and management system on a Likert scale. A profile showing the management system existing within an organization is developed through this survey of opinion (Figure 12-1). For example, when the

Operating Characteristics		System 1 Exploitative— authoritative	System 2 Benevolent— authoritative	System 3 Consultative	System 4 Participative Group	Item No.
Motivations	1a					1
	b					2
	c					3
	d					4
	e					5
	f					6
	g					7
Communication	2a					8
	b					9
	c(1)					10
	(2)					11
	d(1)					12
	(2)					13
	(3)					14
	(4)					15
	(5)					16
	e					17
	f					18
	(1)					19
Interaction	3a					20
	b					21
	c(1)					22
	(2)					23
	d					24
	e					25
Decision making	4a					26
	b					27
	c					28
	d					29
	e(1)					30
	(2)					31
	f					32
Goal setting	5a					33
	b					34
	c					35
Control	6a					36
	b					37
	c					38
	d					39
Performance	7a					40
	b					41
	c					42
	d					43
Total						

FIGURE 12-1
Likert chart —
management systems

SOURCE Rensis Likert, *The Human Organization* (New York: McGraw-Hill, 1967). Reprinted by permission of author and publisher.

NOTE: Management system used by the most productive plant (Plant L) of a well-managed company, as seen by middle and top managers.

question, "To what extent are superiors willing to share information with subordinates?" is asked, the employee can answer on the continuum from "provide minimum information" all the way to "seeks to give subordinates all relevant information and all information they want." (See question 3c2 in Figure 12-2.) It has been found that the positions on these scales can be significantly altered through organizational and management development programs. (See Chapter 15.)

Blake and Mouton's Managerial Grid

managerial grid

Perhaps the most widely known of all leadership theories is the **managerial grid** developed by Robert R. Blake and Jane S. Mouton:[8] The managerial grid is illustrated in Figure 12-3. The two dimensions of the 9×9 grid are labelled "concern for people" and "concern for production." A score of 1 indicates low concern and a score of 9

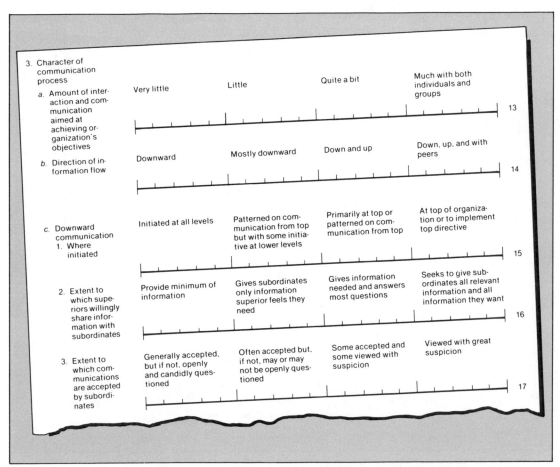

FIGURE 12-2   Sample of questions on Likert scale relating to organization communications

SOURCE   Rensis Likert, *The Human Organization* (New York: McGraw-Hill, 1967). Reprinted by permission.

shows a high concern. The grid depicts five major leadership styles representing the degree of concern the leader has for "people" and "production."

- 1,1 *Impoverished Management*: The manager has little concern for either people or production.
- 9,1 *Authority-Obedience*: The manager stresses operating efficiently through controls in situations where human elements cannot interfere.

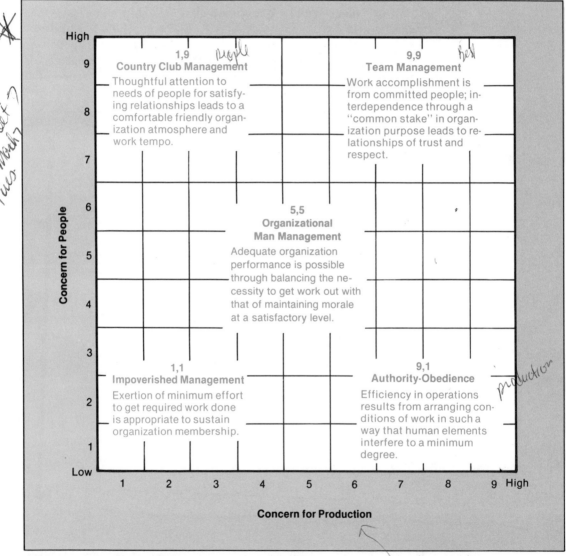

FIGURE 12-3   Blake and Mouton's managerial grid

SOURCE   Robert R. Blake and Jane Nrygley Mouton, *The New Managerial Grid* (Houston: Gulf Publishing Company, 1978): 11. Reprinted by permission of the authors and publisher.

- 1,9 *Country Club Management*: The manager is thoughtful, comfortable, and friendly, and has little concern for output.
- 5,5 *"Organizational Man" Management*: The manager attempts to balance and trade off concern for work in exchange for a satisfactory level of morale — a compromiser.
- 9,9 *Team Management*: The manager seeks high output through committed people, achieved through mutual trust, respect, and a realization of interdependence.[9]

According to Blake and Mouton, the first four styles listed are not always effective leadership styles. They strongly suggest that the 9,9 position of maximum concern for both output and people is the most effective. They argue that using the 9,9 team approach will result in improved performance, lower employee turnover and absenteeism, and greater employee satisfaction. The use of job enrichment and subordinate participation in managerial decision making contributes to this 9,9 situation, where both the organization and its members are accorded maximum and equal concern. The managerial grid concept has been introduced to many managers throughout the world since its development in the early 1960s and has influenced the management philosophies and practices of many of them.

SITUATIONAL THEORIES OF LEADERSHIP

Generally speaking, situational leadership theories are a recent development. They assume that the leadership issue is so complex that one style of leadership is unlikely to be universally effective. These theories have identified a wide variety of factors that determine the effectiveness of a given leadership style at a given point in time. The most popular situational leadership theories are: (1) The Ohio State leadership studies, (2) House's Path-Goal theory of leadership, (3) Tannenbaum and Schmidt's leadership continuum, (4) Fiedler's contingency leadership model, (5) Hersey and Blanchard's situational leadership theory, and (6) Vroom and Yetton's decision-making model.

The Ohio State Leadership Studies

Beginning in 1945, researchers in the Bureau of Business Research at Ohio State University made a series of detailed studies of the behavior of leaders in a wide variety of organizations.[10] The key concern of the **Ohio State leadership studies** was the leader's behavior in directing the efforts of others toward group goals. After many studies, researchers identified two important dimensions of leader behavior: (1) **Initiating structure** is the extent to which leaders establish goals

Ohio State leadership studies

initiating structure

consideration

and structure their roles and the roles of subordinates toward the attainment of the goals, and (2) **Consideration** is the extent to which leaders have relationships with subordinates characterized by mutual trust, respect, and consideration of employees' ideas and feelings.

Initiating structure and consideration were identified as separate and distinct dimensions of leadership behavior. As illustrated in Figure 12-4, there are four basic leadership styles representing different combinations of leadership behavior. A manager can be high in both consideration and initiating structure, low in both, or high in one and low in the other. Although the Ohio State studies are often cited as a universalist theory of leadership, the one most effective combination that meets the needs of all situations is not suggested in their model. Rather, the combination or appropriate level of initiating structure and consideration is determined by the demands of the particular situation.

Among the many situational variables that must be related to leadership behavior are:

- Expectations of the people being led
- Degree of task structuring imposed by technology
- Pressures of schedules and time
- Degrees of interpersonal contact possible between the leader and subordinates
- Degree of influence of the leader outside of the group
- Congruency of style with that of one's superior.

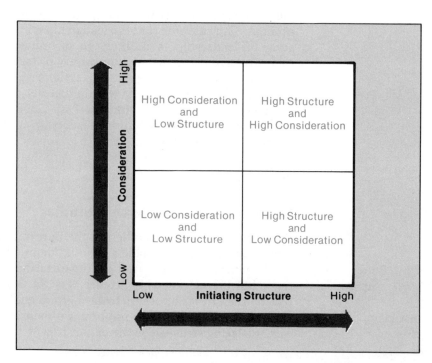

FIGURE 12-4
Ohio State
leadership model

The following observations can be made with regard to the type of leadership styles proposed in the Ohio State model:

- If a group expects and wants authoritarian leadership behavior, it is more likely to be satisfied with that type of leadership.
- If group members have less authoritarian expectations, a leader who strongly emphasizes initiating structure will be resented.
- If the work situation is highly structured by technology and the pressures of time, the supervisor who is high in consideration is more likely to meet with success, when measured by good attendance, low turnover, and few grievances.
- If task structuring precludes individual and group self-actualization, it will be useless to look for motivation from this source.
- When subordinates have little contact with their supervisor, they tend to prefer a more autocratic style.
- If employees must work and interact continuously, they usually want the superior to be high in consideration.

The Path-Goal Theory of Leadership

path-goal theory

Robert House developed what he termed the path-goal theory of leadership.[11] This approach to leadership is also closely related to the expectancy theory of motivation discussed in Chapter 11. **Path-goal theory** is the proposition that managers can facilitate job performance by showing employees how their performance directly affects their receiving desired rewards. In other words, a manager's behavior causes, or contributes to, employee satisfaction and acceptance of the manager if it increases goal attainment by employees. According to the path-goal approach, effective job performance results if the manager clearly defines the job, provides training for the employee, assists the employee in performing the job effectively, and rewards the employee for effective performance.

Four distinct leadership behaviors are associated with the path-goal approach:

- *Directive:* The manager tells the subordinate what to do and when to do it (no employee participation in decision making).
- *Supportive:* The manager is friendly with and shows interest in employees.
- *Participative*: The manager seeks suggestions and involves employees in decision making.
- *Achievement oriented*: The manager establishes challenging goals and demonstrates confidence that employees can achieve these goals.

Following the path-goal theory, a manager may use all four of the leadership behaviors in different situations. For instance, a manager may use directive behavior when supervising an inexperienced employee and supportive behavior when supervising a well-trained, experienced worker who is aware of the goals to be attained. The primary focus of the path-goal approach is on how managers can increase employee motivation and job satisfaction by clarifying performance goals and the path to achieve those goals.[12]

The Leadership Continuum

leadership
continuum

The **leadership continuum** is the graphical representation developed by Robert Tannenbaum and Warren H. Schmidt showing the trade-off between a manager's use of authority and the freedom of subordinates as leadership style varies from boss-centered to subordinate-centered. Tannenbaum and Schmidt described a series of factors that they thought influenced a manager's selection of the most appropriate leadership style. Their approach advocates a continuum of leadership behavior based on the notion that choosing an effective leadership style depends on the demands of the situation. As illustrated in Figure 12-5, leadership behavior ranges from boss-centered to subordinate-centered. Tannenbaum and Schmidt emphasized that a manager should give careful consideration to the following factors before selecting a leadership style:

- Characteristics of the manager: Background, education, experience, values, knowledge, goals, and expectations.
- Characteristics of the employees: Background, education, experience, knowledge, goals, values, and expectations.
- Requirements of the situation: Size, complexity, goals, structure, and climate of the organization, as well as the impact of technology, time pressure, and nature of the work.

According to Tannenbaum and Schmidt, a manager may engage in a more participative leadership style when subordinates:

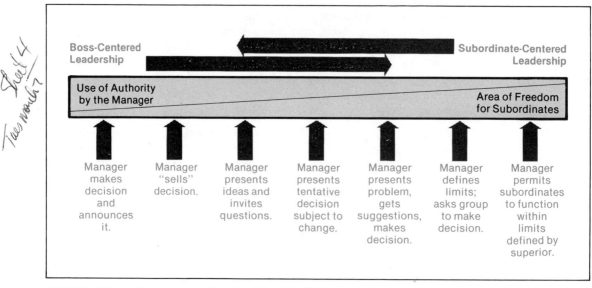

FIGURE 12-5   Continuum of leadership behavior

SOURCE   Reprinted by permission of the *Harvard Business Review*. Exhibit from "How to Choose a Leadership Pattern" by Robert Tannenbaum and Warren H. Schmidt (May/June 1973). Copyright © 1973 by the President and Fellows of Harvard College.

- Seek independence and freedom of action
- Understand and are committed to the goals of the organization
- Are well educated and experienced in performing the jobs
- Seek responsibility for decision making
- Expect a participative style of leadership.

If the above conditions do not exist, managers may need to adopt a more autocratic or "boss-centered" leadership style. In essence, managers must be able to diagnose the situations confronting them and then choose a leadership style that will improve their effectiveness. The most effective leaders are neither "task centered" nor "people centered" but, rather, are flexible enough to select a leadership style that fits their needs as well as the needs of their subordinates and of the situation.

Fiedler's Contingency Leadership Model

Fiedler's contingency leadership model

leader-member relations

task structure

leader position power

The contingency theory developed by Fred E. Fiedler has received considerable recognition as a situational approach to leadership.[13] **Fiedler's contingency leadership model** suggests that there are a number of leadership styles that may be appropriate, depending on the situation. His model's framework is made up of eight significantly different situations and two basic styles of leadership. Three major elements determine whether a given situation is favorable to a leader:

- **Leader-member relations**: The degree to which the leader feels accepted by subordinates. The culture may be friendly or unfriendly, relaxed or tense, threatening or supportive.
- **Task structure**: The extent to which goals are clearly defined and solutions to problems are known.
- **Leader position power**: The degree of influence over rewards and punishments, as well as the official authority possessed by the leader.

The concept of leader-member relations is similar to the consideration or relationship behavior concepts, while task structure and position power are closely related to initiating structure or task behavior, discussed previously. By mixing these three elements, eight situations can be identified. (See Table 12-2.)

The eight situations are ranked in terms of their degree of favorableness to a leader, as indicated by the amount of influence and control the leader has over the group. A leader has maximum influence in situation 1 and very little in situation 8. Research evidence indicates that a task-oriented, controlling leader will be most effective when the situations are either very favorable (1, 2, and 3) or very unfavorable (8). The more permissive, considerate leader performs more effectively in the intermediate situations, which are moderately favorable to the leader (4, 5, 6, and 7). Another way to illustrate Fiedler's framework is shown in Figure 12-6. The task-oriented style of leader is more effective in situations 1, 2, 3, and 8 while the

TABLE 12-2   Framework of Fiedler's Contingency Leadership Model

Situation	Degree of Favorableness of Situation to Leader	Leader-Member Relations	Task Structure	Position Power of Leader
1	Favorable	Good	Structured	High
2	Favorable	Good	Structured	Low
3	Favorable	Good	Unstructured	High
4	Moderately Favorable	Good	Unstructured	Low
5	Moderately Favorable	Poor	Structured	High
6	Moderately Favorable	Poor	Structured	Low
7	Moderately Favorable	Poor	Unstructured	High
8	Unfavorable	Poor	Unstructured	Low

SOURCE   Edwin B. Flippo and Gary M. Munsinger, *Management*, 5th ed. (Newton, Mass.: Allyn and Bacon, 1982): p. 342.

FIGURE 12-6

Appropriateness of leadership styles to situation

SOURCE   Adapted from Edwin B. Flippo and Gary M. Munsinger, *Management,* 5th ed. (Newton, Mass.: Allyn and Bacon, 1982): 342.

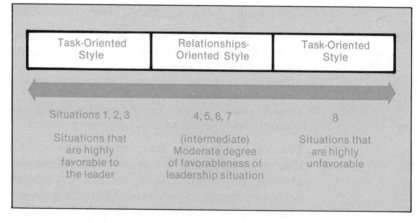

Task-Oriented Style	Relationships-Oriented Style	Task-Oriented Style

Situations 1, 2, 3 | 4, 5, 6, 7 | 8

Situations that are highly favorable to the leader | (intermediate) Moderate degree of favorableness of leadership situation | Situations that are highly unfavorable

relationship-oriented style is more effective in situations 4, 5, 6, and 7. As demonstrated by Fiedler's theory, the most effective leadership style is contingent on several situational factors.

Hersey and Blanchard's Situational Leadership Theory

situational leadership theory

Paul Hersey and Kenneth Blanchard have developed a situational leadership theory that has attracted considerable attention on the part of managers.[14] **Hersey and Blanchard's situational leadership theory** is based on the notion that the most effective leadership style varies according to the level of maturity of the followers and demands of the situation. Their model uses two dimensions of leadership behavior — task and relationship. These are similar to the classifications used in the Ohio State leadership model and Blake and Mouton's managerial grid. Hersey and Blanchard argue that an effective leader is one who can diagnose the demands of the situation and the level of maturity of the followers and use an appropriate leadership style. Their theory is based on a relationship among these factors:

task behavior

relationship behavior

task-relevant maturity

- The amount of **task behavior** the leader exhibits — providing direction and emphasis on getting the job done
- The amount of **relationship behavior** the leader provides — consideration of people, level of emotional support for people
- The level of **task-relevant maturity** followers exhibit toward the specific goal, task or function that the leader wants accomplished.

The key concept of their leadership theory is the level of task-relevant maturity of the followers. Maturity is not defined as age or psychological stability. The maturity level of the followers is defined as:

- A desire for achievement — level of achievement motivation based on the need to set high but attainable goals
- The willingness and ability to accept responsibility
- Education and/or experience and skills relevant to the particular task.

A leader should consider the level of maturity of his or her followers only in relation to the work or job to be performed. Employees are mature when they have the experience and skills as well as the desire to achieve and are capable of assuming responsibility. For example, an accountant may be very mature when preparing quarterly tax reports for Revenue Canada, but may not exhibit the same level of maturity when preparing written audits of the company's operations. The accountant does not need much direction (task-related behavior) from the manager when preparing tax reports, but may require considerably more supervision and direction when preparing and writing audits. He or she may not have the skills and/or motivation to prepare audits but, with proper training, direction, and encouragement, can assume greater responsibility in this area.

As illustrated in Figure 12-7, the appropriate leadership style varies according to the maturity level (represented by M1 through M4) of the followers. There are four distinct leadership styles that are appropriate given different levels of subordinate maturity. As the task-relevant maturity level of followers increases, the manager should reduce task behavior and increase relationship behavior. These changes are illustrated as follows:

FIGURE 12-7
Situational
leadership
SOURCE Paul Hersey and
Kenneth Blanchard,
Center for Leadership
Studies, California
American University,
1977. Reprinted by
permission.

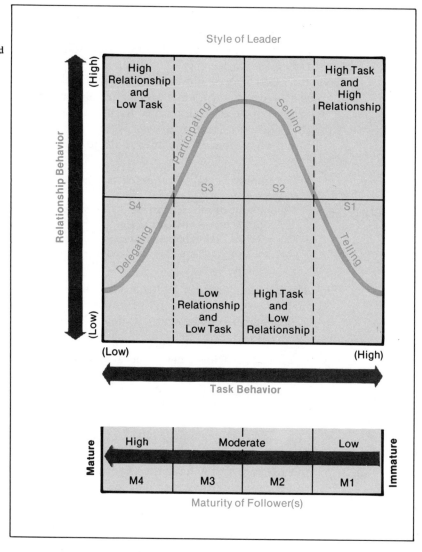

S1 — Telling	High task
	Low relationship
S2 — Selling	High task
	High relationship
S3 — Participating	High relationship
	Low task
S4 — Delegating	Low relationship
	Low task

With the S1 (Telling) leadership style, the leader uses one-way communication, defines the goals and roles of employees, and tells them what, how, when, and where to do the work. This style is very appropriate when dealing with subordinates who lack task-relevant maturity. For example, in supervising a group of relatively new, inexperienced employees, a high level of task-directed behavior and low-relationship behavior may be an appropriate leadership approach. Inexperienced employees need to be told what to do and how to accomplish their assigned tasks.

As employees learn their jobs, the manager begins to use an S2 leadership style. There is still a need for a high level of task behavior, since the employees do not yet have the experience or skills to assume more responsibility, but the manager provides a higher level of emotional support — high-relationship behavior. The manager encourages the employees and demonstrates greater trust and confidence in them.

The S3 leadership style is suitable when employees possess considerable task-relevant maturity. As employees become more experienced and skilled, as well as more achievement motivated and more willing to assume responsibility, the leader should reduce the amount of task behavior but continue the high level of emotional support and consideration. A continuation of a high level of relationship behavior is the manager's way of reinforcing the employees' responsible performance. Thus, S3 — high-relationship and low-task behavior — becomes the appropriate leadership style.

The S4 leadership style is for followers with the highest level of task maturity. At this stage, the employees are very skilled and experienced, possess high achievement motivation, and are capable of exercising self-control. The leadership style that is most appropriate for this situation is S4 — low relationship and low task. At this point the employees no longer need or expect a high level of supportive or task behavior from their leader.

Hersey and Blanchard argue that leadership style and effectiveness can be measured, and they have designed an instrument for this purpose — the Leader Effectiveness and Adaptability Description (LEAD). The LEAD provides feedback on leadership style and the effectiveness of the individual completing the instrument.[15]

You should not conclude from this discussion that it is easy to determine the appropriate leadership style. It can be difficult to diagnose the maturity level of followers, as well as the specific needs of a situation. A leader must have insight into the abilities, needs, demands, and expectations of the followers and be aware that these can and do change over time. Also, managers must recognize the need to adapt or change their style of leadership whenever the level of maturity of followers changes. Maturity levels can change for many reasons — for instance, a change in jobs, personal or family problems, or a switch in the present job to new technology. For example, a sales manager has been using an S4 leadership style in supervising John, who is normally a highly productive sales representative. But suppose that John's pending divorce has recently been adversely affecting his

MANAGEMENT IN PRACTICE

Employee Maturity

Andrew Grove is president of Intel Corporation, one of North America's premier high-technology companies. He notes that there is no single style of leadership which works best in all situations. Rather, a subordinate's task-relevant maturity (TRM) determines the style a leader should adopt in order to be effective. Task-relevant maturity is a combination of a person's achievement orientation and readiness to take responsibility, as well as his or her education, training, and experience. A person could have high maturity in one task and low maturity in another.

Grove says that managers should strive to increase the TRM of their subordinates because they need to spend less time with a high TRM subordinate. As well, high TRM subordinates are internally motivated and work more effectively for the company.

SOURCE Adapted from Andrew S. Grove, "What Kind of Boss Works Best?" *Canadian Business* (March 1984): 82-86.

performance. In this situation, the sales manager might increase both the level of task and relationship behavior in order to provide John with the direction, support, and confidence he may need to cope with his personal problems and improve his sales performance.

In a recent review of contingency leadership theories, Graeff found that, for situational leadership to be effective, the leader must come to two conclusions: (1) the leader must be flexible in behavior; habitual patterns must be broken, and (2) the subordinate must be recognized as a major situational determinant. Drawing these conclusions involves not only careful observation of behavior, but the ability to interpret that behavior in a meaningful way.[16]

In summary, Hersey and Blanchard's theory provides a useful and understandable framework for situational leadership. In essence, their model suggests that there is no one best leadership style that meets the needs of all situations. Rather, a manager's leadership style must be adaptable and flexible enough to meet the changing needs of employees and situations. The effective manager is one who can change styles as employees develop and change or as required by the situation.

Vroom and Yetton's Leadership Decision-Making Model

leadership decision-making model

Vroom and Yetton's **leadership decision-making model** is based on the idea that a leader must decide how much participation subordinates should be allowed when making decisions.[17] Such participation can range widely. At one extreme, the manager might allow no participation and simply make the decision: an autocratic style. At the other extreme, the manager might stress group problem solving and allow subordinates total freedom to make the decision: a participative style.

Vroom and Yetton suggested that each of these leadership styles can be effective, depending on the leader's answers to five work-related questions:

- Do I [the leader] have sufficient information to make a good decision?
- Is there a quality requirement in the decision?
- Is the decision problem-structured?
- Is subordinate acceptance of the decision important?
- Do subordinates share the organization's goals?

Vroom and Yetton have developed a detailed model to guide managers through this process. To give you a general idea of how their model works, consider this case. A leader of a group of clerks in an insurance company is dissatisfied with the present filing system and wants to introduce a new one. The leader doesn't really know much about alternative filing systems, but she does know that the clerks must be comfortable with any new system or their productivity will decline. Her relations with the clerks are good and the clerks identify with the company, but they are consistently quite vocal about the routine procedures in their department.

What style of leadership should be used in this situation? Before the leader decides, she must ask herself the questions Vroom and Yetton pose. In this case, the answers would probably be:

- No, I (the leader) do not have sufficient information to make the decision alone.
- Yes, there is a quality requirement because I want to have a good system.
- No, the decision is not problem-structured — how to go about introducing a new filing system is not obvious.
- Yes, because subordinates want a say in how the department operates.
- Yes, subordinates identify readily with the goals of the organization.

Based on this series of answers, Vroom and Yetton would say that the leader should exhibit a highly participative style of leadership and should let subordinates actually make the decision. In the context of this situation, their suggestion seems to make good practical sense.

What happens if one of the situational features changes? Suppose subordinates did not identify with the goals of the organization. The best leadership style then would still be a participative style, but the leader must make the final decision based on the organization's goals.

Vroom and Yetton's theory is that several leadership styles may be effective or feasible for certain problems, but for other problems only one style will work. Their theory is clearly situational because the leader cannot decide on the appropriate leadership style until the specific situation has been analyzed.

GENERAL FACTORS AFFECTING CHOICE OF LEADERSHIP STYLE

The notion that there is one best leadership style has been criticized as being unrealistic and simplistic. It is illogical to assume that the same leadership style would be equally effective in managing such diverse groups as auto assemblers, research scientists, clerk-typists, college professors, lawyers, or construction workers. The most effective leadership style is one that meets the needs of each particular situation. This requires a careful consideration of characteristics of the leader, the followers, and the specific situation (see Figure 12-8).

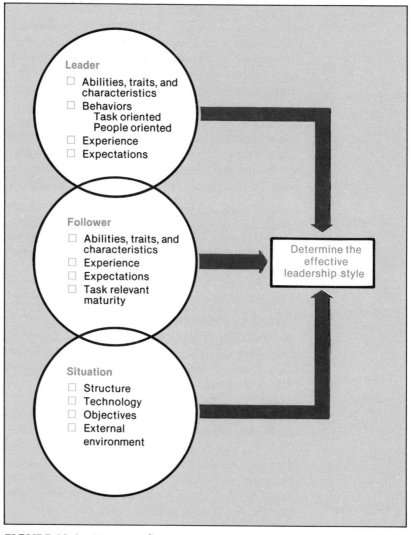

FIGURE 12-8 Factors influencing leadership style

MANAGEMENT IN PRACTICE

A Change in Leadership Style at CN

On January 1, 1987 chairperson Maurice Le-Clair unexpectedly resigned from CN. Ronald Lawless, the man passed over for the job when LeClair was originally appointed, took over. Insiders note that the management styles of the two men are quite different. Lawless, who has worked for CN for 46 years, is confident and friendly and seen as a "people's man" who understands the needs of the corporation and its customers. LeClair was seen as aloof and unconcerned about profit (but he disagrees with that assessment).

The two men had quite different work histories and this contributed to their different management styles. Lawless started as a CN clerk and worked his way up the ladder by developing his skills in marketing. LeClair, on the other hand, was originally a medical doctor and then a federal bureaucrat before he was appointed chairperson of CN in 1982.

The two men also differed over what role CN should play in the Canadian economy.

LeClair felt the company should work closely with the federal government to address issues like regional disparities, and that the corporation was putting too much emphasis on profitability. Lawless felt the opposite.

LeClair considered himself to be the head of a holding company with many diverse interests. He gave managers a free hand to run their operations as they wanted, as long as they met predetermined goals. He did not get involved in day-to-day operations. By contrast, Lawless has a hands-on style and works with managers not only to set goals, but to develop plans to achieve them. He will therefore be closer to the day-to-day operations of the company. Perhaps Lawless is better able to do this since he came up through the ranks and understands many of the details of company operations.

SOURCE   Adapted from Cecil Foster, "Lawless Putting Personal Stamp On CN," *The Globe and Mail* (May 4, 1987): B1–B2.

Factors Related to the Manager

Self-knowledge is important to effective leadership. Leaders have different abilities and goals; they have also had different experiences. Through those experiences, they develop basic beliefs about people. Some think that people must be threatened to make them work. Others believe in encouraging workers and rewarding them for performance. Although managers should be flexible in the choice of a leadership style, they usually perform better if they use a style consistent with their personal beliefs.

The manager's professional and technical competence also affects leadership style. Not only are competent managers more confident, but workers are also less likely to challenge or question them. Although this might suggest that the manager would be more autocratic, in fact, it permits the manager more flexibility in leadership styles. Thus, a leader could be a gentle, supportive manager in certain situations and a stern disciplinarian in others.

Factors Related to the Workers

Characteristics of subordinates must also be taken into account when deciding on leadership style. One important consideration is the work ethic of subordinates. Some workers feel that work is, in and of itself, satisfying, pleasurable, and fulfilling. Such workers are easy to motivate. Others see work as an unpleasant way to get money. Perhaps rewards and punishments are the only effective motivators for these workers.

Workers' attitudes toward authority must also be considered. Some believe that the job of the manager is to tell them what to do. They do not want to help make decisions. Others wish to make all the decisions; they resist any exercise of authority by the leader.

The maturity level of subordinates influences leadership style. Some workers are mature in the way they approach their work. They exercise initiative not only in doing their job but also in self-development. Others may have to be watched quite closely to obtain even minimum performance. Workers may handle one aspect of their job maturely yet be quite immature in other aspects.

Another factor is the experience level and skill of subordinates. The leadership style used with a trainee will be different from that used with an experienced craftsperson. A more directive style may prove best for the trainee, while the craftsperson may need no direction at all.

For some employees an autocratic style will work best. This may be particularly true in extremely favorable or extremely unfavorable situations. Studies have shown, however, that workers generally respond more favorably to a participative approach. This appears to be true for subordinates exhibiting a very wide range of characteristics.[18] Even at companies with a strong authority structure, workers tend to be more highly motivated if they take part in the decision-making process.

Factors Related to the Situation

Many situational factors affect the supervisor's leadership style. Some of the major situational factors are described below.

- *Number of people in the work group:* Managers can give more individualized attention in smaller work groups. As group size increases, management by exception may tend to be used.
- *Kinds of tasks:* Jobs involving simple repetition may permit the manager to be more autocratic. Workers with creative or complex jobs require more freedom.

- *Situational stress:* Managers often shift to a more autocratic style when the going gets tough. The firm may be in financial difficulties, and the management may be experiencing unusual pressure to increase output. The supervisor should be careful in changing leadership styles and should not do so as a reflex action.
- *Objectives of the unit:* The specific objectives the manager is expected to accomplish affect leadership style. If the only objective is to get the job done immediately, the use of strong authority may be justified, even though it may make workers unhappy. When there is an important rush project, subordinates are more likely to accept simply being told what to do.
- *Whether or not the company has a union:* Union workers often do not want to participate in management. They may believe that supervisors should supervise and workers should work. Managers in nonunion firms are able to adopt a wider range of leadership styles. Being able to maintain nonunion status has been a major strength of IBM management.
- *Leadership style of the manager's boss:* Managers tend to lead as they are led. If the boss is autocratic, managers may lean toward this leadership style. The example set by Thomas Watson, Sr., still guides managers throughout IBM.
- *Relationship of the manager with subordinates:* If the relationship is one of mutual respect, the manager will usually let workers take part in managing themselves. Workers, too, are likely to contribute more when they are respected and liked by their supervisor. Because of a careful selection process at IBM, employees tend to be "a cut above average" and thus can be given extra responsibility.

After reading the preceding list, your first reaction might be to throw up your hands in despair. You might say, "I want to know exactly what leadership style to use." There is no absolute answer. We question those who say there is. In the 1980s, organizations are moving toward flatter, more decentralized structures. This has increased, not decreased, the need for interdependence, collaboration, communication and flexibility in leadership style.[19]

One final aspect of the situation that may have an impact on leadership is the possibility that there are "substitutes for leadership." Leadership may not be crucial if certain other characteristics of the work place help employees get their work done properly even without much guidance. Clearly defined jobs, a strong informal organization, and a professional orientation on the part of employees are examples of substitutes for leadership. They can help employees to know what to do even though the leader may not give them direction. These substitutes for leadership may be very important in some situations, and unimportant in others. For example, in mass-production, jobs on the production line may be rigidly defined and leadership may not have a dramatic impact on employees. In an unstructured work atmosphere, however, the leader should have a major impact on employee job satisfaction and output.

MANAGEMENT IN PRACTICE

Employee Involvement at Ford Canada

There has been a big change in management's attitude at Ford Motor's engine plant at Windsor, Ontario. Management has discovered that workers have excellent ideas about how to improve production operations. The change in thinking is called Employee Involvement (EI), and means that supervisors and employees work as a team to come up with better ways to make automobile engines.

Employee involvement is a change from the adversarial system (labor vs management) that existed at Ford for so many years. Changing to the EI system has involved training people to change their old views of the company. So far, Ford has spent more than $1 million on training. For example, hourly workers get 20 hours of training in problem solving and 20 hours in statistical process control. Managers are also being trained to deal with their new employee relations.

The EI program has yielded very positive results. Ford has experienced a 59 percent improvement in quality (as measured by a reduction in customer warranty claims), and absenteeism has dropped sharply at the plants that use EI. For example, in November 1982 (before the EI program was introduced), 400 workers were absent from work at the Windsor plant; by November 1983, only 144 workers were absent during the month. The program has also had an impact on workers' compensation claims. During November 1983, Windsor's five plants had only 37 people on workers' compensation, while the Oakville plant (which has far fewer workers) had 125.

SOURCE Adapted from Daniel Stoffman, "Blue-Collar Turnaround Artists," *Canadian Business* (February 1984): 38.

OPENING INCIDENT REVISITED

Mission Chapel

At the Mission Chapel, Carolyn Barnes was concerned about whether her leadership style was appropriate for the chapel choir. What do the leadership theories discussed in this chapter suggest?

The situational leadership theory says that subordinate maturity levels are the key to determining effective leader behavior. Ten members of the choir are mature (they know what to do technically) while 35 are in various stages of immaturity. The theory suggests that different styles are appropriate for these two groups. Unfortunately, it is not feasible for Barnes to treat the high and low maturity people differently because the choir must perform as a group. Perhaps the maturity level of the inexperienced members will improve as time passes and they become technically more capable. Barnes can then use a more participative

style. For the moment, however, the theory suggests that an autocratic style is most appropriate.

Using Fiedler's contingency model to analyze Barnes's situation, the following criteria can be established. Leader-member relations are good, task structure is high (music is very structured), and leader position power is low (the choir members are volunteers). Given this combination, an autocratic style is most appropriate.

The path-goal model says that the leader should help subordinates get to their goals. The choir members have good performance as one of their goals; the nonprofessional singers would probably welcome guidance from a professional. As their leader, Barnes should probably adopt an autocratic style. Presumably, the professional members of the choir will be less satisfied with this style as they know what to do, but, as noted above, the trained and untrained members cannot be treated differently because of the nature of the task.

On balance, the analysis of the situation using these contingency leadership theories suggests that Barnes continue with her present directive style. The absenteeism may simply be an effect of the volunteer nature of the choir, while the talking and joking may indicate the interest and enthusiasm of the members. In neither case is Barnes's leadership style causing problems.

SUMMARY

Effective leadership is essential to the survival and growth of every organization. Leadership guides the process of motivating and directing others toward the accomplishment of goals. The requirements for being an effective manager and the definition of the most effective leadership style have been of concern to managers for generations and have been the subject of thousands of research studies. However, no simple list of traits or behaviors has been identified that is consistently related to effective leadership. In fact, the basic conclusion of these studies is that there is no one most effective leadership style.

The early studies of leadership attempted to identify universal traits and characteristics of effective leaders. Traits relating to physical characteristics, personality, or intelligence were studied to determine if they were related to effective leadership. For the most part, research has not shown that traits alone can distinguish effective from ineffective leaders. Despite these findings, the trait approach to the study of leadership has continued. Ghiselli has identified traits that his extensive research indicates are related to effective leadership. These include supervisory ability, need for occupational achievement, intelligence, decisiveness, self-assurance, and initiative.

Dissatisfaction with the trait approach to the study of leadership caused the research emphasis to shift to the behavior and actions of leaders. The behavioral theories identified two basic dimensions of leadership behavior. Although these behaviors have been referred to by several different names, they are the leader's behavior and concern for (1) the accomplishment of tasks (task behavior) and (2) the relationship with people (relationship behavior). One of the most widely known leadership theories is Blake and Mouton's managerial grid. The two dimensions of leadership behavior identified in the 9 × 9 managerial grid are "concern for people" and "concern for production." Five basic styles of leadership on the grid were: do nothing (1,1), task centered (9,1), country club (1,9), "organizational man" (5,5) and team builder (9,9). Blake and Mouton suggest that the 9,9 style of leadership is the most effective and achieves the best results in performance.

In recent years, considerable attention has been given to the situational approach to the study of leadership. The basic conclusion of this approach is that the most effective leaders are neither task centered nor people centered. Rather, effective leaders must be flexible enough to adopt a leadership style that fits their needs as well as the needs of their subordinates and the situation.

The theories of Fiedler, Hersey and Blanchard, House, and Vroom and Yetton suggest there is no one most effective style of leadership that is appropriate to every situation. In Fiedler's theory, the degree of favorableness or unfavorableness of the situation determines the style of leadership that is most effective. Hersey and Blanchard's theory is based on the notion that the most effective leadership style varies according to the level of maturity of the followers and the demands of the situation. Their theory offers four basic combinations of the task and relationship behavior of the leader. For instance, if the leader is dealing with "highly mature followers" the appropriate leadership style might be low emphasis on both relationships and task behavior. House's path-goal theory says that the role of the leader is to clarify the subordinates' performance goals and how these goals can be achieved. Vroom and Yetton's decision-making model requires managers to answer several work-related questions before they decide which leadership style to use.

Perhaps the most realistic approach to leadership is an integrated one that carefully considers the forces in the leader, the followers, and the situation. To be truly effective in achieving goals, the leader must recognize that no one approach will be effective in all circumstances.

REVIEW QUESTIONS

1. What is meant by the term "leadership"? Why is it important to management?
2. What is the distinction between management and leadership? How is it possible to be a good leader but an ineffective manager?
3. In the chapter, how did leadership cause the bankruptcy of the mobile home company?
4. Briefly describe and contrast the types of power a leader may possess to influence the behavior of others.
5. What is the trait approach to the study of leadership? To what extent are universal traits related to effective leadership?
6. List several significant traits identified by the research of Edwin Ghiselli as important for effective leadership.
7. What are the four basic styles or systems of management identified by Rensis Likert? Explain each.

8. Describe the five leadership styles presented in the managerial grid. Which style is recommended as most effective by Blake and Mouton?

9. What were the Ohio State leadership studies? What basic dimensions of leadership behavior were identified? What were some of the factors that determined the most effective style of leadership?

10. What basic conclusion can be derived from the Tannenbaum and Schmidt leadership continuum? What factors should be considered before choosing a given style of leadership?

11. What is the basic contention of Fiedler's theory of leadership? In what situations are task-centered leaders most effective? people-centered leaders?

12. Briefly explain Hersey and Blanchard's situational leadership theory. What is the key concept of their theory?

13. Briefly explain Vroom and Yetton's leadership decision-making idea. How does their approach contrast and compare with Hersey and Blanchard's theory?

14. Describe what is meant by an integrated approach to leadership.

EXERCISES

1. Assume you have just been promoted to the position of office manager in charge of 12 clerical personnel — eight typists and four general clerks. The previous manager was removed from the position because the office staff members were not able to complete their work on schedule. In addition, the office experienced excessive turnover of employees, and several of the employees had expressed concern about poor quality of work and the bad attitude of the clerical staff. Under the previous manager, the employees showed little interest in their jobs and generally viewed the office manager as a "soft touch."
   a. What style of leadership would you utilize as you assume the position of office manager?
   b. Explain, in terms of situational leadership theory presented in this chapter, how your leadership style might change, should output improve and employee turnover decrease.

2. Go to the library and make a copy of the article "So You Want To Know Your Leadership Style?" by Paul Hersey and Kenneth Blanchard, *Training and Development Journal* (February 1974): 22–32. Complete the Leader Adaptability and Style Inventory (LASI) instrument contained in the article. Then read the article. What is your leadership style as per the LASI? Discuss in class.

3. Assume you are a newly appointed manager over the following types of workers. What leadership style would you suggest? De-

fend your response in view of the leadership theories you have studied.

a. New, untrained machine operator.
b. Skilled, highly motivated mechanic.
c. Research scientist.
d. Tenured full professor at a major university.

CASE STUDY

A Natural-Born Leader

"Phil is a natural-born leader," said Jim Hollis, the plant manager, as he looked out over the factory floor from the production manager's office.

"Yes," said the production manager. "I believe those carpenters would follow him off the end of the earth."

Phil Granger is the carpentry supervisor in the shipping department at the Jacobs Castings Company. He is a big man, six-foot-four, 240 pounds. He has a booming voice. His size and the steel-blue sternness of his eyes belie a gentle spirit. He avoids confrontations and is known to be patient and lenient with subordinates. Phil and his crew of six make wooden boxes for packaging the several hundred custom-made castings that Jacobs ships every day. The work requires little skill, but it is vital to the plant.

Before Phil took over, the carpentry division was a bottleneck. Shipments were often delayed for days because the carpentry work just did not seem to get done. Turnover in the department had been high. The carpenters seemed to have more personal problems than other workers in the plant.

When Phil took over, everything seemed to change almost immediately. The work was caught up within a few days, and castings no longer had to wait for more than a day to be shipped. The carpenters also seemed happier. During the first two months that Phil was in charge, there was not a single complaint and only one day was lost because of absenteeism.

As Phil sketched the boxes to be made the next morning, he thought, "I sure would like to go home a little early today, but I want the others to know I'm trying as hard as they are. Anyway, I need to finish these sketches so I'll have time to help with the boxes in the morning. I also want to check with Brad about his new baby before he leaves today. Since I took him around and showed him how our work affected the rest of the plant, he sure has done a great job."

QUESTIONS

1. Is Phil a natural-born leader? Explain.
2. What accounts for the success of the carpentry division? Defend your answer.

CASE STUDY

The Unhappy Salesman

Art Cranston was a regional sales manager for a major computer manufacturer. In this position he supervised 22 industrial salespeople who sold computers, word processors, and other office equipment to business and educational organizations. Supervising the sales force involved setting sales quotas and targets after discussion with the salespeople, checking on performance levels, developing and monitoring compensation programs, allocating salespeople to different territories, as well as the usual duties performed by sales managers. Salespeople were paid on a salary-plus-commission basis, with the salary portion being small enough that it did not provide an adequate standard of living. Cranston assumed that the commission component would motivate the salespeople to sell more aggressively.

On balance, the performance of the sales force was quite good, although two problems surfaced. One of these was turnover, which was averaging 23 percent per year. Cranston was concerned about this, but he also knew that high turnover was a common problem in selling occupations where incentive compensation schemes were used. His major concern about turnover was the time and money he had to spend looking for new salespeople and then training them to do the job the right way.

The other problem concerned two salespeople who chronically failed to reach their objectives. In an attempt to overcome this problem, Cranston had instituted a Management by Objectives system. He felt that, if goals were mutually decided on by the salesperson and the boss, the salesperson would be more committed to the goals and would work harder to achieve them. This system improved the performance of salespeople who were already satisfactory, but it had no effect on the two low performers. Over a period of several years Cranston had developed a detailed system that all salespeople used when they called on prospects. The feedback he received from salespeople was that the system was helpful in improving their sales. Cranston also heard comments such as: "Art, you're very task-oriented, but we're happy because what you're doing puts more money in our pockets." These views were widely held by the sales staff but not by the two problem employees.

At a sales convention in Banff during October, Cranston happened to overhear Jim Brewer (a top salesman) arguing loudly with Mike O'Donnell (one of the poor performers) about the nature of incentive schemes:

Brewer: I think our compensation scheme is really good. It forces a guy to keep moving. If he does that, he makes a lot of money and the company also benefits.

O'Donnell: That's easy for you to say! What about me? I can't make big money with the compensation scheme we're using.

Brewer: That's because you're not working hard enough.

O'Donnell: What do you know about how hard I work? We hardly ever see each other except at these conventions!

Brewer: You must not be working hard enough if you aren't making much money.

O'Donnell: I'm working very hard! The problem is that Cranston doesn't have any feeling for people. All he thinks about is sales volume. This incentive scheme just won't work for everyone, because each person is unique.

Brewer: Are you saying Cranston should develop a unique incentive scheme for each salesperson?

O'Donnell: Yes.

Brewer: That's ridiculous. Then everyone would be running around worrying about whether their deal was better or worse than someone else's. Besides, the paperwork would be outrageous.

O'Donnell: Well, the present system isn't working!

Brewer: That's not what most of the people here would say. You're out in left field on this one!

After hearing this conversation, Cranston was both pleased and disturbed. He felt that most of the salespeople would agree with Brewer, but he also knew that O'Donnell firmly believed what he was saying. He wondered what all this meant for his leadership of the salesforce.

QUESTIONS

1. Should Cranston try to use different leadership styles with different salespeople? Is this feasible?
2. What can Cranston do to improve the performance of O'Donnell and other low performers?
3. Use the leadership theories in this chapter to draw some conclusions about the most appropriate style of leadership for Cranston. What are the shortcomings of these schemes?

ENDNOTES

[1] A. Zaleznik, "Managers and Leaders: Are they Different?" *Harvard Business Review* (May 1977): 67–68.

[2] R. J. House, "A 1976 Theory of Charismatic Leadership," in J. G. Hunt and L. L. Larson (eds.), *Leadership: The Cutting Edge* (Carbondale, Ill.: Southern Illinois University Press, 1976): 189–207.

[3] N. M. Tichy and D. O. Ulrich, "The Leadership Challenge — A Call for the Transformational Leader," *Sloan Management Review* (Fall, 1984): 59–68.

[4] George Kozmetzky, *Transformational Management* (Cambridge, Mass.: Ballinger Publishing, 1985).

[5] Edwin Ghiselli, *Explorations in Managerial Talent* (Pacific Palisades, Cal.: Goodyear, 1971).

[6] R. W. Rice, D. Instone, and J. H. Adams, "Leader Sex, Leader Success, and Leadership Process: Two Field Studies," *Journal of Applied Psychology* (February 1984): 27.

[7] Rensis Likert, *The Human Organization* (New York: McGraw-Hill, 1967).

[8] Used with permission of Robert R. Blake and Jane S. Mouton, *The New Managerial Grid* (Houston: Gulf Publishing, 1978): 11.

[9] Blake and Mouton.

[10] A. W. Halpin and B. J. Winer, "A Factorial Study of the Leader Behavior Descriptions," in R. M. Stogdill and A. E. Coons (eds.), *Leader Behavior: Its Description and Measurement* (Columbus: Ohio State University, Bureau of Business Research, 1957.)

[11] Robert House, "A Path-Goal Theory of Leadership Effectiveness," *Administrative Science Quarterly* 16 (September 1971): 321–338."

[12] Alan C. Filley, Robert House, and Steven Kerr, *Managerial Process and Organizational Behavior* (Glenview, Ill.: Scott, Foresman, 1976): 256–260.

[13] Fred E. Fiedler, *A Theory of Leadership Effectiveness* (New York: McGraw-Hill, 1967).

[14] Paul Hersey and Kenneth Blanchard, *Management of Organizational Behavior: Utilizing Human Resources*, 3d ed. (Englewood Cliffs, N.J.: Prentice-Hall, 1977): 94–95.

[15] See Paul Hersey and Kenneth Blanchard, "So You Want to Know Your Leadership Style?" *Training and Development Journal* (February 1974): 22–32. This article contains the Leader Adaptability and Style Inventory (LASI), an instrument that can be used to examine your leadership behavior, style adaptability, and effectiveness. Since this article, the LASI has become the Leader Effectiveness and Adaptability Description (LEAD). Information, LEAD inventories and training materials may be obtained from the Center for Leadership Studies, 17253 Caminito Canasto, Rancho Bernardo, San Diego, CA 92127.

[16]C. L. Graeff, "The Situational Leadership Theory: A Critical View," *Academy of Management Review* (April 1983): 290.

[17]V. Vroom and P. Yetton, *The Leadership Decision Making Model* (Pittsburgh: University of Pittsburgh Press, 1973).

[18]M. E. Heilman, H. A. Hornstein, J. H. Cage, and J. K. Herschdag, "Reactions to Prescribed Leader Behavior as a Function of Role Perspective: The Case of the Vroom-Yetton Model," *Journal of Applied Psychology* (February 1984): 50.

[19]R. Lippitt, "The Changing Leader-Follower Relationships of the 1980s," *Journal of Applied Behavioral Science* 18 (March 1982): 396.

REFERENCES

Adams, Jerome; Rice, Robert W.; and Instone, Debra. "Follower Attitudes Toward Women and Judgements concerning Performance by Female and Male Leaders." *Academy of Management Journal* 27, no. 3 (September 1984): 636–643.

Burke, Michael, and Day, Russell. "A Cumulative Study of the Effectiveness of Managerial Training." *Journal of Applied Psychology* 71, (May 1986): 232–246.

Burke, W. W. "Leadership: Is There One Best Approach?" *Management Review* 69 (November 1980): 54–56.

Butler, Mark C., and Jones, Allan P. "Perceived Leader Behavior, Individual Characteristics, and Injury Occurrence in Hazardous Work Environments." *Journal of Applied Psychology* 64, no. 3 (June 1979): 299–304.

Carbone, T. C. "Theory X and Theory Y Revisited." *Managerial Planning* 29 (May-June 1981): 24–27.

Chitayat, Gideon, and Venezias, Itzhak. "Determinants of Management Styles in Business and Nonbusiness Organizations." *Journal of Applied Psychology* 69, (August 1984): 437–447.

Deszca, Gene, and Burke, Ronald. "Leader Behaviour in Managing Day-to-Day Job Performance and Subordinate Work Experiences." *Canadian Journal of Administrative Sciences* 2, (June 1985): 211–227.

Fiedler, F. E. "Job Engineering for Effective Leadership: A New Approach." *Management Review* 66 (September 1977): 29–31.

Fiedler, F. E. and Mahar, Linda. "The Effectiveness of Contingency Model Training: A Review of the Validation of Leader Match." *Personnel Psychology* 32, no. 1 (Spring 1979): 45–62.

Foster, Cecil. "An Iconoclastic Boss Is Turnaround Artist for Gray Coach." *The Globe and Mail* (March 2, 1987): B6.

_____."Lawless Putting Personal Stamp on CN." *The Globe and Mail* (May 4, 1987): B1–B2.

Fox, W. M. "Limits to the Use of Consultative-Participative Management." *California Management Review* 20 (Winter 1977): 17–22.

Green, S. G., and Nebeker, D. M. "Effects of Situational Factors and Leadership Style on Leader Behavior." *Organizational Behavior and Human Performance* 19 (August 1977): 368–377.

Greene, Charles N. "Questions of Causation in the Path-Goal Theory of Leadership." *Academy of Management Journal* 22, no. 1 (March 1979): 22–41.

Griffin, R. W. "Relationships among Individual, Task Design and Leader Behavior Variables." *Academy of Management Journal* 23 (December 1980): 665–683.

Grove, Andrew S. "What Kind of Boss are You?" *Canadian Business* 57, no. 3 (March 1984): 82.

Himes, G. K. "Management Leadership Styles." *Supervision* 42 (November 1980): 9–11.

Katz, R. "Influence of Group Conflict on Leadership Effectiveness." *Organizational Behavior and Human Performance* 20 (December 1977): 265–286.

Kimber, Stephen. "Rescue at Sea." *Canadian Business* 59, (October 1986): 68–73, 148.

Klimoski, R. J., and Hayes, N. J. "Leadership Behavior and Subordinate Motivation." *Personnel Psychology* 33 (Autumn 1980): 543–545.

Komaki, Judith. "Toward Effective Supervision: An Operant Analysis and Comparison of Managers at Work." *Journal of Applied Psychology* 71, (May 1986): 270–279.

Leister, A., et al. "Validation of Contingency Model Leadership Training: Leader Match." *Academy of Management Journal* 20 (September 1977): 464–470.

Likert, R. "Management Styles and the Human Component." *Management Review* 66 (October 1977): 23–28.

McNeil, Art. "Containing Chaos." *Canadian Business* 60, (January 1987): 62–65.

Meindl, J. R., and Ehrlich, S. "The Romance of Leadership and the Evaluation of Organizational Performance." *Academy of Management Journal* 30 (1987): 91–109.

Miner, Frederick C. Jr. "A Comparative Analysis of Three Diverse Group Decision Making Approaches." *Academy of Management Journal* 22, no. 1 (March 1979): 81–93.

Misumi, Jyuji. *The Behavioral Science of Leadership: An Interdisciplinary Japanese Research Program.* Ann Arbor, Michigan: University of Michigan Press, 1985.

Peters, Thomas J. "Leadership: Sad Facts and Silver Linings." *Harvard Business Review* 57, no. 6 (November-December 1979): 164–172.

Schriesheim, C. A., and Schriesheim, J. F. "Test of the Path-Goal Theory of Leadership and Some Suggested Direction for Future Research." *Personnel Psychology* 33 (Summer 1980): 368–370.

Sheridan, John E.; Vredenburgh, Donald J., and Abelson, Michael A. "Contextual Model of Leadership Influence in Hospital Units." *Academy of Management Journal* 27, no. 1 (March 1984): 57–78.

Sinetar, M. "Developing Leadership Potential." *Personnel Journal* 60 (March 1981): 193–196.

Stoffman, Daniel. "Blue Collar Turnaround Artists." *Canadian Business* 57, no. 2 (February 1984): 38.

Tichy, Noel, and Devanna, Mary Anne. *The Transformational Leader.* New York: Wiley and Sons, 1986.

Tjosvold, Dean; Andrews, Robert; and Jones, Hale. "Alternative Ways Leaders Can Use Authority." *Canadian Journal of Administrative Sciences* 2 (December 1985): 307–317.

Vroom, V., and Yetton, P. *The Leadership Decision Making Model.* Pittsburgh: University of Pittsburgh Press, 1973.

Wall, Jim. *Bosses.* Lexington: D. C. Heath and Co., 1986.

Yukl, Gary A. *Leadership in Organizations.* Englewood Cliffs, N.J.: Prentice-Hall, 1981.

Zaleznik, A. "Managers and Leaders: Are They Different?" *Harvard Business Review* 55 (May 1977): 67–68.

Zierden, William E. "Leading Through the Follower's Point of View." *Organizational Dynamics* 8, no. 4 (Spring 1980): 27–46.

Zwarun, Susan. "The Peter Principle." *Canadian Business* 59, (May 1986): 28–33.

13

Communication

KEY TERMS

communication	lateral	marginal listening
source (sender)	communication	evaluative listening
encoding	diagonal	nonevaluative
channel	communication	listening
decoding	barriers	body language
feedback	to communication	transactional
conceptual noise	technical barriers	analysis
communication	timing	Parent ego state
channels	communication	Child ego state
formal communica-	overload	Adult ego state
tion channels	filtering	teleconferencing
informal communi-	perception set	artificial
cation channels	empathy	intelligence

LEARNING OBJECTIVES

After completing this chapter you should be able to
1. Describe the basic components of the communication process and state what should be communicated to workers.
2. Describe the formal downward channels of communication.

3. Describe the formal upward channels of communication.
4. Describe the informal communication channels.
5. Identify the barriers that can cause breakdowns in communication.
6. Describe the facilitators that are available to improve communication.

OPENING INCIDENT

The Business School

Vincent Carletti was the associate dean of the business school at a large western Canadian university. In addition to his regular duties as associate dean, he was required to inform students whose grades were too low in person that they must withdraw from the business school. Late one afternoon Carletti's secretary informed him that Randall Lane, a fourth-year student, had arrived for his interview. Carletti had mixed feelings about Lane. Through the student grapevine, he had learned that Lane was the only member of his family ever to attend university and that Lane was very impressed with this fact. In addition, Lane was pleasant, hard working, and enthusiastic. Unfortunately, his grades had deteriorated to the point where he could not be allowed to graduate. Carletti therefore had the unpleasant task of informing Lane that, although he had reached fourth year, he was now required to withdraw.

Carletti asked Lane to step into his office, and the following conversation took place:

Carletti: Mr. Lane, I have been examining your scholastic records in some detail during the last few days. I regret to inform you that your grade point average has dropped too low for you to be allowed to graduate from the business school.

Lane (calmly): I admit I've been having grade trouble lately, but I believe I can raise them in time to graduate.

Carletti: I'm afraid you didn't understand me. You see, your grade point has dropped to a level where you must withdraw from the business school. It will be impossible for you to graduate with a business degree.

Lane (still calmly): But I only have four courses left before I graduate. Just let me complete those four courses and then I'll be able to graduate.

Carletti (getting slightly annoyed): Even if you do complete those four courses, you can't graduate because your grade point average is too low. Just forget the four courses; you're going to have to withdraw.

Lane (remaining calm): But once I complete the four courses, I will have satisfied all the requirements for graduation. That will solve the problem, won't it?

Carletti (getting angry): No, it won't solve the problem! Forget about those four courses! We have a requirement here that you must maintain a certain grade point average to graduate. You've known about it for three years. You haven't maintained it, so you won't be allowed to graduate. It's very simple. Can't you see that?

Lane (remaining very calm): But I only have four courses left before I graduate. I don't feel that it's reasonable to require me to withdraw when I'm so close to graduation.

Carletti (totally exasperated): I give up! You can sit there all day pretending everything is fine and you only have "four courses to complete and then you'll graduate," but that won't change reality. You'll get your ejection notice from the registrar and that will be that! Goodbye!

The exchange between Vincent Carletti and Randall Lane is an example of an unfortunate communication breakdown. Breakdowns in communication occur frequently in all types of organizations, and they have a negative effect on both interpersonal relationships and overall effectiveness. Even in organizations with a participative management attitude, with good leadership, and high employee motivation — poor communication can have a negative effect on production. Good communication and the ability to handle conflict effectively are essential to positive managerial influence. Given these facts, it is important that practicing managers and students aspiring to management positions understand how good communication skills can enhance their own careers and the performance of the organizations for which they work.

Managers spend a large portion of their time communicating with others — as much as 75 percent by some estimates. Accordingly, one of the worst criticisms that a manager can receive from peers, superiors, and subordinates is that he or she cannot communicate effectively. In a previous chapter, we defined management as the accomplishment of objectives through the efforts of other people. In order for an employee to achieve the goals of the manager, he or she must know what the supervisor wants to accomplish. When the goals of the manager do not match what has actually been completed, a breakdown in communication is often found to be the source of the difficulty. When a frustrated manager says: "You did what you thought I meant very effectively; unfortunately, that was not what I wanted you to do" — clearly communication did not take place.

communication

Communication is the transfer of meaning and understanding between people through verbal and nonverbal means in order to affect behavior and achieve desired results. In an organization, communication has two primary purposes. First, it provides the means by which the objectives of the firm are accomplished. The manner in which plans are to be implemented and actions coordinated to achieve a particular goal must be communicated to the individuals who must accomplish the task. Second, communication provides the means by which members of the firm may be stimulated to accomplish organization plans willingly and enthusiastically.

The inability to communicate effectively can severely hamper a manager in the accomplishment of his or her duties. In fact, a person cannot be effective as a manager unless he or she possesses good communication skills. Consider the manager who performs tasks that a subordinate should be doing, claiming that he or she is doing the job because the worker is incapable of doing the assigned job. This is often not really the case; the manager may actually be incapable of communicating his or her goals effectively. Rather than risk giving unclear instructions, the manager decides to do the work of the subordinate. In this instance, the failure to communicate has caused the efficiency of the unit to deteriorate because neither the subordinate nor the manager are doing the work for which they were hired.

A crucial aspect of communication is that it is a learned quality. A person who truly wants to improve his or her ability to communicate can do so. In this chapter we first address the issue of communication through the communication process. Once each phase of the process is understood, existing problem areas and weaknesses in your own or other people's communications can be identified and corrected. Second, we note what should be communicated to employees to enhance their motivation and productivity. Third, we discuss the main organizational channels of communication. Fourth, barriers and facilitators to communication are examined in some detail to help managers to avoid poor communication practices.

THE COMMUNICATION PROCESS

Communication takes place only when two or more people are involved. Shouting for help on a desert island is not communication; similarly, if a professor lectures and no one listens or understands, there is no communication. The basic elements in the communication process are shown in Figure 13-1. Each step in the sequence is critical to the ultimate success of the process.

source

The **source**, or sender, is the person who has an idea or message to communicate to another person or group. The credibility of the source's communication depends on the characteristics of the source. A communicator can use a number of tactics to convince the receiver to accept the communication. These include playing on the emotions of the receiver, using logical arguments, or asking the receiver to accept what is being said because the source is trustworthy.

encoding

Once the source has decided what message is to be conveyed, the message must be put in a form that the receiver can understand. The message emerges as a result of **encoding**. Senders must encode their messages or ideas into symbols that their receivers will understand. Words on a page are symbols to readers. The sound of a siren on a busy highway may mean that there is traffic trouble ahead.

channel

The actual means by which the message is transmitted to the receiver is the communication **channel**. A number of channels may be used to transmit a message. The spoken word can be used through such channels as face-to-face communication, telephone, radio, and television. Books, articles, memos, and letters can serve as channels for the written word. The senses of sight, sound, touch, smell, and taste also assist in communication. Senders must select the appropriate channel to avoid problems that may occur in either the understanding or the retention of a message. To explain a complex mathematical problem to students, an instructor may use a variety of methods: lecture, graphs, and formulas. Similarly, a manager who wants to increase the probability that a message will be retained by subordinates may follow a verbal instruction with a written memorandum.

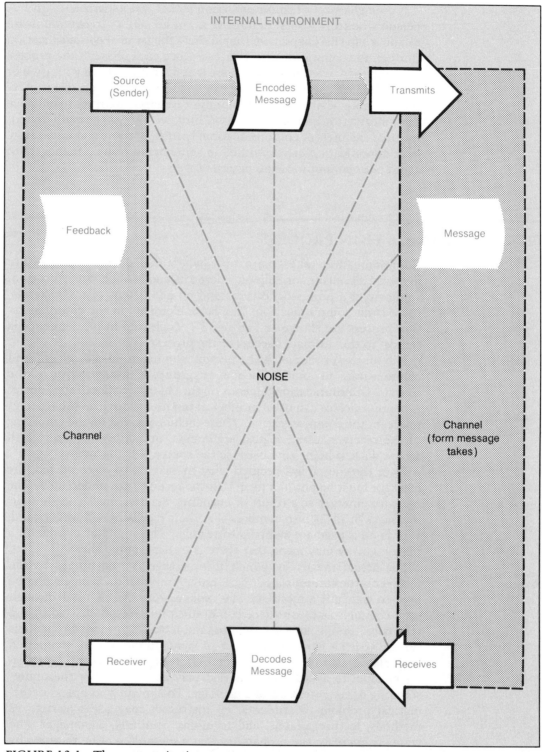

FIGURE 13-1 The communication process

SOURCE Adapted from H. Joseph Reitz, *Behavior in Organization* (Homewood, Ill.: Irwin, 1977): 342. Reprinted by permission of the author and publisher.

decoding

The receiver of the message must convert the encoded symbols into meaning through the process of **decoding**. How accurately decoding is done depends very much on how similar the receiver is to the sender. The greater the similarity in the background or status factors of the communicator and the receiver, the greater the likelihood that the message will be understood as it was intended. One reason why communication between organizational levels is so often misinterpreted is that many background differences exist among the individuals who are communicating. For example, the company president may have difficulty communicating with first-line supervisors because of decoding problems caused by status differences.

feedback

The sender of a message will observe one of three reactions to a message: agreement, disagreement, or apathy. These various forms of **feedback** tell the sender whether the message was accurately received and whether proper action was taken. The speed at which feedback occurs varies with each situation. In face-to-face conversation, feedback may be practically instantaneous, whereas in the case of mass advertising, many weeks or months may pass before the source (the advertiser) knows how effective the communication was. Feedback can also take many forms — verbal, written, or facial expressions.

conceptual noise

At each step in the communication process, both senders and receivers must cope with "noise." Although the term noise may be taken literally (for example, two factory workers trying to talk over the noise of machines), the term is generally used to refer to **conceptual noise** — those personality, perceptual, and attitudinal differences in individuals that reduce their ability to communicate effectively. Noise can be powerful enough to block communication between senders and receivers. Consider a manager who is doing a performance appraisal of an employee who the manager thinks is lazy. The manager makes the criticisms in a threatening manner; the employee reacts defensively to these words. They do not actually discuss the problem area. These two people will probably never reach the point of deciding how to resolve whatever problem exists between them because of communication noise.

WHAT SHOULD BE COMMUNICATED?

In the past, managers often communicated only enough information to give subordinates clear orders. With the increasing education levels of the work force, and the higher expectations that go along with increased education, managers are finding that employees often want to know far more than simply what to do. They also want to know why they should do a certain task, if there are better ways of doing it, and other information that will make them feel better about their job. Behavioral science research has demonstrated that when job-related information is provided, employee motivation to do the job well often increases. This research also points out the importance of subordinates feeling that their managers hear, understand, and value their ideas.

Determining what specific topics are to be communicated is often very difficult. The manager who believes that everything is suitable for transmission will not only clog the channels with trivia but may harm operations by releasing information that should be retained. The National Association of Manufacturers has suggested that the following should be communicated to employees:

- Information about the company — its operations, products, and prospects
- Information about company policies and practices related to personnel and their jobs, such as vacations, seniority, and pay systems
- Information about specific situations that arise in the company, such as a change in management or a change in plant layout
- Information about the general economic system in which a company and its employees operate.

Within these broad areas, many specific details must be considered. For example, management should inform its employees of the company's products, believing that their understanding will inspire interest, loyalty, and cooperation. But disclosure of future product plans may jeopardize the company's chances in a highly competitive industry. In matters more closely related to the employee's interests, such as seniority and pay, the tendency is toward providing all information that could possibly be desired. The two best guides for determining what information to provide are the responses to these questions: (1) What must personnel know in order to relate effectively to others and to the organization as a whole? and (2) What do employees want to know before they cooperate willingly and enthusiastically? The typical employee usually wants to know:

- His or her standing in relation to the official, formal authority structure
- His or her standing in relation to the informal organization (individual status, power, and acceptance)
- Events that have bearing on future economic security
- Operational information that will enable him or her to develop pride in the job.

ORGANIZATIONAL CHANNELS OF COMMUNICATION

communication channels

formal communication channels

Organizations provide many channels for communication. **Communication channels** are the means by which information is transmitted. Communication channels may be classified as formal and informal. **Formal communication channels** are those that are officially recognized by the organization. Instructions and information are passed downward along these channels, and information flows upward.

Information also travels through informal channels. **Informal communication channels** are ways of transmitting information within an organization that bypass formal channels.

informal communication channels

Formal Downward Channels

The traditional manager is likely to emphasize the importance of the downward channels of communication. Managers are aware of the necessity for conveying top management's orders and viewpoints to subordinates. They believe that the logic of these orders will stimulate desired action. Some of the various channels available to carry the information downward are indicated in Table 13-1. Many other channels are used every day by management to communicate with subordinates. Middle- and lower-level managers are usually contacted pesonally by written memos, policy manuals, and authorized schedules. External means, such as radio, television, and the press, can be used to communicate with employees as well as the general public.

Formal Upward Channels

Advocates of participative management and leadership have emphasized the stimulation of upward communication from subordinate to supervisor. This channel is necessary not only to determine if subordinates have understood the information that was sent downward, but also to meet certain needs of people. A communication effectiveness survey of thousands of employees showed that only half believed that significant upward communication was present. The others saw little chance of discussion or dialogue with top management.[1] An upward flow of information is also necessary if management is to coordinate the various activities of the organization. As shown in Table 13-2, there are several upward channels of communication to choose from.

Informal Communication Channels

Informal communication channels are not included in the formal organizational structure. If a manager has a problem that is affected by another department, the two managers may get together informally. When managers are at the same organizational level, this channel is **lateral communication**; it results from established personal relationships. Mutual trust must first be developed, and this can take time. But effective lateral communication can improve the productivity of both departments. Some companies even provide for lateral communication as a part of the formal organizational structure.

lateral
communication

Another type of informal channel is diagonal communication, which also bypasses the formal chain of command. In **diagonal communication**, communication channels are established with peo-

diagonal
communication

TABLE 13-1. Downward Channels of Communication

The chain of command	Orders and information can be given face-to-face or in written fashion and transmitted from one level to another. The most frequently used channel, this one is appropriate on either an individual or a group basis.
Posters and bulletin boards	Many employees do not read such boards; this channel is useful only as a supplementary device.
Company periodicals	A great deal of information about the company, its products, and policies can be disseminated in this manner. To attract readership, a certain percentage of space must be devoted to items about employees; thus, the periodical plays a part in developing the social life of the organization.
Letters and pay inserts	This form of direct mail contact is ordinarily used when the president of the organization wishes to present something of special interest. Letters are usually directed to the employee's home address. The use of pay inserts ensures exposure to every employee.
Employee handbooks and pamphlets	When special systems are being introduced, such as a pension plan or a job evaluation system, concise, highly illustrated pamphlets are often prepared to facilitate understanding and stimulate acceptance.
Loudspeaker system	The loudspeaker system is used not only for paging purposes but also to make announcements while they're hot. Such systems can also be misused, as in the case when the president of a company sent his summer vacation greetings from his cool place in the mountains to the sweating workers on the production floor.
Annual reports	A review of typical annual reports would indicate that they are increasingly being written for the benefit of the employee and the union as well as the shareholder. It is a channel that appears to be designed for one group, the owners, to which others tap in, hoping to obtain information not intended for them.
The labor union	The union can be helpful in communicating certain philosophies to company employees. The union voice, added to the management voice, can be highly persuasive.

TABLE 13-2. Upward Channels of Communication

The chain of command	Theoretically, the flow of communications is two-way between superior and subordinate. The superior should have an open-door attitude as well as some of the skills of a counselor. More courageous managers may opt to hold group meetings, in which employees are encouraged to air gripes and suggestions.

The grievance procedure	A systematic grievance procedure is one of the most fundamental devices for upward communication. The subordinate knows that there is a mechanism for appeal beyond the authority of the immediate supervisor. If this grievance procedure is backed up by the presence of a labor union, the subordinate will be even more encouraged to voice grievances.
The complaint system	In addition to grievance procedures, some firms encourage upward communication by preserving the identity of the complainant. Gripe boxes may be established, into which an employee can place a written complaint or rumor that management will investigate. In one firm, a blackboard was divided into halves, one side being for employee complaints or rumors, the other for management's replies. An answer of some sort was guaranteed within a 24-hour period.
Counseling	Though all supervisors have a counseling obligation, the authority barrier makes true communication difficult. For this reason, special staff counselors may be provided to allow employees to discuss matters in privacy and confidence.
Morale questionnaires	This channel also preserves the identity of the employee when answering specific questions about the firm and its management.
An open-door policy	An open-door attitude on the part of each supervisor toward immediate subordinates is to be highly commended. Higher management seldom use it because the employee is usually reluctant to bypass his or her immediate supervisor.
Exit interview	If the employee leaves the organization, there is one last chance in the exit interview to discover feelings and views about the firm in general and reasons for quitting in particular. Follow-up questionnaires are also used at times, because employees are reluctant to give full and truthful information at the time of departure.
Labor union	A prime purpose of the labor union is to convey to management the feelings and demands of employees. Collective bargaining sessions constitute a legal channel of communication for any aspect of employer/employee relations.
Special meetings	Special employee meetings to discuss particular company policies or procedures are sometimes scheduled by management to obtain employee feedback. The keystone of teamwork in the Pitney Bowes Company is monthly meetings in all departments involving all employees. In addition, a central employee council of 13 employee representatives meets with top executives on a monthly basis. Employees on this main council are elected for two-year terms and devote full time to investigating problems and improving communication processes.

The ombudsman

Though little used in North America, the ombudsman's role is to ensure corporate justice in nonunionized firms. In essence, the ombudsman acts as a complaint officer to whom employees may go when they feel they have exhausted the typical avenues of receiving an acceptable hearing. An ombudsman has only the rights of acceptance or rejection of complaints, investigation, and recommendation of action to the top organizational official. Most complaints center around salary, performance appraisal, layoff, and fringe benefits. In many instances, lower-level managers make voluntary adjustments precluding specific recommendations from the ombudsman. Though the position has existed for about 150 years, only a few North American business firms have adopted the concept. Xerox Corporation inaugurated the position in 1972 and reports that 40 percent of the final decisions clearly favored the employee, 30 percent were against the employee, and 30 percent represented some type of compromise.[2]

---

[2]Information on Xerox Corporation from "Where Ombudsmen Work Out," *Business Week* (May 3, 1976): 114-116.

ple whose levels are higher or lower in the organization but not directly in the formal chain of command. Again, this process is not automatic. Trust must first develop. Care must be taken in using diagonal communication because immediate superiors might take offense. However, used carefully, diagonal communication can be an important information source for the manager.

As noted in Chapter 8, the grapevine is the system of personal relationships and contacts that does not follow the firm's formal communication channels. The grapevine does not respect formal lines of authority and often extends throughout an organization. However, it does get much of its information from the formal organization. It usually transmits this information more rapidly than the formal system, although sometimes not as accurately. Employees generally rate the grapevine as one of the primary sources of current information.[2] A much simplified representation of the grapevine is shown in Figure 13-2.

The grapevine has four basic characteristics. First, it transmits information in every direction throughout the organization. Information on the grapevine can move down, up, laterally, and diagonally, all at the same time. It can connect organization units that have distant or indirect formal relationships. Second, the grapevine transmits information rapidly because it is not restricted by any formal policies and procedures. The chain of command does not have to be followed. Once a message gets into the grapevine, it can be moved

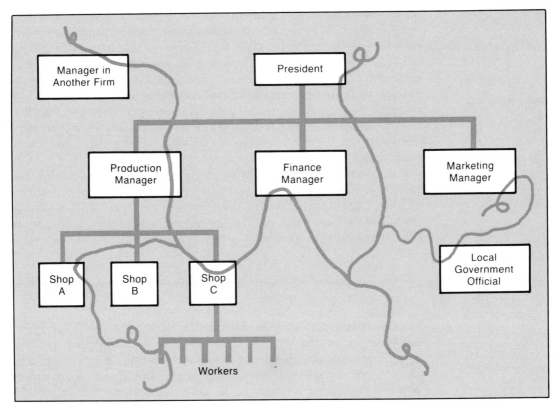

FIGURE 13-2 The grapevine

MANAGEMENT IN PRACTICE

Communicating with Employees

AT&E Corporation has developed a wrist pager — a wristwatch that will receive messages from standard telephones anywhere in the world and will give the wearer a brief message like "call the office" or other such information. A person in head office will no longer have difficulty locating, say, a travelling salesperson who is between flights at an airport or visiting a customer.

Wearers would register with the AT&E clearing house in their local area. Anyone wish-ing to reach the person when he or she is away would call the clearing house, and the message would be relayed. The wearer would be alerted that a message was coming by a beep.

Messages have to be fairly short — about 24 characters. The wearer will be charged a monthly service fee of about $5, plus 25 cents per message received.

SOURCE Adapted from Barbara Aarsteinsen, "If Your Watch Is Still On, This Paging Will Reach You," *The Globe and Mail* (December 12, 1986): B5.

instantaneously to any point in the organization. Third, the grapevine is selective about who receives information. Some people are tuned in to it and others are not. Some people regard grapevine information as gossip and, therefore, disregard or disapprove of it. Consequently, some managers are not even aware of the grapevine. Finally, the grapevine extends beyond the formal organization. Considerable communication about the firm occurs off the job. Employees who are friends may talk shop among themselves, or workers at a party may pass on or receive information about the company to people who don't work for it.

Managers should not ignore the grapevine: it can be useful and cannot be eliminated. Wise managers tune in to the grapevine. Not only will they obtain useful information, but they will be able to correct inaccurate messages. The grapevine is a prominent channel in the communication process.

BARRIERS TO COMMUNICATION

Effective communication means that the receiver correctly interprets the message of the sender. Often this does not happen because various breakdowns can occur in communication. If a manager tells an employee to "produce a few more parts," and the employee makes two but the manager wanted 200, communications certainly broke down. If a manager is to develop his or her communication ability, the reasons communication breaks down must be fully understood.

barriers to communication

As illustrated in Figure 13-3, successful management decisions must pass through the bottleneck, or **barriers to communication** if the organization's goals are to be achieved. If the barriers are excessive, communication may be reduced to the point where the firm's objectives cannot be achieved. Barriers may be classified as technical, language, or psychological. Knowledge of these possible communication barriers helps managers avoid them or minimize their impact.

Technical Barriers

technical barriers

Barriers to communication that derive from the work place are referred to as **technical barriers**. Some of these include timing, communication overload, and cultural differences.

Timing

timing

Timing means determining when a message should be communicated. Managers need to determine the most appropriate time to transmit a message. For instance, a manager who must reprimand a worker for excessive tardiness must speak with the worker as soon as

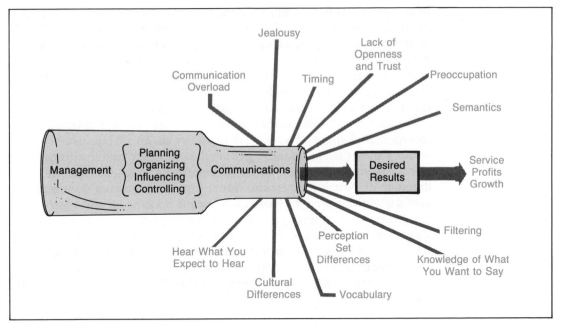

FIGURE 13-3 Successful management decisions must pass through the bottleneck – or barriers to communications – prior to achieving desired results

possible after the event happens. As another example, a firm might want to announce to the general public that it has a new product only when economic factors are most favorable.

Communication Overload

communication overload

Communication overload occurs when the sender attempts to present too much information to the receiver at one time. A person can absorb only so many facts and figures at one time. When excessive information is provided, a major breakdown in communication can occur. In any organization, the number of channels of communication is likely to be profuse; the demands on employees can become excessive. One professor experienced overload while teaching statistics in a four-hour class. For the first hour, students were eager and alert. By the fourth hour, however, few students were able to grasp what was taught.

Cultural Differences

In North America, time is usually a highly valuable commodity and a deadline suggests urgency. In the Middle East, however, giving a deadline to a person is considered to be rude; the deadline is likely to be ignored. If a client is kept waiting for 30 minutes in Canada, it may mean that he or she has low status. In Latin America, a 30-minute wait means nothing. If a contract offer has not been acted on in North America over a period of several months or a year, the conclusion is that the party has lost interest. In Japan, long delays mean no slackening of interest; delay is often a highly effective negotiation tactic when used on impatient North Americans.

Canadians and Americans conduct most face-to-face business at an interpersonal space of about 1.5 m to 2.5 m; an interpersonal space under a meter suggests more personal or intimate undertakings. The normal business distance for Latin Americans is closer to the personal distance of North Americans. Some highly interesting communication difficulties arise as North Americans back-pedal and their Latin American counterparts press ever closer. Regarding status symbols, a Canadian manager's office that is spacious, well furnished, and located on the top floor conveys high prestige. In the Middle East, size and decor of office mean little or nothing and, in France, the manager is likely to be located in the midst of subordinates in order to control them.

Language Barriers

Barriers to communication can occur when language problems result from vocabulary or from different meanings being applied to the same word (semantic differences).

Vocabulary

Managers must understand the audience being addressed if they are to be effective communicators. In one business organization, a market researcher, a supervisor, and a janitor will likely have different vocabulary sets. Words that the market researcher understands may have little meaning for the janitor, and vice versa, even though they both work in the same organization. Breakdowns in communication often occur when the sender does not tailor the message to match the knowledge base of the receiver.

All of us have a common level of vocabulary. (See Figure 13-4 for an illustration.) If we speak using level four words, both the market researcher and the janitor will understand. As we speak or write above this base level, less and less people will be able to comprehend the message. If the market researcher uses words above the scale of six, communication with the supervisor is lost. It will cease at level 4 with the janitor. Naturally, there will be times when higher-level words must be used to communicate a technical concept but, if managers can concentrate their messages in the common vocabulary base, they have a better chance of being understood.

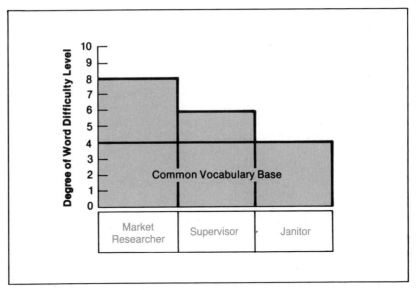

FIGURE 13-4   Common vocabulary base

Two systems for measurement of reading ease are the fog index developed by the late Robert Gunning and the Flesch system developed by Rudolph Flesch. The purpose of the fog index is to determine the reading level of writing. A fog index of 10 would mean that tenth graders can understand what you write.[3] The Flesch system helps you determine whether your writing is interesting to read. The means by which both systems are used may be seen in the "Management in Practice" insert on fog indexes.

The objective of both of these systems is to reduce the amount of pompous jargon and inflated prose. Of course, there is more to communication than can be revealed by counting syllables and sentence lengths. Each communicator must have a clear and coherent grasp of the idea he or she hopes to transmit. The Flesch and Gunning indexes help the writer to keep the reader in mind.

Semantics

When a sender sends words to which a receiver attaches different meaning from the one intended by the sender, a semantic — or meaning of words — communication breakdown has occurred. A major difficulty with the English language is that multiple meanings may be attached to a word. Take, for instance, the word *charge*. A manager may place an employee *in charge* of a section. The company *charges* for its services. A person gets a *charge* out of a humorous event. When two individuals attach different meanings to a word, a breakdown in communication can occur.

MANAGEMENT IN PRACTICE

Measure your Fog Index

Is your writing hard to understand? Do eyeballs glaze after a glance at your prose? Experts have devised measurements of reading ease, and you can rate your own performance.

One of the simplest and most consistent tests is the "fog index" developed by the late Robert Gunning. Here's how it works: Choose at random a medium-length paragraph of your own writing. A paragraph of about 120 words is ideal, says Douglas Mueller, president of the Gunning-Mueller Clear Writing Institute in Santa Barbara, Calif. Dates and other number combinations are single words. Count the number of words in your sample, then the number of sentences. Divide the word total by the sentence total to obtain the average number of words per sentence.

Step two is slightly more complex. Skim your sample and note each word of three or more syllables. Don't count words that are made by combining common short words, such as butterfly. And don't count verbs that acquire their extra syllable from tense endings, -es or -ed. Don't count words that begin with capital letters — place names, for example. And exclude the first word of any sentence. "I don't know why, but it works," says Mueller. "If you start a sentence with a polysyllable, it lowers the fog index. Magazines such as *The New Yorker* do it constantly."

Once you have your polysyllable count, add it to the word average and multiply the total by 0.4. The product will be a number corresponding to a reading comprehension grade level. A nine means that a ninth-grader can understand what you write. If you score 17 or more, then your prose is so densely wrapped in fog that only a graduate student will be able to grope

through it. The Gettysburg Address has a fog index of 10. Most news magazines manage 11 (*Business Week* averages 10). The article that you are now reading scores eight.

If you want to know whether your prose is interesting to read, Rudolph Flesch, one of the most eminent of reading and writing specialists, has devised a human-interest score. Using a sample of 100 words, count the personal words, which Flesch defines as pronouns — I, you, he, she, them, but not it or a plural pronoun referring to a thing. Count all words with gender, such as father or sister, actress, businessman, and proper names. And count collective nouns such as people and folks.

Next, count up your sample's personal sentences: any sentence containing speech set off by quotation marks or by references such as "she said"; sentences addressed directly to the reader as a question, a command, a suggestion; a sentence cast as an exclamation; any incomplete sentence of a conversational nature. (Flesch's examples: "Doesn't know a word of English. Handsome though." Those are two incomplete but comprehensible sentences.)

Once you have done all this, the arithmetic is a little complicated. Multiply the number of personal words in your 100-word sample by 3.635. Multiply the number of personal sentences by 0.314, and add the two products. The total is your human interest score, which runs from dull at 5, through interesting at 30, to dramatic at 80. What you have been reading, by the way, scores about 21: mildly interesting.

SOURCE Reprinted from the July 6, 1981 issue of *Business Week* by special permission, ©1981 by McGraw-Hill, Inc., New York, NY 10020. All rights reserved.

The use of jargon can also create a barrier to communication. Virtually every industry develops certain jargon that is used in everyday business. The statistician, computer programmer, typist, or ditch digger likely develops expressions peculiar to his or her specific profession. When speaking to an individual not associated with the trade, a breakdown in communication may occur. For this reason, many firms provide new personnel with a list and definition of terms associated with the particular industry.

Psychological Barriers

Although technical factors and semantic differences are credited with causing breakdowns in communication, psychological barriers tend to be the major reasons for miscommunication and communication breakdowns. These include various forms of distortion and problems involving interpersonal relationships.

Knowledge of What You Want to Say

The expression "The mouth was going before the mind was in gear" illustrates one form of breakdown in communication. Directives, orders, and even comments that are not well thought out can convey a

---

MANAGEMENT IN PRACTICE

The Sorry State of Communication in Business

The corporate world is awash in a sea of paper. One survey of 100 large corporations revealed that managers write memos that are too long, too self-serving, and sent to too many people. Memos are used to postpone work (assuring the boss something will be done so the boss stops bothering you), to show efficiency (writing memos that show you are organized), to make someone else feel guilty (writing a memo to remind them they haven't done something they promised to do), and to show the boss how hard you're working (describing in detail your work progress).

Don Ricks runs a Calgary-based company that holds business writing workshops for corporations. Billings run about a half a million dollars per year. Ricks says it is important to improve the writing skills of managers because they spend about 20 percent of their time writing. For many managers, writing is a threatening activity; they get little praise for doing it well, but *can* get a lot of criticism for doing it badly.

Rapid increases in technology make clear writing all the more important. The Bank of Montreal discovered a few years ago that many employees couldn't understand the technicians who were computerizing the company's operations. So they hired Ricks' company to teach the computer staff how to write business reports, letters, and memos. The program was successful, and has been expanded. Now, about 250 bankers volunteer each year to take the course.

SOURCE Adapted from Angela Barnes, "Memo To The Staff: Send Fewer Memos, Please," *The Globe and Mail* (April 28, 1987): B1.

message that the sender did not intend. A manager who asks for one thing but expects another has caused a breakdown in communication.

Filtering

An attempt to alter and color information to present a more favorable image to the manager is referred to as **filtering**. Managers often discover that information given to them by subordinates has been filtered. As subordinates contribute information to superiors, they know that it will be used for at least two purposes: (1) to aid management in controlling and directing the firm (and therefore the worker), and (2) to evaluate the worth of their performance. Managers at all levels are tempted to filter information as it progresses up the chain of command. Even the president may filter information before it goes to the board of directors.

Because the data have been filtered, an incorrect impression of the actual situation may develop. There have been many managerial attempts to reduce both the number and thickness of the authority filters that clog organization communication channels. It should be apparent that decentralization reduces the number of managerial levels, with a consequent speeding up of the communication process. Such reorganizations are drastic and require considerable effort in the areas of retraining and establishing realistic control standards.

A consultant can serve as a means of reducing communication filters. One company noticed a steady decrease in productivity for no reason that could be identified by management. A consultant systematically interviewed all employees over a six-month period. The results of these interviews indicated strong feelings on the part of many employees that work standards were too high, older employees resented the high wage scales of the new employees, and temporary transfers to new jobs to avoid layoffs were widely resented. In each case, management thought that it had effectively communicated its intent to the employees.

Lack of Trust and Openness

Openness and trust on the part of managers and employees must exist if orderly changes in the organization are to occur. When employees feel that openness and trust do not exist, barriers to communication are present.

As was illustrated in Figure 13-1, the sender needs feedback to know whether communication has occurred. If employees perceive the manager is open and receptive to their ideas, communication is encouraged. Should managers give the impression that feedback is not desired and that their statements should never be questioned, communication tends to be stifled.

One of the major factors in the success of Japanese businesses is

MANAGEMENT IN PRACTICE

Information and the Company President

Information is crucial to the president of a corporation. The president must use information to decide what changes are necessary in the way the organization is operating. Without accurate information, the president is in big trouble. Yet corporate presidents are often isolated from important information because subordinates are fearful of being the bearers of bad news. However, subordinates are eager to communicate good news, so the president may get, from them, a very distorted view of how the company is actually faring in the marketplace.

Even presidents who consciously try to avoid this problem may have difficulty. Jim McDonald, president of National Silicates in Toronto, found that out. He had first worked for the

company 30 years ago as a student, then returned and eventually became president. He found that the people who knew him previously think of him as "Jim," while the people who didn't know him earlier think of him as "Mr. McDonald." In an attempt to overcome this distinction, he holds periodic meetings with senior management as a group to get their views. He feels that this is less threatening than one-on-one confrontations, and that people will communicate more openly if they have peer support.

SOURCE Adapted from Andrew Weiner, "Stay in Control by Mastering the Art of Listening Well," *Executive* (September 1983): 14–18.

---

that managers trust not only their workers but also their peers and superiors. As a result, a simpler organizational structure evolves. For instance, Ford Motor company has 11 layers of management between the factory worker and the chairperson, while Toyota Motor Company has only six. Japanese firms assume that personnel at all levels are trustworthy, and they do not have to employ highly paid executives to review the work of other highly paid executives.[4]

Jealousy

It is perhaps difficult for managers to accept, but not everyone, especially peers and subordinates, will be pleased to see them perform successfully. Competence and effective performance may actually be viewed as a threat to the security of peers and subordinates. Individuals may attempt to diminish the accomplishments of another person because they are jealous. If jealous people are able to gain the attention of the supervisor, there is a possibility that when their peers attempt to communicate, they may find a less receptive ear. Because of jealousy, the effectiveness of communication may be reduced.

Perception Set Differences

perception set
A **perception set** is a fixed tendency to interpret information in a certain way. Differences in past experiences, educational back-

ground, emotions, values, and beliefs — to name just a few — affect each person's perception of a message or of words. The word *management*, for example, may be defined by two individuals as planning, organizing, influencing, and controlling the activities of others. If one person's parents were managers and the second's parents were labor union organizers, the word *management* will evoke drastically different meanings. It is difficult enough if words are representative of tangible objects such as *chair, pencil,* or *hat.* But the difficulties increase with such terms as *liberal, conservative, philosophy, group dynamics,* or *communication.*

FACILITATING COMMUNICATION

Once managers recognize that communication can break down, they can work toward improving their ability to communicate. As previously mentioned, the point to remember is that communication is learned. If managers truly want to improve their communication ability, means are available to assist them. Empathy, listening, reading skill improvement, observation, word choice, body language, actions, and transactional analysis are discussed in the following sections.

Empathy

empathy

You have likely heard the expression "I hear you," by which one person expresses empathy for what has been said. Empathy is the ability to identify with the various feelings and thoughts of another person. It does not mean that you necessarily agree with the other person but, while you are with the individual, you can appreciate why that person speaks and acts as he or she does. If a person is bitter, you are able to relate to this bitterness; if he or she is scared, you understand this fear.

Taken in its broadest meaning, an empathetic person is communicating. It is for this reason that managers should take the time to understand as much as possible about the people with whom they must work daily. With this information, the manager is in a much better position to understand why people act as they do. The manager may not agree with the individual but, if he or she takes the time to understand the reason for certain action, problems may be easier to resolve.

Listening

One of the most effective communication tools a manager has at his or her disposal is the ability to listen. A person who is constantly talking is not listening or learning. Listening assists a manager in discovering problems and determining solutions to problems.

Communication cannot take place unless messages are received and understood by the other party. The average speaking speed is 120 words per minute, yet people are able to listen at the rate of 480 words per minute. What does the listener do with the excess time that results from this difference in speeds?

At least three types of listening have been identified: marginal, evaluative, and projective. The speed of listening provides the opportunity for **marginal listening**, which can cause the listener to misunderstand and even insult the speaker. For instance, most people can tell, if they are speaking to a person, when the listener's mind is elsewhere. The listener may occasionally hear some words, but the majority of the message will not be understood.

Evaluative listening requires the listener to allocate full attention to the speaker. The excess time is devoted to evaluating and judging the nature of the remarks heard. Often, a listener is forming rebuttal remarks while the sender is still speaking, thus moving into a type of marginal listening. As soon as the sender says something that is not accepted, communication ceases and the receiver begins to develop a response mentally. Such thoughts as "this person does not know what he is talking about" can significantly reduce, or even eliminate, the communication process. Instead of one idea being transmitted and held by two people, the result may be two ideas, neither of which is really communicated to the other. If the listener allocated too much time to disapproving or approving of what is heard, it is doubtful whether he or she has the time to understand fully. This is particularly true when the remarks are loaded with emotion or concern over the security and status of the receiver.

Projective or **nonevaluative listening** holds the greatest potential for effective communication. Listeners attempt to project themselves into the position of the speaker and understand what is being said from the speaker's viewpoint. We should first listen without evaluation. After feeling that we understand what has been said, we can then evaluate what we have heard. Rogers suggested a rule to be followed to ensure some degree of projective listening: "Each person can speak for himself only *after* he has related the ideas and feelings of the previous speaker accurately and to that speaker's satisfaction."[5] There is no need to agree with the statements, but there is a need to understand them as the speaker intended. Only in this way is it possible to frame a reply that will actually respond to the speaker's remarks. Effective listening is empathic listening. It requires an

marginal listening

evaluative listening

nonevaluative listening

ability to listen for feeling as well as for words. The person attempts to place himself or herself in the shoes of the other person.

Improved Reading Skills

Reading skills have received great attention in our society. The amount of written material a manager must cover has increased significantly, and some attempt should first be made to consolidate and reduce it. However, the ability to read rapidly and with understanding is an essential communication skill, particularly in larger organizations. It has been found that reading speeds can be doubled and tripled with little or no loss in comprehension.

Observation

As in the case of listening, managers make too few attempts to increase skill in observation, outside of training for law enforcement. Most people have heard reports where there were many witnesses to a traffic accident. When the police arrive and question the witnesses, there are many different versions about what actually occurred. "The blue car went through the stop light," says one witness. "No, that's not correct," says another, "the light was green." Most people miss a great deal by not carefully observing important elements in their surroundings. Some managers are very adept at assessing the general atmosphere of an organization by merely strolling through its work places. Observation of furnishings, housekeeping, dress of personnel, and activities can convey much information. Using our powers of observation to supplement listening and reading will add immeasurably to an understanding of what is actually going on.

Word Choice

As mentioned previously, virtually everyone can understand a certain threshold of words. If a manager wants to communicate effectively, he or she must make certain that the choice of the words transmitted by the sender is in the vocabulary set of the receiver. Generally, simple or common words provide the best means through which communication is accomplished. However, readers tend to be impressed with complex words. Studies have shown that hard-to-read journals are more highly rated than those containing the same information written in simpler language.[6]

Body Language

body language

Most subordinates do not have to be told when their manager is displeased with them. A frown and crossed arms may communicate this message clearly. **Body language** is a nonverbal method of communication in which physical actions, such as motions, gestures, and facial expressions, convey thoughts and emotions.

Appreciation of the significance of understanding body language in the communication process is also quite important for a manager. All people — managers, superiors, and subordinates — give off unintentional signals that can provide insight into the exact meaning that a person is attempting to communicate. The manager particularly must be constantly aware of the signals that he or she is presenting. Employees grasp at these small symbols to determine what the "boss" means. A frown, even though the words were positive in nature, may result in the words being taken the wrong way. A sarcastic smile when "you did a good job" was mentioned will likely be interpreted to mean that the worker actually did not do a good job. A blank stare in a conversation may communicate to the employee that the manager is not interested.

A manager must also be aware of the signals that a subordinate may be giving off. Sweaty hands or nail biting in the presence of the supervisor may mean that the worker feels ill at ease. Managers need to recognize these signs and be prepared to adjust their behavior accordingly.

Most nonverbal signals are given subconsciously. Hence it takes considerable effort to change them. Such changes may be particularly hard for women. In today's corporate environment, women have risen in status and responsibility-levels, but studies show that their unconscious communications tend to indicate that they still perceive their status as lower than that of male managers in similar positions.[7]

Actions

The manager must also recognize that people communicate by what they do, or don't do. If a person comes to work one day and finds her or his desk moved from a location in a private office to one in an open area, communication of a sort has taken place. If no verbal explanation accompanies the action, people will interpret it their own way; the missing symbol or signal will be supplied by the observer. And despite any verbal statement to the contrary, such a move will likely be interpreted as a demotion for the person.

In one company, management introduced a change in procedure for a small crew of employees. The new method was timed and piece rates were established. None of the personnel produced more than half of the standard amount and were therefore on a time-wage basis rather than piece rates. They all filed grievances protesting the unfairness of the standard. Management tried everything it could think of to correct the problem, from all-day time studies to providing each employee with a private instructor in the new method. A check on similar jobs in other companies revealed that the standard was in line. Thus, management concluded that a concerted work restriction conspiracy was taking place.

The next move was one of communication by action. An engineer was sent to the production department, and he proceeded to measure various angles and spaces on the floor. He volunteered no information to the group. Finally, one man's curiosity got the best of him and he asked the engineer what he was doing. The engineer indicated that management wanted to see if there was sufficient room to locate certain machinery that could do the work of this crew. He continued about his business of measuring. The next day, all work crew members were producing amounts well above the established standard.

Transactional Analysis

transactional analysis

One recently proposed system for facilitating communication involves analyzing transactions among people. **Transactional analysis** (TA) proposes that there are three ego states constantly present and at work within each individual: the Parent, the Adult, and the Child.[8] The manner in which these individual ego states interact can have a significant effect on interpersonal communication.

Parent

Parent ego state

The **Parent ego state** may take on the characteristics of either the Nurturing or the Negative Parent. When the Nurturing Parent dominates, the person gives praise and recognition, comfort in time of distress, and reassurance in time of need. Statements such as "you have done a good job" or "I am certain the problem will work out all right" might be associated with the Nurturing Parent. Conversely, the Negative Parent is overcontrolling, suffocating, critical, and oppressive. Comments such as "children should be seen and not heard" or "be careful, you can hurt yourself with the knife" might be associated with the Negative Parent. When the Negative Parent dominates, the person tends to lecture, believes that his or her moral standard is best for everyone, and often will not accept other ideas.

Child

Child ego state

The **Child ego state** may take on the characteristics of either the Natural Child, the Little Professor, or the Adaptive Child. The Natural Child is spontaneous, impulsive, untrained, expressive, self-centered, affectionate, and curious. The Little Professor tends to be intuitive, manipulative, and creative. The Adaptive Child tends to react in a way determined by parental figures.

Adult

Adult ego state

A person who tends to evaluate the situation and attempts to make decisions based on information and facts is in the **Adult ego state**. No emotions are involved, and the individual tends to function like a computer, with all decisions based on logic.

The interaction of ego states can have a significant impact on communication behavior in organizations. The manager must recognize that a person will not always be in the Adult state and therefore will not always make decisions based entirely on logic. In fact, the greatest amount of creativity is associated with the Child state. Also, the manager will be able to recognize when communication is impossible. For instance, the manager who is in the Adult state may attempt to speak to the Adult state of the employee. The Child state of the employee returns the conversation to the Parent state of the manager. The following dialogue illustrates such a communication problem:

Manager: This task needs to be completed today.
Employee: Why are you always pushing me to work harder?

Communication has broken down because the employee is not addressing the problem that the manager was attempting to communicate.

Managers should also be aware of the ego state that they themselves are speaking in. If the state is properly interpreted, managers can recognize and possibly change their actions. Should you recognize that you are in one state and an employee is in a state that precludes effective communication, it may be best to postpone discussion. For instance, if the manager is in the Child state and the employee is in the Adult state, communication perhaps should be postponed. The employee who is in the Adult state is serious about his or her work at this time and may misinterpret, for instance, joking remarks.

Applying TA concepts on a broad basis may prove valuable in producing desired organizational change. As individuals in a firm learn to analyze their own social interactions, better communication and greater overall effectiveness can occur.

EFFECTS OF NEW TECHNOLOGIES

As a consequence of the electronic revolution, communication methods in today's organizations are rapidly changing. Information processing is becoming increasingly automated, with word processors, micro-, mini-, and mainframe computers, as well as new developments in telecommunication and video technology. One reason for the electronics explosion is the tumbling cost of the technology.

Company video, or private television, has had its ups and downs

Michael Cowpland
Mitel Corp.

Mitel Corp., a manufacturer of telecommunications equipment and semiconductors, is growing at the exponential velocity exclusive to high-tech organizations. Launched on $12 000 capital in the basement of an Ottawa home in 1975, it was ringing up annual sales of $1.5 million the following year, $11.5 million by 1978, $43.4 million by 1980, and $204 million in 1982. In a recent American study of 2400 publicly listed companies, Mitel was ranked third-equal among the North American corporations predicted to grow fastest during the mid-1980s. Creators of this startling success story are two English-born engineers, Terry Matthews and Michael Cowpland, both now in their late 30s. When they started in Cowpland's basement they vowed they'd be the world's best at whatever they did, and they seem to have kept that promise.

Q: Is there something in this industry that makes it not only possible but also necessary to grow so fast?
Cowpland: To a certain extent there is. We're looking at the world market and, if we don't grab whatever markets are available, somebody else will. After that they would be building on the strength of their position. We would be at a competitive disadvantage.

Q: Don't you now have to translate the company from entrepreneurial type management into something that will work for a large stable "corporate giant"?
Cowpland: I think that change has been underway almost continuously. Our management approach has changed almost every 6 or 12 months. One of the good things is that we're used to changing. There are thresholds at $1 million in sales; $10 million; $50 million; $100 million. It's a process of almost continuous change.

Q: Although you have grown so fast, Northern Telecom, for example, is a heck of a lot bigger. Does its size give it a considerable advantage? Or do you gain by having flexibility?
Cowpland: All things being equal it's a disadvantage to be big. Our biggest challenge now is to avoid accumulating the disadvantages that we could pick up. Fortunately, having been small so recently, we know how good it is to be small. Therefore we try to organize the company so that we stay responsive and fast-moving.

Q: Every company wants to cut red tape, and keep things informal. Yet they don't manage to do so.
Cowpland: One of the things we've done pretty successfully is keep an open-door policy. You'll notice when you're walking around here that things are open, there are no secrets. That's a policy I push very strongly throughout the company. We don't have a "need-to-know" policy — yet a lot of companies do, even small high-tech companies. They say: "You have no need to know this, therefore I'm not going to give this piece of information to you."

We have the attitude, on the other hand, that if you want to know something you *can* know it. There are only about two or three things that are confidential — they're mainly salaries and maybe the odd pricing deal on special marketing contracts. Apart from that everything is wide open. We flow the information as broadly as possible thoughout the company for two reasons. One is that people want to know what's going on from a satisfaction point of view. Nobody wants to be a mushroom. Secondly it's a good training tool because the more that people can see the big picture the better decisions they're going to make in terms of what's good for the whole company.

Q: You can only share information like that if you're enormously self-confident. Traditional corporation people hang on to knowledge as a source of power.

Cowpland: That's right. A lot of people do that just for that purpose. Their knowledge base is their security blanket. The more people share their knowledge base, the less security they have because then they're dispensable. We push very hard to avoid letting that attitude creep in, because it's a real danger. When people are hiding information it can cause real problems. That's why we purposely promote and select people who have a lot of self-confidence. We try to avoid office politics. We try to continue to think about what's best for the company, not what's best for an individual. And we move people around and give them more or less power according to whether they feel that way.

Q: Does your engineering background help you handle the management job? Do these things link?

Cowpland: Not necessarily. But the open, team approach we've taken from Day One is very healthy because we all automatically learn from each other. Even though we have an organizational chart, we all look at each other's areas. There's very little sense of empire because everybody feels free to discuss and even criticize an area that's not his or her own, freely looking over the fence, as it were. Everybody worries about everybody else's area and that's good because it gives people peripheral vision and they don't get tunnel vision. The finance people thus know a lot about our engineering and our marketing guys know a lot about finance. We tend to make people more generalists than specialists, even though they're com-

ing from a pretty specialized knowledge base.

Q: There's periodic talk in Canada about the need for an industrial strategy. Do you think we really need such a thing? Or might that just lead us into all the traps that usually go with central planning?

Cowpland: An industrial strategy as such is a waste of time. What we should have is an encouraging environment. "Strategy" sounds too detailed. If they would just recognize what's obvious to almost everybody, that high tech is going to be a tremendous thing for the future, then they could simply help create an environment which encourages that, recognizing the United States as the standard against which you're going to measure yourself. We have to have an environment which is better than the one in the States. We must have a better environment for raising money for these industries by virtue of better tax arrangements or whatever. We must have a better environment for education. Those are the main things.

Q: Is there a chance of Canada developing its own robotics industry?

Cowpland: We could; but I'm not convinced it's the area we should concentrate on. We now lead in the communications area. Robotics to me sound inherently quite mechanical and the Japanese are so good at mechanical stuff that they'd be tough to compete with. Where the Japanese have been so successful is mainly mechanical — the cars, the cameras, the motorbikes, the videotape recorders. Take one of those apart and you see mechanical wizardry more than anything else. The electronics involved are pretty straightforward. It's a big mistake to try to compete with the mechanical wizardry of the Japanese.

On the other hand, communications technology is almost all electronics and software and it's a much more natural fit for us. In Canada you can't get good craftsmen; they all get imported from eastern Europe and there's only a limited supply. There's no apprentice scheme here to train people who can lathe and machine beautiful parts. That's one reason why robotics would never be a big industry for Canada.

SOURCE Excerpted from Dean Walker, "Michael Cowpland of Mitel", *Executive* (April 1983): 26–32. Reprinted by permission.

since the late 1960s. Now, though, the problems caused by lack of standardization and compatibility between components have largely been overcome. With the advent of the video-cassette in 1972, video has become an inexpensive alternative for communication. Increasing numbers of managers are turning to this medium for information dissemination.[9] Since many persons are accustomed to, and even prefer, getting information through television, more emphasis is being placed on using video for transmitting corporate information. This medium "puts the face behind the memo."[10] Private television breaks through communication barriers and delivers the message straight, with no filtering by intermediate managers and less chance of misunderstanding through inappropriate prose.

Converging technologies in data and word processing, voice and data communications, networking, electronic mail and computer graphics have made communications more effective and efficient. Large data bases within management information systems (MIS) have speeded up data processing and information flows.[11] Communication networks connect various office machines together, making possible instantaneous electronic transfers of messages, images and data. Contrasted with traditional communication processes, these devices are fast, are convenient, and integrate a variety of communication tasks. "Information democracy" — equal access to information by all organization members — is arriving, as larger numbers of online terminals are installed in corporations.[12]

teleconferencing

A new development, combining video, computer, and telecommunication technologies, is **teleconferencing.** Uses of teleconferencing run from the simple speaker phone to full-blown satellite-transmitted video.[13] The middle part of this spectrum, audiographics, combines graphics-oriented visual displays with vocal teleconferencing facilities to provide the opportunity for enhanced multisite dialogues.[14] As computer hardware and software become more sophisticated, the machines are becoming more cost effective and user friendly. Fewer skills are required to use the latest systems, facilitating their adoption.

artificial intelligence

A new technology on the horizon is artificial intelligence (AI). **Artificial intelligence** involves the attempt to make machines (e.g., computers) which display intelligent behavior.[15] AI computers have been developed to think and learn somewhat as human beings do. Expert systems are computers which can draw highly specialized conclusions from huge stores of data, much as the human brain does. Scientists predict their increasing use in routine management tasks.[16]

The new technologies have, in effect, changed the methods used in organization communications. Many of these devices decrease barriers to communications. However, they have their built-in limitations. Used ingeniously, they hold immense potential to enhance communication capabilities.

OPENING INCIDENT REVISITED

The Business School

After Lane had left his office, Carletti felt remorseful at having lost his temper and began to think of ways that he could make it up to Lane. However, the more he thought about it, the more he realized that he was completely constrained by university regulations and, in fact, could do nothing about Lane's withdrawal. Carletti reasoned that he could apologize for losing his temper but that would probably be little consolation to Lane. The more he thought about it, the more he became convinced that Lane understood him perfectly well but was simply feigning ignorance. Carletti therefore decided to do nothing.

One week later, Carletti received formal notification from the registrar that Lane had been required to withdraw. Carletti was later told by another student that Lane had transferred into liberal arts. He wondered why Lane had so readily accepted the brief written notice from the registrar but had refused to accept his detailed verbal communication in the interview.

This incident is typical of situations where one of the parties in the interview (Lane) simply does not allow understanding to develop. Lane's behavior is not surprising since he has a lot to lose if he is required to withdraw. How should Carletti have dealt with Lane's behavior? First, he should not have attempted to ram the required withdrawal idea down Lane's throat. Rather, he should have explained it clearly and, if Lane did not seem to understand, he should then have asked him to explain the policy on withdrawals. By listening to what Lane was saying, Carletti could have developed a strategy for overcoming Lane's objections and communicating this unpleasant news to Lane without becoming exasperated.

Second, Carletti should have remained calm throughout the interview. After all, he knew that, in the final analysis, the registrar would deny Lane the right to register for courses in the business school, so he need not have got excited about it at that stage. If he had remained calm, Carletti may have been able to get through to Lane.

SUMMARY

Communication is defined as the achievement of meaning and understanding between people through verbal and nonverbal means in order to affect behavior and achieve desired results. The source (sender) is the person who has an idea or message to communicate to another person or persons. Encoded messages are transmitted through such means as speaking, writing, acting, and drawing. A number of channels may be used to transmit the message. The receiver of the message must decode it by converting the symbols into meaning. Communication effectiveness is determined by the extent to which the receiver's interpretation matches the sender's intention.

There are numerous channels of communication through which a manager transmits information. Downward channels provide means through which management's orders and viewpoints are transmitted to subordinates. Upward channels provide means through which subordinates can communicate with their superiors.

Effective communication is often not achieved because of various breakdowns that can affect the communication process. Barriers may cause communication to be reduced to the point that the firm's objectives cannot be achieved. Barriers may be classified as technical, language, or psychological. Technical barriers include improper timing, communication overload, and cultural differences. Language barriers result when different meanings are applied to the same word or when inappropriate vocabulary is used. Psychological barriers include various forms of distortion and problems involving interpersonal relationships.

Although there are many barriers to communication, there are means available to eliminate or reduce these breakdowns. The use of empathy and the development of good listening skills can facilitate good communication. In addition, improved reading and observation skills, as well as a careful choice of words can aid the manager in better communication with employees. Studying transactional analysis and developing the ability to read body language have also been used to improve a manager's ability to communicate.

REVIEW QUESTIONS

1. Define communication. Describe the elements in the communication process.
2. Distinguish between downward and upward communication. What are examples of both types of communication channels?
3. What is the difference between formal and informal communication channels? Give examples of each.
4. What is meant by the phrase "barriers to communication"? Distinguish among technical, language, and psychological barriers.
5. List the communication facilitators discussed in this chapter. Briefly define each.
6. Explain how empathy may be used to assist a person to become a better listener.
7. What is transactional analysis? How can it be used to improve communication?
8. What has been the effect of the new technologies on the communication process?

EXERCISES

1. Over a 24-hour period, identify factors and situations that create barriers to communication in your life. Attempt to secure at least one example of each of the barriers to communication identified in the chapter. What aids to communication could have been used to reduce these barriers to effective communication?

2. Visit a business of your choice. Attempt to identify the various means of both downward and upward communication.
3. Try this exercise regarding observation skills. With one of your classmates, go to the window and observe what is occurring outside for 10 seconds. Each of you then write down what you saw. After completing the list, compare your list with your partner's list. Compare the differences.

CASE STUDY

A Failure to Communicate

"Could you come to my office for a minute, Bob?" asked Terry Geech, the plant manager. "Sure, be right there," said Bob Glemson. Bob was the plant's quality control director. He had been with the company for four years. After completing his degree in mechanical engineering, he worked as a production supervisor and then as maintenance manager, prior to promotion to his present job. Bob thought he knew what the call was about.

"Your letter of resignation catches me by surprise," began Terry. "I know that Wilson Products will be getting a good man, but we sure need you here, too." "I thought about it a lot," said Bob, "but there just doesn't seem to be a future for me here." "Why do you say that?" asked Terry. "Well," replied Bob, "the next position above mine is yours. With you only thirty-nine, I don't think it's likely that you'll be leaving soon."

"The fact is that I am leaving soon," said Terry. "That's why it's even more of a shock to know that you are resigning. I think I'll be moving to the corporate offices in June of next year. Besides, the company has several plants that are larger than this one. We need good people in those plants from time to time, both in quality control and in general management."

"Well, I heard about an opening in the Hamilton plant last year," said Bob, "but by the time I checked, the job had already been filled. We never know about job opportunities in the other plants until we read about them in the company paper."

"All this is beside the point now. What would it take to get you to change your mind?" asked Terry. "I don't think I can change my mind now," replied Bob. "I've already signed a contract with Wilson."

QUESTIONS

1. Evaluate the communication system at this company.
2. What actions might have prevented Bob's resignation?

CASE STUDY

The Management Trainee

Lois Atkins, a recent graduate, had just joined Bellingham Electric Company as a management trainee. Bellingham was a manufacturer of electric light bulbs, transformers, and generators. Bellingham had been successful over a period of many years in recruiting management trainees through university and community college placement offices. In a typical year, the company would hire 200 management trainees from their recruiting efforts.

The company had a well-established one-year management training program during which the trainee was assigned to a branch location to learn various phases of company operations. The program, designed to prepare individuals for branch management, included training in: shipping and receiving, inventory control, purchasing, personnel, production, order service, and outside sales. In addition to this on-the-job experience, the trainee returned to headquarters four times during the year for one week of classroom-type instruction and to compare notes and review individual progress with members of upper management.

Atkins was assigned to a branch operation in Hamilton and was under direct supervision of Clayton Thomas, the branch manager. Thomas, 55, had been with Bellingham for 35 years. He had not attended college but had worked his way up and believed this way of making it into management provided better training than the company's one-year rotation program. Atkins was assigned to perform various jobs in the branch but not according to the planned program. Atkins was asked to fill in as needed: she became concerned about not receiving the type of training required to prepare her for her first management position.

During her second trip to headquarters for a one-week training session, Atkins discussed her problem with the coordinator of management training and development, John Wilson. Wilson assured Atkins that he would look into the matter. On her return to the branch, Atkins was reprimanded by Thomas for discussing the problem with Wilson. The conversation proceeded as follows:

Thomas: Lois, why did you discuss your problems with John Wilson? You work for me, at least as long as you're at this branch.

Atkins: I don't know — I guess I was just frustrated with the training I've received.

Thomas: You're just like a lot of young college graduates. You think your degree should entitle you to special treatment. Well, I'm sorry, but in my book it doesn't mean a thing.

Atkins: What should I do now?

Thomas: Go back to work and don't cause any more trouble.

QUESTIONS

1. What action do you think Lois Atkins should take?
2. To what extent should John Wilson have discussed Atkins's problem with the local branch manager, Clayton Thomas?
3. What evidence is there of a breakdown in communication between the branch office and the intentions of headquarters? Discuss.

CASE STUDY

Assuming the Worst

Springfield Products Company is a medium-sized manufacturer of small outboard motors. The motors are supplied to major retailing chains, which sell them under their own brand names. For the past few years, sales had been falling. The decline was industry wide. In fact, Springfield was faring better than its competitors and had actually been able to increase its share of the market slightly. While forecasts indicated that the demand for the company's outboards would improve in the future, Anne Goddard, the company's president, believed that something needed to be done immediately to help the company maintain its financial health through this temporary slump. As a first step, she employed a consulting firm to determine if a reorganization might be helpful.

A team of five consultants arrived at the firm. They told Goddard that they would like to get a thorough understanding of the current situation before they made any recommendations. She told them that the company was open to them. They could ask any questions that they thought appropriate.

The grapevine was full of rumors virtually from the day the consulting group arrived. One employee was heard to say, "If they shut down the company, I don't know if I could take care of my family." Another worker said, "If they try to move me away from my friends I'm going to quit."

When workers questioned their supervisors, they received no explanation. No one had told the supervisors what was going on either. The climate began to change to one of fear. Rather than being concerned about their daily work, employees worried about what was going to happen to the company and their jobs. Productivity dropped as a result.

A month after the consultants left, an informational memorandum was circulated through the company. It stated that the consultants had recommended a modification in the top levels of the organization to achieve greater efficiency. No one would be terminated. Any reductions would be the result of normal attrition. By this time, however, some of the best workers had already found other jobs, and company operations were disrupted for several months.

QUESTIONS

1. What part did the informal organization play in what happened at Springfield Products? (Review Chapter 8 before answering this question.)
2. Why did the employees assume the worst about what was happening?
3. How could this difficulty have been avoided?

ENDNOTES

[1] R. Foltz and R. D'Aprix, "Survey Shows Communication Problems," *Personnel Administrator* (February 1983): 8.

[2] Foltz and D'Aprix.

[3] Robert Gunning, "How to Improve Your Writing," *Factory Management and Maintenance* 110 (June 1952): 134.

[4] "Trust: The New Ingredient in Management," *Business Week* (July 6, 1981): 104.

[5] Carl R. Rogers and F. J. Roethlisberger, "Barriers and Gateways to Communication," *Harvard Business Review* 30 (July-August 1952): 48.

[6] D. K. Denton, "Protecting Against Communication Fallout," *Management World* (April 1983): 28–30.

[7] L. R. Cohen, "Minimizing Communication Breakdowns Between Male and Female Managers," *Personnel Administrator* (October 1982): 57–58.

[8] For an expanded coverage of transactional analysis, see Thomas A. Harris, *I'm O.K.—You're O.K.* (New York: Harper, 1969).

[9] J. M. Brush and D. P. Brush, "Companies Tune in to Video," *Management World* (January 1984): 25.

[10] Brush, 25.

[11] P. F. Calise and M. Locke, "Office Automation: Who's in Control?" *Management World* (March 1984): 17.

[12] Z. K. Quible, and R. A. Ankerman, "Office Connections," *Management World* (December 1983): 31.

[13] Quible, 31.

[14]L. G. A. Graham, "Audiographics for Sound Teleconferencing," *Computer World* 17:394 (September 28, 1983): 63.

[15]C. W. Holsapple and A. Whinston. *Business Expert Systems* (Homewood, Ill.: Irwin, 1987): 4.

[16]"Artificial Intelligence Is Here," *Business Week* (July 9, 1984): 54.

REFERENCES

Aarsteinsen, Barbara. "If Your Watch Is Still On, This Paging Will Reach You." *The Globe and Mail* (December 12, 1986); B5.

Allen, T.H. "Communication Networks: The Hidden Organizational Chart." *Personnel Administrator* 21 (September 1976): 31–35.

Axley, Stephen R. "Managerial and Organizational Communication in Terms of the Conduit Metaphor." *Academy of Management Review* 9, no. 3 (July 1984): 428–437.

Barnes, Angela. "Memo to the Staff: Send Fewer Memos, Please." *The Globe and Mail,* (April 28, 1987): B1.

Collins, Anne. "Making It in the Media." *Canadian Business* 60, (March 1987): 38–44.

Davis, Keith, "Cut Those Rumors Down to Size." *Supervisory Management* 20 (June 1975): 2–6.

Deutsch, A. R. "Does Your Company Practice Affirmative Action in Its Communication?" *Harvard Business Review* 54 (November-December 1976): 16.

Donath, Bob. "Corporate Communications." *Industrial Marketing* 65 (July 1980): 52–53.

Ewing, David W., and Banks, Pamela M. "Listening and Responding to Employees' Concerns." *Harvard Business Review* 58 (January-February 1980): 101–114.

Foltz, Roy G. "Internal Communications, Give Them Facts." *Public Relations Journal* 36 (October 1980): 35.

Gildea, Joyce A., and Emanuel, Myron. "Internal Communications: The Impact of Productivity." *Public Relations Journal* 36 (February 1980): 8–12.

Hargreaves, J. "Six Keys to Good Communications." *International Management* 31 (December 1976): 54–56.

Hyseman, R. C. "Managing Change Through Communication." *Personnel Journal* 57 (January 1978): 20–25.

Kikoski, John F. "Communication: Understanding It, Improving It." *Personnel Journal* 59 (February 1980): 126.

Laing, G. J. "Communication and Its Constraints on the Structure of Organizations." *Omega* 8 (1980): 287–301.

Leavitt, Harold J. *Managerial Psychology.* 2d ed. Chicago: University of Chicago Press, 1964.

Levine, Edward. "Let's Talk: Breaking Down Barriers to Effective Communication." *Supervisory Management* 25 (August 1980): 3–12.

Lewis, Carl B. "How to Make Internal Communications Work." *Public Relations Journal* 36 (February 1980): 14–17.

McMaster, J. B. "Getting the Word to the Top." *Management Review* 68 (February 1979): 62–65.

Miles, James M. "How to Establish a Good Industrial Relations Climate." *Management Review* 67 (August 1980): 42–44.

Muchinsky, P. M. "Organizational Communication: Relationships to Organizational Climate and Job Satisfaction." *Academy of Management Journal* 20 (December 1977): 592–607.

Roberts, Karlene H., and O'Reilly, Charles A. III. "Failures in Upward Communication in Organizations: Three Possible Culprits." *Academy of Management Journal* 17 (June 1974): 205–215.

Schuler, Randall S. "Effective Use of Communication to Minimize Employee Stress." *Personnel Administrator* 24 (June 1979): 40–44.

Snyder, Robert, and Morris, James. "Organizational Communication and Performance." *Journal of Applied Psychology* 69, (August 1984): 461–465.

Tavernier, Gerard. "Improving Managerial Productivity: The Key Ingredient Is One-on-One Communication." *Management Review* 70 (February 1981): 13–16.

Weiner, Andrew. "Stay in Control by Mastering the Art of Listening Well." *Executive* (September 1983): 14.

14

Organizational Conflict, Change, and Stress

KEY TERMS

conflict	mediation	stress
conflict	superordinate goal	executive burnout
management	problem solving	
arbitration		

LEARNING OBJECTIVES

After completing this chapter you should be able to
1. Distinguish between the traditional and current views of conflict.
2. Explain why conflict develops and identify various means of effectively managing it.
3. Identify and describe the change sequence.
4. Describe the sources of resistance to change and the approaches that can be used to reduce resistance to change.

5. Explain the causes of stress and executive burnout.
6. Describe actions which can be taken to reduce the impact of stress and executive burnout.

OPENING INCIDENT

Craig Ltd.

Lorna Kasian was the assistant to the president of Craig Ltd., a manufacturing firm located in Halifax. Her job occasionally included overseeing special projects that were given to her by the president. Recently, he had asked her to draw up plans for renovations to the company's administrative offices, and to see that the renovations proceeded efficiently and on time. Kasian was looking forward to this project because one of the outcomes would be a new office for her.

Because Kasian wanted to make a good impression on the president, she immediately put the project at the top of her priority list. She gave considerable thought to what should be included in the renovations; then she contacted a local architect and had him draw up renovation plans. When the blueprints were ready, Kasian circulated a memo to all those who would be affected by the renovation and invited them to a meeting to announce the changes that would be made.

At the meeting, everything went wrong. Several secretaries who were going to have to move their work stations as a result of the renovation were very upset. After they had received Kasian's memo, they had got together on their own time and drawn up an alternate plan, which Kasian could immediately see was better than hers. They argued that the renovations should be delayed until everyone had a chance to comment on them.

Several other groups were also upset. The drafting department members, for instance, complained that their proposed new quarters were unacceptable and that no one had consulted them about the specialized type of space they needed. The marketing people complained that there was no area where sales meetings could be held. They reminded Kasian that the president had promised that, when renovations were made, a large meeting room would be included.

Kasian was exhausted by the time the meeting ended. She was concerned that the president would hear about the negative tone of the meeting, and that it would reflect badly on her. She also felt obliged to consult with several of the more vocal groups at the meeting. She realized that she would need more time and that the renovations project could not possibly be completed by the time the president wanted. Kasian thought to herself: "If only I had talked to some of these people before I had the renovation plans drawn up!"

The opening incident clearly demonstrates how the topics of change, conflict, and stress are related. In attempting to introduce a major change, Lorna Kasian was confronted with considerable conflict during an informational meeting. Both the employees and Lorna were put under stress because of this conflict.

We begin this chapter by defining organizational conflict, and noting the two basic views of conflict that exist in our society. Next, a model of the conflict process is presented. We then discuss both interpersonal and structural conflict management techniques. The second major section of the chapter deals with organizational change. We describe the change sequence, and note the reasons people resist change. We also offer suggestions on how to reduce resistance to change. The chapter concludes with a discussion of management stress and executive burnout, and how organizations can help individuals cope with these problems.

ORGANIZATIONAL CONFLICT

conflict

Conflict occurs when an individual or group purposely inhibits the attainment of goals by another individual or group. This purposeful inhibition may be active or passive. For example, in a sequential production line, if one group does not do its job and its output is the input for another department, the other department will be blocked from reaching its goal of, say, producing at standard. Alternatively, the blocking behavior may be active, like two fighters trying to knock each other out. The key issue in defining conflict is that of incompatible goals. When one person or group deliberately interferes with another person or group with the purpose of denying the other goal achievement, conflict exists.[1]

Two Views of Conflict

Looking back over this century, it becomes obvious that assumptions about whether conflict is good or bad for organizations have changed substantially. There are two distinct phases of thinking about conflict: the traditional view and the current view.

The Traditional View

This view of conflict, which was popular until the early 1940s, assumed that conflict was bad for organizations. In the view of the traditionalists, organizational conflict was proof that there was something wrong with the organization. The Hawthorne studies (discussed in Chapter 1) were probably important in shaping the traditional view because in those studies the dysfunctional consequences of conflict were noted. Another likely factor in the traditional view was the development of labor unions and the often violent conflict between labor and management. During the early twentieth century, labor unions were struggling for the legal right to bargain collectively. It was not until the 1940s that this goal was reached. Along the way, many confrontations occurred between labor and management. These were almost always viewed as bad for both the organization and the individual, and it is therefore not surprising that the traditionalists viewed conflict as undesirable. Overall, the traditional view assumed that the organization's performance declined steadily as conflict increased (see Figure 14-1).

Because conflict was viewed as bad, considerable attention was given to reducing or eliminating it. Perhaps the most general reaction was to suppress it. This was done in an obvious way by simply demanding that people in conflicting situations change their behavior for the good of the company. It was also done indirectly by rigidly prescribing the limits of authority of each job so that individuals would be less likely to be in conflict. While these tactics sometimes worked, they were largely ineffective because: (1) they did not get at the exact cause of the conflict, and (2) suppressing the conflict did not allow any of the positive aspects of conflict to come out.

The traditional view of conflict appears to be losing ground as time passes, yet it still describes the views of many people. Why should

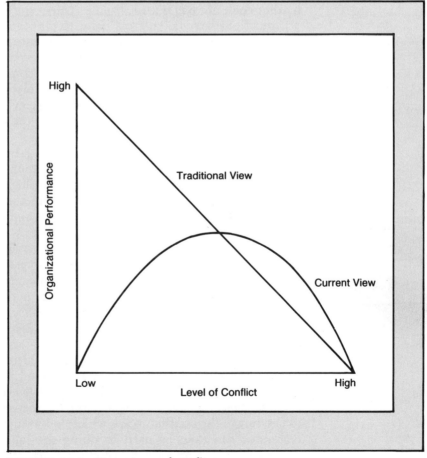

FIGURE 14-1 Two views of conflict

this view be so widespread, given that some conflict has been shown to be beneficial? One researcher answers this question by saying that the important institutions in our society — the home, church, and school — are founded on the traditional view of conflict, and these institutions have a powerful influence on society.[2] Since these institutions are very influential when we are young, we are subtly influenced to have a particular view of conflict. In the home, for example, parents suppress conflict by telling their children to stop fighting. In schools, teachers are assumed to have the correct answers, and exams are a check to see whether students are deviating from these. Most churches stress brotherhood and peace, not conflict. If this argument is correct, the change in the view of conflict from traditional to current will take many years.

The Current View

The view which prevails among researchers at present (and which is gaining ground in the rest of society) is that organizational conflict is neither good nor bad but inevitable. Thus, conflict will occur even if organizations have taken great pains to prevent it. Recall the discussion in Chapter 8, where we noted that the informal organization will emerge and be active irrespective of management's attempts to suppress it. Thus, organizations will experience conflict even if they have carefully defined employee jobs and their managers are reasonable people who treat employees well. There are even some instances in which conflict is purposely created, such as the project management structure discussed in Chapter 7.

The current view of conflict (see Figure 14-1) is based on the idea that there is an optimum level of conflict which maximizes performance. This optimum level is neither low nor high. In an organization where there is too little conflict, little impetus for innovation and creativity exists. Employees are comfortable and not concerned about improving performance. As a result, things which might improve performance get very little attention. At the other extreme, organizational conflict is so disruptive that employees cannot give proper attention to performance goals because interpersonal or intergroup conflict saps employee energy. Here again, performance suffers. At moderate levels of conflict, however, employees are motivated to resolve conflicts, but these conflicts do not disrupt the normal work activities.

There are two crucial implications of the current view. First, much of the conflict in organizations may be good because it stimulates people to find new ways of doing things. If two employees are in conflict about the best way to do a job, the manager might be advised to encourage the conflict to see which individual is correct. The best technique can then be used in doing the job in the future. This approach should be used sparingly because it usually results in a winner and a loser and this has implications for the organization. As another example, consider two departments that are in conflict. Each department tries to get its own way and engages in whatever blocking behavior it thinks is necessary to prevent the other department from attaining its goals. Top management may see this as dysfunctional; but, instead of trying to suppress the conflict (the traditional approach), management might try to induce the departments to find a solution which allows each to get its way.

Second, management of conflict, not suppression, becomes a key activity. If conflict can be good or bad, constructive conflict should be encouraged and destructive conflict should be resolved. But what criterion should be used to make this decision? Robbins suggests that the most practical and important criterion is group performance.[3] Organizations exist to achieve goals, and high performance by groups in the organization increases the likelihood that the organization's goals will be reached. Thus, if the criterion of group performance is used, managers must view conflict in terms of its effect on group performance before they move to resolve it or encourage it. Specific methods for encouraging and discouraging conflict are discussed later.

Sources of Conflict

The sources of conflict within organizations are numerous. Conflict is caused by limited resources (each person or group wants more resources than are available); interdependent work activities (people interfere with each other's work); the formal organizational structure (people in different departments see the world differently); and communication difficulties (people don't say what they mean or they are not understood). These factors motivate people to block the goal attainment of others and open conflict is the result. (See Figure 14-2.) Once open conflict has occurred, some decisions must be made about how it will be resolved (see box 5). These resolution techniques may be functional, and the conflict may be truly resolved; or they may be dysfunctional, in which case the conflict will remain, or simply reappear later in a different form. In either case, the resolution arrived at will have an influence on the sources of future conflicts.

conflict
management

Since conflict can be either positive or negative, managers should not simply suppress it but should manage it. **Conflict management** involves dealing with conflict in such a way that the organization and the individuals working in it will benefit from it. It also involves knowing when to stimulate conflict and when to resolve it quickly. Communication is a prominent aspect of conflict management because so many misunderstandings occur when individuals or groups are in conflict. The two basic approaches to the management of conflict are: (1) managing the human (interpersonal) aspects of conflict, and (2) managing the structural aspects of conflict. Several methods that are used in each of these approaches are discussed below.

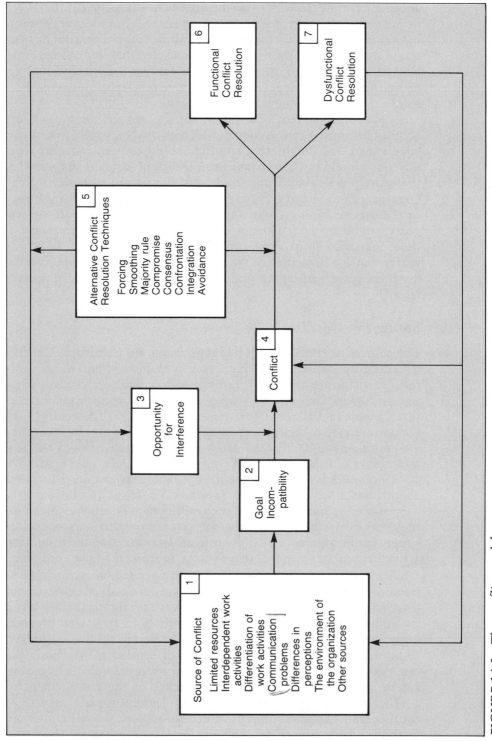

FIGURE 14-2 The conflict model

Interpersonal Conflict Management

The techniques for dealing with interpersonal conflict are numerous. They range from the use of force by a superior over a subordinate to the problem-solving approach. Possible ways of managing interpersonal conflict are discussed below.

Force

When force is used in the resolution of conflict, official authority may compel one party to accept a solution. The expression "he may not be right but he's still the boss" applies in this instance. The party for which the decision was directed may not agree with the results, but if he or she wants to stay within the organization, the directive must be accepted.

Withdrawal

A solution that some individuals use in resolving conflict is to withdraw, or avoid the person with whom the conflict exists. Conflict is reduced, but the reason for the conflict remains. It would be the same as seeing a person you do not want to speak to approaching you on the street, and walking around the block to keep from having to speak to the individual.

Smoothing

When smoothing is used, a manager attempts to provide a semblance of peaceful cooperation by presenting an image that "we're one big happy family." With this approach, problems are rarely permitted to come to the surface, but the potential for conflict remains.

Compromise

Neither party gets all it wants when compromise is used. This is the most typical way of dealing with labor/management conflict. For example, management may offer to increase wages by 8 percent, while the union may be seeking a 12 percent pay hike. A compromise figure of 10 percent may result in a settlement of the conflict, but neither side may be happy with it.

Mediation and Arbitration

arbitration

mediation

Both arbitration and mediation call for outside neutral parties to assist in resolving the conflict. **Arbitration** is frequently used in union/management grievance conflicts. The arbitrator is given the authority to act as a judge in making a decision. The decision rendered is binding on both parties. In **mediation**, a mediator can only suggest, recommend, and attempt to keep the two parties talking in the hope of reaching a solution.

Superordinate Goals

superordinate goal At times, a **superordinate** goal may be encountered that overrides the conflict of two opposing factions. If the firm is in danger of going out of business, both union and management may put aside conflict and work toward the common goal of survival. There have been instances where union members have taken a decrease in pay and benefits in order to assist in the survival of the firm. On a broader level, nations have often banded together to achieve a superordinate goal even though they normally don't get along with each other. Many Arab states in the Middle East, for example, do not see eye-to-eye, but their common concern about the price of oil induces them to work together.

Problem Solving

problem solving Another approach to conflict management is problem solving. As usually practiced, **problem solving** is characterized by an open and trusting exchange of views and facts. A person realizes that conflict is caused by relationships among people and is not within a person. With the problem-solving approach, two individuals can disagree and still remain friends. It is a healthy approach which recognizes that rarely is one person completely right and the other person completely wrong, that granting a concession is not a sign of weakness and that a person does not have to win every battle to maintain his or her self-respect.

With the problem-solving approach, a person recognizes that a certain amount of conflict is healthy. For instance, if a difference of opinion exists between two individuals and they openly discuss their difficulties, a superior solution often results. A person is encouraged to bring difficulties into the open without fear of reprisal. Often, a situation that initially appeared to be a major problem may evolve into only a minor incident, which is easily resolved.

Structural Conflict Management

Conflict can also be managed by changing procedures, organizational structure, physical layout, or expanding resources. These methods for resolving conflict are discussed next.

Procedural Changes

There are times when conflict can occur because a procedure is illogically sequenced. When a credit manager and a sales manager were both about to be fired because of an irreconcilable personality conflict, it was discovered that the processing of credit applications too late in the procedure was the cause of the difficulty. The credit manager was forced to cancel too many deals already made. When the credit check was placed earlier in the procedure, most of the conflict disappeared. In another instance, the personnel director and the production manager were in continuous disagreement. At times the conflict actually came to blows. Then it was discovered that the production manager was not being permitted to review the applicants at an early stage of the hiring sequence and provide input regarding an applicant. When the procedure was changed, many of the difficulties were resolved.

Organizational Changes

The organization can be changed to either promote or reduce conflict. There are times when a department becomes too complacent and, although there is little conflict, very little is accomplished. To reduce undesired conflict within an organization, transfers of incompatible personnel can be made. Often this procedure is quite acceptable, but a manager must be careful that the workers are transferred for the proper reason. To transfer a worker who is incompetent merely because a manager is afraid to deal with the individual does an injustice to the overall goals of the organization. Some managers begin to suspect an employee who is transferred to their department with too glowing a recommendation. The issue for them is, if the employee is that good why is he moving? If transfers are handled on a professional basis, both the company and the employee benefit.

When the conflict is between two units of the organization, special liaison personnel can be assigned. A traditional problem exists between production and marketing. Production personnel have been taught to cut costs, and the technique used most often to accomplish this goal is to produce as few variations of a product as possible. Marketing personnel want products of different colors, styles, and shapes. A person who understands and appreciates the problems of both departments can greatly assist in resolving conflict.

Physical Layout Changes

Changes in the design of the physical work place have been used effectively to reduce or eliminate conflict. Office space can be designed to either force interaction or to make it difficult. Personnel can use desks as barriers and buffers. Some offices have dividers to separate workers. However, if a manager wants to stimulate a problem-solving atmosphere, a more open office arrangement may be permitted. When known antagonists are seated in conference directly across from each other, the amount of conflict increases. When they are seated side by side, the conflict tends to decrease.

A detrimental conflict involving physical layout existed between two groups of workers in a truck assembly plant. Working at different phases on the assembly line, the two groups came into conflict because both had to obtain parts from the same shelving unit. Each group would deliberately rearrange the other group's supply of parts, which sometimes resulted in fights. The conflict was resolved by moving the shelving unit between the two groups so as to set up a barrier between them. Thus, each group had its own supply area or territory. As a result of this change, mistakes were reduced by 50 percent within two days.[4]

Expand Resources

A source of conflict caused by incompatibility of goals can be reduced if resources can be expanded. Thus, in a growing organization everything seems to run smoothly. When hard times come, competition among employees for a possibly diminishing job supply can cause conflict. As enrollment goes down in some colleges and universities, the battle for graduate assistants begins. Should everyone get a graduate assistant? Should the senior faculty members get one? Or should the most productive (but junior) member get the assistant? The same question must be asked when summer teaching assignments are made. Under these conditions, skills in conflict management of the highest order are demanded. Whatever the situation, the effective use of conflict management will have a major impact on overall organizational effectiveness.

ORGANIZATIONAL CHANGE

The topic of managing change is perhaps the one that comes closest to describing the totality of a manager's job. Practically everything a manager does is in some way concerned with implementing change. Hiring a new employee (changing the work group), purchasing a new piece of equipment (changing work methods), and rearranging work stations (changing work flows) all require knowledge of how to manage change effectively. Virtually every time a manager makes a decision some type of change occurs.

Change is a fact of life in all organizations. One study showed that most companies or divisions of major corporations find that they must undertake moderate changes at least once a year and major changes every four or five years. There are different levels of change, ranging from a minor change in a work procedure to a major revamping of the organization's structure.

Recognizing that change occurs frequently should not imply that it should be introduced for its own sake. Managers should ask themselves: "Is this change really necessary?" Managers who make changes for the sake of change may have a disruptive effect on their section. When one of the authors was working as a consultant for a manufacturing firm, he inadvertently noticed a note on the desk of a new vice-president who had been brought in from the outside to improve the poor performance of a division. The note said: "Do not

MANAGEMENT IN PRACTICE

The Impact of Change in the Field of Management

The magnitude of change facing corporations is immense. Of the 10 most profitable firms on a *Forbes* magazine list from 1972, three are no longer in existence, one is involved in bankruptcy proceedings, and four others have poor returns on equity. These figures show how important it is for companies to manage change effectively.

Edward Priestner is president and CEO of Westinghouse Canada Inc. He has overseen a major change in the company, which shifted it away from the centralized structure it formerly had. The firm has also reduced its workforce by 2000 people, and eliminated 14 business divisions.

One specific change has come in the area of quality control. Westinghouse instills in workers the idea that quality is every worker's responsibility, not just the quality control inspector's. In this environment, supervisor's roles are changing from an emphasis on controlling and disciplining to an emphasis on clearing obstacles, finding resources, and communicating. Some supervisors are having difficulty adapting to these new conditions.

SOURCE   Adapted from Margot Gibb-Clark, "Managing Change A Long, Tough Road But A Key To Survival, Executive Warns," *The Globe and Mail* (April 30, 1987): B8.

---

make any major changes for three months." The new executive obviously wanted to be aware of the total situation before she acted. Obviously, she realized that if she acted too quickly, inappropriate changes could be made and an entire division could be further damaged. Organizations and people need some degree of stability in order to accomplish their assigned tasks. But there are times when changes are necessary and failure to make them effectively can have a disastrous effect.

The Change Sequence

The sequence of events needed to bring about change in an organization is shown in Figure 14-3. Management must first recognize that there is a need for change. Then the appropriate method(s) must be chosen. The actual change process cannot begin until these stages are completed.

Recognition of the Need for Change

Managers must train themselves constantly to seek areas for change and improvement. This is not always easy because of the tendency to permit existing conditions to continue; if something was successful in the past, it is tempting to believe it will likely continue to be successful in the future. Managers and employees who view their ongoing performance as successful often resist any changes because the old way is comfortable. If their system is modified, people fear for

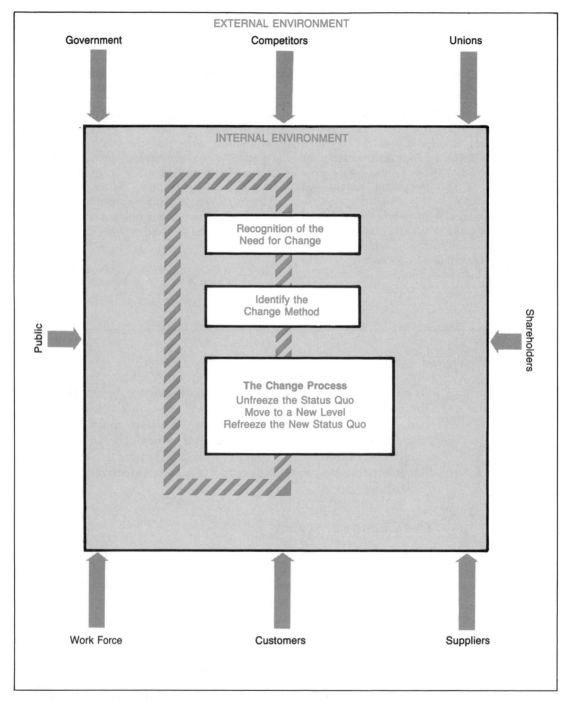

FIGURE 14-3   The change sequence

MANAGEMENT IN PRACTICE

Introducing Change at IBM

Recently, IBM Canada has been experiencing some difficulties. In 1986, computer hardware sales in the industry climbed six percent, but at IBM sales dropped eight percent. The company is introducing some major changes in an attempt to return to an upward growth spiral. For example, nearly 1000 IBM employees are being offered early retirement. In addition, 300 employees who used to work in manufacturing are going through a 17-week retraining program to learn how to write software. Many employees are also being asked to relocate to different branches across the country.

The man heading up the change is John Thompson, president and chief executive officer. He says that the magnitude of the change is the greatest in his 21 years with the company. However, he believes change is good because it keeps people motivated. Thompson notes that IBM is a full-employment company,

so employees aren't worried about actually losing their job. They may have to learn some new skills, however. Thompson also notes that since IBM employees are rotated through different jobs as a normal condition of work, they are more used to change than employees at some other companies.

Some experts think positive assessments like these are naive. Warren Shepell, a Toronto industrial psychologist, argues that employees usually greet changes with some fear because the change may call their competence into question. As well, if employees are unhappy in their new job, productivity could go down and the very reason for the change could be frustrated.

SOURCE   Adapted from Karen Howlett, "IBM Canada Realigns: Staff Go Back to School," *The Globe and Mail* (March 17, 1987): B1–B2.

their job, status, power, or whatever is meaningful to them. There are three basic characteristics a manager must develop in order to recognize that change is needed and to have the courage to implement the change. They are 1) curiosity and discontent, 2) openmindedness, and 3) respect for oneself.[5]

A person should have sufficient curiosity to ask searching questions regarding why a task is being performed in a certain manner; it is vital in recognizing where change for improvement is needed. Discontent, on the other hand, has the implication that a person should fight the system. He or she is not satisfied merely to let things go along in their established pattern and concede that the old way is the best way. Through curiosity and discontent, managers place themselves in a position to recognize when a change may be needed.

Donaldson and Lorsch argue that all companies must change or die, though the change may be revolutionary or evolutionary.[6] There are five possible reasons for imposing rapid cultural change:

- If your company has strong values that don't fit a changing environment
- If the industry is very competitive and moves with lightning speed
- If your company is mediocre or worse
- If the company is about to join the ranks of the very largest companies
- If it is smaller, but growing rapidly.[7]

Managers who believe that their way is always the best will recognize that a change is needed only if they personally make the discovery. Subordinates' opinions are not considered. Managers who are open-minded permit subordinates to make suggestions. They believe that, many times, two heads are better than one and that useful ideas can evolve from lower-level personnel if they are provided the opportunity.

Managers understand that any change is likely to be met with some resistance. However, managers who have respect for themselves do not fear to attempt a modification that may draw initial resistance but will eventually result in a better operation. These individuals believe in their ability.

Identifying the Change Method

Management has at its disposal numerous techniques that can be used to implement organizational change. Specific techniques include survey feedback, team building, process consultation, management by objectives, job enrichment, and sensitivity training. (Several of these are discussed in Chapter 15, in the context of organization development.) The technique chosen should meet the needs of the organization; it should also identify the type of culture that will provide for the greatest productivity in the organization.

Unfreezing the Status Quo

If individuals are to change their present attitudes, current beliefs must be altered or unfrozen.[8] Resistance to change must be eliminated or reduced if a change is to be effective. Once resistance to change has been reduced, the manager is in a position to implement the desired change. Sources of resistance to change and approaches to reduce resistance to change are discussed later in this chapter.

Unfreezing in the change process generates self-doubt and provides a means of remedying the situation. Employees must be made to feel that ineffectiveness is undesirable, but it can be remedied. If organization members are to be receptive to change, they must feel that they can change.

Moving to a New Condition

The initiation of a change can come from an order, a recommendation, or a self-directed impetus. A manager with authority can command that a change be made and enforce its implementation by threats, punishments, and close supervision. If this manner of implementing change is taken, the manager will likely find that the change must be constantly monitored. Change is more permanent and substantial if employees want and feel a need to change.

The most effective approach to initiating change is for a two-way relationship to exist between the person who is attempting to implement the change and the person(s) who must change. Rather than a one-way flow of commands or recommendations, the person implementing the change should make suggestions, and the changees should be encouraged to contribute and participate. Those initiating the change should be responsive to suggestion, either by reformulating the change or by providing explanations as to why the suggestions cannot be incorporated.

Refreezing to Create a New Status Quo

If a person changes to a new set of work habits for a week and then reverts to former practices, the change has not been effective. Too often changes that are introduced do not stick. If the change is to be permanent, employees must be convinced that it is in their own and the organization's best interest. One of the best ways to accomplish this is to collect objective evidence of the success of the change. A manager who sees production increase because of a change in leadership style has obtained excellent evidence of the success of the change. People should have feelings of competence and pleasure in adopting the new behavior. But the change will be completely accepted only if the reward system of the organization is geared to the new form of behavior. If a university states that all its faculty must begin to publish articles and there is no reward attached to publishing, it is likely that few faculty members could be motivated to make this change. An employee's job may be substantially enriched in terms of content and self-supervision, but if the change is not accomplished by properly enriched pay and status symbols, dissatisfaction is likely to result. People tend to repeat behavior that they find rewarding.

Sources of Resistance to Change

A change may involve some loss to the person who is affected by it. Attachments to familiar habits, places, and people must be given up. In major and unexpected changes, there is often daze, shock, recoil, and turmoil.[9] Some of the many sources of resistance to change are described next.

Insecurity

Once people have operated in a particular atmosphere for a long time, they begin to feel comfortable. Change often brings with it uncertainty; workers do not know exactly what to expect. For example, many students experience insecurity as they make the transition from high school to college. A similar sense of insecurity is felt by individuals who move from one job to another or from one city to another. Perhaps because of this feeling of insecurity, many people resist change, both in their personal and professional lives.

Possible Social Loss

A change has the potential to bring about social losses. As we discussed in Chapter 8, the informal work group may be extremely powerful. If change causes individuals in the group to be transferred, the power of the group is likely to be diminished. A change may cause established status symbols to be destroyed or an individual of lower status may even be awarded a high-status symbol.

The impact a change can have on social atmosphere is illustrated by the case of a small hospital that decided to expand from 100 to 300 beds. In one department, all personnel reported directly to the department head, and a close rapport had developed among the members. On a rotating shift, staff members would have to work the evening and night shift, but they still maintained close contact with the other department members. Because of the great increase in workload the work force was expanded; a decision was made to have three shifts with a shift supervisor for each. The department head now had only three people reporting directly to him, and it was believed that the work could be performed much more efficiently. But the social loss was drastic. Subordinates no longer had a close relationship with the department head; some, because they were on a different shift, rarely saw him. This created a tremendous social loss to several long-term employees and resulted in over 50 percent of the personnel quitting within six months.

Economic Losses

Technology may be introduced that can produce the same amount of output with fewer personnel. While most companies make an honest attempt to transfer or retain employees who have been affected by technological change, the fear remains. When the computer was first introduced into business firms, the number of clerical personnel needed was often drastically reduced. The computer firms attempted to lessen this fear by claiming that the number of jobs had actually increased through the use of the computer. This claim was not very convincing to clerical employees, many of whom resisted the retraining necessary. To them, the new computer technology was a major threat. Use of robots on production lines has caused similar concern for assembly-line workers.

Inconvenience

Even if there is no social or economic loss associated with a change, it may still be resisted simply because it represents a new way of doing things. New procedures and techniques may have to be learned. This means that physical and mental energy must be expended — for some people this is not an enjoyable task. When a new phone system is installed in an organization, there initially can be many complaints. The new system means that time and effort must be expended in learning how to use it. It can take months for the system to be accepted by a majority of the firm's personnel at all levels of the structure.

Resentment of Control

Taken as a whole, Canadians are rather independent. When employees are told that a change must take place, they realize that they do not have control over an aspect of their lives. Even though the change may be for the better, a certain amount of resentment may develop. For instance, one government agency decided to implement a management by objectives (MBO) system. While management pointed out the many benefits of the new MBO system, many employees resented the new approach to planning and goal setting because they perceived it as a threat to their way of life in the organization.

Unanticipated Repercussions

Because the organization is a system, a change in one part is likely to have unforeseen repercussions in another portion. For example, a newly enriched job is likely to demand a change in supervisory behavior. The supervisor may resist this change in behavior even though he or she initially supported the concept of job enrichment.

Union Opposition

Labor union representatives in an adversarial atmosphere are inclined to oppose on principle any change suggested by management. Employees are often more comfortable with a fighting union than they are with one that cooperates with management on changes designed to promote organizational interests.

Reducing Resistance to Change

One of the authors, while working as a personnel administrator for a large insurance company, observed that an anticipated introduction of computers brought about considerable employee resistance. Management of the company had announced that a new computer system with greatly increased capacity would be installed in about six months. The new computer would bring substantial changes in many of the clerical jobs performed by office personnel. Uncertain as to what to expect from the change in computer systems, numerous employees began expressing fears and concern about the impact of the change.

Before management took any action, the employees caused a severe slowdown in work flow in the office. Customer and agent complaints rose substantially during the six-week period after the announced change. Management therefore took action to correct the situation by holding a series of small group meetings to explain the new computer

MANAGEMENT IN PRACTICE

Introducing Change at Cardinal

In 1982, Cardinal Meat Specialists Ltd. of Mississauga, Ontario wanted to introduce a change involving the way its employees were paid. The change involved introduction of a major productivity gain-sharing program that was designed to improve employee productivity and to satisfy employee requests for higher income.

The change was introduced in four phases. First, consultants did a feasibility study to determine whether the work the company did would allow the setting of quantitative standards which could be used to measure productivity accurately. Second, a plan was developed to implement the new system. All employees

who were affected by the change were consulted and their views listened to. Third, both employees and management of the company got involved in implementing the change. All actions were explained to employees in small group sessions and in regular written communications. Finally, follow-up discussions were conducted with both employees and management to determine if the program was operating to the company's satisfaction.

SOURCE Adapted from Sandra Bernstein, "Morale Booster: Productivity Gain-Sharing Helps You Get More From Your Workers," *Canadian Business* (April 1984): 122.

---

system and how it would affect each job and each work group. While there would be several major changes in job functions affecting some individuals and work groups, management made a commitment to all employees that no one would be dismissed as a result of the installation of the new computer. The company would provide retraining programs to increase the affected employees' skills, thereby improving their adaptability to the new system.

This incident demonstrates the importance of having a change strategy worked out before any change announcements are made. In the insurance company, management had not anticipated employee uncertainty; it had to scramble around on short notice to come up with a program that would reduce employees' fears and get them to concentrate on their normal work. Fortunately, everything worked out all right, but the change was not planned very well.

When developing the change strategy, several principles should be kept in mind to reduce resistance. We will discuss each of these in turn.

Make Only Necessary Changes

Changes should be made only when the situation demands, not because of a whim on the part of a manager. A manager who gains a reputation for making change for the sake of change will discover that the support for any change, whether beneficial or not, will be minimal.

Attempt To Maintain Useful Informal Relationships

We noted in Chapter 8 that the informal work group is a powerful force in organizations. Therefore, when introducing change, every effort must be made to ensure that crucial informal relationships, status hierarchies, or group norms are not disrupted. When safety shoes were first introduced, for example, few workers would wear them willingly because of their appearance. When they were redesigned to resemble dress shoes, resistance faded. The granting of fictional rank to civilian consultants who are to work with military personnel makes their integration into ongoing operations more acceptable. A staff expert who wants a change introduced may find it advisable to have the announcement made by a line executive and to allow the line executive to share some of the credit. Changes that go against established customs and informal norms will likely cause resistance and reduce the chance of acceptance.

Build Trust

If a manager has a reputation for providing reliable and timely information to employees, the explanation as to why a change is to be made will likely be more believable. The change may still be resisted, but if the manager is trusted by the employees, problems will be minimized. On the other hand, managers who have gained a reputation for providing incomplete or inaccurate information will experience considerable resistance as they attempt to institute change.

Provide Information in Advance

Whenever possible, the manager should provide in advance the reasons for the change, its nature, planned timing, and the possible impact on the organization and its personnel. Withholding information that could seriously affect the lives and futures of particular individuals, such as keeping secret the planned closure of a plant in order to maintain the work-force level until the last possible moment, should be avoided. The firm that gains a reputation for such actions will have a difficult time making future changes. There are occasions when competitive survival requires that information be closely held until shortly before introduction. In these cases, the information should be provided on an as-required basis.

Encourage Participation

When possible, subordinate participation should be encouraged in establishing a change. A person who is involved in implementing new procedures will likely be more supportive of the change. Recall from Chapter 11 that Theory Y assumes abilities are widespread in the population. Thus, many valuable ideas may be gained by permitting employees to help in implementing change.

Guarantee Against Loss

To promote acceptance of technological changes, some organizations guarantee no layoffs as a result of such changes. In cases of a change in methods and output standards, employees are often guaranteed retention of their present level of earnings during the learning periods.

Provide Counseling

At times some form of nonthreatening discussion and counseling may be required. Nondirective counseling has been used effectively in many change situations. The approach rests on a fundamental belief that people have the ability to solve their problems with the aid of a sympathetic listener. The role of a counselor is to understand rather than pass judgment. This type of counseling requires a permissive, friendly atmosphere, with actions and statements that exhibit continuing interest but not judgment. In most instances, managers with authority are unable to establish this type of atmosphere. Successful nondirective counseling must usually be undertaken by staff psychologists. What the manager can do is to permit some ventilation of feelings by subordinates, particularly those of frustration and anger. Discovering that others have similar feelings and doubts will often make the transition less painful.

STRESS MANAGEMENT

stress

A by-product of some change is the stress that can develop in workers. **Stress** is the nonspecific response of the body to any demands made on it. Over a period of time or under intense conditions, stress can take its toll on the body. A vast array of ailments ranging from lower back pains and headaches to coronary problems and cancer are considered to be by-products of stress. If stress is strong enough and lasts long enough, it can damage both mental and physical health. Unmanaged stress can create anxiety, depression, paranoia, and other mental difficulties for the individual. The cost and pain of stress are enormous. Although costs are difficult to state exactly, stress-related absenteeism, illness, and premature death cost Canadian companies millions of dollars each year.

Fortunately, managers are now beginning to realize that effective stress management is important to them, to their employees, and to the organization. Job-related stress can be as disruptive and as costly to the corporation as any accident that occurs to an employee. In fact, many employee accidents are considered to be stress-related. Managers must recognize employee behavior patterns that may indicate excessive stress.

MANAGEMENT IN PRACTICE

Stress and Organizational Change

At one time or another, most executives have had to deal with an employee who breaks down and cries on the job. Studies in this area show that the person doing the crying generally isn't trying to manipulate the boss. Rather, the person has simply crossed the threshold of what he or she can tolerate. Studies show that women cry about four times as often as men on the job.

Emotional reactions on the part of employees are particularly noticeable during major organizational changes. Theodore Williams, chairperson of Bell Industries Inc. noted that his firm is in the midst of a major move to computerization, and many employees are feeling insecure. When he is confronted with an employee who is crying, he usually invites the person into his office to talk with them privately.

Most business executives say crying and business don't mix. One executive was telling a supervisor that performance in her department had to show improvement. When the supervisor began crying, the executive simply left the room. He argues that dealing with anyone who is crying — male or female — is not productive. He talks to them later when they have calmed down. A crying worker may also trigger resentment among those workers who don't cry at work. They feel if *they* can control themselves, so should other people.

People who are prone to tears worry that it will negatively affect their careers. And in some companies it does. A common assumption is that a person who cries in a professional situation is weak, or is trying to manipulate others.

SOURCE Adapted from Kathleen A. Hughes, "Bosses May Wince, But Crying Helps," *The Globe and Mail*, (March 5, 1987): B1–B2.

- Working late more than usual, or increased tardiness or absenteeism
- Difficulty in making decisions
- Increase in the number of careless mistakes
- Missing deadlines or forgetting appointments
- Problems interacting and getting along with others
- Focusing on mistakes and personal failure.[10]

Management can anticipate or try to reduce stress for employees through preventive attitudes. For example, if management recognizes that the corporate culture is causing problems, a conscious effort can be made to change it. Perhaps it should be made more open and less threatening so that workers can do their jobs without stress. Another way to reduce stress is to redesign jobs so that workers feel that they are doing something exciting and worthwhile rather than boring and unimportant. Changes can also be made to the physical layout by reducing excessive noise, heat, or other poor working conditions. Some companies have introduced physical fitness programs for their employees, which help improve their physical condition and allow them to cope more effectively with the stress that is unavoidable on the job.

Joanne Klassen
Human Resources Consultant

Joanne Klassen is a human resources consult-ant, training specialist, and writer. During the past 15 years, she has developed and presented over 600 programs spanning a wide range of professional and personal development topics. Ms. Klassen is currently the Executive Director of the Employee Assistance Centre, a division of Blue Cross. The centre provides counseling services in many areas, including marriage, careers, alcohol and drug abuse, stress, and smoking cessation. Ms. Klassen is also the Di-rector of the Human Development Centre, a private consulting group. She is the author of *Learning to Live, Learning to Love* (1985), a book about self-esteem and communication, and is the co-author of *Minding Her Own Business*, a study of female entrepreneurs. One of her major interests is the impact of stress on individuals in their personal and professional lives. We asked her several questions related to stress.

Q: How do you define stress?
Klassen: I believe Hans Selye's definition is very useful. He says that stress is the nonspe-cific response of the body to any demand made on it. We all must deal with demands from our external environment. It's *how* we deal with these demands that is important. Stated an-other way, stress is not what happens to you, but how you deal with what happens to you.

Q: Are there obvious signs that a person is under stress?
Klassen: Yes. The major one is any marked change in behavior in an individual. For exam-ple, if a person who is known to be uncon-cerned about the way they dress suddenly be-gins to dress very smartly, that person could be under stress. Or, if a person who is always on time for meetings suddenly begins to be late for everything, this is also a warning signal. These warning signs don't tell us what is caus-ing the change in behavior, but they suggest that there may be some new stress in the per-son's life that they are having difficulty dealing with.

Q: Are there other, more specific signs of stress?
Klassen: There are quite a few specific things that suggest that a person is under stress (hunching up the shoulders or tensing the muscles in the jaw), but I think the more general signs of stress are better indicators. Most fundamentally, when people try to be something they aren't, this causes stress. Much has been written about Type A and Type B individuals. If a Type A tries to be a Type B, this may cause stress and vice versa. To use an illustration developed by Hans Selye, a "racehorse" type of person is going to find it very difficult to behave like a "turtle" in every-day activities. We each have certain personali-ties that influence how we respond to demands made on us, and trying to behave in an artificial way is stressful.

Q: Do Type A people experience more stress than Type B people?
Klassen: Yes, but any person can experience stress. Type A's generally experience more stress because they are achievement-oriented and deadline-oriented. They are therefore more likely to be under self-imposed pressure. But Type B's can also experience stress. Re-member, it's not how many demands are placed on you by your environment that is

harmful, it's how you deal with those demands.

Q: Various lists of major "stress events" (such as losing your job) have been developed. Are these lists accurate, and are they helpful in dealing with stress?

Klassen: Let's take the example of a person losing their job. If they were basically unhappy with the job, that will cause them far less stress than if they lost a job they loved. The lists you are referring to do not include these kinds of refinements. In addition, certain important stress events are not even included on these lists (for instance, suicide of a coworker). Further, minor chronic stressors such as noise, smoke, or crowding can have a significant cumulative effect over time, yet they are not on these lists. But the lists are useful for showing us that excessive stress can develop when too many stressful events occur at one time. Since the lists contain many events that are commonly experienced by people, each person can identify with them.

Q: Are there data on the costs of stress to organizations in Canada?

Klassen: It is difficult to be precise about the costs of stress, but the Canadian Institute of Stress in Montreal estimates that Canada loses over $20 million per work day because of the stress that our work force is experiencing. We also estimate that stress-related disabilities cost Canada approximately $13 billion a year in lowered productivity, lost work days, and disability and medical payments.

Q: How can people reduce the stress they are experiencing?

Klassen: There are four basic things that can be done. First, recognize that everyone has demands put on them. You can't easily change these demands because they are part of your role as a manager, or a parent, or whatever. You can, however, change the way you react to these demands. This involves updating your value system. Things you learned as a child may no longer be appropriate or realistic, yet you may feel compelled to pursue them. For example, many young men are raised to believe they should make more money than their father did. Many young women think they should be a first-rate homemaker and hold down a full-time job. Both of these situations create stress because unrealistic demands may

be placed on the individual. Second, re-examine your priorities. You can't do everything well, yet over time, people keep adding tasks to their list of things to do without ever considering whether these tasks are still important to them. Prioritizing activities prevents stress by focusing your attention on important things; it also keeps you from worrying about unimportant things.

Third, after you have decided what is important, choose a task you have control over and finish it. Being involved in a lot of projects that are in various stages of completion can lead to a feeling of lack of accomplishment and this increases stress.

Finally, make sure you spend some time doing things that are fun. There must be a balance between things you have to do and things you want to do. Some people are fortunate because the things they have to do are the things they want to do. These people can, for example, take work along on their holidays and be very happy.

Q: What is the relationship between exercise and stress?

Klassen: Exercise reduces the harmful effects of stress. When a person is stressed, adrenalin is produced. Although adrenalin is an integral part of the "fight or flight" response, it is harmful to the heart if it builds without release. Exercise is an excellent way to get excess adrenaline out of the body.

Q: What can managers do to help subordinates who are experiencing stress?

Klassen: Stress management training programs benefit managers as well as employees. Increasingly, there are formal employee assistance programs (EAP's) that are available in organizations. Managers must be well-versed about the services these programs offer so they can direct employees to the appropriate help. As part of this process, the manager must determine whether the problem is job-related or is being caused by something off-the-job. If the stress is job-related, then coaching, training, or clarifying work expectations may reduce the level of stress. Help is available in many companies, and this help is professional. Many managers feel uncomfortable about dealing with certain kinds of employee problems, so the existence of confidential professional help is very valuable to both the manager and the employee.

EXECUTIVE BURNOUT

executive burnout

Although related to stress, executive burnout is a distinct concept. **Executive burnout** has been defined as "a state of fatigue or frustration brought about by devotion to a cause, way of life, or relationship that failed to produce the expected reward."[11] Burnout may affect as many as 1 in 10 managers. A major problem with burnout is that it is contagious. If one executive is a burnout victim, he or she may influence others to become cynical, negative, and pessimistic. The result is an entire group which is unhappy, unproductive, and resistant to improvements.[12]

Some of the symptoms of burnout include: (1) chronic fatigue, (2) anger at those making demands, (3) self-criticism for putting up with the demands, (4) cynicism, negativism, and irritability, (5) a sense of being besieged, and (6) a hair-trigger display of emotions.[13] Other symptoms might include recurring health problems, such as ulcers, back pain, and frequent headaches. The burnout victim is often emotionally changeable; unwarranted hostility may occur in completely inappropriate situations.

Burnout often occurs among talented, achievement-oriented workers. Many of these people are business executives. Perhaps they have set their standards too high and then refuse to admit that they cannot achieve them. Sometimes the organization itself designs situations that are capable of causing burnout. Giving a manager a job to do and then making it virtually impossible for the person to do the job is an example. Burnout is the "consequence of a work situation in which the person gets the feeling he's butting his head against the wall day after day, year after year."[14]

The problem can be corrected. Some firms are arranging for full-time staff counselors to help employees who are experiencing burnout. Seminars can be given to help managers help their workers overcome the problem. Some firms are granting disability leaves until the worker recovers.

Firms can also take measures to prevent burnout among their employees. For example, workers should not be permitted to work too much overtime, even on critical problems. Often the best people are called on first in times of crisis. These are the very people who are likely to burn out. Another method to avoid overburdening good workers is to rotate employees who are working on stressful jobs. Some firms are starting physical exercise programs and counseling programs. Moving people to a new project can relieve stress, and breaks in the business routine are often helpful.[15] The job at hand should not be allowed to overshadow all other aspects of living.

OPENING INCIDENT REVISITED

Craig Ltd.

Lorna Kasian ran into a hornet's nest when she tried to implement a major renovation at Craig Ltd. Now that you have been exposed to some material on organizational change, it is easy to see why this problem arose and what should have been done to implement the change properly.

Why have these groups objected so vigorously to the change? In the chapter, several reasons were given and one or more of them may apply here. The people may be insecure about their new work stations, how the proposed renovations will affect their informal social relationships, or how much inconvenience the renovation will cause.

How could this vocal opposition have been avoided? Again, the chapter makes several suggestions. Generally speaking, Kasian would have to demonstrate first that the change was necessary and, second, that it recognized and maintained important informal relationships. If Kasian hoped to gain general acceptance for the project from the other empoyees, she should have provided information in advance and encouraged participation in the plans along the way. Any concerns people may have had about social or status losses would have

been dealt with; technical requirements for groups like the drafting department and promises made to marketing would have been noted earlier in the process. More specifically, Kasian should have consulted with each group before trying to have a renovation plan drawn up by an architect. Consultations would undoubtedly reveal good ideas for the renovation plan. Recall that the secretaries came up with a good idea that Kasian hadn't thought of.

What about the president's unhappiness at Kasian's inability to complete the renovations on time? If Kasian had consulted with various people right at the start, she would have known that renovations could not possibly be finished when the president wanted. Kasian could therefore have told him that he had two options: impose renovations without consultation and face the consequences, or proceed with consultations so that the renovations are enthusiastically accepted. The president could then decide what he wanted, but Kasian would not be to blame if he chose the first alternative. More than likely, he would have seen the wisdom of consultation and he would have increased the time allotment for the renovations.

SUMMARY

Conflict occurs when an individual or group purposely inhibits the goal attainment efforts of another individual or group. The traditional view assumes that conflict is bad and must be immediately resolved, while the current view assumes that some level of conflict may be desirable in organizations.

There are many sources of conflict, including limited resources, interdependent work activities, differentiation of work activities, communication problems, differences in perceptions, and the environment of the organization. These sources can lead to goal incompatibility. If an opportunity for interference exists, open conflict can develop.

Various conflict management devices have been proposed. Interpersonal conflict management techniques include forcing, withdrawal, smoothing, compromise, mediation/arbitration, superordinate goals, and problem solving. Structural conflict management techniques include procedural changes, organizational changes, physical layout changes, and the expansion of resources. The application of these techniques may lead to either functional or dysfunctional resolution of conflict.

The sequence of events needed to bring about change in an organization begins with management's recognition of the need for a change. Next, the method to be used is identified. The next steps consist of unfreezing the status quo, moving to a new level, and freezing to create a new status quo. A change may cause some loss to the person who is affected by it, and thus generate resistance. Some of the possible reasons for resistance to change include insecurity, possible social loss, economic losses, inconvenience, resentment of control, unanticipated repercussions, and union opposition. Approaches that may be used to reduce resistance to change include providing information in advance, encouraging participation, guaranteeing against loss, providing counseling, making only necessary changes, attempting to maintain useful customs and informal relationships, building trust, and allowing for negotiation.

Stress management and executive burnout are of increasing concern to managers. Stress is the nonspecific response of the body to any demands made upon it. A person experiencing executive burnout is someone in a state of fatigue or frustration brought about by devotion to a cause, way of life, or relationship that failed to produce the desired reward. There are numerous ways to identify and treat both stress and executive burnout.

REVIEW QUESTIONS

1. What is conflict? What two factors must exist before open conflict is evident?
2. What major factors in organizations are sources of conflict?
3. What is the difference between the traditional and current views of conflict?
4. List and describe the structural conflict management techniques.
5. List and describe the interpersonal conflict management techniques.
6. List and describe the steps in the change sequence.
7. What is the primary reason for introducing a change in an organization?
8. What are the sources of resistance to change?
9. Describe the approaches that may be used to reduce resistance to change.
10. Define and distinguish between stress and executive burnout.
11. What can organizations do to help individuals cope with stress and burnout?

EXERCISES

1. Think of a conflict situation that you have recently experienced. Analyze it using the conflict model in Figure 14-1.
2. Identify the major changes that have occurred in your life in the past year. How did you react to these changes?
3. Assume that you are the president of a community college and that you would like to make the following changes:
   a. Students must be professionally attired at all times
   b. Faculty members must be in their office daily by 9 a.m.
   Assuming that these changes are being made for a logical reason, what type of resistance to these changes could you expect? How could you deal with resistance to these changes?
4. Interview three practicing managers. Determine the level of stress they perceive in their job and how they cope with stress. Ask them to speculate on other jobs that are more stressful than theirs and why they see them as more stressful.

CASE STUDY

Rumors of a Change at Duncan Electric

Donna Pichet is a supervisor for Duncan Electric Corporation, a manufacturer of high-quality electrical parts. Pichet has been with the firm for five years and has a reputation for having one of the best teams in the plant. Pichet picked the majority of these employees herself and was proud of the reputation they had achieved. But a problem was now brewing that had the potential to destroy her department.

For weeks, rumors of a substantial reduction in personnel at Duncan Electric have been circulating. Pichet has not received any confirmation from the corporate office regarding the reduction. The rumors, all claiming to be from reliable sources, range from minor reductions to a large-scale reduction in personnel. Every day someone claims to have the inside story, and every day the story changes. Pichet, who has a reputation for leveling with her people, successfully discounted the rumors for a while. But, as the doubts grew, work output began to suffer. Her employees were now spending time trying to verify the latest rumor. Speculation increased to the point where the best-qualified employees were starting to shop around.

The action by these employees did not make sense unless there was to be a very large-scale layoff. Pichet was convinced that a minor layoff was the worst that could possibly happen and she was demoralized to see her department falling apart for no good reason.

On Friday, two of the most skilled employees in the department told Pichet that they had taken a job with a competitor. This situation was what she had feared most; the best qualified workers would leave and the least qualified workers would remain. Instead of having one of the best departments at Duncan Electric, she may now have one of the worst.

QUESTIONS

1. Why have the rumors damaged the morale of the employees in Donna Pichet's department?
2. What should management do to reduce the fear of the anticipated change?
3. What should Pichet do in a situation like this?

CASE STUDY

A Line-Staff Conflict

Hutton Solvents manufactures a group of products which includes paint thinner, liquid cleaners, and automobile windshield de-icer. The company owns a large plant in Ontario where these products are manufactured on a mass-production basis. Most of the production line-supervisors have been with the company for many years, although they do not have a lot of formal schooling.

The company was having problems with quality control and machine breakdowns, and in an attempt to resolve these, a quality control/engineering department (QC/E) was formed to monitor manufacturing processes. The department was staffed with individuals with expertise in quality control and industrial engineering. In fact, most of the people in the new department were industrial engineers. The department had two main functions: (1) to run quality control checks on the finished products, and (2) to keep up on the latest developments in specialized, high-speed machinery for the manufacture and packaging of solvents.

Within a few months of the new department's formation, problems became evident. Brendan MacDuff, the head of the QC/E department, indicated to the vice-president of production that his department was being largely ignored, and that the supervisors of the various production lines in the plant were working as they had always worked. He argued that this was not what had been intended when

the QC/E department had been set up. The quality control and engineering expertise in the QC/E department was being totally wasted, he claimed, because production line-supervisors were ignoring advice from his department. MacDuff supported his arguments by noting that quality control and machine breakdown problems were still very much in evidence. He concluded by saying that the only way to resolve these problems was to give the QC/E department functional authority over the supervisors with respect to quality control and new machinery decisions.

The vice-president said he would have to think that over very carefully. He agreed that the quality control problem had to be solved, but he wasn't sure that the machinery question was as clear-cut. He noted that the production line-supervisors were very valuable to the company because they "got the product out the door." He was therefore reluctant to institute changes that would make them unhappy. He promised to get back to MacDuff after speaking with the production line-supervisors.

QUESTIONS

1. Use Figure 14-2 to analyze the development of this conflict.
2. Develop a plan for resolving the problem. Describe each action that should be taken, including the use of specific conflict management techniques.

ENDNOTES

[1] This view of conflict was proposed in S. Schmidt and T. Kochan, "Conflict: Toward Conceptual Clarity," *Administrative Science Quarterly* 17 (1972): 359–370.

[2] S. Robbins, *Organizational Behavior* (Englewood Cliffs, N.J.: Prentice-Hall, 1979): 289.

[3] Robbins, 288.

[4] H. Kenneth Bobele and Peter J. Buchanan, "Building a More Productive Environment," *Management World* 8 (January 1979): 8.

[5]Addison C. Bennet, "The Manager's Responsibility for Work Improvement," in *Improving the Effectiveness of Hospital Management* (New York: Preston, 1972): 161–162.

[6]Gordon Donaldson and Jay Lorsch, *Decision Making at the Top* (New York: Basic Books, 1983).

[7]Bro Uttal, "The Corporate Culture Vultures," *Fortune* (October 17, 1983): 66–72.

[8]Kurt Lewin, *Field Theory and Social Science* (New York: Harper, 1964): Chapters 9 and 10.

[9]Ralph G. Huschowitz, "The Human Aspects of Managing Transition," *Personnel* 51 (May-June 1974): 13.

[10]John M. Ivancevich and Michael T. Matteson, *Stress and Work: A Managerial Perspective* (Glenview, Ill.: Scott, Foresman, 1980): 208.

[11]Herbert J. Freudenberger, *Burnout: The High Cost of High Achievement* (Garden City, N.Y.: Anchor Press, 1980): 13.

[12]Gary Cherniss, "Job Burnout: Growing Worry For Workers, Bosses," *US News and World Report* (February 27, 1980): 72.

[13]Harry Levinson, "When Executives Burn Out," *Harvard Business Review* 59 (May-June, 1981): 76.

[14]Freudenberger, *Burnout*: 17–18.

[15]Levinson, "When Executives Burn Out," 78–81.

REFERENCES

Allen, R. F., and Silverzweig, S. "Changing Community and Organizational Cultures." *Training and Development Journal* 31 (July 1977): 28–34.

Baron, Robert. "Reducing Organizational Conflict: An Incompatible Response Approach." *Journal of Applied Psychology* 69, (May 1984): 272–279.

_____. "Reducing Organizational Conflict: The Role of Attributions." *Journal of Applied Psychology* 70, (August 1985): 434–441.

Bensahel, J. G. "How to Overcome Resistance to Change." *International Management* 32 (September 1977): 66–67.

Bhagat, Rabi S. "Effects and Stressful Life Events on Individuals Performance Efforts and Work Adjustment Processes with Organizational Settings: A Research Model." *Academy of Management Review* 8, no. 4 (October 1983): 660–671.

Biggart, N. W. "Creative-Destructive Process of Organizational Change: The Case of the Post Office." *Administrative Science Quarterly* 22 (September 1977): 410–426.

Carlson, H. C. "Organizational Research and Organizational Change." *Personnel* 54 (July 1977): 11–22.

Cosier, Richard A. "Equity Theory and Time: A Reformulation," *Academy of Management Review* 8, no. 2 (April 1983): 311–319.

Davis, L. E. "Individuals and the Organization." *California Management Review* 22 (Spring 1980): 5–14.

Fennell, Mary L. "Synergy, Influence and Information in the Adoption of Administrative Innovations." *Academy of Management Journal* 27, no. 1 (March 1984): 113–129.

Frese, Michael. "Stress At Work and Psychosomatic Complaints: A Causal Interpretation." *Journal of Applied Psychology* 70, (May 1985): 314–328.

Gaertner, Gregory H.; Gaertner, Karen N.; and Akinnusi, David M. "Environment, Strategy and the Implementation of Administrative Change: The Case of Civil Service Reform." *Academy of Management Journal* 27, no. 3 (September 1984): 525–543.

Ganster, Daniel; Fusilier, Marcelline; and Mayes, Bronston. "Role of Social Support in the Experience of Stress At Work." *Journal of Applied Psychology* 71, (February 1986): 102–110.

Gibb-Clarke, Margot. "Managing Change a Long, Tough Road But a Key to Survival." *The Globe and Mail* (April 30, 1987): B8

Govier, Katherine. "Eminence Gray." *Canadian Business* 59, (March 1986): 30–34, 107–112.

Howlett, Karen. "IBM Canada Realigns: Staff Go Back to School." *The Globe and Mail* (March 17, 1987): B1–B2.

Hughes, Kathleen. "Bosses May Wince, But Crying Helps." *The Globe and Mail* (March 5, 1987): B1–B2.

Jackson, Susan; Schwab, Richard; and Schuler, Randall. "Toward An Understanding of the Burnout Phenomenon." *Journal of Applied Psychology* 71 (November 1986): 630–640.

Jamal, Muhammad; and Ahmed, Syed. "Job Stress, Stress-Prone Type A Behavior, and Personal and Organizational Consequences." *Canadian Journal of Administrative Sciences* 2 (December 1985): 360–374.

Kimberly, John; and Quinn, Robert. *Managing Organizational Transitions.* Homewood, Ill.: Irwin, 1984.

Motowidlo, Stephen; Packard, John; and Manning, Michael. "Occupational Stress: Its Causes and Consequences for Job Performance." *Journal of Applied Psychology* 71 (November 1986): 618–629.

Oriorne, George S. "The Change Registers." *Personnel Administrator* 26 (January 1981): 57–63.

Peters, James W.; and Mabry, Edward A. "The Personnel Officer as Internal Consultant." *Personnel Administrator* 26 (April 1981): 29–32.

Seers, Anson; McGee, Gail W.; Serey, Timothy T.; and Graen, George B. "The Interaction of Job Stress and Social Support: A Strong Inference Investigation." *Academy of Management Journal* 26, no. 2 (June 1983): 273–284.

Tichy, Noel M. *Managing Strategic Change: Technical, Political and Cultural Dynamics.* New York: Wiley, 1983.

15

Corporate Culture and Organization Development

KEY TERMS

corporate culture
participative culture
organization
  development

change agent
survey feedback
  method
team building

process consultation
sensitivity training
management
  development
  programs

LEARNING OBJECTIVES

After completing this chapter you should be able to

1. Explain the concept of corporate culture and describe the factors that determine it.
2. Describe a participative culture and identify the values and limitations of participation.

3. Define the term "organization development" (OD) and explain the role of the change agent in OD programs.
4. Describe the OD techniques that can be used to assist in changing the culture of an organization.
5. Distinguish between "management development" and "organization development."

OPENING INCIDENT

The Toronto Experience

Albert Arnot is the president of Fun-Time Ltd. The firm manufactures playground equipment which is sold by major retail outlets across Canada. Most of the firm's 200 employees are production workers; there are about 15 managers, including the president and vice presidents. Fun-Time is a small firm, and has a rather informal atmosphere. Arnot encourages this, and insists that everyone call him by his first name. Some of the managers are not comfortable with this informality, but they go along with it.

A few months ago, the president of the company finally decided to attend a management development seminar in Toronto that he had been considering for a long time. After he returned from the three-day experience, he was very enthused about what he had learned. When asked about the details, the president had some difficulty saying exactly what had happened, other than that he had "learned more about himself as a person." Some of the vice-presidents didn't know quite what to make of this.

A few weeks later, the managers in the firm received a memo which summarized the president's "Toronto Experience." The memo talked in glowing terms about "increasing awareness of one's capabilities" and "gaining insights into one's real being." It also talked about the importance of interpersonal relationships and how improvements in this area could benefit the performance of the organization as a whole. The memo concluded by saying that all managers in the firm would profit from such an experience and that each manager should consult with the president on when he or she wanted to attend the seminar.

Over the next two days, small groups of executives were seen talking in anxious, animated tones about the president's memo.

The opening incident demonstrates the importance of corporate culture to the organization and the individuals within it. In this chapter, we first define the term "corporate culture" and identify the factors that influence it. Two basic cultures often found in organizations are described next. The second major section of the chapter deals with organization development. The term is defined and a variety of OD techniques are discussed. The chapter concludes with a discussion of management development.

CORPORATE CULTURE

corporate culture

Corporate culture is the complex set of values, beliefs, assumptions, and symbols that define the way in which a firm conducts its business.[1] Corporate culture is composed of such factors as friendliness, supportiveness, and risk taking. Employees' perceptions of the organization's culture are gradually formed by each individual in the course of performing assigned activities under the general guidance of a superior and a set of organizational policies. The culture existing within a firm has an impact on the employees' degree of satisfaction with the job, as well as on the level and quality of their performance. The assessment of how good or poor the organization's culture is may differ for each employee. One person may perceive the environment as bad, and another may see the same environment as good. An employee may actually leave an organization in the hope of finding a more compatible culture.

Antony Jay stated, "It has been known for some time that corporations are social institutions with customs and taboos, status groups and pecking orders, and many sociologists and social scientists have studied and written about them as such. But they are also political institutions, autocratic and democratic, peaceful and warlike, liberal and paternalistic."[2] What Jay was writing about, although the term had not then achieved broad usage, was corporate culture.

MANAGEMENT IN PRACTICE

Corporate Culture at Hewlett-Packard (Canada) Ltd.

Malcolm Gissing is president and general manager of Hewlett-Packard Canada Ltd. Like everyone else at the company, he wears a name tag. Everyone calls him Malcolm. The practice of using first names is what the people who work at Hewlett-Packard call "the HP way."

The Canadian subsidiary of HP is headquartered in Mississauga, Ontario. The company has a distinctive corporate culture that seems to work as well in Mississauga as it does in Palo Alto, California, the US headquarters. The company throws beer bashes for employees several times a year, and employees can go to several resorts the company operates for employees.

The HP way is based on the idea that people want to do a good job and be creative, and that they will perform well if they are given the proper environment in which to work. At HP, each employee is treated with consideration and respect, and their personal achievements are recognized. The company emphasizes communication among employees. One way this is done is the "mandatory coffee break." Employees are urged to take two coffee breaks a day so they get to know other employees.

The company believes that employees should benefit if the firm does well. The company has a profit sharing plan and in recent years employee salaries have been supplemented by 7 to 9 percent as a result of profit sharing.

SOURCE   Adapted from Daniel Stoffman, "Great Workplaces and How They Got That Way," *Canadian Business* (September 1984): 30–33, 34, 36, 38.

Identifying A Corporation's Culture

The culture of an organization may be difficult to determine by casual observation. A detailed knowledge of what goes on in an organization is generally necessary before an accurate assessment can be made of its culture. One obvious way to assess culture is to observe how new employees are oriented to the firm. What employees are told when they first begin work gives a good indication of whether or not a firm has a strong culture, and just what that culture is. Organizations with strong cultures make sure that the key values in the firm are communicated to new employees.

A firm's culture can also be determined by analyzing the behavior, attitudes, and values of the top executives in the firm. Their views about what is important, as well as their reactions to crises or opportunities facing the firm, give a good idea of the firm's culture. The culture of a firm is strongly influenced by the top executive's values.[3] In many firms with strong cultures stories are widely circulated about how the leader responded to a certain situation. These stories convey to employees what the key values of the firm are. Rites and ceremonies can also be used to assess the culture of the firm, as can an examination of the firm's philosophy or values statements.

MANAGEMENT IN PRACTICE

Corporate Culture at Principal Group

Principal Group of Edmonton was one of the most technologically advanced financial services companies in Canada. It also had some of the most imaginative sales campaigns. Work was never boring at this company. In 1983 president Donald Cormie auctioned off 10 of his prize Maine Anjou heifers — on the 29th and 30th floors of the Principal building. On another occasion, one executive arrived for a meeting on horseback.

The culture of the company attracted "doers" instead of bureaucrats, in Cormie's view. Employees generally felt that the company was a friendly place to work; the impersonal environment that exists in many large companies was not evident here. Staff togetherness was encouraged at the Cormie Ranch Field Day, when staff members travelled to the ranch to enjoy a cattle show, steak dinner, and Western band.

As part of its culture, the company placed great emphasis on goal achievement by employees. Employees who reached sales goals were given gifts such as vacations, records, and champagne. On one occasion, 37 people were flown to Paris to celebrate a successful sales campaign.

Unfortunately, the positive corporate culture at Principal was not enough to save the company. On June 30, 1987, two of Principal's subsidiaries — First Investors Corp. and Associated Investors of Canada, Ltd. — collapsed. On August 10, 1987, Principal declared bankruptcy. Interestingly, many employees had no idea the company was in trouble. One sales rep said he heard of the collapse on the evening news.

SOURCE Adapted from Daniel Stoffman, "Great Workplaces and How They Got That Way," *Canadian Business* (September 1984): 30–33, 34, 36, 38. Also, "Principal Failures Shock Salesman," *Winnipeg Free Press* (Nov. 13, 1987): 17.

In spite of the fact that the culture may be somewhat elusive, it can have a very strong influence on the people working in the firm. Employees may have a difficult time describing in words exactly what the corporate culture is, but they know what behaviors are consistent with it.

Some firms have so effectively developed their culture that they have achieved a certain reputation. Procter and Gamble, for example, is known for having a culture that stresses high quality products. IBM is world renowned for a culture that stresses customer service. Matsushita's emphasis on good quality at low prices is also well-known.

Corporate Culture and Organizational Performance

In the early 1980s, several best-selling books on corporate culture appeared, including *In Search of Excellence, Theory Z*, and *Corporate Culture*.[4] These books relate many anecdotes, stories, and legends about various organizations and how they conduct their business. In *Corporate Culture*, for example, the authors refer to the biographies and speeches of leaders at IBM, NCR, General Motors, and Kellogg's as support for their arguments about corporate culture. They also describe many of the corporate rituals and ceremonies that are evident in organizations with strong corporate cultures.

The theme of these books is that a strong corporate culture leads to success for the firm. The argument is that a strong culture stimulates employees to work harder and pay attention to what matters in the firm. In an organization that does not have a strong culture, each major area of the firm may pursue its own interests without sufficient concern for the goals of the organization as a whole. In a firm with a strong culture, however, congruent goals are more likely to develop between the various units in the organization because each unit knows what the key goals and values in the firm are. Subunits can have their own culture but it must be consistent with the overall culture.

A strong corporate culture will not automatically lead to sustained high financial performance in a firm. In order for a culture to be a source of sustained high performance, a firm's culture must be: (1) valuable (it must help the company do those things which result in high sales, low costs, high margins, etc.); (2) rare (its attributes must not be commonly found in other firms), and (3) imperfectly imitable (other firms will have difficulty trying to imitate the successful firm's culture).[5]

FACTORS THAT DETERMINE CORPORATE CULTURE

Chapters 11, 12, and 13 concentrated on the topics of motivation, leadership, and communication. Each of these topics has an impact on a firm's psychological environment. For example, the following factors can greatly affect corporate culture: work groups, organizational characteristics, supervision, and administration.[6] These factors are shown in Figure 15-1. As you can see, it would be difficult to discuss these topics without a good understanding of the concepts of motivation, leadership, and communication.

The nature of the immediate work group will affect a person's perception of the corporate culture. The level of commitment of the group refers to whether or not its members are just going through the motions associated with a job. If so, it would be difficult for a particular individual to derive high levels of output and satisfaction. The factor "hindrance" is concerned with the degree to which a great deal of busywork of doubtful value is given to the group. Morale and friendliness within the group are factors with which you should also be familiar.

The leadership style of the immediate supervisor will have a noticeable impact on the culture of the group. If the manager is aloof

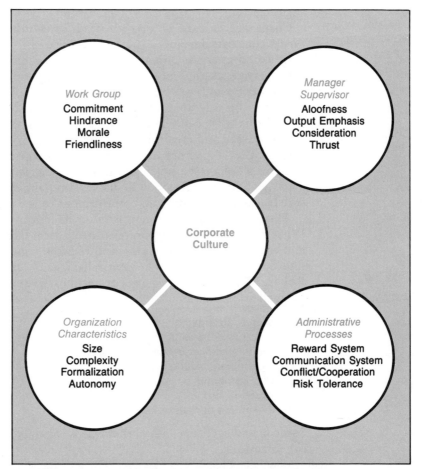

FIGURE 15-1   Factors that determine corporate culture

and distant in dealing with subordinates, the atmosphere will tend toward coolness. If the supervisor is always pushing for more output, this pressure will also influence the culture. Thrust refers to supervisory behavior characterized by working hard and setting an example. As we saw in Chapter 12, consideration is a leadership characteristic.

Organizational characteristics may also affect a firm's corporate culture. Organizations vary on such attributes as size and complexity. Large organizations tend toward higher degrees of specialization and greater impersonalization. Labor unions often find that large firms are easier to organize than smaller ones because employees in smaller firms tend to be closer and have more informal relations with management. Complex organizations tend to employ a greater number of professionals and specialists, who formalize the general approach to problem solving. Organizations also vary in the degree to which they write memos and attempt to program behavior through rules, procedures, and regulations. They can also be distinguished on the basis of the degree of decentralization of decision-making authority, which affects the degree of autonomy and freedom of personnel within the organization.

Corporate culture is also affected by administrative processes. Firms that can develop a direct link between performance and rewards tend to create climates conducive to achievement. Communication systems that are open and free-flowing tend to promote participation and creativity. General attitudes toward the handling of risk and the tolerance of conflict will, in turn, have considerable impact on the type of teamwork effected. They also affect the amount of innovation and creativity exhibited by the organization.

From the 16 factors in Figure 15-1, organization members will develop a subjective impression of the kind of place they work in. This general impression will have some impact on performance, satisfaction, creativity, and commitment to the organization.

At times an organization must alter its culture in order to survive. What are the types of corporate culture a firm might wish to emulate, and why should one particular culture prove superior to another? The one advocated by most behavioralists, such as Rensis Likert and Robert Blake, is the open and/or **participative culture**, characterized by such attributes as:

participative
culture

- Trust in subordinates
- Openness in communications
- Considerate and supportive leadership
- Group problem solving
- Worker autonomy
- Information sharing
- Establishment of high output goals.

Some behavioralists contend that this is the only viable culture for all organizations.

The opposite of this open and supportive culture is a closed and threatening one. It, too, is characterized by high output goals. But such goals are more likely to be declared and imposed on the organization by autocratic leaders through threats. There is greater rigidity in this culture, which results from strict adherence to the formal chain of command, narrower spans of management, and stricter individual accountability. The emphasis is on individual work rather than on teamwork. Employee reactions are often characterized by going through the motions and following orders.

Despite support by behavioralists, a more participative philosophy may not work on all occasions. In one instance involving the packaging of inexpensively priced china, low productivity of the work group was caused by excessive and unnecessary interaction among employees during working hours. Management found that the threat of termination did not prevent the unproductive talking. In this situation space allocated to the china packaging process was redesigned by building cubicles for each worker. These cubicles, constructed of sound-proofing material, virtually eliminated the unproductive con-

MANAGEMENT IN PRACTICE

What is Acceptable When Trying to Change Corporate Culture?

Many organizations hire outside consultants to train their workers to be more motivated and productive. Until recently, there were few objections to this practice. But some employers are now encountering resistance to certain types of training programs because employees either don't like what they are learning or they feel that "mind control" is being used on them.

Many of the complaints are directed against training programs that use methods such as meditation, self-hypnosis, inducements to trance-like states, or instructions to visualize events in the mind. All these approaches are loosely related to the "human potential" or "New Age" movement. The movement combines Eastern mysticism, the occult, and a Norman Vincent Peale type of positive thinking.

Large sums of money may be spent on training of this type. A senior official at the California Utilities Commission estimated that Pa-

cific Bell may be spending as much as $100 million a year on these programs in an effort to change its corporate culture. The change in culture is considered necessary as Pacific Bell moves from a monopoly situation to a competitive market as a result of recent deregulation in the telephone industry.

Representatives of companies selling "personal growth" seminars claim there is nothing sinister about them and that they allow a company to change its corporate culture faster than would otherwise be possible. Jack Gordon, the editor of *Training* magazine, says these types of seminars are likely to increase in popularity because they promise quick results to executives.

SOURCE   Adapted from Robert Lindsey, "Not All Workers Entranced By The Motivational Guru," *The Globe and Mail* (April 21, 1987).

versation between workers. As a result, productivity increased substantially and employee turnover was reduced. The total cost was $3200 — recovered during the first three weeks.[7]

The Participative Culture

The prevailing managerial approach in most organizations is to impose considerable structure on the work environment. Consequently, most of the attempts to alter corporate culture have been directed toward creating a more open, flexible, and participative culture. The theme of participation developed by individuals such as McGregor, Herzberg, and Maslow relates primarily to self-actualization, motivation factors, consultative and democratic leadership, job enrichment, and management by objectives.

Values of Participation

The possible values of involving more people in the decision-making process within a firm relate primarily to productivity and morale. Increased productivity can result from the stimulation of ideas and from the encouragement of greater effort and cooperation. If employees are psychologically involved, they will often respond to shared problems with innovative suggestions and extra effort. Open and participative cultures are often used to improve the levels of morale and satisfaction. Specific goals in this area include:

- Increased acceptability of management's ideas
- Increased cooperation with members of management
- Reduced turnover
- Reduced absenteeism
- Reduced complaints and grievances
- Greater acceptance of changes
- Improved attitudes toward the job and the organization.

In general, the development of greater employee participation appears to have a direct and immediate effect on employee morale. Employees take a greater interest in the job and the organization. They tend to accept, and sometimes initiate, changes not only because of their understanding of the necessity for change but also because their fear of insecurity has been reduced by knowing more about the change. Unfortunately, there is little evidence that suggests a positive relationship between job satisfaction and productivity. If productivity is not harmed by participation, it would appear that merely improving morale would make a program worthwhile. If productivity decreases, then management will have to make some tough decisions about the use of participation.

Limits of Participation

There are certain prerequisites and limits to greater employee participation in decision making. The requirements for greater participation in decision making are: (1) sufficient time; (2) adequate ability and interest on the part of the participants; and (3) restrictions generated by the current structure and system.

If immediate decisions are required, time cannot be spared for group participation. The manager decides what to do and issues the order accordingly. Should management decide to switch from a practice of autocracy to one of increased participation, some time for adjustment on the part of both parties will be required. Participation calls for employees to gain some measure of ability to govern themselves instead of leaning on others. In addition, time is required for subordinates to learn to handle this new-found freedom and for supervisors to learn to trust subordinates.

Whether greater involvement in decision making can be developed largely depends on the ability and interest of the participants, both subordinates and managers. This concept is not easy to implement. Obviously, if the subordinate has neither knowledge of nor interest in a subject, there is little need to consult. As organizations and technology become increasingly complex and as management becomes more professionalized, it is likely that employee participation will become more characterized by cooperation seeking or information gathering. We should also note that not all employees are equally interested in participation. Managers must face the fact that some workers do not seek more responsibility and greater involvement in their jobs.

Finally, as indicated in Figure 15-2, some restrictions to participative culture are caused by the organization's structure. An individual employee's task may be governed by management directives, organi-

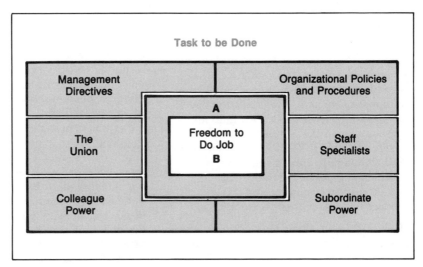

FIGURE 15-2 Limits to participative freedom

SOURCE Edwin B. Flippo and Gary M. Munsinger, *Management*, 5th ed. (Boston: Allyn and Bacon, 1982): 360. Reprinted by permission.

Judith Jossa
Personnel Administration Office

Judith Jossa is the Executive Director of the Organization Development Division of the Alberta Personnel Administration Office. The division, which contains 21 full-time employees, provides management and organization development (OD) services to various individuals and departments in the Alberta public service. These services include specialized career planning and training for women and native people employed in the public service, management and executive officer training, and OD consulting services to departments on request.

Q: Talk a little bit about how your division deals with other public service organizations that want OD work done.
Jossa: Our clients come from departments, boards, or commissions in the Alberta government. We are a centralized staff department supplying a specialized service in the field of human resource and organization development. Our services are not based on forced compliance but, rather, are offered on request from user departments. Credibility in the consulting services we provide has been built over a number of years. This is an important factor in that we must demonstrate that what we do is useful before other departments or divisions will request our services. We are involved in both custom designing of OD interventions and in the delivery of standardized management development programs. In 1986, over 10 000 employees — one third of the public service — were offered a "training event." A training event can range from a short workshop to a one-week management course.
Q: Can you give an example of a custom-designed OD program that was developed for a client?
Jossa: A couple of months ago, I received a call from an executive director in another government department. He felt that some substantial changes needed to be made in his division before it could really be effective in what it was attempting to do. He thought that it was important to get employees more involved in planning the department's activities; then they would be more enthusiastic and creative when making decisions about the day-to-day operations of the department. This was important, because the department dealt regularly with the private-sector business community and was really trying to serve it instead of being seen as an unresponsive, rules- and regulations-oriented government agency. Our first step was to do a needs survey to determine what employees really thought about their individual jobs and about the goals and objectives of the department. A summary of employee views was then analyzed and reviewed by management. At that point, it became clear that employees wanted some things that management hadn't thought of — for example, training in report writing and public speaking. After the data from the needs survey had been analyzed, the managers heading the department decided that our division should conduct a major "team building" exercise and put on several other educational programs that would deal specifically with employee needs as noted in the survey. Because of the success of this OD program, it was later provided on a department-wide basis.

Q: Can you give an example of services that are not custom designed but are repeated frequently with a different client each time?

Jossa: We offer 30 standardized management/supervisory development programs — such as Situational Leadership or Management, Leadership and Motivation — plus a supervisory development program for technical people who are ready to move into the first line of the management ranks. We have 13 supervisory modules that start off with theory and then bridge the gap to the job. These modules will be offered on a regular basis from the central agency; however, departments are encouraged to deliver these modules in-house. Modularized training programs offer choices, and each is based on an individual topic, such as discipline, motivation, or performance appraisal. Employees can take a particular module or all 13. In terms of pure OD services, on a regular basis, we provide mediation and process consultant services where techniques in needs surveys to team building are offered.

Q: Do you charge clients for the services you provide?

Jossa: We do not charge for the development of custom-designed OD programs because we want to encourage the various government departments to learn about OD and how it can be helpful to them. A charge-back system for the programs in our calendar has been in effect for several years.

Q: How do you ensure that people attending either custom-designed or standardized seminars actually get something that they can use when they return to their jobs?

Jossa: Our division is very concerned about precisely that point; as a result we require each person who attends a training course to sign a "learning contract." This contract indicates the practical skills or knowledge employees need to learn in the course and how these skills will be applied once they return to their regular job. Both employees and their supervisors sign the learning contract before any employee goes to the seminar. We have found that this contract really focuses attention on the course objectives and increases the chance that people will actually use the new skills or knowledge once they return to the job.

Q: Is there ever a shortage of demand for the services your division provides?

Jossa: In previous years, we had more business than we could comfortably handle. In fact, we sometimes had to turn down requests because we did not have enough staff to deliver all the programs requested. When demand exceeds our ability to supply it, we usually refer and/or contract the work to private consultants. This is particularly true for the standardized seminars. Recently, the trend has reversed itself and this is directly attributable to the restraint program in the Alberta Public Service.

Q: Suppose a line manager from a government department approaches you about doing some OD work and you don't agree with what the line manager wants. Since you are a staff division and don't have authority over line managers, how do you resolve disagreements like this when they arise?

Jossa: We don't usually have disagreements like that, because, after we do a needs analysis, it is pretty clear what employees need by way of training and what management needs to accomplish. Our emphasis is on total integration of organization and employee needs. If a manager originally felt that "X" should be done and then the needs analysis suggests that "Y" is necessary instead, it's our experience that most managers are very interested in doing what will maximize productivity for the benefit of all.

Q: Do you practice OD actively within your own division?

Jossa: Definitely. I feel that our division should continually be looking for new and creative ways to manage. This will help employees in this division to enrich their own job and to enhance their overall career prospect. Originally, the division focus was directed at providing centralized training and development programs. Today, the focus is on decentralized services and moving away from packaged programming to meeting the needs of the client. Flexibility and responsiveness are necessary in delivering tailored programs. As an example of this type of thinking, several consultants in this division who formerly taught management development programs on a regular basis are now managing those programs. In order to do that, they had to develop such new skills as process consulting, administration, program management, or consulting skills as a change agent. Today the division provides both expert and process consulting with an emphasis on organization behavior.

zation policies and procedures, the union contract, relations with the union steward, staff specialists, and the degree to which the manager can obtain the cooperation of subordinates. The greater the area in the Freedom To Do Job section of Figure 15-2, the greater the degree of participative freedom available. In the illustration, *A* would have more freedom to accomplish the job than *B*.

ORGANIZATION DEVELOPMENT

Change that involves the entire organization is called organization development (OD). Although the term has come into use only recently, practicing managers have been trying to improve organizations for many decades. OD is thus not a new activity but rather an extension of efforts that have been made during the long history of organizations. In the most general sense, OD is the attempt to improve the overall effectiveness of an organization. Since it is such a broad concept in practice, many different definitions have been proposed. However, we think the following definition conveys its important features: **organization development** is the systematic effort to improve the overall, long-term functioning of the organization, with emphasis usually placed on participative decision making and the development of a collaborative culture. The person who is responsible for assuring that the planned change in OD is properly implemented is referred to as a **change agent.** This individual may be either an external or an internal consultant. Change agents are knowledgeable about OD techniques and they use this knowledge to assist organization change.

When an organization first attempts to change, outside consultants are often used. An outside expert may bring more objectivity to a situation and be better able to obtain acceptance by and trust from organization members. With time, internal consultants may move into the role of a change agent.

organization development

change agent

Organization Development Techniques

Among the many organization development techniques available to management are: survey feedback, team building, process consultation, sensitivity training, management by objectives, job enrichment, and Blake and Mouton's managerial grid.

The Survey Feedback Method

The method of basing organizational change efforts on the systematic collection and measurement of subordinate attitudes by anonymous questionnaires is referred to as the **survey feedback method.** The three basic steps in the process are shown in Figure 15-3. First, data are

survey feedback method

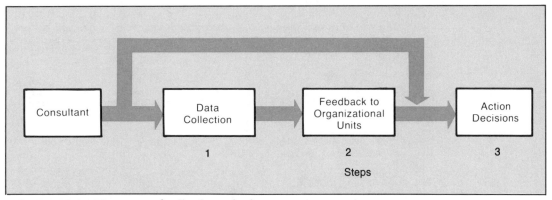

FIGURE 15-3   The survey feedback method

SOURCE   Adapted from Michael E. McGill, *Organization Development for Operating Managers.*
(New York: AMACOM, a division of American Management Associations, 1977).

collected from members of the organization by a consultant. Surveys are typically either the objective multiple-choice type (see Figure 15-4) or a scaled answer to suggest agreement or disagreement with a particular question (see Figure 15-5). Normally, questionnaires are answered anonymously. If management wishes to obtain truthful information concerning attitudes, the employee must feel comfortable, secure, and confident in responding.

In the second step, the results of the study are presented to concerned organizational units. In the final step, the data are analyzed and decisions are made. Some means by which the data may be compared and analyzed include:

FIGURE 15-4
Examples of multiple-choice responses to survey questions

Why did you decide to do what you are now doing?

a.   Desire to aid or assist others

b.   Influenced by another person or situation

c.   Always wanted to be in this vocation

d.   Lack of opportunity or interest in other vocational fields

e.   Opportunities provided by this vocation

f.   Personal satisfaction from doing this work

What do you like least about your job?

a.   Nothing

b.   Pay

c.   Supervisor relations

d.   Problems with fellow workers

e.   Facilities

f.   Paperwork and reports

SOURCE   R. Wayne Mondy and Robert M. Noe, III, *Personnel: The Management of Human Resources,* 2nd ed. (Newton, Mass.: Allyn and Bacon, Inc., 1984): 583-84.

Considering all aspects of your job, evaluate your compensation with regard to your contributions to the needs of the organization. Circle the number that best describes how you feel.

Pay too Low		Pay Low		Pay Average		Pay Above Average		Pay Too High	
1	2	3	4	5	6	7	8	9	10

What are your feelings about overtime work requirements? Circle the number that best indicates how you feel.

Unnecessary			Necessary on Occasion				Necessary		
1	2	3	4	5	6	7	8	9	10

FIGURE 15-5   Examples of scaled responses to survey questions

SOURCE   R. Wayne Mondy and Robert M. Noe, III, *Personnel: The Management of Human Resources* (Boston: Allyn and Bacon, 1981): 493.

- Scores for the entire organization now and in the past
- Scores for each department now and in the past
- Scores by organizational level
- Scores by seniority
- Relative scores on each question
- Scores for each question for each category of personnel cited above.

The decisions are directed at improving relationships in the organization. This is accomplished by revealing problem areas and dealing with them through straightforward discussions.

Team Building

team building

One of the major techniques in the arsenal of the organizational development consultant is **team building**, a conscious effort to develop effective work groups throughout the organization.[8] The purpose of team building is the development of effective management teams. These work groups focus on solving actual problems in building efficient management teams. The team-building process begins when the team leader defines a problem that requires organizational change. Next, the group analyzes the problem to determine the underlying causes of the problem. These factors may be related to such areas as communication, role clarifications, leadership styles, organizational structure, and interpersonal frictions. The next step is to propose alternative solutions and then select the most appropriate one. Through this process, the participants are likely to be committed to the solution. Interpersonal support and trust develops. The overall improvement in the interpersonal support and trust of group members enhances the implementation of the change.[9] The concept of the quality circle, imported from Japan, is a modern example of team building.

Process Consultation

Edgar Schein defines **process consultation** as "a set of activities on the part of the consultant which help the client to perceive, understand, and act upon process events which occur in the client's [culture]."[10] As the definition suggests, this particular OD program starts from the assumption that the outside consultant does not merely conduct an analysis of the organization and then suggest a remedy for the problem that is identified. Rather, the consultant and management jointly discuss and diagnose organizational processes (both structural and human) and decide what problems need to be solved. According to Schein, this approach to problem solving is based on the following assumptions:

- Management often has difficulty deciding what is wrong with the organization. Special diagnostic help is therefore needed.
- While most managers honestly wish to improve organization effectiveness, they may need help in deciding how to do so.
- When organizations learn to diagnose their own strengths and weaknesses, they can be more effective.
- The outside consultant cannot hope to get a clear understanding of the organization's culture in a short period of time; therefore, joint consultation with management, which does know the culture, is necessary.
- The client, not the consultant, must come to a conclusion regarding the problem, its causes, and its remedy. Decision-making authority about organizational changes remains with the client.

Process consultation differs from two other typical OD models: the purchase model and the doctor/patient model. When the purchase model is used, the organization defines its problems without outside help and then hires an expert to solve them — for example, how to design a new plant, how to improve employee morale, or how to determine if consumers are satisfied with company products. This approach is often not optimal because the organization may have incorrectly defined its needs or because the consultant chosen is not technically competent. When the doctor/patient model is used, the consultant (doctor) diagnoses the organization (the patient) and then suggests a cure for the problem. The major difficulties here are that the unit that is diagnosed as having problems may reject the diagnosis and/or may resist implementing the solutions proposed by the consultant.

The limitations of these two OD models are overcome by the use of process consultation, since the consultant's main role is not to suggest solutions but instead to help management understand its organizational problem as clearly as possible. Once understood, the problem can be tackled properly by management. Solutions generated from within the organization are less likely to meet resistance.

Senstivity Training

sensitivity
training

Sensitivity training is designed to increase the awareness of individuals about their own motivations and behavior patterns as well as those of others.[11] This is accomplished through the use of leaderless training groups (T-groups). In the extreme, the technique uses the group confrontation method to achieve its fundamental goal of increased awareness. The T-group operates as follows. Individuals who volunteer for, or are sent to, the T-group meet at a predetermined location away from the normal place of work. These individuals may be complete strangers coming from many different organizations (stranger groups) or they may all come from the same organization (family groups). The groups, usually composed of 10 to 15 individuals, meet for approximately 7 to 10 days. There is no set agenda or required material to cover as there is in a structured seminar. Instead, the members are faced with a very unstructured atmosphere in which the decision as to what direction to take must be made by the group. The sessions are moderated by a trainer, whose function is to clarify the basic goal of the session and to assist the group in its function. The trainer generally assumes no leadership role, although this can vary.

In an atmosphere like this, it is not surprising that high anxiety levels develop in the group as some members attempt to impose structure on the others. Conflicts of this sort are ideal for increasing members' awareness of their own feelings and behaviors during conflict or consensus situations. Although the actual conduct of a T-group varies considerably because of the lack of structure, it generally involves group discussions of individual behavior patterns as they relate to particular problems. For example, a group of executives who work together may decide to engage in a T-group session to improve their effectiveness as a team. Each individual might describe how he or she sees the behavior of others, and the group might suggest possible improvements. Afterward, group members diagnose their own feelings and pursue ways of changing interpersonal relationships.

Sensitivity training is not as widely used in business today as it formerly was. It has been labeled "psychotherapy" rather than proper business training. Leaders of T-groups have been criticized for having an insufficient background in psychology. It has been suggested that individual defense mechanisms built up to preserve the personality over a period of years may be destroyed without replacing them with more satisfactory behavioral patterns.

In business organizations, managers frequently must make unpleasant decisions that work to the detriment of particular individuals and groups. Excessive empathy and sympathy will not necessarily lead to a reversal of the decision, but may exact an excessively high emotional cost for the decision maker. Many business organizations have an internal atmosphere characterized by competition and autocratic leadership. The power structure may not be compatible with openness and trust. In some instances, managers may feel that they should practice diplomacy by telling only part of the truth, or perhaps even telling different stories to two different persons or groups. Truth is not always most conducive to effective interpersonal and group relations. Sensitivity training tends to ignore organizational values that are derived from aggressiveness, initiative, and the charismatic appeals of a particular leader.

Management by Objectives

In Chapter 4, we described management by objectives as a systematic approach that facilitates achievement of results by directing efforts toward attainable goals. MBO is a philsophy of management that encourages managers to plan for the future. Because MBO emphasizes participative management approaches, it has been called a philosophy of management. Within this broader context, MBO becomes an important method of organization development. The participation of individuals in setting goals and the emphasis on self-control promote not only individual development but also development for the entire organization.

Job Enrichment

The deliberate restructuring of a job to make it more challenging, meaningful, and interesting is referred to as job enrichment. As we suggested in Chapter 11, the individual is provided with an opportunity to derive greater achievement, recognition, responsibility, and personal growth in performing the job.

The Managerial Grid

One of the best known OD programs is the managerial grid of Blake and Mouton. As we discussed in Chapter 12, they suggest that the most effective leadership style is that which stresses maximum concern for both output and people. The managerial grid provides a systematic approach for analyzing managerial styles and assisting the organization in moving to the best style.

Management Development

management
development
programs

Organization development techniques are designed to change the entire organization. **Management development programs** (MDP) are formal efforts to improve the skills and attitudes of present and potential managers. Managers learn more effective approaches to managing people and other resources. With MDP, specific areas that have been identified as possible organization weaknesses are included in the program. Some of these areas might relate to leadership style, motivation approaches, or communication effectiveness.

The training programs may be administered by either company personnel or external consultants. A typical management development program is illustrated in Figure 15-6. The intent of MDPs is not only to teach managers new methods and techniques, but also to develop in them an inquisitive thought process. Too often personnel within a firm become so accustomed to performing the same task day after day that they forget to think. A properly designed management development program places a person in a frame of mind to analyze problems and is often used to provide the foundation for a change to occur.

FIGURE 15-6
Course content for a management development program

I. **Management Development Program Title:**
"Improving Group Effectiveness and Team Building"

II. **Objectives:**
(1) To identify the reasons for group formation
(2) To understand the types of groups and their attributes
(3) To discover the implications of research on group dynamics
(4) To acquire an understanding as to forces in intra- and inter-group processes
(5) To learn the characteristics of teamwork and ways to achieve it
(6) To provide experience in analyzing and diagnosing work group dimensions
(7) To acquire an appreciation for various team-building techniques

III. **Description and Evaluation:**
The course is designed to provide greater understanding of, and ability to work with and through, groups. Special emphasis is given to understanding the various need levels of groups and what can be done to appeal more effectively to those levels. Actual practice in team-building techniques is given, as well as experience in analyzing work groups. Evaluation is made of the major contingencies affecting groups. Observing group behavior through various media is a portion of the course content.

IV. **Size of Class:**
The class should have a maximum enrollment of 20 participants so as to allow the group process to be seen in action in the group itself, yet small enough to allow for active participation.

V. **Assignment of Instructor:**
The instructor allocates an equal amount of time to lecture and active class discussion with approximately one-third of the time devoted to various media presentations and group involvement. The course is designed for a two- or three-day session.

VI. **Enrollment Requirements:**
Middle- and upper-level managerial experience desired

OPENING INCIDENT REVISITED

The Toronto Experience

Arnot obviously is very enthusiastic about creating an organization that is informal, open, and supportive. Unfortunately, several people in the organization do not share Arnot's enthusiasm. In the jargon of corporate culture literature, there are no "shared values"; the behavioral norms that Arnot is hoping for have therefore not materialized. Although most discussions of corporate culture imply that top management is holding back on the development of an open, participative culture, this incident demonstrates that if either party is reluctant, the change will not happen.

With regard to training, Arnot has let his enthusiasm cloud his judgment. He has not consulted with any of his subordinates about their goals. Rather, he has decided unilaterally that they would all benefit from the program he took. His subordinates would probably be much more enthsiastic about training if they were allowed to assess their own needs and goals and pick an appropriate program to at-

tend. They are obviously dubious about Arnot's "experience," and his decision to make them all attend the same seminar has raised real concerns in their minds. They feel under pressure to attend, yet some of them are clearly uncomfortable about the prospect of doing so.

What is required is an assessment of the kind of training that Arnot's subordinates want. Once that is clear, a decision can be made about which kind of seminar would best suit their needs. The president also needs to recognize that managers in this company may be anxious because they perceive that they may be required to change their attitudes and behavior as a result of the seminar. As we saw in the preceding chapter, resistance to change is an obvious reaction to something new. Arnot can increase the chance that executives will be enthusiastic about *some* kind of training if he follows the change sequence noted in the preceding chapter.

SUMMARY

Corporate culture is the system of shared values, beliefs, and habits within an organization that interacts with the formal structure to produce behavioral norms. The culture existing within a firm has an impact on the employee's degree of satisfaction with the job, as well as on the level and quality of their performance. Typical factors that affect corporate culture are: the work group, organizational characteristics, supervisors, and administrative processes. The culture advocated by most behavioralists is the open and/or participative culture, which is characterized by such attributes as trust in subordinates, openness in communications, considerate and supportive leadership, group problem solving, worker autonomy, information sharing, and the establishment of high output goals.

Efforts to change that involve the entire organization are referred to as organization development (OD). OD is a planned and calculated attempt to change the organization, typically to a more open and participative culture. Some of the OD techniques available include survey feedback, team building, process consultation, sensitivity training, management by objectives, job enrichment, and the managerial grid approach. The person who is responsible for ensuring that the planned change in OD is properly implemented is referred to as a change agent.

Whereas organization development techniques are designed to improve the entire organization, management development programs are specifically tailored to benefit managers. Some of the areas for development include leadership style, motivation approaches, and communication effectiveness.

REVIEW QUESTIONS

1. Define the term "corporate culture." What are the factors that interact to determine the type of corporate culture that exists in an organization?
2. Identify the values and limitations of a participative culture.
3. Define the following terms: (a) organization development, (b) sensitivity training, and (c) process consultation.
4. List and briefly describe the steps in the survey feedback method.
5. What is team building?
6. How does process consultation differ from many other OD techniques?
7. What is the difference between organization development and management development?

EXERCISES

1. Visit three business firms. Attempt to assess the culture that exists in each of the firms. Identify the reasons for your assessment in each case.
2. Interview the human resources manager of an organization of your choice. Determine what type of management development/organization development programs the organization is currently involved in. Also determine how the organization assesses the effectiveness of these programs.

CASE STUDY

A Change of Culture

Until one year ago Wayne daCosta, Don Pio, and Roberta Vine were supervisors with a chain of 39 grocery stores. Each supervisor had responsibility for 13 stores and reported directly to the company president. All three supervisors worked well together, and there was a constant exchange of information, which was useful in coordinating the activities of the stores. Each supervisor had specific strengths that were useful in helping the others. DaCosta coordinated the deployment of the part-time help at all 39 stores. Pio monitored the inventories, and Vine interviewed prospective new employees prior to sending them to daCosta and Pio for review. It was a complete team effort directed toward getting the job done.

One year later, the chain had undergone some changes. The president, wishing to relieve himself of many daily details, decided to promote Vine to vice-president. Another supervisor, Phillips, was hired for Vine's position. Vine had a completely different idea of how the activities of the supervisors should be conducted. Under Vine's leadership each supervisor was now responsible for the activities at only his or her 13 stores. If a problem occurred, the supervisor was to discuss it with Vine, who would provide the solution. When any of the three supervisors attempted to solve problems on their own, they were reprimanded by Vine. After a few reprimands, daCosta, Pio and Phillips decided not to fight the system and did as Vine wanted; they rarely saw each other any more. If Pio had a problem at his stores that caused him to work all night that was not any concern of daCosta or Phillips.

The main problem with the new system was that efficiency dropped drastically. For instance, daCosta was a good coordinator of part-time help. He had the type of personality that could talk a person into coming to work at 17:00 on Saturday evening when the individual had a date at 18:00. DaCosta's stores remained well staffed with part-time help, but the others suffered. Many times the part-time help did not show up, and either Pio or Phillips had to act as the replacement if the store manager could not be convinced to work overtime. On the other hand, daCosta's inventory control suffered because Pio was best qualified in this area.

Vine accused the three supervisors of working against her and threatened them with dismissal if operations did not get better. DaCosta, Pio, and Phillips thought that they could not be productive in this atmosphere and found other positions. When the president discovered what had occurred, Vine was fired. It took the president two years to get operations back to the level of efficiency that had existed previously.

QUESTIONS

1. What different corporate culture was created as a result of promoting Vine to vice-president?
2. How do you think that this situation could have been avoided?

CASE STUDY

Creighton Ltd.

Creighton Ltd. was established in 1912. It manufactured power and hand tools for the industrial and consumer market. The company had been very successful for many years, and was the dominant firm in the industry. However, by the late 1970s serious problems were beginning to be evident. Industry analysts noted that as the firm matured, it had become very conservative and was not generating many new products or ideas. The analysts felt the firm was trying to coast along on its past accomplishments.

The company's profitability declined sharply during the recession of the early eighties, and in 1984 the board of directors decided that something significant needed to be done if the firm was to regain its dominant position in the industry. One of the actions taken to achieve this goal was the hiring of Ferris Lambert as president. Lambert was hard-driving but personable, and had a reputation as a "turnaround artist"; that is, a person who could take a company that was in trouble and make it a viable market force again.

Lambert threw himself into his work with great vigor. He made sweeping changes in the executive ranks, instituted a new product development group, and, like Lee Iacocca at Chrysler and Victor Kiam at Remington, began appearing in the company's advertisements.

One of the things Lambert discovered in his analysis of Creighton was that the firm did virtually no management training. He immediately met with the vice-president of personnel and, after informing him of the importance of training for managers, asked the vice-president to institute a major training program for all managers in the firm. He indicated that he expected a detailed training plan on his desk in two weeks. When the vice-president asked exactly what the president had in mind, the vice-president was told to begin work on the plan and to use his judgment.

QUESTIONS

1. How is the corporate culture going to change as a result of the new president's actions?
2. Comment on the president's handling of the training issue.

ENDNOTES

[1] Jay Barney, "Organizational Culture: Can It Be A Source Of Sustained Competitive Advantage?" *Academy of Management Review*, (1986): 656–665.

[2] Antony Jay, *Management and Machiavelli* (New York: Holt, Rinehart, and Winston, 1967).

[3] E. H. Schein, "The Role of the Founder in Creating Organizational Culture," *Organizational Dynamics* (Summer 1983): 13–28.

[4] Thomas J. Peters and Robert H. Waterman, *In Search of Excellence* (New York: Harper and Row, 1982); William G. Ouchi, *Theory Z* (New York: Avon Books, 1982); Terrence E. Deal and Allan A. Kennedy, *Corporate Culture* (Reading, Mass.: Addison Wesley, 1981).

[5] Barney, "Organization Culture," p. 658.

[6] Many of the factors were taken from the Organizational Climate Description Questionnaire generated by Halpin and Croft as described in Andrew W. Halpin, *Theory and Research in Administration* (New York: Macmillan, 1966), chap. 4. Another widely used measure is that of Litwin and Stringer found in G. Litwin and R. Stringer, *Motivation and Organizational Climate* (Cambridge, Mass.: Harvard University Press, 1968).

[7] H. Kenneth Bobele and Peter J. Buchanan, "Building a More Productive Environment," *Management World* 1 (January 1978): 8.

[8] Edgar F. Huse, *Organization Development and Change* (St. Paul, Minn.: West, 1975): 230.

[9] Michael A. Hitt, R. Dennis Middlemist, and Robert Q. Mathis, *Effective Management* (St. Paul, Minn.: West, 1979): 462–464.

[10] Edgar Schein, *Process Consultation: Its Role in Organization Development* (Reading, Mass.: Addison-Wesley, 1969): 9.

[11] For a detailed review of 100 research studies on sensitivity training, see P. B. Smith, "Control Studies on the Outcome of Sensitivity Training," *Psychological Bulletin* (July 1975): 597–622.

REFERENCES

Baird, John E. Jr. "Supervisory and Managerial Training through Communication by Objectives." *Personnel Administrator* 26 (July 1981): 28–32.

Barney, Jay. "Organizational Culture: Can It Be A Source of Sustained Competitive Advantage?" *Academy of Management Review* 11, (July 1986): 656–665.

Baysinger, Rebecca T., and Woodman, Richard W. "The Use of Management by Objectives in Management Training Programs." *Personnel Administrator* 26 (February 1981): 83–86.

Beck, Robert. "Visions, Values, and Strategies: Changing Attitudes and Values." *Academy of Management Executive*, (February 1987): 33–42.

Cobb, Anthony. "Political Diagnosis: Applications in OD." *Academy of Management Review* 11, (July 1986): 482–496.

Gordon, G. G., and Goldberg, B. E. "Is There a Climate for Success?" *Management Review* 66 (May 1977): 37–44.

Greiner, Larry E. "Evolution and Revolution as Organizations Grow." *Harvard Business Review* 50 (July 1971): 37–46.

Hellriegel, Don, and Slocum, John W. Jr. "Organizational Climate: Measures, Research, and Contingencies." *Academy of Management Journal* 17 (June 1974): 255–280.

Hornstein, Harvey. *Managerial Courage: Revitalizing Your Company Without Sacrificing Your Job.* New York: Wiley and Sons, 1986.

Howe, R. J., et al. "Introducing Innovation Through Organizational Development." *Management Review* 67 (February 1978): 52–56.

Huse, E. F. *Organization Development and Change.* St. Paul, Minn.: West, 1980.

Jennings, Eugene E. "How to Develop Your Management Talent Internally." *Personnel Administrator* 26 (July 1981): 20–23.

Kelly, Joe, and Khozan, Kamiran. "Participative Management: Can It Work?" *Business Horizons* (August 1980): 74–79.

Margerison, Charles, and New, Colin. "Management Development by Intercompany Consortiums." *Personnel Management* 12 (November 1980): 42–45.

Miles, James M. "How to Establish a Good Industrial Relations Climate." *Management Review* 67 (August 1980): 42–44.

Miller, Danny, and Friesen, Peter H. "Momentum and Revaluations in Organizational Adaptation." *Academy of Management Journal* 23 (December 1980): 591–614.

Mintzberg, Henry. "Organizational Design: Fashion or Fit?" *Harvard Business Review* 59 (January-February 1981): 103–116.

Monat, Jonathan S. "A Perspective on the Evaluation of Training and Development Programs." *Personnel Administrator* 26 (July 1981): 47–52.

Nicholas, Jon, and Katz, Marsha. "Research Methods and Reporting Practices in OD: A Review and Some Guidelines." *Academy of Management Review* 10, (October 1985): 737–749.

Olivas, Louis. "Using Assessment Centers for Individual and Organizational Development." *Personnel* 57 (May-June 1980): 63–67.

Scott, Walter B. "Participative Management at Motorola — The Results." *Management Review* 70 (July 1981): 26–28.

Schein, Edgar. *Organizational Culture and Leadership.* San Francisco: Jossey-Bass, 1985.

Stoffman, Daniel. "Blue Collar Turnaround Artists." *Canadian Business* 57, no. 2 (February 1984): 38.

Lindsey, Robert. "Not All Workers Entranced By The Motivational Guru." *The Globe and Mail* (April 21, 1987): B1–B2.

Schein, Edgar. "Coming to a New Awareness of Corporate Culture." *Sloan Management Review* (Winter 1984): 3–16.

V

Controlling

16

The Controlling Process

KEY TERMS

controlling	quality standards	statistical sampling
standards	behavioral standards	process controls
time standards	control tolerances	comparison controls
productivity	disciplinary action	quality
standards	progressive discipine	strategic control
cost standards	input controls	points

LEARNING OBJECTIVES

After completing this chapter you should be able to
1. Define controls and describe the control process.
2. Describe four types of standards.
3. Explain the importance of disciplinary action and describe what is meant by the concept of progressive discipline.
4. Relate controlling to the business system.
5. Describe and identify the characteristics of strategic control points.

6. Relate the reasons for employees' negative reactions to controls.
7. Describe ways of overcoming negative reactions to controls.

OPENING INCIDENT

Can-Mark Manufacturing

Henry Friesen was a foreman at Can-Mark Manufacturing, which manufactured a wide array of consumer products. Recently Friesen had been put in charge of a group of nine people who were to produce the company's latest addition to its product line. The production process for the new product required use of state-of-the-art equipment, and the company's industrial engineers had just completed a lengthy series of tests to determine reasonable production standards for the new machines.

The production line experienced trouble right from the start. The workers had considerable difficulty getting the machines to work properly, and rejects were running substantially above the level that was considered acceptable. One afternoon, as Friesen was sitting in his office wondering how to resolve this problem, the plant superintendent, Peter Jansen, appeared at his door. Friesen invited him in and the following conversation took place:

Jansen: Henry, what's the problem with our new line? You know this product is high profile; I'm already getting pressure from the vice-president. He says the new product is crucial to our company and he wants these production problems resolved immediately. There's a lot of demand out there for this product and we've got to get your production volume up.

Friesen: After talking to the workers, I'm convinced those production standards are way out of line. My people are very motivated and experienced but they can't meet the standards the engineering people have set.

Jansen: Now, Henry, you know our engineers have a very good reputation for setting realistic job standards.

Friesen: I know that, but in this case they have made a big mistake. This state-of-the-art equipment we're using is more difficult to work with than they could have imagined.

Jansen: We've got to get output on this line up to standard or we'll both be in trouble with top management.

At this point one of Friesen's workers entered his office and told him of another problem with the new equipment, so Friesen had to cut the meeting short. For the rest of the day his discussion with Jansen weighed heavily on his mind.

The incident at Can-Mark Manufacturing portrays an all-too-common occurrence in organizations: a manager and a subordinate disagree about whether or not the employee's performance is up to standard. The incident reveals how sensitive managers and workers are when it comes to making conclusions about employee performance. Given this sensitivity, organizations need to have a reasonable control system that will make objective performance assessment possible.

A properly designed control system alerts managers to the existence of potential problems and permits them to take corrective actions when necessary. The control function, therefore, is a valuable part of the management process. Controlling is concerned with ensuring that results are achieved according to plan. Stated another way, controls provide management with the means of finding out if tasks have been performed properly.

Some managers believe that, if the functions of planning, organizing, and influencing are performed satisfactorily, they have little need for the control function. This belief is not wisely held for two reasons. First, unexpected events often occur that make the best of plans inoperable. Second, people do not always do what management expects them to do; that is, they don't work the way the plan says they should work. Therefore, managers must perform the control function to ensure that plans become reality.

In this chapter, we first describe the control function and the control process. Second, we examine the basic types of controls that are applied as organizations convert inputs to output. Third, we note the importance of establishing strategic control points, and analyze the nature of control at different management levels. The fourth section examines the reasons why employees in organizations so often resist control measures, and the fifth section offers suggestions on how to reduce this resistance.

THE CONTROLLING PROCESS

controlling

Controlling is the process of comparing actual performance with standards and taking any necessary corrective action. The control process involves four critical steps: (1) setting standards and control tolerances, (2) observing or measuring, (3) comparing actual performance to standard, and (4) taking corrective action if necessary. This process is shown in Figure 16-1. A discussion of each phase follows.

Establishing Standards

standards

Managers must know what is expected before the controls can be implemented. **Standards** are established levels of quality or quantity used to guide performance. For example, if a shaft has a standard diameter, the machinist must try to cut it to that specific size. Standards are sometimes viewed as goals. Wherever possible, standards should be expressed numerically to reduce subjectivity and depersonalize the control process.[1] The most frequently used types of standards are:

time standards

- **Time standards:** Time standards state the length of time it should take to make a certain product or perform a certain service. An airline pilot has a

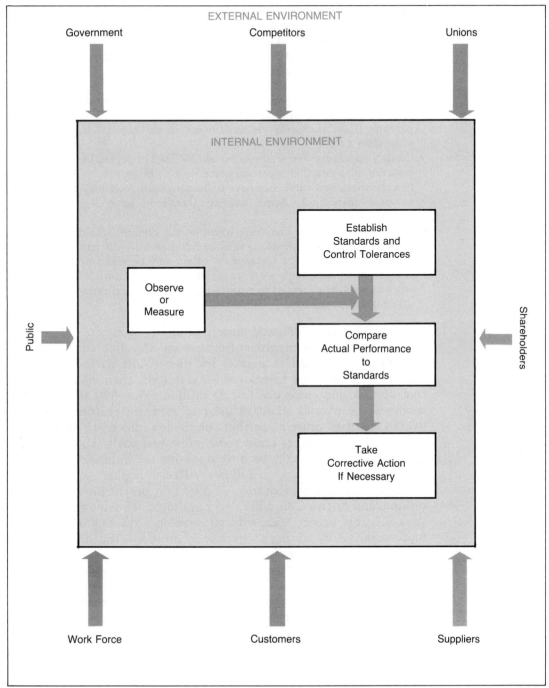

FIGURE 16-1   The controlling process

standard time span in which to make a certain trip. Most organizations have a standard lunch time and a standard work week.

productivity standards

- **Productivity standards:** These standards are based on the amount of product or service produced during a set time period. For instance, a productivity standard might be to produce 10 units per hour or to serve 150 customers per hour in a fast-food restaurant.

cost standards

- **Cost standards:** These standards are based on the cost associated with producing the goods or service. For example, the material cost might be $10 per unit. Cost standards are usually set in the expense budget for the supervisor's unit.

quality standards

- **Quality standards:** These are based on the level of perfection desired. For instance, no more than a certain percentage of impurities may be allowed in a chemical, or a valve may have to hold pressure for 10 minutes in order to pass inspection. Some quality standards have legal minimum requirements.

behavioral standards

- **Behavioral standards:** These are based on the type of behavior desired of workers in the organization. It is sometimes difficult to express these standards precisely. For instance, workers may be asked not to curse in front of customers, some workers may have to follow a strict dress code, or workers may be expected to maintain a level of cheerfulness or pleasantness toward customers.

Standards must be related closely to an organization's objectives. Suppose a clothing manufacturer has an objective of getting 10 percent of the Canadian market for men's suits. If industry sales across the country are forecast at $200 million, then the sales objective of this one company is $20 million. This $20 million then becomes the overall standard used to measure performance; this overall standard must be further subdivided into more manageable units so that employees know their individual goals. To begin with, specific standards might be developed for the company's regional sales managers, perhaps as follows: Atlantic region — $2 million, Quebec — $5 million, Ontario — $6 million, prairie provinces — $2 million, and British Columbia — $5 million. Each sales manager will then take his or her standard and develop a quota for each sales representative. By stating progressively more specific standards, the company is able to plan its objectives systematically.

Standards must be appropriate for the type of work that is being done. For example, in a research and development laboratory, controls are normally less specific than those on an automated production line. This is because it is usually not possible to specify work procedures as exactly in a research lab as it is on an automated production line. An attempt to overspecify controls might result in negative outcomes (lower morale, emphasis on the wrong activities, and so forth).

control tolerances

Even when standards are clear, control tolerances also need to be established. **Control tolerances** are specifications of how much deviation will be permitted before corrective action will be taken. For

TABLE 16-1 Standard and Control Tolerances

Standard	Tolerance
7.9 cm Shaft diameter	∓0.13 cm Difference
0 Absences	2 Unexcused absences per month
08:00 Starting time	08:05 Starting time
1 min Waiting time	1 min 15 sec Waiting time
Clear polished surface	2 Visible defects
130 over 80 Blood pressure	∓20 points for either pressure

instance, a standard of quality for the shaft diameter of a particular part may be 7.9 cm. (See Table 16-1.) However, a tolerance of ±0.13 cm may be permitted. If a part is produced with a shaft diameter within the ranges of 7.77 cm and 8.03 cm, it is acceptable. If the shaft diameter falls outside this range, the part is rejected. As another example, a company might allow only two unexcused absences per month. A standard work day might be eight hours, but most managers have a certain tolerance for deviation, perhaps five minutes later than starting time. Whether the standard relates to a product, a service, or to behavior, both the standard and the control tolerances should be communicated to workers. If managers make standards and tolerances clear, most workers will control themselves accordingly.

Observing or Measuring

The next phase in the controlling process — observation or measurement — is an important one. Managers need to determine what has actually taken place. In some work places, this phase may require only visual observation. In other situations, more precise determinations are needed. For example, a quality control inspector may use a micrometer or other instrument to take physical measurements in order to assess performance.

Managers should be careful to observe and measure accurately. For instance, a supervisor may believe that a worker has missed too many days from work. A check of attendance records may show that the worker has only averaged missing one day a month. One of the authors, as a young Navy personnel officer, reprimanded a clerk for working too slowly. The leading chief petty officer showed the young officer that, although the clerk appeared to be working slowly, he was actually doing more than his share. The manager should be careful to measure accurately before taking corrective action.

Comparing Performance with Standards

If the first two phases have been done well, the third phase of the controlling process — comparing performance with standards — should be straightforward. For example, quality control inspectors keep in mind the standards and control tolerances as they make measurements. Often a quality control checklist such as the one shown in Table 16-2 is used. As another example, telephone operator supervisors keep strict count of calls handled and length of time per call; the manager knows immediately if an operator is working within time standards.

Behavorial standards are usually not as exact as other standards. Therefore, it is more difficult to make the required comparisons. Because of this problem some managers prefer to keep their subordinates guessing; for instance, they will not tell employees that being five minutes late is all right. However, since workers like to know where they stand, this may not be the best procedure.

Correcting Deviations if Necessary

The final phase of the controlling process occurs when managers must decide what action to take to correct performance when deviations occur. Often the real cause of the deviation must be found before corrective action can be taken. For instance, if the number of allowable defects has exceeded standard, the cause may be a defective machine or a careless operator. Each cause requires a different corrective action.

Not all deviations from standard justify corrective action. Suppose that a usually dependable worker is 15 minutes late for work (a deviation from the standard), but the manager realizes the lateness was unavoidable. The manager may decide to take no action, even though a deviation occurred. The standard is to be on time, but some flexibility is allowable in this case.

There are two general types of corrective action — immediate and permanent. The type most frequently recognized is the immediate;

TABLE 16-2 Quality Control Tire Tread Checklist

	Minimum	Maximum	Actual
Width	56.0 cm	57.0 cm	56.2 cm
Length	183.0 cm	184.0 cm	183.2 cm
Thickness	2.08 cm	2.21 cm	2.16 cm
Mass	3.90 kg	3.99 kg	3.94 kg
Number of Visible Defects	0	2	0

something must be done now to correct the situation and get back on track. For example, a particular project is a week behind schedule and, if not corrected, will seriously affect other projects. The first problem is not to worry about who or what caused the difficulty but rather to get the project back on schedule. Depending on the authority of the manager, the following corrective actions may be ordered: (1) overtime hours may be authorized, (2) additional workers and equipment may be assigned, (3) a full-time director may be assigned to push the project through personally, (4) an extra effort may be requested of all employees, or (5) if all these fail, the schedule may have to be readjusted, thereby requiring changes all along the line.

After the degree of stress has lessened through any of the above measures, attention can be devoted to the second type of corrective action. Just how and why did events stray from their planned course? What can be done to prevent a recurrence of this difficulty? Many managers fail at this phase. Too often they find themselves putting out daily fires but not discovering the actual cause of the problem. For instance, managers may find themselves constantly having to interview and hire new people to replace those who are leaving the firm. A manager may be working 12 hours a day attempting to locate new employees, but he or she must recognize that high turnover is not solved merely by employing new workers. Managers must take some type of corrective action after they have determined what has actually caused the high turnover. A supervisor may be extremely difficult to work with, or the pay scale may not be competitive for the area. Whatever the problem, it must be identified and corrected or the high turnover problem is likely to continue. The work of permanent corrective action must be done for the sake of economical and effective future operations.

The Dynamics of Corrective Action

In order to deal effectively with situations requiring corrective action, a manager must possess (1) a good understanding of why the problem has arisen, and (2) good interpersonal skills with which to resolve it. Since individuals will often respond negatively to data showing that their work is not up to standard, the manager must possess considerable sensitivity when applying corrective action.

It is generally best to begin with a positive approach. If a worker's output is not up to standard, for example, the manager will have to determine why the deviation occurred and attempt to reach an agreement with the worker about how to avoid this type of situation in the future. It is important that work that is being done correctly is praised. This improves the worker's self-image and reduces the chance that the worker will resist taking corrective action. Once a positive environment has been established, it is easier to work toward a resolution of the problem at hand.

TALKING TO MANAGERS

Sharon Matthias
Alberta Occupational Health & Safety

Sharon Matthias is manager of the Standards and Projects Section in the Occupational Hygiene Branch, Alberta Occupational Health and Safety Division. In the province of Alberta, the division is the government agency responsible for matters concerning health and safety in the work place, including administration of the Occupational Health and Safety Act and its regulations. Matthias believes controlling is an important function both externally — ensuring that companies adhere to worker health and safety standards — and internally — ensuring that employees reporting to her achieve the objectives of the section.

Matthias has a BSc in pharmacy, an MSc in pharmaceutical chemistry, and an MBA. She worked for eight years in the Crime Detection Laboratory of the Royal Canadian Mounted Police as an alcohol specialist and was head of the Alcohol Section. Following two years in residential real estate, she joined the Occupa-

tional Health and Safety Division as an occupational hygienist. Matthias has been promoted through several positions of increasing responsibility to her present position.

Q: What activities does your section perform?

Matthias: There are five basic areas of activity. First, we review the plans for major new plants in the province; "major" is anything exceeding $100 000 000 in capital costs. We examine these plans at the design stage to be sure that proper health and safety controls are scheduled to be built into the plant. Second, we develop worker health regulations; for example, there are about 750 substances, such as asbestos, coal dust, and chemicals, for which we have specific standards. When working on new regulations, we first develop a draft proposal for public comment by workers and employers. Third, we have a Chemical Hazards Information Program which disseminates information on chemicals and trade name products and their potential hazards. Fourth, our major projects program evaluates work-place hazards on an industry-wide basis; for example, we might research the status of health-hazard controls in welding shops in Alberta. Finally, we administer the Work Site Internal Responsibility Systems program, which ensures that employers develop and maintain a systematic approach to the protection of workers. These five programs are all external control programs, since they deal with ensuring compliance with provincial health and safety legislation.

Q: What is the province's view of the most effective way to be certain that health and safety standards are met?

Matthias: The position is currently in transition. Historically, regulations have been prescriptive. They have primarily regulated the process by which the objectives of workplace health and safety are to be achieved. We are now moving toward a more performance-oriented approach where the objective is clearly stated, but exactly how it is to be achieved is not. For example, whereas formerly a regulation might have read "a guard rail must be at least 58 cm high," the regulation would now say "an employer must ensure that workers are protected from falling." The key is to identify the objective and then let the companies decide how to achieve it. A company might find that a guard rail is not the best way to achieve a particular safety objective. Under the former system, when accidents occurred, the government took the blame for not imposing the proper safety standards. Under the new system, the company is given the freedom to institute programs that will reduce accidents. Since they control the process, they also take the responsibility for the outcome of their safety programs. Also, since work places vary, one single approach may not be best. Some prescriptive-type regulations actually create more of a hazard on some work sites.

Q: What about the internal controlling function? What are your thoughts on the most effective way to carry out your controlling responsibilities, so that your subordinates perform at a high level?

Matthias: Actually, I have a strong philosophical interest in the controlling aspect of management. I am particularly interested in control systems — what works and what doesn't. The work we do on external control has influenced my behavior in performing my internal control responsibilities. I've learned that improper control systems can actually subvert good planning. I've learned that I cannot control without an objective or a sense of direction; otherwise, people focus on busy work.

Q: Do the characteristics of subordinates affect the type of control you use?

Matthias: Yes, to some extent. The people who work for me are professionals; they have a lot of technical training and considerable experience. Many managers set objectives for workers and also tell the workers how to get to those objectives, but I don't feel that approach works very well — especially with professionals. When I have professionals or competent people working for me, I'm concerned about making sure our objectives are achieved but I do not over-control the process. So, I set the objectives with the people who work for me, but they can achieve those objectives in a variety of ways. I find that this approach makes them more motivated, and they often find creative ways of doing their work that I wouldn't have thought of.

Q: Can you give us an example of your "control the result but not the process" philosophy?

Matthias: One of the outputs of this section is information brochures. When we are making up a new brochure, I set out the specific message we want to get across and the target audience. The person responsible for the brochure then writes a first draft and discusses it with me. To be consistent with my philosophy, I suppress the urge simply to tell the person how to fix it; instead, I try to tell the writer conceptually what is missing and then allow him or her to fill in the specifics. For example, instead of saying "add this sentence on respiratory equipment in the third paragraph," I say "we need to say something to identify clearly to the worker why it's important to wear respiratory equipment."

Staff control systems are another example. I work much harder, more effectively, and more creatively if I operate with a control system that says "achieve the objectives of the year plan within these dollar and person/year restrictions" than I do under a system which controls specifically each individual position I can recruit.

Q: What is the effect on the control process if the manager has the same technical training as his or her subordinates?

Matthias: If a manager knows the technical aspects of a subordinate's job, there is a tendency for the manager to tell the subordinate not only what the objective is but also how to achieve it. I have technical training in the same areas as some of my subordinates and I have to watch out that I don't overcontrol them. This reduces their decision-making discretion, their authority, and their motivation.

Q: Are you really saying that management by exception is the way to go?

Matthias: I think management by exception has some advantages; but, in practice, it too often leads to emphasis on negative outcomes because the only time the worker hears from management is when something goes wrong. We need a more positive approach to the controlling function of management. I agree that the manager should not get involved in the details of subordinates' work, but a manager shouldn't have dealings with workers only when work isn't going well. There must be positive feedback. I know that many managers think of a control system as a dirty word, but it's essential. Properly designed and properly administered, it can really make a difference in how people view their jobs and how they carry out their work.

disciplinary
action

This approach will not always work, however. In some cases, workers will simply not accept being told that they are causing difficulties. In extreme cases, disciplinary action will be necessary. **Disciplinary action** is the process of invoking a penalty against an employee who fails to adhere to some work-related standard: for instance, production requirements, rules, or policies. Managers regularly deal with disciplinary actions. Many of the grievance cases appealed to arbitrators by labor unions involve disciplinary action, and management decisions are often overturned. Evidently, some managers do not apply disciplinary action in an acceptable manner.

Disciplinary action begins with a clear understanding of organization objectives. Standards should be created to facilitate accomplishment of these objectives, and they should be clearly communicated to employees. Performance is then observed and compared to standards. No difficulty exists if performance is in line with standards. However, disciplinary action may be needed when excessive performance deviations exist. Once disciplinary action has been taken, it serves to reinforce the importance of the standard to other employees.

progressive
discipine

At all times, the penalty must be appropriate to the violation or accumulated violations. This process is known as **progressive discipline** and its sequence is shown in Figure 16-2. Once a manager observes improper behavior, he or she asks a series of questions about it. The discipline required gets progressively more severe with each affirmative answer. Notice that the mere fact of a violation does not mean that disciplinary action must be taken. The manager may use discretion and decide that no action should be taken in one case but must be taken in another. Certain violations (for example, fighting on the job) may result in automatic suspension, while others (for example, failing once to inspect a product properly) may not.

Discipline Principles

There are several useful principles that managers should use when disciplining employees:

- The manager should act on the assumption that all employees want to conform to reasonable organizational requirements.
- The act, rather than the person, should be condemned.
- Although the act may be the basis for penalty, a model of future acceptable behavior should be communicated to employees.
- Prompt action is important, so that the employee connects the penalty to the violation.
- A managerial listening role is highly recommended to: (a) effect greater understanding of the reasons for the act, and (b) prevent hasty decisions that may lead to unjustified penalties.
- Negative disciplinary action should be administered in private so that an employee can save face among colleagues.
- Definite, but tactful, follow-up should occur to determine the degree of success of the conditioning effort.

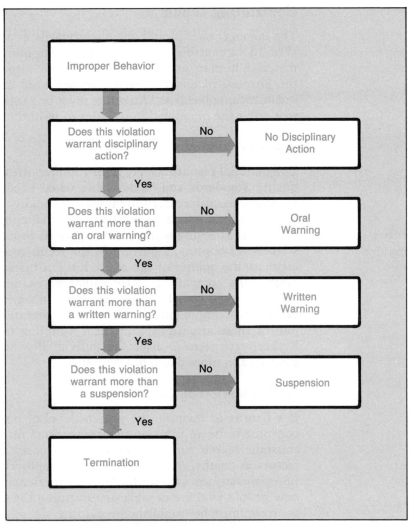

FIGURE 16-2
Progressive
discipline

SOURCE   R. Wayne Mondy and Robert M. Noe, III, *Personnel: The Management of Human Resources* (Boston: Allyn and Bacon, 1981): 493.

• Consistency and flexibility, though apparently contradictory, are both desirable elements of a superior's style of disciplining.

CONTROLLING AND THE BUSINESS SYSTEM

Recall from Chapter 2 that the business system was illustrated by the input-process-output model (see Figure 2-1). Controlling efforts by management may concentrate on inputs, the process itself, or outputs.

Controlling Inputs

input controls

The manager uses input controls primarily as a preventive measure. With **input controls,** an attempt is made to monitor the resources — material, human, and capital — that come into the organization, for the purpose of ensuring that they are used effectively to achieve organization objectives. An effort must be made to control resources that enter the organization in order to monitor these inputs.

Materials Controls

statistical sampling

The material resources an organization requires must meet specified quality standards and be available when needed by the firm. If a furniture manufacturer purchased low-quality wood, the company could not maintain its reputation for producing excellent furniture. **Statistical sampling** is often used to assist in material control. With statistical sampling, a portion of the items received are checked to estimate the quality of the entire lot. For instance, 5 percent of the lumber the company receives might be examined. In many cases, failure of even a small percentage of the incoming items could create difficulty. Components for commercial aircraft engines are an example. In these situations, statistical sampling is not typically used. Rather, each item is inspected individually. Statistical sampling is discussed in more detail in Chapter 17.

Personnel Selection Controls

If a firm is to maintain its present level of operations, there must continue to be an infusion of new workers into the company. This constant search for new employees is necessary because of such factors as deaths, retirements, loss of employees to other organizations, and any growth that the firm is experiencing. In order to obtain new people who are capable of sustaining the organization, certain controls must be established regarding the selection of individuals employed by the firm. Skill requirements of each job must be determined, and new employees should meet or exceed these skills before being employed. These activities were discussed in Chapter 10.

Capital Controls

The firm must have sufficient capital available to achieve its objectives. Equipment and people must be obtained and financed. However, when funds are expended on capital goods, the firm exchanges today's dollars in the anticipation of future profits. A firm wants to purchase capital equipment and pay people in such a way that the greatest benefit will accrue to the company — no easy matter because the future contains much uncertainty. However, there are techniques available to assess the value of various capital outlays. One of the most useful approaches — the net present value method — takes into account the fact that a dollar today is worth more than a dollar not to be received until next year. The procedure for using net present value is described in Chapter 17.

Controlling the Process

process controls

Process controls are used to monitor the actual creation of products or services, largely by observation and by interactions between supervisors and subordinates. Process controls occur as the actual work activities are being performed. A large portion of the operating manager's time is devoted to this function.

The greatest opportunity for the discovery and correction of undesirable deviations takes place while the work is being performed. If an entire lot of 50 units is completed by a worker, and inspection reveals that all 50 have the same defect, the process controls have failed. If someone had at least done a spot check while the first few units were being produced, the error would have been found and much time, energy, and raw materials would have been saved. The amount of overseeing necessary depends on such factors as the skill and attitudes of the workers, the confidence the manager has in the workers, the past work record of the employees, and the extent to which the job is carefully specified to reduce the chance of errors.

Controlling Output

Comparisons determine the degree of agreement between performance results and performance standards. They can take place at or away from the work site. They can be applied to the cumulative performance results of departments or of the entire organization. The objective of **comparison controls** is to determine whether deviations from plans have taken place and, if necessary, to bring the deviations to the attention of the managers who are responsible.

comparison controls

There are several differences between the process and comparison phases of control, even though both involve relating what is going on to what should be going on. First, process control occurs while the work is in progress, while comparison comes later and relies either on information received after a step in a project is completed, or on the results of an entire project.

A second difference between the two controls occurs as a result of the timing. Process controlling must be done by the immediate supervisor. Comparison, however, can be done not only by the supervisor but also by higher line managers or various staff officials. Because it relies on reporting, it can be separated physically from the place where the actual work was done.

Finally, process control requires face-to-face contact and personal observation as the method of obtaining information. The manager must evaluate work in both qualitative and quantitative terms and must be adept in human relations skills. Comparison, however, is usually concerned with only a quantitative and statistical evaluation of actions that have reached some state of completion.

There are several types of comparison controls, including employee performance evaluation, quality and quantity controls, and financial analysis. A brief description of each follows.

Evaluation of Employee Performance

Given a particular task to be accomplished, different people would likely perform at different levels of efficiency. One manager may be quite proficient in planning techniques and another in communication skills. But if each is to improve, each must know his or her specific deficiencies and determine what can be done to overcome them. An effective employee performance system is a means of control whereby individuals learn of their strengths and weaknesses and are told what they should do to overcome them. Collaborative approaches to performance appraisal done in an objective, realistic manner help subordinates grow and become more effective.[2] Employee performance evaluation systems that give each worker the same ratings do not benefit the individual who is a superior performer nor do they assist the substandard worker who wants to improve.

Quality and Quantity Controls

Since the Japanese have developed such a reputation for producing high-quality goods, they have set standards for all competitors. The issue of quality in manufactured goods has become very salient for most Canadians. Anyone who hears a buyer state that he or she got a "lemon" understands that the product was of inferior quality. But what exactly is meant when the term "quality" is mentioned? **Quality** is the degree of conformity to a certain predetermined standard. Standards result ultimately from the establishment of objectives. If the company's objective is to gain a reputation for manufacturing high-quality products, standards will have to be high. In order to meet these high standards, there will have to be a very rigid quality control program. On the other hand, another firm may not have high quality as its objective. Increased quality generally results in higher prices; therefore, some firms may target their appeal to a market that desires lower prices and will accept lower quality. Certain standards remain, but they are not as rigid.

A common approach to evaluating quality is to seek comparison with other organizations or subunits. Figure 16-3 shows how three shift crews compare in terms of the acceptable parts they produce. The supervisor for Shift III probably feels that his or her shift is deficient in comparison to the other two and that corrective action is necessary. (The issue of quality control is discussed in more detail in Chapter 17.)

FIGURE 16-3
Monthly quality
comparison report,
by shifts

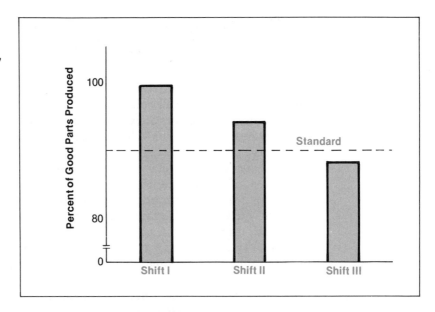

Productivity is normally thought of in terms of the quality of output. Most companies expect a certain amount of production from each individual or organizational unit, often expressed in terms of a quota. Sales quotas specify the amount of sales an individual, district, or region is expected to meet. Production quotas specify the amount or number of an item that needs to be produced. Control of quotas at every level is important if the organization is to achieve its objectives.

Controls through Financial Analysis

The financial statement provides valuable information with regard to whether a company, department, or unit is effectively utilizing its financial resources. Intelligent interpretation of financial data provides an excellent means through which management can control its financial welfare. In order to analyze its financial position, a firm would likely begin with ratio analysis. Financial ratio analysis provides management with a basis for comparing current to past performance. In addition, financial ratios can be compared not only to past trends within the company but also to other divisions within the company and to other firms in the industry. If the ratios are not in line with what is considered acceptable, the manager is in a position to make corrections. These analyses are discussed in more detail in Chapter 17.

ESTABLISHING STRATEGIC CONTROL POINTS

Management through controls is concerned with monitoring a system comprised of resources, processes, activities, and outputs. Management may have difficulty deciding which phases of the system should be monitored. Theoretically, every resource, processing activity, and output should be measured, reported, and compared to some predetermined standard. This can be extremely costly and time-consuming since all activities are not equally significant. A manager must decide what to measure and when to measure it. These critical areas are **strategic control points**, areas that must be monitored if the organization's objectives are to be achieved.

A strategic control point has a number of basic characteristics. First, it is a point established to regulate key operations or events. If a difficulty occurs at a strategic control point, the entire operation may grind to a halt. For instance, if the manager of the word-processing center for Sun Life Insurance Company does not have control of the type and quality of equipment purchased, inaccurate and untimely information may be sent to policyholders. The problem created by poor-quality equipment may have a detrimental impact on the sales of the company even though the word-processing personnel and sales force are of exceptional quality.

A second major characteristic of a strategic control point is that it must be set up so that problems can be identified before serious damage occurs. If the control point is properly located, action can be taken to stop or alter a defective process before major harm is done. Testing for defects early in the process typically cuts costs and improves production and quality.[3] It does little good to discover after the fact that a million defective parts have been produced. The control point should be located so deviations can be quickly identified and corrections made.

One of the authors had the opportunity to observe how the improper selection of strategic control points almost caused a major tire manufacturer to cease operations. In the manufacture of a tire, four basic phases were required. (See Figure 16-4.) The mixing department had to obtain the proper blend of rubber for the type of tire that was being produced. The tread was then shaped with specific attention given to length, width, and thickness. The next phase, building, required placing the various components such as the tread, steel belting, and whitewalls together. In the molding department, the tires were heated and shaped into final form.

The former system of control consisted only of inspecting tires after they had been molded. Because there was already a large investment in the product at this stage, a tire would have to have a major defect before it would be rejected. Recognition of the deficiency in the control process occurred when the tire manufacturing firm received an order for several million dollars from a company that purchased tires and sold them at retail outlets under a different brand name. The retail chain, after careful inspection of the tires, rejected the order and demanded that the entire batch be redone. The tire manufacturing firm nearly went out of business because of this

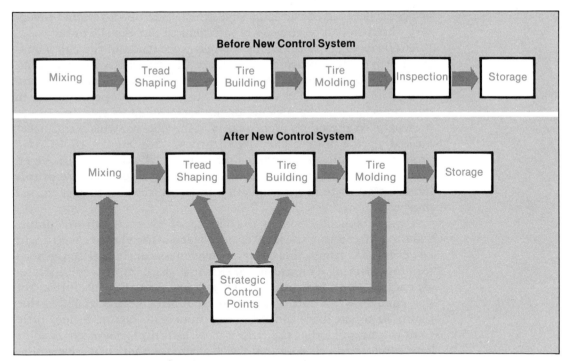

FIGURE 16-4   Example of placement of strategic control points

---

MANAGEMENT IN PRACTICE

Control Difficulties at Ontario Hydro

For the past several years, Ontario Hydro has been experiencing trouble controlling certain aspects of its operations. The first problem area is an inability to predict demand for electricity. Until 1976, demand for electricity grew at an annual rate of 7 percent, but, since the formation of OPEC and rising energy costs, consumers have been conserving with a vengeance. In 1982, electricity demand was actually down 0.8 percent from the previous year. To make matters worse, Hydro's generating capacity in 1983 was 42 percent above the highest expected peak load.

A second major problem is Hydro's inability to control costs. In 1983, Hydro's total debt was $18 billion, and the debt-service bill alone is $2 billion. For three years in a row, Hydro

has paid out more interest to foreign bondholders than all the foreign-controlled oil companies combined have paid out in dividends. Cost-plus contracts are also a problem. In 1978, Hydro signed contracts to buy uranium from the high-cost operations of Denison and Rio Algom. If Hydro goes through with its part of the bargain, it could end up paying $1.2 billion more than if it got its uranium from Saskatchewan's lower priced mines. The biggest embarrassment, however, is the Darlington Nuclear Generating Station. Originally estimated to cost $3.5 billion, it is now expected that $11.4 billion will be necessary to complete it.

SOURCE   Adapted from Robert Bott, "Power Failure," *Canadian Business* (January 1984): 96–101.

decision. Because of the large investment tied up in rejected inventory, the firm had to go heavily into debt to remake the order.

After this experience, major changes were made in the tire manufacturer's control process. A separate quality control department, reporting directly to the president, was established. Quality control inspectors were hired and given authority to stop operations, even over the advice of the production superintendent, if they felt it was necessary to maintain high quality. Strategic control points were located in the four major departments. (See Figure 16-4.) If a problem occurred in the mixing department, it would be discovered before the tire progressed through the other stages. Because of this intensive effort to improve quality, the firm was able to survive and prosper.

A third consideration in the choice of strategic control points should be to indicate the level of performance for a broad spectrum of key events. At times, this comprehensiveness conflicts with the need for proper timing. Net profit, for example, is a comprehensive strategic control point, indicating the progress of the entire enterprise. Yet if a manager waits until the regular accounting period to obtain this figure, he or she loses control of the immediate future. It does little good to recognize that the firm is now bankrupt; managers need to have some accounting figures ahead of time so that corrective action may be taken.

MANAGEMENT IN PRACTICE

Control at Mirvish's Restaurants

Edwin ("Honest Ed") Mirvish is an entrepreneur who owns and runs retail stores, restaurants, real estate operations, and theatres which employ over 1000 people. He has a very hands-on style of management and has strong views about what a company must do to be successful. One reason for his success is his concern for the customer.

Mirvish's four restaurants serve more than one million meals a year. In the restaurant business, tight controls are necessary since there are so many things to look after. One of his control strategies was to serve only roast beef, even though other restaurateurs said you couldn't have only one item on the menu. The key control element in a restaurant is the chef, who is often a very individualistic person who doesn't like anyone meddling in the kitchen — Mirvish says chefs have chased him out of the kitchen with knives. Mirvish now has one chef controlling all the kitchens; the control strategy involves making the food consistent across locations.

Mirvish visits his restaurants regularly and talks to people to see if they have any complaints. He feels that, if he is visible, people will talk to him or send him letters saying what they really think of the restaurant. He responds quickly to any complaints that he receives. He also talks to the employees of the restaurant to get their views of the operation. In this way, the performance of individuals is kept up to his standard.

SOURCE Adapted from Dean Walker, "From Discounts to Show Biz, Ed Mirvish Does It His Way," *Executive* (November 1983): 34–38. Reprinted by permission.

Economy is the fourth consideration in the choice of proper control points. With computer and management information systems available, managers may be tempted to demand every conceivable bit of information. But there is a limited amount of information that any executive can effectively use. If every bit of information is available, critical information may be lost in the mass of data.

Finally, the selection of various strategic control points should be balanced. If only credit losses are watched and controlled, for example, sales may suffer because of an overly stringent policy in accepting credit risks. If sales are emphasized, then credit losses may mount. There is a tendency to place tight control over tangible functions, such as production and sales, while maintaining limited control over the intangible functions, such as personnel development and other staff services. This often leads to an imbalance where production line executives are held to exact standards and staff executives are apparently given blank cheques.

CONTROL AND LEVELS OF MANAGEMENT

Managers, unless they are the top officers in the firm, link two levels of organization. As illustrated in Figure 16-5 each management level plans for, organizes and influences the level below it. Lower levels of

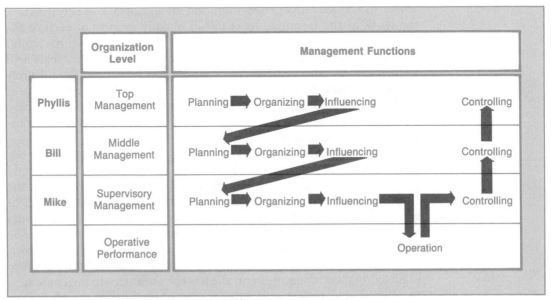

FIGURE 16-5 Organization levels and linking management functions

SOURCE   Adapted from Edwin B. Flippo and Gary M. Munsinger, *Management*, 5th ed. (Boston: Allyn and Bacon, 1982): 384. Reprinted by permission.

management require more specific planning, organizing, and influencing. Higher-level managers issue orders to lower-level supervisors to accomplish tasks generally planned by top management. As tasks are accomplished, results are communicated to both the immediate supervisor and other levels of management. This enables immediate supervisors to operate within the limits of their specific plan. The immediate supervisor must then provide the information to higher management to ensure that higher-level plans are being fulfilled. This information enables each level of management to determine if the actions of the lower levels are conforming to general plans and objectives and if corrective measures need to be taken.

Consider the types of controls a person would confront as he or she moved from a supervisory management position to a top management position. Mike Miller is a shift foreman for a firm that manufactures aluminum window and door frames. Each Monday, he is given a schedule of items that must be produced each day for that week. With this schedule, Miller plans, organizes, and directs the activities that must be accomplished that week. He knows the standards that have been established for each piece of equipment and monitors each of his employees to ensure that the correct number of frames are being manufactured. If an employee is deficient in any task, Miller must take immediate corrective action to ensure that the daily and weekly schedules are achieved. Each day, Miller sends a report of activities to the general manager, Bill Alexis.

Bill Alexis supervises the activities of 10 shift foremen within a division. He must plan, organize, and influence their efforts. He works in a much longer timeframe and views his task as coordinating the work of the foremen; he studies the daily reports of each of the foremen and determines if they need help to solve particular problems. If a foreman is consistently below standard, Alexis will analyze the situation to determine what action must be taken. Rarely will any decision be made entirely on one day's performance of one of the shifts, but the general overall trend is studied. Alexis submits a weekly performance report of his sections to Phyllis Towne, the vice-president of operations.

Towne also performs the various functions of management but from a different perspective. She has five divisions reporting directly to her. She uses control to ensure that the overall objectives of the firm are achieved. She attempts to ensure that a consistent level of quality is maintained, but she must also consider the cost of reaching the quality standard. Her view is even longer than Bill Alexis's. She sees controls as assisting her in solving problems that the divisions may be unable to handle. For instance, if quality is declining because of an aging piece of equipment, she has the authority to purchase new machinery. She monitors the day-to-day operations of the plants but is not as involved as Bill Alexis or Mike Miller.

MANAGEMENT IN PRACTICE

Controlling Executive Salaries

Much has been written about how managers at various companies have tried to control costs. Recent efforts have been motivated by the recession of 1981-82. But the latest data about managers' salaries show that there have been few restrictions in this regard. Salary increases for executives have outpaced those of all other employee groups as well as increases in the rate of inflation, according to a study by Hansen Consultants Ltd. of Toronto.

The study found that the average annual salary increase for managers in 1986 was 7.6 percent, which was almost double the inflation rate. Not surprisingly, these results made organized labor unhappy. Michel Cleroux, media relations officer with Labour Canada, noted that labor settlements averaged about 3.5 percent in 1986.

SOURCE   Adapted from Gail Lem, "Top Executives Fare Well Despite Cost-Cutting," *The Globe and Mail* (December 18, 1986): B6.

REASONS FOR NEGATIVE REACTIONS TO CONTROLS

Although strategic control points and the various types of control that we have discussed are important in effective management, controls are often viewed in a negative way by employees. When controls are mentioned, it makes some workers realize that other people have the power to regulate their activities. There is a natural resistance to controls because a certain amount of individual freedom has been taken away. Employees may not like to be controlled, but they will likely accept the fact that some controls are necessary if the organization is to function successfully. When controls are inappropriate, unattainable, unpredictable, uncontrolled, or contradictory, major resistance is encountered.[4]

Inappropriate Controls

Controls that do not conform to the needs of the situation are inappropriate. In many instances, workers recognize better than management where controls need to be placed if efficiency is to be increased. Inappropriate controls can inhibit the accomplishment of the goals of a department or unit within the organization. For example, in one firm, because of an immediate need for more machine operators, the control system was changed from a measurement of skill level to one that measured the number of machine operators regardless of their skill level. Many more workers completed the training program, but there was considerable grumbling among the production foremen because the skill level of the machine operators had actually declined. True, more people were available to run the machines, but performance had dropped to the point that the quality level could not be maintained. The controls that had been established were inappropriate to meet the needs of the situation.

Unattainable Standards

Employees realize when a standard is unrealistic. When unattainable controls are established, it may actually cause some employees to work below their capabilities. Suppose that a machine operator has been producing effectively at a standard of 20 units an hour. If management arbitrarily increases the standard to 40 units, the operator may feel that the standard is unattainable, and output may decline to less than 20 units per hour.

Unpredictable Standards

When the control system is unpredictable and is constantly changed, much frustration and resentment can result. For instance, if a production manager is told that he or she should strive to achieve maximum output and, once this high output level has been achieved, is then told that quality is more important, resentment toward the control process can result. The production manager could not predict what standard he or she was to be evaluated on.

No Control of the Situation

All workers find it frustrating to be reprimanded for something they cannot control. Suppose that a manager is told that he or she will be evaluated on the profit performance of his or her division, but is not given the right to determine employees' compensation or the right to hire and fire people. This manager will rightfully feel that the control process is unfair because he or she is given no authority over what influences how profitable the division can be. This may lead the manager to resent other kinds of controls, even those which are reasonable and necessary.

Contradictory Standards

At times, various controls may be established that do not complement each other. It may appear to the manager that, if one standard is achieved, it will be impossible to accomplish the other. For instance, it might appear to some managers that high quality and maximum output are contradictory in nature. To a marketing manager, a control system that stresses both increased sales and reduced advertising expenditures may appear contradictory.

OVERCOMING NEGATIVE REACTIONS TO CONTROLS

While the reasons why people resist controls are numerous, managers can find ways to reduce this resistance. A good control system should be justifiable, understandable, realistic, timely, and accurate. If controls have these characteristics, adverse reaction by employees will be minimal.

Justify Controls

If employees believe that there is a need for a particular control system, compliance is much easier to obtain. For instance, the firm may have to increase the quality of its product in order to obtain future contracts. These contracts will mean not only profit for the firm but job stability for the employees. A control system will have higher acceptability if the reason for the control appears justifiable to those who must comply.

Make Controls Understandable

Employees who know exactly what is expected of them with regard to a control system tend to exhibit less resistance. A statement by a manager that quality should increase does not clearly convey what is expected. A requirement that the number of defects should decrease by 10 percent is precise and understandable. When workers do not understand what is expected of them, frustration and resentment can occur.

Establish a Realistic System

A realistic control system is one that permits the organization to achieve its goals without straining employee output. At times it may appear that controls are established merely to harass workers. Excessive standards that are higher than needed to accomplish the purpose of the organization are not only expensive but are likely to be resisted by employees.

Give Timely Feedback

For a control system to be effective, information regarding deviations needs to be communicated to employees as quickly as is practical. It does little good to tell workers that their performance was below standard three weeks ago. If a problem is to be corrected, it must receive immediate attention.

Give Accurate Feedback

A control system must provide accurate feedback to employees. If information feedback has been incorrect in the past, it may be difficult to convince individuals that their effort is below standard. If workers consistently find errors made by supervisors, belief in their ideas may be questioned. An employee who receives a low performance evaluation under such circumstances may have reason to suspect the evaluation is inaccurate even if it is not.

To attain organization objectives, managers perform their basic functions of planning, organizing, and influencing. To be effective with the fourth basic function — controlling — managers should always bear in mind two points: (1) that the controlling process is vital to organizational success, and (2) that workers will often resist controls if they are poorly designed or improperly implemented. A successful manager performs all four basic functions well.

OPENING INCIDENT REVISITED

Can-Mark Manufacturing

Production foreman Henry Friesen was under pressure to get production levels up to standard on a new product using state-of-the-art equipment. The new product is crucial to the company. The production workers were complaining that the output standards were not reasonable, even though they had been set by engineering experts.

This situation portrays one of the classic controlling problems that management faces. Are the standards really unreasonable? Are the workers trying to take advantage of the uncertainty associated with a new production process to get lower standards established? Why are the workers objecting to the standards that were set by the industrial engineering department?

In the chapter, several causes of negative reactions to standards were noted. At Can-Mark, apparently, the workers genuinely believe that the standard is unattainable. They may also feel that they do not have sufficient control over the situation because they have to work with state-of-the-art machinery.

What can be done to reduce these negative reactions and get production back on track?

The chapter notes that standards should be justifiable, understandable, and realistic. Can-Mark's management has a perception problem here because the standards for this new product are not perceived as either justifiable or realistic by the production workers who have good past records with the company. As a show of good faith, management will probably have to retime the jobs — taking into account the newness of the process — to see if any unreasonable assumptions were originally made by the industrial engineers. Management will also have to deal with the quality issue. Perhaps quality standards were not clear enough to workers who may be worrying excessively about quality and not enough about volume. This imbalance would make the standards seem unreasonably high to them.

Overall, management personnel need to show the workers that they are concerned about the problem and want to cooperate with the workers to resolve it. If the workers who actually use the machines are encouraged to analyze the problem and work with management, they will undoubtedly come up with some suggestions for increasing output.

SUMMARY

Control is the process of comparing actual performance with established standards for the purpose of taking corrective action. However, before standards can be established, objectives and plans must be developed. Thus, standards serve as the link between planning and control.

The controlling process involves four critical activities: establishing standards, observing and measuring, comparing performance to standards, and taking corrective action. In an organization, the most important means by which performance can be compared to standards relate to quantity, quality, time, and costs. Corrective action is needed to straighten out deviations from planned performance or to alter the plan to allow for obstacles that cannot be removed. A natural byproduct of corrective action is discipline, the process of invoking a penalty against an employee who fails to adhere to standards.

There are three basic types of controls: inputs, process, and comparison controls. Input controls take place as resources enter the organization. They are relevant for materials, people, and financial resources. Process controls are used during the process when the products and services are being produced. Comparison controls are used after the final product or service has been produced. Comparison controls include quality control; certain products and services require very high quality, with little margin for defects, while others can be sold at lower quality and cost.

Strategic control points are areas that must be monitored closely if the organization is to achieve its objectives. Strategic control points should (1) regulate key operations, (2) identify major problems before serious damage occurs, (3) indicate organizational performance for a broad range of important operations, (4) develop economical information on which to base decisions, and (5) not overemphasize one factor at the expense of others.

Lower-level managers require more specific controls than middle- or upper-level managers. At the supervisory level, the time frame for controls is very short and corrective action must be taken immediately if performance is not up to standard. At the middle levels of management, the time frame is somewhat longer. A person managing supervisors would look for trends in their work, but would not take corrective action on the basis on one day's activities. An upper-level manager has the longest time frame for the controlling function. Top managers use controls to ensure that the overall objectives of the firm are being met.

Managers must realize that there will sometimes be negative reactions to controls. These negative reactions may be caused by inappropriate controls, or by unattainable, unpredictable or contradictory standards. However, there are means by which negative reactions to controls may be overcome. If controls are justifiable, understandable, realistic, timely, and accurate, they will likely cause little resistance.

REVIEW QUESTIONS

1. Define *control* as a process for assisting managers to accomplish their objectives.
2. Explain in your own words why the functions of planning and controlling are so closely related.
3. What are the phases involved in the controlling process?
4. What are the four means by which actual performance may be compared to standards? Briefly discuss each.
5. What are some guidelines that a manager should follow when disciplinary action must be used?
6. Distinguish input controls, process controls, and comparison controls. When would each type be used?
7. What factors should a manager consider in establishing strategic control points?
8. What effect does the level of management have on the control process?
9. Why do employees sometimes resist controls?
10. What characteristics should a control system have in order to overcome employee resistance to controls?

EXERCISES

1. Develop objective(s), plans, and standards for obtaining an A in this course. What type of control measures must be developed for you to accomplish this goal?
2. Consider the following types of businesses and managers. What types of controls do you believe they must have to ensure that they accomplish their objectives?
   a. A small convenience store
   b. A community college or university
   c. A firm that manufactures a high-quality hand calculator
   d. An insurance agency
   e. An automobile repair shop.

CASE STUDY

A Question of Standards

Steven Dowling was a regional sales manager for McGavin-Shane Ltd., a firm that manufactured and sold hydraulic and pumping equip-

ment for industrial uses. Dowling supervised seven salespeople in Southern Ontario.

To ensure good performance from the sales

people, Dowling met with each one twice a year to set sales goals for his or her territory. At the end of each month, he received sales reports from each salesperson. Every six months, he met with each salesperson and discussed the reports, then set goals for the next six-month period. Whenever a salesperson fell short of a six-month goal, Dowling tried to be positive and to encourage him or her to do better during the next period.

Recently he had become quite concerned about Mike Litvin's sales performance. Litvin had worked for another firm in the same business for 17 years, but he had been with McGavin-Shane for only five months and Dowling didn't yet know him very well. For the last three months, Litvin had failed to reach his targeted sales; worse, the shortfall in each succeeding month had increased. In Dowling's mind, a trend had developed that he ought to investigate. Once he found out what was wrong, he could help Litvin. At the regular six-month meeting with Litvin, Dowling raised the issue of the shortfall. The following conversation took place:

Dowling: Mike, I'm concerned about your sales volume during the last few months. You haven't been up to standard for three months now, and you know I can't let that continue.

Litvin: I've been meaning to speak to you about my sales territory and some of the things that are going on there. You know, you're very fortunate that I'm in that territory and have experience in this business.

There has been a big drop in demand for our equipment, but I'm getting at the sales that are out there.

Dowling: I'm very surprised to hear you say that, Mike. The other salespeople aren't reporting any problems.

Litvin: Well, maybe they just don't want to worry you. I've never experienced so much difficulty in getting sales as I have during the last three months.

Dowling: But Mike, the sales figures of the other people are right up to standard. Yours aren't.

Litvin: Steve, if anybody else was in my territory, they wouldn't have sold nearly as much as I have.

Dowling: Mike, aren't you missing the point? Your performance has fallen below our standard.

Litvin: That's one way of looking at it. Another way is to say that my performance is very good given the tough sales atmosphere out there.

At this point, Dowling terminated the interview. He was astonished that Litvin would not even admit the obvious fact that his sales were not up to standard.

QUESTIONS

1. What is Litvin really saying about the sales standard that has been set for him?
2. What should Dowling do to resolve this problem?

CASE STUDY

Flextime

Kathy Collier is a supervisor in a government office in Ottawa. Morale in her office has been quite low recently. The workers have gone back to an 8:30 a.m. to 4:30 p.m. work schedule after having been on flextime for nearly two years.

When the directive came down allowing Kathy to place her office on flextime, she

spelled out the rules carefully to her people. Each person was to work during the core period from 10:00 a.m. to 2:00 p.m.; however, they could work the rest of the eight-hour day at any time between 6:00 a.m. and 6:00 p.m. Kathy felt her workers were honest and well motivated, so she did not set up any system of control.

Everything went along well for a time. Morale improved, and all the work seemed to get done. In November, 1987 however, an auditor found that Kathy's workers were averaging six hours a day. Two employees had been working only during the core period for more than two months. When Kathy's department manager reviewed the auditor's report, Kathy was told to return the office to regular working hours. Kathy was upset and disappointed with her people. She had trusted them and felt they had let her down.

QUESTIONS

1. What type of controls should Kathy have used to prevent the problem: input, process, or comparison controls? Explain your answer.
2. Should Kathy be disappointed with her people? Why or why not?

ENDNOTES

[1] S. M. Klein and R. R. Ritti, *Understanding Organizational Behavior* (Boston: Kent Publishing Co., 1984): 509.

[2] R. L. Taylor and R. A. Zawachi, "Trends in Performance Appraisal: Guidelines for Managers," *Personnel Administrator* 29 (March 1984): 71.

[3] Jon Turino, "Test Strategies That Cut Manufacturing Costs," *SAM Advanced Management Journal* 49 (Winter 1984): 53.

[4] Robert N. Anthony and Regina E. Herzlinger, *Management Control in Non-Profit Organizations* (Homewood, Ill.: Irwin, 1975): 222–226.

REFERENCES

Buffa, Elwood S. *Modern Production-Operations Management.* 6th ed. New York: Wiley, 1980.

Camillus, John C. "Six Approaches to Preventive Management Control." *Financial Executive* 48 (December 1980): 28–31.

Chase, Richard B., and Aquilano, Nicholas J. *Production and Operations Management: A Life Cycle Approach.* Homewood, Ill.: Irwin, 1981.

Dalton, Dan R., and Todor, William D. "Win, Lose, Draw: The Grievance Process in Practice." *Personnel Administrator* 26 (March 1981): 25–29.

DeWelt, R. L. "Control: Key to Making Financial Strategy Work." *Management Review* 66 (March 1977): 18–25.

Flamholtz, Eric. "Organizational Control Systems as a Managerial Tool." *California Management Review* 22 (Winter 1979): 50–59.

Gitman, Lawrence J. *Principles of Managerial Finance.* 2d ed. New York: Harper, 1979.

Hayhurst, B. "Proposal for a Corporate Control System." *Management International Review* 16 (1976): 93–103.

Horovitz, J. H. "Strategic Control: A New Task for Top Management." *Long Range Planning* 12 (June 1979): 2–7.

Lem, Gail. "Top Executives Fare Well Despite Cost-Cutting." *The Globe and Mail* (December 18, 1986): B6.

Lissy, William E. "Necessity of Proof to Support Disciplinary Action." *Supervision* 40 (June 1978): 13.

Machin, John L., and Wilson, Lynn S. "Closing the Gap between Planning and Control." *Long Range Planning* 12 (April 1979): 16–32.

Mittelstaedt, Arthur H., and Berger, Henny A. "The Critical Path Method: A Management Tool for Recreation." *Parks and Recreation* 7 (July 1972): 14–16.

Mondy R. Wayne, and Noe, Robert M. III. *Personnel: The Management of Human Resources.* Boston: Allyn and Bacon, 1981.

Nelson, E. G., and Machin, J. L. "Management Control: Systems Thinking Applied to Development of a Framework for Empirical Studies." *Journal of Management Studies* (October 1976): 274–287.

Ouchi, W. G. "Relationship between Organizational Structure and Organizational Control." *Administrative Science Quarterly* 22, no. 1 (March 1981): 95–113.

Pearce, Jone, and Porter, Lyman. "Employee Responses to Formal Performance Appraisal Feedback." *Journal of Applied Psychology* 71, (May 1986): 211–218.

Pingpank, Jeffery C., and Mooney, Thomas B. "Wrongful Discharge: A New Danger for Employers." *Personnel Administrator* 26 (March 1981): 31–35.

Schroeder, Roger G. *Operations Management: Decision Making in the Operations Function.* New York: McGraw-Hill, 1981.

Shortell, Ann. "The Auditors." *Canadian Business* 59, (November 1986): 38–44.

Solomon, Ezra, and Pringle, John J. *An Introduction to Financial Management.* Santa Monica, Cal.: Goodyear, 1980.

Swann, James P. Jr. "Formal Grievance Procedures in Non-Union Plants." *Personnel Administrator* 26 (August 1981): 66–70.

17

Control Techniques

KEY TERMS

socialization
management audit
management by
  exception
exception principle
statistical quality
  control
acceptance sampling
variable sampling
attribute sampling
control chart
inventory
obsolescence
economic order
  quantity
  (EOQ)
ordering costs
carrying costs
ABC inventory
  method

just-in-time
  inventory system
  (JIT)
PERT
event
activity
expected time
critical path
critical path method
  (CPM)
budget
operating budget
financial budget
cash budget
capital budget
Planning-
  Programming
  Budgeting System
  (PPBS)

zero base budgeting
  (ZBB)
break-even
  analysis
fixed costs
variable costs
net present value
profit center
ratio analysis
balance sheet
income statement
liquidity ratios
leverage ratios
activity ratios
profitability ratios
audit

LEARNING OBJECTIVES

After completing this chapter you should be able to
1. Explain the difference between financial and nonfinancial control techniques.
2. Identify nine nonfinancial and six financial control techniques.
3. Understand the concepts and techniques involved in quality control.
4. Understand the concepts and techniques involved in inventory control.
5. Explain the key elements in the just-in-time inventory system.
6. Describe how budgets are used to facilitate the controlling function.
7. Do a break-even analysis.
8. Explain how ratio analysis helps managers determine how effective an organization is.
9. Explain the difference between financial audits and management audits.
10. Indicate the manager's responsibility in choosing appropriate control techniques.

OPENING INCIDENT

Cam's Corner

Cameron McIntyre opened a variety store called Cam's Corner in Charlottetown, PEI in 1970. During the first few years of operations, business was very good and McIntyre continually found himself having to expand to meet customer demand. He began adding more product lines and salespeople in the early 1970s and this continued through 1979. By that time he had opened two new stores and employed 22 people.

In 1979, interest rates began increasing substantially, and demand for the products he sold began to decline. Like most business people, McIntyre responded by tightening up operations in obvious areas like inventory control or employee overtime. This strategy did reduce costs somewhat, but not enough to make up for substantially declining sales. By 1981, his net profit after taxes was virtually zero; McIntyre was deeply concerned because he knew he couldn't carry on much longer without an improvement in sales and profits. He wanted to continue in business, but he didn't know what else to do.

In an attempt to resolve his problems, McIntyre asked his business acquaintances in Charlottetown how they were coping with the recession, and they were able to give him some additional ideas on better ways to control his business. By early 1984, the general Canadian economy was recovering and McIntyre's profits began to increase once again. McIntyre became very busy with the day-to-day operations of his three stores and didn't have much time to think about his earlier problems. However, in his quiet moments at home in the evening, he still had nagging doubts about the effectiveness of the control devices he was using in his business. He wondered what would happen if another economic downturn occurred.

In Chapter 16, we analyzed the control process and the importance of the controlling function to management. In this chapter, we present several of the most commonly used control techniques. Some of these techniques require formalized management activity, while others do not. Some focus on the total organization, while others focus on individuals or small groups. Some of them require quantitative data, while others do not.

In order to simplify the discussion of the numerous control techniques that companies actually use, we divide them into two categories: nonfinancial and financial. As the names imply, nonfinancial techniques are used to control employee behavior without specific reference to corporate financial data. Financial control techniques can be used only when financial data like costs, profit, or sales revenue are available. Neither category of techniques should be considered more important than the other; rather, they complement each other. In total, they give management a good idea of what is going on in an organization.

NONFINANCIAL CONTROL TECHNIQUES

The most widely used nonfinancial control techniques are: rewards and punishments, selection procedures, socialization and training, the management hierarchy, management audits, management by exception, inventory and quality control, and PERT. These control techniques can be used in any area of the firm, but corporate policy and the personality of the managers in the organization will determine how vigorously they are pursued. We discuss each of these techniques next.

Rewards and Punishments

Every organization has some systems for rewarding behavior that is desirable and punishing behavior that is undesirable. The systems may be formal or informal, but their purpose is to convey to employees how management prefers them to behave. Individual managers usually administer these systems, so, typically, they are not used consistently across all departments or divisions of a company.

The effectiveness of rewards and punishments as a control device depends heavily on the individual manager. The manager must: (1) identify what employees find rewarding and punishing, (2) be consistent in the application of rewards and punishments, and (3) be able to measure employee performance accurately in order for the system to work. If these criteria are not satisfied, managers may experience difficulty trying to control employee behavior with rewards and punishments. For example, in one company, management thought they were doing workers a favor by not making them work overtime, but they later found out that workers wanted to work overtime to earn extra money. Thus, management thought they were rewarding workers when in fact they were punishing them.

Rewards and punishments can have a powerful influence on employee behavior, so they are a potentially useful control device. However, they must be applied carefully or significant problems may arise. The role of rewards and punishments in motivation was discussed in some detail in Chapter 11.

Selection Procedures

Organizations also control employees by controlling the type of employee that is hired in the first place. When the personnel department recruits people for various jobs in the organization, it stipulates certain characteristics that applicants must have. The net effect is to control the types of people that come into the organization. For example, if a company is hiring electrical engineers, it might require applicants to have a degree in electrical engineering. When newly hired electrical engineers begin working, they will find that they have something in common with other electrical engineers at the company because of their educational background.

This kind of control can, of course, have a negative effect on a company. Over time, individuals with a similar perspective may narrow their views; without infusion of new perspectives, they may come to dominate the firm, and it may have difficulty being innovative or creative. Further, if this stagnation happens, the company may find itself unable to respond to changes in its markets; the firm may experience these difficulties precisely because it is efficient in controlling the type of people it hires.

Socialization and Training

When a new employee comes into a company, he or she is given information about both the formal and informal activities of the firm. One of the subtle, but powerful, control techniques that new employees experience is **socialization** — the gradual change of attitudes and behavior of individuals so that they fit into the organization.

socialization

The influence of socialization is evident in the public school system in Canada. Graduates often don't realize that the way they view the business and social aspects of their lives is partially a result of how they were taught in school. Over the period of years in grade school and high school, students are socialized to fit into the Canadian economic and social systems. A similar process of socialization happens in organizations. Each organization has certain attitudes and procedures it wants employees to accept and, over a period of time,

Stephen B. Butler
Miles Laboratories, Ltd.

Stephen B. Butler has a BA from University of Toronto and an MBA from York University. He is manager of operations/logistics, for Miles Laboratories, Ltd., a pharmaceutical manufacturer and distributor, situated in Rexdale, Ontario, a suburb of Toronto. The Canadian company is a subsidiary (see Chapter 17) of Miles Laboratories, Inc. of the United States, which in turn is owned by Bayer ag, a German multinational pharmaceutical company.

Q: How do you handle materials management at Miles Laboratories?

Butler: Our manufacturing process actually begins with a sales forecast generated by the marketing department. We translate that sales forecast into production requirements needed to replenish inventories to the level that will be

required. The goal of materials management is to have the right product in the right place at the right time, but we need to do this in a cost-efficient manner. We must decide how to translate the forecast demand for all our products into a plan for using our production facilities — equipment, labor force, etc. — to the best advantage. We don't want to try for perfect customer service at the cost of supporting huge inventories. On the other hand, we don't want to produce something on Monday, change over the production line, and then change back to produce it again on Thursday. We have to try to find that optimal blend of investment, efficiency, and customer service standards that will allow us to be effective as a business.

One of the most difficult things that we must establish, then, is an acceptable level of customer service. There are conflicting objectives on this matter. Marketing and sales want to have enough stock in inventory to fill all orders as they come in. That level of service is unachievable; we would need cities of warehouses. On the other side, finance people want to minimize the amount of money we have tied up in inventory. What our customers really expect is consistency. They want to know that, if they order from Company X, they can expect delivery in three days — not in two days the first time, ten days the second time, five days the third time.

Q: Once you establish standards, how do you control the process to get the results you want?

Butler: There are so many variables involved in the whole process that efficient control is extremely difficult. One thing we know about market forecasts is that they are always wrong. What we have to do is continuously monitor how wrong they are. We then establish a guideline that we can expect a given forecast to be wrong by a variation of, say, 20 percent. So instead of continually adjusting our production plans to meet changing market forecasts, we establish a safety margin that allows for likely inaccuracy. If you are dealing with only one product, the variables become fairly easy to handle in determining appropriate reactions; and, unfortunately, what we usually do is react rather than pro act. As a company grows and develops more products, the combinations of possibilities become so numerous that it is impossible to evaluate them all using traditional methods in time to take meaningful action. Only the computer can do that job, and that fact has led to the universal acceptance of the computer as *the* control device.

Computerized manufacturing resource planning systems are designed specifically to provide timely control of the execution of the production plan. Once you have established your basic guidelines, the computer can turn them into a detailed plan of action in a very short time. For each product we manufacture, the computer contains a bill of material; this is a list of all the components or ingredients required to make one unit of the product. If we know we need 10 000 units to replenish inventory, the computer can quickly compare what we need to produce with our existing supplies in inventory, and generate a list of products we need to order. An additional power of the system is that it has a lead time built into each item so that it can generate a master schedule for reordering supplies from outside or from our production floor, if we produce it ourselves. Production control managers don't need to spend all their time pushing a pencil against a piece of paper to make the plan; they can devote their time to making the plan happen.

Q: How do you react to the antagonism some managers feel toward computers?

Butler: When looking at computer control systems, managers must remember that a computer does not erase the need for human interface. A computer should be used as a mechanism for getting rid of the drudgery of number tumbling and number crunching, so that people can use their intelligence and skills to analyze situations and make decisions. So many times, I've seen people struggle to make a decision, because they didn't have all the data available to them. After a while, they may develop intuition, gut reactions, that give them appropriate answers. I prefer to have the relevant data available when making decisions. To me, the essence of a good system is that it not be person-specific. If a company is relying on the decisions of a manager who happens to have an exceptional intuitive feel for the products and the marketplace, then that company is extremely vulnerable should that person leave. The company is safer with a system that allows anybody with particular analytical skills to handle the situation.

Q: Can you discuss the other aspect of your job, controlling people?

Butler: People are so diverse that in my experience I need a variety of management styles in controlling people. About 25 people report to me — production and inventory control, purchasing, warehousing, and distribution staff. I regard people as my most important resource in managing my functional area. It is easy for managers to assume they have a system that works and to leave it static, but I prefer to challenge people to create improvements. There are people out there who are not motivated solely by money. They need challenge; they need standards of quality; they need to feel they are part of the thinking process, not just scribes.

Q: Computers can make it tempting to apply very tight controls to the productivity of individual workers; for instance, a manager can use a word processor to track the keystrokes of each operator and can push slower operators to meet the standards set by the fastest ones. How do you feel about that?

Butler: I think that monitoring results is an important task for a manager, but the attitude in which this is done is also important. I could quantify the efforts of my purchasing manager and use my information as a whip to beat him with — a Theory X approach; but, I would rather take the data to him and say there must be something in the system that we can change to improve this. I would encourage the employee to make suggestions. The whole range of activity associated with Management by Objectives must be endorsed. I have found that to be a very useful method of providing people that extra opportunity to improve themselves and their worth to the company.

We can learn a lesson from the Japanese and try to reduce the number of tiers of management so that a manager is closer to the workers. This improves the opportunities for communication. The Japanese have had success in using quality circles to generate ideas from employees. We can learn from the Japanese to change in an evolutionary rather than revolutionary manner. Sometimes we develop control systems that are more complex than the original problems. The Japanese approach is to stand back from the problem and to try to understand it in simple terms so they can find simple solutions.

employees are socialized into accepting that these attitudes and procedures are good. Socialization can be a very powerful form of control over employees.

Training is also used to change employee attitudes and behavior so that they are in line with overall goals of an organization. For instance, if a company has quality as a top priority, it may require all production-line employees to take a course in quality control. Or, if a company is a leader in technological innovation, it may systematically train its employees to be effective in that area. Whatever the company's strategic goal is, it may want to control its employees through training. An employee who resists being trained will probably experience considerable difficulty.

The Management Hierarchy

One of the most fundamental and obvious control techniques is the management hierarchy. Employees in all organizations know that they are responsible to the manager above them in the chain of command. That manager, in turn, knows that he or she is responsible to the next manager up in the formal structure. In some companies the hierarchy is rigidly defined, while in others it is not. In either case, the hierarchy is a control device because each person must account for personal performance and behavior to the next person up the line.

Organizations have developed various control techniques, which are an integral part of the management hierarchy. Rules, policies, procedures, and objectives are examples of control techniques embedded in the management hierarchy. Each controls employee behavior in some way. Rules, for example, limit employee behavior with respect to specific activities, while policies allow considerable flexibility. Objectives may have a restrictive connotation, in that individuals are responsible for reaching certain objectives, but they also can motivate employees toward positive achievements — for example, higher wages if objectives are exceeded. All of these hierarchical controls allow management to predict what employees might do and how they might be motivated to do better while they are working for the company.

The Management Audit

management
audit

A **management audit** is designed to analyze systematically the strengths and weaknesses of the managerial talent in a company. The goal is to improve the organization by making sure that weaknesses in management can be identified and corrected. Some areas of the firm that might be subject to a management audit are economic performance, the state of research and development, production efficiency, sales effectiveness, and earnings growth. All these areas can reflect how well top management has been doing its job of strategic planning, organizing, staffing, and controlling the activities of the organization.

The audit is usually done by an outside consulting firm because the areas to be assessed are politically very sensitive. They may also be difficult to measure objectively, so an organization with no vested interest in the results should be used. The management audit is a control device because it measures how well the managers in a firm have been able to get actual corporate performance up to the desired level. This level may be an industry standard, or it may have been set by the company's own top management. In either case, the management audit compares actual performance against some standard.

Management by Exception

management by exception

Perhaps the most fundamental of all control techniques is **management by exception** (MBE). The basic idea of MBE is that a manager should exercise general management of an area of responsibility, not detailed supervision of each worker. Management by exception is a control technique because it requires the manager to watch overall trends and take action when certain aspects of the operation become exceptions.

exception principle

The **exception principle** — the idea that employees should handle routine matters and the supervisor should handle exceptional matters — is the basis for MBE. For example, a manager might require that employees inform him or her when quality checks on products are below standard more than 10 percent of the time. Otherwise, employees would have the right to continue production without consulting the supervisor. In a service organization, a manager might want to know about customer complaints only when they exceed a certain percentage of customers handled.

The use of MBE results in two advantages for organizations. First, it means a better use of the manager's time. We saw in Chapter 1 that some managers fail to confine themselves to managerial work; instead, they involve themselves in the same kinds of activities as their subordinates. This behavior is not appropriate for management, and use of MBE increases the likelihood that a manager will perform managerial duties, not operative duties. Second, MBE encourages workers to exercise judgment when doing their work. They need not continually consult the manager to check that their work performance is appropriate. As long as they are within the guidelines that have been established, they can continue working as they see fit.

Management by exception is both a motivational and a control technique. Generally speaking, when workers operate under an MBE system, they feel that management has a higher opinion of them and this feeling is motivating. At the same time, control is exercised by management, but only when unusual circumstances merit it.

Quality Control

We saw in the last chapter that quality is the degree of conformity to predetermined standards. This means that quality can vary across firms and amongst products or services. But what constitutes an acceptable range of quality standards? The range is narrow for firms in the pharmaceutical, nuclear, aircraft, and genetic engineering industries, but it is much broader for firms that make nails, garbage cans, and household furniture. Determining the proper quality levels in service firms can be quite difficult. How does a customer know whether a lawyer, doctor, accountant, or architect has rendered a service where the quality is equal to the price? While there are professional groups in each province that deal with issues like this, many consumers have the perception that these groups simply protect their members, not consumers.

Some firms traditionally insist on buying the highest quality materials available and telling about it in their advertising. For example, some firms advertise that they could reduce their costs by using cheaper ingredients but say that that would hurt their reputation for quality. There is little doubt that a lot of the success of Japanese car makers is a result of the image they have created for using strict quality control standards.

Quality standards may also vary within a firm. A manufacturer of canned foods is likely to exercise great care to ensure the highest

---

MANAGEMENT IN PRACTICE

Quality Control at Moldcraft Plastics

If a company hopes to be successful in the custom molding business it needs high-precision molding skills and strict quality control. One of the handful of Canadian firms that has made the grade is Moldcraft Plastics Ltd., which sold over $6 million worth of components to the telecommunications industry in 1984.

The company's president, Frank Zotter, notes that the products Moldcraft supplies to companies like IBM, Northern Telecom, Mitel, and NCR must have reliability levels that were unheard of a few years ago. A two percent rejection rate used to be acceptable, but even that is no longer good enough. Now, almost any rejection rate is unacceptable.

The only way to meet this kind of demand from buyers is to stress quality control from the factory floor up. Top management exhortations to produce high quality will not work. The Moldcraft system is as follows: When an order is received, a sheet listing the critical specifications of the mold is posted so that all workers can see what needs to be done. As the job progresses, both workers and management keep track of how well the specifications are being met. The result has been a slight increase in paperwork, but a very low rejection rate.

SOURCE   Adapted from Judith Nancekivell, "The Pursuit of Excellence," *Canadian Plastics* (June 1984): 24–25.

MANAGEMENT IN PRACTICE

Quality Control at McDonald's

McDonald's has 7500 restaurants worldwide and had sales of almost $8 billion in 1983. In Canada, there are 425 restaurants and sales were $650 million. McDonald's sells the equivalent of one meal every three weeks to each Canadian.

Quality control plays a crucial role at McDonald's. In a Canadian franchise operation, quality control is important because consistency must be maintained in 425 diverse locations. Take meat, for example. It is purchased from independent suppliers that McDonald's doesn't own or control. McDonald's specifies the quality of meat that it wants, and the independent supplier makes sure that quality control at the meat plant is up to McDonald's standards. People from McDonald's purchasing department visit these plants on a regular basis to ensure that standards are being maintained. These activities are in addition to the inspection process that is required by the government.

McDonald's is a loyal buyer. If a relationship with a supplier has been going on for a long time, McDonald's will not suddenly curtail it without a very good reason. McDonald's has found that suppliers come up with innovative ways of doing things that benefit both the supplier and McDonald's. The Canadian president, George Cohon, says that the company would never sacrifice quality just to save a fraction of a cent on an item.

SOURCE   Dean Walker, "Conversation With George Cohon of McDonald's," *Canadian Business* (June 1983): 32–36.

quality for products it sells under its own brand. For those it sells as unbranded or generic products, meeting the minimum government standards for quality may be enough. Kitchenaid sets higher standards for its top-of-the-line dishwasher than for its bottom-of-the-line model.

There are numerous ways to maintain quality of a product. A company could make the decision to inspect 100 percent of the items manufactured but, even with a total inspection program, some defects will not be discovered. When you insert the human element into quality control, mistakes will occasionally be made. Some items that are good may be rejected and other items that are defective will be accepted.

In many instances, it is impossible to have a 100 percent inspection. For instance, if the standard for the life of a light bulb were 200 hours, you would have to burn the light for the assigned number of hours to determine if it met standards. Naturally, you would have no product to sell in this situation. Tire manufacturing companies set standards for their tires in order that they can be driven a certain number of kilometres. If each tire were placed on a machine and run the assigned number of kilometres to determine if it met standards, there would be no product to market. In still other instances, the cost to inspect each item to determine if it conforms to standard is prohibitive. If each nail in a keg were inspected separately, the cost to inspect might be higher than the price of the nails.

The technique that is available to overcome the above problems is known as **statistical quality control**, in which a portion of the total number of items is inspected. For instance, five out of 100 items may be selected and an estimate made as to the characteristics of the other 95. Naturally, some degree of error exists. For instance, if there are five defective items in a batch of 100, and the five defective ones just happened to be chosen, the entire batch would be rejected. Likewise, if there were only five good items in a batch of 100, these five might all be chosen and the quality control inspector would erroneously conclude that all items in the batch were good. However, both these situations are very unlikely, so the benefits of sampling far outweigh the costs.

Acceptance Sampling

Acceptance sampling is the inspection of a portion of the output or input of a process to determine acceptability. Assume that it has been statistically determined that taking a sample of 15 items from each batch of one hundred and limiting defective units to two will result in the desired quality. If two or more items are defective, the entire lot is rejected. When a lot is rejected, every item in that batch may be inspected. Or the lot may be returned to the supplier and the supplier required to straighten out the problem.

There are two basic approaches to sampling: sampling by variables and sampling by attributes. Both are appropriate for use but under different circumstances.

A plan developed for **variable sampling** consists of determining how closely an item conforms to an established standard. In essence, degrees of goodness and degrees of badness are permitted. For instance, a stereo speaker is designed to project a certain tone quality. All speakers will not project precisely the same tone quality. Some speakers will have quality that is above the established standard, and some will have tone quality that is below standard. The variance does not necessarily mean that the speaker will be rejected. Only when the quality is outside a certain established limit will it be rejected.

With sampling by variables, degrees of conformity are considered; with **attribute sampling**, the item is either acceptable or unacceptable. The product is either good or bad; there are no degrees of conformity to consider.

Control Charts

A **control chart** is a graphic record of how closely samples of a product or service conform to standards over time. The chart is used with both variable and attribute sampling, although the statistical proce-

FIGURE 17-1
Example of control
chart

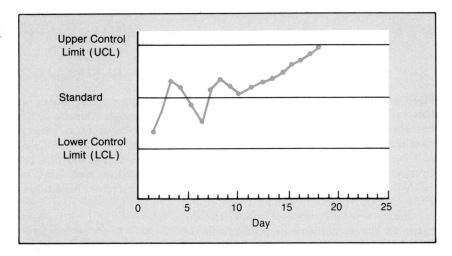

dure for developing the charts is different. In both instances, the standard is determined (Figure 17-1). A variable sampling plan in the manufacture of tire treads might have standards that test thickness, weight, length, and width. If the average thickness of a certain tire tread is expected to be 0.87 inch, this becomes the standard.

Once the standard has been established, the manager must determine the amount of deviation that will be acceptable. The maximum level that will be allowed is referred to as the *upper control limit* (UCL), and the minimum level is called the *lower control limit* (LCL). In the tire tread example, the UCL might be 0.89 inch and the LCL might be 0.84 inch. If the thickness of a tread being evaluated falls within the two extremes, it will be accepted. If it falls outside the limit, it will be rejected.

Another benefit that accrues through the use of control charts is that potential problems may be recognized prior to their actual occurrence. Figure 17-1 shows that from day 10 until day 17, the quality of the product progressively worsened. Although the item is still within the limits of acceptability, if the problem is not corrected, the process may soon go above the upper control limit. When managers see this pattern developing, they are in a position to take corrective action.

Inventory Control

inventory

Inventory refers to the goods or materials that are available for use by a business. The general public is exposed to inventory almost daily. You might hear that a car dealer has excessive inventory and it will offer you a special deal if you buy a car. A furniture dealer provides you with a similar offer. While there may also be a bit of sales promotion in these offerings, inventory does represent a cost that

MANAGEMENT IN PRACTICE

Inventory Control at Phillips Cables

Phillips Cables' construction division manufactures low-voltage electrical wires for the household and construction market. The division has improved customer service 20 percent and cut inventory in half by introducing a Computerized Inventory Management System (CIMS) and a Transportation Service Plan (TSP). CIMS forecasts product demand and centralizes inventory control, while TSP ensures the timely delivery of products to the company's regional warehouses. These two systems now link the eight regional and two central warehouses and factories together through a central computer.

With a centralized inventory, the amount of safety stock that needs to be held can be reduced. The risk of accumulating back orders is also decreased. CIMS and TSP have resulted in an increase in customer satisfaction.

SOURCE Adapted from David Wong, "High Inventory Headache — How Phillips Relieved It," *Canadian Transportation and Distribution Management* (August 1983): 22–23.

must be controlled. A product in inventory constitutes an idle but valuable resource. Suppose that the car dealer keeps a million dollars in extra inventory for one year. At a 10 percent interest rate, $100 000 would be lost because items in inventory do not draw interest. Much of the resources of some major companies are in inventory, and failure to control inventories can mean the difference between a profit or a loss to a firm.

One of the major advantages of inventory is that it permits independence of operations between two activities. For instance, if Machine A makes a product that will be used in a later stage by Machine B and Machine A breaks down, Machine B will have to cease operation unless inventory of the product has been previously built up. Inventories also provide for continuous operations when demand for the product is not consistent. Electric razors are sold primarily during the Christmas buying season, but manufacturers of electric razors typically keep production going through the entire year. Stability is assured, in that a skilled work force can be maintained and equipment usage can be kept at an optimum level. Another advantage of inventory is that it allows the company to fill orders when they are received, thereby maintaining customer satisfaction. If orders arrived on a constant basis, there would be no need to maintain inventory. But if five orders come in this month and 100 next month, a company might be hard pressed to fill the 100 requests unless an inventory had been maintained.

There are some equally good reasons for keeping inventories low, however. First, inventories require an investment of funds. A factory which operates with a lower inventory is operating more efficiently — that is, it is producing profits with a smaller investment than a factory with large inventories. Second, inventories take up scarce space. Third, goods in inventory may decrease in value because of deterioration, theft, or damage. Inventory goods also may be subject **obsolescence** to **obsolescence**: this is what happens when something is out of date or not as efficient as newer products. New inputs or new finished goods may be invented or found which would make inventories obsolete. Many firms keep as little inventory as possible.

Economic Order Quantity (EOQ)

economic order quantity

ordering costs

carrying costs

The **economic order quantity** (EOQ) method of inventory control is a procedure for balancing ordering costs and carrying costs so as to minimize total inventory costs. **Ordering costs** are administrative, clerical, and other expenses incurred in initially obtaining inventory items and placing them in storage. **Carrying costs** are the expenses associated with maintaining and storing the products before they are sold or used. Taxes, insurance, interest on capital invested, storage, electricity, and spoilage are some of the items associated with carrying costs. The purchase price is the price of the product multiplied by the number of items ordered. Thus, the total cost associated with a particular order is calculated according to the following general formula:

Total cost = Ordering cost + carrying cost + purchase cost.

The task of the manager is to purchase in amounts that will minimize total cost. If you order less frequently, ordering costs will go down, but carrying costs go up. If you submit frequent orders, ordering costs go up but carrying costs are reduced. This balancing process is graphically presented in Figure 17-2. The optimum number of items to order at any one time is at the lowest point on the total cost curve. The lowest point is where carrying costs and ordering costs intersect.

In order to determine the EOQ, calculus is used in the development of the mathematical model. Again, the manager does not have to be a quantitative wizard to determine EOQ. A manager, however, must be capable of identifying two primary costs: carrying (C) and ordering (O). Through the power of calculus, an EOQ formula is then determined from the total cost equation. The basic equation for EOQ is presented below:

$$\text{EOQ} = \frac{2\left(\begin{array}{c}\text{ordering}\\ \text{cost}\end{array}\right)\left(\begin{array}{c}\text{annual}\\ \text{demand}\end{array}\right)}{\text{carrying costs}} = \frac{2(O) \times (D)}{C}$$

If we assume that annual demand is 1000 units, carrying cost is $2 per unit, and ordering cost is $4, we will determine that the optimum

FIGURE 17-2
Economic order
quantity illustration

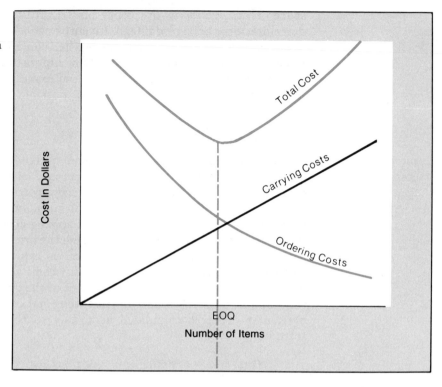

number to order is 63.25, or 63 when rounded to the nearest unit. We cannot choose another order quantity that would lower the total cost.

The model described is one of the simplest to develop. The sophistication level of the model depends on the actual need of the company and the demands of the environment. The manager must be capable of realizing when inventory control procedures may be useful and must identify what costs may be associated with the problem. Then specialists such as accountants and mathematicians are called upon to assist in the development of the model. The manager provides the guidelines and ensures that necessary output is received.

ABC Inventory Method

Sometimes it is impractical to monitor every item in inventory with the same degree of intensity. In such cases it is useful to categorize the items of inventory according to the degree of control needed. The **ABC inventory method** is the classification of inventory items for control purposes into three categories according to unit costs and number of items kept on hand. The usual categories are:

ABC inventory method

- A — Small number of items but high unit cost
- B — Moderate number of medium-cost items
- C — Large number of low-cost items

A manager using the ABC classification is able to develop a sophisticated system to monitor Category A items. Items in the category might include automobiles, machinery, and tractors. Category B items would have a less sophisticated inventory control system. Category C items might not even be controlled if the cost associated with monitoring the items would be prohibitive, as may be the case for pencils and paper. Through the ABC method, a manager is capable of monitoring inventory in an optimum manner.

The Just-in-Time Inventory System

just-in-time
inventory
system
(JIT)

During the last few years, a completely new concept of inventory management, which was started in Japan, has begun to gain ground in North America. It is called the **just-in-time inventory system**, or JIT. When the JIT system is used, inventory is scheduled to arrive just in time to be used in the production process. This system is based on the idea that very little inventory is necessary if it is scheduled to arrive at precisely the right time. If it is properly managed, the JIT system saves the company considerable money because inventory levels can be drastically reduced. All the risks associated with inventory — such as obsolescence, theft, or destruction by fire — can therefore be avoided.

The JIT system requires a major change in the way managers think about inventory. It requires great precision in the scheduling of production and in the delivery of inventory. Some companies that use it have found that they are able to schedule arriving inventory almost to the minute if they are very careful in their planning. Drastic inventory reductions are therefore possible, but only if control of the system is tight. One expert suggests that the JIT system can result in zero inventory.[1]

MANAGEMENT IN PRACTICE

The Just-in-Time Inventory System at Omark Canada

Omark Canada Ltd., a manufacturer of chain saw bars and sprockets, began using JIT in 1982. In the past, Omark's American supplier took three or four days to make deliveries, partly because drivers had to be changed at the border. As well, loads were often over or underweight. The company solved both these problems by leasing a truck. Its driver picks up the steel needed to make the saw bars and sprockets and delivers it on the same day. He also synchronizes his arrival with the time the load is required at the plant. The new method has meant savings of $30 000 per year. The company is also planning to ship finished goods on the return trip, in order to save even more money.

SOURCE   Adapted from Shelley Boyes and Michelle Ramsay, "Just-In-Time — The New Eastern Philosophy," *Canadian Transportation & Distribution Management* (June 1984): 33.

MANAGEMENT IN PRACTICE

Just-in-Time Inventory Management at Chrysler Canada

The JIT inventory system is highly refined at Chrysler Canada's Windsor, Ontario plant. Since the plant receives up to 300 truckloads a day of raw materials, much care must be taken to ensure that shipments arrive on a precise timetable.

At present, 120 of the 300 arriving shipments are made just in time. Suppliers must work to a strict schedule. For example, Chrysler might tell a supplier to deliver 260 units of a certain raw material to delivery dock "A" at 09:00, and another 340 units at 14:00. Chrysler expects a call from the supplier 30 minutes before the load is scheduled to leave the supplier's dock. If Chrysler doesn't get the load, it calls the supplier and asks what is wrong.

It took some suppliers time to accept that Chrysler meant business. One shipment arrived 12 hours ahead of schedule because the truck driver hadn't stopped to sleep. He had to wait 12 hours to unload. Overall, however, suppliers are responding positively to the system because it also makes them more efficient. Since they know exactly what is expected of them, they are able to schedule their own people more efficiently.

SOURCE Adapted from Shelley Boyes and Michelle Ramsay, "Just-In-Time — The New Eastern Philosophy," *Canadian Transportation & Distribution Management* (June 1984): 33–34.

Substantial changes are also necessary outside the company. For example, the JIT system requires suppliers to time deliveries with much greater precision than formerly. Achieving this precision requires a very close working relationship between suppliers and manufacturers, perhaps by having a manufacturer purchase a given raw material from only one supplier. This motivates the supplier to be more careful when scheduling deliveries because the supplier knows how much business is at stake. In the past, many manufacturers purchased a certain part from several different suppliers. This kept competition up among suppliers, but it also meant that the business available to a given supplier was small. Under this system, manufacturers often experienced difficulties with uniformity of parts because they came from three or four different suppliers. If a manufacturer uses the JIT system and purchases from only one supplier, both of these problems are solved.

Some managers feel very uncomfortable about the JIT system because they are used to carrying inventory and feel good about having buffer stocks in case anything goes wrong. During the strike against General Motors of Canada in October 1984, thousands of American workers were laid off because their plants were using the JIT system. Their plants ran out of parts very quickly when the Canadian strike occurred, so management laid off the workers. But with increasing numbers of companies adopting the JIT system and gaining the financial benefits from it, other companies may have no alternative but to follow suit.

MANAGEMENT IN PRACTICE

Just-in-Time and Plant Design

The just-in-time (JIT) inventory system, so named because its use requires that inventory arrive literally "just-in-time" to be used in the manufacturing process, saves firms money because they do not have to store inventory. But JIT also affects manufacturing firms in other ways. First, because inventory storage space is reduced, plant size can also be reduced. With serviced industrial land selling for up to $400 000 per acre in Vancouver, a company which could build a smaller plant because of JIT could save considerable money.

Second, since inventory is not stored, savings can be achieved in automated storage equipment. Since automated storage and retrieval systems can run into the millions of dollars, JIT can save considerable money in this area.

Third, since JIT requires that suppliers de-liver inventory on a very tight schedule, they want to be located near major highways. There is also a trend for suppliers to move closer to the manufacturing facility they are supplying so that inventory delivery is simplified. Manufacturers are also interested in developing closer ties and more business with a few key suppliers to guarantee that inventory is delivered on time. Finally, because inventory is delivered frequently, more loading docks are needed than in the typical factory. In Japan, loading docks are often found on all four sides of a factory, not just at the back as is customary in North America.

SOURCE "Just-In-Time Gives Whole New Look To Plant Design," *The Financial Post* (September 14, 1985): P1.

Network Models

The number of separate tasks that must be accomplished to build a skyscraper or a dam across a river are almost impossible to conceive for the average person. We are often fascinated at how the construction manager in charge of a project of this magnitude is able to coordinate all the tasks and arrive at a finished product. When the project is nonrecurrent, large, complex, and involves multiple organizations, the manager needs a tool that will assist in coordinating this complicated network of interdependencies. He or she needs to be able to think through the project in its entirety and see where resources can be shifted or rescheduled to ensure that the project is completed within the time and cost constraints. The primary techniques available to accomplish these tasks are program evaluation and review technique (PERT) and critical path method (CPM). PERT was developed to assist in the rapid development of the United States Polaris submarine program. At approximately the same time, researchers at DuPont and computer specialists at Remington Rand's Univac division combined their talents to develop a method to schedule and control all activities involved in constructing chemical plants. The result of their effort was a network model termed the critical path method.

Both PERT and CPM have received widespread acceptance since their introduction in the late 1950s. They are used primarily in construction projects, but some firms use the technique to assist in the development of new products. Network analysis is common to both PERT and CPM. Because of their similarity, only PERT will be discussed in detail.

PERT

PERT

PERT (program evaluation and review technique) is a planning and control technique that involves the display of a complex project as a network of events and activities with three time estimates used to

event

calculate the expected time for each activity. An **event** is the beginning or completion of a step. It does not consume time or resources. An event is represented by a circle or node, as shown below:

activity

An **activity** in a PERT network is the time-consuming element of the program. It is represented by an arrow in a PERT diagram.

In order to demonstrate how PERT works, we consider the case of a company which is trying to get a government contract to build a certain type of aircraft. The main steps that must be taken by a project manager are as follows:

1. Define the objective of the project and specify the factors (time, cost) that must be considered as the variables to be controlled — for instance, how quickly the project must be completed or how much money is allocated for completion of the project.
2. List all of the significant activities that must be performed for the project objectives to be achieved:
   Preparing specifications
   Establishing quantity requirements
   Negotiating contract
   Preparing test facilities
   Developing airframe
   Developing engine
   Assembling airframe
   Installing engine
   Preparing test

Testing
Obtaining headquarters approval
Evaluating by contractor
Negotiating contract.

3. Develop a statement of the relationship among project activities. The order in which each task is to be accomplished is also specified. A PERT network is then developed through this information. (See Figure 17-3.) As may be seen, the prototype airframe and the prototype engine must be completed before the test model is completed.

4. Determine the expected times that will be required to complete each activity. PERT requires that three time estimates be provided:
Optimistic time: If everything goes right and nothing goes wrong, the project can be completed in this amount of time.
Most likely time: The most realistic completion time for the activity.
Pessimistic time: If everything goes wrong and nothing goes right, the project will be completed in this amount of time.

The expected time for the completion of each activity may be seen in Figure 17-4, on page 618. For instance, the optimistic time for the activity "developing airframe" is 36 weeks, the pessimistic time is 56 weeks, and the most likely time is 40 weeks. Inserting these figures into the expected time formula below, we determine that 42 weeks is the expected time to complete the activity. **Expected time** is then computed by applying the three time estimates to the following formula:

expected time

$$\text{Expected time } (te) = \frac{\text{Optimistic time} + 4 \text{ (most likely time)} + \text{pessimistic time.}}{6}$$

critical path

5. Determine the **critical path,** that is, the longest path from start to finish of the project. (The actual work of the manager terminates once the three time estimates have been obtained.) There are numerous computer programs that are available to perform the mechanics of this task. The critical path for this project is represented by the broken line seen in Figure 17-5 (see page 619). If any activity along the critical path is a week late, the entire project will be delayed an additional week.

6. Determine the probability of completing the entire project or a particular activity on time. This in itself is a major feature of PERT. Because of the three estimates, the manager is able to obtain an estimate of whether the project will be completed on schedule. The optimistic and pessimistic times have been determined to assist in this operation. If there were but one time estimate — the most likely time — probabilities could not be computed.

A manager usually finds it beneficial to compare the optimistic and pessimistic times to the most likely time. For instance, the

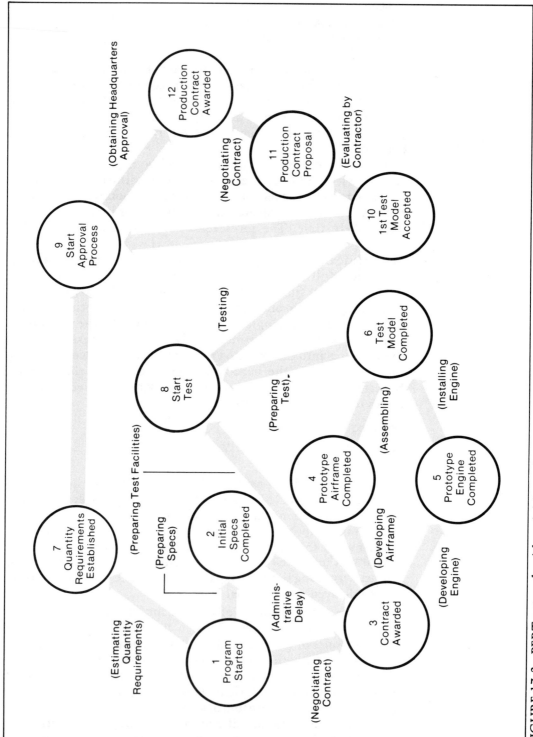

FIGURE 17-3 PERT network with activities and events

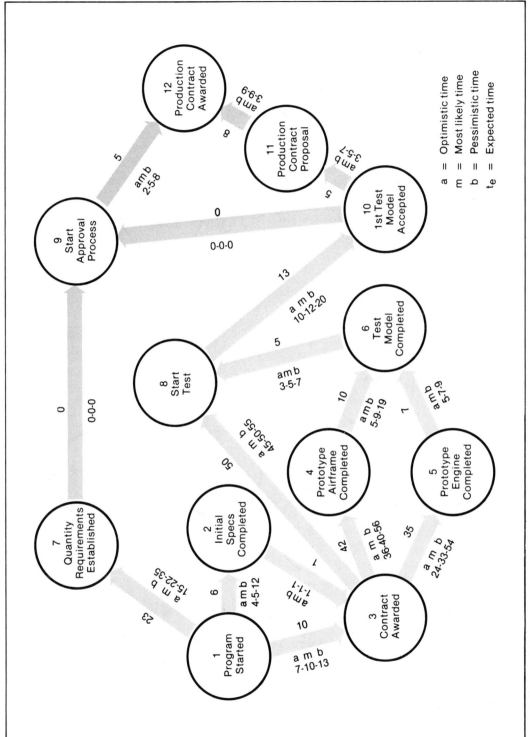

FIGURE 17-4 Expected times to complete each activity

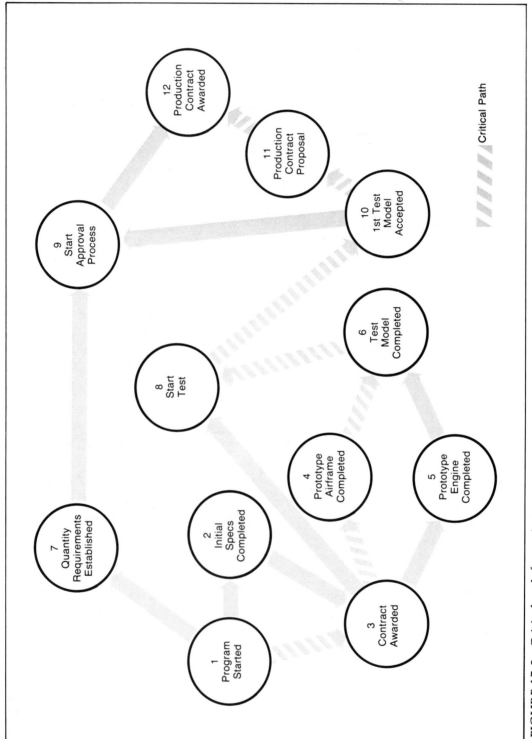

FIGURE 17-5 Critical path for project

activity "developing engine" would likely cause greater concern to the manager than the activity "developing airframe." The difference between the optimistic time and pessimistic time for "developing engine" is 30 weeks (54 − 24), while the difference for the activity "developing airframe" is but 20 weeks (56 − 36). A manager will likely monitor the activities that have the greatest difference between optimistic and pessimistic time because they provide the greatest potential for not meeting the completion date.

Once the critical path has been identified, the manager is able to determine quickly what activities must be carefully monitored. If an activity along the critical path slips one day, the entire project will be delayed one day. Activities that are not on the critical path may not have to be monitored as carefully as those on the critical path. The manager is also in a position to determine which activities are not likely to be completed on time and to monitor them carefully.

PERT may serve both as a planning and a control tool. It forces a manager to think through a project thoroughly and identify the tasks that must be accomplished and how they interrelate in the completion of the project. It serves as a control tool in that a critical path (the longest path from start to finish of the project) is identified. Thus, a manager is able to work with extremely complex projects and still maintain control over the project.

The Critical Path Method

critical path
method
(CPM)

CPM (critical path method) is a planning and control technique that involves the display of a complex project as a network with one time estimate used for each step in the project. The developers of CPM were dealing with projects for which the time and cost of tasks (activities) required to complete the project were known. In CPM the points or nodes of the CPM network represent activities rather than events. Also, there is but one time estimate in CPM because it was designed to accommodate situations in which sets of standardized activities were required for the completion of a complex project. Time for completion of a task was relatively easy to determine accurately. Because there was but one time estimate, probabilities of completing the project on time were not available. With these minor exceptions, PERT and CPM provide for accomplishment of similar functions.

FINANCIAL CONTROL TECHNIQUES

The most widely used financial control techniques are: budgets, break-even analysis, net present value, profit centers, ratio analysis, and accounting audits.

Budgets

budget

Though there are many devices that managers can use in controlling costs or expenditures, the most widely known and used is the budget. A **budget** is a formal statement — in dollar-and-cents terms — of the firm's planned expenditures in a future time period, usually one year. Budgetary control requires comparison of actual and planned expenditures.

Types of Budgets

Budgets are important documents used by managers in planning and controlling operations. There are two broad categories of budgets: financial budgets, and operating budgets. An overview of the components of these two types of budgets is provided in Figure 17-6.

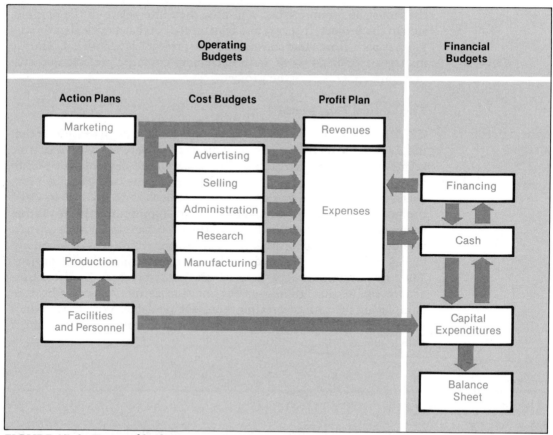

FIGURE 17-6   Types of budgets

SOURCE   Gordon Shillinglaw, *Managerial Cost Accounting*, 4th ed. (Homewood, Ill.: Irwin, 1977): 137. Reprinted by permission of author and publisher.

operating budget

financial budget

cash budget

capital budget

- **Operating budgets** indicate the revenues and expenses the business expects from producing goods and services during a given year. As illustrated in Figure 17-6 these budgets consist of action plans, cost budgets, and a profit plan.
- **Financial budgets** indicate the amount of capital the organization will need and where it will obtain the capital. Two financial budgets are usually developed: the cash budget and the capital budget. The **cash budget** summarizes planned cash receipts and disbursements, while the **capital budget** indicates planned capital acquisition, usually for the purpose of purchasing additional facilities or equipment.

An Illustration of Budgetary Control

The use of a budget as a control device is relatively simple. Table 17-1 shows the monthly budget for a keypunch department. The major expense items include direct labor (wages for the unit's keypunch operators), indirect labor (the department manager's salary), operating supplies (keypunch cards), maintenance expenses (repair of machines), and miscellaneous expenses. As shown in Table 17-1 actual expenditures are compared with budgeted or planned expenditures. In this department, actual expenditures exceeded budgeted expenditures for direct labor and operating supplies by $800 and $250, respectively. Actual spending for maintenance and miscellaneous was under the budgeted amount by $440. Budgetary control enables the manager of the department to identify significant deviations in actual versus budgeted or planned expenses and to take corrective action when necessary. For example, the $800 over budgeted expenses for the wages of keypunch operators may have been caused by the necessity to pay overtime wages. This cost may have resulted from ineffective work scheduling or the sudden appearance of a rush job. This situation, if it occurred in several successive periods, may cause the manager to take such actions as requesting

TABLE 17-1   Department operating budget

BUDGET KEYPUNCH DEPARTMENT
January 131

Item	Budget	Actual	Over	Under
Director labor	$10 000	$10 800	$800	
Indirect labor	1 800	1 800		
Operating supplies	1 250	1 500	$250	
Maintenance	1 800	1 400		$400
Misc. expense (telephone)	190	150		40
Total	$15 040	$15 650	Over $610	

additional personnel or improving the scheduling of work to correct the problem. In any event, budgeting control is a very useful tool of managers at virtually every level of an organization.

Benefits of the Budgeting Process

The fact that most profit and not-for-profit organizations operate within the framework of budgets attests to their benefits. Budgeting is a very significant part of both the planning and controlling processes. Budgets are widely used by managers to plan, monitor, and control various activities and operations at every level of an organization. There are several important advantages in preparing and using budgets. Some of the benefits of the budgeting process are that it:

- Provides standards against which actual performance can be measured. Budgets are quantified plans that allow management to measure and control performance more objectively. If, for instance, a department manager knows that the budgeted expenditure for supplies is $1000 per month, the manager is then in a position to monitor and control the expenses for supplies.
- Provides managers with additional insight into actual organization goals. Monetary allocation of funds as opposed to lip-service more often than not is the true test of a firm's dedication to a particular goal. For instance, suppose that two firms of relatively similar size had a stated policy of hiring minority personnel. Firm A allocates $100 000 and Firm B provides $10 000. A personnel agent will realize that a much stronger commitment to minority hiring is expressed by Firm A than by Firm B.
- Tends to be a positive influence on the motivation of personnel. People typically like to know what is expected of them, and budgets clarify specific performance standards.
- Causes managers to divert some of their attention from current to future operations. To some extent, a budget forces managers to anticipate and forecast changes in the external environment. For example, an increase in transportation costs created by higher-priced petroleum might force the firm to seek an alternative transportation or distribution system.
- Improves top management's ability to coordinate the overall operation of the organization. Budgets are blueprints of the company's plans for the coming year and greatly aid top management in coordinating the operations/activities of each division or department.
- Enables management to recognize and/or anticipate problems in time to take the necessary corrective action. For example, if production costs are substantially ahead of the budgeted amount, management will be alerted to make changes that may realign actual costs with the budget.
- Facilitates communications throughout the organization. The budget significantly improves management's ability to communicate the objectives, plans, and standards of performance which are important to the organization. Budgets are especially helpful to lower-level managers by letting them know how their operations relate to other units or departments within the organization. Also, budgets help pinpoint managers' responsibility and improve their understanding of the goals of the organization. This process usually results in increased morale and commitment on the part of managers.

- Helps managers recognize when change is needed. The budgeting process requires managers to review carefully and critically the company's operations to determine if the firm's resources are being allocated to the right activities and programs. The budgeting process causes management to focus on such questions as: What products appear to have the greatest demand? What markets appear to offer the best potential? What business are we in? Which business(es) should we be in?[2]

Limitations of the Budgeting Process

Although numerous benefits can be attributed to the use of budgets, potential problems may also arise. If the budgetary process is to achieve its maximum effectiveness, these difficulties must be recognized and an attempt made to reduce the potential damaging side-effects associated with the use of budgets. Some of the major problems are:

- The attitude by some managers that all funds allocated in a budget must be spent may actually work against the intent of the budgetary process. Some managers have learned from experience that, if they do not spend the funds that have been budgeted, their budget will be reduced the following year. Managers have found that they can actually hurt their department because of their conscientious cost-effectiveness approach. A manager who operates in this type of budget atmosphere may make an extraordinary effort to spend extra funds for reasons that may be marginal at best.
- A budget may be so restrictive that supervisors are permitted little discretion in managing their resources. The actual amount that can be spent for each item may be specified, and funds cannot be transferred from one account to another. This inflexibility may result in, for instance, funds being available for word processor paper, but not for word processor repairs.
- Budgets may be used to evaluate the performance of a manager as opposed to evaluating the actual results accomplished. If this philosophy is prevalent within the firm, a poor manager may gain recognition because he or she met the budget, but a good manager may be reprimanded for failure to follow exact budgetary guidelines. With this corporate philosophy, the amount of risk a manager will be willing to take may be severely reduced. Managers may spend a majority of their time ensuring that they are in compliance with the budget when their time might be better spent in developing new or innovative ideas.

PPBS and ZBB

In recent years, two specific budgeting systems have received considerable attention: planning-programming budgeting system (PPBS) and zero base budgeting (ZBB). To date, these two techniques have been used more frequently in public-sector firms than they have in private-sector firms.[3]

Planning-
Programming
Budgeting
System
(PPBS)

The **planning-programming budgeting system** (PPBS) was designed to aid management in identifying and eliminating costly programs that were duplicates of other programs and to provide a means for the careful analysis of the benefits and costs of each program or activity. The essential elements of PPBS include:

- Careful analysis and specification of basic objectives in each major program area. A vital starting point for PPBS is to answer such questions as: "What is the firm's basic purpose or mission?" or "What, specifically, is it trying to accomplish?"
- Analysis of the output of each program in terms of the specific objectives. In other words, how effectively is the firm achieving its goals?
- Measurement and analysis of the total costs of the program over several years. For example, in budgeting for additional buildings, management would need to consider not only the initial costs of construction but also costs of operating and maintaining the facilities in future years.
- Determination of which alternatives are the most effective in achieving the basic objectives at the least cost.
- Implementation of PPBS in an organized and systematic manner so that, over time, most budgetary decisions are subject to rigorous analysis.

zero base budgeting (ZBB)

The approach of **zero base budgeting** (ZBB) requires management to take a fresh look at all programs and activities each year, rather than merely building on last year's budget. In other words, last year's budget allocations are not considered as a basis for this year's budget. Each program, or decision package, must be justified on the basis of a cost-benefit analysis. The three main features of zero base budgeting are:

- The activities of individual departments are divided into decision packages. Each decision package provides information so that management can compare costs and benefits of the program or activity.
- Each decision package is evaluated and ranked in the order of decreasing importance to the organization. Priorities are established for all programs and activities. Each of these is evaluated by top management to arrive at a final ranking.
- Resources are allocated according to the final rankings of the programs by top management. As a rule, decisions to allocate resources for high-priority items will be made rather quickly, whereas greater analysis or scrutiny will be given lower-priority programs or activities.[4]

ZBB is not a panacea for solving all problems associated with the budgeting process. Organizations may experience problems in implementing ZBB, as most managers are reluctant to admit that all of their activities are not of the highest priority or to submit their programs to close scrutiny. However, ZBB does establish a system whereby an organization's resources can be allocated to the higher-priority programs. Under this system, programs of lower priority are reduced or eliminated. Thus, the benefits of zero base budgeting appear to outweigh the costs.[5]

Break-Even Analysis

break-even analysis

The technique used to determine the amount of a particular product that must be sold if the firm is to generate enough revenue to cover costs is **break-even analysis.** In order to do a break-even analysis, the manager must know: (1) the fixed cost, (2) the variable cost, and (3) the selling price of the product.

fixed costs

variable costs

Fixed costs are costs that do not change with the level of output. Items that normally are considered fixed are the salaries of top management, rent, property taxes, and similar expenses. **Variable costs** are those costs that are directly related to changes in output. Items included as variable costs are direct materials and labor expenses needed in making a product or completing a service. As production output increases, these costs increase.

To demonstrate how break-even analysis works, consider the following problem. Suppose a product is priced at $15, the variable cost is $10 per unit, and total fixed costs are $1000. The following formula can be used to determine the break-even point (in units of output):

$$\text{Break-even point} = \frac{\text{Total fixed costs}}{\text{Price} - \text{Variable cost}} = \frac{\$1000}{\$15 - \$10} = 200.$$

Thus, according to break-even analysis, 200 units would have to be sold before profit can be registered.

The break-even point can also be illustrated graphically. (See Figure 17-7.) The vertical axis shows costs and revenues, while the horizontal axis shows the units of output. Since the $1000 fixed costs

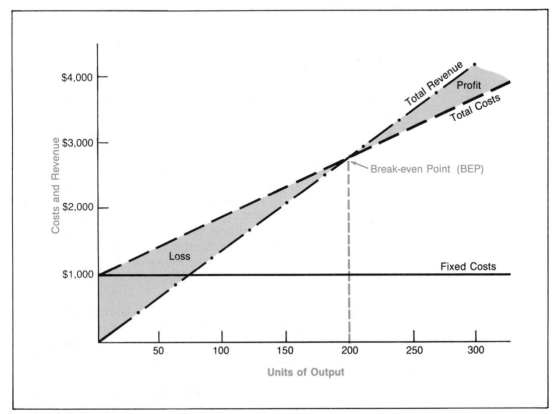

FIGURE 17-7 Break-even analysis

do not change, they are represented as a straight line. The $10 variable costs change with the level of production, so the total cost line (fixed plus variable cost) slopes upward accordingly. The variable cost line is drawn starting at the point where fixed costs intercept the vertical axis. Next, the total revenue line is drawn showing the total amount of revenue (price multiplied by the number of units sold) at all possible combinations of production. When the total revenue line intersects the total cost line, the break-even point has been reached at 200 units.

How reliable is this one point in space? Would you risk your firm's survival on its accuracy? Not likely, because there are some uncertainties associated with fixed and variable costs. However, break-even analysis is an effective technique because it forces a manager to plan. An individual who plans is in a position to make better decisions than a nonplanner.

Net Present Value

net present value

The **net present value** approach assesses the value of goods in order to help managers when purchasing capital equipment. A dollar earned today does not have the same value as a dollar to be received one year from today because it can be invested today and a year later it will be worth the dollar plus interest. The time value of money is important in planning and controlling business activity in all businesses.

This idea is used when capital investment decisions are made in a manufacturing firm. Consider the case of Brian Slater, vice-president of production, who is trying to decide which of two machines to purchase for his factory. One piece of equipment costs $200 000 and is capable of providing a savings of $50 000 a year over the next seven years. The other machine costs $150 000 and will generate $60 000 in savings each year for the next four years. (Assume Slater has to pay an interest rate of 15 percent.) Referring to Table 17-2, you can see that, based on the discounted cash flow method, Slater should purchase Machine B because cash savings would be $21 360 as compared to Machine A's savings of only $8050. This illustration demonstrates the importance of the time value of money and the need for managers to evaluate carefully the various alternatives facing them.

Profit Centers

profit center

A **profit center** exists when a department or division in an organization is given the responsibility of making a profit, of making sure that its revenues exceed its costs. A profit center is both a motivational and a control technique. It is motivational because the people in the unit know that their unit's profitability, or lack of it, can be identified; they will therefore work to ensure that revenues exceed costs. It is also a control device because, at the end of the fiscal year, both top

TABLE 17-2 Slater's Purchase Decision

Year	Savings per Year Machine A	Machine B	Present Value of $1	Machine A	Machine B
1	$50 000	$60 000	0.870	$ 43 500	$ 52 200
2	$50 000	$60 000	0.756	$ 37 800	$ 52 200
3	$50 000	$60 000	0.658	$ 32 900	$ 45 360
4	$50 000	$60 000	0.572	$ 28 600	$ 39 480
5	$50 000		0.497	$ 24 850	$ 34 320
6	$50 000		0.432	$ 21 600	
7	$50 000		0.376	$ 18 800	
				208 050	171 360
		Less cost of equipment		200 000	150 000
		Net discounted cash flow		8 050	21 360
		Difference in cash flow		$13 310	

NOTE Machine A costs $200 000; Machine B costs $150 000.

management and the unit in question can tell whether the established objectives have been achieved.

Top management personnel must ensure that the profit center concept makes sense before they implement it. For example, in a functional organization (refer to Figure 7-4 in Chapter 7), a profit center would cause great difficulty because none of the functional areas — for example, production, marketing, or finance — can make a profit by itself. Rather, they must coordinate their efforts so that the total company can make a profit.

A profit center would, however, be very appropriate for a company with a divisional structure. (Refer to Figure 6-4 in Chapter 6.) Each of the divisions — consumer products, government products, and industrial products — can be held accountable for its profit picture because each is operating as a separate division. Each has the resources it needs to conduct business independently.

Ratio Analysis

ratio analysis

When a company wants to assess how effective its performance has been, it may use **ratio analysis.** This analysis involves taking two financial figures from the company's balance sheet or income statement and dividing one figure by the other. The resulting ratio is then assessed to see if it is indicative of good management. Since the figures used for ratio analysis come largely from the firm's income statement and/or balance sheet, we describe these two documents briefly.

balance sheet

The **balance sheet** is a key financial document that describes the company's financial position with respect to assets, liabilities, and owners' (or shareholders') equity at a particular point in time. It is therefore a snapshot of the company's financial position at that time. The balance sheet is divided into three main sections. (See Figure 17-8.) The first section contains information about the company's assets. These are subdvided into current assets (for example, cash, inventory, and accounts receivable) and fixed assets (for example, plant and equipment). The second section shows the company's liabilities, or debts. These are divided into short- and long-term liabilities; the former must be paid within one year, while the latter do not come due for at least one year. The final category is shareholders' equity, which is the residual value of the corporation after liabilities have been subtracted from assets.

income statement

The **income statement,** in contrast to the balance sheet, shows the company's financial performance over a period of time (usually one year). Income statements contain two parts: a revenue section and a costs section. (See Figure 17-9.) Although income statements can be very complex for large organizations, they basically show the revenue the organization had and the expenses which were incurred to obtain that revenue. The difference between revenue and expenses is profit.

The balance sheet and income statement provide valuable information with regard to whether a company, department, or unit is effectively utilizing its financial resources. Intelligent interpretation

---

NORCAN LTD.
Balance Sheet
as of December 31, 198X

Current Assets:		Current Liabilities:	
Cash	$ 60 000	Accounts Payable	$100 000
Accounts Receivable	180 000	Accrued Expenses Payable	10 000
Inventory	100 000	Estimated Tax Liability	70 000
Prepaid Expenses	20 000		
Total Current Assets	$360 000	Total Current Liabilities	$180 000
Fixed Assets:		Long-Term Liabilities:	
Land	$ 40 000	Bond Payable	$100 000
Building	80 000		
Less Depreciation	40 000	Shareholders' Equity:	
		Common Stock (25 000 shares)	250 000
Other Assets:		Retained Earnings	10 000
Goodwill	100 000		
Total Assets	$540 000	Total Liabilities and Equity	$540 000

FIGURE 17-8 A balance sheet

MANAGEMENT IN PRACTICE

Financial Control at the Pattison Group

James Pattison is the president of the largest solely owned Canadian company, with 1983 revenues of $772 million. He controls a diverse set of companies in areas such as real estate, communications, food and beverages, and financial services. Because these are such diverse businesses, he has adopted certain financial controls to assess their performance.

The measure which he believes best pinpoints short-term performance in using assets wisely is Return On Invested Capital (ROIC). To calculate ROIC, he takes the value of company assets less accounts receivable and divides the figure by pretax profit added to the cost of financing. This percentage is called the "hurdle rate". Each company he controls is assigned a hurdle rate annually and managers are assessed on their ability to meet or exceed this goal.

A company in a stable industry is expected to achieve a rate of 16 or 17 percent, while a company in an extremely volatile industry and with a small asset base might be expected to achieve as much as 35 or 40 percent.

SOURCE Adapted from David Cruise and Alison Griffiths, "Japanese-Style Tactics Work for the Shogun from the West," *Executive* (April 1984): 28–32.

of financial data provides an excellent way for management to control its financial welfare. Financial ratio analysis provides management with a basis for comparing current to past performance. In addition, current financial ratios can be compared not only to past trends within the company but also to other divisions within the company

NORCAN LTD.
Income Statement
Year Ending December 31, 198X

Sales		$2 670 000
Less Cost of Goods Sold		1 520 000
Gross Profit		$1 150 000
Less Expenses:		
Wages Paid	$682 000	
Administrative Expenses	380 000	
Interest Expenses	15 000	
Operating Profit		$1 077 000
Net Profit before Taxes		$ 73 000
Taxes		20 000
Net Profit after Taxes		$ 53 000
Less Dividends		40 000
Added to Retained Earnings		$ 13 000

FIGURE 17-9   An income statement

and to other firms in the industry. If the ratios are not in line with what is considered acceptable, the manager is in a position to make corrections. There are four basic types of ratios:

liquidity ratios

leverage ratios

activity ratios

profitability ratios

- **Liquidity ratios** measure a firm's ability to meet its current obligations.
- **Leverage ratios** measure whether a firm has effectively used outside financing.
- **Activity ratios** measure how efficiently the firm is utilizing its resources.
- **Profitability ratios** measure the overall operating efficiency and profitability of the firm.

Names of ratios, the formula for their calculation, and the meaning and definition of the ratios are shown in Table 17-3.

TABLE 17-3 Summary of Financial Ratio Analysis

Type of Ratio	Name of Ratio	Formula for Calculation	Meaning and Definition of Ratio
Liquidity	Current ratio	$\dfrac{\text{current assets}}{\text{current liabilities}}$	Measures ability to meet debts when due — short-term liquidity
	Quick ratio	$\dfrac{\text{current assets — inventory}}{\text{current liabilities}}$	Measures ability to meet debts when due — very short-term liquidity
Leverage	Debt to total assets	$\dfrac{\text{total debt}}{\text{total assets}}$	Measures percentage of total funds that have been provided by creditors (debt = total assets – equity)
	Times interest earned	$\dfrac{\text{profit before tax + interest charges}}{\text{interest charges}}$	Measures the extent to which interest charges are covered by gross income
Profitability	Return on sales (net profit margin)	$\dfrac{\text{net income}}{\text{sales revenue}}$	Measures percent of profit earned on each dollar of sales
	Return on total assets	$\dfrac{\text{net income (after tax)}}{\text{total assets}}$	Measures the return on total investment of a firm
	Return on equity	$\dfrac{\text{net income (after tax)}}{\text{shareholder equity}}$	Measures rate of return on shareholders' investment
	Earnings per share	$\dfrac{\text{net income (after tax)}}{\text{number of common shares outstanding}}$	Measures profit earned for each share of common stock
Activity	Total asset turnover	$\dfrac{\text{revenues}}{\text{total assets}}$	Measures effectiveness of assets in generating revenues
	Collection period	$\dfrac{\text{receivables}}{\text{revenues per day}}$	Measures amount of credit extended to customers
	Inventory turnover	$\dfrac{\text{sales}}{\text{inventory}}$	Measures number of times inventory is used to generate sales

Auditing

audit

Corporations in Canada are required by law to conduct an **audit**, an independent analysis of their financial statements. Auditing is done by chartered accountancy firms. They analyze a corporation's financial statements and give an opinion on whether or not a company has followed generally accepted practices in developing its financial statements. A chartered accountancy firm does not develop a firm's financial statements; rather, it assesses them after they have been prepared by the corporation's internal accounting staff.

The audit is one of the best-known control techniques used by organizations. Even though it looks back on the financial transactions of a firm for the last year, it influences the day-to-day operations of the firm because managers know that the books will be examined. This acts as a deterrent against fraud. The audit is also a good control device as far as investors and the general public are concerned. They can examine the company's audited statements in order to make reasonable decisions about where to invest their money.

THE USE OF CONTROL TECHNIQUES BY MANAGERS

The control techniques discussed in this chapter are widely used by Canadian companies. There are, of course, numerous other controls that organizations might use. This profusion creates the problem for management of deciding which technique should be used for a given situation. Since managers are always looking for ways to simplify their options, they may be tempted to ask which of these control techniques is best or most suitable.

There is no simple answer to either of these issues because no single technique can solve the multitude of control problems that managers face in their work. Rather, each of the control techniques is intended for a different purpose. For example, the profit center is designed to identify costs and revenues for a division, while ratio analysis retrospectively shows how well the organization as a whole has performed. Both these control techniques focus on financial data, but neither is sufficient by itself to fulfill the demands of the controlling function. Likewise, rewards and punishments are designed to motivate employees to perform in certain ways, while selection controls are designed to recruit certain types of individuals into a firm. Both of these non-financial controls are necessary; management cannot choose only one of them and hope it will do an adequate job of controlling behavior.

The major job of management, therefore, is to decide which control technique is appropriate for which job. When making this decision, the manager must balance the need for control against the potential employee resistance to controls. Generally speaking, controls should not convey to employees that they are not trusted; rather, they should indicate that certain fundamental checks on the work system exist so that the organization can continue to function and provide employment opportunities.

In order to make rational choices about which control techniques to implement, managers must understand what a given control technique can and cannot do. Unfortunately, there is often misunderstanding about controls. For instance, consider corporate financial statements. When certain profit figures are reported in the newspaper, some reporters may comment about "windfall profits," intimating that the company made an "excessive" amount of profit. But how do they measure what is excessive? The profit figures reported on the company's income statement are arrived at only after many judgments have been made about which costs are associated with the revenue the company generated. The amount of profit reported therefore depends to a considerable degree on the assumptions that are made when the income statement is prepared. It is beyond the scope of this chapter to get into a detailed analysis of this issue but, as a general comment, we can say that the dollar figures shown on the company balance sheets and income statements are often not as clear cut as they appear. If people inside and outside the company make unreasonable assumptions about what the profit figure means, this particular control device will not have served a useful purpose.

The problem of misunderstanding control techniques is not restricted to financial statements. Take budgets, for example. Some managers assume that once the budget is set, everything is under control. But they fail to realize that people may overexpend their budgets, even though safeguards are supposed to prevent this from happening. Once an overexpenditure has occurred, what should be done? Since the money has probably already left the company, there is not much that can be done except to try to make sure that it doesn't happen again. A similar general problem is evident with other controls like policies, rules, and procedures. These are frequently violated in organizations, yet some managers seem to assume that, because these controls exist, all the potential problems have been dealt with. Managers must recognize that simply having controls in place does not guarantee that everyone will abide by them.

Managers must also deal with negative reactions to controls on the part of employees. As we noted in Chapter 16, there are a variety of reasons why employees resist controls. The manager must therefore: (1) spend some time thinking about what controls are necessary, and (2) explain these necessary controls and how they work to employees. If the manager and the employees can come to a consensus about what kind of controls are required for the work they are doing, the possible resistance to controls can be minimized. Obviously, the kinds of controls that are necessary at the Canadian Mint are different from the controls needed at a restaurant that serves tacos. Yet, for both organizations, controls are necesssary.

Managers must assess the kind of work that is being performed and then choose control systems that are appropriate for that work. Managers must also recognize that, while one specific control technique may be necessary to control certain activities, a variety of controls may be required for the entire function of controlling. In the typical private-sector firm, for instance, all of the control techniques discussed in this chapter would be used. This demonstrates the diversity of activities of most firms and the need to use a variety of controlling techniques.

OPENING INCIDENT REVISITED

Cam's Corner

Cameron McIntyre experienced severe problems in controlling his variety store business during the 1979-1983 recession. Afterward, he wondered what he could do to ensure that he would not have similar problems if another recession occurred.

We purposely did not give much detail in the opening incident so that we can talk generally about the appropriateness of the control techniques presented in the chapter. In keeping with the organization of the chapter, we suggest that Cameron McIntyre systematically look at the controlling function in his organization from both the nonfinancial and the financial perspective.

Several illustrative questions McIntyre should ask himself regarding nonfinancial controls are:

- What kinds of rewards and punishments are being given to salespeople, and do these rewards and punishments motivate them to exercise self-control and behavior that is in the best interest of the company?
- What kind of controls is McIntyre using to ensure that the people he hires for his stores are appropriate?
- What kind of training is he giving employees?
- Is the reporting function clear to employees?
- Is he doing any auditing of management activities to see if they are effective?

- Is he trying to do all the work, or is he delegating a significant amount of day-to-day work so that he can concentrate on strategic planning for the business?

Questions like these deal with the nonfinancial aspects of the business — although what management does in these areas certainly shows up on the income statement and balance sheet. If McIntyre answers these questions honestly, he will see where improvements in nonfinancial controls are necessary.

Some illustrative questions in the financial area that McIntyre should ask himself are:

- Does he have an adequate budgeting system that gives him timely information on cost control?
- Are each of his stores profit centers, or is all activity in the three stores considered together?
- Does he know if all three stores are profitable, or is one store a problem?
- What do his liquidity, leverage, activity, and profitability ratios look like? Would these ratios give some clue regarding where potential problems exist?

As suggested in the chapter, McIntyre must consider the activity performed by employees and then adopt appropriate control techniques. These illustrative questions should help him get started on this task.

SUMMARY

Managers can choose from a wide variety of control techniques to increase the probability that planned objectives can be achieved. These control techniques can be divided into two main categories: financial and nonfinancial. As the terms imply, nonfinancial control techniques do not require financial data to be used, while financial control techniques require some form of financial data such as profits, costs, or revenues.

There are several types of nonfinancial control techniques. Rewards and punishments are designed to shape employee behavior by rewarding desirable behavior and punishing undesirable behavior. Selection procedures control the type of employee that is hired in the first place. Socialization and training gradually changes the attitudes and behaviors of new employees so they learn what is acceptable in the organization. The management hierarchy controls employee behavior by making employees responsible to the manager above them in the chain of command. The management audit systematically assesses the strengths and weaknesses of the management group in an organization. Management by exception is a very basic control device which allows the manager to give only general supervision to workers unless some major deviation from standards is evident.

Quality is the degree of excellence of a product or service. The purpose of quality control is to make sure the product or service is likely to serve the purpose for which it is intended. With statistical quality control, a portion of the total number of items is inspected. Acceptance sampling is the inspection of a portion of the output or input of a process to determine acceptability. There are two basic types of acceptance sampling: sampling by variables and sampling by attributes. Variable sampling determines how closely an item conforms to an established standard. With sampling by attributes, the item is either acceptable or unacceptable. A control chart is a graphic record of how closely samples of a product or service conform to standards over time.

Inventory refers to the goods or materials available for use by a business. One of the major purposes of inventory is that it permits relative independence of operations between two activities. Inventory also provides for continuous operations when demand for the product is not consistent. Another purpose of inventory is to enable orders to be filled when they are received. The economic order quantity (EOQ) method of inventory control is a procedure for balancing ordering costs and carrying costs so as to minimize total inventory costs. With the ABC inventory method of control, inventory is categorized according to the degree of control needed. The just-in-time inventory method is the practice of having inputs to the production process delivered precisely when they are needed and assigning responsibility to suppliers for keeping inventories to a minimum.

When a project is nonrecurring, large, complex, and involves multiple organizations, the manager needs a tool that will assist in coordinating this complicated network of interdependencies. The primary techniques available to organize and coordinate this type of project are program evaluation and review technique (PERT) and the critical path method (CPM).

There are also a variety of financial control techniques which managers can use. A budget is a formal statement — in dollar-and-cents terms — of the firm's planned expenditures for a future time period. There are two broad categories of budgets: financial and operating. The former indicates the amount of capital the firm will need and where it will get it, while the latter indicates the revenues and expenses the firm will experience during a given year. Budgets are control devices because they tell people how much money is available for expenditures in a given time period. Budgets help in making planned activities actually occur. They may, however, make some people feel unduly constrained in their activity.

Break-even analysis allows a firm to determine the level of operations that will have to be achieved if it hopes to make a profit. Break-even analysis is a control technique because it shows management where actions need to be taken to improve the efficiency of the firm's operations. In order to do a break-even analysis, management must have a knowledge of fixed costs, variable costs, and the selling price of the product. The break-even point in units can be determined by dividing total fixed costs by the selling price minus the variable costs.

A profit center exists when a division of an organization is given the responsibility of ensuring that its revenues exceed its costs. It is a control technique because it allows management to determine if the goals that were set have been reached.

Ratio analysis helps managers to determine if their actions have led to an effective operation of the firm. A ratio can be computed by taking any two figures from the balance sheet or income statement and dividing one by the other. The most commonly used ratios are liquidity, leverage, activity, and profitability ratios.

An accounting audit involves analysis by a chartered accountancy firm of an organization's financial statements. The chartered accountancy firm gives an opinion on whether the firm has followed generally accepted accounting principles in the preparation of its annual financial statements. Because the firm's managers know an audit will be conducted, they must control the day-to-day finances.

Because there are so many control techniques available to managers, they must decide which ones are appropriate for each function that must be controlled. Managers must also try to use the techniques in such a way that employees do not feel threatened by them and, therefore, resist the controls. Most large organizations use all the control techniques presented in this chapter, but they use each of them in situations that demand the particular strength that the specific control technique has.

REVIEW QUESTIONS

1. What is the difference between financial and nonfinancial control techniques?
2. What determines how effective rewards and punishments will be in controlling behavior of employees?
3. What are the benefits and costs of personnel selection procedures as a control device?
4. Why are socialization and training considered to be control techniques?
5. The management hierarchy acts as a controlling mechanism. What other organizational controlling devices are embedded in the management hierarchy?
6. How is a management audit different from an accounting audit?
7. Explain the concept of management by exception as a control technique.
8. What is statistical quality control? Give three examples of statistical quality control and explain why a 100 percent inspection could not be used instead.
9. What is the purpose of a control chart?
10. What are some advantages and disadvantages of the traditional North American inventory system and the Japanese just-in-time inventory system?
11. What is the EOQ procedure used for?
12. In what circumstances is the ABC inventory method used?
13. Distinguish between PERT and CPM.
14. What kind of businesses use PERT or CPM network controls? Explain how PERT helps to control a complicated project.
15. How does an operating budget differ from a financial budget?
16. What are some benefits and limitations of budgets?
17. What potential problem exists in using break-even analysis?
18. In what situations are profit centers appropriate? inappropriate?
19. Describe what each of the basic types of ratios — liquidity, leverage, activity, and profitability — are designed to measure. Give an example of each kind of ratio.
20. What is management's responsibility when choosing control techniques?

EXERCISES

1. Examine the financial statements of several different kinds of companies and compute the profitability, leverage, activity, and liquidity ratios for each of them. What differences do you see across these companies?
2. Interview three managers in different types of organizations. What kinds of control techniques does each one use? Why do they use the control techniques? What problems do they have when using the techniques?
3. Discuss the uncertainties associated with an accounting audit with a chartered accountant. How much confidence can investors put in the opinion of chartered accountants?
4. What specific control techniques would be most obvious in a convenience store? a community college? an insurance company? an automobile repair shop?
5. Assume that ordering costs are $6.00 per order, carrying costs are $1.50 per unit per year, and the annual demand is 1000 units. What would be the economic order quantity (EOQ) for this situation?
6. Assume that you are responsible for monitoring inventory control for the following types of firms:
   a. Fancy restaurant
   b. Automobile dealership
   c. Bookstore
   Using the ABC method of inventory control, identify inventory items that would be in each class.
7. Develop a small PERT network for a task with which you are very familiar. The task that is chosen should have at least two people performing different tasks at the same time.

CASE STUDY

Pooling Our Knowledge

"This is the third batch of sticks we've gotten back from Brunswick this quarter," said Jerry Hodges, "and it's been different problems each time." Jerry and his shop manager, John Kenner, were looking over the checklist of defects Brunswick had provided with the returned pool sticks. The sticks had been made by Jerry's company, Hodges' Woodworks. Brunswick is a major manufacturer of recreation equipment of all kinds, and Hodges had contracted to provide the company 5000 pool sticks per month during 1985.

The defects in the 200 sticks in the returned batch ranged from misaligned leather tips on two of the sticks to four thread defects where the sticks screwed together in the middle, to an incomplete covering of varnish on the wood sections of four others. Altogether 16 faults were noted in the batch.

"The costs are just too high to inspect every piece of every stick," said Jerry. "Yeah, I know," replied John, "but it's not as expensive as having to rework an entire batch. Anyway, Brunswick uses 100 percent inspection. Why shouldn't we?" Jerry replied, "We may have to do that. But if the number of defectives is below two percent, Brunswick will accept the batch. Let's see if we can figure out a cheaper way to accomplish that."

The manufacturing process for pool sticks is complex. The wood parts are cut from solid maple and machined to shape on numerically controlled lathes. Then they are drilled and shaped on other machines to fit plastic, metal, and rubber parts purchased from other manufacturers. After being assembled, the pool cues are varnished in batches of twenty with a spray gun. Because of the small volume, most of the assembly work is done by hand.

After some discussion, John and Jerry determined that, except for the varnish problem, all of the defects in the present batch resulted from parts purchased from others. "Obviously," said Jerry, "we should do the same thing to our suppliers that Brunswick is doing to us: check the parts when we get them, and return them if they are defective."

QUESTIONS

1. What techniques are available to help Hodges' Woodworks get the defective rate down below two percent?
2. Should the company attempt to prevent any defective cue sticks at all from leaving the factory? Explain.

CASE STUDY

A New Product Decision

Carolyn Loewen is the vice-president of marketing for Novelties Ltd., a small firm that manufactures and sells promotional material, such as buttons, decals, and book covers. She recently came up with the idea of producing miniature Canadian flag decals that could be sold to companies for conventions or sales meetings.

Loewen is familiar with break-even analysis, so she developed some cost figures for producing the flags. She estimates that the fixed cost for the project will be $2000; the variable cost will be $0.50 per flag, and the company should be able to sell them for $1 each.

QUESTIONS

1. How many flags must Novelties Ltd. sell in order to break even?
2. How many flags must the company sell to make a profit of $1000?
3. If Carolyn Loewen thinks that the maximum number of flags the company can sell is 5000, do you think that Novelties Ltd. should begin manufacturing the flags?
4. What uncertainties exist in this situation?

CASE STUDY

Ratio Analysis at Norcan Ltd.

Norcan Ltd. is a Saskatoon-based manufacturing firm that produces oil field equipment. At the last meeting of the board of directors, one of the outside board members expressed some concern about the company's financial condition. Several long-standing board members expressed surprise and said that they believed the company was doing very well. The outside member persisted in his questions, however, and a lengthy discussion took place regarding the company's activities over the last year.

After approximately 45 minutes of listening to various opinions and very few facts, the chairperson appointed a subcommittee to analyze Norcan's financial statements and report back to the board regarding the firm's financial condition. As part of this responsibility, the subcommittee was asked to do a thorough ratio analysis.

QUESTIONS

1. Assume that you are the chairperson of the subcommittee. Use the balance sheet and income statement shown in Figures 17-8 and 17-9 to compute the liquidity, leverage, profitability, and activity ratios for Norcan. (Refer to Table 17-3 for ratios; for the collection period ratio, assume revenues are collected 365 days a year.)

2. Based on this ratio analysis, what can you say about the company's financial condition?

3. What additional information do you need to make an overall judgment of the financial condition of the company?

ENDNOTES

[1] William E. Dollar, "The Zero Inventory Concept," *Purchasing* (September 29, 1983): 433.

[2] Robert N. Anthony and Regina E. Herzlinger, *Management Control in Non-Profit Organizations* (Homewood, Ill.: Irwin, 1975): 222–226.

[3] Anthony and Herzlinger, *Management Control in Non-Profit Organizations.*

[4] James A. Stoner, *Management* (Englewood Cliffs, N.J.: Prentice-Hall, 1978): 600–677.

[5] Gordon Shillinglaw, *Managerial Cost Accounting: Analysis and Control* (Homewood, Ill: Irwin, 1977): 142–143.

REFERENCES

Adam, N., and Surkis, J. "Comparison of Capacity Planning Techniques in a Job Shop Control System." *Management Science* 23 (May 1977): 1011–1015.

Bott, Robert. "Power Failure." *Canadian Business* 57, no. 1 (January 1984): 96.

Boyes, Shelley, and Ramsay, Michelle. "Just-In-Time — The New Eastern Philosophy." *Canadian Transportation and Distribution Management* (June 1984): 33.

Brennan, J. M. "Up Your Inventory Control." *Journal of Systems Management* 28 (January 1977): 39–45.

Buffa, Elwood S. *Modern Production-Operations Management.* 6th ed. New York: Wiley, 1980.

Chase, Richard B., and Aquilano, Nicholas J. *Production and Operations Management: A Life Cycle Approach.* Homewood, Ill.: Irwin, 1981.

Clay, M. J. "Evaluating the Production Function." *Journal of Accountancy* 148 (May 1977): 82.

Cummings, L. L. "Needed Research in Production/Operations Management: A Behavioral Perspective." *Academy of Management Review* (July 1977): 500–504.

Green, T. B. "Why Are Organizations Reluctant to Use Management Science/Operations Research? An Empirical Approach." *Interfaces* 7 (August 1976): 69–72.

Harwood, G. G., and Hermanson, R. H. "Lease or Buy Decisions." *Journal of Accountancy* 147 (September 1976): 83–87.

Hostage, G. M. "Quality Control in a Service Business." *Harvard Business Review* 53 (July-August 1975): 98–106.

"Just-in-Time Gives Whole New Look to Plant Design." *The Financial Post* (Sept. 14, 1985): 1.

Lefrançois, Pierre. "Selecting a Forecasting Method for Inventory Control: A Safety Stock Based Criterion." *Canadian Journal of Administrative Sciences* 3 (December 1986): 348–358.

Moore, Giora. "A Multiperiod Breakeven Analysis." *Canadian Journal of Administrative Sciences* 3, (June 1986): 123–130.

Morey, R. "Operations Management in Selected Non-manufacturing Organizations." *Academy of Management Journal* 19 (March 1976): 120–124.

Petry, Glenn H. "Effective Use of Capital Budgeting Tools." *Business Horizons* 18 (October 1975): 57–65.

Plossl, G. W., and Welch, W. Evert. *The Role of Top Management in the Control of Inventory.* Reston, Va.: Reston Publishing, 1979.

Remick, Carl. "Robots: New Faces on the Production Line." *Management Review* 68 (May 1979): 27.

Ritter, Richard, and Cutt, James. "A Policy Implementation Analysis of Zero-Base Budgeting." *Canadian Journal of Administrative Sciences* 1, (December 1984): 352–366.

Schmenner, Roger W. *Production/Operations Management: Concepts and Situations.* Chicago: Science Research Associates, 1981.

Smith, Martin R. "A 10-point Guide to Making Quality Control Management Effective." *Management Review* 64 (April 1975): 52–54.

Solomon, Eyra, and Pringle, John J. *An Introduction to Financial Management.* Santa Monica, Cal.: Goodyear, 1980.

VI

Situational
Applications

Managing Small Businesses

KEY TERMS

small business   nepotism   Counselling
entrepreneur   financial assistance   Assistance to Small
franchising   programs   Enterprises
     (CASE)

LEARNING OBJECTIVES

After completing this chapter you should be able to
1. Describe what is meant by a small business and identify why some people want to have their own business.
2. Describe franchising and some of its advantages to franchisees and franchisers.
3. Describe some of the factors affecting the management of small business.
4. Identify some of the pitfalls of starting a small business.

5. Describe the types of assistance available to small businesses from the federal and provincial governments.
6. Identify some of the inconveniences caused for managers of small businesses by government regulations.

OPENING INCIDENT

Kent Computers

Evan Kent always had an entrepreneurial streak. After graduating from a British Columbia business school, he decided to go into business for himself. Kent considered several possibilities and decided to open a retail outlet which sold home computers. He reasoned that the rapid growth in the use of computers by both business and consumers would almost guarantee high demand for his products.

Kent opened his store, Kent Computers, in New Westminster. Right from the start customer interest was high. At once, Kent noticed that each customer required a very long time because everyone had many questions about the computers and what they could do. Kent was particularly discouraged when, after he had spent a lot of time with a customer, the customer would decide not to buy anything.

Competition astonished Kent. Apparently, a lot of other people had the same idea as Kent because he noticed more and more home computer stores springing up. Price competition was severe, and he was continually faced with customers pressuring him to give them a price deal that he couldn't afford. He also experienced irritation from customers who wanted to buy software that he didn't have in stock. Everyone seemed to want everything immediately. Kent was trying to keep his inventory to a minimum, but he was discovering that customers would go elsewhere when he didn't have a particular item in stock.

Kent found himself working extremely long hours both at the store and at home. In his non-store hours, he tried to keep up with the new developments in the computer field so that he could talk knowledgeably to customers. He also found he had to do all sorts of work that he hadn't anticipated. One evening after a particularly hectic day, he looked at the floor and saw what a mess it was. As he picked up a broom and began sweeping, he realized that he was mentally and physically exhausted. Somehow, running his own business wasn't the excitement or challenge he'd expected. Kent wondered whether it was worth the effort, particularly since he had yet to make his first dollar of profit.

Every year, thousands of individuals motivated to be their own boss and to earn a better income launch a new business venture. These individuals, often called entrepreneurs, are essential to the growth and vitality of the Canadian economic system. Entrepreneurs develop or recognize new products or business opportunities, secure the necessary capital, and organize and operate various kinds of businesses. Most people who start their own business get a great deal of satisfaction from owning and managing their own firm.

However, even with assistance provided by various government agencies, the failure rate of small businesses is extremely high. As we noted in Chapter 1, approximately half of all new businesses fail within the first four years of operation, and over 60 percent fail within six years. In spite of this high failure rate, people continue to challenge the odds. The entrepreneurial spirit is alive and well in Canada.

In this chapter we examine the important role that small business plays in the Canadian economy. We first define small business. The role of the entrepreneur is described and the advantages and disadvantages of owning a small business are noted. We also discuss the impact of franchising on small business. Second, we present the key factors affecting the management of small business. These factors include the external environment peculiar to small businesses as well as internal factors. Third, the pitfalls of owning a small business are described in some detail. Since the failure rate for new businesses is so high, the potential owner must be aware of them. We discuss the role government plays in assisting and regulating small business. We conclude the chapter with a lengthy checklist for individuals considering starting their own business.

At times in our discussion, we may appear quite negative. Do not think that the authors are trying to dissuade people from starting their own business. This is definitely not the case; we are simply trying to paint a realistic picture of small business in Canada and how successful management of such firms takes a special type of person. If you are fully aware of the difficulties you might encounter, you are more likely to avoid the classic problems small business owners face. It is not very difficult to start a business, but to operate one at a profit over a period of years requires knowledge and application of the fundamentals of management. This chapter is designed to give you realistic expectations about small business management.

SMALL BUSINESS IN CANADA

Although most of the media attention in Canada is directed at large business enterprises, the fact is that small businesses are thriving and are making a significant contribution to the economic well-being of Canada. A small business may be a corporation, sole proprietorship, or a partnership. Small businesses include those operated by professionals, such as doctors, lawyers, and accountants, and self-employed owners, such as mechanics, television repairmen, and restaurateurs. They are found in virtually every industry; they are particularly prominent in the retail trade.

In terms of numbers, small business is the dominant type of business in Canada. Assuming for the moment that a firm is "small" if its sales are less than $2 million per year, over 90 percent of all business firms in Canada are small businesses. These small businesses account for approximately 30 percent of the total sales of Canadian business firms and approximately 40 percent of employment.

The importance of small business in Canada can also be seen by examining organizations in terms of the number of employees they have. As shown in Figure 18-1, by far the most common size of firm in Canada in the manufacturing sector is one with fewer than five employees. Many other firms have between 5 and 15 employees, but only a very small number have over 500 employees. In the manufacturing sector, only 121 firms in all of Canada have over 1000 employ-

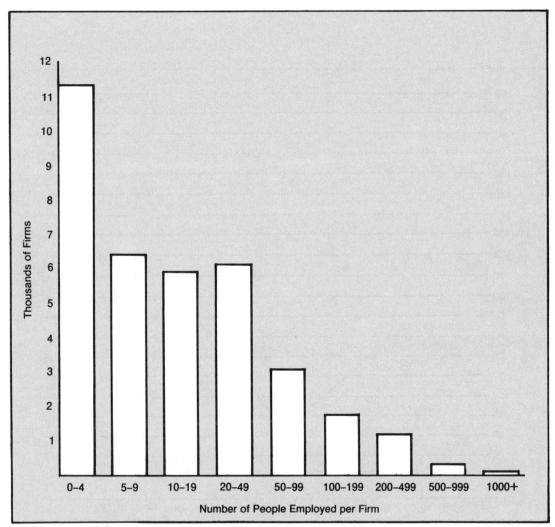

FIGURE 18-1   Number of people employed by size of firm in the
                manufacturing sector

SOURCE   Manufacturing Industries in Canada (31-203, 198*): 254. Used by permission of the
          Minister of Supply and Services Canada.

ees. In other sectors of the economy, such as retailing, small businesses are even more dominant.

Compared to large organizations, the resources possessed by small businesses are limited. This means that small businesses are susceptible to fluctuations in the economy, and are often not able to survive during economic downturns. In Figure 18-2, the failure rate for Canadian businesses is depicted over the last 60 years. Note that the rate fluctuates widely. During World War II, when the economy was heavily influenced by the war effort, very few firms failed; but during the recession of the early 1980s, the failure rate reached an all-time high. Many of these failures are small businesses.

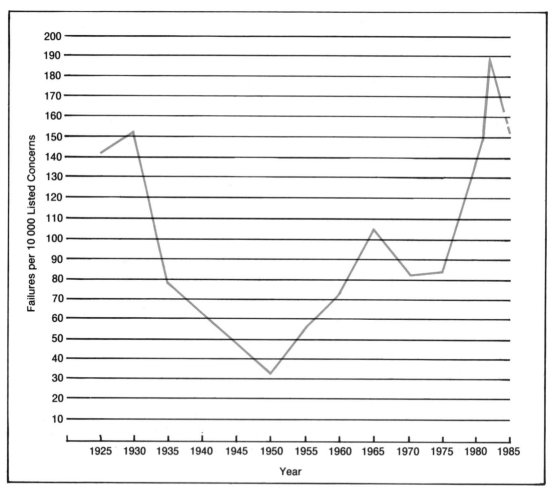

FIGURE 18-2 Business failure rate, 1925–1985, selected years

SOURCE The Canadian Business Failure Record (1985): 2. Used by permission of Dun and Bradstreet Canada Ltd.

What Is a Small Business?

There is no simple definition of the term *small business*. Different groups have developed definitions of small business largely for administrative convenience. For instance, Industry, Trade, and Commerce Canada defines small business as manufacturing firms with less than 100 employees and firms in other sectors with less than 50 employees. For purposes of the Small Business Loans Act, a small business is one whose gross revenue for the year does not exceed $1.5 million dollars. For purposes of management consulting assistance from the government, a firm cannot have more than 75 employees if it is to be classified as a small business.

small business

Note that all of these definitions use different criteria, so no single definition can be deduced. For our purposes, we define a **small business** as one with the following characteristics:

- The owner is actively involved in the day-to-day management of the business.
- The company is localized in its operation.
- The company is not a dominant force in the industry.

The Role of the Entrepreneur

entrepreneur

The key individual in most small businesses is the owner. Because of the nature of the factors in establishing small businesses, the small business owner is often referred to as an **entrepreneur.** In fact, the small business is a natural haven for the entrepreneur. The entrepreneur is a unique person whose major characteristic is the ability to create an ongoing enterprise where none existed before. He or she brings ideas, skills, money, equipment, and markets together into a profitable combination. It has been suggested that this type of person strongly feels that security cannot be found in working for others in a well-structured situation. Rather, security is found only in working for oneself with minimum external restraints.

Entrepreneurs desire to control their own lives and have a tremendous need for independence. They possess a constant drive to remove all restrictions and threatening persons. Any other person in the small firm who appears to bid for power will likely be quickly removed. For this reason, some small businesses fail when their owners die or retire; no one has been developed to take their place.

This yearning for security through independence demands a great deal of self-confidence. An entrepreneur finds it exceedingly difficult to accept leadership from others. Such a person often makes a poor member of a large enterprise. In addition, entrepreneurs have little fear of failure; they seek risks eagerly. Venturesomeness is almost an obsession; their level of activity is steadily high, and they take great joy in winning.

MANAGEMENT IN PRACTICE

Turning Young People Into Entrepreneurs

Sunil Kayal is an economist who runs Operation Youth, an organization devoted to turning unemployed young people into entrepreneurs, and to helping them start their own businesses. Kayal felt that unemployment among young people couldn't be solved merely by relying on economic growth. And, in fact, unemployment among young people dropped very little after the recent recession ended (from 19.9 percent to 16.5 percent). Kayal's view is that to be successful, young people must be given training and encouragement so they will not be deterred by the high failure rate of new businesses.

The first graduates of the program have started a wide variety of businesses: a print-on-wheels company, an instant photo shop, an advertising agency, and a chimney cleaning company, to name a few. The main characteristics Mr. Kayal looks for in an applicant are keenness, enthusiasm, and entrepreneurial attitude — the desire to get rich fast. Applicants must be under 25 years of age.

Trainees are given a five-day seminar on how to start and run a business. They also are helped in preparing a business plan and in making contact with bankers, accountants, and lawyers — people who are helpful in starting a business. Once they are in business they can turn to Operation Youth for further assistance when they need it.

SOURCE   Adapted from Peter Cook, "Turning Young People Into Entrepreneurs Free Of Charge," *The Globe and Mail* (December 24, 1986): B3.

The management style of the entrepreneur is generally not one that fits well into structured and orderly organizations. Entrepreneurs often show great reluctance to formalize structure and processes. Leadership is primarily based on their charismatic attraction. Entrepreneurs are organization starters rather than organization builders. As a consequence, their level of mobility is great; they move from one deal to another, all of which are rationalized in the name of profit. They may have few qualms about severing relationships with people or with organizations. They would rather leave intolerable situations than stay and resolve problems. Because of these characteristics, many people become annoyed with entrepreneurs. However, they provide a dynamic and innovative element in the Canadian economic system.

There are both benefits and costs of entrepreneurship. On the positive side, entrepreneurs get a tremendous sense of satisfaction from being their own boss. They also derive ego satisfaction from successfully bringing together the factors of production (land, labor, and capital) to make a profit. Perhaps the greatest benefit, however, is the fact that entrepreneurs can make a fortune if they have carefully planned what the business will do and how it will operate.

On the negative side, entrepreneurs can go bankrupt if their business fails. Customers can demand all sorts of services or inventory that small businesses cannot profitably supply. Entrepreneurs must

MANAGEMENT IN PRACTICE

Houseboating in Alberta

It seems unlikely that a houseboat manufacturing company would have much success in arid and landlocked Alberta, but Dave Steele and Phil Carroll are doing just fine. In the first 18 months of their business, they grossed $800 000 in sales.

The two men got the idea for the company when they saw all the houseboats in Sicamous, BC and thought that it was a great recreational idea. They tried to get one for the summer, but they were all booked up. Seeing this demand, they decided to get into the manufacturing end of the business. They set up shop in Airdrie, Alberta and hired 15 craftsmen to build the boats, which sell for approximately $55 000. Currently, the plant produces about one houseboat per week at a cost of $30 000 to $40 000 per boat.

Steele and Carroll expect to have an active market for some time to come because older houseboats that other companies are renting to customers will have to be replaced. Sales to these organizations should keep demand high.

SOURCE Adapted from Alister Thomas, "Holiday Houseboating Gives Two Albertans a Place in the Sun," *Canadian Business* (July 1983): 147.

work long hours and often get little in return during the first few years their business is in operation. An entrepreneur may find that he or she is very good at one particular aspect of the business — for example, marketing — but knows little about managing the overall business. This imbalance can cause serious problems; in fact, poor management is the main reason small businesses fail.

Becoming a Small Business Owner

Most people become involved in a small business in one of three ways: (1) taking over the family business, (2) buying out an existing firm, or (3) starting their own firm. Taking over the family business was very common in Canada until recently; it still happens, of course, but not as often as in the past, when it was often assumed that the eldest son would take over a business from his father. This trend was especially true for family farms.

Buying out an existing firm has become more common during the twentieth century. Entrepreneurs often keep a sharp eye out for business firms that are poorly run but that have good profit potential. They believe that if they buy them out, they can make the firms profitable using their entrepreneurial expertise.

It has become increasingly common for individuals to start their own businesses from scratch. A new firm does not come with the built in problems that a bought or inherited firm does, but the owner must build it up from nothing. Building a business can take many years; but, managed properly, it can produce large profits.

Dick Smeelen
Astley-Gilbert Productions Ltd.

Dick Smeelen is the president of Astley-Gilbert Productions Ltd. The company primarily supplies architects and engineers with reproductions of engineering drawings and specifications. The whole industry providing this type of service is called "Reprographics" and it combines the science, the art, and the technology by which documents can be copied. Astley-Gilbert is the largest volume white printer in Toronto.

Q: Can you tell me about your own background?
Smeelen: I was born in Holland and came to Canada with my parents at the age of seven. I graduated from Central Technical School in Toronto, majored in machine-design drafting,

and spent seven years as a tool-design draftsman for T & D Designs Ltd. While working at that job, I happened to be the draftsman who was sending out some reproduction work — the same type of work I receive now. I asked for the invoice to be extended by the reproduction company we were using, and when it came back it said $78. I said to my employers: "$78? Why don't we buy a blueprint machine and rent a Volkswagen and go into the blueprint business?" Later, they did decide to start Astley-Gilbert Reproductions, and they asked me to be the new company's manager.

One of the reasons I was approached to do the job was that I looked pretty dependable. Within a seven-year period I was never late once and had never missed a day's work. A year and a half later I was offered some shares and, over the next three or four years, I kept buying more shares. In 1976, I offered to buy them out and I made the final payment in 1982. Astley-Gilbert started from absolutely nothing, now we're doing about $3.5 million in business a year.

Q: Did you ever formulate a goal to own your own business?
Smeelen: Unfortunately, or fortunately depending on how you want to look at it, no. I came from parents who worked very hard for very little and I just assumed that that was how things were. Fortunately, I worked for people who saw my potential and used it for our mutual benefit. You may find this hard to believe, but for the first eight years of being in business I did not know that a company had to survive on profits. The profits came — but it was a result of hard work and luck rather than actual strategy. For a certain time the business ran me instead of me running the business. Once again, fortunately, I had the physical stamina to put in the long hours, and the mental attitude to meet the customers' deadlines no matter what it took because my reward was seeing jobs done and on time. The excited customer who bubbled with enthusiasm every time you delivered the impossible was all the adrenalin I needed to keep going and at the same time ask for more. There were many

times I asked myself why, and I concluded that half of me hates what I do but the other half thrives on how well I cope with the part that I hate. Every day I go home a winner.

Q: How did you develop the drive you obviously have?

Smeelen: I think my Dutch background and the fact that I saw my parents work so hard for so little helped me a lot in later years, when I actually got into business. But there was an incident in my youth which taught me an unforgettable lesson in life. I failed grade 8, not because I was stupid, but because I was the "class clown." At the same time, the school bully would pick on me and I would run away. In my second year of grade 8 I discovered I was getting twice as much attention by being the smartest kid in the class. I realized if you want to stay on top you have to work hard and be aggressive. Every day I assumed I would bump into the previous year's school bully but he never showed up. I created an effective defense — it's called aggressive offense — and discovered how many people want to associate with positive rather than negative people. The other valuable lesson I learned was never to avoid a potential problem and try to put it off. Meet it head on, solve it and get on with your life. Avoid your problems and they will eat away at you like a cancer and you will eventually fail.

Q: What major difficulties do you see from your position?

Smeelen: I sometimes get so wrapped up in the day-to-day production I lose track of the original goal. Fortunately I have two older, wiser men that I constantly confer with. Every time I get uptight they remind me that happiness is the journey not the destination. The destination should be a goal, but certainly not at any cost.

Q: Can you describe your ownership structure?

Smeelen: Originally, I worked for three partners who had been in business together for a long time. They owned T & D Designs Ltd., then started this reproduction business. Now I'm the sole owner. However, I do have a rather unique arrangement, in which I'm very fortunate. I have two advisers who meet regularly with me. One of these gentlemen, Jim Jones, is a certified industrial accountant whom I stumbled across in 1980 through the Federal Business Development Bank, when I was in financial hot water. He was instrumental in getting me through my toughest period and has worked for me ever since as a salaried employee, aside from providing invaluable advice. The other gentleman is one of the original owners of the company, Tom Fox. The three of us form what you might call an informal board, although these two gentlemen have no financial interest in the business. Sometimes I can't see the forest through the trees; with these two older, wiser men, I'm very fortunate, because they provide me with crucial guidance and direction.

Q: On a day-to-day basis, how much do you operate according to strategies and plans you've worked out, and how much do you operate on gut feeling?

Smeelen: There's an overall plan we try to follow to stay on top of technological changes. We get literature and we go to reproduction/reprographic shows to see what's coming down the road in that area and then try to plan toward that. In the day-to-day operations, I will deviate from the plan if I see something worthwhile. I'll present it to the board, which will either shoot it down or say "Yeah, let's pursue it." If I've got a gut feeling for something, I'll pursue it. As an example, I bought some equipment which wasn't in the plan. I presented the idea to my advisers, and at first they shot me down. I said: "I can see that. That's worth just too much money. But if I don't buy it, and my competition does, I'll lose existing business to them." So their reply was: "Well, you have a gut feeling on this, and you're the only one who can tell. If that's what you feel, then okay, we'll back you up 100 percent. Go for it." It turned out to be one of the best moves we ever made; that equipment has earned us over $250 000 in sales over the last two and a half years.

Why Some People Want their own Business

Many thousands of Canadians start their own businesses each year. Why? While there are probably dozens of reasons, some of the more common ones are as follows:

- *A strong desire to be one's own boss.* Entrepreneurs long to be independent, able to set their own direction, and reliant on their own talents, skills, and hard work.
- *The opportunity to work at something enjoyable.* Instead of settling for a possibly more secure job in a large organization, some people choose the freedom, and risks, of ownership.
- *The desire to achieve financial success.* Earning a profit is a primary motivator for wanting to own a business.
- *An ego identification with their business.* Most small business owners have a close identification with their business and demonstrate a pride of ownership. The business often represents an extension of themselves and their ideals and values. Or a business may allow a family to maintain a historic tradition of ownership of a particular business firm.
- *A strong motivation for recognition and prestige.* Business owners may gain considerable prestige or status from owning and operating a small business. A small business gives owners a base of power in the community and an opportunity to wield political and economic influence.
- *A feeling they are controlling their own destiny.* To many individuals, controlling their own firm is tremendously rewarding.
- *A desire for achievement.* One of the most prevalent characteristics of the entrepreneur is a strong drive for achievement. Most studies of the motives of individuals who own their own firm indicate that they are achievers — they prefer to set their own goals and like to try to control their future.

Figure 18-3 sets forth the rewards and the contributions of the small-business owner.

Franchising and Small Business

franchising

Franchising became popular during the 1960s and has continued to increase in economic importance. Franchising involves drawing up a contract between a manufacturer and a dealer that stipulates how the manufacturer's product or service will be sold. The dealer, called a franchisee, agrees to sell the product or service of the manufacturer, called the franchisor, in return for royalties. Franchising organizations that are well known in Canada include Holiday Inn, McDonald's, Weight Watchers, Kentucky Fried Chicken, Midas Muffler, and Canadian Tire.

The franchising arrangement can be beneficial to both the franchisee and the franchisor. For the franchisee, the following benefits are evident:

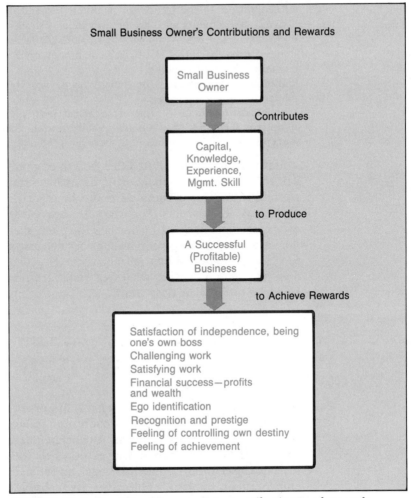

Small Business Owner's Contributions and Rewards

Small Business Owner

Contributes

Capital, Knowledge, Experience, Mgmt. Skill

to Produce

A Successful (Profitable) Business

to Achieve Rewards

Satisfaction of independence, being one's own boss
Challenging work
Satisfying work
Financial success—profits and wealth
Ego identification
Recognition and prestige
Feeling of controlling own destiny
Feeling of achievement

FIGURE 18-3 Small business owner's contributions and rewards

- Recognition — the franchise name gives the franchisee instant recognition with the public.
- Standardized appearance of the franchise — customers know that consistency exists from one outlet to another.
- Management assistance — the franchisee can obtain advice on how to run the franchise effectively.
- Economies of scale in buying — the head office of the franchise buys in large volume and resells to the franchisee at lower prices than he or she could get buying personally.
- Promotional assistance — the head office of the franchise provides the franchisee with prepared advertising and other promotional material.

The franchisee is not the only party who benefits in franchising. The following benefits are available to the franchisor:

- Recognition — the franchisor is able to expand its area of operation by signing agreements with dealers in widely dispersed places.
- Promotion savings — the various franchisees can decide on local advertising efforts; this saves the franchisor money on wasted coverage in areas where it has no franchise.
- Franchisee payments — the franchisees pay the franchisor for the right to operate their franchises.
- Attention to detail — since franchisees own their franchises, they are motivated to do a good job and to sell the franchisor's product or service aggressively.

Franchising has facilitated the growth of small business in Canada. The financial and management assistance franchisees can receive from the franchisor removes many of the risks that typically face small business owners. For example, few McDonald's outlets have ever closed for lack of business. However, many entrepreneurs are not interested in becoming franchisees because their behavior will be too closely regulated by the franchisor. They would rather start their own business and take whatever risks are necessary in return for freedom to do what they want.

FACTORS AFFECTING THE MANAGEMENT OF SMALL BUSINESSES

The small business offers challenges, opportunities, and difficulties that are different from those encountered in larger businesses. To be successful, the small business owner/manager must cope with a variety of factors internal and external to the firm. These factors include the economic, political/legal, and social factors in its external environment, the firm's objectives, its technology, its organizational structure, and the personnel working in the firm. We next discuss each of these important factors.

Economic Factors

Unlike the large corporation, the small business can concentrate on a restricted economic market in one locale or in one segment of an industry. This condition is a double-edged sword; if economic conditions become depressed in one portion of the industry, the small business may suffer severely, whereas the large, diversified firm may be capable of relying on other segments of the firm to offset the adverse conditions. However, in some situations the small business may be able to choose more favorable economic conditions in which to operate.

In numerous instances a small business may find itself in competition with a large enterprise. When it does, it often will seek to protect itself by serving a particular market segment. Microcomputer and minicomputer manufacturers competing against IBM often decide not to go head-to-head against IBM's strength. Rather, they might direct their effort at a market segment IBM hasn't pursued. The same situation exists for a small grocery store competing for sales against the major chains such as Safeway or Dominion. Because of the volume sales of the chains, the small stores may find it difficult to engage in strong price competition. Factors such as staying open late, offering shorter service lines, selling unusual products, and allowing customers to charge their purchases frequently provide the means for the small business to survive.

The flexibility of being small is somewhat offset by the weaker power resulting from limited resources. On occasion a major customer can take advantage of the small company by insisting on excessively favorable terms in price, quality, or delivery. A small business owner may feel he or she cannot withstand pressure from a supplier larger than the small firm itself. Small businesses often find it more difficult to secure adequate financing from institutional lenders. Lenders are aware of the fact that the small business has less depth in management. They are also aware of the statistics with respect to small business failure. However, many small businesses are able to secure a loan simply on the basis of the personal reputation of the owner.

Unlike many large enterprises, the small business is typically unable to exert a major influence on the economic market. Whereas some suggest that large enterprises are engaged in closed enterprise, there is usually little doubt that the small firm is involved in a highly competitive free enterprise system. In this atmosphere, the small business that is able to maintain lower operational costs will be the most profitable and have the greatest chances of remaining in business.

Political/Legal Factors

Both large and small businesses in Canada must adhere to provincial and federal laws that regulate business firms. For the small firm, however, adherence may be difficult because it does not have a staff of experts to make sure that government regulations are being properly followed. The small business owner may find that a certain action — such as paying a young relative less than the minimum wage — is against the law, even though it makes sense for the business. Because the small business owner/manager is totally occupied with running the business, he or she may not be well versed in the myriad laws that have been passed in the last decade.

Three major areas have become prominent for small business firms in the last few years: personnel practices, ecology, and paper burden. With regard to personnel practices, many small business owners may be unaware of provincial workplace health and safety regulations. When visited by a safety inspector, owners may be distressed to find that they must spend money to bring the workplace up to provincial or municipal standards, for instance by installing fire alarms and extinguishers or improving electrical wiring.

Ecological considerations can cause small business owners to pay huge costs to meet legal requirements or to pay fines for contravening them. Some small firms have been charged with excessively polluting sewer systems, waterways, and the air. Prevailing winds can carry animal and waste odors generated from hog and cattle feedlots as far as three kilometers. Small laundries that bleach blue jeans have added blue water and sludge to municipal sewer systems. Most small businesses operate on thin margins and may be tempted to reduce their operating costs by pouring wastes into available streams, air, land, and sewers. This, combined with the lack of expert staff and alternative production facilities, makes coping with ecological demands a critical problem.

In a few instances, the owner/managers of small businesses have found ways to cope with ecological problems, and at a profit. For example, animal waste solids from feedlots have been collected, sterilized, and sold as organic fertilizer or converted to gas to heat homes. Some laundry managers who were forced to buy special tank trucks to remove excessive sludge have expanded into the septic tank drainage business. The pressing necessity for ecological cleanup applies to both small and large enterprises.

Another political/legal factor in the external environment of small businesses is the variety of government reports that managers must fill out: forms for federal sales tax collection, workers' compensation, business licences, Statistics Canada surveys, and employee hiring procedures. Small business managers complain that this "paper burden" takes precious time away from the running of their businesses and reduces the chance that they will be successful.

Social Factors

The small business typically has fewer problems in coping with social factors in the external environment than does the large corporation. First, the small firm usually has only one community with which to deal. Also, the small firm's manager, being part of the local community, is better able to understand its customs than is the manager of a large corporation. Customers in the community may patronize the business because they know the owner. A small grocery store may find that some of its customers will pay a higher price for their groceries because they know and trust the owner.

Another positive social factor is the close relationship that usually exists between small business owners and their workers. While there is no guarantee that work will always go smoothly, generally speaking a closer working relationship exists between the owner and the workers because the business is small and everyone is on a first-name basis. Because the owner/manager knows each employee well and works closely with them, the employees are usually motivated to do a good job. Also, problems that turn up in daily work are likely to be worked out quickly and openly.

Objectives

The objectives of a small business are no different from those of a large enterprise, although the priorities that the owner places on them may be different. As we discussed in Chapter 3, the major objectives that a firm has are survival, profit, service, and growth.

For a small business, survival of the enterprise is the most crucial and the most difficult goal to attain. Since a significant percentage of new business ventures fail in the first year of existence, earning a profit is absolutely essential to long-term business survival. But a newly formed small business must be prepared, both financially and psychologically, to lose money during the early phases of operation. The profit objective provides incentive to assume business risks and, without the profit motive, few people would start their own businesses. But the survival objective constantly haunts the small business. A small business is limited in what it can do, being short on capital, being subject to competitive destruction, and often operating on a hand-to-mouth basis. With respect to the service objective, the typical small business is highly customer oriented. The large enterprise must also adapt to customer requirements, but such adaptation is not usually as specific or as rapid. Whereas the large enterprise can manipulate and control products and markets with its vast resources, the small firm must immediately be attuned to specific customer wishes and requirements. In this way, a unique market niche can be gained.

The small business has the advantage of being able to specialize by concentrating on a limited number of services. Though real estate agents often concentrate on a particular type of property, such as residential or commercial, one particular agency carved out a niche by concentrating solely on providing faculty housing in a city that contained a major university. A retail supermarket may develop special excellence in providing unusually good meat products. One small pharmaceutical company prospered in competition with larger firms by concentrating on the needs of one type of medical specialty — the ophthalmologic surgeon.

Another basic objective of most small businesses is growth. However, certain limitations to growth must be considered. Unlimited growth cannot be an objective of the small business if:

- The owner/manager seeks to retain direct and personal control of the firm.
- The firm wishes to sell only selected products or services.
- Management wants the firm to remain highly flexible.
- The owner does not value growth.

MANAGEMENT IN PRACTICE

Sun Ice Ltd.

Calgary-based Sun Ice Ltd. is a manufacturer of ski outerwear. The company is a newcomer to the highly competitive ski wear marketplace, but has been performing well because its garments have "fit, fashion, and function" — industry buzzwords that sum up excellence.

Sylvia Rempel, the president of the company, had always sewed her family's clothes. She had also taken a course in making recreational outerwear. She made ski wear for her children and it caught the eye of a Calgary retailer who volunteered to sell her apparel. But she wanted to expand, so in 1978 she and her husband Vic sold their retirement property, borrowed money from their lawyer to buy used sewing machines, and started their business. They hired a dozen seamstresses to turn out the product.

At the beginning, Rempel worked 16 hours a day, seven days a week to make the business a success. Her husband, a school principal, took a sabbatical and went on the road to sell. Her children modeled, did office chores, and helped out on the production line. Sales in the first (partial) year totalled $50 000, and increased to $325 000 by 1979. By 1986, the company employed 165 people and was turning out six lines of outerwear that were sold in both the US and Canada.

Sun Ice's success has led to pirating of their designs by offshore companies. Sylvia Rempel has vowed to prosecute these firms, even though it will be expensive and time-consuming.

SOURCE   Adapted from Suzanne Zwarun, "Parrying Unkind Cuts: The Battle is On," *Canadian Business* (February, 1987): 21–24.

The personal values and stage in life of the small business owner have a significant effect on the growth rate of the firm. If the owner is satisfied with the volume of the business and wants to spend more time with his or her family, growth will likely be slow. On the other hand, an ambitious entrepreneur with few commitments outside the business may work long hours trying to increase the growth rate of the business.

Technology

Technology exerts a significant impact on the types of products and services provided by small business firms. These products and services tend to possess characteristics that distinguish them from those of larger enterprises:

- The technology needed to create products and services in small businesses is characterized by shorter processing cycles. This enables promptness of service and does not require extensive investment in facilities.
- The demand for products and services of many small businesses tends to show greater seasonal variations.
- Small businesses are often in a better position to produce higher-quality products than are larger firms.

- The technology used to produce the products and services tends to be relatively stable. The small firm does not have the resources to be constantly bringing out new products as markets for old products disappear.

Because of these technological characteristics, there will always be a place for small business to provide products and services adapted to its particular capabilities. Since the majority of small businesses in Canada are engaged in retailing, wholesaling, and services, the most commonly needed technology is that of dealing directly with customers. Because customers are not completely controllable, great flexibility and sensitivity are needed.

Many small businesses were started because of a single technological innovation by its owner. Once the owner deals with the day-to-day operations of the business, he or she often does not have sufficient time to devote to continued research and development. The reason for the creation of the small business may also be the cause of its failure. Should the competition develop a superior product, the small business may find itself in severe difficulties.

Organizational Structure

The major characteristics of small business organizational structure are: (1) an emphasis on informality, (2) the critical importance of the owner/manager, and (3) the necessity for increased departmentalization with growth. Small firms tend to operate in a somewhat informal manner. The small size permits it; the need for flexibility demands it. High degrees of formalization, in terms of organizational charts, job descriptions, and procedures, are not evident; this contrasts sharply with the large firm where much formalization exists. (Recall structural discussions in Chapter 7.)

Because of the size of the small business, its owner and/or operator is of critical importance. There has been a tendency for operators of successful small firms to remain in the position for long periods of time — sometimes as much as 20 to 40 years. In large enterprises, a president remains for a much shorter period, typically fewer than 10 years. Heads of small businesses almost always wear two or more hats; for instance, they must perform several important functions. Not only do they manage the total enterprise, but they almost always perform a second or third function, frequently the finance function. In some small manufacturing firms, owners personally handle the major sales, placing themselves in competition with subordinate sales representatives. If a labor union is present, the owner/manager often handles the negotiations personally. If the owner has an engineering degree, he or she may be the firm's only machine maintenance person; management problems may have to wait until a machine is back in operation.

As the small business grows, the variety, number, and complexity of functions and relationships increases. The typical span of control in the small firm ranges from four to seven subordinates, whereas in the large company it ranges from five to over eleven. Thus, in the small business, communication distances are short and personal contacts frequent.

Not only do the typical small business manager and virtually all personnel wear two or more hats, they are expected to perform many activities that would normally be handled by a staff of experts in a large organization. For example, consider a small business employing six people. One day all six may be sales personnel, the next day they may spend time seeking financing, and the next day they all may be on the production line. The limited number of different departments and specialization of personnel enables the small business to operate with speed and flexibility.

There also tend to be fewer rigid or formal rules to follow in small firms. Employees may leave assigned work places without permission, have more flexible starting and quitting times, and have a more flexible dress code. The culture of the organization is more personalized. Names are more important than time clock numbers. It is likely that there are neither time clocks nor codified rule books. When instances calling for disciplinary action do arise, there is more individualized handling of the case. The less-rigid scheduling of tasks permits greater degrees of interaction among employees.

The nature of the job assignment combined with the friendly culture that can be developed in a small business leads to greater employee identification with the enterprise. There is an excitement in being actively involved in daily operations, of having personal contact with managers and customers. Individuals' impact on the total organization is greater, and they can see what they have personally accomplished. Absence rates are often significantly lower in the small firm. There is also considerably less likelihood that a labor union will be present.

Personnel

There are many noneconomic reasons for a person to prefer to work in a small business. While work in a large organization is often highly specialized, the typical task assignments in the small firm offer variety, challenge, and a greater degree of self-control. This flexibility may explain why many recent graduates are beginning to seek jobs with small businesses. At times, an employee has an opportunity to carry a job through from the original idea to its introduction into the market. Experience is gained at an accelerated pace. The opportunities provided by a small business are of great significance to many people.

Although there are exceptions, larger organizations usually pay their employees higher salaries than do small businesses. Most small firms tend to view salary as an expense rather than the employee as an asset. If the owner of a small business had to choose between a $25 000 accountant and one costing $35 000, the odds are heavily in favor of the former. If the owner were choosing between a $25 000 piece of machinery and one costing $35 000, however, considerably more deliberation would go into the decision. The owner may be aware that the more expensive machine might have certain advantages over the less expensive one, which would make the additional expenditure worthwhile.

nepotism

Quite often, an employee in a small firm may be a member of the owner/manager's family. The practice of hiring one's own relatives is **nepotism**. In the past this family member was often the son or son-in-law of the owner. (One writer states that the most lethal of all situations in small businesses is where all three — father, son, and son-in-law — are key people in the enterprise.[1]) More recently, a number of daughters of successful small business owners have gone to work in the family business.

Using family members has some advantages to the small business. Identification with "our business" should be great, thereby leading to increased effort and dedication. In addition, family members may constitute sources for funds to finance the enterprise. Bringing a son or daughter into the firm enables retention of control by the family in the years ahead. However, if a firm rigidly follows a policy of nepotism in its hiring or promotion practices, competent nonfamily personnel will leave the firm because they see little opportunity for advancement.

Employing family members can cause a number of interpersonal problems. Family quarrels can and do spill over into the everyday operations of the firm. In one instance, the introduction of the son initially caused few problems in a small hardware business. As the firm prospered, the standard of living of the son's family exceeded that of his sister and her husband. His sister brought pressure on their father to bring her husband into the firm. After this was done, head-on competition began to develop between the son and the son-in-law. Ultimately the father was forced to dissolve the firm because of family warfare. In another company run by a father and his four sons, a disagreement about business procedures led to a fist fight between two of the brothers on the front steps of the business.

PITFALLS IN STARTING A SMALL BUSINESS

A person who wants to start a small business should be aware of a number of potential pitfalls.[2] All of these can be avoided, although many small business owners fail to do so. Several of the most important pitfalls are discussed below.

Lack of Experience in the Business

A good rule of thumb for anyone thinking of starting a small business is: "You don't enter a business that you know nothing about." Much more experience is needed than merely a knowledge of the product or service that will be provided. Experience relates also to such areas as purchasing, marketing, and finance. It is because of lack of balanced experience that many small businesses fail.[3] An engineer who has a tremendous idea for a new product will find that, before the product can be manufactured, capital must be available to secure parts required to produce the item. The engineer must also determine what quantities and quality levels are needed. Once the item has been manufactured, it must be marketed. A certain amount of personal selling is necessary. Thus, in order to go into business for oneself, a person should ask if he or she has the package of experience that is necessary to operate the business successfully.

Lack of Capital

A good idea does not guarantee the success of a small business. A person should also evaluate carefully the amount of capital that will be required both to start and to maintain a business. Often these calculations are much too optimistic, and a person can actually fail before the business has opened. One individual decided to take over the operation of a small convenience store. All expenses were carefully calculated: salaries, rent, utilities, and advertising. The only thing that was forgotten was that additional inventory had to be purchased for the successful operation of the business because the previous owner had reduced inventory to a very low level prior to selling the store. The new owner was not aware of this and did not have funds to purchase the inventory required. The store was never re-opened.

Poor Location

Since a large percentage of small businesses are retail store operations, a major factor that should be considered is the selection of the proper location. Low rent in the wrong location may be high; high rent in the right location may be low. Factors that should be considered might be:

- Population: What is the traffic volume surrounding the store? Are the types of customers who will potentially purchase the product located within the trading area? For instance, approximately 70 percent of all convenience store customers reside within two kilometers of the store.
- Accessibility: Do cars have to cross traffic to get to the location? How fast is the traffic generally moving past the location? Are car parks nearby?
- Competition: Are there a large number of similar types of businesses in

the marketing area? How will the competition affect the proposed location?

- Economic stability: The site must be considered not only for its current location but also for potential considerations. The anticipated move of a large supermarket across the street may have a detrimental effect on a new family-owned grocery.

Inadequate Inventory Management

Inventory represents a debt for a small business; it ties up funds that could be used for other purposes. Inventory management is crucial to successful operation. If a business attempts to get by on minimum inventory, its customers may begin shopping at other locations where all of the items they want are available. On the other hand, if excessive inventory is carried, funds cannot be used for other purposes. Also, if the items cannot be sold, they represent a complete loss for the business.

Another major factor related to inventory mismanagement is internal theft. Often the greatest number of thefts are committed by in-house personnel. A manager of a small business is often so closely involved with the personnel that he or she never believes that they would steal. There have been instances where an employee was making more than the owner because of internal theft. An inventory control system should be established to discover shortages before they become excessive.

Excessive Investment in Fixed Assets

Fixed assets, such as buildings and equipment, cannot be converted into cash easily, if at all. If sales are increasing, the owner may decide to purchase additional equipment, and to hire additional personnel. If sales decline again, payment on the equipment may prove difficult. Because of this, the business may be forced into bankruptcy — even though at one time it had an excellent chance for success. The small business owner must consider this factor much more carefully than do large, well-established firms.

Poor Credit Policies

One sure way to make a sale is to give credit. But small business owners have discovered that one of the fastest ways to go out of business is to give excessive credit. In many instances, credit is granted based on whether the owner likes a person. The owner has not determined if the individual is a poor credit risk. With this approach, an owner may find that sales are increasing but there is little cash inflow. Because the owner may feel uncomfortable about asking people to pay their debts, the debt owed by the customer may not be collected.

MANAGEMENT IN PRACTICE

Success and Failure in Small Business

In the 1970s, Billy Hitzig started Pierre de Paris Fashions Ltd., a women's fashion manufacturing company. He expanded quickly and moved into the United States market. He got the contract to produce clothes bearing the logo of the 1980 Moscow Olympics, and sales rose to $4 million by 1979. Then the United States announced that it was boycotting the Olympics, and the stores he had contracts with backed out. He was left with obsolete inventory valued at half a million dollars. The banks foreclosed on his business.

Mr. Hitzig has now started another business — Bohtogs Industries Ltd. — and he is experiencing much more success on his second try. He accepts most of the blame for the failure of his first business and says that it was his poor management that caused it to fail. This time around, he is being much more cautious and trying to keep his operation manageable. For example, until recently, his line of credit was only $10 000. When he decided he needed more, he paid for the services of a large accounting firm to draw up his application. This resulted in a more thorough financial analysis than if he had done it himself.

He is looking at the American market again, but this time much more carefully. He has decided simply to export to the United States rather than to set up operations there. He also has turned to the Ontario government's trade offices in the United States to help him explore that market more systematically.

Billy Hitzig isn't bitter about his initial failure in the garment business. He says that experience helped him to do a much better job of managing his business the second time around.

SOURCE Adapted from "Chapter Two: The Resurrection of an Entrepreneur," *Canadian Business* (May 1984): 108.

Taking Too Much Cash Out of the Business

Money that is spent by the owner cannot be used to make the business grow. When a small business is just starting to develop, it is likely that a major problem will be that of securing sufficient capital. If the owner takes too much cash out of the business to maintain a high lifestyle, growth may be stymied. Sacrifices must be made at first to enjoy future success.

Unplanned Expansions

If one business location is doing fine, the owner may be tempted to add an additional location and do twice as well. Growth by acquisition has often caused major problems for owners of small businesses. When rapid expansions occur, difficulties are often experienced. The manager will discover that running two locations is much more difficult than one. He or she may not be accustomed to delegating authority, which must be done if there is more than one location. If the owner has been making all the decisions, efficiency may drop when additional locations are involved.

Having the Wrong Attitude

Let's face it; starting your own business is difficult. There is a good possibility it will fail. It is certainly not a structured job, where you can leave the problems behind at quitting time. If a business is to be successful, it will take a lot of hard work. The responsibilities of the business will likely mean that many outside interests will have to be reduced. Small business owners must assess the personal value of such outside interests, because the assessment is not merely a matter of money. Personal time, family life, and nonbusiness relationships may suffer. If the owner decides to go on a holiday, this decision could reduce business. Sacrifices will be necessary, but to see a business survive and grow can also be very rewarding.

GOVERNMENT AND SMALL BUSINESS

Federal and provincial governments in Canada have a two-sided impact on small business. On the one hand, many government assistance programs are available for small businesses; on the other, small businesses must cope with many government regulations, some of which seem unnecessarily intrusive. We look at each of these issues in this section.

Government Assistance to Small Business

Unlike the United States, where the federal Small Business Administration coordinates the available aid to small business, in Canada a variety of federal and provincial programs exist. These programs show how strong the belief is in Canada that small business is something that should be encouraged at various levels of government. These aid programs are also an attempt to keep large firms from dominating markets. Government programs provide aid in two distinct areas: (1) financial assistance, and (2) management consulting assistance.

financial assistance programs

The **financial assistance programs** for small business are numerous, so only illustrative programs are presented here. One of the best-known programs was established in 1978, with the passage of the federal Small Business Loans Act. Under this Act, small business owners can get loans up to $75 000 to purchase fixed and movable assets. The Federal Business Development Bank (FBDB) also encourages loans to small businesses; the interest rates it charges increase as the size of the loan increases. The Income Tax Act also assists small business because it allows Canadian-controlled private corporations to pay a low tax rate on the first $150 000 of income each year.

Financial assistance to small business is also prominent at the provincial level. The specific agencies and laws differ somewhat, but

MANAGEMENT IN PRACTICE

Profiting from Garbage

Oonagh McNerney is president of Extrufix Inc., a Markham, Ontario firm that has Canadian sales of $5 million and export sales to the United States, Australia, Britain, and other countries totalling $1.25 million. The company manufactures and sells the "Roll and Rack," a device that dispenses small garbage bags for kitchen use.

The company started in 1970 with $20 000 from a remortgaged home and $50 000 from a venture capitalist. McNerney spent many hours demonstrating the product in Eaton's and Simpsons in the early years of the company. The marketing strategy was carried out in three phases: first, sell to stores like Eaton's to establish product credibility; second, sell to the large discount stores like Woolco; third, sell to grocery stores after the product's workability was established.

Sales doubled annually during the 1970s. The company eventually built a manufacturing facility on two hectares of land in Pefferlaw, Ontario and hired 17 people with the help of a Federal Business Development Bank loan of $200 000. The company began selling in the American market some years ago, but the operation there became profitable only in 1983. The company now has a very bright future in both countries.

SOURCE Adapted from Helen Kohl, "Mother Finds Marketing Gold in Patented Garbage Bag Gizmo," *Small Business* (November 1983): 6–7.

the aim in each province is to encourage small business activity. Examples are the Enterprise Development Group of Manitoba, the Alberta Opportunity Company, and the Industry Development Branch of Saskatchewan. These provincial agencies usually give financial aid to individuals wanting to establish a small business or to those wanting to improve an existing small business.

An important part of financial aid to small business is the incentive aspect of the aid. The federal Department of Regional Industrial Expansion (DRIE), for example, gives incentive grants to certain firms if they are located in such designated slow-growth areas as the Atlantic provinces, most of Quebec, northern Ontario, Manitoba, Saskatchewan, northern Alberta and BC, and the two territories. By giving incentive grants, the federal government hopes to influence entrepreneurial decision making. When considering these grants, the entrepreneur must ask whether the short term financial benefit of the grant more than offsets the potential negative effects of locating in a slow-growth area.

The owner/manager of a small business must give careful consideration to government aid. The role of an entrepreneur is to bring together land, labor, and capital to earn a profit. Government aid does not come without strings attached, and the entrepreneur must consider how much these strings will inhibit his or her ability to do what is necessary to run a profitable business. If the government aid requires setting up a business in a certain geographic area, the entrepreneur must ask hard questions about whether or not the area can support the business he or she has in mind. Or, if the aid requires a certain pay-back schedule, the entrepreneur must consider whether the business can meet the schedule.

Overall, government assistance to small business changes the payoffs to owner/managers. From the managerial perspective, the nature of these payoffs must be considered in relation to the performance the business would be capable of without the aid.

Counselling Assistance to Small Enterprises (CASE)

The other area of government assistance to small business involves low cost advice on how to manage a small business. The **Counselling Assistance to Small Enterprises** (CASE) program brings retired business executives into contact with entrepreneurs as consultants to small businesses. The small business owner can discuss problems in marketing, production, finance, and personnel with these consultants and also discuss the value of new ideas on how to improve productivity and the general effectiveness of the business. To be eligible for CASE, a firm must have less than 100 employees and sales less than $5 million per year.[4]

Government Regulation of Small Business

We noted earlier in the chapter that small business owners often feel resentment toward government involvement. Governments must protect consumers and the ecology; they cannot allow even small businesses simply to do whatever they please. Entrepreneurs, conversely, often believe that government is unnecessarily strict in the regulation of small business.

As we discussed in Chapter 2, the federal, provincial, and municipal governments control business in several major areas. One involves the requirement that all businesses must procure certain licenses and permits before they are allowed to operate. For example, a restaurant must have a food and liquor license before the business can serve food and alcohol. Businesses must also collect sales tax, carry workers' compensation insurance, and pay employer taxes. Most small business owners would agree that these kinds of things are necessary and desirable, but they do consume valuable time.

Small business owners must usually provide pertinent information to the municipal, provincial and federal governments. For example, small business owners might be required to fill out a questionnaire indicating how many employees the business has, how much they are paid, and other aspects of their operation. Many entrepreneurs feel that being required to provide information of this sort intrudes unreasonably into their activities. One survey by the Canadian Federation of Independent Businesses found that government-required paperwork was identified as the number one problem in 10 percent of the firms that responded; overall, it ranked fourth.

MANAGEMENT IN PRACTICE

Government and Small Business

John Brady is the owner of an ice cream parlor called "After All" on Mount Pleasant Road in uptown Toronto. From the time he conceived of the idea until he actually opened the store, he encountered a series of obstacles that had to be overcome. In addition to the usual managerial problems, he was faced with many government requirements. Consider the following:

- When he took his architectural drawings to City Hall for approval, he discovered that many building code requirements had not been considered by the architect who had drawn up the plans (a friend of his). He consulted the Building Code, added the changes he thought were necessary, and waited for approval. He received approval of his building plans, but had to make many changes that cost him a significant amount of money. For example, he had to add a sink on the main floor of the store so that employees could wash their hands.
- He could have got a loan from the Federal Business Development Bank, but it would have taken too much time to process; he wanted to get going immediately.
- As construction neared completion, a parade of public health, fire, electrical, and building inspectors toured the building. By and large,

though, they were reasonable people.
- Other problems were not so easily solved. One concerned the sign he wanted to hang on his building. Since it extended 15 cm beyond his building, he was told he would have to pay a city tax on the sign. He also had much difficulty getting a permit to use a strip of land 1m by 9m next to his building for a patio. Thirteen different groups had to approve of the idea before he was allowed to set up his patio. That process took two months.
- Because he wanted to serve liquor, he had to get a liquor permit. When he went to the liquor commission to apply, he was confronted by two people who were concerned abut his having a liquor license. One was a tenant who lived over his store and was concerned about excessive noise, and the other was the Baptist church across the street. After several compromises, Brady got his license.

In spite of all this, John Brady says it was worth it. The freedom of owning your own business is, after all, better than working for someone else.

SOURCE Adapted from Tony Leighton, "The Emperor of Ice Cream," *Canadian Business* (March 1984): 32–38.

CHECKLIST FOR GOING INTO BUSINESS

A person considering starting a business should carefully and critically evaluate a number of factors. The two most important attributes that determine profitability, according to highly successful small business managers, are the ability to manage cash, and the ability to solve problems innovatively.[5] The Small Business Administration in the United States has developed a comprehensive checklist of questions that assist in this evaluation process. These questions are relevant for any small business owner. (See Table 18-1.) As can be seen, these questions are organized under such topics as: "Before You Start," "Getting Started," and "Making It Go."

If you have carefully answered the questions posed in the table, you have done some hard work and serious thinking. That's good! But you have probably found some things you still need to know more about or do something about.

Do all you can for yourself, but don't hestiate to ask for help from people who can tell you what you need to know. Remember, running a business takes courage. You've got to be able to decide what you need and then go after it.

Good luck!

TABLE 18-1   Checklist for Going into Business

Before You Start	
How about you?	• Are you the kind of person who can get a business started and make it go?
	• Think about why you want to own your own business. Do you want it badly enough to keep working long hours without knowing how much money you'll end up with?
	• Have you worked in a business like the one you want to start?
	• Have you worked for someone else as a foreman or manager?
	• Have you had any business training in school?
	• Have you saved any money?
How about the Money?	• Do you know how much money you will need to get your business started?
	• Have you counted up how much money of your own you can put into the business?
	• Do you know how much credit you can get from your suppliers — the people you will buy from?
	• Do you know where you can borrow the rest of the money you need to start your business?
	• Have you figured out what net income per year you expect to get from the business? Count your salary and your profit on the money you put into the business.
	• Can you live on less than this so that you can use some of it to help your business grow?
	• Have you talked to a banker about your plans?
How about a Partner?	• If you need a partner with money or know-how that you don't have, do you know someone who will fit — someone you can get along with?
	• Do you know the good and bad points about going it alone, having a partner, and incorporating your business?
	• Have you talked to a lawyer about it?
How about Your Customers?	• Do most businesses in your community seem to be doing well?
	• Have you tried to find out whether stores like the one you want to open are doing well in your community and in the rest of the country?
	• Do you know what kind of people will want to buy what you plan to sell?
	• Do people like that live in the area where you want to open your store?
	• Do they need a store like yours?
	• If not, have you thought about opening a different kind of store or going to another neighborhood?
Getting Started	
Your Building	• Have you found a good building for your store?
	• Will you have enough room when your business gets bigger?
	• Can you fix the building the way you want it without spending too much money?
	• Can people get to it easily from parking spaces, bus stops, or their homes?
	• Have you had a lawyer check the lease and zoning?

TABLE 18-1 cont'd.: Checklist for Going into Business

Equipment and Supplies	• Do you know just what equipment and supplies you need and how much they will cost? • Can you save some money by buying second-hand equipment?
Your Merchandise	• Have you decided what things you will sell? • Do you know how much or how many of each you will buy to open your store with? • Have you found suppliers who will sell you what you need at a good price? • Have you compared the prices and credit terms of different suppliers?
Your Records	• Have you planned a system of records that will keep track of your income and expenses, what you owe other people, and what other people owe you? • Have you worked out a way to keep track of your inventory so that you will always have enough on hand for your customers but not more than you can sell? • Have you figured out how to keep your payroll records and take care of tax reports and payments? • Do you know what financial statements you should prepare?

Getting Started

Your Records (continued)	• Do you know how to use these financial statements? • Do you know an accountant who will help you with your records and financial statements?
Your Store and the Law	• Do you know what licenses and permits you need? • Do you know what business laws you have to obey? • Do you know a lawyer you can go to for advice and for help with legal papers?
Protecting Your Store	• Have you made plans for protecting your store against thefts of all kinds — shoplifting, robbery, burglary, employee stealing? • Have you talked with an insurance agent about what kinds of insurance you need?
Buying a Business Someone Else Has Started	• Have you made a list of what you like and don't like about buying a business someone else has started? • Are you sure you know the real reason why the owner wants to sell the business? • Have you compared the cost of buying the business with the cost of starting a new business? • Is the stock up to date and in good condition? • Is the building in good condition? • Will the owner of the building transfer the lease to you? • Have you talked with other business people in the area to see what they think of the business? • Have you talked with the company's suppliers? • Have you talked to a lawyer about it?

Making It Go

Advertising	• Have you decided how you will advertise? (Newspapers, posters, handbills, radio, by mail?) • Do you know where to get help with your ads? • Have you watched what other stores do to get people to buy?
The Prices You Charge	• Do you know how to figure what you should charge for each item you sell? • Do you know what other stores like yours charge?
Buying	• Do you have a plan for finding out what your customers want?

- Will your plan for keeping track of your inventory tell you when it is time to order more and how much to order?
- Do you plan to buy most of your stock from a few suppliers rather than a little from many, so that those you buy from will want to help you succeed?

Selling
- Have you decided whether you will have salesclerks or self-service?
- Do you know how to get customers to buy?
- Have you thought about why you like to buy from some sales representatives while others turn you off?

Your Employees
- If you need to hire someone to help you, do you know where to look?
- Do you know what kind of person you need?
- Do you know how much to pay?
- Do you have a plan for training your employees?

Credit for Your Customers
- Have you decided whether to let your customers buy on credit?
- Do you know the good and bad points about joining a credit-card plan?
- Can you tell a bad risk from a good credit customer?

A Few Extra Questions

- Have you figured out whether you could make more money working for someone else?
- Does your family go along with your plan to start a business of your own?
- Do you know where to find out about new ideas and new products?

OPENING INCIDENT REVISITED

Kent Computers

In the opening incident, Evan Kent was having second thoughts about his decision to start his own small business. He was working extremely long hours, yet he had virtually nothing to show for all his efforts so far. The problems experienced by Kent are very typical in newly formed small businesses. In the chapter, we noted that a person starting a business from scratch would probably have to spend several years building up the business to the point where it was a viable entity. Kent has only been in business a few months, yet he is already thinking about quitting. His lack of a longer-run perspective could seriously damage his chances for success.

Since Kent is not involved in manufacturing, he does not have a key problem that some small businesses face — shortage of cash. He keeps as little inventory as possible and in this way is able to avoid cash problems. However, the kind of product he is selling requires intensive discussions with customers, so he is going to have to spend considerable time with customers if he hopes to make sales. He therefore has time problems, which can be just as serious as cash problems.

Kent's two major problems are: (1) no experience in the business, and (2) poor inventory management. His lack of experience can be overcome, but he is going to have to spend many hours becoming well-versed in the computer business. His inventory problems are probably going to cost him customers if he doesn't get a more complete line of products in the store. However, to do this will cost money. Kent seems to have successfully avoided most of the other pitfalls noted in the chapter, yet he still is wondering whether he made the right decision to go into business for himself.

Kent should have asked himself the kinds of questions contained in the checklist in the last section before he started a small business. Perhaps he is not suited to owning his own business, or at least not a business that sells this particular product.

SUMMARY

Thousands of Canadians dream of owning and managing their own business — of being their own boss. While the freedom to start and manage one's own business is available to everyone, each year thousands of new businesses fail. In fact, statistics reveal that half of all new businesses in Canada fail within the first four years of operation, and over 60 percent fail within six years. Despite these grim statistics, virtually every large, successful business began as a small business. Also, it is important to note that small businesses make significant contributions to the health and vitality of the Canadian economy.

Franchising has facilitated the growth of small business in Canada. In franchising, a contract is drawn up between a manufacturer and a dealer stipulating how the manufacturer's product or service will be sold. The franchisee pays the franchisor a fee to get into the franchise; then the franchisee collects royalties based on sales revenue.

The small business enterprise offers challenges, opportunities, and considerable problems that differ from those encountered by large businesses. The large firm usually has the resources to withstand adverse circumstances. Limited resources may make it difficult for the small business to exert a major influence on the economic or political/legal aspects of its external environment. However, a small business may be more flexible and responsive to changing conditions. A small firm, for example, may be able to offer more personalized service and maintain lower operational costs.

The high failure rate for small businesses is caused primarily by ineffective management. Some of the major pitfalls that small businesses encounter include the owner's lack of experience in the business, lack of capital, a poor location, inadequate inventory management, excessive capital investment in fixed assets, poor credit policies, the owner taking too much cash out of the business, unplanned expansions, and having the wrong attitude. Many small business owner/managers also spend much time and money complying with government regulations — coping with the paper burden or tailoring their business to meet legal requirements. However, to help prospective, new, and established small businesses avoid and/or overcome problems that might cause failure, federal and provincial assistance in the areas of finance and management is available.

REVIEW QUESTIONS

1. What is a small business? What is a franchise and how does it differ from small business ownership?

2. What is considered to be a small business in Canada in manufacturing? in other sectors?
3. What are the failure rates for small businesses in Canada? Why?
4. What external environment factors affect the management of small businesses? Do each of these factors affect small firms more than large companies?
5. What are the basic objectives of the typical small business? Is growth always an objective of a small business? Why or why not?
6. Products and services of small businesses tend to have characteristics that distinguish them from those of larger enterprises. Discuss any three of these characteristics.
7. What are the major characteristics of small business organizational structures?
8. What is meant by nepotism? Briefly discuss how the practice can affect a small business.
9. What is an entrepreneur? What are the major personality characteristics of entrepreneurs?
10. List and briefly discuss five of the more prominent pitfalls often encountered in starting a small business.
11. Briefly describe the various types of regulations that affect new small businesses and the types of assistance available to small businesses from the federal and provincial governments.
12. Review the Checklist for Going into Business for Yourself. What areas covered in the checklist are most significant?

EXERCISES

1. Using the Checklist for Going into Business for Yourself, evaluate the feasibility of starting your own restaurant specializing in steak and seafood entrées.
2. Visit three successful small businesses in your local area. Discuss with the owner/manager of each business the reasons for their success. Ask them if they would advise a person to start up his or her own small business.

CASE STUDY

The New Business

Greg Forrest had worked for Eaton's for eighteen years when he decided to go into business for himself. He was 47 years old. He and his wife, Joyce, had two grown sons and another 15 years old. He knew the kind of business he wanted to be in — furniture and appliances. He had been the general merchandise manager for an Eaton's store, and before that he had managed the appliance department in another larger store.

Forrest felt that he was well qualified to run his own business. He had worked for years as a commission sales representative. As a manager, he had managed other salespersons and had been responsible for product displays, inventory turnover, credit approvals, and many other aspects of management. He had saved $10 000 in cash and his home was paid for. He also had 300 shares of stock valued at $30 000.

Forrest had been actively looking for a business to buy for about three months when he learned of Marsdon Appliance Company. The company was owned by Ronald Marsdon, who was 68 years old and had decided to retire. Marsdon was offering his business for sale for only $25 000, although monthly sales averaged about $30 000.

The business was in a rented store in a small shopping center. When Forrest talked with Mr. Marsdon he found that the furniture inventory of about $80 000 was financed with a local bank and the appliance inventory was floor planned by Canadian General Electric. Under the floor planning arrangement, General Electric finances the appliances in full and charges no interest as long as the inventory is turned over every 90 days. Forrest knew that what he would really be purchasing with the $25 000 was a small amount of office equipment, a three-year-old delivery truck, and the company's good will.

After going over the financial statements for Marsdon Appliance with his C.A., Forrest decided that the business was a good deal. It was exactly what he had been looking for. His wife could keep the books and help out part time, and he could be the main sales representative. Mr. Marsdon had said he would stay and help four hours a day until Forrest felt that he could get along without him.

QUESTIONS

1. What sources of financing do you think are available to Forrest?
2. What kinds of problems is Forrest likely to encounter in his new business venture? How would you recommend that he prepare to handle the problems which occur?

CASE STUDY

The Lethbridge Inn

For many years, Joan Goodson had thought that Lethbridge, Alberta needed a first-class motel, restaurant, and private club. Although there was limited industry in the city, Lethbridge was a growing community. It was also the home of the University of Lethbridge. The building of a quality motel, restaurant, and club facility in Lethbridge had long been a dream of Goodson. She became particularly enthusiastic about the potential success of the motel facility after discussing her plans with local business people and university officials. The business and university leaders pledged their support and encouraged Goodson to continue with plans for the creation of the facility. Goodson, the president of a retail chain, was able to interest her brother-in-law, Charles Jones, and two of Jones's business associates,

Paula Prince and Bob Johnson, in the venture. Jones was a vice-president with an encyclopedia company and Prince and Johnson were highly successful sales managers. All three lived in Calgary.

After considerable discussion, the four people — Goodson, Jones, Prince, and Johnson — formed a partnership and began serious preparations for entering the motel business. While none of the partners had any previous experience in the motel, restaurant, or club business, each was considered a successful business person. The partners hired a nationally known consulting firm specializing in hotel/motel operations, to conduct a study to determine the feasibility of the project. Prior to engaging the consulting firm, the four partners agreed on the location and size of the proposed facility.

The consulting firm recommended the creation of the proposed motel, restaurant, and club facility on the location specified by the partners. The study was completed in 10 days at a cost of $5000 to the partners. The consultants based their recommendation on the following factors:

- Favorable general business conditions and projected growth of Lethbridge and the university.
- Apparently favorable supply of and demand for motel rooms.
- A lack of quality motel and/or restaurant facilities in Lethbridge.
- Excellent financial projections — a forecast of $50 000 net income during the first year of operation.
- The excellent location of the proposed site: close to a major highway and to the university.

Much of the consultants' study consisted of interviewing business and university leaders to obtain their estimate of the potential for such a venture.

After reviewing the feasibility study, the partners decided to proceed immediately with plans for the facility, which was to be named the Lethbridge Inn. An architectural firm completed plans for the facility and construction began in September; the inn opened for business the next September, with 60 rooms, a restaurant, and a private club. The total capital invested in the facility was $800 000 with $100 000 being contributed directly by the partners. A $700 000, 20-year loan at 14 percent annual interest provided the remainder of the capital.

Almost immediately on opening, the Lethbridge Inn began experiencing operational and financial difficulties. None of the partners was interested in managing the facility, so a professional manager was hired, as well as a staff of several full- and part-time personnel. During the first two years of operation, the inn had five managers and experienced losses totaling over $200 000. The occupancy rate was much lower than the level predicted by the feasibility study, and expenses for food and salaries were far out of line.

When questioned about the lack of success of the inn, Goodson stated: "Our poor results during the first two years of operation resulted from poor management — particularly in the areas of control of salaries and food expenses. Also, we haven't had the business we were promised from the university or from local townspeople. We've also had a tough time finding competent managers."

QUESTIONS

1. What were the primary problems experienced by the Lethbridge Inn? What were the causes of these problems?
2. Do you think that Goodson and her partners should have entered the business? Discuss.
3. Do you spot any apparent weaknesses in the consultants' feasibility study? If so, what are they?
4. What do you predict in the future for the Lethbridge Inn?

CASE STUDY

The Photography Studio

The Clark Photography Studio located in Regina has an excellent reputation for high-quality photography. The studio specializes in bridal, family, and executive portraits. In addition, the studio is very active in photographing weddings. Raymond Clark is the owner and manager of the studio. He started the business in his garage 30 years ago, and it has since grown to become one of the leading photography studios in Regina, with revenues in excess of $150 000 annually and five full-time employees. Clark has earned a reputation as a highly creative and innovative photographer.

Clark was the first portrait photographer to take outdoor garden color portraits some

15 years ago. Most of his bridal portraits and many of the individual and/or family portraits are taken in his outdoor garden studio. Because of the unique features of the studio's portraits, the studio has as much business as Clark believes he wants. He has never advertised in any form — he depends on word-of-mouth to carry his reputation for quality photography. Throughout the history of the business, Clark's goal has been to be a high-quality photographer. In recent years, he has raised prices considerably, but has noticed no overall decrease in revenues.

The Clark Photography Studio has five key employees: Ray Clark; his wife, Joan, who handles customers and manages the office; Ray and Joan's son, Ken, who is also a professional photographer; Hilda, a professional spotter who does touch-up work on negatives and prints; and Cathy, who performs such duties as framing pictures and working with customers. Ken, 32, is one of three sons. He is interested in someday owning the business. Unfortunately, Ken has had a history of instability and unpredictability, especially with regard to work. He has either quit or been fired by his father several times and has not always been a very conscientious employee. Recently, however, he seems to have taken a more responsible attitude. Clark's other sons have never been interested in the photography business.

In recent years, Ray Clark has been spending less and less time in the business. Several years ago, he decided to close the studio on Mondays — which meant that the business was open from 9-5 Tuesday through Friday and from 9-noon on Saturday. Although the studio is currently operating on this schedule, Ray Clark, who is 60 and is interested in retiring from the business, has chosen to work fewer days. His typical work week is as follows: Wednesday: 9-5; Thursday: plays golf; Friday: 9-5; and every other Saturday: 9-noon.

While not at the studio, Ray Clark spends most of his time at his ranch located about 145 km from Regina. Six years ago, he bought 60 hectares of land and built a large, beautiful retirement home. He has 25 head of cattle on the ranch and enjoys having a garden. Ray Clark and his friend, Bob Schroeder, have frequent discussions about the future of the Clark Photography Studio. One of their recent conversations was as follows:

Schroeder: Ray, how are your plans for retirement coming along? Do you think that Ken is ready to take over the business?

Clark: I'm ready to get out now, but I don't believe that Ken can handle the business on his own yet. He is doing a good job, but if Joan and I leave the studio, I'm not sure he could make it. Ken wants to buy the business but I think that he would have a difficult time making the payments. Just the other day I was offered $300 000 for the studio property by a group of investors who want to build condominiums on the land. That's an excellent price, don't you think?

Schroeder: The $300 000 offer sounds good to me, especially when you consider the interest income from that amount of money. But your annual earnings from the business are more than the interest on the $300 000.

Clark: I want out of the city and the pressures of the business. I have been able to work two or three days a week now for two years and still earn almost what I earned when I was spending five days in the studio. Our business has declined some during the past year, but not drastically. Besides, I enjoy my golf day on Thursdays with the boys and Joan likes to come in to Regina to visit friends — so I'll probably continue the two- or three-day schedule for a while longer.

QUESTIONS

1. What are the present goals of Ray Clark as a small business person? Have they changed over time?
2. Why has the Clark Photography Studio been successful in the past? Do you believe its current goals ensure continued success in the future?
3. In view of what we discussed in this chapter, evaluate the effectiveness of Ray Clark as an owner/manager.
4. Since Clark wants to retire, would you advise that he accept the $300 000 offer for the studio property?
5. Why do you think Ray Clark does not have much confidence in his son Ken's ability to run the studio when he retires?

OPENING INCIDENT

Canadian Implements Ltd.

Two years ago, Dan Shelton went to work for Canadian Implements Ltd., a firm with manufacturing and sales operations in several Far Eastern countries. Dan was originally hired to shape up the company's production facility in Hamilton, Ontario. Management felt that the operation was not running nearly as efficiently as possible; Shelton was hired away from Braxton Manufacturing because he had a good track record there. In less than a year, he successfully straightened out the Hamilton plant.

Late last year, Shelton was asked whether he would be interested in an overseas assignment. The situation was similar to the one he had originally encountered in Hamilton: one of the company's Far Eastern manufacturing facilities was not operating as effectively as management had hoped. Shelton was chosen to go there and straighten production out. Shelton realized that, if he could be as successful there as he was in Hamilton, his reputation as a top-notch troubleshooter would be assured. This strategy would dramatically improve his long-run career prospects at Canadian Implements.

Shelton accepted the assignment almost immediately, considering it a challenge.

Shelton was extremely busy during his first two months in the Far East, as he tried to learn all the important facts about why the production facility there was not functioning properly. Many of the key personnel spoke English well enough that he experienced few language misunderstandings. Once he felt comfortable with his new situation, Shelton planned what actions he believed were necessary to resolve the production problems. He decided to begin by firing one supervisor who was notoriously incompetent. When he advised his assistant, a foreign national, to terminate the man in question, Shelton was told: "You can't fire that person. Our government will not permit the dismissal of a long-term employee unless the company agrees to continue paying his salary."

Shelton was amazed. Suddenly, he wondered how many other rules like this one would restrict him. Would he be able to turn the plant around and complete his new assignment?

Dan Shelton's experience illustrates just one of the many problems facing organizations conducting business in more than one country. But in spite of significant problems, more and more organizations are getting involved in business activities on an international basis.

Many people believe that, with resources, technology, food, and trained personnel unevenly distributed throughout the world, international business activities have the potential for distributing goods and services more equitably and for improving standards of living for all people. A dissenting view is that international business activities will lead to exploitation of developing countries and will benefit only the companies themselves. The one certain result is that international business activity has caused the countries of the world to become more closely interrelated; people in all countries are more aware of what is happening in other parts of the world.

Gilbreath, J. D., and Humphries, N. J. "Aggressive Contracting Strategies for Small Business Owners." *Journal of Small Business Management* 17 (October 1979): 30–36.

Higgins, Christopher; Irving, Richard; and Rinaldi, Saverio. "Small Business and Office Automation." *Canadian Journal of Administrative Sciences* 2, (December 1985): 375–381.

House, W. C. "Dynamic Planning for the Smaller Company — A Case History." *Long Range Plan* 12 (June 1979): 38–47.

"How to Start a Sideline Business." *Business Week* (August 6, 1979): 94–95.

Knight, Russell. "The Role of Franchisee Associations." *Canadian Journal of Administrative Sciences* 3, (June 1986): 114–122.

McKenna, J. F., and Oritt, P. L. "Small Business Growth: Making a Conscious Decision." *Advance Management Journal* 45 (Spring 1980): 45–53.

Petrof, J. V. "Small Business and Economic Development: The Case for Government Intervention." *Journal of Small Business Management* 18 (January 1980): 51–56.

Robinson, R. "Forecasting and Small Business: A Study of the Strategic Planning Process." *Journal of Small Business Management* 17 (July 1979): 19–27.

"Small Business Process a Passport to Profits." *Nation's Business* 67 (April 1979): 48.

"Study Shows Companies in Trouble Invariably Lack Planning and Control." *Management Review* 70 (February 1981): 38–39.

Timmins, S. A. "Large-Firm Forecasting Techniques Can Improve Small Business Decision-Making." *Journal of Small Business Management* 17 (July 1979): 14–18.

Walker, Gene C. "Starting a New Business — Pitfalls to Avoid." *U.S. News & World Report* (July 13, 1981): 75–76.

Zwarun, Susan. "Parrying Unkind Cuts: The Battle Is On." *Canadian Business* (February 1987): 21–24.

19

Managing Multinationals

KEY TERMS

multinational company (MNC) parent country host countries	developing nations parent country nationals host country nationals	third country nationals repatriation plan

---

LEARNING OBJECTIVES

After completing this chapter you should be able to
1. Describe the characteristics of a multinational enterprise and briefly explain the history and development of multinationals.
2. Explain how the external environment, objectives, and technology affect managing international operations.
3. State how the organizational structure may change when firms are engaged in international operations.
4. Describe personnel requirements and management approaches for a multinational company.

ENDNOTES

[1]Howard J. Klein, *Stop! You're Killing the Business* (New York: Mason and Lipscomb, 1974).

[2]*Pitfalls of Starting a Small Business* (New York: Dun and Bradstreet, 1980).

[3]R. A. Peterson, G. Kozmetsky, and N. M. Ridgway, "Perceived Causes of Small Business Failures: A Research Note," *American Journal of Small Businesses* 8 (July-September 1983): 18.

[4]For a detailed description of federal and provincial government taxation assistance to small business in the areas of taxation, management assistance, and government grants, see the Commerce Clearing House (Canada) *Small Business Guide*, pp. 4001–4952.

[5]R. Chaganti and R. Chaganti, "A Profile of Profitable and Not-So-Profitable Small Businesses," *Journal of Small Business Management* 21 (July 1983): 49.

REFERENCES

Black, Debra. "Strength in Numbers: The Joy of Franchising." *Canadian Business* 57, no. 5 (May 1984): 111.

———. "The Importance of Raising Money." *Canadian Business* 57, no. 5 (May 1984): 115.

Bruckman, J. C., and Iman, S. "Consulting with Small Business: A Process Model." *Journal of Small Business Management* 18 (April 1980): 41–47.

Carland, James W.; Hoy, Frank; Boulton, William R.; and Carland, JoAnn C. "Differentiating Entrepreneurs from Small Business Owners: A Conceptualization." *Academy of Management Review* 9, no. 2 (April 1984): 354–359.

Charan, Ram; Haber, Charles W.; and Mahan, John. "From Entrepreneur to Professional Manager: A Set of Guidelines." *Journal of Small Business Management* 18 (January 1980): 1–10.

Clugston, Michael; Ferguson, Ted; and Wells, Jennifer. "Small Business Report: An Entrepreneur's Handbook." *Canadian Business* 59, (October 1986): 84–140.

Clute, R. C. "How Important is Accounting to Small Business Survival?" *Journal of Commercial Bank Lending* 62 (January 1980): 24–28.

Cook, Peter. "Turning Young People Into Entrepreneurs Free of Charge." *The Globe and Mail* (December 24, 1986): B3.

Drucker, Peter. *Innovation and Entrepreneurship.* New York: Harper and Row, 1985.

In this chapter we examine the phenomenon of international business and the importance of effective management to the success of firms doing business in two or more countries. The chapter is divided into two main parts. First, we define the term multinational company and note the rapid development of multinational companies since World War II. Second, the actual management of multinational companies is examined in some detail. Included in this discussion is an assessment of the external environment factors the multinational company faces when it enters a foreign country. The management of objectives, technology, structure, and personnel in the multinational firm is also treated.

WHAT IS A MULTINATIONAL COMPANY

multinational
company
(MNC)

A **multinational company** (MNC) is a firm engaged in business in two or more countries. These firms typically have sales offices and sometimes manufacturing plants in many different countries. MNCs are instrumental in improving the world economy and the standards of living of many people; they can also significantly affect the technology, culture, and customs of the countries in which they operate. Peter Drucker refers to the multinational company as "the outstanding social innovation of the period since World War II."[1]

Technically speaking, any company conducting business in two or more countries is a multinational. However, this criterion is too simplistic because it does not give adequate recognition to the size and scope of operations of many such organizations. Some experts in the field of multinational business believe that organizations designated as multinationals should meet the following criteria:

- Operations are conducted in at least six different countries.
- At least 20 percent of the firm's assets and/or sales from business are in countries other than that where the parent company is located.
- Management has an integrated, global orientation.
- Resources are allocated without regard to national boundaries.
- National boundaries are viewed as merely a constraint that enters into the decision-making process.
- The firm's organizational structure cuts across national boundaries.
- Personnel are transferred throughout the world.
- Management takes on a broad, global perspective — it views the world as interrelated and interdependent.

A list of the world's 20 largest multinational companies is

presented in Table 19-1. The largest Canadian multinationals are listed in Table 19-2. To illustrate the impact of the multinational, one Massey-Ferguson executive states: "We combine French-made transmissions, British-made engines, Mexican-made axles, and United States-made sheet metal parts to produce in Detroit a tractor for sale in Canada."[2]

It is clear from Table 19-1 that firms headquartered in the United States dominate the list of the world's significant MNCs. This dominance has caused considerable concern in Canada during the last 20 years, since much of the industry activity in certain Canadian industries is controlled by American MNCs. The issue is that American firms may not have any interest in the well-being of Canada other than to ensure that Canadian consumers continue to buy their products so that they can make a profit.

TABLE 19-1 The Top Twenty Multinational Companies

Company	Home Country
Exxon	USA
Royal Dutch/Shell Group	Netherlands/GB
Mobil	USA
General Motors	USA
Texaco	USA
British Petroleum	GB
Standard Oil of California	USA
Ford Motor	USA
ENI	Italy
Gulf Oil	USA
IBM	USA
Standard Oil (Indiana)	USA
Fiat	Italy
General Electric	USA
Francoise des Petroles	France
Atlantic Richfield	USA
Unilever	GB/Netherlands
Shell Oil	USA
Renault	France
Petroleos de Venezuela	Venezuela

SOURCE Adapted from "The Largest Industrial Companies in the World," *Fortune* (August 10, 1981): 205. Reprinted by permission.

TABLE 19-2   20 Large Canadian Industrial Multinationals

	Sales[1]	Employees	Foreign Sales to total Sales (%)	No. of Foreign Nations in which active[2]
Alcan	$5 879	70 000	84	28
Seagram	3 169	14 000	92	20
Noranda	2 867	51 700	63	17
Hiram Walker	2 867	10 200	42	5
NOVA	2 665	8 600	29	4
Northern Telecom	2 573	39 318	79	11
Massey-Ferguson	2 542	27 609	91	33
MacMillan Bloedel	2 143	15 472	79	7
Moore	2 141	26 100	90	39
Inco	1 929	24 866	85	14
Genstar	1 861	15 000	60	1
Domtar	1 684	15 151	29	2
Abitibi-Price	1 577	15 000	63	1
AMCA	1 515	15 408	76	7
Molson	1 434	11 100	32	35
John Labatt	1 432	9 000	na	3
Consolidated-Bathurst	1 386	14 787	54	3
Cominco	1 349	10 466	73	12
Bombardier	419	4 600	67	4
National Sea	339	7 000	71	5
Average	2 279	21 874	66	13

[1]Average 1979–1983, billions of dollars.
[2]1983 (slightly different for some companies whose accounting periods differ).

SOURCE   Alan Rugman, Megafirms: Strategies for Canada's Multinationals (Toronto: Methuen, 1985).

Several government inquiries have been conducted since 1950 and all have pointed out the potential problems of excessive foreign ownership of Canadian business. Recommendations have been made that the amount of foreign ownership be reduced, but how this is to be accomplished is not clear. Interestingly, recent statistics do show a decline in the dominance of American companies in certain sectors of the Canadian economy. Table 19-3 shows the changes that occurred during the period 1977–1983. While most of the changes are not dramatic, if they continue, substantial reductions of foreign ownership in Canada may occur.

TABLE 19-3   Degree of Foreign Ownership by the United States and Others in Canada, as Measured by Assets, 1977-1983

Industry	Assets of Foreign-Controlled Corporations, as a Percentage of Total Industry Assets		
	1977	1980	1983
Agriculture, forestry, and fishing	7.4	4.3	3.5
Mining:			
Metal mining	37.7	31.3	22.7
Mineral fuels	60.2	53.3	39.5
Other mining	55.0	40.4	38.1
Total mining	51.1	45.1	35.3
Manufacturing:			
Food	39.2	29.4	30.4
Beverages	31.1	31.7	27.7
Tobacco products	99.8	99.7	99.9
Rubber products	94.1	91.0	91.5
Leather products	20.3	22.8	21.1
Textile mills	58.1	54.1	51.4
Knitting mills	17.7	14.8	20.8
Clothing	16.2	14.1	12.2
Wood industries	21.0	19.0	13.4
Furniture industries	16.2	12.0	17.4
Paper and allied industries	41.5	35.3	25.6
Printing, publishing, and allied industries	11.2	11.5	12.4
Primary metals	14.0	13.4	15.4
Metal fabricating	40.1	34.5	30.7
Machinery	64.0	51.7	47.7
Transport equipment	76.9	70.7	73.0
Electrical products	69.0	53.9	50.9
Nonmetallic mineral products	70.0	70.4	70.9
Petroleum and coal products	92.3	69.8	60.6
Chemicals and chemical products	67.2	77.4	70.9
Miscellaneous manufacturing	48.0	42.9	39.0
Total manufacturing	53.8	47.6	44.5
Construction	11.7	10.0	9.6
Utilities:			
Transportation	12.2	7.3	4.2
Storage	6.4	5.2	5.8
Communication	14.3	13.0	12.9
Public utilities	2.1	0.3	0.3
Total utilities	7.3	4.5	3.5
Wholesale trade	26.1	24.0	21.6
Retail trade	15.6	13.0	12.9
Services	17.4	14.6	15.4
Total nonfinancial industries	30.4	27.3	24.3

SOURCE   Statistics Canada, Corporations and Labour Returns Act, *Annual Report* (1978): 147; (1980): 149; (1986): 149. Reprinted by permission.

THE DEVELOPMENT OF MULTINATIONALS

Modern communications systems and jet travel have been a powerful incentive for the development of MNCs since World War II. With increasingly sophisticated technology and information about people in foreign lands, organizations began to think about the possibility of conducting business beyond the borders of their home countries.

The first MNC established with a global orientation grew out of a merger in 1929 between Margarine Unie, a Dutch firm, and Lever Brothers, a British company. The company became Unilever, and it has since become one of the largest companies in the world, with approximately 500 subsidiaries operating in about 60 nations. Unilever even has two headquarters, one located in Rotterdam and the other in London.

Multinationals usually operate through subsidiary companies in countries outside their home nation. Some of the names of the largest multinationals have become household words; these include General Motors, Ford, IBM, General Electric, Gulf Oil, and Exxon. The worldwide impact of these companies is very significant. Their operations create interrelationships among countries and cultures, as well as among economic and political systems.

The economic output of MNCs contributes a major portion of the total economic output of the world. Some economists have estimated that by the year 2000, about 200 to 300 multinationals will account for half of the world's total output of goods and services. In recent years, there has been a rapid growth of direct investment by multinational firms averaging about 10 percent per year. MNCs based in the United States account for more than half of this worldwide investment.

MANAGEMENT IN PRACTICE

Connaught Labs Goes Multinational

Connaught Laboratories at the University of Toronto is where insulin was first produced in quantity in 1923. The lab continues to be very active, and sales in 1983 were nearly $70 million. The goal is to boost sales to $200 million by 1989; this objective is to be met by expanding into the international market with several new products.

As part of its international expansion strategy, Connaught has entered into joint ventures with firms in Denmark and the United States. The international game is rough because the competitors in it are so big. All of them have sales in excess of $1 billion, and their research and development budgets are in the $100 million to $300 million per year category. No Canadian firm can match these figures.

With this kind of competition, Connaught Labs must carefully pick the niche where it can profitably operate. It must also get involved in joint ventures which will allow it to acquire the kind of technology needed to compete on an international basis.

SOURCE Adapted from Elizabeth Highstead, "Connaught Goes Multinational," *Financial Post* (April 14, 1984): 28.

FACTORS AFFECTING THE
MANAGEMENT OF MULTINATIONALS

Companies that conduct business in only one geographic region have relatively few problems understanding their external environment. However, the MNC, because it operates in many different countries, may find management of its activities is enormously complicated. MNCs face a staggering array of economic, cultural, and political issues. It is difficult for individuals or entire firms to be knowledgeable in all of these areas, but the external environment must be studied or the firm can find itself in major difficulties. During the past decade, many stories have appeared in newspapers indicating how MNCs angered people in host countries by behaving in a way that was considered inappropriate or insulting to the people in the host country. North American business styles are not universal, as we noted in Chapter 12. On a more subtle level, managers in MNCs must know how to conduct themselves in their day-to-day business dealings or they will not be successful in a host country.

In this section we examine the important external and internal factors that influence the management of MNCs. Included are the corporate objectives, technology, structure, and personnel practices of the MNC, as well as its external environment. The success or failure of the MNC is determined largely by how it responds to its external environment. As portrayed in Figure 19-1, the MNC must deal with the environment not only of the **parent country** (location of headquarters) but of all **host countries** (location of operational units) as well. As with small businesses, most of the external environment problems can be summarized as: (1) economic, (2) political/legal, and (3) social. As shown in Figure 19-1, an MNC's external environment is characterized by great complexity, variety, and uncertainty. Such a situation requires that managers develop sophisticated skills to deal effectively with this environment.

parent country

host countries

Economic Factors

The economic factors of the external environments of the various host countries is of prime importance to the management of multinational companies. A number of crucial questions must be answered:

- What are the income levels, growth trends, inflation rates, balance of payments, gross national product, and the number and nature of economic institutions in the host country?
- Is there a local banking and financial resource that can be tapped?
- Are there organized labor unions, planning agencies, and the necessary service structures for power, water, housing, and communication?
- How politically stable is the country, and how stable is its currency?

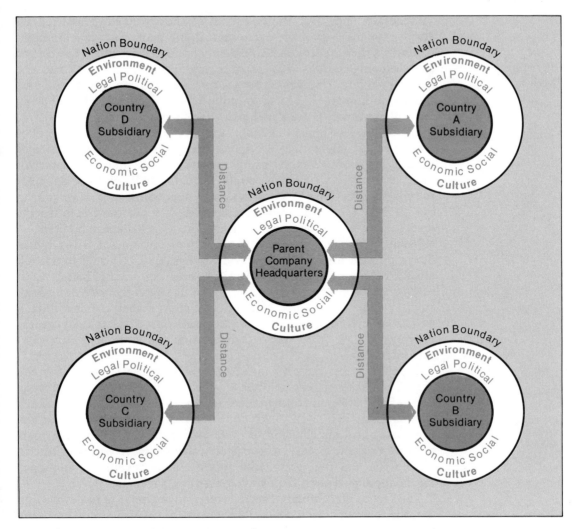

FIGURE 19-1   The multienvironments of MNCs

SOURCE   Edwin B. Flippo and Gary M. Munsinger, *Management*, 4th ed. (Boston: Allyn and Bacon, 1978): 583. Reprinted by permission.

A major economic issue that affects multinationals is the stability of the host country's currency. Many different events (for example, a change in governments, a war, or economic difficulties) can cause the currency to fluctuate and this may reduce the MNC's ability to extract profits from the host country. MNCs must constantly assess the prospects for the host country's currency or they may experience large losses as the currency is exchanged for that of the home country. In 1976, for example, the Canadian dollar was on a par with the US dollar, but since that time it has dropped to US $0.75. This difference affects both Canadian firms doing business in the United States and American firms doing business in Canada.

developing
nations

Generally speaking, the countries of the world are classified according to their level of technological and economic development. Countries that are less technologically advanced are often referred to as **developing nations**. This term is now replacing Third World as a descriptive label. However, both terms are laden with implied value judgments and ethnocentric connotations. (For lack of a better term, we will continue to use *developing nation* in this text.)

Developing nations are generally characterized by a lower level of technological sophistication and a correspondingly lower level of output per person. As well, there is usually an unequal distribution of income, with very few rich people, a small middle class, and a great number of poor. The MNC provides an opportunity for a fast start in building the economies of such countries. The objective is to reach a level where the economy can grow on a self-sustaining basis. A substantial percentage of the MNC's total investment is located in developing nations. Often, the country has strong feelings of nationalism. Although it needs the MNC to exploit its natural resources, it often perceives the MNCs as a threat to its sovereignty. When a host country feels that it has effected sufficient transfer of skills in a particular technology, it might expropriate or confiscate the business organization. An MNC must consider this risk in making an investment decision.

Experts in the field of multinational business suggest that the degree of risk is increasing. One group predicts that some developing nations will attempt to form resource-based cartels like OPEC. They also say that they will make continued attempts to take over the processing and distribution of their own resources, even where cartels do not exist. Finally, it is expected that pressure will continue to renegotiate existing agreements because many developing countries are disappointed with the experiences they have had.[3]

The fact that so much of total foreign investment is in developing nations is evidence that possible returns are worth the risk. If the most important resources of a multinational are technological and managerial skills, rather than property and goods, some companies can reduce the risk of expropriation or host country take-overs by one or more of the following means: (1) licensing agreements, (2) contracts to manage host country-owned installations, and (3) turnkey operations — constructing and developing the unit to the point where the key of ownership can be turned over to nationals of the host country. It is far more difficult to expropriate people skills than property. There are also far fewer conflicts of interest between this type of MNC and the various countries in which it operates.

Political/Legal Factors

MNCs operate in an environment with a variety of political factors. We have already noted host country nationalism. Perhaps the most important aspect that MNCs look for is political stability.[4] Without it, the conduct of business becomes very risky. Since so many countries gained independence only in the 1960s and 1970s, there remains much concern about political stability in those areas.

Analyses of the political factors in the MNC's external environment increasingly take into account how competing political philosophies or social unrest in a host country may affect the conduct of business. There have been numerous instances of terrorism and the kidnapping of multinational executives in some parts of the world, and these dramatically increase the stress levels of executives working in those areas. For example, a Goodyear Tire and Rubber executive was held hostage and then murdered in Guatemala. Some executives are reluctant to accept assignments in certain parts of the world because of these threats to their security.

Because there is no comprehensive system of international law or courts, the MNC must become acquainted in detail with the laws of each host-country. The United States, England, Canada, Australia, and New Zealand have developed their legal requirements by means of English common law; judges and courts are extremely important, for they are guided by principles declared in previous cases. In most of continental Europe, Asia, and Africa, the approach is the civil law; the judges play a lesser role because the legal requirements are codified. Civil servants or bureaucrats have greater power under the civil law than under the common law.

Regardless of their country of origin, MNC managers must take care to comply with the legal requirements of the host country. And if any laws should be contravened, the MNC must be prepared for the legal consequences. The costs of settling with victims of a lethal gas leak from the Union Carbide pesticide plant in India may bankrupt the MNC involved. These costs will undoubtedly have an impact on future class action suits regarding MNCs, as well as on safety and ecological procedures in MNC work places. In addition, managers of MNCs must be knowledgeable about:

- Laws governing profit remission to the parent country
- Import and export restrictions and investment controls
- Degree of foreign ownership permitted.

Although Canada is a highly legalistic country and MNC executives tend to carry Canadian law with them, they must realize, for instance, that the Japanese dislike laws, lawyers, and litigation. In France, lawyers are prohibited from serving on boards of directors by codes of the legal profession. The vastness and sheer complexity of varying legal systems throughout the world demonstrate quite clearly the intricate and demanding political/legal factors in the external environment of the MNCs.

Social Factors

The culture of each nation in the world is unique. Managers of MNCs are not citizens of each country they do business in; rather, they are outsiders who are trying to mobilize resources effectively, so that a profit can be made. Managers of MNCs must be very careful not to superimpose their views of the world on the host country. If the MNC is to operate in many nations, it will of necessity be required to adapt some of its managerial practices to the specific and unique situation of each nation. Attitudes will differ concerning such subjects as work, risk taking, introducing change, time, authority, and material gain. It is unwise to assume that the attitudes within the parent country will be found in all other countries.

In some nations, authority is viewed as a manager's natural right and is not questioned by subordinates. In other cultures, authority must be earned and is provided to those who have demonstrated their ability. Our western attitudes toward achievement are not universal either. It may be hard for some westerners not to pass judgment on some of these attitudinal differences. To be sure, David McClelland has discovered that the fundamental attitude toward achievement in a country correlates somewhat with rates of economic development. If a nation's citizens are willing to commit themselves to the accomplishment of tasks deemed worthwhile and difficult, a country will

---

MANAGEMENT IN PRACTICE

A Problem in International Fashions

Saul and Joseph Mimram own Monaco Group, Inc., a firm specializing in women's clothing. In 1978, Joseph Mimram met Alfred Sung, a designer. The Mimrams needed a designer, and Sung needed marketing expertise to sell his designs. So they combined their talents and went after a share of the big United States market.

They thought they had done their homework. They contacted all the key people, spent thousands of dollars preparing for the American market, and even got Saks Fifth Avenue to buy Sung's collection. Success seemed just around the corner. But they had forgotten one thing: American sizes are larger than Canadian sizes — for example, an American size 10 is a Canadian size 12. American women who had always bought a size 10 were unhappy when they had to buy a size 12. As a result, the merchandise had to be marked down a quarter of a million dollars in order to make it move.

The story has a happy ending, however. The owners quickly adjusted their sizes to fit the American market. The strategy paid off in Canada, too, because Canadian women like buying a size smaller. Everyone is happy. By the end of 1984, sales for Monaco Group Inc. were soaring, with 40 percent of the total coming from the American market.

SOURCE Adapted from Patrick Pardoe, "Selling Alfred Sung," *Canadian Business* (July 1984): 23–24.

benefit economically. As previously discussed in Chapter 11, McClelland contends that the achievement motive can be taught.[5] However, managers should be aware of the reasons for the apparent lack of motivation of some workers. Certainly, cultural beliefs concerning an individual's ability to influence the future will have an impact on the behavior of a company's work force. If the basic belief is fatalistic — what will be, will be — then the importance of planning and organizing for the future is downgraded. Cultures also vary as to interclass mobility and sources of status. If there is little hope of moving up to higher classes in a society, then fatalism and an absence of a drive for achievement are likely.

In many instances, the MNC managers will have to adapt and conform to the requirements of the local culture. A multinational must introduce new technology and skills into a host nation's culture if economic development is to occur. Some changes proposed are revolutionary. There must be one common language and system of measurements when communicating between a subsidiary and its headquarters. English and French are currently the two most commonly chosen MNC languages. Despite the slowness of Canada and the United States to adapt, the metric system will be the common method of measurement.

This brief review of the differences in the economic, political/legal, and social factors of the external environments of MNCs serves to highlight the enormous complexity of the task of managing an MNC. It is apparent that sophisticated approaches to managing are necessary.

Objectives of the Multinational

In some ways, the objectives of multinational companies are not any different from the objectives of businesses operating exclusively within Canada. The typical goals of survival, profit, and growth are indeed similar. An MNC seeks to produce and distribute products and services throughout the world in return for a satisfactory profit. It seeks to survive and grow by maintaining its technological advantages and minimizing risks. However, the MNC differs from the domestic firm because of the potential clash of its goals with the objectives of the economic and political systems of the host countries within which each operates. Some of the objectives of countries may coincide with the objectives of the MNC and some may not. Most countries want improved standards of living for their people, as well as, for instance, a trained labor force, full employment, reasonable price stability, a favorable balance of payments, and steady economic growth. Canadians, too, have had numerous debates about the advantages and disadvantages of MNCs operating in Canada.

In some of these goals, the interests of the MNC and the host country will overlap. (See Figure 19-2.) For example, a new MNC in

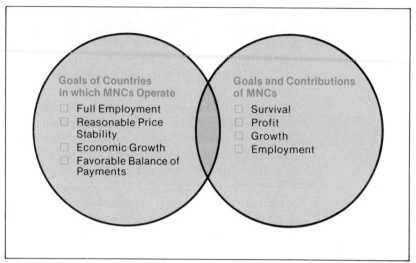

FIGURE 19-2   Overlapping interest of MNC and host countries

a country will usually create jobs, thereby contributing to a higher level of employment, increased income, and economic growth. Inviting MNCs in often provides an escape for political leaders accused of having contributed to unemployment in their countries.[6] While the company contributes to the accomplishment of these goals, it may not do so at the rate expected by the host country.

MANAGEMENT IN PRACTICE

The Impact of International Events on Canadian Business

An example of how international events can affect Canadian business is evident in the agricultural sector. Over the last decade, the European Community (EC) has heavily subsidized its farmers in order to increase food exports. The US has reacted strongly to this challenge and passed the Food Security Act in an attempt to regain its historical dominance.

The US is spending $25 billion a year to subsidize food exports. However, the EC has responded with additional subsidies and a price war has developed. The net effect of this stalemate is to drive grain prices way down.

The price of grain and oilseeds, for example, fell 30 percent during the last half of 1986. If the trend continues, farm incomes in Canada will decline substantially. The outlook is particularly bad on the Prairies, where farm incomes in Manitoba and Alberta may fall as much as 50 percent. Canada is unable to protect itself from this kind of action because the EC and the US are apparently too big to influence.

SOURCE   Adapted from Oliver Bertin, "US Policies Bedevil Canadian Farmers," *The Globe and Mail* (December 22, 1986): B1.

In the pursuit of some objectives, there will be conflicts of interest. A multinational may close a plant in one country to streamline its worldwide production facilities. Considerable controversy can arise when an MNC increases its international activities, but decreases its activities in the home country of the company. For example, when Inco announced it would reduce the output of its Canadian operations and increase the output of its foreign mines, there was much concern in Canada about unemployment for Inco's Canadian workers. Or, a company may subsidize a beginning assembly operation in Country A by underpricing component parts produced in Country B. In effect, Country B's economy is required to make a sacrifice to enable the plant in Country A to get started.

If the MNC is to achieve its return-on-investment objective, some portion of subsidiary earnings must be returned to headquarters in the parent country. This arrangement could adversely affect the host country's balance of payments, particularly if the subsidiary unit does not export its products. Funds may also be shuffled among various countries so that profits are maximized in countries having the most stable political systems and the lowest tax rates.

Some of the complaints various countries have regarding multinationals are that MNCs:

- Restrict or allocate markets among subsidiaries and do not allow manufacturing subsidiaries to develop export markets
- Extract excessive profits and fees because of their monopolistic advantages
- Enter the market by taking over existing local firms rather than developing new productive investments
- Finance their entry mainly through local debt and maintain a majority of the equity with the parent company
- Divert local savings away from productive investments by nationals, hire away the most talented personnel, and exhaust resources of the host country
- Restrict access to modern technology by centralizing research facilities in the home country and by licensing subsidiaries to use only existing or even outmoded technologies
- Restrict the learning-by-doing process by staffing key technical and managerial positions with managers from the home country
- Fail to do enough in the way of training and development of host country personnel
- Ignore the host country's social customs or frustrate the objectives of the host country's economic planning
- Contribute to price inflation
- Dominate key industrial sectors
- Answer to a foreign government
- Undermine the host country's culture by operating according to standards developed in other countries.[7]

In response to such complaints as these, many countries have moved toward applying restrictions upon the operations of multinationals. For example, one of the guidelines in the Andean Common

MANAGEMENT IN PRACTICE

Doing Business in China

The People's Republic of China, with one-quarter of the world's population, is viewed with great enthusiasm by business firms wishing to tap that immense market. But there are monumental problems for Canadian firms wishing to do business in China.

In 1983, there were 10 Canadian business firms, four banks, and three media bureaus with business offices in China. Unfortunately, commercial transactions are few, bureaucratic red tape is excessive, prices are outrageous, and air pollution is bad. Patience is the main characteristic that a Canadian firm must possess to be successful. For example, if a company wants to set up a joint venture in oil exploration, it must deal with several different organizations, including the China National Oil Corporation, the Ministry of Petroleum Industry, the Ministry of Foreign Relations and Trade, and the

Bank of China. Identifying the individual in these organizations who actually makes the approval decision can be quite difficult.

Business expenses are also very high in China. Massey-Ferguson Ltd. pays $3500 per month for a small, one-room office in the Peking Hotel. The Bank of Montreal pays $8400 per month for a two-room office at the Jianguo Hotel. The changes Canadian managers must make to their personal lives also leave something to be desired. Executives know that in a police state they must be careful about what they say; Jianguo Hotel residents are told that the hotel cannot guarantee that their rooms are not bugged.

SOURCE Adapted from Gayle Herchak, "Behind the Bamboo Curtain: The Awful Truth about Doing Business in China," *Canadian Business* (August 1983): 15–16.

Market (Bolivia, Chile, Colombia, Ecuador, and Peru) is that 51 percent of the stock in manufacturing subsidiaries should be held by nationals of the host country within 15 to 20 years of start-up. When extremely discontented with the MNC or in response to a rising tide of nationalism, subsidiaries may be expropriated or confiscated by the host country. France gained control over its telephone system by purchasing a controlling interest from International Telephone & Telegraph Corporation of the United States and Sweden's L. M. Ericsson Group.[8] In other instances, the host country has seized the subsidiary unit without compensation.

Although the host has power as a result of national sovereignty, the multinational is not helpless. Its power lies in its ability to grant or withhold needed economic resources and technological knowledge. Other MNCs will observe the kind of treatment given MNCs by the host country, and this treatment may influence whether or not they invest in that country. Should the host country have enterprises with investments in the parent country, retaliation can be threatened. If the parent country provides foreign economic aid, this can also be used as leverage in promoting equitable treatment for the MNC subsidiary.

In most instances, the economic power of the MNC and the political power of the host country will lead to accommodations whereby both parties can achieve some of their goals. Host country governments realize, for example, that the intense emotions of national sovereignty exhibited by some of their citizens do not always coincide with long-term national interests. For their part, MNCs will have to alter objectives to suit the requirements of the host country if operations are to be conducted there. If such requirements do excessive damage to global objectives, the MNC may choose to conduct its business elsewhere in the world.

To head off an effort by some developing countries to establish, through the United Nations, a tough set of restrictions on MNCs, the governments of 24 developed, noncommunist nations have proposed a code of ethics. Important aspects of the code of ethics are:

- MNCs are not to meddle in the political processes of the countries in which they operate.
- No bribes are permissible under any conditions.
- No donations to political parties are proper unless national laws allow them.
- MNCs should make full disclosure of local sales and profits, number of employees, and expenditures for research and development for major regions of the world.
- MNCs should refrain from participating in cartels and avoid "predatory behavior toward competitors."
- The proper amount of taxes in the countries in which they are earned should be paid. One should not seek to avoid taxes by switching money from high-tax to low-tax countries.
- MNCs should respect the right of their employees to organize into unions.[9]

Technology and Multinationals

Technological expertise is the primary advantage of the multinational enterprise. Many of the MNCs operate in such high-technology industries as oil, computers, pharmaceuticals, electronics, and motor vehicle manufacturing. There are fewer MNCs in such fields as cotton, textiles, and cement. It is the technological gap in other nations that provides the opportunity for the MNC to transfer high technology from the parent country. The simpler industries are likely to be developed by each country for itself.

The more important the economies of scale to be derived from a particular technology, the greater the opportunity for an MNC to transfer knowledge to other countries: If the market size of a particular country is not such that it can absorb the output of an advanced economic unit, then many nations must be interlocked. MNCs in many small European countries started before those in Canada and the United States for just this reason. The development of the European Economic Community constitutes an attempt to develop a wide market area.

Bernard Lamarre
Lavalin Inc.

In Canadian business, sadly, the two solitudes still exist. Until recently, few English-speaking Canadian executives knew of the existence, let alone the startling business skills and success, of Bernard Lamarre, chairman, president, chief executive and largest of four shareholders of Montreal-based Lavalin Inc., one of the biggest consulting engineering firms in the country.

Lavalin and its 40 divisions and affiliates are currently working on engineering projects worth about $3 billion in 56 countries. That includes work handled through its 25 Canadian offices, which supply about half of the firm's total fees. It lists its special strengths as mass-transportation systems, power generation and transmission, petroleum-product processing facilities, telecommunications, large mining complexes and public works. But the company, started by Lamarre's father-in-law, can and does handle just about everything in engineering. Total revenue in 1984 was about 15 percent higher than in 1983 at

$575 million, generated by 5000 employees. About $280 million of that is the result of the company's overseas assignments.

Q: Can you explain the reasons for Lavalin's overseas success?

Lamarre: In any country, you first have to find out who makes the contract decisions — and that's not an easy task. It might be a minister, a tribal chief, or a chief engineer. It always takes three or four years before you identify contracts that suit your specializations, and before you are identified by the people making decisions.

We started in French Africa, a natural hunting ground for us because of language. In one very small country there, Benin (it used to be Dahomey), we have been working continually since 1967. It's a very, very poor country but all the contracts are financed by international organizations such as the World Bank.

We expanded in West Africa, then went to North Africa, and then into English-speaking Africa. When we knew how to sell our services there, we started to sell in Latin America, and then Asia. We have 20 offices in 16 countries, each with somebody from Canada who knows exactly what we can do. In Asia, we have permanent representatives in Indonesia, Malaysia, the Philippines, and Singapore. And we are just starting in China.

It costs about $300 000 a year to start in any country so it usually costs $1 million before we get our first contract. At the beginning, when we were just getting small fees for small projects, that was an important investment for us. Now we have about $80 million a year in overseas consulting fees and about $200 million in construction.

We haven't stuck to one area of expertise. In Algeria, for example, we are doing mostly building construction. In Nigeria we are doing water wells all over the country. In Kenya we are mostly in oil and gas. In Cameroon it's roads and water-treatment plants. In Indonesia we are involved in a transmigration project, taking an island that has never been inhabited and putting in an infrastructure so farmers and others can be sent in to relieve congestion elsewhere.

Q: When you put it all together, are the margins sufficiently higher than what you'd earn in North America to justify the effort?

Lamarre: I wish that were true, but it's really more profitable to work here in Canada. However, because it's a cyclical business, we fill in the downside through business elsewhere. Moreover, it's very difficult to structure a good team, and when you have one you don't want to lose it.

In Canada in 1982-83 there was a very deep crisis in engineering. For the first time in my business career, I saw contracts cancelled or suspended after we had already started them. Until then, you would not get new contracts when there was a slowdown, but at least you'd complete those you already had. Before 1982 we were doing 85 percent of our business in Canada. Now it's about half and half.

Q: Canadian businessmen have been criticized for years for not getting out and hustling on the world scene. Is that still true?

Lamarre: Canadians have always been out there because Canada has had to trade to survive. In the past, however, we had big corporations like Alcan and the pulp and paper companies selling outside of the country. In those days engineering and other aspects of industry were not exporting much. So this is a new phenomenon. We are selling very hard now because we have realized that we have to do that to survive.

Q: How important is bribery in Third World business? How do you cope with that?

Lamarre: I cannot say we have a problem. There are countries, such as Saudi Arabia, where by law you have to give a local agent a commission. That's not bribery, it's the law. On the other hand, in Algeria, for example, that sort of thing is completely forbidden. If you do something wrong there, you'll be kicked out of the country. Then there are the in-betweens.

It has not been a problem for us. I'm not saying that we don't pay some local agents sometimes, but when we do it's a commission. We receive a bill and we pay. There is no cash under the table because cash is very hard to get. About 25 years ago you could get a lot of cash, but now it's very difficult.

It is all watched very carefully. When we are putting in financing with the Export Development Corp., for example, or the World Bank, they're also looking at what we are doing. The only problem we might have is in Latin America. There's always a local consultant who gets 50 percent of the fees although he doesn't do much. But it's understandable. The governments want their people to be able to

transfer technology. That's a far bigger problem than the one you were mentioning. We have worked in Africa for a long time and bribery has never been a problem. That doesn't mean you don't have to send a Christmas gift sometimes, but it's reasonable — a book or something of that sort.

Q: You have dozens of subsidiaries and affiliated companies and joint enterprises. How do you personally control and manage the whole structure?

Lamarre: We have profit-centered divisions and it's very rare for a division to have more than 150 people. So the president of each division knows his people. He knows exactly what he is talking about and he reports to a group vice president who will have six to eight divisions. The group vice presidents report to me. It is very easily managed.

Q: What's your personal role in this?

Lamarre: Marketing and monitoring. As chief executive my role is to establish the company's policies; to look after the corporate position of a new division when we want to extend technologically or geographically; to monitor the policies of our clients; to check on the profitability of all these areas; to get after my group vice presidents when I sense that one of the divisions is not doing as well as it should. We have a good corporate financial reporting system. We see any trends in time for something to be done.

Q: You're a professional engineer. Is that a particularly suitable background for the chief executive of a major corporation?

Lamarre: I've never asked myself that. I've always liked what I've done. To run an engineering construction firm you have to know engineering and you have to know construction. My father was an engineer, a contractor. My grandfather was a contractor. My great grandfather was a contractor. So I've been talking about engineering all my life.

Q: You don't miss being out on the construction site?

Lamarre: I often go out on the construction site. Sometimes on Sundays I visit sites. When my family was younger we'd visit sites every Saturday or Sunday for fun, and at the same time I'd be taking notes. I'm still very much aware of what's going on. I'm not there all the time but enough to be able to know where we are, how the job is coming.

MANAGEMENT IN PRACTICE

International Business Activity at LeBlanc & Royle

George Patton is president of LeBlanc & Royle Communications Ltd., an Oakville, Ontario multinational company which builds communications towers. The company has an outstanding record for quickly reconstructing towers that have fallen down because of ice storms or vandalism. Since 1974, 49 towers have fallen in Canada alone, and LeBlanc & Royle has reconstructed 47 of them.

The company's success in the international market is based partly on the needs of developing nations for microwave towers to intercept satellite transmissions. But there are many unexpected costs which are incurred when a Canadian company goes international. For example, distance can create big problems. When LeBlanc & Royle was constructing communications towers in Rwanda, Africa, a small engineering error was discovered that necessitated the shipment of reworked parts to the site. This would have presented no problem in Canada, but it took three weeks to get the parts to the site in Africa. While the workers were waiting for the parts, they ran up a bill of $25 per person per day for drinking water. That simple error ate up most of the profit on the job.

SOURCE Adapted from Mike Macbeth, "Towering Triumph," *Canadian Business* (October 1983): 64–65.

The situation existing within a country will dictate the nature of the technology required to accomplish the work. There are a wide range of external environment factors, objectives, and technologies that preclude any significant general statements that would apply to all multinationals. It should be noted, however, that the strength of most MNCs lies in their ability to operate highly complex technologies.

Multinational Organizational Structures

The organizational structure of a multinational firm must be designed to meet its international needs. Normally the first effort of a firm to become a multinational is the creation of an export unit in the domestic marketing department. At some point, the firm may perceive the necessity of locating manufacturing units abroad. After a time, these various foreign units are grouped into an international division.

The international division then becomes a profit center with status equal to other major domestic divisions. It is typically headed by a vice-president and operates on a fairly autonomous basis from the domestic operations. The reasons for this approach are: (1) the necessity of obtaining managerial and technical expertise in the diverse external environments of many countries, and (2) the reduction of control from the often larger domestic divisions. Of course, this approach to organization has the disadvantage of decreased coordination and cohesion of the international division with the rest of the company.[10]

As the international division grows, it usually becomes organized on either a geographical or product base of specialization. In giant MNCs the international division is often a transitional stage in moving toward a worldwide structure that discounts the importance of national boundaries. As portrayed in Figures 19-3, 19-4, and 19-5, any such global structure requires a careful balance of three types of specialization: functional, geographical, and product. When the primary base is any one of the three, the other two must be present in the form of specialized staff experts or coordinators. A clear-cut decision that is heavily in favor of any one base is usually inappropriate.

Figure 19-3 illustrates a global-functional organizational structure for a multinational. The executive in charge of the production function has a worldwide responsibility. Together with the presidents and executives in charge of sales and finance, a small group of managers enables worldwide centralized control of the MNC to be maintained.

MNCs with widely diversified product lines requiring a sophisticated technology to produce and distribute tend to use the area base in their global structures. This form is shown in Figure 19-4. During the 1960s, General Electric adopted this structure. Four regional managers were established in Europe, Canada, Latin America, and the rest of the world. These executives were General Electric's eyes and ears in the countries assigned. They advised on the most suitable

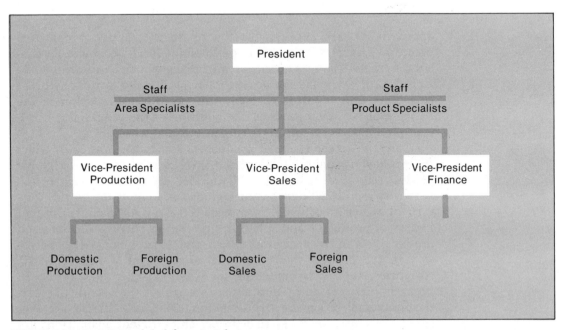

FIGURE 19-3 MNC global-functional structure

SOURCE Edwin B. Flippo and Gary M. Munsinger, *Management*, 4th ed. (Boston: Allyn and Bacon, 1978): 588. Reprinted by permission.

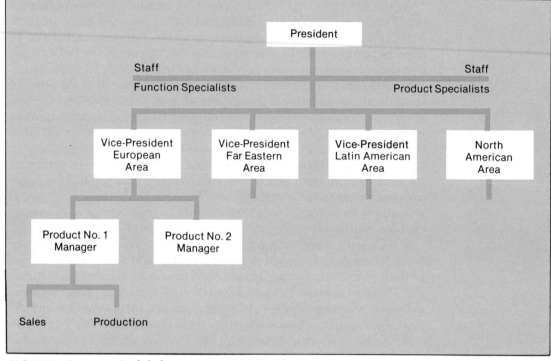

FIGURE 19-4   MNC global-area structure

SOURCE   Edwin B. Flippo and Gary M. Munsinger, *Management*, 4th ed. (Boston: Allyn and Bacon, 1978): 588. Reprinted by permission.

approach in each country for the product executives, identified potential partners, and aided in establishing locally oriented personnel programs. The area executive might be given line authority when a product division had not yet sufficient skill in the region or when a subsidiary unit reported to many product divisions. Although the basic emphasis is on product, the addition of the geographical concept produced a type of matrix organizational structure.

Finally, when the range of products is somewhat limited or when the product is highly standardized, MNCs tend to use the global product structure, as shown in Figure 19-5. Executives with true line authority are placed over major regions throughout the world. This type of structure is used by international oil companies (limited variety of products) and soft-drink producers (highly standardized product). As in the other instances, some supporting staff is necessary in the product and functional areas. In all forms of MNC structures, top management makes sure: (1) that the product is properly managed and coordinated throughout the world; (2) that the functional processes of production, sales, and finance are executed efficiently; and (3) that proper and efficient adaptations are made in response to the external environments in the host countries.

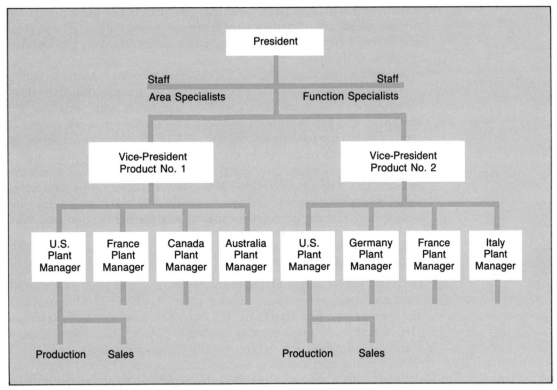

President

Staff
Area Specialists

Staff
Function Specialists

Vice-President
Product No. 1

Vice-President
Product No. 2

| U.S. Plant Manager | France Plant Manager | Canada Plant Manager | Australia Plant Manager | U.S. Plant Manager | Germany Plant Manager | France Plant Manager | Italy Plant Manager |

Production   Sales

Production   Sales

FIGURE 19-5   MNC global-product structure

SOURCE   Edwin B. Flippo and Gary M. Munsinger, *Management*, 4th ed. (Boston: Allyn and Bacon, 1978): 588. Reprinted by permission.

Personnel Management in Multinationals

Successful management of an MNC requires that the manager understand the needs, values, and problems of personnel in the countries where the company operates. But a study of 300 managers in 14 countries found that parent country managers had a low opinion of their subordinates' ability to take an active role in the management process.[11] Management must recognize that there is no one style of leadership that will be equally effective in all countries. People in the various countries will have widely divergent backgrounds, education, cultures, languages, and religions and live within a variety of social conditions and economic and political systems. All of these factors must be considered by managers because they can have a dramatic effect on work atmosphere and performance.

The requirements for effective leadership of personnel in Canada, the United States, Great Britain, Australia, or many western European countries differ significantly from those in such countries as Turkey, Mexico, Malaysia, Taiwan, Thailand, or certain African,

Asian, or Latin American countries. Research has shown that the needs and values of people vary from nation to nation. These often result from differences in economic living standards, or cultural or religious influences.

As we discussed in Chapter 10, unsatisfied needs motivate behavior. In Canada and other developed countries, people's basic needs — physiological, security, and social — are fairly well satisfied. Research on the application of Maslow's hierarchy of needs theory of human behavior has shown considerable differences concerning the dominant needs of people in different countries. So, in some developed countries, managers must try to satisfy employee needs for esteem and self-actualization. However, in developing countries, appeals to physiological and safety needs may prove to be not only appropriate but the primary means for motivating desired behavior.

Types of MNC Employees

parent country
nationals

host country
nationals

third country
nationals

In filling key managerial, technical or professional positions abroad, multinationals can choose among three basic types of personnel: (1) **parent country nationals** (PCN), (2) **host country nationals** (HCN), and (3) **third country nationals** (TCN). Until the 1950s, it was very common for MNCs to fill their key foreign posts with trusted and experienced personnel from home (PCNs). Recently, stronger nationalistic feelings have led countries to alter their policies and require MNCs to employ more people from host countries (HCNs). Some firms have used personnel from countries other than the parent country or host country. Such personnel are known as third country nationals (TCNs); for example, a Canadian firm might build a highway in Saudi Arabia using personnel from Turkey and Italy. Still, many companies attempt to keep parent country personnel in at least half of the identified key positions, particularly in the financial function.

Using personnel from the parent nation of the multinational ensures a greater degree of consistency and control in the firm's operations around the world. This policy is not without its costs because these personnel may experience considerable difficulty with linguistic and cultural differences. In an attitude survey of personnel in 49 multinationals, personnel from the host country contended that parent country personnel tended not to question orders from headquarters even when appropriate to do so.[12] This enabled them to advance their own long-term interests in the firm by getting better headquarter evaluations and facilitating repatriation at the end of their tour of duty. In addition, the common practice of frequent rotation of key personnel intensified the problem of understanding and adapting to local cultures. However, employing the PCN can facilitate communications with headquarters because both parties are likely of the same country and language.

Utilizing personnel from the host country in key positions will improve the MNC's relations with the host country government. It will also enable a quicker and more accurate adaptation to requirements of the local culture. Disadvantages include a lessened degree of central control and increased communication problems with headquarters. In addition, if the HCNs perceive that the opportunity for higher positions is blocked for ethnic reasons, they will use the MNC to gain experience so they may transfer to higher positions in local national firms.

Personnel Problems in MNCs

One of the most difficult personnel problems for multinationals is that of selecting the appropriate people to be sent on foreign assignments. Careful plans should be made to assure that selectees possess certain basic characteristics, among them:

- A very real desire to work in a foreign country
- Spouses and families who have actively encouraged the person to work overseas or are willing to accompany him or her
- Cultural sensitivity and flexibility
- A high degree of technical competence
- A sense for politics.

MANAGEMENT IN PRACTICE

Briefing Employees on Overseas Assignments

When Canadian workers get an overseas posting, they can run into considerable difficulty if they are unprepared for the significant cultural differences they encounter. One Christian couple stationed in Saudi Arabia experienced problems when they advertised a prayer meeting in their home. The Saudi government promptly requested that they be sent home. A consulting engineer working in Africa demanded to be sent back to head office because he didn't like the fact that his children, who were the only white students in the local school, were being teased by the local children.

Difficulties like this caused Kim Harker and Michael Miner to form International Briefing Associates (IBA), a Vancouver-based firm which specializes in offering informational seminars to people who are going overseas. They believe that situations like those noted above can be avoided if the transferred employee knows what to expect. They point out that it costs the typical company approximately $150 000 to send someone overseas, so the firm should be concerned about properly preparing people to take up foreign posts.

Harker and Miner got the idea for the company while they were working in Indonesia for Canada World Youth. They saw the frustration and depression some Canadians experienced after the euphoria of their foreign posting wore off. IBA had first year sales of $35 000, and by 1984 it had 500 course participants and sales of $400 000. Increasingly, companies are becoming convinced of the need to do the kind of training IBA offers before sending employees to foreign countries.

SOURCE Adapted from Anne Templeman-Kluit, "IBA's Briefings Help Make Foreign Jobs Fun", *Canadian Business* (January, 1985): 141–142.

Several surveys of overseas managers have revealed that the spouse's opinion and attitude should be considered the number one screening factor. Cultural sensitivity is also essential.

A second major problem that confronts MNCs is the establishment of equitable compensation systems for personnel given international assignments. Typically, personnel from the parent country receive a salary plus an overseas premium of up to 50 percent plus moving expense allowances and certain living allowances. Personnel from the parent country of the MNC receive a higher pay than personnel employed from the local country. This imbalance can create resentment and reduce cooperation. Many MNC managers have found their standard of living and social status to be considerably improved in foreign countries, so that they may experience some difficulties when they return to Canada. In addition to financial rewards, the foreign assignment usually provides career advancement opportunities.

Despite the company's intention to provide career advancement opportunities, there is still some danger that skilled personnel will come to feel that their career progress has suffered by leaving their home country. Some personnel have returned from foreign assignments to find no job available or a job that does not utilize skills obtained during the overseas service. To solve this problem, some **repatriation plan** companies develop a **repatriation plan** that includes a statement about the duration of the assignment and what job the appointee will do on his or her return. During the assignment, the individual is kept informed of major ongoing events occurring in the unit of future assignment. In this way, not only is there a logical career plan worked out, the person overseas does not feel lost in the vast international shuffle of the company.

The chief executive officer of each foreign subsidiary is confronted by the opposing flows of corporate uniformity and cultural fragmentation. If the officer is from the parent country, uniformity is likely to be emphasized. If the manager is from the host country, cultural adaptation may take precedence. Because of growing nationalistic tendencies of many countries, there is an increased chance that the top manager will be from the host country. Each of these host countries has a particular view of what constitutes a good chief executive officer. In Germany, for instance, the chief executive officer must have an engineering degree to be accepted and respected. In France, graduates of the Grandes Écoles are favored. If third country nationals are to be used as chief executive officers, varying mobilities must also be considered. A married Frenchperson living in Paris is almost unmovable. However, German managers are often quite enthusiastic about working in other countries. The English and Scandinavians are typically willing to relocate, but they usually require assurance of return to their native lands.

Adaptation is not all one way. Local nationals will usually make an effort to understand and adapt to the culture of the MNC, which inevitably requires some understanding of the culture of the parent country of the MNC. This learning, too, will require considerable effort and time. In dealing with executives from headquarters of Canadian MNCs, the local national should learn to get to the point quickly because North Americans are notoriously impatient with lengthy and detailed explanations. Nationals must be positive in their approach, and they should avoid constantly criticizing. They must also learn to question Canadian executives, but know just how far they can go. For their part, Canadian managers should foster understanding and cooperation to help local nationals.

Effective managers of multinational operations must develop a style of leadership consistent with the needs of the situation existing in the host country. The appropriate style of leadership can be determined only after a careful assessment is made of the external environment of the host country, the type of personnel to be managed, the level of existing technology, and the specific goals and operational requirements of the company.

A FINAL WORD ON MULTINATIONALS

Academic research has not kept pace with internationalization of industry.[13] Much that is said concerning the appropriate management approach for international businesses must therefore be based on common sense and informed conjecture. It seems reasonable that a successful international manager should possess the following qualities, among others:

- A knowledge of basic history, particularly in countries of old and homogeneous cultures
- A social background in basic economics and sociological concepts as they differ from country to country
- An interest in the host country and a willingness to learn and practice the language
- A genuine respect for differing philosophical and ethical approaches.

The multinational company is faced of necessity with a wide variety of situations: differing cultures, economic and political systems, and religions. Management must capitalize on its unique strength of being able to make worldwide decisions in the selection of markets and the allocation of resources. Yet each market has different environmental constraints. Thus, multinational managers must adapt to and work with the varying cultures of a multiplicity of nations throughout the world.

One study showed that global-centered MNCs generally perform better than country-centered ones. Global-centered companies see the world marketing effort as an integrated set of activities. Country-centered ones follow the portfolio approach to their overseas subsidiaries, treating operations in each country as a separate investment. Global companies tend to think more in the long term. They are organized to achieve economies of scale.[14]

OPENING INCIDENT REVISITED

Canadian Implements Ltd.

In the opening incident, Dan Shelton had run into a problem when he tried to implement a troubleshooting plan by dismissing an incompetent employee. He suddenly realized that customs and rules he knew nothing about might prevent him from improving Canadian Implement's Far Eastern plant operations. Not completing this assignment will make him look less effective as a plant manager and may thwart Shelton's career aspirations.

Shelton's dilemma clearly demonstrates the kinds of difficulties Canadian managers can face when they go on a foreign assignment. These Canadian managers take with them a set of assumptions that may or may not be relevant in the country where they are assigned. The material in the chapter dealing with the economic, political, and social factors of another country's external environment demonstrates that managers must learn as much as possible about the country in which they will be working before their arrival.

In Dan Shelton's case, Canadian Implements should have provided him with information it must already have had on the cultural and political/legal factors of the Far Eastern country before he went there. However, since Shelton sees himself as a troubleshooter, he could have helped himself by finding out what kind of restrictions might affect his assignment. Failure to investigate the external environment meant that Shelton assumed that actions taken at the Hamilton plant could also be taken in the Far Eastern country.

What can Dan Shelton do now? First of all, he can rely far more heavily on his local national assistant for information that is critical to his troubleshooting plans. The assistant can tell him about any other customs, laws, rules, or regulations that will influence his plans to improve the Far Eastern facility. The assistant can also convey a sense of the culture of the country and how Shelton might proceed with his reorganization plans so that he has the greatest chance for success. Shelton is probably going to have to allow much more time to acclimatize himself and then solve this plant's problems than he had taken to help the Hamilton plant.

SUMMARY

Canada is now in the age of the multinational corporation (MNC). Few other developments have had the overall impact of multinationals, which have caused the countries of the world to become more closely related to each other. An MNC is a firm engaged in business in two or more countries. These firms typically have sales offices and sometimes manufacturing plants in many different countries. The MNCs are not only instrumental in improving the world economy and thereby standards of living of many people but also can significantly affect the technology, culture, and customs of the countries in which they operate.

The multinational corporation is the type of enterprise that provides a special challenge to managers. Effectiveness in managing an MNC requires the manager to give careful consideration to such factors as the external environment, objectives, technology, structure, and personnel. The external environment that confronts multinational enterprises consists primarily of the economic, political/legal, and social factors in the various countries in which the MNC operates. This external environment characterized by complexity, variety, and uncertainty requires that managers develop sophisticated skills to deal effectively with these conditions. Objectives of the MNC would not seem to be any different from the objectives of businesses operating exclusively within Canada. However, the MNC differs from domestic firms because of the potential clash of its goals with the objectives of the economic and political systems of the various countries within which it operates.

Technological expertise is the primary advantage of the MNC. Many MNCs operate in such high-technology industries as computers, oil, pharmaceuticals, electronics, and motor vehicles. Another major factor to be considered in managing the MNC is the organization of the firm. The organizational structure of an MNC must be designed to meet its international needs. Such a structure may differ significantly from that found in the company's domestic operations.

Successful management of an MNC requires that the manager understand the needs, values, and problems of personnel in the countries where the company operates. Management must recognize that there is no one style of leadership that will be equally effective in all countries. People in the various countries have widely divergent backgrounds, educations, languages, cultures, and religions and live in a variety of social conditions and economic and political systems.

Effective managers of MNCs must develop a style of leadership consistent with the needs of the situation existing in the host country. The appropriate style of leadership can be determined only after a careful assessment is made of the external environment of the host country, the type of personnel to be managed, the level of existing technology and the specific goals and operational requirements of the company.

REVIEW QUESTIONS

1. What is a multinational corporation? List three of the major criteria used to classify multinationals.
2. Name four of the world's largest multinational corporations (MNCs).
3. "The success or failure of the MNC is determined largely by how it responds to the external environment." Comment.
4. List the major factors affecting the management of multinationals.
5. Described two major economic factors that often cause difficulty for multinationals.

6. Distinguish between developed and developing countries from the perspective of top management of a Canadian MNC.
7. How does the political/legal factor affect an MNC?
8. What specific types of laws or local regulations must a multinational corporation be concerned with?
9. How may the objectives of the MNC differ from domestic firms?
10. Identify five of the more typical complaints host countries have against MNCs.
11. Is a code of ethics needed for MNCs? Why or why not? Give examples of what might be included.
12. "Technological expertise is the primary advantage of the multinational enterprise." Explain.
13. Describe the types of personnel used by MNCs and any potential problems with these personnel.

EXERCISES

1. Assume that you have agreed to accept a two-year position in Helsinki, Finland effective in 60 days. You are married and have a six-year-old daughter. What would you do to prepare yourself and your family (who are staying at home) for this assignment?
2. If you were selecting MNC personnel to be sent on international assignments, what qualities, experience, and characteristics would you look for in prospective personnel?
3. Review two current journal articles on the problems multinational companies have in recruiting and placing Canadian managers and/or technical personnel in assignments in foreign countries. Make a list of the problems and how the companies are able to overcome them.

CASE STUDY

The Overseas Transfer

In college, Pat Marek majored in industrial management and was considered by his teachers and peers to be a good all around student. Marek not only took the required courses in business, but he also learned French. After graduation, Marek took an entry-level management training position with Tuborg International, a multinational corporation with offices and factories in 30 countries, including Canada. Marek's first assignment was in a plant in Toronto. His supervisors quickly identified Marek for his ability to get the job done and still maintain good rapport with subordinates, peers, and superiors. In only three years, Marek had advanced from a manager trainee to the position of assistant plant superintendent.

After two years in this position, Marek was called into the superintendent's office one day and told that he had been identified as ready for a foreign assignment. The move would mean a promotion. The assignment was for a plant in France; but Marek wasn't worried about living and working there. Marek was excited and wasted no time in making the necessary preparations for the new assignment.

Prior to arriving at the plant in France, Marek took considerable time to review his French textbook exercises. He was surprised by how quickly the language came back to him. He thought that there wouldn't be any major difficulties in making the transition from Canada to France. However, Marek found, on arrival, that the community where the Tuborg plant was located did not speak the pure French that Marek had learned. There were many expressions that meant one thing to Marek but had an entirely different meaning to the employees of the plant.

While meeting with several of the employees a week after arriving, one of the workers said something to Marek that Marek interpreted as uncomplimentary; in actuality, the employee had greeted him with a rather risqué expression but in a different tone than Marek had heard before. All of the other employees interpreted the expression to be merely a friendly greeting. Marek's disgust registered in his face.

As the days went by, this type of misunderstanding occurred a few more times, until the employees began to limit their conversation with Marek. In only one month, Marek managed virtually to isolate himself from the workers within the plant. He became disillusioned and thought about asking to be relieved from the assignment.

QUESTIONS

1. What problems had Pat Marek not anticipated when he took the assignment?
2. How could the company have assisted Marek to reduce the difficulties that he confronted?
3. Do you believe the situation that Marek confronted is typical of a Canadian going to a foreign assignment? Discuss.

CASE STUDY

International Expansion

James Cartwright is the marketing manager for communications products for National Systems Limited, a Canadian company based in Halifax with sales in all 10 provinces. Sales revenues are in the area of $210 million annually. National Systems had indicated its intention to expand its marketing efforts to countries other than Canada.

In Canada, the communications products division had a 28 percent market share. Its product competes against products imported from other countries. It is regarded as having one of the better products for the Canadian market.

Issues that Cartwright is considering, in determining whether to enter international markets and how to enter them, include the product he offers, what markets he should attempt to sell in, what personnel he can utilize to develop these market opportunities, and what arrangements if any he should make with organizations in potential foreign markets.

Regarding the product, Cartwright knew that the National Systems product competed well in Canada. He wondered whether the same product features and characteristics would be equally well accepted in various foreign markets. He also wondered whether it was necessary to develop new products for each foreign market or whether he should follow an approach of testing and proving his products in Canada and not offering them for sale in other countries until they were proven successful in Canada.

Regarding the market, Cartwright was concerned whether he should attempt to penetrate the United States market right away, or focus on developing the market for his product in developing countries. His major concern about the United States was that competition was fierce. Offsetting this concern was the fact that this very large market was geographically and culturally the most similar to the Canadian market, with which he was most familiar. Regarding markets in developing countries, he felt that the Canadian reputation and the quality of his products were particularly strong points. He would be able to use products that had been tried, tested, and proven in the Canadian market, some of them for a number of years. Cartwright had reports indicating certain cultural and market development problems associated with the sophistication of product use in many of the developing countries.

Another issue was the personnel he had available to develop these markets. He had what he considered to be five key senior marketing people in Canada, along with 15 other people at the level immediately below them. They were all fully engaged in their present jobs and none had any international marketing experience. Cartwright himself had no international marketing expertise other than a two-week seminar he attended on international marketing. One option was to recruit a new graduate from a university program in business administration. His concern in this instance was that the individual would not have sufficient experience to be able to handle the area. Another option was to recruit someone from a major consulting firm which specialized in international marketing. However, this approach would not lead to long-run development of an international marketing team.

Another issue was to decide how to enter different foreign markets. Should they export from plants in Canada? Should they license people to manufacture the product in foreign markets? Should they enter into a joint venture agreement to market the product in these other countries?

There was also the general issue, raised by the board of directors of National Systems Limited, of whether or not expansion from the Canadian market was wise. On the one hand, international expansion would mean increases in sales and potential for profit, and the chance to learn about business in other countries. (Many of their domestic competitors were from other countries, and international experience would make it easier for National Systems to compete in the Canadian market.) On the other hand, some of the disadvantages to international expansion were the investment that would be required to develop these markets, the fact that other companies had a considerable lead on National Systems in the international market, and the fact that they were already doing well and were profitable in serving only the Canadian market.

QUESTIONS

1. Are there other considerations that James Cartwright should take into account in formulating his recommendation about whether to advise National Systems to go into foreign markets?
2. Are there other issues that are important to Cartwright if the company does decide to enter foreign markets?
3. Considering the issues he faces regarding products, markets, personnel, and business arrangements, what are the options available and what are the pros and cons of each option? Where can Cartwright look for information that will be useful to him in addressing these issues?

ENDNOTES

[1]Peter F. Drucker, *Management* (New York: Harper, 1973): 729.
[2]Robert W. Stevens, "Scanning the Multinational Firm," *Business Horizons* 14 (June 1971): 53.
[3]Peter Wright, David Townsend, Jerry Kindard, and Joe Iverstine, "The Developing World to 1990: Trends and Implications for Multinational Business," *Long Range Planning* 15 (1982): 122.

[4]Geert Hofstede, "The Cultural Relativity of Organizational Practices and Theories," *Journal of International Business Studies* 24 (Fall 1983): 75.

[5]David C. McClelland, *The Achieving Society* (Princeton, N.J.: Van Nostrand, 1961).

[6]J. O. Enitame, "Do Multinationals Create Wealth?" *International Management* 37 (January 1983): 48.

[7]R. Hal Mason, "Conflicts between Host Countries and Multinational Enterprise," *California Management Review* 17, no. 1 (1974): 6 and 7, by permission of the Regents of the University of California.

[8]"France Seizing Control of Technical Industries," *Business Week* (May 17, 1976): 47.

[9]United Nations information.

[10]L. Drake Rodman and Lee M. Caudill, "Management of Large Multinationals: Trends and Future Challenges," *Business Horizons.*

[11]Abdulrahman Al-Jafary, and A. T. Hollingsworth, "Practices in the Arabian Gulf Region," *Journal of International Business Studies* 14 (Fall 1983): 144.

[12]Yoram Zeira, "Overlooked Personnel Problems of Multinational Corporations," *Columbia Journal of World Business* 10 (Summer 1975): 96–103.

[13]Nancy J. Adler, "The Ostrich and the Trend," *Academy of Management Review* 8 (April 1983): 23.

[14]Michael Porter, "Why Global Businesses Perform Better," *International Management* 38 (January 1983): 40.

REFERENCES

Alpander, Guvenc G. "Multinational Corporations: Home-based Affiliate Relations." *California Management Review* 20, no. 3 (Spring 1978): 47–56.

Beamish, Paul, and Munro, Hugh. "The Export Performance of Small and Medium Sized Canadian Manufacturers." *Canadian Journal of Administrative Sciences* 3, (June 1986): 29–40.

Bertin, Oliver. "US Policies Bedevil Canadian Farmers." *The Globe and Mail* (December 22, 1986): B1.

Capstick, R. "The Perils of Manufacturing Abroad." *International Management* 33 (March 1978): 43–46.

Davis, S. M. "Trends in the Organization of Multinational Corporations." *Columbia Journal of World Business* II (Summer 1976): 54–71.

Davis, Stanley M., and Lawrence, Paul R. "Problems of Matrix Organizations." *Harvard Business Review* 56, no. 3 (May-June 1978); 131–142.

Davidson, Frame J. *International Business and Global Technology.* Lexington, Mass.: D. C. Heath and Co., 1983.

Duncan, Robert. "What is the Right Organization Structure?" *Organizational Dynamics* 7, no. 3 (Winter 1979): 59–80.

Evans, William A. *Management Ethics: An Intercultural Perspective.* Hingham, Mass.: Martinus Nyhoff Publishing, 1981.

Fitzpatrick, Mark. "The Definition and Assessment of Political Risk in International Business: A Review of the Literature." *Academy of Management Review* 8, no. 2 (April 1983): 249–254.

Galbraith, J. K. "The Defense of the Multinational Company." *Harvard Business Review* 56 (March 1978): 83–93.

Galbraith, J. K., and Edstrom, A. "International Transfer of Managers: Some Important Policy Considerations." *Columbia Journal of World Business* 11 (Summer 1976): 100–112.

Ghymn, K. I., and Bates, T. H. "Consequences of MNC Strategic Planning: An Empirical Case Study." *Management International Review* 17 (1977): 83–91.

Gladwin, Thomas N., and Walter, Ingo. *Multinationals Under Fire: Lessons in the Management of Conflict.* New York: John Wiley and Sons, 1980.

Harbron, John D. "How International Executives Have Responded to the New Challenges of World Recession." *Business Quarterly* 48, no. 4 (Winter 1983): 77–79.

Lawrence, Paul R.; Kolodny, Harvey F.; and Davis, Stanley M. "The Human Side of the Matrix" *Organizational Dynamics* 6, no. 1 (Summer 1977): 43–61.

May, W. F. "Between Ideology and Interdependence." *California Management Review* 19 (Summer 1977): 88–90.

Milner, Brian. "Firms Find South Africa Not Worth The Hassle." *The Globe and Mail* (November 29, 1986): B1, B4.

Mitchell, J., and Shawn, A. "All Multinationals Aren't the Same." *Financial World* (January 1977): 36.

Morris, James H.; Steers, Richard M.; and Koch, James L. "Influence of Organization Structure on Role Conflict and Ambiguity for Three Occupational Groupings." *Academy of Management Journal* 22, no. 1 (March 1979): 58–70.

Paul, Karen and Barbato, Robert. "The Multinational Corporation in the Less Developed Country." *Academy of Management Review* 10, (January 1985): 8–14.

Paulson, Steven K. "Organizational Size, Technology, and Structure: Replication of a Study of Social Service Agencies among Small Retail Firms." *Academy of Management Journal* 23, no. 2 (June 1980): 341–346.

Pazy, Asya, and Zeira, Yoram. "Training Parent Country Professionals in Host Country Organizations." *Academy of Management Review* 8, no. 2 (April 1983): 262–272.

Pohlman, R. A. "Policies of Multinational Firms: A Survey." *Business Horizons* 19 (December 1976): 14–18.

Prahalad, C. K. "Strategic Choices in Diversified MNCs." *Harvard Business Review* 54 (July 1976): 67–78.

Ross, Alexander. "Free Trade's Mr. Tough Guy." *Canadian Business* 59 (March 1986): 22–29, 101–102.

Sharpe, Andrew. "Can Canada Compete?" *Canadian Business Review* 12 (Winter 1985): 34–37.

Siggins, Maggie. "The Big Fortune Cookie." *Canadian Business* 59, (July 1986): 16–18, 21–29.

Sparkman, J. "Economic Interdependence and the International Corporation." *California Management Review* 20 (Fall 1977): 88–92.

Stoffman, David, "How to Make Deals in Japan." *Canadian Business* 59, (January 1986): 20–25, 90–91.

Templeman-Kluit, Anne. "IBA's Briefings Help Make Foreign Jobs Fun." *Canadian Business* (January 1985): 141–142.

Vernon, R. "Multinational Enterprises and National Governments: An Uneasy Relationship." *Columbia Journal of World Business* 11 (Summer 1976): 9–16.

Walker, Dean. "The World is His Oyster." *Executive* (April 1985): 56–60.

Zeira, Yoram. "Management Development in Ethnocentric Multinational Corporations." *California Management Review* 18 (Summer 1976): 34–42.

Zeira, Y., and Harari, E. "Managing Third Country Nationals in Multinational Corporations." *Business Horizons* 18 (October 1977) 83–88.

Social Responsibility and Business Ethics

KEY TERMS

social contract
economic function
social
   responsibility
organizational
   constituency

organizational
   stakeholder
social audit
iron law of
   responsibility
ethics

Type I ethics
Type II ethics
business ethics
ethical dilemma
managerial code of
   ethics

LEARNING OBJECTIVES

After completing this chapter you should be able to
1. Describe corporate social responsibility.
2. Explain the role of business in society.
3. Identify the arguments both for and against social responsibility of business.

4. State some of the current corporate practices regarding social responsibility and explain what is meant by a social audit.
5. Define business ethics and describe why it is important for an industry and/or company to establish codes of ethical behavior.

OPENING INCIDENT

Papeterie Boulanger

Adrian Kulik is the plant superintendent of a paper mill, Papeterie Boulanger, located in a northern Quebec town. During the 1970s the mill received a great deal of negative publicity because it was polluting the air and water. The mill has been fined regularly for violating air and water quality standards. Until recently, opinion among local townspeople was mixed. Most didn't like the pollution, but they didn't complain much because the mill provided most of the jobs in town. Over the past year, however, people have become increasingly critical of the company's refusal to install air and water pollution control devices.

Kulik has lived in the town for 14 years and has a good reputation. He is very involved in local volunteer and civic activities. He knows most of the workers at the mill personally, and he coaches a local minor league hockey team. During the past few years, he has grown depressed about the pollution issue partly because he has some doubts about what his company is doing, but also because complaints about pollution are getting more obvious. He is aware of the health threats and wonders if his work might be a potential danger to his children.

Two years ago, he made a presentation to the company's head office requesting that additional pollution control equipment be installed at the plant. Kulik made this request based on the fact that the mill should be able to operate at its present site for many years to come, allowing the company time to recoup their pollution control costs. Head office is now considering three alternatives: (1) install the pollution control equipment, (2) continue to pay the regular (but affordable) fines the company incurs for air and water quality violations, or (3) close the plant. Despite repeated applications, head office can get no help from governments in Ottawa or Quebec City to defray costs of the needed equipment.

Kulik has been assured that, if the plant is closed, he will have a good job elsewhere in the company. He knows that, from a strictly financial perspective, doing nothing and continuing to pay the fines is the best alternative because it avoids both a plant closure and a costly bill for installing pollution control equipment. But that doesn't make Kulik feel any better about the situation.

The opening incident demonstrates what is perhaps the most fundamental dilemma facing Canadian business firms: should they pursue profit to the exclusion of all else, or should they consider what they perceive as their social responsibilities when they make business decisions? There are no easy answers to this question, as we shall see in this chapter. In the areas of social responsibility and business ethics, management often has to agonize over which course of action is best. In many situations, managers find themselves doing a juggling act as they try simultaneously to adhere to government regulations, to pursue their profit objectives, and to meet the competing demands of employees, customers, shareholders, and suppliers.

Because there are no easy resolutions to many of the issues that arise with regard to corporate social responsibility and business ethics, our goal in this chapter is to sharpen your awareness of the issues; with this knowledge, you will be better prepared to deal with these issues in your work as a manager. The chapter is divided into two main parts. The first part examines corporate social responsibility. We note how the role of business has changed in Canadian society during the twentieth century and what the concept of corporate social responsibility means. We also examine the arguments for and against corporate social responsibility. The second part of the chapter deals with business ethics. We present a model of ethics, and describe some typical ethical dilemmas facing managers. The factors which determine the level of ethical behavior of managers are also discussed. Overall, this chapter demonstrates some of the difficult decisions that managers must make in their day-to-day work. The fact that there are no straightforward formulas for handling such matters further reinforces the dynamic nature of the manager's job, which we have tried to convey throughout the first 19 chapters of this book.

THE SOCIAL CONTRACT

social contract

In effect, organizations and society enter into a contract. This **social contract** is the set of rules and assumptions about behavior patterns among the various elements of society. Much of the social contract is embedded in the customs of society. For example, society has come to expect companies to do more than the law requires to integrate minorities into the work force. When one company behaves in an especially commendable way, its actions tend to increase the expectations society has concerning other companies.

Some of the provisions in the contract result from practices between parties. Like a legal contract, the social contract often involves a *quid pro quo* (something for something) exchange. One party to the contract behaves in a certain way and expects a predictable pattern of behavior from the other. For example, a relationship of trust may have developed between a manufacturer and the community in which it operates. Because of this, each may inform the other well in advance of any planned action that might cause harm, such as the closing of the plant by the company or the imposition of a new dumping regulation by the community.

The social contract concerns relationships with individuals, government, other organizations, and society in general. This is illustrated in Figure 20-1. Let us consider these relationships individually.

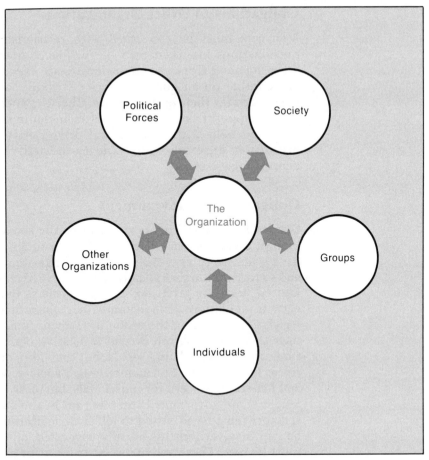

FIGURE 20-1   The social contract

Obligations to Individuals

Individuals often find healthy outlets for their energies through joining organizations. From their church, they expect guidance, ministerial services, and fellowship, and they devote time and money to its sustenance. From their employers, they expect a fair day's pay for a fair day's work — and perhaps much more. Many expect to be paid for time off to vote, perform jury service, and so forth. Clubs and associations provide opportunities for fellowship and for community service. Customers expect to be catered to. Most of our society still subscribes to the notion that the customer is king. To the extent that these expectations are acknowledged as responsibilities by the organization, they become part of the social contract.

Obligations to Other Organizations

Managers must be concerned with relationships involving other organizations like their own — such as competitors — and vastly differing ones. Commercial businesses are expected to compete with one another on an honorable basis, without subterfuge or reckless unconcern for their mutual rights. Charities such as the United Way expect support from businesses, often including the loaning of executives and help with annual fund drives. At the same time, such institutions are expected to come hat in hand, requesting rather than demanding assistance.

Obligations to Government

Government is an important party to the social contract for every kind of organization. Under the auspices of government, companies have a license to do business, along with patent rights, trademarks, and so forth. Churches and other charitable organizations, such as the United Way, are given tax-exempt status as long as they adhere to certain regulations. Labor unions have benefited from government legislation regarding the union movement, but they must also conduct themselves within certain legislative bounds. Crown corporations are very visible in Canada, but they, too, operate under certain rules. In the interest of maintaining a society which functions well and has some concern for individuals, business firms are expected to accept some government intervention in their activities. Safety inspectors must be admitted to job sites, legislation limiting what can be said in advetisements must be respected, and pollution standards must be met. These and many other facets of organizational life are part of the social contract.

Obligations to Society in General

Traditionally, the responsibility of the business firm has been to produce and distribute goods and services in return for a profit. Businesses have performed this function effectively. Largely as the result of our economic system and the important contributions of business firms, Canada enjoys one of the highest overall standards of living in the world. Rising standards of living have enabled a high percentage of Canadians to have their basic needs for food, clothing, shelter, health, and education reasonably well satisfied. Businesses can take pride in these accomplishments because they have had a great deal to do with making the higher standards of living possible.

Business has been able to make significant contributions to rising living standards primarily because of the manner in which the free enterprise economic system operates. The profit motive provides incentive to business to produce products and services efficiently.

Business firms try to improve the quality of their products and services, reduce costs and prices, and thereby attract more customers. The successful profit-making firm pays taxes to the government. It may also make donations to provide financial support for charitable causes. Because of the efficient operations of business firms, an ever-increasing number of people have increasing wealth and leisure time.

Businesses operate by public consent with the basic purpose of satisfying the needs of society. Despite significant improvements in standards of living in recent years, society has begun expecting — even demanding — more of all of its institutions, particularly large business firms. Goals, values, and attitudes in society are changing to reflect a greater concern for improvements in the quality of life. An indication of these concerns would include such goals as the following.[1]

- Eliminating poverty and providing quality health care.
- Preserving the environment by reducing the level of pollution.
- Providing a sufficient number of jobs and career opportunities for all members of society.
- Improving the quality of working life of employees.
- Providing safe, livable communities with good housing and efficient transportation.

THE CHANGING ROLE OF BUSINESS IN SOCIETY

economic
function

Society's expectations of North American business have broadened considerably in recent years to encompass more than just the traditional economic function. This is illustrated in Figure 20-2. Inner circle I represents the traditional economic functions of business. The **economic function** is the primary responsibility of businesses to society; in performing the economic function, businesses produce needed goods and services, provide employment, contribute to economic growth, and earn a profit. Level II represents the responsibility of business to perform the economic functions with an awareness of changing social goals, values, and demands. Management must be aware of such concerns as: the efficient utilization of resources, reducing pollution, employing and developing skills of minorities and females, providing safe products, and providing a safe work place. Level III is concerned with the corporation's responsibility for assisting society in achieving such broad goals as the elimination of poverty and urban decay through a partnership of business, government agencies, and other private institutions. While the responsibilities in Level III are not primary obligations of businesses, there is increasing interest by business in voluntary social action programs.

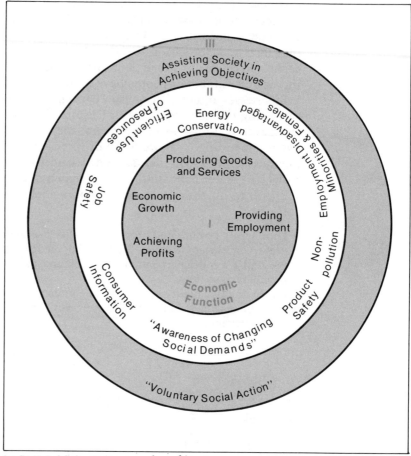

FIGURE 20-2   Primary roles of business

MANAGEMENT IN PRACTICE

Corporate Support for the Arts

Several years ago, American Express Toronto launched an unusual marketing effort. Each time a customer used an American Express card, the company donated $0.01 to the National Ballet School, the National Theatre School, and the National Youth Orchestra. Each time a customer purchased American Express Travellers Cheques, the company donated $0.05 to the three Canadian arts organizations. For each new card member signed, the company contributed $2.

The company openly stated that it was benefiting from the program through increased sales, but it pointed out that the three arts groups were also benefiting, both by the money they received and by the exposure the campaign generated. The company introduced the campaign in Canada after successfully using it in the United States.

SOURCE   Adapted from "American Express Tries an Arts Tack," *Marketing* (March 15, 1982): 7.

MANAGEMENT IN PRACTICE

Investment in South Africa

During the last decade, many Canadian companies have ceased doing business in South Africa for reasons that are both economic and social. A major concern is how much the company image may suffer in other countries if they retain their investments. At the end of 1986, only 14 Canadian companies had any significant South African involvement. Anti-apartheid lobbyists are now focusing their attention on the three major companies that still remain — Ford of Canada, Falconbridge, and Varity Corp. Lobbyists expect that the worsening economic environment in the country will help their cause.

Until recently, many companies argued that their presence in the country was good for the local people because they provided jobs. Most companies are now retreating from that position, as the financial rewards for continuing to carry on business in South Africa are outweighed by the hassles.

Clearly, the financial returns of South African operations are not enough, for most Canadian firms, to offset the politics and pressuring from anti-apartheid groups.

SOURCE   Brian Milner, "Firms Find South Africa Not Worth The Hassle," *The Globe and Mail* (November 29, 1986): B1, B4.

CORPORATE SOCIAL RESPONSIBILITY

Modern corporations need to develop an opinion about what they consider right or wrong in particular issues. Many companies develop patterns of concern for moral issues, through policy statements, through practices over time, and through the leadership of morally strong individuals. Some companies have programs of community involvement for their employees and managers. Many cooperate with fund drives such as the United Way. Open-door policies, grievance procedures, and employee benefit programs often stem as much from a desire to do what is right as from a concern for productivity and avoidance of strife. Managers have great influence over whether corporate behavior is conscientious or not because they are the ones who establish policies, develop the company's mission statement, and listen to employees' concerns.

A Definition of Social Responsibility

social
responsibility

When a corporation behaves as if it had a conscience, it is said to be socially responsible. **Social responsibility** is the implied, enforced, or felt obligation of managers, acting in their official capacities, to serve or protect the interests of groups other than themselves. Acceptance of the social responsibility concept means that a primary obligation of an organization is to ensure that its decisions and operations meet the needs and interests of society. Some people argue that the corporation can have a conscience.[2]

If a business firm contributes large amounts of money to charity, institutes a training program for the chronically unemployed, is actively involved in civic affairs, or gives scholarship money to a university or community college, it is behaving voluntarily in a socially responsible fashion because these activities are not required by law. When an organization behaves in this way, it usually does so without regard for the effect of this action on its profit. However, if the organization is involved in these activities because they will increase profits, the public may still think highly of the firm, but technically the organization is not adhering to the spirit of social responsibility.

If the definition of social responsibility quoted above is accepted, we could conclude that most business firms have historically not behaved in a socially responsible way. The general nature of business — and it is perfectly legal — is to mobilize the factors of production efficiently in the hope of making a profit. But the general public seems to be increasingly suspicious of businesses that follow the historical pattern. Surveys conducted during the 1960s and 1970s show a substantial decline in the public's confidence in business. However, these same surveys also show a decline in the public's confidence in various other groups — for example, doctors.

Managers in modern corporations should be very concerned about misperceptions that the general public may have about business. The most prominent misperception deals with consumer beliefs about business profits. As we noted in an earlier chapter, if you ask the typical consumer how much profit a business firm earns on each

MANAGEMENT IN PRACTICE

Socially Responsible Corporate Behavior

Many Canadian corporations have been actively involved in social responsibility programs. Consider the following:

- Imperial Oil's annual report details the kinds of community activities the organization is involved in. These include the formation of teams to deal with the problem of oil spills, programs for upgrading job safety and reducing accident rates, continued support for higher education, and reduction in energy costs incurred by the company.
- John Labatt Ltd. spends hundreds of thousands of dollars each year on such social programs as recreational facilities in communities where Labatt's has production

plants; creating summer jobs for students; the establishment of a Social Responsibility Committee within the board of directors; and an exchange program for children of Labatt's employees, which allows them to visit other areas of Canada.
- Gaz Metropolitan opened a training center where firefighters were taught how to contain natural gas leaks. They also offer employees a free medical examination and, for those who are nearing retirement, free courses on how to make the important transition from work to retirement.

SOURCE Adapted from Louis Demers and Donald Wayland, "Corporate Social Responsibility," *CA magazine* (February 1982): 59–60.

dollar of sales, they will generally say between $0.25 and $0.30. If he or she is then asked how much is a reasonable amount, the answer will usually be about $0.10. The actual profit that business makes on each dollar of sales is only about $0.05. Unless misconceptions like this one are corrected, business will continue to get very little sympathy from the general public.

Another major problem regarding consumer misconceptions of business is how people perceive the level of ethical behavior demonstrated (or not) by top management of businesses. Various surveys show that the public has a relatively low opinion of the calibre of the business executive's ethical behavior. Typically, such surveys show that while a majority of the public believes business firms have an obligation to help society, even if it means making less profit, fewer than half of those surveyed accept the notion that executives actually have a social conscience.

These two public perceptions — excessive concern for profits on the part of businesses and a low level of ethical behavior on the part of business managers — constitute a major image problem for business. If the general public has serious reservations about the role of business and the people who carry it out, Canadian society cannot function as effectively as it should. In Japan, for example, this kind of problem seems almost nonexistent; employees and management have worked together to become a formidable economic force in the world. Studying the Matsushita company, the largest manufacturer of electrical appliances in the world,[3] two American scholars attributed part of the company's success to the basic business principles of its founder. Commitment to the following principles are expected from every Matsushita employee:

> To recognize our responsibilities as industrialists, to foster progress, to promote the general welfare of society, to devote ourselves to the further development of world culture.[4]

One way to increase the effectiveness of the Canadian economic system is to create proper expectations of the role of business in the mind of the average Canadian.

Socially responsible decision makers within corporations consider both the economic and social impact of their decisions and the firm's operations on affected groups in society. Keith Davis, a professor who has written extensively about the concept of corporate social responsibility, believes that, in meeting its responsibilities to society, a firm must be concerned with more than the narrow technical and legal requirements.[5] It should recognize that an obligation exists to protect and enhance the interests and welfare not only of the corporation but of society.

Modern business organizations are often expected to assume broader and more diverse responsibilities than ever before. However, critics argue that there is more lip-service than real action, more public relations programs than concrete activities. Nevertheless, social responsibility is an area in which the modern business firm must develop a stance, accompanied by appropriate policies and activities.

Factors Affecting Corporate Social Responsibility

The factors that affect corporate social responsibility are illustrated in Figure 20-3, which depicts the relationship of a business firm to its external environment. How business conducts itself with regard to each of these groups will greatly affect its opportunities for survival, growth, and profitability. Labor unions and government units are among the most powerful groups in the firm's external environment. Consumer groups are gaining increased power, as are special interest groups, such as the Acid Rain Coalition, Nader's Raiders, and the Canadian Consumers' Association. On occasion, even shareholders have organized to try to alter the existing management of an organization when the firm has not conducted business in a socially responsible manner. (Recall Chapter 2.)

Managers must assess the power of each group in the external environment and its potential impact on the organization's activities. They should pursue what they deem to be the primary goals of the enterprise, but always with an eye out for constraints imposed by forces in the external environment. When managers go too long without responding or when they fundamentally disagree with actions demanded by various groups, they can risk boycotts, picketing, adverse media attention, new legislation, government hearings, proxy contests, and strikes. However, demands made by groups in society will keep the organization from becoming too selfish or irresponsible. Actions by these groups, rather than profits or conscience, have often led a firm to pursue socially responsible actions.

More and more executives see themselves as legitimate servants of a variety of constituencies. In a political sense, constituency means a body of citizens or voters that is entitled to elect a representative to a legislative or other public body. An **organizational constituency** is any identifiable group that organizational managers have, or acknowledge, a responsibility to represent. The intention of political constituents is that they will be represented by the person they elect. The constituents of corporate managers, however, may or may not have the power to elect those managers.

Every business or other organization has a large number of stakeholders, some of which are recognized as constituents and some of which are not. An **organizational stakeholder** is an individual or group whose interests are affected by organizational activities. Remember that although the interests of all stakeholders are affected by the corporation, managers may not acknowledge any responsibility to

organizational constituency

organizational stakeholder

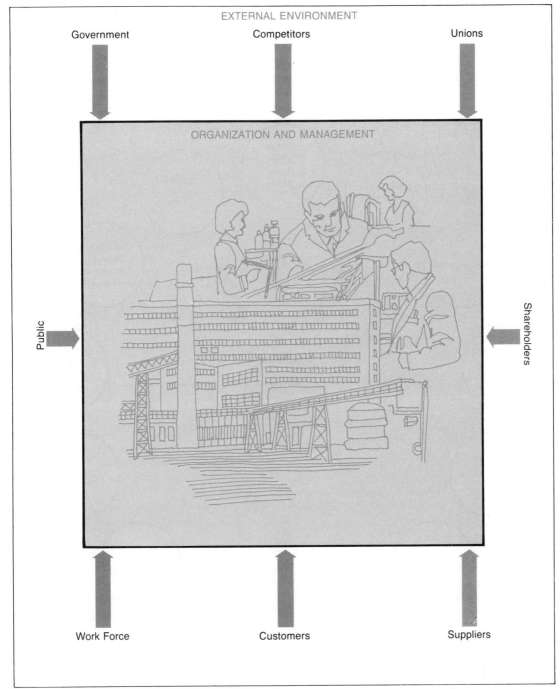

FIGURE 20-3   Relationship of the firm to groups in society

them. The stakeholders of a manufacturer of metal furniture might be as shown in Figure 20-4.

Representing such a diversity of interests requires answering questions such as the following: During an economic downturn, should employees be afforded continuous employment even when this is not

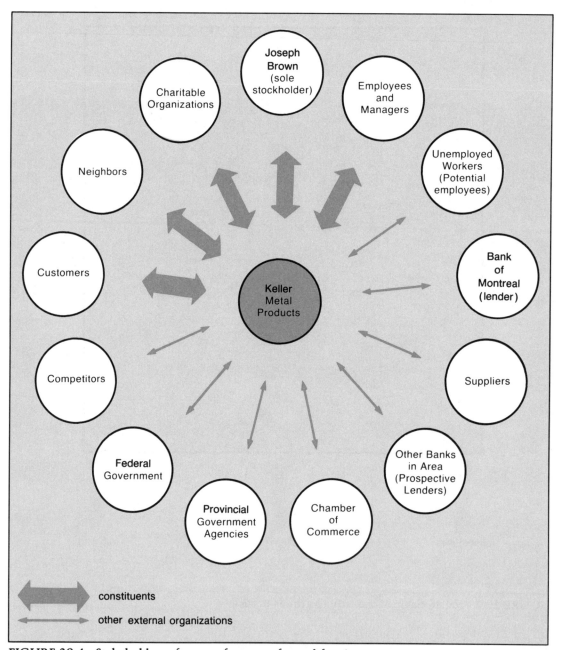

FIGURE 20-4 Stakeholders of a manufacturer of metal furniture

MANAGEMENT IN PRACTICE

A Problem at Key Lake

Key Lake Mining Corporation operates a uranium mine at Key Lake, Saskatchewan, 600 km north of Saskatoon. In January 1984, 100 million litres of radium-contaminated water escaped from a reservoir into the lake. The open-pit mining operation had been in operation only three months before the accident. It was later learned that eight smaller spills had preceded the big accident, and two smaller spills followed it.

Company officials concede that these accidents have not created an image of competence about the operations of the mine. Neal Hardy, the Environment Minister for Saskatchewan, called the company's president and bluntly asked him what the province could expect from the company in the future.

It appears that the company wasn't prepared for the spill or for the publicity surrounding it.

After the incident occurred, the company hired a public relations specialist to help deal with the publicity problem. Because the site is so isolated, reporters had a hard time getting to the mine. At one point, the company denied landing permission to two reporters who had flown in to investigate the spill. This incident created further concerns about the company. The bad publicity has also caused the union, the United Steelworkers of America, to question safety at the mine.

After the incident became well known, the company's president offered the opinion that the media had sensationalized the incident. This comment brought forth further criticism of the company.

SOURCE   Adapted from Edward Greenspan, "Key Lake Spills Will Mean Some Public Relations Repairs," *Financial Post* (January 28, 1984): 23–24.

---

in the long-term best interest of the owners of the corporation and does not accord with their preferences? Should managers be concerned about whether suppliers receive a reasonable profit on the items purchased from them, or should management simply buy the best inputs at the lowest price possible?

The Social Audit

social audit

A **social audit** is a commitment to systematic assessment of and reporting on some meaningful, definable domain of a company's activities that have social impact. Some firms have demonstrated their concern for the area of social responsibility by periodically surveying and assessing their activities through social auditing. Systematic social auditing is only in its infancy, and relatively few firms do periodic appraisals. However, a social audit does provide information to management that contributes toward decision making; it also provides information to the general public in response to pressures on the enterprise.

Four possible types of audits are currently being used: (1) a simple inventory of activities, (2) compilation of socially relevant expenditures, (3) specific program management, and (4) determination of social impact. The inventory, generally a social audit's starting point, consists of a simple listing of activities undertaken by the firm over

MANAGEMENT IN PRACTICE

Does Business Give Enough to Charity?

During the last few years, the number of charitable causes has grown, while federal and provincial subsidies to them have been shrinking. Many business firms, with problems of their own to worry about, are becoming more tight-fisted about giving to charities. Mr. Ken Wyman, national secretary of the Canadian Society of Fund Raising Executives, notes that although corporations are giving more money in total to charity each year, the amount they give as a percentage of their pre-tax profit is declining.

The business sector donates about 15-20 percent of the total funds contributed to charities in Canada. Foundations represent about 8 – 12 percent, and individuals give about 70-80 percent of the total. On average, Canadian companies give less than one-half of one percent of their pre-tax income to charities. In the US, on the other hand, companies average more than 1.5 percent. There is also a movement in the US to get charitable giving up to 5 percent of pre-tax income.

There are two reasons for the low level of giving in Canada. First, companies are themselves caught in financial squeezes and don't feel they can contribute to outside agencies when their own financial house isn't in order. Second, they are concerned that giving to one charity will cause others to request support. In 1984, business concerns received an average of 490 requests for help; that is up from 184 a decade earlier.

SOURCE Adapted from Barbara Aarsteinsen, "Business Giving Outpaced By Needs," *The Globe and Mail* (December 10, 1986): B1, B2.

and above what is required. For example, firms have itemized the following types of activities: (1) minority employment and training, (2) support of minority enterprises, (3) pollution control, (4) corporate donations to charities and educational institutions, (5) involvement in selected community projects by firm executives, and (6) programs for the chronically unemployed. The ideal social audit would help determine the benefits to society of socially oriented business activity.

THE DEBATE ABOUT SOCIAL RESPONSIBILITY

To this point, we have noted that: (1) the general public perceives that the role of business has changed during the twentieth century, and (2) the majority of Canadians think that business firms should behave in a socially responsible fashion. Corporate social responsibility has some forceful opposition, however. Its critics argue that forcing business into a socially responsible role will not benefit society and will, in fact, harm it. The debate that has arisen during the last decade disputes the role business should play in North American society. In this section we examine the major arguments from both sides of this debate.

Arguments Favoring Social Responsibility

Various groups and individuals have argued that business should be involved in socially responsible activities. Proponents of corporate social responsibility stress such areas as provision for better jobs and promotion opportunities for minorities and women, financial support for education, charitable donations to civic organizations, financial and managerial support for improving health and medical care, a safer work place, leadership and financial support for urban renewal, and means to reduce ecological pollution. The major arguments for the acceptance of social responsibility by business are:

- People expect businesses and other institutions to be socially responsible.
- It is in the best interest of business to pursue socially responsible programs; consumers are likely to continue buying from businesses with good reputations.
- Socially responsible activities improve the image of the firm.
- Business should be involved in socially useful projects because it has the resources to see that they succeed.
- Corporations must be concerned about society's interests and needs because society sanctions business operations.
- If business is not responsive to society's needs, the general public will press for more government regulation requiring more socially responsible behavior.
- Socially responsible actions may increase profits in the long run.
- Business firms have a great deal of power; with this power goes the responsibility to exercise it in a socially responsible fashion.

iron law of
responsibility

Keith Davis summarizes these arguments with what he terms the **iron law of responsibility:** "in the long-run, those who do not use power in a manner in which society considers responsible will tend to lose it."[6] Thus, if business firms are to retain their social power, they must be responsive to society's needs.

Arguments against Social Responsibility

There are numerous arguments against businesses assuming an active role of social responsibility. A leading opponent is Dr. Milton Friedman, a Nobel Prize-winning economist. Friedman's view of social responsibility is:

> There is one and only one social responsibility of business — to use its resources and engage in activities designed to increase its profits so long as it stays within the rules of the game, which is to say, engages in open and free competition without deception and fraud. . . Few trends could so thoroughly undermine the very foundations of our free society as the acceptance by corporate officials of a social responsibility other than to make as much money for their stockholders as possible.[7]

Dorothy Dobbie,
Association Publications Ltd.

Dorothy Dobbie is a successful business-woman with 17 years experience as the senior vice-president of a printing and publishing company, which she helped build to an international corporation with over 200 employees. Currently the president of the Winnipeg Chamber of Commerce, Dobbie is also the president of her own company, Association Publications Ltd. She has always been deeply involved in community activities and believes that a well-developed social consciousness makes good business sense.

Q: In your position as president of the Chamber of Commerce, you have the opportunity to observe a wide variety of corporate behavior. Could you give us some specific examples of behavior that you feel demonstrates what social responsibility is all about?

Dobbie: There are really two broad areas of socially responsible behavior by business firms. The first is the responsibility business firms feel toward their employees. Most businesses go beyond the simple "I pay you to work" attitude and exhibit genuine concern for their employees as people. Companies will often react in a very generous way to unexpected problems that employees experience. For example, they may give an employee a paid leave to care for a sick child, or they may pay medical bills for employees who aren't sufficiently covered by insurance, or they may provide low-cost daycare service, or give other help to employees.

The second area of social responsibility relates to business involvement in the community. Once again, most businesses that I am familiar with feel a strong responsibility to be a good corporate citizen and to support the community in which they operate. This involves all the usual things like charitable donations to various organizations, air and water pollution control, support for community projects, funds for education, sponsoring a Christmas party for disadvantaged children, providing uniforms for a community hockey team, and so forth. But it also involves much more that the general public is often not aware of. For example, a business might contribute toward landscaping a boulevard close to its plant because it wants to maintain a good appearance in the neighborhood. Or a company may let an employee work for the city, or do volunteer work on company time, or use sales and marketing people to head up a fund drive for a volunteer organization. Business firms often receive little publicity for this type of work, but it is very important in the local community and it indicates the concern that business has for the community.

I think it is important to make a distinction between what the company wants to do and what individuals in the company want to do, but sometimes this distinction is blurred. This is particularly true in small firms, where the owner may have a very strong interest in doing socially responsible things for the community. In these cases, it is hard to tell where individual preferences end and company policy begins.

Q: What can you tell us about corporate donations to charity, the arts, and education?

Dobbie: Some large companies have specific policies about giving money. Many give between one-tenth and one-half of one percent of net income. The smaller firms generally don't have specific policies, but give in response to both perceived needs and "salesmanship," often in the form of peer pressure. Many companies feel that giving the time and expertise of their people (on company time) is as important and perhaps more effective than giving money.

Q: Does a firm's financial position influence how much it gives?

Dobbie: Generally speaking, yes. If a firm has a good year, it may give not only its stated policy amount, but something extra. If it has a bad year with no profits, it will probably reduce its giving rather sharply. But I've seen firms that were in bad financial shape keep on giving because they felt strongly about their duty to the community. At the same time, it is also true that some profitable organizations give nothing, even though they could easily afford to. However, we must remember that organizations that don't give money may contribute to the community in other ways. This is most noticeable when the managerial talent that exists in a business firm is used to organize and run an important volunteer or fund-raising program in a community.

Business firms are becoming increasingly concerned about the effectiveness of the money they give. The press has recently focused considerable attention on charities that use up much of the money they receive in administration. Business firms avoid organizations that have large administrative overhead. They are also wary of organizations that ask for money and do not have a clear plan for using it, or who do not have a track record of effective use of funds. When a business firm does not feel comfortable giving money, it often decides to do something socially responsible on its own. In this way, it can more closely control what is done, and it can clearly see the results of its contributions and activity.

Q: Do some businesses behave in a socially responsible way because they think it will improve their image and profitability?

Dobbie: That's probably true in some cases, but less frequently than is commonly thought. Corporate giving occurs at a variety of levels. In certain instances, one level of management may wish to take a socially responsible action for purely altruistic reasons, but may feel compelled by shareholders, upper management, or even the firm's banks to provide some justification for doing so. Management may then develop a justification, and it may contain the argument that behaving in a socially responsible fashion will lead to better sales and profits through image enhancement or other advertising-related benefits.

Q: What do you think of the argument made by some economists that the sole purpose of business is to make a profit, and that business firms shouldn't get involved in a lot of peripheral activities because managers haven't been trained to make decisions in those areas?

Dobbie: Well, theoretically that sounds good, but in practice it doesn't work. Let us keep one important fact in mind: Business firms are made up of people, and human emotions therefore enter into all business decisions. The stereotyped cold-hearted corporation in which business decisions are ruthlessly made on strictly rational grounds is a myth. People in all organizations — public or private, profit or not-for-profit — sometimes do good things and sometimes do bad things. Social concern and socially responsible actions are two of the good things. In business firms, these decisions are often not made on the basis of their effect on profit, but rather on very personal grounds that may be rooted in a variety of reasons. In cases where the coldly administered, unbreakable rules apply, it is usually where decisions are made by disinterested third parties and handed down without regard for, or personal knowledge of, the recipient.

Q: What kinds of problems arise if a firm is actively involved in doing things that are socially responsible?

Dobbie: I think the major problem is that management finds it hard to predict whether their desire to behave in a socially responsible way will actually have the desired effect. Let me give you an example. One company that was in some economic difficulty reluctantly came to the conclusion that it would have to lay off a substantial number of long-service employees. Since it felt a responsibility for these employees, it hired a placement firm to help them find new jobs. The employees had little difficulty finding new jobs, but the companies that hired them soon found that they stayed only a few months before quitting. In this case, management made an honest effort to be socially responsible but found that their good intentions did not have much effect. When things like this happen, business firms may become frustrated and confused and feel that their attempts to be socially responsible are not recognized. Business is constantly being told to "do more," but the more it does, the greater the potential for problems such as those in the example I've just cited.

Friedman goes on to assert that social responsibility is a "fundamentally subversive doctrine." He argues that managers are agents of the owners of an enterprise and that for them to engage in any activities not related to earning profits may be illegal. Diverting funds to social projects without shareholder approval is, in effect, "taxation without representation." He says that business performance is economic, not social.

Concentrating resources in the social area could lead to less economic efficiency and therefore actually be detrimental to society. Friedman and others who argue against the assumption of social responsiblity by business believe that government should deal with the social demands of society. The major arguments against social responsibility are:

- Concern for social responsibility violates sound business decision making and diverts the attention of managers from the pursuit of profit.
- Social responsibility might be illegal, in that executives do not have the legal right to use corporate resources (the property of the shareholders) to pursue activities like giving to charity.

MANAGEMENT IN PRACTICE

Socially Responsible Investing

There is a trend toward providing investors with investment opportunities that fit with their view of ethical business practice. Larry Trunkey is the founder of the Canadian Network for Ethical Investing, an organization which is attempting to develop workable criteria for evaluating corporate behavior in areas like employment practices, human rights, opportunities for women and minorities, product quality, and environmental pollution.

The first open-ended socially responsible mutual fund was launched by Vancouver City Savings Credit Union in October 1986. The fund uses five criteria to determine investment: a company must be Canadian and public; it must practice progressive industrial relations; it must not do business with countries that promote racial inequality; it must not

manufacture armaments; it must not do business with firms that are involved in nuclear energy. Investors Group of Winnipeg started a socially responsible mutual fund in January 1987. The fund will not invest in firms with significant involvement in tobacco, pornography, gambling, or weapons.

One study of the performance of socially responsible mutual funds indicates that they do not perform as well as traditional mutual funds. This study of US mutual funds (the Canadian funds have not been established long enough to make an assessment) shows that their returns to investors were slightly to substantially below traditional mutual funds.

SOURCE Adapted from Margaret Inwood, "Ethical Investors Opt For Principles Over Profits," *The Globe and Mail* (January 2, 1987): B5

- The cost of socially responsible behavior exceeds the benefits; the net result is higher prices to consumers.
- Managers aren't trained, nor do they possess the skills or resources, to determine which socially responsible projects to pursue.
- Too much power is concentrated in the hands of business executives, none of whom is elected by the public.
- An emphasis on social responsibility leads to a deterioration in the free enterprise system.

An Evaluation of the Debate

Both the positions for and against corporate social responsibility make logical arguments to support their case. Often, business executives themselves are proponents of corporate social responsibility when profits are high or social conditions unfavorable, and are opponents when the economy is under great pressure, when the company is in financial difficulty, or when social conditions do not warrant a great deal of concern.

Friedman's arguments against the assumption of social responsibility by business firms have been criticized on a number of grounds. First, Friedman implies that business should engage in open and free competition as part of its basic operations. However, open and free competition does not exist in most sectors of the North American economy. A second and more fundamental point is that business firms, particularly large ones, cannot avoid making decisions that influence society. Almost every major decision made in a corporation affects various groups in and outside the organization. Problems confronting society — employment discrimination, pollution, unsafe products, corporate bribery, illegal political contributions, price fixing — are all practices of some companies that are not in the best interest of society.

Because of the social undesirability of such acts, there has been an increasing amount of government regulation. Some managers have concluded that "if it's legal, it's ethical" — if it is not in violation of the law, one is free to act as one wishes. This managerial philosophy will invite more and more outside regulation and may be self-defeating in the long run. Being socially responsible means more than just following the law. It means considering the consequences of actions and asking if such actions are socially responsible. Social responsibility starts where the law ends. Keith Davis stresses this point:

> A firm is not being socially responsible if it merely complies with the minimum requirements of the law, because this is what any good citizen would do. A profit maximizing firm under the rules of classical economics would do as much. Social responsibility goes one step further. It is a firm's acceptance of a social obligation beyond the requirements of the law.[8]

ETHICS

ethics

Closely related to social responsibility is the concept of ethics. **Ethics** is the discipline dealing with what is good and bad or right and wrong or with moral duty and obligation. Whereas social responsibility is primarily concerned with how the total corporation conducts itself, ethics deal with the contemporary standards or principles of conduct that govern the actions and behavior of individuals within the organization. Each of us must make ethical (or unethical) decisions every day. Should we tell the clerk that we have received too much change? What should we do if the professor makes a mistake in our favor in calculating our grade?

A Model of Ethics

A model of ethics is presented in Figure 20-5. It shows that ethics consist mainly of two relationships, indicated by arrows in the figure. A person or organization is ethical if these relationships are strong and positive. There are a number of sources that one might use to determine what is right or wrong, good or bad, moral or immoral behavior. These include the Bible, the Koran, and a number of other holy books. They also include the "still small voice" that many refer to as conscience. Millions believe that conscience is a gift of God or the voice of God. Others see it as a developed response based on internalization of societal mores.

Another source of ethical guidance is the behavior and advice of what psychologists call "significant others" — our parents, friends, role models, and members of our churches, clubs, and associations. For organized professionals especially, there are often codes of ethics that proscribe certain kinds of behavior. Any type of act sufficiently hurtful to others is often prohibited by law. Thus, enacted laws offer guides to ethical behavior.

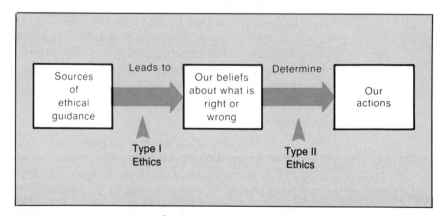

FIGURE 20-5 A Model of Ethics

Notice in Figure 20-5 that the sources of ethical guidance lead to appropriate beliefs or convictions about what is right and wrong. Most would agree that people have a responsibility to avail themselves of these sources of ethical guidance. In short, individuals should care about what is right and wrong and not just be concerned with what is expedient. The strength of the relationship between what an individual or an organization believes to be moral and correct and what available sources of guidance suggest is morally correct is **Type I ethics**. For example, suppose a student believes it is acceptable to copy another student's exam paper despite the fact that almost everyone condemns this practice. This student is unethical in a Type I sense.

Type I ethics

Simply having strong beliefs about what is right and wrong and basing them on the proper sources does not make one ethical. Figure 20-5 illustrates that behavior should conform with what we believe about right and wrong. **Type II ethics** is the strength of the relationship between what one believes and how one behaves. Generally a person is not considered ethical unless possessed of both types of ethics. Everyone would agree that to do what one believes is wrong is unethical. For example, if a student knows that it is wrong to look on another's examination answer sheet while taking a test and does so anyway, the student has been unethical in a Type II sense. If a business manager knows that it is wrong to damage the environment yet dumps poisonous waste in a nearby stream, this behavior is unethical also.

Type II ethics

BUSINESS ETHICS

business ethics

One can usually provoke a lively discussion by simply mentioning the words business ethics. **Business ethics is the application of ethical principles to business relationships and activities.** Reading the newspapers or watching the evening news provides ample ilustrations of illegal and/or unethical practices of individuals within large corporations. Particularly ethical practices seldom make the news.

The ethical norms provided by society in general are not so specific and long lasting that they always give clearly defined guidelines for everyone to follow. The difference between conduct that is barely tolerated and conduct that is clearly indefensible is sometimes blurred. Elected representatives have been known to take foreign trips on taxpayers' money to attend conferences that seem little more than paid holidays. Highly respected business people hire professional accountants and lawyers to identify loopholes in tax laws. Business executives engage in a variety of practices that are often viewed with suspicion by the general public. Yet there is seldom agreement in public opinion that these and similar activities are unconditionally unethical.

Ethical Dilemmas Facing Managers

ethical dilemma

Today's managers are continually confronted with situations where difficult ethical choices must be made. An **ethical dilemma** exists when a manager has difficulty making a decision because he or she feels uncomfortable about the morality of one of the alternatives. Very often the alternative that makes the manager feel uncomfortable is weighted with financial or career-advancement benefits offered to the manager. Consider these examples of ethical dilemmas:

- Suppose you are a sales manager attending a regular meeting of your sales staff. Three senior salespeople report that salespeople employed by two major competitors are paying customers under the table to accept their contracts. The meeting breaks into a chaotic debate over what should be done. Several salespeople state without hesitation that your company should follow the competitors' example. You argue that your company has never used such tactics. What decision do you make? What do you tell your sales staff to do? Will you suspect some of your salespeople will act contrary to a recommendation not to pay kickbacks?
- Suppose you are the vice-president of marketing for a consumer products company and you've been with the company for 27 years. You've worked all your life for the presidency of the company; you've been assured it's yours if you can make the latest new product successful in the marketplace. You have received a letter from a parent noting that this new product has some questionable features that make it potentially unsafe for the small children who will use it. Would you suppress these safety problems in order to assure your selection as president?
- Suppose you are a department head in a government agency and a vacancy has just opened in your department. Your boss asks you to lunch one day and makes an extraordinary suggestion. He notes how tight your department's budget has been for the past couple of years and offers to increase it substantially for next year. In return, he wants a female friend of his promoted into the vacant position, without going through the usual procedures of advertising and interviewing. Can you afford to turn down the offer? Will your boss be willing or able to protect you from awkward questions from other departments? What do you decide to tell your boss? What do you actually do?

Ethical dilemmas like these frequently confront managers in their work. In trying to resolve these ethical dilemmas, managers would like simultaneously to feel good about the decision and to have the decision further their career. Unfortunately, this combination is often impossible because the decision that they consider unethical may be the one that will further their career. For example, if you are the marketing vice-president mentioned above and you ignore the safety warnings, your product likely will be a success; you will probably become president, but you may feel uneasy because you promoted a product for children that had safety problems.

We do not mean to imply by these examples that managers can never feel that, by making ethical decisions, they may be restrained in pursuit of their careers. But it is true that managers continually face ethical dilemmas that create mental anguish for them. Unfortunately, we cannot provide easy answers for students aspiring to be managers. We can, however, warn you that these kinds of circumstances will arise and that you will often feel you are in an untenable position.

Illegal versus Unethical Behavior

It is important to make the distinction between illegal behavior and unethical behavior. If there is a law prohibiting an action, it is illegal; most people will also consider such actions to be unethical. For example, most people would say that murder is not only illegal but also unethical. However, some people argue that some conduct that is illegal is not automatically to be considered unethical. They argue that some laws — like abortion or marijuana possession — should not be on the books. The classic example of this dichotomy is the law that was passed prohibiting the consumption of alcohol in the United States in the 1920s. Many people were forced to recognize that the consumption of alcohol was illegal, but they did not consider it unethical.

As we noted earlier, different people may view one issue with differing ideas about its degree of properness. Assessing whether or not behavior is unethical is therefore a difficult task. Is the behavior portrayed in the following examples unethical or not?

- A manager has objective evidence that he is underpaid. He consistently pads his expense account to make up for some of the shortfall in his regular salary.
- A broker quietly hints to a relative about a major stock deal involving the company where the relative works as a manager. The manager quickly sells his own shares and tips off one or two of his close friends in the company.
- A manager creates doubts about the competence of some of her peers in order to enhance her chances for a promotion. She does so without ever lying about her peers; rather, she selectively passes on unfavorable information about them.
- A purchasing agent takes a gift from a supplier in return for purchasing some of the supplier products. The purchasing agent is not sure in her own mind whether or not the gift influenced her purchasing decision.
- A manager discovers a computer programmer has been using the company computer to program harassing telephone calls in a personal vendetta. The programmer has saved the company money and works well, so the manager decides to ignore the discovery.
- An employee gives industrial secrets to a competitor of the company she works for. She was induced to divulge the secrets after being encouraged to work for the competitor at a large increase in salary.

If a list of examples like these were given to a sample of practicing managers, it is likely that there would be considerable disagreement about which practices are unethical and which ones are acceptable. This is sometimes the difficulty with business ethics — each individual considers the facts of the situation and makes a judgment about whether the behavior in question is unethical. If a firm has no policy statements or has shown no strict intolerance of certain conduct, individual managers must depend on their personal perspective to reach a consensus on what constitutes ethical behavior.

Factors Affecting Managerial Ethics

Although we cannot predict what decision an individual manager will make when confronted with an ethical dilemma, we can identify what influences the levels of managerial ethics. These factors are discussed below.

Government Regulation

Laws may be viewed as the results of a trend of what society expects in terms of acceptable behavior. Behavior can be made illegal if society views it as excessive or unethical. The law defines and clarifies acceptable standards or practices in a given area. For example, if contributions to political candidates from corporations are illegal, then firms either obey the law or violate it. However, in either case the guidelines or standards are clear, and a violator may be punished for engaging in the illegal activity. Laws regarding corporate behavior are often passed as a result of long-standing low ethical standards or the failure of corporations to recognize their social responsibilities.

Beyond explicit laws, governments also form regulations to define acceptable and unacceptable practices. For example, the areas of minimum product safety, fire precautions, acceptable levels for auto emissions, safe working conditions, and nondiscriminatory employment practices are all supported by government regulation. The interpretation of the laws by the courts and the development of guidelines by government agencies assist managers in understanding what constitute acceptable practices in the work place.

Codes of Ethical Behavior

Many industries and individual companies have formal, written codes of ethics that provide specific guidelines for managers and other employees to follow. The key issue in this regard is whether individuals within organizations are truly governed by the code of ethics or simply give lip-service to it. Another issue is whether the company or industry enforces the code if individuals or companies violate it. In any event, these codes of ethics define or clarify the

MANAGEMENT IN PRACTICE

Guiding Principles — Great-West Life Assurance Company

1. Great-West Life's management recognizes that, to prosper, the company must serve its customers, staff members and sales representatives, shareholders, and the community at large to the best of its ability. Moreover, this is based on a conviction that those elements which make Great-West Life an outstanding company for its customers are beneficial to all its constituencies.

2. We will maintain an environment of confidence in, and respect for, the dignity of the individual. We will strive to select superior people. We will build and maintain a dynamic organization through an open and participative style of management. We will give staff members and sales personnel every opportunity to make the most of their abilities and reward them according to their contribution to meeting our objectives.

3. We will distribute our products and services in the best interests of our customers through distribution systems that are con-

temporary, innovative, and socially responsible.

4. Our investment program will carefully balance the quality, terms, and rate of return on our investments. We will strive to achieve a consistently superior rate of return to meet our overall financial objectives and obligations to our customers.

5. We will find new and better ways to serve our customers by offering products and services that are both contemporary and innovative to satisfy their changing needs and desires. We will maintain their goodwill by meeting our commitments to them both in spirit and letter with particular emphasis upon the financial management and security of their funds.

6. We will work to increase the long-term value of shareholders' investment to maintain our reputation as a sound and growing financial institution.

SOURCE   Guiding Principles of Great-West Life Assurance Company, Winnipeg. Reprinted by permission.

ethical issues and allow the individual to make the final decision. An example of a code of ethics is presented in the Great-West Life insert.

There are advantages in having each industry form industry associations which develop their own codes of ethics. It is difficult for a single firm to follow ethical practices if its competitors undercut them by taking advantage of unethical shortcuts. But if an entire industry agrees that certain behavior will not be tolerated, there is a much greater chance for an improvement in the level of ethical conduct in that industry.

A particularly difficult ethical problem currently exists in international trade. Several highly publicized cases have appeared in recent years where business executives or "middlemen" companies paid bribes to foreign government officials in return for major sales contracts. In Canada, bribery is considered to be highly unethical, but in some other parts of the world it is viewed by people in authoritative government posts as acceptable business practice. If Canadian multinational companies cannot get some agreement from other multinationals that this practice should be stopped, they may find themselves at a disadvantage when they try to get business in some foreign countries.

Social Pressures

Social forces and pressure groups have considerable impact on ethics or acceptable standards of behavior. Examples of pressure groups seeking to make organizations more responsive to the needs and desires of society are numerous. Removal of lead paint from baby furniture, the banning of urea formaldehyde home insulation, and stopping of fraudulent practices by transmission dealerships are all results of action by pressure groups. They have also actively promoted more employment of women and minorities, some have boycotted products, and others have tried to prevent the construction of nuclear arms devices. Such actions by pressure groups may, in fact, cause management to alter certain decisions by taking a broader view of ecological and consumer needs.

At the same time, however, there may be strong social pressures within the firm urging managers to band together to ward off the pressures from external groups, particularly if these external pressures are seen as unreasonable or too costly. Most managers are more susceptible to pressure from their peers than they are to pressures from outsiders; thus, even desirable change may be very slow to occur. For example, reducing air pollution is certainly a desirable objective, but installation of control devices may be an excessive cost for management to consider as a quick solution.

Individual Ethics
versus Corporate Demands

The needs and goals of the firm may conflict with the values and ethical standards of a manager. This dilemma between organizational goals and personal ethics or values greatly complicates the life of the typical manager. There is often considerable pressure on managers to increase performance and generate higher profits. At times, this objective may create pressures to compromise personal ethics to meet the goals of the company. For example, a manager in an autocratic firm may be given what he or she considers to be an impossibly high sales goal; that manager, unable to persuade superiors to change the goal and unable to quit, may feel forced to engage in practices like getting together with managers from other firms and fixing prices so that they can all make their profit goals. This practice is, of course, illegal and unethical. It reduces competition and harms the consumer, but it can happen when individual managers in a nonparticipative corporation become desperate enough or are driven far enough by a conflict between individual and organizational goals.

One study found that managers can feel a great deal of pressure to compromise their personal ethical standards in order to achieve organizational goals. A. B. Carroll's study, representing the response of 258 American managers, revealed that 50 percent of top-level managers, 65 percent of middle-level managers and 84 percent of lower-level managers felt "under pressure to compromise personal standards to achieve company goals."[9]

A Managerial Code of Ethics

managerial code
of ethics

The medical and legal professions have established codes of ethics that provide guidelines and standards for conduct. These codes are known to everyone in the profession but may or may not be practiced to the letter. Managers do not have an established code of ethics, but in recent years there have been numerous attempts to develop and promote one. The following list provides an example of such an attempt to formulate what might be included in a **managerial code of ethics**:

- I will recognize that management is a call to service with responsibilities to my subordinates, associates, supervisors, employer, community, nation, and world.
- I will be guided in all my activities by truth, accuracy, fair dealings, and good taste.
- I will earn and carefully guard my reputation for good moral character and citizenship.
- I will recognize that, as a leader, my own pattern of work and life will exert more influence on my subordinates than what I say or write.
- I will give the same consideration to the rights and interests of others that I ask for myself.
- I will maintain a broad and balanced outlook and will look for value in the ideas and opinions of others.
- I will regard my role as a manager as an obligation to help subordinates and associates achieve personal and professional fulfillment.
- I will keep informed on the latest developments in the techniques, equipment, and processes associated with the practice of management and the industry in which I am employed.
- I will search for, recommend, and initiate methods to increase productivity and efficiency.
- I will respect the professional competence of my colleagues and will work with them to support and promote the goals and programs of the industry.
- I will support efforts to strengthen professional management through example, education, training, and a lifelong pursuit of excellence.[10]

To be realistic, we must admit that such a code of ethics will have very little effect on some managers, and a substantial effect on others. The statements contained in the code are general, allowing each individual to interpret the statements according to his or her own view of the world. For example, in the first statement, the word "responsibility" would undoubtedly be interpreted in many different ways; given that, any manager could probably say in good conscience that he or she was acting responsibly toward subordinates.

A final comment on the difficult subject of ethics: remember that human beings are capable of infinite amounts of self-delusion. This means that if a certain manager does something that 99.9 percent of his or her peers think is unethical, we should not be surprised if that manager remains convinced that what he or she did was perfectly all right. If students aspiring to management positions expect this kind of behavior, they will be able to recognize it and deal more effectively with it.

OPENING INCIDENT REVISITED

Papeterie Boulanger

Adrian Kulik, the plant superintendent of Papeterie Boulanger, was very concerned about the water and air pollution his paper mill was creating in the northern Quebec town where it operated. He was not sure what should be done to resolve the problem. Like most managers, Kulik believes he is a reasonable person. Yet he finds himself at the center of a major controversy and he is experiencing considerable anxiety because of it. What alternatives are open to him? At one extreme, he could demand that the company do something to protect the people of the town, many of whom are its own employees, or he will quit the company. If he is truly a top-notch plant superintendent, the company may give serious consideration to his request. At the other extreme, he could continue to do his job and not make waves. He'll probably never be blamed personally for the air and water pollution and, even if someone challenges him, Kulik can point to the request he sent to head office. Kulik can say that he did all he could, even if he isn't persuaded of it himself.

The positions that the supporters and opponents of social responsibility will take on this issue are fairly clear. The supporters will say that the pollution control equipment should be installed immediately, while the opponents will point out that, if the company is forced to install the equipment, it may have to close the plant and many jobs will be lost.

What should Kulik do? We're not sure.

If you are uncomfortable with our answer, perhaps you should ask yourself what you would do in Kulik's position. Be honest with yourself when you think about this issue and try to imagine what Kulik is going through. You have worked for this company for many years; are you going to demand that they do something about this problem and threaten to quit? Is it realistic to think that a company will spend millions of dollars on pollution control equipment just to keep one valued employee? Are you going to throw away your career over an issue like this? On another level of thought, can you live with yourself if you don't do something? If you truly want to act, you might petition your MNA and MP to help the company. Only you can answer these questions. When you realize that tough decisions like this one are made by managers every day, you begin to realize why the occupation of management is so important to our society.

Perhaps it is appropriate to end this text with a problem that leaves much uncertainty in your mind. In the first 19 chapters we have tried to give answers to a wide range of important questions facing managers. But we must recognize that the practice of management is filled with uncertainties and that clear-cut answers are simply not possible in all cases. If you can accept that, and if you can make a decision on a tough issue and live with the consequences, perhaps you have what it takes to be a good manager.

SUMMARY

Managers in today's organizations have the difficult job of trying to meet the demands of employees, shareholders, government, customers, the public, and other groups in their external environment. The social contract is the set of rules and assumptions about behavior patterns among the various elements of society. When a corporation behaves as if it had a conscience, it is said to be socially responsible. Social responsibility is the implied, enforced, or felt obligation of managers, acting in their official capacities, to serve or protect the interests of groups other than themselves. Social responsibility can be understood in terms of the social contract that exists between a firm and its environment.

Values are changing with regard to social responsibility. The iron law of responsibility states that "in the long run, those who do not use power in a manner in which society considers responsible will tend to lose it." Traditionally, however, companies were not expected to have social goals, except indirectly. Recently, more and more corporate executives see themselves as legitimate servants of a variety of constituencies. An organizational constituency is any identifiable group that organizational managers either have or acknowledge a responsibility to represent.

A social audit is a systematic assessment of a company's activities in terms of their social impact. Although few companies have ever attempted to conduct a rigorous social audit, most make efforts to respond to the public's desire to know how they are doing in social areas. Four possible types of audits are currently being utilized: (1) a simple inventory of activities, (2) a compilation of socially relevant expenditures, (3) specific program management, and (4) determination of social impact.

While business firms have contributed greatly to the high standards of living enjoyed in Canada, many people expect them to do more. But how much responsibility for society's problems should business assume? Those favoring increased corporate social responsibility advance arguments that: (1) it is in the best interest of the firm to pursue socially responsible programs, (2) they have the resources to do so, (3) society expects business to be socially responsible, (4) long-run profits for the business may increase, and (5) if business is not responsive to society's needs, the public may press for more government regulation.

There are several arguments against business assuming social responsibility. Dr. Milton Friedman, a leading opponent of business assumption of social responsibility, asserts that there is one and only one social responsibility of business: to generate profits within the rules of the game by engaging in open and free competition without deception and fraud. The major arguments against social responsibility include: (1) it misdirects resources and violates sound business decision making that should concentrate on making profits, (2) costs are excessive relative to benefits and therefore may cause prices to increase, (3) managers do not have the resources or skills to engage in social projects, (4) it concentrates too much power in the hands of business executives, and (5) it may lead to the deterioration of the free enterprise system.

Ethics is the discipline dealing with what is good and bad or right and wrong or with moral duty and obligation. The strength of the relationship between what an individual or an organization believes to be moral and correct and what available sources of guidance suggest is morally correct is Type I ethics. Type II ethics is the strength of the relationship between what one believes and the way one behaves. Generally a person is not considered ethical unless possessed of both types of ethics. Business ethics is the application of ethical principles to business relationships and activities.

REVIEW QUESTIONS

1. In general, how is North American business viewed by the general public? Provide examples. Do you think the perception is accurate? Why or why not?
2. What is meant by corporate social responsibility? Define and describe the relationships a firm has with groups in its external environment.
3. What traditionally has been the primary role of business in society? Explain. Should this role change? Why or why not?
4. Compare and contrast two opposing views of corporate social responsibility. Which, in your view, is more correct or appropriate?
5. Can corporate social responsibility be legislated? If so, give examples of such laws.
6. What are some examples of current practices of companies engaging in social responsibilities? Be specific. Are there others you are aware of from your own experience or reading?
7. What is a social audit?
8. What is meant by the term *ethics*? What determines ethical norms for managers?
9. Briefly discuss several examples of unethical practices by business managers. What factors affect managerial ethics?
10. What are some examples of ethical dilemmas faced by managers? How can they cope with these dilemmas?
11. What is the difference between illegal behavior and unethical behavior?

EXERCISES

1. Visit two local companies that have formal codes of ethics. Evaluate the code of ethics, bearing our discussion of ethics in this chapter in mind.
2. Select what you consider to be a local social or ecological problem — such as water or air pollution. Make a list of the groups or businesses within the community that are concerned about the problem. Analyze the impact of the problem on the various segments of the community. Develop a proposal for solving the problem, giving consideration to the benefits and costs of your solution.
3. Interview a manager about an ethical dilemma that he or she has faced. How did the manager resolve it?

CASE STUDY

Dilemma at Can-Roc Ltd.

Sandi Bentley is the chairperson of the board of Can-Roc Ltd., a manufacturing firm with headquarters in a large Canadian city. During the past few years the company has been under considerable but polite pressure from the business school at the local university to contribute to a scholarship fund for promising students. The dean of the business school argues that, since business firms like Can-Roc are one of the prime beneficiaries of university business schools, they should help with the cost of training students.

The university is not the only organization applying pressure for funds. The symphony and the ballet are also asking for charitable donations so that they can continue to contribute to the cultural richness of the city. Their representatives suggest that business firms like Can-Roc should contribute to the arts — like patrons in past eras — because they have a responsibility for the cultural development of the city where they carry on business activities.

After several years of this pressure, the board of directors agreed to establish a $10 000 university scholarship and to contribute $5000 each to the ballet and the symphony on a one-year trial basis. The board hoped that these

donations would demonstrate the firm's good citizenship. Sandi Bentley has pointed out that Can-Roc would get considerable free publicity from these philanthropic actions.

At the annual meeting at the close of the fiscal year, these contributions were mentioned by Bentley. At that point, Peter Illych stood up and, noting that he represented a group of 40 shareholders, said that they were unhappy with the donations. Illych claimed that the board had no right to give $20 000 to scholarships and cultural activities; he argued that the board was supposed to run the business well and see that it made a good profit. By giving to charity, the board was taking money out of the shareholders' pockets because less money could be distributed as dividends. Illych stated that shareholders had bought Can-Roc shares to get good dividend payments; with this kind of behavior, the board was preventing them from achieving their financial goals. Illych also questioned the board's competence to make decisions on charitable donations.

At the conclusion of this negative speech, several other shareholders stood up to say that they disagreed with the sentiments Illych expressed. While they agreed that the board's action meant a slight reduction in dividends, they felt that the decisions were reasonable. These shareholders agreed with the university and the arts groups that Can-Roc could not ignore important organizations in the city that were in real need of funds and that the corporation had a responsibility to consider requests for charitable donations.

The meeting ended with a promise by Bentley that the board would examine the issue of corporate charity and would report to the shareholders at the next annual meeting.

QUESTIONS

1. What kinds of arguments can you pose in favor of and opposed to corporate charitable donations?
2. What should the board of directors do about this issue? How should they defend their decision to shareholders represented by Illych? to the shareholders not opposed to charitable donations?

CASE STUDY

The Hiring of a Friend's Daughter

Petra Underys recently graduated from university with a degree in general business. Petra was quite bright, although her grades might lead a person to think otherwise; her education had been funded by her parents and she'd felt no pressure to excel. When she graduated from university, Petra did not find a job immediately. When he discovered this, Petra's father, Stan Underys, took it on himself to see that Petra became employed. Underys was executive vice-president of a medium-sized manufacturing firm. One of the people he contacted in seeking employment for his daughter was Bill Garbo, the president of another firm in the area. Underys's firm purchased many of its supplies from Garbo's company. On telling Garbo his problem, Underys was told to send Petra to his office for an interview. Petra duly presented herself and was surprised that, before she left Garbo's firm that day, she had a job. Petra may have been lazy but she certainly was not stupid. She realized that this job was obtained because of the hope of future business from her father's company.

It did not take long for the employees in the department to discover the reason she had been hired — Petra told them. When a difficult job was assigned to her, Petra normally got one of the other employees to do it, inferring that Garbo would be pleased with them for helping her out. She developed a pattern of coming in late, taking long lunch breaks, and leaving early. When her department manager attempted to reprimand her for these unorthodox activities, Petra would bring up the close relationship that her father had with Garbo. The department manager was at his limits when he asked for your help.

QUESTIONS

1. From an ethical standpoint, how would you evaluate the merits of Garbo employing Petra Underys? Discuss.
2. Now that she is employed and not behaving well on the job, Petra presents a problem to her department manager. How can the manager handle her in order to get her to work more productively?
3. Do you believe that a firm should have policies regarding such hiring practices? Discuss.

ENDNOTES

[1] Adapted from the Committee for Economic Development and from Sandra Holmes, "Corporate Social Performance and Present Areas of Commitment," *Academy of Management Journal* 20 (1977): 435.

[2]Kenneth E. Goodpaster and John B. Matthews, "Can A Corporation Have A Conscience?" *Harvard Business Review* 60 (January-February 1982): 132-141.

[3]Matsushita Electric Annual Report, 1979.

[4]Richard Tanner Pascale and Anthony G. Athos, *The Art of Japanese Management* (New York: Simon and Schuster, 1981): 51.

[5]Keith Davis, "The Case for and against Business Assumption of Social Responsibilities," *Academy of Management Journal* (June, 1973). Reprinted in Archie B. Carroll, *Managing Corporate Social Responsibility* (Boston: Little, Brown, 1977) p.35.

[6]Davis, 36.

[7]Milton Friedman, "The Social Responsibility of Business Is To Increase its Profits," *New York Times Magazine* (September 1970): 33, 122-126.

[8]Davis, 36.

[9]Archie B. Carroll, "Managerial Ethics: A Post Watergate View," *Business Horizons* (April, 1975): 77. See also Archie B. Carroll, "A Survey of Managerial Ethics: Is Business Morality Watergate Morality?" *Business and Society Review* (1976): 58-63.

[10]Code of Ethics of the Institute of Certified Professional Managers.

REFERENCES

Aarsteinsen, Barbara. "Business Giving Outpaced by Needs." *The Globe and Mail* (December 10, 1986): B1, B2.

Alvarez, Rodolfo; Lutterman, Kenneth G.; et al. *Discrimination in Organizations: Using Social Indicators to Manage Social Change.* San Francisco: Jossey-Bass, 1982.

Archer, Lawrence. "The Moral Minority." *Canadian Business* 59, (January 1986): 56–59.

Armandi, B. R., and Tuzzolino, F. "Need Hierarchy Framework for Assessing Corporation Social Responsibility." *Academy of Management Review* 6 (January 1981): 21–28.

Aupperle, Kenneth; Carroll, Archie; and Hatfield, John. "An Empirical Examination of the Relationship Between Corporate Social Responsibility and Profit." *Academy of Management Journal* 28, (June 1985): 446–463.

Behrman, Jack N. *Discourses on Ethics and Business.* Cambridge Mass.: Oelegschlager, Gunn and Hain, 1981.

Brady, F. Neil. "Aesthetic Components of Management Ethics." *Academy of Management Review* 11, (April 1986): 337–344.

Cannon, Margaret. "Doing Well by Doing Good." *Canadian Business* 60, (March 1987): 92–94.

Carroll, Archie B. "A Three-Dimensional Conceptual Model of Corporate Performance." *Academy of Management Review* 4, no. 4 (October 1979): 497–505.

Clutterbuck, D. "Blowing the Whistle on Corporate Misconduct." *International Management* 35 (January 1980): 14–16.

Drory, Amos, and Gluskinos, Uri M. "Machiavellianism and Leadership." *Journal of Applied Psychology* 64, no. 1 (February 1980): 81–86.

Ford, Robert, and McLaughlin, Frank. "Perceptions of Socially Responsible Acts and Attitudes: A Comparison of Business School Deans and Corporate Chief Executives." *Academy of Management Journal* 27, no. 3 (September 1984): 666–674.

Greenough, William Croan. "Keeping Corporate Governance in the Private Sector." *Business Horizons* 23, no. 1 (February 1980): 71–81.

Grunig, James E. "A New Measure of Public Opinions on Corporate Social Responsibility." *Academy of Management Journal* 22, no. 4 (December 1979): 738–764.

Henderson, H. "Changing Corporate-Social Contract in the 1980s: Creative Opportunities for Consumer Affairs Professionals." *Public Relations Quarterly* 24 (Winter 1979): 7–14.

Hipp, H. "Business Ethics and Society's Future." *National Underwriter* 3 (property ed.) (September 14, 1979): 7–14.

"How Business Treats Its Environment." *Business and Society Review* 33 (Spring 1980): 56–65.

Inwood, Margaret. "Ethical Investors Opt for Principles Over Profits." *The Globe and Mail* (January 2, 1987): B5.

Jones, T. M. "Corporate Social Responsibility Revisited, Redefined." *California Management Review* 22 (Spring 1980): 59–67.

Lippin, P. "When Business and the Community Cooperate." *Administrative Management* 42 (February 1981): 34–35.

Marusi, A. R. "Balancing Power Through Public Accountability." *Public Relations Journal* 35 (May 1979): 24–26.

Milner, Brian. "Firms Find South Africa Not Worth the Hassle." *The Globe and Mail* (November 29, 1986): B1, B4.

"Privacy Issue Arouses Concern about Ethics in Marketing Research." *Sales and Marketing Management* (December 8, 1980): 88–89.

Rosen, G. R. "Can the Corporation Survive?" *Duns Review* 114 (August 1979): 40–42.

Shapiro, I. S. "Accountability and Power: Whither Corporate Governance in a Free Society?" *Management Review* 69 (February 1980): 29–31.

Sonnenfeld, Jeffrey, and Lawrence, Paul R. "Why Do Companies Succumb to Price Fixing?" *Harvard Business Review* 56, no. 4 (July-August 1978): 145–156.

Waters, James A. "Catch 20.5: Corporate Morality as an Organizational Phenomenon." *Organizational Dynamics* 6, no. 4 (Spring 1978): 3–19.

White, B. J., and Montgomery, B. R. "Corporate Codes of Conduct." *California Management Review* 22 (Winter 1980): 80–87.

White, Louis P., and Wooten, Kevin C. "Ethical Dilemmas in Various Stages of Organizational Development." *Academy of Management Review* 8, no. 4 (October 1983): 690–697.

Comprehensive
Management
Case Studies

HOW TO ANALYZE
COMPREHENSIVE CASES

This section of the text contains 14 comprehensive management cases, which are considerably longer than those at the end of the chapters. In these comprehensive cases, you are given a great deal of information about a real company that has certain management problems. Your task is to analyze the information and then make suggestions that will resolve the management problems facing the company.

There are two basic approaches that can be used with case studies. Your instructor may ask you to answer the questions found at the end of each case. These questions focus on specific topics that have been covered in the text, such as leadership, communication, conflict, or change. To answer the questions, reread the relevant section in the text and then decide how it can be applied to the practical problems that are evident in the case. Using the text material to answer the case questions will help you bridge the gap from management theory to management practice.

The second approach to case analysis is a more general one and involves using a four-step problem solving process. Your instructor may suggest that you ignore the questions provided for you. Instead, you will be required to:

1. *Define the problem or opportunity:* In each case you will be able to observe either a problem that needs to be solved or an opportunity that can be exploited. When defining problems, don't be side-tracked by symptoms of the problem. For example, if a company's employees have low productivity, this is not the problem but a symptom of the problem. What you must do is discover specifically what is causing low employee productivity. Be careful about the assumptions you make. For example, don't automatically assume that something is wrong with the employees just because their productivity is low; management may not have designed the work system properly, and employees therefore might not be able to be productive even if they are highly motivated.

2. *Develop plausible alternative solutions:* Once you have defined the problem or opportunity, you must develop several plausible alternatives that might solve the problem or help management exploit the opportunity. Make sure that your alternatives will actually improve the situation; a "do nothing" suggestion is generally not worthwhile. Creative thinking is also important when you are developing alternatives. Try to think of unconventional ways to solve the problem or exploit the opportunity. Some of the most successful managers are those who are able to see alternatives that other, more traditional, managers cannot see.

3. *Evaluate the alternatives:* Each alternative that you develop must be evaluated. This is probably the most difficult part of case analysis. Do not start this step with an opinion about which alternative is best and then try to find information to support that opinion. Rather, develop a list of pros and cons for each alternative through a systematic assessment of the material in the case. This takes time, but when you have completed this step you will be able to decide which alternative(s) should be chosen.

4. *Choose the best alternative(s):* Select the alternative which, considering all the pros and cons, promises to do the best job of resolving the problem or exploiting the opportunity you have defined. More specifically, pick the alternative which best satisfies the specific criterion you think is important to the company — for example, profit, employee satisfaction, or product quality. In some situations, there will be multiple and conflicting criteria that should be satisfied. In these situations, the decision will be much tougher. Be aware that, no matter which alternative you choose, some individuals or groups in the case are going to be unhappy. From a management perspective, your job is to decide what will benefit the organization as a whole.

Keep in mind that, while there is no simple answer to a case study, some solutions are better than others. Therefore, the emphasis should be on working through the four steps to reach a workable solution to a problem or a workable strategy for exploiting an opportunity. If the process rather than the outcome of decision making is stressed, you will become adept at analyzing any management problem with which you are confronted. Developing the ability to solve management problems is one of the key elements in the manager's job.

CASE STUDY 1

Westcorp

Westcorp, located in Rosslyn, Ontario, is a waferboard plant employing some 120 people. It has been in operation for 15 years and has always been managed in a traditional style. The structure of the organization is illustrated in Exhibit 1.

Waferboard is a product made with compressed layers of wood. The layers are produced from trees that have been cut into fine wafers, then dried and compressed into sheets of waferboard. Waferboard is frequently used as a substitute for the more expensive ply-

EXHIBIT 1   Partial organization chart of the Rosslyn plant

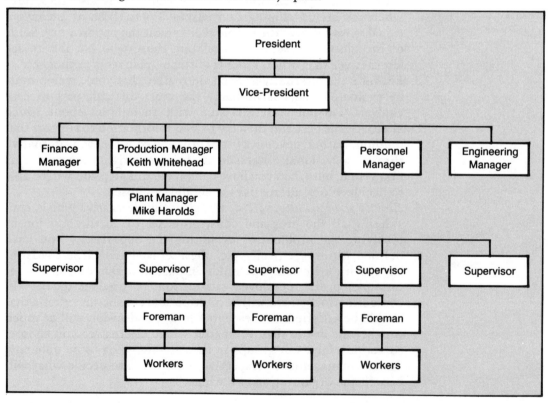

wood. The production process is reasonably simple, though regular technology changes occur because the industry is highly competitive.

The plant manager, Mike Harolds, was an oldtimer at Westcorp and had risen through the ranks. He had started with the company 25 years before as a shift supervisor in a British Columbia plant. He came to the Rosslyn plant 10 years ago. He believed in a rigid style of supervision and let the staff know who was the boss. He also encouraged his supervisors to use a firm hand when dealing with workers. "This is an excellent company," he would say, "with the best benefits in the province. We deserve good employees and good work and we are going to get it."

The senior management team recognized the fact that Harolds would be reaching retirement in a few years and so they left the plant floor supervision pretty much to him. However, the management team had been college-educated, and they preferred a more informal, participative style of management among themselves.

The turnover rate at the Rosslyn plant had risen steadily over the last five years. It was a good plant, relatively new, and paid hourly employees very well. Unlike most other plants in the town, it did not have a union. "The union boys just never seem to last long in my plant," said Harolds, who had loyal followers in the plant, workers he had hired and who stayed with him over the years. Most were now in their 50s and 60s. They kept a close watch on the operations of the plant for Harolds and acted as observers.

The younger workers in the plant were well aware of the older group and its members, and while there was no overt hostility, the group was recognized as "Mike's gang." They controlled the operation on the floor in a way which some younger workers feared, but few respected. Occasionally, the younger workers managed to get the ear of one or two of the management team and complained about the treatment, but not much could be done because of the firm grip Harolds had on the plant floor. Many of the senior managers liked Harolds, but the new personnel manager, Tim Stone, found Harolds' military style of leadership very difficult to cope with.

Harolds and Stone had tangled on several occasions. "I am running the plant," Harolds told Stone. "You can run the personnel office and stay out of my business." Stone felt that this style of leadership was outdated. His training had been in the "new" school of management thought that emphasized participation and involvement by workers. This was the polar opposite of what Harolds practised in the plant; he wanted robot-like response and would never have dreamed of asking workers for their ideas.

The problems in the plant remained under control in the short run, largely because Harolds managed to keep them under wraps and out of the view of the senior management people. However, a new cost control system was installed, and it revealed many problems with materials wastage. The profitability of the plant had been high until recently, with very strong markets and good demand for the product. Harolds prided himself on this performance. But the market had been saturated in recent months because of a proliferation of new waferboard plants. The cost system had been installed at the Rosslyn plant to tighten the control of the operations in the face of this new competition. The computer analysis showed that the Rosslyn plant was really very inefficient compared with other similar plants owned by the company.

Formation of a Task Force

Once it became clear to management that there were problems, a task force was set up by head office to examine the situation. It was comprised of managers from both the head office of Westcorp and from the local management team. The task force initially complimented Harolds on the loyalty he received from his men and the respect that management had for him in the company. But after the task force had conducted a more intensive review, it was clear that respect for Harolds was largely found among the older workers and that the young workers disliked Harolds' style and found him difficult to work with. The task force found serious problems in the quality control section of the plant and a great deal of spoilage and wasted material. This finding was confirmed by the accounting group who were helping with the analysis.

The management team was perplexed and spoke with Harolds about this. He explained that this had been going on for some time, and that the wastage occurred because he could not get the younger men to cooperate with him and do as they were told. "No matter how many times I tell them what has to be done and how to do it, they won't listen. They're late to work, and I find it difficult to find good men who will take orders and live up to my expectations. We have lost four quality control supervisors in the last three months. The basic problem is that in a waferboard plant of this kind, good communication has to take place among a number of key people to keep the manufacturing process running smoothly. I don't seem to be able to get the degree of commitment I need to run the plant efficiently. We get the job done, but it's very frustrating."

In a discussion with one of the foremen, it was revealed that it was very difficult to pin down the major problems. "The plant runs day in and day out, but there's an attitude of resentment and antagonism that is very discouraging," said the foreman.

The inquiry continued, with the task force conducting a series of intensive questionings and probings. "We pay them good money and give them an excellent benefit package and there's no union here. Why are we getting so little commitment and cooperation?" lamented one of the supervisors who was interviewed. At the end of its inquiry, the task force concluded that something had to be done, since the performance indicators were below par for a plant of this kind, and competition was increasing. The task force recommended that a more flexible style of leadership be introduced in the plant. They concluded that the problems of poor productivity and low worker morale were caused by the stern and forceful leadership style of Mike Harolds.

Stone Proposes Job Enrichment

Tim Stone, encouraged by Keith Whitehead, the production manager, found the time opportune to present some new ideas to management. He had been thinking about the possibility of job enrichment for many weeks and had even made a presentation on this subject to a local service group. However, his thoughts were not complete. He and Whitehead were adding ideas to the basic principle and trying to produce an adaptive strategy for the Rosslyn plant.

The management team, with the exception of Mike Harolds and his supervisors, received the idea with enthusiasm and interest. Could job enrichment work at Westcorp? This was the question on the minds of the management team. The indication was that it could, but substantial changes were going to be necessary. Stone felt that it would take some time to modify the basic job enrichment idea and adapt it to the Rosslyn plant. He intended to develop his plans in more detail and then introduce them to his colleagues, including Mike Harolds. He felt strongly that what management needed was a way of running the organization that recognized the importance of treating people differently and placing them in work situations suited to their unique needs, skills, and abilities. This, he felt, would have a beneficial effect on the profit picture. Mike Harolds would require convincing on this change, and Stone was willing to undertake the task.

The New Style

"The first thing we need to do," Tim asserted in a management meeting, "is to combine tasks. We are somewhat limited by our technology, but I think we can divide the plant into four major sections" (see Exhibit 2). Stone continued: "We will move away from the high task specialization dictated by the scientific management approach. We can combine highly specialized tasks into larger work modules. Our sectioning of the plant will undergo a further breakdown into specific jobs, and we will use job rotation within each section. In the wood prep room for example, we will describe about four or five jobs, and the workers will learn each job and rotate every two hours. This will not give us the full job enrichment we want, but it is as much as we can do given the constraints imposed on us by the design of the plant. The work teams will be able to hire and fire people and have considerable discretion on the job. The books will be open and people can have all the accounting information they want. Our profit picture will be available to anyone. Everyone will know whether we are profitable or not."

In a discussion with Mike Harolds, Tim Stone tried to point out the stregths of the new approach. Predictably, Harolds became more entrenched. His comments were as follows: "That textbook stuff is difficult to understand and is not how the factory is managed," said Harolds. "Job rotation, natural work units, feedback — what has all this got to do with running the plant? You are about to make the workplace far more complicated than it should be. My men don't want this nonsense!"

The Worker Response

The younger workers on the production floor responded favorably to the new ideas Stone was proposing. The older workers, on the other hand, were uncertain about the changes and made their feelings known to Harolds. The split opinion on job enrichment resulted in problems for the production operation. Stone pushed hard for planning and developing this new approach. He urged all the men to remain grouped and to have team meetings as much as possible to solidify the new program. Some workers did not like the new techniques of team work and group discussion. It annoyed

EXHIBIT 2   Proposed reorganizaiton of the Rosslyn plant

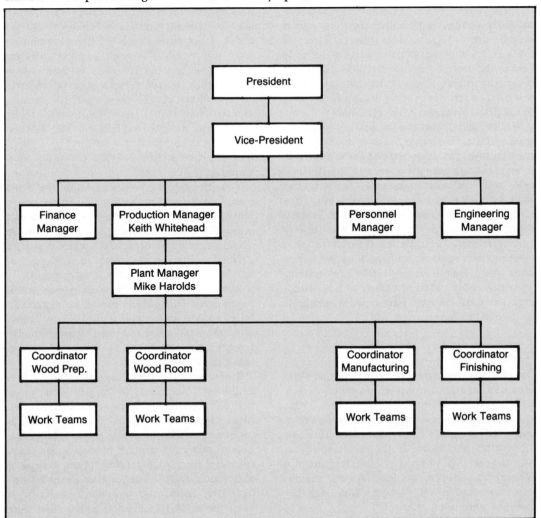

them to have to rotate jobs and learn new routines. Some men seemed genuinely confused. Tim Stone's frequent pep talks helped, but, as he himself recognized, the new system would need time to take hold.

Harolds was skeptical from the very beginning and made this fact known. However, he went along with the system, knowing that Keith Whitehead and senior management wanted the change. He intensely resented the loss of authority in this more "democratic" environment, and thought job rotation was a joke.

Under the new system production output varied from week to week, with some good days and many bad ones. The evening shift was proving to be most successful in adapting to the new system, possibly because it was dominated by younger and newer workers, and it seemed more a time to relax from the hurry of the day shift. Production meetings, usually held in the morning before the 8:00 a.m. shift, revealed this fact. The other managers picked this pattern up very quickly and pointed it out to the plant manager, Mike Harolds.

Weeks passed, and the pattern continued of good production during the evening and night shift, followed by a down trend in the day time. It was a significant difference. Typically Harolds and "his" men dominated the day shift with their ideas and approach to the job. They reluctantly held group meetings and seldom rotated through the series of jobs within a particular area. Their participation at the team meetings was sporadic and when present, they were quite skeptical about the new system. They paid only token attention to job enrichment and the related participative methods introduced by Stone.

Other New Ideas

Over the next several months, the evening shift showed a dramatic improvement in production and employee morale. The contributions of the workers from this shift were being accepted and introduced into the system. One idea (an innovation in technical design) saved the company a great deal of money. Management was pleased, and adopted the idea in other plants. Stone breathed a sigh of relief and knew his energies were not wasted.

Some workers were responding well to the program in other ways, too. The evening shift workers now had the opportunity to hire personnel for their team and they performed this function with maturity and commitment. New candidates were brought into the workplace and were interviewed by the team members individually and as a group. Those ultimately hired on the recommendation of the team worked out exceptionally well. "Management", a term now somewhat vague to the plant personnel, left most of the decisions to the team and to the team reps.

Training the new employees generally proceeded smoothly as the team members pitched in to assist new personnel. As well, on-the-job training, previously an unstructured exercise, now became far more routinized. Training was seen as an opportunity rather than a threat or a chore. Time during each shift was set aside to train the workers in each of their different tasks. While much of it was equipment maintenance work, it still very much interested the shift workers. At the same time, the training was structured into the promotion of the workers, adding a further incentive. The workers could, after completing a training unit, move to the other sections of the plant for more training.

The group cohesiveness within the work teams was slower to develop. When necessary, workers would cover for each other and a team atmosphere was beginning to emerge. On the occasions where an employee was not participating or sharing the work load, the group would discipline the individual accordingly. And when necessary the work group would recommend firing if the individual repeatedly failed to live up to expectations. Harolds usually supported these recommendations, but he resented the fact that he was not allowed to make the decision.

Turnover was reduced somewhat. Some men could not fully adjust to the new system and they left the company. The senior people under Mike Harolds still resisted the new ideas. In one incident, Harolds hotly protested to senior management the attempt by one of the teams to discipline an older worker for not discussing some mechanical changes that he had introduced. It seems the individual preferred to keep the matter to himself rather than share the change with the group. Fortunately, the matter did not get out of hand, but was smoothed over by management. Incidents like this bothered Stone and slowed down the effective implementation of job enrichment.

Overall, Stone's ideas were taking hold, but the situation was still very tenuous. There was a rumor that Mike Harolds was now talking to union people and had sworn to resist changes that were being implemented. Stone knew that his own approach was sound, and that in time it would be better for the plant. His task now was to swing the older production workers over to his side and get their commitment. Profit performance improved, but only marginally. There was still a lethargy in the organization that bothered Stone.

SOURCE   Professor Peter McGrady, Administrative and Policy Studies, Trent University, Peterborough, Ontario.

QUESTIONS

1. What principles of job enrichment are evident in this case?
2. What shortcomings were evident in Stone's introduction of the change?
3. Describe in detail the specific points that Tim Stone should have made in his presentation to the people involved in the plant.
4. What effect did the new management style have on Harolds? Why?
5. Why was Tim Stone successful with the younger workers and not the older workers?
6. Could Stone have converted Mike Harolds to his way of thinking? If not, why not? If yes, how?

CASE STUDY 2

Maids, Maids, Maids Inc.

Following the sale of his small business, Corporate Janitorial Services, Desmond Kennedy decided to move to Edmonton. After three months of relative inactivity, he became itchy for an entrepreneurial challenge. Not long afterward he noticed an advertisement for Minit Maids, a franchised residential-cleaning operation. After a brief conversation with a Minit Maid representative, Kennedy determined that, if he wanted to enter this field, he would be better to strike out on his own.

A search through *The Entrepreneur* magazine revealed a May 1979 article entitled "Maid Service Mops Up Money." The article described high first-year profits, low start-up costs, and rapid growth. Experience indicated that teams of two to four maids could clean seven to ten apartments or houses in one day. The team-cleaning approach was found to be price-competitive with traditional single housecleaners and, with better training and technology, could result in a better job.

Kennedy decided that, before investing any more time or money on this opportunity, he should try to find out something about the competition. From the telephone directory he identified 12 firms currently serving the Greater Edmonton market. All of the competitors performed the same set of standard services:

- Washing and waxing floors
- Vacuuming rugs and furniture
- Cleaning fridges and stoves
- Cleaning appliances and countertops
- Cleaning bathroom and kitchen tiles and fixtures
- Cleaning kitchen sink and cupboard fronts
- Dusting and polishing wood furniture
- General tidying
- Changing bed linen
- Washing inside windows and window sills.

Of the 12 identified competitors, Desmond Kennedy was able to obtain information from eight. (See Exhibit 1.) One telephone number was no longer in service; at two companies no answer could be obtained after repeated calls; and one firm used an automatic answering

EXHIBIT 1   Companies Competing in the Home Cleaning Market in Greater Edmonton

Company	Price	Contract	Bonding	Team/ Individuals	Training
Molly's Home Cleaning Service Ltd.	$10.00/1st hour $8.00/each add. hour per person	no	no—insured	teams of 3	on-the-job
Edmonton Personnel	$4.50-$5.00/h plus carfare	no	no	individuals (placement agency)	no
Classical Personnel	$6.00/h	yes, bring girls from overseas to work for 12 months	yes	individuals	no
Helping Hands Agency	$7.50/h minimum $30.00	no	no—unnecessary expense— checks refs., checks up new employees with customers	individuals, sometimes teams	community college fall, spring sessions
Broomhilda's Services	$17/wk. 1-bd. apt. $25/wk. 2-bd. apt. $30-$50 houses windows $15-$20 extra	no	insured	both individuals and teams	yes
OMO Maid Service	makes estimates for ea. job; 3 bdm. 2 bth. home $45/wk.	no	yes	teams of 2 or 3	yes
Ajax Home Services	quotation basis	no	no—checks refs.	individuals	yes
Mop Squad	$30/1st visit $24/subsequent visit	no	yes	not available	n.a.
Girl Tuesday	n.a.	n.a.	n.a.	n.a.	n.a.
Overseas Home Help	n.a.	n.a.	n.a.	n.a.	n.a.
Top Notch Services	n.a.	n.a.	n.a.	n.a.	n.a.
Exquisite	n.a.	n.a.	n.a.	n.a.	n.a.

device but did not respond to the message. Kennedy wondered what implications these data had for corporate life expectancy in this industry.

Although he was surprised by the number of competitors, he was not discouraged. He felt that there was a large opportunity in the residential-cleaning business. From his conversations with the various cleaning firms, he identified a number of different pricing schemes. None of the companies reported formal contracts with customers. Two firms bonded their employees and two said they were insured to cover security problems. Four of the eight firms contacted operated on a team basis, while the other four sent out individual cleaners. Three cleaning companies provided training, another one sent its people to a community college course, and a fifth firm had an on-the-job training program.

Kennedy was convinced that his background in the office-cleaning field gave him an advantage in terms of technology, selection and training of personnel. He believed the market would continue to grow. Kennedy cited the following factors:

- The increasing number of women in the workforce
- The growth in household incomes
- The decrease in family size (for instance, more singles and more childless couples)
- Changing values, which place more emphasis on keeping fit, being creative, doing important things, and which give less importance to mundane household activities
- More people living in apartments
- The growing intensity of life with family members involved in a multitude of activities.

In evaluating the home-cleaning business, Desmond Kennedy concluded that there were a number of needs satisfied. First, and perhaps most important, is the natural need to be clean. This is perhaps magnified in Canada by the Protestant Ethic and by the concern that someone might see one's home is not tidy. Another important need satisfied by a maid service is the desire to have time free to satisfy other needs, such as recreation and creative activities. There is also a sense of social status to be derived from being able to say, or perhaps just to think, "I have someone do my house cleaning for me." In a household where both husband and wife are employed, having a cleaning service may reduce the friction among spouses and children. Kennedy was also made aware of a modern aspect of this problem, described by a young woman. Before hiring a maid service, this young working woman had shared the cleaning chores with her husband. If he didn't perform his share well, and they had guests arrive, she felt that the guests would see her as a poor homemaker, not thinking that the husband was at fault.

In considering a target market for his proposed operation, Kennedy wondered whether he would be best to target on particular geographic areas, particular types of residences, or particular types of people. These factors obviously intertwined. There were a number of areas in the city with large family homes occupied by high-income professional and managerial people. There were a few districts with concentrations of apartment buildings where, in many cases, both spouses worked. Most of these people were at the extremes of the family life cycle. In other areas, there were multitudes of average-sized homes within which resided households with a number of employed members. For example, it seemed to Kennedy that there were many families in which both the parents and one or more adult children were employed.

Should Maids, Maids, Maids — the first name which popped into Kennedy's head and which he was stuck on — go into geographic areas where there was competition or try to identify an area that was not now serviced heavily? Should Kennedy try to take customers away from current services or identify people who were not now using a cleaning company?

Kennedy envisioned his service taking the form of a number of two-person crews, carefully trained and motivated to work with efficiency. Each worker would be bonded. Teams would travel on a pre-set route in an economy car. They would be equipped with tote-boxes of cleaning materials and highly efficient vacuum cleaners. Each worker would wear a distinctive smock with large pockets to carry cleaning tools and chemicals. Arrangements would be made with customers to be admitted to their homes by means of a key, apartment manager, or neighbor. The cleaners would be trained to move through each room in a predetermined time and fashion. Teams would operate systematically; each member would specialize in certain rooms of the residence. One team member would be designated as lead hand and would be responsible for the team's performance. The prime orientation would be to do an extremely good cleaning job very quickly. This would be the major selling point for Maids, Maids, Maids, according to Kennedy.

To ensure quality control, Kennedy was considering an inspection form that the lead hand would complete for each customer's home. It would list the standard and extra services performed and have an area for comments. The team would leave a copy of this inspection form behind for the customer and turn a copy in to the office. Unannounced spot checks would be made by Kennedy, who would also telephone a selected group of customers each week to ascertain whether they were satisfied.

Kennedy was also thinking about a set of extra functions which could be performed on a complimentary basis. Such things as polishing

EXHIBIT 2   Kennedy's Variable and Fixed Costs

Variable costs, calculated as follows:	Per hour	
Wages:		
Lead hand $5.00 + 5 percent for benefits	$5.25	
Cleaner $4.75 + 5 percent for benefits	4.99	
Total for crew		$10.24 /h
Materials:		
Gas and oil	$0.40	
Cleaning materials	$0.60	1.00
Total variable costs		$11.24 /h
Fixed costs, estimated to be:	**Per month**	
Fixed costs per crew:		
Leased vehicle	$130	
Insurance and handling	40	
Equipment depreciation	50	
	$220 /month	
General fixed costs:		
Office rent	$150	
Telephone and answering service	105	
Leased vehicle	130	
Advertising	40	
Business license	30	
Miscellaneous	20	
	$475 /month	
Assuming each crew would work 160 hours per month, fixed costs per crew per hour would be:		
One crew		$4.34
Two crews		2.86
Three crews		2.36
Four crews		2.12
Five crews		1.97
Six crews		1.87

silverware, cleaning the oven, or washing a wall could be done at no charge every once in a while to surprise the customer. Kennedy felt that this would be valuable for retention of customers.

Determining what price to charge was difficult. Based on his analysis of the competition, and considering it would take about 1½ hours for a crew of two to clean a unit, the average competitive price might be between $25 and $30. Competitive prices ranged between $17 for a one-bedroom apartment to $50 for a large house.

Kennedy assembled the information in Exhibit 2.

With an average cleaning job taking three person-hours and 30 minutes travelling between assignments (a lapsed time of two hours), the variable and fixed costs per job would be:

One crew	$2 \times \$11.24 + 2 \times \$4.34 = \$31.16$
Two crews	$2 \times \$11.24 + 2 \times \$2.86 = \$28.20$
Three crews	$2 \times \$11.24 + 2 \times \$2.36 = \$27.20$
Four crews	$2 \times \$11.24 + 2 \times \$2.12 = \$26.72$
Five crews	$2 \times \$11.24 + 2 \times \$1.97 = \$26.42$
Six crews	$2 \times \$11.24 + 2 \times \$1.87 = \$26.22$

If the operation was to generate a surplus of $10 000 to compensate Kennedy for his work and risk, the average price to customers would have to be:

One crew	$\$31.16 + \$10.42 = \$41.58$
Two crews	$\$28.20 + \$ 5.21 = \$33.41$
Three crews	$\$27.20 + \$ 3.47 = \$30.67$
Four crews	$\$26.72 + \$ 2.60 = \$29.32$
Five crews	$\$26.42 + \$ 2.08 = \$28.50$
Six crews	$\$26.22 + \$ 1.74 = \$27.96$

Clearly, Kennedy would have to have a number of crews operating to bring the price in line with the market. Attracting customers, he felt, would be based on an aggressive marketing campaign emphasizing superior cleaning, speed, efficiency, and trustworthiness. He considered that a direct mail campaign followed up by personal selling would be the best way to kick off his marketing program. He was convinced that, once the operation was off the ground, word of mouth would result in fast growth.

The personnel area was one which Kennedy considered to be key to the success of this venture. Should he recruit people experienced in cleaning or just try to attract willing and able individuals? Would it be best to advertise for employees, work through an employment agency, or contact Employment Canada? Kennedy knew that turnover would likely be high at first, and he wanted to reduce this as much as possible by careful selection, good training and supervision, and some form of incentive. Based on comments in the article in *The Entrepreneur*, Kennedy planned to use his own home as a training center for the first teams. Once a number of clients had been obtained, on-the-job training with lead hands would be possible.

Desmond Kennedy was not sure what success the Minit Maids organization had had in selling franchises, but he felt that this was a fast-developing opportunity. He believed he should decide right away whether to enter this market or not.

SOURCE   Robert G. Wyckham from Beckman, Good and Wyckham, *Small Business Management: Concepts and Cases* (Toronto: Wiley, 1982). Reprinted by permission of the publisher.

QUESTIONS

1. What are the strong and weak points of Desmond Kennedy's idea?
2. What kinds of supervision and control problems might Kennedy encounter?
3. What will be involved in performing the four basic functions of management?
4. Should Kennedy start the proposed company? Indicate how you reached this decision.

CASE STUDY 3

City of Fasofurn, Ontario

Fasofurn is a mid-sized municipality located in southern Ontario. The Planning and Development Department is one of eight municipal government departments integrated into a well-defined hierarchy. This department is responsible for the administration of the majority of bylaws and actions which affect private property. The department is comprised of urban planning, land use control (zoning), building and plumbing inspection, and property maintenance. (See the area within the dotted line in Exhibit 1.) The enforcement of all municipal bylaws (with the exception of municipal taxes), the inspection of all building and property, and all short-term and long-range planning that affects private property is controlled by this department.

By the fall of 1976 the director of planning and development had become concerned that his department was not functioning as effectively as it should. He felt that increasing staff dissatisfaction represented an important symptom of this problem. The following is an initial report which the director submitted to a firm of management consultants who were retained by the city to study the municipal government.

"Unlike all other city departments, which are directly responsible solely to the city administrator, some employees of my department are responsible not only to me, and thus to the city administrator, but also to boards and committees that may or may not be responsible to city council.

EXHIBIT 1   Planning and development department showing liaison with city council boards and committees

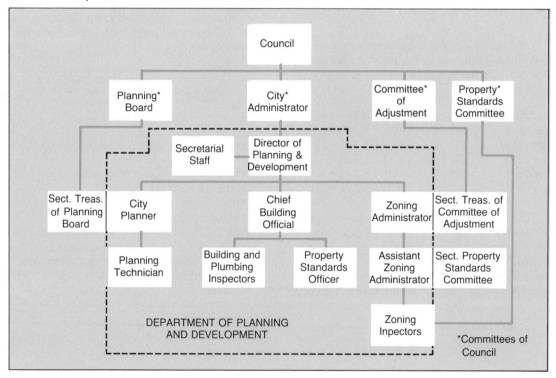

There are occasions when council opposes a committee decision and staff are requested to testify before the Ontario Municipal Board (OMB), the provincial government's body that regulates municipalities. Staff try to maintain their professionalism and testify in accordance with their prior decision. However, conflicts of interest may arise because council pays all staff wages. Over the years, some staff planners have found themselves unemployed for some minor reason after testifying too many times for the side opposing council. Our professional staff thus learned the hard way and now strive to reach a compromise when disputes arise. They are still left in an untenable position regarding some matters.

One recent case found planning board and department staff supporting an official plan amendment for a commercial development project which would have benefitted a neighborhood. The residents had been using the area as a private park and did not want the developer to build on his property. The ratepayers association raised such a commotion that council reversed the board's recommendation and the developer appealed to the OMB. The city solicitor requested council to hire an outside planner to support the city's negative decision, since staff had favored the proposal. Council gave instructions to the solicitor to discredit its own planning staff — which he did, and won the case for council.

One cannot help but notice the ramifications of this type of situation, which occurs frequently. Despite these instances, which impair relations between staff and council, the department generally operates more smoothly than other city departments and has far more real output.

Procedures

"The rules and regulations within the city government are very rigid. All bylaws and amendments thereto which it enforces are prepared by solicitors. All procedures and terms of reference are to be updated regularly to ensure all aspects of any work are covered. There are very few gray areas. When one is discovered, it must be clarified through either a legal interpretation, a policy statement, or an amending bylaw.

The degree of discretion for municipal employees would appear limited or nil. However, depending upon council's attitude (which will be discussed below), the staff acquire a sense of where discretion may be used. In gray areas or where procedures are not spelled out, the staff use their own discretion, as long as their decisions can be substantiated, if necessary, at a later date. This department has, on occasion, told council not to enforce its bylaws and constantly recommends amendments to make these bylaws and documents more flexible. Although our bylaws and procedures have rigid time requirements for staff action spelled out, discretion regarding enforcement is left to the accused and the staff member, provided his or her action can be justified if required.

Flexibility and discretion is a dangerous thing for staff. When one works for 13 elected members, one soon learns that 13 interpretations of a single issue will arise. If the issue is black and white, staff can avoid trouble by a strict interpretation. But, when staff provide flexibility to better serve the public, their job positions or chances for promotion are placed in jeopardy if their discretionary decisions do not sit favorably with the elected. Staff can always make decisions which meet the approval of 90 percent of council. However the opposing 10 percent is not the same 10 percent for each case. It only takes seven members of the 13-member council to remember some instance when staff did not support their view. They return the favor when staff are reviewed for promotion or for a salary increase. This is the one major reason government employees do not desire discretionary powers.

Recently, I was verbally attacked by an alderman for having a charge laid against a person for a zoning violation. The accused had cleaned up an abandoned eyesore building in an industrial zone and opened a commercial venture, which was not permitted. The alderman accused our department of being cold, inflexible, harassing, and forcing individuals onto the welfare roll. The following day the same alderman accused us of using no discretion when we legally issued a building permit for a house addition along his street, which he felt would devalue the streetscape. These are perfect examples of staff following the bylaws of their council and being accused on both occasions of using no discretion, because the outcome did not agree with one member of council.

The degree of impersonality in administering the regulations could have been described as extreme at one time. However, our department is now trying to create a more positive city attitude. When proposals do not comply to regulations, we do not use the "that's it — like it or not" attitude. We say, "Sure you can do it if you get these extra approvals," such as from the Committee of Adjustment or council. We also explain how the system works, how long it will take, what the cost will be, what the chances are, and whether or not we will support the request. We attempt to treat members of the public in the way we would want to be treated, if we were in their position.

Several months ago, a professional engineer visited our offices to obtain a building permit to renovate a house into offices for his staff. He was given a firm reply that he could not do that. Although the zone in which the house was located was zoned commercial, conversions from residential to commercial had to meet certain criteria, such as off-street parking and lot size, which his property could not do. He stormed out of the office, only to advise us by letter the following day that he was suing the municipality. I had the staff member reply to his letter, stating that he had not said the engineer could not renovate the house but that Committee of Adjustment permission was needed before he could renovate. The gentleman returned to our office. We explained the procedure, supported his application, and we lost. But he did go away happier, with an understanding of the system, and the feeling that he had received all the help and support that could be expected.

Goals and Objectives

"In January of this year, the department established long-range goals for the first time. (See Exhibit 2.) We did have policy established for our day-to-day procedures, but we had not previously formulated goals that our department could strive to realize. The goals were established by senior people and basically apply to our public image. These goals cover such items as achieving better communication with the public, being more sensitive to the public, encouraging more public input, and advising the public of the management of land, water, and air.

Although we realized it would take years of effort to change the public's thinking about municipal employees, the goals were established provisionally for one year. Many employees immediately noticed a change of attitude at the senior level, and they changed also.

EXHIBIT 2   Goals and objectives of the Department of Planning and Development

1. Advise council on the means of implementing its goals which affect this department through recommending bylaws, policy procedures, and related programs and setting department goals, objectives, and planned actions.

2. Achieve and maintain an open and mutual system of communication through which information can pass between this department and the general public. Members of council and other administrative staff are to create a climate of understanding and cooperation.

3. Strive to project an image of courteousness, friendliness, and sensitivity to members of the general public so as to overcome their apprehensions; provide the service in the manner we would expect if we were on the other side of the counter.

4. Provide information to members of the general public to expand their knowledge about the use and regulation of land; stimulate their input and interest in development in order to encourage their involvement in the future of the community.

5. Advise council, its boards, and the public on the management, development, conservation, and protection of our municipal resources of land, water, and air as they relate to the quality of life.

6. Keep abreast of improved techniques and concepts that pertain to the operation of this department to provide improved information, optimum efficiency, and a desirable standard of service, all at an acceptable cost.

Some remained the way they were. All knew that goals existed, but many did not know how this would affect them, or even what the goals meant to the overall operation of the department. The senior staff failed to explain adequately the overall philosophy.

I am now in the process of explaining the reasons for our goals to each employee and am receiving startling feedback as a result. Although the younger, more aggressive, intermediate staff agree with the goals, the older, longer-term employees do not want the public knowing more than absolutely necessary, for fear that the public might challenge an administrative decision. This same group also wants to discourage, instead of encourage, public input. They appear to be afraid that they, the staff, will be proven wrong, instead of adopting the intended attitude that the public's feelings are a necessary consideration in every proposed change. At the other end of the scale, we have employees who are not in the least interested in goals. These are the younger ones, people who work in the department just because it is a job, and who would move on for better money. There are also a few in this group who do not care about the department goals since only senior staff prepared them and they had no input. These differences in opinion seem defined by age group. The older, more established employees do not want change. The intermediate level, who are career oriented, strive to reach established goals. The younger, alienated employees do not care in the least what goals are established.

Policy has previously been established through tradition and authoritarian decree. Along with the municipality's general change in attitude to lessen the degree of bureaucracy and our department's internal goal setting, we are now beginning to review and revise policies to use wider staff participation. On one recent occasion, a task force was established. Although the task force created much strife at the senior level (because I did not explain my motives clearly enough), it did facilitate the required communication links.

I had decided it was time to review our policy for accepting building permit applications, because the requirements set down by the Ontario government had changed and it had been years since the policy's last review. The chief official was appalled at the thought of changing a policy he had established earlier. He saw nothing wrong with it as it was. The head secretary, whose clerk was responsible for accepting the permits, was of the opinion that the policy did not reflect today's requirements, was difficult to follow, and created unnecessary paperwork and confusion for the public. The two were at loggerheads. I established a task force comprised of the clerks in the secretarial staff who receive permits and the inspectors under the chief building official for whom the applications were received. I wanted fresh ideas from these people, who were actually involved in the process. I thought both divisions would keep their superiors informed of what was happening, so I did not take time to explain my action to the division heads whose employees were involved in the task force.

Unforeseen problems occurred. The chief building official was infuriated that only clerks and inspectors were being allowed to establish policy. He ordered his inspectors to prepare the policy by themselves, submit it, and say the other division was involved. The inspectors then told the chief official that they were selected without him because I had lost my confidence in him as a leader. The head secretary was upset because she thought the policy had been established without her clerks' input, which was not what had been decided earlier when the task force was established. And the lonely clerk who reported to the head secretary was still anxiously awaiting the first task force meeting to put forward a collection of ideas.

After the task force staff were assembled and the motives explained, the task force quickly established the policy, implemented it without senior staff ratification, and established a communication link which had never existed before. The chief official, however, still will not recognize the new policy and continues to work with the old.

Communication

"Our organization could be described as a typical hierarchy, and the chain of command attitude is enforced to show authority. We have always stressed two-way communication because upward communication keeps senior staff aware of what is happening at the lower levels and serves as a motivator for the worker. With our tall organization, supervisors are more accessible than with a flat organization, because fewer people report to each manager. It is not unusual to find the worker, senior staff, and department head sitting together to find a solution.

To encourage upward communication to our council, I attempt to call bimonthly meetings of the council committee I report to. Most departments object to such committee meetings. They do not appreciate the elected representatives dealing in matters over which they feel departments should have control. Our staff enjoy the meetings because they let the elected representatives know what we are thinking and vice versa. Whether or not they implement our recommendations is not as important as the continuing contact.

Lateral communication between departments has been encouraged to reduce senior staff's workload. Formerly, most communications were directed through the hierarchy, leaving most senior staff no time except to handle communications. With the present system, the communication travels laterally, and a copy of the letter or a verbal report is given to the supervisor to keep him or her informed. Some departments ask that their employees remain at the department for all business, but I encourage physical movement for face-to-face discussion if the other department is within easy reach. As a social builder it is great; for immediate feedback it is even better. It consumes more time, but usually more relevant information is volunteered, which may help in any decision.

Like most organizations, we have an unofficial network which can be of great benefit if department heads could tap into it. Usually, however, I do not become involved unless a disgruntled employee complains about a circulating rumor. I found this system very informative prior to becoming part of management but, since my promotion, I have been entirely cut out. Most of the information circulating within this network did have to do with management decisions. Because that information

was so informative when I was working my way through the ranks, I now circulate minutes of senior staff meetings to my own employees, which in turn are fed into the unofficial network. The idea is not to control this system but to ensure undistorted information is received by it.

Downward authoritarian communication is avoided wherever possible because of the coldness and demoralizing effect of the order. However, I do have one long-term employee who can be moved in no other manner. He hates change and even verbal direction has no effect. Anything of any importance must be written to him giving full directions. I do not know whether this is a result of his having spent so much time in the navy, or whether it is a result of him wishing to cover himself for every move or decision he makes.

Our channels of communication are among divisions within the organization, among our department and other city departments, and between our department and the general public. At one time our means of transmission was by personal letter. Now, we stress telephone calls to the public or to other departments and personal contact within the department. We have found that this method has cut down on distortion as well as providing immediate feedback. We follow up any out-of-the-ordinary telephone conversation with a confirming letter. We have also attempted to hire qualified technical help, on a part-time basis, which costs a little more per week, but has drastically cut down on training time and errors caused by the misunderstanding of technical matters.

External Relationships

"Since we are a department within a municipal body, we have dealings with city council, provincial government departments, programs and legislation, public wants and needs, other city departments, and the housing market and construction industry. Also important, though indirectly, are the influence of federal legislation on provincial policies; provincial legislation on municipal programs and policy; federal and provincial legislation and municipal policy regarding other city departments; market conditions and the construction industry; and the public's influence on municipal, provincial, and federal representatives.

To keep abreast of this complex external environment, we meet regularly with council, provincial departments, and other municipal departments to discover what types of legislation, policies, and programs are being proposed. We also monitor government newsletters, local papers, and opinion polls. We have even developed a system to provide this type of information to any external person or organization who requests it. Good communication links exist to our federal and provincial members of parliament, and we have a former provincial government employee on staff with numerous contacts within the provincial civil service.

Thus we were able to discover one funding program prior to its release by the federal government and quickly take the necessary steps to take full advantage of it. This will result in the city receiving close to $1.5 million in grants. Similarly, an Ontario program resulted in a $5.58 million noninterest loan to the city. During one of our regular meetings with the provincial government representatives, they had accidentally mentioned that the new program was forthcoming.

To keep the provincial and federal bureaucrats informed of our interests, we have established an arrangement with our mayor whereby we prepare a letter for his signature, which is sent to our local MP or MPP. This has been very effective, since the elected representatives respond far better to other elected officials than they do to civil service staff.

Although committees of our council meet almost daily, council, the legislating body, meets only twice per month. Some member of the public might ask permission of council to do something for which council's permission is needed. Two weeks later they meet and refer it to staff for a recommendation. We respond and they adopt it one month after the original letter was received. If they need more information, there is a delay of another two weeks. The public are also very slow to respond. We publicize apartment rezonings on radio, on television, and in the newspaper. We mail notices to everyone within 122 m but few respond. After perhaps a six- to nine-month period, the builder is ready to start construction and moves onto the site. The public then respond with complaints, but it is too late. The majority of politicians will stick with their original decision but are always sensitive to public pressure and critical of their own staff. They quietly check to see if we carried out the proper procedures. It is hard on staff morale to have politicians asking demeaning questions of our personnel in front of the televised council sessions, with staff given little opportunity to respond in depth.

Because of the complexity of our work, 80 percent of our staff are professionals; but the strong lines of authority that would be required to force the adoption of current government ideology do not exist. Government bodies are typically slow to act, leaving their staff much time to prepare for any response to the elected. Municipal staff personnel have an advantage over those reporting to the higher levels of government. Our aldermen are elected every two years, and the average turnover is about 40 percent. This forces staff to adapt to a different government philosophy every other year, instead of becoming entrenched and stale as provincial and federal bureaucrats may. Yet this periodic change of bosses may also be a source of hostility and conflict.

One former council always viewed staff as working hand-in-hand with developers against council. A large apartment complex was being designed and a road widening was required as a final condition. A recent transportation study had called for a 3 m widening. The old official plan, which had never been updated, called instead for a grass strip about 1.5 m in width. Normally staff would recommend the result of the latest study. But because of constant criticism by council, the problem was referred to the elected representatives to make a decision. We quietly supported the 3 m widening. After two months, they chose the opposite for no apparent reason. They indicated staff was not telling them what to do. Had it been a cooperative council, staff would have made the decision and had council ratify it, thus saving two months of interest carrying charges for the builder."

SOURCE Randy Hoffman, *Canadian Management Policy* (Toronto: McGraw-Hill Ryerson, 1981): 168–176. Reprinted by permission.

QUESTIONS

1. Comment on the goal-setting system used by this organization.
2. What are the important organizations in the external environment of the Planning and Development department? How can the de-partment more effectively cope with city council?
3. What kind of leadership style is being exhibited by the Director of Planning and Development?

CASE STUDY 4

Electronics Unlimited

Mike Craig, an economics major from Laurentian University, was employed by Agriculture Canada for three years and worked at the government offices for this department in the downtown area of Hamilton, Ontario. His work was assessed as above average and his ability to organize and present work efficiently as noteworthy. His job involved preparing reports and statistics based on current trends and developments in farm management. Mike had a number of colleagues with whom he worked on a cooperative basis, each supplying the others with pertinent data for their studies. The organizational hierarchy under which he worked was a traditional bureaucratic structure; supervisors tended to be formal and impersonal and there was strict adherence to procedure. It was within this atmosphere that Mike performed his research and administrative activity.

Mike's role was very clearly defined: he was assigned a supervisor to whom he reported directly. His research work was submitted at various intervals, but current progress was frequently examined. While there was cooperative effort among the workers, there was very little enthusiasm for the work. The challenge seemed to be missing from the required task, for seldom were the results of his research implemented into a strategy for action. Instead, much of the work was collated with other material for government reports and sent to Ottawa.

Mike had been dissatisfied with his job for about six months. He felt he had nowhere to go in this government position and, since he was still single and without family responsibility, he thought it was time to look for a more challenging job. He watched the newspapers for an interesting position and consulted a Toronto placement agency for opportunities. His interests, as he described them to an interviewer, were in joining a growing and dynamic company, possibly a young company looking for people to train as managers in an expanding operation.

Eventually the placement agency in Toronto uncovered an opportunity for Mike in a Montreal firm with a new subsidiary company in northern Toronto, called Electronics Unlimited. The company was new and growing in the field of electronic equipment for the home and office. It had a growing sales and distribution network with production to follow in the near future. The product line the company distributes is broad and serves both the industrial and commercial markets. There are many new and innovative developments in this field and in this organization. For example, the Toronto plant is organizing for a more sophisticated warehousing and distribution operation, and plans are forthcoming for a fully integrated Marketing Department.

Frank Wilson, the personnel manager, interviewed Mike Craig for an opening at Electronics Unlimited. Mike was immediately impressed not only with the organization but with the personal style of Frank Wilson who, as a manager, appeared innovative and progressive. He was quite empathetic to Mike's predicament and understood the value of growth opportunities in any company; also, the discussion of money and potential advancement in the organization seemed very promising. Wilson further discussed the young company's need for energetic managers with ambitious goals for achievement. As he suggested: "We have outlets to develop, contacts to be made, people to recruit, and many more activities that will challenge a young college graduate."

Mike was very excited about his meeting with Frank Wilson and his application to the company. He felt sure that Wilson liked him and would offer him a job with the company. The situation, too, he thought would be a complete change from his current position and a welcome relief from the routine. For the first time in three years Mike was enthusiastic about his life and the prospects it held for him. The job offer came through three weeks later, and he accepted the position with a substantial increase in salary. He was due to begin in early September, and he proceeded to resign from his government position and to find an apartment in Toronto.

The first two months on his new job were a real learning experience, as Mike Craig made himself acquainted with the people and the situation. Three other recent college graduates were hired from the area at about the same time. One of these was John Corrigon, a marketing major from the University of Western Ontario, a very aggressive, outgoing individual. The other two co-workers had degrees from McMaster in engineering and were studying for the MBA degree in the evening. The four new employees to the company all seemed to hit it off well at the start.

For the first six months the four young men were expected to get acquainted with the firm's operation and make themselves available to do reports and other tasks as required by the managers. (See the firm's organizational chart in Exhibit 1.) Mike Craig and John Corrigon became involved with the distribution and sales side of the organization. Their first task was to generate a report on potential users of electronic equipment in the area on a commercial basis. Their guidelines were to examine demographic trends, store openings, potential volumes, and customer needs. The existing group had made some contacts in this area but a thorough report and strategy were required. The managers of various departments indicated they would be available for consultation and enquiries. Craig felt very confident about this new assignment. His economics background provided him with all the knowledge to complete a thorough analysis of the area. Though he and Corrigon kept each other informed about their activities, they worked independently in different areas. Their plan was to meet before the date of submission and review their efforts.

Mike followed a steady pattern of work in the next week, confining much of his efforts to written material and research. Statistics Canada, *Financial Post* surveys of markets, and other books were among his sources of information. He gained confidence as the time passed. Corrigon, to avoid duplication, spent much of his time out of the office and in the field. He visited people and talked to them of their needs and requirements.

EXHIBIT 1 Organizational chart of Electronics Unlimited

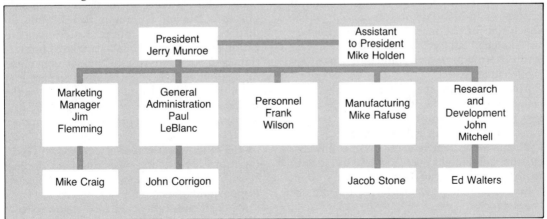

When Corrigon was in the office, he frequently visited the executive offices to gather information and to learn about the operation. Mike, for his part, conversed with the managers only at lunch. He would also take work home with him at night and on weekends. Many of the avenues he was pursuing were of great interest to him, and he wanted to follow them through in what was now becoming a lengthy report.

Craig and Corrigon met at the end of the month just prior to their submission to management. It was a brief meeting, with Corrigon flipping through Craig's typed pages of report material. Then, behind closed doors on a Friday afternoon, two of the managers, Flemming and LeBlanc, discussed the research and activities with the two new employees. The meeting was expected to take most of the afternoon, a rather formal atmosphere prevailing throughout the early part of the encounter. Later, over coffee, the meeting became more relaxed. Jerry Munroe, the president, came in for a moment and exchanged casual comments with the group. It seemed as though Corrigon had got to know Munroe, since they were on a first-name basis. Much of the discussion centered around Corrigon's ideas. He quoted names of people in key locations and presented an understanding of the needs and requirements of the area. Corrigon did not hesitate to initiate discussion and when necessary to focus the direction of the meeting. Craig, on the other hand, spoke infrequently and made vague references to his written report, his confidence dwindling as the time passed. Mike was continually forced to confirm by figures much of what Corrigon was expressing in his ideas and proposals. At the conclusion of the meeting, a short summary was sketched out by Flemming and LeBlanc on a flip chart summarizing much of what Corrigon had suggested.

Mike Craig left the office that afternoon somewhat dismayed by the results of the meeting. He felt Corrigon had dominated the discussion and not contributed Mike's ideas as he had expressed them in their pre-meeting discussion. He thought over Corrigon's ease with managers and the way they responded to him. Ideas and action were clearly the bywords of this company.

In the next few weeks many of the major ideas of the meeting were broken down into smaller areas of focus; both Craig and Corrigon were left alone on their jobs without too much direction. The managers continued to hurry through one task, then address another. Potential customers were given full details of the company aspirations and frequently Corrigon was asked to entertain customers and show them the operations. His aggressive and outgoing style seemed most suited to this task. Craig was given small reports to make and was generally left to muddle in the details. He would ask Corrigon for support from time to time on some of the matters, but seldom could he sit Corrigon down long enough for a meaningful exchange of ideas or plans. At the bimonthly meetings, Corrigon was never short of a comment or an idea for a particular project.

The manufacturing side of Electronics Unlimited was now coming on-line for full production. The two engineers who had been hired were working well under Rafuse and Mitchell in their departments. They had settled in their own offices and were very productive in their field, developing changes and ideas for the product line. Both Rafuse and Mitchell were satisfied with the new employees, particularly since they provided current ideas for their work. They had already been invited to Montreal to visit the main plant and production operation.

Flemming and LeBlanc continued to make good use of Corrigon and Craig, who were busy on the marketing side of the operation. However, nothing was clearly defined in this company. John Mitchell, for example, frequently provided data and reports for Paul LeBlanc on distribution networks for the area. The organization was run on a flexible pattern of interactions and responsibilities. Corrigon continued his aggressive style and developed an excellent rapport with Jim Flemming. They were in the process of hiring salespeople for the field and Corrigon was given an opportunity to conduct the interviewing and initial screening. Craig, on the other hand seemed always to be preparing more reports and analyzing data, largely because he had not been asked to take other responsibility.

Mitchell and Rafuse had also begun to take

advantage of Craig's report writing. By now, however, Craig had had enough and had become quite discouraged at these frequent requests. He began to wonder just what he was going to be expected to do on this "dynamic job." This uncertainty bothered him. At the same time, Corrigon was now beginning to annoy him with his abrasive style. He would ask for information and request of Craig routine jobs a secretary could do. Craig resented these requests but, in the interest of the company, would complete the tasks. Despite Craig's increased efforts at establishing rapport with the Marketing Manager, Flemming, he couldn't seem to produce results.

After six months on the job Craig had still not found it a satisfying experience. He was determined not to give up, however, and proceeded to present lengthy and detailed studies of market trends and other reports that would help the company. All the managers took advantage of his services to the point where Craig was frequently working on weekends.

Corrigon, well on his way to organizing a sales staff, also requested a lengthy analysis of sales potential for the company. Craig had worked himself into complete frustration. He refused Corrigon's request. He didn't feel he was there just to write reports but rather to become more involved with managing the company. He felt he was receiving little recognition for his contribution, while Corrigon and the two engineers were progressing much more rapidly. However, his refusal to write the report for Corrigon earned him a sharp rebuke from Flemming. This upset Craig and he felt he had to redeem himself.

Electronics Unlimited had been growing and stabilizing in the months that had passed. The retail outlets had been contacted and connections organized to complete the network of distribution. New products had been developed by the company and were marketed in an effective manner. The administrative staff had been growing to meet the requirements of the production and sales force. An incentive system for the sales force had been designed in the Toronto office and had received wide recognition from the Montreal company. Corrigon was instrumental in this effort and was appropriately rewarded for his contribution. A small achievement award was presented to Corrigon for his part in the design of the plan that had been implemented. The award was presented to him at an office get-together.

The event further deflated Craig's self-image in the growing company. What little spirit of camaraderie that had existed among the four employees who had arrived almost together had been lost by this time. Mike Craig had retreated into a gloomy silence, anticipating a difficult time in an upcoming evaluation that had been announced. The notice had come to the desks of the respective employees that they would be evaluated in the next month by the managers. It would be a formal evaluation, one that would take place in their offices over coffee. It would be verbal and based on discussion rather than a written document channelled through personnel.

Craig looked glum as he peered up from his desk after reading the memo, the first of its kind. Corrigon, with his usual cockiness, suggested that he would have to get the boss a bottle of good Scotch but that he really didn't have much to worry about.

Craig had less secure feelings about the whole procedure. He had this terrible feeling that he would handle himself poorly. In a brief discussion with Flemming one afternoon, he made enquiries about the method of evaluation, pointing out the traditional function of personnel administration. Flemming laughed at this idea, responding that around here they worked to get things done and did not worry too much about who did the evaluations.

The evaluation day arrived and Craig was assigned to Rafuse, the person he felt was least involved with his work. The interview and discussion went smoothly and very cordially. There were many silent moments during the course of the interview, and he went away feeling that his work was regarded as less than satisfactory. Rafuse had hinted that the company's interest lay in more outgoing individuals. Craig was left with mixed feelings about the company and his future.

Indeed, Craig felt the time had come for a confrontation with the management of the company and he proceeded to make an appointment with the personnel officer for a lengthy discussion about his future. He felt he might be able to get some straight answers from Frank Wilson, but he knew that he was taking a chance of finding out the worst. Some hard discussions would follow.

SOURCE Peter McGrady, Administrative and Policy Studies, Trent University, Peterborough, Ontario.

QUESTIONS

1. What kinds of problems is Mike Craig having at Electronics Unlimited? Discuss in detail why you think Craig is having these problems.
2. What can Craig do to increase his job satisfaction? What can he do to make his performance look better to management?
3. What factors might limit Craig's ability to improve his situation?

CASE STUDY 5

Atlantic Store Furniture

Atlantic Store Furniture (ASF) is a manufacturing operation in Moncton, New Brunswick. The company, located in an industrial park, employs about 25 people, with annual sales of about $2 million. Modern shelving systems are the main product and these units are distributed throughout the Maritimes. Metal library shelving, display cases, acoustical screens and work benches are a few of the products available at ASF. The products are classified by two distinct manufacturing procedures which form separate sections of the plant. (See Exhibit 1 for ASF's organizational chart.)

The Metalworking Operation

In the metalworking part of the plant, sheet metal is cut and formed into shelving for assembly. The procedure is quite simple and organized in an assembly-line method. Six or eight stations are used to cut the metal to the appropriate length, drill press, shape, spotweld, and paint the final ready-to-assemble product. The equipment used in the operation is both modern and costly, but the technology is quite simple.

The metalworking operation employs on average about 8 or 10 workers, located along the line of assembly. The men range in age between 22 and 54 and are typically francophone Canadians. Most have high school education or have graduated from a technical program. The men as metalworkers are united by their common identity in the plant and have formed two or three subgroups based on common interests. One group, for example, comprising the foreman and three other workers has season tickets to the New Brunswick Hawks home games. Another group bowls together in the winter and attends horse races in the summer months.

The foreman's group is the most influential among the workers. The men in this group joined the company at the same time and James Savoie, the foreman, was once a worker with

EXHIBIT 1 Partial organizational chart for Atlantic Stove Furniture

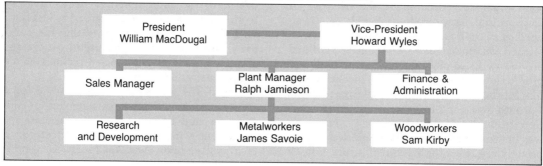

the three other men in the group. The group characteristically gets to the lunch counter first, sits together in the most comfortable chairs, and punches the time clock first on the way out of work. Conrad LeBlanc, another group member, has a brother who plays professional hockey in the NHL and he frequently describes the success of the team and his brother's large home.

The metalworkers as a group operate on one side of the plant and work at a very steady pace. The demand for the products in this section is high and the production is usually constant. The group adjusts well to changes in the order requests and the occasional overtime pressures. The salespeople on the road provide a constant flow of orders, to the point where there is a small backlog of requisitions to be filled. The products vary in size and style but for the most part they are standardized items. A small amount of work is performed on a customized basis.

Woodworking Operations

The woodworking operation differs considerably from the metalworking operation. It is a new addition to the plant and has had some success. It is separated from the metal production unit by a wide sliding door.

The organization of the wood shop is haphazard because the majority of its work is customized. Some areas are organized to produce standard products like screening, but the majority of the woodworking section is organized around a particular project. Typically tools, equipment, and supplies are left in the area of the partially completed projects. Custom cabinets and display cases are made for large department and retail stores. A small line of products are produced as a regular line while the rest of the products are custom designed. The flow of work is basically steady in the shop, but there are stages when the work orders become intermittent. Though the appearance of the woodworking shop is quite disorganized and messy, reflecting the nature of the operations, the workers in this section of the plant see themselves as real craftsmen and take considerable pride in their work. Typically, two or three projects are in progress simultaneously along with the normal run of standard

products. The metalworkers store some of their completed units in the woodworking area, to the dislike of the woodworkers and to the disorganization of the section.

Unlike the metalworkers, there is a distinct hierarchy among the woodworkers based on seniority and ability. Sam Kirby is the quick-tempered but fiercely loyal foreman; most of the full-time woodworkers have come through apprenticeship programs or have similar backgrounds to the metalworkers'. Most are middle-aged anglophone Canadians and beyond an occasional after-work beer at the local tavern, they do not spend time together. Through Kirby's persistence, an apprenticeship program within the company has produced a number of good carpenters. This section of the company, though still relatively young, has produced good work and has a reputation for quality craftsmanship.

The morning coffee break for the woodworkers follows that of the metalworkers. Lunch hour is staggered by 20 minutes as well. Only a minimal amount of interaction occurs between the woodworkers and metalworkers, as there tends to be rivalry and competition between the two groups.

Recent Events

The supervisor who oversees these two sections of the plant (plant manager) is Ralph Jamieson, a production engineer from a local university. As plant manager he reports to the vice-president. At the time of his hiring, ASF had not developed the woodworking section of the plant. Jamieson's work at the university became integrated into the production line when he discovered a method of galvanizing the metal product in final stages of production. He spends a good deal of his time in the metalworking operation planning and discussing problems in production with the foreman, James Savoie. Laboratory research is another occupation assigned to Jamieson, who enjoys experimenting with new methods and techniques in design and fabrication of metal products. Jamieson and Savoie are good friends and they spend a good deal of time together both on and off the job. James Savoie is quite happy with the way his operation is running. His boisterous, good-humored attitudes have created a very good rapport with his men and absenteeism is minimal.

A recent personnel change that has occurred within ASF is the addition of two new salesmen who are on the road in New Brunswick and Nova Scotia. Their contribution to the company is most notable in the metalwork area. They have placed many orders for the company. The new sales incentive program has motivated these people to produce and their efforts are being recognized.

Sam Kirby, the woodworking foreman, blew up at Jamieson the other day. Some metalworkers had pushed open the sliding doors with an interest in storing more excess shelving units in the woodworking area, without seeking Kirby's advice or permission. Sam is a hothead sometimes and has become quite annoyed with all the intergroup rivalry between the metalworkers and the woodworkers. Storage space has been a sore point between the groups for the last six months or so, ever since the metalworkers became very busy. Jamieson and Howard Wyles, the vice-president, were asked to settle the problem between the two shops and decided that the metalworkers were only to enter the woodworking shop if absolutely necessary and with consent of the foreman.

This latest incident really upset the fellows in the woodworking shop. The woodworkers feel intimidated by the metalworkers, who are taking space and interrupting their work. They grumble among themselves about the shouting and joking from the francophone assembly lines next door.

In a later conversation Kirby and Jamieson smoothed things over somewhat. It was explained to Kirby that it was the metalworkers who were really turning out the firm's work and that they needed the extra space. The area that metalworkers want to use is not really needed by the woodworkers; rather it is simply an area around the perimeter of the room by the walls.

Kirby did not like Jamieson's response, knowing full well his commitment to the metalworking operations. With this decision, the metalworkers proceeded to use the area in the woodworking shop and never missed an opportunity to insult or criticize the woodworkers in French. The effect of the situation on the re-

spective groups became quite obvious. The metalworkers became increasingly more jocular and irritating in their interactions with the woodworkers. The woodworkers grew resentful and their work pace slowed.

The infighting continued and became of concern to the president and vice-president. For example, the large sliding doors separating the shops were too hastily closed one afternoon on a metalworker who was retreating from a practical joke he was playing on a woodworker. The resulting injury was not serious but it did interrupt a long series of accident-free days the company had been building up. This incident further divided the two groups. Meetings and disciplinary threats by management were not enough to curtail the problems.

The woodworkers were now withdrawing all efforts to communicate. They ate lunch separately and took coffee breaks away from the regular room. Kirby became impatient to complete new products and to acquire new contracts. He urged management to hire personnel and to solicit new business. The work atmosphere changed considerably in the woodworking shop as the workers lost their satisfying work experience. Much of the previous friendly interaction had ceased. Kirby's temper flared more frequently as small incidents seemed to upset him more than before. After-work get-togethers at the tavern were no longer of much appeal to the men.

The metalworkers were feeling quite good about their jobs as the weeks passed. Their orders remained strong as demand continued to grow for their products. The metalworkers complained about the woodworkers and demanded more space for their inventory. The metalworkers were becoming more cohesive and constantly ridiculed the woodworkers. The woodworkers' concern for the job decreased as back orders filled up and talk of expansion developed for the metalwork operation.

Just as the metal shop became more confident, there were more difficulties with the woodworking shop. The woodworkers were completing the final stages of an elaborate cabinet system when information came regarding a shipping delay. The new store for which the product was being built was experiencing problems, causing a two- or three-month delay before it could accept the new cabinet system. Kirby was very disturbed by this news, as his woodworkers needed to see the completion of their project and the beginning of a new one. The predicament was compounded somewhat by the attitude of the metalworkers, who heard of the frustration of the woodworkers and added only more jeers and smart remarks. Morale at this stage was at an all-time low. The chief carpenter, an integral member of the woodworkers, was looking for a new job. One or two of the casual workers were drifting into new work or not showing up for work they had. Contracts and orders for new products were arriving but in fewer numbers, and casual workers had to be laid off. Defective work was beginning to increase, to the embarrassment of the company.

Management was upset with the conditions of the two operations and threatened the foreman. Kirby was disturbed at the situation and was bitter about the deteriorating state of the woodworking shop. Despite many interviews he was unable to replace the head carpenter, who had left the company attracted by a new job prospect. Efforts to reduce the intergroup conflict were tried but without success.

The president of ASF, William MacDougal, was alarmed with the situation. He recognized some of the problems with the different operations. One operation was active and busy while the other section worked primarily on project work. The organization was designed, he thought, with the normal structure in mind. The men in the company, he thought to himself, were very much of the same background and what little diversity there was should not have accounted for this animosity. As president, he had not developed a culture of competition or pressure in the company.

The disorganization and chaos in the woodworking shop was alarming and there was very little that could be done about it. Kirby had been discussing the problem with the president, trying to identify some of the alternatives. This had been the third meeting in as many days and each time the conversation drifted into a discussion about current developments in Jamieson's metalworking pursuits. James Savoie had told the president he felt that there was too much worrying going on "over there"! Plans for expanding the building at ASF were developing at a rapid pace. The president felt that more room might alleviate some of the problems, particularly with respect to inventory, warehousing, and storage.

Kirby became enthusiastic about the prospects of some relief for his side of the operation. He was very much aware of the fact that the performance of his operation was quite low. The president of the company felt satisfied that the woodworking concern was going to improve its performance. One or two new contracts with large department stores inspired an effort to improve the operation.

The men in the woodworking section became somewhat more relaxed. A few positive interactions between the woodworkers and metalworkers became evident. One afternoon about two weeks after the disclosure by the president of the new plant development, Kirby observed blueprints for the new expansion. The plans had been left on Jamieson's desk inadvertently and, to the surprise of Kirby, revealed full details of the expansion for the new building. Kirby sat down and examined the details more carefully and recognized that the woodworking area was not to be included in the expansion plans.

Kirby left the office in a rage and stormed into the president's office to demand an explanation. Kirby shouted that he had changed things around in the woodworking shop on the promise of more room and possibility of expansion. The president shook his head and apologized; he explained Kirby was going to be told but nothing could be done. The market demand was simply not that great for wood products. Kirby left the office and went straight for his car and drove off.

SOURCE   Peter McGrady, Administrative and Policy Studies, Trent University, Peterborough, Ontario.

QUESTIONS

1. List and analyze the factors which have led to intergroup conflict between the woodworkers and the metalworkers.
2. What negative outcomes have occurred because of this conflict? Are any positive outcomes evident?
3. Assess management's handling of the intergroup conflict so far.
4. Develop an action plan for resolving the problems at Atlantic Store Furniture.

CASE STUDY 6

Scott Trucks

"Mr. McGowan will see you now, Mr. Sullivan," said the secretary. "Go right in."

Sullivan looked tired and tense as he opened the door and entered McGowan's office. He had prepared himself for a confrontation and was ready to take a firm approach. McGowan listened as Sullivan spoke of the problems and complaints in his department. He spoke of the department's high personnel turnover and the difficult time he had attracting and keeping engineers. McGowan questioned Sullivan as to the quality of his supervision and direction, emphasizing the need to monitor the work and control the workers.

"You have got to let them know who is boss and keep tabs on them at all times," said McGowan.

"But, Mr. McGowan, that is precisely the point; my engineers resent surveillance tactics. They are well-educated, self-motivated people. They don't want to be treated like soldiers at an army camp."

McGowan's fist hit the table. "Listen, Sullivan, I brought you in here as a department manager reporting to me. I don't need your fancy textbook ideas about leading men. I have 15 years as a navy commander and I have run this plant from its inception. If you can't produce the kind of work I want and control your men, then I will find someone who can. I don't have complaints and holdups from my other managers. We have systems and procedures to be followed and so they shall, or I will know the reason they aren't."

"But that is just the point," continued Sullivan, "my men do good work and contribute good ideas and, in the face of job pressures, perform quite well. They don't need constant supervision and direction and least of all numerous and unnecessary interruptions in their work."

"What do you mean by that?" demanded McGowan.

"Well, both Tobin and Michaels have stated openly and candidly that they like their work but find your frequent visits to the department very disconcerting. My engineers need only a minimal amount of control and our department has these controls already established. We have weekly group meetings to discuss project and routine work. This provides the kind of feedback that is meaningful to them. They don't need frequent interruptions and abrasive comments about their work and the need to follow procedures for change."

"This is my plant and I will run it the way I see fit," shouted McGowan. "No department manager or engineer is going to tell me otherwise. Now I suggest, Mr. Sullivan, that you go back to your department, have a meeting with your men, and spell out my expectations."

Sullivan was clearly intimidated by this time and very frustrated. He left the office hastily and visibly upset. McGowan's domineering style had prevailed and the meeting had been quite futile. No amount of pleading or confrontation would change McGowan's attitude.

Sullivan returned to his department and sat at his desk quite disillusioned with the predicament. His frustration was difficult to control and he was plagued with self-doubt. He was astonished at McGowan's intractable position and stubbornness. He posted a notice and agenda for a meeting to be held the next day with his department. He left the plant early that day, worried about the direction he should take, and thought over the events that had led to this situation.

Background at Scott Trucks

The operation at Scott Trucks is housed in an old aircraft hangar in the Debert Industrial Park, near Truro, Nova Scotia. The government of Nova Scotia sold the building for a modest sum as it no longer had use for the hangar after the armed forces had abandoned it. The facility, together with the financial arrangements organized by McGowan, the president of Scott, made the enterprise feasible. (See the organizational chart in Exhibit 1.)

EXHIBIT 1   Partial organizational chart for Scott Trucks

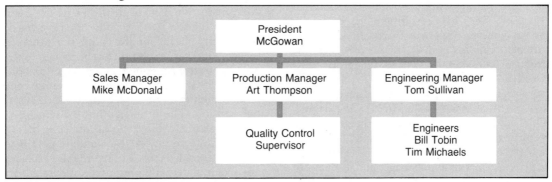

Inside the building, renovations have provided for an office area, a production operation, and an engineering department. The main offices are located at the front of the building, housing the sales team and the office clerks. The sales manager, Mike McDonald, and two assistants make up the sales team at the Debert location of Scott Trucks. Three or four field representatives work in southern Ontario and the United States. Mike is considered a good salesman and often assumes a role much broader than sales. Customer complaints, ordering, and replacement parts also fall into his domain. The production manager frequently makes reference to Mike's ability to talk on two phones at the same time!

Art Thompson has been production manager at Scott Trucks for eight years. The area he manages is behind the sales office and takes up most of the space in the building. The engineering department comprising small offices is located behind the production department, which is divided into two areas by a long narrow corridor. The shop floor is divided into basic sections of assembly, with a paint, a welding, and a cab section as well as other areas used to assemble the large Scott trucks.

Owing to the limited capacity of the plant only two or three truck units are in production at any one time. Another constraint on capacity is the nature of the system used to produce the trucks. There are no pulleys, belts, or assembly lines used in the system; rather, the production takes place in large bays, where sections of the truck are individually completed in preparation for the final assembly.

The truck units are used for a variety of functions, particularly where a heavy truck requirement is in demand. Fire trucks, highway maintenance trucks, and long-distance hauling trucks are some of the units produced by Scott. To some extent the trucks are custom-made as each purchaser will request changes on the basic design. The engineers are also adapting the trucks to meet the various standards and specifications of the Canadian government and of the vigorous and changeable Canadian climates.

Tom Sullivan, who is a recent engineering graduate from Nova Scotia Technical Institute, is the newest of the managers at Scott. He shows good promise as an engineer but, as with his predecessor, Tom Sullivan is having adjustment problems as a manager. Tom also received an MBA from Dalhousie University and majored in management science and organizational behavior. He completed project work in participative management styles under the direction of a specialist in this area. He tries to practice this approach in his new position and enjoys the ideas and flow of discussion at the department meetings. Tom works in a department with men much his senior and is the youngest of the department managers at Scott Trucks. He works hard and is well liked by his subordinates. Personal satisfaction, though infrequent, comes as a direct result of the open and participative management style he uses.

The Engineers

The composition of the group of engineers at Scott is unusual. One of the members is not an engineer by qualification but has many years of practical experience. He moved from Detroit to Truro, having worked with Ford Trucks for 15 years. Since his recruitment by McGowan he has worked with Scott for eight years. Retirement for this man is not far off, a fact he frequently makes known to the group. His work is good, and he seems to have many answers to difficult problems, a redeeming factor in the absence of an engineering degree. Don Jones, another member of the group, is a good engineer. His work day is solid; however, most evenings are spent at a local tavern. His wife was killed six months ago, and he does not seem to care any more about anything. The remainder of the group is a combination of senior and junior men who have been with the company for a number of years. Two engineers left the group for better jobs and for a "less confining atmosphere," as they put it. Tom Sullivan's efforts to lead the group are proving to be a difficult task.

The Production Workers

Work for the men in the production plant is reasonably stable. A well paying job in production in Truro is difficult to find, a situation of which the men are fully aware. Many of them experienced the monotony of unemployment and job hunting before this opening presented itself.

With the exception of a few francophone Canadian welders, the workers are Maritimers whose experience and skills range from those of a skilled tradesman to those of a casual laborer. The local trade school in Truro has provided the organization with a number of good machinists, welders, and painters that the foreman hired and began to develop.

The morale on the plant floor has been very good, particularly since the company has improved its sales position. The once frequent layoffs resulting from work shortage have ceased in the presence of higher demand for the trucks. The new field sales group contributes significantly to the situation by their efforts in southern Ontario and the northern United States. The pay scale is above average for the area and there is a good rapport between the production manager and the workers.

Administrative Control

Administrative control in the plant has been accomplished by two methods; one in terms of the quality of the product and the other in terms of its cost. Attention has been paid to the quality control function through a quality control supervisor, whose task it is to examine the end product in a thorough manner using rigorous criteria. The other method of control is that implemented by the accounting office. Through the adoption of a standard cost program, material, labor, and overhead variances are accumulated and presented on data report sheets.

The production manager, Art Thompson, is responsible for collecting cost data and for sending it to the office on a weekly basis. Art is not an easy-going person; he frequently gets upset when problems occur on the shop floor. He is closely watched by McGowan, the president. Consequently, to Art, the monthly meetings of the managers are a real ordeal, since McGowan, as owner, tries to watch the costs very carefully and to make sure the plant is running as efficiently as possible.

McGowan uses three approaches to managing the operation at Scott Trucks: (1) a monthly meeting with the three managers, (2) a series of interdepartmental memos that interpret the results of cost figures presented to him throughout the month, and (3) frequent plant visits and observations.

None of these controls is favorably received by the managers as they feel they are being watched too carefully. Interdepartmental memos may read as follows:

> May 12, 198X
> To: Mr. Art Thompson, Production
>   Manager
> From: Mr. McGowan, President, Scott
>   Trucks
> Re.: Materials Quantity Variance
> I noticed a considerable amount of material quantity variance in your production reports for last week. The standard cost system has been implemented for six weeks now, and it no longer suffices to say that you are still "working the bugs out of the system." It is time you paid closer attention to the amount of materi-

als going into the production process and to avoiding any spoilage.

Another example of an interdepartmental memo reads as follows:

May 20, 198X
To: Mr. Art Thompson, Production Manager
From: Mr. McGowan, President, Scott Trucks
Re.: Inaccurate Recording of Time and Use of Time Cards
I noticed last week on your labor cost submissions that a number of employees have been neglecting to punch time cards. Please see that this system is properly followed.

Art Thompson's reaction to these memos has been one of apprehension and concern. It is the practice of the foreman and himself to try to resolve the problems as quickly as possible and together, they have been able to rectify these difficulties quite rapidly, as the men are eager to cooperate.

The plant visits to the production area made by McGowan are frequent and effective. He has been known to come out in shirt sleeves and literally assume the worker's job for a period of time. This is particularly true in the case of a new worker or a young worker, where McGowan will dig in and instruct the individual on how he should be doing his job. On such occasions, McGowan will give specific instructions as to how he wants things done and how things should be done.

It makes McGowan feel right at home when he is involved with the workers. He spent 15 years as a navy commander, and he often used to remark that there was only one way to deal with his subordinates. The reaction of the workers to this approach is mixed. Some of the production people dislike this "peering over the shoulders"; others do not seem to mind and appreciate McGowan's concern for a "job well done." The workers grumble at McGowan's approach but feel most of his criticisms to be constructive.

McGowan's management approach in the monthly meetings with his managers is not considerably different. As with the production workers, McGowan assumes a very authoritarian style in dealing with his managers. The monthly meetings are an integrative effort by engineering, sales, and production, with the purpose of ironing out difficulties both on a personality basis and on a work basis. The work load in the engineering department has been growing for the last six months at a considerable rate. This reflects the increase in production and the need for people in the area of engineering and design to provide a high quality of technical expertise.

The number of engineers currently working at Scott is eight. Relations with the engineering department have been less than satisfactory and a good deal of conflict has occurred over a number of issues. For example, the reports from quality control at Scott have been poor from time to time and, increasingly, the problem has been traced to unclear engineering specifications. Upset about these conditions, McGowan has expressed his feelings in his memos to the department.

Lately, the engineers have been bombarded with McGowan's memos, the results of more frequent complaints about the engineering department from the quality control supervisor and the production manager. Along with other factors, they have provided the ammunition McGowan needed to confront the engineering department. The engineers, however, have resisted, refusing to accept these memos in the same way that the production people have. As a result of these memos, complaints and misunderstandings have arisen. The engineers have responded by suggesting that the production people cannot interpret the blueprints and that they never bother to question them when a change is not understood or unclear.

Disturbed by this situation, McGowan has made it a point to visit the engineering department at regular intervals and his tactics have been much the same as with the production people. Unfortunately, the engineering manager, Tom Sullivan, was feeling the pressure and could not seem to keep his department running smoothly. Being new to the job, he did not know how to handle McGowan. Two engineers had quit recently, apparently to leave the "confining atmosphere," going to better jobs elsewhere.

Tom Sullivan had reacted poorly to his new job situation and had been in a somber mood for about two months. His work and his adjustment had not been successful. The veterans in the department, though understanding his frustration, could not help Sullivan, who felt he was better off trying to accommodate McGowan than resisting him. To make matters worse, the two engineers who had recently quit had left a large backlog of work incomplete, and efforts to recruit new engineers had been a strain on Sullivan. The marketplace quickly absorbed all the engineers graduating from Nova Scotia Tech, and Debert had few attractions available to enable it to compete with larger centers.

Tom did get a big break in his recruiting drive when he discovered, through a contact in Montreal, two engineers who wished to return to the Maritimes. Both men were young and had experience and good training in engineering. In their interview, they discussed their experiences and their ability to work independently. Moreover, both were looking for a quiet work atmosphere. Sullivan liked their credentials and hired the two men: Bill Tobin and Tim Michaels.

McGowan had been on vacation at the time and had not met the new engineers until a month after they had been on the job. His first encounter, however, was a cordial meeting with the two engineers and, although the atmosphere in the department was always unpredictable and changing, activities and relations were smooth for a month or two, much to the relief of Sullivan. McGowan maintained his surveillance of the plant, including the engineers. Tim Michaels and Bill Tobin, the new engineers, felt uncomfortable with McGowan around but just proceeded with their work and ignored the long stares and the continued presence of the boss.

One Friday afternoon McGowan walked into the engineering department with a smug look on his face. It was near the end of the month just prior to the monthly meeting. Sullivan looked up immediately as McGowan moved toward Tobin's drafting table. McGowan was irate. He began talking to Tobin in a loud voice. Shaking his fist, he threw down a report on a change proposed by Tobin for the interior of the cabs made at Scott.

"What gives you the right to implement such a change without first going to Sullivan, then to me?" shouted McGowan. "You have only been with this company for two and a half months and already you feel you can ignore the system."

"Well, Mr. McGowan, I thought it was a good idea, and I have seen it work before," responded Tobin, flustered by McGowan's attack.

Sullivan came out from his office to see what the problem was about. McGowan turned to him and asked him why he couldn't control his men, adding that the changes were totally unauthorized and unnecessary. Sullivan glanced at the blueprint and was taken by surprise as he examined it more carefully. In the meantime, McGowan raved on about Tobin's actions. Sullivan roused himself to reply.

"Oh, um, ah, yes, Mr. McGowan, you're right; this should have been cleared between, uh, you and me before production got it but, ah, I will see that it doesn't happen again."

McGowan stormed out, leaving Tobin and Sullivan standing by the desk. Tobin was upset by "this display of rudeness," as he put it. "Tom," he went on, "this was a damn good idea and you know it."

Sullivan shook his head, "Yes, you're right. I don't know how to deal with McGowan; he wears me down sometimes. But you and Bill have to channel your changes through the system."

Tobin turned back to his table and resumed his afternoon's work.

For the next six weeks the plant operated smoothly as production picked up and more people were hired. Work in the engineering department increased correspondingly as people wanted new and better parts on their trucks. New engine and cab designs were arriving and put an increased burden on the engineering department. In fact, it fell well behind in its efforts to change and adapt the truck specifications to meet the Canadian marketplace. The lengthy review process required to implement change put an added burden on the operations at Scott. Moreover, summer was approaching, which meant decreased personnel, owing to the holidays.

McGowan's frequent visits added to the difficult situation in the engineering department.

Sullivan had initiated group meetings once a week with the engineers in an attempt to solve engineering problems and personal conflicts. At each meeting, Tobin and Michaels discussed their work with the group and showed signs of real progress and development. They were adjusting well and contributing above expectations. At these meetings, however, they both spoke openly and frankly about McGowan's frequent visits and his abrasive style. A month had passed since they first suggested to Sullivan that he talk to McGowan about the problems he presented to the engineers by his visits to the department. At first the rest of the group agreed passively to the idea that Sullivan confront McGowan on this issue but, by the fourth week, the entire group was very firm with Sullivan on this issue, insisting he have a talk with McGowan.

Tom Sullivan knew the time had come and that he had to face McGowan. Only that morning he had received a call from a local company inquiring about Bill Tobin and the quality of his work. Presumably Tobin had been looking for work elsewhere. This was the last straw. Sullivan had made and kept his appointment with McGowan.

SOURCE Peter McGrady, Administrative and Policy Studies, Trent University, Peterborough, Ont.

QUESTIONS

1. Contrast in detail the leadership styles of Sullivan and McGowan.
2. Describe the communication processes at Scott Trucks. What areas are most effective? What areas are ineffective? What can be done to improve the ineffective areas?
3. What is the most effective leadership style for the engineering manager at Scott Trucks? Support your choice fully.
4. What should Sullivan do now? What limitations exist in the engineering department that might constrain Sullivan's alternatives?

CASE STUDY 7

Eastern Tel

Mary Jacobs has been with Eastern Tel in Amherst, Nova Scotia, for 10 years, ever since the opening day of the telephone unit assembly plant in 1974. She speaks highly of the company, which has always served her well, the management, and her friends. She is a member of an informal work group in the plant that has developed over the years. A native of Amherst, Mary Jacobs left her job at Margolians, a local department store, to join a better paying operation at Eastern Tel. The clerical job she left had little future for her, while the new position appeared more demanding and less confining. A new opportunity, more salary, and a fresh start prompted her move to the factory position.

Testing and Getting Acquainted

A routine testing procedure is part of the job application system at Eastern Tel, and Jacobs met the requirements well. Hand and finger dexterity are needed for the job of soldering small wires together in preparation for further assembly of the telephone units; Mary Jacobs demonstrated a good capacity in these job requirements. A short personality test is also administered as part of the application procedure, and Mary performed well on this too. Of the original group hired, Mary Jacobs showed the greatest ability on the job, reaching the hourly quota output in the early days of her new job. A pleasant personality is also one of her characteristics. Her supervisor was impressed with her and Mary quickly won the respect and the liking of the management. Her satisfaction with the job and the factory atmosphere is very gratifying to her, particularly the informal status afforded to her by management, who frequently ask for ideas and advice. Jacobs' energetic style is evident in the plant where she is often asked to introduce a new worker to the operation. Not only is her help very valuable to many of the new workers but, also, most of the Amherst employees follow Jacobs' direction on the job and in other activities.

Indeed, Eastern Tel is not faced with a large number of personnel problems. The company pays well and relations are kept favorable with a good basic salary and frequent increases. Moreover, the reputation of the company is good in the area and the personnel manager often boasts about how many applications he has on file and the numerous job interviews he carries out during the week.

Production is usually on schedule, and the product is in high demand. Currently, the production comprises partial assembly of telephone units. Work is done at independent tables that resemble large drafting boards. Material parts are brought to the tables by stock clerks, and the product is subsequently shipped to Montreal for completion.

Company Image

To foster good morale in the plant and a good image in the community of Amherst, the company sponsors bowling teams, baseball teams, and other sports teams. The Eastern Tel logo is frequently seen in the community on sports sweaters and jackets. Mary Jacobs, as convenor of the bowling league in town, participates actively in organizing and administering the league. A good deal of camaraderie is evident within the plant, centering around the bowling results or playoffs in the league. Someone on the plant floor is frequently congratulated or made fun of regarding the scores in a previous night's game. Thomas, one of the stock clerks, has just begun to bowl and takes a considerable amount of ribbing from the plant workers.

The company has taken the time to develop supervisors and managers in the plant who understand the value of worker satisfaction on the job. As a result, production quotas are not compromised and satisfaction is very high. (A partial organizational chart can be found in Exhibit 1.)

Company and Workers' Background

Eastern Tel, which is associated with Bell Canada and Maritime Tel and Tel, has a steady supply of customers willing to purchase the

EXHIBIT 1 Partial organizational chart for Eastern Tel

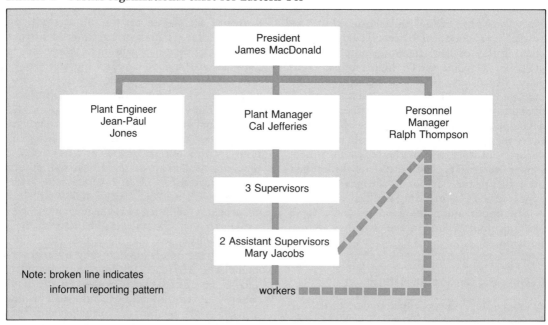

President
James MacDonald

Plant Engineer
Jean-Paul
Jones

Plant Manager
Cal Jefferies

Personnel
Manager
Ralph Thompson

3 Supervisors

2 Assistant Supervisors
Mary Jacobs

Note: broken line indicates
informal reporting pattern

workers

products. The operation at Eastern Tel is one of subassembly, as mentioned, with the units completed at the Montreal plant. Costs and market structures make this approach viable.

Eastern Tel was attracted to Nova Scotia and the Amherst Industrial Park on the basis of location incentive and lower wage rates. There had been more promise for the industrial park than had materialized, but a number of reputable companies had come to town. Amherst is a small town on the border of Nova Scotia and New Brunswick with a population of about 10 000 people. It is well located in terms of direct accessibility to other parts of Nova Scotia, but the economy is not fast developing. Other nearby centers, such as Springhill and Oxford, have very few industries or manufacturing operations.

Eastern Tel has a number of workers from Springhill who travel in a large van to and from the plant each day. The workers who come from Springhill can typically be found playing cards with their group over lunch or chatting about a previous night's hockey game. This group is usually quite friendly with the other workers but is notorious for its lunch-hour gossip. Pam Walters is one woman who comes in to the plant from Springhill. She is best described as an excellent worker, who rarely misses a day's work.

Pam Walters, though an excellent worker, is easily excited when things go wrong. An incident occurred not long ago that upset Pam, as she got into a fight with the stock boy over a shortage which prevented her from doing what she preferred for her afternoon's work. Pam became upset when the stock clerk gave the last carton of parts to Karen Henderson, a new worker and a friend of Mary Jacobs. The clerk refused to recognize Walters' seniority in the situation and gave the box to the new worker. It was not a serious incident, but it did mean Pam would have to work at a less desirable job for the afternoon. A few problems emerged from this dispute, but nothing serious. Pam's group supported her in this conflict, and much of the talk on the way home was about the foolishness of the stock clerk.

The group from Springhill occasionally found itself being slighted by one incident or another, though their common transportation difficulties and hometown kept them together and looking out for one another. Moreover, their success on the job kept them in good standing with most of the workers and management at Eastern Tel; one or two of the foremen were from the Springhill area, which added some support during the occasional conflict.

The culture in the plant at Eastern Tel could be described as relaxed and noncompetitive. The shop is clean and, though it is not tidy, a sense of organization and accomplishment exists. Country music is heard throughout the shop as the women work away at their large tables. An informal atmosphere prevails on the floor. Managers and workers speak freely, discussing and resolving problems. At one large table, four women sit facing one another, working on an output quota, soldering minute wires into an exact pattern to form the innards of a telephone unit.

The main composition of the work force at Eastern Tel is women. Many of these women support their families. The productivity of the plant is usually quite high, the morale is likewise fairly good; the women have good opportunities to interact and socialize both on and off the job. The hourly wage is high, in relation to that of the community in general — the minimum rate being typical in many of the adjoining plants. The company holds barbecues and skating parties to keep people active and involved with the company.

Plant Changes at Eastern Tel

One morning the plant manager, Cal Jefferies, walked into the plant and called the supervisors together to inform them of a meeting that would take place in his office in 30 minutes. The three supervisors, the plant engineer, and the personnel manager collected in the manager's office. Jefferies introduced Mel Pardoe, the chief engineer from the Montreal plant, who informed them about an important proposed plan for changing the layout of the plant floor. The operation was going to be changed because head office wanted the Amherst plant to complete the telephone units to the full assembly stage. The Maritime market was beginning to grow and demand for the telephone units was increasing. The more complex process of shipping the partially completed units to Montreal would soon be ended. Pardoe elaborated very carefully on the new changes that would take place on the shop floor.

"You see, ladies and gentlemen, the new design is more efficient and it will reduce the time required to assemble each unit. Floor space will be utilized to a greater extent, and the system is designed to require fewer workers. This is the rationale behind the plan. Our operations in Montreal and California are much more efficient. Now you may be thinking that the operations are not comparable since we are just putting in the new plan, but my point is that overall the plants are more efficient with this line assembly. Allowing Amherst to complete the task from start to finish will fulfill this objective. The cost structures of production in the plant are forcing us to make this decision. We expect to produce 30 complete units an hour initially, then move to 50 units at full capacity. The line assembly you will see is quite efficient.

"The diagram on this chart," Pardoe continued, showing them Exhibit 2, "illustrates the changes we will make adding this new line and allowing us to complete the product here in Amherst. This method will eliminate the work tables altogether. The work tables are okay for the work in the early stages of assembly, when the product is small and the operation simple and precise. However, when the telephones reach more complete stages of assembly, moving them from table to table will become difficult and so the line method will be more efficient.

"We will eliminate the stock boys' moving partially completed units from table to table," the engineer explained. "The units will now move down the assembly line with each worker adding a part to the unit.

"Are there any questions, ladies and gentlemen? Do you understand the concepts? It is basically a simple rearrangement of the existing operation."

The personnel manager, Ralph Thompson, smoked his pipe as he examined the chart. "How many people are we going to need to work on this new line assembly?" he asked. "How many lines are we going to have? Do you think this is the best system? Our workers are not used to or may not adjust to this kind of a system. You know as well as I do the pace of the shop is not all that high."

"That is precisely the reason we need to increase the production output! Your workers will adjust," said the engineer. "The change is

EXHIBIT 2   Eastern Tel's new production set-up

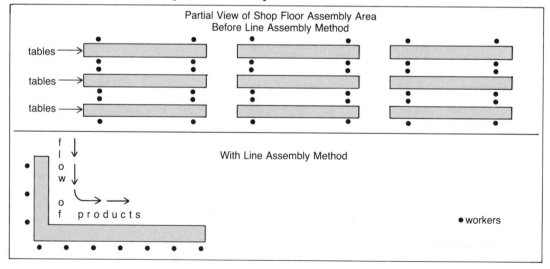

not all that great. If they don't adjust, get rid of them. Don't be soft."

The plant manager, Jefferies, interjected, "Now wait a minute. We don't deal with our workers that way. We've established good worker relations here in Amherst and we have loyal employees."

Questions and discussions followed, but the plans were in place. The changes were introduced over a long weekend in May by a team from Montreal. The work tables were replaced with a new line assembly system.

First Four Weeks of Production

The first four weeks of production proved to be very discouraging with the new line setup. The supervisors tried to appease higher management by saying the problems were all the result of learning and the workers were still trying to get the bugs out of the new system.

Jefferies could not accept the excuses, as pressure was being put on him from Montreal head office to get production on stream. Jefferies recalled also the details of that promotion for Mary Jacobs. Thompson had pushed hard for it, emphasizing Jacobs's spark and enthusiasm on the job. It hadn't been part of the original plans for change, but Thompson felt that she deserved the position since she'd been so helpful and cooperative in the past. Jefferies had thought it might ease the change for the workers.

Jefferies tried to find the answer to the problems by interviewing the supervisors and the key people on the assembly line. Thompson followed up by approaching Jacobs. Their findings were revealing.

Jefferies's Reaction

Jefferies was upset with the developments. A month had passed and the change was taking longer to implement than anticipated. Interpersonal conflicts had erupted throughout the plant. The once-present congeniality among the workers was decreasing noticeably. Rumors were rampant about layoffs that were forthcoming. In a conference one morning, Jefferies and one of the supervisors discussed the situation.

Jefferies: What's going on out there? The line is 50 percent below production levels. How do you explain it?

Supervisor: Well, I don't know. I'm used to the old system of the women working on individual tables and working at their own pace — enough to meet the quota. The workers seem so discontented. You kid with them now and they complain. The job seems the same but not as relaxed as before. One woman told me she feels pressured all the time and hates not being able to leave her position when she wants to get a cup of coffee. Others complain of having to wait until 12:30 to eat lunch. I don't know; I can handle the paperwork on this job but the damn complaints are driving me crazy. Mary Jacobs argues a lot with those two women from Springhill you hired for the line job. You should have heard the remarks the other day. Wow!! I guess we'll give it a few more weeks and see what happens. But the situation could blow up any time. The Springhill group is upset about Jacobs and her new title and increase. Assistant supervisor might have been a hasty move. I mean she is good . . . but!

Jefferies: That was really more Thompson's decision than mine! But we have to live with it now.

Supervisor: I am telling you quite frankly, Mr. Jefferies, I feel the trouble is going to worsen. Pam Walters is a very capable and respected worker. Many feel she should have been promoted.

Ralph Thompson Reacts

Ralph Thompson, the personnel manager, walked back and forth in his office with signs of concern showing on his face. He too did not like the feel of the change that was in place. As usual in times of difficulty, he called Mary Jacobs into his office to talk over the situation. He tried to keep things on an informal basis and spoke in a light-hearted way about the problems with the change, but he was visibly concerned about the production figures and the discord he observed among the workers.

He felt Mary's experience would help to establish this new system of telephone assembly. Thompson felt that by taking workers from the existing work force and training them on the system, a stable situation would develop.

These workers, together with ten new workers, made up the new group. A small pay differential was used to attract the workers from existing jobs in the plant. After a briefing and a number of trial runs, production had begun. There was going to be difficulty with the new layout, Thompson could feel it.

Thompson: Mary, I'm surprised things are not running more smoothly than they are. The boys in Montreal think we're asleep out here in Amherst, and the boss would like to get to the bottom of the problem pretty quickly. The line's organized to produce 50 units an hour and we're doing 20 units. What's the problem?

Mary: Mr. Thompson, nothing seems to be going very well. We get the telephones down the line, but the people at quality control constantly reject the units for one reason or another. I don't know! The women on the line are an odd bunch. They don't seem to want to listen and they do not like the pace of the line. They don't seem to be involved with their job and those two you hired from Springhill are hopeless. All the job requires them to do is add a small element to the unit as it comes down the line, and they get it wrong a lot of the time. I've told them to concentrate on the job rather than talking, but they don't seem to listen. The work is not that hard, just boring and tedious. And at lunch hour, no one talks or jokes any more. The idea of having to produce so many units an hour as a group is different from individual quotas. The women don't seem to like it much. I guess too, Mr. Thompson, it's the freedom we miss. It's so confining on the assembly line. Morale is really low and the complaints among the workers are tremendous. It's not the same as before the change. People are quitting now and those late to work are also on the increase. That van from Springhill is always 10 or 15 minutes late.

Thompson: Well, I don't know! You are one of our more experienced workers. I've given you more responsibility with this change hoping you could lead the group. Try to keep it together and reduce the number of defective units the quality control turns back. The executives from head office are due to come down next month for a review.

The difficulties in the plant worsened in the next week. Production runs were behind schedule, bickering among the workers was very noticeable and quality control became backed up with rejects. The pressure continued with missing inventory, and flattened tires on employees' automobiles. The supervisors were at a loss to know what to do. Employees from Springhill were arriving late more frequently and some days not at all. Jacobs approached Thompson with her concerns, but he was too overworked with hiring new people to replace those who had left.

SOURCE   Peter McGrady, Administrative and Policy Studies, Trent University, Peterborough, Ont.

QUESTIONS

1. What is the central problem at Eastern Tel? Why has it developed?
2. Assess in detail management's handling of the change in production methods.
3. List the steps that can be taken to improve the morale and productivity of the workers at Eastern.

CASE STUDY 8

Kryzowski and Sons Ltd.

Art Kryzowski, one of three sons of an immigrant tradesman, was in his final year of pre-law studies at University of Manitoba in 1941. In more ordinary times he would have looked forward to staying in school, working for admission to the bar, and an eventual comfortable living in a local general practice. His father, a sheetmetal worker by training, had built up a moonlight business repairing and reselling industrial salvage. By the early 1930s, it had grown into a full-time business, which brokered used machinery to small business owners, providing the family with a stable and substantial income. Kryzowski senior was the personification of the work ethic, pouring countless hours, heart and soul, into running the family business. He dreamed, like so many of his generation, of a company which would become Kryzowski and Sons and allow his children and grandchildren to enjoy the advantages in life that he and his wife had missed.

By 1941, Kryzowski senior's dreams were well on the way to realization. All three sons had been exposed to the business through summer and part-time work. Carl, just finishing high school, was a dismal student and rather easy-going, but had a natural bent for mechanical objects. His good nature and empathic touch with lathes, pumps, and presses made him popular among the shop hands and an obvious candidate for running the production activities of the company. The oldest brother, Alfred, was tall, handsome, and outgoing; Alfred frequently accompanied his father on visits to customers. Persuasive and likeable, Alfred was visualized by all concerned as the future sales director of Kryzowski and Sons, although his interests clearly lay more in enjoying the good life than setting sales records. Nominally in his fourth year in business studies at McGill, Alfred was active in fraternity life, a dinnertime companion of young men whose fathers ran major corporations, but a ''Gentleman's C'' scholar only by dint of numerous purchased papers. Art was nearly the opposite of his older brother; short, stocky, intense, and introverted, Art inherited his father's tendency to be a workaholic. He was regarded by fellow students as a greasy grind, but one whose constant efforts were grudgingly respected. Art had comparatively little social life during those years, instead spending most of his spare time helping out in the company office.

1941 was a year of decision for the Kryzowski family. As the war effort moved into high gear, the family business prospered. With new components and virgin materials in short supply, new customers and orders were added. However, the war effort also made its demands on the company's staff. Early in the year, Alfred surprised the family with a dinnertime announcement that he had resigned from the university and enlisted in the RCAF. Three weeks later, Alfred reported for training as a pilot officer and, except for short home furloughs, he was absent until demobilization in July 1945. From his infrequent letters, it was evident that Alfred cut a dramatic circle in the RCAF. He flew Wellingtons and later Lancaster bombers on night operations over occupied Europe until late 1944, completing three tours of duty and accumulating several decorations before being posted to an operational training unit in the north of England. What came through less clearly in his letters was the taste Alfred had acquired for reinforcing his battered nerves with whisky, which accounted for his failure to advance beyond Flight Leader rank.

Late in 1941, against the protests of the entire family, Carl enlisted in the Navy. Carl's mechanical aptitude was quickly recognized, and he was assigned to a service school for machinists, fitters, and artificers after an initial tour in Corvettes, small anti-submarine crafts. Carl was retained as an instructor by the service school and passed the remainder of the war as a petty officer. He was able to take most of his furloughs at home, at the cost of many sleepless nights on the train between Halifax and Winnipeg, but was lost as a contributor to the firm for the duration of the conflict. By 1945, Carl was a chief instructor at the technical school and received superlative service evaluations. However, a few stints filling in for the director while the latter was on leave convinced both Carl and his superiors that he would never be an effective administrator.

1941 was also the year in which Kryzowski senior had his first heart attack. A bull of a man in his mid-50s, Kryzowski rebounded well, but it was a bad portent and forced him to reduce his activities drastically. The brunt of the extra work fell directly on the shoulders of Art Kryzowski. The shop hands were typically older men who had been with the company for years and required little supervision. However, the onus of inspecting, estimating, and haggling on lots and prices, keeping fences mended with established customers, and running the financial side of the business also fell increasingly on Art Kryzowski. Despite his ambitions for law school, and accompanied by sub rosa entreaties from Mrs. Kryzowski, Art began to spend mornings — then afternoons and weekends — making calls, visiting suppliers, and troubleshooting for client firms.

By the Christmas holidays, Art Kryzowski found himself hooked. Every day he spent at the office uncovered new problems and crises which only he had the stamina to unravel. He could count on his father's advice, but all of the footwork and a growing proportion of the key decisions had to be handled alone. In the process, Art also burned bridges behind him. The long hours at the office included many cut classes, late assignments, and a barely passing average for the semester despite dropping one course. When Kryzowski senior had his second heart attack in February 1942, Art, who was already hopelessly behind in his coursework at Manitoba, spoke with his faculty advisor and dropped out of school.

Art Kryzowski's youth was all that sustained him through the next three years. With Kryzowski senior now partially handicapped, although mentally alert, Art not only took over the leadership of the firm, but assumed the equal burden of negotiating every minor change or decision past a suddenly conservative and reluctant Kryzowski senior. In the months before the end of the war and the return of his brothers, Art learned first-hand the folly of running a firm out of one's hip pocket. Records were disorganized or absent entirely. Scheduling was nonexistent. Every supplier and nearly every customer had been demanding and receiving special concessions, and much of the machinery had been jury-rigged so many times that repairs were a nightmare. Art managed. He managed, however, only by putting in still more hours, gradually learning all the peculiarities and wrinkles of the business on a case-by-case basis, and looking forward to the day his brothers would return and share the responsibility. Having learned the hard way how overextended and harassed one can become running a business as a one-man band, Art entered into a career which for the most part emulated his father's example.

This is not to say that Art did not make any changes, or that the firm did poorly in his hands. With Mrs. Kryzowski too distraught and occupied with caring for her husband, Art found it necessary to hire a full-time bookkeeper and office assistant. He wondered at times if it was the right decision, but it did free him from a lot of routine activities and brought

a semblance of order to the financial records. He also engaged a general accountant to handle tax matters and give him periodic financial advice. Art was frankly surprised when he examined the financial statements. The company, despite years of seat-of-the-pants management, was financially healthy. The building, machines, and trucks were owned outright, and there were no outstanding long term debts. The short-term picture was equally good. The company was paying salaries to himself, both parents, his brothers in absentia at reduced scales, and 18 hourly employees, and was turning a surplus, which his father had been plowing back into inventory. The inventory, in turn, secured any credit necessary to fund new purchases. Nominally valued at $30 000 in 1944, the inventory was a mixed blessing, as many of the items stocked were obsolete and unlikely to sell except as scrap. Looking ahead, although little could be done under wartime conditions, the entire physical plant and truck fleet would require replacement within a few years.

The return of Carl and Alfred was initially unremarkable. Alfred was furloughed on terminal leave in July 1945, and Carl in October of the same year. Carl slid unobtrusively into his old activities in the shop, where his knowledge and energy measurably improved output. His old Navy and seaport contacts were extremely useful in obtaining war surplus tools and equipment to modernize the shop and expand the inventory. The shop and warehouse became Carl's personal domain over the years, and on a day-to-day basis he ran them well. Although his title was a more grandiose "vice-president of production," Carl was in fact a glorified foreman, referring any unusual decisions directly to Art Kryzowski.

The Post-war Years

The decision to move away from the scrap and salvage business into the provision of new and used pumps and air compressors tended to change the nature of the business. Although the company continued to stock scrap and salvage, the emphasis was on pumps, pipe, and hoses. The company became known as the source for used specialized pipe (stainless steel, copper, natural gas, and hoses for pumping chemicals and corrosive liquids). The pumps sold and, remanufactured by the company, were used in the pulp and paper industry, gas transmission, chemicals, and manufacturing. Air compressors provided power for equipment in construction, manufacturing, and assembly work. The importance of pumps and air compressors to the various firms meant that a breakdown required prompt repairs. Often plants or construction sites were shut down for lack of a pump or the failure of an air compressor.

Under the direction of Art Kryzowski, the firm responded to the needs of its customers. Air compressors and large pumps were not only sold and rebuilt, but rented. A 24-hour service department was added. The company prided itself on being able to deliver new or used pumps or air compressors anywhere in the province within 24 hours. The trucking fleet was expanded. As the industries which Kryzowski and Sons served grew after the war, the company prospered along with them.

Art, although he welcomed the reduced workload made possible by Carl's return, was still more hopeful about what Alfred could do for the firm. He looked to his outgoing and imaginative older brother as someone who would be a more active managing partner and who would help to redirect and expand the firm to exploit post-war opportunities. Alfred concurred, at least verbally, and agreed to work as rapidly as possible at taking over the entire marketing and customer relations function.

In a business sense, the company did well indeed. The company's reputation for quality repairs and used machines carried over into the new enterprises, often with the same customers. The building was modernized and expanded to include a showroom and a second warehouse. Sales continually grew and the firm grew with them. Over the next 30 years, the Kryzowskis pursued a conservative and prudent course, building the firm into one of the dominant forces in the regional market. The general economic decline of the late 1970s saw sales peak and then slip, but business remained both comfortable and profitable.

The firm also did well by the Kryzowski family. With the business apparently well in hand, Mr. and Mrs. Kryzowski gradually relaxed their vigilance, slipping by 1950 into unofficial retirement on very healthy executive

paycheques. The Kryzowski brothers, as they acquired family responsibilities and their own children grew into their teens, also did well. At the behest of their tax accountant, a real estate subsidiary was formed to rent the Kryzowskis' homes to them, and most of their families were put on the payroll in one or another capacity. It was only when one looked at the internal dynamics of the firm that any cause for concern might have arisen.

In that initial period of reorganization and expansion after the war, everyone was on unusually good terms. There was so much work to be done that the Kryzowski brothers all worked horrendous hours to keep the growing business together. But Art Kryzowski gradually became aware of a sense of disengagement by Alfred. Alfred dutifully made calls on all of his regular customers and took over the supervision of the one, and then the three, young men Alfred and he brought in to keep up with customers relations, direct sales, and running the showroom. However, his initiative in seeking out new clients and trying to broaden offerings gradually trailed off. Alfred spent more and more time in sales lunches with old customers and commensurately less at the office. His conversations with Art increasingly centered on taking more out of the firm. He regularly suggested bringing in bright young professional managers so that he, Art, and Carl could have more time for their families, and seemed to be as concerned with how to set up tax sheltered benefits for family members as with making the company grow. As Art put the situation in a family argument in 1974, Alfred was acting more like a paid employee and less like one of the family team, leaving Art to work ever more hours and make all of the tough, important decisions virtually on his own.

Alfred's version of the story was substantially different. Like Art, he looked back fondly on the rush and bustle of the post-war period, when everyone was too busy to worry about family politics or titles or the like. And in his off-guard moments Alfred would ocasionally admit to confidants that he was not going to "kill himself" for the company, like Art. However, Alfred's major objection was the behavior of Art Kryzowski. In Alfred's terms, Art was treating the company more and more as his personal property, which had to be protected at all costs from mistakes by Alfred or Carl. He insisted that they adopt his viewpoint on all significant decisions, intervened in their deliberations with major customers, and in general acted as though he were the father and they were his teenaged, impulsive offspring. So if Art wanted to run the show, let him. Alfred was making a good living, doing a fair share of the work for what he earned and, if he felt excluded from the corridors of power, he more than compensated by a fuller family and social life.

Carl was largely oblivious to all of this, although the issue occasionally arose in family arguments. He ran his shop and ran it well. And until Art started making mistakes which hurt his shop, he would stick by him.

This process continued for years, never emerging into open confrontation, but never existing far below the surface. Art became the man who dominated the firm, made the key contacts, and met with customers. Customers called Art almost any time of the day or night when a pump failed or an air compressor broke down. During the construction season, customers often demanded immediate service, and Art grew accustomed to staying at the office for extended periods of time.

On July 17, 1980, Art Kryzowski had a fatal heart attack. He was alone in his office and was not found until the next morning. He was 59 years old.

The death of Art Kryzowski was duly noted in the local obituary column, but it did not cause much of a stir. The company closed for the funeral, and all 30 employees attended. Everyone knew Art as an intense and likeable workaholic. It was only after the funeral that Carl and Alfred looked at one another helplessly and asked each other: "What do we do with the company?"

SOURCE Ronald L. Crawford from Harold A. Gram, *Facts & Figures: Cases in Business Policy* (Toronto: Wiley, 1982): 193-197. Reprinted by permission of the author.

QUESTIONS

1. Describe the management problems that are evident in Kryzowski and Sons Ltd.
2. Create a plan that will allow Carl and Alfred Kryzowski to remedy these problems and put the company on a solid, long-term footing.
3. What role has organization and family politics played in this company?

CASE STUDY 9

Central Decal, Ltd.

Late in the evening of January 20, 1981, Roger McIntyre sat in his hotel room in Calgary thinking about one of the most significant business decisions he had ever faced. During the last several months, McIntyre and his business partner, John Altman, owners of Central Decal, Ltd., had been having difficulties with their business. McIntyre attributed some of these difficulties to Altman. At dinner earlier in the evening, McIntyre had told Altman that either Altman had to leave the firm or he would. Altman expressed shock and surprise at this comment and asked why McIntyre felt this way. McIntyre replied that Altman's work in the finance area of the firm was completely unsatisfactory and that unless this problem

was resolved the company could not survive. As he sat in his hotel room, McIntyre wondered if he had been right to give Altman the ultimatum.

Company Background

In June 1978, Roger McIntyre and Bill Merrill formed Central Decal, Ltd., a private corporation with McIntyre and Merrill as the shareholders. Each man had put $15 000 into the business. As well, they received a $40 000 federal grant after they promised to create 11 new jobs with the money. The company manufactured four products: decals, point-of-purchase displays for retailers, displays for trade shows, and plastic forming products. Most of the sales of the firm were to retailers and manufacturers in the prairie provinces, eastern Canada, and the upper midwest in the United States.

The company has $200 000 worth of machinery (book value) in the plant. The equipment is as modern as any in western Canada. In fact, there is only one other firm in Canada that can compete with the ultraviolet screen printing process used at Central.

Marketing. The basic marketing problem is to avoid getting into contracts that consume significant amounts of production time but don't give much financial return. Since screen printing can be done on almost any material, there is a temptation to accept a wide diversity of jobs. Specialization and high volume in a few areas are the key to both production and marketing success. McIntyre doesn't know what the total market potential is, but the company has never had any trouble generating sales.

The marketing strategy involves both personal and mass selling. The company employs five industrial sales reps, including McIntyre and Altman, who are paid a salary plus bonus. The company also spends approximately $600 per month on advertising in the Yellow Pages and elsewhere. The company does extensive direct mail advertising and regularly attends trade shows. Sales are often made to other exhibitors at trade shows. The emphasis in all these areas is on what Central can do for the customer. To demonstrate this, the company is actively involved in making up samples of their work that are relevant to a potential customer. Sales contracts are often signed after the customer sees these samples.

Finance. The relevant financial information for the company is contained in Exhibits 1 and 2.

Personnel. Employees are hired if they are experienced in screen printing and if their personal interview is successful. There is no union at the company. No formal personnel testing is done. Performance appraisal is also informal. Wage rates for production workers are based on their performance and aggressiveness as determined by Roger McIntyre. Thus, workers with more seniority may make less than workers with less seniority. McIntyre feels that there will be no need to hire any production or administrative staff (excluding replacement for resignations) for at least one year.

Recent Developments

In December 1979, Bill Merrill left the business for personal reasons. Roger McIntyre was left as the only shareholder, so he began looking for someone who wanted to join the firm and share the management responsibilities. After some searching, John Altman was brought into the firm as one of the shareholders because he was both a chartered accountant and a management consultant for small business.

Central was growing very rapidly, and McIntyre felt that some financial control was necessary. Altman came into the company on the understanding that he would produce the firm's financial statements, conduct financial dealings with the bank, and share management responsibilities with McIntyre. Shortly after Altman joined the firm, however, two problems arose. First, Altman had difficulty delegating authority. As a result, many jobs were not being completed on time because Altman would not delegate the work, nor could he do it all himself. There was also some uncertainty among the workers in the company as to who they reported to — McIntyre or Altman.

Second, it became clear that Altman was actually more interested in production and marketing than he was in finance and accounting. The cash flow projections and financial statements which Altman was supposed to produce rarely got done. Relations with the bank were also less than satisfactory. In May 1980, several of Central's cheques were returned because of insufficient funds. McIntyre felt certain that Altman knew a cash flow crunch was imminent, but Altman had made no plans to cope with it. Promises had been made to the bank that they would get monthly financial reports on the firm's condition but this had not been done either. When the crunch came, Altman put about $50 000 of his own money into the business to resolve the crisis; he was able to do this because he came from a wealthy family. After this incident, McIntyre and Altman had a meeting, when it was agreed that Altman would not let this happen again. However, after about two months it became clear that

EXHIBIT 1

CENTRAL DECAL, LTD.
Balance Sheet as of April 30

Assets

	1981	1980	1979
Current Assets			
Cash	$ 100	—	—
Accounts receivable	235,407	$160,943	$ 62,719
Inventories	134,032	81,239	25,057
Prepaid expenses	1	626	978
	$369,540	$242,808	$ 88,754
Other Assets			
Shareholder loans receivable	—	—	$ 6,015
Development incentives grant receivable	$ 5,352	$ 5,352	$ 5,352
Deposits	—	3,521	6,868
	$ 5,352	$ 8,873	$ 18,235
Fixed Assets			
Equipment and leasehold improvements	$210,070	$175,761	$ 88,874
Less accumulated depreciation & amortization	57,702	31,549	7,950
	$152,368	$144,212	$ 80,924
Total Assets	$527,260	$395,893	$187,913

Liabilities

	1981	1980	1979
Current Liabilities			
Bank advances, secured by demand debenture over all assets	$198,949	$155,440	$ 76,160
Bank loan	—	58,946	—
Accounts payable and accrued liabilities	135,514	119,276	67,409
Taxes payable	13,366	10,658	4,425
Principal due within one year on long-term debt	8,002	8,002	8,002
Cheques in excess of cash on hand	45,966	—	—
	$401,797	$352,322	$155,996
Long-Term Debt			
GMAC loans, payable $867 monthly including principal, interest, secured by chattel mortgages	$ 17,194	$ 24,262	$ 31,598
Less principal included in current liabilities	8,002	8,002	8,002
	$ 9,192	$ 16,260	$ 23,596
Shareholders' Loan	151,334	108,484	—
Deferred Development Incentives Grant	1,784	10,706	21,413
Total Liabilities	$564,107	$487,772	$201,005

Share Capital & Deficit

	1981	1980	1979
Share Capital	$ 63,000	$ 31,000	$ 46,000
Deficit	(99,847)	(122,879)	(59,092)
Excess of deficit over share capital	(36,847)	(91,879)	(13,092)
	$527,260	$395,893	$187,913

EXHIBIT 2

CENTRAL DECAL, LTD. **Statement of Profit and Loss** Year Ending April 30			
	1981	**1980**	**1979**
Sales	$855,653	$583,605	$192,992
Cost of goods sold	556,174	416,032	145,781
Gross profit	$299,479	$165,573	$ 47,211
Expenses	276,447	229,360	106,303
Net profit (loss)	$ 23,032	$(63,787)	$(59,092)

finances were returning to their former disorganized state. A second meeting was held, and McIntyre basically demanded that Altman either do the job properly or get someone who could.

When the second crunch came in September 1980, Altman put in another $50 000 to resolve the problem. McIntyre felt that this behavior on Altman's part merely hid the real financial problems the firm was facing. McIntyre discovered, for example, that Altman had not increased the firm's line of credit even though monthly sales volumes had nearly tripled. Altman had not pursued further grants either, even though these were likely to be approved because the company had more than fulfilled its obligation to create a certain number of jobs with its first grant. In addition, the bank had sent a very critical report to McIntyre detailing other shortcomings in the financial affairs of the company.

After the second incident, McIntyre had reached the end of his rope. He knew that Altman would be financially solvent even if the business folded, because he was wealthy; Altman also had a CA degree which was very marketable. McIntyre, on the other hand, had nothing to fall back on. He felt that he had several alternatives: (1) buy out Altman's shares, (2) drop out of the business and sell Altman his shares, or (3) start a new screen-printing company. With regard to the first alternative, McIntyre had approached several individuals about financing who had agreed to put up $250 000 in return for being made shareholders. McIntyre could then use this money to buy Altman's shares and to put the firm on a more solid financial footing. McIn-

tyre felt this was a very desirable alternative except that Altman probably would resist selling his shares.

With regard to option 2, McIntyre felt that Altman could not keep the business going by himself, because during the last few months Altman had been showing signs of extreme anxiety and emotional stress; also, in spite of Altman's management consulting background, McIntyre felt Altman couldn't manage the firm. McIntyre felt uncomfortable about leaving the company because he felt he had a moral obligation not to put Altman in a position which would cause him even more stress than he had been experiencing.

With regard to option 3, McIntyre was confident that he could start a new business. He also felt that many of Central's customers would bring their work to his new firm once it got started. Once again, however, he felt something of a moral obligation to Altman; the increased competition of another screen-printing company would make it even harder for Altman alone to keep Central going.

As he considered these alternatives, McIntyre had great difficulty deciding what to do. He wondered if there were other alternatives to be considered or if he should make the decision and get it over with.

SOURCE Frederick A. Starke, from Beckman, Good, and Wyckham, *Small Business Management: Concepts and Cases* (Toronto, Wiley, 1982). Reprinted by Permission.

QUESTIONS

1. Assess McIntyre and Altman as managers of Central Decal.

2. How are the functions of management oper-

ating at Central Decal? Debate the possibilities that:

a. McIntyre and Altman could split the functions to perform more effectively.

b. McIntyre or Altman could each run the company alone.

3. As a management consultant, what would you advise McIntyre to do now? What would you advise Altman to do?

CASE STUDY 10

North Hill Regional Centre

The director of North Hill Regional Centre, Paula Cox, drew in a deep breath and pulled her shoulders forward in an attempt to relieve the mounting tension in her back and neck. The activity was futile. The problems at the North Hill Regional Centre (NHRC) seemed to be overwhelming.

Paula had been with NHRC since its inception five years ago. Prior to that time she was an assistant director at Lady Minto Psychiatric Hospital. While she was there, the decision was made to develop a separate operation, within the same building, at the North Hill Centre for the developmentally handicapped. Paula jumped at the offer to become director of the new centre.

In her new position Paula was responsible for supervising the professional and non-professional staff, and for planning, staffing, and controlling the NHRC. She reports to the Board of Directors. She had some influence in the management structure, although it was basically the same tall structure that was standard in institutional settings. Paula had an assistant director reporting directly to her. Covering the eight wards she had two level-five residential counsellors (R.C.-V). Each ward had a level-four supervisor (R.C.-IV), two assistant supervisors (R.C.-III), and approximately twelve R.C.-II's (see Exhibit 1 for the organization structure of the Centre).

Services needed by the Centre, such as laundry, pharmacy, cleaning staff, workshops, recreation facilities, and the cafeteria, were all shared with the Psychiatric Hospital. This caused some conflict at first, and many slowdowns were blamed on the new Centre.

Paula did not have a wide selection of qualified counsellors to choose from. The NHRC was in a relatively isolated area in Northern Ontario, and the community college in the area did not have a program to train residential counselors. Paula did what she could to attract staff. For example, she offered upgrading through a staff development program to persons with a background in psychiatric or nursing care.

No such recruiting problems were evident with regard to nurses and nurses aides, however. They flocked to the new centre from the Psychiatric Hospital, to take advantage of the upgrading and to fill supervisory positions it would take them years to achieve if they stayed at the hospital. Competition had begun between the old and new facilities. The staff in the mutual departments acted as a buffer between the two sides (the mutual departments service both centres and include activities like the laundry and pharmacy).

Changing Attitudes

Things eventually fell into place and for the next few years the Centre ran fairly smoothly. Gradually, however, Paula was beginning to feel pressured by the changing ideas involving care of the developmentally handicapped. Parents were demanding that more be done with their children. They were no longer satisfied that their children were simply being cared for; they expected to see development.

The Centre was expanding and offering more and more services. Social workers, psychiatrists, psychometrists (psychologists involved with testing), and program directors joined the staff. The concepts they introduced were new to Paula and most of her staff. As well, Paula was very busy and felt that she was no longer in direct control of activities at the Centre. She

EXHIBIT 1   Organization structure of North Hill Regional Centre

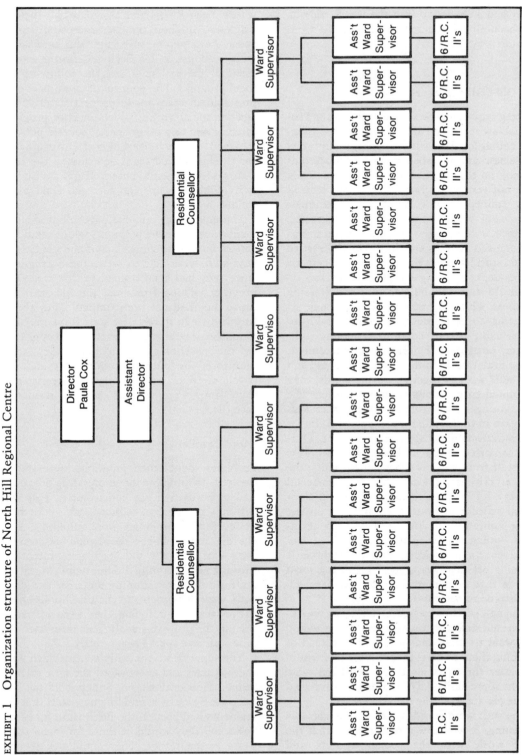

rarely had a chance to visit the wards and she was becoming more and more isolated from her staff.

The Old Staff versus the New Staff

Staffing requirements were also changing. Provincial law required Paula to hire only residential counselor II's with a college diploma. These new staff members had a much different outlook on the care of the handicapped. They were not trained to nurse people, but instead were trained in developmental techniques. They were young, ambitious, and energetic, and they wanted to see the residents do things for themselves. This was in direct contrast to the old staff, who felt their duty was to care for the residents by doing everything for them.

The old staff were busy feeding and dressing residents while the new staff were busy attempting to implement developmental programs using token economies, shaping techniques, positive and negative reinforcement, and stimulation techniques. Since both old and new staff worked together on the wards, they attempted to get along with each other. The new, younger staff usually made concessions and gave in to the older, more senior staff.

Frustrations were apparent, however. During the coffee breaks with the social workers and staff from various other departments, the old staff criticized the new staff (to the neutral parties) for their unrealistic ideas and their casual attitudes toward their nursing duties. They pointed out habits the new staff developed — such as signing off medication so they could leave a little earlier after the night shift (signing off involves a nurse signing a form stating that certain medication has been administered to patients).

The new staff expressed puzzlement regarding the old staff's attitudes, asking "why would you want to dress and feed people instead of teaching them to do it themselves? Life would be easier for all of us if the residents were taught some skills." They constantly referred to the old staff as "the babysitters."

The staff were worlds apart and the gap was widening. It was now a requirement that the staff work with the social workers and psychometrists to assess the residents on the wards. Each R.C.II was assigned two to four residents, to whom they became parent surrogates. As a parent surrogate, the counselors were responsible for both the initial assessment of the residents and the follow-up on their progress. The counselors were part of a professional team made up of the resident's teacher, social worker, psychometrist, program director and any other special service persons required (speech pathologist, neurologist, etc.). This special team determined the resident's developmental potential and devised an individual program plan for each resident to follow.

The counselors and the psychology department then wrote the programs which would be carried out by the counselors on the wards. The new staff were able to write these programs since they had been trained in this area. The program writing frustrated the old staff because they had not been trained. They therefore had to go to the new staff for assistance. Once the programs were written and approved by the psychology department, they were monitored by both the counselors and the psychometrists. Baseline data, progress, and regressions were charted on each resident's case file.

More Conflict

Problems arose when programs were implemented. In order to be successful, programs had to be carried out consistently. This was difficult to achieve, as new staff were firm believers that programs were valuable, while the old staff believed they were "hogwash." New staff felt the old staff were intent on proving programming did not work. Many old staff did the programming on paper and dutifully wrote comments in the case books about the programs, but, in fact, they were not carrying out the programs at all. This infuriated the new staff and sparks began to fly.

The supervisors generally sympathized with the old staff and encouraged the new staff to reduce their enthusiasm. Supervisors tried to keep the peace by reminding new staff that the residents had been in the institution for many years and they would be there for many more years in the future. They could not see the point in programming either. The supervisors felt that the most that could be done was to make the residents' lives as comfortable as possible by keeping them clean, dry and fed. The new staff therefore had no support group to turn to. Their training was not being utilized, yet they knew that the only jobs available that paid well in their field were in institutions like the NHRC. Many of them expressed anger that the college program had misled them. They thought they would be helping people to develop and grow, but they ended up doing what they felt were menial tasks. Their dissatisfaction was becoming increasingly evident.

Many of the new staff developed outside relationships. The time spent together was usually spent complaining about the work situation. New staff lost pride in their work and began to neglect their ward duties. This caused more problems as shifts coming on duty complained that work was being left behind for them. No one appeared to be happy. Accidents among the residents increased. Some of these accidents were serious, one involving the loss of a finger that was slammed in a door by another resident. Many accidents were caused by fighting between residents when staff were not around.

Because of the intergroup conflict, many staff members (both old and new) were becoming careless about coming to work on time and absenteeism increased. Supervisors therefore did not have enough staff to cover the wards appropriately. This meant staff that were working could not take breaks as there was no one to cover the floor during their absence. The inevitable began to happen. Slowly at first, a few staff began to leave the Centre. Then the trend accelerated. Paula had lost twelve staff members in the last six months. The staff that were leaving now were trained staff that had been with the Centre for a number of years.

Because there was a problem with scheduling enough trained staff to cover the floors, the quality of care the residents were receiving was deteriorating. The staff that were working were too busy with shift reports, accident reports, physicians' orders and programming to spend any quality time with the residents. It seemed to Paula that as the professional support staff grew, and as the potential developed for a more progressive and up-to-date developmental centre, things appeared to be deteriorating. Paula could not get a firm grasp on the situation. She knew this could be an excellent centre but didn't know how to gain control over the situation. She was at a loss as to where to begin to solve the Centre's numerous problems.

SOURCE   Peter McGrady and Janet Jardine, Administrative and Policy Studies, Trent University, Peterborough, Ontario.

QUESTIONS

1. Explain the reasons for the air of competition that has emerged between the old staff and the new staff at the North Hill Regional Centre.
2. Why are the old staff resisting the new ideas?
3. Develop a proposal for motivating the old staff to accept the ideas that are being proposed by the new staff.

CASE STUDY 11

Duke and Noble

Richard Duke leaned back in his chair and peered out of the window, thinking about a decision that had to be made sometime the following week. He had gone over the pros and cons many times in the last months, trying to understand the implications of the proposal that faced him.

Duke and Noble, a Chartered Accounting firm, was considering the addition of two part-

ners and their clients to the company. Mr. Duke hoped to strengthen the firm by adding partners. There were also some prospects of organizing a consulting group within the firm which would broaden the line of services the company could offer to its clients. The addition of two new partners was a big step for a firm that had traditionally maintained a small town, small business profile, and

Duke was concerned that the amalgamation might have a negative effect on his staff. As well, he was thinking about refurbishing the office to develop a new image for the expanded firm. He had to make a decision on both these issues very shortly.

Company Background

Duke and Noble was located in Peterborough, Ontario (Mr. Noble is retired). The firm's office was located in a converted home in the residential section of the city. This had been a satisfactory arrangement over the years, as it provided a relaxed atmosphere in which to conduct business. The organizational structure of the firm is shown in Exhibit 1.

As well as offering the usual array of accounting, auditing, and tax services, Duke and Noble employed the normal contingent of accounting students who were working toward their CA (Chartered Accountant) designation. A number of students had successfully completed their articling and Uniform Final Examination (UFE) under the direction of Richard Duke, the senior partner. The success rate of the students in the firm was due in part to Mr. Duke's interest in his students. He kept himself informed of their progress throughout the articling period. He also provided Saturday morning tax seminars for the students, at which time they would study complex tax situations. While the students performed much of the routine and detailed work of the firm, at the same time they gained valuable practical experience. They would move from client to client in their work and be exposed to many different business environments.

Employee relations in the past had been very smooth; Mr. Duke had never experienced any problems with people not getting along with one another. He felt that any negative effects of the amalgamation could be offset if the office was refurbished. The extra business the new partners would bring in meant that much of the expense of redecorating could be distributed over a broader base. Moreover, the two large clients the new partners were bringing with them would mean increased income for Duke and Noble. It also meant exposure to a wider variety of business people and potential clients.

EXHIBIT 1   Organizational chart for Duke and Noble

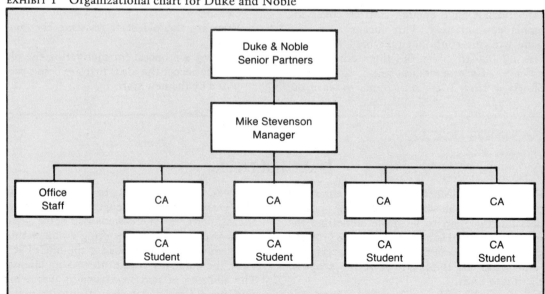

After a period of further inquiry and discussion, the decision was made to go ahead with the amalgamation and refurbishing. The changes that occurred in the office were substantial and reflected the "modern interpretation" of a well-known interior decorator. The changes were not superficial; new wallpaper, desks, office equipment, carpet and filing systems were added to the decor. Modern calculators were purchased as well. Many of the clients commented on the "new look" and wondered how much their bills would increase that year!

A relaxed relationship existed between the company and the clients, many of whom had become very friendly with Mr. Duke over the years. At lower levels in the organization, junior people were encouraged to bring in clients requiring tax services or other accounting needs, since it was important to expand the client base of the organization. Competition was keen, and accounting firms solicited not only good clients but also good students.

The New Partners Arrive

Not long after the office was renovated, the new partners arrived with their contingent of senior and junior people and their files on two large manufacturing companies in the area (see Exhibit 2 for the organizational structure of the firm after the amalgamation). These two clients were of particular interest to the organization. For the next six weeks, Mr. Duke immersed himself in the files on these companies. It was imperative that he become acquainted with the new clients as their "year ends" approached. At the same time, the new partners were becoming acquainted with the clients of Duke and Noble.

The computer audit of the manufacturing companies presented many points of study and inquiry for Duke and Noble. The original partners' limited experience in this area presented some difficulties. At the same time, the incoming partners were not well versed in the auditing of small operations, which had been the mainstay of Duke and Noble.

Problems Begin

At the partner level, the reception of the new people went fairly well. At lower levels in the organization, however, conflict erupted. This was most evident at the level of the senior students, largely because the new partners had brought four students into the company with them.

John Kreighoff and Bill Whitmore, two senior students already working at Duke and Noble, felt threatened by the presence of the four new students, two of whom were due to write their UFE's in the near future. It was expected that they would pass their examinations and eventually seek a career in industry. This would thin out the personnel at that level in the firm. Both Krighoff and Whitmore, a once congenial pair, now became quite concerned about their future. This "new scene," as Kreighoff called it, was not that "cool." The new office arrangement required them to sit at their own desks separated from other desks by accoustical screening. The shirt, tie, and suit atmosphere was too formal for their tastes.

Practical experience was becoming a more important part of the training program for chartered accountants and both Kreighoff and Whitmore felt they were being deprived of this experience. Moreover, the amount of work was being diluted considerably by the presence of the new staff. When it came time for job assignments and workload allocations, the selection procedure was based solely on seniority and availability. This meant that both Kreighoff and Whitmore were bumped from jobs on which they had previously worked.

Kreighoff was particularly upset with the situation since he was being replaced on a job involving an old client. This client had been his for two years after he joined the firm as a junior student. For the last two years he had continued to work on this account and had developed a good rapport with the managers and owners of the company. The problem was further complicated because the owner of the company being audited wanted Kreighoff to do the audit. He felt the new team coming into his company meant delay and greater cost. The problems would be resolved, the owner thought, by a telephone call to Mr. Duke, but Duke could not be reached. The change took place, and the audit proceeded as scheduled without Kreighoff.

Problems were also evident elsewhere in the firm. The secretaries were involved in a battle

EXHIBIT 2 Organization structure after amalgamation

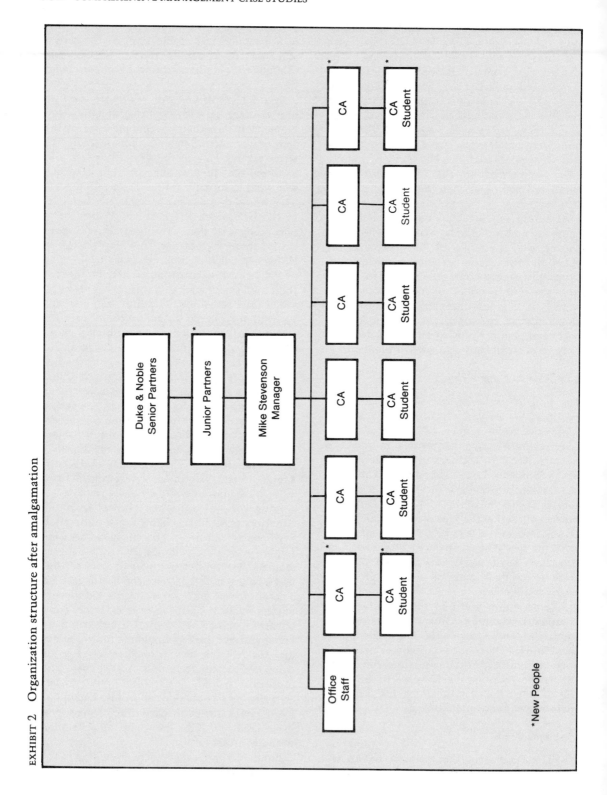

*New People

for position. Two women had arrived with the new group, and both were older and more experienced than the existing group of secretaries at Duke and Noble. A shortage of space and typewriters meant that some sharing had to take place. This left one woman idle for alternate mornings. She was asked to do some menial work which would have pleased no one.

There were personality conflicts as well. One secretary, Miss LaVoie, was extremely domineering and soon became alienated from the group. The secretaries also complained of not being able to communicate. They felt the desk dividers cut them off from one another and from the group. Thus, the once relaxed and informal office became tense and uncomfortable.

The work flow, which had been predictable at one time, was now less clear. This left the secretaries feeling confused and discontented. New clients were also making demands on the organization, and the firm was not adjusting very well. Chris Rose, a junior partner, tried to resolve this problem by having group discussions which were designed to give eveyone a chance to air his or her views.

At a social gathering at his home on a Saturday night, Richard Duke, who had been absent from the office during the last month, explained to the employees that the firm was moving ahead very nicely. Two large companies had just been acquired as clients as a result of the merger, and the company was expanding its business. He said that he was aware of the difficulties and inconvenience the merger was causing. He assured the employees that things would settle down over the next few months.

Further Pressures

Mike Stevenson, the manager of the firm, thought to himself that they might be replacing him soon if he didn't settle down! Mike functioned as the coordinator of the firm's CA's and CA students. He also acted as liaison between clients and the firm's accountants, coordinating activities and identifying needs. Mike was ambitious and had an excellent record in the organization.

He had been left with the coordinating job for all the "year ends" then in progress. It was the firm's busiest time, and they were least prepared for it. Clients' tax forms had also started to arrive, and for the first time, new clients were arriving at the office unannounced, with forms to be completed and sent to Revenue Canada. In fact, on many days there was a waiting room full of clients, and some of the old clients were put off by the hasty treatment they received. Even the junior and senior students were now responsible for the interviewing of clients and the determination of their tax service requirements. Although this treatment dissatisfied some clients, it was a much welcomed responsibility for the students because they were allowed to do different tasks from the ones they had become accustomed to.

The timing, however, was not good for the students since they were all studying for the UFE. This represented the difference between obtaining or not obtaining the CA designation, a qualification that was crucial in the competitive accounting field. Everyone was aware of the difficulty of passing the exam. It also became apparent that Mr. Duke was too busy to provide Saturday morning taxation seminars as he had done in previous years.

A concurrent problem was also developing into a serious situation. Mike Stevenson was in the middle of preparing a prospectus for a client who was considering a merger with another company. The client had been with Duke and Noble for 15 years and both a business and social relationship had developed. Mr. Duke knew the company, a sound financial operation with assets of over $550 000. Even so, he turned the matter over to Mr. Stevenson, disregarding the request for his own personal attention. The inquiry and procedures for the prospectus followed without difficulty. The matter was straightforward, and after a week of the appropriate tests and measures, the final documents were drawn up for endorsement by the firm. The normal procedure at this stage involved a lengthy series of discussions between partners, senior people and the chief administrative officers of the company. Intensive meetings and discussions were required, but like the rest of the encounters of the last few months, it was hurried. It broke up about an hour after it began with apologies from Mr. Duke and an excuse about a trip to Toronto on business.

Two weeks after the meeting, Mike Stevenson received a call from this client, who indicated that he was very upset about the prospectus for the proposed merger. A considerable amount of questioning had centered on the prospectus, and it was discovered that a large contingent liability existed that had not been properly presented. Other news had arrived regarding the examination results of the senior students. John Krieghoff had failed his UFE, and two of the junior people had failed their summer courses. It was 7:30 at night when Mike Stevenson, after spending a hectic day sorting out problems, decided that the time had come for a long discussion with Mr. Duke about the direction of the firm.

SOURCE Professor Peter McGrady, Administrative and Policy Studies, Trent University, Peterborough, Ontario.

QUESTIONS

1. Comment on Duke's management of the change. What should have been done differently?
2. Why did the climate within the organization change so much after the amalgamation? Is it a matter of adjustment and time, or will the problems become more serious? Explain.
3. What should Richard Duke do now?

CASE STUDY 12

Slow Wheeling

Fred Mills paced the floor in his office wondering why operations in the railyard were so backlogged. This was March, the time of highest demand for rail services, and the company could ill afford delays. Fred had been supervisor of yard operations at C & R Rail's Thunder Bay location for twelve years and had never seen the yard so disorganized. Worse, the yard crew workers were very displeased with working conditions. Fred recalled that the new computers that were recently installed at the various terminals in the yard were supposed to make operations more efficient and decrease the cost of operations. To his dismay, the reverse had occurred. Conflict between workers and complaints from customers were rampant. The dreariness and chill of winter added to the problems as Fred slumped behind his desk trying to fight his gloomy feelings.

The Thunder Bay Terminal

Thunder Bay is an active railway center and a crucial link in the Canadian rail transportation system. The operations at the terminal commence with the arrival of freight trains from the east (Toronto) or the west (Winnipeg).

Trains from the west stop at the Westfort terminal. These trains include grain cars destined for the various grain elevators in Thunder Bay, wood cars for Great Lakes Paper, and miscellaneous cars containing merchandise for the various businesses in Thunder Bay.

Trains from the east terminate at the East End terminal. These contain cars with merchandise for businesses in Thunder Bay, as well as empty grain cars that are to continue further on to western Canada. Approximately one-quarter of the arrivals are run-through trains; i.e., they simply stop at the main station where new road crews take over for the continuation of the trip. Trains that enter Thunder Bay have an average of 175 cars per train.

Operations Prior to Computerization

Before computers were installed, the yard supervisor (who was located in the central office) obtained a master car list for each arriving train (a car list indicates the contents of each rail car as well as its destination). This list was then given to the yard master (who was located within the yard limits). Using this list, the yard master then wrote out by hand four separate lists — one for each of the four yard crews that were responsible for a specific territory in the yard (see Exhibit 1).

Each yard crew was made up of one engineer and two switchmen. After receiving their lists, the yard crews switched out the various cars from the main train and delivered them (via spur lines) to designated customers in Thunder Bay. The cars that were left either contained special goods or were designated for depots outside of Thunder Bay. Train cars were checked by car-checkers and the list given to the supervisor for verification and distribution of work assignments.

Operations After Computerization

With the introduction of computers, programs now format the various trains and their cars on computer printouts. These printouts have all the necessary information that the yard masters require to allocate work assignments to the yard crews. The system provides the yard master with a detailed switch list and increases the speed of distribution of the work assignments. The yard master no longer has to write out the switch lists by hand (which requires writing the car numbers, contents, weights, track numbers and destination). Instead, the computer prints all this information on a list, and the yard master simply distributes the list to the appropriate crews. This system is designed for greater accuracy, speed, and control and should mean better service for customers. Unfortunately, the system doesn't always work.

Problems Begin

Before the installation of the computers, the yard crews finished their required work list in six or seven hours. Upon completion of their switch list, they were allowed to leave the premises and were not required to return to work until their next scheduled shift. The full eight-hour work day was seldom needed to complete the work list. This was a well-established and understood work norm among the railway workers. At present, even with the new computers, the switch crews are not completing their required work in the eight hour shifts. Delays of all kinds have developed, even with the best crews. Under these circumstances, the yard master either has to instruct the crews to

EXHIBIT 1   Workflow at the C & R terminal

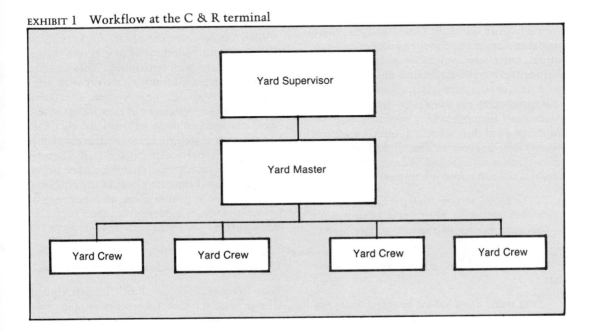

work overtime or call in a spare crew. Since yard crews consist of an engineer and two switchmen, the overtime and spare crew creates substantial extra cost for the company. Also, the various businesses in Thunder Bay are beginning to complain about late arrivals and missing shipments.

There is a rumor among the office staff that the yard crews are "slow wheeling" (working slower than normal) because they are no longer able to achieve the hour to an hour-and-a-half "quits" (yard jargon for leaving early). There is also a rumor that the yard crews are deliberately placing cars on the wrong tracks after switching them out. This creates an error in the computer list that the yard master uses to assign work. Because certain cars are not on the appropriate switch crew list, the customer in Thunder Bay receives the wrong merchandise. There is a chance that a rail car can be placed at Great Lakes Forest Products, for example, and really be designated for Fitzsimmons Food Company. On occasion, rail cars examined by the company car-checkers have also been found emptied of their contents.

A lost car incident creates extra paper work for the office staff and also requires investigation by company police and insurance personnel. The yard crews seem to enjoy these incidents. They feel good about getting even with management for disrupting their previously enjoyable work schedule. Unfortunately, these incidents disrupt the delivery process and customers must seek out other alternatives for their delivery and distribution needs. The end result is that company relations with the business community are frequently strained.

Company management is presently addressing the issue of slow wheeling, but they are not sure what to do about it. The United Transportation Union of Railroad Workers handbook contains the following references:

> "The speed at which all switching movements are to be performed is to be left entirely to the discretion of the switch crew members."

The company and union agreement stipulates that:

> "the speed of switching movements is not to exceed that of restricted speed."

> "Restricted speed is defined as the speed which allows stopping an engine within half the vision of the line of sight and to have complete control of all movement and able to stop movement within a safe distance in regard to public transportation."

Switching Operations

In the past, car-checkers monitored every track within the yard limits at various times during the day to determine an accurate listing of the car numbers, contents and destination in the order that they were positioned on the correct track. The introduction of the computer relieved the car-checker of this duty, a fact that the union has watched very carefully because it does not want to see a reduction of jobs in the rail yards.

The computer controls the various cars using an elimination process. If a car is assigned to a crew on one of its computer listings, then that specific car is simply removed from the computer terminal listing. The sequence of the cars on that track is assumed to be in the same order minus the car that is switched out. Over a three- or four-day period, the cars on a track may not match the updated computer printout because the crews have not properly carried out their switching moves.

With the involvement of car-checkers under the old system, switchmen knew exactly where a required car was positioned. This enabled them to plan their switching moves with great efficiency. With the new system, the trains containing the switched out cars are often disorganized, and on many of them, a crew member must go searching for a specific car that is needed by a particular business in Thunder Bay. Consequently, the switchmen are beginning to feel as if they are glorified car-checkers. This does not appeal to them, and their lack of job satisfaction is evident from their increased absenteeism.

The Road Crew Situation — More Problems

The Brotherhood of Rail Transportation Union requires that the company give road crews (an engineer and three brakemen) a two-hour notice before they go on duty. It is the responsibility of switch crews to have the road crews' trains made up and ready for the road crews to depart Thunder Bay. The slow wheeling of the yard crews makes it difficult for the company to plan the departure time. As a result, road crews are waiting at the station while on duty.

This costs the company money. For every twenty minutes a road crew is delayed at a station while on duty, the company is required to compensate that crew for twenty-five miles. All workers are paid on a per mile basis. The older workers like the extra money they get when they have to wait. The younger, single members, who are not as concerned about the extra money, are unhappy with the delayed departures because it makes it difficult for them to know exactly when they will be back in Thunder Bay after completing a trip. This, in turn, creates havoc with their social lives. Their frustrations are evident in the radio conversations between them and the switch crews. The messages are mostly verbal hassling, but on occasion there has been pushing and shoving in the locker room on this issue. The hostile behavior and crude language in some conversations are detrimental to the company image and reflect poorly on the management of the company.

An observer would be surprised to learn that yard crews and road crews both belong to the same union. The comradeship is deteriorating, the cooperation between the two units is decreasing, and the overall morale of the switchmen is diminishing. The high cohesiveness of each group is a contributing factor in the conflict as each group attempts to protect its own interests.

The disruptions at the workplace are affecting the workers, management, and customers. The problem is compounded by the fact that the economic stituation in Thunder Bay is not good at the moment, and the transportation business has many new entries. Trucking companies have become very aggressive in this region, particularly since highways have been improved and the trucking industry has been deregulated.

Since Fred Mills was a switchman prior to moving up to management, he knows the impact that yard crews have on operations. He also knows that it is his responsibility to analyze the situation and restore operations to an efficient and controlled level. Top management from the operations area is scheduled to arrive in Thunder Bay at the end of the month for inspections. They will also do a performance evaluation of the supervisors. Fred is feeling stress and frustration in his job for the first time. It is a complex situation and the latest correspondence from the union expressing concern about the unrest among the workers has compounded the difficulties facing him.

SOURCE   Professor Peter McGrady and Dennis Humphreys, Administrative and Policy Studies, Trent University, Peterborough, Ontario.

QUESTIONS

1. List and briefly discuss the factors that are causing the conflict between the yard crews and the road crews.
2. Assuming that the yard crews are "slow wheeling," why are they doing so?
3. What actions might Fred Mills take in an attempt to resolve the "slow wheeling" of the yard crews?
4. What should Fred Mills do?

CASE STUDY 13

Aggravation at ANC

Mrs. Peterson, the personnel clerk, strode briskly along with the assurance that she knew exactly where she was headed. Nervous and more than a little apprehensive, Valerie Gallant followed closely behind, not at all assured about where she was going. They moved abruptly from the smooth white walls and carpeted floors of the offices into a rather large, dingy and cold corridor with a cement floor and cinderblock walls. Valerie's eyes darted to the numerous doorways lining the corridor. Each doorway led into some cavernous room where men moved among machines which clanked and roared. And from each doorway came some new and often putrid smell. Valerie was able to get only a quick glance into each of the rooms.

The corridor opened into a colossal room where forklifts zipped back and forth among pallets loaded with cardboard cylinders. Although the walled corridor was behind them, a path of sorts was outlined by parallel strips of yellow paint about six feet apart. Glancing ahead, Valerie could see that off in the distance the path wound on into another room — sort of like following the yellow brick road, she thought. Unexpectedly, Mrs. Peterson turned to the right onto a connecting path and their road ended at a door marked, "Order Department."

Opening the door, Mrs. Peterson motioned for Valerie to enter the office beyond. Valerie's gaze swept the room. The floor was tiled; the walls painted industrial green and yellow. Pipes ran across the ceiling, and through a small, square opening in one wall she could see into the next office. Just inside the door, a young woman sat at a secretary's desk. Directly ahead, from another desk, an older man with greying hair and a neatly trimmed moustache looked up as the door opened. Rising from his chair with a crisp, "Good morning, Mrs. Peterson," he purposefully locked his hands behind his back and advanced to meet the pair of visitors.

"Good morning Charles. This is your new clerk, Valerie Gallant." Turning to the young woman at the desk, Mrs. Peterson completed her introduction with, "And this is Cynthia." Valerie and Cynthia exchanged hello's.

Charles, who had meanwhile closed the distance between himself and Valerie, came to a halt within two feet of her, took a military style "at ease" pose and fixed her with a steely-eyed glare. Valerie managed a stammered, "H-Hello . . Sir."

"Ah, so this is my new recruit, eh? Well, welcome to the order department Miss Gallant." Looking past Valerie, he spoke directly to Mrs. Peterson, "Is there anything you need from us?"

"No Charles. I just wanted to see that Valerie found her way here."

"Yes. Well thank you for bringing her down. I expect you have work to do. Certainly, we can put Miss Gallant to work right away. Bye for now!"

With a parting smile for Valerie, Mrs. Peterson accepted her dismissal and retreated out the door.

Turning back to Charles, Valerie thought she had never, outside the movies, met anyone who so neatly fit the picture of an army drill sergeant.

About ANC

ANC manufactured cellophane for use in packaging products such as cigarettes and potato chips. A wholly-owned subsidiary of a British parent, ANC was a little bit of England dropped down in Ontario. Many of the senior staff and plant employees were British — either imported from the parent firm or hired locally from the immigrant population.

Offices at ANC were distributed in three areas within the building. The front office contained a reception area with the main switchboard, personnel and accounting downstairs, and executive offices upstairs. At the opposite end of the building, the lab incorporated a research and development group and a customer service department. The latter dealt with special orders, as well as coordinating sales, research and quality control in investigating and responding to customer complaints. In the center of the plant, a string of offices contained the progress and planning, order, computer services, and shipping departments.

About Charles

Charles, an emigrant from England, worked as a bookkeeper for several years until he joined ANC as supervisor of the order department. As supervisor, Charles was responsible for receiving and logging orders from sales offices located in Toronto, Montreal and Vancouver. He had been in this position for about one year.

A "company man," Charles took pride in running what he considered an efficient department. He paid close attention to accuracy in processing all orders, personally assigning order numbers, pricing, and checking each order before it was distributed to the other departments.

Although Charles' position was included in the staff bargaining unit, he had taken steps to distance himself from the unionized staff. He took no active part in union affairs, took his coffee breaks with the non-union staff from his area and openly criticized unions in general, especially when any of the brass from upstairs was around.

The Situation in the Order Department

The previous supervisor had passed away suddenly. Anne, the senior order clerk, had managed to run the department with the help of Cynthia for two months until Charles was hired to take over. Three months later, Anne transferred to a secretarial position in the front office. Although Charles immediately put in a request for a replacement, his boss, the sales manager, thought the workload wasn't sufficient in the department to warrant two clerks, and convinced Charles to try operating the office with only himself and Cynthia. Charles kept a close tally of the overtime hours needed to cover the extra work and made repeated but unsuccessful attempts to justify the second clerical position. After several months, however, a new opportunity presented itself to him.

More and more manual work was being transferred onto computerized systems. With only two terminal operators in the computer department, backlogs developed so that more and more orders were not processed on the same day that they were received. This played havoc with lead-times set by the planning and shipping personnel. Without the necessary paperwork coming through quickly, promised delivery dates could not be met.

Charles was finally able to justify the addition of a second clerk by convincing the sales manager to install a new terminal in the order department so that his staff could directly key in the orders. There would be sufficient workload to keep both clerks busy, and no need for overtime hours. To Charles, it seemed that this solution would resolve many difficulties, especially his problems with Cynthia.

The Trouble with Cynthia

Cynthia could only be termed by Charles as a recalcitrant employee. She did her work, but was easily distracted and frequently stopped to chat through the passway with the planning secretary. At first she complied when Charles demanded that she "get back to work," but recently she had become quarrelsome and uncooperative.

Although the department was able to cope without a second clerk, the less important tasks of filing and typing envelopes for order confirmations were left for slack periods. When things piled up over several days, Charles arranged for the work to be done on overtime, staying to supervise Cynthia himself, and to catch up on statistical reports he generated each week for the sales manager. Cynthia became increasingly resistant to requests that she work overtime, and had in fact retorted to Charles on one occasion that maybe *he* needed the extra money, but *she* didn't and all this overtime was ruining her social life! Their heated arguments grew to a fevered pitch and as the connecting passway to the planning department was ordinarily open, the staff in that office were well aware of the conflicts.

The whole question of overtime culminated when Ernie, one of the fellows from the planning office and the union steward for their area, drew Charles aside and suggested that he lay off for a while on demands that Cynthia work overtime. Charles discovered that she had spoken with the union president, seeking to lodge a grievance against him for making unreasonable requests for overtime and alleging that he was "making work" in order to earn extra money. Ernie related that Cynthia had been told that the grievance procedure was not meant to deal with disputes between union members, but that someone would speak to Charles about it. Ernie's point was that if Cynthia made the same allegation to management, Charles might be in hot water with the people upstairs.

Charles was furious. It had been bad enough enduring the jabs of the planning staff, who frequently referred to him as the "slavedriver of the order department," but to have the union meddle in his affairs was too much. On returning to the office he told Cynthia in no uncertain terms, "Fine, you don't want to work overtime, there will be no overtime. But be prepared to work as you've never worked before, my girl, because hell will freeze over before you get any overtime work in this department again!"

Since then, Cynthia had found new ways to irritate Charles. As the postage meter and photocopier were located in the front office, at least one trip a day had to be made to take outgoing mail up. Cynthia was only too happy to make the mail run, and inevitably took an inordinately long time to get back. Charles was sure that she stopped to chitchat and gossip with anyone who was willing to pass the time of day and was positive that she was spending time with Anne, who was now secretary to the sales manager. It took little analysis on Charles' part to predict the outcome if the sales manager should observe Cynthia as frequently idle, apparently without sufficient work.

Charles disliked giving Cynthia opportunities to be out of the office as he knew she would use each occasion to waste time, to her advantage and his detriment. However, he liked to be available at his desk in case something came up which required his attention. He never knew when one of the sales offices might call with an urgent request for an improved delivery date on an order. Charles always made such requests personally to the planning department, haggling with the planners to shorten the lead-time or shuffle stock. Frequently, several days could be shaved off the shipment date, and the salespeople were quick to praise Charles for his efforts.

A Possible Solution

The addition of a second clerk meant that Cynthia would become senior order clerk and receive an increase in salary. Charles was sure that her attitude toward him and her work stemmed from the fact that she had not been promoted when Anne had left. This was not Charles' doing, but was a result of the union contract. To have a senior clerk in the office, there must be a junior clerk. Until a second clerk was added, Cynthia had remained at the junior clerk level. Now that the new junior clerk (Valerie) was on board, Charles was sure that Cynthia would straighten out.

Valerie's Observations

Charles assigned Valerie to train with Cynthia on the order desk, and advised that as soon as the new terminal was set up in the computer department she and Cynthia would in turn go over there to train. When both girls were competent, the terminal would be moved to their office and the order department would take charge of keying in all orders.

Cynthia took Valerie along on a jaunt to the lab on the morning of her first day of work, followed by a mail run to the front office in the afternoon. Valerie was introduced by Cynthia to the staff in each area and they chatted briefly with several people. Cynthia did spend a considerable amount of time talking with one girl in the lab, and again, in the front office, with another. While in the front office, they sauntered upstairs to see Anne, whom Cynthia introduced as secretary to the sales manager, and a previous coworker in the order department. Anne informed Cynthia that she had heard "nothing new" about whether or not Barbara was leaving. Valerie did not meet Barbara, but got the impression that she was another secretary who worked upstairs. It seemed to Valerie that working upstairs must be very prestigious. The furnishings and panelled offices, in themselves, certainly made the order offices seem shabby by comparison.

At 10:00 a.m. that first day, a girl with short, dark hair leaned through the passway. With a "Hi, I'm Penny!" for Valerie, she asserted, "Break time girls. Let's go." The three of them met outside the offices, where another girl who introduced herself as Hannah joined them.

On their way to the cafeteria, it was explained to Valerie that Penny was the planning department secretary, while Hannah was the secretary to the production supervisor. "And our Cynthia," Hannah pointed out to Valerie, "is now senior order clerk!" Although that sounded impressive to Valerie, Cynthia merely snarled, "Yeah, soon to be glorified machine operator!" Valerie was puzzled by Cynthia's outburst, but Penny launched into a story about this fabulous dress she had seen, and the subject of the jobs was agreeably dropped.

Three weeks passed before they were advised that the new terminal was set up and training could begin the following Monday. During that time, Valerie took her breaks each day with Cynthia, Penny and Hannah, and had been invited each payday to go downtown with the group over the lunch break. Lunch was one and one-half hours and their routine was to cash cheques, shop for clothes, then grab a quick sandwich before rushing back to work. Valerie began adding to her wardrobe, buying business suits, blouses and shoes from the same exclusive shops that Cynthia and the other girls frequented. The talk during Monday morning coffee breaks was always filled with a rehash of weekend exploits, although Cynthia was less often able to hold the floor, since Charles usually insisted that Valerie make the runs to the lab and the front office. Valerie was privy to all the details the girls shared, but they had not yet asked her along on one of their "nights out."

One day, while Charles was on break, Cynthia took the stack of outgoing mail and told Valerie that if Charles returned before she did, Valerie should tell him that she had taken the mail since she was going up front to use the washroom. When Charles returned and asked where Cynthia had gone, Valerie dutifully related just what Cynthia had told her.

Charles exploded with a "Bloody Hell! The moment my back is turned . . .," and got on the phone to someone in the front office right away. Valerie was so frightened, she stood rigid while Charles roared over the phone to Cynthia, whom he had managed to locate. His stern manner made Valerie apprehensive at the best of times, but to see him angry made her tremble. Poor Cynthia! He was sure to tear a strip off her when she returned.

And return she did; but, not as the apologetic prodigal that Valerie assumed. Instead, she stormed into the office, railing at Charles for embarrassing her by telephoning around the front office! Charles declared that she was sneaky and lazy, while she retorted that he was a slavedriver who wished to keep her caged in the office. He asserted that there was a perfectly good washroom nearby and it was absurd to go all the way to the front office to relieve oneself. She countered that they (the female

office staff) didn't have a washroom: the only washroom nearby belonged to the plant girls and it was a pigsty and not fit for office girls who paid good money for their clothes. On and on they went. Valerie was astounded both by Cynthia's posture in the confrontation and by the fact that none of the yelling was directed at her. Finally, one of the planners came to the passway. After yelling, "Will the two of you keep it down!" he slammed the passway door shut. That ended the argument, but not the conflict.

The very next day, when the girls gathered outside the offices to go on their break, Cynthia declared that she was "sick of getting her clothes dirty in that crummy cafeteria." "I'm going up front for my break. Are you coming?" Although someone objected that there wouldn't be time, Cynthia pooh-poohed that notion, and they all followed her to the front offices. The girls there were pleased to welcome them into their "coffee room" and the tea-lady asked whether she could expect them every day, so that she could be sure to have enough coffee and cups available. "Sure, we'll be here every day from now on," Cynthia advised.

They were a few minutes late returning, and Valerie suffered all the way back, knowing that Charles would be very annoyed. Cynthia seemed jubilant. Both Penny and Hannah seemed to think that nobody would say anything to them, but Valerie knew that their bosses weren't depending on the girls' return in order to take their coffee breaks.

Just as Valerie had feared, Charles greeted them with, "Bloody Hell! Where have you two been? Don't you realize you've made me miss half of my break?" Cynthia replied without apology that they had gone to the front office for their break and had lost track of time. Valerie said nothing, waiting for the axe to fall.

"The front office! Since when do you take breaks in the front office? You are to take your breaks in the cafeteria, Cynthia, and well you know it. Let this be the last time I need to speak to you about this." With that Charles marched out of the office.

To Valerie's surprise, Cynthia was unperturbed by Charles' remarks. "He can't tell us where to take our breaks!" she told Valerie. "There's no rule that says we can't go to the front office, and if he thinks he can stop us, he can talk to the union about it."

So it was that a few days later, when Charles announced that one of them would begin training on the computer terminal the following Monday, Valerie volunteered to be first. She knew that another big row would ensue if Charles insisted that Cynthia go first. Also, it would take her out from under Charles' rule for a while and that would be a great relief, since she had been living in fear that it was only a matter of time before he discovered that they had gone back to the front office for breaks several times.

She had been introduced to both of the terminal operators before, but had never really got to know them. They always sat at a different table during breaks in the cafeteria and were never part of the payday lunches. For some reason, they were never included in anything that Cynthia and the girls did.

When she reported to the computer room on Monday morning, all of the staff were friendly, and both operators were helpful and patient. Valerie took breaks with two operators, Enid and Francis, in the cafeteria. She knew Cynthia and the other girls must be taking their breaks in the front office, since they didn't show up in the cafeteria at their regular break times. Although she was sure Cynthia wouldn't approve of her associating with the machine operators, they were both so nice that she could hardly refuse to join them for breaks.

Things were fine until Thursday afternoon, when she was asked to take the computer print-out over to the order department. Charles was on break when she arrived, and Cynthia asked where she had been all week. Valerie avowed that she had looked for the girls each day in the cafeteria and wondered why they hadn't shown up for breaks. Cynthia explained that they were now taking all of their breaks in the front office and suggested that Valerie join them. Friday afternoon was especially important, since the girls were bringing in sandwiches and sweets to celebrate the engagement of one of the girls in accounts receivable. It promised to be a lot of fun, and Cynthia implied the party would likely spill over into a "night out" after work.

The Last Straw

Charles had planned to send Cynthia over to the computer department first, partly to get her out of his hair for a few days, and partly to separate Valerie and have her completely under his influence. He had seen that she was following in Cynthia's footsteps, but knew that if she was alone, she would do as he instructed. The fact that she had volunteered to train first indicated to Charles that she took an interest in her work, and that was more than he could say for Cynthia.

During the week that Valerie was in training, Cynthia did her work and returned only a few minutes late from her breaks. She dallied a little on runs to the lab and the front office, but not to the extremes to which she had previously gone. Charles thought that her promotion was having a positive effect, and was content to let her have her little chats, since she wasn't slacking off on her work. According to reports from the computer department, Valerie was learning quickly and would be fully trained in another week.

On Friday afternoon, Cynthia left as usual at 3:00 p.m. At 3:15 p.m., when John from the shipping department called in for Charles, Cynthia was not yet back. "Go ahead John. "You'll likely pass Cynthia in the hallway. Ask her to hurry along please. I'll see you shortly." So Charles thought, but when John looked in at 3:30, wondering why Charles hadn't gone on break, Cynthia had still not returned. Adding fuel to the fire, Frank from the computer department telephoned to ask whether Valerie would be back that afternoon. It seemed she had not taken her break with his subordinates and since she hadn't turned up in the computer department after break, he assumed she was back in the order department.

Charles immediately telephoned Harold in the accounting office. "Sure, Cynthia and Valerie are up front. In fact all of the girls are still in the coffee room. There's a celebration going on." Charles very politely asked Harold to interrupt the festivities and call Cynthia to the telephone. When she came on the line, he yelled, "You are to report back to the office at once! If the two of you are not here in five minutes, I shall come up there and drag you back!" With that he hung up.

This was it. This was the last time his subordinates would make a laughing stock of him in the eyes of the other men. Blast them anyway. They couldn't disregard his orders and get away with it. This was definitely the last straw!

SOURCE Gail Lawrence, Thunder Bay, Ontario; and Peter McGrady, Administrative and Policy Studies, Trent University, Peterborough, Ontario.

QUESTIONS

1. What are the sources of conflict between Charles and Cynthia?
2. What should Charles do to improve Cynthia's attitude toward her work?
3. How can the conflict between Charles and Cynthia be resolved? Be specific.

CASE STUDY 14

Good Samaritan Services

Good Samaritan Services (GSS) is a national voluntary agency founded in Canada approximately 100 years ago to direct geriatric health care services and training to the public. The Good Samaritans deliver first aid training to thousands of Canadians each year; they also provide a program of health care courses. Some of the organization's activities are financed by contributions from the United Way, and some revenue is derived from the training courses provided.

Organizational Structure

GSS is divided into two basic structural units — the branch and the unit. The branch is the administrative arm of the organization and exercises control through the guidance of the board of directors. Branches are located across Canada; the larger ones usually have a full-time paid secretary and one full-time paid training coordinator. Generally, branch members are volunteers from the community with some background in business or finance.

The unit provides at-home visits and first-aid services for shut-ins and the elderly. Unit members are well trained in first aid and cardiopulmonary resuscitation (CPR). They conduct the courses that the organization offers to the public. The first aid course instructors receive a nominal fee for teaching the courses.

The Sudbury, Ontario Branch

The structure of the Sudbury branch of the Good Samaritans is shown in Exhibit 1. Jim Stanley (a volunteer) is the chairman of the board of directors. The board of directors, which is comprised of representation from both the branch and the unit, meets monthly and is open to all members of the Samaritans. The management committee is composed of selected members of the board of directors and functions as an executive committee of the board. The management committee was set up to address management issues that continually arose as the branch grew. Its membership is restricted so that it can handle issues quickly as they arise. At the present time, the Sudbury branch has no general manager. (This position is found only in the larger branches.) If the Sudbury branch grows, it could require such a position.

The Sudbury branch has operated out of several different older buildings during the past 20 years. In 1980, the building that housed the branch burned down, so the branch moved to the former residence of a local hospital. During this time, public interest in the first aid classes declined, as did the morale of Samaritan volunteers. It became obvious that the organization's effectiveness was slipping.

Dan Foster, the head of the unit, therefore spearheaded a campaign to raise funds for a new building to be called the Samaritan Centre. The project was successful, and, in January 1985, the Sudbury Good Samaritans moved into the new premises. Everyone was pleased with the new building and morale improved. The unit members were particularly elated with their new quarters.

EXHIBIT 1   Organization structure of the Sudbury, Ont. Good Samaritans branch

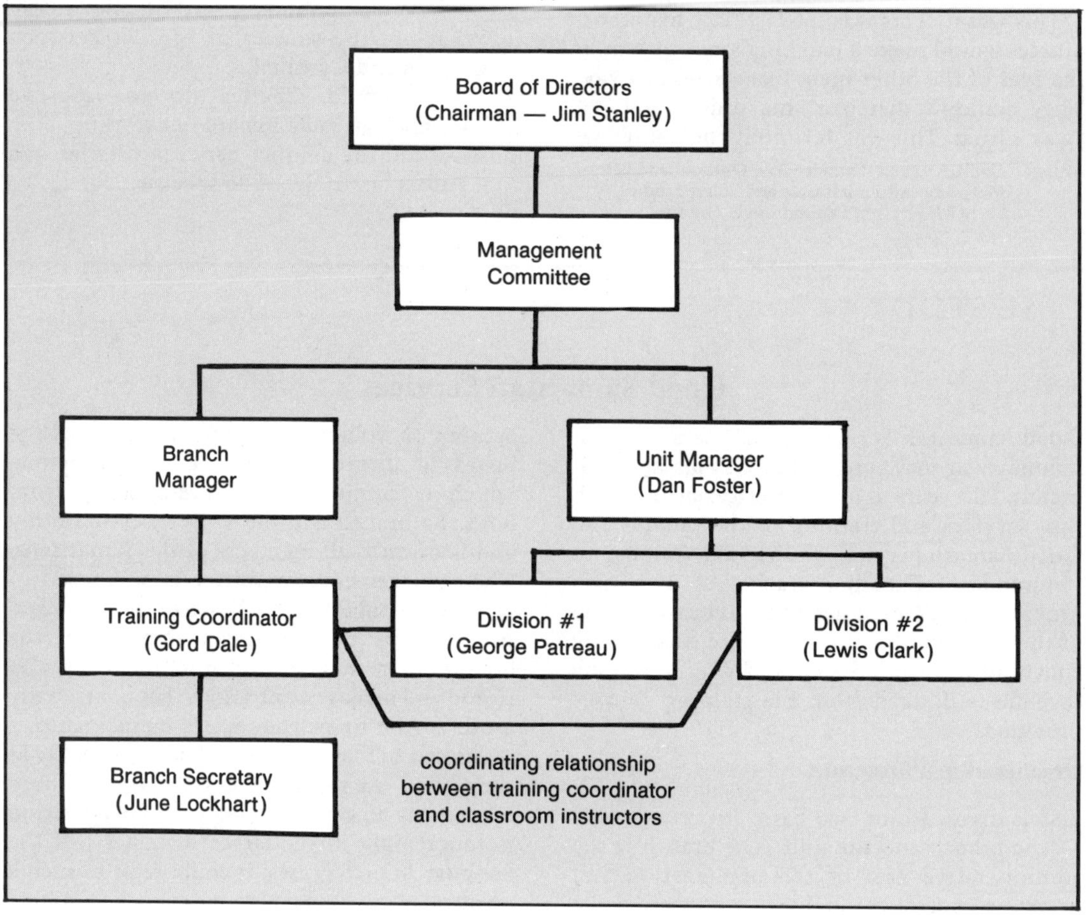

The chart shows:
Board of Directors (Chairman — Jim Stanley) → Management Committee → Branch Manager and Unit Manager (Dan Foster). Branch Manager → Training Coordinator (Gord Dale) → Branch Secretary (June Lockhart). Unit Manager → Division #1 (George Patreau) and Division #2 (Lewis Clark). coordinating relationship between training coordinator and classroom instructors

The Problem Begins

When the vice-chairman returned to Sudbury in January 1985 after the Christmas vacation, he was summoned to the Samaritan Centre for a special meeting. Dan Foster wanted the board to enlist the services of Tom Jennings, a consultant, to act for the branch to raise money.

The branch, in its move to the new site, quickly realized it did not have the kind of operating money it needed. It also required substantially more time commitment and managerial skill than had been available in the past. Foster had known Jennings for many years and believed that he had the management skills that were necessary to put GSS on its feet.

These were much needed skills, as the majority of people in the organization were there on a voluntary basis, only one or two nights a month. Restructuring and organizing were necessary if the organization was to meet its potential and become a more useful non-profit enterprise. Foster believed the organization needed to improve its marketing of courses to the general public. Therefore, he proposed to the board that Jennings be hired as a full-time consultant for $30 000 a year.

Jennings was asked questions about his plans and his ideas for GSS. He responded in a capable and professional manner and presented pro forma statements that made the financial picture look very promising. He believed that the

Samaritans should increase course offerings by 60 percent and that doing so would put the operation in the black within six months. Jennings forecast high utilization rates for the classrooms, including a program of evening and weekend rentals. These figures were projected over a three-year period to show GSS on an exceedingly firm financial footing. He also made clear that he would cover his consulting fee with the money he generated from donations and fund raising.

The board was concerned about Jenning's fee but, after considerable discussion, decided to hire him. Several board members considered that $30 000 was too much money for a non-profit organization to spend in the face of financial stress. These concerns turned out to be well founded.

Open Conflict

Almost immediately on beginning his work, Jennings had disagreements with Gord Dale, the branch training co-ordinator. Jennings, Dale, and the branch secretary, June Lockhart, had moved into the new office. They were supposed to work together to set up operations and begin selling the courses to produce some much-needed revenue. Dale was older than Jennings and resented the fact that Jennings was being paid more than he was. Jennings's manner was brusque and tactless. He had no knack for diplomatically persuading Dale to change his job. The arguments between Jennings and Dale were heated, and Dale began to think about resigning.

The disagreements between Dale and Jennings were to some extent aggravated by the volunteer nature of the organization. According to the formal structure of the branch, Dale reported to Jim Stanley, the chairman of the board of directors. (See Exhibit 1.) However, because Stanley was a volunteer, he was in the office only once a week or so. Dale made it clear to Jennings that Jennings was not his boss and that Dale would not take orders from him. However, Dale did need some direction because the whole complexion of his job was changing. A much more aggressive style of selling the courses and marketing the organization was needed; he had to go to the public and

consequence, the financial affairs of the organ-sell, not wait for the public to come to him. Despite these realities, Dale sat behind his desk waiting for business to come in. This refusal of Dale to alter irked Jennings. Lockhart had to work tirelessly to keep peace in the office.

Unit versus Branch

The conflict between Dale and Jennings also caused a split to develop between the unit and the branch. The unit comprised the grass roots of the organization. Its members put in thousands of volunteer hours every year. Even though Dale was the branch training coordinator (see Exhibit 1), he felt aligned with the unit. The unit members usually received their teaching assignments from Dale.

Dale made his negative feelings about Jennings known to unit members, who listened attentively and watched the changes taking place around them. As the verbal battles between Dale and Jennings continued, both Stanley and Foster became increasingly concerned. At the monthly meetings of the Sudbury branch, this conflict was discussed frequently. It was always a strained affair. Foster had taken a dislike to Dale because Dale constantly complained about Jennings's behavior and insensitivity. The management committee tended to side with Jennings, who it considered was getting the office organized. Jennings, now signing himself as "Director of Good Samaritan Services," had the support of the volunteer branch members. Dale sensed this support and felt that his efforts to perform well and get ahead in the organization were in vain. Dale began drinking heavily to escape these stressful developments.

Dale wanted to earn more money and decided to investigate the possibility of becoming the branch manager. Foster, who had the most informal influence with the management committee, would not hear of it. Foster was a popular man, both in GSS and in the community. He had lived in Sudbury all his life and had recently retired from Ontario Hydro.

By now, the conflict between Dale and Jennings was full-blown. Dale was taking time off from work on doctor's orders and Jennings was taking time off to pursue other interests. As a

ization were suffering and courses were not being solicited as planned. The official opening of the Samaritan Centre was drawing closer and plans were in place for a gala affair, which the Lieutenant Governor of the province would attend. Tension in the office was very high.

During this time of crisis, unit members generally defended the struggling Dale, who tried to avoid having to deal with Jennings. Unit members complained to branch management committee members that Jennings did not know how to handle people and that communication in the organization was deteriorating. George Patreau, one of the officers of the unit, became very annoyed one evening when his division was left without a place to prepare for the opening ceremonies. It seems that Jennings had booked the hall for a meeting of an outside group. Patreau, a senior man in the organization and a well-respected leader, was beside himself when Jennings flippantly told him that he should have read the notice board in advance.

As another example of poor communication, Dale returned the wine glasses for the formal opening dinner to the caterer because there was no invoice with the delivery. This occurred while Jennings was out of the office, and earned Dale a sharp rebuke from Foster after Jennings complained.

At the monthly meetings of the board of directors, unit members became tight-lipped and sullen about the situation. They complained about the need for more money and new equipment. They claimed they could not run good quality classes with audio-visual equipment that broke down frequently. At the same time, they were asked to vote on motions for money to go to the branch office for the "big party" (the formal opening) that was coming up. The unit became increasingly defensive and upset. They participated at tag day with limited enthusiasm, which showed in the final tally of money.

The unit held private meetings to discuss their concerns. Dale participated actively in these discussions and pleaded that something be done about Jennings. The members of the unit, who normally followed Foster's direction on most matters, elected to ignore him and proceed with a letter signed by all unit members asking to have the problems in the branch office attended to immediately. The letter of complaint was addressed to Stanley and read at a management committee meeting. The committee was upset by this gesture and the conflict deepened. Many members of the unit also approached Foster independently to mention the struggle and the lack of co-operation.

Foster sadly had to admit that Jennings had not raised one cent since he had been hired as a consultant. Course offerings and a few rentals were up, but produced insufficient revenue to resolve the financial problems facing the branch. Nevertheless, Jennings was perceived as a good business manager, and the plans were in place for the formal opening of the new centre.

However, behind the scenes business at Good Samaritan Services was changing. Foster was forced to spend more time on administrative duties than with his normal unit duties. Disenchantment among unit members grew as new office furniture arrived, including a rather expensive microcomputer for Jennings's exclusive use. The unit was extremely envious. Members wondered why they were wearing old uniforms and why fund raising was meeting only branch needs, while the unit went without. Dale made it known that Jennings was spending more time pursuing outside interests. There was also a rumor that Jennings was negotiating with a company to purchase a small gas station and diner near the edge of town.

The conflict reached its peak when Dale refused delivery of the printed programs for the opening day events. The printing company required payment in full and there was no money available. Jennings was off on another jaunt to assess his latest business operation. Word was out that he was planning to run both Good Samaritans and the diner at the same time. Jennings claimed that he could make both operations successful.

The president of the Ontario council for Good Samaritan Services called on the Tuesday before the grand opening and was told that everything was in readiness for Saturday's activities. But the office was in turmoil. To make matters worse, on Wednesday morning, the Royal Bank manager called Foster and Stanley to his office to have a discussion about the branch's financial status. He told them that their line of credit had reached its limit of $10 000 and that no further money would be forthcoming until the branch developed a realistic financial plan. Then, on Wednesday afternoon, Lockhart called Foster to tell him that Dale had been admitted to hospital suffering from chest pains and shortness of breath. She had driven him there after he had collapsed at the branch. The doctors said that Dale was near exhaustion and needed a rest.

Foster called Stanley and told him to convene an emergency meeting of the board of directors as soon as possible. Swift action was needed if a complete breakdown of the organization was to be averted.

SOURCE   Professor Peter McGrady, Administrative and Policy Studies, Trent University, Peterborough, Ontario.

QUESTIONS

1. What kind of structural problems are evident at GSS?
2. Construct a new organization chart for the Sudbury branch that will solve the structural problems you've noted.
3. What kind of people problems are evident at Sudbury's branch of GSS?
4. Suggest ways to solve the people problems you've noted.

Glossary

ABC inventory method The classification of inventory items for control purposes into three categories according to unit costs and number of items kept on hand.

acceptance sampling Inspection of a portion of the output or input of a process to determine its acceptability.

accountability Any means of ensuring that the person who is supposed to do a task actually performs it and does so correctly.

action plans Require clear delineation of what specifically is to be accomplished and when it is to be completed.

activity In PERT, it is the time-consuming element of a network.

activity ratios Measure how efficiently the firm is utilizing its resources.

activity trap The state in which personnel are so enmeshed in performing assigned functions that they lose sight of the goal or reasons for their performance.

Adult ego state The ego state of transactional analysis that identifies the person who tends to evaluate situations and attempts to make decisions based on information and facts.

advisory staff Advise line managers in areas where the staff has particular expertise.

arbitration Calls for outside neutral parties to assist in resolving the conflict. The arbitrator is given the authority to act as a judge in making a decision.

Artificial intelligence The attempt to develop computers that are able to make decisions that are similar to those that would have been made by humans in the same situation.

assessment center Designed to provide systematic evaluation of the potential of individuals for future management positions.

attribute sampling Quality control method which does not allow degrees of conformity.

audit An assessment of the financial condition of a company, conducted by an external group such as a chartered accountancy firm. *See also* management audit.

authority The right to decide, to direct others to take action, or to perform certain duties in achieving organization goals.

autocratic leader Person who tells subordinates what to do and expects to be obeyed without question.

backward integration Taking control of any of the sources of a firm's inputs.

balance sheet A financial statement that describes the company's financial position with respect to assets, liabilities, and owners' equity at a particular point in time.

barriers to communication Factors that can reduce communication effectiveness between the sender and the receiver.

behavioral school of management The approach to management thought that is primarily concerned with human psychology, motivation, and leadership as distinct from simple mechanical efficiency.

behavioral science Gives primacy to psychological considerations but treats fulfillment of emotional needs mainly as a means of achieving other, primarily economic, goals.

behavioral standards Standards based on the type of behavior desired of workers in an organization.

board of directors A group of people who are given the power to govern a corporation's affairs and to make general policy; they are elected by the corporation's shareholders.

body language Nonverbal communication in which physical actions such as motions, gestures, and facial expressions convey thoughts and emotions.

brainstorming An idea-generating technique wherein a number of persons present alternatives without regard to questions of feasibility or practicality.

break-even analysis Approach used to determine the amount of a particular product that must be sold if the firm is to generate enough revenues to cover costs; the point at which revenues and costs are equal.

budget A formal statement in dollar and cents terms of the firm's planned expenditures in a future time period, usually one year.

business ethics The application of ethical principles to business relationships and activities.

business firm An entity that seeks to make a profit by gathering and allocating productive resources to satisfy consumer demand.

capital budget Indicates planned capital acquisition, usually for the purpose of purchasing additional facilities or equipment.

carrying costs The expenses associated with maintaining and storing the products before they are sold or used.

cash budget Summarizes planned cash receipts and disbursements.

cash cows In BCG analysis, businesses with high market share in a slow growth market.

centralization Individual managers and workers at lower levels in the organization have a narrow range of decisions or actions they can initiate.

centralized The type of situation in which decision-making authority is concentrated at the upper levels of the organization.

chain of command The line along which authority flows from the top of the organization to any individual in it.

change agent The person who is responsible for ensuring that the planned change in organization development is properly implemented.

channel The means by which the message is transmitted to the receiver.

Child ego state The ego state of transactional analysis that identifies the person who bases decisions primarily on personal satisfaction.

classical school of management School of management thought, evolved in the early twentieth century, which attempted to provide a rational and scientific basis for the management of organizations.

coercive power Derived from the ability to punish or to recommend punishment.

cohesiveness The degree of attraction that the group has for each of its members.

common stock Those shares showing ownership in a corporation, the holder of which has voting rights.

communication The transfer of meaning and understanding between people through verbal and nonverbal means in order to affect behavior and achieve desired results.

communication overload Exists when a sender attemps to present too much information to the receiver at one time.

comparison controls Used to determine whether deviations from plans have taken place and, if necessary, to bring them to the attention of the responsible managers.

compensation All rewards which individuals receive as a result of their employment.

compromise Conflict resolution technique which involves giving each party in a conflict some of what it wants.

concentration Growth by producing and selling more of what a company has always produced.

concentric diversification Developing businesses that are related to the firm's current businesses.

conceptual noise The personality, perceptual, and attitudinal differences in individuals that reduce their ability to communicate effectively.

conceptual skill The ability of the manager to understand the complexities of the overall organization and how each department or unit fits into it.

conflict Occurs when an individual or group purposely inhibits the attainment of goals by another individual or group.

conflict management Dealing with conflict in such a way that the organization and the individuals working in it will benefit.

conglomerate diversification Developing businesses that are not related to the firm's current business.

consideration The extent to which leaders have relationships with subordinates characterized by mutual trust, respect, and consideration of employee ideas and feelings.

contact chart Identifies the informal connections that an individual has with other members of the organization.

contingency planning The development of different plans to be placed in effect if certain unexpected events occur.

control The established standard against which actual performance is compared for the purpose of taking action to correct deviations.

control chart Graphic record of how closely samples of a product or service conform to standards over time.

control staff Responsible for controlling some aspect of organizational performance (e.g., quality control).

control tolerances Specifications of how much deviation will be permitted before corrective action will be taken.

controlling The process of comparing actual performance with standards and taking any necessary corrective action.

coordination The process of ensuring that persons who perform interdependent activities work together in a way that contributes to overall goal attainment.

corporate culture The complex set of values, beliefs, assumptions, and symbols that define the way in which a firm conducts its business.

corporate level strategic planning The process of defining the overall character and purpose of the organization, the businesses it will enter or leave, and how resources will be distributed among those businesses.

corporation An artificial organization, existing only in contemplation of law, that is composed of shareholders, managers, employees, and a board of directors.

corporation bylaws The rules by which the corporation is run.

cost standards Standards based on the cost associated with producing a good or service.

Counselling Assistance to Small Enterprises

(CASE) Federal government program to aid small business, which uses retired business executives to give management consulting advice.

critical path In PERT and CPM, it is the longest path from start to finish of a project.

critical path method (CPM) A network control technique developed by industry. Only one time estimate is used, thereby making the network a deterministic model.

cyclical variation Variation around a trend line.

data Unanalyzed facts about an organization's operations.

decentralization Individual managers and workers at lower levels in the organization have a wide range of decisions or actions they can initiate.

decentralized The type of situation in which decision-making authority has been delegated to lower levels in the organization.

decision maker The person who has the responsibility for choosing the course of action that will solve a problem or take advantage of an opportunity within the area for which he or she is accountable.

decision making The process by which managers evaluate alternatives and make a choice among them to solve a problem or take advantage of an opportunity.

decision matrix A decision-making technique useful for problems in which the alternatives are known but the criteria for making the decision are numerous and the weights for these criteria are disputed.

decisional role Requires the manager to use the information available to make decisions that will help the manager's unit function effectively.

decoding Converting communication symbols into a message; it requires a receiver to determine what the sender meant.

delegation The process of granting specific work assignments to individuals within the organization and providing them with the right or power to perform these functions.

Delphi technique Procedure for obtaining consensus among a number of experts through the use of a series of questionnaires.

demand forecasting An attempt to estimate the demand for a firm's products or services.

democratic leader A person who tries to do what the majority of subordinates desire.

departmentation Grouping related functions or major work activities into manageable units.

developing nations Countries which lack modern industry and supporting services.

diagonal communication Communication between people who are at different levels in the organization, but who are not in a superior-subordinate relationship.

disciplinary action The process of invoking a penalty against an employee who fails to adhere to standards.

diversification Increasing the variety of products or services made and sold.

divisional structure An organizational structure composed of divisions, in which each division performs all the functions necessary for it to reach its objectives. Each division operates as a profit center.

dogs In BCG analysis, businesses in low growth, low market-share situations.

economic function Businesses' production of needed goods and services, provision of employment, contribution to economic growth, and earning of profit.

economic order quantity Method of inventory control that uses a procedure for balancing ordering costs and carrying costs so as to minimize total inventory costs.

effectiveness Achieving the goals that have been set.

efficiency Achieving the greatest output possible with a given amount of inputs.

empathy The ability to identify with the various feelings and thoughts of another person.

employment application Form that collects objective, biographical information about an applicant, such as education, work experience, special skills, general background, and references.

employment requisition Issued to activate the recruitment process; typically includes such information as job title, starting date, pay scale, and summary of job duties.

encoding Putting a communications message in a form that the receiver can understand.

entrepreneur A person who has the ability to create an ongoing enterprise where none existed before.

equity theory Assumes that individuals consider the ratio of their inputs on the job to the outcomes they receive and then compare this ratio with the input/outcome ratio of others doing similar work.

E-R-G Theory Motivation theory developed by Alderfer that attempts to make Maslow's theory more consistent with knowledge of human needs. Alderfer's classification of needs is *Existence, Relatedness,* and *Growth.*

ethical dilemmas Situations involving questionable moral issues that confront managers and are often difficult to resolve or avoid.

ethics The discipline dealing with what is good and bad, or right and wrong, or with moral duty and obligations.

evaluative listening Requires the listener to allocate full attention to the speaker, while evaluating and judging the nature of the remarks heard.

event The beginning or completion of a step in a PERT network.

exception principle The belief that employees should handle routines matters and the supervisor should handle exceptional matters.

executive burnout State of exhaustion and frustration brought about by devotion to a cause, way of life, or relationships that failed to produce the expected reward.

expectancy An individual's perception of the chances or probability that a particular outcome will occur as a result of certain behavior.

expectancy theory Attempts to explain behavior in terms of an individual's goals,

choices, and the expectations of achieving those goals.

expected time In PERT, it is calculated by using a formula consisting of 3 time estimates: optimistic, most likely, and pessimistic.

expert power Comes from a person possessing special knowledge or skill.

exponential smoothing Technique using the forecast from the previous period, the actual demand that resulted from this forecast period, and a smoothing constant.

extrinsic motivation Exists when a person works on a task because of the promise that some obvious reward will be forthcoming if a good job is done.

feedback Tells the sender of a communication message whether it was properly decoded and acted on by the receiver.

Fiedler's contingency model Suggests that there is no one most effective style that is appropriate to every situation.

filtering Attempts to alter or edit information to present a more favorable message.

financial assistance programs Various forms of financial assistance to small businesses, on a provincial or federal level.

financial budget Indicates the amount of capital the organization will need and where it will obtain it.

fixed costs Costs that do not change with the level of output.

flextime A system which requires all workers to be at the workplace at certain core hours during the day, but which allows workers flexibility in choosing the remaining hours they will work.

force Using official authority to compel one party in a conflict to accept a solution.

forecasting Attempts to predict what will occur in a firm's future.

formal communication channels Means by which information is transmitted that are officially recognized by the organization.

forward integration Integration toward the final user of a product.

franchising Establishment of a small business through a contract between a manufacturer and a dealer that stipulates how the manufacturer's products or services will be sold.

Friedman's view of corporate social responsibility Businesses have one and only one social responsibility: to earn maximum profits for their shareholders.

function A type of work activity that can be identified and distinguished from other work activities.

functional authority Occurs when a staff person is given authority over a line person; limited to the staff person's area of expertise.

functional-level strategic planning The process of developing policies and procedures for relatively narrow areas of activity that are critical to the success of an organization.

functional structure Departments are structured formally on the basis of the key functions an organization must perform in order to reach its objectives.

grand strategy The overall plan of major actions the firm has decided upon as a means to reach its long-term objectives.

grapevine The informal means by which information is transmitted in an organization.

group Two or more people who join together to accomplish a desired organization goal.

Hawthorne effect The influence of behavioral researchers on the people they study.

health An employee's physical and mental well being.

Hersey and Blanchard's situational leadership theory Theory based on the notion that the most effective leadership style varies according to the level of maturity of the followers and the demands of the situation.

hierarchy of needs Maslow's theory that human needs such as psychological, safety, so-

cial, esteem, and self-actualization are arranged in a hierarchy.

horizontal differentiation The creation of different departments at the same structural level in an organization.

horizontal integration Buying or taking control of competitors at the same level in the marketing and production process.

host country Country where a multinational company is operating away from its home base.

host country nationals Personnel in an MNC from the host country.

human relations movement Treating satisfaction and psychological needs as the primary management concern.

human resource planning The analysis of future personnel requirements.

human skill The ability to understand, motivate, and get along with other people.

hygiene factors Relate to the environment in which a job is performed; their absence causes dissatisfaction, but their presence does not lead to satisfaction.

hypothesis A tentative statement of the nature of existing relationships.

income statement A financial statement that shows the company's financial performance over a period of time — usually one year.

influencing The process of determining or affecting the behavior of others.

informal communication channels Ways of transmitting information within an organization that bypass formal channels.

informal group Two or more persons associated with one another in ways not prescribed by the formal organization.

informal organization The patterns of behavior and influence that arise out of the human interaction occurring within the formal structure.

information Anything relevant and useful to practicing managers.

informal role Requires the manager to both gather and disseminate information.

initiating structure The extent to which the leader establishes goals and structures the roles of subordinates.

input controls Methods used to monitor resources — material, human, and capital — that come into the organization.

integration The unified control of a number of successive or similar operations.

interpersonal role Requires the manager to interact with other significant people both inside and outside the organization.

interview Face-to-face method of assessing the qualifications of job applicants.

intrinsic motivation Exists if a person performs a task in the absence of any obvious external reward for doing so.

intuition Insight acquired through experience and accomplishment rather than through a formal decision-making process.

inventory Stored goods or materials available for use by a business.

iron law of responsibility States that, if business firms are to retain their social power and role, they must be responsive to society's needs.

job analysis The process of determining the human qualifications required to perform each job.

job description Summarizes the purpose, principal duties, and responsibilities of a job.

job design The process of altering the nature and structure of a job for the purpose of increasing productivity.

job enlargement A horizontal expansion of duties that involves an increase in the number of tasks an employee is required to perform.

job enrichment Refers to basic changes in the content and level of responsibility of a job to provide additional satisfaction of the motivation needs of personnel.

job rotation Employees are rotated through several similar jobs.

job specification Statement of the minimum acceptable human qualities necessary to perform the job.

just-in-time inventory system Inventory system developed in Japan, in which supplies arrive just in time to be used in the production process. Cuts down on the need for inventory storage, but requires accurate delivery schedules.

laissez faire leader Leader who is uninvolved in the work of the unit.

lateral communication Communication between managers at the same level in the organization.

leader Anyone who is able to influence others to pursue certain goals.

leader-member relations According to Fiedler, the degree to which the leader feels accepted by the subordinates.

leader position power The degree of influence over rewards and punishments, as well as the official authority possessed by the leader.

leadership The ability to motivate followers to pursue the goals the leader wishes to achieve.

leadership continuum As developed by Tannenbaum and Schmidt, suggests that choosing an effective leadership style depends on the demands of the situation. The continuum ranges from boss-centered, autocratic management to subordinate-centered, participative management.

leadership decision-making model Vroom and Yetton's model, based on the idea that a leader must decide how much participation subordinates should be allowed when making decisions.

legitimate power Results from a person being placed in a formal position of authority.

leverage ratios Measure whether a firm has effectively used outside financing.

Likert's systems of management Universal theory of leadership consisting of a continuum of styles ranging from autocratic to participative.

line and staff organizations Those organizations that have direct, vertical relationships between different levels and also specialists responsible for advising and assisting other managers.

line departments Those directly involved in accomplishing the primary purpose of the organization.

line organization Structure that shows the direct, vertical relationships between different levels within the firm.

liquidity ratios Measure a firm's ability to meet its current obligations.

lower-level managers Usually referred to as supervisors or first-line supervisors, they are responsible for managing employees in the performance of daily operations.

mainframe computers Computers at the large end of the spectrum which are able to handle vast amounts of data.

management The process of planning, organizing, influencing, and controlling to accomplish organization goals through the coordinated use of human and material resources.

management audit Is used to assess systematically the strengths and weaknesses of the managerial talent in an organization.

management by exception The general management of an area of responsibility, not detailed supervision of each worker.

management by objectives (MBO) A philosophy of management that emphasizes the setting of agreed-on objectives by superior and subordinate managers and the use of these objectives as the primary basis of motivation, evaluation, and control efforts.

management development programs Formal efforts to improve the skills and attitudes of present and potential managers.

management information system (MIS) A system for collecting, analyzing, organizing, and disseminating information from both internal and external sources so that managers can use it to make decisions beneficial to the organization.

manager A person who performs the functions of planning, organizing, influencing, and controlling, and who occupies a formal position in an organization.

managerial code of ethics Provides guidelines and standards for conduct of managers.

managerial grid Leadership theory developed by Blake and Mouton that depicts 5 primary styles of leadership described according to the leader's concern for people and production.

marginal listening Allowing the mind to wander while listening to someone.

market development Marketing the firm's existing products to customers similar to the firm's current customers.

matrix organization The structure created when a temporary project structure is continued on a more permanent basis; it is used when a firm must be responsive to rapidly changing external environment conditions.

mediation Assistance in resolving organization conflict from outside neutral parties.

microcomputer The smallest computers.

middle managers Situated between supervisors and top managers, they are concerned primarily with the coordination of programs and activities necessary to achieve the overall goals of the organization.

minicomputers Computers a step above microcomputers that are larger and more powerful.

mission The organization's continuing purpose or reason for being.

motivation The perseverence and enthusiasm employees exhibit as they work toward organizational goals.

motivators According to Herzberg, these consist of factors intrinsic to the job, such as recognition, responsibility, achievement, and opportunities for growth and advancement.

moving averages Forecasting technique for smoothing the effects of random variation.

multinational company (MNC) A firm engaged in business in 2 or more countries.

need for achievement According to McClelland, the need for achievement is concerned with an individual's desire for excellence.

need for affiliation According to McClelland, this need is concerned with the desire for affection and establishing friendly relationships.

need for power According to McClelland, this need is concerned with an individual's desire for influence and control over others.

nepotism The practice of hiring relatives.

net present value Assesses the value of goods in order to help managers when they are purchasing capital equipment.

nominal grouping An approach to decision making that involves idea generation by group members, group interaction only to clarify ideas, member rankings of ideas presented, and alternative selection by summing ranks.

non evaluative listening Listeners attempt to project themselves into the speaker's position and to understand what is being said from the speaker's point of view.

nonroutine decisions Those decisions that are designed to deal with unusual problems or situations.

norms Standard of behavior that is expected from group members.

not-for-profit organizations Organizations that do not pursue profit as a goal; they generally have service goals instead.

objectives The results a person or organization wants to accomplish.

obsolescence The state of products or services that are no longer as useful or as efficient as they once were.

Ohio state leadership studies Detailed studies of the behavior of leaders in a wide variety of organizations.

open system Any system (including a business organization) which depends on interaction with other systems.

operating budget Indicates the revenues and expenses the business expects from producing goods and services during a given year.

ordering costs Include administrative, clerical, and other expenses incurred in initially obtaining inventory items and placing them in storage.

organization Two or more people working together in a coordinated manner to achieve group results.

organization development The systematic effort to improve the overall, long-term functioning of the organization, with emphasis usually placed on collaborative decision making.

organization politics The activities of individuals as they try to develop and use power to get their own desired outcomes.

organizational behavior modification The application of Skinner's reinforcement theory to organizational change efforts.

organizational chart Diagram which depicts the firm's formal structure at a point in time.

organizational constituency Any identifiable group that managers have, or acknowledge, a responsibility to represent.

organizational stakeholder An individual or group whose interests are affected by organizational activities.

organizational structure The formal relationships among groups and individuals in the organization.

organizing The process of prescribing formal relationships among people and resources to accomplish goals.

orientation The process of introducing the new employee to the organization.

parent country Home base or headquarters for a multinational firm.

parent country nationals Personnel in a multinational from the parent country.

Parent ego state The ego state in transactional analysis that identifies the person who bases decisions primarily on what the individual has heard or learned in the past.

participative culture An open type of culture characterized by trust in subordinates, openness in communication, considerate and supportive leadership, group problem solving, worker autonomy, information sharing, and establishment of high output goals.

participative leader A person who involves subordinates in decision making but may retain the final authority.

partnership A form of business that comes into being when two or more individuals agree to combine their financial, managerial, and technical abilities for the purpose of earning a profit.

path-goal leadership theory Developed by House, this theory stresses that managers can facilitate job performance by showing employees how their performance directly affects them in receiving rewards.

patterned interview Interviewer follows a predetermined series of questions in interviewing an applicant.

payroll relationships Situations in which costs or profits of various courses of action and benefits that may be obtained can be measured.

perception set A fixed tendency to interpret information in a certain way.

performance appraisal An evaluation of employees that determines how well they are performing their assigned tasks.

performance results standards Standards that are straightforward to measure accurately; used to specify what results are required.

personal staff Assist specific line managers, but generally do not act for them in their absence.

PERT (program evaluation and review technique) A control technique that is used to think through a project in its entirety, as a network of events and activities. Three time estimates are used, which permit the user to develop probabilities of occurrences.

planning The process of determining in advance what should be done and how to do it.

planning-programming budgeting system (PPBS) A budgetary aid to management in identifying and eliminating costly duplicative programs and in providing a means for the careful analysis of the benefits and costs of each program or activity.

plans Specifications for the manner in which objectives are to be accomplished.

policy The predetermined general guide established to provide direction in decision making.

power The ability of one person to influence the behavior of another person.

preferred stock Those shares showing ownership in a corporation, holders of which generally do not have voting rights.

problem content Includes the situation within which the problem exists, the decision maker's knowledge of that situation, as well as the situation that will exist after a choice is made.

problem solving Approach to conflict management characterized by an open and trusting exchange of views and facts.

procedure A series of steps established for the accomplishment of some specific project or endeavor.

process consultation A set of activities on the part of the consultant which help a client to perceive, understand, and act on a process events that occur in the client's organization.

process controls Used to monitor the actual creation of products and services, largely by observation and by interactions between supervisors and subordinates.

process standards Standards that attempt to evaluates a function for which accurate measurements are difficult or impossible to quantify.

product development Involves introducing changes in the company's current products or creating entirely new products.

product life cycle The general pattern of introduction, growth, maturity, and decline that all products go through.

production The conversion of inputs into outputs, which results in the creation of goods and services.

productivity standards Standards based on the amount of product or service produced during a set time period.

profit The difference between the cost of inputs and the revenue from outputs.

profit center A department or division in an organization that is given the responsibility of making profit.

profitability ratios Measure the overall operating efficiency and profitability of a firm.

program evaluation and review technique (PERT) A control technique that is used to think through a project in its entirety as a network of events and activities. Three time estimates are used, which permit the user to develop probabilities of occurrences.

progressive discipline Efforts made to make the penalty appropriate to the violation(s).

project organization Temporary organizational structure designed to achieve specific results by using a team of specialists from different functional areas within the organization.

quality The degree of conformity to a certain predetermined standard.

quality circles Groups of employees who meet periodically to brainstorm ways to improve the quality and quantity of their work.

quality standards Standards based on the level of perfection desired.

question marks In BCG analysis, businesses with low market share in a high-growth market.

random demand Variations in demand that cannot be anticipated.

ratio analysis An assessment of a firm's performance made by taking two financial figures from the balance sheet or income statement and dividing one figure by the other.

recruitment Encouraging individuals with the needed skills to make application for employment with a firm.

referent power Based on a liking for, or a desire to be like, the power holder.

regression analysis Used to predict one item through knowledge of another.

reinforcement theory The idea that human behavior can be explained in terms of the previous positive or negative outcomes of that behavior.

relationship behavior Managerial behavior designed to provide consideration of people and emotional support for them.

reliability Concerned with the degree of consistency of test results.

repatriation plan A statement about the length of an assignment a multinational executive will have in a foreign country and the kind of position that executive will have when he or she returns to Canada.

responsibility An obligation of personnel to perform certain work activities.

résumé A written description that a job applicant provides to a prospective employer with such information as career objectives, education, work experience, and other biographical data.

retrenchment Reduction in the size or scope of a firm's activities.

reward power Derived from a person's ability to reward another individual.

risk The probability that a particular decision will have an adverse effect on a company.

role The total pattern of expected behavior, interactions, and sentiments of an individual.

routine decisions Daily decisions made by managers that are governed by policies, procedure, and rules of the organization, as well as the personal habits of the manager.

rule A specific and detailed guide to action that is set up to direct or restrict action in a fairly narrow manner.

safety Protection of employees from injuries caused by work-related accidents.

SBU-level strategic planning The process of determining how an SBU will compete in a particular line of business.

scalar principle Authority and responsibility should flow from top management downward in a clear, unbroken line.

scientific management The name given to principles and practices that grew out of the work of Frederick Taylor and his followers and that are characterized by concern for efficiency and systematization in management.

scientific method A four part decision-making method which includes observation of events, hypothesis formulation, experimentation, and verification.

screening interview Used to eliminate obviously unqualified applicants.

seasonal demand Demand patterns within the short term (less than one year).

selection The process of identifying those recruited individuals who will best be able to assist the firm in achieving organization goals.

self-fulfilling prophecy What one expects to happen actually occurs. A manager's expectations often determine employee performance.

sensitivity training Technique used to develop awareness of sensitivity to oneself and others.

service staff Provide a specific service to line managers (e.g., testing and interviewing prospective employees).

Seven S model A model that attempts to identify what makes an enterprise successful or unsuccessful; factors include: strategy, structure, systems, staff, skills, style, and superordinate goals.

shareholders People who are owners and who share in a corporation's profit or loss.

single accountability The concept that each person should be answerable to only one immediate supervisor — one boss to each employee.

situational approach The ability to adapt to meet particular circumstances and constraints that a firm may encounter.

small business A business that is independently owned and operated and is not dominant in its field.

smoothing Conflict resolution technique which attempts to play down the level of conflict and stress peaceful cooperation.

social audit A commitment to systematic assessment of and reporting on some meaningful, definable domain of a company's activities that have social impact.

social contract The set of rules and assumptions about behavior patterns among the various elements of society.

social responsibility The implied, enforced, or felt obligation of managers, acting in their official capacities, to serve or protect the interests of groups other than themselves.

socialization The gradual change of attitudes and behavior of an individual so that he or she fits into a society or an organization.

sociogram Illustrates how the members of a group interact with each other; it is developed by observing the actual behavior of group members.

sole proprietorship A business owned and managed by one person.

source The person who has an idea or message to communicate to another person or group.

span of management The limit to the number of employees a manager can effectively supervise.

specialization of labor The division of a complete job into simpler tasks so that one person or group may carry out only identical or related activities.

staff departments Provide line people with advice and assistance in specialized areas.

staffing The process of ensuring that the organization has qualified workers available at all levels in order to achieve company objectives.

staffing process Involves planning for future personnel requirements, recruiting individuals, and selecting from those recruited individual employees who fulfill the needs of the firm.

standard A norm, or criterion, to which something can be compared.

standard operating procedures The stable

body of policies and procedures, written and unwritten, that governs an organization.

standards Established levels of quality or quantity used to guide performance.

standing plans Plans that remain roughly the same for long periods of time.

stars In BGG analysis, businesses with high market shares in high growth-rate industries.

state of nature Refers to the various situations that could occur and the probability of each happening.

statistical quality control Technique that allows for a portion of the total number of items to be inspected.

status A person's rank or position in a group.

status symbol A visible, external sign of a person's position in society or in an organization.

strategic business unit (SBU) Any part of a business organization that is treated separately for strategic planning purposes.

strategic control points Critical areas that must be monitored if the organization's overall objectives are to be achieved.

strategic planning The determination of overall organizational purposes and objectives and how they are to be achieved.

stress The nonspecific response of the body to any demands made on it.

stress interview Puts the interviewee under stress and then observes the interviewee's reaction.

structure The manner in which the internal environment of the firm is organized or arranged formally.

superordinate goal Goal that supersedes the conflict of two parties.

survey feedback method An organization development technique based on the systematic collection and measurement of subordinate attitudes through the use of anonymous questionnaires.

synergism The whole is greater than the sum of its parts. When 2 or more people work together, they can often produce more than if each worked separately.

system An arrangement of interrelated parts designed to achieve objectives.

systems approach Sees the organization as a set of interrelated parts which must be coordinated.

task behavior Behavior of the manager designed to provide direction and emphasis on getting the job done.

task-relevant maturity The desire for achievement, willingness and ability to do a job, and the education and/or experience relevant to a job that subordinates possess.

task structure The extent to which goals are clearly defined and solutions to problems are known.

team building A conscious effort to develop effective work groups throughout the organization.

technical barriers Barriers to communication that derive from the workplace; include timing, communication overload, and cultural differences.

technical skill Ability of a manager to use specific knowledge, methods or techniques in performing work.

technology All of the skills, knowledge, methods, and equipment required to convert resources into desired products and services.

telecommuting Computer hookups in a home from an office.

teleconferencing Combines video, computer, and telecommunication technologies to convey meaning.

theory X Traditional philosophy of human nature, suggests that motivation of employees requires managers to coerce, control, or threaten employees in order to achieve maximum results.

theory Y A theory of human nature that provides an alternative to Theory X, Theory Y suggests that people are capable of being responsible and mature.

theory Z Label for the type of company that

creates a strong relationship between management and workers. The company demonstrates great responsibility toward its workers, and the workers in turn show great loyalty to the company.

third country nationals Personnel in multinationals from countries other than the parent or host countries.

time series analysis Mathematical approach in which the independent variable is expressed in units of time.

time standard Monitoring of the time required to complete the project.

timing Selecting the most appropriate time to transmit a message.

top management Referred to by such titles as president, chief executive officer, vice-president, or executive director, these managers are responsible for providing the overall direction of the firm.

training and development Programs which help indiviuals, groups, and the entire organization to become more effective.

trait approach Study of leadership that focuses on leader's physical, intellectual, and personal characteristics.

transactional analysis (TA) A method that assists individuals in understanding both themselves and the people with whom they work. TA consists of three ego states that are constantly present and at work within each individual: the Parent, the Adult, and the Child.

transactional managers Stress planning for the future, setting up a structure to achieve the plans, and controlling the system so that it performs well.

transformational managers Stress activities like revitalizing the organization, communicating the organization's vision and culture to employees, molding employees into effective performers, and getting employee commitment to organizational goals.

trend line Projects the long-run estimate of the demand for the product being evaluated.

type I ethics The strength of the relationship between what an individual or an organization believes to be moral and correct and what available sources of guidance suggest is morally correct.

type II ethics The strength of the relationship between what one believes and how one behaves.

union A group of employees who have joined together for the purpose of presenting a united front in dealing with management.

unity of command principle Each person should answer to only one immediate superior.

unstructured interview No predetermined interviewing strategy or list of questions used.

valence How much value an individual places on a specific goal or result he or she is seeking.

validity Concerned with the relationship between the score on the test and performance on the job. Questions whether the test measures what it was intended to measure.

variable costs Costs that are directly related to changes in output.

variable sampling Consists of determining how closely an item conforms to an established standard, allowing for degrees of goodness and badness.

vertical differentiation The creation of multiple levels of authority and activity in an organization. Work at one level may be managerial, while at another level may be operative.

withdrawal Conflict resolution technique which involves withdrawing from the situation or avoiding the person with whom the conflict exists.

work-force analysis Process of identifying the skills of current personnel to determine if work loads can be accomplished by these employees.

work-load analysis Process of estimating the type and volume of work that need to be performed if the organization is to achieve its objectives.

zero base budgeting (ZBB) A budgetary system that requires management to take a fresh look at all programs and activities each year, rather than merely to build on last year's budget.

Index

ABC inventory method 612
accountability
defined 263
in divisional structure 272
in line and staff organization 277
single 263
actions plans (MBO) 118
activity trap (MBO) 114
Alderfer, Clayton 402
Allan, Gordon 32
antidiscrimination laws 353-354
arbitration 517
Argyris, Chris 31, 397-398
motivation theories 399-412
Art of Japanese Management, The (Pascale and Athos) 422-423
artificial intelligence 502-503
assessment center (for managerial talent) 375-376
authority 258-263; *see also* power
in centralized organization 259
in decentralized organization 259
and delegation 256-257
functional 279-280
informal 283
in line organization 273-274
and responsibility 257-258

Barnard, Chester 30
behavioral school of management
described 30-32
Hawthorne experiments 30-31
human relations movement 30
modern 31-32
behavioral science 31
Beyond Freedom and Dignity (Skinner) 409
Blake, Robert, and Mouton, Jane
managerial grid of 447
board of directors 9-11
legal obligation 10-11
body language 497
brainstorming 202; *see also* quality circles
breakeven analysis 627-628
budgets; *see also* financial controls
benefits of 624
capital 622
cash 622
defined 622
financial 622
limits of 625
operating 622
PPBS 625-626
ZBB 626
burnout 534

business; *see also* corporate social responsibility, ethics, *and* profit
economic function of 721-722
failure rate of 4
firm, described 4-12
mission of 96-98, 145-147
profit objective of 99-100
public view of as negative 75
small; *see* small business
and social role 722
system 75-77

careers in management 43-55
centralized organization 83, 259
chain of command 263; *see also* managerial levels
change; *see also* organization development
decision making for 521-525
job redesign 415-422
resistance management 527-530
resistance to, sources of 525-527
sequence for 521-525
technological 83, 85
classical school of management 27-30
climate, organizational; *see* corporate culture
communication; *see also* feedback, information, *and* language
barriers to 487-294; *see also* conflict
channel 477
diagonal 485
downward channels of 480
encoding/decoding 476-477
facilitation of 494-499
filtering 492-493
Fog Index 490
grapevine 305, 485-486
lateral 481
noise 479
overload 487
process of 477-479
source 477
teleconferencing 502; *see also* high-tech industries
timing 487
trust and 493
upward channels of 480
compensation 350, 412-414
laws 356
competitors
as external environment factor 64-66
for small business 656-657
computers 215-217; *see also* change, high-

tech industries, *and* technology
and MIS 215-216
mainframe 216
micro- 215
mini- 216
personnel uses for 213-214
telecommuting 217
conflict; *see also* change
arbitration for 517
compromise 517
current view of 514-515
force 517
management of 517-520
mediation for 517
problem solving 518
smoothing 517
sources of 515-516
superordinate goal 518
traditional view of 512
withdrawal 517
consideration 450
contact chart 300
contingency planning 111-112
controlling
comparison controls 581-583
defined 19
financial techniques 621-633
input controls 580-581
management of resistance to 591-592
nonfinancial techniques 600-621
process controls 581
process of 570-579
resistance to, sources of 589-590
strategic control points 583-586
techniques, managerial use of 633-635
coordination
defined 19-20, 245
corporate culture
defined 544
factors determining 546-548
identifying 545-546
Japanese 423-424
participative 548-550; *see also* managerial style
and performance 546
Corporate Cultures (Deal and Kennedy) 546
corporate social responsibility; *see also* ethics
defined 75, 723
and external environment 606-608
opponents' views 731, 734-735
proponents' views 730

and social audit   728-730
social pressures for   718-722
corporation   7-11
bylaws   10
critical path method   621
customers
boycott pressure   74
as external environment factor   74
and small businesses   656-657
cyclical variation (demand forecasting)
   150-151

data   209
decentralized organization; see also corporate
   culture
and decision making   259-263
defined   83, 259
factors determining extent   261-263
decision making; see also change
approaches to   185-187
defined   21
factors affecting process   195-197
individual vs. group   205-208
intuitive approach   185-186
and intelligence   186
and intuition   185
nonroutine   182-183
and organization politics   197
personal   181
process of   187-194
professional   181
requirements for   183-185
and risk   197
routine   182
systematic approach to   186-187
techniques for   197-205
time for   197

decision matrix   197-202
decision trees   202-203
delegation   256-257; see also authority and
   responsibility
Delphi technique   205
demand forecasting
cyclical variation   150
long-term trends   151
random   151
seasonal   151
trend line   150
departmentation   235-243; see also structure
combination approach to   244
by customer   238

by function   237
by geographic territory   238
by product   237-238
by project   239
developing nations   690
differentiation; see also functions and
   management, span of
horizontal   241
vertical   241
discipline   578-579
diversification strategy   166-168; see also
   planning
divisional structure   272-273; see structure
division of labor: see specialization
Drucker, Peter (MBO)   114

economic order quantity   611
effectiveness   13
efficiency   13
Emerson, Harrington   28
empathy   494
employment application   364
employment requisition   363
encoding/decoding   476-477
entrepreneur   649-651
equity theory (Adams)   412
E-R-G theory (Alderfer)   402
ethics
business   737
codes of   740-742
defined   75, 736-737
dilemmas   738
factors affecting   740-743
and government regulation   740
managerial code of   743-744
MNC code of 697
exception principle of management   605
executive burnout   534
executives: see managerial levels
expectancy theory (Vroom)   408-409
expectancy   408
valence   408
exponential smoothing forecasting   151
external environment
factors of, defined   58-75
forecasting of   150-151
and leadership   460-463
of MNCs   688-693
in situational management approach   82
of small businesses   656-659

Fayol, Henri   30

feedback; *see also* performance appraisal
defined   479
Fiedler, Fred
contingency leadership model   453-454
filtering   492-493
financial controls; *see also* budget,
   compensation *and* money
audits   633
balance sheet   630
break-even analysis   626-628
budgets   622-626
cost standards   105
income statement   630
net present value   628
profit centers   272
ratio analysis   629-632
in small businesses   667
flextime   421-422
forecasting
demand   150-151; *see* demand forecasting
described   150
exponential smoothing   151
moving averages   151
regression analysis   151
time series analysis   151
foreign control   684
franchising   654-656
Friedman, Milton   731, 734-735
functional authority   279-280
functional similarity   236
functional structure   269-272; *see* structure
functions; *see also* structure
basic management: *see* controlling,
   influencing, organizing, *and* planning
coordination of   19-20
defined   230
specialization   232-234
Functions of the Executive, The (Barnard)
30

Gantt, H. L.   28
general public; *see also* corporate social
   responsibility *and* ethics
employees as members of   67-71
as external environment factor   74-75,
   720-721
negative view of business   725
Ghiselli, Edwin
trait approach to leadership   441-442
Gilbreth, Frank and Lillian   29-30
 goals   114-121, 152-153
 government

and business ethics   740
business legislation, summary   60-63
controversial intervention   62-63
as external environment factor   60-63, 657-
   658, 690-691
financial aid to small business   667-669
legislation affecting MNCs   690-691
regulation affecting small business   669
staffing legislation   353-356
Graicunas, A. V.
formula for span of management   266
grand strategies
concentration   165
defined   164
diversification   166-167
integration   165-166
joint venture   168
market development   165
product development   165
retrenchment   168
grapevine   305, 485-486
group, defined   295
cohesiveness   302
norms   297
size   302
structure   299
synergism   303

Hawthorne Effect   31
health and safety   355
Hersey, Paul, and Blanchard, Kenneth
situational leadership theory   454-458
Herzberg, Frederick   31, 402-405
high-tech industries; *see also* computers
communication in   502-503
MNCs in   697-700
planning in   107
House, Robert
path-goal leadership theory   451
human relations movement   30-31
human resource planning   350
hygiene factors (Herzberg)   403
hypothesis   186-187

influencing; *see also* change, communication,
   corporate culture, leadership, managerial
   style, *and* motivation
defined   18-19
through leadership   435-437
through motivation   388
informal organization   296
benefits   303-306

costs 306-307
information, *see also* computers, data, grapevine, *and* management information systems
for change 529
for communication 480
and creation of alternatives 192
vs data 209
initiating structure 449
inputs 76
In Search of Excellence (Peters and Waterman) 546
integration strategy 165-166; *see also* planning
backward 166
forward 166
horizontal 166
interviewing 365
patterned 365
stress 370
unstructured 365
intuition 185
inventory 609-614
defined 609
just-in-time system 613-614
obsolescence 611
in small businesses 665
iron law of responsibility 731

Japanese management 29, 422-423, 613-615
job
analysis 359
description 359
design 415-422
enlargement 416, 417
enrichment 417-418
quality circles on 418-420
rotation 416
specification 360

Kondrasuk, Jack 129
Koontz, Harold 32-33

labor force: *see* work force
language
body 497
fog index 490
and reading skills 496
semantic differences 489
vocabulary 488-491
leadership; *see also* managerial style
defined 19, 436
integrated approach to 460-463

situational theories 449-459
traits 441-442
universalist theories about 440-449
vs. management 436-437
Likert, Rensis 32, 442-446
line and staff organization 275-280; *see* structure
line organization 273-275; *see* structure
line and staff organization 275-280
listening 495-496

mainframe computer 216
management
audit 604-605
behavioral school of 30-32
careers in 43-55
by exception 605
classical school of 27
defined 13
functions 15, 18-19
functions and polar exploration 20
Japanese: *see* Japanese management
Koontz's classifications 33-34
by objectives 113-129
scientific 27-30
theoretical schools of 26-34
transactional 439
transformational 439
universality of 5
management by objectives (MBO) 113-129
activity trap 114
action plans 118
advocates of 114
background of 114
benefits of 124-128
business example of 121-127
commitment of top management 113
defined 113
effectiveness of 129
evaluation 129
long-range planning 115
potential problems 128
management development programs 559-560
management information system (MIS) 208-217; *see also* communication, feedback, *and* information
computers and 215-217
defined 208
development of 210-211
information vs data 209
misconceptions about 211-212
personnel example of 213-214

management, span of 265-268
defined 265
factors affecting 267-268
Graicunas's formula for 266
in tall/flat organizations 267-268
manager
defined 13-15
lower-level 14
middle 14
top 14
managerial levels
authority/responsibility at 257-259
and basic functions 21-22
and computer use 217
information needs of 209-210
and managerial skills 23-26
and nonroutine decisions 182-183
managerial roles
decisional role 23
informational role 22
interpersonal role 22
managerial skills
and basic functions 26
conceptual 24
human 25
technical 24-25
managerial style; *see also* corporate culture
    and leadership
and centralized/decentralized organizations
    259-260
autocratic 440
laissez-faire 440
participative 440
Theory X/Theory Y 396-397
Maslow, Abraham 31, 400-402
matrix organization 280-283; *see* structure
Mayo, Elton (Hawthorne studies) 31
McClelland, David (motivation) 406-407
McGregor, Douglas 31, 396-397
mediation 517
metrication 63
microcomputers 215-216
minicomputer 216
Mintzberg, Henry
managerial role theories 22-24, 34
mission 96, 98, 145, 147
money, as motivator 412-414
and equity theory 412
motivation
defined 18-19
extrinsic 392-394
intrinsic 392-394

money as 412-414
motivators 403
process of 388-392
productivity and 395
profit sharing and 413
theories about 398-412
moving averages forecasting 151
multinational company (MNC)
Canadian-based 685
defined 683
described 683-684
development of 687
external environment(s) of 688-693
host country of, defined 688; Canada as: *see*
    foreign control
host country nationals 704
objectives of 693-697
parent country nationals 704
personnel for 703-707
political factors for 690-691
socio-cultural factors for 692
stucture of 700-702
technology and 697
third country nationals 704

nature, state of 184-185
needs 389-392
for achievement (*n Ach*) 406
for affiliation (*n Aff*) 407
existence-relatedness-growth (Alderfer)
    402
hierarchy of (Maslow) 400-402
for power (*n Pow*) 406
net present value 628
network controls 615-621
critical path method (cpm) 621
PERT 616-621
    activity 616
    critical path 617
    event 616
    expected time 617
    most likely time 617
    optimistic time 617
    pessimistic time 617
networks: *see* organization politics
noise 479
nominal grouping 204-205
norms 298; *see* standards
not-for-profit organization
described 11-12
economic objective of 11

objectives; *see also* MBO, planning, policies, *and* standards
  defined 82, 98
  development of 101-102
  distortion of 103
  economic 99-100
  establishment of 101-102
  group 120-121
  individual (MBO) 119-120
  of MNCs 693-697
  multiple 103
  personal 100-101
  problems in establishing 102-104
  real vs stated 102
  service 100
  for small businesses 659-660
  team (MBO) 120-121
Odiorne, George (MBO) 114
Ohio State leadership studies 449-451
open system 76
organizational behavior modification (OBM) 409-412
  critics of 411-412
  defined 409
  examples of 410
  Skinner's reinforcement theory 409
organizational chart 269; *see* structure
organization development
  change agent 554
  defined 554
  management development programs 559-560
  process consultation 557-558
  sensitivity training 558-559
  survey feedback 554-555
  team building 556-557
organization, informal 296-309; *see next entry*
organization politics
  benefits and costs of 336-340
  and decision making 197
  defined 328
  negative aspects 335-341
  positive aspects 335-341
  universality of 329, 332
organizing; *see also* functions *and* structure
  authority 258-263
  defined 18, 228
  delegation 256-257
  responsibility 257-258
orientation 372

participative style: *see* corporate culture *and* managerial style
partnership 7
payoff relationships 184
perception set differences 494
performance appraisal 350
personnel; *see also* functions; management, span of; performance appraisal; selection processing; staffing; unions; *and* work force
  and ethical decisions 353; *see* antidiscrimination laws
  executives: *see* managerial levels
  in MNCs 703-707
  planning for 361
  repatriation 706
  as resource/input 6
  in small business 662-663
  specialized staff 277
PERT 616-621
planning; *see also* MBO, objectives, policies, *and* standards
  contingency planning 111-112
  defined 15, 18
  examples of 144
  forecasting 150-151
  grand strategies 164-170
  process of 96-104
  statement of mission for 96, 97, 145, 146
  strategic 145-156
plans 106; *see* planning
  standing 108
policies 108-109
politics, corporate/office: *see* organization politics
power; *see also* leadership *and* status
  and authority 323-327
  business example of 332-333
  coercive 324
  described 323
  expert 324
  legitimate 325
  referent 324
  reward 324
PPBS 625
Practice of Management, The (Drucker) 114
Prince, The (Machiavelli) 81
problem content 184
procedures 109
  standard operating 109

productivity 66
professional sports
functions in 231-232
motivation in 394
profit
center 272
defined 6; *see also* business
and payoff relationships 184
project organization 280-283

quality circles
brainstorming in 418
business examples of 418-421
described 418-421
quality control 582-583, 606-609
defined 582
standards 105, 606-608
statistical 608
Quebec language laws 63

Raia, Anthony (MBO) 120
random demand (forecasting) 151
real estate industry
motivation in 390-391
planning in 107
recruitment 362
reinforcement theory (Skinner) 409-412
reinforcers (OBM) 409
reliability 365
repatriation plan 706
responsibility 257-258; *see also* authority
and delegation 256-257
retrenchment strategy (planning) 168, 170
risk 195
Roethlisberger, F. J. 31
roles
in informal organization 298, 299
managerial (Mintzberg) 22-23
rules 109-110
scalar principle 265
scientific management
defined 28
seasonal demand (forecasting) 151
selection process (personnel) 364-372
application 364
as control 601
interviews 365
  patterned 365
  screening 364
  stress 370
  unstructured 365-370

management approval 372
physical check-up 372
reference checks 371
testing 364-365
self-fulfilling prophecy 398-399
service organizations 12
Seven S Model 422-423; *see* Japanese
  management theories
Shareholders
as activists 74
defined 8
as external environment factor 73-74
union members as 8
situational management approach 79-85
Skinner, B. F. (OBM) 409
small business; *see also* entrepreneur
CASE 669
checklist for 671-673
defined 649
drawbacks to 650-651
DRIE 668
external environment of 656-659
FBDB 667
financial assistance programs 667-668
and franchising 654-656
nepotism 663
objectives of 659-660
owner/manager motivation 645, 649, 654
personnel in 662-663
structure of 661-662
technological effects on 660-661
social audit 729-730
social contract 718
social responsibility of business: *see*
  corporate social responsibility
socialization 601
sociogram 301
sole proprietorship 7
source (communication) 477
span of management 265
factors affecting 267-268
specialization; *see also* structure
advantages of 233-234
defined 232
disadvantages of 234-235
by function 235-236
in line and staff organizations 275-278
for major projects 280-283
staff
advisory 277
control 277

personal 277
service 277
staffing 357-372
defined 350
legislation, re. 353-356
process for 357-372
recruitment 363-364
selection 364-372; *see* selection process
standards
behavioral 571
contradictory 590
and control tolerances 571, 573
correction 574-575, 578-579
cost 571
defined 104-106, 570-571
performance results 104
process 104
productivity 571
quality; *see* quality control
quantity 105
time 105
unattainable/unpredictable 590
state of nature 184
status; *see also* power
defined 310
functions of 314
sources 310-311
symbols of 312-313
stock, common/preferred 8-9
strategic control points 583-586
strategic management techniques
BCG Matrix 158-161
G. E. Grid 161-162
McKinsey Seven S Model 163-164
product life cycle 162-163
strategic planning 142-145
assessing external environment 148-149
assessing internal environment 147-148
corporate level 156
mission statement 145, 147
monitoring strategy 153
selecting a strategy 151-152
strategic business unit 156
stress 530-534
structure; *see also* change
centralized/decentralized 83, 259
defined 83
departmentation 235-240
divisional 272-273
flat 267
functional 269-272

by functional similarity 235-236
global 701
line 273-275
line and staff 275-280
matrix 280-283
of MNCs 700-702
organization, informal 296-301
project 280-283
in situational management approach 83
and small businesses 661-662
tall 267
suppliers
as external environment factor 74
synergism 303
system 76
systems approach 75-77

Tannenbaum, Robert, and Schmidt, Warren H.
leadership continuum 452-453
Taylor, Frederick
Bethlehem Steel study 28
monetary incentive views 412
and scientific management 27-28
technology; *see also* change, computers, high-tech industries, *and* personnel
defined 82
and job design 415
in host countries 697, 700
as MNC resource 697, 700
in situational management approach 82
and small businesses 660-661
telecommuting 217
teleconferencing 502
testing (personnel) 364-365
Theory X, Y, Z
X 396
Y 396
Z 422-423
Theory Z (Ouchi) 423
time series analysis (forecasting) 151
training and development 350, 373-377
trait approach 441
transactional analysis 498-499
transactional management 439
transformational management 439
Adult ego state 499
Child ego state 499
Parent ego state 498
trend line (demand forecasting) 150

unions
at Eaton's   72
as external environment factor   71-72
and job design   415-416
legislation, re.   355-356
unity of command   264

validity   365
Vroom, Victor, and Yetton, P.
leadership decision-making model   458-459
Vroom, Victor (motivation)   408-409

women
in work force   67-70
work (labor) force
analysis of   361-362
Canadian composition   67-71
as external environment factor   67-71
women in   67-70
work load analysis   361
Work Redesign (Hackman and Oldham)
   415
work simplification: *see* specialization

zero-base budgeting   626